Cases on Torts

Cases on Torts

Fifth edition

Barbara McDonald

Professor of Law, The University of Sydney

Ross Anderson

Senior Lecturer in Law, The University of Sydney

THE FEDERATION PRESS
2012

Published in Sydney by
    The Federation Press Pty Ltd
    PO Box 45, Annandale, NSW, 2038.
    71 John St, Leichhardt, NSW, 2040.
    Ph (02) 9552 2200. Fax (02) 9552 1681.
    E-mail: info@federationpress.com.au
    Website: http://www.federationpress.com.au

First edition   1992
Second edition   1994
Third edition   2002
Fourth edition   2007
Fifth edition   2012

National Library of Australia
Cataloguing-in-Publication entry

    McDonald, Barbara
    Cases on torts / Barbara McDonald; Ross Anderson.

    5th ed.

    978 186287 885 3 (pbk)

    Torts – Australia – Cases.

346.9403

Typeset by The Federation Press, Leichhardt, NSW.
    Printed by Ligare Pty Ltd, Riverwood, NSW.

PEFC™

PEFC/21-31-17

This publication has been printed on paper certified by the Programme for
the Endorsement of Forest Certification (PEFC). PEFC is committed to
sustainable forest management through third party forest certification of
responsibly managed forests. For more info: www.pefc.org

Preface to the Fifth Edition

As in previous editions, the editors' aim is to provide a collection of cases illuminating the principles of Australian tort law. This edition also includes a number of non-Australian cases of historical or doctrinal importance in the development of modern Australian law or which, in the editors' view, are likely to represent Australian law on an issue where there is no Australian case in point. It is also the editors' aim to allow the cases to speak for themselves in order to give university teachers flexibility in the design of individual torts courses around a core of significant cases, and to provide students with, as much as is practicable, experience in reading and comprehending primary sources of law.

The significant case law developments since the fourth edition have required the addition and deletion of material throughout the book. A development of particular significance in Australian tort law in the past decade has been the civil liability legislation enacted in each State and Territory and by the Commonwealth parliament in response to recommendations contained in the *Final Report of the Review of the Law of Negligence* submitted to the Commonwealth government in September 2002 by a panel chaired by Justice David Ipp. In varying degrees this legislation, sometimes in convoluted language, seeks to modify or abrogate aspects of the common law of negligence particularly (but not exclusively) in cases of personal injury and death. The editors of this book believe that an understanding of the common law, especially its principled exposition by the High Court of Australia, continues to be essential in the interpretation of this legislation, and in the education of law students who may practise in other common law jurisdictions.

Regrettably, and contrary to the recommendation of the Ipp panel, the civil liability legislation is not uniform throughout Australia, limiting the national relevance of case law on particular provisions. An example is the decision in *Wicks v State Rail Authority of New South Wales; Sheehan v State Rail Authority of New South Wales* (2010) 241 CLR 60 where, in the context of a claim for damages for psychiatric injury suffered by police officers who attended the scene of a rail accident, the High Court of Australia was called upon to construe particular provisions of the *Civil Liability Act 2002* (NSW). However, while some other Australian jurisdictions have identical provisions, others have a modified version of the New South Wales legislation or no equivalent provisions at all.

As with previous editions, this edition will have the benefit of the publisher's website where edited versions of new cases within the scope of the book may be accessed under "Book Supplements". The publisher's website address is: <www.federationpress.com.au>.

The editors wish to thank Edward Anderson, BA, LLB (Syd), for his research assistance in the preparation of this edition. Finally, the editors wish to acknowledge the substantial contribution to the previous editions of this book by Associate Professor Jane Swanton who, on her retirement after a working life of common law scholarship, elected not to participate in the preparation of new editions, and by our former colleague, Professor Stanley Yeo, now of the Faculty of Law at the National University of Singapore.

Barbara McDonald
Ross Anderson
May 2012

Contents

Table of Cases

(References in **Bold** are to extracts of cases)

Table of Statutes

Chapter 1

Historical Background

1. TRESPASS AND CASE

Scott v Shepherd
(1773) 96 ER 525
Court of Common Pleas

The settled distinction is that, where the injury is immediate (direct), an action for trespass will lie. Where the injury is consequential (indirect), it must be an action on the case.

[The defendant Shepherd threw a lighted squib (a kind of exploding firework containing gun powder) into a crowded market-house at Milborne Port, Somerset on fair day. The squib fell on Yates' gingerbread stand. Willis, instantly and to prevent injury to himself and damage to Yates' goods, picked up the squib and threw it across the market-house where it fell on Ryal's gingerbread stand. Ryal, instantly and to prevent damage to his goods, picked up the squib and threw it to another part of the market-house where it struck the plaintiff Scott in the face and exploded causing Scott to lose sight in one eye.

In the plaintiff's action for trespass, the jury found a verdict for the plaintiff and awarded him £100 damages subject to the opinion of the court as to whether trespass was maintainable on these facts.

A majority of the Court of Common Pleas, De Grey CJ, Nares and Gould JJ, gave judgment for the plaintiff. Although De Grey CJ and Blackstone J agreed on "the settled distinction" between trespass and an action on the case they disagreed on the application of that distinction to the facts of the case, Blackstone J being of the opinion that Shepherd had committed no trespass against Scott.]

> BLACKSTONE J. [dissenting] … . **[526]** The settled distinction is that, where the injury is immediate, an action of trespass will lie; where it is only consequential, it must be an action on the case: *Reynolds v Clarke* (1725) 2 Ld Raym 1399 at 1401 … . [I]t is held by the Court in the same case, that if I throw a log of timber into the highway, (which is an unlawful act), and another man tumbles over it, and is hurt, an action on the case only lies, it being a consequential damage; but if in throwing it I hit another man, he may bring trespass, because it is an immediate wrong. **[527]** [T]he solid distinction is between direct or immediate injuries on the one hand, and mediate or consequential on the other. And trespass never lay for the latter. If this be so, the only question will be whether the injury which the plaintiff suffered was immediate or consequential only; and I hold it to be the latter.

1

The original act was as against Yates a trespass; not as against Ryal or Scott. The tortious act was complete when the squib lay at rest upon Yates's stall. He, or any bystander, had, I allow, a right to protect themselves by removing the squib, but should have taken care to do it in such a manner as not to endamage others. But Shepherd, I think, is not answerable in an action of trespass and assault for the mischief done by the squib in the new motion impressed upon it and the new direction given it by either Willis or Ryal, who both were free agents and acted upon their own judgment. ...Here the instrument of mischief was at rest till a new impetus and a new direction were given it, not once only, but by two successive rational agents. ...

But it is said, if Scott has no action against Shepherd, against whom must he seek his remedy? I give no opinion whether Case would lie against Shepherd for the consequential damage, though, as at present advised, I think upon the circumstances it would. But I think, in strictness of law, Trespass would lie against Ryal, the immediate actor in this unhappy business. Both he and Willis have exceeded the bounds of self-defence and not used sufficient circumspection in removing the danger from themselves. The throwing it across the market-house, instead of brushing it down or throwing it out of the open sides into the street ... was at least an unnecessary and incautious act. ...

[528] It is said by Lord Raymond, and very justly, in *Reynolds v Clarke* (1725) 1 Stra 635 [in another report of the case], 'we must keep up the boundaries of actions, otherwise we shall introduce the utmost confusion.' As I therefore think no immediate injury passed from the defendant to the plaintiff, (and without such immediate injury no action of trespass can be maintained), I am of opinion that in this action judgment ought to be for the defendant. ...

DE GREY CJ. **[528]** This case is one of those wherein the line drawn by the law between actions on the case and actions of trespass is very nice and delicate. Trespass is an injury accompanied with force, for which an action of trespass vi et armis lies against the person from whom it is received. The question here is whether the injury received by the plaintiff arises from the force of the original act of the defendant or from a new force by a third person. I agree with my Brother Blackstone as to the principles he has laid down, but not in his application of those principles to the present case. ... [T]he true question is whether the injury is the direct and immediate act of the defendant: and I am of opinion that in this case it is. ...

Every one who does an unlawful act is considered as the doer of all that follows. ... **[529]** I look upon all that was done subsequent to the original throwing as a continuation of the first force and first act, which will continue till the squib was spent by bursting. And I think that any innocent person removing the danger from himself to another is justifiable; the blame lights upon the first thrower. The new direction and new force flow out of the first force, and are not a new trespass. ... It has been urged that the intervention of a free agent will make a difference: but I do not consider Willis and Ryal as free agents in the present case, but acting under a compulsive necessity for their own safety and self-preservation. On these reasons I concur with my Brothers Gould and Nares, that the present action is maintainable.

Judgment for the plaintiff

Hutchins v Maughan
[1947] VLR 131
Supreme Court of Victoria

In applying the settled distinction between trespass and case, an interference with the plaintiff will be direct when it follows so immediately in terms of causation upon the defendant's act as to be part of that act.

HERRING CJ. **[132]** This is an order to review a decision of a police magistrate in which, on a special complaint, he awarded the complainant the sum of £50. The claim arose out of the loss by the complainant of two sheep dogs. They both died as a result of picking up poisonous baits laid by the defendant. The baits were laid on unfenced land at Balwyn. On this land the defendant was accustomed to graze his horses.

The complainant is a drover and on Easter Saturday 1944 he was droving in the vicinity 2,000 ewes. On his way to some unfenced land north of the land where the baits were picked up he met the defendant, and was told by him that the paddock north of the Sanctuary in the vicinity was poisoned. With regard to the land where the baits were picked up he was also warned that there were baits all along the creek. The complainant apparently thought the defendant was bluffing about the poison along the creek, and a day or so later rode down along the creek with his dogs. He saw no sign of baits and two days later moved his sheep in and brought his dogs with him. Shortly after the dogs picked up baits and died.

The complainant's claim was laid alternatively in negligence, nuisance or trespass. The police magistrate upheld the defences taken so far as negligence and nuisance were concerned, but gave judgment for the complainant for his trespass claim. Before me it was conceded that the police magistrate was right in his decision as to negligence and nuisance. And the only question argued before me was whether on the facts of the case the police magistrate could properly enter judgment as he did for the complainant on his trespass claim. The laying of the baits was admittedly an unlawful act, and consequently it was not disputed that the complainant had a cause of action for the injuries he suffered as a consequence thereof. But it was contended for the defendant that such cause of action sounded only in case and not in trespass, and that the complainant having failed in his claims in case, viz, those for nuisance and negligence, is now without remedy.

The basis of the defendant's contention was that the injury suffered by the complainant in the present case was not occasioned by but was merely consequential upon the defendant's act complained of, viz, the laying of the baits, and so was not a trespass. The principle was thus stated in 1725 in *Reynolds v Clarke* (1725) 2 Ld Raym 1399, at p 1402: "The distinction in law is, where the immediate act itself occasions a prejudice, or is an injury to the plaintiff's person, house, land, etc, and where the act itself is not an injury, but a consequence from that act is prejudicial to the plaintiff's person, house, land, etc. In the first case trespass *vi et armis* will lie; in the last it will not, but the plaintiff's proper remedy is by an action on the case."

[133] In 1773 in the famous case of *Scott v Shepherd* (1773) 2 Wm Bl 892, at p 894, Blackstone J said he "took the settled distinction to be that where the injury is *immediate*, an action of trespass will lie; where it is only *consequential*, it must be an action on the case." And he cited the example of a man's throwing a log into the highway; an example later made use of by Le Blanc J in 1803 in *Leame v Bray* (1803) 3 East 593, at pp 602-3 where the learned Judge said: "But in all the books the invariable principle to be collected is that where the injury is immediate on the act done, there trespass lies; but where it is not immediate on the act done, but consequential, there the remedy is in case. And the distinction is well instanced by the example put of a man's throwing a log into the highway; if at the time of its being thrown it hit any person, it is trespass; but if after it be thrown any person going along the road receive an injury by falling over it as it lies there, it is case … trespass is the proper remedy for an immediate injury done by one to another; but where the injury is only consequential from the act done, there it is case."

And that the question whether the injury is immediate or consequential is still vital, in spite of procedural reforms, and that the old rule still applies that injury that is consequential is not a trespass, is made clear in an article by Professors Goodhart and Winfield in the *Law Quarterly Review* for 1933, vol 49 p 359 at p 366. See, too, *Salmond on Torts* (7th ed 1928), p 230, where the learned author says: "To constitute a trespass, however, it is not enough that the injury should be forcible; it must be also direct and not merely consequential. An injury is said to be direct when it follows so immediately upon the act of the defendant that it may be termed part of that act; it is consequential on the other hand, when, by reason of some obvious and visible intervening cause, it is regarded, not as part of the defendant's act, but merely as a consequence of it. In direct injuries the defendant is charged in an action of trespass with having done the act complained of; in consequential injuries he is charged in an action of case with having done something else, by reason of which (*per quod*) the thing complained of has come about." The learned author in a footnote to p 231 points out that the distinction does not seem to possess any logical basis. And he adds – "The distinction between an act and its consequences – between doing a mischief and causing one – seems to be nothing more than an indeterminable difference in degree."

Each case must, of course, be determined on its own facts and in the present case the question is whether on its facts the injury the complainant suffered in the loss of his dogs was immediate or consequential, that is to say, whether it was directly occasioned by the defendant's act in laying the baits or was merely consequential upon that act. Now [134] the baits were laid by the defendant before the complainant took his dogs on to the land in question. They may even have been laid before he arrived in the vicinity. And had he not chosen to come into the vicinity and bring his dogs with him he would have suffered no injury from the defendant's act. Nor indeed would he have done so, had he not taken his dogs on to the land where the baits were laid. The doing of the act therefore of itself did him no mischief. Before he could suffer an injury, he had himself to intervene by coming to the land and bringing his dogs thereon.

In these circumstances the injury he suffered cannot, in my opinion, be said to have followed so immediately in point of causation upon the act of the defendant as to be termed part of that act. It should rather be regarded merely as consequential upon it and not as directly or immediately occasioned by it. And so trespass does not lie in respect of defendant's act in laying the baits. Had the baits been thrown by the defendant to the complainant's dogs, then no doubt the injury could properly have been regarded as directly occasioned by the act of the defendant, so that trespass would lie. As it was, it was necessary for the complainant himself to bring his dogs with him to the baits in order that the injurious consequences, of which he complains, should result from the defendant's act. His position is like that of the man who, going along the road upon which a log has been thrown, receives an injury by falling over it. In such a case the man who threw the log upon the road has, of course, caused the mischief, but trespass does not lie, as the injury is consequential upon his act and not immediately or directly occasioned thereby. Had the man who fell over the log not passed that way, he would have suffered no injury from the other's act. …

[136] In my opinion in the present case the police magistrate was wrong in holding that the complainant's claim in trespass was maintainable. The order *nisi* will be made absolute and the complaint dismissed.

Order absolute

Bird v Holbrook
(1828) 130 ER 911
Court of Common Pleas

A person who does an act intending to cause injury to another person may be liable in damages in an action on the case where the injury caused was an indirect consequence of the act.

[The plaintiff brought an action on the case for damages for personal injuries suffered when he entered the defendant's walled flower garden for the innocent purpose of retrieving a stray pea-hen and was shot in the leg by a spring gun, set by the defendant, after a recent theft of valuable flowers, in the hope of catching any intending thief.]

BEST CJ. [916] I am of the opinion that this action is maintainable. …

It has been argued that the law does not compel every line of conduct which humanity or religion may require; but there is no act which Christianity forbids, that the law will not reach; if it were otherwise, Christianity would not be, as it has always been held to be, part of the law of England. I am therefore, clearly of opinion that he who sets spring guns, without giving notice, is guilty of an inhuman act, and that, if injurious consequences ensue, he is liable to yield redress to the sufferer. But this case stands on grounds distinct from any that have preceded it. In general, spring guns have been set for the purpose of deterring; the Defendant placed his for the express purpose of doing injury; for, when called on to give notice, he said, "If I give notice, I shall not catch him." He intended therefore, that the gun should be discharged, and that the contents should be lodged in the body of his victim, for he could not be caught in any other way. On these principles the action is clearly maintainable, and particularly on the latter ground. …

[917] But we want no authority in a case like the present; we put it on the principle that it is inhuman to catch a man by means which may maim him or endanger his life, and, as far as human means can go, it is the object of English law to uphold humanity, and the sanctions of religion. It would be, indeed, a subject of regret, if a party were not liable in damages, who, instead of giving notice of the employment of a destructive engine, or removing it, at least, during the day, expressed a resolution to withhold notice, lest, by affording it, he should fail to entrap his victim.

BURROUGH J. The common understanding of mankind shews [sic], that notice ought to be given when these means of protection are resorted to … The Plaintiff was only a trespasser: if the Defendant had been present, he would not have been authorised even in taking him into custody, and no man can do indirectly that which he is forbidden to do directly. …

[918] Here, no notice whatever was given but the Defendant artfully abstained from giving it, and he must take the consequence. …

[Park and Gaselee JJ concurred.]

Judgment for the plaintiff

Williams v Holland
(1833) 131 ER 848
Court of Common Pleas

Where the plaintiff is injured by the defendant's direct (or immediate) act, the plaintiff may elect to bring an action on the case (rather than trespass) provided that the defendant's act is negligent. However, where the defendant's act is both direct and intentional, the only cause of action available to the plaintiff is trespass.

TINDAL CJ. [849] This was an action on the case, in which the declaration states that the Plaintiff was possessed of a cart, and horse drawing the same, in which cart were the Plaintiff's son and daughter, and that Defendant was possessed of a gig, and horse drawing the same, "which gig and horse were then under the care, &c of Defendant, who was driving the same in and along the highway": nevertheless Defendant "so carelessly, unskilfully, and improperly drove, &c his said gig and horse," that through the carelessness of the Defendant the said gig and horse of Defendant ran and struck with great violence upon and against the horse and cart of Plaintiff, and thereby broke to pieces the same, and the son and daughter of Plaintiff were greatly hurt, &c. The Defendant pleaded the general issue; and on the trial the question left to the jury was, whether the injury was occasioned by the negligence and carelessness of the Defendant; which question the jury found in the affirmative, and gave their verdict for the Plaintiff, with £12 damages. After the trial, the present rule [*nisi*] was obtained for setting aside the verdict and entering a nonsuit, under leave given for that purpose, upon the ground that the injury having been occasioned by the immediate act of the Defendant himself, the action ought to have been trespass, and that the case [sic] was not maintainable; and amongst other cases cited by the Defendant's counsel in support of this objection, that of *Leame v Bray* (1803) 3 East 593 was principally relied upon as an authority in point.

The declaration, in this case, states the ground of action to be an injury occasioned by the carelessness and negligence of the Defendant in driving his own gig; and that such carelessness and negligence is, strictly and properly in itself, the subject of an action on the case, would appear, if any authority were wanting, from Com Dig tit Action upon the Case for Negligence; and the jury have found in the very terms of the declaration, that the injury was so occasioned. Under such a form of action, therefore, and with such a finding by the jury, the present objection ought not to prevail, unless some positive and inflexible rule of law, or some authority too strong to be overcome, is brought forward in its support. If such are to be found, they must, undoubtedly, be adhered to; for settled forms of action, adapted to different grievances, contribute much to the certain administration of justice.

But upon examining the cases cited in argument, both in support of, and in answer to, the objection, we cannot find one in which it is distinctly held, that the present form of action is not maintainable under the circumstances of this case.

For as to *Leame v Bray*, on which the principal reliance is placed by the Defendant, in which the form of action was trespass, and the circumstances very nearly the same as those in the case now under consideration, the only rule established is, that an action of trespass might be maintained, not that an action on the case could not. The case of *Savignac v Roome* (1794) 6 TR 125, in which the Court held that case would not lie where the defendant's servant wilfully drove against the plaintiff's carriage, was founded on the principle, that no action would lie against the master for the wilful act of his servant; and in that of *Day v Edwards* (1794) 5 TR 648, in which it was ruled that trespass was the proper remedy, and not case, it should be observed that the question arose upon a special demurrer to the declaration; and that the declaration stated that the defendant "so furiously, negligently, and improperly drove his cart and horse, that through the furious, negligent, and improper conduct of the defendant, the cart and horse were driven and struck with great force and violence upon and against the carriage of the plaintiff;" the question therefore arising upon a special demurrer, where the Court could look to nothing but the legal construction of the declaration, is very differently circumstanced from this, where the jury have found that negligence was the ground of the injury. On the other hand, the cases of *Rogers v Imbleton* **[850]** (1806) 2 NR 119, and *Ogle v Barnes* (1799) 8 TR 188, are simply in favour of the proposition, that the present form of action, is, under the circumstances, maintainable.

We hold it, however, to be unnecessary, to examine very minutely the grounds of the various decisions; for the late case of *Moreton v Hardern* 4 B&C 223, appears to us to go the full length of deciding, that where the injury is occasioned by the carelessness and negligence of the Defendant, although it be occasioned by his immediate act, the Plaintiff may, if he thinks proper, make the negligence of the Defendant the ground of his action, and declare in case. …

We think the case last above referred to has laid down a plain and intelligible rule, that where the injury is occasioned by the carelessness and negligence of the Defendant, the Plaintiff is at liberty to bring an action on the case, notwithstanding the act is immediate, so long as it is not a wilful act; and, upon the authority of that case, we think the present form of action maintainable to recover damages for the injury.

Rule nisi discharged

Williams v Milotin
(1957) 97 CLR 465
High Court of Australia

The principle in Williams v Holland is part of Australian law.

THE COURT. [DIXON CJ, McTIERNAN, WILLIAMS, WEBB and KITTO JJ] … **[469]** The action was brought by an infant by his next friend to recover damages for personal injuries sustained by the plaintiff in consequence, as he alleged, of being struck while riding his bicycle in the street by a motor truck which was driven by the defendant in a negligent manner. The date assigned by the statement of claim for the occurrence is 7th May 1952. The writ of summons in the action was issued on 19th July 1955, that is to say more than three years after the alleged cause of action arose but less than six years. By a paragraph of the defence the defendant pleaded that the action was barred by s 36 of the *Limitation of Actions Act 1936-1948* (SA). The question referred to the Full Court was the validity of this plea. The Court decided against the validity of the plea and declared that the action was not barred by s 36 of the *Limitation of Actions Act 1936-1948*. At the same time the court ordered that the defendant should have leave to appeal to this Court.

Section 36 provides that all actions for assault trespass to the person menace battery wounding or imprisonment shall be commenced within three years next after the cause of such action accrued but not after. Section 35 enumerates a number of actions which must be commenced within six years next after the cause of action accrued and not after. The list includes actions on the case. The material parts of s 35 are as follows – "35. The following actions namely – ... (*c*) actions which formerly might have been brought in the form of actions called actions on the case: ... (*k*) actions for libel malicious prosecution arrest or seduction and any other actions which would formerly have been brought in the form of actions called trespass on the case: shall, save as otherwise provided in this Act, be commenced within six years next after the cause of such action accrued but not after." The contention for the plaintiff is that the action he has brought falls within s 35 as one which might have been brought in the form of action called action on the case or trespass on the case. The defendant's contention is that s 35 operates only subject to the qualification expressed by the words "save as otherwise provided in this Act" and that, even if the action could have been brought in case, it could have been brought in trespass as an action of trespass to the person so as to fall under s 36.

In support of this contention the defendant's starting point is that the action the plaintiff has brought could formerly have been properly framed as an action of trespass to the person.

The word "formerly" seems to mean prior to the passing of the *Supreme Court Act 1878* of South Australia, by which the "judicature **[470]** system" was adopted: cf definition in s 5 of the *Supreme Court Act 1935* (SA).

At that time the present action might have been framed as an action of trespass. For it seems that the facts which the plaintiff, by his next friend, intends to allege are that he was immediately or directly hit by the motor car driven by the defendant as a result of the negligence of the defendant himself. There is no suggestion that the defendant intended to strike him. If that had been the allegation the action could have been brought in trespass and not otherwise. But as only the negligence of the defendant is relied upon, while the cause of action might have been laid as trespass to the person, the action might also have been brought as an action on the case to recover special or particular damage caused by the defendant's negligence. Had the damage been caused indirectly or mediately by the defendant or by his servant (a state of things to be distinguished from violence immediately caused by the defendant's own act) the action must have been brought as an action on the case and not otherwise. See *Leame v Bray* (1803) 3 East 593; *Williams v Holland* (1833) 10 Bing 112; *Sharrod v London and NW Railway Co* (1849) 4 Ex 580; and *Holmes v Mather* (1875) LR 10 Ex 261; cf *Stanley v Powell* [1891] 1 QB 86 and the comment thereon in *Fifoot: History and Sources of the Common Law (Tort and Contract)* (1949), pp 188, 189. See too the note in *Smith's Leading Cases* in the sixth (1867) and previous editions under *Scott v Shepherd*. ...

[472] It is indisputable that the facts, had they occurred a century ago, would have supported a count framed in trespass to the person, if it had been included in the declaration. Does that mean that, by reason of the words "save as otherwise provided in this Act", the limitation of six years contained in s 35 is inapplicable and the limitation of three years contained in s 36 applies?

We do not think the words "save as otherwise provided in this Act" have any application to the problem. They were not directed in any way to the possibility that it should be found that causes of action fell under s 36 although they also fell under s 35. ...

[473] When you put aside the suggestion that these words affect the matter, the problem is reduced to the simple position that on the same set of facts two causes of action arose to which different periods of limitation were respectively affixed. In saying that two causes of action arose no more is meant than that two traditional categories continue to exist in the contemplation of the material provisions of s 35(*c*) and (*k*) and s 36 and that there is no difficulty in distinguishing between the categories either notionally or historically.

[474] Plainly enough the plaintiff relies on the category which we commonly call negligence but which the statute looks at as an action of the kind which once was brought for the recovery of special or particular damage caused by conduct on the part of the defendant making it actionable, in this instance negligence. Why should the plaintiff's action be limited by any other period of time than that appropriate to the cause of action on which he sues? The two causes of action are not the same now and they never were. When you speak of a cause of action you mean the essential ingredients in the title to the right which it is proposed to enforce. The essential ingredients in an action of negligence for personal injuries include the special or particular damage – it is the gist of the action – and the want of due care. Trespass to the person includes neither. But it does include direct violation of the protection which the law throws round the person. It is true that in the absence of intention of some kind or want of due care, a violation occurring in the course of traffic in a thoroughfare is not actionable as a trespass. It is unnecessary to inquire how that comes about. It is perhaps a modification of the general law of trespass to the person. But it does not mean that trespass is the same as actionable negligence occasioning injury. It happens in this case that the actual facts will or may fulfil the requirements of each cause of action. ...

In our opinion the decision of the Supreme Court is right and the appeal should be dismissed.

Appeal dismissed

[In *New South Wales v Lepore; Samin v Queensland; Rich v Queensland* (2003) 195 ALR 412 (cases concerned with the liability of school authorities for the sexual assault of primary school pupils committed by teachers at school), Gummow and Hayne JJ observed at 480:

270. As *Williams v Milotin* (1957) 97 CLR 465 at 470 makes plain, negligently inflicted injury to the person can, in at least some circumstances, be pleaded as trespass to the person, but the intentional infliction of harm cannot be pleaded as negligence. ...]

2. FAULT IN TRESPASS

Weaver v Ward
(1616) 80 ER 284
Court of Common Pleas

There is no liability in trespass where the trespassory act was committed without fault by the defendant.

[The plaintiff, Thomas Weaver, alleged that the defendant, George Ward, had shot and wounded him during a military training exercise on 18 October 1614 in the parish of St Mary-le-Bow, London. The full text of the report by Sir Henry Hobart CJCP, who presided at the trial, follows.]

Weaver brought an action of trespass of assault and battery against Ward. The defendant pleaded, that he was amongst others by the commandment of the Lords of the Council a trained soldier in London, of the band of one Andrews captain; and so was the plaintiff, and that they were skirmishing with their musquets charged with powder for their exercise in re militari, against another captain and his band; and as they were so skirmishing, the defendant casualiter & per infortunium & contra voluntatem suam, in discharging of his piece did hurt and wound the plaintiff, which is the same, &c. absque hoc, that he was guilty aliter sive alio modo. And upon demurrer by the plaintiff, judgment was given for him; for though it were agreed, that if men tilt or turney in the presence of the King, or if two masters of defence playing their prizes kill one another, that this shall be no felony; or if a lunatick kill a man, or the like, because felony must be done animo felonico: yet in trespass, which tends only to give damages according to hurt or loss, it is not so; and therefore if a lunatick hurt a man, he shall be answerable in trespass: and therefore no man shall be excused of a trespass (for this is the nature of an excuse, and not of a justification, prout ei bene licuit) except it may be judged utterly without his fault.

As if a man by force take my hand and strike you, or if here the defendant had said, that the plaintiff ran cross his piece when it was discharging, or had set forth the case with the circumstances, so as it had appeared to the Court that it had been inevitable, and that the defendant had committed no negligence to give occasion to the hurt.

Judgment for the plaintiff

Venning v Chin
(1974) 10 SASR 299
Supreme Court of South Australia, Full Court

As a general rule, in trespass the onus is on the defendant to disprove fault. However, in trespass for injury caused in a highway accident, the onus is on the plaintiff to prove fault on the part of the defendant.

[The plaintiff (appellant) suffered personal injuries when she was struck by a car, driven by the defendant (respondent), while crossing a public road.

In the plaintiff's action for damages the trial judge found the plaintiff guilty of contributory negligence in crossing the road without due regard for her own safety. In respect of the defendant's conduct the trial judge was unable to find positively that the defendant was guilty of negligence. However, the trial judge also was unable to find positively that the defendant was *not* guilty of negligence. Accordingly, on the ground that the defendant had failed to prove absence of fault on his part, the trial judge held that the plaintiff was entitled to recover damages for trespass to the person. The trial judge also held that the amount of the damages should be reduced by 60% under the apportionment legislation, s 27a of the *Wrongs Act 1936-1971* (SA), on account of the plaintiff's contributory negligence.

The plaintiff appealed and the defendant cross-appealed. The Supreme Court (In Banco) disagreed with the trial judge's findings of fact in respect of the defendant's conduct. The Court held that the defendant was guilty of negligence causing the plaintiff's injuries. A majority of the Court (Bray CJ and Bright J; Jacobs J dissenting) also held that the correct apportionment of responsibility for the plaintiff's injuries was 40% to the plaintiff and 60% to the defendant. Jacobs J would not have disturbed the trial judge's apportionment of responsibility.

In respect of the operation of the apportionment legislation, the Court was of the opinion that the legislation applied whether the plaintiff's action was framed as one of trespass to the person or as an action on the case for negligence. However, in reaching this conclusion the Court was required to consider the availability of an action of trespass to the person and the onus of proof.]

BRAY CJ. ... **[306] Is trespass still available for injuries caused by negligence?** ...
I think this question is concluded in Australia in favour of an affirmative answer.

Under the old system the boundary lines between trespass and case were not easy to draw, though the Judges insisted that they should be drawn and that "the boundaries of actions" should be kept up (*Reynolds v Clarke* (1725) 1 Str 634, at p 635, per Lord Raymond CJ). The true criterion was whether the injury was immediate on the act of the defendant himself or only consequential on that act or was caused by the act of his servant. But confusion was introduced by another suggested distinction, that between wilful and negligent injuries. However, in 1803 in *Leame v Bray* (1803) 3 East 593, it was held that trespass would lie for a highway accident caused by the direct act of the defendant in driving his carriage against the carriage of the plaintiff, even though that driving was negligent, not wilful. From then on trespass was not infrequently brought for highway accidents without demur (*Cotterill v* **[307]** *Starkey* (1839) 8 C&P 691; *Holmes v Mather* (1875) LR 10 Ex 261), though in more recent times its use for such a purpose has been deprecated (*Elliott v Barnes* (1951) 51 SR (NSW) 179; *Australian National Airways Ltd v Philips* [1953] SASR 278), though not denied (see *Elliott v Barnes* (1951) 51 SR (NSW) 179, per Maxwell J at p 182) until 1965, and case for various reasons was the normal remedy for negligent injuries caused by highway accidents, whether the injuries were direct or consequential.

But in *Letang v Cooper* [1965] 1 QB 232, 162 years after *Leame v Bray* (1803) 3 East 593, Lord Denning MR is reported as saying that if the injury was inflicted unintentionally the plaintiff had no cause of action today in trespass but "his only cause of action is in negligence" (p 239). I must say, with respect, that this seems to me to be judicial legislation. In *Admiralty Commissioners v SS Amerika* [1917] AC 38 the House of Lords refused to disturb a common law rule of venerable antiquity, though of dubious justice or utility. Lord Loreburn said at p 41: "When a rule has become inveterate from the earliest time, as this rule appears to have been, it would be legislation pure and simple were we to disturb it." I realise that there will always be disagreement between judges as to the respective claims of authority and progressive innovation and that the earliest times of the law are considerably anterior to the year 1803. Nevertheless I do not think, with respect, that the courts have power to legislate so as to deprive plaintiffs of a remedy which they have enjoyed for over a century and a half. ...

Anyhow it seems to me that we are concluded in this matter by the decision of the High Court in *Williams v Milotin* (1957) 97 CLR 465. ...

[308] *Williams v Milotin* (1957) 97 CLR 465 and *Letang v Cooper* [1965] 1 QB 232 cannot stand together. ... It is the High Court's decision which binds us and it is immaterial that I would have come to the same conclusion in its absence. ... In my view, an action for trespass was open to the appellant on the present facts. ...

[310] Onus of proof

There was for long a dispute about whether or not trespass to the person was an absolute wrong in the sense that if there was a direct unjustified voluntary act of force on the part of the defendant against the plaintiff's person or property the defendant was liable, whether his action was intentional or negligent or neither. That controversy was finally put to rest, I think, by *Stanley v Powell* [1891] 1 QB 86. It is true that that decision was only the decision of a single Judge, Denman J. It is true also that it did not relate to a highway accident, though highway accidents, I should think, were *a fortiori*. But it was approved by the Court of Appeal in *National Coal Board v Evans & Co (Cardiff) Ltd* [1951] 2 KB 861 and by Windeyer J in *McHale v Watson* (1964) 111 CLR 384, at pp 387-388. Indeed, I think the principle that the defendant is not liable in trespass if his act was neither intentional nor negligent is implicit in the famous case of *Weaver v Ward* (1616) Hob 134 [where the court said: "No man shall be excused of a trespass except it be judged utterly without his fault"]. I do not pause, therefore, to enter into the academic controversy about the matter and I take it that there is no liability in trespass for the use of force against the person which is neither intentional nor negligent.

In my view there is no doubt that under the old system it was for the defendant in trespass to allege and prove any justificatory or excusatory matter by a special plea. ...

[311] At this time [the early 19th century] the onus of disproving negligence was clearly on the defendant but, as the learned [trial] Judge said, in the course of time various heresies have arisen and heresies sometimes become orthodoxies, and there is a prevalent view that, whatever the position may once have been, the law now is that if the plaintiff sues in trespass he must prove that the act of the defendant was either intentional or negligent. There are two varieties of this doctrine, a general doctrine applying to all cases, and a particular doctrine applying to highway accidents only.

The wider doctrine was upheld by Diplock J, as he then was, in *Fowler v Lanning* [1959] 1 QB 426. That was not a case of a highway accident but a case of shooting on private property and the learned Judge held that the onus lay on the plaintiff to prove that the shooting was either intentional or negligent and that, as the statement of claim alleged neither, it disclosed no cause of action. It will be obvious from what I have said about the pleading point that, with great respect, I do not agree. The learned Judge held further that there was no difference between highway cases and other cases, and he relied on dicta from highway cases. This is an illustration of how authorities for an exception to a rule can be used to subvert the rule entirely on the ground that there is no difference between the cases covered by the exception and the remainder of the cases covered by the rule. With respect, I cannot agree with this approach, but I will revert to the topic.

Again, however, I think that in Australia the matter is concluded. In **[312]** *McHale v Watson* (1964) 111 CLR 384, Windeyer J held that the onus of proof was on the defendant. That, too, was not a highway case but a case of the throwing of a piece of sharp metal on private property. The learned Judge held that the onus was on the defendant to prove that the throwing in question was neither intentional nor negligent. He followed the decision of the Full Court of New South Wales in *Blacker v Waters* (1928) 28 SR (NSW) 406. He refused to follow *Fowler v Lanning* [1959] 1

QB 426 or other authorities to the like effect. His view has the weighty support of the Supreme Court of Canada in *Cook v Lewis* [1952] 1 DLR 1, and it was followed by Walters AJ in this State in *Tsouvalla v Bini* [1966] SASR 157. In *Stanley v Powell* [1891] 1 QB 86 itself the learned Judge seemed to assume that if the action lay in trespass the onus was on the defendant to disprove negligence; see at p 94.

It is true that in *McHale v Watson* (1964) 111 CLR 384, Windeyer J was sitting in the original jurisdiction of the High Court. The case went to appeal on another point ((1966) 115 CLR 199), but the learned Judges expressed no dissent from the remarks of Windeyer J about the onus of proof. However, I think that I should follow his decision, the more so because, with respect, I agree with it. It seems to me to be clearly in accord with the older authorities and I do not know of any binding authority to the contrary before *Fowler v Lanning* [1959] 1 QB 426 except highway cases.

It remains, however, to consider whether or not there is an exception with regard to highway accidents. There are dicta which seem to say that those who use the highway or have premises adjoining the highway must be taken to have impliedly accepted the risk of injury from contacts on the highway caused neither intentionally nor negligently. The difficulty is that it is often hard to ascertain whether the remarks in question are directed to onus of proof at all, or are rather directed to the question of whether liability exists for a trespass to the person or to property which is neither intentional or negligent. ...

[314] In *Australian National Airways Ltd v Phillips* [1953] SASR 278, at p 280, Ligertwood J said that the law was clear "that the overall onus was on the plaintiff to prove negligence on the part of the defendant". That was a case of alternative claims in trespass and negligence and a case of a vehicle running off the highway into a window. With respect, it is not so clear to me. But on the whole I think that he was right and that the exception has become established in the case of claims in trespass arising out of highway accidents. ...

[315] But I see no reason, with respect, to extend the assumption of risk to all cases of trespass as did Diplock J in *Fowler v Lanning* [1959] 1 QB 426, at p 439 on the ground that "the plaintiff must today in this crowded world be considered as taking upon himself the risk of inevitable injury from any acts of his neighbour which, in the absence of damage to the plaintiff, would not in themselves be unlawful." In the first place, I think it is contrary to authority to do so and that the exception cannot eat up the rule. In the next place, I doubt, with respect, the reality of any implied acceptance of the risk of being shot. ...

If I am right, it will have to be decided some day what is a highway accident for this purpose. A collision between vehicles or between a vehicle and a pedestrian on the highway here is clearly covered; so, in view of the dicta previously referred to, are damage to property adjoining the highway caused by a vehicle running off the highway and contacts [316] between things lowered or carried out of such property with people using the highway. But I need not pursue the matter here.

In summary, I think that I am bound by *McHale v Watson* (1964) 111 CLR 384 and the other authorities to which I have referred to hold that in trespass generally the onus lies on the defendant to disprove negligence, but also I think that the weight of authority favours the proposition that highway accidents are an exception to this rule and that in trespass for injury on the highway the onus is on the plaintiff to prove either intention or negligence on the part of the defendant. ...

[323] In my opinion the cross-appeal should be dismissed and the appeal should be allowed. ...

[Bright and Jacobs JJ agreed with Bray CJ's exposition of the law on the issue of onus of proof of fault in an action for damages for personal injuries sustained in a highway accident.]

Appeal allowed. Cross-appeal dismissed

[A further appeal by the defendant to the High Court of Australia was dismissed: *Chin v Venning* (1975) 49 ALJR 378. The High Court held that the Supreme Court of South Australia, Full Court had been correct in finding that the defendant was guilty of negligence causing the plaintiff's injuries. The High Court also agreed with the apportionment of responsibility for the plaintiff's injuries made by the Full Court. Although onus of proof of fault in trespass was not argued in the High Court, Gibbs J observed at 379 that the proposition that "a person injured in a running-down accident on the highway may, by suing in trespass, succeed in recovering damages without proving that the defendant driver was guilty of negligence or intentional wrongdoing" would be "contrary to the assumption on which thousands of collision cases have been conducted in Australia in recent years".]

Platt v Nutt
(1988) 12 NSWLR 231
Supreme Court of New South Wales, Court of Appeal

Onus of proof of the trespassory act is an issue distinct from onus of proof of fault. The plaintiff in trespass must prove that the defendant committed the trespassory act of which the plaintiff complains.

[The facts are stated in the judgment of Clarke JA. In a dissenting judgment, Kirby P found, on the evidence, that the plaintiff had proved the defendant's trespassory act and that the plaintiff also had proved the defendant's negligence in relation to that act (an issue the majority of the Court found unnecessary to decide). Kirby P's judgment is extracted on the issue of onus of proof of fault in trespass.]

KIRBY P. **[232]** … In *Fowler* [*v Lanning* [1959] 1 QB 426], his Lordship [Diplock J] supported the proposition that, in an action for trespass to the person, it was for the plaintiff to aver and prove that the act of the defendant was either intentional or negligent. More than three centuries earlier in *Weaver v Ward* (1616) 80 ER 284 it had been said that "no man shall be excused of a trespass … except it may be judged utterly without his fault". This appeal raises the question whether in an action framed in trespass to the person, on the one hand, is it for the plaintiff to prove that the defendant intended the acts constituting the trespass or that the damage suffered arose out of the defendant's negligence, or, on the other, is it for the defendant to prove, once the happening of the physical acts is established, that he did not intend to hit the plaintiff or that he was not negligent in acting as he did?

In *McHale v Watson* (1964) 111 CLR 384, Windeyer J, sitting as a single judge in the High Court of Australia, adhered to his conception of the traditional and historical approach in answering these questions. The relevant acts being proved, he held that the onus of establishing an absence of intent or negligence lay upon the defendant. More recently in *Hackshaw v Shaw* (1984) 155 CLR 614 at 619, Gibbs CJ expressed the view that the contrary opinion, as established in England in *Fowler*, was "the preferable one". In that case his Honour observed that it was perhaps unfortunate that "we are not now called upon to resolve this difference of opinion". …

[235] Burden of proof in trespass:
Neither the decision of Windeyer J in *McHale* nor the remarks to differing effect of Gibbs CJ (and also of Dawson J) in *Hackshaw* bind this Court to find one locus of the burden of proof in trespass in preference to the other. …

[236] One of the cases to which Bowie DCJ [primary judge in the present case] referred, and on which also Windeyer J relied in his decision in *McHale,* was the decision of the Full Court of the Supreme Court of New South Wales in *Blacker v Waters* (1928) 28 SR (NSW) 406. Like many such cases, *Blacker* involved an injury to a person caused by a bullet. The bullet in question had been fired by the defendant at a shooting gallery. It struck the plaintiff in the eye. P W Street CJ (with whom Ferguson and James JJ concurred) held that, once a prima facie case of trespass had been established, on the proof of the fact that the event which caused injury had arisen from the conduct of the defendant, the burden of proving that the act complained of was neither intentional nor negligent lay upon the defendant … .

In support of the principle expounded in *Blacker* and *McHale* it must be said that it has stood for some time and has been applied on several occasions not only by Windeyer J in the High Court but also by the Full Courts of other Supreme Courts in Australia: see, eg, *Exchange Hotel Ltd v Murphy* [1947] SASR 112 at 117; *Venning v Chin* (1974) 8 SASR 397 at 400, 410; reversed (1974)

10 SASR 299 at 310; *Lord v Nominal Defendant* (1980) 24 SASR 458 and *Shaw v Hackshaw* [1983] 2 VR 65 at 97, 113-114.

Quite apart from this weight of authority, some (although it must be said minority) academic opinion, and some policy considerations favour the approach adopted in *Blacker* and followed in *McHale*, notwithstanding developments to the contrary in other jurisdictions.

For example, in Professor Heuston's 16th edition of *Salmond on the Law of Torts* (1973) at 138, several points are made in defence of holding to this statement of the law. These included the fact that the distinction between trespass and case (the action in negligence being an example of the latter) is one deeply embedded in the history of the common law and should not therefore be abolished merely for reasons of symmetry or convenience. It is a distinction which "has always been the understanding of the profession". It has certain practical consequences, particularly "when the defendant is an infant of tender years against whom it will be difficult to establish intent or negligence"; or where a defendant, having denied fault on the pleadings, fails to appear in the trial: see *Tsouvalla v Bini* [1966] SASR 157. There may, moreover, be differences which concern the proper test for remoteness of damages; the accrual of the cause of action; the running of time under limitation statutes; the availability of contributory negligence as a defence; the necessity (or otherwise) to show actual damage or the entitlement to succeed without proof of damage.

In addition to these considerations which are of concern to the lawyer and [237] legal historian, there is a policy consideration which is rarely mentioned. The law of trespass dates back to the earliest times of the establishment of the legal system of England. Even in the most primitive of societies, it is necessary to establish criminal and civil remedies against violent conduct which not only harms the individual but endangers the peace. Accordingly, if people do dangerous things and what they do causes injury to others (or contributes to such injury), by putting the onus upon them to show the "innocence" of their conduct, the law may achieve both a general and a particular objective. The general is the discouragement of violent conduct in society. Thus, in an action for damages, it is necessary for the defendant to justify the conduct by proving that it was neither intentional nor negligent. The particular objective is to protect the victims of such trespatory conduct. Sometimes all that they will know is that they have suffered an injury. Frequently, they will not be in the position affirmatively to prove the intention of the person whose trespass causes the injury. Nor may they be in as good a position to prove negligence, as the alleged trespasser will be to negative both negligence and intention. In short, the objective of trespass, as a cause of action, remains the same today as it was in the beginning. It is to provide remedies to a person harmed by the trespass and, by the provision of such remedies and the assignment to the defendant of the burden of proof, to promote a peaceful society and discourage the kind of violent, aggressive or dangerous activities which may lead, with intent or negligence, to the injury of others. The principle in *Blacker* and *McHale* may contribute to the attainment of those objectives.

Those who assert must prove:
Although the foregoing arguments have force, the weight of judicial and academic opinion nowadays favours the contrary conclusion. The decision of Diplock J in *Fowler* followed the long established position in the United States of America by assigning the burden of proof of negligence to the plaintiff: see *Brown v Kendall* 60 Mass 292 (1850): see also Gregory, "Trespass to Negligence to Absolute Liability" 37 Va L Rev 359 (1951) and J G Fleming, *The Law of Torts*, 7th ed (1987) at 20. It also conformed to a decision of the Supreme Court of British Columbia in *Walmsley v Humenick* [1954] 2 DLR 232. It was immediately followed in New Zealand: see *Beals v Hayward* [1960] NZLR 131. ...

According to Professor Fleming (at 21) the reluctance of courts in Australia (and some parts of Canada) to follow the law as now long established in the United States (and as established since 1959 in England) finds its explanation "less in policy-tilt towards stricter liability than a misplaced cult of historicism". Certainly, an examination of the cases in the Australian courts adds strength to the accusation that the reasons for the differing approach taken by the courts of this country is rooted in the history of the causes of action in trespass to the person and in negligence and specifically in the history of the pleading of the forms of action which continued to follow their common law forms in this State until 1970. ...

[238] The only way of restoring a satisfactory conceptual approach and consistency in the assignment of the burden of proof in cases of trespass to the person in Australia is to bring other such cases into line with the law now clearly established as applicable in respect of trespass to the person by the use of a motor vehicle. The development of a different law on the burden of proof in motor vehicle collisions and in other cases of trespass is simply unprincipled.

If a more coherent approach is sought, it can be found by resort to the general rule which obtains in our courts, namely that those who assert must prove. That principle applies throughout the law. The uniform application of the principle in all cases of trespass to the person would have a number of advantages. In a stroke, it would remove the inconsistency which has arisen in the treatment of motor vehicle and non-motor vehicle trespasses. It would remove the tactical advantages which may arise if a plaintiff is free to choose whether to characterise and plead his action as one of trespass or negligence: see H Luntz, D Hambly and R Hayes, *Torts: Cases and Commentary* (2nd ed) (1985) at 572. It might also encourage the law to a reformulation of [239] the respective functions of trespass and negligence in the law of tort, reconciling the ancient cause of action in trespass to the more modern tort of negligence. ...

[240] In my opinion the time has come for this Court to take the step which Diplock J took in *Fowler* in England in 1959 and which McGregor J took in *Beals* in New Zealand in 1960. Such a change may readily be adopted by the Court, in the development of the common law. It involves not the definition of the cause of action itself but the assignment by the Court of the responsibility of proving it. By assigning the burden of proof to the person who asserts the wrong, the Court, far from departing from ordinary principle, is bringing this cause of action into conformity with the normal principle applied elsewhere. ...

CLARKE JA. [243] In the course of an emotional domestic upheaval the respondent [plaintiff] was injured when her hand penetrated a glass panel in the front door of a house which had until that day been the family home of her daughter and her son-in-law who is the appellant [defendant].

She sued the appellant for trespass to the person upon the basis that he had caused her injury by slamming the door on her.

The trial judge accepted the respondent's case that the appellant had slammed the door but rejected the contention that he had done so with the intention of injuring the respondent.

Accordingly he concluded the respondent could only succeed if her injury resulted from negligent conduct on the part of the appellant. There is nothing controversial about this conclusion. It is established that if injury to a person is the direct result of a defendant's act the plaintiff will be entitled to succeed in trespass although the injury was not intended by the defendant if it resulted from his negligence.

There has however been much controversy on the question of onus. On one view, which was articulated with much force by Diplock J, as he then was, in *Fowler v Lanning* [1959] 1 QB 426, the plaintiff bears the onus of establishing negligence on the part of the alleged trespasser. According to this view the onus is similarly placed whether the cause of action is trespass or negligence. The opposing view is that once the plaintiff has shown that she was injured as a direct consequence of the defendant's act she is prima facie entitled to succeed in trespass. In order to defeat the claim the defendant bears the onus of establishing justification, for instance, self-defence, lack of intent or an absence of negligence.

The latter view, which was recently applied by Windeyer J in *McHale v Watson* (1964) 111 CLR 384 at 389, was, at least until *Fowler*, the traditional view in both England and Australia.

The trial judge's conclusion that the appellant had not intended to injure the respondent led him to consider whether negligence, or an absence of negligence, had been shown and, as an incident of this task, the onus question.

In the event the judge followed *Blacker v Waters* (1928) 28 SR (NSW) 406; 45 WN 111, a decision of the Full Supreme Court of New South Wales which applied the traditional view, and concluded that the onus lay on the appellant to prove the absence of negligence. This onus the appellant failed to discharge and accordingly the learned judge found a verdict for the plaintiff. In his reasons for judgment his Honour pointed to an apparent anomaly that because he was unable positively to conclude that the appellant had been negligent he would have been bound to find for the appellant if the action had been framed in negligence.

The appellant has challenged this determination contending that the onus [244] of proof of negligence lay upon the respondent and that his Honour should have found that trespass had not been made out.

It is necessary at the outset that some detailed reference be made to the facts as found by the trial judge before attention can be directed to an analysis of the legal consequences of the factual findings.

Prior to the incident the respondent had been standing on the porch outside the front door of the house with her back to an external wire gauze door holding it open to enable her daughter to pass through the doorway while she carried luggage to her parents' car. Both the front door and the wire gauze door were hinged on the one side with the front door opening inwards into the hall of the house and the wire gauze door swinging out.

After the respondent had been standing in that position for half to three quarters of an hour the appellant's wife left the house followed by their daughter Kylie and the appellant slammed the front door shut. When he did this the respondent, who was still holding the wire gauze door open, put out her right hand which hit and broke the glass in a panel of the door and she sustained lacerations and some nerve damage to her hand.

I have already indicated that the learned judge concluded affirmatively that the appellant did not intend to strike the respondent with the door. But he also held that neither Kylie, who was then on the porch, nor the respondent would have been struck by the closing door if they had remained still and that the respondent's action in putting her hand out brought about her injury. These findings appear to me to be irrefutable as the movement of the door was necessarily restricted by the door jamb and both Kylie and the respondent were standing on the porch well beyond the limit of the possible path of the closing door.

The respondent claimed in evidence that she put out her hand to prevent the door striking her in the face and also to prevent it striking Kylie. The learned judge rejected this evidence and stated that he was unable to determine whether the respondent put out her hand in an attempt to thwart the appellant in his desire to close the door or as a reflex action in response to a sensation of danger.

What emerges clearly from these findings is the fact that the respondent would not have suffered injury unless she had put out her hand to impede the passage of the closing door.

The immediate question which arises is whether in these circumstances the learned judge erred in concluding that the appellant was liable in trespass.

The cause of action pleaded was that the appellant assaulted the respondent by slamming a door on her causing her injuries. If the evidentiary findings were to the effect that the appellant slammed the door *on her* and thereby caused her injuries then it would be clear in my view that trespass had, subject to the question of negligence, prima facie been made out. While it is true to say that trespass lies even where no harm results from the conduct complained of the present context is one in which the respondent contended that the appellant caused her injury by his trespass, or assault (and battery).

In these circumstances, and putting to one side questions of intention and negligence, the respondent would make good her claim if she established that [245] her physical injury resulted from the trespassing, or forceful, conduct of the appellant.

This is basal principle. In the 7th edition of *Bacon's Abridgement* (1832), Trespass (D) (at 659) the following appears:

If one man have received corporal injury from the voluntary act of another, an action of trespass lies, provided there was a neglect or want of due caution in the person who did the injury, although there were no design to injure.

Again in *Fowler*, Diplock J said (at 435):

… Since trespass to the person only lay where the injury to the plaintiff was the direct consequence of the personal act of the defendant, proof that the defendant did the act and that the plaintiff was thereby injured would normally be prima facie evidence of the defendant's negligence.

His Lordship was of course concerned with the onus question and his reference to *direct* was intended to distinguish trespass vi et armis with an action on the case which lay for consequential damage. Nonetheless the passage emphasizes the need in a case such as the present one to establish that the personal act of the defendant caused the plaintiff's injury.

This does not mean, of course, that the defendant must personally strike the plaintiff with his fist or another part of his body. It extends to situations in which a plaintiff is struck by a missile, or indeed any object set in motion by a defendant (for instance, a bullet fired from a rifle).

It may also be accepted that where a defendant sets in motion an unbroken series of continuing consequences the last of which ultimately caused injury to a plaintiff he may be liable in trespass: *Hillier v Leitch* [1936] SASR 490 at 494. For instance, in the celebrated Squib case (*Scott v Shepherd* (1773) 2 Wm Bl 892; 96 ER 525) a wag who threw a lighted firework into a market whence it was tossed from one stall to another in order to save the wares until it exploded in the plaintiff's face was found liable in trespass.

Likewise if the respondent had been in a position of danger from the closing door and had received the injuries to her hand when acting in self-protection there can be little doubt but that the appellant would have been liable. Her injuries would have resulted from the forceful act of the appellant. Even if she had merely apprehended danger from the swinging door and had raised her hand in a reflex action and thereby suffered injury it can be accepted, at least for the purposes of this decision, that she would sustain her claim.

On the other hand if she had not been in a position of danger and received her injuries in the course of taking positive action designed to thwart the appellant then, so it seems to me, she would fail in her action.

This is because her injuries resulted from her own independent actions and not the conduct of the appellant. ...

[246] The conclusion that it is necessary for the respondent to establish that her injuries were caused by the actions of the appellant necessarily means that the onus of showing this lay on her. If she failed to discharge the onus then she failed, in my opinion, to make out the trespass with which the appellant was charged.

I have already referred to the fact that the trial judge was unable to determine on the evidence whether the respondent in thrusting out her arm did so as a reflex action to a threatening situation or in order to thwart the appellant. The consequence is that the respondent failed to establish that her injury resulted from, or was caused by, the act of the appellant.

She failed to establish on the balance of probabilities that her injuries were caused by the appellant's use of force rather than as consequence of her own wilful act. ...

[248] Accordingly I am of opinion that the judgment below should be set aside. This conclusion renders it unnecessary to deliberate upon the vexed question whether *Fowler* should now be followed in New South Wales and the onus of establishing negligence placed on the plaintiff.

The question is not an easy one and there are many considerations in favour of the traditional view which was, after all, applied in *Blacker*. Proof that the plaintiff's injury was the direct result of the defendant's force has historically been regarded as sufficient to give rise to a prima facie case of trespass. In accordance with this approach lack of intent, absence of negligence and self-defence, inter alia, were regarded as matters of justification and excuse on which the defendant bore the onus.

In my opinion there is much to be said for this view despite the dicta of Lord Diplock in *Fowler* (which has itself been described as a doubtful authority – *Salmond on Torts*, 17th ed (1977) at 6) and, whilst I recognise the considerations which support Lord Diplock's conclusion I prefer to [249] reserve for another day the question whether this Court should decline to follow *Blacker*. ...

[Hope JA agreed with Clarke JA.]

Appeal allowed

Chapter 2

Interference with the Person

1. BATTERY

Rixon v Star City Pty Ltd
(2001) 53 NSWLR 98; [2001] NSWCA 265
Supreme Court of New South Wales, Court of Appeal

Physical contact which is generally acceptable in the ordinary conduct of daily life does not constitute battery. Assault requires an intention to create in another person an apprehension of immediate harmful or offensive contact.

[The plaintiff, Mr Brian Rixon, was the subject of an exclusion order issued by the defendant, Star City Pty Ltd, a casino operator, pursuant to the *Casino Control Act 1992* (NSW) ("the Act") which authorised a casino operator to prohibit a person from entering or remaining in a casino.

The plaintiff was identified playing roulette in the defendant's casino in breach of the exclusion order issued to him. The plaintiff was approached by one of the defendant's employees who placed his hand on the plaintiff's shoulder, without using any degree of force or causing any injury, and asked the plaintiff if he was Brian Rixon.

In the plaintiff's action for damages in the District Court of New South Wales, the trial judge, Balla ADCJ, rejected the plaintiff's claims for assault and battery in respect of the conduct of the defendant's employee. Her Honour found that these torts were negatived because the defendant's employee who touched the plaintiff lacked "the requisite intention in relation to assault and the requisite anger or hostile attitude in relation to battery". The plaintiff appealed.]

SHELLER JA. ...

[112] Battery ...
51. The placing of the hand on the shoulder could be a battery. As Holt CJ said in *Cole v Turner* (1704) 87 ER 907 "the least touching of another in anger is a battery". On the other hand, as the Chief Justice said, "if two or more meet in a narrow passage, and without any violence or design of harm, the one touches the other gently, it will be no battery".

52. However the absence of anger or hostile attitude by the person touching another is not a satisfactory basis for concluding that the touching was not a battery. In *In re F* [1990] 2 AC 1 at 73 Lord Goff of Chieveley said:

In the old days it used to be said that, for a touching of another's person to amount to a battery, it had to be a touching 'in anger' (see *Cole v Turner* per Holt CJ); and it has recently been said that the touching must be 'hostile' to have that effect (see *Wilson v Pringle* [1987] QB 237, 253). I respectfully doubt whether that is correct. A prank that gets out of hand; an over-friendly slap on the back; surgical treatment by a surgeon who mistakenly thinks that the patient has consented to it – all these things may transcend the bounds of lawfulness, without being characterised as hostile. Indeed the suggested qualification is difficult to reconcile with the principle that any touching of another's body is, in the absence of lawful excuse, capable of amounting to a battery and a trespass.

53. In *Collins v Wilcock* [1984] 1 WLR 1172 Lord Goff (then Robert Goff LJ) sitting in the Divisional Court, at 1177-8 referred to the fundamental principle, plain and incontestable, that every person's body is inviolate, and that any touching of another person, however **[113]** slight may amount to a battery. His Lordship referred to *Cole v Turner* and to Blackstone's Commentaries, 17th ed (1830) Vol 3, 120:

the law cannot draw the line between different degrees of violence, and therefore totally prohibits the first and lowest stage of it; every man's person being sacred, and no other having a right to meddle with it, in any the slightest manner.

His Lordship continued:

But so widely drawn a principle must inevitably be subject to exceptions. For example, children may be subjected to reasonable punishment; people may be subjected to the lawful exercise of the power of arrest; and reasonable force may be used in self-defence or for the prevention of crime. But, apart from these special instances where the control or constraint is lawful, a broader exception has been created to allow for the exigencies of everyday life. Generally speaking, consent is a defence to battery; and most of the physical contacts of ordinary life are not actionable because they are impliedly consented to by all who move in society and so expose themselves to the risk of bodily contact. So nobody can complain of the jostling which is inevitable from his presence in, for example, a supermarket, an underground station or a busy street; nor can a person who attends a party complain if his hand is seized in friendship, or even if his back is, within reason, slapped: see *Tuberville v Savage* (1669) 1 Mod 3. Although such cases are regarded as examples of implied consent, it is more common nowadays to treat them as falling within a general exception embracing all physical contact which is generally acceptable in the ordinary conduct of daily life. We observe that, although in the past it has sometimes been stated that a battery is only committed where the action is 'angry, revengeful, rude, or insolent' (see Hawkins, Pleas of the Crown, 8th ed (1824), vol 1, cl 5, section 2), we think that nowadays it is more realistic, and indeed more accurate, to state the broad underlying principle, subject to the broad exception. Among such forms of conduct, long held to be acceptable, is touching a person for the purpose of engaging his attention, though of course using no greater degree of physical contact than is reasonably necessary in the circumstances for that purpose. So, for example, it was held by the Court of Common Pleas in 1807 that a touch by a constable's staff on the shoulder of a man who had climbed on a gentleman's railing to gain a better view of a mad ox, the touch being only to engage the man's attention, did not amount to a battery: see *Wiffin v Kincard* (1807) 2 Box & Pul 471; for another example, see *Coward v Baddeley* (1859) 4 H & N 478. But a distinction is drawn between a touch to draw a man's attention, which is generally acceptable, and a physical restraint, which is not. So we find Parke B observing in *Rawlings v Till* (1837) 3 M & W 28, 29, with reference to *Wiffin v Kincard*, that 'There the touch was merely to engage [a man's] attention, not to put a restraint upon his person'.

54. This distinction is explained in Clerk & Lindsell on Torts, 17th ed, 12-06 where the question is posed whether the physical contact imposed on the plaintiff was in excess of that "generally acceptable in everyday life". It is pointed out in a footnote **[114]** that acceptable conduct must be considered in the context of the incident in dispute.

For an adult to jump on another and snatch her shoulder bag is clearly unacceptable. Between 13-year-old schoolboys it might perhaps be seen as 'as unremarkable as shaking hands'.

55. No error has been demonstrated which would entitle this Court to interfere with the trial Judge's finding that the touching lacked "the requisite anger or hostile attitude". More accurately, … it could not be said that the conduct of [the defendant's employee] in the circumstances found [by the trial judge] and clearly for the purpose of engaging Mr Rixon's attention, was not generally acceptable in the ordinary conduct of daily life.

Assault …

58. Proof of assault requires proof of an intention to create in another person an apprehension of imminent harmful or offensive contact; see, for example, *Hall v Fonceca* [1983] WAR 309. … The trial Judge rejected the case in assault by finding "that the actions of the defendant's employee lacked 'the requisite intention in relation to assault'". By this her Honour must have meant the intention to create in Mr Rixon an apprehension of imminent harmful or offensive contact. Having rejected Mr Rixon's account of being grabbed or spun round, her Honour's finding that [the defendant's employee] placed his hand on Mr Rixon's shoulder without using any degree of force and said "Are you Brian Rixon?" led her to conclude that [the defendant's employee] had no intention of creating in Mr Rixon an apprehension of imminent harmful or offensive conduct.

59. In my opinion, the evidence left it open to her Honour to find that the necessary intention to create in Mr Rixon an apprehension of imminent harmful or offensive contact was lacking. The appeal against the trial Judge's decision that neither battery nor assault was made out accordingly fails. …

[Priestley and Heydon JJA agreed with Sheller JA. The trial judge and the New South Wales Court of Appeal also rejected the plaintiff's claim for false imprisonment in respect of the one and a half hours he was detained by the defendant in an interview room at the casino until the police arrived. This detention was authorised in "unmistakably clear" (Sheller JA) language by the Act.]

Appeal dismissed

2. ASSAULT

ACN 087 528 774 Pty Ltd (formerly Connex Trains Melbourne Pty Ltd) v Chetcuti
(2008) 21 VR 559; [2008] VSCA 274
Supreme Court of Victoria, Court of Appeal

Where the mental element in assault is an intention on the part of the defendant to cause the plaintiff to apprehend the immediate application of unlawful force, the requisite intention is subjective, not objective. Further, the plaintiff's apprehension of the imminent application of unlawful force must be a reasonable one.

[The defendant (appellant) was a public transport company operating rail services in Melbourne. The plaintiff (respondent), Mr Joseph Chetcuti, entered the defendant's railway station for the purpose of catching a train. An incident then occurred in which the plaintiff engaged in "offensive and highly confrontational behaviour" (Hargrave AJA at [6]) towards two officers (inspectors) employed by the defendant. During this incident, the plaintiff spat in the face of one of the officers and committed a number of offences contrary to the *Transport Act 1983* (Vic). In the course of running away with the defendant's officers in pursuit, the plaintiff fell and fractured his right wrist before physically being restrained. It was the plaintiff's contention that he had run away from the defendant's officers because he expected and feared they would "bash" him as retaliation for the act of spitting.

In the plaintiff's action in the County Court of Victoria (*Chetcuti v Connex Trains* [2007] VCC 166) to recover damages for assault and battery, the defendant, for reasons unexplained, did not rely on any statutory defence of justification. The trial judge awarded the plaintiff substantial damages for assault reflecting the fact that the plaintiff's wrist injury was serious and permanent. The trial judge also held that the physical restraint of the plaintiff by the defendant's officers constituted battery but that this had not caused "any compensable injury" (trial judge at [51] of her reasons).

The Victorian Court of Appeal allowed the defendant's appeal on the ground that the trial judge had acted on a misapprehension of the elements of the tort of assault. However, the proceedings were remitted for re-trial on all issues because the trial judge had failed to address the entirety of the plaintiff's case as presented at the trial.]

HARGRAVE AJA. ...

[564]Errors of law

16. A plaintiff seeking to establish a cause of action for the tort of assault, in circumstances where no physical contact or battery in fact takes place, must prove the following elements:

    [565](1) A threat by the defendant, by words or conduct, to inflict harmful or offensive contact upon the plaintiff forthwith: *Barton v Armstrong* [1969] 2 NSWR 451, 454-5; *Rixon v Star City Pty Ltd* (2001) 53 NSWLR 98, 114. It is enough if the threat is to make contact to the body of the plaintiff without the plaintiff's consent or without any legal justification: *Rixon v Star City Pty Ltd* (2001) 53 NSWLR 98, 112-3. (In this case, the threat to "catch" and detain the plaintiff, by holding him, was a sufficient threat to satisfy this element of the tort.)

    (2) A subjective intention on the part of the defendant that the threat will create in the mind of the plaintiff an apprehension that the threat will be carried out forthwith: *Rozsa v Samuels* [1969] SASR 205, 207; *Rixon v Star City Pty Ltd* (2001) 53 NSWLR 98, 114. It is not necessary to prove that the defendant in fact intends to carry out the threat: *Rixon v Star City Pty Ltd* (2001) 53 NSWLR 98, 114.

    (3) The threat must in fact create in the mind of the plaintiff an apprehension that the threat will be carried out forthwith: *ibid*. It is not necessary for the plaintiff to fear the threat, in the sense of being frightened by it. It is enough if the plaintiff apprehends that the threat will be carried out without his or her consent: *Brady v Schatzel* [1911] St R Qd 206, 208 (a case of criminal assault) as discussed in F Trindade, P Cane and M Lunney, *The Law of Torts in Australia* (4th ed, 2007) 53.

    (4) The apprehension in the mind of the plaintiff must be objectively reasonable. *Barton v Armstrong* [1969] 2 NSWR 451, 455; R P Balkin and J L R Davis, *Law of Torts* (3rd ed, 2004) 48.

    (5) The plaintiff's reasonable apprehension caused injury, loss or damage to the plaintiff. This requirement attracts the ordinary common law concept of causation by reference to commonsense and, where appropriate, consideration of normative factors such as value judgements and policy considerations: *March v E & M H Stramare Pty Ltd* (1990) 171 CLR 506, 516-7 ... .

18. The trial judge erred in two important respects. First, the judge said that it was sufficient to satisfy the first two elements of the tort of assault, as stated above, for a defendant to engage in an intentional act which creates in the mind of a plaintiff an apprehension of imminent physical attack or harm. That is a statement of objective intention, and ignores the requirement that the defendant must subjectively intend to create such an apprehension. Second, the trial judge made no reference to the fourth element of the tort stated above. Nowhere in her **[566]** reasons is there any consideration of the reasonableness of Mr Chetcuti's [the plaintiff's] belief that the two Connex officers [the defendant's officers] intended to cause him harmful or offensive contact if their chase resulted in him being caught.

19. It must be said that, on the material presented to this Court, the trial judge did not receive the assistance from counsel to which she was entitled. During the course of argument on appeal,

counsel provided this Court with the brief written submissions made to the trial judge on behalf of Mr Chetcuti and extracts from the transcript of oral submissions. Nowhere in those submissions was the judge's attention drawn to the appropriate mental elements of intention and apprehension which are necessary to establish in order to prove the tort of assault. ...To the extent that the tort of battery may require intent, it is enough that the defendant intends to do the act which constitutes the battery: *McClelland v Symons* [1951] VLR 157, 166; *Rixon v Star City Pty Ltd* (2001) 53 NSWLR 98, 112-4; RP Balkin and JLR Davis, *Law of Torts* (3rd ed, 2004) 35-8 ... .

[Ashley and Dodds-Streeton JJA agreed with Hargrave AJA.]

Appeal allowed. Proceedings remitted for re-trial on all issues

[The High Court of Australia refused the plaintiff's application for special leave to appeal from the Victorian Court of Appeal on the ground there were "insufficient prospects of success": *Chetcuti v ACN 087 528 774 Pty Ltd (formerly Connex Trains Melbourne Pty Ltd)* [2009] HCATrans 114.]

Barton v Armstrong
[1969] 2 NSWR 451
Supreme Court of New South Wales

Words spoken over the telephone may constitute assault where those words cause the listener to apprehend the immediate application of unlawful force.

[The plaintiff and defendant were members of the Sydney business community who had been engaged in an acrimonious equity suit in the Supreme Court of New South Wales in relation to the acquisition of shares in a public company. One of the allegations made by the plaintiff in the equity suit was that he had executed a certain deed under the duress of the defendant.

In the present proceedings, in which the plaintiff claimed damages for assault, the defendant made application for an order striking out the plaintiff's declaration on the ground that the proceedings were frivolous, vexatious and an abuse of the process of the court.

In response to a request by the defendant, the plaintiff had provided written particulars of the assault in his declaration. However senior counsel for the defendant (Mr Staff) submitted that the matters alleged in the particulars, if true, were not capable in law of constituting assault.]

TAYLOR J. ... **[454]** If I am satisfied that the plaintiff cannot succeed in this action because the only facts on which he can rely are not capable in law of amounting to an assault, then I ought to make the order.

Mr Staff referred to the definition of "assault" in *Fleming*, 3rd ed at p 26 and to *Salmond*, 15th ed at pp 158, 159 and the various authorities there cited. He examined all these cases and claimed that they established (1) there must in every case be a present ability on the part of the defendant to carry out the threat; (2) threatening acts do not constitute an assault unless they are of such a nature as to put the plaintiff in fear or apprehension of immediate violence; (3) words accompanying an act may render harmless that which otherwise would be an assault; and (4) the intent to do violence must be expressed in the threatening acts not merely in threatening speech. Nowhere, he continued, in these particulars is there alleged an occasion on which all these elements are present. The allegation of threats by the defendant over the telephone cannot amount to an assault because the defendant was not, nor was any agent of his, in such physical proximity to the plaintiff at the time the threat was made as would cause the plaintiff to fear that physical violence would follow, that is, that the threat would be carried out. On occasions when the defendant did convey to the plaintiff a threat of violence if he did not sign the deed, he made it clear to the plaintiff that what he wanted was the deed to be executed, and unless and until this was prepared and ready to be executed there could not be any apprehension of violence on the plaintiff's part.

It is apparent from a perusal of the voluminous matter supplied as particulars that the plaintiff does not rely upon any particular single act or single occasion as constituting the basis of his claim that the defendant assaulted him. What he alleges, as I understand the particulars – and this is gathered not from any one particular but from the effect of a number of them – is that the defendant on very many occasions threatened to do or to have done to him physical violence, to the extent of having him killed; that the defendant had engaged men to carry out these threats; that these men had been supplied with details of the plaintiff's home, his house, his car number and his office and that from time to time they followed him, watched his house, his office and were in a position to attack him; that this produced in the plaintiff's mind a fear that his life was in danger.

There was not in the particulars, as I read them, any allegation that at a particular time that a threat was made by the defendant over the telephone there was any person near enough to the plaintiff to carry out the threat. The question I have to decide is whether these allegations are clearly incapable in law of constituting an assault, so that an action based on them is vexatious in that it never could succeed. I am not concerned at this stage with difficulties of proof which the plaintiff might have, nor am I concerned with questions of estoppel that might arise between the parties as a result of certain findings of the learned judge in equity.

Many of the decisions that are cited by the text-writers are, of course, very old cases. This branch of the law was developed at a time when means of communication and means of inflicting harm by physical violence were more restricted than they are today. However, the earlier cases seem to establish that the gist of the offence of assault is putting a person into apprehension of impending physical contact. The effect on the victim's mind is the material factor, and not whether the defendant actually had the intention or the means to follow it up. The essence of assault is the expectation raised in the mind of the victim of physical contact from the threat of the defendant. "An assault **[455]** is the threat by one man to inflict unlawful force upon another. It is a civil wrong and a crime where the threat by some physical act has intentionally caused the other to believe that such force is about to be inflicted. The *actus reus* of assault thus consists in the expectation of physical contact which the offender creates in the mind of the person whom he threatens": *Russell on Crime*, 11th ed, p 724. Thus it has been held in Canada it is enough for the plaintiff on reasonable grounds to believe that he is in danger of violence. He does not have to show that there was any actual intention or power to use violence: *Bruce v Dyer* 58 DLR (2d), pp 211 and 216, cited by *Salmond*, 15th ed, 159.

Mr Staff's first and second propositions can, I think, be best dealt with together. They are the ones upon which he most strongly relied. There are, undoubtedly, many authorities which show that mere words do not constitute an assault, however insulting or even menacing they may be, and that the intention to do violence must be expressed in acts. It has been said that: "the origin of this rule lay not in law but in the fact that in the early days the King's Courts had their hands full when they intervened at the first threatening gesture or, in other words, when the fight was about to start, and taking cognizance of all the belligerent language which the foul mouths of merrie England could dispense was simply beyond their capacity. Threats for the future and insults for the present are simply not present breaches of the peace so never have fallen within the narrow boundaries of this rather antiquated tort": *Law of Torts*, William J Prosser, 3rd ed, at p 39. Whatever the reason may be, it is clear from the many authorities cited on this subject that mere words themselves are not sufficient to constitute an assault and that the threatening act must put the victim in immediate fear or apprehension of violence. For these reasons Mr Staff contended that all threats over the telephone could not in law be capable of constituting an assault.

I am not persuaded that threats uttered over the telephone are to be properly categorized as mere words. I think it is a matter of the circumstances. To telephone a person in the early hours of the morning, not once but on many occasions, and to threaten him, not in a conversational tone but in an atmosphere of drama and suspense, is a matter that a jury could say was well calculated to not only instil fear into his mind but to constitute threatening acts, as distinct from mere words. If, when threats in this manner are conveyed over the telephone, the recipient has been led to believe that he is being followed, kept under surveillance by persons hired to do him physical harm to the extent of killing him, then why is this not something to put him in fear or apprehension of immediate violence? In the age in which we live threats may be made and communicated by persons remote from the person threatened. Physical violence and death can be produced by acts done at a distance by people who are out of sight and by agents hired for that purpose. I do not think that these, if they result in apprehension of physical violence in the mind of a reasonable person, are outside the protection afforded by the civil and criminal law as to assault. How immediate does the fear of physical violence have to be? In my opinion the answer is it depends on the circumstances. Some threats are not capable of arousing apprehension of violence in the mind of a reasonable person unless there is an immediate prospect of the threat being carried out. Others, I believe, can create the apprehension even if it is made clear that the violence may occur in the future, at times unspecified and uncertain. Being able to immediately carry out the threat is but one way of creating the fear of apprehension, but not the only way. There are other ways, more subtle and perhaps more effective.

Threats which put a reasonable person in fear of physical violence have always been abhorrent to the law as an interference with personal freedom and integrity, and the right of a person to be free from the fear of insult. If the threat produces the fear or apprehension of physical violence then I am of opinion that the law is breached, although the victim does not know when that physical violence may be effected. I would for these reasons reject Mr Staff's first and second propositions and hold that there is material in these particulars which a trial judge might think fit to be submitted to the jury as evidence of an assault. As to the fourth proposition, I have in these reasons already made it clear that it would be open to a jury to take the view that [456] there was more involved in the threats made over the telephone than mere words.

The remaining submission is that at all times it was made clear to the plaintiff that what the defendant, assuming he made these threats, was seeking to do was to procure his assent to the deed and that there could not be any fear of physical violence in the mind of the plaintiff, as a reasonable person, until the time for executing the deed had arrived and, since this had not arrived at the time that the threat was made, then it was not capable of being an assault. It is said that this submission is supported by decisions such as *Tuberville v Savage* (1669) 86 ER 684: "If it were not Assize time I would not take such language from you. Held: no assault since the judges were in town". Presumably it was held no assault because the plaintiff knew the judges were in town and knew there was no real threat. I do not think that the principle decided by this case excludes an assault where the defendant has threatened physical harm to the plaintiff unless he does what the defendant requires him to do. It would well be open to the jury to conclude that no matter that the plaintiff be given, as it were, an alternative to the suffering of physical harm, he might nevertheless entertain a real fear that he would suffer physical violence. There is no doubt that the purpose of the threat would be to instil such fear in the mind of the plaintiff that he would do the will of the person making the threat. It would be for the jury to say if it were, in the circumstances, an assault. …

Defendant's application dismissed

3. FALSE IMPRISONMENT

Balmain New Ferry Company Ltd v Robertson
(1906) 4 CLR 379
High Court of Australia

There is no false imprisonment where a person has consented to a restraint on liberty. Query whether the occupier of land may impose a condition, such as the payment of a sum of money, for allowing a person on the land to leave.

[The defendant (appellant) conducted a harbour steam ferry between Sydney and Balmain. Fares were collected only at turnstiles at the defendant's Sydney wharf. The system for collection was that persons entering the wharf paid one penny to the defendant's employee at the entry turnstile which conferred the right to travel to Balmain and persons leaving the wharf paid one penny to the defendant's employee at the exit turnstile and passed through to the street. A noticeboard above the turnstiles read as follows: "Notice. A fare of one penny must be paid on entering or leaving the wharf. No exception will be made to this rule, whether the passenger has travelled by the ferry or not."

The plaintiff (respondent) entered the defendant's Sydney wharf through the turnstile, after payment of one penny, with the intention of travelling on the defendant's ferry. When he reached the water side he found that he had missed the ferry. The plaintiff then sought to leave the wharf but refused to pay another penny to pass through the exit turnstile, which was the only means of egress to the street. The defendant's employees, who insisted on the requirement for payment of another penny, used force (not excessive) to prevent the plaintiff from squeezing through the space between the exit turnstile and the bulkhead. However, after about twenty minutes the plaintiff succeeded in gaining the street.

In an action in the Supreme Court of New South Wales for false imprisonment and assault the plaintiff obtained a verdict for £100 damages. The defendant appealed to the High Court of Australia.]

GRIFFITH CJ. [386] I have had the opportunity of reading the judgment which will be delivered by my learned brother *O'Connor*, in which I fully concur. I will therefore only say a few words for myself. The first question that arises for consideration is: On what terms did the plaintiff ask for and obtain admittance to the defendants' premises? It is clear that the invitation which the defendants offered to members of the public to come upon their premises was conditional, and it must be taken that members of the public, who availed themselves of the permission, agreed to be bound by the terms on which it was granted so far as they were acquainted with them. There is no doubt that in fact the terms were that persons should obtain admittance on payment of one penny, and when admitted should be free to depart from the premises by water, but should not be entitled to egress by land except on payment of another sum of one penny. If the plaintiff was aware of these terms he must be held to have agreed to them when he obtained admission. If he had been a stranger who had never before been on the premises, it would have been sufficient for the defendants to prove that they had done what was reasonably sufficient to give the plaintiff notice of the conditions of admittance: *Parker v South Eastern Railway Co* (1877) 2 CPD 416, cited with approval in *Richardson v Rowntree* [1894] AC 217. In this case, however, it appeared that the plaintiff had been on the premises before, and was aware of the existence of the turnstiles and of the purpose for which they were used. It was therefore established that he was aware of the terms on which he had obtained admittance, and it follows that he had agreed to be bound by them.

This agreement involves, in my opinion, an implied promise by the plaintiff that he would not ask for egress by land except on payment of one penny, and, further, a consent on his part that the defendants should be entitled to prevent him from departing in that way until he paid the penny. In the case of *Butler v Manchester, Sheffield and Lincolnshire Railway Co* (1888) 21 QBD 207, it was taken for granted, and, I think rightly, that, if such an [387] agreement existed, the use of any necessary force to prevent a breach of it would be justified. As the plaintiff was free to leave the premises by water I think that there was no imprisonment: *Bird v Jones* (1845) 7 QB 742. And as to the alleged assault, there was no evidence that anything was done which was not authorized by the agreement to which the plaintiff was a party. ...

O'CONNOR J. ... [388] It is admitted on this appeal that the company are responsible for what was done by their officers, so that there is left for our decision substantially one question only, namely, whether, on the facts, the company are liable to the plaintiff for false imprisonment and assault. The legal position on which the plaintiff relies may be thus stated:- He entered the wharf under a contract to be carried in the company's steamer from Sydney to Balmain. Before the contract was performed he decided to abandon it, and, having no further business on the wharf, became entitled to pass out to the street through the turnstiles, or, if not through them, at least through the eight and a-half inch space between the turnstile and the bulkhead. The company's officers by force prevented him from doing so, refused to allow him to pass out through the turnstile except on payment of a penny at the exit turnstile, and thus kept him imprisoned as a means of enforcing payment of that demand. He maintains that, even if he were bound to pay the extra penny as a matter of contract and it became a debt recoverable in the Courts, the company could not thus take the law into their own hands and deprive him of his liberty in order to enforce payment. If that were an accurate statement of the position the plaintiff's contention would be unanswerable. But it is not an accurate statement of the position. Undoubtedly it is not permissible for a creditor, except under due process of the law, to abridge the liberty of his debtor for the purpose of enforcing payment. But the abridgment of a man's liberty is not under all circumstances actionable. He may enter into a contract which necessarily involved the surrender of a portion of his liberty for a certain period, and if the act complained of is nothing more than a restraint in accordance with that surrender he cannot complain. Nor can he, without the assent of the other party, by electing to put an end to the contract, become entitled at once, unconditionally and irrespective of the other [389] party's rights, to regain his liberty as if he had never surrendered it. A familiar instance of such a contract is that between a passenger and the railway company which undertakes to carry him on a journey. If the passenger suddenly during the journey decided to abandon it and to leave the train at the next station, being one at which the train was not timed to stop, he clearly would not be entitled to have the train stopped at that station. However much he might object, the railway company could lawfully carry him on to the next stopping place of that particular train. In such a case the passenger's liberty would be for a certain period restrained, but the restraint would not be actionable, because it is an implied term of such a contract that the passenger will permit the restraint of his liberty so far as may be necessary for the performance by the company of the contract of carriage according to the time table of that train. Or a person may conditionally, by his own act, place himself in such a position that he cannot complain of a certain restraint of his liberty. Take an illustration which was used in the course of the argument. Assume that the turnstiles on the company's wharf completely closed the opening between the bulkheads, that they were worked on the penny in the slot system, and would not open except when a penny dropped in the slot operated the mechanism. If under these circumstances the plaintiff, having opened the entry turnstile by his penny and entered the wharf, changed his mind about crossing in the company's steamers, and wished to return at once to the street, could he claim that he was not bound to use the ordinary means of opening the exit turnstile by dropping in his penny, but was entitled to break his way through it, or to demand from the company's officers that they should specially unlock the apparatus to enable him to pass out? If, under the circumstances, the officers refused to comply with his request, could it possibly be contended that the company would be liable to an action for false imprisonment? *Prima facie*, no doubt, any restraint of a person's liberty without his consent is actionable. But, when the restraint is referable to the terms on which the person entered the premises in which he complains he was imprisoned, we must examine those terms before we can [390] determine whether there has been an imprisonment which is actionable. The fallacy in the plaintiff's legal position lies in the assumption that, immediately he abandoned the contract to be carried to Balmain by the company's steamer, he was in the same position as if the wharf was one to which the public had free right of access, that, finding his exit barred by the turnstiles, he was entitled either to squeeze past them, or to demand from the company's officers that they should be specially released to let him through. Whether that assumption is or is not justifiable depends upon the terms on which the plaintiff was permitted to enter the wharf. In ascertaining those terms it must be remembered that the wharf was not a place to which the public had free right of access. If it had been so no one could legally place upon the wharf any bar or obstruction to the free entry or exit of any member of the public. But it was not a public place in that sense. It was private property. No one had a right to enter there without the company's permission, and they could impose on the members of the public any terms they thought fit as a condition of entering or leaving the premises. What were the terms on which the plaintiff entered the company's wharf? There was no express contract, and the terms must therefore be implied from the circumstances. In dealing with the circumstances I leave the question of the notice board out of consideration. In my view, it is immaterial whether the company did what was reasonable to direct public attention to the notice, or whether the plaintiff ever read it until his attention was called to it by the officer at the turnstile. But as to the material facts from which the contract must be implied there is no dispute. The plaintiff was aware that the only entrance to and exit from the wharf on the land side was through the turnstiles, and that, to quote his evidence, "When the turnstile was not released there was a complete barrier stretching across the whole entrance," in other words, entrance to and exit from the wharf were completely barred except when by the action of the officer in charge the turnstile was released. He also knew that the turnstiles were so constructed as to admit only persons entering the wharf through the entry turnstile, and only persons leaving the wharf through the [391] exit turnstile, that the passing through of every passenger was automatically registered by the turnstile, and that the automatic register was a check on the cash taken by the officer. He himself in speaking to one of the officers said, "If it is the question of putting out the tally of your turnstiles I can squeeze through there," referring to the eight and a-half inch space before mentioned. Having travelled on many occasions backward and forward by the company's boats, and, as he says, paid his fare to the officers at the turnstiles, he must have been aware that the company's method of conducting their business was to release the turnstiles only on payment of a penny, and that in every case where there was a departure from that method "the tally of the turnstile," as he terms it, would be thrown out.

Such being the condition of the company's premises, and such being their method of carrying on their business, the plaintiff paid his penny to the officer and went through the entry turnstile on to the wharf. The first question is, what is the contract to be implied from the plaintiff's payment at and passing through the turnstiles under these circumstances? It is that in consideration of that payment the company undertook to carry him as a passenger to Balmain by any of their ferry boats from that wharf. That is the only contract which could be implied from those circumstances, and the plaintiff was permitted to enter the wharf for the purpose of the contract being performed. It is not denied that the company were ready to perform their part, but the plaintiff, as far as one party can do so rescinded the contract and determined to go back from the wharf to the street. What then were his rights? They were, in my opinion, no more and no less than they would have been if he had landed from his own boat at the company's wharf. He was on private property. He had not been forced or entrapped there. He had entered it of his own free will and with the knowledge that the only exit on the land side was through the turnstile, operated as a part of the company's system of collecting fares in the manner I have mentioned. If he wished to use the turnstile as a means of exit he could only do so on complying with the usual conditions on which the company opened them. The company were lawfully entitled to impose the condition of a penny payment on all who [392] used the turnstiles, whether they had travelled by the company's steamers or not, and they were under no obligation to make an exception in the plaintiff's favour. The company, therefore, being lawfully entitled to impose that condition, and the plaintiff being free to pass out through the turnstile at any time on complying with it, he had only himself to blame for his detention, and there was no imprisonment of which he could legally complain. Next, had he the right to force his way through the narrow space between the turnstile and the bulkhead? Clearly he had not. If the turnstile had filled the whole space between the bulkheads, it could not be contended that the plaintiff would have been entitled to break it open in order to pass through. The company's officers were in my opinion, entitled to regard the turnstile as blocking the whole space, not only for the necessary protection of the mechanism of the turnstiles from injury, but also because it was a necessary part of their system of collecting fares on entry and exit that the turnstile should be an effective barrier against entry and exit of any person except on the company's conditions. They were therefore entitled to prevent the plaintiff from squeezing through the space in question, and were justified in meeting the plaintiff's forcible attempt with as much force as was reasonably necessary to defeat it. It is not alleged that they did more, and any assault they may have committed on the plaintiff under these circumstances was justified. In this connection I may observe that it is not necessary to determine whether or not this justification is, strictly speaking, open to the company on the pleadings. The case has been conducted all through on the footing that it is open, and, if it were necessary, the Court would make any amendment required to formally shape the issues in accordance with the way in which both parties regarded them at the trial. ...

[394] The verdict ought therefore to have been entered for the defendants, and this Court must now order accordingly that the verdict for the plaintiff be set aside and judgment be entered for the defendants.

[Barton J agreed with O'Connor J.]

Appeal allowed

[A further appeal by the plaintiff to the Privy Council was dismissed: *Robinson* (sic) *v Balmain New Ferry Co Ltd* [1910] AC 295. Lord Loreburn LC, who delivered the judgment of the Privy Council, stated (at 298) that "their Lordships entirely agree with the conclusion of the High Court".]

Symes v Mahon
[1922] SASR 447
Supreme Court of South Australia, Full Court

False imprisonment does not require the application of physical force by the defendant to the plaintiff. It is sufficient if the plaintiff has submitted completely to the control of the defendant.

MURRAY CJ. **[448]** This is a motion to make absolute a rule *nisi* to show cause why a judgment **[449]** entered for the plaintiff for £60 damages in an action for false imprisonment in the Local Court of Adelaide should not be set aside and a new trial had between the parties, or why judgment should not be entered or varied in favour of the defendant on the grounds (1) that there was no evidence of any unlawful arrest or false imprisonment of the plaintiff; (2) that the damages awarded were excessive. The action was tried before Mr Commissioner Mitchell and a jury. The objection taken to the amount of damages was not pressed. We indicated at the hearing that we should not interfere with the judgment on that ground. The only question, therefore, is whether there was evidence on which the jury could, as reasonable men, have found that there was an imprisonment of the plaintiff.

"A prison," said Coleridge J, in the leading case of *Bird v Jones* (1845) 7 QB 742, at p 744, "may have its boundary large or narrow, visible and tangible, or, though real, still in the conception only; it may itself be moveable or fixed; but a boundary it must have; and that boundary the party imprisoned must be prevented from passing; he must be prevented from leaving that place within the ambit of which the party imprisoning would confine him, except by prison-breach. Some confusion seems to me to arise from confounding imprisonment of the body with mere loss of freedom; it is one part of the definition of freedom to be able to go whithersoever one pleases; but imprisonment is something more than the mere loss of this power; it includes the notion of restraint within some limits defined by a will or power exterior to our own." Mr Justice Patteson, in the same case, said, at p 752:- "Imprisonment is, as I apprehend, a total restraint of the liberty of the person, for however short a time, and not a partial obstruction of his will, whatever inconvenience it may bring on him." Lord Macnaghten, delivering the judgment of the Privy Council in *Syed Mahamad Zusuf-ud-din v Secretary of State for India* (1903) 19 TLR 496, quoted these passages, and summarized them in this sentence, at p 497:- "Nothing short of actual detention and complete loss of freedom would support an action for false imprisonment."

The evidence showed that a warrant had been issued in Adelaide for the arrest of Michael Hillary McMahon on a **[450]** charge of having failed to maintain an illegitimate child of which he was the father by a young woman name White. The plaintiff's name was William James Mahon. He lived at Lower Light, where he was a school teacher. The defendant, a police constable, at Two Wells, which is 18 miles from Lower Light, drove to the plaintiff's house on the evening of 23rd September 1921, and said to him, "Do you know a girl in Adelaide by name of White?" The plaintiff replied, "Yes, I knew a Miss White for about two years." The defendant said, "There's a warrant out for your arrest for the maintenance of an illegitimate child." The plaintiff replied, "This cannot be possible, as I know Miss White to be an honourable girl." The defendant said, "I have your photo down at Two Wells." The plaintiff asked, "Is the hair parted down the middle?" The defendant replied, "Yes; your're the man, all right," adding, "You'll have to come to town with me, but it can be done quietly, if you don't wish your wife to know." The plaintiff said, "I shall certainly tell my wife; I'm not the father of any illegitimate child. I've a man calling for me to-morrow at six in the morning to drive me to Roseworthy to catch the Morgan train." The defendant said, "I am very sorry, but you'll have to come to town." The plaintiff then went away to speak to his wife. On his return the defendant said to him, "Will you give me your word to be at Two Wells tomorrow morning?" The plaintiff replied, "I suppose I'll have to." The defendant said, "You can buy your own ticket if you wish, but, if you don't wish to, you can travel for nothing, but you'll have to travel with me." The plaintiff replied, "I'll buy my own ticket, as I don't want everyone to know I am under arrest." During the conversation the defendant also said, "When we get to town we will drive in the police trap from the station to the watch-house." The plaintiff inquired, "What about my wife?" The defendant replied, "She will not be able to come with you." He further said, "On the back of the photograph are written the words 'Michael Hillary McMahon,' but we do not take any notice of the name." The defendant, who had remained in his trap all the time, then drove away.

Pausing here, I agree with the Crown Solicitor that there was no evidence of an imprisonment up to this point. The most that can be said is that the defendant impressed upon [451] the plaintiff that there was a warrant out for his arrest, and that he would have to go to town with him from Two Wells on the following day. There may have been some coercion of his will, but there was no restraint of his person, nor anything from which the jury could infer that the plaintiff reasonably thought that any attempt on his part to go to such a distance from the railway station that he could not be there when the train started would be futile.

On the following morning the plaintiff went to Two Wells railway station with his wife. He bought two tickets for Adelaide. The defendant was sitting inside the ticket office. Producing a little book, he said to the plaintiff, "This is a copy of the warrant," and "Here is your photo." The plaintiff looked at the photograph, and said, "It's not anything like me; this man wears a soft collar, and I never wore a soft collar in my life." The defendant, looking first at the photograph and then at the plaintiff, said, "I think it's you, all right. You'll have to come to town to have matters cleared up." The plaintiff and his wife then got into the train. The defendant entered another compartment. On the journey to Adelaide the train stopped at several stations, but the plaintiff and defendant did not speak to one another.

The Crown Solicitor contended that there was no evidence on which the jury could find as reasonable men that there was any imprisonment of the plaintiff at Two Wells or during the journey to Adelaide. To that I cannot assent. A warrant for arrest is a command addressed to all constables and peace officers to apprehend the person named in the warrant. The defendant told the plaintiff that he thought he was the man who was wanted, and said that he must come to Adelaide. After that the plaintiff got into the train, and the defendant got into the train also. On these facts the jury might reasonably hold, in my opinion, that the plaintiff was wholly deprived of his liberty by being required to enter the train, although he had paid for his own fare. I think they might also hold that the restraint continued throughout the journey, for, though the plaintiff might have got out at an intermediate station, the defendant was close at hand and might have prevented him from escaping. The defendant denied that he saw the plaintiff or his wife during the journey, but it might fairly have been inferred that he kept an eye on the carriage [452] at each station, for he had arranged that the police trap should meet the train at Adelaide and he would have looked very foolish if he had arrived without the plaintiff. Besides, the only object of his visit to Adelaide was to take the plaintiff to the watch-house to have the matter cleared up.

There was this further evidence after the arrival of the train in Adelaide. The police trap was at the station. The defendant spoke to the driver and then came to the plaintiff. He said, "We are not going to drive to the watch-house. We will walk." The plaintiff asked, "What about my luggage? Can I leave it at the Grosvenor?" The defendant replied, "Yes; you can take it across. I will wait for you opposite the station." The plaintiff took his wife and his luggage to the Grosvenor Hotel, and returned to the defendant. They then walked together to the Beehive Corner, where they boarded a tram-car to take them to the watch-house. Before they entered the car the defendant said, "You are not under arrest now. I am only taking you up for identification." The plaintiff asked, "What if the girl says I am the man?" The defendant replied, "You can bail yourself out or get someone else to bail you out." They reached the watch-house at about noon. Miss White was not there. The defendant told the plaintiff she would come at a quarter to one. The plaintiff asked if he might go to the Grosvenor and bring his wife. The defendant said, "Yes." Mahon left the watch-house and returned with his wife. They were shown into a room where the woman was sitting. She looked at the plaintiff and said, "No, that is not the man; I haven't seen him before." After a pause, the plaintiff said to his wife, "Well, we had better go," and to the defendant, "Thank you for spoiling my holiday. I should be along the Murray now." The defendant replied, "I am very sorry, but don't forget I told you all along you were not under arrest." The plaintiff rejoined, "Yes, you told me when I was getting on the electric car that I was not under arrest." He then left.

It will be observed that the defendant approached the plaintiff almost immediately after the train reached Adelaide, and walked off with him. At the top of the stairs in North Terrace he give him leave to take his wife over to the Grosvenor Hotel on the opposite side of the road, but said he would wait for him. On the plaintiff's return he accom**[453]**panied him to the Beehive Corner and got into a tram-car with him. He told him that he was not under arrest, but that he was only taking him up for identification. The sense in which these words were used was for the jury to determine. "Taking up" is an ambiguous term, but there was other evidence which could be treated by the jury as showing what the defendant meant by the expression. He admitted having said at Lower Light, "You can buy your own ticket, if you like, but you'll have to be in the carriage with me if you don't want to, but then anyone will know I am taking you down." Clearly the jury might rightly have considered that in the mouth of the defendant the expression "Taking you up for identification" meant compelling the plaintiff to go in custody for identification.

In a case of this description, where there has been no application of physical force to the person alleging imprisonment, there must be evidence of complete submission by him to the control of the other party, for it is obvious that if he evaded, or refused to go with the latter, it could not be said that he had been deprived of his freedom: *Grainger v Hill* (1838) 4 Bing NC 212. This requirement was abundantly satisfied here. After being told at Lower Light that there was a warrant out for his arrest, and that he would have to come to town with the defendant, the plaintiff was asked if he would give his word to be at the Two Wells station next morning. He replied, "I suppose I'll have to," showing an intention to submit. And he did submit, for he went next morning and placed himself in the power of the defendant. He was there told again that he would have to come to town to have matters cleared up, and he got into the train. Arrived in Adelaide, he went with the defendant from the railway station to the watch-house, and, although he was allowed at two different times to go to the Grosvenor Hotel by himself, he did not attempt to do so without asking for and obtaining the leave of the defendant. From all these circumstances the jury might properly infer that he submitted himself to the defendant's power, reasonably thinking that he had no way of escape which could reasonably be taken by him.

There are, no doubt, parts of the evidence of the defendant in contradiction of those which I have above quoted. But it was for the jury to say which version they believed. If they **[454]** accepted the account I have given, which is mainly that of the plaintiff, they would be justified in finding that there was an imprisonment when the plaintiff rendered himself up to the defendant at Two Wells, when he got into the train, and when he was taken to the watch-house at Adelaide.

I am therefore of opinion that the appeal should be dismissed, and the rule discharged with costs.

[Gordon and Poole JJ agreed.]

Appeal dismissed. Rule nisi discharged

South Australia v Lampard-Trevorrow
(2010) 106 SASR 331; [2010] SASC 56
Supreme Court of South Australia, Full Court

The plaintiff's awareness of deprivation of liberty is not an element of the tort of false imprisonment. However, the care and protection given by the carer of a child is not a deprivation of the child's liberty in the sense required to constitute false imprisonment.

[In 1957, at the age of 13 months, the plaintiff, Bruce Trevorrow, an indigenous Australian living in a remote rural community in South Australia with his family, was admitted to hospital suffering gastroenteritis. After he had recovered, South Australian government officials, acting without statutory or other lawful authority and without the knowledge of the plaintiff's family, placed him in foster care with a white family with whom he remained for 10 years, unaware of his natural family, before being returned by the State to his natural mother. During this period, South Australian government officials responded to inquiries by the plaintiff's mother as to his whereabouts by saying he was still sick and needed further treatment.

In proceedings by the plaintiff against the State of South Australia on the basis of its responsibility for the conduct of its officials, the primary judge, Gray J, held that the State was in breach of a relevant duty of care it owed the plaintiff. In addition, the conduct of the government officials constituted misfeasance in public office and breach of fiduciary duty, and the plaintiff had been falsely imprisoned. Compensatory damages were assessed at $450,000 and exemplary damages were assessed at $75,000: *Trevorrow v South Australia (No 5)* (2007) 98 SASR 136.

Although the Full Court dismissed the State of South Australia's appeal, the Full Court disagreed with Gray J's finding that the plaintiff had been falsely imprisoned. This aspect of the judgment of the Full Court (which did not affect the final disposition of the appeal) is extracted below. The Full Court also disagreed with Gray J's finding that there had been a breach of fiduciary duty by the State.

After the judgment of the Full Court, the South Australian government announced that it would not seek leave to appeal to the High Court of Australia.]

DOYLE CJ, DUGGAN and WHITE JJ.[some footnotes in whole or part omitted] ...

[391] 282. We agree with counsel for the State that the fostering of Bruce Trevorrow does not readily fall under the heading of false imprisonment or wrongful imprisonment. In part this is attributable to the use of the word "imprisonment" to capture the factual essence of the cause of action. The factual essence of the cause of action is the placing of a "total restraint" on the plaintiff's movement. That restraint need bear no similarity to what one would normally describe as imprisonment. The law has moved on from any such limitation. ...

284. The State argues that Bruce Trevorrow's liberty was not totally restrained. He was able to move about (once he reached a certain age) as he wished subject **[392]** only to the normal limits placed on children. He was not imprisoned within a defined area. The fact that Mr and Mrs Davies [the foster carers with whom the plaintiff was placed] would have controlled and monitored his movements did not amount, the State argues, to imprisonment.

285. It might be added that if this is a case of total restraint or total deprivation of freedom of movement, then all small children are, as a matter of fact, equally subject to the same restraint. Infants can go only where their parents or guardians take them, or allow them to go. It is true that Bruce Trevorrow, when fostered by Mrs Davies, had the same freedom of movement, or absence of freedom as the case may be, as other children of a like age.

286. In those circumstances can it be said that the fact of total restraint on the freedom of movement was proved? Having posed this question, the State argued that other legal remedies could equally well or better protect the interests at stake here. The law of wrongful imprisonment should not be stretched to cover this case. The State relied on an appeal to coherence in the law to argue that treating this case as a case of wrongful imprisonment would be to allow the tort to invade areas of law better regulated in other ways: cf *Sullivan v Moody* (2001) 207 CLR 562 at [55]. The State argues that Bruce Trevorrow's parents had available to them administrative law remedies to enable them to challenge the actions of the Secretary [of the Aborigines Protection Board] and of the APB [the Aborigines Protection Board]. It is true that in theory they did, however remote the prospect of that happening might be.

287. But an order by the Court quashing or declaring invalid the act of the Secretary or of the APB in placing Bruce Trevorrow with Mrs Davies would not vindicate the interest of Bruce Trevorrow in his freedom, such as it was. Such an order would not compensate Bruce Trevorrow for harm caused to him by the act of the APB. It would restore him to his parents' custody, but would not compensate him for the intrusion on his freedom. As an infant that freedom might be described as latent, but as he grew up it became real.

288. We will return to the question of whether the APB imposed on Bruce Trevorrow, or through Mrs Davies caused to be imposed on him, a restraint of the required kind. Before we do so, we will deal with some other issues.

289. There is a solid body of authority supporting the conclusion that the fact that a plaintiff is not aware of a restraint on him or her, or is not physically able to exercise his or her freedom of movement, does not mean that wrongful imprisonment cannot be made out.

290. In *Meering v Grahame-White Aviation Co Ltd* (1919) 122 LT 44 Atkin LJ said at 53-54:

I think a person can be imprisoned while he is asleep, while he is in a state of drunkenness, while he is unconscious, and while he is a lunatic ... though the imprisonment began and ceased while he was in that state. ...

Warrington LJ said nothing on this point, Duke LJ expressed a contrary opinion. But as we understand the case law, it is the view of Atkin LJ that has subsequently been preferred, when the issue has arisen. ...

[393] 292. In *Murray v Ministry of Defence* [1988] 1 WLR 692 the House of Lords considered a claim for damages for false imprisonment arising from an arrest. Lord Griffiths, with whom the other members of the House of Lords agreed, denied that it was "an essential element of the tort of false imprisonment that the victim should be aware of the fact of denial of liberty": at 701. ...

294. In *Myer Stores Ltd v Soo* [1991] 2 VR 597 two members of the Court said that a person can be imprisoned without knowing and appreciating that fact: Murphy J at 599, O'Bryan J at 615, cf McDonald J at 626.

295. It follows that it should not matter that the victim of the alleged unlawful restraint lacks the mental capacity, permanently or temporarily, to choose to resist the restraint in question. ... A person who is asleep or unconscious, as postulated by Atkin LJ, is temporarily incapable of making the choice to resist or protest the unlawful restraint, but can be the subject of wrongful detention. ...

[394] 297. Although there is no case on point, in our opinion it should not matter that the person who complains of wrongful detention lacks or lacked the physical capacity to exercise the freedom of movement that was denied by the restraint in question. For example, assume a person confined to bed by reason of serious injury or illness, the person being completely unable to leave the bed in the room in which the person is placed. Assume that that person, against his or her will, is removed in the bed to another place and kept there against his or her will. Being unable to move from the bed, that person is incapable of exercising any freedom of movement. But, once again, surely the fact of removal and detention in another location would amount to wrongful detention, even though the person was incapable of moving from the bed in which the person remained at all times.

298. There is another point to be made. We have already commented on the fact that Bruce Trevorrow was subject to no greater restraint than that applied to many infants in his position. The restraint arose from his infancy, rather than being imposed on him, at least for a number of years. But from one point of view, the fact that other children were the subject of a like restraint would appear to be no answer to a claim of wrongful detention. It appears to be accepted that a prisoner who is kept in prison after the date when the prisoner should have been released has a claim for wrongful detention. The prisoner in question is in no different circumstances from other prisoners in the prison. The only difference is that this prisoner should have been released on the release date. Most childcare centres have substantial fences and a gate that children cannot open. A child will usually be allowed to leave the centre only with the permission of a staff member and when collected by an authorised person. All children in the childcare centre are subject to that restraint. Drawing on the decision in *Herring v Boyle* (1834) 149 ER 1126, if the person in charge of the childcare centre refused to release a particular child until fees owing to the centre had been paid, that surely would be a wrongful detention, even though the restraint was no different from the restraint imposed on other children.

299. For these reasons, the fact that Bruce Trevorrow was not aware of any relevant restraint is not decisive, nor is the fact that he was incapable of opposing or consenting to his placement with Mrs Davies. Nor is the fact that he was incapable, at least for some time, of exercising freedom of movement. The fact that he was unaware, for a number of years, of his natural parents, and so practically incapable of expressing any wish to be with them, is also neither here nor there.

300. But the question remains of whether, in all the circumstances, it is right to find in a case like this that there was a total restraint of the kind required to establish liability. ...

301. As we have said, while an infant he [Bruce Trevorrow] could go only where Mrs Davies or a family member took him. As he grew a little older he could go only where Mrs Davies or a family member permitted him to go. No doubt as he grew older, the restraints on his movements lessened. At first, the restraint arose from his own physical incapacity. Later it was attributable to his immaturity, and the [395] duty of Mrs Davies as his carer to take care for his safety. There is nothing to suggest that at any time he was more or less restrained than the average child. There were no set boundaries to his movements, beyond those imposed by Mrs Davies or a family member from time to time. ...

305. There is no decision that covers the situation now before us.

306. We appreciate the force of the argument that the tort of wrongful detention should extend to a situation like the present one. That is a way of vindicating Bruce Trevorrow's interest in the custody and care of his natural parents, and of compensating him for the removal from their custody and care.

307. However, in our opinion the required element of restraint is not made out here. It is artificial to treat the placement of Bruce Trevorrow with Mrs Davies as a restraint. While Bruce Trevorrow was an infant, he needed care and nurture. That is what Mrs Davies gave him. There was no restraint. It is artificial to describe him, while an infant, as under any restraint. As he grew a little older, and could walk and talk, it can be said that there was a restraint on his movements. But the restraint was one attributable to the obligation of [396] Mrs Davies to care for him, and attributable to his immaturity. We do not think it is realistic to describe the care and protection given by the carer of a child as a restraint on the child, in the relevant sense of the term. Bruce Trevorrow was separated from, and denied, the care of his mother, but that does not establish the fact of a restraint. It seems to us that if the notion of restraint for the purposes of the tort of wrongful detention were taken this far, the potential would arise for the tort to expand into previously untouched areas and situations, with unpredictable consequences.

308. The State does not challenge the finding that Bruce Trevorrow's fostering by Mrs Davies, and his removal from his natural parents, resulted in injury that caused loss. Nor does the State challenge the assessment of damages. ...

Appeal dismissed

4. INTENTIONAL INFLICTION OF PSYCHIATRIC INJURY

Wilkinson v Downton
[1897] 2 QB 57
Queen's Bench Division

A person who wilfully does an act calculated to cause physical harm to the plaintiff, including psychiatric injury, is liable to the plaintiff in damages for the harm inflicted.

WRIGHT J. [58] In this case the defendant, in the execution of what he seems to have regarded as a practical joke, represented to the plaintiff that he was charged by her husband with a message to her to the effect that her husband was smashed up in an accident, and was lying at The Elms at Leytonstone with both legs broken, and that she was to go at once in a cab with two pillows to fetch him home. All this was false. The effect of the statement on the plaintiff was a violent shock to her nervous system, producing vomiting and other more serious and permanent physical consequences at one time threatening her reason, and entailing weeks of suffering and incapacity to her as well as expense to her husband for medical attendance. These consequences were not in any way the result of previous ill-health or weakness of constitution; nor was there any evidence of predisposition to nervous shock or any other idiosyncrasy.

In addition to these matters of substance there is a small claim for 1*s* 10 1/2*d* for the cost of railway fares of persons sent by the plaintiff to Leytonstone in obedience to the pretended message. As to this 1*s* 10 1/2*d* expended in railway fares on the faith of the defendant's statement, I think the case is clearly within the decision in *Pasley v Freeman* (1789) 3 TR 51. The statement was a misrepresentation intended to be acted on to the damage of the plaintiff.

The real question is as to the 100*l*, the greatest part of which is given as compensation for the female plaintiff's illness and suffering. It was argued for her that she is entitled to recover this as being damage caused by fraud, and therefore within the doctrine established by *Pasley v Freeman* and *Langridge v Levy* (1837) 2 M & W 519. I am not sure that this would not be an extension of that doctrine, the real ground of which appears to be that a person who makes a false statement intended to be acted on must make good the damage naturally resulting from its being acted on. Here there is no injuria of that kind. I think, however, that the verdict may be supported upon another ground. The defendant has, as I assume for the moment, wilfully done an act calculated to cause physical **[59]** harm to the plaintiff – that is to say, to infringe her legal right to personal safety, and has in fact thereby caused physical harm to her. That proposition without more appears to me to state a good cause of action, there being no justification alleged for the act. This wilful injuria is in law malicious, although no malicious purpose to cause the harm which was caused nor any motive of spite is imputed to the defendant.

It remains to consider whether the assumptions involved in the proposition are made out. One question is whether the defendant's act was so plainly calculated to produce some effect of the kind which was produced that an intention to produce it ought to be imputed to the defendant, regard being had to the fact that the effect was produced on a person proved to be in an ordinary state of health and mind. I think that it was. It is difficult to imagine that such a statement, made suddenly and with apparent seriousness, could fail to produce grave effects under the circumstances upon any but an exceptionally indifferent person, and therefore an intention to produce such an effect must be imputed, and it is no answer in law to say that more harm was done than was anticipated, for that is commonly the case with all wrongs. The other question is whether the effect was, to use the ordinary phrase, too remote to be in law regarded as a consequence for which the defendant is answerable. Apart from authority, I should give the same answer and on the same ground as the last question, and say that it was not too remote. Whether, as the majority of the House of Lords thought in *Lynch v Knight* (1861) 9 HLC 577, at pp 592, 596, the criterion is in asking what would be the natural effect on reasonable persons, or whether, as Lord Wensleydale thought ((1861) 9 HLC 577 at p 600), the possible infirmities of human nature ought to be recognised, it seems to me that the connection between the cause and the effect is sufficiently close and complete. …

[61] There must be judgment for the plaintiff for 100*l* 1*s* 10 1/2.

Judgment for the plaintiff

Bunyan v Jordan
(1937) 57 CLR 1
High Court of Australia

Under the principle in Wilkinson v Downton, the defendant's wilful act must be such as to cause harm to a "normal" person in the plaintiff's position unless the "peculiarly susceptible" disposition of the plaintiff is known to the defendant.

[The plaintiff went into the office of the defendant, her employer, and noticed a revolver lying on the table from which she watched him extract the cartridges. She walked out of the office and overheard him say that he was going to shoot himself or someone. A shot was then heard. The plaintiff alleged that she had suffered a nervous illness brought about by the shock she had sustained and sued the defendant for negligence, breach of contract, assault and for causing harm with wilful intent.

The trial judge entered judgment by direction for the defendant, which was upheld by the Full Court of the Supreme Court of New South Wales. The plaintiff appealed to the High Court on the issue of whether it was open to a jury to find facts constituting any cause of action against the defendant.]

LATHAM CJ. ... **[9]** [I]t is said that [the pleadings disclose] three possible causes of action.

In the first place it is said that the evidence shows that the defendant deliberately uttered words, namely, "I am going to shoot someone" and discharged a revolver and that thereby the **[10]** plaintiff sustained a shock which produced illness. This suggested cause of action is independent of any intention to injure the plaintiff and of any negligence and of any special relationship between the parties which could be the foundation of any legal duty. It would involve the principle that the mere fact that a man is injured by another's act gives him a cause of action. No such principle is known to the law. If authority is required for this negative proposition it may be found in *Grant v Australian Knitting Mills Ltd* [1936] AC at p 103; *Farr v Butters Bros & Co* [1932] 2 KB at p 613.

In the second place it is argued that the evidence shows that the defendant deliberately spoke the words mentioned and fired a revolver with the intention of frightening his sons: that in fact he frightened the plaintiff, and that his wrongful act in attempting to frighten his sons caused the personal injury of which the plaintiff complains. If a person deliberately does an act of a kind calculated to cause physical injury for which there is no lawful justification or excuse and in fact causes physical injury to that other person, he is liable in damages (*Wilkinson v Downton* [1897] 2 QB 57). ... In *Janvier v Sweeney* [1919] 2 KB 316 also there was an intention to injure and it was obvious that the act done was likely to cause harm. In that case it was held that threats addressed to a person which were calculated to cause injury, which were uttered with the knowledge that they were likely to cause such injury, and which actually caused **[11]** such injury, were actionable. The result of the threats made to the woman plaintiff in that case was that she was extremely frightened so that she suffered very severe nervous shock and had a long period of serious illness. The fact that one link in the causation was mental in character was held not to affect the plaintiff's right of action. The threats found by the jury to have been uttered were directed against the woman plaintiff and also against the man to whom she was betrothed. ...

In *Wilkinson v Downton* [1897] 2 QB 57 and in *Janvier v Sweeney* [1919] 2 KB 316 the person suffering the injury was the person to whom the words were uttered, and the words spoken were of such a character and were spoken in such circumstances that it was naturally to be expected that they might cause a very severe nervous shock with serious results to the health of the person to whom the words were said. In the present case the words were not uttered to the plaintiff and they were not even uttered in her presence. According to her own evidence she overheard them being uttered to someone else after she had left the room in which the defendant was at the time. ...

[12] None of the cases has gone so far as to suggest that a man owes a duty to persons who merely happen to overhear statements that are not addressed to them. There is the additional fact of the revolver shot, but there is no reason to suppose or anticipate that the firing of a revolver shot, even following upon a threat of shooting somebody, will cause serious illness to a person who hears it fired. The acts of the defendant, taken all together, cannot be said to be calculated or likely to cause harm to any person – even to his sons, if they were normal persons.

[13] In the third place it is urged that the defendant is liable as for negligence. It is said that he owes a duty to the plaintiff to take care to avoid doing acts in relation to her which might damage her personal safety unless there was some lawful justification or excuse for doing those acts. ... In the present case it is difficult to define the duty upon the breach of which the plaintiff must rely in order to succeed in an action for negligence. It cannot be said that there is a simple absolute legal duty to avoid frightening people, or even to avoid causing injury to them by frightening them (See *Wilkinson v Downton* [1897] 2 QB 57 and *Janvier v Sweeney* [1919] 2 KB 316). Where there is any duty to take care, the duty is to take reasonable care in all the circumstances of the case, and, in defining the extent of the duty, it is necessary to consider what results may reasonably be expected to follow from the act in question in a particular case. ...

[14] In this case the application of this principle reduces itself to finding the answer to the question whether it can fairly be said that the defendant might reasonably have expected that after the plaintiff had seen him with the revolver she might overhear what she subsequently did overhear and, hearing the revolver shot soon afterwards, might get such a fright as to suffer personal injury. In the case of a person known to the defendant to be highly nervous it might be said that such a result could be expected. There is, however, no evidence that, if the plaintiff was peculiarly susceptible to nervous shock, the defendant was aware that that was the case. In the case of ordinary persons, if a man said to them that he was going to shoot somebody and they then heard a shot or even saw the speaker shoot himself or someone else, they would be disturbed or upset in varying degrees, but they would not suffer from illness producing a nervous breakdown. Such a consequence is not within the scope of reasonable anticipation. Accordingly I am of opinion that there was no evidence upon which any jury could properly hold that the defendant was guilty of negligence in this case. ...

I think the judgment of the Supreme Court ... should be affirmed ...

DIXON J. ... [15] Upon the evidence as it stands the jury might find, I think, that, under the influence [16] of drink, the defendant produced a bottle labelled "Poison" and a revolver, threatened to commit suicide, and afterwards fired a shot, all with the intention of promoting among those about him feelings of interest, surprise, pity and horror. With the same view, on his reappearance unharmed, he proceeded to tear up pound notes, saying that he would not be there in the morning. The plaintiff was one of those about the defendant at the time he exposed the poison and the revolver to view and when he threatened suicide. When he fired the shot he was outside, but the distance was not great and she could plainly hear the shot.

The jury would not be at liberty to find that he had a specific intention of frightening the plaintiff, but they might conclude that he intended to arouse the feelings I have described in all those who were at hand, including the plaintiff. On the medical evidence, the jury might find that the defendant's actions threw the plaintiff into a sufficiently emotional condition to lead to a neurasthenic breakdown amounting to an illness.

I have no doubt that such an illness without more is a form of harm or damage sufficient for the purpose of any action on the case in which damage is the gist of the action, that is, supposing that the other ingredients of the cause of action are present. But I do think that upon facts like those I have stated it is impossible to formulate any cause of action in which the reasonable likelihood of harm of some such nature resulting from the act done does not form an essential element. ...

[17] On the facts of the present case I am of opinion that this element is not established. It is, of course, quite clear that the defendant did not intend to bring upon the plaintiff a nervous breakdown or any physical harm. He may have intended to frighten those surrounding him, but, if so, it was only for the purpose of sensationalism. The shock he intended to give or the emotions he intended to arouse could not in a normal person be more than transient. The harm which is said in fact to have ensued is not a consequence which might reasonably have been anticipated or foreseen.

Upon this ground I am of opinion that the appeal should be dismissed.

[Rich and McTiernan JJ delivered concurring judgments. Evatt J dissented.]

Appeal dismissed

Carrier v Bonham
[2002] 1 Qd R 474; [2001] QCA 234
Supreme Court of Queensland, Court of Appeal

The phrase "calculated to cause harm" under the rule in Wilkinson v Downton means objectively "likely to have that effect" rather than "intended to have that effect".

[The appellant (defendant) was a mentally ill patient who had escaped from hospital and stepped in front of a moving bus with the intention of committing suicide. The respondent (plaintiff) was the bus driver who, as a result of the experience, suffered nervous shock. The respondent sued the appellant in negligence and under the rule in *Wilkinson v Downton* [1897] 2 QB 57. The trial judge dismissed the action in negligence on the ground that the appellant had not breached the standard of care expected of him. According to the judge, the standard was not the purely objective standard of an ordinary person but someone with a mental illness. However, the trial judge held the appellant liable under the rule in *Wilkinson v Downton*. The appellant challenged this latter ruling in the Court of Appeal of the Supreme Court of Queensland. With regard to the action in negligence, the court held that the trial judge had erred in lowering the standard of care by taking into account the appellant's mental illness. In respect of the action based on the rule in *Wilkinson v Downton*, the court held that the trial judge had correctly applied the rule. Accordingly, the appellant was liable to the respondent both in negligence and under the rule. The following extracts are primarily concerned with the said rule.]

McMURDO P. ... **[480]** I am ... of the view that the appellant was liable for the tort described as an action on the case, the principles of which were first set out in *Wilkinson v Downton* [1897] 2 QB 57 and referred to with approval in *Bunyan v Jordan* (1936) 36 SR (NSW) 350 and *Northern Territory of Australia v Mengel* (1995) 185 CLR 307. The mental element of the tort was described in *Wilkinson v Downton* as established where:

"The defendant has ... wilfully done an action [sic] *calculated* to cause physical harm to the plaintiff – that is to say to infringe her legal right to personal safety and has in fact thereby caused physical harm to her ... This wilful injuria is in law malicious, although no malicious purpose to cause the harm which was caused nor any motive of spite is imputed to the defendant.

... One question is whether the defendant's act was so plainly *calculated* to produce some effect of the kind which was produced that an intention to produce it ought to be imputed to the defendant, regard being had to the fact that the effect was produced on a person proved to be in an ordinary state of health and mind." *(my emphasis)*

The key to the required intention is the meaning of "calculated" in this context. In *Mengel*, which involved the tort of misfeasance of public office, Brennan J concluded that the mental element in that tort is satisfied either by malice or by knowledge, adding:

"Another state of mind which is inconsistent with an honest attempt to perform the functions of public office is reckless indifference as to the availability of power to support the impugned conduct and as to the injury which the impugned conduct is *calculated* to produce. The state of mind relates to the character of the conduct in which the public officer is engaged – whether it is within power and whether it is *calculated* (that is, naturally adapted in the circumstances) to produce injury." *(my emphasis)*

[481] The same meaning should be given to "calculated" in the context of the intention required for liability under *Wilkinson v Downton*. Where "calculated" describes a set of words, as in *Wilkinson v Downton*, "calculated" describes the quality of those words and means "likely to have that effect", rather than "intending to have that effect": *Howard v Gallagher* (1989) 85 ALR 495 and cf *O'Sullivan v Lunnon* (1986) 163 CLR 545.

On the facts of this case, the appellant's actions were calculated (that is, likely, naturally adapted in the circumstances) to cause injury to the respondent driver. The appellant was liable to the respondent in both negligence and on an action on the case ...

McPHERSON JA. ... **[482]** [T]he learned judge went on to hold that the first defendant was liable to the plaintiff on the authority of *Wilkinson v Downton*. That is the well known case in which the defendant as a practical joke told the plaintiff's wife that the plaintiff had been seriously injured in an accident, with the consequence that she suffered shock and illness, pain and suffering. Saying that the defendant would be liable for having "wilfully done an act calculated to cause physical harm to the plaintiff", and which had in fact done so, R S Wright J held (at 58-59) that the defendant's act was "so plainly calculated to produce some effect of the kind which was produced that an intention to produce it ought to be imputed to the defendant". He added that it was no answer in law to say that more harm was done than was expected or anticipated "for that is commonly the case with all wrongs".

The decision has since been applied throughout the common law world on occasions too numerous to mention. In *Bunyan v Jordan* (1936) 36 SR (NSW) 350, Jordan CJ said (at 353):

"Whenever a person does an act which has the effect of causing physical injury to another in circumstances which do not amount to trespass to the person, he is legally responsible if the act was done negligently (that is, if it was done carelessly in circumstances which created a legal duty to be careful) and the injury was attributable to the negligence."

It was not a case involving unsoundness of mind on the part of the defendant, except perhaps in the limited sense that, if there was madness, then as with Prince Hamlet there was method in it. On appeal in *Bunyan v Jordan* (1937) 57 CLR 1 at 10, Latham CJ said that if a person "deliberately does an act of a kind calculated to cause physical injury ... and in fact causes physical injury to that other person, he is liable in damages". In *Northern Territory v Mengel* (1995) 185 CLR 307 at 347, **[483]** their Honours referred to *Wilkinson v Downton* as conceptually illustrative of "acts which are calculated in the ordinary course to cause harm ... or which are done with needless indifference to the harm that is likely to ensue". See also *Khorasandjian v Bush* [1993] QB 727, 735.

The appellant Bonham seizes on the word "calculated" in these passages as demonstrating a need to show an intention to cause, or at least actual foresight of the likelihood of causing, harm of some kind. From there he submits that no such intention or foresight can, because of his mental condition, be attributed or imputed to him. Dr Joan Lawrence, whose evidence on this matter was accepted by the trial judge, considered that Bonham would not have been capable of being aware of the fact that his actions might cause injury to people on the bus. She did not believe, she said, that that would have been in his mind at all; he would have had absolutely no concept of what his actions might do to someone else.

To my mind, however, the problem is that the expression "calculated" which is used in those passages is one of those weasel words that is capable of meaning either subjectively contemplated and intended, or objectively likely to happen. See, for example, *O'Sullivan v Lunnon* (1986) 163 CLR 545 at 549. The implication I draw from the context in which the word appears in the passages quoted is that it was being used in the latter and not the former sense. That seems plainly to be so in what was said by Latham CJ in *Bunyan v Jordan* (1937) 57 CLR 1 at 11, where, reverting to *Wilkinson v Downton*, his Honour remarked that the words in that case were of such a character and spoken in such circumstances that "it was naturally to be expected that they might cause a very severe nervous shock". Certainly that seems to have been the view of Dixon J who, in contrasting the facts of *Bunyan v Jordan* (1937) 57 CLR 1 with those of *Wilkinson v Downton*, concluded at 17 that the harm which was said in fact to have ensued in the case before the High Court, was "not a consequence which might reasonably have been anticipated or foreseen". It must be recalled that in 1937 the common law was still labouring to some extent under the shadow of the decision in *Victorian Railways Commissioners v Coultas* (1888) 13 App Cas 222, which appeared to deny liability for damages for "pure" fright or nervous shock on the ground that it was too "remote": see *Wilkinson v Downton* at 59-61. From that particular species of intellectual bondage, courts in Australia were perhaps not completely set free until the decision in *Jaensch v Coffey* (1984) 155 CLR 549. It is considerations of that kind that also explain the rather cautious tone of Dean Roscoe Pound's statement, to which Dixon J referred in his judgment in *Bunyan v Jordan* (1937) 57 CLR 1 at 16.

Wilkinson v Downton is still sometimes described as being an action "on the case", as if that would serve to distinguish it from actions for negligence. The implication seems to be that it does not quite fit the traditional dichotomy between liability in trespass for intentional wrongs, and liability in negligence for those that involve conduct that is merely inattentive. Despite the debate generated by *Fowler v Lanning* [1959] 1 QB 426, the distinction that was recognised by the late 18th century did not correspond to that between intentional and unintentional harm. As is evident from the differences of judicial opinion in the famous case of *Scott v Shepherd* (1773) 2 Wm Black 892; 96 ER 525 (the Squib Case), the difference was between harm that was immediate and direct, and harm that was caused indirectly. See *Platt v Nutt* (1988) 12 NSWLR 231. Even **[484]** that distinction has been shown by Professor Milsom to be historically astray, in (1954) 12 CLJ 105, where the learned author points out that trespass was originally the generic name for all "wrongs" or, as we would now say, torts. See also JH Baker *Introduction to English Legal History* (3rd ed) at 71-75, 454. In that broader sense of the word, we still ask to be forgiven our "trespasses".

The feature that is often singled out as peculiar about *Wilkinson v Downton* is that it was an intentional act which had reasonably foreseeable consequences that were apparently not in fact foreseen by the defendant in all their severity; but that is, as RS Wright J pointed out in *Wilkinson v Downton*, "commonly the case with all wrongs". Most everyday acts of what we call actionable negligence are in fact wholly or partly a product of intentional conduct. Driving a motor vehicle at high speed through a residential area is an intentional act even if injuring people or property on the way is not a result actually intended. *Wilkinson v Downton* is an example of that kind. The defendant intended to speak the words in question to the plaintiff's wife. Even if he did not intend to inflict the harm on her that followed, or perhaps any harm at all, he was plainly negligent as regards the result that followed. It is only when injury ensues from inaction or omission to act that problems may still arise at common law about whether the wrong is, properly speaking, the act or conduct of the defendant. Otherwise, since the Judicature Act which, in Maitland's famous phrase, buried the forms of action, it no longer matters whether the act was done intentionally or negligently, or partly one and partly the other. What matters is whether the consequences of the conduct, whether foreseen or not, were reasonably foreseeable and are such as should have been averted or avoided. What we really have now is not two distinct torts of trespass and negligence, but a single tort of failing to use reasonable care to avoid damage however caused. Negligence, if narrowly understood, is something of a misnomer.

It follows, in my opinion, that if the defendant Bonham in this case was, because of his mental condition, not legally responsible for the foreseeable consequences of his action in throwing himself at or under the bus, he was no more liable under the decision in *Wilkinson v Downton* than he was according to ordinary principles of the law of negligence ...

[486] What is in issue here is the significance of the defendant's mental incapacity to foresee that his actions might cause injury to someone else. Ever since the decision in *Vaughan v Menlove* (1837) 3 Bing (NC) 468; 132 ER 490, the established rule of our law has been that the standard for judging negligence is "the conduct of a man of ordinary prudence" (Tindal CJ, at 474). The decision is directly relevant here because the defendant who, against all advice, had risked spontaneous combustion in his hayrick, obtained a rule nisi for a new trial on the ground (at 471) that "he had acted bona fide to the best of his judgment; [and] if he had, he ought not to be responsible for the misfortune of not possessing the highest order of intelligence". It also appears from the report (at 472) that, a few years before, he had been successfully sued for burning weeds so near the boundary of his land as to set fire to and destroy his neighbour's wood. The point being made by the defendant there was that he was a man of reduced intelligence; but the rule nisi for a new trial was nevertheless discharged by the Common Pleas. The decision has been "generally recognised ever since" as having set an objective standard of conduct that is independent of the idiosyncrasies of particular individuals: *McHale v Watson* (1964) 111 CLR 384, 396-397 (Windeyer J) ...

[488] For these reasons I would, for the findings made by the learned trial judge, substitute findings that the first defendant's mental condition had no effect on the standard of care owed by him to the plaintiff, which, on the contrary, is to be judged by the standard of the ordinary and reasonable person, and that it did not diminish or reduce his liability in negligence to the plaintiff.

This has the consequence that, as to liability, the appeal must be dismissed ...

[Moynihan J agreed with McPherson JA.]

Appeal dismissed

Nationwide News Pty Ltd v Naidu
(2007) 71 NSWLR 471; [2007] NSWCA 377
Supreme Court of New South Wales, Court of Appeal

The Wilkinson v Downton line of authority provides a basis of claim where harassment, racial vilification and personal abuse cause psychiatric injury.

[The plaintiff (respondent), Mr Devandar Naidu, was employed as a security guard by ISS Security Pty Ltd ("ISS"). Pursuant to a contract between ISS and the defendant (appellant),

Nationwide News Pty Ltd, ISS made the plaintiff available to provide security services at the defendant's premises. As a result of the humiliating and harassing treatment, racial vilification and personal abuse to which the plaintiff was subjected by his supervisor, the defendant's fire and safety officer, Mr Lance Chaloner, the plaintiff suffered psychiatric injury. In the plaintiff's claim against the defendant, the New South Wales Court of Appeal upheld the primary judge's award of damages in favour of the plaintiff, including exemplary damages of $150,000, for breach of the duty of care owed him by the defendant.

Although the other members of the court found it unnecessary to decide whether Mr Chaloner's conduct constituted an intentional tort, this issue was considered by the Chief Justice.]

SPIGELMAN CJ. ...

[485] The intentional tort ...

67. His Honour's [the primary judge, Adams J] findings of fact are that Mr Chaloner wilfully committed a series of acts calculated to cause Mr Naidu physical harm, being a recognised psychiatric injury. This could constitute an intentional tort of the character identified in *Wilkinson v Downton* [1897] 2 QB 57 affirmed in *Janvier v Sweeney* [1919] 2 KB 316 and accepted, albeit without affirmation, by the High Court in *Bunyan v Jordan* (1937) 57 CLR 1 and *Northern Territory v Mengel* (1995) 185 CLR 307 at 347. ...

[486] 70. A conclusion in a particular case that what was involved was the intentional infliction of personal injury is a matter of significance, for example, for deciding whether to award exemplary damages and also for determining any question of contribution between joint tort feasors. Indeed, with respect to a range of matters, notably the availability of exemplary damages, the distinction between an intentional tort and negligence will be of growing significance by reason of the exemption of the intentional torts by s 3B of the *Civil Liability Act 2002* [NSW] from the provisions of that Act, which modify the common law of negligence in a number of significant respects. ...

71. Observations have been made which suggest that the reasons that led the courts to develop the *Wilkinson v Downton* line of authority have been superseded by the tort of negligence and that therefore *Wilkinson v Downton* has "no leading role in the modern world": *Wainwright v Home Office* [2004] AC 406 at 425; see generally the analysis per Lord Hoffmann (at 424 [36]-[47]).

72. In Australia it has been suggested that the *Wilkinson v Downton* line of authority has been "subsumed under the unintentional tort of negligence". See *Magill v Magill* (2006) 226 CLR 551 at 589 [117]. However, this Court should follow the acceptance by the High Court of the authority of *Wilkinson v Downton* in *Bunyan v Jordan* and in the joint judgment in *Northern Territory v Mengel*. ...

[487] 74. Although in some respects an intentional tort is more difficult to establish than negligence, it is not confined by a test of foreseeability and does not involve an inquiry into reasonableness of response. ...

76. One issue that arises is what is meant by the word "calculated" in the *Wilkinson v Downton* and *Janvier v Sweeney* formulation of the tort. For the reasons I have set out above [at 478], psychiatric injury was reasonably foreseeable on the test of conceivable foreseeability adopted for the law of negligence. Clearly something substantially more certain is required for the intentional tort.

77. The word "calculated" is notoriously ambiguous: it can either mean a subjective, actual, conscious desire to bring about a specific result or it can mean what is likely, perhaps overwhelmingly likely, to occur considered objectively. [The Chief Justice referred to the judgment of McPherson JA in *Carrier v Bonham* [2002] 1 Qd R 474 at 483 and continued.] ...

79. This issue has not been determined authoritatively. It does appear that an actual subjective intention is not required. Indeed, the formulation in *Wilkinson v Downton* (at 59) refers to an "imputed intention". (See also the reference by Latham CJ to the result that was "naturally to be expected" in *Bunyan v Jordan* (at 11).)

80. It is not necessary, in this case, to decide, as McMurdo P suggests in *Carrier v Bonham* (at [12]), that "calculated" means "likely to have that effect". It may be that it is sufficient if the

result satisfied a test of "substantial certainty". … However, a test of reckless indifference to a result will, in this context, satisfy the requirement of intention. … In the present case, the findings of Adams J establish such reckless indifference and that is sufficient to establish intention, just as it is in the criminal law.

81. The High Court has authoritatively established the test for recovery of consequential loss in the case of an intentional tort in terms of asking whether the particular head of damage is a natural and probable result of conduct. (See *Palmer Bruyn & Parker Pty Ltd v Parsons* (2001) 208 CLR 388 especially at 396 [13], 411 [73], 425 [114]. See also *TCN Channel Nine Pty Ltd v Anning* (2002) 54 NSWLR 333 at 352 [100].)

82. There is no finding that Mr Chaloner did actually intend to inflict psychiatric damage. However, the nature and scale of his conduct was such, as the expert evidence confirmed, as to constitute a recognised psychiatric injury as a natural and probable consequence of that course of conduct. The limitations of foresight and remoteness are not applicable. (See *Palmer Bruyn* (at 396 [13], 413 [78]).)

83. If sued, Mr Chaloner would, in my opinion, have been liable to pay the damages awarded to Mr Naidu on the basis of the intentional infliction of psychiatric injury. …

Appeal dismissed

Chapter 3

Interference with Land

1. TRESPASS

(a) Scope of the Tort

Halliday v Nevill
(1984) 155 CLR 1
High Court of Australia

Trespass to land comprises a direct interference without lawful authority. The occupier may expressly or impliedly authorise entry or revoke that authority.

[Police Constable Nevill and Police Constable Brida were on patrol in a police car when they saw the appellant, who was known to Police Constable Brida as a disqualified driver, reversing a car out of the driveway of private residential premises, 375 Liberty Parade. After driving into the street the appellant saw the police car and drove back into the driveway. The police officers stopped their car and walked down the open driveway where Police Constable Nevill arrested the appellant for driving while disqualified. Prior to the arrest the police officers did not seek and were not given express permission by the occupier of the premises, a person known to the appellant, to enter on the driveway.

The appellant was charged with various offences on informations laid by the police officers. However, the informations were dismissed by the magistrate on the ground that the arrest of the appellant was unlawful because the police officers were trespassers at the time of the arrest.

In the Supreme Court of Victoria, Brooking J made absolute orders nisi to review the magistrate's decision.

The appellant appealed to the High Court of Australia.]

GIBBS CJ, MASON, WILSON and DEANE JJ. ... **[6]** It is common ground that the appeal must fail unless Police Constable Nevill was, at the time he arrested the appellant in the driveway of premises at 375 Liberty Parade, a trespasser on that driveway. The evidence on that question is sparse. On that evidence however, we consider that the only conclusion which is open as a matter of law is that Police Constable Nevill had an implied licence from the occupier of the premises to be upon the driveway.

While the question whether an occupier of land has granted a licence to another to enter upon it is essentially a question of fact, **[7]** there are circumstances in which such a licence will, as a matter of law, be implied unless there is something additional in the objective facts which is capable of founding a conclusion that any such implied or tacit licence was negated or was revoked: cf *Edwards v Railway Executive* [1952] AC 737, at p 744. The most common instance of such an implied licence relates to the means of access, whether path, driveway or both, leading to the entrance of the ordinary suburban dwelling-house. If the path or driveway leading to the entrance of such a dwelling is left unobstructed and with entrance gate unlocked and there is no notice or other indication that entry by visitors generally or particularly designated visitors is forbidden or unauthorized, the law will imply a licence in favour of any member of the public to go upon the path or driveway to the entrance of the dwelling for the purpose of lawful communication with, or delivery to, any person in the house. Such an implied or tacit licence can be precluded or at any time revoked by express or implied refusal or withdrawal of it. The occupier will not however be heard to say that while he or she had neither done nor said anything to negate or revoke any such licence, it should not be implied because subjectively he or she had not intended to give it: see, generally, *Robson v Hallett* [1967] 2 QB 939, at pp 950-952, 953-954; *Lipman v Clendinnen* (1932) 46 CLR 550, at pp 556-557; *Lambert v Roberts* (1980) 72 Cr App R 223, at p 230. Nor, in such a case, will the implied licence ordinarily be restricted to presence on the open driveway or path for the purpose of going to the entrance of the house. A passer-by is not a trespasser if, on passing an open driveway with no indication that entry is forbidden or unauthorized, he or she steps upon it either unintentionally or to avoid an obstruction such as a vehicle parked across the footpath. Nor will such a passer-by be a trespasser if, for example, he or she goes upon the driveway to recover some item of his or her property which has fallen or blown upon it or to lead away an errant child. To adapt the words of Lord Parker CJ in *Robson* [1967] 2 QB, at p 950, the law is not such an ass that the implied or tacit licence in such a case is restricted to stepping over the item of property or around the child for the purpose of going to the entrance and asking the householder whether the item of property can be reclaimed or the child led away. The path or driveway is, in such circumstances, held out by the occupier as the bridge between the public thoroughfare and his or her private dwelling upon which a passer-by may go for a legitimate purpose that in itself involves no **[8]** interference with the occupier's possession nor injury to the occupier, his or her guests or his, her or their property.

The evidence indicates that the premises at 375 Liberty Parade were residential premises with an open driveway to the roadway. There is no suggestion that the driveway was closed off by a locked gate or any other obstruction or that there was any notice or other indication advising either visitors generally or a particular class or type of visitor that intrusion upon the open driveway was forbidden. That being so, a variety of persons with a variety of legitimate purposes had, as a matter of law, an implied licence from the occupier to go upon the driveway. The question which arises is whether, in those circumstances, the proper inference as a matter of law is that a member of the police force has an implied or tacit licence from the occupier to set foot on the open driveway for the purpose of questioning or arresting a person whom he had observed committing an offence on a public street in the immediate vicinity of that driveway. The conclusion which we have reached is that common sense, reinforced by considerations of public policy, requires that that question be answered in the affirmative. That conclusion does not involve any derogation of the right of an occupier of a suburban dwelling to prevent a member of the police force who has no overriding statutory or common law right of entry from coming upon his land. Any such occupier who desires to convert his path or driveway adjoining the public road into a haven for minor miscreants can, by taking appropriate steps, preclude the implication of a licence to a member of the police force to enter upon the path or driveway to effect an arrest with the result that a police officer's rights of entry are restricted to whatever overriding rights he might possess under some express provision or necessary implication of a statute (cf *Crimes Act 1958* (Vic), s 459A and note generally *Morris v Beardmore* [1981] AC 446 and the discussion in the judgment of Kennedy J in *Dobie v Pinker* [1983] WAR 48 of the common law). All that conclusion involves is that, in the absence of any indication to the contrary, the implied or tacit licence to persons to go upon the open driveway of a suburban dwelling for legitimate purposes is not so confined as to exclude from its scope a member of the police force who goes upon the driveway in the ordinary course of his duty for the purpose of questioning or arresting a trespasser or a lawful visitor upon it. It follows that Police Constable Nevill was lawfully upon the driveway of 375 Liberty Parade when he arrested the appellant. ...

[9] We would dismiss the appeal.

[Brennan J delivered a dissenting judgment.]

Appeal dismissed

Plenty v Dillon
(1991) 171 CLR 635
High Court of Australia

There are only limited exceptions to the fundamental common law principle that entry onto land without the authority of the occupier is a trespass. The action in trespass to land serves to vindicate an occupier's right to exclusive use and occupation.

[The plaintiff (appellant) was the owner and occupier of a farm near Port Pirie, South Australia. The defendants (respondents) were police officers who entered the farm, without the plaintiff's express or implied consent and contrary to his known will, for the purpose of serving notices on the plaintiff and his wife and a summons on their daughter aged 14 issued pursuant to the *Juvenile Courts Act 1971* (SA).

In respect of this entry the plaintiff sued the defendants in the Supreme Court of South Australia for damages for trespass. The trial judge gave judgment for the defendants and this was affirmed by the Full Court. The plaintiff appealed to the High Court of Australia.]

MASON CJ, BRENNAN and TOOHEY JJ. ... **[639]** The starting point is the judgment of Lord Camden LCJ in *Entick v Carrington* (1765) 19 St Tr 1029 at 1066:

By the laws of England, every invasion of private property, be it ever so minute, is a trespass. No man can set his foot upon my ground without my licence, but he is liable to an action, though the damage be nothing ... If he admits the fact, he is bound to shew by way of justification, that some positive law has empowered or excused him.

And see *Great Central Railway Co v Bates* [1921] 3 KB 578 at 582; *Morris v Beardmore* [1981] AC 446, at 464. The principle applies to entry by persons purporting to act with the authority of the Crown as well as to entry by other persons. As Lord Denning MR said in *Southam v Smout* [1964] 1 QB 308 at 320, adopting a quotation from the Earl of Chatham:

"The poorest man may in his cottage bid defiance to all the forces of the Crown. It may be frail – its roof may shake – the wind may blow through it – the storm may enter – the rain may enter – but the King of England cannot enter – all his force dares not cross the threshold of the ruined tenement." So be it – unless he has justification by law.

And in *Halliday v Nevill* (1984) 155 CLR 1, Brennan J said (at 10):

The principle applies alike to officers of government and to private persons. A police officer who enters or remains on private property without the leave and licence of the person in possession or entitled to possession commits a trespass and acts outside the course of his duty unless his entering or remaining on the premises is authorised or excused by law.

The proposition that any person who "set[s] his foot upon my ground without my licence ... is liable to an action" in trespass is qualified by exceptions both at common law and by statute. The first ground relied on to authorise or excuse the entry of Constables Dillon and Will on Mr Plenty's farm on the occasion of the attempted service of the fresh summons was the common law rule known as the third rule in *Semayne's Case* (1604) 5 Co Re 91a at 91b (77 ER 194 at 195) which reads:

In all cases when the King is party, the sheriff (if the doors be not open) may break the party's house, either to arrest him, or to do other execution of the [King]'s process, if otherwise he cannot enter. But before he breaks it, he ought to signify the cause of his coming, and to make request to open doors.

[640] The scope of the third rule in *Semayne's Case* is stated in *Tomlins' Law-Dictionary* (4th ed, 1835), vol I, tit Execution, III 3:

It is laid down as a general rule in our books, that the sheriff, in executing any judicial writ, cannot break open the door of a dwelling-house; this privilege, which the law allows to a man's habitation, arises from the great regard the law has to every man's safety and quiet, and therefore protects them from the inconveniences which must necessarily attend an unlimited power in the sheriff and his officers in this respect; hence, every man's house is called his castle. *5 Co 91: 3 Inst 162: Moor, 668: Yelv 28: Cro Eliz 908: Dalt Shar 350.*

Yet in favour of executions, which are the life of the law, and especially in cases of great necessity, or where the safety of the king and commonwealth are concerned, this general case has the following exceptions:

1st. That whenever the process is at the suit of the king, the sheriff or his officer may, after request to have the door opened, and refusal, break and enter the house to do execution, either on the party's goods, or take his body, as the case shall be. *5 Co 91b.*

The third rule in *Semayne's Case* provides justification for more than a mere entry onto land; in terms it relates to breaking into a dwelling-house. The justification afforded by the rule is needed only when the alleged trespass is of that kind: see, for example, *Penton v Brown* (1664) 1 Keb 698 (83 ER 1193); *Southam v Smout*, at 321 et seq. Of course, justification for breaking into a dwelling is justification for entering on the land on which the dwelling stands. However, the third rule in *Semayne's Case* affords justification for an entry, whether by breaking into a dwelling-house or not, only when the purpose of the person making the entry is either "to arrest ... or to do other execution of the [King]'s process". It is not suggested that the defendant police officers proposed to arrest Mr Plenty's daughter. They had no authority to do so. ... So the question is whether the police officers were engaged in "execution of the [King]'s process". ...

[641] We take the third rule's reference to execution of process to relate to the enforcement of process which is coercive in nature, that is, to the execution of process against person or property. ... The service of a summons is not an execution of process of that nature. ...

[644] It follows that the common law gave no authority to Constables Dillon and Will to go onto Mr Plenty's farm in an attempt to serve the fresh summons on Mr Plenty's daughter.

[Their Honours also found that there was no statutory authority for the defendants' entry on the plaintiff's farm.]

[645] The grounds advanced by the defendants to justify their entry fail. Their entry was wrongful, and the plaintiff is entitled to judgment and an award of some damages. ... At first instance, Mohr J said that, even if trespass had occurred, the trespass was "of such a trifling nature as not to sound in damages". But this is an action in trespass not in case and the plaintiff is entitled to some damages in vindication of his right to exclude the defendants from his farm. As the subject of damages was not argued before us, it will be necessary to remit the assessment of damages to the Supreme Court. ...

GAUDRON and McHUGH JJ. ... **[647]** The policy of the law is to protect the possession of property and the privacy and security of its occupier: *Semayne's Case* (1604) 5 Co Rep 91a at 91b (77 ER 194 at 195); *Entick v Carrington* (1765) 2 Wils KB 275 at 291 (95 ER 807 at 817); *Southam v Smout* [1964] 1 QB 308 at 320; *Eccles v Bourque* [1975] 2 SCR 739 at 742-743; (1974) 50 DLR (3d) 753 at 755; *Morris v Beardmore* [1981] AC 446 at 464. A person who enters the property of another must justify that entry by showing that he or she entered with the consent of the occupier or otherwise had lawful authority to enter the premises: *Entick*, at 291 (817); *Morris v Beardmore*, at 464; *Southam v Smout*, at 320; *Halliday v Nevill* (1984) 155 CLR 1 at 10. Except in the cases provided for by the common law and by statute, constables of police and those acting under the Crown have no special rights to enter land: *Halliday*, at 10. Consent to an entry is implied if the person enters for a lawful purpose. In *Robson v Hallett* [1967] 2 QB 939, Lord Parker CJ said (at 951):

the occupier of any dwelling-house gives implied licence to any member of the public coming on his lawful business to come through the gate, up the steps, and knock on the door of the house.

This implied licence extends to the driveway of a dwelling-house: *Halliday*. However, the licence may be withdrawn by giving notice of its withdrawal. A person who enters or remains on property after the withdrawal of the licence is a trespasser. In *Davis v Lisle* [1936] 2 KB 434, police officers who had lawfully entered a garage for the purpose of making inquiries were held to have become trespassers by remaining in the garage after they were told by the proprietor to "get outside".

The common law has a number of exceptions to the general rule that a person is a trespasser unless that person enters premises with the consent, express or implied, of the occupier. Thus, a constable or citizen can enter premises for the purpose of making an arrest if a felony has been committed and the felon has been followed to the premises. A constable or citizen can also enter premises to prevent the commission of a felony, and a constable can enter premises to arrest an offender running away from an affray. Moreover, a constable or citizen can enter premises to prevent a murder occurring. In these cases there is power not only to enter premises but, where necessary, to break into the premises. However, it is a condition of any lawful breaking of premises that the person seeking **[648]** entry has demanded and been refused entry by the occupier: see *Swales v Cox* [1981] QB 849 at 853. Furthermore, a constable, holding a warrant to arrest, may enter premises forcibly, if necessary, for the purpose of executing the warrant provided that the constable has first signified "the cause of his coming, and … [made] request to open doors": *Semayne's Case*, at 91b (195); *Burdett v Abbot* (1811) 14 East 1 at 158, 162-163 (104 ER 501 at 561, 563); *Lippl v Haines* (1989) 18 NSWLR 620 at 631. But no public official, police constable or citizen has any right at common law to enter a dwelling-house merely because he or she suspects that something is wrong: *Great Central Railway Co v Bates* [1921] 3 KB 578 at 581-582. Nor, except in the instances to which we have referred, can any person enter premises, without a warrant, to apprehend a fugitive who may be on the premises: *Lippl v Haines*, at 636. Another exception to the general rule that a person who enters premises without the express or implied consent of the occupier is a trespasser is the rule that the sheriff can enter premises, by force if necessary, for the purpose of executing process in cases where the Sovereign is a party to the action: see the third resolution in *Semayne's Case* at 91b (195). Moreover, if the door of premises is open the sheriff may enter "and do execut[ion] at the suit of any subject, either of the body, or of the goods" (at 92a (197)). But the right to execute at the suit of a subject does not extend to breaking open the outer doors of a dwelling-house: *Semayne's Case* at 92a, 92b (197, 198); *Burdett v Abbot*, at 154-155 (560); *Southam v Smout*, at 322-323, 326, 329; *Tomlins' Law-Dictionary* (4th ed, 1835), vol 1, tit Execution, III 3. It has been held, however, that, for the purpose of executing process at the suit of any subject, the sheriff may break open a barn or outhouse which is not part of a dwelling-house: *Penton v Brown* (1664) 1 Keb 698 (83 ER 1193).

A number of statutes also confer power to enter land or premises without the consent of the occupier. But the presumption is that, in the absence of express provision to the contrary, the legislature did not intend to authorise what would otherwise be tortious conduct: *Morris v Beardmore*, per Lord Diplock, at 455. …

[Their Honours considered *Semayne's Case* (1604) 5 Co Rep 91a and the *Justices Act 1921* (SA) and concluded that the defendants' entry on the plaintiff's farm was unauthorised.]

[654] The matter must be remitted to the Supreme Court for the purpose of assessing the appellant's damages.

In his judgment, the learned trial judge said that, even if a trespass had occurred, it was "of such a trifling nature as not to sound in damages". However, once a plaintiff obtains a verdict in an action of trespass, he or she is entitled to an award of damages. In addition, we would unhesitatingly reject the suggestion that this trespass was of a trifling nature. The first and second respondents deliberately entered the appellant's land against his express wish. True it is that the entry itself caused no damage to the appellant's land. But the purpose of an action for trespass to land is not merely to compensate the plaintiff for damage to the land. That **[655]** action also serves the purpose of vindicating the plaintiff's right to the exclusive use and occupation of his or her land. Although the first and second respondents were acting honestly in the supposed execution of their duty, their entry was attended by circumstances of aggravation. They entered as police officers with all the power of the State behind them, knowing that their entry was against the wish of the appellant and in circumstances likely to cause him distress. It is not to the point that the appellant was unco-operative or even unreasonable. The first and second respondents had no right to enter his land. The appellant was entitled to resist their entry. If the occupier of property has a right not to be unlawfully invaded, then, as Mr Geoffrey Samuel has pointed out in another context, the "right must be supported by an effective sanction otherwise the term will be just meaningless rhetoric": "The Right Approach?" (1980) 96 *Law Quarterly Review* 12 at 14, cited by Lord Edmund-Davies in *Morris v Beardmore* at 461. If the courts of common law do not uphold the rights of individuals by granting effective remedies, they invite anarchy, for nothing breeds social disorder as quickly as the sense of injustice which is apt to be generated by the unlawful invasion of a person's rights, particularly when the invader is a government official. The appellant is entitled to have his right of property vindicated by a substantial award of damages. ...

Appeal allowed

[The judgments of Mason CJ, Brennan and Toohey JJ and Gaudron and McHugh JJ in *Plenty v Dillon* (extracted above) were referred to with approval in the joint judgment of Gleeson CJ, Gummow, Kirby, Heydon and Crennan JJ in *New South Wales v Ibbett* (2006) 229 CLR 638. In *Ibbett* the High Court upheld awards of $20,000 in aggravated damages and $20,000 in exemplary damages against the State of New South Wales, on the basis of the State's vicarious liability, for trespass to land (and assault) committed by two police officers who, in pursuit of the plaintiff's son, entered the plaintiff's home in the early hours of the morning without lawful authority or justification dressed in casual clothing, shouting commands and brandishing a service pistol which was pointed at the plaintiff. These awards of damages were in addition to the award of $10,000 in aggravated damages and $25,000 in exemplary damages for assault. On aggravated damages, the court observed:

[646] 31. Aggravated damages are a form of general damages, given by way of compensation for injury to the plaintiff, which may be intangible, resulting from the circumstances and manner of the wrongdoing: *Uren v John Fairfax & Sons Pty Ltd* (1966) 117 CLR 118 at 129-130. The interest of the plaintiff against invasion of the exclusive possession of the plaintiff extends to the freedom from disturbance of those [647] persons present there with the leave of the plaintiff, at least as family members or as an incident of some other bona fide domestic relationship. The affront to such persons may aggravate the infringement of the right of the plaintiff to enjoy exclusive and quiet possession. ...

32. The decision of the majority in the [New South Wales] Court of Appeal to uphold the award of aggravated damages partly by reference to the affront to Mrs Ibbett of the treatment of her son as well as herself was consistent with basic principle. The same is true ... of the award of exemplary damages for the trespass. ...

On exemplary damages, the court observed:

[648] 38. An action for trespass to land and an award of exemplary damages has long been a method by which, at the instance of the citizen, the State is called to account by the common law for the misconduct of those acting under or with the authority of the Executive Government: *Commissioner of Australian Federal Police v Propend Finance Pty Ltd* (1997) 188 CLR 501 at 558; *Enfield City Corporation v Development Assessment Commission* (2000) 199 CLR 135 at 143-144 [17]. ...

A factor taken into account in *Ibbett* in the award of exemplary damages against the State was the "perfunctory in the extreme" re-education program of the offending police officers after the incident in question.]

Coco v The Queen
(1994) 179 CLR 427
High Court of Australia

"Statutory authority to engage in what otherwise would be tortious conduct must be clearly expressed in unmistakable and unambiguous language."

[Under s 43(1) of the *Invasion of Privacy Act 1971* (Qld) ("the Act"), the use of a listening device to record a private conversation was an offence. However, s 43(2)(c) of the Act conferred on a judge of the Supreme Court of Queensland the power to approve the *use* of a listening device by a police officer. The Act also provided, in s 46(1), that evidence obtained through the unlawful use of a listening device was inadmissible in civil or criminal proceedings.

Pursuant to an approval given by a judge for the use of a listening device in connection with a criminal investigation, police officers entered, without the knowledge or consent of the occupier, private factory premises where the appellant, Mr Coco, had an office and installed a listening device for the purpose of recording Mr Coco's private conversations. At Mr Coco's criminal trial, recordings of these private conversations over a period of 200 hours were admitted in evidence and his conviction for the offence of offering a bribe to Commonwealth officers was upheld by the Court of Appeal of the Supreme Court of Queensland.

On appeal to the High Court, the respondent, the Crown, conceded that the conviction could not be sustained in the absence of the evidence obtained by the use of the listening device.]

MASON CJ, BRENNAN, GAUDRON and McHUGH JJ. ... [435] Every unauthorised entry upon private property is a trespass, the right of a person in possession or entitled to possession of premises to exclude others from those premises being a fundamental common law right (... *Halliday v Nevill* (1984) 155 CLR 1 at p 10 per Brennan J; *Plenty v Dillon* (1991) 171 CLR 635 at p 639 per Mason CJ, Brennan and Toohey JJ, p 647 per Gaudron and McHugh JJ. ...) In accordance with that principle, a police officer who enters or remains on private property commits a trespass unless the entry or pres- [436] ence on the premises is authorized or excused by law (*Halliday v Nevill* (1984) 155 CLR 1 at p 10 per Brennan J; *Plenty v Dillon* (1991) 171 CLR 635 at p 639 per Mason CJ, Brennan and Toohey JJ, p 647 per Gaudron and McHugh JJ.) Statutory authority to engage in what otherwise would be tortious conduct must be clearly expressed in unmistakable and unambiguous language. ...

[438] Section 43 of the ... Act does not contain express words conferring power upon a Supreme Court judge to authorize conduct which would otherwise be tortious and involve inter- ference with a fundamental common law right. In this case, the installation of the listening device in the [private factory] premises ... infringed the fundamental right of a person to exclude others from his or her property. ...

[439] In our view, it cannot be said that there is to be implied in s 43 power in a judge to authorize conduct which otherwise would amount to a trespass. ...

[445] It follows ... that the evidence of the appellant's private conversations was obtained by means of the use of a listening device contrary to s 43 of the ... Act and was inadmissible. ...

[Deane and Dawson JJ, in a joint judgment, and Toohey J, in a separate judgment, agreed with Mason CJ, Brennan, Gaudron and McHugh JJ.]

Appeal allowed. Conviction quashed. New trial ordered

TCN Channel Nine Pty Ltd v Anning
(2002) 54 NSWLR 333; [2002] NSWCA 82
Supreme Court of New South Wales, Court of Appeal

There is no implied licence to enter land in use as business premises for the purpose of filming, as distinct from requesting permission to film, the occupier or the occupier's activities on the land. The test for recovery of consequential damage after trespass to land, an intentional tort, is whether the damage is the natural and probable consequence of the tort.

[The respondent (plaintiff), Mr Henry Anning, was the lessee in occupation of 92 acres of fenced rural land on which he had built a motor cycle race track. On this property was a large quantity (about 70,000) used tyres which the respondent had purchased. The Environment Protection Authority, which was concerned that an offence in relation to waste disposal may have been committed, conducted a "raid" of the respondent's property accompanied by a television journalist and camera crew employed by the appellant (defendant), a television network which produced a program titled "A Current Affair". The appellant's employees entered the respondent's property, with cameras rolling, through a gate which had been unlocked by the respondent to allow a delivery truck to enter.

Upon confronting the television journalist and camera crew, the respondent told them to leave the property, which the appellant's employees immediately did. A subsequent broadcast of "A Current Affair" contained three separate segments of film taken by the appellant's employees on the respondent's property during the "raid". A prosecution of the respondent by the Environment Protection Authority for environmental offences was dismissed.

In proceedings by the respondent in the District Court of New South Wales, English DCJ found that the appellant had committed the tort of trespass to land. Although there was no evidence of damage to the respondent's property, the trial judge awarded the respondent a single figure amount of $100,000 for general, aggravated and exemplary damages in respect of hurt to the respondent's feelings, humiliation, affront to dignity and mental trauma. The trial judge's finding and award of damages were the subject of this appeal.]

SPIGELMAN CJ. ...

[339] Trespass and Purpose of Entry
23. The tort of trespass is committed whenever there is interference with possession of land without lawful authority or, relevantly, the licence or consent of the person in possession. In the present case, there was no issue about the Appellant's physical entry onto, or its remaining on, land in the Respondent's possession. The issue was whether the acts of the Appellant, by its employees, were authorised by the Respondent, either impliedly or expressly. [His Honour the Chief Justice referred to *Halliday v Nevill* (1984) 155 CLR 1, *Plenty v Dillon* (1991) 171 CLR 635 and *Coco v The Queen* (1994) 179 CLR 427.] ...

[341] 28. The Appellant relied on the reference in *Halliday v Nevill* to a "purpose of lawful communication" with, relevantly, the Respondent and to the reference to "a lawful purpose" in *Plenty v Dillon*. ...

[343] Implied Licence
38. The Appellant submitted that the entry of its employees occurred pursuant to an implied licence to enter. It relied in this regard on two alternatives:
- The use of the land as a tyre dump and/or as a racing track necessarily involved permission for members of the public to enter.
- Any member of the public has a right to enter a property in an attempt to lawfully communicate with the occupier, specifically to approach the occupier to ask if he or she will give an interview. ...

43. Whatever may have been the scope of a permission for entry with respect to the conduct of the used tyre business or the conduct of a race track, nothing the Appellant did was referable to any such purpose. If there was an implied licence to enter for any such purpose, the Appellant did not avail itself of such a licence. ...

[346] 58. Persons conducting business on private property are entitled to do so without others intruding for purposes unrelated to the business activities they are conducting. This includes those who wish to enter with a view to publicly exposing aspects of their business.

59. Although the law has been particularly protective of persons from intrusion on the part of the organs of government, it should be no less protective in the case of other powerful sections of society of which, in contemporary conditions, the mass media is one. ...

[348] 69. Alternatively, the Appellant relied on an implied permission to enter in order to ask the occupier for permission to film. Such a licence will be implied. ...

70. ... However, I do not see any evidence of any request for permission. ...

[349] 78. ... It [the Appellant] entered the land for the purposes of filming the raid, recording the Respondent's use of the land, conducting such interviews as it could with a view to broadcasting a programme. It was wholly outside any implied licence. ...

[350] 84. The appeal against the finding of trespass should be dismissed.

Scope of Damages

85. The Appellant submitted that her Honour [the trial judge, English DCJ] erred in awarding damages for personal injury, specifically mental trauma. It submitted that the tort of trespass to land protects the interest of the plaintiff in possession of land. It does not protect a plaintiff's right to bodily integrity. ...

[352] 100. The High Court has recently explained recovery for consequential loss in the case of intentional torts by invoking a general test. Damages can be recovered for harm that is intended or that is the natural and probable consequence of the tortious act. (See *Palmer Bruyn & Parker Pty Ltd v Parsons* [2001] HCA 69; 76 ALJR 163 esp at [13], [14], [73], [75]-[76], [114].) Damage that is the "natural and probable consequence" of conduct is within the "presumed intent" of the actor. (*Palmer Bruyn & Parker* at [73] and [80] per Gummow J.) Although this case involved injurious falsehood, the High Court's reasoning is of more general application to intentional torts. The issue in the present case is best approached on this more general test. *Palmer Bruyn & Parker* establishes that reasonable foreseeability is not an element of the test for recoverable damages, a proposition which had been left open in earlier cases (eg *Lippl v Haines* (1989) 18 NSWLR 620 at 639.) ...

[353] 102. In *Mayfair Ltd v Pears* [1987] 1 NZLR 459, a trespasser who had parked his car on premises without authority, was found to be not responsible for the damage to the building caused by a fire that started in the car. The references to reasonable foreseeability in some of the judgments in this case would now have to be rejected in view of the High Court's decision in *Palmer Bruyn & Parker*. However, the reasoning of the New Zealand Court of Appeal encompassed a natural and probable consequence test finding the fire not to be such a consequence of the trespass. ...

103. In the light of the reasoning in *Palmer Bruyn & Parker*, the relevant test for recovery of consequential loss after an intentional tort in terms of "natural and probable consequence" is the preferred formulation in Australia. ...

104. What is a natural and probable consequence arising from a trespass to land must depend on all the circumstances of a case. It is essentially a question of fact. Personal injury to an occupier was a natural and probable consequence of the kind of trespass that occurred in *Wormald v Cole* [1954] 1 QB 614 ie the escape of cattle from the defendant's land onto adjoining property. Similarly, injury to a plaintiff's horse was a natural and probable consequence of the act of trespass in *Hogan v AG Wright Pty Ltd* [1963] Tas SR 44 ie destroying a fence with a bulldozer which allowed horses to escape, one of which was injured in the subsequent roundup. Finally, injury to olive trees on an adjoining property was a natural and probable consequence of permitting cattle to enter it. (*Svingos v Deacon* [1971] 2 SASR 126.)

105. It is unnecessary to decide whether or not damages for personal injury and, specifically, psychiatric injury may, as a matter of law, be recovered in an action for trespass to land. It is undesirable to lay down a general rule that such damages cannot be recovered. I have come to the

conclusion that personal injury, including mental trauma, was not, in the circumstances of this case, a "natural and probable" result of the trespass. ...

106. ... **[354]** It is possible to conceive of a trespass to land in which psychiatric harm is actually intended or is within the trespasser's "presumed intent" under the "natural and probable consequence" test. This may be the case if a trespass occurred by way of leaving a cobra snake in a bedroom. Similarly, in the case of a stalker who enters property. (Although in such cases, a cause of action based on *Wilkinson v Downton* [1897] 2 QB 57 and *Janvier v Sweeney* [1919] 2 KB 316 may be more appropriate.)

107. A video camera, however damaging it may prove on occasions, is not a cobra, although there may be circumstances in which the stalker analogy is apt. Humiliation, injured feelings and affront to dignity may be a natural and probable consequence of intrusion by the media on private property. Such damage is compensable as aggravated damages. Such damage is different in kind to mental trauma. In my opinion, mental trauma – or indeed any form of personal injury – does not flow "naturally" and "probably" from a trespass to land committed in the way the Appellant acted, in all of the circumstances of this case. I reach this conclusion even though the nature of the intrusion carried with it the implicit prospect of broadcast to the public at large of the recording made during the trespass. ...

114. ... **[355]** I would allow the appeal insofar as damages were awarded for mental trauma. ...

[His Honour the Chief Justice found that the trial judge was in error in awarding a single figure amount for general, aggravated and exemplary damages. As a matter of principle, exemplary damages should be awarded as a discrete amount in order to mark the court's disapproval of the defendant's conduct and to deter the defendant and others from acting in that way (at [166]). However, this was not an appropriate case for an award of exemplary damages because "the Appellant's conduct was not, in the circumstances of this case, of sufficient gravity to be described as contumelious disregard of the Respondent's rights" (at [185]).

Spigelman CJ concluded that the respondent's damages should be reassessed. The respondent was entitled to a substantial award ($25,000) of general damages to "reflect the significant purpose of vindicating the Respondent's right to exclusive occupation" (at [178]). The respondent also was entitled to an award of aggravated damages ($25,000) in respect of the hurt to feelings, humiliation and affront to dignity experienced by the respondent by the way in which the appellant acted in the course of the trespass (at [179]).

Mason P and Grove J agreed with Spigelman CJ.]

Appeal allowed in part in respect of damages

(b) Aerial and Underground Trespass

LJP Investments Pty Ltd v Howard Chia Investments Pty Ltd
(1989) 24 NSWLR 490
Supreme Court of New South Wales

Trespass may be committed by an interference to airspace above the occupier's land.

[The plaintiffs were respectively the owner (with a right to possession) and the tenant of property at 38 Cross Street, Double Bay. The defendant was the owner of adjoining property, 36 Cross Street.

In the course of carrying out a commercial development of its property the defendant, without the plaintiffs' consent and after negotiations for payment by the defendant to the first plaintiff of a substantial sum in return for consent had broken down, erected scaffolding along 16 metres of the boundary between the properties. The scaffolding began at a height of about 4.5 metres above ground level and extended about 1.5 metres into the air space above the plaintiffs' property. At ground level, two posts supporting the scaffolding were located 100 millimetres inside the plaintiffs' property.

The plaintiffs commenced proceedings for a mandatory injunction.]

HODGSON J. ... [494] In these circumstances, Mr Jacobson for the plaintiffs submitted that a mandatory injunction should be granted. The defendant had committed a deliberate trespass. It had been told by the landowner that consent was not given, and nevertheless went ahead. The defendant did not seek to negotiate a payment, but on the contrary went ahead, and until the morning of the final hearing made no offer of payment whatsoever to the landowner.

Mr Jacobson submitted that the incursion into and occupation of airspace in this case was a trespass, and he referred me to *Kelsen v Imperial Tobacco* [1957] 2 QB 334, particularly at pp 343-347. He referred me to the discussion of discretionary matters at pp 346-347 of that report, and submitted that in this case the grant of an injunction was appropriate because the defendant had acted with reckless disregard of the plaintiffs' rights, and it would not be oppressive to grant the injunction because the defendant had deliberately placed itself in its present situation.

Next Mr Jacobson referred me to *Woollerton v Costain* [1970] 1 WLR 411, where a crane jib being used for the erection of a building on occasions overhung the plaintiff's premises at a height of about 50 feet above roof level. In that case, the defendant admitted trespass. Stamp J considered that an injunction should be granted, but its operation suspended until the end of November in the following year, that being the time by which the building operations were expected to be finished. His reasons were that the plaintiff's airspace had no value, until it suddenly acquired artificial value by reason of the defendant's proposed works; the plaintiff had been offered a substantial sum for the right to intrude; accordingly, when the plaintiff commenced the proceedings nominal damages were not the only alternative to an injunction; it was not a case where the defendant was claiming to have the right to do what it did; and evidence was led by the defendant that there had never previously been problems in relation to this sort of matter, so that Stamp J considered that the defendant was in its present position by inadvertence.

The correctness of that decision was questioned in *Charington v Simons & Co Ltd* [1971] 1 WLR 598 at p 603. In *Graham v KD Morris & Sons Pty Ltd* [1974] Qd R 1, in somewhat similar circumstances a different result was arrived at. In that case, the defendant was constructing a building on land adjoining the plaintiff's house. When the crane being used for the building was not in use, the wind sometimes caused its jib to extend as much as 62 feet over the plaintiff's land, apparently at a height of about 80 feet above the ground. Campbell J held that this constituted a trespass (following *Kelsen*) and also that the crane jib was unsightly and a cause of some nervousness in the plaintiff. He considered that the defendant's conduct was negligent, cavalier and high-handed, and noted that it had offered merely to negotiate "reasonable compensation". In those circumstances an injunction was granted.

Mr Emmett QC for the defendant submitted that the intrusion in this case did not constitute a trespass. He submitted that entry into airspace above land is a trespass only if it occurs at a height and in a manner which interferes with the occupier's use of the land: see *Bernstein v Skyviews and General Limited* [495] [1978] QB 479. He submitted that if *Kelsen* was against this, it was wrong; and in support of that proposition he referred me to *Pickering v Rudd* (1815) 4 Camp 219 and *Clifton v Bury* (1887) 4 TLR 8. He submitted that contrary statements in *Wandsworth District Board of Works v United Telephone Co* (1884) 13 QBD 904 were obiter only. He further referred me to *Salmond on Torts*, 19th ed pp 52-53; and to *Evans v Finn* (1904) 4 SR (NSW) 297, where an action concerning bullets straying on to and over the plaintiff's land from a rifle range was treated as a case of nuisance, and not of trespass. Since no damage was proved, nuisance was not shown in this case.

Alternatively, even if there was a trespass in this case, damages were an adequate remedy, because the interference with the plaintiff's right was trivial. He referred me to *Cooper v Laidler* [1903] 2 Ch 337, *Behrens v Richards* [1905] 2 Ch 614 and *Armstrong v Shepherd and Short* [1959] QB 384. In this case, the interference was both temporary and trivial. There was no danger to life or limb, and indeed the scaffolding protected the occupiers from the dangers of the building operations. The property was an investment property of the first plaintiff, and the second plaintiff had indicated that for herself she was not particularly concerned about the scaffolding.

Furthermore, even if the interference was not trivial, the Court should decline or postpone the injunction, because the scaffolding was necessary in order to comply with safety requirements imposed under the Construction Safety Act. The building had commenced, so that the defendant was bound to maintain the scaffolding to complete it. If the scaffolding had to be removed, one would have the unsafe and undesirable situation of the building remaining uncompleted. An injunction would impede the reasonable use of the defendant's land without conferring any practical benefit on the plaintiffs. The practical consequences of injunctions being granted in these circumstances would be ruinous to development in commercial areas, and would in effect mean that buildings would have to be set well back from boundaries in order to avoid the extraction of exorbitant fees.

The first question to be determined is whether this is a case of trespass. If the defendant's submission is to the effect that entry into airspace is a trespass only if it occurs at a height and in a manner which actually interferes with the occupier's actual use of land at the time, then I think it is incorrect. In my view, the rule stated in the *Skyviews case* by Griffiths J was rather that a trespass occurred only if the incursion was at a height which may interfere with the ordinary user of land, or is into airspace which is necessary for the ordinary use and enjoyment of the land and structures upon it: see [1978] 1 QB 479, at pp 486 and 488. It was held in that case that there was no trespass by an aeroplane flying many hundreds of feet above the land. On the other hand, in *Woollerton v Costain* [1970] 1 WLR 411 and *Graham v KD Morris & Sons Pty Ltd* [1974] Qd R 1, the incursions of crane jibs at heights of the order of 50 feet above the plaintiff's roof were treated as trespasses.

I think the relevant test is not whether the incursion actually interferes with the occupier's actual use of land at the time, but rather whether it is of a nature and at a height which *may* interfere with any ordinary uses of the land which the occupier *may* see fit to undertake. Such a rule has the advantages [496] stated by Griffiths J in *Skyviews* in [1978] 1 QB 479 at p 486:

> Adjoining owners then know where they stand; they have no right to erect structures overhanging or passing over their neighbours' land and there is no room for argument whether they are thereby causing damage or annoyance to their neighbours about which there may be much room for argument and uncertainty.

I also think the weight of authority is against the view adopted in *Pickering v Rudd* (1815) 4 Camp 219, that the incursion into the plaintiff's airspace of an overhanging sign is a nuisance rather than a trespass. Weight must be given to the considered dicta of the Court of Appeal in the *Wandsworth District Board of Works case* (1884) 13 QBD 904, and such matters have been treated as trespasses in *Gifford v Dent* [1926] WN 336, *Kelsen v Imperial Tobacco* [1957] 2 QB 334, *Woollerton v Costain* [1970] 1 WLR 411 and *Graham v KD Morris & Sons Pty Ltd* [1974] Qd R 1. I refer also to Fleming, *The Law of Torts*, 7th ed at p 42, where the learned author states:

> The weight of authority clearly favours the view that direct invasion by artificial projections, like a swinging crane, advertising signs, electric cables, or the overlap of a wall, constitutes trespass actionable per se and, in suitable cases, warranting a mandatory injunction to compel removal. In contrast, protruding branches, even of artificially planted trees, are treated as consequential, not direct, encroachment for which the remedy is in nuisance, requiring proof of damage or actual inconvenience except in support of the privilege to abate by cutting back the offending branch.

The other question for determination is whether I should grant a mandatory injunction. In *Kelsen v Imperial Tobacco* [1957] 2 QB 334, McNair J treated as applicable the principles stated by Smith LJ in *Shelfer v City of London Electric Lighting Co* [1895] 1 Ch 287 at p 322, to the following effect. The plaintiff is prima facie entitled to an injunction. However, there may be cases where damages are the appropriate remedy, for example where the plaintiff is disentitled by his acts or by laches. Furthermore, if the injury to the plaintiff's rights is small, capable of being estimated in money and adequately compensated by a money payment, and if the grant of an injunction would be oppressive to the defendant, then an injunction may be refused. However, the defendant may be disentitled to this approach, for example by reckless disregard of the plaintiff's rights.

Furthermore, as pointed out by Buckley J in *Cooper v Laidler* [1903] 2 Ch 337 at p 341, the jurisdiction to give damages instead of an injunction is not to be exercised so as "to enable the defendant to purchase from the plaintiff against his will his legal right to the easement".

In the present case, the plaintiffs are not disentitled from an injunction by laches, and the only act which could be considered to disentitle the plaintiffs is what is said to be the unreasonable demand for payment. There is no substantial injury caused to the plaintiffs, and compensatory damages would probably be nominal only. I do not think an injunction could be said to be greatly oppressive to the defendant: the defendant knowingly put itself in a position where it needed to use the first plaintiff's land in order to carry out a commercial development, and I think the law establishing that what the [497] defendant did was a trespass was reasonably clear, so that the defendant has not been taken by surprise in this regard.

In my view, the case really comes down to the question of whether one person should be permitted to use the land of another person for considerable commercial gain for himself, simply because his use of the other person's land causes no significant damage to that other person's land. As a matter of general, though not universal, principle, I would answer this question no. I think this approach is reflected in the principles applied in relation to exemplary damages: it is considered appropriate to award exemplary damages in cases where a defendant shows high-handed disregard for the plaintiff's rights, and by breaching those rights secures a great advantage to himself while causing little damage to the plaintiff. In those circumstances, it is sometimes considered appropriate to seek to deter that kind of conduct by awarding damages which bear some relationship to the advantage which the defendant sought to gain for himself.

In a case such as the present, where one landowner is seeking to effect a commercial development of his land which is more profitable or less expensive if use can be made of the land of an adjoining owner, it is not unreasonable in my view for that adjoining owner to require payment which bears some relationship to the financial gain or saving which the developing landowner achieves by use of the adjoining land. It may be that if the landowner effecting the development makes an offer to the adjoining landowner to pay, for the use of his land, a sum of money which bears some relationship to the gain or saving which the landowner effecting the development will thereby make, and the adjoining landowner refuses that offer, then there may be circumstances in which a court might find the adjoining owner's conduct unreasonable so that a mandatory injunction would be refused, particularly if a similar unconditional offer of payment is made at the hearing of the case. What relationship the amount offered should have to the gain or savings made by the landowner effecting the development will depend on all the circumstances: it could, I suppose, in some circumstances be as much as one half the gain or savings, although it may be some other and lesser proportion.

In the present case, there is no evidence from the defendant as to the difference in value between the development actually being undertaken and the development which could be undertaken without any use of the plaintiffs' land, or of the savings in the cost of development which can be achieved by using the first plaintiff's land rather than not using it. There is no basis upon which I could find, on this approach, that the first plaintiff's initial demand was unreasonable, or that the first plaintiff's non-acceptance of the defendant's most recent offer is unreasonable.

For these reasons, in my view the plaintiff is entitled to a mandatory injunction. The precise form of the injunction will need to be a matter for further submissions, because it would not, I think, be reasonable to grant an injunction which requires the defendant's development to forever remain in an unfinished state. What I would propose would be an injunction which would enable completion of an amended development which involves the absolute minimum of trespass on the first plaintiff's property. ...

Judgment for the plaintiffs

[An appeal to the New South Wales Court of Appeal was dismissed: see Editorial Note (1989) 24 NSWLR 490. In a subsequent phase of the proceedings, Hodgson J awarded the first plaintiff in the earlier proceedings (the owner in possession of the affected land) "restitutory damages" of $37,380 for the use the defendant had made of the airspace above the plaintiff's land: *LJP Investments Pty Ltd v Howard Chia Investments Pty Ltd* (1990) 24 NSWLR 499. In relation to the basis of assessment of restitutory damages, Hodgson J made the following observations (at 507):

[I]n my view, if what is used has peculiar value for a defendant, then damages under this head should reflect that value, rather than the general market value. For example, if a plaintiff is the last tenant in a development site, and is forcibly ejected and the building immediately demolished; and if the defendant acted on incorrect legal advice that he was entitled to do this, so that he may be able to escape exemplary damages; then I think the plaintiff's damages should not be limited to the general market value of the plaintiff's tenancy, but should reflect the price which the plaintiff and defendant would reasonably have negotiated, having regard to the plaintiff's position and the defendant's wish to develop the site.

An appeal from this subsequent phase of the proceedings also was dismissed by the New South Wales Court of Appeal: see Editorial Note (1990) 24 NSWLR 499.]

Di Napoli v New Beach Apartments Pty Ltd
(2004) Aust Torts Reports ¶81-728; [2004] NSWSC 52
Supreme Court of New South Wales

Trespass to land may be committed beneath the surface.

[The plaintiff and the defendant were adjoining occupiers of land. In the course of constructing a building on its land, the defendant placed rock anchors which projected beneath the plaintiff's land and were visible in the excavation on the defendant's land. Young CJ in Eq, in an interlocutory hearing of the plaintiff's claim in trespass, granted a mandatory order in favour of the plaintiff for the removal of the rock anchors.]

YOUNG CJ in Eq. ... **[65,399]** 13. The plaintiff's substantial case is that she is the registered proprietor of the land, or alternatively has the best right to possession of the land and that these rock anchors constitute a trespass.

14. The defendant in its defence, as filed, seems to say that the rock anchors are below the usable subterranean space of the plaintiff's land and that they are in a location too distant or the depth too great to be available to the plaintiff for the ordinary use and enjoyment of her land. That seemed to be the sole defence. ...

[65,400] 17. So far as the ... defence is concerned, it did not seem to me that it had any validity. It is certainly the case that the old adage, that the person with title to the land owns the land usque ad coelum et ad infernos [up to the sky and down to the depths], is not to be taken literally. It is also true that, especially so far as the air space above land is concerned, there have been pronouncements of courts which make it clear that flying an aircraft over a person's land is not necessarily of itself a trespass: see for instance *Bernstein v Skyviews and General Ltd* [1978] QB 479.

18. However, a series of cases in Kentucky involving caves which have been accepted by most of the sound academic writing on real property in this State make it clear that, at least for subterranean rights, a person has substantial control over land underneath his or her soil for a considerable depth. Cases such as *Cox v Colossal Cavern Co* 276 SW 540 (1925); *Edwards v Sims* 24 SW (2d) 619 (1929) and *Edwards v Lee* 96 SW (2d) 1028 (1936) are in this category and deal with caves some 360 feet below the surface. In Australia, the same flavour comes through in cases such as *Graham v KD Morris & Sons Pty Ltd* [1974] Qd R 1 and *Stoneman v Lyons* [1974] VR 797, 802 (reversed on another point (1975) 133 CLR 550). ...

[65,401] 28. In connection with cases of trespass to land, the authorities do seem to have taken a consistent line. That is that where a person seeks to develop their land by utilising neighbouring land for their convenience without consent ... then the court will, almost as a matter of course, grant an injunction to restrain it. This is because people are entitled to the exclusive use of their land and it is no answer to say that that person is not suffering financial loss by the defendant's use and that it is extremely important to the defendant to be able to make use of the plaintiff's land for its purposes; see *LJP Investments Pty Ltd v Howard Chia Investments Pty Ltd* (1989) 24 NSWLR 490, 496... .

30. It seems to me that I should grant an order in favour of the plaintiff. ...

Order accordingly

Bocardo SA v Star Energy UK Onshore Ltd
[2010] 3 All ER 975; [2010] UKSC 35
United Kingdom Supreme Court

An intrusion beneath land may constitute trespass even although the intrusion occurs at a depth beyond the effective control of the occupier of the surface.

[Part of an oilfield extended beneath land, the Oxted estate in Surrey, England, owned and occupied by the claimant, Bocardo SA. The defendant, Star Energy UK Onshore Ltd, was the holder of a licence from the Crown, the owner of the oil, to search and extract petroleum from the oilfield. The defendant carried out drilling operations from land adjoining the claimant's land. Three wells drilled by the defendant penetrated beneath the claimant's land at a depth of 800–2800 feet.

In respect of the defendant's subterranean intrusion, the claimant sought damages in trespass. Although the defendant abandoned an argument that its subterranean intrusion was authorised by statutory authority, it contended that the subterranean intrusion was at a depth "too far removed" from the claimant's occupation of the surface to be actionable as a trespass.

The primary judge, Peter Smith J, citing *Bulli Coal Mining Co v Osborne* [1899] AC 351 and *Edwards v Sims* 24 SW (2d) 619 (1929), held that the defendant's subterranean intrusion constituted a trespass to the claimant's land for which the defendant was liable in damages. The defendant appealed to the English Court of Appeal which agreed with the primary judge's finding that the defendant's subterranean intrusion constituted a trespass to the claimant's land. However, the English Court of Appeal allowed the defendant's appeal as to the amount of damages payable under the relevant statutory scheme. A further appeal by the claimant to the United Kingdom Supreme Court on the issue of the amount of damages was dismissed but the Supreme Court, dismissing a cross-appeal by the defendant, agreed with the primary judge and the English Court of Appeal on the trespass issue. The judgment of Lord Hope DP, with whom Lord Walker, Lord Brown, Lord Collins and Lord Clarke SCJJ agreed on the trespass issue, is extracted only on this issue.]

LORD HOPE DP. ... **[984]** 8. There is, of course, nothing new in one person carrying out works under land whose surface is in the ownership or the possession of another. Operations of that kind have been familiar since at least Roman times. They ranged from great public works such as catacombs on the one hand to modest cellars for the storage of wine or other commodities on the other. What is new is the depth at which the operations that are said to constitute a trespass in this case have been carried out. The advance of modern technology has led to the discovery of things below the surface, and the desire to obtain access to and remove them, that were unimaginable when the depths to which people could go were limited by what manual labour could achieve.

9. Bocardo's case is that it is trite law that a conveyance of land includes the surface and everything below it, unless there have been exceptions from the grant such as commonly occurs in the case of minerals. The respondents [defendant] do not dispute this proposition as a general rule that applies where the rights of the surface owner are interfered with. But they maintain that it does not extend to the depth at which the operations were and are being carried out in this case. ...

10. It has often been said that prima facie the owner of the surface is entitled to the surface itself and everything below it down to the centre of the earth: see, for example ... **[985]** *Elwes v Brigg Gas Co* (1886) 33 ChD 562, 568, per Chitty J ... . The proposition that prima facie everything below the surface belongs to the surface owner is often linked to the proposition that everything above it belongs to him too. ...Plainly, the source for these remarks was the well-known Latin brocard *cuius est solum, eius est usque ad coelum et ad inferos* [the person with title to land owns up to the sky and down to the depths]. ...

[986] 15. The particular relevance of the brocard to the dispute in this case is that, taken literally, it answers Mr Driscoll's [senior counsel for the defendant] point that the wells in question were too [987] deep for the landowner's interest in his land to be affected. If the brocard is accepted as a sound guide to what the law is, there is no stopping point. This makes it unnecessary to speculate as to how it can be applied in practice as one gets close to the earth's centre. The depths to which the wells in question were drilled in this case do not get anywhere near to approaching the point of absurdity. The fact that there were substances at that depth which can be reached and got by human activity is sufficient to raise the question as to who, if anybody, is the owner of the strata where they are to be found. The Crown has asserted ownership of the petroleum, but it does not assert ownership of the strata that surround it. The only plausible candidate is the registered owner of the land above, which is exactly what the brocard itself indicates. ...

[988] 20. As for the position above the surface, the development of powered flight has made it impossible to apply the brocard *usque ad coelum* literally. In *Bernstein of Leigh (Baron) v Skyviews & General Ltd* [1978] QB 479 Baron Bernstein failed in his claim that the defendants, who had flown over his land to take an aerial photograph of his property which they then offered to sell to him, were guilty of trespass. Griffiths J noted at p 485 that the proposition that an owner has certain rights in the air space above his land was well established by authority. In *Kelsen v Imperial Tobacco Co (of Great Britain and Northern Ireland) Ltd* [1957] 2 QB 334, for example, a mandatory injunction was granted ordering the defendants to remove a sign which projected 8 inches over the plaintiff's property on the ground that, applying the brocard, this was a trespass. Griffiths J was willing to accept, as a sound and practical rule, that any incursion into air space at a height which may interfere with the ordinary user of land was a trespass. But he said that wholly different considerations arise when considering the passage of aircraft at a height which in no way affects the user of the land. In his judgment, at p 488, the balance was best struck by restricting the rights of the owner to such height as necessary for the ordinary use and enjoyment of his land and the structures upon it, and declaring that above that height he has no greater rights in the air space than any other member of the public.

21. The respondents say that this analysis should be applied to subsurface ownership too. They submit that a sensible and pragmatic solution would be for each surface owner to own directly down beneath the boundaries of his land as far down as is necessary for the use and enjoyment of the surface, the buildings on the surface and any minerals which have not been excluded from his ownership by conveyance, common law or statute which lie beneath it. ...

[990] 24. ... In Canada, Griffiths J's approach in *Bernstein of Leigh (Baron) v Skyviews & General Ltd* [1978] QB 479 to the right to use air space above the land was described by the Alberta Court of Appeal as most persuasive in *Didow v Alberta Power Ltd* [1988] 5 WWR 606, 613. But we were not referred to any Canadian or Australian authority that extends that approach to ownership below the surface. ...

[991] 27. The better view, as the Court of Appeal recognised [at] para 59, is to hold that the owner of the surface is the owner of the strata beneath it, including the minerals that are to be found there, unless there has been an alienation of them by a conveyance, at common law or by statute to someone else. .... There must obviously be some stopping point, as one reaches the point at which physical features such as pressure and temperature render the concept of the strata belonging to anybody so absurd as to be not worth arguing about. But the wells that are at issue in this case, extending from about 800 feet to 2,800 feet below the surface, are far from being so deep as to reach the point of absurdity. Indeed the fact that the strata can be worked upon at those depths points to the opposite conclusion.

28. I would hold therefore that the appellant's [claimant's] title extends down to the strata through which the three wells and their casing and tubing pass. ...

29. The next question is whether possession or a right to possession is a pre-condition for bringing a claim in trespass. The respondents maintain that possession, not ownership, is essential and that the claim should fail because the appellant is not in possession of the substrata where the wells entered the substrata at least 800 feet below the surface of its land. ...

30. In *Powell v McFarlane* (1977) 38 P & CR 452, 470 Slade J said:

In the absence of evidence to the contrary, the owner of land with the paper title is deemed to be in possession of the land, as being the person with the prima facie right to possession. The law will thus, without reluctance, ascribe possession either to the paper owner or to persons who can establish a title as claiming through the paper owner.

31. As Aikens LJ said in the Court of Appeal, it is difficult to say that the appellant has actual possession of the strata below the Oxted Estate as it has done nothing to reduce those strata into its actual possession: para 66. But he held that the appellant, as the paper title owner to the strata and all within it (other than any gold, silver, saltpetre, coal and petroleum which belong to the Crown at common law or by statute), has the prima facie right to possession of those strata so as to be deemed to be in factual possession of them. I think that he was right to conclude that this was the effect of Slade J's dictum. As the paper title carries with it title to the strata **[992]** below the surface, the appellant must be deemed to be in possession of the subsurface strata too. ...

[993] 36. For all these reasons I would hold, in agreement with the Court of Appeal, that the respondents have trespassed on Bocardo's land and that, subject to their submissions as to the amount of the damages, they have no defence to Bocardo's claim. I would dismiss the [defendant's] cross-appeal.

Appeal as to damages dismissed
Cross-appeal on the trespass issue dismissed

(c) Title to Sue

Rodrigues v Ufton
(1894) 20 VLR 539
Supreme Court of Victoria

The occupier is the only person with title to sue for trespass. However, an owner out of posses-sion may bring an action on the case in respect of damage to the owner's reversionary interest.

[The plaintiff was the owner of property comprising a dwelling house and back yard which was in the possession and occupation of her tenants. The defendant, who was the owner of adjoining property, disputed the plaintiff's title to a strip of land forming part of the back yard of the plaintiff's property.

The defendant entered the plaintiff's property, destroyed a part of the existing fence and erected a new fence which excluded the plaintiff from enjoyment of the disputed strip of land.]

HODGES J. [His Honour declared that, as against the defendant, the plaintiff was owner of the disputed strip of land.]

[543] There was further a claim by the plaintiff for damage sustained by the trespass committed by the defendant knocking through from his property, which adjoins her property, and erecting a fence, digging holes to erect it, removing pitchers, and so forth. Though the objection was not taken by the pleadings, it was taken at the trial, that inasmuch as the plaintiff was not herself in possession, she could not maintain an action of trespass; that the only person who could maintain an action of trespass was the person who was in possession of the property, and a number of authorities were cited for the plaintiff to show that a person not in possession can maintain an action of trespass. I have carefully examined those authorities to see whether any of them support a proposition which is certainly at variance with what might be called a fundamental notion, that an action of trespass is an action for the disturbance **[544]** of possession, and that the persons who can maintain it are those whose possession is disturbed. I propose to examine only those authorities cited for the plaintiff, and I think that, with the exception of one case, they show that an action of trespass can be maintained only by a person in possession, and I think that possibly a mistake may have arisen in not distinguishing between the statement that an action of trespass can only be maintained by a person who has possession, and that an action may be maintained by a reversioner for an injury to the reversion done by a trespasser, which are two totally different things. It has not been doubted for nearly a century that a reversioner can sue for an injury to the reversion which has been done by a trespasser. The first case cited by the plaintiff was *Baxter v Taylor* (1832) 4 B & Ad 72. Now in that case the action was not one of trespass; it was an action, as it was then called, on the case, and it is distinctly shown in the declaration that it was a claim by a reversioner, not for disturbance of the possession, but for an injury to the reversion, and the marginal note states the effect of the judgment as follows:- "A reversioner cannot maintain an action on the case against a stranger for merely entering upon his land held by a tenant on lease, though the entry be made in exercise of an alleged right-of-way; such an act during the tenancy not being necessarily injurious to the reversion." So that it was there held that an action on the case could not be maintained by a reversioner unless there was an injury to the reversion; if there was such an injury, it appears to be conceded that an action on the case would lie – but not an action of trespass. Taunton J, referring to the authority of *Jackson v Pesked* (1813) 1 M & S 234, says that it shows "that if a plaintiff declare as reversioner for an injury done to his reversion, the declaration must allege it to have been done to the damage of his reversion, or must state an injury of such a permanent nature as to be necessarily prejudicial thereto, and the want of such an allegation is cause for arresting the judgment"; and he adds, "if such an allegation must be inserted in a count, it is material, and must be proved." There was then the case of *Jackson v Pesked* (1813) 1 M & S 234. In that case again the action was not an action of trespass, but an action upon the case, and it is clear from the language of Lord Chief Justice Ellenborough that the only matter they were then considering was under what circumstances a reversioner could bring an action on the case; but the Court never suggested that a reversioner could bring an action of trespass. I was then referred to *Metropolitan Association for Improving the Dwellings of the Industrious Classes v Petch* (1858) 5 CB (NS) 504. In that case the declaration was for an injury to the reversionary interest of the plaintiff by obstructing ancient lights. In that case again it was not an action of trespass, it was an action on the case, and the declaration sets out that one person was in possession and that the other had a reversionary interest, and the question was whether the reversionary interest was injured. Then comes an authority which should, I think, set the matter at rest – the authority which was cited to me of *Cooper v Crabtree* (1881) 19 Ch D 193. In that case in the course of the argument, Fry J says: "*Baxter v Taylor* (1832) 4 B & Ad 72 shows that a reversioner cannot maintain an action of trespass, because he is out of possession." That is the whole matter at once stated in one sentence – the whole of the proposition. In answer to that counsel says, "the possession of the tenant is that of the landlord," to which Fry J says, "not for all purposes"; and the argument goes on – "This must not be treated as a mere common law action of trespass," and it is answered by Fry J, "If it is an action on the case for an obstruction or nuisance, you must show a substantial injury to the reversion." In that case there was an examination of the authorities by Fry J, but he never departs from that statement in the course of the argument that a reversioner cannot maintain an action of trespass. I was then referred to a case of *Mayfair Property Company v Johnston* [1894] 1 Ch 508, a decision of North J. In that case there was some language used in dealing with the counterclaim which, if not closely read, might lead one to suppose that a reversioner could bring an action of trespass. At page 516 North J said: "It was said on behalf of the plaintiffs that the counter-claiming defendants are not entitled to sue in respect of the trespass, because they are only reversioners, they having let the house to the other defendants. In my opinion that is not the law." But he does not say he is entitled to bring an action of trespass, but only to maintain an action in respect of a trespass. It was not **[546]** disputed before me that the plaintiff could not recover damages if her reversionary interest were damaged by the defendant's trespass, but only whether she could bring an action of trespass. "In some cases," North J adds, "no doubt, a reversioner cannot sue for a trespass; but in many he can." He then proceeds to discuss these cases, but as far as I understand his judgment he did not for one moment maintain that a reversioner could bring an action of trespass. There is one authority in the plaintiff's favour to which Mr Davis referred me. It is the case of *O'Grady v Boulter* (1871) 2 AJR 118. In that case, as reported, the Court did hold that the reversioner could bring an action of trespass. It is true the note of the judgment says that the Court held that "the action was properly brought as for trespass," but the statement of the case looks as if it were an action of trespass, and as if the Court held that a reversioner could bring an action of trespass. I do not think that that can be a correct report. It is in direct violation of every case that I have ever read on the subject of pleadings, and every case that has been cited, and of every principle. I must think that that case is misreported, and not that Fry J is wrong when he says that it is common knowledge that a reversioner cannot bring an action of trespass. I entertain no doubt that a reversioner cannot bring an action of trespass. He can bring an action, and can recover damages, if a trespass will injure his reversion.

I have discussed the subject at some length, but I do not know that it makes any very material difference in this case. Forms of action are gone, but while the forms of action are gone, and trespass as a form of action is gone, parties may so state their case in their pleadings as to show the damage claimed is damage for a trespass. In the pleadings in this case it certainly looks like an action of trespass, but the whole dispute between the parties was unmistakeable, and if it be necessary to alter the pleadings in any way I think I ought to allow such amendment. I propose to dispose of the case as if any doubt on that subject was removed, and as the plaintiff was in possession of the land by her tenants, and as a fence was permanently put up which would interfere with her possession, I think I ought to give some damages for the obstruction. …

Judgment for the plaintiff

Newington v Windeyer
(1985) 3 NSWLR 555
Supreme Court of New South Wales, Court of Appeal

Actual possession, not ownership as such, confers title to sue in trespass and the plaintiff must prove actual possession of the land at the date of the trespass. Possession is a question of fact.

[The respondents (plaintiffs) owned and occupied all the land adjoining the eastern and southern boundaries of The Grove, a rectangular area of land 200 feet by 60 feet, registered under the *Real Property Act 1900* (NSW), consisting of lawn, trees, gardens and a path. For many years the respondents had used The Grove, to the exclusion of others, as a common garden. The owner of The Grove appeared to be a deceased estate which was not a party to the present proceedings.

The appellant (defendant) owned two blocks of land adjoining the western boundary of The Grove. In or about February 1979 the appellant replaced the fence which ran along the western boundary of The Grove and effectively prevented access from that direction with one which contained two gates giving access from her land to The Grove.

The question was whether the respondents had title to maintain an action of trespass and deny the appellant any right to use The Grove.]

McHUGH JA. … **[563]** The respondents are not the owners of the registered title of The Grove, but that fact does not prevent them maintaining an action of trespass against the appellant. The modern law of real property continues to invoke the medieval doctrine that possession is prima facie evidence of seisin in fee and that an estate gained by wrong is nevertheless an estate in fee simple: *Wheeler v Baldwin* (1934) 52 CLR 609 at 632; *Allen v Roughley* (1955) 94 CLR 98 at 108. Seisin gives ownership good against everyone except a person who has a better, because older, title: *Wheeler v Baldwin* (at 632-633); *Perry v Clissold* [1907] AC 73 at 79. A person who is in possession of land adverse to the true owner has a legal interest in the land even though the twelve year limitation period has not expired: *Perry v Clissold*. As long as a person does not abandon possession, possession for less than twelve years enables him to exclude from the land any person who does not have a better title: *Allen v Roughley* (at 109-110, 115, 131, 135, 143). The above cases and principles relate to Old System title. But in *Spark v Whale Three Minute Car Wash (Cremorne Junction) Pty Ltd* (1970) 92 WN (NSW) 1087, Slattery J held that those principles are equally applicable to land held under the provisions of the *Real Property Act 1900*. Counsel for the parties accepted that the common law principles concerning adverse possession apply to land under the Torrens System. In my opinion the agreement of counsel was correct. *Spark v Whale* **[564]** *Three Minute Car Wash* was correctly decided. …

The learned trial judge held that the respondents were in possession of the land at the time when the appellant sought to use it. Conduct which indicates the taking of possession of land varies with the type of land concerned: *Wuta-Ofei v Danquah* [1961] 1 WLR 1238; [1961] 3 All ER 596. The evidence proved that the [respondents] had engaged in many acts of ownership over a period of nearly fifty years. They employed a man to mow the lawn. They engaged in the maintenance of the trees, garden and rockeries. They cut down trees when necessary. They used The Grove as a common garden. Individual residents held birthday parties and wedding receptions in The Grove, used it for displays of sculpture, for exhibitions, and, on a number of occasions, for the entertainment of Dental Congresses. Since 1978 the [respondents] have been assessed for and paid rates in respect of the land. They blocked off attempts by Dr Kelly [another occupier of land adjoining the western boundary] and the appellant to use The Grove. On many occasions the [respondents] told uninvited visitors that The Grove was private land and that they were trespassing. In my opinion, his Honour was correct in finding that the respondents were in possession of The Grove.

[Kirby P and Hope JA agreed with McHugh JA. However, Kirby P noted that counsel for the parties had agreed that the common law principles governing adverse possession applied to Torrens System land. His Honour stated that, in the absence of argument, he wished to reserve the correctness of this concession.]

Appeal dismissed

2. PRIVATE NUISANCE

(a) Interests Protected and Title to Sue

Victoria Park Racing and Recreation Grounds Co Ltd v Taylor
(1937) 58 CLR 479
High Court of Australia

The action in nuisance protects an occupier from unreasonable interference with certain legally recognised aspects or incidents of use and enjoyment of the land. Nuisance provides only limited protection to an occupier from being overlooked by others.

LATHAM CJ. **[492]** This is an appeal from a judgment for the defendants given by Nicholas J [in the Supreme Court of New South Wales] in an action by the Victoria Park Racing and Recreation Grounds Co Ltd against Taylor and others.

The plaintiff company carries on the business of racing upon a racecourse known as Victoria Park. The defendant Taylor is the owner of land near the racecourse. He has placed an elevated platform on his land from which it is possible to see what takes place on the racecourse and to read the information which appears on notice boards on the course as to the starters, scratchings, &c, and the winners of the races. The defendant Angles stands on the platform and through a telephone comments upon and describes the races in a particularly vivid manner and announces the names of the winning horses. The defendant the Commonwealth Broadcasting Corporation holds a broadcasting licence under the regulations made under the *Wireless Telegraphy Act 1905* and carries on the business of broadcasting from station 2UW. This station broadcasts the commentaries and descriptions given by Angles. The plaintiff wants to have the broadcasting stopped because it prevents people from going to the races and paying for admission. The evidence shows that some people prefer hearing about the races as seen by Angles to seeing the races for themselves. The plaintiff contends that the damage which it thus suffers gives, in all the circumstances, a cause of action.

The plaintiff's case is put as an action upon the case for nuisance affecting the use and enjoyment of the plaintiff's land. ...

The first contention is that the plaintiff's land has been made suitable for a racecourse, that by reason of the action of the defendants it has been deprived of at least some measure of that suitability, **[493]** and that therefore this is a case of nuisance – an unlawful interference with the use and enjoyment of land. No analogous case has been cited to the court. I agree that the category of nuisance is not closed and that if some new method of interfering with the comfort of persons in the use of land emerges the law may provide a remedy. For example, the increasing use of electricity, with the possibility of the escape of electricity into an adjoining property, has provided a new possible source of interference with the use of land and the law provides a remedy in such a case.

In this case, however, in my opinion, the defendants have not interfered in any way with the use and enjoyment of the plaintiff's land. The effect of their actions is to make the business carried on by the plaintiff less profitable, and they do so by providing a competitive entertainment. It is unnecessary to cite authorities for the proposition that mere competition (certainly if without any motive of injuring the plaintiff) is not a cause of action. The facts are that the racecourse is as suitable as ever it was for use as a racecourse. What the defendants do does not interfere with the races, nor does it interfere with the comfort or enjoyment of any person who is on the racecourse. The alleged nuisance cannot be detected by any person upon the land as operating or producing any effect upon the plaintiff's land. It is consistent with the evidence that none of the persons on that land may, at any given moment, be aware of the fact that a broadcast is being made. The only alleged effect of the broadcast is an effect in relation to people who are not upon the land, that is, the people who listen in or have the opportunity of listening in and who therefore stay away from the land. In my opinion the defendants have not in any way interfered with the plaintiff's land or the enjoyment thereof. ...

[495] The claim under the head of nuisance has also been supported by an argument that the law recognizes a right of privacy which has **[496]** been infringed by the defendant. However desirable some limitation upon invasions of privacy might be, no authority was cited which shows that any general right of privacy exists. The contention is answered, in my opinion, by the case of *Chandler v Thompson* (1811) 3 Camp 80; 170 ER 1312; see also *Turner v Spooner* (1861) 30 LJ Ch 801, at p 803: "With regard to the question of privacy, no doubt the owner of a house would prefer that a neighbour should not have the right of looking into his windows or yard, but neither this court nor a court of law will interfere on the mere ground of invasion of privacy; and a party has a right even to open new windows, although he is thereby enabled to overlook his neighbour's premises, and so interfering, perhaps, with his comfort"; see also *Tapling v Jones* (1865) 11 HLC, at pp 305, 311; 11 ER, at pp 1350, 1352, 1353. ...

[498] In my opinion the appeal should be dismissed.

RICH J. [dissenting] ... **[500]** Nuisance covers so wide a field that no general definition of nuisance has been attempted but only a classification of the various kinds of nuisance. Courts have always refrained from fettering themselves by definitions. ... **[501]** An action on the case in the nature of nuisance was one of the flexible remedies capable of adaptation to new circumstances falling within recognized principles. This case presents the peculiar features that by means of broadcasting – a thing novel both in fact and law – the knowledge obtained by overlooking the plaintiff's racecourse from the defendants' tower is turned to account in a manner which impairs the value of the plaintiff's occupation of the land and diverts a legitimate source of profit from its business into the pockets of the defendants. It appears to me that the true issue is whether a non-natural use of a neighbour's land made by him for the purpose of obtaining the means of appropriating in this way part of the profitable enjoyment of the plaintiff's land to his own commercial ends – a thing made possible only by radio – falls within the reason of the principles which give rise to the action on the case in the nature of nuisance. There is no absolute standard as to what constitutes a nuisance in law. But all the surrounding circumstances must be taken into consideration in each case. As regards neighbouring properties their interdependence is important in arriving at a decision in a given case. An improper or non-natural use or a use in excess of a man's right which curtails or impairs his neighbour's legitimate enjoyment of his property is "tortious and hurtful" and constitutes a nuisance. A man has no absolute right **[502]** "within the ambit of his own land" to act as he pleases. His right is qualified and such of his acts as invade his neighbour's property are lawful only in so far as they are reasonable having regard to his own circumstances and those of his neighbour (*Law Quarterly Review*, vol 52, p 460; vol 53, p 3). The plaintiff's case must, I am prepared to concede, rest on what is called nuisance. But it must not be overlooked that this means no more than that he must complain of some impairment of the rights flowing from occupation and ownership of land. One of the prime purposes of occupation of land is the pursuit of profitable enterprises for which the exclusion of others is necessary either totally or except upon conditions which may include payment. In the present case in virtue of its occupation and ownership the plaintiff carries on the business of admitting to the land for payment patrons of racing. There it entertains them by a spectacle, by a competition in the comparative merits of racehorses, and it attempts by all reasonable means to give to those whom it admits the exclusive right of witnessing the spectacle, the competition and of using the collated information in betting while that is possible on its various events. This use of its rights as occupier is usual, reasonable and profitable. So much no one can dispute. If it be true that an adjacent owner has an unqualified and absolute right to overlook an occupier whatever may be the enterprise he is carrying on and to make any profitable use to which what he sees can be put, whether in his capacity of adjacent owner or otherwise, then to that extent the right of the occupier carrying on the enterprise must be modified and treated in law as less extensive and ample than perhaps is usually understood. But can the adjacent owner by virtue of his occupation and ownership use his land in such an unusual way as the erection of a platform involves, bring mechanical appliances into connection with that use, ie, the microphone and land line to the studio, and then by combining regularity of observation with dissemination for gain of the information so obtained give the potential patrons a mental picture of the spectacle, an account of the competition between the horses and of the collated information needed for betting, for all of which they would otherwise have recourse to the racecourse and pay? …

[503] There can be no right to extend the normal use of his land by the adjoining owner indefinitely. He may within limits make fires, create smoke and use vibratory machinery. He may consume all the water he finds on his land, but he has no absolute right to dirty it. Defendants' rights are related to plaintiff's rights and each owner's rights may be limited by the rights of the other. *Sic utere tuo* is not the premise in a syllogism but does indicate the fact that *damnum* may spring from *injuria* even though the defendant can say: "I am an owner." All the nuisance cases, including in that category *Rylands v Fletcher* (1868) LR 3 HL 330, are mere illustrations of a very general principle "that law grows and … though the principles of law remain unchanged, yet (and it is one of the advantages of the common law) their application is to be changed with the changing circumstances of the times. Some persons may call this retrogression, I call it progression of human opinion" (*R v Ramsay and Foote* (1883) 48 LT NS 733, at p 735). I adapt Lord Macmillan's words and say: "The categories of 'nuisance' are not closed" (*Donoghue v Stevenson* [1932] AC 562, at p 619). Nuisance is not trespass on the case and physical or material interference is not necessary. The "vibration" cases and the "besetting and eavesdropping" cases are certainly against such a contention. **[504]** What appears to me to be the real point in this case is that the right of view or observation from adjacent land has never been held to be an absolute and complete right of property incident to the occupation of that land and exercisable at all hazards notwithstanding its destructive effect upon the enjoyment of the land overlooked. In the absence of any authority to the contrary I hold that there is a limit to this right of overlooking and that the limit must be found in an attempt to reconcile the right of free prospect from one piece of land with the right of profitable enjoyment of another. The unreported case of the Balham dentist mentioned by Professor Kenny in his *Cases on the Law of Tort*, 4th ed (1926), p 367, would, if correctly decided, be discreditable to English law. This is what Professor Winfield, in an article on Privacy, *Law Quarterly Review*, vol 47, at p 27, says:

> A curious invasion of privacy, recorded by the late Professor Kenny, was a case of 1904 in which a family in Balham, by placing in their garden an arrangement of large mirrors, were enabled to observe all that passed in the study and operating room of a neighbouring dentist, who sought in vain for legal protection against 'the annoyance and indignity' to which he was thus subjected. This is all that is given of the case, and, as there is no further reference, it is worthless as an authority. Why should it not have been actionable as a nuisance? It was something very like watching and besetting the dentist's house so as to compel him to do or not to do something which he was lawfully entitled not to do or to do; and this was held to be

a common law nuisance in *Lyons & Sons v Wilkins* [1899] 1 Ch 255. Subsequent trade union legislation may have affected the decision in that case, but not the principle underlying it, which is that such conduct seriously interferes with the ordinary comfort of human existence and the ordinary enjoyment of the house beset. Indeed, the Balham family behaved worse than the defendants in *Lyons' Case* [1899] 1 Ch 255, for there was some economic excuse for the acts of the trade union officials there, while none whatever existed in the Balham case.

In 1904 the unneighbourly neighbours of Balham were forced to adopt an elaborate system of mirrors to vent their ill feeling. But it is easy to believe that half a century later they would be able to do all they desired **[505]** by means of television. Indeed the prospects of television make our present decision a very important one, and I venture to think that the advance of that art may force the courts to recognize that protection against the complete exposure of the doings of the individual may be a right indispensable to the enjoyment of life. For these reasons I am of opinion that the plaintiff's grievance, although of an unprecedented character, falls within the settled principles upon which the action for nuisance depends. ...

I think that the appeal should be allowed.

DIXON J. ... **[506]** The plaintiff's counsel relied in the first instance upon an action on the case in the nature of nuisance. The premises of the plaintiff are occupied by it for the purpose of a racecourse. They have the natural advantage of not being overlooked by any surrounding heights or raised ground. They have been furnished with all the equipment of a racecourse and so enclosed as to prevent any unauthorized ingress or, unless by some such exceptional devices as the defendants have adopted, any unauthorized view of the spectacle. The plaintiff can thus exclude the public who do not pay and can exclude them not only from presence at, but also from knowledge of, the proceedings upon the course. It is upon the ability to do this that the profitable character of the enterprise ultimately depends. The position of and the improvements to the land thus fit it for a racecourse and give its occupation a particular value. The defendants then proceed by an unusual use of their premises to deprive the plaintiff's land of this value, to strip it of its exclusiveness. By the tower placed where the race will be fully visible and equipped with microphone and line, they enable Angles to see the spectacle and convey its substance by broadcast. The effect is, the plaintiff says just as if they supplied the plaintiff's customers with elevated vantage points round the course from which they could witness all that otherwise would attract them and induce them to pay the price of admission to the course. The feature in which the plaintiff finds the wrong of nuisance is the impairment or deprivation of the advantages possessed by the plaintiff's land as a racecourse by means of a non-natural and unusual use of the defendants' land.

This treatment of the case will not, I think, hold water. It may be conceded that interferences of a physical nature, as by fumes, smell and noise, are not the only means of committing a private **[507]** nuisance. But the essence of the wrong is the detraction from the occupier's enjoyment of the natural rights belonging to, or in the case of easements, of the acquired rights annexed to, the occupation of land. The law fixes those rights. Diversion of custom from a business carried on upon the land may be brought about by noise, fumes, obstruction of the frontage or any other interference with the enjoyment of recognized rights arising from the occupation of property and, if so, it forms a legitimate head of damage recoverable for the wrong; but it is not the wrong itself. The existence or the use of a microphone upon neighbouring land is, of course, no nuisance. If one, who could not see the spectacle, took upon himself to broadcast a fictitious account of the races he might conceivably render himself liable in a form of action in which his falsehood played a part, but he would commit no nuisance. It is the obtaining a view of the premises which is the foundation of the allegation. But English law is, rightly or wrongly, clear that the natural rights of an occupier do not include freedom from the view and inspection of neighbouring occupiers or of other persons who enable themselves to overlook the premises. An occupier of land is at liberty to exclude his neighbour's view by any physical means he can adopt. But while it is no wrongful act on his part to block the prospect from adjacent land, it is no wrongful act on the part of any person on such land to avail himself of what prospect exists or can be obtained. Not only is it lawful on the part of those occupying premises in the vicinity to overlook the land from any natural vantage point, but artificial erections may be made which destroy the privacy existing under natural conditions. ...

[508] When this principle is applied to the plaintiff's case it means, I think, that the essential element upon which it depends is lacking. So far as freedom from view or inspection is a natural or acquired physical characteristic of the site, giving it value for the purpose of the business or pursuit which the plaintiff conducts, it is a characteristic which is not a legally protected interest. It is not a natural right for breach of which a legal remedy is given, either by an action in the nature of nuisance or otherwise. ...

[511] In my opinion the judgment of Nicholas J is right and the appeal should be dismissed.

EVATT J. [dissenting] ... **[513]** It is quite unnecessary to cite or discuss authorities which repeat or illustrate the well-known principle that the plaintiff must affirmatively establish that the defendants have been guilty of a tort, and that the damage which they have caused to be inflicted upon the plaintiff may be *damnum absque injuria*. At the same time, it is practically conceded that, if a legal wrong has been committed, the case is one for the application of the remedy of injunction.

The defendants have argued that the damage and loss of the plaintiff have been sustained by it rather in its character as racing entrepreneur than as occupier of land. But the plaintiff's profitable conduct of its business cannot be dissociated from its occupation of the land, and damage to the plaintiff's business is necessarily reflected by some diminution in the value of the land of the plaintiff. It has been said with accuracy that:

> nuisance does not convey the idea of injury to the realty itself. It means rather an interference with some right incident to the ownership or possession of realty. The law of nuisance is an extension of the idea of trespass into the field that fringes property. It is associated with those rights of enjoyment which are, or may become, attached to realty. Ownership or rightful possession necessarily involves the right to the full and free enjoyment of the property occupied (Street, *Foundations of Legal Liability* (Tort), vol 1, p 211). ...

[515] Here the plaintiff contends that the defendants are guilty of the tort of nuisance. It cannot point at once to a decisive precedent in its favour, but the statements of general principle in *Donoghue v Stevenson* [1932] AC 562 are equally applicable to the tort of nuisance. A definition of the tort of nuisance was attempted by Sir Frederick Pollock, who said:

> Private nuisance is the using or authorizing the use of one's property, or of anything under one's control, so as to injuriously affect an owner or occupier of property – (*a*) by diminishing the value of that property; (*b*) by continuously interfering with his power of control or enjoyment of that property; (*c*) by causing material disturbance or annoyance to him in his use or occupation of that property. What amounts to material disturbance or annoyance is **[516]** a question of fact to be decided with regard to the character of the neighbourhood, the ordinary habits of life and reasonable expectations of persons there dwelling, and other relevant circumstances. (*Indian Civil Wrongs Bill*, c VII, s 55)

At an earlier date, Pollock CB had indicated the danger of too rigid a definition of nuisance. He said:

> I do not think that the nuisance for which an action will lie is capable of any legal definition which will be applicable to all cases and useful in deciding them. The question so entirely depends on the surrounding circumstances – the place where, the time when, the alleged nuisance, what, the mode of committing it, how, and the duration of it, whether temporary or permanent (*Bamford v Turnley* (1862) 3 B & S, at p 79; 122 ER, at p 31).

In the present case, the plaintiff relies upon all the surrounding circumstances. Its use and occupation of land is interfered with, its business profits are lessened, and the value of the land is diminished or jeopardized by the conduct of the defendants. The defendants' operations are conducted to the plaintiff's detriment, not casually but systematically, not temporarily but indefinitely; they use a suburban bungalow in an unreasonable and grotesque manner, and do so in the course of a gainful pursuit which strikes at the plaintiff's profitable use of its land, precisely at the point where the profit must be earned, viz, the entrance gates. Many analogies to the defendants' operations have been suggested, but few of them are applicable. The newspaper which is published a considerable time after a race has been run competes only with other newspapers, and can have little or no effect upon the profitable employment of the plaintiff's land. A photographer overlooking the course and subsequently publishing a photograph in a newspaper or elsewhere does not injure the plaintiff. Individuals who observe the racing from their own homes or those of their friends could not interfere with the plaintiff's beneficial use of its course. On the other hand, the defendants' operations are fairly comparable with those who, by the employment of moving picture films, television and broadcasting would convey to the public generally (i) from a point of vantage specially constructed; (ii) simultaneously with the actual running of the races, (iii) visual, verbal or audible representations of each and every portion of the races. If such a plan of campaign were [517] pursued, it would result in what has been proved here, viz, actual pecuniary loss to the occupier of the racecourse and a depreciation in the value of his land, at least so long as the conduct is continued. In principle, such a plan may be regarded as equivalent to the erection by a landowner of a special stand outside a cricket ground for the sole purpose of enabling the public to witness the cricket match at an admission price which is lower than that charged to the public bodies [sic] who own the ground, and, at great expense, organize the game.

In concluding that, in such cases, no actionable nuisance would be created, the defendants insist that the law of England does not recognize any general right of privacy. That is true, but it carries the defendants no further, because it is not merely an interference with privacy which is here relied upon, and it is not the law that every interference with privacy must be lawful. The defendants also say that the law of England does not forbid one person to overlook the property of another. That also is true in the sense that the fact that one individual possesses the means of watching, and sometimes watches what goes on on his neighbour's land, does not make the former's action unlawful. But it is equally erroneous to assume that under no circumstances can systematic watching amount to a civil wrong, for an analysis of the cases of *J Lyons & Sons v Wilkins* [1899] 1 Ch 255 and *Ward Locke & Co (Ltd) v Operative Printers' Assistants' Society* (1906) 22 TLR 327 indicates that, under some circumstances, the common law regards "watching and besetting" as a private nuisance, although no trespass to land has been committed. ...

[520] It should be appreciated that the plaintiff does not question the general principle that it is a legitimate use of property to erect and extend homes for the purpose of obtaining or improving favourable prospects or "views". A number of cases bearing upon such question have been collected and discussed by Professor Winfield in a learned article on "Privacy", published in the *Law Quarterly Review*, vol 47, p 23. The Balham case there discussed illustrates not only what Paley called the "competition of opposite analogies," but also, in my opinion, how the competition might fairly be resolved. It appeared that, by an arrangement of large mirrors, "neighbours" succeeded in observing all that went on in the surgery of a near-by dentist. Professor Winfield rightly asks: "Why should it not have been actionable as a nuisance?" In my opinion, such conduct certainly amounted to a private nuisance and should have been restrained by injunction, although the sole object of the "peeping [521] Toms" of Balham was to satisfy their own degraded curiosity and not to interfere with the dentist's liberty of action. In truth, no normally sensitive human being could have pursued his profession or business under so intolerable an espionage, and the result would have been to render the business premises practically uninhabitable.

The motive of the wrongdoers at Balham was to satisfy their curiously perverted instincts. But let us suppose that, by such devices as broadcasting and television, the operating theatre of a private hospital was made inspectable, so that a room outside the hospital could be hired in order that the public might view the operations on payment of a fee. It would not be any the less a nuisance because in such a case the interference with the normal rights of using and enjoying property was accentuated and aggravated by the wrongdoers making a profit out of their exhibition. Let it be also supposed that medical students, who would otherwise pay a fee to the hospital in order to witness the operations, stayed away because they were able to see them performed elsewhere but simultaneously for a smaller fee, the result being that damage is sustained by the hospital.

My opinion is that an action would lie, not only in the Balham case but in the instances I have suggested and that a court of equity would grant the additional remedy of an injunction. If this conclusion is right, the following propositions may be suggested: (*a*) Although there is no general right of privacy recognized by the common law, neither is there an absolute and unrestricted right to spy on or to overlook the property of another person. (*b*) A person who creates or uses devices for the purpose of enabling the public generally to overlook or spy upon the premises of another person will generally become liable to an action of nuisance, providing appreciable damage, discomfort or annoyance is caused. (*c*) As in all cases of private nuisance, all the surrounding circumstances will require examination. (*d*) The fact that in such cases the defendant's conduct is openly pursued, or that his motive is merely that of profit making, or that he makes no direct charge for the privilege of overlooking or spying will provide no answer to an action. ...

[522] Thus the plaintiff is entitled to maintain an action for damages for private nuisance, and, if so, it is indisputable that it is also entitled to an injunction against all three defendants.

In my opinion the appeal should be allowed.

[McTiernan J agreed with Latham CJ and Dixon J that the activities of the defendants did not constitute an actionable nuisance.]

Appeal dismissed

Raciti v Hughes
(1995) 7 BPR 14,837
Supreme Court of New South Wales

Illumination and surveillance of the plaintiff's land may amount to an actionable nuisance.

YOUNG J. ... [14,837] The defendants' property and the plaintiffs' property adjoin. ...

The defendants have installed on their property (a) floodlights; and (b) camera surveillance equipment. The floodlights and surveillance equipment are so positioned that they respectively illuminate the plaintiffs' backyard and may record on video tape what occurs in the plaintiffs' backyard. On the evidence to date, the [14,838] equipment does not just provide light or security for the defendants' yard, indeed, it may be inferred from the evidence that its purpose is to record what happens in the plaintiffs' backyard.

The plaintiffs say that they are accustomed to use their backyard for hanging up their clothes, doing their gardening, sitting and listening to the radio and for their children to play. They say they have become distressed since July 1995 when the electronic equipment was installed, and no longer feel that they can use their backyard in the way in which they have theretofore. The floodlight system appears to be activated by a sensor, which switches the floodlights on with movement or noise, such as movement in the backyard or perhaps even a dog barking. When the equipment is activated the lights come on and the camera may be activated because there is sufficient light to film what is happening. ...

Although to a degree they are interconnected, there are really two quite separate acts of nuisance in the instant case: (a) the lights; and (b) the surveillance equipment. Although it is necessary to look at the total effect, it is convenient, at least in the first instance, to deal with these separately.

(a) **The lights.** Early cases tended to deny that the use of bright lights was a nuisance. ...

However, even last century the American courts came to the view that the concentration of light onto the plaintiff's yard could constitute a nuisance. In New [14,839] Jersey in *Cleveland v Citizens' Gas Light Company* (1869) 20 New Jersey Equity 201 at 205, the Court of Chancery in New Jersey held that there was little doubt that light radiating from lamps of intensity could become a nuisance if they materially interfered with the ordinary comfort of human existence. ...

In Australasia in more recent times the law has perhaps tended to be more sympathetic to plaintiffs than the older cases.

In *Abbott v Arcus* (1948) 50 WALR 41, the defendants constructed a tennis court in a residential area with floodlights. Wolff J held that the use of the floodlit court after sunset and before 7 am was a nuisance, and granted an injunction and gave damages of £5.

The leading Australasian case is *Bank of New Zealand v Greenwood* [1984] 1 NZLR 525. In that case the defendant built a two storey shopping arcade in the shopping centre at Christchurch. The top of the building was constructed of glass with a slope of 60 degrees and this at certain times of the day produced a dazzling glare across the road into the windows of BNZ House, where the plaintiff conducted its business. M Hardie Boys J, analysing the English and Australian cases at

532, considered that there could be a nuisance, but considered that the interference was intermittent and slight and it was up to the plaintiff to guard against it and buy proper blinds. Accordingly, he stood the matter over to see whether the installation of blinds would remedy the problem. He did not seem, however, to have any doubt that provided the proper degree of inconvenience was established, there was a nuisance. ...

In the present case the evidence shows that the lights are automatically switched on by noise or movement on the plaintiffs' land. They come on day or night. There is evidence that the plaintiffs are suffering real health problems as a result of the continued illumination of their land. In my view, the cases show that lights of this nature may well constitute a nuisance. ...

[14,840] (b) The surveillance equipment. There is no doubt that as a general rule what one can see one can photograph without it being actionable: *Sports & General Press Agency Ltd v Our Dogs Publishing Co Ltd* [1917] 2 KB 125; *Victoria Park Racing & Recreation Grounds Co Ltd v Taylor* (1937) 58 CLR 479; *Bathurst City Council v Saban* (1985) 2 NSWLR 704 and *Lincoln Hunt Australia Pty Ltd v Willesee* (1986) 4 NSWLR 457. ...

I digested some of the United States authorities in *Saban's* case and the *Lincoln Hunt* case. I there indicated that the general liberty to photograph was at least subject to not deliberately photographing people in embarrassing situations. ...

Although the United States law has developed far more tenderly towards the right of privacy than Australian law, nonetheless some of the American cases are applicable here. An illustration of a case that would be applied here is *Daily Times Democrat v Graham* 169 So (2d) 474 (1964) (Alabama), where an injunction was granted to prevent publication without the plaintiff's consent of a picture showing the plaintiff with her dress blown up as she was leaving a fun house operating at the county fair. ...

On the evidence before me at the moment there is a deliberate attempt to snoop on the privacy of a neighbour and to record that on video tape. It seems to me that this is an actionable nuisance. This view fits in with the attitude of the courts to what is now called "telephone nuisance". Thus in *Alma v Nakir* [1966] 2 NSWR 396, McLelland CJ in Eq held that where a defendant persistently dials the plaintiff's telephone number and then when the telephone is answered deliberately refrains from replacing the receiver at the dialling end, as a result of which distress and serious inconvenience is caused to the plaintiff, there is a nuisance for which injunctive relief will lie. ...

[14,841] [T]he facts of this case show that the surveillance and accompanying recording by video camera of what occurs in the plaintiffs' backyard gets sufficiently close to watching and besetting, and which, on analogy with cases such as *Alma's* case, are an actionable nuisance. ...

Injunction granted

Hunter v Canary Wharf Ltd
[1997] AC 655
House of Lords

"More is required than the mere presence of a neighbouring building to give rise to an actionable private nuisance". Title to sue in nuisance is actual and exclusive possession of the land affected. A mere licensee does not have title to sue.

LORD GOFF of CHIEVELEY. ... **[683]** [T]here are ... appeals in two actions, which raise fundamental questions relating to the law of private nuisance.

In the first action, *Hunter v Canary Wharf Ltd*, the appellant plaintiffs claim damages in respect of interference with the television reception at their homes. This, they claim, was caused by the construction of the Canary Wharf Tower, which was built on land developed by the defendants. The tower is nearly 250 metres (about 800 feet) high and over 50 metres square. The source of television transmissions in the area is a BBC transmitter at Crystal Palace; and the plaintiffs claim that, because of its size and the metal in its surface (it has stainless steel cladding and metallised windows), it has caused interference with the television signals from Crystal Palace. The plaintiffs all lived at the material time in an area on the Isle of Dogs affected by the interference, which has been called "the shadow area". They claim that the interference began in 1989, during the construction of the tower. A relay transmitter was then built to overcome the problem of interference in the shadow area. This came into operation in April 1991, and it is claimed that the aerials at the plaintiffs' homes were adjusted or replaced between July 1991 and April 1992 to achieve satisfactory reception. The plaintiffs claim damages in respect of the interference with their television reception during the intervening period. Their claim was framed in nuisance and in negligence, though their claim in negligence has since been abandoned.

In the second action, *Hunter v London Docklands Development Corporation*, the respondent plaintiffs claim damages in respect of damage caused by what they claim to be excessive amounts of dust created by the construction by the defendants of a road 1,800 metres in length, known as the Limehouse Link Road, which was constructed by the defendants between November 1989 and May 1993. The plaintiffs are residents in the affected area, and they advanced their claims in negligence and nuisance [684] and under the rule in *Rylands v Fletcher* (1868) LR 3 HL 330, though this last head of claim has been abandoned. ...

The preliminary issues in the two actions were considered by Judge Havery QC at separate hearings. ... [I]n the first action, he held (1) that interference with television reception is capable of constituting an actionable nuisance, but (2) that a right of exclusive possession of land is necessary to entitle a person to sue in private nuisance. He later held that his answer on the second issue was applicable in the case of the same issue in the second action. The Court of Appeal ... reversed the decision of Judge Havery on both issues, holding (1) that the creation or presence of a building in the line of sight between a television transmitter and other properties is not actionable as an interference with the use and enjoyment of land, but (2) that occupation of property as a home provided a sufficiently substantial link to enable the occupier to sue in private nuisance. The plaintiffs in the first action now appeal to your Lordships' House against the first of these answers, and the defendants in both actions appeal or cross-appeal against the second.

Interference with television signals

I turn first to consider the question whether interference with television signals may give rise to an action in private nuisance. This question was first considered over 30 years ago by Buckley J in *Bridlington Relay Ltd v Yorkshire Electricity Board* [1965] Ch 436. That case was concerned not with interference caused by the presence of a building, but with electrical interference caused by the activities of the defendant electricity board. Buckley J held that such interference did not constitute a legal nuisance, because it was interference with a purely recreational facility, as opposed to interference with the health or physical comfort or well-being of the plaintiffs. He did not however rule out the possibility that ability to receive television signals free from interference might one day be recognised as "so important a part of an ordinary householder's enjoyment of his property that such interference should be regarded as a legal nuisance:" p 447. Certainly the average weekly hours for television viewing in this country, which your Lordships were told were 24 hours per week, show that many people devote much of their leisure time to watching television, even allowing for the fact that it is not clear whether the relevant statistic is based more on the time when television sets are turned on, rather than being actually watched. Certainly it can be asserted with force that for many people television transcends the function of mere entertainment, and in particular that for the aged, the lonely and the bedridden it must provide a great distraction and relief from the [685] circumscribed nature of their lives. That interference with such an amenity might in appropriate circumstances be protected by the law of nuisance has been recognised in Canada, in *Nor-Video Services Ltd v Ontario Hydro* (1978) 84 DLR (3d) 221, 231.

However, as I see the present case, there is a more formidable obstacle to this claim. This is that the complaint rests simply upon the presence of the defendants' building on land in the neighbourhood as causing the relevant interference. The gravamen of the plaintiffs' case is that the defendants, by building the Canary Wharf Tower, interfered with the television signals and so caused interference with the reception on the plaintiffs' television sets; though it should not be overlooked that such interference might be caused by a smaller building and moreover that, since it is no defence that the plaintiff came to the nuisance, the same complaint could result from the simple fact of the presence of the building which caused the interference. In this respect the present case is to be distinguished from the *Bridlington Relay* case, in which the problem was caused not just by the presence of a neighbouring building but by electrical interference resulting from the defendant electricity board's activities.

As a general rule, a man is entitled to build on his own land, though nowadays this right is inevitably subject to our system of planning controls. Moreover, as a general rule, a man's right to build on his land is not restricted by the fact that the presence of the building may of itself interfere with his neighbour's enjoyment of his land. The building may spoil his neighbour's view (see *Attorney-General v Doughty* (1752) 2 Ves Sen 453 and *Fishmongers' Co v East India Co* (1752) 1 Dick 163); in the absence of an easement, it may restrict the flow of air on to his neighbour's land (*Bland v Mosely* (1587) 9 Co Rep 58a, cited in *Aldred's Case* (1610) 9 Co Rep 57b, and *Chastey v Ackland* [1895] 2 Ch 389); and, again in the absence of an easement, it may take away light from his neighbour's windows (*Dalton v Angus* (1881) 6 App Cas 740, *per* Lord Selborne LC, at pp 794-795, *per* Lord Blackburn, at p 823): nevertheless his neighbour generally cannot complain of the presence of the building, though this may seriously detract from the enjoyment of his land. ... From this it follows that, in the absence of an easement, more is required than the mere presence of a neighbouring building to give rise to an actionable private nuisance. Indeed, for an action in private nuisance to lie in respect of interference with the plaintiff's enjoyment of his land, it will generally arise from something emanating from the defendant's land. Such an emanation may take many forms – noise, dirt, fumes, a noxious smell, vibrations, and suchlike. Occasionally activities on the defendant's land are in themselves so offensive to neighbours as to constitute an actionable nuisance, as in *Thompson-Schwab v Costaki* [1956] 1 WLR **[686]** 335, where the sight of prostitutes and their clients entering and leaving neighbouring premises were held to fall into that category. Such cases must however be relatively rare. In one New Zealand case, *Bank of New Zealand v Greenwood* [1984] 1 NZLR 525, the glass roof of a verandah which deflected the sun's rays so that a dazzling glare was thrown on to neighbouring buildings was held, prima facie, to create a nuisance; but it seems that the effect was not merely to reflect the sunlight but to deflect it at such an angle and in such a manner as to cause the dazzling glare, too bright for the human eye to bear, to shine straight into the neighbouring building. One expert witness explained that the verandah glass diffused the light, as if from a multitude of mirrors, into what he described as a high intensity dazzle, which was extremely difficult to look at. On that basis, such a case can be distinguished from one concerned with the mere presence of a building on neighbouring land. At all events the mere fact that a building on the defendant's land gets in the way and so prevents something from reaching the plaintiff's land is generally speaking not enough for this purpose. ...

In the result I find myself to be in agreement on this point with Pill LJ, who delivered the judgment of the Court of Appeal ... when he expressed the opinion ... that no action lay in private nuisance for interference with television caused by the mere presence of a building. ...

[687] For these reasons I would dismiss the appeal of the plaintiffs in the first action on this issue.

Right to sue in private nuisance

I turn next to the question of the right to sue in private nuisance. In the two cases now under appeal before your Lordships' House, one of which relates to interference with television signals and the other to the generation of dust from the construction of a road, the plaintiffs consist in each case of a substantial group of local people. Moreover they are not restricted to householders who have the exclusive right to possess the places where they live, whether as freeholders or tenants, or even as licensees. They include people with whom householders share their homes, for example as wives or husbands or partners, or as children or other relatives. All of these people are claiming damages in private nuisance, by reason of interference with their television viewing or by reason of excessive dust. ...

The basic position is, in my opinion, most clearly expressed in Professor Newark's classic article on "The Boundaries of Nuisance" (1949) 65 LQR 480 when he stated, at p 482, that the essence of nuisance was that "it was a tort to land. Or to be more accurate it was a tort directed against the plaintiff's enjoyment of rights over land ..." The historical origin of the tort lay in the fact that:

> Disseisina, transgressio and nocumentum [nuisance] covered the three ways in which a man might be interfered with in his rights over land. Wholly to deprive a man of the opportunity of exercising his **[688]** rights over land was to disseise him, for which he might have recourse to the assize of novel disseisin. But to trouble a man in the exercise of his rights over land without going so far as to dispossess him was a trespass or a nuisance according to whether the act was done on or off the plaintiff's land: p 481.

Later, when distinguishing cases of personal injury, he stated, at pp 488-489:

> In true cases of nuisance the interest of the plaintiff which is invaded is not the interest of bodily security but the interest of liberty to exercise rights over land in the amplest manner. A sulphurous chimney in a residential area is not a nuisance because it makes householders cough and splutter but because it prevents them taking their ease in their gardens. It is for this reason that the plaintiff in an action for nuisance must show some title to realty.

Finally, he proclaimed four theses which should be nailed to the doors of the Law Courts and defended against all comers. The first was that: "The term 'nuisance' is properly applied only to such actionable user of land as interferes with the enjoyment by the plaintiff of rights in land." There are many authoritative statements which bear out this thesis of Professor Newark. I refer in particular to *Sedleigh-Denfield v O'Callaghan* [1940] AC 880, 902-903, *per* Lord Wright; *Read v J Lyons & Co Ltd* [1947] AC 156, 183, *per* Lord Simonds; *Tate & Lyle Food and Distribution Ltd v Greater London Council* [1983] 2 AC 509, 536-537, *per* Lord Templeman; *Fleming, The Law of Torts*, 8th ed (1992), p 416.

Since the tort of nuisance is a tort directed against the plaintiff's enjoyment of his rights over land, an action of private nuisance will usually be brought by the person in actual possession of the land affected, either as the freeholder or tenant of the land in question, or even as a licensee with exclusive possession of the land (see *Newcastle-under-Lyme Corporation v Wolstanton Ltd* [1947] Ch 92, 106-108, *per* Evershed J); though a reversioner may sue in respect of a nuisance of a sufficiently permanent character to damage his reversion. It was however established, in *Foster v Warblington Urban District Council* [1906] 1 KB 648, that, since jus tertii is not a defence to an action of nuisance, a person who is in exclusive possession of land may sue even though he cannot prove title to it. That case was concerned with a nuisance caused by the discharge of sewage by the defendant council into certain oyster beds. The plaintiff was an oyster merchant who had for many years been in occupation of the oyster beds which had been artificially constructed on the foreshore, which belonged to the lord of the manor. The plaintiff excluded everybody from the oyster beds, and nobody interfered with his occupation of the oyster beds or his removal and sale of oysters from them. It was held by the Court of Appeal that he could sue the defendant council in nuisance, notwithstanding that he could not prove his title. ...

[689] Subject to this exception, however, it has for many years been regarded as settled law that a person who has no right in the land cannot sue in private nuisance. For this proposition, it is usual to cite the decision of the Court of Appeal in *Malone v Laskey* [1907] 2 KB 141. In that case, the manager of a company resided in a house as a licensee of the company which employed him. The plaintiff was the manager's wife who lived with her husband in the house. She was injured when a bracket fell from a wall in the house. She claimed damages from the defendants in nuisance and negligence, her claim in nuisance being founded upon an allegation, accepted by the jury, that the fall of the bracket had been caused by vibrations from an engine operating on the defendants' adjoining premises. The Court of Appeal held that she was unable to succeed in her claim in nuisance. ...

[690] The decision in *Malone v Laskey* on nuisance has since been followed in many cases, of which notable examples are *Cunard v Antifyre Ltd* [1933] 1 KB 551 and *Oldham v Lawson (No 1)* [1976] VR 654. ...

[692] It follows that, on the authorities as they stand, an action in private nuisance will only lie at the suit of a person who has a right to the land affected. Ordinarily, such a person can only sue if he has the right to exclusive possession of the land, such as a freeholder or tenant in possession, or even a licensee with exclusive possession. Exceptionally however, as *Foster v Warblington Urban*

District Council shows, this category may include a person in actual possession who has no right to be there; and in any event a reversioner can sue in so far his reversionary interest is affected. But a mere licensee on the land has no right to sue.

The question therefore arises whether your Lordships should be persuaded to depart from established principle, and recognise such a right in others who are no more than mere licensees on the land. At the heart of this question lies a more fundamental question, which relates to the scope of the law of private nuisance. Here I wish to draw attention to the fact that although, in the past, damages for personal injury have been recovered at least in actions of public nuisance, there is now developing a school of thought that the appropriate remedy for such claims as these should lie in our now fully developed law of negligence, and that personal injury claims should be altogether excluded from the domain of nuisance. The most forthright proponent of this approach has been Professor Newark, in his article … from which I have already quoted. Furthermore, it is now being suggested that claims in respect of physical damage to the land should also be excluded from private nuisance: see, eg, the article by Mr Conor Gearty on "The Place of Private Nuisance in a Modern Law of Torts" [1989] CLJ 214. In any event, it is right for present purposes to regard the typical cases of private nuisance as being those concerned with interference with the enjoyment of land and, as such, generally actionable only by a person with a right in the land. Characteristic examples of cases of this kind are those concerned with noise, vibrations, noxious smells and the like. The two appeals with which your Lordships are here concerned arise from actions of this character.

For private nuisances of this kind, the primary remedy is in most cases an injunction, which is sought to bring the nuisance to an end, and in most cases should swiftly achieve that objective. The right to bring such proceedings is, as the law stands, ordinarily vested in the person who has exclusive possession of the land. He or she is the person who will sue, if it is necessary to do so. Moreover he or she can, if thought appropriate, **[693]** reach an agreement with the person creating the nuisance, either that it may continue for a certain period of time, possibly on the payment of a sum of money, or that it shall cease, again perhaps on certain terms including the time within which the cessation will take place. The former may well occur when an agreement is reached between neighbours about the circumstances in which one of them may carry out major repairs to his house which may affect the other's enjoyment of his property. … But the efficacy of arrangements such as these depends upon the existence of an identifiable person with whom the creator of the nuisance can deal for this purpose. If anybody who lived in the relevant property as a home had the right to sue, sensible arrangements such as these might in some cases no longer be practicable.

Moreover, any such departure from the established law on this subject, such as that adopted by the Court of Appeal in the present case, faces the problem of defining the category of persons who would have the right to sue. The Court of Appeal adopted the not easily identifiable category of those who have a "substantial link" with the land, regarding a person who occupied the premises "as a home" as having a sufficient link for this purpose. But who is to be included in this category? It was plainly intended to include husbands and wives, or partners, and their children, and even other relatives living with them. But is the category also to include the lodger upstairs, or the au pair girl or resident nurse caring for an invalid who makes her home in the house while she works there? If the latter, it seems strange that the category should not extend to include places where people work as well as places where they live, where nuisances such as noise can be just as unpleasant or distracting. In any event, the extension of the tort in this way would transform it from a tort to land into a tort to the person, in which damages could be recovered in respect of something less serious than personal injury and the criteria for liability were founded not upon negligence but upon striking a balance between the interests of neighbours in the use of their land. This is, in my opinion, not an acceptable way in which to develop the law.

It was suggested in the course of argument that at least the spouse of a husband or wife who, for example as freeholder or tenant, had exclusive possession of the matrimonial home should be entitled to sue in private nuisance. … But I do not see how a spouse who has no interest in the matrimonial home has, simply by virtue of his or her cohabiting in the matrimonial home with his or her wife or husband whose freehold or leasehold property it is, a right to sue. No distinction can sensibly be drawn between such spouses and other cohabitees in the home, such as children, or grandparents. Nor do I see any great disadvantage flowing from this state **[694]** of affairs. If a nuisance should occur, then the spouse who has an interest in the property can bring the necessary proceedings to bring the nuisance to an end, and can recover any damages in respect of the discomfort or inconvenience caused by the nuisance. Even if he or she is away from home, nowadays the necessary authority to commence proceedings for an injunction can usually be obtained by telephone. Moreover, if the other spouse suffers personal injury, including injury to health, he or she may, like anybody else, be able to recover damages in negligence. The only disadvantage is that the other spouse cannot bring an independent action in private nuisance for damages for discomfort or inconvenience.

I would allow the appeal or [695] cross-appeal of the defendants in both actions and restore the order of Judge Havery on this issue.

[Lord Lloyd of Berwick, Lord Hoffman and Lord Hope of Craighead, in separate judgments, agreed with Lord Goff of Chieveley. Lord Cooke of Thorndon, although agreeing with the other Law Lords that, as a matter of principle, interference with television signals may give rise to an action in private nuisance, dissented on the question of title to sue. His Lordship agreed with the Court of Appeal that occupation of property as a home provided a sufficiently substantial link to enable the occupier to sue in private nuisance, at least with respect to interference with amenities as distinct from injury to the land.]

Appeal of plaintiffs in Hunter v Canary Wharf Ltd dismissed.
Cross-appeal allowed

Appeal of defendants in Hunter v London Docklands Development Corporation
allowed

(b) Unreasonable and Substantial Interference

St Helen's Smelting Co v Tipping
(1865) 11 ER 1483
House of Lords

Whether an interference with comfort and quiet enjoyment amounts to an actionable nuisance will depend on the locality. An interference which causes material damage will be an actionable nuisance.

[In 1860 the plaintiff (respondent) purchased property consisting of a manor house and 1300 acres in an area of Lancashire where there were numerous manufacturing works. At the time of purchase the plaintiff was aware of the presence, about a mile and a half away, of the defendants' (appellants') copper smelting works.

Noxious vapours from the defendants' works caused damage to trees and crops on the plaintiff's property. In the plaintiff's action to recover damages for nuisance, the trial judge (Mellor J) directed the jury that an actionable nuisance was one producing sensible discomfort, trifling inconveniences being disregarded; that every person was bound to use his or her property in such a manner as not to injure other property in the neighbourhood; that all the circumstances (including time and locality) must be looked at from a reasonable point of view; and that the nuisance from noxious vapours in the present case was actionable if it visibly diminished the value of the plaintiff's property and the comfort and enjoyment of it. The jury returned a verdict in favour of the plaintiff and judgment was entered for him. This judgment was affirmed by the Exchequer Chamber, from which the defendants appealed to the House of Lords on the ground that Mellor J had misdirected the jury.]

LORD WESTBURY LC. ... [1486] My Lords, in matters of this description it appears to me that it is a very desirable thing to mark the difference between an action brought for a nuisance upon the ground that the alleged nuisance produces material injury to the property, and an action brought for a nuisance on the ground that the thing alleged to be a nuisance is productive of sensible, personal discomfort. With regard to the latter, namely, the personal inconvenience and interference with one's enjoyment, one's quiet, one's personal freedom, anything that discomposes or injuriously affects the senses or the nerves, whether that may or may not be denominated a nuisance, must undoubtedly depend greatly on the circumstances of the place where the thing complained of actually occurs. If a man lives in a town, it is necessary that he should subject himself to the consequences of those operations of trade which may be carried on in his immediate locality, which are actually necessary for trade and commerce, and also for the enjoyment of property, and for the benefit of the inhabitants of the town and of the public at large. If a man lives in a street where there are numerous shops, and a shop is opened next door to him, which is carried on in a fair and reasonable way, he has no ground for complaint, because to himself individually there may arise much discomfort from the trade carried on in that shop. But when an occupation is carried on by one person in the neighbourhood of another, and the result of that trade, or occupation, or business, is a material injury to property, then there unquestionably arises a very different consideration. I think, my Lords, that in a case of that description, the submission which is required from persons living in society to that amount of discomfort which may be necessary for the legitimate and free exercise of the trade of their neighbours, would not apply to circumstances the immediate result of which is sensible injury to the value of the property. ...

[1487] [T]he jurors have found the existence of the injury; and the only ground upon which your Lordships are asked to set aside that verdict, and to direct a new trial, is this, that the whole neighbourhood where these copper smelting works were carried on, is a neighbourhood more or less devoted to manufacturing purposes of a similar kind, and therefor it is said, that inasmuch as this copper smelting is carried on in what the appellant contends is a fit place, it may be carried on with impunity, although the result may be the utter destruction, or the very considerable diminution, of the value of the plaintiff's property. My Lords, I apprehend that that is not the meaning of the word "suitable", or the meaning of the word "convenient", which has been used as applicable to the subject. The word "suitable" unquestionably cannot carry with it this consequence, that a trade may be carried on in a particular locality, the consequence of which trade may be injury and destruction to the neighbouring property. Of course, my Lords, I except cases where any prescriptive right has been acquired by a lengthened user of the place.

On these grounds ... I advise your Lordships to affirm the decision of the Court below, and to refuse the new trial, and to dismiss the appeal with costs.

[Lord Cranworth and Lord Wensleydale agreed with the Lord Chancellor.]

Appeal dismissed

Munro v Southern Dairies Ltd
[1955] VLR 332
Supreme Court of Victoria

In order to be an actionable nuisance, an interference with comfort and convenience must be substantial according to the ordinary standards of comfort to be expected in the locality. It is no defence to say that the activity is socially useful or that the defendant took reasonable care.

[The plaintiff was the owner and occupier of a house and land at Hampton, a suburb of Melbourne. The defendant, which carried on the business of a milk distributor, kept permanently about five to seven horses on adjoining premises for use in drawing vehicles engaged in retail delivery of milk.

In proceedings founded on private nuisance, in which he claimed an injunction and damages, the plaintiff alleged that the keeping of horses on the defendant's premises with associated noise, smell and flies interfered with the quiet enjoyment of his premises and had done so since 1952.]

SHOLL J. … [334] The defendant does not deny that there is some smell from the horses, or that there is some noise. It does deny that there is any substantial quantity of flies, and it says that such smell or noise as is caused by the keeping of the horses on the premises is insufficient to amount to a nuisance – that is, insufficient to amount to a substantial interference with the comfort and convenience of the plaintiff as the occupier of his property, so as to constitute a nuisance in law. …

[Private nuisance] is defined in one of the text books as "An unlawful interference with a person's use or enjoyment of land, or of some right over, or in connection with it," but that definition of itself is so wide that it is necessary to add to it and qualify it in order to set out clearly what it is that will constitute an actionable private nuisance of the kind here complained of. In the first place, there must be a substantial degree of interference with the comfort and convenience of the occupier who complains of a private nuisance, or with some other aspect of the use or enjoyment of his land. The interference must be so substantial as to cause damage to him. On that matter I may refer to what is said in *Winfield on Torts* (2nd ed), p 482. Dealing with the subject of interference, the learned author says:

> The forms of this are innumerable. Noise, smells, pollution of air or water, are the most usual instances, but there are many others. The two main heads are injury to property and interference with personal comfort. The escape of fumes which kill vegetation and cattle is an illustration of the first, and excessive tolling of church bells of the second. But whatever be the type, it does not follow that any harm [335] constitutes a nuisance. The whole law on the subject really represents a balancing of conflicting interests. Some noise, some smell, some vibration, every one must endure in any modern town, otherwise modern life would be impossible.

And later he continues:

> Where the interference is with personal comfort, it is not necessary in order to establish a nuisance that any injury to health should be shown. It is enough that there is a material interference with the physical comfort of human existence reckoned "not merely according to elegant or dainty modes and habits of living, but according to plain and sober and simple notions among the English people".

The last phrase, of course, is a quotation from the well known judgment of Knight-Bruce V-C, as he then was, in *Walter v Selfe* (1851) 4 De G & Sm 315, at p 322. I think Mr Jacobs [counsel for the plaintiff] was right in his submission that the loss of even one night's sleep may amount to such a substantial interference with personal comfort as to constitute a nuisance, and I adopt with respect what was said by Sir Wilfrid Greene MR in a case to which Mr Jacobs referred me, *Andreae v Selfridge & Company Ltd* [1937] 3 All ER 255, at p 261. Speaking there of interference with rest caused by the defendant's working of cranes, his Lordship said:

> There were other occasions on which it conducted noisy operations at night. I do not propose to go through them. There are a number of letters of complaint, and those complaints were either attempted to be explained away or they were remedied. But that the complaints were substantial complaints I, for one, am satisfied, and I certainly protest against the idea that, if persons, for their own profit and convenience, choose to destroy even one night's rest of their neighbours, they are doing something which is excusable. To say that the loss of one or two nights' rest is one of those trivial matters in respect of which the law will take no notice appears to me to be quite a misconception, and, if it be a misconception existing in the minds of those who conduct these operations, the sooner it is removed the better.

I have already said something in the remarks I have just made about the standard of comfort which a land owner is entitled to expect. The test which the law applies is not the test of an abnormal sensitiveness. A man is not entitled to relief merely because he may happen to be unduly sensitive to noise or smell or any other form of interference with his property. Nevertheless a man who lives next door to premises from which some interference emanates may get relief when another man some distance away will fail to obtain it. That, after all, is only commonsense, because the degree of interference may and frequently does vary with the distance of the plaintiff's premises from the source of the interference. A good deal of evidence was led in the present case to show that the defendant's use of the premises was in accordance with accepted standards, and evidence was called from an inspector of the Department of Agriculture and from the Senior Health Inspector of the City of Sandringham on that point. That evidence was, of course, relevant insofar as it tended to negative the facts alleged by the plaintiff and his witnesses, but it was irrelevant, in my opinion, insofar as it was relied on, if it was relied on, for the purpose of the submission that reasonable use of the premises was sufficient to negative nuisance. On that point there are a number of authorities. I need, I think, refer only to three. In *Broder v Saillard* (1876) 2 Ch D 692, at pp 700-702, Sir George Jessel MR was dealing with a case in which a nuisance of noise from a stable was complained of, among other things, and at pp 700-701 he said:

[336] I come now to the second branch of the case – the noise. It is very hard on the defendant, who is a gentleman with three horses in his stable, and whose horses do not appear to make more than the ordinary noise that horses do, if he is not to be allowed to keep his horses in his stable. On the other hand, it is very hard on the plaintiffs if they cannot sleep at night, and cannot enjoy their house, because the noise from the stables is so great as seriously to interfere with their rest and comfort. The question is, on which side the law inclines? If there were no authority on the question I should have felt no difficulty about it, because I take it the law is this, that a man is entitled to the comfortable enjoyment of his dwelling-house. If his neighbour makes such a noise as to interfere with the ordinary use and enjoyment of his dwelling-house, so as to cause serious annoyance and disturbance, the occupier of the dwelling-house is entitled to be protected from it. It is no answer to say that the defendant is only making a reasonable use of his property, because there are many trades and many occupations which are not only reasonable, but necessary to be followed, and which still cannot be allowed to be followed in the proximity of dwelling-houses, so as to interfere with the comfort of their inhabitants. I suppose a blacksmith's trade is as necessary as most trades in this kingdom; or I might take instances of many noisy and offensive trades, some of which are absolutely necessary, and some of which, no doubt, may not only be reasonably followed, but to which it is absolutely and indispensably necessary for the welfare of mankind that some houses and some pieces of land should be devoted; therefore I think that is not the test. If a stable is built, as this stable is, not as stables usually are, at some distance from dwelling-houses, but next to the wall of the plaintiffs' dwelling-house, in such a position that the noise would actually prevent the neighbours sleeping, and would frighten them out of their sleep, and would prevent their ordinary and comfortable enjoyment of their dwelling-house, all I can say is, that is not a proper place to keep horses in, although the horses may be ordinarily quiet.

At p 702 his Lordship added:

The test, therefore, is whether the stables are unluckily so situated as that the noise from the horses, not being uncommon horses in any way, materially disturbs the comfort of the plaintiffs' dwelling-house, and prevents the people sleeping at night.

In *Rapier v London Tramways Company* [1893] 2 Ch 588, a nuisance from stables was again complained of. In that case the London Tramways Company was carrying on its undertaking under statutory authority, and Lindley LJ, at pp 599-600, says this:

Unless the Act of Parliament is so worded as to limit their duty to that extent, I think the common law must prevail, that they must exercise their power so as not to commit a nuisance. At common law, if I am sued for a nuisance, and the nuisance is proved, it is no defence on my part to say, and to prove, that I have taken all reasonable care to prevent it.

Lastly, in *Painter v Reed* [1930] SASR 295, Richards J had to deal with a case involving allegations of nuisance of noise and smell from horses. He held that the alleged nuisance by smell had not been proved, but that the nuisance by noise had been, and the head note, I think, accurately represents the substance of his judgment. It is to this effect:

In an action for nuisance, where it was shown that the defendant had taken much trouble to make the carrying on of his business as unobjectionable as possible, and had carried on his business in a fair and reasonable way, and at a site proper for such a business, *Held*, on the evidence, that noises caused in the early mornings by the movements and stamping of horses, which disturbed the sleep of the plaintiff, constituted an actionable nuisance, and should be restrained by injunction.

[337] In the same way, it has been held that the mere fact that a business may be so carried on as to be useful to the public, or even important from the point of view of public benefit, is insufficient to justify what otherwise would be a nuisance. On that I need only make a brief reference to a case cited during the argument before me, *Shelfer v City of London Electric Lighting Company* [1895] 1 Ch 287. The relevant passage is in the judgment of Lindley LJ, at pp 315-316. His Lordship said:

The Court has always protested against the notion that it ought to allow a wrong to continue simply because the wrongdoer is able and willing to pay for the injury he may inflict. Neither has the circumstance that the wrongdoer is in some sense a public benefactor (eg, a gas or water company or a sewer authority) ever been considered a sufficient reason for refusing to protect by injunction an individual whose rights are being persistently infringed. Expropriation, even for a money consideration, is only justifiable when Parliament has sanctioned it. Courts of Justice are not like Parliament, which considers whether proposed works will be so beneficial to the public as to justify exceptional legislation, and the deprivation of people of their rights with or without compensation.

In one paragraph of the defence reference was made to the carrying on of the stabling of horses in their present position on the Willis Street property since the year 1934 or thereabouts. I do not think that Mr Frederico [counsel for the defendant] in his final address really advanced the contention that it was a defence to show that the plaintiff had in any sense "come to the nuisance," as the common phrase is, and it is sufficient to refer to the authorities collected in *Winfield: Law of Tort* (2nd ed), at pp 511-512, to show that the mere fact that a plaintiff can in a sense be said to have "come to a nuisance" is not of itself a defence. The locality, however, is of importance and, as Professor Winfield observes at p 512:

If a man chooses to make his home in the heart of a coal-field or in a manufacturing district, he can expect no more freedom from the discomfort usually associated with such a place than any other resident can.

In the present case it is, of course, material to consider the general nature of the locality of Willis Street, Hampton, and particularly whether the discomfort or inconvenience of which the plaintiff now complains is so characteristic of the general neighbourhood that he ought not to be heard to complain of what other people are accustomed habitually to put up with. Evidence was also led before me as to the general nature of the retail milk distribution trade in Melbourne and the economic necessity for the use of horses for milk delivery in this city. I allowed that evidence, though I had some doubt as to its true relevance. I allowed it because I thought it was necessary to consider an allegation of nuisance against the social background of the time, and there is some authority for the view that the operations of a trade in a locality where it is essential cannot be complained of. Even if that proposition, however, can be maintained to its full extent, which I greatly doubt, it can extend only to what can be shown to be essential and unavoidable in the particular locality. I therefore take into account only within the limits stated the evidence given as to the necessity for horse delivery. ...

[His Honour considered the facts of the case and continued:]

[338] I have now referred to all the witnesses called in this lengthy hearing, and I am in a position to state my conclusions of fact and of law in the light of the legal principles which I enunciated earlier. In my judgment, there has been caused by the defendant's keeping of horses on its Willis Street premises a substantial nuisance of [339] noise, smell of manure and urine, and flies, to the plaintiff, as occupier of the premises at 23 Willis Street, from at least the latter part of 1952 onwards.

Judgment for the plaintiff

(c) Basis of Liability

Fennell v Robson Excavations Pty Ltd
[1977] 2 NSWLR 486
Supreme Court of New South Wales, Court of Appeal

A person may be liable for a nuisance which he or she created whether or not as occupier of the land from which the nuisance emanates.

[The plaintiffs were the owners of land at Gosford. The second defendant ("the developer") was a developer and builder in occupation of adjoining land which it was developing as a home unit site. In the course of this development the developer engaged the first defendant ("the excavator"), an independent contractor, to carry out excavation work, which the excavator performed competently and in accordance with proper practice.

Upon completion of the excavation work the excavator had reasonable grounds for believing that the developer would carry out retaining work on its land to protect the plaintiffs' land from possible future subsidence. However, the developer became insolvent before the retaining work could be performed.

About six months after completion of the excavation work the plaintiffs' land began to subside along its boundary with the developer's land. In proceedings founded on private nuisance in which the developer, now in liquidation, took no part, the plaintiffs were awarded damages against the excavator. The excavator appealed.]

GLASS JA. ... [490] The first submission for the excavator founds upon the findings of fact made by the trial judge that the excavator was not in possession or occupation of the premises where the excavation was carried out. It is submitted that in those circumstances the excavator cannot incur liability in private nuisance. The principal authority relied upon is contained in a passage in *Beaudesert Shire Council v Smith* (1966) 120 CLR 145, at p 152, which reads as follows: "We have also considered whether the facts, as proved, disclose an actionable nuisance. Patrick Reilly Smith was the owner and occupier of land, and it was from adjoining land that the appellant removed the gravel, thus causing him damage. The appellant was not, however, the occupier of the adjoining land; the damage suffered by Smith was simply inability to water his land from a river belonging, in effect, to the Crown; and the removal of gravel from a river cannot be regarded as a public nuisance such as is constituted by interference with a public right of way or by the pollution of waters. Smith, so far as it appears, was the only one adversely affected by the unlawful removal of the gravel. There was, therefore, no public nuisance and the facts do not bring the case within the category of private nuisance. So far as nuisance is concerned, the respondents appear to us to be in a much less favourable position than the unsuccessful respondent in *Esso Petroleum Co Ltd v Southport Corporation* [1956] AC 218. There the jettisoning of the oil did pollute the sea, and the foreshore at Southport was damaged by the oil which was brought on to it by the sea."

It will be seen that, in the course of giving reasons why the plaintiffs' claim in private nuisance failed, three separate matters were referred to. The first was that the defendant was not the occupier of the adjoining land. The second was that the plaintiffs' damage did not involve any inability to enjoy his land, but an inability to draw water for his land from a public river. The third was that the plaintiff was worse off than the plaintiff corporation in the *Esso Petroleum* case [1956] AC 218, which was able to show that the enjoyment of its land was adversely affected. Two of the three constituent findings suggest that the fatal defect in the plaintiffs' claim to private nuisance was that the loss of the flow of water was not an invasion of his interest in land such as would ground an action of private nuisance. It is true that the status of the defendant as a non-occupier is also mentioned, and the construction for which the defendant contends has been adopted by others, Dworkin & Harari, 40 ALJ 297, at p 302; Higgins, *Elements of Torts in Australia*, 177-178. But I think it is not possible to distil from the passage what the appellant seeks, namely an authoritative pronouncement that a party who creates a nuisance cannot be liable, unless he is in occupation of the land where the nuisance was created. Reliance was also placed on a statement in *Sedleigh-Denfield v O'Callaghan* [1940] AC 880, at p 903, where Lord Wright, discussing the nature of an action for private nuisance, said: "The ground of responsibility is the possession and control of the land from which the nuisance proceeds." But it is to be observed that on the same page the sentence appears: "With possibly certain anomalous exceptions, not here material, possession or occupation is still the test." The third principal authority cited to us by counsel for the defendant was *Kraemers v Attorney-General (Tas)* [1966] Tas SR 113. In that decision, the three judges of the Supreme Court of Tasmania found as a fact that the defendant was in **[491]** actual control of the premises where the nuisance was created. In those circumstances, this was held to be sufficient. They deemed it, therefore, to be unnecessary to decide whether liability can be visited upon a party who creates a nuisance on land without being in occupation.

There is no doubt that liability in nuisance normally attaches to the occupier. The question is: Whether liability may also be incurred by a party who creates a nuisance on land in the occupation of another? There is a considerable body of authority to this effect. In *Thompson v Gibson* (1841) 7 M & W 456; 151 ER 845, the defendants were charged in an action on the case with continuing a nuisance to the plaintiff's market by a building which had been erected under their superintendence and direction, but not on their land. The court held that they could be held liable for continuing the nuisance, and with respect to their responsibility for the original erection of the building had this to say ((1841) 7 M & W 456, at p 460; 151 ER 845, at p 846): "That the defendants were responsible for some consequences of the original erection of the building to the then owner of the market, though the defendants were not acting for their own benefit, but for that of the corporation, is not disputed; nor could it be. If they are considered merely as servants of the corporation, they would be liable, just as the servant or an individual is if he is actually concerned in erecting a nuisance; ..."

I take this to be a clear statement that a person who erects a nuisance, whether he be the occupier of the land, or a contractor, or servant acting on behalf of the occupier, incurs personal responsibility for it. *Wilson v Peto and Hunter* (1821) 6 Moore 47 was an action on the case for the obstruction of the plaintiff's lights. Peto was the contractor carrying out the building work in question and Hunter was his managing clerk supervising the works. Lord Chief Justice Dallas said ((1821) 6 Moore 47, at p 48): "The action was therefore properly brought against him (Hunter) as the manager; and even if it had been brought against him alone, I think the plaintiff would have been entitled to recover."

There are in numerous cases obiter statements to the effect that persons who are on premises with the authority of the occupier may be held liable for the nuisances which they create: *Hall v Beckenham Corporation* [1949] 1 KB 716, at p 723; *Southport Corporation v Esso Petroleum Co Ltd* [1953] 2 All ER 1204, at pp 1207, 1208, per Devlin J; per Denning LJ ([1954] 2 QB 182, at p 196); *Hargrave v Goldman* (1963) 110 CLR 40, at p 60. The text writers are unanimously of the view that responsibility for nuisance devolves on anyone who actively creates it, whether or not he is in occupation of the land from which it emanates: Fleming, *The Law of Torts*, 5th ed, pp 409, 410; *Clerk & Lindsell on Torts*, 14th ed, p 822, par 1418; *Winfield and Jolowicz on Tort*, 10th ed, p 335; *Salmond on Torts*, 16th ed, p 69. It was put to us that a non-occupier should not be liable upon the general footing that he may lack the power to abate the nuisance which has been created. This, however, is inconsistent with decisions which make the creator of a nuisance liable for its continuance, even after he has ceased to be in occupation: *Thompson v Gibson* (1841) 7 M & W 456; 151 ER 845. Although there appears to be no direct authority fastening liability on a complete stranger to the occupier of land upon which the nuisance is created, the weight of authority, it seems to me, attaches liability to any person who creates a nuisance **[492]** while present on land with the authority of its occupier. ...

[493] For these reasons, I would dismiss the appeal.

MAHONEY JA. ... **[500]** The excavator argued, first, that it was not liable in nuisance because, when the excavation was carried out, it was not in possession or control of the company's land. It based this submission upon the view that, for a person to be liable in private nuisance at all, it must be shown that the acts of which complaint are made were done by him whilst in possession or control of land.

I do not think that it is necessary, for present purposes, to decide that general question. In my opinion, it has long been established that, where a nuisance has been caused by a person acting, not for his own benefit, but for that of one in possession of the land from which the nuisance emanates, that person is liable for that nuisance, and remains liable for it, even though he has ceased to act for him who is in possession of the land. This was the basis of the decision of the Court of Exchequer in *Thompson v Gibson* (1841) 7 M & W 456; 151 ER 845; see also *Dalton v Angus* (1881) 6 App Cas 740, at p 791. This, in my opinion, is a sufficient answer to the excavator's first argument.

I do not express any view upon the question whether, in general, a defendant in private nuisance must be shown to be in possession or control of the land from which the nuisance originates. Different views have been expressed in this regard: see *Halsbury's Laws of England*, 3rd ed, vol 28, pp 126(f), 128(c), 155(c) and the cases there referred to; see also *Eastern Asia Navigation Co Ltd v Fremantle Harbour Trust Commissioners* (1951) 83 CLR 353, at pp 394, 397. The term "nuisance" covers a number of different kinds of actions and, whilst it may be that, in respect of some of the actionable interferences with a plaintiff's use and enjoyment of his land which are properly described as nuisances, it is not necessary that the defendant be in possession or occupation of land: cf, for example, Shawcross & Beaumont, *Air Law*, 4th ed, vol 1, p 501; I would reserve the question whether, in relation to some of the acts which constitute a nuisance, the defendant's possession or occupation of the land may be a necessary ingredient of the cause of action. ...

[501] In my opinion, the appeal should be dismissed with costs.

[Samuels JA agreed with Glass JA.]

Appeal dismissed

[In *Southern Properties (WA) Pty Ltd v Executive Director of the Department of Conservation and Land Management* [2012] WASCA 79, McLure P, with whom Buss JA agreed, made the following observations on the basis of liability for private nuisance:

118. Nuisance protects a claimant's interest in the beneficial use of land. It is not confined to the actual use of the soil but extends to the pleasure, comfort and enjoyment which a person normally derives from occupancy of land. Thus, nuisance covers physical damage to property and non-physical damage. To constitute a nuisance, the interference must be unreasonable. In making that judgment, regard is had to a variety of factors including: the nature and extent of the harm or interference; the social or public interest value in the defendant's activity; the hypersensitivity (if any) of the user or use of the claimant's land; the nature of established uses in the locality (eg residential, industrial, rural); whether all reasonable precautions were taken to minimise any interference; and the type of damage suffered.

119. This exercise involves weighing the respective rights of the parties in the use of their land to make a value judgment as to whether the interference is unreasonable. Although the 'fault' of the defendant may be a relevant consideration in an assessment of whether the interference with the claimant's enjoyment of land is unreasonable, the duty not to expose one's neighbours to nuisance is not necessarily discharged by the exercise of reasonable care. Liability in nuisance is strict. Once a prima facie case has been established, it is for the defendant to prove its defence.]

Goldman v Hargrave
(1966) 115 CLR 458
Privy Council

An occupier of land comes under a general duty to neighbours to take reasonable measures, according to his or her circumstances, to remove or reduce natural hazards arising on the land.

LORD WILBERFORCE delivered the judgment of their Lordships. [459] This consolidated appeal from a decision of the High Court of Australia, reversing that of the Supreme Court of Western Australia, arises out of a bush fire, which developed in the grazing area of Gidgegannup, Western Australia, and did extensive damage to the respondents' [plaintiffs'] properties. The High Court decided that the appellant [defendant], on whose property the fire started, was liable for the damage, and this decision the appellant now contests.

The circumstances in which the fire started are concisely stated in the judgments of the High Court, which accepted the findings of the trial judge. There was an electrical storm on 25th February 1961, and a tall redgum tree, about one hundred feet in height, in the centre of the appellant's property, was struck by lightning. This tree was about two hundred and fifty yards from the western boundary of the appellant's property (in which direction the respondents' properties lie) and rather less from the eastern boundary. The redgum caught fire in a fork eighty-four feet from the ground and it was evidently impossible to deal with the blaze while the tree was standing. Early in the morning of 26th February, the appellant telephoned the district fire control officer, appointed as such under the *Bush Fires Act 1954-1958* (WA), and asked for a tree feller to be sent. Pending his arrival the appellant cleared a space round the tree of combustible material and sprayed the surrounding area with water.

The tree feller arrived at midday on 26th February, at which time the tree was burning fiercely, and it was cut down. The trial judge found, and the High Court accepted the finding, that up to this point the appellant's conduct in relation to the fire was not open to criticism.

[460] But the judge also found that if the appellant had taken reasonable care he could, on the Sunday evening (26th February), or at latest early on the next morning, have put out the fire by using water on it. The appellant indeed claimed that he spent two hours on Monday, 27th February, in extinguishing the fire, but his evidence as to this was rejected. …

On Tuesday 28th February, the appellant was away from the property for a substantial part of the day, and it was found that he did not at any time after 27th February take any steps which could be regarded as reasonable to prevent the fire from spreading. On Wednesday 1st March there was a change in the weather; the wind, which had previously been light to moderate, freshened to about 20 mph with stronger gusts. The air temperature rose some 10° to 105°F. The fire revived and spread over the appellant's paddock towards the west and on to the respondents' properties: it was not observed by the appellant until about noon on 1st March and by then it could not be stopped. The damage to the respondents' properties followed. …

The result of the evidence, in their Lordships' opinion, is that the appellant both up to 26th February and thereafter was endeavouring to extinguish the fire; that initially he acted with prudence, but that there came a point, about the evening of 26th February or the morning of 27th February, when, the prudent and reasonable course being to put the fire out by water, he chose to adopt the method of burning it out. That method was, according to the findings of the trial judge, unreasonable, or negligent in the circumstances: it brought a fresh risk into operation, namely the risk of a revival of the fire, under the influence of changing wind and weather, if not carefully watched, and it was from this negligence that the damage arose. That a risk of this character was foreseeable by someone in the appellant's position **[461]** was not really disputed. …

This conclusion has an important bearing upon the nature of the legal issue which has to be decided. It makes clear that the case is not one where a person has brought a source of danger on to his land, nor one where an occupier has so used his property as to cause a danger to his neighbour. It is one where an occupier, faced with a hazard accidentally arising on his land, fails to act with reasonable prudence so as to remove the hazard. The issue is therefore whether in such a case the occupier is guilty of legal negligence, which involves the issue whether he is under a duty of care, and if so, what is the scope of that duty. Their Lordships propose to deal with these issues as stated, without attempting to answer the disputable question whether if responsibility is established it should be brought under the heading of nuisance or placed in a separate category. As this Board has recently explained in *Overseas Tankship (UK) Limited v Miller Steamship Co Pty Limited* (*Wagon Mound (No 2)*) [1967] 1 AC 617, the tort of nuisance, uncertain in its boundary, may comprise a wide variety of situations, in some of which negligence plays no part, in others of which it is decisive. The present case is one where liability, if it exists, rests upon negligence and nothing else; whether it falls within or overlaps the boundaries of nuisance is a question of classification which need not here be resolved.

What then is the scope of an occupier's duty, with regard to his neighbours, as to hazards arising on his land? With the possible exception of hazard of fire, to which their Lordships will shortly revert, it is only in comparatively recent times that the law has recognized an occupier's duty as one of a more positive character than merely to abstain from creating, or adding to, a source of danger or annoyance. It was for long satisfied with the conception of separate or autonomous proprietors, each of whom was entitled to exploit his territory in a "natural" manner and none of whom was obliged to restrain or direct the operations of nature in the interest of avoiding harm to his neighbours.

This approach, or philosophy, found expression in decisions both in England and elsewhere. In *Giles v Walker* (1890) 24 QBD 656 a claim that an occupier had a duty to protect his neighbour against the invasion of thistledown was summarily rejected by the Queen's Bench Division. And, in a similar field, it was held in 1908 by the High **[462]** Court of Australia (*Sparke v Osborne* (1908) 7 CLR 51) that an occupier was not under a duty to prevent a noxious weed, prickly pears, from attacking a neighbour's fence. The case was decided on a demurrer to a pleading in which negligence was not alleged. In relation to fires, there were similar decisions. In Australia, in 1879 the Supreme Court of Victoria decided on a demurrer to a pleading which alleged negligence, that an occupier of land on which a fire accidentally occurs is not under any duty to put it out (*Batchelor v Smith* (1879) 5 VLR (L) 176). In New Zealand, in 1888, the Supreme Court in Banco held that there is no legal duty cast upon the owner of land upon which a fire originates to prevent it from spreading to the land of another, though he was present immediately after it was lighted and might have put it out (*Hunter v Walker* (1888) 6 NZLR 690). ...

That, at common law an occupier of premises from which fire escapes was liable if either the origin, or the escape, of the fire was due to his negligence seems also to have been the opinion of Sir John Salmond – see *Eastern Asia Navigation Co Ltd v Fremantle Harbour Trust Commissioners* (1951) 83 CLR 353, where Fullagar J in the High Court of Australia left the point open (p 393).

Lastly in 1905 the Supreme Court of South Australia in *Havelberg v Brown* [1905] SALR 1 held that an occupier who remains passive is under no responsibility, and that if he interferes, he is liable only upon proof of negligence. ...

[463] These three decisions relating to fires were followed by the learned trial judge in the present case.

A decision which, it can now be seen, marked a turning point in the law was that of *Job Edwards Ltd v Birmingham Navigations* [1924] 1 KB 341. The hazard in that case was a fire which originated in a refuse dump placed on land by the act of a third party. When the fire threatened to invade the neighbouring land, the owners of the latter, by agreement, entered and extinguished the fire at a cost of some £1,000. The issue in the action was whether the owners of the land, where the fire was, were liable to bear part of the cost. The Court of Appeal by a majority answered this question negatively, but Scrutton LJ's dissenting judgment contained the following passage (at pp 357, 358): "There is a great deal to be said for the view that if a man finds a dangerous and artificial thing on his land, which he and those for whom he is responsible did not put there; if he knows that if left alone it will damage other persons; if by reasonable care he can render it harmless, as if by stamping on a fire just beginning from a trespasser's match he can extinguish it; that then if he does nothing, he has 'permitted it to continue,' and becomes responsible for it. This would base the liability on negligence, and not on the duty of insuring damage from a dangerous thing under *Rylands v Fletcher* (1868) LR 3 HL 330. I appreciate that to get negligence you must have a duty to be careful, but I think on principle that **[464]** a landowner has a duty to take reasonable care not to allow his land to remain a receptacle for a thing which may, if not rendered harmless, cause damage to his neighbours". One may note that this passage is dealing with a different set of facts from that involved in the case then under consideration: the one referring to a fire just beginning which can be extinguished by stamping on it, the other concerned with a smouldering dump to extinguish which involves both effort and expense, so that it is quite possible to approve both of the majority decision and of the passage quoted from the dissenting judgment.

This was followed in 1926 by *Noble v Harrison* [1926] 2 KB 332. The damage there was caused by an overhanging tree with a latent defect and the decision was against liability. The judgment of Rowlatt J in the Divisional Court contains this passage (at p 338): "a person is liable for a nuisance constituted by the state of his property: (1) if he causes it; (2) if by neglect of some duty he allowed it to arise; and (3) if, when it has arisen without his own act or default, he omits to remedy it within a reasonable time after he did or ought to have become aware of it".

It will be seen that the learned judge in the third category makes no distinction according to whether the "nuisance" is caused by trespassers or by natural causes, and that he does not enter into any question as to the limits of the effort or expenditure required of the occupier. As a general statement of the law it was cited with apparent approval by Dixon J in *Torette House Pty Ltd v Berkman* (1940) 62 CLR 637, at p 657.

In 1940 the dictum of Scrutton LJ passed into the law of England when it was approved by the House of Lords in *Sedleigh-Denfield v O'Callaghan* [1940] AC 880. Their Lordships need not cite from this case in any detail since it is now familiar law. It establishes the occupier's liability with regard to a hazard created on his land by a trespasser, of which he has knowledge, when he fails to take reasonable steps to remove it. It was clear in that case that the hazard could have been removed by what Viscount Maugham described as the "very simple step" of placing a grid in the proper place. The members of the House approved the passage just cited from Scrutton LJ's judgment, and Viscount Maugham and Lord Wright also adopted the statement of the law in *Salmond on Torts* 5th ed (1920) pp 258-265: "When a nuisance has been created by the act of a trespasser or otherwise without the act, authority, or permission of the occupier, [465] the occupier is not responsible for that nuisance unless, with knowledge or means of knowledge of its existence, he suffers it to continue without taking reasonably prompt and efficient means for its abatement."

The appellants [sic], inevitably, accept the development, or statement, of the law which the *Sedleigh-Denfield Case* [1940] AC 880, contains – as it was accepted by the High Court of Australia. But they seek to establish a distinction between the type of hazard which was there involved, namely one brought about by human agency such as the act of trespasser, and one arising from natural causes, or act of God. In relation to hazards of this kind it was submitted that an occupier is under no duty to remove or to diminish it, and that his liability only commences if and when by interference with it he negligently increases the risk or danger to his neighbour's property.

Their Lordships would first observe, with regard to the suggested distinction, that it is well designed to introduce confusion into the law. As regards many hazardous conditions arising on land, it is impossible to determine how they arose – particularly is this the case as regards fires. If they are caused by human agency, the agent, unless detected in flagrante delicto, is hardly likely to confess his fault. And is the occupier, when faced with the initial stages of a fire, to ask himself whether the fire is accidental or manmade before he can decide upon his duty? Is the neighbour, whose property is damaged, bound to prove the human origin of the fire? The proposition involves that if he cannot do so, however irresponsibly the occupier has acted, he must fail. But the distinction is not only inconvenient, it lacks, in their Lordships' view any logical foundation.

Within the class of situations in which the occupier is himself without responsibility for the origin of the fire, one may ask in vain what relevant difference there is between a fire caused by a human agency such as a trespasser and one caused by act of God or nature. A difference in degree – as to the potency of the agency – one can see but none that is in principle relevant to the occupier's duty to act. It was suggested as a logical basis for the distinction that in the case of a hazard originating in an act of man, an occupier who fails to deal with it can be said to be using his land in a manner detrimental to his neighbour and so to be within the classical field of responsibility in nuisance, whereas this cannot be said when the hazard originates without human action so long at least as the occupier merely abstains. The fallacy of this argument is that, as already explained, the basis of the [466] occupier's liability lies not in the use of his land: in the absence of "adoption" there is no such use; but in the neglect of action in the face of something which may damage his neighbour. To this, the suggested distinction is irrelevant.

On principle therefore, their Lordships find in the opinions of the House of Lords in *Sedleigh-Denfield v O'Callaghan* [1940] AC 880 and in the statements of the law by Scrutton LJ and Salmond, of which they approve, support for the existence of a general duty upon occupiers in relation to hazards occurring on their land, whether natural or man-made. But the matter does not rest there. First, the principle has been applied to the specific hazards of fire by the more recent decision of the Supreme Court of New Zealand in *Boatswain v Crawford* [1943] NZLR 109. That was a case of a fire of unknown origin which could easily have been controlled in its initial stages.

The Court held the defendant liable for breach of duty following expressly *Sedleigh-Denfield v O'Callaghan* [1940] AC 880 and applying the passage above quoted from *Salmond on Torts*. The High Court of Australia, which may be taken to be aware of the present-day conditions as regards bush fires considered that this decision is now to be preferred to the older cases as in accordance with the trend of the law, and their Lordships agree with their view. A still later case in New Zealand, *Landon v Rutherford* [1951] NZLR 975, followed *Boatswain v Crawford* [1943] NZLR 109, though, as was pointed out by Taylor J and Owen J in their judgment in the High Court of Australia, it placed too heavy an onus of proof on the defendant ((1963) 110 CLR, at p 52). Secondly, it appears that the movement of American decisions has been towards the development of a duty of care on the part of occupiers in relation to hazards arising on their land both generally and of fire. Their Lordships were referred to three successive series of the American Law Reports Annotated in the years 1926, 1937 and 1951 referring to a number of decided cases in various jurisdictions, all of which, save one, point in the same direction. The cumulative result of these is to establish the occupier's duty of care towards his neighbour to a similar extent as the English and New Zealand cases. Their Lordships were also referred to the *Restatement of the Law of Torts* the relevant portion of which (vol iv, par 839-840) dates from 1939. This makes a distinction between invasions of a neighbour's interest arising from a natural condition of land and other invasions, which is expressed in somewhat general terms and which is of less direct application to such a case as the present than the American decisions.

[467] Thirdly their Lordships have considered the modern text books of authority on the law of torts, *Clerk and Lindsell* 12th ed (1961), *Salmond* 13th ed (1961), *Winfield* 7th ed (1963), *Fleming* (1965), as well as a formative article by Dr AL Goodhart in *4 Cambridge Law Journal* (1932) p 13. All of these endorse the development which their Lordships find in the decisions, towards a measured duty of care by occupiers to remove or reduce hazards to their neighbours.

So far it has been possible to consider the existence of a duty, in general terms. But the matter cannot be left there without some definition of the scope of his duty. How far does it go? What is the standard of the effort required? What is the position as regards expenditure? It is not enough to say merely that these must be "reasonable" since what is reasonable to one man may be very unreasonable, and indeed ruinous to another: the law must take account of the fact that the occupier on whom the duty is cast, has, ex hypothesi, had this hazard thrust upon him through no seeking or fault of his own. His interest, and his resources whether physical or material, may be of a very modest character either in relation to the magnitude of the hazard, or as compared with those of his threatened neighbour. A rule which required of him in such unsought circumstances in his neighbour's interest a physical effort of which he is not capable, or an excessive expenditure of money would be unenforceable or unjust. One may say in general terms that the existence of a duty must be based upon knowledge of the hazard, ability to foresee the consequences of not checking or removing it, and the ability to abate it. And in many cases, as for example in Scrutton LJ's hypothetical case of stamping out a fire, or the present case, where the hazard could have been removed with little effort and no expenditure, no problem arises. But other cases may not be so simple. In such situations the standard ought to be required of the occupier what it is reasonable to expect of him in his individual circumstances. Thus, less must be expected of the infirm than of the able bodied: the owner of a small property where a hazard arises which threatens a neighbour with substantial interests should not have to do so much as one with larger interests of his own at stake and greater resources to protect them: if the small owner does what he can and promptly calls on his neighbour to provide additional resources, he may be held to have done his duty: he should not be liable unless it is clearly proved that he could, and reasonably in his individual circumstance should, have done more. ... [468] In the present case it has not been argued that the action necessary to put the fire out on 26th to 27th February was not well within the capacity and resources of the appellant. Their Lordships therefore reach the conclusion that the respondents' claim for damages, on the basis of negligence, was fully made out. ...

[469] Their Lordships will humbly advise Her Majesty that the appeal should be dismissed.

Appeal dismissed

Peden Pty Ltd v Bortolazzo
[2006] 2 Qd R 574; [2006] QCA 350
Supreme Court of Queensland, Court of Appeal

A lessor is not liable for a nuisance created by a tenant unless the lessor expressly authorised the nuisance or the nuisance was certain to result from the purpose for which the land was leased.

[The plaintiff (respondent) was the occupier of premises used as a motel.

The defendant (applicant) was the owner of adjacent property on which there was a house divided into two residential flats. The plaintiff contended that the defendant was liable for nuisance (comprising excessive noise, smoke from burning off and unruly and drunken behaviour at all hours of the day) created by the tenants to whom the defendant had leased one of the flats under a lease containing an express prohibition on the tenants creating a nuisance.

The District Court at Cairns upheld the plaintiff's claim and the defendant applied for leave to appeal. The Queensland Court of Appeal granted leave to appeal and allowed the defendant's appeal.]

McMURDO P and PHILIPPIDES J. … [some footnotes omitted] **[581] When is a lessor liable for the nuisance created by a tenant?**
12. An occupier of land commits a nuisance if, with knowledge or presumed knowledge of a nuisance initially committed by another, the occupier fails to take reasonable means to end a nuisance within a reasonable time: *Sedleigh-Denfield v O'Callaghan* [1940] AC 880. The law is reluctant to impose a duty on one person to control the conduct of another for whom the first person has no primary responsibility; the general rule is that one person is under no duty to control another person to prevent doing damage to a third: *Smith v Leurs* (1945) 70 CLR 256, Dixon J, 262 … .
13. Consistent with that general rule, a lessor (who is necessarily not in occupation having leased the premises to a tenant) will not ordinarily be liable for a nuisance created by the tenant (*Rich v Basterfield* (1847) 4 CB 783; *Harris v James* (1876) 35 LT 240) and is under no obligation to put an end to the tenancy when he or she discovers that a tenant is creating a nuisance (*Sykes v Connolly* (1895) 11 WN (NSW) 145). The primary judge was concerned that, because of the antiquity of *Sykes v Connolly*, it may no longer accurately state the law. However, the principle behind that case and the decisions of *Rich v Basterfield* and *Harris v James* has been followed in *Smith v Scott* [1973] 1 Ch 314. In that case, the plaintiff, the owner of a home neighbouring premises owned by the defendant, brought an action against the defendant arising out of actions of the defendant's tenants. As in the present case, the terms of the tenancy expressly prohibited the creation **[582]** of a nuisance. Pennycuick V-C made the following pertinent observations concerning a landlord's liability for a nuisance created by a tenant (at 321):

It is established beyond question that the person to be sued in nuisance is the occupier of the property from which the nuisance emanates. In general, a landlord is not liable for nuisance committed by his tenant, but to this rule there is, so far as now in point, one recognized exception, namely, that the landlord is liable if he has authorized his tenant to commit the nuisance: *Harris v James* (1876) 35 LT 240. But this exception has, in the reported cases, been rigidly confined to circumstances in which the nuisance has either been expressly authorised or is certain to result from the purposes for which the property is let: *Rich v Basterfield* (1847) 4 CB 783 … . I have used the word 'certain,' but 'certainty' is obviously a very difficult matter to establish. It may be that … the proper test in this connection is 'virtual certainty' which is another way of saying a very high degree of probability, but the authorities are not … altogether satisfactory in this respect. Whatever the precise test may be, it would, I think, be impossible to apply the exception to the present case. The exception is squarely based in the reported cases on express or implied authority: see in particular the judgment of Blackburn J in *Harris v James* (1876) 35 LT 240, 241. The exception is not based on cause and probable result, apart from express or implied authority. …

14. Pennycuick V-C also rejected the proposition that a duty of care was owed by a landlord to a neighbour when selecting a tenant and made the following additional observations (at 322):

... the relationship of landowner, tenant and neighbour is, in its nature, of the most widespread possible occurrence, and the introduction of the duty of care in this connection would have far reaching implications in relation to business as well as to residential premises.

15. Pennycuick V-C's statement of the law relating to a lessor's liability for a nuisance created by a tenant has been recently followed by the English Court of Appeal in *Hussain v Lancaster City Council* [2000] QB 1, 23-24 ... and was even more recently referred to with approval by the New South Wales Court of Appeal in *Wilkie v Blacktown City Council* (2002) 121 LGERA 444, per Davies AJA (Heydon JA and Young CJ in Eq agreeing). Pennycuick V-C's conclusions concerning the absence of a duty of care in a landlord in selecting tenants were endorsed in *WD & HO Wills (Aust) v SRA* (1998) 43 NSWLR 338, Mason P, 360. Mason P (Beazley JA agreeing) noted that Pennycuick V-C's approach was **[583]** "nothing more than a particular application of judicial restraint based upon the fear of creating 'liability in an indeterminate amount for an indeterminate time to an indeterminate class'", consistent with McHugh J's observations in *Pyrenees Shire Council v Day* (1998) 72 ALJR 152, 171. ...

17. The District Court judge was influenced in reaching a contrary conclusion by the case of *R v Shorrock* [1994] QB 279. Shorrock appealed against his conviction for public nuisance arising out of him granting a licence to use his premises over a weekend for an "acid house party". Between 3,000 and 5,000 people attended and paid £15 admission each. The event caused very extensive noise and greatly disturbed the local populace; 275 telephone complaints were received from nearby residents disturbed by the music and speech relayed over a public address system. Shorrock accepted that a public nuisance was caused but contended he was not liable for it. The English Court of Appeal relied on a passage from *Sedleigh-Denfield v O'Callaghan* [1940] AC 880, 904-905 where Lord Wright considered the liability in private nuisance of a landowner for a nuisance created on the land by a trespasser and concluded that the occupier will be liable even though the occupier did not create the nuisance if the occupier knowingly leaves the nuisance on the land or if with ordinary care in the management of the property the occupier should have realised the risk of the existence of the nuisance. The Court of Appeal concluded that the mental element of the offence of public nuisance was established if Shorrock knew, or ought to have known in the sense that the means of knowledge were available to him, that there was a real risk that the consequences of the licence granted by him in respect of his field would be to create the sort of nuisance that in fact occurred.

18. *Shorrock* is plainly distinguishable from the present case because he [Shorrock] was not a lessor; it does not state the law relating to the responsibility of a lessor for a nuisance created by a tenant. ...

[587] 29. In our view the relevant legal principles applicable here are as follows. A lessor is not responsible for a nuisance created by a tenant unless the lessor let the premises for a purpose calculated to cause a nuisance, that is, by express authorization of the nuisance or in circumstances where the nuisance was certain to result from the purposes for which the property was being let. ...

[McMurdo P and Philippides J found that there was no evidence that the applicant had expressly authorized the tenants to create a nuisance or that a nuisance was certain to result from the residential lease to the tenants.]

Conclusion

[590] 49. The District Court judge erred on an important question of law. This Court should correct that error which could have wide-ranging effects. That error has also resulted in substantial injustice to the applicant. For those reasons leave to appeal should be granted, the appeal allowed with costs to be assessed and the decision of the District Court judge set aside. ...

[White J agreed with McMurdo P and Philippides J.]

Appeal allowed

(d) Statutory Authority and "Coming to the Nuisance"

Allen v Gulf Oil Refining Ltd
[1981] AC 1001
House of Lords

Statutory authority to carry out an activity may provide a defence to an action in nuisance.

[The plaintiff (respondent) lived in the village of Waterston in south west Wales. She brought an action against the defendants (appellants) complaining that the operation by the defendants of an oil refinery on four hundred acres of land immediately adjoining the village constituted a private nuisance by smell, noise and vibration.

The defendants sought to rely on the *Gulf Oil Refining Act 1965* as authorising the operation of the refinery and providing the defendants with the defence of statutory authority for any inevitable nuisance caused by such operation.

The proceedings came before the House of Lords for determination of a preliminary point of law.]

LORD WILBERFORCE. ... [1011] The question as framed by Kerr J reads "Can the defendants rely on the *Gulf Oil Refining Act 1965* as having authorised the construction and operation of an oil refinery at Waterston ...?" In this House both sides accepted that this is incomplete and they have endeavoured to recast, or at least to expand it. I quote from the respondent's printed case:

> The issue arising in this appeal is whether the appellants, Gulf Oil Refining Ltd ("Gulf") can rely upon the *Gulf Oil Refining Act 1965* ("the Act") as having authorised the construction and operation of an oil refinery at Waterston, Milford Haven in the county of Dyfed. Gulf seek to rely on the Act as providing the defence of "statutory authority" to Mrs Allen's claims for nuisance arising out of the operation of the refinery in fact constructed and operated by Gulf at Waterston. Gulf contends, in effect, that by reason of the Act any inevitable nuisance caused by the construction or operation of the refinery must be borne by Mrs Allen without compensation.

The appellants' formulation is much to be the same effect. I think that these at any rate give your Lordships a workable indication of what is needed. That must be in the form of a direction of law on which the judge who is to try the case can proceed.

The case, as a matter of law, depends upon the construction of the Act of 1965.

We are here in the well charted field of statutory authority. It is now well settled that where Parliament by express direction or by necessary implication has authorised the construction and use of an undertaking or works, that carries with it an authority to do what is authorised with immunity from any action based on nuisance. The right of action is taken away: *Hammersmith and City Railway Co v Brand* (1869) LR 4 HL 171, 215 *per* Lord Cairns. To this there is made the qualification, or condition, that the statutory powers are exercised without "negligence" – that word here being used in a special sense so as to require the undertaker, as a condition of obtaining immunity from action, to carry out the work and conduct the operation with all reasonable regard and care for the interests of other persons: *Geddis v Proprietors of Bann Reservoir* (1878) 3 App Cas 430, 455 *per* Lord Blackburn. It is within the same principle that immunity from action is withheld where the terms of the statute are permissive only, in which case the powers conferred must be exercised in strict conformity with private rights: *Metropolitan Asylum District v Hill* (1881) 6 App Cas 193.

What then is the scope of the statutory authority conferred in this case? The Act was a private Act, promoted by the appellants, no doubt mainly in their own commercial interests. In order to establish [1012] their projected refinery with its ancillary facilities (jetties, railway lines, etc), and to acquire the necessary land, they had to seek the assistance of Parliament. And so they necessarily had to satisfy Parliament that the powers they were seeking were in the interest of the public to whom Parliament is responsible. The case they undertook to make, and which, as the passing of the Act shows, they did prove, is shown by the preamble. This recites "increasing public demand for (the company's) products in the United Kingdom" and that "it is *essential* that further facilities for the importation of crude oil and petroleum products and *for their refinement* should be made available" (emphasis supplied). It proceeds to recite the intention of the company to establish a refinery at Llanstadwell, that it was expedient that in connection therewith the company should be empowered to construct works including jetties for the accommodation of vessels (including large tankers) and for the reception from such vessels of crude oil and petroleum products for the proposed refinery and for conveying oil and petroleum products therefrom: that it was expedient for the company to be empowered to acquire lands: and that "plans ... showing ... the lands which may be taken or used compulsorily under the powers of the Act for the purposes thereof ... have been deposited."

My Lords, all of this shows most clearly that Parliament considered it in the public interest that a *refinery*, not merely the works (jetties etc), should be constructed, and constructed upon lands at Llanstadwell to be compulsorily acquired.

To show how this intention was to be carried out I need only quote section 5:

(1) Subject to the provisions of this Act, the company may enter upon, take and use such of the lands delineated on the deposited plans and described in the deposited book of reference as it may require for the purpose of the authorised works or *for the construction of a refinery* in the parish of Llanstadwell in the rural district of Haversfordwest in the county of Pembroke or for purposes ancillary thereto or connected therewith. (2) The powers of compulsory acquisition of land under this section shall cease after the expiration of three years from October 1, 1965.

The lands in question were the specific lands – about 450 acres in extent – shown with precise detail in the deposited plans.

I cannot but regard this as an authority – whether it should be called express or by necessary implication may be a matter of preference – but an authority to construct and operate *a refinery* upon the lands to be acquired – a refinery moreover which should be commensurate with the facilities for unloading offered by the jetties (for large tankers), with the size of the lands to be acquired, and with the discharging facilities to be provided by the railway lines. I emphasize the words *a refinery* by way of distinction from *the refinery* because no authority was given or sought except in the indefinite form. But that there was authority to construct and operate *a* refinery seems to me indisputable.

The respondent's contention against this is a curious one. She points to the sections (mainly s 15) dealing with works: these specify in great **[1013]** detail what is to be carried out in the way of construction of jetties and of railway lines. Here, she says, is plain statutory authority of the kind conferred in the well-known cases concerned with railways. By contrast there is no authority to construct or operate a refinery – not even by implication. There is nothing but power to acquire lands. The construction of the refinery is left entirely to the promoters – there is no specification of the size or nature of the refinery, they have "carte blanche" and therefore the intention must be that they must construct it with regard to private rights. The case is similar, she says, to that of *Metropolitan Asylum District v Hill* (1881) 6 App Cas 193. This argument has remarkable consequences. It follows that if the plaintiff, or any other person, can establish a nuisance, he or she is entitled (subject only to a precarious appeal to Lord Cairns' Act) to an injunction. This may make it impossible for the refinery to be operated: that in turn would leave the appellants as the owners and occupiers of a large area of land which they have compulsorily acquired under the Act of 1965 for the purpose of a refinery, and which, in accordance with well-known principles, they could not use for any other purpose. Such consequences must be accepted if they clearly flow from the terms of the Act.

But I must say that I find the construction which would give rise to this result to be not only far from clear but a most artificial reading of the enactment. It is true, and at one time I was impressed by the point that, by contrast with the detailed specification given to the "works" by description, plans, levels, etc, the Act conspicuously does not define or specify the refinery even in general terms, and this might appear to support an argument that this was left altogether outside the Parliamentary authority. But I think it was answered by the case in this House of *Manchester Corporation v Farnworth* [1930] AC 171. In that case the statutory authority was simply, in general terms, for the erection of a generating station, without specification, but nevertheless it was held that, subject to the "negligence" exception, the usual rule applied: see particularly Viscount Dunedin, p 183. There could be "no action for nuisance caused by the making or doing of that thing" (ie the thing authorised) " if the nuisance is the inevitable result of the making or doing so authorised." That, in my opinion, describes the situation in the present case. It is true that the Act of 1965 does not, as did the relevant Act considered in the *Manchester Corporation* case, confer express authority to use or operate any refinery which might be installed on the site, but the preamble refers to "refinement" – ie operation of the refinery – and authority must in this case carry authority to refine. The two cases are entirely parallel.

If I am right upon this point, the position as regards the action would be as follows. The respondent alleges a nuisance, by smell, noise, vibration, etc. The facts regarding these matters are for her to prove. It is then for the appellants to show, if they can, that it was impossible to construct and operate a refinery upon the site, conforming to Parliament's intention, without creating the nuisance alleged, or at least a nuisance. Involved in this issue would be the point discussed by Cumming-Bruce LJ in the Court of Appeal, that the establishment of an oil refinery, etc, was bound to involve some alteration of the environment **[1014]** and so of the standard of amenity and comfort which neighbouring occupiers might expect. To the extent that the environment has been changed from that of a peaceful unpolluted countryside to an industrial complex (as to which different standards apply – *Sturges v Bridgman* (1879) 11 ChD 852) Parliament must be taken to have authorised it. So far, I venture to think, the matter is not open to doubt. But in my opinion the statutory authority extends beyond merely authorising a change in the environment and an alteration of standard. It confers immunity against proceedings for any nuisance which can be shown (the burden of so showing being upon the appellants) to be the inevitable result of erecting a refinery upon the site – not, I repeat, the existing refinery, but any refinery – however carefully and with however great a regard for the interest of adjoining occupiers it is sited, constructed, and operated. To the extent and only to the extent that the actual nuisance (if any) caused by the actual refinery and its operation exceeds that for which immunity is conferred, the plaintiff has a remedy.

For myself I would respond in this sense to the question asked, rather than in the purely negative sense favoured by the Court of Appeal, and to that extent I would allow the appeal.

[Lord Diplock, Lord Edmund-Davies and Lord Roskill agreed with Lord Wilberforce. Lord Keith of Kinkel dissented.]

Appeal allowed

Campbelltown Golf Club Ltd v Winton
[1998] NSWSC 257
Supreme Court of New South Wales, Court of Appeal

It is no defence to say that the nuisance was in existence before the plaintiffs' occupation of their land.

[In 1990 the respondents (plaintiffs) purchased vacant land at Glen Alpine, a suburb in the Campbelltown area, on which they built a house. The respondents' land adjoined a fairway of the appellant's (defendant's) golf club. Over a period, a large number of golf balls (including 421 in the period 1 January – 17 May 1995), emanating from the appellant's property, struck the respondents' land causing damage to their house and, on one occasion, hitting their infant son. On numerous occasions, golfers wishing to recover their balls would climb the boundary fence and enter the respondents' garden.

In the District Court, the trial judge (Backhouse DCJ) held that the respondents were entitled to succeed in an action for private nuisance. Her Honour found that the intrusion of golf balls and golfers constituted an unreasonable interference with the use and enjoyment of the respondents' land.

On appeal, the appellant sought to challenge the trial judge's award of general damages ($15,000) but not her Honour's finding on liability and award of damages for the cost of repairs to the respondents' house.]

SHEPPARD AJA. ... The essential submissions made on behalf of the appellant ... were that her Honour failed to take into account:

  (a) that the respondents built their house with full knowledge of the existence of the golf course; and

  (b) that the respondents' house was built on land included in a plan of subdivision in which the golf course was designed as the focal point.

Undoubtedly the respondents bought into a subdivision which bordered a golf course. The benefit of this to them was that they overlooked a degree of open space at the rear of the premises. If it were not for the problems created by golf balls coming on to their land, the outlook would have been a pleasant one increasing their enjoyment of the property.

The problem with the appellant's submission is that it endeavours to relegate houses built on land in the subdivision to an inferior position to that occupied by the golf course. In the appellant's submission, the golf course was the focal point. If it created a problem for residents, that was something which the residents had to tolerate. That is not the law.

What was required was that the golf course should so adjust its activities as not to interfere unreasonably with the peaceful enjoyment by residents of their land. At the same time, the residents, bordering as they did a golf course, had to accept the fact that the game of golf was going to be played on land adjoining their properties and that it could be expected that from time to time some golf balls might come on to their land. But what they were not bound to accept was a situation such as was suffered by the respondents in which their property was peppered with golf balls on a daily basis, thus posing a threat, not only to the respondents' property but also to their physical safety. ...

As was conceded by counsel for the appellant during the argument, the submission upon which the golf course relied really brought into play the suggestion that the respondents should not recover as much as they otherwise might have done because they came to the nuisance. It is clear, of course, that it is no defence to an action for nuisance that a plaintiff came to it. Reference may be made to *Kerr on Injunctions*, 6th ed (1927) 189 and to *The Law of Torts*, JG Fleming, 9th ed (1998) at 491. The authority cited for this proposition by Kerr is *Attorney-General v Corporation of Manchester* [1893] 2 Ch 87 where Chitty J said (at 95) that the doctrine of coming to a nuisance had long been "excluded". Kerr refers to the doctrine as having been exploded. That is the expression used by Fleming. Fleming also says that, in the absence of a prescriptive right, a purchaser or lessee is entitled to the reasonable use and enjoyment of his land to the same extent as any other occupier since a defendant would otherwise be able, by his wrongful conduct, to diminish the value of neighbouring land without compensation. Amongst other authorities he refers to *Sturges v Bridgman* (1879) 11 ChD 852 where the party committing the nuisance unsuccessfully endeavoured to establish a prescriptive right to carry on a manufacturing process which amounted to a nuisance to neighbouring occupiers.

Counsel for the appellant acknowledged that the law was as I have stated it, but submitted that the authorities and texts referred to dealt with the question of liability, not the question of damages. We were referred to no authority dealing with the question whether a plaintiff who had come to a nuisance might suffer a reduction in damages because of having come to it. I have not found any authority dealing with the matter. In principle, however, if coming to a nuisance provides no defence to an action, it seems difficult to conclude that that circumstance could have some application in relation to the assessment of damages. To give effect to the submission would, in my opinion, negate the clear principle that parties complaining of a nuisance are not deprived of an action because the nuisance complained of was in existence before they entered into occupation of their properties. Accordingly, I would reject the submission. ...

[Sheller and Powell JJA agreed with Sheppard AJA.]

Appeal dismissed

[In *Campbelltown Golf Club Ltd v Winton* (extracted above), the court did not consider the basis of liability of the club for the nuisance created by the golfers in hitting balls on to the plaintiff's land. This issue was considered in *Challen v McLeod Country Golf Club* (2004) Aust Torts Reports ¶81-760, a decision of the Queensland Court of Appeal.

The facts in *Challen* were similar to *Campbelltown Golf Club Ltd v Winton*. Over a period of years a large number of golf balls (at least 526 in one year) landed on the plaintiff's residential property after being hit by players using, with permission, the defendant's golf course. Some of the balls caused actual damage to the plaintiff's property, including broken tiles and windows. In respect of this private nuisance, the court held that the defendant was liable from the date the defendant first became aware or ought to have become aware of the nuisance. With regard to the basis of liability of the defendant, McPherson JA made the following observation:

> [65,956] 2. The incorporated defendant golf club appears at one stage to have adopted the stance that it was only the individual player who struck the errant golf ball who incurred liability for the nuisance to the plaintiff. If the club took that view, it was mistaken. If an occupier of land permits a nuisance to be conducted on its land of which it knows or ought to know, it becomes liable for that nuisance and its potentially harmful consequences to others from the time at which it acquired that knowledge or ought to have done so.]

3. TORT OF INVASION OF PRIVACY?

Australian Broadcasting Corporation v Lenah Game Meats Pty Ltd
(2001) 208 CLR 199; [2001] HCA 63
High Court of Australia

Victoria Park Racing and Recreation Grounds Co Ltd v Taylor (1937) 58 CLR 479 does not stand in the path of the development of a tort of invasion of privacy.

[The plaintiff (respondent), Lenah Game Meats Pty Ltd, operated premises in Tasmania where brush tail possums were killed and processed for export. An unknown trespasser entered the plaintiff's premises and installed video cameras which recorded the killing of the possums. The video tapes were retrieved from the plaintiff's premises, without its knowledge or consent, by an unknown person. A video tape with sound, which had been made in these circumstances, was handed to the defendant (appellant), Australian Broadcasting Corporation, by Animal Liberation Ltd. It was not alleged that the defendant was implicated in or privy to the trespasses on the plaintiff's premises.

The plaintiff commenced proceedings against the defendant and Animal Liberation Ltd in the Supreme Court of Tasmania seeking a mandatory injunction for the delivery up of the video tapes and damages. A majority of the Full Court of the Supreme Court of Tasmania (Wright and Evans JJ; Slicer J dissenting), reversing the primary judge (Underwood J), granted the plaintiff an interlocutory injunction restraining the defendant from broadcasting the video tape. The interest which the plaintiff sought to protect by this remedy was the goodwill of its business which was likely to be damaged if there was publicity about its method of killing possums.

The High Court (Gleeson CJ, Gaudron, Gummow, Kirby and Hayne JJ; Callinan J dissenting) allowed the defendant's appeal.

In argument before the High Court, the plaintiff contended that broadcasting of the video tape by the defendant would constitute an actionable invasion of a right of the plaintiff to "privacy". Although the Court found it unnecessary to decide whether Australian law recognises a general tort of invasion of privacy, the Court discussed the continuing authority and relevance of its earlier decision in *Victoria Park Racing and Recreation Grounds Co Ltd v Taylor* (1937) 58 CLR 479. Some footnotes are omitted in the extract which follows.]

GLEESON CJ. [His Honour held that the primary judge in the Supreme Court of Tasmania was correct to dismiss the plaintiff's application for an interlocutory injunction on the ground that, by reference to the alleged facts, there was no serious question to be tried.] ... [224] 34. A photographic image, illegally or improperly or surreptitiously obtained, where what is depicted is private, may constitute confidential information. ...

[225] 39. If the activities filmed were private, then the law of breach of confidence is adequate to cover the case. I would regard images and sounds of private activities, recorded by the methods employed in the present case, as confidential. There would be an obligation of confidence upon the persons who obtained them, and upon those into whose possession they came, if they knew, or ought to have known, the manner in which they were obtained. ...

41. But the lack of precision of the concept of privacy is a reason for [226] caution in declaring a new tort of the kind for which the respondent contends. Another reason is the tension that exists between interests in privacy and interests in free speech. I say "interests" because talk of "rights" may be question-begging, especially in a legal system which has no counterpart to the First Amendment to the United States Constitution or to the *Human Rights Act 1998* (UK). The categories that have been developed in the United States for the purpose of giving greater specificity to the kinds of interests protected by a "right to privacy" illustrate the problem. See, e.g. Prosser, "Privacy", *California Law Review*, vol 48 (1960) 383; *Restatement of the Law Second, Torts*, §652A. The first of those categories, which includes intrusion upon private affairs or concerns, requires that the intrusion be highly offensive to a reasonable person. Part of the price we pay for living in an organised society is that we are exposed to observation in a variety of ways by other people.

42. There is no bright line which can be drawn between what is private and what is not. Use of the term "public" is often a convenient method of contrast, but there is a large area in between what is necessarily public and what is necessarily private. An activity is not private simply because it is not done in public. It does not suffice to make an act private that, because it occurs on private property, it has such measure of protection from the public gaze as the characteristics of the property, the nature of the activity, the locality, and the disposition of the property owner combine to afford. Certain kinds of information about a person, such as information relating to health, personal relationships, or finances, may be easy to identify as private; as may certain kinds of activity, which a reasonable person, applying contemporary standards of morals and behaviour, would understand to be meant to be unobserved. The requirement that disclosure or observation of information or conduct would be highly offensive to a reasonable person of ordinary sensibilities is in many circumstances a useful practical test of what is private.

43. It is unnecessary, for present purposes, to enter upon the question of whether, and in what circumstances, a corporation may invoke privacy. ... However, the foundation of much of what is protected, where rights of privacy, as distinct from rights of property, are acknowledged is human dignity. This may be incongruous when applied to a corporation. ... [227] The problem for the respondent is that the activities secretly observed and filmed were not relevantly private. ...

[229] 51. There is judicial support for the proposition that the trespassers, if caught in time, could have been restrained from publishing the film. In *Lincoln Hunt Australia Pty Ltd v Willesee* (1986) 4 NSWLR 457 some representatives of a producer of material for television entered commercial premises, with cameras rolling, and harassed people on the premises. Their conduct amounted to trespass. Young J had to consider whether to restrain publication of the film. Because of the effrontery of the conduct of the defendants, he concluded this was a case for large exemplary damages, and that damages were an adequate remedy. On that ground, he declined an injunction. In accordance with settled practice, and principle, however, the first question he asked himself was as to the plaintiff's equity. Because of the ground on which he declined relief, he did not need to decide that question which, he said, took him "into very deep waters". However, he expressed the following tentative opinion, which has been taken up in later cases:

> In the instant case, on a prima facie basis I would have thought that there is a lot to be said in the Australian community where a film [230] is taken by a trespasser, made in circumstances as the present, upon private premises in respect of which there is some evidence that publication

of the film would affect goodwill, that the case is one where an injunction should seriously be considered.

52. If, in the present case, the appellant had been a party to the trespass, it would be necessary to reach a conclusion about the question which Young J thought should seriously be considered. I would give an affirmative answer to the question, based on breach of confidence, provided the activities filmed were private. I say nothing about copyright, because that was not argued. But the case [*Lincoln Hunt*] was one against the trespassers. That was why exemplary damages were available, and constituted a sufficient remedy. ...

55. ... I regard the law of breach of confidence as providing a remedy, in a case such as the present, if the nature of [231] the information obtained by the trespasser is such as to permit the information to be regarded as confidential. But, if that condition is not fulfilled, then the circumstance that the information was tortiously obtained in the first place is not sufficient to make it unconscientious of a person into whose hands the information later comes to use it or publish it. ...

GUMMOW and HAYNE JJ. ... [237] 79. ... The interest of Lenah [the plaintiff/respondent] is in the profitable conduct of its business. Its sensitivity is that of the pocket book. This provides an important point of distinction between the present case and [238] the situation where an individual is subjected to unwanted intrusion into his or her personal life and seeks to protect seclusion from surveillance and to prevent the communication or publication of the fruits of such surveillance. ...

81. The fundamental difficulties facing Lenah's case are twofold. It has not pleaded or presented its case as one raising a recognised cause of action which attracts injunctive relief at the interlocutory level. Then Lenah submits that this deficiency is not fatal because, in effect, that interlocutory remedy is at large; the only touchstone of relief is said to be "unconscionable conduct". ...

[248] 106. ... Lenah suggested in its submissions that to date the Australian courts most probably had not developed "an enforceable right to privacy" because of what generally was taken to follow from the failure of the plaintiff's appeal in *Victoria Park Racing and Recreation Grounds Co Ltd v Taylor* (1937) 58 CLR 479.

107. *Victoria Park* does not stand in the path of the development of such a cause of action. The plaintiff in that case was a company which [249] carried on for profit the business of conducting race meetings at a racecourse owned by it in a Sydney suburb. Signals and noticeboards within the grounds displayed information respecting each race about 20 minutes before it commenced. There were three defendants: the owner and occupier of nearby land on which an observation platform was erected; a radio broadcasting station; and an employee of that station who, from the platform, observed the races and the information displayed on the racecourse and broadcast these matters to the public. The plaintiff sought injunctive relief to restrain the actions of the defendants but failed before Nicholas J: (1936) 37 SR (NSW) 322. On appeal directly to this Court, the plaintiff submitted that it should succeed on the ground of infringement of copyright and in an action on the case which it said might be divided into common law nuisance and the rule in *Rylands v Fletcher* (1868) LR 3 HL 330. The appeal was dismissed.

108. In the course of his judgment, Latham CJ rejected the proposition that under the head of nuisance the law recognised a right of privacy: *Victoria Park* (1937) 58 CLR at 495-496. But the decision does not stand for any proposition respecting the existence or otherwise of a tort identified as unjustified invasion of privacy. Writing in 1973, Professor W L Morison correctly observed (New South Wales, Parliament, *Report on the Law of Privacy*, Paper No 170, (1973), par 12):

> The plaintiff in the case was a racecourse proprietor [which] was not seeking privacy for [its] race meetings as such, [it] was seeking a protection which would enable [it] to sell the rights to a particular kind of publicity. [Its] sensitivity was 'pocket book' sensitivity ... . The independent questions of the rights of a plaintiff who is genuinely seeking seclusion from surveillance and communication of what surveillance reveals, it may be argued, should be regarded as open to review in future cases even by courts bound by the High Court decision.

[250] 111. The litigation in *Victoria Park* is significant in the present case in a further respect. Not only did the "privacy" in that case concern the opposition by the plaintiff to the turning to commercial account by the defendants of the business operations of the plaintiff, but the plaintiff

itself was a corporation. As will be mentioned later in these reasons, at that time, and subsequently, existing authority in the United States did not accept that corporations, as distinct from individuals, enjoyed the interests which a tort of unjustified invasion of privacy protected. In those circumstances, it is perhaps not surprising that "privacy" was not at the forefront of the arguments by the plaintiff in *Victoria Park*. ...

[256] 126. ... Lenah is endowed with legal personality only as a consequence of the statute law providing for its incorporation. It is "a statutory person, a *persona ficta* created by law" which renders it a legal entity "as distinct from the personalities of the natural persons who constitute it": *Chaff and Hay Acquisition Committee v J A Hemphill and Sons Pty Ltd* (1947) 74 CLR 375 at 385. Lenah's activities provide it with a goodwill which no doubt has a commercial value. It is that interest for which, as indicated earlier in these reasons, it seeks protection in this litigation. But, of necessity, this artificial legal person lacks the sensibilities, offence and injury to which provide a staple value for any developing law of privacy. ...

[258] 132. For these reasons, Lenah's reliance upon an emergent tort of invasion of privacy is misplaced. Whatever development may take place in that field will be to the benefit of natural, not artificial, persons. It may be that development is best achieved by looking across the range of already established legal and equitable wrongs. On the other hand, in some respects these may be seen as representing species of a genus, being a principle protecting the interests of the individual in leading, to some reasonable extent, a secluded and private life, in the words of the *Restatement*, "free from the prying eyes, ears and publications of others": *Restatement of Torts*, 2d, s 652A, comment b. Nothing said in these reasons should be understood as foreclosing any such debate or as indicating any particular outcome. Nor, as already has been pointed out, should the decision in *Victoria Park*. ...

KIRBY J. ... [274] 178. ... [T]he reasoning adopted by Young J in *Lincoln Hunt* [*Lincoln Hunt Australia Pty Ltd v Willesee* (1986) 4 NSWLR 457], that equitable jurisdiction exists to restrain the publication of a videotape or photograph made by a trespasser, is in my view equally applicable where such materials have passed into the hands of a third party, itself innocent of the trespass, who threatens to publish it. It was not essential to Young J's reasoning that the publication in *Lincoln Hunt* was by the trespasser. The essence of his reasoning was that the material was acquired in consequence of a trespass upon private property; that its publication would be unconscionable; and that it would affect the material interests (there, as here, the goodwill) of the plaintiff. ...

[276] 183. ... Apart from the other cases where a cause of action can be shown to sustain the grant of an interlocutory injunction, in my view a court, such as the Supreme Court, has the statutory power [*Supreme Court Civil Procedure Act 1932* (Tas)] to grant an injunction to restrain the use of information which has been obtained by a trespasser or by some other illegal, tortious, surreptitious or improper means where the use of such information would be unconscionable. ...

[277] 186. Since the majority decision of this Court in *Victoria Park Racing and Recreation Grounds Co Ltd v Taylor* (1937) 58 CLR 479, it has generally been accepted that a cause of action for breach of privacy does not exist in the common law of Australia, any more than it existed in the common law of England. Some of the values that might be described as aspects of privacy could be defended by invoking other, established, causes of action. But in consequence of *Victoria Park*, a general tort of privacy did not develop in Australia, as it did in the United States of America and elsewhere.

187. It may be that more was read into the decision in *Victoria Park* than the actual holding required. However, because of the general understanding of what the decision stood for (encouraged by the wide language in which Latham CJ, at least, expressed his opinion), legislatures and law reform bodies have, for more than 50 years, proceeded on the footing that no enforceable general right to privacy exists in the law of this country. Indeed the Australian Law [278] Reform Commission concluded that a general statutory right to privacy, as had been enacted in some places overseas, should not be recommended in Australia: Australian Law Reform Commission, *Privacy*, Report No 22, (1983). Instead, the Commission proposed that specific legislation should be enacted which defined the values to be protected, the circumstances of the protection and the defences that would be applicable. ...

189. Whether, so many years after *Victoria Park* and all that has followed, it would be appropriate for this Court to declare the existence of an actionable wrong of invasion of privacy is a difficult question. I would prefer to postpone an answer to the question. Upon my analysis, no answer is now required. ...

[279] 190. *Privacy and corporations*: The fact that the respondent is a corporation is a further reason for delaying a response to this question. This is because doubt exists as to whether a corporation is apt to enjoy any common law right to privacy. ...

[Kirby J concluded that the exercise of discretion by the Full Court of the Supreme Court of Tasmania in granting the interlocutory injunction had miscarried. In granting the interlocutory injunction the Full Court had not given appropriate consideration of the constitutional principle in *Lange v Australian Broadcasting Corporation* (1997) 189 CLR 520 protecting the freedom of communication concerning governmental and political matters, specifically animal welfare issues in the present case.]

CALLINAN J. ... **[315]** 297. Equity should ... regard the relationship created by the possession of the appellant of a tangible item of property obtained in violation of the respondent's right of possession, and the exploitation of which would be to its detriment, and to the financial advantage of the appellant, as a relationship of a fiduciary kind and of confidence. ... The film was brought into existence, and the appellant acquired it, in circumstances in which it cannot in good conscience use it without the permission of the respondent. If the facts remain at the trial as they appear to be now, the appellant should then be obliged to deliver up the film to the respondent. There is therefore an underlying remedy sufficient to support an interlocutory injunction. ...

[320] 313. It is not necessary, because of my conclusion as to unconscionability, to deal with the respondent's alternative claim for relief based upon an intrusion upon its privacy but out of deference to the careful arguments of the parties, I will express some tentative views about it.

314. It is correct, as the appellant submits, that in *Victoria Park Racing* **[321]** *and Recreation Grounds Co Ltd v Taylor* (1937) 58 CLR 479 (Latham CJ, Dixon and McTiernan JJ; Rich and Evatt JJ dissenting), the Court held that a racecourse owner and operator could not prevent the observation and broadcasting of, from a tower on land adjoining the course, the progress and results of races conducted on the racecourse; and that the case has been regarded as authority for the proposition that there is no tort of intrusion of privacy in this country. ...

316. It [*Victoria Park*] was decided by a narrow majority. The decision was a product of a different time, a time when sporting events and sporting people did not, as today, attract large payments from sponsors and advertisers, a time before statutory corporations and public companies conducted remunerative, on- and off-course and off-site betting businesses on sporting events, and a time when television was in its infancy, and the regular payment of vast sums of prize and other money to sports people whose public profile enabled them to earn further income by associating their names and images with advertisers of goods and services, was unknown. Those different conditions of that very different era may go some way to explaining why Latham CJ was so dismissive of a "quasi-property" in a spectacle. ...

[322] 317. Even if there be no, or there is to be no, tort of intrusion of privacy as such, the law may need to devise a remedy to protect the rights of the "owners" of a spectacle, at least against unauthorised reproduction of it by broadcast, telecast or publication of photographs, or other reproductions of it, under the rubric of nuisance or otherwise. ...

[324] 323. In the United States, a tort based upon the right to privacy has been developed and is still evolving in response to encroachments upon **[325]** privacy by the media and others. The history of its development is traced in *Prosser and Keeton on the Law of Torts* 5th edn 1984, at pp 850-851. As early as 1960, William Prosser ("Privacy", (1960) 48 California Law Review 383 at 389) said:

It is not one tort, but a complex of four. The law of privacy comprises four distinct kinds of invasion of four different interests of the plaintiff, which are tied together by the common name, but otherwise have almost nothing in common except that each represents an interference with the right of the plaintiff, in the phrase coined by Judge Cooley, 'to be let alone'. Without any attempt to exact definition, these four torts may be described as follows:

1. Intrusion upon the plaintiff's seclusion or solitude, or into his private affairs.
2. Public disclosure of embarrassing private facts about the plaintiff.
3. Publicity which places the plaintiff in a false light in the public eye.
4. Appropriation, for the defendant's advantage, of the plaintiff's name or likeness."

Prosser's categorisation has been accepted by the United States Supreme Court (*Time Inc v Hill* 385 US 374 (1967) at 383; *Cox Broadcasting Corporation v Cohn* 420 US 469 (1975) at 488) and the *Restatement of Torts*, 2d, s 652A. ...

[328] 335. It seems to me that, having regard to current conditions in this country, and developments of the law in other common law jurisdictions, the time is ripe for consideration whether a tort of invasion of privacy should be recognised in this country, or whether the legislatures should be left to determine whether provisions for a remedy for it should be made. ...

[Gaudron J agreed with Gummow and Hayne JJ.]

Appeal allowed

Chapter 4

Interference with Goods

1. TRESPASS AND CONVERSION

Fouldes v Willoughby
(1841) 151 ER 1153
Court of Exchequer Chamber

A simple asportation or removal of goods with no denial of the plaintiff's right to possession may constitute trespass but not conversion.

[The defendant was the manager of a steam ferry on the River Mersey. The plaintiff paid the fare for the journey from Birkenhead to Liverpool and boarded the ferry with his two horses. Before the ferry had departed Birkenhead, the defendant informed the plaintiff that he would not carry the plaintiff's horses and that the plaintiff should take them ashore. When the plaintiff refused, "the defendant took the horses from the plaintiff, who was holding one of them by the bridle, and put them on shore on the landing slip". In the plaintiff's action of trover for conversion of the horses, the defence was that "the plaintiff had misconducted himself and behaved improperly on board, and that the horses were sent on shore in order to get rid of the plaintiff, by inducing him to follow them". The jury found a verdict for the plaintiff, and awarded £40 damages representing the value of the horses, after the trial judge (Maule J) instructed them that the defendant's conduct in putting the horses ashore constituted conversion unless the plaintiff's behaviour justified his removal from the ferry. The defendant appealed.]

LORD ABINGER CB. **[1155]** This is a motion to set aside the verdict on the ground of an alleged misdirection; and I cannot help thinking that if the learned Judge who tried the case had referred to the long and frequent distinctions which have been taken between such a simple asportation as will support an action of trespass, and those circumstances which are requisite to establish a conversion, he would not have so directed the jury. It is a proposition familiar to all lawyers, that a simple asportation of a chattel, without any intention of making any further use of it, although it may be a sufficient foundation for an action of trespass, is not sufficient to establish a conversion. I had thought that the matter had been fully discussed, and this distinction established, by the numerous cases which have occurred on this subject; but, according to the argument put forward by the plaintiff's counsel to-day, a bare asportavit is a sufficient foundation to support an action of trover. I entirely dissent from this argument; and therefore I think that the learned Judge was wrong, in telling the jury that the simple fact of putting these horses on shore by the defendant, amounted to a conversion of them to his own use. In my opinion, he should have added to his direction, that

96

it was for them to consider what was the intention of the defendant in so doing. If the object, and whether rightly or wrongfully entertained is immaterial, simply was to induce the plaintiff to go on shore himself, and the defendant, in furtherance of that object, did the act in question, it was not exercising over the horses any right inconsistent with, or adverse to, the rights which the plaintiff had in them. Suppose, instead of the horses, the defendant had put the plaintiff himself on shore, and on being put on shore, the plaintiff had refused to take his horses with him, and the defendant had said he would take them to the other side of the water, and had done so, would that be a conversion? That would be a much more colourable case of a conversion than the present, because, by separating the man from his property, it might, with some appearance of fairness, be said the party was carrying away the horses without any justifiable reason for so doing. Then, having conveyed them across the water, and finding neither the owner nor any one else to receive them, what is he to do with them? Suppose, under those circumstances, the defendant lands them, and leaves them on shore, would that amount to a conversion? The argument of the plaintiff's counsel in this case must go the length of saying that it would. Then, suppose the reply to be, that those circumstances would amount to a conversion, I ask, at what period of time did the conversion take place? Suppose the plaintiff had immediately followed his horses when they were put on shore, and resumed possession of them, would there be a conversion of them in that case? I apprehend, clearly not. It has been argued, that the mere touching and taking them by the bridle would constitute a conversion, but surely that cannot be: if the plaintiff had immediately gone on shore and taken possession of them, there could be no conversion. Then the question, whether this were a conversion or not, cannot depend on the subsequent conduct of the plaintiff in following the horses on shore. Would any man say, that if the facts of this case were, that the plaintiff and defendant had had a controversy as to whether the horses should remain in the boat, and the defendant had said, "If you will not put them on shore, I will do it for you," and in pursuance of that threat, he had taken hold of one of the horses to go ashore with it, an action of trover could be sustained against him? There might, perhaps, in such a case, be ground for maintaining an action of trespass, because the defendant **[1156]** may have had no right to meddle with the horses at all: but it is clear that he did not do so for the purpose of taking them away from the plaintiff, or of exercising any right over them, either for himself or for any other person. The case which has been cited from Strange's Reports, of *Bushell v Miller* (1718) 1 Stra 128, seems fully in point. There the plaintiff and defendant, who were porters, had each a stand on the Custom House Quay. The plaintiff placed goods belonging to a third party in such a manner that the defendant could not get to his chest without removing them, which he accordingly did, and forgot to replace them, and the goods were subsequently lost. Now suppose trespass to have been brought for that asportation, the defendant, in order to justify the trespass, would plead, that he removed the parcels, as he lawfully might, for the purpose of coming at his own goods; and the Court there said, that whatever ground there might be for an action of trespass, in not putting the package back in its original place, there was none for trover, inasmuch as the object of the party in removing it was one wholly collateral to any use of the property, and not at all to disturb that plaintiff's rights in or dominion over it. Again, suppose a man puts goods on board of a boat, which the master thinks are too heavy for it, and refuses to carry them, on the ground that it might be dangerous to his vessel to do so, and the owner of the goods says, "If you put my goods on shore, I will go with them," and he does so; would that amount to a conversion in the master of the vessel, even assuming his judgment as to the weight of the goods to be quite erroneous, and that there really would be no danger whatever in taking them? In order to constitute a conversion, it is necessary either that the party taking the goods should intend some use to be made of them, by himself or by those for whom he acts, or that, owing to his act, the goods are destroyed or consumed, to the prejudice of the lawful owner. As an instance of the latter branch of this definition, suppose, in the present case, the defendant had thrown the horses into the water, whereby they were drowned, that would have amounted to an actual conversion; or as in the case cited in the course of the argument, of a person throwing a piece of paper into the water; for, in these cases, the chattel is changed in quality, or destroyed altogether. But it has never yet been held, that the single act of removal of a chattel, independent of any claim over it, either in favour of the party himself or any one else, amounts to a conversion of the chattel. In the present case, therefore, the simple removal of these horses by the defendant, for a purpose wholly unconnected with any the least denial of the right of the plaintiff to the possession and enjoyment of them, is no conversion of the horses, and consequently the rule for a new trial ought to be made absolute … .

[Alderson, Gurney and Rolfe BB concurred.]

Order that the verdict for the plaintiff be set aside
for misdirection and that there be a new trial

[In *Bunnings Group Limited v CHEP Australia Limited* [2011] NSWCA 342, the plaintiff owned and had the right to immediate possession of pallets which it hired for the carriage and storage of goods. A number of these pallets came into the possession of the defendant and were used by the defendant in the course of its retail hardware business without the plaintiff's consent in circumstances amounting to conversion. In this context, Allsop P (with whom Giles and Macfarlan JJA agreed) made the following observations on the continuing authority of *Fouldes v Willoughby* (1841) 151 ER 1153:

124. The framing of a precise definition of the tort of conversion has been described as "well nigh impossible": Lord Nicholls of Birkenhead in *Kuwait Airways Corporation v Iraqi Airways Co (Nos 4 and 5)* [2002] 2 AC 883 at 1084 [39]… . The essential elements, or basic features, involve an intentional act or dealing with goods inconsistent with or repugnant to the rights of the owner, including possession and any right to possession. Such an act or dealing will amount to such an infringement of the possessory or proprietary rights of the owner if it is an intended act of dominion or assertion of rights over the goods: see generally *Penfolds Wines Pty Ltd v Elliott* (1946) 74 CLR 204 at 217-221 (Latham CJ), 228-230 (Dixon J, with whose statements of principle Starke J agreed at 221), 234-235 (McTiernan J), and 239-244 (Williams J); and *Kuwait Airways* at 1084 [39]-[42] (Lord Nicholls of Birkenhead), 1104 [119] (Lord Steyn) and 1106 [129] (Lord Hoffmann).

125. The tort is one of strict liability and thus a mental element in knowing that a wrong is being committed is not required. Nevertheless, intention is not irrelevant. The act or dealing in question must be intentional; further, the intention must be the exercise of such dominion as is repugnant to the rights of the owner. Thus, in *Fouldes v Willoughby* (1841) 151 ER 1153 the ferry manager did not commit trover by taking the plaintiff's horses off the ferry and putting them ashore after the plaintiff had refused to remove them. This was so because the acts were to take the horses to the river bank, not to take them to his own use or some other person's, but merely to remove them from his ferry. Whilst there can be a conversion for a limited period of time, this would occur only if there was an intention to exercise dominion over the goods inconsistent with the rights of the owner, including the right to possession. As Rolfe B said in *Fouldes* at 1157:

"In every case of trover, there must be a taking with the intent of exercising over the chattel an ownership inconsistent with the real owner's right of possession."

126. Whilst criticised by J W Salmond in a note in (1905) 21 Law Quarterly Review 43, *Fouldes v Willoughby* retains its authority being cited in *Penfolds Wines,* as does the distinction it makes between trespass and conversion: *Penfolds Wines*, at 218 per Latham CJ.]

The Winkfield
[1902] P 42
English Court of Appeal

"As against a wrongdoer, possession is title". Thus, a bailee in possession of goods may recover the full value of those goods from a wrongdoer who has interfered with them. However, the bailee is under an obligation to account to the true owner.

[Following a collision off the coast of South Africa between two steamships, "The Winkfield" and "The Mexican", in which "The Mexican" sank and a large quantity of parcels and mail on board was lost, "The Winkfield" admitted limited liability and paid money into court. The Postmaster-General filed a motion claiming as bailee the value of certain letters and parcels, which he undertook to distribute among the senders or addressees. The motion was dismissed and the Postmaster-General appealed.]

COLLINS MR. [After noting that, in view of the course followed by the parties on the hearing of the motion, it was not now open to the respondents (the owners of "The Mexican") to take the point that the Postmaster-General was not in actual occupation of the things bailed at the time of the loss, his Honour continued:]

[54] I assume, therefore, that the subject-matter of the bailment was in the custody of the Postmaster-General as bailee at the time of the accident. For the reasons which I am about to state I am of opinion that … the law is that in an action against a stranger for loss of goods caused by his negligence, the bailee in possession can recover the value of the goods, although he would have had a good answer to an action by the bailor for damages for the loss of the thing bailed.

It seems to me that the position, that possession is good against a wrongdoer and that the latter cannot set up the jus tertii unless he claims under it, is well established in our law, and really concludes this case against the respondents. As I shall shew [sic] presently, a long series of authorities establishes this in actions of trover and trespass at the suit of the possessor. And the principle being the same, it follows that he can equally recover the whole value of the goods in an action on the case for their loss through the tortious conduct of the defendant. I think it involves this also, that the wrongdoer who is not defending under the title of the bailor is quite unconcerned with what the rights are between the bailor and the bailee, and [55] must treat the possessor as the owner of the goods for all purposes quite irrespective of the rights and obligations as between him and the bailor.

I think this position is well established in our law, though it may be that reasons for its existence have been given in some of the cases which are not quite satisfactory. I think also that the obligation of the bailee to the bailor to account for what he has received in respect of the destruction or conversion of the thing bailed has been admitted so often in decided cases that it cannot now be questioned; and, further, I think it can be shewn [sic] that the right of the bailee to recover cannot be rested on the ground suggested in some of the cases, namely, that he was liable over to the bailor for the loss of the goods converted or destroyed. It cannot be denied that since the case of *Armory v Delamirie* 1 Stra 504, not to mention earlier cases from the Year Books onward, a mere finder may recover against a wrongdoer the full value of the thing converted. That decision involves the principle that as between possessor and wrongdoer the presumption of law is, in the words of Lord Campbell in *Jeffries v Great Western Ry Co* 5 E & B 802, at p 806, "that the person who has possession has the property." In the same case he says (at p 805): "I am of the opinion that the law is that a person possessed of goods as his property has a good title as against every stranger, and that one who takes them from him, having no title in himself, is a wrongdoer, and cannot defend himself by shewing [sic] that there was title in some third person, for *against a wrongdoer possession is title*. The law is so stated by the very learned annotator in his note to *Wilbraham v Snow* 2 Wms Saund 47f." Therefore it is not open to the defendant, being a wrongdoer, to inquire into the nature or limitation of the possessor's right, and unless it is competent for him to do so the question of his relation to, or liability towards, the true owner cannot come into the discussion at all; and, therefore, as between those two parties full damages have to be paid without any further inquiry. The extent of the liability of the finder to the true owner not being relevant to the discussion between him and [56] the wrongdoer, the facts which would ascertain it would not have been admissible in evidence, and therefore the right of the finder to recover full damages cannot be made to depend upon the extent of his liability over to the true owner. To hold otherwise would, it seems to me, be in effect to permit a wrongdoer to set up a jus tertii under which he cannot claim. But, if this be the fact in the case of a finder, why should it not be equally the fact in the case of a bailee? Why, as against a wrongdoer, should the nature of the plaintiff's interest in the thing converted be any more relevant to the inquiry, and therefore admissible in evidence, than in the case of a finder? It seems to me that neither in one case nor the other ought it to be competent for the defendant to go into evidence on that matter …

[60] The chattel that has been converted or damaged is deemed to be the chattel of the possessor and of no other, and therefore its loss or deterioration is his loss, and to him, if he demands it, it must be recouped. His obligation to account to the bailor is really not ad rem in the discussion. It

only comes in after he has carried his legal position to its logical consequence against a wrongdoer, and serves to soothe a mind disconcerted by the notion that a person who is not himself the complete owner should be entitled to receive back the full value of the chattel converted or destroyed. There is no inconsistency between the two positions; the one is the complement of the other. As between bailee and stranger possession gives title – that is, not a limited interest, but absolute and complete ownership, and he is entitled to receive back a complete equivalent for the whole loss or deterioration of the thing itself. As between bailor and bailee the real interests of each must be inquired into, and, as the bailee has to account for the thing bailed, so he must account for that which has become its **[61]** equivalent and now represents it. What he has received above his own interest he has received to the use of his bailor. The wrongdoer, having once paid full damages to the bailee, has an answer to any action by the bailor …

[Stirling and Matthew LJJ concurred.]

Appeal allowed

Penfolds Wines Pty Ltd v Elliott
(1946) 74 CLR 204
High Court of Australia

Title to sue for trespass to goods requires the plaintiff to be in possession of the goods at the time of the trespassory interference. Title to sue for conversion of goods requires the plaintiff to be in possession or have a right to immediate possession of the goods at the time of the wrongful interference. The wrongful use of another person's goods may constitute the tort of conversion.

[In proceedings in the Supreme Court of New South Wales, the plaintiff (appellant), Penfolds Wines Pty Ltd, sought an injunction restraining the defendant (respondent), James Peter Elliott, the licensee of the Central Hotel, Singleton, "from collecting or disposing of, or parting with the possession of or in anywise dealing with or handling the plaintiff company's bottles except such of them as contained at the time wine or brandy put on the market and bottled by the company, and from placing any other liquor in any of the bottles". Further facts appear in the judgment of Latham CJ. In essence, the principal issue was whether the defendant had committed a tortious interference with two of the plaintiff's empty wine bottles, supplied to the defendant by his brother, when, on 7 November 1944, the defendant refilled the bottles with wine other than the plaintiff's wine and delivered the bottles (but did not purport to sell them) to a third party, Spencer Claude Gascoyne Moon, in exchange for the payment of eight shillings, being the cost of the wine in the refilled bottles.

The plaintiff's application for an injunction was refused by the primary judge (Nicholas CJ in Eq) and by the Full Court of the Supreme Court of New South Wales (Jordan CJ, Street and Roper JJ). A further appeal by the plaintiff to the High Court of Australia (argued by two future judges of the Court, Barwick KC for the plaintiff and Kitto KC for the defendant) was dismissed by majority (Starke, Dixon and McTiernan JJ; Latham CJ and Williams J dissenting). Starke and McTiernan JJ dismissed the plaintiff's appeal on the ground that, in the absence of evidence of systematic dealing by the defendant with the plaintiff's bottles, the equitable remedy of injunction (as opposed to the common law remedy of damages) was not appropriate. Dixon J dismissed the plaintiff's appeal on the ground that the defendant had committed no legal wrong. Latham CJ was the only member of the court to find that the defendant had committed trespass to goods. Williams J, together with Latham CJ and McTiernan J, found that the defendant had committed conversion. Although Starke J agreed with Dixon J's exposition of the common law, his Honour was prepared to assume, but did not decide, that the evidence supported a finding that the defendant had committed conversion.]

LATHAM CJ. [208] The appellant company carries on business as a vigneron and wine and spirit merchant in New South Wales and elsewhere. The respondent, Elliott, is a licensed victualler carrying on business at a hotel at Singleton, New South Wales. The company uses large numbers of bottles in its business. All bottles used in [209] New South Wales have, at least since 1922, borne upon them in raised letters moulded upon the glass the words, "This bottle is the property of Penfolds Wines Limited" or "This bottle always remains the property of Penfolds Wines Limited." It was proved that the company never sold bottles so branded, but only the contents of the bottles. When it supplied wine &c to any persons (as it did to the defendant in 1942) in such bottles an invoice was always delivered which referred to the brand and stated that bottles so branded "are not sold, but remain the sole property of Penfolds Wines Limited, from which Company they have been loaned, and such bottles have been delivered by such Company solely for purposes of enabling the contents to be used once only for retailing, consuming or using Australian Wine or Brandy made, distilled or vended by this Company and contained in such bottles. When the contents are once used, the bottles must be forthwith on demand handed or given over or returned to the said Company or its agents. The bottles must not be destroyed or damaged or parted with, or must not be used for any but the foregoing purposes. NB It should be thoroughly understood that this will still allow for a bonus being paid for the prompt return of our branded bottles." The plaintiff alleged that the defendant without its consent had been receiving, collecting and handling branded bottles and using them in connection with his business and placing and delivering in those bottles to his customers liquids not manufactured and put upon the market by the plaintiff company. The plaintiff claimed an injunction against the continuance of this practice.

The plaintiff satisfied the learned trial judge (Nicholas CJ in Eq) that the defendant filled two of the plaintiff's branded bottles (proved to have been manufactured not earlier than 1930) with wine other than Penfold's wine, and delivered them to one Moon, who was a paid employee of the Brand Protection Association with which the Branded Bottle Association of New South Wales Ltd was "affiliated". Moon also had authority to act as an honorary pure foods inspector. It was not found by the learned judge that the defendant actually sold the bottles to Moon, though it was found that the defendant delivered them to Moon in return for a sum of eight shillings. The plaintiff relies upon the transaction with Moon as involving an assumption of dominion over the bottles which amounts to a conversion; but the plaintiff also relies upon the fact that the defendant used the bottles for a purpose inconsistent with the terms upon which the bottles were delivered to purchasers or other persons, namely for containing wine other than Penfold's. The learned judge accepted the evidence of the defendant that the two bottles delivered [210] to Moon were brought to the defendant by his brother to be filled with wine other than Penfold's and that they were so filled.

The defendant admitted in his evidence that he had "for years" and on a subsequent occasion followed the same practice of filling branded bottles with wine other than Penfold's and delivering them in the way of trade to his brother. He admitted that he knew that some bottles were branded and that others were unbranded, and he said that he would not purport to sell a branded bottle, but that if a man brought his own bottle to be filled he did not have to worry about the brand, and that he considered that he was entitled, if a customer brought a bottle to him, to fill a branded bottle "with anything." He admitted that he would fill a bottle, even though he knew that it was Penfold's bottle. The learned judge was not satisfied that the defendant did not also put wine into branded bottles other than those which his brother and certain other customers brought to him. But there was no finding that he did so supply wine. ...

The learned trial judge accepted the [211] position that there was a trespass to chattels but held that "in the absence of any evidence of intent by the defendant to make a business of selling the bottles or to refuse to return them if called upon to do so" it was not a case for an injunction.

Upon appeal to the Full Court it was held that there was evidence of trespass to the plaintiff's goods by the defendant and some likelihood of further trespass. But the Court was of opinion that the plaintiff should be left to its common law rights, and that the case was not one for an injunction ....

[214] In this Court ... The argument for the defendant was directed against the view adopted in the Supreme Court that there was a trespass by the defendant to the plaintiff's goods when he filled the plaintiff's bottles with wine other than Penfold's. It was pointed out that the defendant obtained the branded bottles from his brother and other customers with their consent. He did not violate their possession in any way. He had their authority to use the bottles as he did in fact use them. It was therefore argued that, there being no trespass as against the brother and other customers, there was no trespass for which the plaintiff could sue, even if the plaintiff by reason of the determination of the original bailment had a right to immediate possession of the bottles.

A bailment is determined by any act of the bailee which is wholly repugnant to the holding as bailee, and thereupon the bailor has an immediate right to possession (*Donald v Suckling* (1866) LR 1 QB 585, at p 615; *Whiteley Ltd v Hilt* [1918] 2 KB 808, at p 819; *Bullen & Leake's Precedents of Pleadings*, 3rd ed (1868), pp 291, 292). In this case the delivery of the bottles to the defendant by his brother for the purpose of having them filled with wine other than Penfold's was repugnant to the express terms of the bailment. The bailment having been determined, the plaintiff as bailor had an immediate right to the possession of the bottles.

A mere taking or asportation of a chattel may be a trespass without the infliction of any material damage. The handling of a chattel without authority is a trespass: *Clerk & Lindsell on Torts*, 8th ed (1929), pp 213, 214; *Pollock on Torts*, 14th ed (1939), p 280. Unauthorized user of goods is a trespass; unauthorised acts of riding a horse, driving a motor car, using a bottle, are all equally trespasses, [215] even though the horse may be returned unharmed or the motor car unwrecked or the bottle unbroken. The normal use of a bottle is as a container, and the use of it for this purpose is a trespass if, as in this case, it is not authorized by a person in possession or entitled to immediate possession.

It is argued, however, that, as the defendant obtained the two bottles from his brother, who had actual possession of them, and used them with his authority, there was no trespass as against either the brother or the plaintiff. Plainly there was no trespass as against the brother. Does this fact conclusively show that there was no trespass as against the plaintiff? See *Clerk & Lindsell on Torts*, 8th ed (1929), pp 213, 214:- "It is apprehended, however, that for a taking to constitute a trespass it must not merely be an unlawful act, but unlawful as against the party from whom possession is taken. Thus, if goods belonging to A, and B being unlawfully possessed of them transfers them to C, the taking of them by C, though it may give a good cause of action in trover, is not a trespass. And it makes no difference, it would seem, if C is aware of the infirmity of B's title. The receiver of stolen goods does not commit a trespass when he takes the goods from the thief with the thief's consent. If it were otherwise every receiver might be indicted for larceny."

The same opinion is expressed in *Pollock & Wright on Possession in the Common Law*, 1st ed (1888), where Mr Justice Wright reaches the conclusion that trespass is always an interference with actual possession. If this is the case, the use by the defendant of the plaintiff's bottle for keeping and disposing of wine in his trade (being an act done with the consent of the person who delivered the bottle to him, such person having the actual possession of the bottle) was not a trespass for which any person can sue. In the work cited at p 145, (after a reference to a contrary view expressed in *Williams Saunders* and other authorities) the following opinion is stated:- "It is submitted that the correct view is that right to possession, as a title for maintaining trespass, is merely a right in one person to sue for a trespass done to another's possession; that this right exists whenever the person whose actual possession was violated held as servant, agent, or bailee under a revocable bailment for or under or on behalf of the person having the right to possession; and that it does not exist for the purposes of trespass and theft, as distinguished from trover and detinue, when the person whose possession was violated was not in any way a delegate or representative of the person having the right to possession, nor when the thing was not in any possession at all."

[216] With all respect, I have difficulty in understanding how it can accurately be said that one person can have a right to sue for a trespass done to another's possession – unless that possession is regarded as being the possession of the plaintiff – and then it is not, in any relevant sense, "another's possession."

The possession of a servant or agent is the possession of the master or principal (as is stated at p 138) who therefore is regarded as having actual possession and not only a right to possession:

See also *Pollock on Torts*, 14th ed (1939), p 275. In the other case mentioned, namely that of a revocable bailment, the bailor has neither possession nor a present right to possession so long as the bailment remains unrevoked. If the possession of a bailee holding under such a bailment is violated it is his possession, and not the possession of his bailor, which is violated. In this case, therefore, the admission that the bailor may sue for trespass depends, as already stated, upon allowing one person A to sue for a wrong done to another person B, who is not the servant or agent or in any other way representative of A. The result is that upon this view A may sue for a wrong though no wrong has been done to him.

The contention for the defendant is that a right to immediate possession, as distinct from actual possession, can never entitle any plaintiff to sue in trespass unless there is an interference with the actual possession of some other person falling within the limited class referred to in the extract which I have quoted.

The law is frequently stated, however, in terms which do not recognize the limitation or qualification developed by Mr Justice Wright: See *Johnson v Diprose* [1893] 1 QB 512 at p 516, per Bowen LJ – "A person who brings an action for trespass to goods must either be in possession of them at the time of the alleged trespass or entitled to the immediate possession." The law is stated in the same terms in *Bullen & Leake's Precedents of Pleadings*, 3rd ed (1868), p 414; *Halsbury's Laws of England*, 2nd ed, vol 33, p 23. In *Jenks, Digest of English Civil Law*, 1st ed (1908), Book II, Part III, articles 854 *et seq*, the law is stated in the following terms:–

"854. Trespass to goods is any direct infringement of the possession by another of corporeal personal chattels by means of an asportation or other physical invasion; whether such infringement is or is not intentional.

855. Subject to the exceptions mentioned in" sections 858 *et al* "the plaintiff, in an action for trespass to goods, must prove that he had actual possession of the goods at the time when the defendant interfered with them."

[217] Article 858 states one of the exceptions in the following terms:- "A bailor of goods has sufficient possession to support an action for trespass against third persons [*Lotan v Cross* (1810) 2 Camp 464 [170 ER 1219]; *White v Morris* (1852) 11 CB 1015 [138 ER 778]; *Johnson v Diprose* [1893] 1 QB at p 515] unless an exclusive possession of the goods for a period not yet expired has been granted by him to the bailee [*Ward v Macauley* (1791) 4 TR 409 [100 ER 1135]; *Gordon v Harper* (1796) 7 TR 9 [101 ER 828]]."

In the present case the period of the bailment had expired – the bailment was determined when the person who brought the bottles to the defendant, having used them once for containing &c the plaintiff's wine, procured the defendant to use them to contain wine other than the plaintiff's wine and therefore in a manner absolutely repugnant to the terms of the bailment. ... The plaintiff then became legally entitled to immediate possession of the bottles. The authorities to which I have referred support the view that the plaintiff could therefore sue in trespass, though I agree that logical argument tends against this view.

It is contended, however, that if there was no trespass by the defendant in receiving and taking possession of the bottles from his brother there could be no conversion in the subsequent use which he made of the bottles. I assume (and I think rightly) in favour of the defendant that his brother, who obtained the bottles from a retailer of the plaintiff's wines, was a sub-bailee of the bottles with the same rights as against the plaintiff as the original bailee (the retailer) including a right to use the bottles for the purpose of once using &c the wine made by the plaintiff contained in the bottles, but not including any right to use the bottles for other wine or to deliver them to any person other than the plaintiff. If the defendant's brother is regarded as being a sub-bailee holding the bottles upon the same terms as the original bailee, his delivery of the bottles to the defendant to be filled with wine other than the plaintiff's wine and to be returned to him was an act which, to use the words of Baron Parke in *Fenn v Bittleston* (1851) 7 Ex 152, at p 159 [155 ER 895, at p 899], was "doing a thing entirely inconsistent with the terms of the bailment, though not amounting to a destruction of the chattel." It was therefore "a determination of the lawful bailment, and caused the possessory title to revert to the **[218]** bailor, and entitled him to maintain an action of trover."

The defendant then used them without any regard to the plaintiff's rights. A taking of the bottles without any intention to exercise permanent or temporary dominion over them, though it might be a trespass, would not be a conversion; but the actual use of the bottles for the benefit of the defendant and his brother was a conversion: see *Fouldes v Willoughby* (1841) 8 M & W 540, at p 546 [151 ER 1153, at pp 1155, 1156], per Lord Abinger CB. The defendant in the present case handled and used the plaintiff's bottles for the purpose of exercising what he regarded as his right to use them for containing any liquid that he chose to put into them and to keep them for that purpose until he delivered them, with their contents, to his customers – his brother or other persons who brought branded bottles to him: See *Pollock* on *Torts*, 14th ed (1939), p 286: "The grievance [in conversion] is the unauthorized assumption of the powers **[219]** of the true owner. Actually dealing with another's goods as owner, for however short a time and however limited a purpose, is therefore conversion." The defendant dealt with the bottles on the basis that he was entitled to hold them when brought to him by his brother or other customers and to use them for the purposes of his trade. In *Burroughes v Bayne* (1860) 5 H & N 296, at pp 305, 306 [157 ER 1196, at p 1200], quoted by Sir William Holdsworth in *History of English Law*, vol 7, p 415, Channell B said:– "Every asportation is not a conversion; and therefore it seems to me that every detention cannot be a conversion. If it were, the mere removal of a chattel, independently of any claim over it in favour of the party himself, or anyone else whatever, would be a conversion. The asportation of a chattel for the use of the defendant or third persons, amounts to a conversion, and for this reason, whatever act is done inconsistent with the dominion of the owner of a chattel, at all times and places over that chattel, is a conversion."

In the present case there was not, in my opinion, a mere removal of the bottles received from the defendant's brother independently of any claim over them in favour of the defendant or anyone else. There was a handling of the bottles, an actual user of them, for the purposes of the defendant's trade – for containing and disposing of the defendant's wine and for the use of the defendant's customer, his brother. Such dealing with bottles, under a claim of right so to deal with them (a claim in which the defendant still persists) was inconsistent with the dominion of the owner of the bottles and was a conversion.

But, further, the defendant treated the bottles as his own when he handed them over to Moon and received eight shillings for them. Nicholas CJ in Eq found there was not a sale on the ground that he was of opinion that the defendant considered that Moon was entitled to take them as a pure foods inspector. If the defendant had disclaimed any control in respect of the bottles, and had in effect said to Moon – "You as a pure foods inspector can do whatever you are entitled to do, but I disclaim any right to deal with these bottles," the case would have been very different. But the admitted facts show that the defendant delivered the bottles to Moon in return for eight shillings, a sum which he evidently kept for himself. He dealt with the bottles (as well as with their contents) as being a person entitled to dispose of them to Moon, that is as owner, and I can see no reason for holding that such a disposition was not a conversion of the bottles.

Thus in my opinion it was shown that the defendant had committed the tort of conversion in respect of two chattels belonging to **[220]** the plaintiff. For reasons already stated, a remedy at common law is inadequate. To leave the plaintiff to its common law rights in the present case would be in effect to deprive the plaintiff of any remedy.

[His Honour concluded that the appeal should be allowed and an injunction granted.]

DIXON J. ... **[224]** What wrong to possession or property on the part of the respondent do these facts disclose? I know of none. It cannot be trespass because there is, on the part of the respondent, no infringement upon the possession of any one. It cannot be conversion, because, on his part, there is no act, and no intent, inconsistent with the appellants' right to possession and nothing to impair or destroy it. It cannot be an innominate injury to the appellants' right to possession for which the remedy would have been a special action on the case, because he did no damage to the appellants' goods, the bottles. Detinue is, of course, irrelevant and so too would have been replevin.

In English law what amounts to an infringement upon the possessory and proprietary rights of the owner of a chattel personal is a question still governed by categories of specific wrong. Trespass was the wrong upon which reliance appeared to be placed in support of the appeal when it was opened, but, in the end, it seemed to be conceded that this cause of action was untenable. I think that it is quite clear that trespass would not lie for anything which the foregoing facts disclose.

Trespass is a wrong to possession. But, on the part of the respondent, there was never any invasion of possession.

[225] At the time he filled the two bottles his brother left with him, he himself was in possession of them. If the bottles had been out of his own possession and in the possession of some other person, then to lift the bottles up against the will of that person and to fill them with wine would have amounted to trespasses. The reason is that the movement of the bottles and the use of them as receptacles are invasions of the possession of the second person. But they are things which the man possessed of the bottles may do without committing trespass. The respondent came into possession of the bottles without trespass. For his brother delivered possession to him of the two bottles specifically in question. In the same way, if any other customer ever left bottles of the appellant with him for wine to be poured into them, those customers must have similarly delivered possession of the bottles to the respondent. His possession of the appellants' bottles was, therefore, never trespassory. That his brother was in possession of the two bottles specifically in question there can be no doubt. If, as his evidence suggests, the latter did obtain the two bottles immediately from a retailer of the appellant's wine, it may be that he held the bottles upon a bailment in which the appellants were bailors and he was bailee. Such a bailment needs a privity between them. But the inference is perhaps warranted that, in the distribution of the appellants' wines, each successive merchant or trader, from the wholesaler to the retailer, had an implied authority from the appellants to create a bailment of the bottles from the appellants to the buyer to whom the merchant or trader sold the wine. There is, however, no importance in the question whether the possession of the respondent's brother, and of any customers in like case with him, is to be considered independent or as that of a bailee from the appellants upon a bailment determinable on demand. For it has been settled for centuries, to quote the language of the *Year Book* (1498), 16 H VII, p 3, pl 7: "that where one comes to the goods by lawful means by delivery of the plaintiff immediately at the first, he shall not ever be punished as a trespasser but by writ of detinue; nor any more shall his donee, vendee or sub-bailee who comes to the plaintiff's goods by such means" (cited by the late Mr Justice RS Wright in *Pollock and Wright's Possession in the Common Law*, 1st ed (1888), p 137) ...

[226] Some misunderstanding appeared to arise during the hearing of the appeal about two matters, which, for that reason, should be mentioned. The first is the rule that, where there has been a trespass *de bonis* an action lies against the person committing the trespass not only at the suit of the person in possession, but also at the suit of a person immediately entitled to possession. Thus, suppose that after a purchaser of the appellants' wine from a retailer had consumed the contents of the bottle, a stranger were to take the bottle out of his possession against his will; in such a case an action of trespass could be maintained against the stranger not only by the purchaser whose possession had been violated, but by the appellants as the persons immediately entitled to possession. It is sometimes said, in stating the rule, that an immediate right to possession is enough to support an action of trespass, meaning when an invasion of possession has taken place. The statement, however, seems to have been misunderstood and treated as if it meant that an owner of a chattel personal out of possession but entitled immediately to resume it could complain in trespass of any use of the chattel which he had not authorized made by the person in possession or by anyone acting under the latter's authority. This is not so. If it were so, conversion would have been an unnecessary remedy and, indeed, a wrong to a right of property would exist going far beyond the limits of that tort, which is confined to acts inconsistent with the right to possession. Further, the whole law of larceny at common law would be different and the statutory offence of larceny as a bailee need never have been created. The error is dealt with at length by the late Mr Justice RS Wright (*Pollock and Wright*, pp 145-147) who states the true principle, which Sir William Holdsworth said was implied in the earlier authorities but had not before been clearly stated (*History of English Law*, vol 7, pp 423, 424). It is, perhaps, desirable to set out a little of Mr Justice Wright's text:- "In some cases," he says, "an owner of a thing who has never yet acquired the possession of it, or an owner who has parted with the possession, is nevertheless, in virtue of his right to possession, entitled to sue or prosecute a stranger who takes the thing; and it is of much practical and theoretical importance to discover in what cases a mere right to possession **[227]** suffices for this purpose, and on what ground. There are expressions in some cases and in text books (see *Wms S 47b*) to the effect that a person with a right to possession of a thing, though without possession, can always maintain trespass, as (except where the right is suspended, eg in a bailment for a term – *Gordon v Harper* (1796) 7 TR 9 [101 ER 828]) he certainly can trover or detinue, against a stranger who takes the thing: and if this is correct the gist of the action of trespass must be the wrong to the right to possession. But it is difficult to see how there can be a forcible and immediate injury *vi et armis* to a mere legal right; and there are some parts of the law of trespass and theft which are inexplicable on such a view. It is submitted that the correct view is that the right to possession, as a title for maintaining trespass, is merely a right in one person to sue for a trespass done to another's possession; that this right exists whenever the person whose actual possession was violated held as servant, agent, or bailee under a revocable bailment for or under or on behalf of the person having the right to possession" (*Pollock and Wright's Possession in the Common Law*, at p 145).

The second matter about which there appeared to be some misunderstanding is the effect of acts repugnant to a bailment and consequently operating as a determination of the bailment. The determination of the bailment may enable the bailor to maintain an action of conversion, but not of trespass.

"Any act or disposition which is wholly repugnant to (*Donald v Suckling* (1866) LR 1 QB 585, at p 615) or as it were an absolute disclaimer of (*Fenn v Bittleston* (1851) 7 Ex, at pp 159, 160 [155 ER, at p 899] per Parke B Cp *Cooper v Willomatt* (1845) 1 CB 672 [135 ER 706] and *Bryant v Wardell* (1848) 2 Ex 479 [154 ER 580]) the holding as bailee revests the bailor's right to possession, and therefore also his immediate right to maintain trover or detinue even where the bailment is for a term or otherwise not revocable at will, and so *a fortiori* in a bailment determinable at will. But in trespass and theft the wrong is not, as in trover, to the plaintiff's right to possession, and the bailment cannot be determined by any tortious act which does not destroy the very subject of the bailment; and the only extension which this doctrine ever received at common law was that a bailee of a package or bulk might by taking things out of the package or breaking the bulk so far alter the thing in point of law that it becomes no longer the same thing – the same package or bulk – which he received and thereupon his possession was held to become trespassory" (*Pollock and Wright* at pp 132-133).

[228] There is some authority for the view that complete destruction of the chattel by the bailee might, for the same reason, amount to trespass. Thus Lord Coke in *Co Ltt,* 71*a*: "If one lends oxen to another to plough his land, and he kills them, the owner may have trespass, or trespass on the case, at his election." After citing this passage, Parke B, in *Fenn v Bittleston* (1851) 7 Ex, at pp 159, 160 [155 ER, at p 899], says:- "It was held, that the act of the bailee in doing a thing entirely inconsistent with the terms of the bailment, though not amounting to a destruction of the chattel, was a determination of the lawful bailment, and caused the possessory title to revert to the bailor, and entitled him to maintain an action of trover. It is true that, if it had been done by the bailee *animo furandi*, it could not have been punishable as a larceny; because, being lawfully in possession of the chattel, the taking it would not be either a trespass *vi et armis* or felony, unless the nature of the article had been changed, as by breaking open a bale; the reason for which distinction is somewhat subtle, but is fully explained in the *Year Book*, 13 Edw 4, fol 9*b*, namely, that the possession of the article in its original state was with the consent of the bailor, and therefore lawful; but there was no consent to the possession of the article in its altered state, so that, after the alteration, the bailment was determined."

There is a third matter which perhaps should be mentioned and that is the supposed distinction between the consequences of the delivery by a bailee of possession of a chattel to a stranger and of the stranger's taking it out of his possession by his licence. There is slender but ancient authority for the position that, in the latter case, the licence of the bailee can be treated as void, if it be wrongful as against the bailor, and since there is a taking, as distinguished from a delivery, there may be found in it a trespassory asportation. Whether this refinement would now be maintained as valid need not be considered. The purpose of mentioning it is to show that the question whether the bailee's act is unauthorized cannot be material unless his act must be relied upon as a justification for what otherwise is a trespass, that is by way of confession and avoidance as under a plea of leave and licence. A delivery of possession by the bailee, however wrongful as against the bailor, could not work an invasion of the bailee's own possession, so as to found trespass.

The plain fact in the present case is that the respondent never did any trespassory act and therefore there is no wrong of which the appellants can complain as a trespass.

Conversion appears to me to be equally out of the question. I put on one side for separate consideration the delivery of the two **[229]** bottles to the inspector under the *Pure Food Act*. Unless that can be construed as a conversion, that tort has no place in the case. It is not out of the case because of the appellants' situation as bailor. On the contrary, if any conversion had been committed by the respondent, clearly the appellants as the persons entitled immediately on demand to the possession of the bottles would be the proper party to complain of it. But nothing in the course pursued by the respondent in receiving and filling bottles and returning them could possibly amount to the tort of conversion. The essence of conversion is a dealing with a chattel in a manner repugnant to the immediate right of possession of the person who has the property or special property in the chattel. It may take the form of a disposal of the goods by way of sale, or pledge or other intended transfer of an interest followed by delivery, of the destruction or change of the nature or character of the thing, as for example, pouring water into wine or cutting the seals from a deed, or of an appropriation evidenced by refusal to deliver or other denial of title. But damage to the chattel is not conversion, nor is use, nor is a transfer of possession otherwise than for the purpose of affecting the immediate right to possession, nor is it always conversion to lose the goods beyond hope of recovery. An intent to do that which would deprive "the true owner" of his immediate right to possession or impair it may be said to form the essential ground of the tort. There is nothing in the course followed by the respondent in supplying wine to his customers who brought bottles to receive it involving any deprival or impairment of property in the bottles, that is of the immediate right to possession. The re-delivery of the bottles to the persons who left them could not amount to a conversion: see per Bigham J in *Union Credit Bank Ltd v Mersey Docks and Harbour Board* [1899] 2 QB 205, at pp 215, 216. The re-delivery could not amount to a conversion because, though involving a transfer of possession, its purpose was not to confer any right over the property in the bottles, but merely to return or restore them to the person who had left them there to be filled. Indeed if they had been withheld from that person, he could have complained, at least theoretically, of an actionable wrong, that is unless it were done as a result of the intervention of the true owners and upon their demand.

To fill the bottles with wine at the request of the person who brought them could not in itself be a conversion. It was not a use of the bottles involving any exercise of dominion over them, however transitory. There was, of course, no asportation and the older cases to the effect that an asportation of chattels for the use of the person taking them, or of a third person, may amount to a **[230]** conversion can have no application. In any event, an intention cannot be imputed to the respondent of taking to himself the property in the bottles or of depriving the appellants thereof or of asserting any title therein or of denying that of the appellants. It was not an act derogating from the proprietary right of the appellant. There was no user on the footing that the respondent was owner or that the appellants had no title, in short no act of ownership. The essential elements of liability in trover are lacking.

Even if it had positively appeared that at times the wrong bottle was returned to the person who left one for filling, it may be doubted whether that would amount to conversion, considering the purpose and nature of the transaction and the absence of any intent to affect the ownership, particularly the ownership of branded bottles.

The special facts of the delivery to the inspector under the *Pure Food Act* of the two bottles, I have reserved for separate consideration. If the respondent had meant to sell these bottles to the inspector, then, apart from the effect of the inspector's authority to act for the appellants, no doubt the delivery to him would involve a conversion. But even so, on the remaining findings, I cannot see that the transaction would have afforded any ground at all for an injunction. It would still remain an isolated instance of a sale and one made to a person in authority. It would afford no evidence of practice or likelihood of repetition. But it has been found that it was not a sale and, in the circumstances, it must be taken that there was no intention to transfer the property in the bottles or to impair the appellants' title to immediate possession. On the side of the inspector, he was obtaining them for the appellants, and, on the side of the respondent, he was giving them over to an official who demanded them in order to examine the wine. There was no conversion, and indeed, having regard to the inspector's employment to act for the appellants, the transaction could not amount to an actual wrong to property.

There remains the remedy for special damage sustained by the owner of a chattel who is out of possession. This was a special action on the case and does not depend on the plaintiff's having the immediate right to possession. More usually the action was brought by an owner whose right to possession was suspended. If the chattel was held upon a bailment for a term or until the fulfilment of a condition, it was the only action available to the bailor, if the chattel was damaged. The foundation of the action is the damage and "permanent" damage to the chattel must have occurred, that is damage which would enure to the "reversioner".

"Probably any temporary damage done while the plaintiff's possession was suspended by her contract with another person, is not the foundation of an action," per Pollock CB in *Tancred v* **[231]** *Allgood* (1859) 4 H & N 438, at p 444 [157 ER 910, at p 913]; cf per Williams J in *Mears v London and South Western Railway Co* (1862) 11 CB (NS) 850 at p 854 [142 ER 1029, at 1031].

Where the right to possession is not suspended the kind of damage of which the person out of possession but having an immediate right thereto is entitled to complain may no doubt be less lasting. But the chattel must have suffered some injury enuring to the detriment of the owner out of possession. Clearly no damage was done to the bottles. The use to which they were put was to clean them and to fill them with wine. When the customer consumed the wine with which the bottle had been replenished, the bottle resumed its former condition. But if an attempt were made to spell out of this some damage for which the appellants might complain at law, it would be, as it seems to me, quite misconceived. For this is a suit in equity and it would not be possible to base an injunction upon anything but either the repeated infringement of a legal right not depending upon special damage or, if the cause of action at law depended on special damage, then upon threatened loss having some reality, so much reality indeed as to demand equitable relief. In my opinion, however, no legal wrong is discoverable in what has been established against the respondent. ...

In point of policy there is no reason why the law should make it a civil wrong to put a chattel to some temporary and harmless use at the request and for the benefit of a person possessed of the chattel ... .

In my opinion there is no foundation for the injunction and other equitable relief sought by the appellants and their appeal should be dismissed.

Appeal dismissed

2. POSSESSION AND FINDING

Armory v Delamirie
(1722) 93 ER 664
Court of King's Bench, Pratt CJ

As between the finder of goods and a person to whom the finder delivers the goods for valuation, the finder has title to the goods.

The plaintiff being a chimney sweeper's boy found a jewel and carried it to the defendant's shop (who was a goldsmith) to know what it was, and delivered it into the hands of the apprentice, who under pretence of weighing it, took out the stones, and calling to the master to let him know it came to three halfpence, the master offered the boy the money, who refused to take it, and insisted to have the thing again; whereupon the apprentice delivered him back the socket without the stones. And now in trover [the technical name for the action for the tort of conversion] against the master these points were ruled:

1. That the finder of a jewel, though he does not by such finding acquire an absolute property or ownership, yet he has such a property as will enable him to keep it against all but the rightful owner, and consequently may maintain trover. ...

3. As to the value of the jewel several of the trade were examined to prove what a jewel of the finest water that would fit the socket would be worth; and the Chief Justice directed the jury, that unless the defendant did produce the jewel, and show it not to be of the finest water, they should presume the strongest against him, and make the value of the best jewels the measure of their damages: which they accordingly did.

Judgment for the plaintiff

Chairman, National Crime Authority v Flack
(1998) 156 ALR 501; [1998] FCA 932
Federal Court of Australia

As between the finder of goods and the occupier of private residential premises on which the goods are found, the occupier has title to the goods.

HEEREY J. [507] The respondent Margaret Elizabeth Flack (Mrs Flack) was the tenant of residential premises at 6 Broughton Street, Glebe. Police officers executed a search warrant on the premises and in so doing they discovered a locked briefcase which was found to contain $433,000 in cash. The search warrant was based on suspicion that Mrs Flack's son, Glen, had been involved in drug-related offences. However, no prosecutions were launched against him.

Mrs Flack brought a proceeding against the first appellant, the Chairperson of the National Crime Authority (NCA), and the second appellant, the Commonwealth of Australia. The trial judge (Hill J) ordered that the Commonwealth deliver up to Mrs Flack the briefcase and cash.

The Glebe premises
Mrs Flack at all material times was a weekly tenant under a residential tenancy agreement with the New South Wales Department of Housing. At the time of the events with which the case is concerned she was aged 55. She was the sole occupant of the premises and had lived alone there since the death of her husband in September 1990. Her son, Glen, who was aged 38, had a few clothes in a back room. According to Mrs Flack, he did not stay at the house but visited "about twice a week". Glen had a key to the house, as also did a Mr Sinclair who lived nearby and who was a close friend of Mrs Flack until he died on 24 February 1994. Her married daughter, Deborah Ann Nichols, had a key as well. Mrs Flack said the various persons who had keys used them "reasonably frequently" and might come into the house when she was not there.

The warrant
On 12 April 1994 a justice of the peace issued a warrant under s 10 of the *Crimes Act 1914* (Cth) to Detective Constable David Stewart of the Australian Federal Police. The justice recited that she was satisfied by information on oath [508] that there were reasonable grounds for suspecting that there were in or upon the Glebe premises things which satisfied all three of the following conditions: first, that the things were one or more of the following, namely, cannabis in leaf form or as cannabis resin, correspondence, diary entries, telephone indexes, messages, receipts, wrappings, money, weighing scales and customer and price lists; secondly, that the things related to Glen Flack; thirdly, that there were reasonable grounds for believing that the things would afford evidence as to the commission of the crime of being in possession of prohibited imports to which s 233B(1)(c) of the *Customs Act 1901* (Cth) applied, that is, narcotic goods reasonably suspected of having been imported into Australia. The warrant authorised the holder to enter at any time the Glebe premises and to seize the things which satisfied all of the three conditions.

Execution of the warrant
At about 8.20 am on 13 April 1994, Detective Stewart and four other police officers attended at the Glebe premises. They were admitted by Mrs Flack. Detective Stewart produced the warrant. The police officers asked Mrs Flack if she had a son named Glen Flack. Upon that being confirmed, they informed her that they had information that he may be storing narcotics in the house. A search of the house took place. During the latter part of the search Detective Stewart and another officer

searched a cupboard in an entrance hallway. In the lower portion of the cupboard were, among other things, an ironing board and a fold-up hammock. The police officers then opened the top half of the cupboard and removed what were described as a Balmain bag, a Balmain Fleggs bag and two travel bags, all of which were empty. When those bags were removed, a large-sized black briefcase was revealed. It was removed and found to be locked with a combination lock. The lock was forced and inside were seen a large number of bundles of Australian currency, predominantly $50 notes. The police officers then came into the hallway with Mrs Flack and showed her the black briefcase in a closed position. Detective Stewart asked her who owned the bag. Mrs Flack said: "I have never seen it before. I don't know whose it is." The police then opened the bag exposing the money inside. The following exchange took place:

MRS FLACK: Oh my God.

DETECTIVE STEWART: Is there anything else you can tell us about that?

MRS FLACK: No, nothing, I've never seen it before, I swear.

DETECTIVE STEWART (pointing to where the bag had been found): It was up there.

MRS FLACK: Well, I never go up there. I don't need to. That's what I use for the linen press there.

She indicated a nearby cupboard in use as a linen press. Mrs Flack said she had no idea how the briefcase came to be in the cupboard and that she had not seen her son with the bag. As to the other bags she said: "They're just old bags of Glen's and that one [indicating a travel bag] is mine. I used it when I travelled." She was asked: "Have you ever seen anyone go to this cupboard?" She said: "No, oh, hang on, only Tony who did the painting, but I don't know if he was there or not. I doubt it."

On 19 July 1994 Mrs Flack was examined before a member of the NCA. She was questioned about the cupboard in which the briefcase was found. The following took place:

[509] Q – Have you ever been up that high in the cupboard yourself? A – I'd say when I first moved into the house, when I first moved in there 12 to 13 years ago, when we put the bags and that up there to have somewhere to put things, but that's about the only time, that I'd ever ever been there.

Q – So there were other bags up there? A – Well, there were, yes. There was old football bags, etcetera, up there.

Q – Did you put them up there? A – Years ago I did. Yes.

Q – I am really asking you this to say that it was you, not your husband or someone else? A – Well, I put a few up there. I don't know if my husband put any up there, I wouldn't have a clue.

Q – The ones that you put up there, when were they put up there? A – When I first moved into the house about 12 or 13 years ago.

Q – And since that time have you had any occasion to go up there? A – No.

Q – To look up there? A – No.

Q – Or to take anything from there? A – No.

A Reserve Bank official gave evidence on affidavit that one of the banknotes in the briefcase had a Westpac Banking Corporation stamp dated 13 January 1994 and that another note was from a series first printed in April 1994.

The judgment below [(1997) 150 ALR 153]

After reciting the facts his Honour discussed well-known authorities and texts on possession, and in particular *Bridges v Hawkesworth* (1851) 21 LJQB 75; *South Staffordshire Water Co v Sharman* [1896] 2 QB 44; *Elwes v Brigg Gas Co* (1886) 33 ChD 562; *Willey v Synan* (1937) 57 CLR 200 and *Parker v British Airways Board* [1982] 1 QB 1004, together with Pollock and Wright's *Essay on Possession in the Common Law*, and Fleming's *The Law of Torts* (7th ed).

His Honour noted as to the events following the raid (at 156):

No action was thereafter taken by the Authority. No person was charged in respect of any offence. Requests on behalf of Mrs Flack that the Authority return the bag and money to her were initially met by the response that they might be needed in evidence. Now that some three and a half years have elapsed since the briefcase was seized [the trial and judgment were in November 1997] it is clear that this excuse can no longer be availed of by the Authority. At the hearing, and indeed only after the luncheon adjournment, the Authority by its counsel conceded that there was "no current operational necessity to retain the money". The Authority, however, maintains that it can retain the bag and money on the basis that Mrs Flack has not established a sufficient title to sue for it. Whether she has is thus the real issue for decision.

His Honour's conclusion and the reasoning for it appear from the following passage (at 162):

It follows, in my view, that the rights of an owner/occupier of premises where goods are found will prevail over the rights of a finder, irrespective of knowledge of the existence of the goods on the part of the owner/occupier and irrespective of an acceptance on the part of the owner/occupier of the obligation to exercise dominion over the goods so long as it can be shown that the owner/occupier manifested an intention to exercise control over the premises in which the goods are and all items in those premises. Such manifestation of intention will be presumed where the premises are residential premises of which the owner/occupier has exclusive possession.

Conversely, where the goods in question are found in a private residence a finder cannot assert a better title that the owner/occupier on the basis that the owner/occupier had no knowledge of the existence of the goods and, they not belonging to the **[510]** owner/occupier, he or she had not accepted an obligation to keep them safe. The owner/ occupier does not need to prove that he or she is the owner of the chattels, nor to prove who the owner is. This is the crux of the present case.

Conclusion on the appeal

Mrs Flack's case is that she manifested an intention to exercise control over any chattels on the Glebe premises, including chattels of whose existence she was not aware: JG Fleming, *The Law of Torts* (8th ed, 1992) Law Book Co, p 69.

The question has to be considered as at a point in time immediately prior to the discovery of the briefcase containing the cash. The issue is whether the occupier manifests a sufficient intention to control all chattels, known and unknown, which are on the premises, subject only to any superior right. Therefore one does not ask: "What was Mrs Flack's intention in relation to the large amount of cash?" All the cases which were contests between occupiers and finders were dealt with on the basis that the occupier was not aware of the existence of the chattel until the finder found it.

Since Mrs Flack was the tenant of an ordinary residential house she had possession in law of those premises. In the circumstances, that fact was sufficient to establish the requisite manifestation of intention to possess all chattels on the premises.

In *Parker v British Airways Board* [1982] 1 QB 1004 the English Court of Appeal had to consider the question of an occupier's intention in relation to the international executive lounge at Terminal One, Heathrow Airport. The plaintiff had found a gold bracelet lying on the floor of the lounge. Donaldson LJ said (at 1018) that, the bracelet not being a fixture, the defendants' claim must "... be based upon a manifest intention to exercise control over the lounge and all things which might be in it".

His Lordship concluded (at 1019):

It was suggested in argument that in some circumstances the intention of the occupier to assert control over articles lost on his premises speaks for itself. I think that this is right. If a bank manager saw fit to show me round a vault containing safe deposits and I found a gold bracelet on the floor, I should have no doubt that the bank had a better title than I, and the reason is the manifest intention to exercise a very high degree of control. At the other extreme is the park to which the public has unrestricted access during daylight hours. During those hours there is no manifest intention to exercise any such control. In between these extremes are the forecourts of petrol filling stations, unfenced front gardens of private houses, the public parts of shops and supermarkets as part of an almost infinite variety of land, premises and circumstances.

This lounge is in the middle band and in my judgment, on the evidence available, there was no sufficient manifestation of any intention to exercise control over lost property before it was found such as would give the defendants a right superior to that of the plaintiff or indeed any right over the bracelet. As the true owner has never come forward, it is a case of "finders keepers".

Eveleigh LJ said (at 1020):

A person permitted upon the property of another must respect the lawful claims of the occupier as the terms upon which he is allowed to enter, but it is only right that those claims or terms should be made clear. What is necessary to do this must depend on the circumstances. Take the householder. He has a key to the front door. People do not enter at will. They come by very special invitation. They are not members of a large public group, even a restricted group of the public, as users of the executive lounge may be. I would be inclined to say that the occupier of a house will almost invariably possess any lost article on the premises. He may not have taken any positive steps to [511] demonstrate his animus possidendi, but so firm is his control that the animus can be seen to attach to it. It is rather like the strong room of a bank, where I think it would be difficult indeed to suggest that a bracelet lying on the floor was not in the possession of the bank. The firmer the control, the less will be the need to demonstrate independently the animus possidendi.

Sir David Cairns said (at 1021):

I agree with both Donaldson LJ and Eveleigh LJ that, in a situation at all similar to that which we are considering, the occupier has a better claim than the finder only if he had possession of the article immediately before it was found and that this is only so (in the case of an article not *in* or *attached to* the land but only *on* it) when the occupier's intention to exercise control is manifest. I also agree that such an intention would probably be manifest in a private house or in a room to which access is very strictly controlled. Where the borderline should be drawn would be difficult to specify, but I am satisfied that this case falls on the wrong side of the borderline from the defendants' point of view [emphasis in original].

Thus all members of the Court of Appeal would readily accept that the occupier of a private home will ordinarily manifest the necessary intention to control chattels therein. In my respectful opinion that accords with common sense. I do not see that any different conclusion should be reached in the present case because Mrs Flack's son and daughter and her good friend, Mr Sinclair, had keys. The inference to be drawn is that keys given or lent by an occupier in such circumstances are provided for the recipients' ease of access and not for the purpose of conferring possessory rights over everything on the premises – at any rate not to the exclusion of, or on an equal basis with, the occupier. It would, for example, be an everyday occurrence for householders to give, or lend, or make available, keys to children, even children of primary school age. Similarly, an occupier may provide a key to guests, or to a house cleaner or other tradespeople.

The fact that the briefcase fairly obviously was not lost or mislaid but deliberately placed in the cupboard by the owner or previous possessor is a circumstance which makes no difference. There may be doubt as to whether it was hidden or cached. The cupboard was not locked. It was a logical place to store, or look for, such bags, irrespective of whether Mrs Flack often used it. Also, whoever put the briefcase there would presumably know that persons other than Mrs Flack had access to the house. And this person need not necessarily have known Mrs Flack did not use the cupboard. But in any event the authorities do not deny a possessory right to an occupier where the article in question has been hidden or deliberately placed on the premises: *Johnson v Pickering* [1907] 2 KB 437 at 444-5; *Re Cohen decd; National Provincial Bank Ltd v Katz* [1953] Ch 88.

If Mrs Flack manifested the necessary intention to control chattels on the premises, how do her rights compare or compete with those of the appellants? If the briefcase containing the cash had been found by a guest on the premises, or a thief, it could hardly be doubted that Mrs Flack would have a superior right. But as against the true owner, Mrs Flack would have to yield.

The police executing the warrant were clothed with statutory rights to seize and take away any property which satisfied the three conditions – regardless of whether any other person had possession, or indeed ownership. But at common law an article seized under warrant cannot be kept for any longer than is reasonably necessary for police to complete their investigations or preserve it for evidence. As Lord Denning MR said in *Ghani v Jones* [1970] 1 QB 693 at 709:

[512] As soon as the case is over, or it is decided not to go on with it, the article should be returned.

Section 3ZV of the *Crimes Act 1914* (Cth) now provides that a thing seized under warrant must be returned if:

the reason for its seizure no longer exists or it is decided that it is not to be used in evidence ... unless the thing is forfeited or forfeitable to the Commonwealth or is the subject of a dispute as to ownership.

Section 3ZV is in Pt 1AA, introduced by the *Crimes (Search Warrants and Powers of Arrest) Amendment Act 1994* (Cth), which did not come into force until after the issue and execution of the warrant in the present case. However, it would appear to be not relevantly different from the common law.

Therefore the appellants' rights to retain the goods taken from Mrs Flack's home ceased once it was conceded that those goods were not required for the purposes of further investigation or prosecution. The power to enter on private property and seize goods is a substantial interference with ordinary liberties and should not be extended beyond limits which the law prescribes: see *Levine v O'Keefe* [1930] VLR 70 at 72; *Challenge Plastics Pty Ltd v Collector of Customs* (1993) 42 FCR 397 at 402-9; 115 ALR 149.

Neither at common law nor under statute is there a general power of the State to forfeit goods simply because they appear "suspicious". The presence of a large amount of cash in a private home is certainly unusual. However, the explanation need not necessarily be criminal conduct on the part of the occupier. It could be an eccentric distrust of banks, or conduct that is unlawful or improper, but not criminal, such as concealment from the tax authorities or a spouse or creditor. Before the learned trial judge the appellants did not attempt to prove any connection between the money and Mrs Flack's son. At most there was the fact that, on some grounds not disclosed at the trial, there had at one stage been sufficient cause disclosed for a warrant to be issued. And, notwithstanding the finding of a large amount of cash in a house to which Mrs Flack's son had access, no proceedings were ever brought against him.

Counsel for the appellants submitted:

> Mrs Flack, having prevented a possible criminal charge against her son by denying knowledge of his possession and having avoided a charge against herself by denying her own possession, is not now entitled to claim possession of the bag and money, simply because the real possessor does not dare to claim the money.

It is not correct in my view to say that Mrs Flack denied possession. She certainly denied prior knowledge, and therefore, implicitly, ownership. However, in the circumstances she had no choice but to allow the police officers to take control of the goods, as they were then lawfully entitled to do. To speak of someone else as the "real possessor" begs the question. Mrs Flack was a real possessor since she was the occupier of a private house and is to be taken to have manifested an intention to control goods within the house. Somebody else was the true owner, and Mrs Flack could not resist a claim by that person to hand over the cash. If as a result such other person was at risk of prosecution and conviction for a criminal offence then the criminal law would have to take its course. ...

[513] The appeal should be dismissed with costs.

[Tamberlin J, in a separate judgment, agreed in general terms with Heerey J. Foster J delivered a dissenting judgment in which his Honour said:

[507] [T]his is a case where a person to whom Mrs Flack had provided means of access to her premises for lawful purposes has, contrary to the licence so bestowed, imposed upon Mrs Flack by depositing in her premises, in a manner that deliberately concealed the fact from her, goods which she would never have consented to take into her custody or control. In these circumstances, I am not prepared to find that possession of these goods in fact passed from the depositor of them to Mrs Flack. It remained with the depositor.]

Appeal dismissed

3. OWNER'S REVERSIONARY INTEREST

Mears v London and South Western Railway Company
(1862) 142 ER 1029
Court of Common Pleas

The owner of goods with no immediate right to possession during the term of a lease or bailment of the goods may bring an action on the case against a third party who has caused permanent damage to the goods, that is, permanent damage to the owner's reversionary interest.

[The plaintiff was the owner of a barge which he let on hire to Mr John Scott Russell "for a certain time". During the period of hire and while the barge was in the possession of the hirer, the defendants' employees, while attempting to raise a boiler out of the barge, negligently allowed the boiler to fall into and cause damage to the barge.]

> ERLE CJ. **[1031]** This is an action brought by the owner of a barge to recover damages for injury done to it by the negligence of the defendants' servants whilst it was out on hire to a third person. The question is, whether the owner of the barge has a right to maintain an action for that injury. In my opinion he has that right, the mere temporary outstanding interest in the hirer of the barge amounting to nothing. That trover will not lie for the conversion of a chattel out on loan, is clear: *Gordon v Harper* (1796) 7 TR 9. But, in *Tancred v Allgood* (1859) 4 H & N 438, it was by implication held that an action for a permanent injury done to a chattel while the owner's right to the possession is suspended, may be maintained. ...

> WILLIAMS J. I am of the same opinion. It is alleged in the [plaintiff's] declaration, and admitted by the [defendants'] demurrer, that the wrongful act of the defendants' servants has caused a permanent injury to the chattel of the plaintiff. It is true that the barge at the time was let out to Scott Russell for an unexpired term. But, subject to Scott Russell's temporary interest in it, the barge still remained the property of the plaintiff: and I see no reason why the plaintiff should not maintain the action. It seems to me ... to be clear that, though the owner cannot bring an action where there has been no permanent injury to the chattel, it has never been doubted that, where there *is* a permanent injury, the owner may maintain an action against the person whose wrongful act has caused that injury.

[Willes J concurred.]

Judgment for the plaintiff

["Permanent damage" in the context of *Mears v London and South Western Railway Company* (extracted above) means that, at the time of the owner's action, as in *Mears*, the damage to the goods has not been repaired. *Mears* was distinguished by the English Court of Appeal in *HSBC Rail (UK) Ltd v Network Rail Infrastructure Ltd* [2006] 1 All ER (Comm) 345 where, during the term of a lease of railway rolling stock by the owner to a train operating company, the rolling stock was destroyed or damaged in a derailment caused by the defendant's negligence. However, the owner of the rolling stock was held to have no action on the case for damage to its reversionary interest because the goods had been replaced or repaired in full by the lessee. In these circumstances the owner had suffered no relevant loss.]

Chapter 5

Negligence: Duty of Care

1. GENERAL PRINCIPLES

Donoghue v Stevenson
[1932] AC 562
House of Lords

The law concerns itself with carelessness only where there is a legal duty to take care. A person owes a legal duty to take reasonable care to avoid acts or omissions which he or she should reasonably have foreseen would be likely to injure his or her "neighbour", that is, another person "closely and directly affected" by that act or omission.

[The appellant (plaintiff) drank part of the contents of a bottle of ginger beer, manufactured by the respondent (defendant), which a friend had bought for her from a retailer. She alleged that the bottle contained the decomposed remains of a snail which could not, because the bottle was opaque, be detected before consumption. As a result she suffered from shock and severe gastro-enteritis. The case came before the House of Lords on the issue of law as to whether these averments disclosed a good cause of action].

LORD ATKIN. ... **[579]** It is remarkable how difficult it is to find in the English authorities statements of general application defining the relations between parties that give rise to the duty. The Courts are concerned with the particular relations which come before them in actual litigation, and it is sufficient to say whether the duty exists in those circumstances. The result is that the Courts have been engaged upon an elaborate classification of duties as they exist in respect of property, whether real or personal, with further divisions as to ownership, occupation or control, and distinctions based on the particular relations of the one side or the other, whether manufacturer, salesman or landlord, customer, tenant, stranger, and so on. **[580]** In this way it can be ascertained at any time whether the law recognizes a duty, but only where the case can be referred to some particular species which has been examined and classified. And yet the duty which is common to all the cases where liability is established must logically be based upon some element common to the cases where it is found to exist. To seek a complete logical definition of the general principle is probably to go beyond the function of the judge, for the more general the definition the more likely it is to omit essentials or to introduce non-essentials. The attempt was made by Brett MR in *Heaven v Pender* (1883) 11 QBD 503, 509, in a definition to which I will later refer. As framed, it was demonstrably too wide, though it appears to me, if properly limited, to be capable of affording a valuable practical guide.

At present I content myself with pointing out that in English law there must be, and is, some general conception of relations giving rise to a duty of care, of which the particular cases found in the books are but instances. The liability for negligence, whether you style it such or treat it as in other systems as a species of "culpa", is no doubt based upon a general public sentiment of moral wrongdoing for which the offender must pay. But acts or omissions which any moral code would censure cannot in a practical world be treated so as to give a right to every person injured by them to demand relief. In this way rules of law arise which limit the range of complainants and the extent of their remedy. The rule that you are to love your neighbour becomes in law, you must not injure your neighbour; and the lawyer's question, Who is my neighbour? receives a restricted reply. You must take reasonable care to avoid acts or omissions which you can reasonably foresee would be likely to injure your neighbour. Who, then, in law is my neighbour? The answer seems to be – persons who are so closely and directly affected by my act that I ought reasonably to have them in contemplation as being so affected when I am directing my mind to the acts or omissions which are called in question. This appears to me to be the doctrine of *Heaven v Pender* (1883) 11 QBD 503, 509 **[581]** as laid down by Lord Esher (then Brett MR) when it is limited by the notion of proximity introduced by Lord Esher himself and AL Smith LJ in *Le Lievre v Gould* [1893] 1 QB 491, 497, 604. Lord Esher says: "That case established that, under certain circumstances, one man may owe a duty to another, even though there is no contract between them. If one man is near to another, or is near to the property of another, a duty lies upon him not to do that which may cause a personal injury to that other, or may injure his property." So AL Smith LJ: "The decision of *Heaven v Pender* (1883) 11 QBD 503, 509 was founded upon the principle, that a duty to take due care did arise when the person or property of one was in such proximity to the person or property of another that, if due care was not taken, damage might be done by the one to the other." I think that this sufficiently states the truth if proximity be not confined to mere physical proximity, but be used, as I think it was intended, to extend to such close and direct relations that the act complained of directly affects a person whom the person alleged to be bound to take care would know would be directly affected by his careless act. That this is the sense in which nearness or "proximity" was intended by Lord Esher is obvious from his own illustration in *Heaven v Pender* (1883) 11 QBD 503, 510 of the application of his doctrine to the sale of goods. "This" (ie, the rule he has just formulated) "includes the case of goods, etc, supplied to be used immediately by a particular person or persons, or one of a class of persons, where it would be obvious to the person supplying, if he thought, that the goods would in all probability be used at once by such persons before a reasonable opportunity for discovering any defect which might exist, and where the thing supplied would be of such a nature that a neglect of ordinary care or skill as to its condition or the manner of supplying it would probably cause danger to the person or property of the person for whose use it was supplied, and who was about to use it. It would exclude a case in which the goods are supplied under circumstances in which it would be a chance by whom they would be used **[582]** or whether they would be used or not, or whether they would be used before there would probably be means of observing any defect, or where the goods would be of such a nature that a want of care or skill as to their condition or the manner of supplying them would not probably produce danger of injury to person or property." I draw particular attention to the fact that Lord Esher emphasizes the necessity of goods having to be "used immediately" and " used at once before a reasonable opportunity of inspection." This is obviously to exclude the possibility of goods having their condition altered by lapse of time, and to call attention to the proximate relationship, which may be too remote where inspection even of the person using, certainly of an intermediate person, may reasonably be interposed. With this necessary qualification of proximate relationship as explained in *Le Lievre v Gould* [1893] 1 QB 491, I think the judgment of Lord Esher expresses the law of England; without the qualification, I think the majority of the Court in *Heaven v Pender* (1883) 11 QBD 503 were justified in thinking the principle was expressed in too general terms. ...

[584] In my opinion several decided cases support the view that in such a case as the present the manufacturer owes a duty to the consumer to be careful.

[His Lordship then reviewed the authorities.]

[599] My Lords, if your Lordships accept the view that this pleading discloses a relevant cause of action you will be affirming the proposition that by Scots and English law alike a manufacturer of products, which he sells in such a form as to show that he intends them to reach the ultimate consumer in the form in which they left him with no reasonable possibility of intermediate examination, and with the knowledge that the absence of reasonable care in the preparation or putting up of the products will result in an injury to the consumer's life or property, owes a duty to the consumer to take that reasonable care. …

LORD MACMILLAN. … **[609]** It humbly appears to me that the diversity of view which is exhibited in such cases as *George v Skivington* (1869) LR 5 Ex 1 on the one hand and *Blacker v Lake & Elliot Ld* (1912) 106 LT 533, on the other hand – to take two extreme instances – is explained by the fact that in the discussion of the topic which now engages your Lordships' attention two rival principles of the law find a meeting place where each has contended for supremacy. On the one hand, there is the well established principle that no one other than a party to a contract can complain of a breach of that contract. On the other hand, there is the equally well established doctrine that negligence apart from contract gives a right of action to the party injured by that negligence – and here I use the term negligence, of course, in its technical legal **[610]** sense, implying a duty owed and neglected. The fact that there is a contractual relationship between the parties which may give rise to an action for breach of contract, does not exclude the co-existence of a right of action founded on negligence as between the same parties, independently of the contract, though arising out of the relationship in fact brought about by the contract. Of this the best illustration is the right of the injured railway passenger to sue the railway company either for breach of the contract of safe carriage or for negligence in carrying him. And there is no reason why the same set of facts should not give one person a right of action in contract and another person a right of action in tort. I may be permitted to adopt as my own the language of a very distinguished English writer on this subject. "It appears," says Sir Frederick Pollock, Law of Torts, 13th ed, p 570, "that there has been (though perhaps there is no longer) a certain tendency to hold that facts which constitute a contract cannot have any other legal effect. The authorities formerly relied on for this proposition really proved something different and much more rational, namely, that if A breaks his contract with B (which may happen without any personal default in A or A's servants), that is not of itself sufficient to make A liable to C, a stranger to the contract, for consequential damage. This, and only this, is the substance of the perfectly correct decisions of the Court of Exchequer in *Winterbottom v Wright* (1842) 10 M&W 109 and *Longmeid v Holliday* (1851) 6 Ex 761. In each case the defendant delivered, under a contract of sale or hiring, a chattel which was in fact unsafe to use, but in the one case it was not alleged, in the other was alleged but not proved, to have been so to his knowledge. In each case a stranger to the contract, using the chattel – a coach in the one case, a lamp in the other – in the ordinary way, came to harm through its dangerous condition, and was held not to have any cause of action against the purveyor. Not in contract, for there was no contract between these parties; not in tort, for no bad faith or negligence on the defendant's part was proved."

[611] Where, as in cases like the present, so much depends upon the avenue of approach to the question, it is very easy to take the wrong turning. If you begin with the sale by the manufacturer to the retail dealer, then the consumer who purchases from the retailer is at once seen to be a stranger to the contract between the retailer and the manufacturer and so disentitled to sue upon it. There is no contractual relation between the manufacturer and the consumer; and thus the plaintiff, if he is to succeed, is driven to try to bring himself within one or other of the exceptional cases where the strictness of the rule that none but a party to a contract can found on a breach of that contract has been mitigated in the public interest, as it has been in the case of a person who issues a chattel which is inherently dangerous or which he knows to be in a dangerous condition. If, on the other hand, you disregard the fact that the circumstances of the case at one stage include the existence of a contract of sale between the manufacturer and the retailer, and approach the question by asking whether there is evidence of carelessness on the part of the manufacturer, and whether he owed a duty to be careful in a question with the party who has been injured in consequence of his want of care, the circumstance that the injured party was not a party to the incidental contract of sale becomes irrelevant, and his title to sue the manufacturer is unaffected by that circumstance. The appellant in the present instance asks that her case be approached as a case of delict, not as a case of breach of contract. She does not require to invoke the exceptional cases in which a person not a party to a contract has been held to be entitled to complain of some defect in the subject-matter of the contract which has caused him harm. ...

[His Lordship then reviewed the authorities.]

[618] The law takes no cognizance of carelessness in the abstract. It concerns itself with carelessness only where there is a duty to take care and where failure in that duty has caused damage. In such circumstances carelessness assumes the [619] legal quality of negligence and entails the consequences in law of negligence. What, then, are the circumstances which give rise to this duty to take care? In the daily contacts of social and business life human beings are thrown into, or place themselves in, an infinite variety of relations with their fellows; and the law can refer only to the standards of the reasonable man in order to determine whether any particular relation gives rise to a duty to take care as between those who stand in that relation to each other. The grounds of action may be as various and manifold as human errancy; and the conception of legal responsibility may develop in adaptation to altering social conditions and standards. The criterion of judgment must adjust and adapt itself to the changing circumstances of life. The categories of negligence are never closed. The cardinal principle of liability is that the party complained of should owe to the party complaining a duty to take care, and that the party complaining should be able to prove that he has suffered damage in consequence of a breach of that duty. Where there is room for diversity of view, it is in determining what circumstances will establish such a relationship between the parties as to give rise, on the one side, to a duty to take care, and on the other side to a right to have care taken.

To descend from these generalities to the circumstances of the present case, I do not think that any reasonable man or any twelve reasonable men would hesitate to hold that, if the appellant establishes her allegations, the respondent has exhibited carelessness in the conduct of his business. For a manufacturer of aerated water to store his empty bottles in a place where snails can get access to them, and to fill his bottles without taking any adequate precautions by inspection or otherwise to ensure that they contain no deleterious foreign matter, may reasonably be characterized as carelessness without applying too exacting a standard. But, as I have pointed out, it is not enough to prove the respondent to be careless in his process of manufacture. The question is: Does he owe a duty to take care, and to whom [620] does he owe that duty? Now I have no hesitation in affirming that a person who for gain engages in the business of manufacturing articles of food and drink intended for consumption by members of the public in the form in which he issues them is under a duty to take care in the manufacture of these articles. That duty, in my opinion, he owes to those whom he intends to consume his products. He manufactures his commodities for human consumption; he intends and contemplates that they shall be consumed. By reason of that very fact he places himself in a relationship with all the potential consumers of his commodities, and that relationship which he assumes and desires for his own ends imposes upon him a duty to take care to avoid injuring them. He owes them a duty not to convert by his own carelessness an article which he issued to them as wholesome and innocent into an article which is dangerous to life and health. ...

[Lord Thankerton delivered a judgment in which he concurred with Lord Atkin. Lord Buckmaster and Lord Tomlin dissented.]

Interlocutor reversed

Home Office v Dorset Yacht Co Ltd
[1970] AC 1004
House of Lords

A defendant may have a duty to supervise third parties and be liable for damage to the plaintiff's property caused by the conduct of the third party which is the very kind of thing that is likely to happen if the duty is breached.

LORD DIPLOCK. [1057] My Lords, this appeal is about the law of negligence. Regrettably, as I think, it comes before your Lordships' House upon a preliminary question of law which is said to arise upon the facts pleaded in the statement of claim. This makes it necessary to identify the precise question of law raised by those facts which are very summarily pleaded. Some of them relate to the acts of seven youths undergoing sentences of Borstal training; others relate to the acts and omissions of persons concerned in the management of Borstals and, in particular, to the acts and omissions of three officers of the Portland Borstal.

It is alleged and conceded that the defendant, the Home Office, is vicariously responsible for the tortious acts of the three Borstal officers and any other persons concerned in the management of Borstals. It is not contended that the Home Office is vicariously liable for any tortious acts of the youths undergoing sentences of Borstal training.

At the relevant time, the seven youths were taking part in a working party on Brownsea Island in the custody and control of the three officers. One night the youths escaped from the island and caused damage to the plaintiffs' yacht which was moored off-shore of the island. In causing the damage the youths were themselves guilty of trespass to the plaintiffs' goods.

The three officers did not take any or any effective steps to prevent the youths from escaping from the island. Although it is not stated in express terms, it is implicit in the language of the pleading that by the time the youths committed the damage they had successfully eluded the custody and control of the officers and had reached a place where it was not physically possible for the officers or anyone concerned with the management of Borstals to exercise any control over the youths' actions.

The only cause of action relied upon is the "negligence" of the officers in failing to prevent the youths from escaping from their custody and control.

It is implicit in this averment of "negligence" and must be treated as admitted not only that the officers by taking reasonable care could have prevented the youths from escaping but also that it was reasonably foreseeable by them that if the youths did escape they would be likely to commit damage of the kind which they did commit to some craft moored in the vicinity of Brownsea Island.

The specific question of law raised in this appeal may therefore be **[1058]** stated as: Is any duty of care to prevent the escape of a Borstal trainee from custody owed by the Home Office to persons whose property would be likely to be damaged by the tortious acts of the Borstal trainee if he escaped?

This is the first time that this specific question has been posed at a higher judicial level than that of a county court. Your Lordships in answering it will be performing a judicial function similar to that performed in *Donoghue v Stevenson* [1932] AC 562 and more recently in *Hedley Byrne & Co Ltd v Heller & Partners Ltd* [1964] AC 465 of deciding whether the English law of civil wrongs should be extended to impose legal liability to make reparation for the loss caused to another by conduct of a kind which has not hitherto been recognised by the courts as entailing any such liability.

This function, which judges hesitate to acknowledge as law-making, plays at most a minor role in the decision of the great majority of cases, and little conscious thought has been given to analysing its methodology. Outstanding exceptions are to be found in the speeches of Lord Atkin in *Donoghue v Stevenson* and of Lord Devlin in *Hedley Byrne & Co Ltd v Heller & Partners Ltd*. It was because the former was the first authoritative attempt at such an analysis that it has had so seminal an effect upon the modern development of the law of negligence.

It will be apparent that I agree with the Master of the Rolls that what we are concerned with in this appeal "is ... at bottom a matter of public policy which we, as judges, must resolve." He cited in support Lord Pearce's dictum in *Hedley Byrne & Co Ltd v Heller & Partners Ltd* [1964] AC 465, 536:

How wide the sphere of the duty of care in negligence is to be laid depends ultimately upon the courts' assessment of the demands of society for protection from the carelessness of others.

The reference in this passage to "the courts" in the plural is significant, for

As always in English law, the first step in such an inquiry is to see how far the authorities have gone, for new categories in the law do not spring into existence overnight (*per* Lord Devlin, at p 525).

The justification of the courts' role in giving the effect of law to the judges' conception of the public interest in the field of negligence is based upon the cumulative experience of the judiciary of the actual consequences of lack of care in particular instances. And the judicial development of the law of negligence rightly proceeds by seeking first to identify the relevant characteristics that are common to the kinds of conduct and relationship between the parties which are involved in the case for decision and the kinds of conduct and relationships which have been held in previous decisions of the courts to give rise to a duty of care.

The method adopted at this stage of the process is analytical and inductive. It starts with an analysis of the characteristics of the conduct and relationship involved in each of the decided cases. But the analyst must know what he is looking for, and this involves his approaching his analysis with some general conception of conduct and relationships which **[1059]** ought to give rise to a duty of care. This analysis leads to a proposition which can be stated in the form:

In all the decisions that have been analysed a duty of care has been held to exist wherever the conduct and the relationship possessed each of the characteristics A, B, C, D, etc, and has not so far been found to exist when any of these characteristics were absent.

For the second stage, which is deductive and analytical, that proposition is converted to: "In all cases where the conduct and relationship possess each of the characteristics A, B, C, D, etc, a duty of care arises." The conduct and relationship involved in the case for decision is then analysed to ascertain whether they possess each of these characteristics. If they do the conclusion follows that a duty of care does arise in the case for decision.

But since ex hypothesi the kind of case which we are now considering offers a choice whether or not to extend the kinds of conduct or relationships which give rise to a duty of care, the conduct or relationship which is involved in it will lack at least one of the characteristics A, B, C or D, etc. And the choice is exercised by making a policy decision as to whether or not a duty of care ought to exist if the characteristic which is lacking were absent or redefined in terms broad enough to include the case under consideration. The policy decision will be influenced by the same general conception of what ought to give rise to a duty of care as was used in approaching the analysis. The choice to extend is given effect to by redefining the characteristics in more general terms so as to exclude the necessity to conform to limitations imposed by the former definition which are considered to be inessential. The cases which are landmarks in the common law, such as *Lickbarrow v Mason* (1787) 2 Term Rep 63, *Rylands v Fletcher* (1868) LR 3 HL 330, *Indermaur v Dames* (1866) LR 1 CP 274, *Donoghue v Stevenson* [1932] AC 562, to mention but a few, are instances of cases where the cumulative experience of judges has led to a restatement in wide general terms of characteristics of conduct and relationships which give rise to legal liability.

Inherent in this methodology, however, is a practical limitation which is imposed by the sheer volume of reported cases. The initial selection of previous cases to be analysed will itself eliminate from the analysis those in which the conduct or relationship involved possessed characteristics which are obviously absent in the case for decision. The proposition used in the deductive stage is not a true universal. It needs to be qualified so as to read:

In all cases where the conduct and relationship possess each of the characteristics A, B, C and D, etc *but do not possess any of the characteristics Z, Y or X etc which were present in the cases eliminated from the analysis*, a duty of care arises.

But this qualification, being irrelevant to the decision of the particular case, is generally left unexpressed.

This was the reason for the warning by Lord Atkin in *Donoghue v Stevenson* [1932] AC 562, itself when he said, at pp 583-584:

... in the branch of the law which deals with civil wrongs, **[1060]** dependent in England at any rate entirely upon the application by judges of general principles also formulated by judges, it is of particular importance to guard against the danger of stating propositions of law in wider terms than is necessary, lest essential factors be omitted in the wider survey and the inherent adaptability of English law be unduly restricted. For this reason it is very necessary in considering reported cases in the law of torts that the actual decision alone should carry authority, proper weight, of course, being given to the dicta of the judges.

The plaintiff's argument in the present appeal disregards this warning. It seeks to treat as a universal not the specific proposition of law in *Donoghue v Stevenson* which was about a manufacturer's liability for damage caused by his dangerous products but the well-known aphorism used by Lord Atkin to describe a "general conception of relations giving rise to a duty of care" ([1932] AC 562, 580):

You must take reasonable care to avoid acts or omissions which you can reasonably foresee would be likely to injure your neighbour. Who, then, in law is my neighbour? The answer seems to be – persons who are so closely and directly affected by my act that I ought reasonably to have them in contemplation as being so affected when I am directing my mind to the acts or omissions which are called in question.

Used as a guide to characteristics which will be found to exist in conduct and relationships which give rise to a legal duty of care this aphorism marks a milestone in the modern development of the law of negligence. But misused as a universal it is manifestly false.

The branch of English law which deals with civil wrongs abounds with instances of acts and, more particularly, of omissions which gave rise to no legal liability in the doer or omitter for loss or damage sustained by others as a consequence of the act or omission, however reasonably or probably that loss or damage might have been anticipated. The very parable of the good Samaritan (Luke 10, v 30) which was evoked by Lord Atkin in *Donoghue v Stevenson* illustrates, in the conduct of the priest and of the Levite who passed by on the other side, an omission which was likely to have as its reasonable and probable consequence damage to the health of the victim of the thieves, but for which the priest and Levite would have incurred no civil liability in English law. Examples could be multiplied. You may cause loss to a tradesman by withdrawing your custom though the goods which he supplies are entirely satisfactory; you may damage your neighbour's land by intercepting the flow of percolating waters to it even though the interception is of no advantage to yourself; you need not warn him of a risk of physical danger to which he is about to expose himself unless there is some special relationship between the two of you such as that of occupier of land and visitor; you may watch your neighbour's goods being ruined by a thunderstorm though the slightest effort on your part could protect them from the rain and you may do so with impunity unless there is some special relationship between you such as that of bailor and bailee.

[1061] In *Hedley Byrne & Co Ltd v Heller & Partners Ltd* [1964] AC 465, which marked a fresh development in the law of negligence, the conduct in question was careless words, not careless deeds. Lord Atkin's aphorism, if it were of universal application, would have sufficed to dispose of that case, apart from the express disclaimer of liability. But your Lordships were unanimous in holding that the difference in the characteristics of the conduct in the two cases prevented the propositions of law in *Donoghue v Stevenson* from being directly applicable. Your Lordships accordingly proceeded to analyse the previous decisions in which the conduct complained of had been careless words, from which you induced a proposition of law about liability for damage caused by careless words which differs from the proposition of law in *Donoghue v Stevenson* about liability for damage caused by careless deeds.

In the present appeal, too, the conduct of the defendant which is called in question differs from the kind of conduct discussed in *Donoghue v Stevenson* in at least two special characteristics. First, the actual damage sustained by the plaintiff was the direct consequence of a tortious act done with conscious volition by a third party responsible in law for his own acts and this act was interposed between the act of the defendant complained of and the sustention of damage by the plaintiff. Secondly, there are two separate "neighbour relationships" of the defendant involved, a relationship with the plaintiff and a relationship with the third party. These are capable of giving rise to conflicting duties of care.

This appeal, therefore, also raises the lawyer's question: "Am I my brother's keeper?" A question which may also receive a restricted reply.

I start, therefore, with an examination of the previous cases in which both or one of these special characteristics are present. ...

[His Lordship then examined the case law.]

[1063] From the previous decisions of the English courts, in particular those in *Ellis v Home Office* [1953] 2 All ER 149 and *D'Arcy v Prison Commissioners*, "The Times," November 17, 1955, which I accept as correct, it is possible to arrive by induction at an established proposition of law as respects one of those special relations, viz:

A is responsible for damage caused to the person or property of B by the tortious act of C (a person responsible in law for his own acts) where the relationship between A and C has the characteristics (1) that A has the legal right to detain C in penal custody and to control his acts while in custody; (2) that A is actually exercising his legal right of custody of C at the time of C's tortious act and (3) that A if he had taken reasonable care in the exercise of his right of custody could have prevented C from doing the tortious act which caused damage to the person or property of B; and where also the relationship between A and B has the characteristics (4) that at the time of C's tortious act A has the legal right to control the situation of B or his property as respects physical proximity to C and (5) that A can **[1064]** reasonably foresee that B is likely to sustain damage to his person or property if A does not take reasonable care to prevent C from doing tortious acts of the kind which he did.

Upon the facts which your Lordships are required to assume for the purposes of the present appeal the relationship between the defendant, A, and the Borstal trainee, C, did possess characteristics (1) and (3) but did not possess characteristic (2), while the relationship between the defendant, A, and the plaintiff, B, did possess characteristic (5) but did not possess characteristic (4).

What your Lordships have to decide as respects each of the relationships is whether the missing characteristic is essential to the existence of the duty or whether the facts assumed for the purposes of this appeal disclose some other characteristic which if substituted for that which is missing would produce a new proposition of law which *ought* to be true.

As any proposition which relates to the duty of controlling another man to prevent his doing damage to a third deals with a category of civil wrongs of which the English courts have hitherto had little experience it would not be consistent with the methodology of the development of the law by judicial decision that any new proposition should be stated in wider terms than are necessary for the determination of the present appeal. Public policy may call for the immediate recognition of a new sub-category of relations which are the source of a duty of this nature additional to the sub-category described in the established proposition, but further experience of actual cases would be needed before the time became ripe for the coalescence of sub-categories into a broader category of relations giving rise to the duty, such as was effected with respect to the duty of care of a manufacturer of products in *Donoghue v Stevenson* [1932] AC 562. Nevertheless, any new sub-category will form part of the English law of civil wrongs and must be consistent with its general principles. ...

[1070] I should therefore hold that any duty of a Borstal officer to use reasonable care to prevent a Borstal trainee from escaping from his custody was owed only to persons whom he could reasonably foresee had property **[1071]** situate in the vicinity of the place of detention of the detainee which the detainee was likely to steal or to appropriate and damage in the course of eluding immediate pursuit and recapture. Whether or not any person fell within this category would depend upon the facts of the particular case including the previous criminal and escaping record of the individual trainee concerned and the nature of the place from which he escaped. ...

If, therefore, it can be established at the trial of this action (1) that the Borstal officers in failing to take precautions to prevent the trainees from escaping were acting in breach of their instructions and not in bona fide exercise of a discretion delegated to them by the Home Office as to the degree of control to be adopted and (2) that it was reasonably foreseeable by the officers that if these particular trainees did escape they would be likely to appropriate a boat moored in the vicinity of Brownsea Island for the purpose of eluding immediate pursuit and to cause damage to it, the Borstal officers would be in breach of a duty of care owed to the plaintiff and the plaintiff would, in my view, have a cause of action against the Home Office as vicariously liable for the "negligence" of the Borstal officers.

I would accordingly dismiss the appeal upon the preliminary issue of law and allow the case to go for trial on those issues of fact.

[Lord Reid, Lord Morris of Borth-y-Gest and Lord Pearson delivered concurring judgments. Viscount Dilhorne dissented.]

Appeal dismissed

Graham Barclay Oysters Pty Ltd v Ryan
Ryan v Great Lakes Council
New South Wales v Ryan
(2002) 211 CLR 540; [2002] HCA 54
High Court of Australia

Perhaps after 70 years of judicial consideration of the test for determining the existence of a duty of care, Australian law has returned to the fundamental principle that "a duty of care will be imposed when it is reasonable in all the circumstances to do so".

[These three cases, heard together, arose out of the contamination by polluted run-off of oysters being cultivated in Wallis Lake, New South Wales, by Graham Barclay Oysters Pty Ltd. Mr Grant Ryan, a consumer of the oysters, contracted hepatitis A after eating them. The principal question in the High Court of Australia was whether the local council in the Wallis Lake area, Great Lakes Council, and the State of New South Wales as public authorities owed Mr Ryan a relevant common law duty of care, a question answered by the Court in the negative. A majority of the Court (Gaudron, McHugh, Gummow and Hayne JJ; Gleeson CJ, Kirby and Callinan JJ dissenting) also held there had been no breach of the duty of care which Graham Barclay Oysters Pty Ltd owed Mr Ryan. In the result, the High Court allowed the appeals by Graham Barclay Oysters Pty Ltd and the State of New South Wales from judgments of the Full Court of the Federal Court in favour of Mr Ryan and upheld the judgment of that court which had negatived any relevant duty of care owed by Great Lakes Council to Mr Ryan. In the following extract, Kirby J discusses the "search for a methodology" for determining the existence of a duty of care in modern Australian tort law.]

KIRBY J. (some footnotes omitted) **[622]** 229. **Search for a methodology**: Actions at common law for negligence probably still constitute the largest segment of civil litigation before Australian courts. It is therefore natural, and efficient if it be possible, for the law to afford a methodology or approach to such cases where liability is in dispute. ...

230. There are certain "standard questions" (*Romeo v Conservation Commission (NT)* (1998) 192 CLR 431 at 475) that dissect the composite notion of common law liability in negligence. Relevantly, those questions analyse the concept in terms of: (1) the duty of care; (2) the scope of the duty; (3) the breach; and (4) the causation of damage. Although these issues are commonly considered separately, it has been pointed out many times that "each element can be defined only in terms of the others" (*John Pfeiffer Pty Ltd v Canny* (1981) 148 CLR 218 at 241-242) and, for example, that "the actual nature of the damage suffered is relevant to the existence and extent of any duty to avoid or prevent it" (*Sutherland Shire Council v Heyman* (1985) 157 CLR 424 at 487). These words teach an important lesson. Excessive analysis and undue intellectual subdivision of what is basically a unitary concept can lead a decision-maker into over-sophisticated elaboration of a notion that is, at its heart, a reflection of practicality and common sense. Long ago and far away, Oliver **[623]** Wendell Holmes Jr said, correctly, that "the general foundation of legal liability in blameworthiness, as determined by the existing average standards of the community, should always be kept in mind" (*The Common Law* (1882), p 125). Although that was said years before Lord Atkin wrote his speech in *Donoghue v Stevenson* [1932] AC 562, it is reflected in what his Lordship said there at (580):

> The liability for negligence ... is no doubt based upon a general public sentiment of moral wrongdoing for which the offender must pay. But acts or omissions which any moral code would censure cannot in a practical world be treated so as to give a right to every person injured by them to demand relief. In this way rules of law arise which limit the range of complainants and the extent of their remedy.

231. **The *Caparo* three-stage test**: Whilst Lord Atkin in *Donoghue v Stevenson*, building on earlier judicial attempts, propounded a unifying concept for liability in negligence at common law,

and specifically for the circumstances giving rise to a legally enforceable duty of care, the defect in his analysis and in its acceptance in later cases as a "general unifying proposition" (*Burnie Port Authority v General Jones Pty Ltd* (1994) 179 CLR 520 at 541) or "statement of principle" (*Home Office v Dorset Yacht Co Ltd* [1970] AC 1004 at 1027) is the generality, even circularity, of the touchstone for defining the "neighbour" relationship (*Donoghue v Stevenson* [1932] AC 562 at 580). The decision in *Donoghue v Stevenson* inevitably gave rise to attempted refinement, so as to retain the advantages of a unifying concept but to flesh out the detail concerning the manner of its application.

232. A major attempt in that direction was made in England in *Anns v Merton London Borough Council* [1978] AC 728. Subsequently, the two-stage test expressed in that case was expanded by the House of Lords in *Caparo Industries Plc v Dickman* [1990] 2 AC 605. That decision was interpreted as establishing a settled approach. In order to decide whether a legal duty of care existed, the decision-maker was obliged to ask three questions. These were: (1) whether it was reasonably foreseeable to the alleged tortfeasor that the particular conduct or omission would be likely to cause harm to a person such as the claimant; (2) whether between that tortfeasor and the claimant a relationship existed that could be characterised as one of "proximity" or "neighbourhood"; and (3) if so, whether it was fair, just and reasonable that the law should impose a duty of a given scope upon that tortfeasor for the benefit of that person.

[624] 233. The *Caparo* test, sometimes worded in slightly different ways, continues to be applied in England. Variants of it are applied in other Commonwealth countries. ...

234. **Competing Australian approaches**: Whilst these developments were occurring in other common law countries, Australian courts, led by this Court, continued with their attempts to propound alternative and different tests for establishing the existence of a duty of care. It was obvious that "foreseeability" alone was insufficient to give rise to the potentially onerous obligations of a legal duty to act. Hence the experiments with other concepts such as "proximity" (*Sutherland Shire Council v Heyman* (1985) 157 CLR 424; *Burnie Port Authority v General Jones Pty Ltd* (1994) 179 CLR 520; *Bryan v Maloney* (1995) 182 CLR 609) and "reliance" – including the fiction of "general reliance" (cf *Pyrenees Shire Council v Day* (1998) 192 CLR 330).

235. One by one these attempts, by single or multiple verbal concepts, to encapsulate what was intended when the law imposed a duty of care, collapsed under the demonstration of the inadequacy of the propounded words to perform all of the functions expected of them. ...

236. **Possible resolution**: During the past five years, after "foreseeability", "proximity" and "general reliance" were rejected by this Court as concepts sufficient to establish a duty of care, a contest emerged as to what would replace them. As I view the cases, at least two approaches or "methodologies" for discerning the existence of a duty of care emerged in this Court's decisions. They were locked in mortal combat, intellectually speaking. They were:

(1) The adoption in this country of the three-stage test proposed in England in *Caparo*. ... [625]; and

(2) The adoption of a notion that a range of other factors, sometimes called "salient factors", must be considered in order to determine the existence of a duty of care in a particular case (*Perre v Apand Pty Ltd* (1999) 198 CLR 180 at 253). ...

237. **Choosing the new approach**: In 2001 in *Sullivan v Moody* (2001) 207 CLR 562 an appeal in which I did not participate, five members of this Court, in a unanimous joint opinion, rejected the three-stage test for a duty of care propounded in *Caparo*. ... [626] The flaw in the *Caparo* approach, discerned in the joint reasons in *Sullivan*, was that the question of liability might be "reduced to a discretionary judgment based upon a sense of what is fair, and just and reasonable as an outcome in the particular care" (*Sullivan* at 579). That, it was concluded, would introduce into judicial decision-making an unacceptable unpredictability based on an inappropriate methodology. ...

[627] 239. The resulting test: ...

240. The development of an approach, hinted at by me in *Pyrenees* [*Shire Council v D*ay] (1998) 192 CLR 330 at 416-417, may provide an answer. The statements I made there acknowledged that the verbal attempts at identifying particular criteria for distinguishing cases where a duty of

care existed (and where it did not) had failed; that candid policy evaluation was uncongenial to Australian judges or considered inappropriate; and that liability should therefore be imposed where it was judged that a reasonable person in the defendant's position *could* have avoided damage by exercising reasonable care and was in such a relationship to the plaintiff that he or she *ought* to have acted to do so. Despite its overt circularity, this formulation might at least offer a return to the substance of Lord Atkin's speech in *Donoghue v Stevenson*. It might afford a broad formula that poses a factual (or jury) question and avoids the chaos into which other attempted formulae have lately led the law.

241. In similar terms, Priestly JA in *Avenhouse v Hornsby Shire Council* (1998) 44 NSWLR 1 at 8 was moved to remark in the New South Wales Court of Appeal:

> Courts ... decide, in case after case, whether or not a duty of care exists in new situations. Consideration of all the cases of authority to date leads me to the view that the position in Australia ... has returned to (or recognised the continuing applicability of) what it was immediately after the decision in *Donoghue v Stevenson*; that is, that the courts make decisions by first asking the question 'is the relationship between plaintiff and defendant in the instant case so close that a duty arose?' and then answering 'yes' or 'no' in light of the court's own experience-based judgment.

242. The difficulty with this formulation is that the reference in it to the [628] relationship of the parties as one "so close that a duty arose" could quite easily slip back into the discredited notion that "proximity", alone, is a sufficient criterion for the assignment of a legal duty. However, so long as the "closeness" of the relationship contemplated is not confined to physical closeness, I see no great difficulty now (and some advantage) in leaving the features of the "relationship" of "neighbourhood" undefined and simply asking whether, in all the circumstances, it is such as to make it "reasonable to impose upon the one a duty of care to the other" (*Pyrenees* at 416). This is always the ultimate question that must be answered in all cases of a disputed duty of care in negligence. ...

244. ... The search for such a simple formula [for determining the existence of a duty of care] may indeed be a "will-o'-the wisp" (*Caparo Industries Plc v Dickman* [1990] 2 AC 605 at 632-633, per Lord Oliver of Aylmerton). It may send those who pursue it around in never-ending circles that ultimately bring the traveller back to the very point at which the journey began. Thus we [629] seem to have returned to the fundamental test for imposing a duty of care, which arguably explains all the attempts made so far. That is, a duty of care will be imposed when it is reasonable in all the circumstances to do so. That is the test that Gummow J and I adopted in our joint reasons in the recent decision in *Tame v New South Wales* (2002) 211 CLR 317 decided after *Sullivan*. Even if the approach of the other members of the Court in that case does not do so explicitly, it is obvious that the "touchstone" of reasonableness is fundamental to the way in which they determined the existence or otherwise of a duty of care (*Tame* at 337, per Gleeson CJ; at 357, per McHugh J; at 410, per Hayne J; at 429, per Callinan J). So after seventy years the judicial wheel has, it seems, come full circle. ...

Graham Barclay Oysters Pty Ltd v Ryan
Appeal allowed in so far as it concerns negligence

Ryan v Great Lakes Council
Appeal dismissed

New South Wales v Ryan
Appeal allowed

2. POLICY-BASED EXCLUSIONS

Giannarelli v Wraith
(1988) 165 CLR 543
High Court of Australia

A barrister does not owe a duty of care to his or her client in respect of the conduct of a case in court.

MASON CJ. [553] The issue in these appeals is whether a Victorian barrister is liable in negligence to his clients who were tried and convicted of perjury, the negligence alleged being his failure to advise them that they had a good defence to the proceedings and his failure to object to certain inadmissible evidence tendered by the Crown. The evidence was essential to the Crown case. ...

The first three appellants [the plaintiffs Emilio, Mario and Giovanni Giannarelli] ... were charged and convicted of perjury under s 314 of the *Crimes Act 1958* (Vic) as a result of evidence which they gave to the Commonwealth and Victorian Royal Commission into the Federated Ship Painters' and Dockers' Union. The first appellant was released on a bond; the second and third appellants were sentenced to imprisonment. The first appellant did not appeal. The second and third appellants appealed unsuccessfully to the Court of Criminal Appeal. They then applied for special leave to appeal to this Court. Their application was successful, their appeal was allowed and their convictions were quashed: see *Giannarelli v The Queen* (1983) 154 CLR 212. The appeal succeeded on the ground that s 6DD of the [554] *Royal Commissions Act 1902* (Cth) rendered the evidence given by the three appellants in the Royal Commission inadmissible in the criminal proceedings. ...

The question whether the respondents [three Victorian barristers who had represented the Giannarellis] could be liable in negligence in the circumstances just outlined was argued as a preliminary question of law. At first instance Marks J held that the respondents were not immune from liability in negligence by reason of s 10(2) of the *Legal Profession Practice Act 1958* (Vic) ("the 1958 Act"). The Full Court (Young CJ, Crockett and Fullagar JJ) came to a different conclusion and allowed the respondents' appeal. The present appeal is brought from the order of the Full Court.

The appellants' case is that s 10(2) of the 1958 Act imposes liability on the respondents for negligence and that, in the alternative, the respondents are subject to a common law duty of care. It is convenient to consider, first, the argument that the respondents are subject to a common law duty of care. That consideration may throw some light on the interpretation of the statute. ...

[555] The immunity of the barrister from liability in negligence to his client, at least in respect of court work, is supported by powerful authority, ancient and modern, in England, Scotland and Ireland: see *Rondel v Worsley* [1969] 1 AC 191, at pp 240-244, 258-263, 277-279, 288-289; *Saif Ali v Sydney Mitchell & Co* [1980] AC 198. ...

Various explanations for the barrister's immunity have been advanced. Historically it has been linked to the barrister's inability to sue the client for his professional fees: see *In re Le Brasseur and Oakley* [1896] 2 Ch 487, at p 494; *Robertson v MacDonogh* (1880) 6 LR Ir 433, at p 438. However, in *Rondel v Worsley* the House of Lords squarely rejected the suggestion that the barrister's inability to sue for his fees could support his immunity in negligence. The reason given for that conclusion is compelling. The negligent performance of a service, even if it be undertaken without consideration, gives rise to liability in negligence, if the person for whose benefit the service is performed relies upon that service.

So the barrister's immunity, if it is to be sustained, must rest on considerations of public policy. Of the various public policy factors which have been put forward to justify the immunity, only two warrant serious examination. The first relates to the peculiar nature of the barrister's responsibility when he appears for his client in litigation. The second arises from the adverse consequences for the administration of justice which would flow from the re-litigation in collateral proceedings for negligence of issues determined in the principal proceedings.

The peculiar feature of counsel's responsibility is that he owes a duty to the court as well as to his client. His duty to his client is subject to his overriding duty to the court. In the performance of that overriding duty there is a strong element of public interest. ...

[556] The performance by counsel of his paramount duty to the court will require him to act in a variety of ways to the possible disadvantage of his client. Counsel must not mislead the court, cast unjustifiable aspersions on any party or witness or withhold documents and authorities which detract from his client's case. And, if he notes an irregularity in the conduct of a criminal trial, he must take the point so that it can be remedied, instead of keeping the point up his sleeve and using it as a ground for appeal.

It is not that a barrister's duty to the court creates such a conflict with his duty to his client that the dividing line between the two is unclear. The duty to the court is paramount and must be performed, even if the client gives instructions to the contrary. Rather it is that a barrister's duty to the court epitomizes the fact that the course of litigation depends on the exercise by counsel of an independent discretion or judgment in the conduct and management of a case in which he has an eye, not only to his client's success but also to the speedy and efficient administration of justice. In selecting and limiting the number of witnesses to be called, in deciding what questions will be asked in cross-examination, what topics will be covered in address and what points of law will be raised, counsel exercises an independent judgment so that the time of the court is not taken up unnecessarily, notwithstanding that the client may wish to chase every rabbit down its burrow. The administration of justice in our adversarial system depends in very large measure on the faithful exercise by barristers of this independent judgment in the conduct and management of the case. In such an adversarial system the mode of presentation of each party's case rests with counsel. The judge is in no position to rule in advance on what witnesses will be called, what evidence should be led, what questions should be asked in cross-examination. Decisions on matters such as these, which necessarily influence the course of a trial and its duration, are made by counsel, not by the judge. This is why our **[557]** system of justice as administered by the courts has proceeded on the footing that, in general, the litigant will be represented by a lawyer who, not being a mere agent for the litigant, exercises an independent judgment in the interests of the court.

There is a real risk that, if counsel were exposed to liability in negligence, the existence of that potential liability would influence the exercise of his independent judgment by making him more mindful of the need to avoid any possibility of liability to his client. In some situations, in order to avoid that possibility, counsel would pursue matters which he would not otherwise pursue if the exposure to liability in negligence did not exist. To expect that counsel's conduct of a case would not be influenced by his exposure to such a potential liability would be little more than a pious hope. Inevitably some counsel would be more inclined to act as mere agents of their clients to the detriment of the interests of the court and of the administration of justice generally. Insurance might alleviate but would not eliminate the problem. Counsel would naturally be concerned to avoid allegations of negligence.

It follows that the exposure of counsel to liability in negligence for breach of a common law duty of care would create a real risk of adverse consequences for the efficient administration of justice. Litigation would tend to become more lengthy, more complex and more costly.

To deny the litigant a cause of action for negligence, even if it be limited to in-court negligence, on the part of his counsel is a serious step. It is to sanction a continuing exception in favour of counsel, as against his client, from the ever-expanding tort of negligence. But the exception which the law creates is not to benefit counsel but to protect the administration of justice. And the exception in favour of counsel is in conformity with the privilege which the law has always conferred in the interests of public policy on those engaged in the administration of justice, whether as judge, juror, witness, party counsel or solicitor, in respect of what they say in court: *Cabassi v Vila* (1940) 64 CLR 130, at p 141; *Munster v Lamb* (1883) 11 QBD 588.

The foundation for that principle is the perception that great mischief would result if those engaged in the administration of justice were not at liberty to speak freely. The immunity is not confined to actions for defamation. As McTiernan J noted in *Cabassi* (1940) 64 CLR, at p 144 with reference to the rule in its application to witnesses:

It is a rule of law that no civil action lies at the suit of any person for any statement made by a witness in the course of **[558]** giving evidence in a judicial proceeding. The rule, which is founded on public policy, is not confined to actions for defamation but applies to any form of action.

The considerations which dictate the need to protect freedom of speech in court likewise dictate the need to protect the advocate's freedom of judgment with respect to what is said and done in court. Just as the principle protects the judge and the juror in relation to what they decide, so it protects the advocate. The advocate is as essential a participant in our system of justice as are the judge, the jury and the witness and his freedom of judgment must be protected: see the discussion by Brett MR in *Munster* (1883) 11 QBD at pp 603-604. The need for that protection arises from "the fear that if the rule were otherwise, numerous actions would be brought against persons who were merely discharging their duty", to repeat the words of Fry LJ in *Munster* (1883) 11 QBD, at p 607.

The second aspect of public policy that calls for attention is the impact on the administration of justice of allowing court decisions to become the subject of collateral attack by means of actions against counsel for in-court negligence. Exposure of counsel to liability for such negligence would unquestionably encourage litigation by unsuccessful litigants anxious to demonstrate that, but for the negligence of counsel, they would have obtained a more favourable outcome in the initial litigation. That would be the central issue for decision in secondary litigation of this kind. If the plaintiff were to succeed, the resolution of this issue by a different court and on materials which might well differ from those presented in the initial litigation, due to lapse of time or other reasons, would undermine the status of the initial decision. Yet an appeal against that decision might not succeed with the result that it would stand, though its status would be tarnished by the outcome of the collateral proceedings. The impact of a successful challenge to a criminal conviction resulting in a sentence of imprisonment would be all the greater. It would be destructive of public confidence in the administration of justice. And for this very reason there would be a strong incentive on the part of a disappointed litigant to sue counsel for negligence as an indirect means of calling in question the decision in the initial litigation. ...

[559] However, the grounds for denying liability for in-court negligence have no application to work done out of court which is unconnected with work done in court: *Saif Ali*. The public policy considerations underlying immunity from in-court negligence have no relevance to a barrister's liability for negligent advice in relation to out-of-court matters, in accordance with the principles expounded in such cases as *San Sebastian Pty Ltd v The Minister* (1986) 162 CLR 340; *Hawkins v Clayton* (1988) 164 CLR 539; and *Hedley Byrne & Co Ltd v Heller & Partners Ltd* [1964] AC 465. The problem is: where does one draw the dividing line? Is the immunity to end at the courtroom door so that the protection does not extend to preparatory activities such as the drawing and settling of pleadings and the giving of advice on evidence? To limit the immunity in this way would be to confine it to conduct and management of the case in the courtroom, thereby protecting the advocate in respect of his tactical handling of the proceedings. However, it would be artificial in the extreme to draw the line at the courtroom door. Preparation of a case out of court cannot be **[560]** divorced from presentation in court. The two are inextricably interwoven so that the immunity must extend to work done out of court which leads to a decision affecting the conduct of the case in court. ...

[Section] 6DD was a matter of defence to the charge. The failure to raise it as a defence, like the failure to raise it as a ground of objection to the reception of the evidence, was an incident of the conduct and management of the case in court. Accordingly, the negligence complained of falls within the common law immunity.

I turn now to s 10 of the 1958 Act. It provides: ...

[561] (2) Every barrister shall be liable for negligence as a barrister to the client on whose behalf he has been employed to the same extent as a solicitor was on the twenty-third day of November One thousand eight hundred and ninety-one liable to his client for negligence as a solicitor.

Twenty-third November 1891 was the date on which the *Legal Profession Practice Act 1891* (Vic) ("the 1891 Act"), the ancestor of the 1958 Act, came into force. The provisions of s 5 of that Act were to all intents and purposes the same as those of the present section, except in so far as that part of s 5 which corresponded with s 10(2) of the 1958 Act referred to "the same extent as a solicitor is now liable to his client for negligence as a solicitor". The enactment of the 1891 Act was the culmination of popular agitation to place the two separate branches of the legal profession in Victoria on the same footing, no doubt with a view to amalgamation. That fusion did not happen. However, the point to be made is that the object of the 1891 Act was to place the two branches of the profession on the same footing. Section 5 should be construed accordingly rather than in the light of any supposed notion that it was intended to subject barristers to common law liability for in-court negligence because solicitors were already subject to that liability. As we have seen, the nineteenth century cases did not establish that a solicitor was liable in negligence to a client in respect of work undertaken by the solicitor as an advocate. The provisions of s 5 and the later provisions of s 10(2) are to be interpreted against that background. ...

In the result I would dismiss the appeals.

WILSON J. ... **[570]** I am ... of the opinion that the proper construction of s 10(2) does not lead to the conclusion that, by virtue of that provision, barristers in Victoria are liable for in-court negligence. They are made liable as barristers "to the same extent" as solicitors were liable in Victoria in 1891. Since solicitors were not then liable for in-court negligence in their work as advocates, so today are barristers immune from liability to that extent. ...

[572] I do not think that the appellants can derive any comfort from the common law. In 1891 the common law recognized that advocates, whether solicitors or barristers, were immune from liability for in-court negligence. Notwithstanding the recognition that an action in professional negligence could lie in tort as well as contract, the important principle underlying the immunity remains compelling. The public interest in the due administration of justice, as enunciated by Brett MR in *Munster v Lamb* in 1883, remains a valid unifying theme for the various issues of public policy canvassed by the House of Lords in *Rondel*. Five distinct grounds of public policy were advanced in *Rondel* in support of immunity: the concern that if counsel could be sued for negligence, they would be tempted to prefer the interests of their clients and would be deflected from observing their duty to the court; the adverse effect that the fear of litigation may have on the barrister's efficient conduct of the court proceedings; the "cab-rank" principle, whereby a barrister is not free within his field of practice to choose whether or not to act for a person who desires his services and can pay his fee; the special character of the judicial process wherein judges, jurors and witnesses are immune from civil action; lastly, the threat to the public interest centred in the finality of litigation.

Not all these considerations are of equal weight. There is no reason to suppose that counsel would be deterred by the possibility of a negligence claim from discharging a clear duty to the court in preference to observing the wishes of the client. Counsel could never be in breach of duty to the client by fulfilling the paramount duty.

Nevertheless, counsel's duty to the court is often easier to state than to apply in specific situations. For example, in a particular case, what will constitute *sufficient* evidence so as to justify counsel attacking the character of an opposing witness? There will be cases **[573]** where it will not be easy to determine when the interests and instructions of the client collide with counsel's duty to the court. It is in those cases that counsel's judgment may be consciously or unconsciously impaired, leading him to favour his client's interests over his paramount duty. Yet the court "has and must continue to have implicit trust in counsel": *Rondel* [1969] 1 AC, at p 272. True it is that counsel who errs on the side of his duty to the court is unlikely to be found liable in negligence even if he has misinterpreted the position and the reality is that there was no relevant duty to the court operating to prevent him from doing something which would be in his client's best interests. Counsel is not negligent merely because of a mere error of judgment. But it is the *threat* of litigation, not the likelihood of defeating such litigation, which is material. The expectation that an action in negligence brought against him would fail does not counter the instinctive motivation of counsel to err on the side of caution by bending to the client's interests and avoiding the possibility of troublesome litigation. For the same reason, counsel may be led, contrary to his view of what the justice of the case requires, to extend his examination of witnesses and submissions on the law, thereby unnecessarily prolonging the proceedings. The administration of justice would be at risk.

Next, there is the "cab-rank" principle; however, important though this principle is in itself, I would not accord it significant weight in considering the question of immunity: see *Saif Ali* [1980] AC, at p 221.

As I have said, the public policy reflected in the immunity from suit for defamation, which is conferred upon participants in the legal process, extends in an analogous way to protect counsel from liability for in-court negligence. It would be odd, to say the least, if counsel was immune from liability for malicious in-court slander yet liable for the negligent conduct of a case in court.

In addition to the foregoing matters, there are the many difficulties associated with relitigation, which would be a common feature of trials of actions against counsel. These difficulties provide a powerful argument for counsel's immunity. The situation is not to be compared with a case where an appeal is allowed, a decision set aside and a re-trial ordered. Such a course of events merely portrays the normal course of appellate review. It is altogether different where a disappointed litigant institutes a civil proceeding in a court of co-ordinate jurisdiction with a view to proving that the original decision was wrong by reason of counsel's negligence. If the negligence action succeeds, then the original decision, notwithstanding that it may have been affirmed on appeal, is necessarily **[574]** tarnished by the later inconsistent decision. Yet nothing can correct the record or interfere with the original judgment. Furthermore, the result will have come about without the successful party to the original action being a party to the negligence action, which will fall to be determined in his or her absence. These situations clearly have a capacity to bring the administration of justice into disrepute: see *Rondel*, particularly at pp 249-251.

The problem would be exacerbated in the case of a client who claimed to have been wrongly convicted by a jury of a criminal offence by reason of counsel's negligence in conducting the trial. The issue of causation in the negligence action where questions of fact for a jury were involved could be a mind-boggling exercise, piling "speculation upon speculation": *Rondel* [1969] 1 AC, at p 250. The issue would have to be joined without any evidence from those most closely connected with it, the judge and members of the jury. Public policy would not permit them to be called as witnesses. There are other fundamental problems. Suppose a person is convicted, the jury being satisfied of guilt beyond a reasonable doubt. All avenues of appeal are pursued without success. The convicted person then institutes an action for negligence against the defence counsel, assuming the onus of proof on the balance of probabilities. If the action succeeds but the conviction remains, public confidence in the integrity of the law must be seriously and adversely affected. Even if a way is found to have the conviction set aside notwithstanding the earlier unsuccessful appeals, the end result is that the civil action is converted into a de facto avenue of appeal outside the carefully constructed statutory framework of criminal appeals. It may be noted that there is a longstanding policy of the common law against allowing the re-trial of criminal cases by collateral means: see the discussion by Harding, "Recent Cases, *Rondel v Worsley*", *Western Australian Law Review*, vol 8 (1968) 242, at pp 248-249.

The common law principle of immunity from civil action for in-court negligence thus derives support from the fundamental principle favouring finality of litigation. This principle has been found necessary to conserve public confidence in the administration of justice. It is this confidence which would be most at risk if the appellants' case were to succeed. ...

[578] I would dismiss the appeals.

DEANE J. [dissenting] **[587]** I agree with the judgment of Toohey J ... .

[588] In the result, it is strictly unnecessary that I form any concluded view on the important general question which is addressed in the judgments of the members of the Court who constitute the majority in the present case. That question is whether, under the common law of this country, a barrister or other legal practitioner is, in the absence of applicable statutory provision and regardless of fees charged and received, immune from any liability to his or her client for "in court" negligence. I would, however, indicate my dissent from the conclusion reached by the majority of the Court in relation to that question.

There is no decided case which requires this Court to treat a barrister or other legal practitioner acting professionally in court for a client as beyond the reach of the modern common law of negligence. Nor, in my view, is any convincing justification of such an immunity to be found in general principle; plainly enough, the traditional view that the relationship between a barrister and his client is non-contractual does not provide one. If the recognition of such an immunity can be justified, it must be by reference to largely pragmatic considerations of public policy: cf *Rondel v Worsley* [1969] 1 AC 191, at pp 244, 280-281, 289; *Saif Ali v Sydney Mitchell & Co* [1980] AC 198, at pp 212, 219, 230-231, 233, 235. In that regard however, I do not consider that the considerations of public policy which are expounded in *Rondel v Worsley* [1969] 1 AC, at pp 227-231, 247-254, 267-276, 281-284 and in the majority judgments in the present case outweigh or even balance the injustice and consequent public detriment involved in depriving a person, who is caught up in litigation and engages the professional services of a legal practitioner, of all redress under the common law for "in court" negligence, however gross and callous in its nature or devastating in its consequences. ...

DAWSON J. ... **[594]** More than one reason was advanced in the speeches in *Rondel v Worsley* and *Saif Ali v Sydney Mitchell & Co*. A barrister, it was said, owes his primary duty to the court and not his client and in following his duty, which at times may involve the immediate determination of difficult questions, he ought not to be hampered by the prospect of liability to his client for a wrong decision. In *Saif Ali v Sydney Mitchell & Co* [1980] AC, at pp 219-221, Lord Diplock did not think this a sufficient reason to differentiate barristers from other professional men who also have to make difficult decisions on the spot. Professional negligence consists of more than a mere error of judgment and I must confess that I find it difficult to see any inconsistency between the existence of a duty to the court and the existence of a duty of care to a client. Nor do I see any great force in the argument that immunity is to be justified by the cab-rank principle which requires a barrister to accept instructions to act on behalf of a client, provided he is free, a proper fee is tendered and he practises in the particular jurisdiction. Again like Lord Diplock (in *Saif Ali v Sydney Mitchell & Co* [1980] AC, at p 221), I have never thought the principle to have as much practical operation as is sometimes suggested and it is hardly enough, to my mind, to differentiate the profession of a barrister from other professions.

Of more weight in terms of public policy is the suggestion that a barrister would be impaired in the exercise of his professional judgment by the prospect of an action against him by a disappointed client. He would, the suggestion continues, be led out of caution to put unnecessary arguments, to take unnecessary defences, to ask unnecessary questions and to call unnecessary witnesses, thereby becoming not only prolix but also less effective in the art of advocacy. Not only might the interests of the client be adversely affected but the efficient conduct of the business of the courts would be likely to be impaired.

But there are weightier considerations than these. The first, to my mind, is that the availability of an action in negligence for the conduct of a case in court would subject the decision of the court to collateral attack by a client who sought to blame his barrister for his loss of the case. Not only would this mean relitigation of issues already decided, but the relitigation would be before a different tribunal after a lapse of time upon evidence which would not necessarily be the same. This would be bad enough after a decision **[595]** in a civil case but would be intolerable after a criminal trial. The verdict of the jury would be impugned in a court of law and yet, assuming all avenues of appeal to have been exhausted, it would remain with all its consequences. True it is that the way in which a trial has been conducted by a practitioner appearing for an accused may afford a ground for appeal if it results in a miscarriage of justice (see, eg *Re Knowles* [1984] VR 751), but to contemplate an attack in collateral proceedings which would be incapable of affecting the verdict, raises quite different considerations. Nothing could be more calculated to destroy confidence in the processes of the courts or be more inimical to the policy that there be an end to litigation. If the decision of a court is wrong, the appeal process is the means by which it should be corrected. To allow the courts to be used to undermine its authority in other proceedings is clearly not in the public interest.

However, the most cogent consideration is, to my mind, more broadly based in policy which is not confined to immunity from liability for negligence in the presentation of a client's case in court. Fundamental to the administration of justice is the opportunity which the law affords to all those who are participants in proceedings in a court to speak and act freely, within the rules laid down, unimpeded by the prospect of civil process as a consequence of their having done so. This privilege against civil liability – for privilege it is – extends beyond the parties and their representatives to witnesses, the court officials and the judge himself. ...

[596] I can see no relevant difference for this purpose whether the action be for damages for defamation or for negligence. And it is to be remembered that in either case it is protection against actions which are ill founded as much as against those which are soundly based which is necessary. It is the contemplation of either type of suit which must be likely to hamper an advocate's efforts so as to deprive the administration of justice of the assistance which it might otherwise expect. In this respect the practice of the profession of an advocate differs from the practice of other professions. To err on the side of caution is not only practicable but ordinarily the best course with other professions. With an advocate this may be fatal, not only to the interests of the client, but also to the proper determination of the case. ...

[His Honour agreed that the 1958 Act did not abrogate the barrister's common law immunity.]

I would dismiss the appeals.

[Brennan J delivered a judgment in which he agreed with Mason CJ on the common law and held that the 1958 Act did not abrogate the barrister's common law immunity. Toohey J (Gaudron J concurring) dissented on the ground that the legislation, on its proper construction, imposed liability on a barrister for the performance of his or her duties as a barrister. Toohey J expressed no opinion on the barrister's common law immunity.]

Appeal dismissed

[*Giannarelli v Wraith* (extracted above) is authority for the proposition that public policy considerations related to the administration of justice, including the imperative of finality of litigation, negative the existence of a common law duty of care owed by an advocate to his or her client in respect of the conduct of the client's case in court. This immunity from suit extends to work done by the advocate outside court which leads to a decision, for example, not to raise a particular defence or object to the admissibility of evidence, which affects the conduct of the case in court.

In *D'Orta-Ekenaike v Victoria Legal Aid* (2005) 214 ALR 92 the High Court, in a joint judgment of Gleeson CJ, Gummow, Hayne and Heydon JJ, McHugh and Callinan JJ agreeing in separate judgments and Kirby J dissenting, affirmed the common law in Australia as stated in *Giannarelli v Wraith*. The court also held that a solicitor is entitled to common law immunity from suit in respect of acts or omissions which, if done by an advocate, would be within the scope of the advocate's common law immunity.

In *D'Orta-Ekenaike v Victoria Legal Aid*, the applicant, Mr Ryan D'Orta-Ekenaike, was charged with rape. The first respondent, Victoria Legal Aid, acted as the applicant's solicitor and retained the second respondent, Mr McIvor, as the applicant's barrister to appear for him at the committal proceedings. The applicant pleaded guilty at the committal proceedings and was convicted at trial and sentenced to three years' imprisonment. Subsequently, the conviction was quashed and the applicant was acquitted at a retrial. The applicant commenced an action for negligence against the first respondent and the second respondent in the County Court in Victoria. The applicant contended that, at a conference two days before the committal proceedings and at a further conference on the day of the committal proceedings, the respondents negligently advised him that he did not have any defence to the charge and placed "undue pressure and influence" on him to plead guilty at the committal proceedings even although he was not bound to enter a plea and the fact of a guilty plea was admissible evidence at trial.

The primary judge (Judge Wodak) ordered that the applicant's action be permanently stayed on the ground that the advice allegedly given the applicant by the respondents "was so intimately connected with the conduct of the trial as to come within the immunity defence principle". The primary judge also held that the advocate's common law immunity from suit applied in the circumstances to the first respondent in its capacity as the applicant's solicitor as well as to the second respondent in his capacity as the applicant's barrister. The Victorian Court of Appeal (Winneke P and Buchanan JA) refused the applicant leave to appeal. Although the High Court granted the applicant special leave to appeal from that order, the court dismissed the applicant's appeal.

In considering the advocate's common law immunity from suit, Gleeson CJ, Gummow, Hayne and Heydon JJ observed at 99 that: "Chief attention must be given to the nature of the judicial process and the role the advocate plays in it." The joint judgment continued:

[103] 45. … [T]he central justification for the advocate's immunity is the principle that controversies, once resolved, are not to be reopened except in a few narrowly defined circumstances. This is a fundamental and pervading tenet of the judicial system, reflecting the role played by the judicial process in the government of society. If an exception to that tenet were to be created by abolishing that immunity, a peculiar type of relitigation would arise. There would be relitigation of a controversy (already determined) as a result of what had happened during, or in preparation for, the hearing that had been designed to quell that controversy. Moreover, it would be relitigation of a skewed and limited kind. No argument was advanced to this Court urging the abolition of judicial or witness immunity. If those immunities remain, it follows that the relitigation could not and would not examine the contribution of judge or witness to the events complained of, only the contribution of the advocate. An exception to the rule against the reopening of controversies would exist, but one of an inefficient and anomalous kind.

46. A justification based on finality has as much force today as it did when *Giannarelli* was decided. …

[112] 84. … [U]nderpinning the [judicial] system is the need for certainty and finality of decision. The immunity of advocates is a necessary consequence of that need. …

[113] 91. Because the immunity now in question is rooted in the considerations described earlier, where a legal practitioner (whether acting as advocate, or as solicitor instructing an advocate) gives advice which leads to a decision (here the client's decision to enter a guilty plea at committal) which affects the conduct of a case in court, the practitioner cannot be sued for negligence on that account. …]

Hill v Chief Constable of West Yorkshire
[1989] AC 53
House of Lords

The police service does not owe a duty of care to members of the public, including potential victims of a serial offender, when discharging its functions of investigating and suppressing crime.

LORD KEITH of KINKEL. [57] My Lords, in 1975 a man named Peter Sutcliffe embarked upon a terrifying career of violent crime, centred in the metropolitan police area of West Yorkshire. All his victims were [58] young or fairly young women. Between July 1975 and November 1980 he committed 13 murders and eight attempted murders upon such women, the modus operandi in each case being similar. Sutcliffe's last victim was a 20-year-old student called Jacqueline Hill, whom he murdered in Leeds on 17 November 1980. By chance, Sutcliffe was arrested in suspicious circumstances in Sheffield on 2 January 1981, and confessed to the series of murders and attempted murders following interrogation. On 22 May 1981, at the Central Criminal Court, Sutcliffe was convicted of inter alia the murder of Miss Hill.

Miss Hill's mother and sole personal representative now sues the Chief Constable of West Yorkshire, claiming on behalf of Miss Hill's estate damages on the ground of negligence, for inter alia loss of expectation of life and pain and suffering. The defendant is sued under section 48(1) of the *Police Act 1964*, enacting that the chief officer of police for any police area shall be liable in respect of torts committed by constables under his direction and control in the performance or purported performance of their functions. The plaintiff in her statement of claim sets out the 20 offences committed by Sutcliffe before the death of Miss Hill and avers that the circumstances of each of these were such that it was reasonable to infer that all were committed by the same man, and further that it was foreseeable that, if not apprehended, he would commit further offences of the same nature. The pleadings go on to allege that it was accordingly the duty of the defendant and all officers in his police force to use their best endeavours and exercise all reasonable care and skill to apprehend the perpetrator of the crimes and so protect members of the public who might otherwise be his future victims. A substantial number of matters are set out and relied upon as indicating that the West Yorkshire police force failed in that duty. It is unnecessary to set out these matters in detail. They amount broadly to allegations of failure to collate properly information in possession of the force pointing to Sutcliffe as a likely suspect, and of failing to give due weight to certain pieces of information while according excessive importance to others.

The defendant, without delivering defences, applied under RSC, Ord 18, r 19 to have the statement of claim struck out as disclosing no reasonable cause of action. That application was granted by Sir Neil Lawson, sitting as a judge of the High Court, on 19 December 1985. Upon appeal by the plaintiff the Court of Appeal (Fox and Glidewell LJJ and Sir Roualeyn Cumming-Bruce) [1988] QB 60, on 19 February 1987, affirmed Sir Neil Lawson. The plaintiff now appeals, with leave given in the Court of Appeal, to your Lordships' House. ...

[59] The question of law which is opened up by the case is whether the individual members of a police force, in the course of carrying out their functions of controlling and keeping down the incidence of crime, owe a duty of care to individual members of the public who may suffer injury to person or property through the activities of criminals, such as to result in liability in damages, on the ground of negligence, to anyone who suffers such injury by reason of breach of that duty.

There is no question that a police officer, like anyone else, may be liable in tort to a person who is injured as a direct result of his acts or omissions. So he may be liable in damages for assault, unlawful arrest, wrongful imprisonment and malicious prosecution, and also for negligence. ...

[60] It has been said almost too frequently to require repetition that foreseeability of likely harm is not in itself a sufficient test of liability in negligence. Some further ingredient is invariably needed to establish the requisite proximity of relationship between plaintiff and defendant, and all the circumstances of the case must be carefully considered and analysed in order to ascertain whether such an ingredient is present. The nature of the ingredient will be found to vary in a number of different categories of decided cases. ...

The *Dorset Yacht* case [*Home Office v Dorset Yacht Co Ltd* [1970] AC 1004] was concerned with the special characteristics or ingredients beyond reasonable foreseeability of likely harm which may result in civil liability for failure to control another man to prevent his doing harm to a third. The present case falls broadly into the same category. It is plain that vital characteristics which were present in the *Dorset Yacht* case and which led to the imposition of liability are here lacking. Sutcliffe was never in the custody of the police force. Miss Hill was one of a vast number of the female general public who might be at risk from his activities but was at no special distinctive risk in relation to them, unlike the owners of yachts moored off Brownsea Island in relation to the foreseeable conduct of the Borstal boys. It appears ... [that in Lord Diplock's] view no liability would rest upon a prison authority, which carelessly allowed the escape of an habitual criminal, for damage which he subsequently caused, not in the course of attempting to make good his getaway to persons at special risk, but in further pursuance of his general criminal career to the person or property of members of the general public. The same rule must apply as regards failure to recapture the criminal before he had time to resume his career. In the case of an escaped criminal his identity and description are known. In the instant case the identity of the wanted criminal was at the material time unknown and it is not averred that any full or clear description of him was ever available. The alleged negligence of the police consists in a failure to discover his identity. But if there is no general duty of care owed to individual members of the public by the responsible authorities to prevent the escape of a known criminal or to recapture him, there cannot reasonably be imposed upon any police force a duty of care similarly owed to identify and apprehend an unknown one. Miss Hill cannot for this purpose be regarded as a person at special risk simply because she was young and female. Where the class of potential victims of a particular habitual criminal is a large one the precise size of it cannot in principle affect the issue. All householders are potential victims of an habitual burglar, and all females those of an habitual rapist. The conclusion must be that although there existed reasonable foreseeability of likely harm to such as Miss Hill if Sutcliffe were not identified and apprehended, there is absent from the case any such ingredient or characteristic as led to the liability of the Home Office in the *Dorset Yacht* case. Nor is there present any additional characteristic such as might make up the deficiency. The circumstances of the case are therefore not capable of establishing a duty of care owed towards Miss Hill by the West Yorkshire Police.

[63] That is sufficient for the disposal of the appeal. But in my opinion there is another reason why an action for damages in negligence should not lie against the police in circumstances such as those of the present case, and that is public policy. ... The general sense of public duty which motivates police forces is unlikely to be appreciably reinforced by the imposition of such liability so far as concerns their function in the investigation and suppression of crime. From time to time they make mistakes in the exercise of that function, but it is not to be doubted that they apply their best endeavours to the performance of it. In some instances the imposition of liability may lead to the exercise of a function being carried on in a detrimentally defensive frame of mind. The possibility of this happening in relation to the investigative operations of the police cannot be excluded. Further it would be reasonable to expect that if potential liability were to be imposed it would be not uncommon for actions to be raised against police forces on the ground that they had failed to catch some criminal as soon as they might have done, with the result that he went on to commit further crimes. While some such actions might involve allegations of a simple and straightforward type of failure – for example that a police officer negligently tripped and fell while pursuing a burglar – others would be likely to enter deeply into the general nature of a police investigation, as indeed the present action would seek to do. The manner of conduct of such an investigation must necessarily involve a variety of decisions to be made on matters of policy and discretion, for example as to which particular line of inquiry is most advantageously to be pursued and what is the most advantageous way to deploy the available resources. Many such decisions would not be regarded by the courts as appropriate to be called in question, yet elaborate investigation of the facts might be necessary to ascertain whether or not this was so. A great deal of police time, trouble and expense might be expected to have to be put into the preparation of the defence to the action and the attendance of witnesses at the trial. The result would be a significant diversion of police manpower and attention from their most important function, that of the suppression of crime. Closed investigations would require to be reopened and retraversed, not with the object of bringing any criminal to justice but to ascertain whether or not they had been competently conducted. I therefore consider that Glidewell LJ, in his judgment in the Court of Appeal [1988] QB 60, 76 in the present case, was right to take the view that [64] the police were immune from an action of this kind on grounds similar to those which in *Rondel v Worsley* [1969] 1 AC 191 were held to render a barrister immune from actions for negligence in his conduct of proceedings in court.

My Lords, for these reasons I would dismiss the appeal.

[Lords Brandon of Oakbrook, Oliver of Aylmerton and Goff of Chieveley agreed with Lord Keith of Kinkel. Lord Templeman delivered a concurring judgment.]

Appeal dismissed

Sullivan v Moody
Thompson v Connon
(2001) 207 CLR 562; [2001] HCA 59
High Court of Australia

The formulation of a comprehensive test for determining the existence of a duty of care has proved elusive not least because "different classes of case give rise to different problems".

Thus, in the present case, taking into account whether the existence of a duty of care would impair the "coherence of the law", State community welfare officers and medical practitioners carrying out statutory functions of investigating allegations of child sexual abuse owed no duty of care to the child's parents in respect of the accuracy of the investigation.

GLEESON CJ, GAUDRON, McHUGH, HAYNE and CALLINAN JJ. **[567]** 1. These two appeals were heard together. In each case the appellant's action for damages, commenced in the Supreme Court of South Australia, was struck out by a Master of the Court on the ground that the Statement of Claim failed to disclose a cause of action. In the case of *Thompson*, an appeal to the Full Court of the Supreme Court of South Australia was dismissed following fully reasoned judgments by the members of the Full Court (Doyle CJ, Duggan and Gray JJ) (*CLT v Connon* (2000) 77 SASR 449). In the later appeal of *Sullivan* it was accepted, subject to one qualification, that the decision in *Thompson* meant that the appeal must fail, and it was dismissed (*Sullivan v Moody* [2000] SASC 340). The qualification concerns one defendant in the action, who was regarded as being in a position different from that of the other defendants. He is not a party to the appeal to this Court.

2. The course that was taken in the Supreme Court of South Australia was influenced by the consideration that, in 1996, in a case that had gone to trial, the Full Court of the Supreme Court of South Australia had dismissed a plaintiff's appeal in circumstances that were conceded to be indistinguishable from those of *Thompson* and *Sullivan*. That case was *Hillman v Black* (1996) 67 SASR 490. The Full Court decided in *Hillman v Black* that the defendants did not owe a duty of care to the plaintiff, upholding the decision of the trial judge. That decision meant that, if the present cases had gone to trial, failure at first instance was certain, and failure in the Full Court was very likely. In the light of authority binding him, the Master's decisions were inevitable. In *Thompson*, the appellant endeavoured to persuade the Full Court that, having regard **[568]** to later authority, it should depart from *Hillman v Black*, but was unsuccessful.

3. The concession that *Hillman v Black* is indistinguishable means that the outcome of the present appeals does not turn upon questions as to the standard of persuasion which a defendant ordinarily needs to satisfy in a strike out application (*General Steel Industries Inc v Commissioner for Railways (NSW)* (1964) 112 CLR 125). That case went to trial. The events in issue occurred at about the same time as the events in *Thompson* and *Sullivan*, the relevant statutory regime was the same, and, except for the identity of the doctors and social workers involved, and other matters of immaterial detail, the same allegations are made. If no duty of care was owed in *Hillman v Black*, none was owed in these two cases. For practical purposes, these appeals are challenges to the decision in *Hillman v Black*, and although they are to be decided by reference to the allegations in the pleadings, it is not argued that those allegations are relevantly different from what was alleged, and found, in the earlier case.

The facts in *Thompson*
4. The plaintiff is the father of three young boys. Each of the first and second defendants is a medical practitioner employed at the Sexual Assault Referral Centre at the Queen Elizabeth Hospital, Woodville, South Australia. The third defendant is the hospital. The fourth defendant, the State of South Australia, operates the Department of Community Welfare. The plaintiff is uncertain whether the first two defendants were employed by the third or fourth defendant.

5. During 1986, the plaintiff's wife, on separate occasions, attended the Sexual Assault Referral Centre with the boys. Doyle CJ noted that it was common ground that the medical practitioners who examined the boys did so at the instigation of a person or persons employed by the Department of Community Welfare. One of the boys was examined by the first defendant. The other boys were examined by the second defendant. Both the first and second defendants concluded, and reported to the Department of Community Welfare, that the boys appeared to have been sexually abused.

6. Further investigations were carried out by officers of the Department of Community Welfare, who also concluded that there had probably been sexual abuse. They, in turn, referred the matter to the police. The police charged the plaintiff with sexual offences. Those charges were ultimately dropped, but, in consequence of the allegations and charges, the plaintiff suffered shock, distress and psychiatric harm, and consequential personal and financial loss.

7. The plaintiff alleges that each of the first and second defendants (the medical practitioners at the Sexual Assault Referral Centre) "owed a duty of care to the plaintiff to carry out her duties and responsibilities **[569]** and in particular the examination and diagnoses of persons and in particular

children suspected of having been sexually abused ... with due care, skill, discretion and diligence."
(The introduction of the concept of discretion was capable of causing some confusion, but it played
no separate role in argument). In a number of respects, those defendants are said to have acted
negligently in their examination, diagnosis, and reporting. The third and fourth defendants are
claimed to be vicariously liable for the negligence of the medical practitioners.

8. The State of South Australia is also alleged to have owed the plaintiff a duty to carry
out its responsibilities in relation to the investigation of sexual abuse of children with due care,
skill, discretion and diligence, and the officers of the Department of Community Welfare who
investigated the matters are alleged to have behaved negligently.

9. Doyle CJ summarised the case as follows:

"In short, it is a case in which the plaintiff alleges that the first and second defendants carelessly
reached a conclusion that the plaintiff's children had been or probably had been subjected to
sexual abuse, and reported that conclusion to members of the Department, in circumstances in
which the plaintiff would be regarded as the probable or possible perpetrator of that abuse. ...

The State is also alleged to be liable on an independent basis. It is claimed that the
employees of the Department owed the plaintiff a duty of care in the course of their employment. ...

It is alleged that employees ... gathered and used information about possible sexual
abuse of the children without making adequate inquiry as to those facts, without exercising
proper care and without following appropriate procedures for such cases. ... It is alleged that
the employees of the Department failed to establish appropriate protocols for the diagnosis of
sexual abuse of children. It is alleged that they failed to establish proper procedures to validate
diagnoses of sexual abuse ... ."

[The Court then summarised the facts in *Sullivan* and continued:]

[570] The facts in *Hillman v Black*
17. In that case the plaintiff was the father of a young daughter. His wife came to suspect him of
sexually abusing the daughter. She raised her accusations with a social worker at Crisis Care, and
was referred to the Sexual Assault Referral Centre at Queen Elizabeth Hospital. The daughter
was examined there by a medical practitioner who formed, and expressed, the opinion that there
had been some form of molestation. This opinion was reported by the medical practitioner and a
social worker to the police. A custody dispute in the Family Court followed. The defendants were
a medical practitioner attached to the Sexual Assault Referral Centre, a psychiatrist at the Adelaide
Children's Hospital, who assessed the child in connection with custody and access claims in the
Family Court, and their employers. There was also a claim against the Department of Community
Welfare. The allegations of negligence and damage were similar to those later made in *Thompson*
and *Sullivan*.

[571] The relevant legislation
18. In all three cases the statutory background was the same. There was a difference of opinion in
the Full Court in *Thompson* as to whether it was conclusive, but it is plainly relevant.

19. The Department of Community Welfare functions pursuant to the *Community Welfare Act
1972* (SA) ("the Act"). Section 10 of the Act provides that the objectives of the Department, and of
the Minister of Community Welfare, include promoting the welfare and dignity of the community,
and of individuals, families and groups within the community, by providing services designed to
assist, amongst others, children to overcome disadvantages suffered by them.

20. Part IV of the Act is concerned with "Support Services for Children". Section 25, which
states certain principles to be observed, provides that a person dealing with a child under the
provisions of Pt IV:

"... (a) shall regard the interests of the child as the paramount consideration;
(b)   shall seek to secure for the child care, guidance and support within a healthy and balanced
      family environment;
(c)   shall deal with the child in a caring and sensitive manner;
(d)   shall have regard to the rights of the child, and to the needs and wishes expressed by him;

and

(e)   shall promote, where practicable, a satisfactory relationship between the child and other members of, or persons within, his family or domestic environment."

[The court spelt out other relevant provisions in the Act, and continued:]

[572] The argument for the appellants

23. The appellants in the present appeals, like the appellant in *Hillman v Black*, had no personal dealings with the medical practitioners, social workers, departmental officers, or hospitals involved in investigating, and reporting upon, the allegations of child sexual abuse. They were family members who were actual or potential suspects in relation to such allegations. Each appellant contended that he had not abused his children and that he had been injured as a result of the respondents' negligence in reaching and reporting an opinion suggesting or asserting the contrary. ...

25. The appellants submit that it was reasonably foreseeable that they would suffer harm of the kind alleged in consequence of negligence on [573] the part of the defendants in investigating and reporting upon the allegations. That is not disputed. But foreseeability of harm is not sufficient to give rise to a duty of care. Conscious of a number of difficulties, including indeterminacy of liability, the appellants disclaimed any suggestion that the fact that they were actual or potential suspects of itself gave rise to a duty owed to them by the defendants of a kind that would give rise to liability in negligence. They did not contend that such a duty would be owed to a neighbour, or a stranger, who was suspected of molesting the children. The parental relationship between the appellants and the children, it was said, distinguished these cases from the ordinary case of an investigation of a possible crime. The appellants did not argue that public authorities or individuals who, in the course of their official or professional duties, or otherwise, investigate, and report upon, possible offences, normally owe a legal duty to take reasonable care not to cause harm to people who might be suspected of being offenders, even though it is obviously foreseeable that such people might be adversely affected by carelessness in investigation and reporting.

26. The appellants pointed out that the Act obliges people dealing with children to consider the familial as well as the personal interests of the child. (See, for example, s 25(e)). The relationship between a child and its parents is an aspect of the welfare of the child. It was argued that, if an opinion is negligently formed that a parent has abused a child, the likely disruption of the parent/child relationship is directly against the interests of the child. In that respect there was said to be a coincidence of interest between parent and child. ...

The decision of the Full Court in *Hillman v Black*

28. Matheson, Prior and Perry JJ all concluded that, on the facts found by the trial judge which, so far as they were material to the issue of duty of care, were not in dispute, and were as alleged by the plaintiff, the defendants owed no relevant duty of care to the plaintiff.

29. The case was decided at a time when proximity was commonly treated in Australian courts as what Deane J described in *Jaensch v* [574] *Coffey* (1984) 155 CLR 549 at 584 as a "broad and flexible touchstone of the circumstances in which the common law would admit the existence of a relevant duty of care to avoid reasonably foreseeable injury to another". More will be said of that later. Matheson J reached the conclusion "that the necessary relationship of proximity was not proved" (*Hillman* at 501).

30. As to the Department, Matheson J was strongly influenced by the decision of the House of Lords in *X (Minors) v Bedfordshire County Council* [1995] 2 AC 633 and, in particular, by what Lord Browne-Wilkinson said about one of the cases which formed part of that litigation ("the *Newham* case") where the facts bore a striking similarity to the facts in *Hillman*. His Lordship said that a "common law duty of care cannot be imposed on a statutory duty if the observance of such common law duty of care would be inconsistent with, or have a tendency to discourage, the due performance by the local authority of its statutory duties" (at 739). He also said (at 750):

"... the task of the local authority and its servants in dealing with children at risk is extraordinarily delicate. Legislation requires the local authority to have regard not only to the physical wellbeing of the child but also to the advantages of not disrupting the child's family environment ... if a liability in damages were to be imposed, it might well be that local authorities would adopt a more cautious and defensive approach to their duties. ... If the authority is to be made liable in damages for a negligent decision ... there would be a substantial temptation to postpone making such a decision until further inquiries have been made in the hope of getting more concrete facts. Not only would the child in fact being abused be prejudiced by such delay: the increased workload inherent in making such investigations would reduce the time available to deal with other cases and other children."

31. Reference was also made by his Lordship to the United Kingdom regulatory scheme which "involves the administrators in exercising discretions and powers which could not exist in the private sector and which in many cases bring them into conflict with those who, under the general law, are responsible for the child's welfare" (at 751).

32. Matheson J considered that the same applied to the South Australian legislation.

33. As to the medical practitioners who examined the child, Matheson J said that they "were not retained to advise the appellant, and did not assume a duty of care to him. It was for [the child] alone that they [575] were invited to exercise their professional skill and judgment. The appellant was not their patient" ((1996) 67 SASR 490 at 502).

34. Prior J reasoned to like effect in relation to the Department. As to the medical practitioners, he emphasised that in those cases there was a similar problem of potential conflict between the interests of the child and the interests of the plaintiff which, in turn, exposed the doctors to a conflict of duty and interest if they were subject to a common law duty of care to the plaintiff (at 510).

35. Perry J approached the case as one of statutory construction, the object being to determine whether the statutory provisions excluded tortious liability (at 515-516). He concluded that they had that effect, not only in relation to the Department and its officers, but also in relation to the medical practitioners to whom the Department referred a child.

The decision of the Full Court in *Thompson*

36. Unlike the other two members of the Full Court and Perry J in *Hillman*, Doyle CJ did not find in the Act any implied intention to exclude the imposition of a duty of care. That, however, did not resolve the issue; it merely left it open. He went on to consider factors tending for and against a conclusion that a duty existed.

37. Factors in favour of the plaintiff were: that the duty alleged related to a positive act, not a mere failure to act; that it would have been known to the defendants that carelessness on their part would result in harm to the plaintiff and loss of contact with the children; that, in the case of the medical practitioners, the duty suggested was a duty to act competently when exercising their professional skills; and that the plaintiff was vulnerable in that there was nothing he could do to protect himself against the consequences of the defendants' lack of care.

38. Factors against the plaintiff were: that the harm suffered by the plaintiff was not the direct result of the conduct of the individual defendants, and complex causation issues were involved; that the legal "relationship" between the plaintiff, the medical practitioners, and the employees of the Department, if there was one, was difficult to define, and not analogous to any existing relationship in which a similar duty of care was found to exist; that as a general rule, professionals such as doctors and social workers owe a duty to those for whom and to whom they make their services available, and in whose interest they act; that the plaintiff had a potentially adverse interest to the children, whose welfare was the primary concern of the defendants; and that there is a potential for indeterminate liability, there being no reason in principle to restrict any duty of care to family members.

39. As to the Department, and its employees, Doyle CJ, like Matheson J [576] in the earlier case, was strongly influenced by the reasoning of Lord Browne-Wilkinson in *X (Minors) v Bedfordshire County Council*.

40. As to the doctors, Doyle CJ considered that their primary duty was to the State which requested the examinations and to the child they were asked to examine. That did not necessarily exclude a duty to other people as well. But here there was no reliance on the doctors by the plaintiff, and no undertaking of responsibility to the plaintiff. He said, concerning the doctors:

"The parents of the child, or at least the parent who was a potential suspect for a conclusion of sexual abuse to be reached, could hardly be regarded as a person whose interests they could be expected or required by law to consider."

41. Gray J, with whose reasons Duggan J agreed, considered the legislative scheme to be critical. The question was whether the provisions of that scheme were incompatible with there being a duty owed to the plaintiff. The statute imposed a duty upon the defendants to protect children, to investigate allegations of child abuse, and to make necessary reports. The interests of the child were to be the paramount consideration. If the Department or its officers owed a duty of care to an alleged abuser, this would discourage or inhibit the performance of their statutory duties. An adverse report would obviously be likely to cause family disruption, but to impose duties to an abuser would put children at risk. Medical practitioners, social workers and others were obliged by the State to report suspicions. From all this there was inferred a statutory intention "that the common law should be excluded in so far as the alleged perpetrator of abuse is concerned".

The supposed duty of care

42. The argument was conducted upon the basis that it was foreseeable that harm of the kind allegedly suffered by the appellants might result from want of care on the part of those who investigated the possibility that the children had been sexually abused. But the fact that it is foreseeable, in the sense of being a real and not far-fetched possibility, that a careless act or omission on the part of one person may cause harm to another does not mean that the first person is subject to a legal liability to compensate the second by way of damages for negligence if there is such carelessness, and harm results. If it were otherwise, at least two consequences would follow. First, the law would subject citizens to an intolerable burden of potential liability, and constrain their freedom of action in a gross manner. Secondly, the tort of negligence would subvert many other principles of law, and statutory provisions, which strike a balance of rights and obligations, duties and freedoms. A defendant will only be liable, in negligence, for failure to take reasonable care to prevent a certain kind of foreseeable harm to a plaintiff, in circumstances where the law imposes a duty to take such care.

[577] 43. In *Donoghue v Stevenson* [1932] AC 562, the House of Lords, by a majority of three to two, held that such a duty was owed by the manufacturer of a beverage to a consumer of the beverage where the manufacturer sold the product to a distributor and it was ultimately sold to the consumer in circumstances such that the consumer could not discover a defect in the beverage by inspection. It was established that it was not necessary for a plaintiff to show that a case was covered by, or closely analogous to, existing precedent, and that there were general principles by reference to which a claim in negligence fell to be decided. The first principle was that, in order to support an action for damages for negligence, a plaintiff must "show that he has been injured by the breach of a duty owed to him in the circumstances by the defendant to take reasonable care to avoid such injury" (at 579 per Lord Atkin).

44. Lord Atkin, noting how difficult it was to find in the authorities statements of general application defining the relations between parties that gave rise to that duty, and pointing out that there must be some element common to all the particular relations which had been held to involve a duty, said (at 580):

"To seek a complete logical definition of the general principle is probably to go beyond the function of the judge, for the more general the definition the more likely it is to omit essentials or to introduce non-essentials. The attempt was made by Brett MR in *Heaven v Pender*, in a definition to which I will later refer. As framed, it was demonstrably too wide, though it appears to me, if properly limited, to be capable of affording a valuable practical guide".

45. In *Heaven v Pender* (1883) 11 QBD 503, Brett MR, addressing the question what is the proper definition of the relation between two persons which imposes on one of them a duty to observe, with regard to the person or property of the other, care to prevent injury, said (at 509):

"... whenever one person is by circumstances placed in such a position with regard to another that every one of ordinary sense who did think would at once recognise that if he did not use ordinary care and skill in his own conduct with regard to those circumstances he would cause danger of injury to the person or property of the other, a duty arises to use ordinary care and skill to avoid such danger."

46. Ten years later, in *Le Lievre v Gould* [1893] 1 QB 491 at 504 AL Smith LJ described that as a statement of principle "that a duty to take due care [arose] **[578]** when the person or property of one was in such proximity to the person or property of another that, if due care was not taken, damage might be done by the one to the other". That statement appears to refer to a limited form of proximity: proximity of person or property. But Lord Atkin said that it was not to be understood as limited to physical proximity. It was intended "to extend to such close and direct relations that the act complained of directly affects a person whom the person alleged to be bound to take care would know would be directly affected by his careless act" (*Donoghue v Stevenson* at 581). Even so, his Lordship was speaking of "close and direct relations". He went on to acknowledge that there will no doubt be "cases where it will be difficult to determine whether the contemplated relationship is so close that the duty arises" (at 582).

47. The references to "relations", and to the problem of deciding which relations are sufficiently proximate to give rise to a duty of care, in part reflects the previous history of the law of negligence, the focus of attention often being particular categories of relationship. The search was for a unifying principle which informed the decisions in respect to those categories. The actual conclusion in *Donoghue v Stevenson* was that, at least in certain circumstances, the manufacturer of a product intended for human consumption stood in a sufficiently proximate relation to an ultimate consumer of the product to attract a duty of care. But Lord Atkin, in his formulation of principle, was seeking to find "a valuable practical guide", and warned against "the danger of stating propositions of law in wider terms than is necessary" (at 583-584). Consistently with his reasoning, he might also have warned against the danger of stating such propositions in more categorical terms than is appropriate.

48. As Professor Fleming said (Fleming, *The Law of Torts*, 9th ed, 1998, p 151), "no one has ever succeeded in capturing in any precise formula" a comprehensive test for determining whether there exists, between two parties, a relationship sufficiently proximate to give rise to a duty of care of the kind necessary for actionable negligence. The formula is not "proximity". Notwithstanding the centrality of that concept, for more than a century, in this area of discourse, and despite some later decisions in this Court which emphasised that centrality (eg *Jaensch v Coffey* especially at 584-585 per Deane J; *Stevens v Brodribb Sawmilling Co Pty Ltd* (1986) 160 CLR 16 at 52 per Deane J), it gives little practical guidance in determining whether a duty of care exists in cases that are not analogous to cases in which a duty has been established (*Hawkins v Clayton* (1988) 164 CLR 539 at 555-556 per Brennan J; *Hill v Van Erp* (1997) 188 CLR 159 at 210 per McHugh J; *Crimmins v Stevedoring Industry Finance Committee* (1999) 200 CLR 1 at 96-97 [270]-[274] per Hayne J). It expresses the nature of what is in issue, and in that respect gives focus **[579]** to the inquiry, but as an explanation of a process of reasoning leading to a conclusion its utility is limited. The present appeals provide an illustration of the problem. To ask whether there was a relationship of proximity between the medical practitioners who examined the children, and the fathers who were suspected of abusing the children, might be a convenient short-hand method of formulating the ultimate question in the case, but it provides no assistance in deciding how to answer the question. That is so, whether it is expressed as the ultimate test of a duty of care, or as one of a number of stages in an approach towards a conclusion on that issue.

49. What has been described as the three-stage approach of Lord Bridge of Harwich in *Caparo Industries plc v Dickman* [1990] 2 AC 605 at 617-618 does not represent the law in Australia (*Perre v Apand Pty Ltd* (1999) 198 CLR 180 at 193-194 [9] per Gleeson CJ, 210-212 [77]-[82] per McHugh J, 302 [333]-[334] per Hayne J; *Modbury Triangle Shopping Centre Pty Ltd v Anzil* (2000) 75 ALJR 164 at 182 [101] per Hayne J). Lord Bridge himself said that concepts of proximity and fairness lack the necessary precision to give them utility as practical tests, and "amount in effect to little more than convenient labels to attach to the features of different specific situations which, on a detailed examination of all the circumstances, the law recognises pragmatically as giving rise to a duty of care of a given scope" (*Caparo Industries* at 617-618). There is a danger that judges and practitioners, confronted by a novel problem, will seek to give the *Caparo* approach a utility beyond that claimed for it by its original author. There is also a danger that, the matter of foreseeability (which is often incontestable) having been determined, the succeeding questions will be reduced to a discretionary judgment based upon a sense of what is fair, and just and reasonable as an outcome in the particular case. The proximity question has already been discussed. The question as to what

is fair, and just and reasonable is capable of being misunderstood as an invitation to formulate policy rather than to search for principle. The concept of policy, in this context, is often ill-defined. There are policies at work in the law which can be identified and applied to novel problems, but the law of tort develops by reference to principles, which must be capable of general application, not discretionary decision-making in individual cases.

50. Different classes of case give rise to different problems in determining the existence and nature or scope, of a duty of care. Sometimes the problems may be bound up with the harm suffered by the plaintiff, as, for example, where its direct cause is the criminal conduct of some third party (eg *Modbury Triangle Shopping Centre Pty Ltd v Anzil*). Sometimes they may arise because **[580]** the defendant is the repository of a statutory power or discretion (eg *Crimmins v Stevedoring Industry Finance Committee*; *Brodie v Singleton Shire Council* (2001) 75 ALJR 992). Sometimes they may reflect the difficulty of confining the class of persons to whom a duty may be owed within reasonable limits (eg Perre v Apand Pty Ltd). Sometimes they may concern the need to preserve the coherence of other legal principles, or of a statutory scheme which governs certain conduct or relationships (eg *Hill v Van Erp* at 231 per Gummow). The relevant problem will then become the focus of attention in a judicial evaluation of the factors which tend for or against a conclusion, to be arrived at as a matter of principle. In *Donoghue v Stevenson*, for example, Lord Buckmaster, in dissent, was concerned that, if the manufacturer in that case was liable, apart from contract or statute, to a consumer, then a person who negligently built a house might be liable, at any future time, to any person who suffered injury in consequence; a concern which later cases showed to have been far from fanciful (at 577). The problem which has caused so much difficulty in relation to the extent of tortious liability in respect of negligently constructed buildings was not only foreseeable, but foreseen, in the seminal case on the law of negligence (cf *D & F Estates Ltd v Church Commissioners for England* [1989] AC 177; *Murphy v Brentwood District Council* [1991] 1 AC 398; *Bryan v Maloney* (1995) 182 CLR 609).

51. In *Dorset Yacht Co Ltd v Home Office* [1970] AC 1004 at 1058, Lord Diplock said:

"…[T]he judicial development of the law of negligence rightly proceeds by seeking first to identify the relevant characteristics that are common to the kinds of conduct and relationship between the parties which are involved in the case for decision and the kinds of conduct and relationships which have been held in previous decisions of the courts to give rise to a duty of care".

52. Conversely, conduct and relationships may have been held not to give rise to a duty of care, and the reasons for that holding may provide an important guide to the solution of the problem in a new case.

53. Developments in the law of negligence over the last 30 or more years reveal the difficulty of identifying unifying principles that would allow ready solution of novel problems. Nonetheless, that does not mean that novel cases are to be decided by reference only to some intuitive sense of what is "fair" or "unfair". There are cases, and this is one, where to find a duty of care would so cut across other legal principles as to impair their proper application and thus lead to the conclusion that there is no duty of care of the kind asserted.

54. The present cases can be seen as focusing as much upon the **[581]** communication of information by the respondents to the appellants and to third parties as upon the competence with which examinations or other procedures were conducted. The core of the complaint by each appellant is that he was injured as a result of what he, and others, were told. At once, then, it can be seen that there is an intersection with the law of defamation which resolves the competing interests of the parties through well-developed principles about privilege and the like. To apply the law of negligence in the present case would resolve that competition on an altogether different basis (cf *Spring v Guardian Assurance plc* [1995] 2 AC 296). It would allow recovery of damages for publishing statements to the discredit of a person where the law of defamation would not.

55. More fundamentally, however, these cases present a question about coherence of the law. Considering whether the persons who reported their suspicions about each appellant owed that appellant a duty of care must begin from the recognition that those who made the report had other responsibilities. A duty of the kind alleged should not be found if that duty would not be compatible with other duties which the respondents owed.

56. How may a duty of the kind for which the appellants contend rationally be related to the functions, powers and responsibilities of the various persons and authorities who are alleged to owe that duty? A similar problem has arisen in other cases. The response to the problem in those cases, although not determinative, is instructive.

57. In *Hill v Chief Constable of West Yorkshire* [1989] AC 53, the House of Lords held that police officers did not owe a duty to individual members of the public who might suffer injury through their careless failure to apprehend a dangerous criminal. Lord Keith of Kinkel pointed out (at 63) that the conduct of a police investigation involves a variety of decisions on matters of policy and discretion, including decisions as to priorities in the deployment of resources. To subject those decisions to a common law duty of care, and to the kind of judicial scrutiny involved in an action in tort, was inappropriate.

58. Earlier, in *Yuen Kun Yeu v Attorney-General of Hong Kong* [1988] AC 175, the Privy Council held that a regulatory authority did not owe a duty of care to corporate depositors. Their Lordships pointed to the responsibilities and discretions of the authority, and concluded that there was no intention on the part of the legislature that, in considering whether to register or deregister a company, there should be a common law duty of care superimposed upon the statutory framework.

59. Reference has already been made to the reasoning of Lord Browne-Wilkinson in *X (Minors) v Bedfordshire County Council* [1995] 2 AC 633.

[582] 60. The circumstance that a defendant owes a duty of care to a third party, or is subject to statutory obligations which constrain the manner in which powers or discretions may be exercised, does not of itself rule out the possibility that a duty of care is owed to a plaintiff. People may be subject to a number of duties, at least provided they are not irreconcilable. A medical practitioner who examines, and reports upon the condition of, an individual, might owe a duty of care to more than one person. But if a suggested duty of care would give rise to inconsistent obligations, that would ordinarily be a reason for denying that the duty exists. Similarly, when public authorities, or their officers, are charged with the responsibility of conducting investigations, or exercising powers, in the public interest, or in the interests of a specified class of persons, the law would not ordinarily subject them to a duty to have regard to the interests of another class of persons where that would impose upon them conflicting claims or obligations.

61. There is also a question as to the extent, and potential indeterminacy, of liability. In the case of a medical practitioner, the range of people who might foreseeably (in the sense earlier mentioned) suffer some kind of harm, as a consequence of careless diagnosis or treatment of a patient, is extensive.

62. The statutory scheme that formed the background to the activities of the present respondents was, relevantly, a scheme for the protection of children. It required the respondents to treat the interests of the children as paramount. Their professional or statutory responsibilities involved investigating and reporting upon, allegations that the children had suffered, and were under threat of, serious harm. It would be inconsistent with the proper and effective discharge of those responsibilities that they should be subjected to a legal duty, breach of which would sound in damages, to take care to protect persons who were suspected of being the sources of that harm. The duty for which the appellants contend cannot be reconciled satisfactorily, either with the nature of the functions being exercised by the respondents, or with their statutory obligation to treat the interests of the children as paramount. As to the former, the functions of examination, and reporting, require, for their effective discharge, an investigation into the facts without apprehension as to possible adverse consequences for people in the position of the appellants or legal liability to such persons. As to the latter, the interests of the children, and those suspected of causing their harm, are diverse, and irreconcilable. That they are irreconcilable is evident when regard is had to the case in which examination of a child alleged to be a victim of abuse does not allow the examiner to form a definite opinion about whether the child has been abused, only a suspicion that it *may* have happened. The interests of the child, in such a case, would favour reporting that the suspicion of abuse has not been dispelled; the interests of a person suspected of the abuse would be to the opposite effect.

63. Furthermore, the attempt by the appellants to avoid the problem of [583] the extent of potential duty and liability is unconvincing. They sought to limit it to parents. But, if it exists, why should it be so limited? If the suspected child abuser were a relative other than a parent, or a

schoolteacher, or a neighbour, or a total stranger, why should that person be in a position different from that of a parent? The logical consequence of the appellants' argument must be that a duty of care is owed to anyone who is, or who might become, a suspect.

64. A final point should be noted. The appellants do not contend that any legal right was infringed. And, once one rejects the distinction between parents and everybody else, they can point to no relationship, association, or connection, between themselves and the respondents, other than that which arises from the fact that, if the children had been abused, the appellants were the prime suspects. But that is merely the particular circumstance that gave rise to the risk that carelessness on the part of the respondents might cause them harm. Ultimately, their case rests on foreseeability; and that is not sufficient.

Conclusion

65. The duty of care for which the appellants contend does not exist.

66. The appeals should be dismissed with costs.

Appeals dismissed

Miller v Miller
(2011) 242 CLR 446; [2011] HCA 9
High Court of Australia

Where the purpose of a statute is both to proscribe as a criminal offence the taking and use of a car without the consent of the owner and to deter and punish such conduct because of its association with dangerous or reckless driving, the law would lack coherence or be inconsistent or incongruent if it recognised that one participant engaged in the proscribed conduct owed a duty of care to another participant jointly engaged in the same conduct.

[The plaintiff (appellant) Danelle Miller, aged 16, decided to steal a car and use it to drive from one Perth suburb to her home in another Perth suburb. After stealing the car, the plaintiff picked up the defendant (respondent) Maurin Miller, a distant relative, aged 27. The defendant got into the driver's seat and began to drive, at first sensibly and then at speed, driving through red lights. The plaintiff twice asked the defendant to be let out of the car but the defendant kept driving, laughing off the plaintiff's concerns. Shortly after the second request, an accident occurred due to the defendant's negligent driving. In the accident the plaintiff suffered serious personal injury. In a negligence action in the District Court of Western Australia, the primary judge found in favour of the plaintiff subject to a 50% reduction of her damages for contributory negligence. On appeal, the Western Australia Court of Appeal held that the plaintiff's claim should fail on the ground that her participation with the defendant in the joint illegal enterprise of using the car without the consent of the owner negatived the existence of a duty of care. On further appeal by the plaintiff, a majority of the High Court of Australia (French CJ, Gummow, Hayne, Crennan, Kiefel and Bell JJ; Heydon J dissenting) allowed the plaintiff's appeal on the ground that, by the time of the accident, the plaintiff, by her requests to be let out of the car, had withdrawn from the joint illegal enterprise and was owed a duty of care by the defendant.

Heydon J agreed with the majority that the defendant owed no duty of care to the plaintiff at least until she made the two requests to be let out of the car. However, Heydon J disagreed with the conclusion of the majority that the plaintiff's requests to be let out of the car constituted a withdrawal by her from the joint illegal enterprise in which she and the defendant were engaged. Heydon J reached this conclusion on the ground that "the withdrawal point", although originally pleaded by the plaintiff, had not been the subject of argument before, or consideration by, the primary judge or the Western Australia Court of Appeal and had not been referred to in her notice of appeal or written submissions in the present appeal. As a result of lack of adequate notice, the withdrawal point had not been the subject of "detailed forensic debate" before the High Court.]

FRENCH CJ, GUMMOW, HAYNE, CRENNAN, KIEFEL and BELL JJ. ...

[453] *Preliminary considerations*

11. It is convenient to begin examination of the issues in the case by making two preliminary points: first, the illegality of a plaintiff's conduct presents the question, but does not provide the answer to, whether the plaintiff can recover damages for negligence for injury suffered in the course of or as a result of that illegal conduct; and secondly, causation alone does not provide a satisfactory principle by which to resolve the issue, and was rejected as a determinative criterion by this Court in *Henwood v Municipal Tramways Trust (SA)* (1938) 60 CLR 438. ...

[454] 15. These reasons will show that the central policy consideration at stake is the coherence of the law. The importance of that consideration has been remarked on in decisions of this Court of this Court (*Sullivan v Moody* (2001) 207 CLR 562 at 576 [42], 580-581 [53]-[55]; *Agricultural and Rural Finance Pty Ltd v Gardiner* (2008) 238 CLR 570 at 602 [100]; *CAL No 14 Pty Ltd v Motor Accidents Insurance Board* (2009) 239 CLR 390 at 406-410 [39]-[42]). ... It is a consideration that is important at two levels. First, the principles applied in relation to the tort of negligence must be congruent with those applied in other areas of the civil law (most notably contract and trusts).

16. Secondly, and more fundamentally, the issue that is presented by observing that a plaintiff was acting illegally when injured as a result of the defendant's negligence is whether there is some relevant intersection between the law that made the plaintiff's conduct unlawful and the legal principles that determine whether the plaintiff should **[455]** have a cause of action for negligence against the defendant. Ultimately, the question is: would it be incongruous for the law to proscribe the plaintiff's conduct and yet allow recovery in negligence for damage suffered in the course, or as a result, of that unlawful conduct? ...

17. The second preliminary observation to make is that the issue cannot be resolved by asking only whether there is a causal connection between the plaintiff's illegal conduct and the occurrence of the damage of which the plaintiff complains. Why not?

18. The fact that a plaintiff was acting contrary to law when he or she suffered damage of which the defendant's negligence is alleged to be a cause does not automatically preclude the plaintiff from recovering damages from the defendant. ...

[456] 22. In *Henwood* (1938) 60 CLR 438 at 457-460, Dixon and McTiernan JJ rejected analysis of the significance of illegality to liability in tort by reference only to questions of causation. In *Henwood,* the plaintiffs sued under legislation enacted on the pattern of Lord Campbell's Act (Fatal Accidents Act 1846 (UK)) in respect of the death of their son, allegedly as a result of the defendant's negligence. The son died as a result of injuries sustained when, contrary to a by-law made under statute, he leaned out of a tram on its off-side, and hit his head on poles erected by the defendant Tramways Trust in the centre of the road. As Dixon and McTiernan JJ pointed out (at 458), there was a direct connection between the illegal act and the injury. The illegal conduct of the deceased was a necessary cause of his injury. But their Honours were of the view (at 460) that the plaintiffs **[457]** should succeed in their claim on the footing that it was not a "part of the purpose of the law against which the plaintiff has offended to disentitle a person doing the prohibited act from complaining of the other party's neglect or default, without which his own act would not have resulted in injury". The analysis made by Latham CJ (at 445-448) was to substantially similar effect.

[The majority judgment then discussed illegality in contract and trusts and the decisions of the High Court in *Smith v Jenkins* (1970) 119 CLR 397, *Jackson v Harrison* (1978) 138 CLR 438 and *Gala v Preston* (1991) 172 CLR 243, all cases concerned with claims founded on negligence to recover damages for personal injury arising out of motor accidents where plaintiff passengers were complicit in offences committed by defendant drivers.]

[472] *Common threads in the decided cases*

70. What has been said about the previous decisions in this Court shows that some propositions can be made. First, the fact that a plaintiff was acting illegally when injured as a result of the defendant's negligence is not determinative of whether a duty of care is owed. Secondly, the fact that plaintiff and defendant were both acting illegally when the plaintiff suffered injuries of which the defendant's negligence was a cause and which would not have been suffered but for the plaintiff's participation in the illegal act is not determinative. Thirdly, there are cases where the parties' joint participation in illegal conduct should **[473]** preclude a plaintiff recovering damages for negligence from the defendant. Fourthly, different bases have been said to found the denial of recovery in some, but not all, cases of joint illegal enterprise: no duty of care should be found to exist; a standard of care cannot or should not he fixed; the plaintiff assumed the risk of negligence. Fifthly, the different bases for denial of liability all rest on a policy judgment. That policy judgment has sometimes been expressed in terms that the courts *cannot* regulate the activities of wrongdoers and sometimes in terms that the courts *should not* do so.

71. Twice [*Smith v Jenkins* (1970) 119 CLR 397; *Gala v Preston* (1991) 172 CLR 243] this Court has held (unanimously in each case) that one illegal user of a motor vehicle cannot recover damages for injuries sustained as a result of the negligent driving of another illegal user of the vehicle. Central to the conclusion in each of those cases was the observation that the negligence alleged was negligence by one criminal in carrying out his part in the unlawful undertaking in which both plaintiff and defendant were engaged. ...

73. Why should courts not regulate the activities of the wrongdoers by requiring of the driver that he or she exercise reasonable care for the safety of other road users and any passenger in the vehicle, whether or not the passenger is complicit in the crime? As explained at the outset of these reasons, the answer must lie in whether it is incongruous for the law to provide that the driver should not be using the vehicle at all and yet say that, if the driver and another jointly undertake the crime of using a vehicle illegally, the driver owes the confederate a duty to use it carefully when neither should be using it at all.

74. Incongruity (whether described by that word or as "contrariety" or "lack of coherence") will not be demonstrated or denied by bare assertion of the answer. More analysis is required. If a statute has been contravened, careful attention must be paid to the purposes of that statute. It will be by reference to the relevant statute, and identification of its purposes, that any incongruity, contrariety or lack of coherence denying the existence of a duty of care will be found. That is the path that was taken in *Henwood*. It is the same as the path that has been taken in relation to illegality in contract and trusts. The same path should be taken in cases where the plaintiff sues the defendant for damages for the negligent infliction of injury suffered in the course of, or as a result of, the pursuit of a joint illegal enterprise.

Relevant statutory provisions ...

[The majority judgment then referred to s 371A of the *Criminal Code* (WA) ("the Code") which made it an offence, punishable by imprisonment, for a person unlawfully to use, or take for the purpose of using, a motor vehicle without the consent of the owner. The majority judgment also referred to the legislative history of this provision and to s 8(2) of the Code which provided that, where two or more persons form "a common intention to prosecute an unlawful purpose", a person is not deemed to have committed the offence if "before the commission of the offence, the person – (a) withdrew from the prosecution of the unlawful purpose."]

[478] *The purposes of the legislation*

88. ... [T]he legislative history behind s 371A of the Code demonstrates that the offence of illegal use of a motor vehicle soon passed from the relatively minor offence created by the *Traffic Act 1919* [WA] to a more serious crime (with the enactment of s 390A of the Code in 1932) and thence (by the enactment of s 371A of the Code, and repeal of s 89(1) of the *Road Traffic Act* [WA] in 1991) to a still more serious crime equated with theft. An association between the illegal use of a motor

vehicle and driving in a manner that was reckless or dangerous was reflected by the introduction of aggravated forms of the offence of illegal use.

89. These changes in the legislation reflected not only a rise in the incidence of illegal use of motor cars, but also a recognition of the dangers to life and limb that often attended the commission of that crime. No doubt the legislation, both as it now stands and as it stood in earlier times, must be understood as effecting a purpose of protecting the property interests of vehicle owners. But in more recent years the legislature also recognised the fact that those who took and used vehicles without the permission of their owners often drove (as Dawson J pointed out in *Gala v Preston* (1991) 172 CLR 243 at 280) with a "concomitant lack of responsibility for the safety of the vehicle involved and the inevitable desire to avoid detection". The legislative purposes of s 371A are not confined to protection of property rights. They include the advancement of road safety.

90. If expressed only as the protection of property rights and the promotion of general road safety, the statutory purposes of s 371A, standing alone, appear not to speak to any question of the liability for negligence of one illegal user to another. But there is a further question that must be considered before concluding that one illegal user can sue another in negligence.

[479] 91. As noted earlier, a critical step in the reasoning in earlier cases in this Court considering the liability in negligence of one illegal user of a vehicle to another was that the negligence has been committed *in the performance* (*Gala v Preston* (1991) 172 CLR 243 at 278 per Dawson J; see also *Smith v Jenkins* (1970) 119 CLR 397 at 416-417 per Windeyer J) of the joint criminal venture. ...

93. If, in a particular case, it were to be shown that a probable consequence of commission of an offence of taking or using a vehicle illegally was the commission of other driving offences (including reckless or dangerous driving) those who were complicit in the initial offence would be criminally liable for the subsequent offences as well. More particularly, if, as here, the driver of the illegally used vehicle drove dangerously, and driving in that manner was a probable consequence of the prosecution of the joint illegal purpose, a person complicit in the crime of illegal use would also be complicit in the offence of driving dangerously. And if, as a result of the dangerous driving, the complicit passenger were injured, it would evidently be incongruous to decide that the offender who drove the vehicle owed that passenger a duty to drive with reasonable care. The passenger would have committed the offence of dangerous driving and yet, if the [480] driver owed the passenger a duty to take reasonable care, the passenger (who would be criminally responsible for the driver's dangerous driving) might sue the driver for damages for driving negligently.

94. The incongruity identified stems immediately from the injured passenger's complicity, not only in the illegal use of the vehicle, but also in the driver's commission of the offence of driving dangerously. To conclude that the driver owed the passenger a duty to take reasonable care when driving would not be consistent with the purpose of the statute proscribing dangerous driving. ...

[481] 101. The refusal to find a duty of care between those complicit in the offence follows from the more precise identification of the way in [482] which the statutory proscription of illegal use of a vehicle seeks to promote road safety. The offence of illegally taking and using a vehicle is dealt with as it is because of its association with reckless and dangerous driving. The statutory purpose of a law proscribing dangerous or reckless driving is *not* consistent with one offender owing a co-offender a duty to take reasonable care. And in a case where two or more are complicit in the offence of illegally using a vehicle, the statutory purpose of the law proscribing illegal use (here, s 371A) is not consistent with one offender owing a co-offender a duty to take reasonable care. The inconsistency or incongruity arises regardless of whether reckless or dangerous driving eventuates. It arises from the recognition that the purpose of the statute is to deter and punish using a vehicle in circumstances that often lead to reckless and dangerous driving. ...

The circumstances of this case

103. As noted at the outset of these reasons, Danelle twice asked to be let out of the car before it ran off the road. She was not.

104. Reference has already been made to the provisions of s 8 of the Code concerning liability for offences committed in prosecution of a common unlawful purpose and to the provisions made by s 8(2) for withdrawal from a joint criminal enterprise. It was not disputed, in this Court, that it

was open to Danelle to submit that she had withdrawn from the common purpose of illegally using the vehicle before the accident, and no positive argument was advanced to demonstrate that she had not done so in the manner required by s 8(2) of the Code. The requirement, in s 8(2)(c) of the Code, that an offender, having withdrawn from an enterprise and communicated that fact to his or her confederates, take "all reasonable steps to prevent the commission of the offence" invites attention in this case to what Danelle could reasonably have done to prevent the continued illegal use of the car. ... There were no *reasonable* steps she could take to prevent the continued illegal use of the vehicle. ...

[483] 106. Because Danelle had withdrawn from, and was no longer participating in, the crime of illegally using the car when the accident happened, it could no longer be said that Maurin owed her no duty of care. That he owed her no duty earlier in the journey is not to the point. When he ran off the road, he owed a passenger who was not then complicit in the crime which he was then committing a duty to take reasonable care. ...

Appeal allowed

3. PRODUCTS AND PREMISES

Minchillo v Ford Motor Company of Australia Ltd
[1995] 2 VR 594
Supreme Court of Victoria, Appeal Division

A manufacturer of goods does not owe a duty of care to a consumer in respect of pure economic loss attributable to the defective quality of the goods.

[The appellants (plaintiffs) had acquired a truck from the respondent (defendant) which vibrated excessively at high speed. The appellants sought to establish that the respondent had breached certain provisions of the *Trade Practices Act 1974* (Cth) providing for consumer protection; had breached its contractual collateral warrant; and had breached its duty of care under the tort of negligence. The trial judge rejected all these claims. The appellants appealed to the Supreme Court of Victoria which dismissed the appeal. The following extracts from the judgments are only concerned with the Supreme Court's reasons for holding that the respondent did not owe the appellants a duty of care.]

BROOKING J. ... [596] Where physical injury to person or property is alleged to have been caused by the dangerous character or condition of goods and the manufacturer is sued, the jury can be asked, or a trial judge sitting alone can ask himself, whether the manufacturer is shown not to have taken reasonable care to avoid the risk of injury, and the design, manufacture or labelling of the goods will be considered in answering that question.

But where no physical injury to person or property has been occasioned by goods, what is the question for the jury? It can hardly be whether the manufacturer took reasonable care in relation to the manufacture of the goods to avoid a reasonably foreseeable and real risk of economic injury to another. Accordingly, attempts to formulate the suggested duty of care of a manufacturer towards consumers generally for the purpose of considering whether it exists have introduced the notion that the goods must be in some sense defective. It has been pointed out, as an obstacle to the adoption of the view that the general duty of care exists, that the notion that goods are defective is itself imprecise, and accordingly, less imprecise formulations have been essayed. But these further formulations themselves introduce a standard or standards liable to create difficulties.

In a passage often since referred to, Stamp LJ in *Dutton v Bognor Regis Urban District Council* [1972] 1 QB 373 at 414-5 distinguished between the careless manufacture of a dangerous bottle of ginger beer which caused injury to person or property and the careless manufacture of what should have been a bottle of ginger beer but turned out to be a bottle of water. The duty of care of [597] a manufacturer did not in his Lordship's view extend beyond the careless putting out of a dangerous thing to the careless putting out of a merely defective or useless or valueless thing. The law of tort did not treat the manufacturer as warranting to the ultimate consumer that what he manufactured was reasonably fit for its purpose.

So in *Junior Books Ltd v Veitchi Co Ltd* [1983] 1 AC 520 Lord Fraser of Tullybelton said this at 533:

> "A manufacturer's duty to take care not to make a product that is dangerous sets a standard which is, in principle, easy to ascertain. ... But a duty not to produce a *defective* article sets a standard which is less easily ascertained, because it has to be judged largely by reference to the contract." ...

[598] Accepting that one could not define a manufacturer's supposed duty of care to consumers as a duty to take reasonable care in relation to manufacture to avoid the risk of economic injury to another, Mr Lenczner [appellants' counsel] hovered uneasily between "defects" and "latent defects" as the missing term to be introduced into the statement of the duty. I confess that I do not know how to define a defect for this purpose. "Defective" in the sense of physically dangerous to person and property I can understand; but "defective" affords no satisfactory standard. One man's meat is another man's poison. The scribbling block bought for a few cents at the supermarket might serve very well for the correspondence of the artisan, but it would not have done for the Duke. Price is an important consideration: generally speaking, as the saying goes, you get what you pay for. ...

[599] We should adopt the view that has now been three times expressed in the House of Lords, beginning with the *Junior Books* case itself, that as regards goods which are merely defective in quality as opposed to dangerous manufacturers are under no general duty of care towards consumers. ...

ORMISTON J. ... **[606]** The difficulty, for present purposes, is that the trial judge accepted Mr Minchillo's evidence as to the excessive vibrations and difficulties in steering and Mr Enkelman's opinion that those vibrations were transmitted through the chassis. He rejected the respondent's evidence that the vibration and steering of **[607]** the truck were acceptable for that type of prime mover and that any apparent excessive vibrations would have been caused by run-out. Further he rejected such of the appellants' evidence which suggested that the vibrations were caused by the positioning of the "fifth wheel". However, for reasons which will be examined, he was not satisfied that the condition of the prime mover was attributable to any defects of materials or workmanship in the manufacturing process but concluded that the deficiencies complained of were caused by defects in the design of that model. He reached that conclusion largely because he was not satisfied that the defect arose from any fault in the manufacturing process, although the respondent's evidence was not truly directed towards the distinction between manufacture and design, inasmuch as it sought to deny that there were any deficiencies in the prime mover. ...

[618] The appellants also sought to allege negligence against Ford in relation to the acquisition of the vehicle but the learned trial judge held, correctly in my opinion, that there was no duty of care made out. The facts and circumstances from which the duty of care was alleged were set out with no great precision in the statement of claim but in substance it was alleged that the appellants acquired from Lanes a prime mover made by Ford which was sold by it to Lanes for re-sale. The particulars of negligence alleged against Ford included "manufacturing a defective vehicle for use by a cartage contractor", "failing to any or any proper inspections or examinations for supply of the vehicle to the first-named defendant" (Lanes), "permitting the vehicle to be supplied to the first-named defendant for supply to" the appellants and "failing to take proper care to safeguard the [appellants'] interests". Each of these means of formulating this cause of action involved claims which, as the trial judge rightly held, were not supportable on a proper understanding of authority. ...

In substance his Honour held that there was no sufficient proximity between Ford and either of the appellants so that no duty of care was owed by Ford as manufacturer to prevent damage of the kind alleged by the appellants. In reaching this conclusion he referred to a number of cases in both the High Court and the House of Lords from *Caltex Oil (Australia) Pty Ltd v The Dredge "Willemstad"* (1976) 136 CLR 529 to *Murphy v Brentwood District Council* [1991] 1 AC 398. ...

My firm conclusion is that a proper understanding of those authorities is that the common law, in both England and Australia, has not yet recognised a general duty of care to prevent economic harm. A careful analysis of this authority appears in the latest, 8th edition of *Fleming on Torts*, (1992), at pp 177-85, showing the specific, but limited, circumstances which have so far given rise to a duty to prevent economic loss. So far as manufacturers and distributors are concerned, the learned author has concluded at p 495:

> "The purpose of this branch of the law being the promotion of safety, its concern is primarily with physical injury".

So, although there can be no doubt that those who suffer personal injury or property damage by reason of negligence in the course of the manufacture and distribution of goods may recover from those responsible, the preferable conclusion, at least until this issue is considered by the High Court, has been expressed by Southwell J, after a detailed examination of the authorities, in *Opat v National Mutual Life Association of Australasia Ltd* [1992] 1 VR 283 at 292:

> "However, I do not see in the High Court judgments support for the proposition that a chattel manufacturer owes a duty to any ultimate user who suffers economic loss from faulty manufacture."

It may be that, if a negligently manufactured article results in physical injury or property loss, the consequential economic loss, in particular by persons obliged to indemnify against such loss or damage, will be treated as damage arising from **[619]** a breach of a duty of care and the relevant tests of proximity will have been satisfied ...

[Fullagar J agreed with Ormiston J.]

Appeal dismissed

Voli v Inglewood Shire Council
(1963) 110 CLR 74
High Court of Australia

A contract under which a defendant renders services to a third party may be relevant to the content of the duty of care that the defendant owes to others in tort, arising out of the manner in which the work is carried out. An occupier may be liable for the work of an independent contractor in some circumstances.

[The plaintiff (appellant), Mr Luigi Voli, was injured when the stage of a shire hall, in which he was attending a meeting, collapsed. The cause of the collapse was that the joists supporting the floor were not strong enough to carry the load that was on it. The building, in Texas, Queensland, was designed by Mr RH Lockwood, the second defendant (second respondent), an architect, and owned and occupied by the first defendant (first respondent), a shire council. Although the plans and specifications prepared by the architect did not comply with the Council's building bylaws, they had been passed by Council employees. The plans and specifications had been approved by the Queensland Public Works Department for the purpose of securing a government subsidy for the building. At the time of the accident the hall was hired out by the Council to the South Queensland Tobacco Growers Co-operative Association Ltd, of which the plaintiff was a member, for a meeting of the members.

The trial judge in the Supreme Court of Queensland (Brown J) gave judgment in favour of the architect on the ground that, although the architect was negligent, the plaintiff's injury was not sufficiently proximate to that negligence because the intervention of the Public Works Department relieved the architect from any duty of care towards a person such as the plaintiff. The trial judge gave judgment in favour of the Council on the ground that the Council had no actual or constructive knowledge of the danger. The plaintiff appealed to the High Court of Australia.]

WINDEYER J. ... **[83]** It will be convenient to consider the appellant's case against the second respondent, the architect, before that against the Council.

[84] An architect undertaking any work in the way of his profession accepts the ordinary liabilities of any man who follows a skilled calling. He is bound to exercise due care, skill and diligence. He is not required to have an extraordinary degree of skill or the highest professional attainments. But he must bring to the task he undertakes the competence and skill that is usual among architects practising their profession. And he must use due care. If he fails in these matters and the person who employed him thereby suffers damage, he is liable to that person. This liability can be said to arise either from a breach of his contract or in tort.

In this case, however, the primary question does not arise from the duty that an architect has to his employer. It is whether the respondent architect had a duty to someone not his employer, a person with whom he had no contract at all, a person unknown to him personally whose only relationship with him was that he went into a building designed by him and built under his supervision. In the abstract the question, and it is an important question for architects, is can an architect be liable for negligence to a person who, after a building is finished and has been taken over by the building owner, lawfully enters it and, by reason of faults in its design and construction, comes to harm. Whatever might have been thought to be the position before the broad principles of the law of negligence were stated in modern form in *Donoghue v Stevenson* [1932] AC 562, it is now beyond doubt that, for the reasonably foreseeable consequences of careless or unskilful conduct, an architect is liable to anyone whom it could reasonably have been expected might be injured as a result of his negligence. To such a person he owes a duty of care quite independently of his contract of employment. Therefore it is appropriate to ask, as a preliminary question, whether there was a duty of care to the plaintiff in a particular case. This approach has been criticized. It is, on final analysis, the need for care lest someone be injured that both creates the duty and determines what amounts to a breach of it. Nevertheless the conventional division of the inquiry is sanctioned by high authority. And it is convenient, because whether a duty of care arises from a particular situation or relationship may be, and often is, a question of law; but whether or not that duty was performed is ultimately a question of fact, to be judged by what, in the circumstances of the particular case and in the light of the apparent risks, a reasonable man would or would not do. In some situations the courts have not left the latter question wholly at large. They have indicated what ordinarily a reasonable man must do, or not do, to satisfy [85] the duty of care that the situation of the parties has created. But the question is really one of fact. And what an architect must do to avoid liability for negligence cannot be more precisely defined than by saying that he must use reasonable care, skill and diligence in the performance of the work he undertakes. …

[N]either the terms of the architect's engagement, nor the terms of the building contract, can operate to discharge the architect from a duty of care to persons who are strangers to those contracts. Nor can they directly determine what he must do to satisfy his duty to such persons. That duty is cast upon him by law, not because he made a contract, but because he entered upon the work. Nevertheless his contract with the building owner is not an irrelevant circumstance. It determines what was the task upon which he entered. If, for example, it was to design a stage to bear only some specified weight, he would not be liable for the consequences of someone thereafter negligently permitting a greater weight to be put upon it. …

The respondent, Lockwood, knew the purpose for which the hall was being built, and the use to which it would be put. His duty of care extended to persons who would come there to use it in the ordinary way. Did he use due care and skill in the performance of this duty? That the stage did not answer the requirement of the Australian Standards Association booklet does not of itself establish that he was negligent. But there is no reason for disagreeing with the decision of the learned trial judge that, in fact, he did not exercise due skill and care. He failed to provide in his plans and specifications for a stage that would bear the number of people who might be expected to assemble there. …

[86] The learned trial judge held that, nevertheless, the architect was exonerated because his plans and specifications had been submitted to the Public Works Department and no objection had been made there to the design and details of the stage. His Honour based his conclusion that this absolved the architect upon the well-known passage in Lord Atkin's judgment in *Donoghue v Stevenson* [1932] AC 562, where his Lordship said that a manufacturer's liability for negligence arises when he sells his products "in such a form as to show that he intends them to reach the

ultimate consumer in the form in which they left him with no reasonable possibility of intermediate examination" ([1932] AC at 559). Analysis and discussion of this statement in later cases have established that what is significant is not whether an intermediate examination of the article was possible. It is whether it was contemplated that, in the ordinary course, the article would be examined, or tested, or in some way treated before it was taken into consumption or use. It was argued here that the examination by the Public Works Department was an "intermediate examination". And that, it was said, ended the matter. But this is much too literal an application of Lord Atkin's statement. We must not, as Scott LJ put it, in *Haseldine v C A Daw & Son Ltd* [1941] 2 KB 343, fall "into the error of assuming that Lord *Atkin* was intending to formulate a complete criterion, almost like a definition in the prolegomena to a new theory of philosophy" ([1941] 2 KB 342 at 362). We were asked to take the language in which Lord Atkin formulated a principle, applicable to cases such as that which he was considering, as if it were as inflexible as a statutory enactment. This is wrong. ...

[87] There is, of course, an obvious difference between making or supplying a thing to be examined, tested or treated before use, and making or supplying a thing to be used without more ado. But, when harm ensues, the problem for a court is whether the proximate cause of it was the negligence of the person who made the faulty thing, or the negligence of a person who was to examine, test, or treat it, or the combined negligence of both persons. In some cases, the failure of the person who was to make the test [88] to do so properly, whether he was himself the contemplated user or a third person, may supersede the initial liability of the manufacturer or supplier of the defective article. But, if separate and independent acts or omissions of several persons have directly contributed to cause an injury, the first wrongdoer does not necessarily escape liability by proving that, though he was to blame, the injury would not have occurred but for the later negligence of another person. ... The problem is one of remoteness; and of finding the cause of the damage in a particular case, not according to some philosophical concept of causation, but "to fix liability on some responsible person" to use the words of Lord Sumner in *Weld-Blundell v Stephens* [1920] AC 956, at 986. It is a realm in which law and philosophy both meet and part company. But we do not have to decide an abstract moot question. The facts of the present case really do not admit of the conclusion that the architect was freed of liability to persons in the position of the appellant when his plans were approved by the Public Works Department. No doubt the fact that his plans were approved by a public authority may, in some cases, be relevant in considering whether or not an architect was in fact negligent; but that is a very different thing from saying that by obtaining approval in this case the architect shed all liability for negligence. The approval of the Public Works Department was required because the building of the hall was to be financed in part by a subsidy from the State. The State Treasury required that the plans be approved before it would advance the money. But that does not mean that the officers who examined the plans undertook to correct the architect's errors. In his evidence he said "as these plans had to go to a final authority I thought that they should find anything that was untoward and that would be pointed out". It was a not unnatural expectation. But it did not excuse a lack of care.

Turning now to the claim against the Shire Council: this was put in various ways based upon the well-known formulations of the duty of the occupier of premises to visitors who come there in differing rights and for varying purposes. These rules do not of themselves provide a final answer in all cases. In some cases a [89] lawyer thinks at once of *Indermaur v Dames* (1866) LR 1 CP 274; (1867) LR 2 CP 311, and only later of *Donoghue v Stevenson* [1932] AC 562. But, even without the aid of a statute such as now exists in England, the trend of judicial authority has been to treat the liability of an occupier for mishaps upon his premises as governed by a duty of care arising from the general principles of the law of negligence. The special rules concerning invitees, licensees and others are ultimately subservient to those general principles. Instead of first looking at the capacity in which the plaintiff comes upon the premises, and putting him into a category by which his rights are measured, the tendency now is to look at all the circumstances of the case, including the activities of the occupier upon, or in respect of, the premises, and to measure his liability against the conduct that would be expected of a reasonably careful man in such circumstances. ... How the visitor comes to be upon the premises is always an important fact. But it is not necessarily decisive.

It seems better to appreciate that the ultimate question is one of fact and governed by general rules, than to create new categories and distinctions.

The hall ... was owned by the Council. ... It was formally admitted by the Council that on the occasion with which we are concerned, the Council "hired for reward the said hall to the South Queensland Tobacco Growers' Co-operative Association Ltd. for the purpose of holding a meeting of the members of the said Co-operative".

It becomes of some importance, or so it was argued, to decide what legal interests were created by this hiring. That is because a landlord who grants a tenancy of a building ordinarily ceases to be the occupier of it and is relieved of liability in tort for harm that may occur because of its defective condition. For that the tenant becomes liable as occupier. "A landlord who lets a house in a dangerous state, is not liable to the tenant's customers or guests for accidents happening during the term; for, fraud apart, there is no law against letting a tumble-down house; and the tenant's [90] remedy is upon his contract, if any." This statement of Erle CJ, in *Robbins v Jones* (1863) 143 ER 768 at p 776, has been often quoted, notably so in *Cavalier v Pope* [1906] AC 428. ...Lord Denning has described *Cavalier v Pope* as a "relic of a worn out fallacy which must be kept in close confinement". He said that in *Green v Chelsea Borough Council* [1954] 2 QB 127 at p 138. There the Court of Appeal held that the limitation upon the liability of a landlord only exists in cases in which the relationship is strictly that of a landlord and tenant. It does not exist in the case of a licensor and licensee. One may accept this proposition as correct ... . [91] [I]n this case the letting of the hall to the Association for the purpose of holding its meeting was no more than the grant of a sole licence to have the use of it for a brief time. During that period the Association could, no doubt, decide who, apart from the caretaker or other representatives of the Council, might go in. But that was all. Therefore *Cavalier v Pope* does not stand in the appellant's way.

Moreover, firmly entrenched positions may be outflanked. Even if the letting of the hall for the meeting did technically create a tenancy, that would not be the end of the matter. That the hall was kept by the Council for the ordinary purposes of a public hall and let out for use for short periods, is a circumstance of overriding importance. It attracts by analogy an ancient principle of the common law concerning things, for example vehicles or boats, kept for hire to the public — a principle that ought not, at this day, to be denied application to buildings and structures merely because they are affixed to land. The matter has been discussed in cases in the United States, especially in the State of New York. There it may be said to be established that a person who lets out property for public purposes, such as an assembly hall, is under a duty to members of the public to see that it is reasonably safe for the purpose for which it is let. ... [92] We are not dealing with a building let as a dwelling-house or for similar private purposes. No departure from the tradition of the common law is involved in asking what does the law require of those who keep halls for hire to the public. Of course we must not put their obligations higher than law and good sense combine to demand. Throughout the land there are public halls of varying type, age and size. Some are vested in local authorities, some in trustees; some are managed by schools of arts committees; some belong to church bodies or other voluntary organizations. Those who control them, the occupiers in point of law, are not insurers of the safety of all those who use them. They have, however, a duty of care. And the measure of that duty (where it is not prescribed by statutory provisions for the licensing and inspection of theatres and halls) is in my opinion the same as that laid down in *Francis v Cockrell* (1870) LR 5 QB 184, affd 501. It is convenient to state the effect of that decision in the words of McCardie J in *Maclenan v Segar* [1917] 2 KB 325 at pp 332-333, a passage that was quoted by Fullagar J in his judgment in *Watson v George* (1953) 89 CLR 409 at 424. It runs: "Where the occupier of premises agrees for reward that a person shall have the right to enter and use them for a mutually contemplated purpose, the contract between the parties (unless it provides to the contrary) contains an implied warranty that the premises are as safe for that purpose as reasonable care and skill on the part of anyone can make them. The rule is subject to the limitation that the defendant is not to be held responsible for defects which could not have been discovered by reasonable care or skill on the part of any person concerned with the construction, alteration, repair, or maintenance of the premises ... But subject to this limitation it matters not whether the lack of care or skill be that of the defendant or his servants, or that of an independent contractor or his servants, or whether the negligence takes place before or after the occupation by the defendant of the premises".

That passage, it will be noticed, places the source of the obligation in an implied term in a contractual right of entry upon the premises. And where the plaintiff who suffered an injury had himself paid to go in, the liability of the owner or occupier whom he paid can be rested on breach of contract. In the early decisions it was usually so put. But Martin B said in *Francis v Cockrell*, **[93]** "if you choose to put it in another form, it is the duty of a person, who so holds out a building of this sort, to have it in a fit and proper state for the safe reception of persons who are admitted" (at p 509). Looked at in that way the involvement of contractual elements in an action of negligence, the curiosity on which Fullagar J remarked in *Watson v George* largely disappears. For, although in *Francis v Cockrell*, the plaintiff had himself paid to enter the grand-stand, would it have made any difference if a friend had bought his ticket for him? Should a person whose ticket was bought for him by a friend, as they went in together, be in a worse position, if they both be hurt by a collapse of the stand, than the friend who paid for them both? Surely not? Then suppose a person had taken all the places so that he might invite whom he liked, would his guests, injured when the stand collapsed, have had no right of action against those who erected it? The shadow that the requirement of privity of contract in the law of contract has cast upon the law of tort is now dispelled, or almost so. Liability in tort always depends upon proximity of relationship, not on privity of agreement. ... It is, however, true that to attract a liability according to the principles of *Francis v Cockrell* (1870) LR 5 QB 184, affd 501 it is generally said that the admission of the public to the premises must be for reward to the defendant occupier. But that, it seems to me, is not because the duty is contractual. Rather it is because in such cases the liability is in effect similar to that in the earliest cases on the law of tort, those concerning the common callings, such as carrier, innkeeper, smith. The liability for negligence in cases of that sort arises from want of care in a public business that the defendant carries on. It matters not whether the plaintiff or someone else was to pay him for his services to the plaintiff. For example, in *Marshall v The York, Newcastle and Berwick Railway Co* (1851) 138 ER 632, in the Common Pleas there was an emphatic rejection of an argument that a passenger on a railway could not recover in an action for negligence because he had not himself paid for his ticket. And in *Wright v Anderton* [1909] 1 KB 209 it was held that the common law liability of an innkeeper for the safe custody of goods of guests, in that case members of a hockey **[94]** team using a room to change their clothes, was not diminished because the room had been reserved and paid for by someone else. It is unnecessary to multiply illustrations. But, as one argument for the Council was that as there was no consideration moving from the appellant to the Council therefore the principle of *Francis v Cockrell* could not apply, it is worth noticing that as long ago as 1897 the very question arose in a case in New York, *Fox v Buffalo Park* (1897) 47 NY Supp 788, affd 57 NE 1109. There the plaintiff was injured by the collapse of a badly constructed grand-stand. It had been built by a builder, who was an independent contractor, under the supervision of an architect. The only difference from the facts of *Francis v Cockrell* was that the plaintiff had not himself bought the ticket by which he had got in. Ward J said (at p 792): "While it is undoubtedly true in ordinary cases in the leasing of buildings that there is no implied warranty on the part of the lessor that the buildings are fit and safe for the purposes for which they are leased, the rule is different in regard to buildings and structures in which public exhibitions and entertainments are designed to be given, and for admissions to which the lessors directly or indirectly receive compensation". The use of the expression "implied warranty" is characteristic of the period when the case was decided. But the facts show that the liability was not considered as dependent on privity of contract between the plaintiff and the defendant, but upon the fact that the defendant's business was keeping premises for hire to the public. ...

In cases of this sort the occupier's liability depends, of course, upon proof of negligence on the part of someone. He is liable only **[95]** for the consequences of negligence, either his own negligence or the negligence of someone employed by him. But the case is one of those in which an employer remains liable to third parties for the consequences of the negligence of an independent contractor, just as he would be if it were his own negligence or that of his servant. This is merely one situation where this obtains. Another is the obligation that an employer has to provide a safe system and conditions of work for his employees. Lord Blackburn's statement in *Dalton v Angus* (1881) 6 App Cas 740 at p 829 is generally taken as a starting point: "Ever since *Quarman v Burnett* (1840) 151 ER 509 it has been considered settled law that one employing another is not liable for his collateral negligence, unless the relation of master and servant existed between them. So that a person employing a contractor to do work is not liable for the negligence of that contractor or his servants. On the other hand, a person causing something to be done, the doing of which casts on him a duty, cannot escape from the responsibility attaching on him of seeing that duty performed by delegating it to a contractor. He may bargain with the contractor that he shall perform the duty, and stipulate for an indemnity from him if it is not performed but he cannot thereby relieve himself from liability to those injured by the failure to perform it." The statement is clear. The difficulty is to know when it is applicable. It has become somewhat the fashion to speak of delegable and non-delegable duties. But apart from true instances of strict liability, the distinction between delegable and non-delegable duties does not, it seems, really amount to more than the adoption of convenient headings for those cases in which defendants have been held not liable for the negligence of independent contractors and cases in which they have. It suffices to quote from Viscount Simonds' speech in *Riverstone Meat Co Pty Ltd v Lancashire Shipping Co Ltd* [1961] AC 807 where his Lordship said (at p 845): "No one, I think, doubts that in some circumstances a defendant can escape liability for the negligence of an independent contractor; nor could he doubt that in other circumstances he cannot so escape … . I do not think it necessary to try to reconcile all the cases on this subject". We need not here attempt what his Lordship there did not. All that we need do is say whether or not the defendant Council here is liable for the negligence of the architect, an independent contractor. For reasons given above, **[96]** I think that it is. …

We can, however, … instead of looking upon the appellant as coming upon premises to which the occupier admitted people for reward, … regard him simply as a gratuitous invitee, in the legal sense of that word. Still substantially the same result follows. …

[97] The architect's negligence was not in some casual or collateral act. It was in the perform-ance of the very work that he was employed to perform. It comes back to the same question. Is the case one of those in which there is vicarious liability for the fault of an independent contractor? In *Thomson v Cremin* [1953] 2 All ER 1185 Viscount Simon, with whom Lord Romer concurred, and Lord Wright expressly approved the decision of Luxmoore LJ in *Wilkinson v Rea Ltd* [1941] 1 KB 688 that the duty of an invitor to an invitee cannot be escaped by delegating its performance to an independent contractor. … **[98]** As the decisions of the [English] Court of Appeal stand at present, there is no absolute rule. It is not enough to find that a plaintiff was an invitee. *Haseldine v CA Daw & Son Ltd* [1941] 2 KB 343, stands on one hand; *Woodward v Mayor of Hastings* [1945] KB 174 on the other. In each of these cases an occupier employed an independent contractor. In the first, the contractor was a firm of skilled electricians employed to repair a lift; in the other, a charwoman employed to sweep the snow off steps at a school. For the negligence of the electrician the occupier was not liable to an invitee; for the negligence of the charwoman he was. The distinction in point of policy and on the differing facts may be clear. Its formulation as a matter of law is not easy. Lord Hodson in the *Riverstone Meat Company's Case*, suggested that it may have to be re-considered. The Council, of course, had to employ an architect. Its own engineer would not, one may assume, have been able to undertake the work even if the Council had wished it. Nevertheless the Council is not like a person who employs a contractor because he does not himself understand what is required and is unable to check what is proposed or examine what is done. …

[100] On the whole case the Council must be held liable; vicariously, for the negligence of the architect it employed; and directly, because of the failure of its officers, who in fact examined and approved the plans and specifications, to ascertain whether by-laws in respect of public buildings had been complied with.

The next question then is, both respondents being liable to the plaintiff, how are the damages to be borne? The question arises for determination in this action because a notice was given by the Council to Lockwood claiming contribution pursuant to the *Law Reform (Tortfeasors' Contribution, Contributory Negligence and Division of Chattels) Act 1952* (Qld). …

In the present case the Council was liable for the consequences of the architect's negligence. If the Council were liable only vicariously and were itself otherwise free of blame, it seems that it would be entitled to recover from the architect any sum that it was liable to pay, and in fact paid, to the appellant as damages. But the Council was not itself free from blame in the matter. It was itself negligent, by its servants, in passing and accepting the architect's plans and specifications without further inquiry or examination than was made. To evaluate the respective degrees of departure from the standard of reasonable care is not easy. But, on the whole, it appears just and equitable, having regard to the responsibility of each for the accident, that the Council and the architect should bear the damages equally. The learned trial judge's assessment of the amount of the damages actually sustained by the appellant should stand. It was not challenged. Both the respondents are liable for this sum.

[Dixon CJ and Owen J agreed with Windeyer J.]

Appeal allowed

[Abolition of classifications and special duties to entrants

Windeyer J's comments in *Voli* (above) on the trend to treat the duty of an occupier as part of the general law of negligence were prescient. However, it was not until 1987 in *Australian Safeway Stores Pty Ltd v Zaluzna* (1987) 162 CLR 479, that the High Court of Australia finally rejected the long-established classification of lawful entrants when determining the existence and content of the duty of the occupier towards each category. The majority of the court, Mason, Wilson, Deane and Dawson JJ (Brennan J dissenting), also rejected any distinction being drawn between the "general" duty in negligence, arising from the *activities* of the occupier, and a "special" duty as occupier arising from the static *condition* of the property:

> [487] ... [T]he special duties do not travel beyond the general law of negligence. They are no more than an expression of the general law in terms appropriate to the particular situation it was designed to address. ...
>
> [488] ... [T]he fact that the respondent was a lawful entrant upon the land of the appellant establishes a relationship between them which of itself suffices to give rise to a duty on the part of the appellant to take reasonable care to avoid a foreseeable risk of injury to the respondent.

The High Court of Australia in the joint judgment of Gleeson CJ, McHugh, Kirby, Hayne and Heydon JJ in *Thompson v Woolworths (Q'land) Pty Limited* (2005) 221 CLR 234 commented as follows on this development:

> [243] ... There was a time when the common law sought to define with precision the duty of care owed by an occupier of land, and treated the content of the duty as variable according to categories fixed by reference to the status of entrants: see, for example *Lipman v Glendinning* (1932) 40 CLR 550 at 554 – 556 per Dixon J The common law has since rejected the approach of seeking to construct a series of special duties by reference to different categories of entrant (*Australian Safeway Stores Pty Ltd v Zaluzna* (1987) 162 CLR 479). The problems involved in the former approach included the rigidity of the classification of entrants, and the artificiality of distinguishing between the static condition of premises and activities conducted on the premises. That is not to say, however, that the law now disregards any aspect of the relationship between the parties other than that of occupier and entrant. On the contrary, other aspects of the relationship may be important, as considerations relevant to a judgment about what reasonableness requires of the defendant, a judgment usually made in the context of deciding breach of duty (negligence).

Duties to trespassers

The liability of an occupier to a trespasser has always been contentious. In *Public Transport Commission (NSW) v Perry* (1977) 137 CLR 107, the plaintiff Mrs Perry had fallen involuntarily from the platform of the defendant's railway station onto the tracks where she was struck and injured by a train. There was evidence that the train driver had been negligent in failing to keep a proper lookout and, in the plaintiff's negligence action in the Supreme Court of New South Wales, the jury returned a verdict in her favour. The High Court of Australia dismissed the defendant's appeal, and rejected the defendant's categorisation of the plaintiff as a trespasser. Stephen J's judgment reflects the treatment of trespassers at the time and the perennial concern of the law not to overburden the occupier:

> [139]The case of the unlawful entrant is a distinct one. If his entry be by stealth and unanticipated, entry alone will not cast any duty of care whatever upon the occupier. His arrival on the premises not being authorized, known or anticipated no duty in respect of the state of the premises will arise upon entry and he [140] will in no sense be any 'neighbour' of the occupier. Once his presence is known the position changes and a duty, which has been described as one of common humanity, is cast upon the occupier. In the view which I take of this case the precise ambit of that duty need not concern me … . It is in the realm of precautions against the as-yet-unidentified entrant that difficult questions of degrees of reasonable anticipation arise, coupled as they necessarily are with fears of unduly burdening occupiers for the benefit of future trespassers.

In many situations, the courts did recognise a duty of reasonable care to trespassers arising out of special circumstances, beyond a mere duty of "common humanity". The modern position is set out in *Hackshaw v Shaw* (1984) 155 CLR 614, in which the High Court of Australia allowed an appeal by the plaintiff in respect of the liability in negligence of the defendant, a farmer, who had shot at the parked car of a thief while the thief was pumping petrol from a bowser on the defendant's property. Unknown to the defendant, the plaintiff was lying out of sight on the front seat of the thief's car and sustained injuries to her arm when struck by a bullet. Deane J observed:

> [663] All that is necessary is to determine whether, in all the relevant circumstances including the fact of the defendant's occupation of premises and the manner of the plaintiff's entry upon them, the defendant owed a duty of care under the ordinary principles of negligence to the plaintiff. A prerequisite of any such duty is that there be the necessary degree of proximity of relationship. The touchstone of its existence is that there be reasonable foreseeability of a real risk of injury to the visitor or to the class of person of which the visitor is a member. The measure of the discharge of the duty is what a reasonable man would, in the circumstances, do by way of response to the foreseeable risk. Where the visitor is lawfully upon the land, the mere relationship between occupier on the one hand and invitee or licensee on the other will of itself suffice to give rise to a duty on the part of the occupier to take reasonable care to avoid a foreseeable risk of injury to her or him. When the visitor is on the land as a trespasser, the mere relationship of occupier and trespasser which the trespasser has imposed upon the occupier will not satisfy the requirement of proximity. Something more will be required. The additional factor or combination of factors which may, as a matter of law, supply the requisite degree of proximity or give rise to a reasonably foreseeable risk of relevant injury are incapable of being exhaustively defined or identified. At the least they will include either knowledge of the actual or likely presence of a trespasser or reasonable foreseeability of a real risk of such presence. Whether, when a duty to take reasonable care exists, reasonable care has been taken is a question of fact….
>
> [664] A trespasser may be a burglar, a traveller in difficulty, a person on an errand of mercy, a person who walks on another's land believing it to be his own, a person who honestly follows a mistaken direction or accepts an unauthorized invitation, a person who cannot see or a child who cannot understand. To classify "all these persons under one doctrinal rubric … makes no sense": see G Hughes, "Duties to Trespassers: A Comparative Survey and Re-evaluation" *Yale Law Journal*, Vol 68 (1959) at p 688 and cf per Windeyer J *Commissioner for Railways (NSW) v Cardy* (1960) 104 CLR 274 at 319.

Duties to entrants under contract

Although Windeyer J noted that the same result would apply whether the plaintiff in *Voli* (above) was classified as an "entrant under contract" or as a "gratuitous invitee", his judgment, at 92, deals with the principles concerning contractual entrants, namely that the contract would be treated as containing an implied warranty that the premises were as safe for the contemplated purpose as reasonable care and skill on the part of anyone could make them and that the occupier would be liable for the negligence of an independent contractor, other than incidental negligence.

In *Calin v Greater Union Organization Pty Ltd* (1991) 173 CLR 33, all members of the High Court of Australia accepted the principles set out in *Watson v George* (1953) 89 CLR 409 as continuing to apply to contractual entrants. In their joint judgment, Mason CJ, Deane, Toohey, and McHugh JJ observed (at 38):

> [T]he Court [in *Australian Safeway Stores Pty Ltd v Zaluzna* (1987) 162 CLR 479] had no occasion to examine, and did not examine, the principles of the common law governing the liability of an occupier of premises who agrees for reward to allow a person to enter the premises for some purpose. In this situation, it would not be right to treat *Zaluzna* and the decisions which preceded it (*Hackshaw v Shaw* (1984) 155 CLR 614 and *Papatonakis v Australian Telecommunications Commission* (1985) 156 CLR 7) as authorities which over-ruled the principle established in *Watson v George*.

Liability of lessors

In his judgment in *Voli* (above) at 89-90, Windeyer J also distinguishes the much-criticised immunity then still accorded, under the rule in *Cavalier v Pope* [1906] AC 428, to a landlord/lessor from liability to a tenant/lessee in negligence in respect of defects in the condition of leased premises. The High Court of Australia accepted in *Northern Sandblasting Pty Ltd v Harris* (1997) 188 CLR 313 and confirmed in *Jones v Bartlett* (2000) 205 CLR 166 that the decision of the House of Lords in *Cavalier v Pope* no longer represented the common law in Australia. Accordingly, no immunity protected a landlord/lessor from a duty of care and liability under the ordinary principles of negligence.]

Bryan v Maloney
(1995) 182 CLR 609
High Court of Australia

The builder of a dwelling house owes a duty of care to a subsequent purchaser in respect of pure economic loss attributable to the defective quality of the building work.

MASON CJ, DEANE and GAUDRON JJ. **[615]** The appellant, Mr Bryan, is a professional builder. In 1979, he built a house for a Mrs Manion on land in Launceston which Mrs Manion owned. Subsequently, Mrs Manion sold the land and the house to a Mr and Mrs Quittenden. In 1986, Mr and Mrs Quittenden sold the land and house to the respondent, Mrs Maloney. Mrs Maloney inspected the house three times before purchasing it. She noticed no cracks or other defects. She said that she specifically looked for cracks on the outside walls and found none. Apparently, she neither knew nor inquired about the identity of the builder. Her evidence was that the house suited her needs, that she thought "it was a good solid house", that she "couldn't find anything **[616]** wrong with it" and that she "thought it would be built properly ... so I bought it". About six months after the purchase, cracks began to appear in the walls of the house. The damage to the fabric of the house became extensive. The reason for the cracks and subsequent damage was that the house had been built by Mr Bryan with footings which were inadequate to withstand the seasonal changes in the clay soil.

Mrs Maloney instituted proceedings in negligence against Mr Bryan in the Supreme Court of Tasmania. The learned trial judge (Wright J) found in Mrs Maloney's favour and awarded damages of $34,464.68, that being the amount which his Honour found would necessarily be expended in remedying the inadequate footings and the consequential damage to the fabric of the house. Mr Bryan appealed to the Full Court of the Supreme Court of Tasmania. His appeal was unanimously dismissed. He now appeals to this Court from the judgment and order of the Full Court. ...

[A] number of matters are now common ground, namely, that Mr Bryan was negligent in building the house with inadequate footings; that the damage sustained by Mrs Maloney was the loss involved in the decrease in the value of the house resulting from the inadequacy of the footings and its consequences; that that damage was sustained by Mrs Maloney when the inadequacy of the footings first became manifest by reason of the cracks appearing in the walls of the house after she had purchased it; and, that that damage was a foreseeable consequence of Mr Bryan's negligence. Moreover, it is not in issue that, in the circumstances of this case, the economic loss involved is the amount which would necessarily be expended in remedying the inadequate footing[s] and their consequences as assessed by the trial judge. In the result, the sole remaining issue is whether Mr Bryan owed Mrs Maloney, as a subsequent purchaser of the house, a relevant duty of care under the law of negligence. ...

[617] [T]he case falls to be decided on the basis that it gives rise to a question which can be stated in abstract terms, namely, whether, under the law of negligence, a professional builder who constructs a house for the then owner of the land owes a prima facie duty to a subsequent owner of the house to exercise reasonable care to avoid the kind of foreseeable damage which Mrs Maloney sustained in the present case, that is to say, the diminution in value of the house when a latent and previously unknown defect in its footings or structure first becomes manifest. ...

[618] One policy consideration which may militate against recognition of a relationship of proximity in a category of case involving mere economic loss is the law's concern to avoid the imposition of liability "in an indeterminate amount for an indeterminate time to an indeterminate class": *Ultramares Corporation v Touche* (1931) 174 NE 441 at 444 per Cardozo CJ; *Caltex Oil (Australia) Pty Ltd v The Dredge "Willemstad"* (1976) 136 CLR at 568, 591; *Hedley Byrne and Co Ltd v Heller and Partners Ltd* [1964] AC at 537; and see also *Sutherland Shire Council v Heyman* (1985) 157 CLR at 465. Another consideration is the perception that, in a competitive world where one person's economic gain is commonly another's loss, a duty to take reasonable care to avoid causing mere economic loss to another, as distinct from physical injury to another's person or property, may be inconsistent with community standards in relation to what is ordinarily legitimate in the pursuit of personal advantage: *Jaensch v Coffey* (1984) 155 CLR at 578; *Sutherland Shire Council v Heyman* (1985) 157 CLR at 503. The combined effect of those **[619]** two distinct policy considerations is that the categories of case in which the requisite relationship of proximity with respect to mere economic loss is to be found are properly to be seen as special. Commonly, but not necessarily, they will involve an identified element of known reliance (or dependence) or the assumption of responsibility or a combination of the two: see, generally, *Sutherland Shire Council v Heyman* (1985) 157 CLR at 466-468, 501-502; *Hawkins v Clayton* (1988) 164 CLR 539 at 545, 576, 593. ...

Mr Bryan and Mrs Manion were the parties to a contract in relation to the building of the house. Whatever may have been the position in earlier times (see, generally, *Midland Bank v Hett, Stubbs and Kemp* [1979] Ch 384 at 405-411; *Central Trust Co v Rafuse* (1986) 31 DLR (4th) 481 at 489-499; *Hawkins v Clayton* (1988) 164 CLR at 574-575), the existence of such a contractual relationship between builder and client did not preclude the existence either of a relationship of proximity between them in relation to that work or of a consequent duty of care under the **[620]** ordinary law of negligence: see, eg, *National Mutual Life Association of Australasia Ltd. v Coffey and Partners Pty Ltd* [1991] 2 Qd R 401 at 406; *Opat v National Mutual Life* [1992] 1 VR 283 at 291-295; *Lowden v Lewis* (1989) Tas R 254 at 266-267; *Brumby v Pearton* (1991) 10 BCL 291 at 294-295 (Supreme Court of Tasmania); *Dutton v Jalapen Pty Ltd* (unreported, Supreme Court of Queensland, 14 March 1991); *Miell v Hatjopoulos* (1987) 4 BCL 226 (Supreme Court of South Australia); *Bowen v Paramount Builders* [1977] 1 NZLR 394. That was made clear by Windeyer J, with the concurrence of the other members of the Court (Dixon CJ and Owen J), in *Voli v Inglewood Shire Council* (1963) 110 CLR 74, at 84 when explaining the liabilities of an architect to his or her client:

"He is bound to exercise due care, skill and diligence. He is not required to have an extraordinary degree of skill or the highest professional attainments. But he must bring to the task he undertakes the competence and skill that is usual among architects practising their profession. And he must use due care. If he fails in these matters and the person who employed him thereby suffers damage, he is liable to that person. This liability can be said to arise either from a breach of his contract or in tort."

Subsequently, when dealing with the question of liability to a third party, Windeyer J commented ((1963) 110 CLR 74, at 84):

"Whatever might have been thought to be the position before the broad principles of the law of negligence were stated in modern form in *Donoghue v Stevenson* [1932] AC 562, it is now beyond doubt that, for the reasonably foreseeable consequences of careless or unskilful conduct, an architect is liable to anyone whom it could reasonably have been expected might be injured as a result of his negligence. To such a person he owes a duty of care quite independently of his contract of employment." ...

[622] Clearly enough, a relationship of proximity existed between Mr Bryan and Mrs Manion with respect to ordinary physical injury to Mrs Manion or her property with the consequence that Mr Bryan was under a duty to exercise reasonable care in relation to the building work, including the footings, to avoid a foreseeable risk of such injury. A more difficult question is whether that relationship of proximity and consequent duty of care with respect to the building work extended to mere economic loss by Mrs Manion of the kind ultimately sustained by Mrs Maloney when the inadequacy of the footings became manifest. In our view, it did.

While the relationship between Mr Bryan and Mrs Manion with respect to physical injury to [623] Mrs Manion's person or property must be distinguished from the relationship between them with respect to mere economic loss, the significance of such a distinction varies according to the particular kind of economic loss which is involved in the relevant category of case. Here, the distinction is between ordinary physical damage to a house by some external cause and mere economic loss in the form of diminution in value of a house when the inadequacy of its footings first becomes manifest by consequent damage to its fabric. Obviously, that distinction, which has only recently attained general acceptance (cf Lord Wilberforce's comment in *Anns v Merton London Borough Council* [1978] AC at 759 to the effect that the correct classification of the damage in a case such as the present was not economic loss but "material, physical damage"), is an essentially technical one. Indeed, even now, it is arguably inapplicable in circumstances where a latent defect in the work of one builder or contractor causes damage to a part of the building constructed by a different builder or contractor: see *Murphy v Brentwood District Council* [1991] 1 AC at 470, 497.

Moreover, the policy considerations underlying the reluctance of the courts to recognize a relationship of proximity and a consequent duty of care in cases of mere economic loss are inapplicable to a relationship of the kind which existed between Mr Bryan and Mrs Manion as regards the kind of economic loss sustained by Mrs Maloney. Thus, there is no basis for thinking that recognition of a relationship of proximity between builder and first owner with respect to that particular kind of economic loss would give rise to the type of liability "in an indeterminate amount for an indeterminate time to an indeterminate class" which the courts are reluctant to recognize. Again, in circumstances where the builder is, in any event, under a duty of care to the first owner to avoid physical injury to that owner's person or property by reason of inadequacy of the footings, there can be no real question of inconsistency between the existence of a relationship of proximity with respect to that [624] particular kind of economic loss and the legitimate pursuit by the builder of his or her own financial interests. Nor, as has been seen, is it legitimate to assert that, as a matter of policy, the sanctity of contract or the compartmentalization of the law dictates that liability under the ordinary principles of negligence in respect of either damages generally or a particular kind of damage must be excluded as between parties in a contractual relationship notwithstanding the absence of any actual agreement between the parties to that effect. Whatever may have been or may be the position in other times or in other places, the law of this country knows no such policy.

On the other hand, there are strong reasons for acknowledging the existence of a relevant relationship of proximity between a builder such as Mr Bryan and a first owner such as Mrs Manion with respect to the kind of economic loss sustained by Mrs Maloney. In particular, the ordinary relationship between a builder of a house and the first owner with respect to that kind of economic loss is characterized by the kind of assumption of responsibility on the one part (ie the builder) and known reliance on the other (ie the building owner) which commonly exists in the special categories of case in which a relationship of proximity and a consequent duty of care exists in respect of pure economic loss. ...There is nothing to suggest that the relationship between Mr Bryan and Mrs Manion was not characterized by such an assumption of responsibility and such reliance.

At least prima facie, a relationship of proximity also existed between Mr Bryan and persons other than Mrs Manion, including Mrs Maloney, who might sustain physical injury to person or property as a consequence of a collapse, as a result of inadequate footings, of part of the house while they or their property were lawfully in the house or in its vicinity: the qualification "lawfully" is added merely for greater caution; cf *Benning v Wong* (1969) 122 CLR 249 at 320; *Burnie Port Authority v General Jones Pty Ltd* (1994) 179 CLR at 546. The relationship between Mr Bryan and such persons corresponded with the relationship between the architect and the injured plaintiff in *Voli v Inglewood Shire Council* (1963) 110 CLR 74; and see also *Hawkins v Clayton* (1988) 164 CLR at 578; *AC Billings and Sons Ltd v Riden* [1958] AC 240; *Gallagher v N McDowell Ltd* [1961] NI 26; *Clay v AJ Crump and Sons Ltd* [1964] 1 QB 533; *Sharpe v ET Sweeting and Son Ltd* [1963] 1 WLR 665; *Rimmer v Liverpool City Council* [1984] 1 All ER 930; *Pantalone v Alaouie* (1989) 18 NSWLR 119; *Murphy v Brentwood District Council* [1991] 1 AC at 475; *Department of the Environment v T Bates Ltd* [1991] 1 AC at 519. ...

[625] It is in the context of the above-mentioned relationships of proximity that one must determine whether the relationship which exists between a professional builder of a house, such as Mr Bryan, and a subsequent owner, such as Mrs Maloney, possesses the requisite degree of proximity to give rise to a duty to take reasonable care on the part of the builder to avoid the kind of economic loss sustained by Mrs Maloney in the present case. It is likely that the only connection between such a builder and such a subsequent owner will be the house itself. Nonetheless, the relationship between them is marked by proximity in a number of important respects. The connecting link of the house is itself a substantial one. It is a permanent structure to be used indefinitely and, in this country, is likely to represent one of the most significant, and possibly the most significant, investment which the subsequent owner will make during his or her lifetime. It is obviously foreseeable by such a builder that the negligent construction of the house with inadequate footings is likely to cause economic loss, of the kind sustained by Mrs Maloney, to the owner of the house at the time when the inadequacy of the footings first becomes manifest. When such economic loss is eventually sustained and there is no intervening negligence or other causative event, the causal proximity between the loss and the builder's lack of reasonable care is unextinguished by either lapse of time or change of ownership.

The only factor which arguably precludes the recognition of a relevant relationship of proximity between builder and subsequent owner for the purposes of the present case is the kind of damage involved, namely, mere economic loss. As has been seen, a relevant relationship of proximity would have existed between the builder [626] and Mrs Maloney with respect to ordinary physical injury to her person or other property caused by a partial collapse of the house due to its inadequate footings even if she had not been the owner. Here again, it is important to bear in mind the particular kind of economic loss involved. As has been said, the distinction between that kind of economic loss and ordinary physical damage to property is an essentially technical one. Indeed, the economic loss sustained by the owner of a house by reason of diminution in value when the inadequacy of the footings first becomes manifest by consequent damage to the fabric of the house is, at least arguably, less remote and more readily foreseeable than ordinary physical damage to other property of the owner which might be caused by an actual collapse of part of the house as a result of the inadequacy of those footings. Again, the policy considerations underlying the reluctance of the courts to recognize a relationship of proximity and a consequential duty of care in cases of mere economic loss are largely inapplicable to the relationship between builder and subsequent owner as regards that particular kind of economic loss. There can be no question of inconsistency with the builder's legitimate pursuit of his or her own financial interests since, as has been seen, the builder owed a duty of care to the first owner with respect to such loss. In circumstances where the particular kind of economic loss is that sustained by an owner of the house on the occasion when the inadequacy of the footings first becomes manifest, there is no basis for thinking that recognition of a relevant relationship of proximity between builder and that owner would be more likely to give rise to liability "in an indeterminate amount ... to an indeterminate class" than does recognition of such an element of proximity in the relationship between builder and first owner. It is true that, in so far as "an indeterminate time" is concerned, the time span in which liability to a subsequent owner might arise could be greater than if liability were restricted to the first owner. Nonetheless, the extent of that time span would be limited by the element of reasonableness both in the requirement that damage be foreseeable and in the content of the duty of care: cf *Askin v Knox* [1989] 1 NZLR 248. In any event, it would prima facie correspond with that applicable to the relationship of proximity which clearly exists as regards physical injury to person or other property. Moreover, any difference in duration between liability to the first owner and liability to a subsequent owner is likely to do no more than reflect the chance element of whether and when the first owner disposes of the house.

[627] Upon analysis, the relationship between builder and subsequent owner with respect to the particular kind of economic loss is, like that between the builder and first owner, marked by the kind of assumption of responsibility and known reliance which is commonly present in the categories of case in which a relationship of proximity exists with respect to pure economic loss. In ordinary circumstances, the builder of a house undertakes the responsibility of erecting a structure on the basis that its footings are adequate to support it for a period during which it is likely that there will be one or more subsequent owners. Such a subsequent owner will ordinarily have no greater, and will often have less, opportunity to inspect and test the footings of the house than the first owner. Such a subsequent owner is likely to be unskilled in building matters and inexperienced in the niceties of real property investment. Any builder should be aware that such a subsequent owner will be likely, if inadequacy of the footings has not become manifest, to assume that the house has been competently built and that the footings are in fact adequate.

Ultimately, it seems to us that, from the point of view of proximity, the similarities between the relationship between builder and first owner and the relationship between builder and subsequent owner as regards the particular kind of economic loss are of much greater significance than the differences to which attention has been drawn, namely, the absence of direct contact or dealing and the possibly extended time in which liability might arise. Both relationships are characterized, to a comparable extent, by assumption of responsibility on the part of the builder and likely reliance on the part of the owner. No distinction can be drawn between the two relationships in so far as the foreseeability of the particular kind of economic loss is concerned: it is obviously foreseeable that that loss will be sustained by whichever of the first or subsequent owners happens to be the owner at the time when the inadequacy of the footings becomes manifest. In the absence of competing or intervening negligence or other causative event, the causal proximity between negligence on the part of the builder in constructing the footings and consequent economic loss on the part of the owner when the inadequacy of the footings becomes manifest is the same regardless of whether the owner in question is the first owner or a subsequent owner. In the case of both relationships, the policy considerations which ordinarily militate against the recognition of a relationship of proximity and a consequent duty of care with respect to pure economic loss are insignificant. Moreover, there are persuasive policy reasons supporting the recognition of a relationship of proximity between the builder and a subsequent owner of an ordinary dwelling house with respect to the particular [628] kind of economic loss. ... They include the consideration that, by virtue of superior knowledge, skill and experience in the construction of houses, it is likely that a builder will be better qualified and positioned to avoid, evaluate and guard against the financial risk posed by latent defect in the structure of a house: *Lempke v Dagenais* (1988) 547 A 2d at 295, quoting Whichard J in *George v Veach* (1984) 313 SE 2d 920 at 923. In all the circumstances, the relationship between builder and subsequent owner as regards the particular kind of economic loss should be accepted as possessing a comparable degree of proximity to that possessed by the relationship between builder and first owner and as giving rise to a duty to take reasonable care on the part of the builder to avoid such loss.

The conclusion that a relationship of proximity existed between Mr Bryan, as the builder, and Mrs Maloney, as subsequent owner, with respect to the particular kind of economic loss is also supported by analogy with the relationship which would have existed between Mr Bryan, as the builder, and any person who suffered physical injury to person or property in the event that the house or part of the house had collapsed at the time when the inadequacy of the foundations first became manifest. It is difficult to see why, as a matter of principle, policy or common sense, a negligent builder should be liable for ordinary physical injury caused to any person or to other property by reason of the collapse of a building by reason of the inadequacy of the foundations but be not liable to the owner of the building for the cost of remedial work necessary to remedy that inadequacy and to avert such damage. ...

[630] [T]he decision in this case is not directly decisive of the question whether a relevant relationship of proximity exists in other categories of case or as regards other kinds of damage. In particular, the decision in this case should not be seen as determinative of the question whether a relationship of proximity can, in some circumstances, exist between the manufacturer and the purchaser or subsequent owner of a chattel in respect of the diminution in the value of the chattel which is sustained when a latent defect in it first becomes manifest: cf *Rivtow Marine Ltd v Washington Iron Works* (1973) 40 DLR (3d) 530.

The appeal should be dismissed.

BRENNAN J [dissenting]. ... **[643]** Where the question is whether a duty of care relating solely to the quality of the building or chattel bought by a purchaser should be imposed by the law of tort or the law of contract, the answer, in my opinion, is that the interests to be protected are appropriately to be governed by the law of contract: but cf Fleming, "Tort in a Contractual Matrix", (1993) 5 *Canterbury Law Review* 269. As between a builder and the original owner of a building, any claim between them relating to the condition of the building is properly to be determined by the contract which governs their relationship, not by the law of tort: see *Tai Hing Ltd v Liu Chong Hing Bank* [1986] AC 80 at 107. The doing of work for reward is a matter governed by the agreement between the party doing the work and the party requesting that the work be done. They fix their own rights and liabilities on issues of purely economic significance. The work to be **[644]** performed, the quality and value of that work and the cost of repairing defects in work ill-done are thus properly the concerns of the law of contract. A claim by a remote purchaser against a vendor relating to the condition of the building is also properly to be determined by the law of contract. But physical damage to person or property arising from the construction of a building or the manufacture of a chattel is properly the concern of the law of tort. That is not to say that damage to person or property might not be produced by breach of contract nor to say that pure economic loss cannot be recovered in certain circumstances in tort. In *Voli v Inglewood Shire Council* (1963) 110 CLR at 84, Windeyer J spoke of an architect's liability as arising "either from a breach of his contract or in tort", but his Honour was there speaking of a liability in respect of physical damage to person or property.

It would be anomalous to have claims relating to the condition of the building by an original owner against the builder determined by the law of contract if the relief claimed by the remote purchaser against the builder would be determined by the law of tort. Such a situation would expose the builder to a liability for pure economic loss different from that which he undertook in constructing the building and would confer a corresponding right on the remote purchaser which the purchaser had not sought to acquire from the vendor. (See *Winnipeg Condominium Corp No 36 v Bird Construction Co Ltd* (1993) 101 DLR (4th) 699 at 711. The observation of Huband JA with reference to "caveat emptor" is apposite to a remote purchaser's rights in respect of mere defects in a building. The decision of the Manitoba Court of Appeal was reversed by the Supreme Court which considered the defects to be a substantial danger to the health and safety of the occupants.) It would be tantamount to the imposition on the builder of a transmissible warranty of quality. In some jurisdictions, Parliament has provided such a remedy by statute. The social question whether building costs should be inflated to cover the builder's obligation under such a transmissible warranty is an appropriate question for parliaments to consider but, in the absence of compelling legal principle or considerations of justice reflecting the enduring values of the community, the courts should not decide to extend remedies not hitherto available to remote purchasers of buildings without considering the cost to builders and the economic effect of such an extension. Those are questions which the courts are not suited to consider. The extension of remedies in that direction is properly a matter for Parliament. ...

[His Honour went on to say that he agreed with the Canadian doctrine that if an owner rectifies *dangerous* defects in order to remove the risk of damage to person or property, the expense of removal can be recovered from the builder who is responsible for the defects. However that was not the situation here.]

[655] I would ... allow the appeal, set aside the judgments in the courts below and in lieu thereof order that judgment be entered for the defendant.

[Toohey J delivered an opinion in which he reached the same conclusion as Mason CJ, Deane and Gaudron JJ that a duty of care was owed and the appeal should be dismissed.]

Appeal dismissed

Woolcock Street Investments Pty Ltd v CDG Pty Ltd
(2004) 216 CLR 515; [2004] HCA 16
High Court of Australia

In the particular circumstances of this case, consulting engineers who designed the foundations of a complex comprising a warehouse and offices did not owe a duty of care to a subsequent owner of the complex who suffered pure economic loss due to the settlement of the foundations or the material below the foundations. There was absent any relevant vulnerability on the part of the subsequent owner to the economic consequences of negligent design of the foundations by the consulting engineers.

GLEESON CJ, GUMMOW, HAYNE and HEYDON JJ. [some footnotes in whole or part omitted]

[523] The issue
1. In 1987, the first respondent [first defendant], a company carrying on the business of consulting engineers, designed foundations for a warehouse and offices in Townsville. The land on which this building (referred to in the pleadings as "the Complex") was to be built was owned by the trustee of a property trust. Some years after the building was finished it was sold by the then trustee of the property trust to the appellant [plaintiff]. The contract for the sale of the land did not include any warranty that the building was free from defect and there was no assignment by the vendor of any rights that the vendor may have had against others in respect of any such defects.

2. More than a year after the appellant bought the land, it became apparent that the building was suffering substantial structural distress. It is agreed that the distress was and is due to the settlement of the foundations of the building, or the material below the foundations, or both. The appellant alleges that the first respondent and its employee, the second respondent [second defendant], each owed it a duty to take reasonable care in designing the foundations for the building. The respondents deny that they owed the appellant any duty of care; they deny that they acted in breach of any such duty; they say that despite advising the then owner of the land to allow them to obtain soil tests, the then owner instructed them to proceed without soil tests and to use structural footing sizes provided by the builder. Did the respondents owe the appellant a duty of care?

The procedural context
3. The appellant commenced proceedings in the Supreme Court of Queensland. After it had delivered a further amended statement of [524] claim and each respondent had filed a defence to that pleading, the parties consented to an order stating a case for the opinion of the Court of Appeal. ...

4. The critical paragraphs of the appellant's statement of claim asserted that the respondents had owed it a duty of care but said very little about why that was so.

5. The appellant's statement of claim took a form that is common enough in claims for negligence. The allegation of duty was rolled up with the allegation of breach. The pleading did allege that the respondents had been engaged to perform engineering work in connection with the construction of the building, a "permanent" structure, and alleged that the adverse consequences of which the appellant complained were foreseeable but it alleged no other matter bearing upon the existence of the asserted duty of care. ...

[525] The Court of Appeal

8. The Court of Appeal answered the question reserved: "On the agreed facts, does the further amended statement of claim … disclose a cause of action in negligence against the defendants?", "No". Both McMurdo P and Thomas JA (with whose reasons Douglas J agreed) concluded that *Bryan v Maloney* (1995) 182 CLR 609 established that the builder of a *dwelling* may owe a duty of care to a remote purchaser. Their Honours concluded, however, that those who built or designed *commercial* buildings did not owe any duty of care to subsequent purchasers. As Thomas JA put the matter, "there is no good reason, in terms of principle or policy, to extend the decision in *Bryan v Maloney* to cases other than residential dwellings". …

[526] *Bryan v Maloney*

10. In *Bryan v Maloney*, the Court (Mason CJ, Deane, Toohey and Gaudron JJ, Brennan J dissenting) decided that the builder of a dwelling house owed a subsequent purchaser, Mrs Maloney, of the house a duty to take reasonable care to avoid the economic loss which the subsequent purchaser suffered as a result of the diminution in value of the house when the fabric of the building cracked because the footings were inadequate. Both Mason CJ, Deane and Gaudron JJ in their joint reasons (at 617, 619), and Toohey J in his separate reasons (at 663), noted that there was no direct relationship between the builder and the subsequent purchaser, but concluded (at 628 per Mason CJ, Deane and Gaudron JJ, 665 per Toohey J) that the necessary relationship of proximity existed to warrant finding that the builder had owed the subsequent purchaser a duty of care. …

12. The joint reasons began by examining the relationship between the appellant (the builder) and the first owner of the house (Mrs Manion). They, of course, were the parties to the contract in performance of which the builder had built the house. That contract was said (at 622) to be "non-detailed and [to contain] no exclusion or limitation of liability". Accordingly, the content of the contract was said not to preclude the existence of a duty of care owed by the builder to Mrs Manion, not only to take reasonable care to avoid injury to her person or property (at 622-623) but also to avoid "mere economic loss by Mrs Manion of the kind ultimately sustained by Mrs Maloney when the inadequacy of the footings became manifest" (at 623). That was because:

> the ordinary relationship between a builder of a house and the first owner with respect to that kind of economic loss is characterized by the kind of assumption of responsibility on the one part (ie the builder) and known reliance on the other (ie the building owner) which commonly exists in the special categories of case in which a **[527]** relationship of proximity and a consequent duty of care exists in respect of pure economic loss (at 624).

There was said (at 624) to be nothing to suggest that the relationship between the builder and the first owner was not characterised by such an assumption of responsibility and reliance.

13. Four considerations were then identified as warranting the conclusion that a relationship of proximity also existed with the subsequent owner. First, the house was identified (at 625) as a "connecting link", it being a permanent structure and a significant investment for a subsequent owner like the respondent. Secondly, it was pointed out (at 625) that it was foreseeable that economic loss would likely result from negligent construction of the house. Thirdly, it was said (at 625) that there was no "intervening negligence or other causative event". Finally, the similarities with the relationship between the builder and the first owner as regards the particular kind of economic loss were said (at 627) to be "of much greater significance than the differences to which attention has been drawn, namely, the absence of direct contact or dealing and the possibly extended time in which liability might arise".

14. It is evident, then, that the conclusion that the builder owed a subsequent owner a duty to take reasonable care to avoid the economic loss which that subsequent owner had suffered depended upon conclusions that were reached about the relationship between the first owner and the builder. In particular, the decision in the case depended upon the anterior step of concluding that the builder owed the first owner a duty of care to avoid economic loss of that kind.

15. Both this anterior step, and the conclusion drawn from it, were considered in the context of the facts of the particular case – in which the building in question was a dwelling house. The propositions about assumption of responsibility by the builder and known reliance by the building owner were said (at 624) to be characteristics of "the *ordinary* relationship between a builder of a

165

house and the first owner" (emphasis added). At least in terms, however, the principles that were said to be engaged in *Bryan v Maloney* did not depend for their operation upon any distinction between particular kinds of, or uses for, buildings. They depended upon considerations of assumption of responsibility, reliance, and proximity. Most importantly, they depended upon equating the responsibilities which the builder owed to the first owner with those owed to a subsequent owner.

[528] Criticisms of *Bryan v Maloney*

16. The decision in *Bryan v Maloney* has not escaped criticism. ... [T]wo points should be made.

17. First, for the reasons given earlier, it may be doubted that the decision in *Bryan v Maloney* should be understood as depending upon drawing a bright line between cases concerning the construction of dwellings and cases concerning the construction of other buildings. If it were to be understood as attempting to draw such a line, it would turn out to be far from bright, straight, clearly defined, or even clearly definable. As has been pointed out subsequently (for example, *Zumpano v Montagnese* [1997] 2 VR 525 at 528-529 per Brooking JA), some buildings are used for mixed purposes: shop and dwelling; dwelling and commercial art gallery; general practitioner's surgery and residence. Some high-rise apartment blocks are built in ways not very different from high-rise office towers. The original owner of a high-rise apartment block may be a large commercial enterprise. The list of difficulties in distinguishing between dwellings and other buildings could be extended.

18. Secondly, the decision in *Bryan v Maloney* depended upon the view (at 619) that "the overriding requirement of a relationship of proximity represents the conceptual determinant and the unifying theme of the categories of case in which the common law of negligence recognizes the existence of a duty to take reasonable care to avoid a reasonably foreseeable risk of injury to another". It was the application of this "conceptual determinant" of proximity that was seen as both permitting and requiring the equation of the duty owed to the first owner with the duty owed to the subsequent purchaser. Decisions of the Court after *Bryan v Maloney* reveal that [529] proximity is no longer seen as the "conceptual determinant" in this area.

Economic loss

19. The damage for which the appellant seeks a remedy in this case is the economic loss it alleges it has suffered as a result of buying a building which is defective. Circumstances can be imagined in which, had the defects not been discovered, some damage to person or property might have resulted from those defects. But that is not what has happened. The defects have been identified. Steps can be taken to prevent damage to person or property.

20. A view was adopted for a time in England that, because there was *physical* damage to the building, a claim of the kind made by the appellant was not solely for economic loss. That view was ... rejected in *Bryan v Maloney* (at 617 per Mason CJ, Deane and Gaudron JJ, 657 per Toohey J; cf at 643 per Brennan J). ... There is no reason now to reopen that debate and neither side in the present matter sought to do so. The damage which the appellant alleges it has suffered is pure economic loss.

21. Claims for damages for pure economic loss present peculiar difficulty. Competition is the hallmark of most forms of commercial activity in Australia. As Brennan J said in *Bryan v Maloney* (at 632):

> If liability were to be imposed for the doing of anything which caused pure economic loss that was foreseeable, the tort of negligence would destroy commercial competition, sterilize many contracts and, in the well-known dictum of Chief Judge [530] Cardozo (*Ultramares Corporation v Touche* (1931) 174 NE 441 at 444), expose defendants to potential liability 'in an indeterminate amount for an indeterminate time to an indeterminate class'.

That is why damages for pure economic loss are not recoverable if all that is shown is that the defendant's negligence was a cause of the loss and the loss was reasonably foreseeable.

22. In *Caltex Oil (Australia) Pty Ltd v The Dredge "Willemstad"* (1976) 136 CLR 529, the Court held that there were circumstances in which damages for economic loss were recoverable. In *Caltex Oil*, cases for recovery of economic loss were seen as being exceptions to a general rule, said to have been established in *Cattle v Stockton Waterworks* (1875) LR 10 QB 453, that even if the loss was foreseeable, damages are not recoverable for economic loss which was not consequential

upon injury to person or property. In *Caltex Oil*, Stephen J isolated a number of "salient features" which combined to constitute a sufficiently close relationship to give rise to a duty of care owed to Caltex for breach of which it might recover its purely economic loss (at 576-578). Chief among those features was the defendant's knowledge that to damage the pipeline which was damaged was inherently likely to produce economic loss (at 576).

23. Since *Caltex Oil*, and most notably in *Perre v Apand Pty Ltd* (1999) 198 CLR 180, the vulnerability of the plaintiff has emerged as an important requirement in cases where a duty of care to avoid economic loss has been held to have been owed. "Vulnerability", in this context, is not to be understood as meaning only that the plaintiff was likely to suffer damage if reasonable care was not taken. Rather, "vulnerability" is to be understood as a reference to the plaintiff's inability to protect itself from the consequences of a defendant's want of reasonable care, either entirely or at least in a way which would cast the consequences of loss on the defendant. So, in *Perre*, the plaintiffs could do nothing to protect themselves from the economic consequences to them of the defendant's negligence in sowing a crop which caused the quarantining of the plaintiffs' land. In *Hill v Van Erp* (1997) 188 CLR 159, the intended beneficiary depended entirely upon the solicitor performing the client's retainer properly and the beneficiary could do nothing to ensure that **[531]** this was done. But in *Esanda Finance Corporation Ltd v Peat Marwick Hungerfords* (1997) 188 CLR 241, the financier could itself have made inquiries about the financial position of the company to which it was to lend money, rather than depend upon the auditor's certification of the accounts of the company.

24. In other cases of pure economic loss (*Bryan v Maloney* is an example) reference has been made to notions of assumption of responsibility and known reliance. The negligent misstatement cases like *Mutual Life & Citizens' Assurance Co Ltd v Evatt* (1968) 122 CLR 556; (1970) 122 CLR 628; [1971] AC 793 and *Shaddock & Associates Pty Ltd v Parramatta City Council (No 1)* (1981) 150 CLR 225 can be seen as cases in which a central plank in the plaintiff's allegation that the defendant owed it a duty of care is the contention that the defendant knew that the plaintiff would rely on the accuracy of the information the defendant provided. ...

The appellant's claim

25. On the facts set out in the Case Stated and alleged in the pleadings neither respondent owed the appellant a duty to take reasonable care to avoid the appellant suffering the economic loss which it alleges it suffered. As counsel for the respondents submitted, it was not alleged that the respondents breached any obligation to the original owner. Unlike *Bryan v Maloney*, it cannot be said, in this case, that the respondents owed the original owner of the land a duty to take reasonable care to avoid economic loss of the kind of which the appellant now complains. It was agreed in the Case Stated that, despite the first respondent obtaining a quotation for geotechnical investigations, the original owner of the land, by its manager, refused to pay for such investigations. (The respondents go further in their pleadings and allege that the original owner directed the adoption of particular footing sizes.) The relationship between the respondents and the original owner of the land was, therefore, not one in which the owner entrusted the design of the building to a builder, or in this case the engineer, under a simple, "non-detailed" contract. It was a relationship in which the original owner asserted control over the investi**[532]**gations which the engineer undertook for the purposes of performing its work.

26. In its pleading the appellant did not allege that the relationship between the respondents and the original owner was characterised by that assumption of responsibility by the respondents, and known reliance by the original owner on the respondents, which is referred to in the joint reasons in *Bryan v Maloney* (at 624). Such further facts as are agreed, far from supporting any inference that this was the nature of the relationship between the respondents and the original owner, point firmly in the opposite direction. There was not, therefore, what was referred to in *Bryan v Maloney* (at 619) as "an identified element of known reliance (or dependence)" or "the assumption of responsibility".

27. It follows that the appellant's contention that the respondents owed it a duty of care cannot be supported by the reasoning which was adopted in *Bryan v Maloney*. What we earlier referred to as the anterior step of demonstrating that the respondents owed a duty of care to the original owner is not made out.

The relevance of the contract with the original owner

28. In this case, as in *Bryan v Maloney*, it is not necessary to decide whether disconformity between the obligations owed to the original owner under the contract to build or design a building and the duty of care allegedly owed to a subsequent owner will necessarily deny the existence of that duty of care. However, as Windeyer J said in *Voli v Inglewood Shire Council* (1963) 110 CLR 74 at 85, the terms of the contract between the original owner and the builder (or, in this case, the respondents) "is not an irrelevant circumstance" in considering what duty a builder or engineer owed others. At the least, that contract defines the task which the builder or engineer undertook. There would be evident difficulty in holding that the respondents owed the appellant a duty of care to avoid economic loss to a subsequent owner if performance of that duty would have required the respondents to do more or different work than the contract with the original owner required or permitted. ...

[**533**] 30. This case can be determined without deciding whether disconformity of the kind we have mentioned would always deny the existence of a duty of care to a subsequent owner. There are other reasons for concluding that the respondents owed no duty of care to prevent the economic loss of which the appellant complains.

No vulnerability

31. Neither the facts alleged in the statement of claim nor those set out in the Case Stated show that the appellant was, in any relevant sense, vulnerable to the economic consequences of any negligence of the respondents in their design of the foundations for the building. Those facts do not show that the appellant could not have protected itself against the economic loss it alleges it has suffered. It is agreed that no warranty of freedom from defect was included in the contract by which the appellant bought the land, and that there was no assignment to the appellant of any rights which the vendor may have had against third parties in respect of any claim for defects in the building. Those facts describe what did happen. They say nothing about what could have been done to cast on the respondents the burden of the economic consequences of any negligence by the respondents. The appellant's pleading and the facts set out in the Case Stated are silent about whether the appellant could have sought and obtained the benefit of terms of that kind in the contract.

32. It may be accepted that the appellant bought the building not knowing that the foundations were inadequate. It is not alleged or agreed, however, that the defects of which complaint now is made could not have been discovered. The Case Stated records that, before completing its purchase, the appellant sought and obtained from the relevant local authority a certificate that the building complied with the *Building Act 1975* (Qld) and some subordinate legislation. That the defects now alleged were not discovered by a local authority asked to certify whether the building was "a ruin or so far dilapidated as to be unfit for use or occupation or [was] ... in a structural condition prejudicial to the inhabitants of or to property in the neighbourhood" (s 53(2)) says nothing about what other investigations might have been undertaken or might have revealed.

33. Finally, if it is relevant to know, as was assumed to be the case in *Bryan v Maloney*, whether buying the building represented a very significant investment for the appellant (at 625), there is nothing in the Case Stated or the appellant's pleading which bears on that question. ...

[**534**] 34. ... Once it is recognised that foreseeability of negligently caused economic loss is a necessary but not sufficient condition for recovery of such loss, the critical question is: what more must be shown? The core of the appellant's contention in this Court was that because there is no difference in principle between a residential house and a purely commercial development like the one now in issue, the appellant was entitled to recover, just as the plaintiff in *Bryan v Maloney* had been held entitled to recover. ...

Conclusion and orders

35. ... No doubt, as recognised earlier in these reasons, the principles applicable in cases of negligently inflicted pure economic loss have evolved since *Bryan v Maloney* was decided. Neither the principles applied in *Bryan v Maloney*, nor those principles as developed in subsequent cases, support the appellant's contention that on the facts agreed in the Case Stated and alleged in its

statement of claim the respondents owed it a duty of care to avoid the economic loss which it alleged it suffered.

36. The appeal should be dismissed … .

[McHugh and Callinan JJ, in separate judgments, agreed that the appeal should be dismissed. Kirby J dissented.]

Appeal dismissed

4. RESCUERS

Wagner v International Railway Co
133 NE 437 (1921)
Court of Appeals of New York

A person who negligently creates a dangerous situation may owe a duty of care to a third party rescuer who responds to the predicament of the primary accident victim.

[The plaintiff, Arthur Wagner, and his cousin, Herbert, were night passengers on the defendant's railway between Buffalo and Niagara Falls. As the carriage in which the plaintiff and Herbert were travelling turned a curve there was "a violent lurch" and Herbert was thrown out of the open door. After the train made an emergency stop, the plaintiff walked back along the track to find his cousin. However, in the dark, the plaintiff lost his footing, fell and suffered personal injury.

In the plaintiff's action to recover damages for personal injury, the jury found in favour of the defendant after a direction by the trial judge that, as a matter of law, the negligence of the defendant towards Herbert did not make the defendant liable to the plaintiff unless the defendant, through its conductor, had invited the plaintiff to walk back along the track to look for his cousin.

The Court of Appeals of New York held that the trial judge had misdirected the jury and a new trial should be granted.]

CARDOZO J. [references omitted] … [437] Danger invites rescue. The cry of distress is the summons to relief. The law does not ignore these reactions of the mind in tracing conduct to its consequences. It recognizes them as normal. It places their effects within the range of the natural and probable. The wrong that imperils life is a wrong to the imperilled victim; it is a wrong also to his rescuer. The state that leaves an opening in a bridge is liable to the child that falls into the stream, but liable also [438] to the parent who plunges to its aid. The railroad company whose train approaches without signal is a wrongdoer toward the traveller surprised between the rails, but a wrongdoer also to the bystander who drags him from the path. … The risk of rescue, if only it be not wanton, is born of the occasion. The emergency begets the man. The wrongdoer may not have foreseen the coming of a deliverer. He is accountable as if he had.

The defendant says that we must stop, in following the chain of causes, when action ceases to be 'instinctive.' By this is meant, it seems, that rescue is at the peril of the rescuer, unless spontaneous and immediate. If there has been time to deliberate, if impulse has given way to judgment, one cause, it is said, has spent its force, and another has intervened. In this case, the plaintiff walked more than 400 feet in going to Herbert's aid. He had time to reflect and weigh; impulse had been followed by choice; and choice, in the defendant's view, intercepts and breaks the sequence. We find no warrant for thus shortening the chain of jural causes. We may assume, though we are not required to decide, that peril and rescue must be in substance one transaction; that the sight of the one must have aroused the impulse to the other; in short, that there must be unbroken continuity between the commission of the wrong and the effort to avert its consequences. If all this be assumed, the defendant is not aided. Continuity in such circumstances is not broken by the exercise of volition.

... The law does not discriminate between the rescuer oblivious of peril and the one who counts the cost. It is enough that the act, whether impulsive or deliberate, is the child of the occasion. ...

[On the question whether the plaintiff had acted reasonably, Cardozo J observed, at 438, that "errors of judgment" would not be counted against the plaintiff if those errors resulted "from the excitement and confusion of the moment". Hiscock CJ, Hogan, Pound, McLaughlin, Crane and Andrews JJ agreed with Cardozo J.]

New trial granted

Chapman v Hearse
(1961) 106 CLR 112
High Court of Australia

A person whose negligent conduct has placed himself or herself (or another person) in a dangerous situation owes a duty of care to a rescuer who responds to the situation.

[A collision occurred between two vehicles one of which was driven by Chapman who was thrown out on to the road and rendered unconscious. Almost immediately after the accident another motorist, Dr Cherry, stopped his vehicle and went to Chapman's assistance. A few minutes later a vehicle driven by Hearse struck Dr Cherry and caused him injuries as a result of which he died. The executor of Dr Cherry's estate instituted proceedings against Hearse pursuant to the *Wrongs Act 1936* (SA) seeking damages for the benefit of the widow and children of the deceased. Hearse claimed that, in the event of liability attaching to him he was entitled to contribution from Chapman to such extent as to the Court should seem just and equitable.

The trial judge found that Hearse was negligent and ordered that judgment be entered against him. He also found that Chapman was liable to make a contribution to Hearse of one quarter of the damages. An appeal by Chapman to the Full Court of the Supreme Court of South Australia was dismissed. Chapman appealed to the High Court.]

THE COURT. (DIXON CJ, KITTO, TAYLOR, MENZIES and WINDEYER JJ) ... **[119]** [T]he principal question for examination is whether, having suffered judgment at the hands of Dr Cherry's executor, Hearse became entitled to recover a contribution from Chapman.

The answer to this question depends upon whether Chapman would have been liable for the "same damage" at the suit of Dr Cherry's executor (*Wrongs Act*, s 25(c)). This enquiry, the appellant somewhat emphatically asserts, must be answered in the negative. First of all, it is said, Chapman owed no duty of care to Dr Cherry. Alternatively, it is asserted that, even if he did, Dr Cherry's death was caused solely by the negligent driving of Hearse and not at all by any breach of duty on Chapman's part and, finally, the contention is raised that, on any view of the matter the death of Dr Cherry, considered as a consequence of Chapman's negligence, was too remote to fix him with responsibility.

In the unusual circumstances of the case the point which calls first for attention is the position which Dr Cherry occupied *vis-à-vis* Chapman. At the time when Dr Cherry was run down he was standing – or stooping – near the centre of the road. It was dark and wet and there seems no doubt that visibility was poor. As a consequence the task of attending to the injured man, with no one present to warn oncoming traffic, involved Dr Cherry in a situation of some danger. But, says the appellant, this was quite fortuitous and not **[120]** a situation reasonably foreseeable by Chapman at the time when, as the result of his negligence, his vehicle collided with that of Emery. Then to emphasize the contention that Chapman owed no duty of care to Dr Cherry the appellant enlarged upon the sequence of events which led to the final result. None of these events, it was said, was reasonably foreseeable. It was not reasonably foreseeable that Chapman would be precipitated on to the roadway, that Dr Cherry should at that moment be in the immediate vicinity, that he, as a doctor, should be first on the scene and proceed to render aid to Chapman with no other person present to warn oncoming traffic or, finally, that within a few minutes Dr Cherry should be run down by a negligent driver. But this argument assumes as the test of the existence of a duty of care with respect to Dr Cherry the reasonable foreseeability of the precise sequence of events which led to his death and it was rejected, and rightly rejected, by the Full Court. It is, we think, sufficient in the circumstances of this case to ask whether a consequence of the same general character as that which followed was reasonably foreseeable as one not unlikely to follow a collision between two vehicles on a dark wet night upon a busy highway. In pursuing this enquiry it is without significance that Dr Cherry was a medical practitioner or that Chapman was deposited on the roadway. What is important to consider is whether a reasonable man might foresee, as the consequence of such a collision, the attendance on the roadway, at some risk to themselves, of persons fulfilling a moral and social duty to render aid to those incapacitated or otherwise injured. ... Whether characterisation after the event of its consequences as "reasonable and probable" precisely marks the full range of consequences which, before the event, were "reasonably foreseeable" may be and no doubt will continue to be, the subject of much debate. But one thing is certain and that is that in order to establish the prior existence of a duty of care with respect to a plaintiff subsequently injured as the result of a sequence of events following a defendant's carelessness it is not necessary for the plaintiff to show that the precise manner in which his injuries were sustained **[121]** was reasonably foreseeable; it is sufficient if it appears that injury to a class of persons of which he was one might reasonably have been foreseen as a consequence. ...

[122] These observations do not, of course, conclude the question whether, as the learned Chief Justice decided, Chapman's negligence was in the proved circumstances of the case a cause of Dr Cherry's death and this must now be considered. At the outset, however, it should be said that the approach to this question in the course of argument was, with some resulting confusion, overlaid by a discussion of the decision of the Judicial Committee in *Overseas Tankship (UK) Ltd v Morts Dock & Engineering Co Ltd (The Wagon Mound)* [1961] AC 388. In effect, the argument of the respondent proceeded upon the basis that if the ultimate damage was "reasonably foreseeable" that circumstance would conclude this aspect of the matter against the appellant. But what this argument overlooks is that when the question is whether damage ought to be attributed to one of several "causes" there is no occasion to consider reasonable foreseeability on the part of the particular wrongdoer unless and until it appears that the negligent act or omission alleged has, in fact, caused the damage complained of. As we understand the term "reasonably foreseeable" is not, in itself, a test of "causation"; it marks the limits beyond which a wrongdoer will not be held responsible for damage resulting from his wrongful act. This distinction is of some importance in cases such as the present where there have been successive acts of negligence and where it is sought to establish, notwithstanding the fact that the ultimate consequence might have been reasonably foreseeable at the time of the earlier act of negligence, that the later negligent act was the sole cause of the damage complained of. This, of course, is what Chapman seeks to do in the present case. Dealing with this aspect as an independent matter he concedes the foreseeability of some event such as that which actually happened, but asserts that as a matter of practical fact, Dr Cherry's death was caused solely by Hearse's negligent driving. It was, it is said, a case of *novus actus interveniens*, or that, otherwise, Hearse's negligent driving operated to break the chain of causation between the original negligent act and Dr Cherry's death. Whether this was so or not must, we think, be very much a matter of circumstance and degree.

In support of the appellant's contention it was initially argued that it was sufficient to enable him to escape liability if, as was held to be the case, Hearse's intervening act was negligent. Some support for this proposition, it was said, was to be found in a **[123]** consideration of the so called "last opportunity" rule and by way of illustration it was pointed out that if Chapman had also been injured by Hearse's driving he would have been in a position to recover his damages in full against Hearse. That being so it would be anomalous if, having recovered his own damages in full, he should then be held liable to make a contribution to Hearse in respect of his liability to Dr Cherry's executor. The whole of the damage, it was said, would have resulted from the same cause and it would be curious indeed if, in the final result, one part of it should be borne by Hearse alone and another part by Hearse and Chapman jointly. But, even assuming that the circumstances were, in general, appropriate to invoke the last opportunity rule, the argument is superficially attractive only. It assumes that notwithstanding the provision for apportionment of liability made by s 27a(3) of the *Wrongs Act* that rule retains full force and effect in South Australia. In terms, what that section requires is an apportionment of damages where a person has suffered damage as the result partly of his own fault and partly of the fault of any other person or persons. The appellant's argument must, therefore, be taken to assume that the last opportunity rule was devised as a test of causation so that whenever it was successfully called in aid by a plaintiff its effect was to brand the defendant's negligence as the sole cause of the plaintiff's injuries. The so-called rule as "authoritatively" stated in *Tuff v Warman* (1858) 5 CB (NS) 573 [141 ER 231] as accepted by this Court in *Alford v Magee* (1952) 85 CLR 437 was that a plaintiff's negligence would not disentitle him to recover "if the defendant might by the exercise of care on his part have avoided the consequences of the negligence or carelessness of the plaintiff". It was, of course, pointed out that the qualification so stated was applicable only in appropriate cases. The statement, however, can have reference only to negligence on the part of a plaintiff which, apart from the so-called rule, would disentitle him to recover, that is to say, negligence which was, in fact, a cause of the damage. This view seems to flow naturally from the history of the development of the rule to which reference is made in *Alford v Magee* (1952) 85 CLR 437 and which is fully traced by Professor *Glanville Williams* in his work on *Joint Torts and Contributory Negligence* (1951) p 260 et seq. We think that the observations in *Alford v Magee* (1952) 85 CLR 437 are conclusive against the appellant on this point. That case regarded as preferable the view that contributory negligence means "negligence on the part of the plaintiff which has been a cause of damage in the same sense in which it is necessary for the plaintiff himself to prove **[124]** that negligence of the defendant was a cause of the damage" ((1952) 85 CLR, at p 451) and it then asserted that "it seems more natural and appropriate to use the term as meaning negligence of the plaintiff which has been a cause of the damage in the above sense and then [*apropos of the last opportunity rule*] to consider what circumstances will preclude such negligence from affording a good defence" ((1952) 85 CLR, at p 452). No doubt, in many cases, the rule has been treated as if it had assumed the role of a test of causation but not, as far as we can see, on any occasion when it was of importance to distinguish between its real and what may, perhaps, be called its apparent character.

Notwithstanding this answer to the argument of the appellant on this point, he insists that the fact that Hearse's later act was wrongful operated to break the chain of causation between his negligence and Dr Cherry's death. Why this should be so, however, does not clearly emerge but as far as we can see the submission rests solely upon the general proposition that there should not be imputed to a wrongdoer, as a reasonable man, foreseeability of subsequent intervening conduct which is, itself, wrongful. One illustration will suffice to show that as a proposition of law this is erroneous. Let it be assumed that X is a passenger in a vehicle driven by A and that he is injured when that vehicle comes into collision with a vehicle driven by B. It is established that A and B were successively negligent but, B, not otherwise negligent, could have avoided the consequence of A's negligence if he had used reasonable care. It would be no answer to a claim by X against A merely to assert that B's conduct which had intervened between the negligence of A and the injuries sustained by X was wrongful. A, of course, could not escape liability unless he established that B's negligence was the sole cause of X's injuries and in seeking to do this the last opportunity rule could be of no assistance to him. Nor, indeed, has it ever been suggested in such a case that because B's subsequent conduct was wrongful A's negligence should be excluded as a cause of X's injuries. From this it will be seen that, on principle, it is impossible to exclude from the realm of reasonable foresight subsequent intervening acts merely on the ground that those acts, when examined, are found to be wrongful. ...

[126] In the result we are of the opinion that the appeal should be dismissed.

Appeal dismissed

5. PSYCHIATRIC INJURY

Tame v New South Wales
Annetts v Australian Stations Pty Ltd
(2002) 191 ALR 449; [2002] HCA 35
High Court of Australia

The "ordinary principles of the tort of negligence, unhindered by artificial constrictions",
determine the existence of a duty of care in respect of negligently inflicted psychiatric injury
(nervous shock).
    Accordingly, a duty of care in respect of psychiatric injury requires reasonable foresee-
ability on the part of a person in the position of the defendant of injury of that kind to a
person in the position of the plaintiff. There is no requirement of "sudden shock" or "direct
perception" by the plaintiff of a distressing phenomenon or its immediate aftermath. However,
in addition to reasonable foreseeability of psychiatric injury, there must be a relationship
between the parties such that the defendant should have had the plaintiff in contemplation
as a person closely and directly affected by the defendant's conduct. Absence of "normal
fortitude" on the part of the plaintiff does not preclude the existence of a duty of care but will
be relevant to whether psychiatric injury was reasonably foreseeable.

GUMMOW and KIRBY JJ. [some footnotes in whole or part omitted] **[484]** 148. These two
proceedings, an appeal from a decision of the New South Wales Court of Appeal (*Morgan v Tame*
(2000) 49 NSWLR 21) and an application for special leave to appeal against a decision of the Full
Court of the Supreme Court of Western Australia (*Annetts v Australian Stations Pty Ltd* (2000) 23
WAR 35), concern liability for negligently inflicted psychiatric harm.

149. In the first proceeding, *Tame v New South Wales*, the appellant [plaintiff] seeks to restore
an award at trial of damages for psychiatric harm consequent on being told that a police traffic
collision report had erroneously recorded that she had been driving while intoxicated; the Court
of Appeal set aside that award. The issue in the second, *Annetts v Australian Stations Pty Ltd*,
is whether the Full Court erred in dismissing an appeal against an adverse determination on a
preliminary issue that certain assumed facts did not give rise to a duty of care on the part of the
respondent [defendant] to exercise reasonable care and skill to avoid causing foreseeable psychiatric
injury to the applicants [plaintiffs]. The applicants had pleaded that they sustained "nervous shock"
when their adolescent son disappeared and subsequently died in the Western Australian desert as a
result of the alleged negligence of his employer, the respondent.

[485] 150. The appeal in *Tame* should be dismissed and the decision of the Court of Appeal
affirmed; the question posed in *Annetts* should have been answered favourably to the applicants;
special leave should be granted and the appeal allowed.

Tame v New South Wales
151. On 11 January 1991, the appellant, Mrs Tame, was involved in a motor vehicle collision at
Richmond, outside the Sydney area. The driver of the other vehicle, Mr Terence Lavender, was
clearly at fault. He had a blood alcohol reading of 0.14 and was driving on the wrong side of the
road. A blood sample taken from Mrs Tame shortly after the accident yielded a nil blood alcohol
reading.

152. Constable Morgan of the Windsor Police Station completed a traffic collision report on
the accident, but left blank those portions of the report relating to the blood alcohol content of the
drivers. Subsequently, in February 1991, Senior Constable Beardsley, the acting traffic sergeant at
Windsor Police Station, completed those portions of the form. However, he mistakenly recorded
the blood alcohol content of both drivers as 0.14. Acting Sergeant Beardsley detected the error
on the form some time between February and late March 1991, at which point he corrected the
original report. ...

153. Mr Lavender had been driving an uninsured vehicle and Mrs Tame sued the Nominal Defendant. The claim was handled by NZI Insurance ("NZI"), which admitted liability on 11 June 1991. The claim against the Nominal Defendant was ultimately settled in August 1994 with a substantial sum being paid to Mrs Tame. By May 1992, NZI became reluctant to continue paying for physiotherapy treatment undertaken by Mrs Tame for significant leg and back injuries she sustained in the collision. This became a source of anxiety for Mrs Tame, who spoke with her solicitor, Mr Weller, about NZI's apparent refusal to meet the ongoing costs of the physiotherapy. Mr Weller contacted NZI's solicitor about the matter.

154. During a conversation in June 1992, Mr Weller asked Mrs Tame whether she had been drinking prior to the accident. She had consumed very little alcohol in the previous 20 years and she was horrified at the suggestion. Mr Weller told her that NZI's copy of the traffic collision report (which bore the error that Acting Sergeant Beardsley had corrected on the original report) indicated that her blood alcohol content at the time of the accident was three times the lawful limit. Mrs Tame was alarmed by this information, and began to worry about how many people would be told of it and the detrimental effect she considered this would have on her reputation.

155. Immediately after speaking with Mr Weller, Mrs Tame telephoned the Windsor Police Station and was told that her blood alcohol reading at the time of the collision had been nil and that the information on the form was a mistake. NZI's solicitor reconfirmed the admission of liability on 29 July 1992. In early 1993, Mr Weller obtained from the Police Service a formal apology and an assurance that the mistake on the traffic collision report had been rectified. However, Mrs Tame continued to believe that NZI's reluctance to pay for her physiotherapy was connected with the false information on the traffic collision [486] report. In fact, NZI believed the treatment was unnecessary. Mrs Tame became obsessed with the mistake on the form. She feared she was being punished for something she had done in the past, and spoke repeatedly about the mistake with her husband and friends. She found it difficult to sleep and experienced shame, guilt, stress and depression, for which she sought counselling. Her psychiatrist, Dr Mitchell, diagnosed Mrs Tame's condition in 1995 as psychotic depressive illness. …

156. Mrs Tame brought proceedings in negligence against Constable Morgan and the State of New South Wales in the District Court. During the trial (before Garling DCJ, without a jury) it became apparent that the mistake had been made by Acting Sergeant Beardsley and not Constable Morgan. The Court held that the State was vicariously liable for Acting Sergeant Beardsley's negligence in completing the traffic collision report. Mrs Tame was awarded $115,692 in damages.

157. An appeal by the State to the New South Wales Court of Appeal (Spigelman CJ, Mason P and Handley JA) was allowed unanimously. The Court held that, in the absence of actual knowledge of a particular susceptibility, the law imposes only a duty to take reasonable care to avoid psychiatric injury to a person of "normal fortitude". Their Honours considered that it was not reasonably foreseeable that a person of normal fortitude might sustain psychiatric injury from a clerical mistake of the type that occurred here. Further, Mason P expressly held that, whether or not one assumed a potential victim of normal fortitude, the risk of psychiatric injury was not reasonably foreseeable. Mason P and Handley JA also allowed the appeal on the additional basis that Mrs Tame did not suffer a sudden affront or assault on her psyche from the perception of a horrifying event, which their Honours considered a necessary pre-condition to recovery in negligence for psychiatric harm. Although, as a matter of law, Spigelman CJ accepted this pre-condition to recovery, he declined to allow the appeal on this ground because there were insufficient findings of fact.

158. By special leave, Mrs Tame appeals to this Court on several grounds. In particular, she contends that the Court of Appeal erred in applying the "normal fortitude" and "sudden shock" requirements. Counsel for Mrs Tame submit that neither of these "requirements" were necessary elements in her cause of action in negligence for pure psychiatric injury.

Annetts v Australian Stations Pty Ltd

159. This application for special leave falls to be decided on a somewhat artificial factual substratum. The case is yet to go to trial. The applicants brought their action in the Supreme Court of New South Wales. Upon the motion of the respondent and with the consent of the applicants, the action was transferred to [487] the Supreme Court of Western Australia. By order dated 5 May 1999, Heenan J

of the Supreme Court of Western Australia directed that a preliminary issue be tried separately from and prior to the trial of any other issues. The preliminary issue was whether, on the assumption that the facts pleaded in specified paragraphs in the applicants' Amended Statement of Claim were true, those assumed facts were "sufficient, at law, to give rise to an independent tortious duty of care owed by [the respondent] to [the applicants] to exercise reasonable care and skill to avoid causing them psychiatric injury". The specified paragraphs of the Amended Statement of Claim contain both assertions of fact and assertions of law. Nonetheless, it is possible to state in a general way the assumed facts upon which the application now before this Court proceeds.

160. In August 1986, James Annetts, the son of the applicants, left the family home in Binya, New South Wales, to work for the respondent as a jackaroo at Flora Valley, a cattle station situated about 40 kilometres south-east of Halls Creek in the Kimberley district of Western Australia. James was then 16 years of age. Before he left home, his mother telephoned Mrs Loder, the wife of the respondent's station manager, and inquired about the conditions under which James would be working. Mrs Loder told Mrs Annetts that James would be working at Flora Valley under constant supervision, that he would share a room with several other men and that he would be well looked after. The respondent admits generally that the applicants made inquiries of its servants or agents in relation to the arrangements that would be made for James' safety and that the applicants were provided with assurances thereof.

161. Notwithstanding these assurances, on 13 October 1986 Mr Loder assigned James to work alone as caretaker at Nicholson Station, about 100 kilometres east of Flora Valley. James had worked at Flora Valley for only seven weeks. On 3 December 1986, the respondent learned that James was missing and had reason to suspect that he was in grave danger of injury or death. The applicants were not informed that their son was missing until 6 December, when a police officer at Griffith, New South Wales, telephoned Mr Annetts and told him that apparently James had run away. Mr Annetts collapsed and Mrs Annetts took over the conversation.

162. Subsequent events were summarised by Ipp J in the Full Court as follows:

At some time, not revealed by the facts before the court, an intensive search was begun for James and another teenager, Simon James Amos, who had been employed by the respond-ent as a jackaroo on another station. Thereafter, [the applicants] had a number of telephone conversations with police officers at Halls Creek police station, Mr Loder, and numerous other persons in the Halls Creek area concerning the whereabouts of their son. In January 1987, [the applicants] went to Halls Creek where they remained for some four to five days. They were then shown some of their son's belongings, including a hat covered in blood. Thereafter, on several occasions until the end of April 1987, [the applicants] went to the Halls Creek area in attempts to obtain information about James.

On 26 April 1987, Mr Annetts was informed by telephone that the vehicle driven by James had been found bogged in the desert but there were no signs of any people around it. Later that day, he was told that two sets of remains had been found nearby. [488] On 28 or 29 April 1987, Mr Annetts, alone, returned to Halls Creek. At the police station, he was shown a photograph of a skeleton and he identified it as being that of James.

The parties accept that, in fact, James 'died on or about 4 December 1986 in the Gibson Desert some 133 kilometres south of Balgo as a result of dehydration, exhaustion and hypo-thermia'. Thus, [the applicants] learned of his death almost five months after it occurred. They were far away from James when he died.

163. By their Amended Statement of Claim, the applicants pleaded that James died as a result of the respondent's negligence. The negligence is identified as the placement of James on his own as caretaker of an isolated property, the provision of a defective and unsuitable vehicle, the failure to train James in the skills necessary for survival in such isolation, and the failures to implement or maintain effective radio communication with James and promptly to notify the police of his disappearance.

164. Although not formulated with specificity, the assumed facts apparently include that the applicants suffered not only a grief reaction, but an "entrenched psychiatric condition". However, as Ipp J explained in the Full Court, the assumed facts did not specify precisely when the applicants sustained this condition. The Full Court postulated two alternative situations. The first was that Mr

and Mrs Annetts sustained psychiatric injury on 6 December 1986, when they were told that James was missing from his place of employment and was believed to have run away. The second was that they sustained psychiatric injury upon ultimately learning of James' death in late April 1987, the injury being caused by that development coupled with the accumulated effect of the earlier events.

165. Heenan J resolved the preliminary issue adversely to Mr and Mrs Annetts. He found that the respondent owed Mr and Mrs Annetts no relevant duty of care, because they did not "directly" perceive their son's death or its aftermath and their psychiatric injury was not the result of a "sudden sensory perception".

166. The Full Court of the Supreme Court of Western Australia (Malcolm CJ, Pidgeon and Ipp JJ) unanimously dismissed an appeal by the applicants. Ipp J, with whom Malcolm CJ and Pidgeon J agreed, held that the respondent did not owe Mr and Mrs Annetts a duty of care to exercise reasonable care and skill to avoid causing them psychiatric injury. Regardless of which of the two alternative situations described above applied, the psychiatric injuries sustained by the applicants were not reasonably foreseeable and the applicants were not in a sufficiently proximate relationship with the respondent to found a duty of care. Ipp J favoured the view that persons of "normal fortitude" in the position of the applicants would not have sustained a psychiatric illness, as opposed to deep anxiety and grief, either upon being informed that their son had run away or upon receiving confirmation of his death. In any event, Ipp J held that, in neither of the postulated situations should the respondent have foreseen that its conduct might result in a "sudden sensory perception" on the part of the applicants of a phenomenon so distressing that a recognisable psychiatric illness would be caused thereby. His Honour further held that the applicants had not established **[489]** the requisite degree of proximity as they did not directly perceive the consequences of the respondent's conduct.

167. In seeking special leave to appeal against the decision of the Full Court, Mr and Mrs Annetts submit that the common law of Australia does not and should not recognise the "sudden shock" or "direct perception" rules as pre-conditions of liability. Further, they submit that the "normal fortitude" stipulation is no more than an aspect of the conventional requirement of reasonable foreseeability, and does not operate as a free-standing control mechanism in cases of negligently inflicted psychiatric harm.

Negligence and "nervous shock" ...

[491] 178. Initially, in 1888, the Judicial Committee of the Privy Council in *Victorian Railways Commissioners v Coultas* (1888) 13 App Cas 222 held that nervous shock, unaccompanied by physical injury, was too remote a consequence of a negligent accident to sound in damages. To permit recovery, their Lordships said (at 226), would have the result that "[t]he difficulty which now often exists in case of alleged physical injuries of determining whether they were caused by the negligent act would be greatly increased, and a wide field opened for imaginary claims." ...

180. In *Dulieu v White & Sons* [1901] 2 KB 669, the King's Bench Divisional Court was dealing with a procedure in the nature of a demurrer. Their Lordships referred to the criticism of *Coultas* by Palles CB in *Bell v Great Northern Railway Co* (1890) 26 LR Ir 428, and permitted recovery in negligence for "nervous shock" occasioned by an apprehension of physical injury to the plaintiff herself, at least where the consequences of the shock were partly physical. Subsequently, in 1924, the English Court of Appeal ordered a new trial where an action under Lord Campbell's Act had been dismissed. The plaintiff in *Hambrook v Stokes Brothers* [1925] 1 KB 141 sued in respect of the death of his wife. Thus, he had to show that, if death had not ensued, his wife would have been entitled to maintain an action in respect of the wrongful act, neglect or default of the defendant. The defendant's lorry had seriously injured her child within her hearing. Atkin LJ spoke in general terms of a "duty to take care to avoid threatening personal injury **[492]** to a child in such circumstances as to cause damage by shock to a parent or guardian then present". This later was transmuted into an apparent rule that only relatives could recover for "nervous shock" caused by perception of physical injury to another. ...

181. The reference by Atkin LJ in *Hambrook* to those "present" also proved to be significant. In 1938, the Court of Appeal in *Owens v Liverpool Corporation* [1939] 1 KB 394 upheld an appeal against the dismissal of an action by four family mourners at a funeral for distress caused by witnessing a collision between a negligently driven tramcar and the hearse. The incident involved

no apprehension, or sight, or sound of physical injury to a human being. However, the decision in *Owens* was doubted by the House of Lords in *Bourhill v Young* [1943] AC 92. In that case, it was held that the defendant motorcyclist owed no duty of care to avoid causing nervous shock to the plaintiff, who was not herself in danger of physical impact, nor related to such person, nor within the defendant's line of vision at the time of the accident. Matters did not end there.

182. *Pusey* [*Mount Isa Mines Ltd v Pusey* (1970) 125 CLR 383], decided by this Court in 1970, upheld an award of damages for mental disorder occasioned by "nervous shock" at the sight of an injured co-worker unknown to the plaintiff. By 1984, both the House of Lords and this Court had permitted recovery for "nervous shock" where the plaintiff was not present at the scene of the accident caused by the defendant's negligent driving. In *McLoughlin v O'Brian* [1983] 1 AC 410 and *Jaensch v Coffey* (1984) 155 CLR 549, the shock resulted from what each plaintiff saw and was told at the hospital shortly after motor vehicle accidents which killed or seriously injured members of their respective families. However, recent authorities in the House of Lords dealing with "nervous shock" (*Alcock v Chief Constable of South Yorkshire Police* [1992] 1 AC 310; *Page v Smith* [1996] AC 155; *White v Chief Constable of South Yorkshire Police* [1999] 2 AC 455), to which further reference will be made, have specified a number of "control mechanisms" which are "additional" or "special", adjectives used by Hale LJ in her summary of the English law in *Hatton v Sutherland* [2002] 2 All ER 1 at 11-13. One such "mechanism" requires "secondary victims" (those who witness injury caused to others) to demonstrate close ties of love and affection with the "primary victim" and propinquity in time and space to the relevant accident or its immediate aftermath.

183. Advances in the capacity of medicine objectively to distinguish the genuine from the spurious, and renewed attention to the need to establish breach, causation and a recognisable psychiatric illness that is not too remote, indicate **[493]** the need for re-accommodation of the competing interests which are in play in "nervous shock" cases. But that accommodation is better achieved by direct attention to, rather than attempts to ignore, the conflict of interests involved. This reflects the preferred approach to defining the limits of liability in negligence, which takes as its starting point, not merely the actions of the defendant, but the interests which are sufficient to attract the protection of the law in this field. ...

Control mechanisms ...

[494] 187. This Court is presently concerned with three control mechanisms which influenced the intermediate appellate courts. They are (i) the requirement that liability for psychiatric harm be assessed by reference to a hypothetical person of "normal fortitude", (ii) the requirement that the psychiatric injury be caused by a "sudden shock", and (iii) the requirement that a plaintiff "directly perceive" a distressing phenomenon or its "immediate aftermath". It is an objection to the adoption of these rules that this would substitute for the consideration in the particular case of the general requirements of duty of care, reasonable foreseeability, causation and remoteness of damage, notions which would foreshorten inquiry into those matters by the imposition of absolutes with no necessary relation to basic principles. ...

188. It should be decided here that the three control mechanisms listed above are unsound. ...

189. None of the three control mechanisms has been accepted by this Court as a pre-condition to liability for negligently inflicted psychiatric harm. The first of the mechanisms, the standard of "normal fortitude", is not a free-standing criterion of liability, but a postulate which assists in the assessment, at the stage of breach, of the reasonable foreseeability of the risk of psychiatric harm. Further, for the reasons that follow, the common law of Australia recognises neither the second nor third, "sudden shock" and "direct perception", as pre-conditions to the recovery of damages for negligently inflicted psychiatric harm.

190. As will become apparent, the requirements of "sudden shock" and "direct perception" of a distressing phenomenon or its "immediate aftermath" have operated in an arbitrary and capricious manner. Unprincipled distinctions and artificial mechanisms of this type bring the law into disrepute. ...

[495] 191. Moreover, the emergence of a coherent body of case law is impeded, not assisted, by such a fixed system of categories. Rigid distinctions of the type required by the "direct perception" rule inevitably generate exceptions and new categories, like the "immediate aftermath" qualification, as the inadequacies of the recognised categories become apparent and "hard cases" are accommodated. The old rule that "nervous shock" sounded in damages only where it arose from a reasonable fear of immediate personal injury to oneself (*Dulieu v White & Sons* [1901] 2 KB 669 at 675), and its subsequent relaxation to permit recovery where the plaintiff feared for the safety of another (*Hambrook v Stokes Brothers* [1925] 1 KB 141), illustrates the point. As the categories and exceptions proliferate, the reasoning and outcomes in the cases become increasingly detached from the rationale supporting the cause of action.

Psychiatric harm

192. Before turning to consider each of the postulated control mechanisms, it is appropriate to identify the justification that is said to support them. At base, the justification lies in a perceived distinction between psychiatric and physical harm. Authorities (*White v Chief Constable of South Yorkshire Police* [1999] 2 AC 455 at 493-494) have isolated four principal reasons said to warrant different treatment of the two categories of case. These are (i) that psychiatric harm is less objectively observable than physical injury and is therefore more likely to be trivial or fabricated and is more captive to shifting medical theories and conflicting expert evidence, (ii) that litigation in respect of purely psychiatric harm is likely to operate as an unconscious disincentive to rehabilitation, (iii) that permitting full recovery for purely psychiatric harm risks indeterminate liability and greatly increases the class of persons who may recover, and (iv) that liability for purely psychiatric harm may impose an unreasonable or disproportionate burden on defendants. ...

193. Several points may be made here. First, the concerns underlying propositions (i), (ii) and (iv) apply, to varying degrees, in cases of purely physical injury, yet it is not suggested that they justify denying a duty of care in that category of case. Secondly, many of these concerns recede if full force is given to the distinction between emotional distress and a recognisable psychiatric illness. ... In Australia, as in England, Canada and New Zealand, a plaintiff who is unable affirmatively to establish the existence of a recognisable psychiatric illness is not **[496]** entitled to recover: *Jaensch v Coffey* (1984) 155 CLR 549 at 587. Grief and sorrow are among the "ordinary and inevitable incidents of life" (*Alcock v Chief Constable of South Yorkshire Police* [1992] 1 AC 310 at 416); the very universality of those emotions denies to them the character of compensable loss under the tort of negligence. Fright, distress or embarrassment, without more, will not ground an action in negligence. ...

194. ... Properly understood, the requirement to establish a recognisable psychiatric illness reduces the scope for indeterminate liability or increased litigation. It restricts recovery to those disorders which are capable of objective determination. To permit recovery for recognisable psychiatric illnesses, but not for other forms of emotional disturbance, is to posit a distinction grounded in principle rather than pragmatism, and one that is illuminated by professional medical opinion rather than fixed purely by idiosyncratic judicial perception. ...

195. Thirdly, the law of negligence already supplies its own limiting devices. In *Bourhill v Young* [1943] AC 92 at 107-108, Lord Wright said that in cases of "nervous shock" a crucial point was that the plaintiff cannot build on a wrong to someone else, such as the victim of the accident observed by the plaintiff. This suggests caution in the use of the terms "primary" and "secondary" victim. It has been observed earlier in these reasons under the heading "Control mechanisms" that, in requiring a plaintiff to establish fault, causation and a lack of remoteness of damage, the ordinary principles of negligence circumscribe recovery. Further, the tort of negligence requires no more than reasonable care to avert reasonably foreseeable risks. Breach will not be established if a reasonable person in the defendant's position would not have acted differently. The touchstone of liability remains reasonableness of conduct.

196. The asserted grounds for treating psychiatric harm as distinctly different from physical injury do not provide a cogent basis for the erection of exclusionary rules that operate in respect of the former but not the latter. To the extent that any of these concerns are not adequately met in particular categories of case by the operation of the ordinary principles of negligence, they may be accommodated, in the manner explained later in these reasons, by defining the scope of the duty of care with reference to values which the law protects.

[497] Normal fortitude

197. The attention given to this notion by both the Court of Appeal in *Tame* and the Full Court in *Annetts* may suggest that a plaintiff has no action unless he or she be an individual of "normal fortitude". The concept is said to derive from a passage in the speech of Lord Wright in *Bourhill v Young* at 109-110. However, it is made plain in that passage that the attention to the notional person of "normal fortitude" is the application of a hypothetical standard that assists the assessment of the reasonable foreseeability of harm, not an independent pre-condition or bar to recovery. His Lordship said at 110:

> It is here, as elsewhere, a question of what the hypothetical reasonable man, viewing the position, I suppose ex post facto, would say it was proper to foresee. What danger of particular infirmity that would include must depend on all the circumstances, but generally, I think, a reasonably normal condition, if medical evidence is capable of defining it, would be the standard. The test of the plaintiff's extraordinary susceptibility, if unknown to the defendant, would in effect make him an insurer. ...

199. However, it does not follow that it is a pre-condition to recovery in any action for negligently inflicted psychiatric harm that the plaintiff be a person of "normal" emotional or psychological fortitude or, if peculiarly susceptible, that the defendant know or ought to have known of that susceptibility. The statement by Spigelman CJ in the Court of Appeal in *Tame* that a plaintiff "cannot recover for 'pure' psychiatric damage unless a person of 'normal fortitude' would suffer psychiatric damage by the negligent act or omission" should not be accepted. Windeyer J observed in *Pusey* (1970) 125 CLR 383 at 405-406 that the notion of a "normal" emotional susceptibility, in a population of diverse susceptibilities, is imprecise and artificial. The imprecision in the concept renders it inappropriate as an absolute bar to recovery. Windeyer J also pointed out that the contrary view, with its attention to "normal fortitude" as a condition of liability, did not stand well with the so-called "egg-shell skull" rule in relation to the assessment of damages for physical harm.

200. Analysis by the courts may assist in assessing the reasonable foreseeability of the relevant risk. The criterion is one of *reasonable* foreseeability. Liability is imposed for consequences which the defendant, judged **[498]** by the standard of the reasonable person, ought to have foreseen: *Overseas Tankship (UK) Ltd v Morts Dock & Engineering Co Ltd (The Wagon Mound)* [1961] AC 388 at 423. ...

201. However, the concept of "normal fortitude" should not distract attention from the central inquiry, which is whether, in all the circumstances, the risk of the plaintiff sustaining a recognisable psychiatric illness was reasonably foreseeable, in the sense that the risk was not far-fetched or fanciful: see *Wyong Shire Council v Shirt* (1980) 146 CLR 40 at 48. It may be that, in some circumstances, the risk of a recognisable psychiatric illness to a person who falls outside the notion of "normal fortitude" is nonetheless not far-fetched or fanciful. If that is so, it is then for the tribunal of fact to determine what a reasonable person would do by way of response to the risk, in the manner indicated in *Wyong Shire Council v Shirt*. Where the plaintiff's response to the defendant's conduct is so extreme or idiosyncratic as to render the risk of that response far-fetched or fanciful, the law does not require the defendant to guard against it. ...

203. Nonetheless, questions of reasonable foreseeability are not purely factual. Expert evidence about the foreseeability of psychiatric harm is not **[499]** decisive. Such evidence cannot usurp the judgment that is required of the decision-maker. Further, it is not necessary that the particular type of disorder that eventuated be reasonably foreseeable; it is sufficient that the class of injury, psychiatric illness, was foreseeable as a possible consequence of the defendant's conduct: *Mount Isa Mines Ltd v Pusey* (1970) 125 CLR 383. So much follows from the proposition that liability does not depend upon "the capacity of a reasonable man to foresee damage of a precise and particular character or upon his capacity to foresee the precise events leading to the damage complained of": *Chapman v Hearse* (1961) 106 CLR 112 at 121. If liability be established by application of these criteria, then, consistently with the approach tentatively favoured by Windeyer J in *Pusey* (at 406), the "egg-shell skull" rule applies to the assessment of damages.

Sudden shock ...

205. In *Jaensch v Coffey* (1984) 155 CLR 549, Brennan J stated (at 565) that:

[a] plaintiff may recover only if the psychiatric illness is the result of physical injury negligently inflicted on him by the defendant or if it is induced by 'shock'. Psychiatric illness caused in other ways attracts no damages, though it is reasonably foreseeable that psychiatric illness might be a consequence of the defendant's carelessness. The spouse who has been worn down by caring for a tortiously injured husband or wife and who suffers psychiatric illness as a result goes without compensation; a parent made distraught by the wayward conduct of a brain-damaged child and who suffers psychiatric illness as a result has no claim against the tortfeasor liable to the child.

Mrs Coffey's psychiatric illness was in fact sustained through the "shock" of seeing her severely injured husband at the hospital shortly after his motor vehicle accident. Accordingly, in a sense, his Honour's remarks were not essential for the decision. Brennan J explained that he understood "shock" in this context to mean (at 567):

the sudden sensory perception – that is, by seeing, hearing or touching – of a person, thing or event, which is so distressing that the perception of the phenomenon affronts or insults the plaintiff's mind and causes a recognizable psychiatric illness. A psychiatric illness induced by mere knowledge of a distressing fact is not compensable; perception by the plaintiff of the distressing phenomenon is essential. If mere **[500]** knowledge of a distressing phenomenon sufficed, the bearers of sad tidings, able to foresee the depressing effect of what they have to impart, might be held liable as tortfeasors.

The last sentence of this passage suggests that a desire to avoid imposing liability on the "bearers of sad tidings" justified, at least in part, the requirements of "sudden shock" and "direct perception" which his Honour identified. As will appear, the approach we favour denies, for policy reasons, liability on the part of bearers of bad news without invoking requirements or distinctions which appear to have an insecure basis in contemporary psychiatry.

206. No other member of the Court in *Jaensch v Coffey* expressly adopted the requirement of "sudden shock". The remarks of Deane J (at 601) (with whom Gibbs CJ agreed generally) are inconclusive and neither Murphy J nor Dawson J directly considered the issue. Subsequent authority in the House of Lords has identified "sudden shock" as a distinct and necessary element of liability: *Alcock v Chief Constable of South Yorkshire Police* [1992] 1 AC 310. ... However, in the absence of acceptance by a majority of this Court of the need to establish "sudden shock", it is not a settled requirement of the common law of Australia.

207. With respect to those who espouse it, a "sudden shock" requirement would have no root in principle and therefore would be arbitrary and inconsistent in application. As a growing body of criticism has pointed out (see *Gifford v Strang Patrick Stevedoring Pty Ltd* (2001) 51 NSWLR 606 at 616), individuals may sustain recognisable psychiatric illnesses without any particular "sudden shock". ... The pragmatic justifications for the rule are unconvincing, for the reasons given earlier at [192] to [196]. The harsh and arbitrary operation of the rule has attracted judicial criticism in various jurisdictions: *Campbelltown City Council v Mackay* (1989) 15 NSWLR 501 at 503-504 per Kirby P. ...

208. Assuming that the other elements of the cause of action have been made out, liability in negligence, for which damage is the gist of the action, should turn on proof of a recognisable psychiatric disorder, not on the aetiology of that disorder. ...

[501] 210. Cases of protracted suffering, as opposed to "sudden shock", may raise difficult issues of causation and remoteness of damage. Difficulties of that kind are more appropriately analysed with reference to the principles of causation and remoteness, not through an absolute denial of duty. ...

[502] 213. The requirement to establish "sudden shock" should not be accepted as a precondition for recovery in cases of negligently inflicted psychiatric illness.

Direct perception and immediate aftermath

214. This related "requirement" has not been authoritatively adopted by this Court as an essential ingredient in an action for negligence for psychiatric harm. ...

[503] 218. Direct perception of a distressing phenomenon or its immediate aftermath appears to be a settled requirement of English law: *Alcock v Chief Constable of South Yorkshire Police*

[1992] 1 AC 310. The "immediate aftermath" includes the journey by ambulance to the hospital and the scene at the hospital itself. It was the lack of direct perception that precluded recovery in *Alcock* by plaintiffs who watched live television footage of the overcrowding at the football stadium at Hillsborough where their loved ones were crushed to death, or who heard of the events from friends or radio reports and only later saw recorded footage. Plaintiffs in that category could not establish the requisite propinquity in time and space to the incident or its immediate aftermath. ...

[504] 221. A rule that renders liability in negligence for psychiatric harm conditional on the geographic or temporal distance of the plaintiff from the distressing phenomenon, or on the means by which the plaintiff acquires knowledge of that phenomenon, is apt to produce arbitrary outcomes and to exclude meritorious claims. ... The rule is also disjoined from the realities of modern telecommunications which have developed greatly since this control factor was propounded. ...

[505] 225. Distance in time and space from a distressing phenomenon, and means of communication or acquisition of knowledge concerning that phenomenon, may be relevant to assessing reasonable foreseeability, causation and remoteness of damage in a common law action for negligently inflicted psychiatric illness. But they are not themselves decisive of liability. To reason otherwise is to transform a factor that favours finding a duty of care in some cases into a general pre-requisite for a duty in all cases. This carries with it the risk of attribution of disproportionate significance to what may be no more than inconsequential circumstances.

Bearers of bad tidings
[506] 228. The content of a putative duty of care in novel categories of case accommodates itself to basic values which the corpus of the law promotes or protects. One relevant interest is that of the individual in the privacy of personal affairs: *Australian Broadcasting Corporation v Lenah Game Meats Pty Ltd* (2001) 185 ALR 1. On the other hand, the loved ones of a person who has been killed, injured or put in peril ordinarily have an interest in being told promptly of that circumstance and the law encourages the free and prompt supply of the relevant information to those persons. It is for this reason that, in the absence of a malign intention, no action lies against the bearer of bad news for psychiatric harm caused by the manner in which the news is conveyed or, if the news be true, for psychiatric harm caused by the fact of its conveyance. The discharge of the responsibility to impart bad news fully and frankly would be inhibited by the imposition in those circumstances of a duty of care to avoid causing distress to the recipient of the news. There can be no legal duty to break bad news gently. This is so even if degrees of tact and diplomacy were capable of objective identification and assessment, which manifestly they are not. Neither carelessness nor insensitivity in presentation will found an action in negligence against the messenger.

229. It is unnecessary here to consider in any detail two further questions. The first is whether carelessness in the accuracy of a message conveyed, as opposed to the manner or fact of its conveyance, may attract liability for negligently inflicted psychiatric illness. *Barnes v Commonwealth* (1937) 37 SR (NSW) 511, decided by the New South Wales Full Court as long ago as 1937, indicates that at least in some situations there may be liability even where the defendant does not know the information is incorrect. In *Barnes*, the Full Court overruled a demurrer to a declaration by the plaintiff that she had suffered "nervous shock" upon being incorrectly informed, by memorandum sent by an officer of the Commonwealth Invalid and Old-Age Pensions Office, that her husband had been admitted to a mental hospital.

230. The second matter is whether, where the tortious conduct may be identified independently from the communication of its consequences, liability attaches to the former but not to the latter. This will be most apparent when the tortfeasor and the messenger are different parties. Why should a separately identifiable tortfeasor be sheltered from liability in the same manner as one who conveys information about the distressing consequences of the tortfeasor's **[507]** conduct? Thus it may be necessary on an appropriate occasion to reconsider the suggestion by Windeyer J in *Pusey* (at 407) that, "[i]f the sole cause of shock be what is told or read of some happening" then, in the absence of intention to cause "nervous shock" no action lies against *the person who caused the event* which the bearer of bad news relates. A proposition of that breadth appears to import a requirement of "direct perception" which, for the reasons given earlier, is an unsound criterion of liability for negligently inflicted psychiatric harm.

The outcome in *Tame v New South Wales*

231. It is unlikely that an investigating police officer owes a duty of care to a person whose conduct is under investigation. Such a duty would appear to be inconsistent with the police officer's duty, ultimately based in the statutory framework and anterior common law by which the relevant police service is established and maintained fully to investigate the conduct in question: *Hill v Chief Constable of West Yorkshire* [1989] AC 53. Counsel for Mrs Tame submitted that Mrs Tame's conduct was not under investigation at the time the traffic collision report was completed. It was said that Mrs Tame was an accident victim in respect of whom there was no suspicion of any criminal offence. However, it is unnecessary to pursue that question, because, for the reasons that follow, Mrs Tame's action fails at the outset.

232. No case in negligence can be made out against the respondent in respect of the conduct of Acting Sergeant Beardsley. This is because a reasonable person in Acting Sergeant Beardsley's position would not have foreseen that his conduct in carelessly completing the traffic collision report involved a risk of causing a recognisable psychiatric illness to the appellant. It may be conceded that it was reasonably foreseeable that such carelessness may cause surprise, distress or anger, particularly as the report was likely to be distributed to the appellant's insurer and could be accessed, for a fee, by members of the public. However, it also was reasonably foreseeable (a) that an erroneous recording of the appellant's blood alcohol level, once detected, would promptly be rectified, given the obvious nature of an error which attributed to both drivers precisely the same blood alcohol content and (b) that, if pressed, the Police Service would offer a formal apology in respect of any such error, as subsequently occurred here.

233. But it was not reasonably foreseeable that a person in the position of Mrs Tame would sustain a recognisable psychiatric illness from a clerical error which she was told was a mistake that had been rectified and in respect of which she received a formal apology. The appellant's reaction was extreme and idiosyncratic. The risk of such a reaction was far-fetched or fanciful and, in the manner indicated in *Wyong Shire Council v Shirt* (1980) 146 CLR 40, was not one which the law of negligence required a reasonable person to avoid. ...

234. ... **[508]** The question of reasonable foreseeability involves an assessment respecting the foresight of a reasonable person in the defendant's position; that foresight may differ from the foresight of qualified psychiatrists. The judgment belongs, ultimately, to a court, not to an expert witness. In making that judgment, a court will draw upon its reserves of common sense and reasonableness.

235. The appeal in *Tame* should be dismissed with costs.

The outcome in *Annetts v Australian Stations Pty Ltd*

236. The Full Court erred in failing to apply the ordinary principles of the tort of negligence, unhindered by artificial constrictions based on the circumstance that the illness for which redress was sought was purely psychiatric. In particular, neither the lack of the applicants' direct perception of their son's death or its immediate aftermath, nor the circumstance that the applicants may not have sustained a "sudden shock", is fatal to the applicants' claims. In accordance with the ordinary principles of negligence applied to the assumed facts, the respondent owed the applicants a duty of care. The preliminary issue formulated by Heenan J should be resolved in the affirmative.

237. The connections between the parties indicate the existence of a duty of care. An antecedent relationship between the plaintiff and the defendant [eg the relationship between employee and employer as in *New South Wales v Seedsman* [2000] NSWCA 119], especially where the latter has assumed some responsibility to the former to avoid exposing him or her to a risk of psychiatric harm, may supply the basis for importing a duty of care. ...

238. A duty to avert psychiatric harm in these circumstances finds some, necessarily imperfect, analogy in cases of negligent misstatement causing pure economic loss, where a duty of care may arise with an assumption of responsibility by the defendant and reasonable reliance by the plaintiff: *Tepko Pty Ltd v Water Board* (2001) 206 CLR 1.

239. In the present case, the applicants sought and obtained from the **[509]** respondent assurances that James would be appropriately supervised. The respondent undertook specifically to act to minimise the risk of harm to James and, by inference, to minimise the risk of psychiatric injury to

the applicants. In those circumstances, the recognition of a duty of care does not raise the prospect of an intolerably large or indeterminate class of potential plaintiffs.

240. The applicants had no way of protecting themselves against the risk of psychiatric harm that eventuated. In that regard, nothing turns upon which of the situations postulated by Ipp J in the Full Court as to the time that harm was sustained may be established at trial of the remaining issues in the action. The control over the risk of harm to James, and the risk of consequent psychiatric harm to the applicants, was held to a significant, perhaps exclusive, degree by the respondent. It controlled the conditions under which James worked.

241. Is there, to adapt what was put and rejected on the facts in *Bryan v Maloney* (1995) 182 CLR 609 at 623-624, any real question of inconsistency between the existence of a duty of care to the parents of James and the legitimate pursuit by the respondent of its business interests? The answer is in the negative. It is likely that the respondent's duty of care to the applicants to exercise reasonable care to avoid causing them psychiatric injury with respect to James' death in the course of his employment by it was, at most, co-extensive with the tortious and express or implied contractual duties that it had owed to James directly as his employer.

242. The application for special leave in *Annetts* should be granted and the appeal allowed. The orders of the Full Court dated 21 November 2000 should be set aside. In their place it should be ordered that the appeal to that Court be allowed, that the question posed by Heenan J in the schedule to his order for the trial of a preliminary issue dated 5 May 1999 be answered "Yes" … .

[In separate judgments, Gleeson CJ, Gaudron, McHugh, Hayne and Callinan JJ agreed that the appeal in *Tame* should be dismissed and that the appeal in *Annetts* should be allowed. However, the members of the court expressed a diversity of reasons for reaching these conclusions.

Gleeson CJ agreed with Gummow and Kirby JJ that "sudden shock" and "direct perception" are not requirements of Australian law and noted that "normal fortitude cannot be regarded as a separate and definitive test of liability".

Gaudron J rejected the requirement of "direct perception" and observed that "ordinarily, 'normal fortitude' will be a convenient means of determining whether a risk of psychiatric injury is foreseeable" and that "no aspect of the law of negligence renders 'sudden shock' critical either to the existence of a duty of care or to the foreseeability of a risk of psychiatric injury".

McHugh, Hayne and Callinan JJ held that a duty of care in respect of psychiatric injury requires reasonable foreseeability of injury of that kind to a person of normal (or, in the words of Hayne J, "reasonable or ordinary") fortitude. In view of the pre-existing relationship between the applicants and the respondent in *Annetts*, McHugh J found it unnecessary to consider whether "the special rules" relating to psychiatric injury represent current Australian law. Hayne J held that "rules requiring direct impact of events upon the senses of the plaintiff" should be discarded in the context of psychiatric injury. Callinan J favoured retention of a requirement of "sudden shock" and a requirement of "direct perception". In Callinan J's opinion both these requirements were satisfied in *Annetts*.]

Tame v New South Wales
Appeal dismissed

Annetts v Australian Stations Pty Ltd
Appeal allowed

[A report published in *The Australian*, 18 March 2003, WA Country Edition, stated that the claim for damages for psychiatric injury by Mr and Mrs Annetts against Australian Stations Pty Ltd had been settled on terms favourable to the plaintiffs.]

Wicks v State Rail Authority of New South Wales
Sheehan v State Rail Authority of New South Wales
(2010) 241 CLR 60; [2010] HCA 22
High Court of Australia

A rescuer coming to the scene of an accident involving death, injury and trauma to many victims is not precluded from claiming damages for psychiatric injury by virtue of legislation in some Australian States which bars recovery by claimants, other than close family members, who were not present at the scene of the accident.

THE COURT. (FRENCH CJ, GUMMOW, HAYNE, CRENNAN, KIEFEL and BELL JJ) **[66]** 1. At about 7.14 am on 31 January 2003, a passenger train operated by "State Rail" left the tracks at high speed near Waterfall Station, south of Sydney. Seven of the almost fifty people on the train died. Many others were injured, some very seriously. All four carriages of the train were very badly damaged.

2. At the time of the accident, the appellant in each appeal (Mr Wicks and Mr Sheehan respectively) was a serving member of the New South Wales Police Force. In response to a radio message, Mr Wicks and Mr Sheehan were among the first to arrive at the scene, soon after the **[67]** accident had happened. What confronted them was death, injury and the wreckage of the train. Because the overhead electrical cables had been torn down, and were lying across the wreckage, it was anything but clear whether it was safe to go close to the wreckage.

3. Some of those on board had been thrown out of the train. Many remained in the wreckage. Mr Wicks and Mr Sheehan each forced his way into damaged carriages. Some passengers were so badly injured that they were obviously dead. Some passengers were trapped, evidently seriously injured, and very distressed.

4. Mr Wicks and Mr Sheehan each did his best to relieve the suffering of the survivors and to get them to a place of safety. As further emergency workers arrived at the scene, Mr Wicks and Mr Sheehan each continued his rescue efforts and, later, undertook other tasks assigned at the scene. Each remained at the scene for a considerable time – Mr Wicks until about 4 pm; Mr Sheehan until about 2 pm.

5. State Rail admits that it was negligent in the operation of the railway and of the particular train that derailed.

6. Mr Wicks and Mr Sheehan each alleges that he was injured as a result of being present at the crash site and what he witnessed there. Each pleaded, as particulars of the injuries he suffered: psychological and psychiatric injuries, post-traumatic stress syndrome, nervous shock and major depressive disorder.

The determinative issue
7. The determinative issue in each appeal is whether, if State Rail owed the appellant a relevant duty of care, and if the appellant suffered a recognised psychiatric illness of which the negligence of State Rail was a cause, State Rail is liable to the appellant. All parties accept that resolution of this issue turns on the construction and application of Pt 3 (ss 27-33) of the *Civil Liability Act 2002* (NSW) ["the Civil Liability Act"]. The issue should be resolved in favour of the appellants, and each matter remitted to the Court of Appeal of New South Wales for its further consideration.

8. To explain how the issue arises, and why it is necessary for this Court to leave the questions of duty of care, recognised psychiatric illness and causation undecided, something must be said about the history of the litigation in the courts below.

Proceedings in the courts below
9. Each appellant commenced an action against State Rail in the Common Law Division of the Supreme Court of New South Wales. ... The parties agreed that there were five issues in the case: [including]
    1.   Did the defendant owe the plaintiff, a rescuer, a duty of care?

2.   Did the plaintiff witness, at the scene, victims of the derailment, being killed injured or
put in peril, in accordance with section 30(2) of [the *Civil Liability Act*]?...

[68] 10. At first instance, Malpass AsJ concluded that liability was not established, and directed
the entry of judgment in each action for the defendant: *Wicks v Railcorp* [2007] NSWSC 1346.
Appeals to the Court of Appeal of the Supreme Court of New South Wales ... against those judgments were dismissed: *Sheehan v State Rail Authority* [2009] Aust Torts Reports 82-028. It is from
the orders of the Court of Appeal that, by special leave, the appellants now appeal to this Court.

11. Both at first instance, and on appeal to the Court of Appeal, the answer to the second issue
identified by the parties, concerning the application of s 30(2) of the *Civil Liability Act*, was treated
as determinative of the liability of State Rail. ... Section 30(1)-(4) of the *Civil Liability Act* provides:
(1) This section applies to the liability of a person (*the defendant*) for pure mental harm to
a person (*the plaintiff*) arising wholly or partly from mental or nervous shock in connection
with another person (*the victim*) being killed, injured or put in peril by the act or omission of
the defendant.
(2) The plaintiff is not entitled to recover damages for pure mental harm unless:
(a)   the plaintiff witnessed, at the scene, the victim being killed, injured or put in peril,
or
(b)   the plaintiff is a close member of the family of the victim...
[69] 12. The outcome of the litigation was treated, both at trial and on appeal to the Court of
Appeal, as turning upon whether Mr Wicks and Mr Sheehan "witnessed, at the scene, the victim
being killed, injured or put in peril" within the meaning of s 30(2)(a). Both Malpass AsJ and the
Court of Appeal concluded that neither appellant witnessed a victim or victims of the derailment
"being killed, injured or put in peril".

13. However, s 30(2) is drawn in negative terms, using the word "unless" to indicate the
operation of the sub-section as an exception to, or reservation from, what otherwise would be the
entitlement of the plaintiff. This use of "unless" appears also in ss 31, 32 and 33, to which further
reference will be made. ...

15. Although State Rail submitted that Malpass AsJ made findings which affect whether State
Rail should be found to have owed each appellant a duty of care, his Honour expressly refrained
from deciding that issue. The Court of Appeal also expressly decided that it was not necessary
to address that issue. To begin inquiries by asking whether s 30(2)(a) of the *Civil Liability Act* is
engaged, without first deciding whether State Rail owed a duty to each appellant to take reasonable care not to cause him psychiatric injury, was to omit consideration of an important anterior
question. To examine the content of the limitation on liability provided by s 30 without a proper
understanding of the provisions affecting duty runs the risk of reading the limitation divorced from
its statutory context.

Part 3 of the Civil Liability Act
16. Part 3 of the *Civil Liability Act* is entitled "Mental harm". That term is defined in s 27 to mean
"impairment of a person's mental condition".

17. Section 28(1) provides that Pt 3, *except s 29*, "applies to any claim for damages for mental
harm resulting from negligence, regardless of whether the claim is brought in tort, in contract,
under statute or [70] otherwise". ... For the purposes of these matters, it is necessary to notice
only that, by operation of s 28(1), the other provisions of Pt 3 apply to any claim for damages
for mental harm resulting from negligence, and thus apply to each appellant's claim against State
Rail. Section 27 identifies two species of "mental harm": "consequential mental harm" and "pure
mental harm". ...The claims made by both Mr Wicks and Mr Sheehan are claims for damages for
pure mental harm. ...

21. Section 32 is entitled "Mental harm – duty of care". It provides:
(1) A person (*the defendant*) does not owe a duty of care to another person (*the plaintiff*) to
take care not to cause the plaintiff mental harm unless the defendant ought to have foreseen
that a person of normal fortitude might, in the circumstances of the case, suffer a recognised
psychiatric illness if reasonable care were not taken.

(2) For the purposes of the application of this section in respect of pure mental harm, the circumstances of the case include the following:

  (a) whether or not the mental harm was suffered as the result of a sudden shock,
  (b) whether the plaintiff witnessed, at the scene, a person being killed, injured or put in peril,
  (c) the nature of the relationship between the plaintiff and any person killed, injured or put in peril,
  (d) whether or not there was a pre-existing relationship between the plaintiff and the defendant. ...

[71] 22. Because s 32 defines or controls what otherwise would be a duty of care arising at common law, it falls for consideration before the limitation upon entitlement to damages imposed by s 30(2). Consideration of the operation of s 32 (in particular sub-ss (1) and (2)) must begin from the observation that neither s 32 itself, nor any other provision of the *Civil Liability Act* (whether in Pt 3 or elsewhere), identifies positively when a duty of care to another person to take care not to cause mental harm to that other should be found to exist. Rather, like s 30(2), s 32(1) is cast negatively. It provides that a duty is *not* to be found unless a condition is satisfied. The necessary condition for establishment of a duty of care, identified by s 32(1), is that the defendant ought to have foreseen that a person of normal fortitude might, in the circumstances of the case, suffer a recognised psychiatric illness if reasonable care were not taken.

23. The determination of whether the defendant ought to have foreseen mental injury to a person of normal fortitude must be made with regard to "the circumstances of the case". Section 32(2) identifies four kinds of circumstance to which regard should be had: whether the mental harm was caused by sudden shock, whether there was "witness[ing], at the scene," of certain types of event, what was the relationship between plaintiff and victim, and whether there was a relationship between plaintiff and defendant. But s 32 does not prescribe any particular consequence as following from the presence or absence of any or all of those circumstances. Section 32, taking the form it does, must be understood against the background provided by the common law of negligence in relation to psychiatric injury as stated by this Court in *Tame v New South Wales* (2002) 211 CLR 317. ...

25. *Tame* held (at 331[12], 335-336 [29] per Gleeson CJ; at 349 [89]-[90] per McHugh J; at 385 [201] per Gummow and Kirby JJ; at 411 [275] per Hayne J) that in deciding whether, for the purposes of the tort of negligence, a defendant owed a plaintiff a duty to take reasonable care to avoid recognisable psychiatric injury, the central question is whether, in all the circumstances, the risk of the plaintiff sustaining such an injury was reasonably foreseeable. A majority of the Court in [72] *Tame* rejected (at 332-333 [16]-[18] per Gleeson CJ; at 340-341 [51]-[52],343-344 [61]-[62], [66] per Gaudron J; at 383-384 [197], 384-386 [199]-[203], 390 [213], 393 [221]-[222], 394 [225] per Gummow and Kirby JJ; at 411-412 [275] per Hayne J) the propositions that concepts of "reasonable or ordinary fortitude", "shocking event" or "directness of connection" were additional pre-conditions to liability.

26. In part, s 32 of the *Civil Liability Act* reflects the state of the common law identified in *Tame*. Consistent with what was decided in *Tame*, s 32 assumes that foreseeability is the central determinant of duty of care. Consistent with *Tame* (at 333 [18] per Gleeson CJ; at 344 [66] per Gaudron J; at 394 [225] per Gummow and Kirby JJ; at 411-412 [275] per Hayne J), "shocking event", and the existence and nature of any connection between plaintiff and victim and between plaintiff and defendant, are considerations relevant to foreseeability, but none is to be treated as a condition necessary to finding a duty of care. But contrary to what was decided in *Tame*, s 32 provides that a duty of care is not to be found unless the defendant ought to have foreseen that a person of normal fortitude might, in the circumstances of the case, suffer a recognised psychiatric illness.

27. For present purposes, there are three important features of s 32. First, "sudden shock" (the expression used in s 32(2)(a)) is no more than one of several circumstances that bear upon whether a defendant "ought to have foreseen that a person of normal fortitude might, in the circumstances of the case, suffer a recognised psychiatric illness if reasonable care were not taken". The occurrence

of "sudden shock" is neither a necessary nor a sufficient condition for a finding that a defendant owed a duty to take reasonable care not to cause a plaintiff pure mental harm.

28. Secondly, witnessing, at the scene, a person being killed, injured or put in peril is also but one of the circumstances that bear upon the central question of foreseeability. Witnessing, of the kind described, is neither a necessary nor a sufficient condition for finding a duty of care.

29. Thirdly, the focus of s 32 is "mental harm" and "a recognised psychiatric illness", not mental or nervous shock. Section 32 does not use the expression "mental or nervous shock". Yet, as noted earlier, the phrase "mental or nervous shock" appears in s 29 of the *Civil Liability Act*, and in s 30(1), the provision which determines whether s 30 is engaged. Section 30 applies to the liability of a person (the defendant) for pure mental harm to a person (the plaintiff) "arising wholly or partly from mental or nervous shock" in connection with another person (the victim) being killed, injured or put in peril by the act or omission of the defendant.

30. The phrase "mental or nervous shock" (as used in both ss 29 and 30) doubtlessly has a meaning different from "sudden shock" (the phrase used in s 32(2)(a)). The expression "mental or nervous shock" may be understood as referring to a consequence, and "sudden shock" may be **[73]** understood as referring to an event or a cause. But the notion of "shock", in the sense of a "sudden and disturbing impression on the mind or feelings; usually, one produced by some unwelcome occurrence or perception, by pain, grief, or violent emotion ([occasionally] joy), and tending to occasion lasting depression or loss of composure" (*Oxford English Dictionary*, 2nd ed (1989), vol xv, p 293, meaning 4a), is central to both expressions.

31. Because neither "sudden shock", nor witnessing a person being killed, injured or put in peril, is a necessary condition for finding a duty to take reasonable care not to cause mental harm to another, s 30 will be engaged in only some cases where a relevant duty of care is found to exist. As s 30(1) makes plain, s 30 will be engaged only where the claim is for "pure mental harm", where the claim is alleged to arise "wholly or partly from mental or nervous shock", and where the claim is alleged to arise from shock in connection with "another person ... being killed, injured or put in peril by the act or omission of the defendant".

32. In considering the application of Pt 3 it would ordinarily be desirable to begin by determining whether State Rail owed the appellants a relevant duty of care.

Duty of care?

33. Although the Court of Appeal expressly declined to decide whether State Rail owed a duty to take reasonable care not to cause mental harm to Mr Wicks and Mr Sheehan, who each came to the scene of this accident as a "rescuer" (the expression used by the parties in their agreed statement of issues), it would be open to this Court to decide that issue. Contrary to the submissions of State Rail, the question of duty of care is a question of law (*Amaca Pty Ltd v New South Wales* (2003) 77 ALJR 1509 at 1514 [26]; 199 ALR 596 at 602; *Cole v South Tweed Heads Rugby League Football Club Ltd* (2004) 217 CLR 469 at 487 [56]; *Vairy v Wyong Shire Council* (2005) 223 CLR 422 at 443 [62]). To resolve this question would require consideration of whether it was reasonably foreseeable that a rescuer attending a train accident of the kind that might result from State Rail's negligence (in which there might be many serious casualties and much destruction of property) might suffer recognisable psychiatric injury as a result of his experiences at the scene. Or to put the same question another way, was it reasonably foreseeable that sights of the kind a rescuer might see, sounds of the kind a rescuer might hear, tasks of the kind a rescuer might have to undertake to try to ease the suffering of others and take them to safety, would be, in combination, such as might cause a person of normal fortitude to develop a recognised psychiatric illness? The question of foreseeability is to be posed in these terms because it must be judged (*Vairy v Wyong Shire Council* (2005) 223 CLR 422 at 461-463 [126]-[129]; *Adeels Palace Pty Ltd v Moubarak* (2009) 239 CLR 420 at 438 [31]) before the accident happened.

[74] 34. Any finding at first instance that there was no singular shocking event encountered by either Mr Wicks or Mr Sheehan would not be determinative of the issue of foreseeability and it would not preclude a conclusion that a duty of care was owed. If Malpass AsJ made such a finding (which is itself a doubtful proposition) the finding would seem, on the face of the matter, not to be consistent with the description given in evidence of the scene and the events to which the appellants were exposed at the site of the accident.

35. Because, however, both parties submitted that this Court should not decide the issue of duty of care, these are not issues that should now be decided. The issue of duty of care should be remitted for consideration by the Court of Appeal.

36. Assuming that State Rail did owe Mr Wicks and Mr Sheehan a duty to take reasonable care not to cause mental harm, was s 30(2) engaged? That turns on whether the claims of the appellants were claims alleged to arise "wholly or partly from mental or nervous shock in connection with another person ... being killed, injured or put in peril" by the negligence of State Rail. The phrase must be construed as a whole. It is, however, convenient to begin by noticing some particular matters about one aspect of it: the reference to "shock" in the composite expression "mental or nervous shock".

"Shock"?

37. There can be little doubt that those who came upon the scene of the derailment were confronted with a scene that would cause a "sudden and disturbing impression on the mind or feelings". But it would be wrong to attempt to confine the "shock" that each rescuer suffered to what he perceived on first arriving at the scene. The sudden and disturbing impressions on the minds or feelings of the rescuers necessarily continued as each took in more of the scene, and set about his tasks. Contrary to what appeared to be an unexpressed premise for much of the submissions on behalf of State Rail, the event capable of causing a shock to observers did not finish when the train came to rest as a twisted collection of carriages. The "shock" which caused a sudden and disturbing impression on the minds and feelings of others was not confined to whatever may have happened, or may have been experienced, in the period between the carriages of the train leaving the tracks and stopping. Rather, the consequences, which each appellant alleged he suffered as a result of what happened on that day, were said to follow from some or all of the series of shocking experiences to which he was exposed at the scene.

38. The claim of each appellant can, then, be said to be a claim arising wholly or partly from (a series of) mental or nervous shock(s). Were they claims arising from mental or nervous shock in connection with another person being killed, injured or put in peril by the negligence of State Rail?

39. The course of argument of all parties, both at trial and in the Court of Appeal, assumed that the claim of each appellant was to be [75] characterised in this way. That assumption depended upon treating each appellant's claims as being that his exposure to the accident scene, while the victims of the accident were still at the scene, amounted to a form of mental or nervous shock in connection with another being killed, injured or put in peril. Only if that were so could s 30(2)(a) be engaged. Did the appellants witness, at the scene, another person or other persons being killed, injured or put in peril?

Section 30(2)(a) – State Rail's submissions

40. The chief weight of the argument for State Rail, that neither appellant had "witnessed, at the scene, the victim being killed, injured or put in peril", was placed on the use in s 30(2)(a) of the expression "*being* killed, injured or put in peril" (emphasis added). State Rail submitted that this expression indicated that, to recover, a plaintiff must have observed, at the scene, an event unfolding which included, perhaps culminated in, another's death, injury or being put in peril. State Rail further submitted that, to satisfy s 30(2)(a), a plaintiff must be able to demonstrate that the psychiatric injury of which complaint was made was occasioned by observation of what was happening to a *particular* victim. It will be convenient to deal with these submissions in the order in which they are set out, but to preface that consideration by one observation about the construction of the relevant provisions.

41. Extrinsic material provides no assistance in this case in construing the relevant provisions. Although the *Civil Liability Act* was enacted after submission of the Review of the Law of Negligence Final Report, published in September 2002 (The Review was conducted by a panel of which Ipp A-JA of the Court of Appeal of the Supreme Court of New South Wales was Chairman. The panel was appointed following ministerial meetings on public liability which were attended by Ministers from the Commonwealth, State and Territory governments), s 30 of the *Civil Liability*

Act does not take a form recommended by that Report. The Second Reading Speech on the Bill which inserted Pt 3 of the *Civil Liability Act* contains no useful statement about why s 30 takes the form it does.

"Being killed, injured or put in peril"

42. The expression "being killed, injured or put in peril" is used in s 30(1) as well as in s 30(2)(a). The evident intention of s 30(2) is to create a particular subset of cases that fall within the general description of claims "for pure mental harm … arising wholly or partly from mental or nervous shock in connection with another person …being killed, injured or put in peril". But the definitions of both the general class, and the particular subset created by s 30(2), hinge about another *being* killed, injured or put in peril. The general class is identified by reference to shock *in connection with* another being killed, injured or put in peril. The subset is fixed by an "unless" clause. The alternative conditions thus fixed, as necessary for membership of the subset, are first, that the plaintiff *witnessed*, at the scene, the victim **[76]** being killed, injured or put in peril, or second, that the plaintiff is a close member of the family of the victim.

43. Although both sub-ss (1) and (2) use the phrase "being killed, injured or put in peril", sub-s (1) applies to claims for pure mental harm arising wholly or partly from mental or nervous shock in connection with that event (another being killed, injured or put in peril); sub-s (2) requires that the plaintiff either witnessed that event or was a close relative of the victim. The reference in sub-s (1) to the event must be read as referring to an event that may (but need not) have been complete before the suffering of nervous or mental shock. By contrast, because sub-s (2)(a) requires witnessing of the event at the scene, it must be read as directing attention to an event that was happening while the plaintiff "witnessed" it.

44. It would not be right, however, to read s 30, or s 30(2)(a) in particular, as assuming that all cases of death, injury or being put in peril are events that begin and end in an instant, or even that they are events that necessarily occupy only a time that is measured in minutes. No doubt there are such cases. But there are cases where death, or injury, or being put in peril takes place over an extended period. This was such a case, at least in so far as reference is made to victims being injured or put in peril.

45. The consequences of the derailment took time to play out. Some aboard the train were killed instantly. But even if all of the deaths were instantaneous (or nearly so), not all the injuries sustained by those on the train were suffered during the process of derailment. And the perils to which living passengers were subjected as a result of the negligence of State Rail did not end when the carriages came to rest.

46. Most, if not all, who were injured suffered physical trauma during the process of derailment. It may readily be inferred that some who suffered physical trauma in the derailment suffered further injury as they were removed from the wrecked carriages. That inference follows from the fact that some were trapped in the wreckage. It would be very surprising if each was extricated without further harm.

47. Further, it may be readily inferred that many who were on the train suffered psychiatric injuries as a result of what happened to them in the derailment and at the scene. The process of their suffering such an injury was not over when Mr Wicks and Mr Sheehan arrived. That is why each told of the shocked reactions of passengers they tried to help. That is why each did what he could to take the injured to safety looking straight ahead lest the injured see the broken body of one or more of those who had been killed. As they were removed from the train, at least some of the passengers were still being injured.

48. If either inference is drawn, Mr Wicks and Mr Sheehan witnessed, at the scene, victims of the accident "being injured".

49. Even if neither of these inferences should be drawn, the fact remains that when Mr Wicks and Mr Sheehan arrived at the scene of the accident, those who had been on the train, and had survived, remained **[77]** in peril. The agreed description of each of Mr Wicks and Mr Sheehan as "a rescuer" necessarily implies as much. Each sought to (and did) rescue at least some of those who had been on the train from peril. The observation of fallen electrical cables draped over the

carriages is but a dramatic illustration of one kind of peril to which those who remained alive in the carriages were subject before they were taken to a place of safety.

50. Contrary to State Rail's submission, the expression "being ... put in peril" should not be given a meaning more restricted than that conveyed by the ordinary meaning of the words used. More particularly, "being ... put in peril" is not to be confined to the kind of apprehended casualty which was at issue in *Hambrook v Stokes Bros* [1925] 1 KB 141, where a mother feared a runaway lorry might have injured her child. It is not to be read as confined to the cases discussed by Evatt J in *Chester v Waverley Corporation* (1939) 62 CLR 1 at 41-42 by reference to the decision in *Hambrook*. Nor is the expression to be read down by reference to how the phrase was to be understood when used in s 4 of the *Law Reform (Miscellaneous Provisions) Act 1944* (NSW). Rather, the expression should be given the meaning which the words ordinarily convey. A person is put in peril when put at risk; the person remains in peril (is "being put in peril") until the person ceases to be at risk.

51. The survivors of the derailment remained in peril until they had been rescued by being taken to a place of safety. Mr Wicks and Mr Sheehan witnessed, at the scene, victims of the accident being put in peril as a result of the negligence of State Rail.

52. State Rail's submission that neither Mr Wicks nor Mr Sheehan witnessed, at the scene, a victim or victims being killed, injured or put in peril should thus be rejected.

53. State Rail's further submission, that the combined effect of s 30(1) and s 30(2) requires that a plaintiff must demonstrate that the psychiatric injury of which complaint is made was occasioned by observation of what was happening to a *particular* victim, should also be rejected.

54. In a case such as the present, where there were many victims, s 30(2) does not require that a relationship be identified between an alleged psychiatric injury (or any particular part of that injury) and what happened to a particular victim. To read the provision as requiring establishment of so precise a connection would be unworkable. It would presuppose, wrongly, that the causes of psychiatric injury suffered as a result of exposure to an horrific scene of multiple deaths and injuries could be established by reference to component parts of that single event. Rather, the reference in s 30(1) to "another person *(the victim)*" should be read *(Interpretation Act 1987* (NSW) s 8 (b)) as "another person or **[78]** persons (as the case requires)". The reference to "victim" in s 30(2)(a) is to be read as a reference to one or more of those persons. In a mass casualty of the kind now in issue, s 30(2)(a) is satisfied where there was a witnessing at the scene of one or more persons being killed, injured or put in peril, without any need for further attribution of part or all of the alleged injury to one or more specific deaths.

Conclusion and orders

55. Each appeal to this Court should be allowed with costs. ... [E]ach matter must be remitted to the Court of Appeal for its further consideration in accordance with the reasons of this Court....

In each matter, appeal allowed

[Victoria and Tasmania have legislation identical to ss 30 and 32 of the *Civil Liability Act 2002* (NSW): *Wrongs Act 1958* (Vic), ss 72 and 73; the *Civil Liability Act 2002* (Tas) ss 32 and 34. The *Civil Liability Act 1936* (SA) s 33 is identical to s 32 of the *Civil Liability Act 2002* (NSW) while s 53(1)(a) of the South Australian legislation provides that damages may only be awarded for mental harm if the injured person "was physically injured in the accident or was present at the scene of the accident when the accident occurred". Section 5S of the *Civil Liability Act 2002* (WA) and s 34 of the *Civil Law (Wrongs) Act 2002* (ACT) are identical to s 32 of the *Civil Liability Act 2002* (NSW). However, neither the Western Australia nor the Australian Capital Territory legislation has the equivalent of s 30 of the *Civil Liability Act 2002* (NSW). Queensland and the Northern Territory do not address liability for mental harm in their civil liability legislation.]

6. PRE-NATAL INJURIES, WRONGFUL BIRTH AND WRONGFUL LIFE

Watt v Rama

[1972] VR 353

Supreme Court of Victoria, Full Court

A duty of care may be owed to a person in respect of pre-natal injury, that is, injury in utero.

WINNEKE CJ and PAPE J. **[353]** This case raises for decision an interesting and important point in the law of torts upon which there is no authority **[354]** which binds this Court. It arises in an action in which the plaintiff is Sylvia Watt, an infant born on 4 January 1968 and the defendant is Halil Rama.

The statement of claim endorsed upon the writ (as amended) alleges that on 15 May 1967 a motor car driven by the defendant came into collision with a motor car driven by the plaintiff's mother, Sylvia Alice Watt; that such collision was caused by the negligence of the defendant; that as a result of injuries received by the said Sylvia Alice Watt she was rendered a quadriplegic; that at the time of the said collision the said Sylvia Alice Watt was pregnant, and that on 4 January 1968 she gave birth to the plaintiff; that as at the date of such birth the plaintiff suffered brain damage and epilepsy, which were caused by the negligence of the defendant in that (a) the damage to the plaintiff whilst unborn on the said 15 May 1967 was a result of the said collision and/or (b) the inability of the said Sylvia Alice Watt to carry the plaintiff whilst pregnant in a normal manner and/or to go into labour and deliver the plaintiff in a normal manner was due to the disabilities and deformities suffered by her and associated with her condition of quadriplegia. ...

[355] [T]he following points of law raised by paras 9 and 10 of the defence were ordered to be disposed of before the trial of the action, namely:–

(a) whether in the circumstances set out in the statement of claim the defendant owed a duty of care not to cause injury to the infant plaintiff who was then unborn;

(b) whether in the circumstances set out in the statement of claim the defendant owed a duty of care to the infant plaintiff not to injure her mother;

(c) whether in the circumstances set out in the statement of claim the damages sought to be recovered by the plaintiffs are in law too remote. ...

[358] The real question posed for our decision is not whether an action lies in respect of pre-natal injuries but whether a plaintiff born with injuries caused by the pre-natal neglect of the defendant has a cause of action in negligence against him in respect of such injuries. To this question the defendant answers "No", because at the time of his neglect the plaintiff **[359]** was not in existence as a living person, had no separate existence apart from her mother, was not capable of suing to assert a legal right, and was not a legal person to whom he could be under a duty. For the purpose of these proceedings it is to be assumed that the plaintiff's injuries as subsisting at the time of her birth were caused by the act or omission of the defendant in the driving of his car. What creates the difficulty is that such act or omission preceded and was, therefore, separated in point of time from the birth of the plaintiff in her injured condition. The difficulty may prove on analysis not to be unrelated to that which evoked the statement by the High Court in *Chapman v Hearse* (1961) 106 CLR 112, at p 120; [1962] ALR 379. "But one thing is certain and that is that in order to establish the prior existence of a duty of care with respect to a plaintiff subsequently injured as the result of a sequence of events following a defendant's carelessness it is not necessary for the plaintiff to show that the precise manner in which his injuries were sustained was reasonably foreseeable; it is sufficient if it appears that injury to a class of persons of which he was one might reasonably have been foreseen as a consequence." ...

[360] In the common case where the act or neglect of the defendant and the injury to the plaintiff are for all practical purposes contemporaneous, the duty attaches to the defendant and is breached when the act or neglect occurs. But where the injury does not occur contemporaneously with the act or neglect, the relationship will not necessarily crystallize so as to create a duty at the time of the act or neglect. Where the injury to the plaintiff occurs only subsequently to the time of the act or neglect in circumstances where the plaintiff is not defined at that time, as for example where he is only one of a class, the relationship and the duty to arise therefrom may be said to be contingent or potential but capable of ripening into a relationship imposing a duty when the plaintiff becomes defined. ...

In the present case the act or omission of the defendant occurred while he was driving a motor car upon a public highway, and it was, we think, then reasonably foreseeable that such act or omission might cause injury to a pregnant woman in the car with which his car collided and might cause the child she was carrying to be born in an injured condition. ...

On the birth the relationship crystallized and out of it arose a duty on the defendant in relation to the child. On the facts which for present purposes must be assumed, the child was born with injuries caused by the act or neglect of the defendant in the driving of his car. But as the child could not in the very nature of things acquire rights correlative to a duty until it became by birth a living person, and as it was not until then that it could sustain injuries as a living person, it was, we think, at that stage that the duty arising out of the relationship was attached to the defendant, and it was at that stage that the defendant was, on the assumption that his act or omission in the driving of the car constituted a failure to take reasonable care, in breach of the duty to take reasonable care to avoid injury to the child. On this view the fact that damage was done to the embryo or foetus before birth, if such was sought [361] to be established, was not an independent element in the plaintiff's cause of action, but merely an evidentiary fact relevant to the issue of causation. ...

For these reasons, we are of opinion that the questions submitted for hearing and disposal by the Court should be answered as follows:–

(a) Yes.
(b) Unnecessary to answer.
(c) No.

[Gillard J delivered a judgment in which he substantially agreed with the reasons and conclusion of the majority. His Honour was prepared, if necessary, to hold that an unborn child was a legal person to whom a duty could be owed at the time of the accident. However, an action could only be brought if the child was born alive.]

Questions answered accordingly

Cattanach v Melchior
(2003) 215 CLR 1; [2003] HCA 38
High Court of Australia

Where negligence by a medical practitioner is a cause of the conception and birth of a child, the liability in damages of the medical practitioner to the parents of the child may include the cost of raising and maintaining the child until the child attains the age of 18.

McHUGH and GUMMOW JJ. [some footnotes in whole or part omitted] [24] 41. By majority (McMurdo P and Davies JA; Thomas JA dissenting), the Queensland Court of Appeal ([2001] QCA 246) dismissed an appeal against a judgment in the Supreme Court of Queensland (Holmes J) ((2001) Aust Torts Rep 81-597) awarding damages against the first and second defendants, Dr Cattanach and the State of Queensland. Dr Cattanach is a specialist obstetrician and gynaecologist. The plaintiffs, Mr and Mrs Melchior, are husband and wife. In this Court, [25] they are the respondents and Dr Cattanach and the State are the appellants.

42. It was admitted on the pleadings that the State was the statutory successor to the Brisbane South Regional Health Authority, which had operated the Redland Hospital. Dr Cattanach was a consultant obstetrician and gynaecologist at the Redland Hospital where, on 13 March 1992, he performed on Mrs Melchior a sterilisation procedure. Thereafter, in 1997, Mrs Melchior gave birth to the couple's third child, a son. At the time of the trial, the child was a healthy, active three year old.

43. Mr and Mrs Melchior had married in 1984 and, prior to the sterilisation procedure, there were two children of the marriage, daughters ... born ... in 1985 and 1988 respectively. The primary

judge described as follows the personal circumstances of Mr and Mrs Melchior before Mrs Melchior was referred to Dr Cattanach by her general practitioner:

They were satisfied with a family of two, and in 1991 discussed together the prospect of taking steps to ensure that they would have no more children. They had planned their finances around bringing up two children, and Mrs Melchior did not wish to continue using oral contraceptives. Mr Melchior said that he was also influenced by the fact that he suffered from Charcot-Marie-Tooth syndrome, a disease causing muscular atrophy in his feet and legs. It was his understanding that while his daughters were unlikely to inherit the condition, a male child would be at risk. ... He was content, therefore to limit his family to the two daughters he had.

44. In 1967, when Mrs Melchior was aged 15, she underwent an appendectomy. The surgical notes indicated that, in the course of the operation, her right ovary was found to be filled with a blood clot and was removed; there was no abnormality in the left ovary or either fallopian tube and those organs were left intact. ...

45. ... The trial judge found that, whilst Mrs Melchior's initial consultation with Dr Cattanach had been as a private patient, she had been admitted to hospital for the sterilisation surgery as a public patient. It was not suggested that at that latter stage there had existed any contractual relationship between Dr Cattanach and either plaintiff. Accordingly, the trial judge determined the plaintiffs' claims as issues in tort. The State admitted its vicarious liability for any negligence established against Dr Cattanach.

46. Holmes J found that Dr Cattanach was negligent after the sterilisation procedure in failing to inform Mrs Melchior of various matters. The first was that the oral history she gave of the removal of the right fallopian tube in 1967 had not been positively confirmed [26] during the sterilisation procedure. The second was that, if the fallopian tube were present, there was a ten-fold increase in the risk of her falling pregnant than was usual after the performance of the sterilisation procedure. The third was that an available procedure ... was likely to disclose the existence of a functioning fallopian tube.

47. The Court of Appeal upheld the finding of negligence against Dr Cattanach and the conclusion that his negligence was the probable cause of Mrs Melchior's pregnancy.

48. The award of damages had three components. The first was an award in favour of Mrs Melchior of $103,672.39 consisting of damages for her pain and suffering in respect of the pregnancy and birth, the effect on her health (including a supervening depression), lost earning capacity (past and future), various hospital, medical, pharmaceutical and travel expenses (both past and future), the cost of maternity clothes and damages ... for care that she might need. The second was an award to Mr Melchior of $3,000 for loss of consortium ... The third was an award in favour of Mr and Mrs Melchior for $105,249.33 for the past and future costs associated with raising and maintaining their child until he reaches the age of 18.

49. No appeal was taken to the Court of Appeal respecting the first and second categories of damages. However, with respect to the third category, Dr Cattanach and the State contended that Holmes J had erred in law in allowing any costs for the rearing of the child and that her Honour had erred in failing to apply the decision of the House of Lords in *McFarlane v Tayside Health Board* [2000] 2 AC 59. Davies JA ... stated the issue thus arising as follows:

Should the parents of a healthy child, born in consequence either of a negligently performed sterilisation operation or of negligent advice or of a negligent omission to advise as to the consequences of that operation be entitled to recover from the negligent doctor the costs of reasonable maintenance of the child during his or her minority?

The majority of the Court of Appeal answered that question in the affirmative and dismissed the appeal with costs.

50. ... [27] [T]his Court granted special leave limited to one ground. This is whether the Court of Appeal erred in holding that damages were recoverable by Mr and Mrs Melchior for the reasonable costs of raising and maintaining their child. ...

51. The appellants would be liable under ordinary principles for the foreseeable consequences of Dr Cattanach's negligence. ... Questions of remoteness or insufficient causal connection between the breach of duty by Dr Cattanach and the claimed loss did not arise. ...

53. In *McFarlane* at 76, Lord Slynn of Hadley said that a doctor undertaking a duty of care in regard to the prevention of pregnancy does not assume responsibility for economic losses imposed on or accepted by parents in bringing up a child. To that, Hale LJ responded in *Parkinson v St James and Seacroft University Hospital NHS Trust* [2002] QB 266 at 289:

> Given that the doctor clearly does assume some responsibility for preventing conception, it is difficult to understand why he assumes responsibility for some but not all of the clearly foreseeable, indeed highly probable, losses resulting. ...

54. The appellants' primary submission to this Court is that there can be no award in damages for the cost of rearing and maintaining a healthy child who would not have been born but for the negligent failure of a gynaecologist to give certain advice. Further, and in the alternative, it is submitted that any such award of damages should be limited in some way, in particular by treating the arrival of the healthy child as a benefit to be set off against the damages.

[28] 55. The appellants based these submissions upon the propositions that, as a matter of the policy of the law, the birth of a healthy child is not a legal harm for which damages may be recovered, and that this result would follow whether action was brought in tort or contract. This policy of the law, the appellants submitted, reflects 'an underlying value of society in relation to the value of human life'. In several of the State jurisdictions in the United States, in decisions upon which the appellants rely, the denial of awards of damages for the expense of raising an unwanted, healthy child has been based upon a public policy against 'meddling' with 'the concept of life and the stability of the family unit' including apprehended harm to a child upon later learning that the money for its nurture has been provided by damages recovered in a 'wrongful birth' action: *Wilbur v Kerr* 628 SW 2d 568 at 570-571 (1982); *Boone v Mullendore* 416 So 2d 718 at 721-723 (1982); *MA v United States* 951 P 2d 851 at 855 (1998). ...

57. Merely to repeat those propositions upon which the appellants rely does not explain why the law should shield or immunise the appellants from what otherwise is a head of damages recoverable in negligence under general and unchallenged principles in respect of the breach of duty by Dr Cattanach. ...

58. In *Brodie v Singleton Shire Council* (2001) 206 CLR 512 at 555-556 [94], Gaudron, McHugh and Gummow JJ referred to the use of the term 'immunity' in various areas of tort law to indicate a protection against action in respect of [29] rights and duties which otherwise exist in the law. In various instances referred to in that passage, including the position of barristers and liability for straying animals, the protection is expressed as the negation of the existence of a duty of care and is founded upon particular views of public policy. ...

59. The protection contended for in the present case would not operate in that way. The subject of the protection is recovery of a particular head of damages for an admitted breach of duty. ... [T]here is, as Callinan J indicates in his reasons at [295], a judicial aversion to the enjoyment of special privilege or advantage in litigation unless strong reason for its retention (as was the issue in *Brodie*) or creation (the present case) can be demonstrated.

60. In *Smith v Jenkins* (1970) 119 CLR 397 at 418, Windeyer J observed that 'public policy' in relation to the common law of torts is not to be thought of as like that public policy which invalidates contracts and, one might add, certain trusts and conditions attached to voluntary dispositions by will or settlement. In those areas, the starting point has been the favour with which the law has looked upon the right of private contract and the performance of contracts, and upon the freedom of disposition of property ... .

[30] 64. The appellants' submissions would bring this case within that general area [concerned with the policy of the law] respecting family relationships. But several points should be made immediately. First, the general considerations advanced by the appellants have not, as in the contract and disposition of property cases, matured into a coherent body of legal doctrine. No doubt that is not a fatal obstacle. The policy of the law cannot be static. Yet the novelty of the outcome for the present case of the appellants' submissions calls for a more careful scrutiny than would be required where there was a developed body of legal principle directly relevant.

65. Secondly, this is a case in tort. Further consideration of the remarks of Windeyer J in *Smith v Jenkins* (1970) 119 CLR 397 at 418 is appropriate. His Honour, after speaking of contract, turned

to tort, observed that public policy 'after all is the bedrock foundation on which the common law of torts stands' and continued:

> Here the question is different. It seems to me a mistake to approach the case by asking whether the plaintiff is precluded by [31] considerations of public policy from asserting a right of action for negligence. The proper inquiry seems to me to be simply: is there for him a right of action? That depends upon whether in the circumstances the law imposed a duty of care; for a right of action and a duty of care are inseparable. The one predicates the other. Duty here does not mean an abstract and general rule of conduct. … It is a concept of the law, a duty to a person, which he can enforce by remedy at law. …

66. It is here that the case for the appellants encounters difficulty. Duty, breach and damage are all conceded. The interest of the respondents which the law of negligence protected in respect of the negligent misstatement or omission by Dr Cattanach was that of each of the respondents in the planning of their family or, as it has been put in the United States, in their reproductive future. The injury to that interest had varied elements. There were those matters reflected in the first award of some $103,000 to Mrs Melchior, but there were also those touching the responsibility the spouses incurred to rear their third child. That responsibility was both moral and legal. The *Child Support (Assessment) Act 1989* (Cth) imposed obligations upon the parents of an 'eligible child' who was under the age of 18 years. It does not advance understanding greatly, one way or the other, to describe the expenditure required to discharge that obligation as 'economic loss'.

67. Nor is it correct to say that the damage that the respondents suffered was the parent-child relationship or the coming into existence of the parent-child relationship. To do so is to examine the case from the wrong perspective. In the law of negligence, damage is either physical injury to person or property or the suffering of a loss measurable in money terms or the incurring of expenditure as the result of the [32] invasion of an interest recognised by the law. The parent-child relationship or its creation no more constitutes damage in this area of law than the employer-employee relationship constitutes damage in an action *per quod servitium amisit*. In the latter case, the employer suffers damage, for example, only when it is forced to pay salary or wages to its injured employee although deprived of the employee's services: *Commissioner for Railways (NSW) v Scott* (1959) 102 CLR 392. It does not suffer damage merely because its employee has been injured. Similarly, for the purpose of this appeal, the relevant damage suffered by the Melchiors is the expenditure that they have incurred or will incur in the future, not the creation or existence of the parent-child relationship. If, for example, their child had been voluntarily cared for up to the date of trial, they could have recovered no damages for that part of the child's upbringing. And, if it appeared that that situation would continue in the future, then the damages they would be able to recover in the future would be reduced accordingly.

68. The unplanned child is not the harm for which recompense is sought in this action; it is the burden of the legal and moral responsibilities which arise by reason of the birth of the child that is in contention. The expression 'wrongful birth' used in various authorities to which the Court was referred is misleading and directs attention away from the appropriate frame of legal discourse. What was wrongful in this case was not the birth of a third child to Mr and Mrs Melchior but the negligence of Dr Cattanach.

69. The submissions by the appellants introduce notions of public policy not in formulating the relevant duty of care … . Rather, as remarked above, the appellants seek the proscription of a particular head of recovery of damages. …

70. In *McFarlane* [2000] 2 AC 59 at 108, Lord Millett treated what was involved as the 'admission of a novel head of damages'; this raised a matter 'not solely a question of principle' because '[l]imitations on the scope of legal liability arise from legal policy'. His Lordship continued:

> Legal policy in this sense is not the same as public policy, even though moral considerations may play a part in both. The court is engaged in a search for justice, and this demands that the dispute be resolved in a way which is fair and reasonable and accords with ordinary notions of what is fit and proper. It is also concerned to [33] maintain the coherence of the law and the avoidance of inappropriate distinctions if injustice is to be avoided in other cases.

71. In this Court, the respondents dispute the first proposition that what was involved in the third category of the award made by Holmes J was a novel head of damages. They refer to the

statement of general principle by McHugh J in *Nominal Defendant v Gardikiotis* (1996) 186 CLR 49 at 54:

> When a defendant has negligently injured a plaintiff, the common law requires the defendant to pay a money sum to the plaintiff to compensate that person for any damage that is causally connected to the defendant's negligence and that ought to have been reasonably foreseen by the defendant when the negligence occurred: *Overseas Tankship (UK) Ltd v Morts Dock & Engineering Co Ltd (The Wagon Mound)* [1961] AC 388 at 423, 425; *Chapman v Hearse* (1961) 106 CLR 112 at 122. The sum of money to be paid to the plaintiff is that sum which will put the plaintiff, so far as is possible, 'in the same position as he would have been in if he had not sustained the wrong for which he is now getting his compensation': *Livingstone v Rawyards Coal Co* (1880) 5 App Cas 25 at 39. Consequently, when a plaintiff asserts that, but for the defendant's negligence, he or she would not have incurred a particular expense, questions of causation and reasonable foreseeability arise. Is the particular expense causally connected to the defendant's negligence? If so, ought the defendant to have reasonably foreseen that an expense of that kind might be incurred?

72. Both questions, posed with respect to the third category of the award at trial in the present case, should be answered in the affirmative. ...

73. In addition, notwithstanding what had been said by Lord Millett in *McFarlane* (in the ... passage set out above), the appellants in the present case displayed no enthusiasm for a distinction between 'legal policy' and 'public policy'; they rightly preferred the term 'policy [34] of the law'. ...

[35] 76. What was put by Isaacs J in *Wilkinson v Osborne* (1915) 21 CLR 89 at 97 may be adapted to the present case by posing two questions. First, are the underlying values respecting the importance of human life, the stability of the family unit and the nurture of infant children until their legal majority an essential aspect of the corporate welfare of the community? Secondly, if they are, can it be said there is a general recognition in the community that those values demand that there must be no award of damages for the cost to the parents of rearing and maintaining a child who would not have been born were it not for the negligent failure of a gynaecologist in giving advice after performing a sterilisation procedure?

77. Allowing an affirmative answer to the first question, nevertheless the answer to the second must be that the courts can perceive no such general recognition that those in the position of Mr and Mrs Melchior should be denied the full remedies the common law of Australia otherwise affords them. It is a beguiling but misleading simplicity to invoke the broad values which few would deny and then glide to the conclusion that they operate to shield the appellants from the full consequences in law of Dr Cattanach's negligence. ...

78. The reliance upon values respecting the importance of life is made implausible by the reference to the postulated child as 'healthy'. The differential treatment of the worth of the lives of those with ill health or disabilities has been a mark of the societies and political regimes we [36] least admire. To prevent recovery in respect of one class of child but not the other, by reference to a criterion of health, would be to discriminate by reference to a distinction irrelevant to the object sought to be achieved, the award of compensatory damages to the parents.

79. To suggest that the birth of a child is always a blessing, and that the benefits to be derived therefrom always outweigh the burdens, denies the first category of damages awarded in this case; it also denies the widespread use of contraception by persons such as the Melchiors to avoid just such an event. The perceived disruption to familial relationships by, for example, the Melchiors' third child later becoming aware of this litigation, is at best speculative. In the absence of any clear and accepted understanding of such matters, the common law should not justify preclusion of recovery on speculation as to possible psychological harm to children. ...

[37] 84. There remains the subsidiary submission by the appellants respecting the 'setting-off' of the emotional satisfaction and other benefits enjoyed by Mr and Mrs Melchior from the birth of their third child. The assumption here is that there is no bar to recovery of damages under the third category recovered at trial; the contention is that those damages should have been limited in some way.

85. Section 920 of the *Restatement (Second) of Torts*, issued in 1977, sets out what in the United States is described as the 'benefit rule':
> When the defendant's tortious conduct has caused harm to the plaintiff or to his property and in so doing has conferred a special benefit to the interest of the plaintiff that was harmed, the value of the benefit conferred is considered in mitigation of damages, to the extent that this is equitable.

Comment *b* to the *Restatement* notes:
> Damages resulting from an invasion of one interest are not diminished by showing that another interest has been benefited.

86. Speaking of section 920, it has been said (Milsteen, 'Recovery of Childrearing Expenses in Wrongful Birth Cases: A Motivational Analysis', (1983) 32 *Emory Law Journal* 1167 at 1180):
> In the wrongful birth context, application of the rule requires an identification of the interest a plaintiff sought to protect in attempting to avoid the conception of a child, and a determination of whether a special benefit to that interest was conferred upon the plaintiff as a result of the defendant's tortious conduct. This 'same interest' limitation prevents damages resulting from the injury to one particular interest from being diminished by a showing that some other interest has been benefited.

In some cases in the United States, for example, *Troppi v Scarf* 187 NW 2d 511 (1971), a broad interpretation has been given to the notion of 'same interest' with the effect of allowing **[38]** an offsetting of what was said to be postnatal non-pecuniary benefits of parenthood, thereby resulting in a significant reduction in the damages recovered. Thus, in *Troppi v Scarf* at 518, a Michigan court said:
> Since pregnancy and its attendant anxiety, incapacity, pain and suffering are inextricably related to child bearing ... it would be [unsound] to attempt to separate those segments of damage from the economic costs of an unplanned child in applying the 'same interest' rule.

87. In other decisions, for example *Custodio v Bauer* 59 Cal Rptr 463 (1967), the contrary result has been reached, it being emphasised that the offsetting benefit must be to the interest protected. A similar point was made in this Court, with reference to section 920 as it appeared in the first *Restatement* issued in 1939, by Dixon J in *Public Trustee v Zoanetti* (1945) 70 CLR 266. His Honour stated as a general proposition at 278:
> [W]hen there are two interests adversely affected you cannot treat recompense for one as a gain arising from the occurrence and operating in relief of the loss of or injury to the other interest.

His Honour continued, with reference to Comment *b* to section 920:
> Indeed, even when one of two separate interests is benefited in consequence of a wrongful act, the benefit cannot be set off against an injury to the other. ... It is not immaterial to notice that in describing some of the various applications given to this principle the *Restatement* includes the proposition that damages to a husband for loss of consortium are not diminished by the fact that the husband is no longer under the expense of supporting the wife.

88. Earlier in his reasons in *Zoanetti*, Dixon J identified the different interests of a wife in the life of her husband, founded upon the economic or pecuniary advantages of the marriage, and her interests founded upon affections and feelings. So in this case the interests of Mr and Mrs Melchior in controlling the size of their family, for the economic and apprehended eugenic reasons referred to above, have a different character or quality to the affection they would give and hope to receive from a child of their marriage, whatever the circumstances in which Mrs Melchior conceived and was brought to term.

89. In argument, reference was made to the case of a parent bringing a 'nervous shock' action for the death of a child and of a widow **[39]** bringing an action under the compensation to relatives statutes. Could it be said that in the first case there was to be an offset for the expenditure saved for future support of a child and, in the second, for the removal of the inconveniences involved in the wife looking after her husband? In each case, there would be no set-off because of the principles indicated by Dixon J in *Zoanetti*. The same is true of the present case.

90. The statement of relevant legal principle by Dixon J also shows why it is an error to think that awarding damages for the cost of raising a child inevitably requires the courts to balance the 'monetary value of the child' (*McFarlane v Tayside Health Board* [2000] 2 AC 59 at 111 per

Lord Millett) against the cost of maintaining the child. In assessing damages, it is impermissible in principle to balance the benefits to one legal interest against the loss occasioned to a separate legal interest. The benefits received from the birth of a child are not legally relevant to the head of damage that compensates for the cost of maintaining the child. A different case would be presented if the mother claimed damages for 'loss of enjoyment of life' as the result of raising the child. If such a head of damage were allowable, it would be correct to set-off against the claim all the benefits derived from having the child. But the head of damages that is relevant in the present case is the financial damage that the parents will suffer as the result of their legal responsibility to raise the child. The benefits to be enjoyed as a result of having the child are not related to that head of damage. The coal miner, forced to retire because of injury, does not get less damages for loss of earning capacity because he is now free to sit in the sun each day reading his favourite newspaper. Likewise, the award of damages to the parents for their future financial expenditure is not to be reduced by the enjoyment that they will or may obtain from the birth of the child.

91. Logically, those persons like Lord Millett who would deny the cost of maintaining the child because of what they see as the immeasurable benefits gained from the birth of the child must deny the right of action itself. If the immeasurability of those benefits denies damages for the cost of maintaining the child, there must also be denied recovery for the hospital and medical costs of the birth and for the attendant pain and suffering associated with the birth. Yet, illogically as it seems to us, those persons permit the action and allow damages to be recovered in respect of these two heads of damage.

92. The appeal should be dismissed with costs.

[In separate judgments, Kirby and Callinan JJ agreed with McHugh and Gummow JJ that the appeal should be dismissed. Gleeson CJ, Hayne and Heydon JJ delivered separate dissenting judgments. Gleeson CJ concluded with the following remarks:

[24] 39. The claim under consideration displays all the features that have contributed to the law's reluctance to impose a duty of care to avoid causing [pure] economic loss. The liability sought to be imposed is indeterminate. It is difficult to relate coherently to other rules of common law and statute. It is based upon a concept of financial harm that is imprecise; an imprecision that cannot be concealed by an arbitrary limitation of a particular claim in subject matter or time. It is incapable of rational or fair assessment. Furthermore, it involves treating, as actionable damage, and as a matter to be regarded in exclusively financial terms, the creation of a human relationship that is socially fundamental. The accepted approach in this country is that 'the law should develop novel categories of negligence incrementally and by analogy with established categories': *Sutherland Shire Council v Heyman* (1985) 157 CLR 424 at 481 per Brennan J. The recognition of the present claim goes beyond that, and is unwarranted.

Heydon J stated the following conclusion:

[145] 404. The various assumptions underlying the law relating to children and the duties on parents created by the law would be negated if parents could sue to recover the costs of rearing unplanned children. That [146] possibility would tend to damage the natural love and mutual confidence which the law seeks to foster between parent and child. It would permit conduct inconsistent with a parental duty to treat the child with the utmost affection, with infinite tenderness, and with unstinting forgiveness in all circumstances, because these goals are contradicted by legal proceedings based on the premise that the child's birth was a painful and highly inconvenient mistake. It would permit conduct inconsistent with the duty to nurture children.]

Appeal dismissed

Harriton v Stephens
(2006) 226 ALR 391; [2006] HCA 15
High Court of Australia

There is no cause of action in negligence for wrongful life – that is, where there is a very high risk that a child in utero will be born with serious congenital disabilities, a medical practitioner looking after the health of the child's mother (and in no way responsible for the serious congenital disabilities) is under no common law duty of care to the child (as distinct from the mother) to advise the mother of this risk and the mother's right to elect to have the pregnancy lawfully terminated.

[The plaintiff/appellant, Alexia Harriton, was born with serious congenital disabilities, including blindness, deafness, mental retardation and spasticity, caused by the rubella virus which had infected her mother in the early stages of pregnancy. At this time the plaintiff's mother, who was concerned that she was pregnant and had contracted the rubella virus, had consulted the defendant/respondent, Dr Stephens, a general medical practitioner. According to the agreed statement of facts, the defendant negligently failed to diagnose the plaintiff's mother's illness, an illness which carried a very high risk that the child in utero would be born with serious congenital disabilities. In an action in the Supreme Court of New South Wales, the plaintiff contended that the defendant owed the plaintiff a duty of care to diagnose her mother's illness and to advise her mother that the only way to prevent the serious congenital disabilities with which the plaintiff would be born was to terminate the pregnancy. According to the agreed statement of facts, if the plaintiff's mother had properly been advised by the defendant the plaintiff's mother would have had the pregnancy lawfully terminated. It was not in contention that any claim in negligence by the plaintiff's mother against the defendant was statute barred.

The plaintiff's claim was dismissed by Studdert J and an appeal was dismissed by a majority of the New South Wales Court of Appeal. A further appeal by the plaintiff to the High Court of Australia was dismissed. Gleeson CJ, Gummow and Heydon JJ agreed with Crennan J whose judgment is extracted below. In separate judgments, Hayne and Callinan JJ agreed that the plaintiff's appeal should be dismissed. In the only dissenting judgment, Kirby J made the following observation:

[428] 153. Denying the existence of wrongful life actions erects an immunity around health care providers whose negligence results in a child who would not otherwise have existed, being born into a life of suffering. Here, that suffering is profound, substantial and apparently lifelong. The immunity would be accorded regardless of the gravity of the acts and omissions of negligence that could be proved. The law should not approve a course which would afford such an immunity and which would offer no legal deterrent to professional carelessness or even professional irresponsibility.]

CRENNAN J. [some footnotes in whole or part omitted]

[440] The issues
216. The main issue is whether the appellant/child who was born disabled has a cause of action in negligence against the respondent/doctor on the agreed facts which stated that the doctor failed to advise the child's mother during her pregnancy of circumstances which would have led the child's mother to obtain a lawful termination of that pregnancy. ...

217. Consideration of the nature of the damage in this case, and the principles relevant to assessment of damages, leads to the result that the appellant has no cause of action against Dr PR Stephens [the defendant/respondent]. ...

[441] 223. The appellant's counsel eschewed labelling the appellant's claim a "wrongful life" claim and emphasised that what was wrong was Dr PR Stephens's failures to diagnose rubella and to advise. It was those failures [442] which were said to have caused or materially or effectively

caused the damage, namely Alexia Harriton's "life with disabilities". However, such claims have come to be recognised internationally for some decades as "wrongful life" claims. …

[443] The position elsewhere

227. In the United Kingdom, the English Court of Appeal in *McKay v Essex Area Health Authority* [1982] QB 1166 unanimously rejected such a claim by a child affected by rubella as disclosing no reasonable cause of action against her local health authority and her mother's doctor. The reasoning deals with objections to such a cause of action which have been raised in numerous courts before and since. In finding neither defendant was under any duty to the child to give the child's mother an opportunity to terminate the child's life, Stephenson LJ said at 1180:

That duty may be owed to the mother, but it cannot be owed to the child.

To impose such a duty towards the child would, in my opinion, make a further inroad on the sanctity of human life which would be contrary to public policy. It would mean regarding the life of a handicapped child as not only less valuable than the life of a normal child, but so much less valuable that it was not worth preserving, and it would **[444]** even mean that a doctor would be obliged to pay damages to a child infected with rubella before birth who was in fact born with some mercifully trivial abnormality.

228. He then went on (at 1181) to recognise that a court could not evaluate non-existence for the purpose of determining whether a disabled child had lost anything by being born … .

230. Ackner LJ said at 1189:

But how can a court begin to evaluate non-existence, 'the undiscovered country from whose bourn no traveller returns?' No comparison is possible and therefore no damage can be established which a court could recognise. This goes to the root of the whole cause of action.

231. Griffiths LJ said at 1192:

To my mind, the most compelling reason to reject this cause of action is the intolerable and insoluble problem it would create in the assessment of damage. …

[Her Honour referred to decided cases in the United States and Canada where, generally speaking, wrongful life claims had been rejected. Her Honour also referred to decided cases in Israel (where a wrongful life claim was allowed by the Supreme Court of Israel), Germany (where a wrongful life claim was rejected by the German Supreme Court), France (where a wrongful life claim was allowed in contract) and the Netherlands (where a wrongful life claim was allowed under the *Dutch Civil Code*).]

[447] Duty of care

242. In *Sullivan v Moody* (2001) 207 CLR 562 in the joint judgment of five Justices, it was stated at 579-580 [50]:

Different classes of case give rise to different problems in determining the existence and nature or scope, of a duty of care. Sometimes the problems may be bound up with the harm suffered by the plaintiff, as, for example, where its direct cause is the criminal conduct of some third party. Sometimes they may arise because the defendant is the repository of a statutory power or discretion. Sometimes they may reflect the difficulty of confining the class of persons to whom a duty may be owed within reasonable limits. Sometimes they may concern the need to preserve the coherence of other legal principles, or of a statutory scheme which governs certain conduct or relationships. The relevant problem will then become the focus of attention in a judicial evaluation of the factors which tend for or against a conclusion, to be arrived at as a matter of principle.

243. In the present appeal, particular significance attaches to the need to preserve the coherence of legal principles, as emphasised in *Sullivan v Moody*. … The conclusion will be reached that the nature of the damage alleged is not such as to be legally cognisable in the sense required to found a duty of care. …

244. It was not Dr PR Stephens's fault that Alexia Harriton was injured by the rubella infection of her mother. Once she had been affected by the rubella infection of her mother it was not possible for her to enjoy a life free from disability. The agreed facts assert that Dr PR Stephens should have treated Mrs Harriton differently, in which case rubella would have been diagnosed. However, on

the agreed facts, it was not possible for Dr PR Stephens to prevent the appellant's disabilities. Dr PR Stephens would have discharged his duty by diagnosing the rubella and advising Mrs Harriton about her circumstances, enabling her to decide whether to terminate her pregnancy ...

245. It is important to an understanding of the right or interest which the appellant is seeking to protect, to maintain the distinction between suing the doctor for causing physical damage, being the disability, and suing the doctor for causing a "life with disabilities", as the case was put by the appellant in this Court. The former is immediately caused by rubella, whereas the latter is said to be immediately, or materially, or effectively caused by the doctor's failure to advise the mother such that her response would have been to obtain a lawful abortion. In the Court of Appeal, Spigelman CJ was of the opinion that it is not "possible to avoid or obfuscate the fact that an action by a disabled child, as distinct from an action by the parents, involves an assertion *by the child* that it would be preferable if she or he had not been born". This raises the difficult question of whether the common law could or should recognise a right of a foetus to be aborted, or an interest of a foetus in its own termination, which is distinct **[448]** from the recognised right of a foetus not to be physically injured whilst *en ventre sa mère*, whether by a positive act (*Watt v Rama* [1972] VR 353; *Lynch v Lynch* (1991) 25 NSWLR 411; *R v King* (2003) 59 NSWLR 472) or by an omission (*X and Y v Pal* (1991) 23 NSWLR 26). ...

249. It is not to be doubted that a doctor has a duty to advise a mother of problems arising in her pregnancy, and that a doctor has a duty of care to a foetus which may be mediated through the mother. However, it must be mentioned that those duties are not determinative of the specific question here, namely whether the particular damage claimed in this case by the child engages a duty of care. To superimpose a further duty of care on a doctor to a foetus (when born) to advise the mother so that she can terminate a pregnancy in the interest of the foetus in not being born, which may or may not be compatible with the same doctor's duty of care to the mother in respect of her interests, has the capacity to introduce conflict, even incoherence, into the body of relevant legal principle: *Sullivan v Moody* (2001) 207 CLR 562. ...

[449] Damage

251. Because damage constitutes the gist of an action in negligence, a plaintiff needs to prove actual damage or loss and a court must be able to apprehend and evaluate the damage, that is the loss, deprivation or detriment caused by the alleged breach of duty. Inherent in that principle is the requirement that a plaintiff is left worse off as a result of the negligence complained about, which can be established by the comparison of a plaintiff's damage or loss caused by the negligent conduct, with the plaintiff's circumstances absent the negligent conduct. In the Court of Appeal, Spigelman CJ recognised that in cases of this kind, to find damage which gives rise to a right to compensation it must be established that non-existence is preferable to life with disabilities. A right capable of being protected by the law of tort, to not exist (or to be aborted), must necessarily require the comparison which Spigelman CJ identified. The appellant's counsel conceded correctly that it is the usual principles of tort liability which compel the appellant to contest her own existence.

252. A comparison between a life with disabilities and non-existence, for the purposes of proving actual damage and having a trier of fact apprehend the nature of the damage caused, is impossible. ...

253. There is no present field of human learning or discourse, including philosophy and theology, which would allow a person experiential access to non-existence, whether it is called pre-existence or afterlife. There is no practical possibility of a court (or jury) ever apprehending or evaluating, or receiving proof of, the actual loss or damage as claimed by the appellant. It cannot be determined in what sense Alexia Harriton's life with disabilities represents a loss, deprivation or detriment compared with non-existence. ...

[450] 254. ... A duty of care cannot be stated in respect of damage which cannot be proved by persons alleging such a duty has been breached, and which cannot be apprehended by persons said to be subject to the duty, and which cannot be apprehended or evaluated by a court (or jury). ...

[451] The value of life

258. ... [I]t is odious and repugnant to devalue the life of a disabled person by suggesting that such a person would have been better off not to have been born into a life with disabilities.

259. In the eyes of the common law of Australia all human beings are valuable in, and to, our community, irrespective of any disability or perceived imperfection. ... While Alexia Harriton's disabilities are described in the agreed statement of facts, her disabilities are only one dimension of her humanity. It involves no denial of the particular pain and suffering of those with disabilities [452] to note that while alive, between birth and death, human beings share biological needs, social needs and intellectual needs and every human life, within its circumstances and limitations, is characterised by an enigmatic and ever-changing mixture of pain and pleasure related to such needs.

260. The Court knows very little about Alexia Harriton but it is possible for the Court to infer that Alexia Harriton is no different in this respect from fellow human beings, despite the fact that her grave disabilities include mental retardation. A seriously disabled person can find life rewarding and it was not contended to the contrary on behalf of the appellant. It was not contended as a fact that Alexia Harriton cannot experience pleasure. The Court was informed Alexia Harriton commanded the devotion of her parents.

261. Arguments giving primacy to the value of Alexia Harriton's life, which are additional to and independent of the arguments based on the forensic impossibility of proving and apprehending the nature of the damage claimed, highlight the lack of certainty about the class of persons to whom the proposed duty is owed. Is it only owed to persons whose disability is so severe they could be said to constitute a group for whom life is not worth living? Other categories of established negligence, in which a duty of care exists, do not discriminate between those damaged by a breach of the duty on the basis of the severity or otherwise of the damage. ...

[456] Conclusion
276. In the present case the damage claimed is not amenable to being determined by a court by the application of legal method. A duty of care cannot be clearly stated in circumstances where the appellant can never prove (and the trier of fact can never apprehend) the actual damage claimed, the essential ingredient in the tort of negligence. The appellant cannot come within the compensatory principle for measuring damages without some awkward, unconvincing and unworkable legal fiction. To except the appellant from complying with well-established and well-known principles, integral to the body of doctrine concerning negligence applicable to all plaintiffs and defendants in actions in all other categories of negligence, would occasion serious incoherence in that body of doctrine and would ignore the limitations of legal method in respect of the appellant's claim.

277. The other considerations, the autonomy of a mother in respect of any decision to terminate or continue a pregnancy, the problematic nature of the right or interest being asserted, the uncertainty about the class of persons to whom the proposed duty would be owed and the incompatibility of the cause of action with values expressed generally in the common law and statute all support the conclusion that the appellant does not have a cause of action against the respondent on the agreed facts. For these reasons *Cattanach v Melchior* (2003) 215 CLR 1 represents the present boundary drawn in Australia by the common law (subject to retreat of the legislatures in New South Wales, South Australia and Queensland) in respect of claims of wrongful birth and wrongful life. Life with disabilities, like life, is not actionable.

278. ... The appeal should be dismissed with costs.

Appeal dismissed

[Wrongful life as a cause of action in negligence also was considered by the High Court of Australia in *Waller v James; Waller v Hoolahan* (2006) 226 ALR 457 which was heard with *Harriton v Stephens* (above). In the *Waller* cases, for substantially the same reasons as in *Harriton v Stephens*, the High Court of Australia, Kirby J dissenting, rejected, as a matter of principle, a wrongful life claim brought on behalf of a child, Keeden Waller, who had been born with serious congenital disabilities attributable to a genetic deficiency inherited from his father. The alleged negligence was on the part of specialist medical practitioners who failed to advise the child's parents in relation to the possibility of transmission to the child in utero of this genetic deficiency thereby denying the parents the opportunity to have the pregnancy lawfully terminated.]

7. SUPERVISION AND CONTROL

Smith v Leurs
(1945) 70 CLR 256
High Court of Australia

A parent is not vicariously liable for the torts of his or her child but has a duty to supervise or control the child. Whether that duty has been breached will depend on the circumstances, including the age of the child.

LATHAM CJ. **[258]** The respondent Brian Leurs is an infant who on 17th December 1943 was 13 years of age. He is the adopted son of the other respondents to this appeal. On the date mentioned he, with other boys, including the appellant William Brian Smith, was engaged in what was apparently semi-hostile play in which two groups of boys chased one another, threw dirt, stones and apricots at each other, and used shanghais. The boy Leurs fired a stone from a shanghai and hit Smith in the eye, seriously damaging his sight. The boy Smith sued the boy Leurs and his parents for damages for assault in the case of the infant defendant, and for negligence in the case of the adult defendants. Judgment was given by Mayo J against all three defendants for the sum of £305 4s 6d damages. Upon appeal to the Full Court, the judgment against the adult defendants was set aside, and the plaintiff now appeals to this Court. No question arises as to the liability of the infant defendant.

The contention of the plaintiff is that the adult defendants were guilty of negligence which caused the injury to the plaintiff. The alleged negligence consisted in allowing their child, aged 13 years, to have a shanghai, though they knew of the possible dangers associated with its use. The particulars of negligence alleged lack of proper or any control or supervision of the boy in the possession or use of the shanghai, and, further, in his possession or use of it outside the limits of his own home; secondly, failure by the parents to take away from the boy or to destroy the shanghai or to prevent him taking possession of it; and, thirdly, allowing him to have the possession or use of the shanghai outside the limits of his own home.

Evidence was given by answers to interrogatories and otherwise which showed that the parents knew that the boy had a shanghai. Evidence was also given by the father that he had warned him of danger in using it, and by the mother and the child that she had told him that he must use it only at the side of the house and must shoot towards the wall. His Honour found that the adult defendants did make an attempt to restrict the use of the shanghai to the premises of the boy's home, but that they did not prevent **[259]** him from taking the shanghai with him away from his home premises. There was evidence that most boys in the district had shanghais. There was no evidence that the infant defendant had any vicious propensities. The question is whether in these circumstances the adult defendants were guilty of negligence. ...

A parent as such is not responsible for the torts of his child, though, if the child is his servant or acts with his authority, the parent will be liable as his employer or principal. But a person who, as a parent, has the control of a child is responsible for negligence in the exercise of that control if injury results. Whether there is negligence depends upon all the circumstances. A baby two years old playing with another baby should not be allowed to have a knife or a box of matches. It may be negligent to allow a particular child to have an air gun (*Bebee v Sales* (1916) 32 TLR 413). Is it negligent to allow a boy of 13 to have a shanghai, after giving him caution and warning about its use? A shanghai does not go off "of itself" by accident – as may happen with a loaded gun. It requires deliberate intention before it can produce any effect. It is a common object in boyhood life. Annoyance rather than actual physical harm is the worst that is normally to be expected from its use. In this case, the boy was warned of the danger: he was old enough to understand the warning: he was told not to use the shanghai away from home: he disobeyed this order: there is no evidence to show that such disobedience was to be anticipated or that any special circumstances existed, such as, for example, a disposition to cause injury to other persons. In my opinion, these facts show that the adult defendants took all the precautions which could reasonably be expected. In the absence of special circumstances, I agree with the learned judges in the Full Court, who were of opinion that to require parents to prohibit absolutely the use of a shanghai by a boy or to take it away from him whenever **[260]** he left home would involve setting up an impracticable and unreasonably high standard of parental duty.

In my opinion, the appeal should be dismissed.

DIXON J. **[261]** The not uncommon error that a parent is responsible for the harm done by his young child is perhaps to be accounted for by the persistence of the notions of early law. But the French *Code Civil* adopted or preserved the rule; "Le père, et la mère après le décès du mari, sont responsables du dommage cause par leurs enfants mineurs habitant avec eux" (Article 1384).

In English law, the development was the other way and, in 1860, Willes J was able to say: "I am not aware of any such relation between a father and a son, though the son be living with his father as a member of his family, as will make the acts of the son more binding upon the father than the acts of anybody else" (*Moon v Towers* (1860) 8 CB NS 611, at p 615 [141 ER 1306, at p 1308]). But, apart from vicarious responsibility, one man **[262]** may be responsible to another for the harm done to the latter by a third person; he may be responsible on the ground that the act of the third person could not have taken place but for his own fault or breach of duty. There is more than one description of duty the breach of which may produce this consequence. For instance, it may be a duty of care in reference to things involving special danger. It may even be a duty of care with reference to the control of actions or conduct of the third person. It is, however, exceptional to find in the law a duty to control another's actions to prevent harm to strangers. The general rule is that one man is under no duty of controlling another man to prevent his doing damage to a third. There are, however, special relations which are the source of a duty of this nature. It appears now to be recognized that it is incumbent upon a parent who maintains control over a young child to take reasonable care so to exercise that control as to avoid conduct on his part exposing the person or property of others to unreasonable danger. Parental control, where it exists, must be exercised with due care to prevent the child inflicting intentional damage on others or causing damage by conduct involving unreasonable risk of injury to others. ...

The standard of care is that of the reasonably prudent man, and whether it has been fulfilled is to be judged according to all the circumstances including the practices and usages prevailing in the community and the common understanding of what is practicable and what is to be expected. ...

[264] The Full Court held that the moderate course the defendants took of telling the boy to use the shanghai only on his own premises sufficed. Though I think that it is not easy to choose between the two points of view adopted in the Supreme Court, on the whole I am not prepared to differ from the view taken in the Full Court.

[Starke and McTiernan JJ delivered concurring judgments.]

Appeal dismissed

Modbury Triangle Shopping Centre Pty Ltd v Anzil
(2000) 205 CLR 254; [2000] HCA 61
High Court of Australia

Whether an occupier of premises owes a duty of care to a person harmed by a third party, such as a criminal, while on the premises depends on factors such as control over the harmful activity, assumption of responsibility by the occupier and reasonable reliance by the plaintiff.

[The appellant (defendant) was an occupier of a shopping centre. The first respondent (plaintiff), an employee of a video rental store in the centre, was injured by assailants at the centre's car park as he was leaving work one night. The appellant controlled the car park lights and normally turned them off before the video store closed. The respondent successfully sued the appellant for negligence in failing to provide adequate illumination of the car park. On appeal, the Full Court of the Supreme Court of South Australia upheld the claim. The appellant then appealed to the High Court, a majority of which (Gleeson CJ, Gaudron, Hayne and Callinan JJ;

Kirby J dissenting) allowed the appeal. The following are extracts from some of the majority judgments discussing the circumstances which give rise to a duty of care owed by persons in positions of supervision or control.]

GLEESON CJ. ... [263] 15. The first respondent suffered personal injury, the direct and immediate cause of which was the deliberate wrongdoing of the three men who attacked him. If the attack had occurred in a nearby street, or anywhere other than on land occupied by the appellant, there would have been no possible basis for attributing liability to the appellant. It is the appellant's occupation of the land on which the attack occurred that is the basis for a claim that the appellant was in breach of a duty of care it owed to the first respondent. The lack of care asserted was an omission adequately to light the place of the attack. The assumption is that leaving the lights on would have prevented the attack.

16. It is not contended that the harm suffered by the first respondent resulted from some defect or danger in the physical state or condition of the car park. This is not a case, for example, where inadequate lighting resulted in the concealment of some dangerous object or condition in the car park, with consequent damage to person or property.

17. That an occupier of land owes a duty of care to a person lawfully upon the land is not in doubt. It is clear that the appellant owed the first respondent a duty in relation to the physical state and condition of the car park. The point of debate concerns whether the appellant owed a duty of a kind relevant to the harm which befell the first respondent. That was variously described in argument as a question concerning the nature, or scope, or measure of the duty. The nature of the harm suffered was physical injury inflicted by a third party over whose actions the appellant had no control. Thus, any relevant duty must have been a duty related to the security of the first respondent. It must have been a duty, as occupier of land, to take reasonable care to protect people in the position of the first respondent from conduct, including criminal conduct, of third parties. People in the position of the first respondent would include employees of tenants of the shopping centre, visitors to the shopping centre, including customers of tenants, users of the automatic teller machines, and, perhaps, any member of the public using the car park at any time for any lawful purpose.

18. The basis of the duty which, as occupier, the appellant owed in relation to the physical state or condition of the premises was control over, and knowledge of, the state of the premises (*Commissioner for Railways v McDermott* [1967] 1 AC 169 at 186).

19. The appellant had no control over the behaviour of the men who attacked the first respondent, and no knowledge or forewarning of what they planned to do. In fact, nothing is known about them even now. For all that appears, they might have been desperate to obtain money, or interested only in brutality. The inference that they would have been deterred by lighting in the car park is at least debatable. The men were not enticed to the car park by the appellant. They were strangers to the parties.

[264] 20. In *Smith v Leurs* (1945) 70 CLR 256 at 262, Dixon J said:

"It is, however, exceptional to find in the law a duty to control another's actions to prevent harm to strangers. The general rule is that one man is under no duty of controlling another man to prevent his doing damage to a third. There are, however, special relations which are the source of a duty of this nature. It appears now to be recognized that it is incumbent upon a parent who maintains control over a young child to take reasonable care so to exercise that control as to avoid conduct on his part exposing the person or property of others to unreasonable danger."

21. Control was the basis of liability in *Dorset Yacht Co v Home Office* [1970] AC 1004, where Lord Morris of Borth-y-Gest at 1038-1039, after citing the above passage, said that the case was one of a special relationship involving a duty to control another's actions.

22. Reliance is sometimes the basis of a duty of care. Here there was no relevant reliance. Why the video shop could not have been closed in sufficient time to enable employees of the shop to walk to their cars before the lights went off (assuming they went off at 10 pm) was not investigated at the trial. There was nothing to prevent the first respondent's employer from making such arrangements for the security of its employees as it saw fit. The lease did not give the appellant the exclusive right to take measures for the safety and security of employees and customers of tenants.

23. The present is not relevantly a case of assumption of responsibility. The respondents submitted that the appellant assumed responsibility for the illumination of the car park. That submission confuses two different meanings of responsibility: capacity and obligation. The appellant owned and occupied the car park, controlled the lights in it, and decided when they would be on and when they would be off. But the relevant question is whether the appellant assumed an obligation to care for the security of persons in the position of the first respondent by protecting them from attack by third parties.

24. In *Kondis v State Transport Authority* (1984) 154 CLR 672, Mason J said (at 687):

"The element in the relationship between the parties which generates a special responsibility or duty to see that care is taken may be found in one or more of several circumstances. The hospital undertakes the care, supervision and control of patients who are in special need of care. The school authority undertakes like special responsibilities in relation to the children whom it accepts into its care. If the invitor be subject to a special duty, it is because he assumes a particular responsibility in relation to the safety of his **[265]** premises and the safety of his invitee by inviting him to enter them. And in *Meyers v Easton* the undertaking of the landlord to renew the roof of the house was seen as impliedly carrying with it an undertaking to exercise reasonable care to prevent damage to the tenant's property. In these situations the special duty arises because the person on whom it is imposed has undertaken the care, supervision or control of the person or property of another or is so placed in relation to that person or his property *as to assume a particular responsibility for his or its safety*, in circumstances where the person affected might reasonably expect that due care will be exercised." (Italics added).

25. The fact that, as occupier of the car park, the appellant had the capacity to decide when, and to what extent, it would be lit at night, does not mean that the appellant assumed a particular responsibility to protect anyone who might lawfully be in the car park against attack by criminals. The policy adopted by the appellant as to the hour at which the lights went off suggests that the purpose of the lights was to attract customers, rather than deter criminals. Whether or not that is so, there is nothing in the evidence to suggest that the appellant assumed a responsibility which, at least in the case of employees of tenants of the Centre, might ordinarily be expected to be a responsibility of their employers. It was the first respondent's employer which decided the hour at which the video shop would close, and what, if any, arrangements would be made for the after-hours security of employees. The argument provides an example of what Gummow J, in *Hill v Van Erp* (1997) 188 CLR 159 at 229, described as "[t]he use of the imprecise and beguiling but deceptively simple terms 'known reliance' and 'assumption of responsibility'."

26. Leaving aside contractual obligations, there are circumstances where the relationship between two parties may mean that one has a duty to take reasonable care to protect the other from the criminal behaviour of third parties, random and unpredictable as such behaviour may be. Such relationships may include those between employer and employee (*Chomentowski v Red Garter Restaurant Ltd* (1970) 92 WN (NSW) 1070), school and pupil (*Trustees of the Roman Catholic Church for the Diocese of Bathurst v Koffman* [1996] Aust Torts Reports ¶81,399), or bailor and bailee (*Pitt Son & Badgery Ltd v Proulefco* (1984) 153 CLR 644). But the general rule that there is no duty to prevent a third party from harming another is based in part upon a more fundamental principle, which is that the common law does not ordinarily impose liability for omissions. ...

[266] 28. As Brennan J pointed out in *Sutherland Shire Council v Heyman* (1985) 157 CLR 424 at 477-479, the common law distinguishes between an act affecting another person, and an omission to prevent harm to another. If people were under a legal duty to prevent foreseeable harm to others, the burden imposed would be intolerable. Referring to Lord Atkin's speech in *Donoghue v Stevenson* [1932] AC 562 at 580, his Honour said at 478:

"The judgment of Lord Esher MR in *Le Lievre v Gould* which Lord Atkin cites makes it clear that the general principle expresses a duty to take reasonable care to avoid doing what might cause injury to another, not a duty to act to prevent injury being done to another by that other, by a third person, or by circumstances for which nobody is responsible." ...

[268] 35. The most that can be said of the present case is that the risk of harm of the kind suffered by the first respondent was foreseeable in the sense that it was real and not far-fetched. The existence of such a risk is not sufficient to impose upon an occupier of land a duty to take reasonable care to prevent harm, to somebody lawfully upon the land, from the criminal behaviour of a third party who comes onto the land. To impose such a burden upon occupiers of land, in the absence of contract or some special relationship of the kind earlier mentioned, would be contrary to principle; a principle which is based upon considerations of practicality and fairness. The principle cannot be negated by listing all the particular facts of the case and applying to the sum of them the question-begging characterisation that they are special. There was nothing special about the relationship between the appellant and the first respondent. There was nothing about the relationship which relevantly distinguished him from large numbers of members of the public who might have business at the Centre, or might otherwise lawfully use the car park. Most of the facts said to make the case special are, upon analysis, no more than evidence that the risk of harm to the first respondent was foreseeable.

36. The appellant is entitled to succeed upon the ground that its duty as an occupier of land did not extend to taking reasonable care to prevent **[269]** physical injury to the first respondent resulting from the criminal behaviour of third parties on that land. ...

HAYNE J. ... **[292]** 111. In those cases where a duty to control the conduct of a third party has been held to exist, the party who owed the duty has had power to assert control over that third party. A gaoler may owe a prisoner a duty to take reasonable care to prevent assault by fellow prisoners. If that is so, it is because the gaoler can assert authority over those other prisoners (cf *Howard v Jarvis* (1958) 98 CLR 177; *Hall v Whatmore* [1961] VR 225). Similarly, a parent may be liable to another for the misconduct of a child because the parent is expected to be able to control the child (*Smith v Leurs* (1945) 70 CLR 256 at 262 per Dixon J).

112. The occupier of land has power to control who enters and remains on the land and has power to control the state or condition of the land. It is these powers of control which establish the relationship between occupier and entrant "which of itself suffices to give rise to a duty ... to take reasonable care to avoid a foreseeable risk of injury" to the entrant (*Australian Safeway Stores Pty Ltd v Zaluzna* (1987) 162 CLR 479 at 488). It is the existence of these powers which lies behind both the particular conclusion in *Hargrave v Goldman* (1963) 110 CLR 40 (affirmed on appeal *Goldman v Hargrave* (1966) 115 CLR 458) that occupiers of land owe a duty to take reasonable care in respect of fire or other hazards originating on the land and general statements, of the kind made by Lord Nicholls of Birkenhead in his dissenting speech in *Stovin v Wise* [1996] AC 923 at 931, that "[t]he right to occupy can reasonably be regarded as carrying obligations as well as rights".

113. The appellant, in this case, did not control what happened to the first respondent. It is not enough to say that the appellant had power to act in a way that may have made the occurrence less likely (by leaving the lights on). That is doing no more than restating, in other words, a conclusion about foresight or, perhaps, causation. The conduct which caused the first respondent's injuries was deliberate criminal wrongdo**[293]**ing. By its very nature that conduct is unpredictable and irrational. It occurs despite society devoting its resources to deterring and preventing it through the work of police forces and the punishment of those offenders who are caught. That is, such conduct occurs despite the efforts of society as a whole to prevent it. Yet the respondents' contention is that a particular member of that society should be held liable for not preventing it.

114. I have emphasised the inability of the appellant to control the conduct of the assailants who injured the first respondent because a duty to take steps to control that conduct should not be found if the person said to owe the duty has not the capacity to fulfil it. ...

116. To hold that the appellant owed a duty to take reasonable steps to prevent or hinder the attack on the first respondent is not only to hold the appellant responsible for conduct it could not control, it is to impose liability on it when its contribution to the occurrence, compared with that of the assailants, is negligible. As Professor Stapleton points out ("Duty of Care: Peripheral parties and alternative opportunities for deterrence", (1995) 111 *Law Quarterly Review* 301 at 317), the coherence of tort law depends upon "the notions of deterrence and individual responsibility". Those values would be diminished if the appellant is held to owe a duty of care of the kind for which the respondents contend. To accept the respondents' submissions would be to impose a duty which does nothing to deter wrongdoing by the appellant or other occupiers. Further, it would shift financial

responsibility for the consequences of crime from the wrongdoer to individual members of society who have little or no capacity to influence the behaviour which caused injury.

117. Established principle provides the answer to the present problem because it reveals that there is no duty to control the criminal conduct of others except in very restricted circumstances. Being an occupier of land should not be added to those exceptional cases, at least where the **[294]** complaint that is made by the plaintiff is not about the occupier failing to control access to or continued presence on the premises (cf *Chordas v Bryant Pty Ltd* (1988) 20 FCR 91; *Public Transport Corporation v Sartori* [1997] 1 VR 168). …

CALLINAN J. … **[301]** 146. The *Dorset Yacht Co Ltd v Home Office* [1970] AC 1004 case is, I think, a very special one. As Lord Reid pointed out, the Borstal Officers **[302]** negligently failed to carry out their orders with respect to the young offenders whom they were obliged to keep under proper supervision and restraint (at 1031). Lord Pearson expressly found a special relationship of an exceptional kind as referred to by Dixon J in *Leurs* (at 1055). It is clearly distinguishable from this case.

147. I have come to the conclusion that the duty owed by the appellant to the first respondent in the circumstances of this case did not extend to a positive obligation to keep the lights illuminated on the towers, or any tower, until after the shop closed. That does not mean that there can never be a duty, whether dischargeable by turning lights on, or otherwise to take precautions to prevent or reduce the chances of criminally inflicted injury or loss by third parties. However, as Dixon J in *Leurs* said, for such a duty to arise, there must be something special in the circumstances, or the nature of the relationship between the plaintiff and the defendant. I do not consider that anything of that kind exists here. …

Appeal allowed

Cole v South Tweed Heads Rugby League Football Club Ltd
(2004) 217 CLR 469; [2004] HCA 29
High Court of Australia

In the particular circumstances of this case, a registered club which supplied alcohol to a patron on club premises was not in breach of any relevant duty of care for the physical safety of the patron after she left the club premises in an intoxicated state and, as a pedestrian, was injured in a motor accident. Query the existence and extent of a duty on the part of an alcohol supplier to take reasonable care to protect an adult consumer from the risk of accidental physical injury or death as the result of self-induced intoxication.

[At about 6.20 pm on a Sunday evening in June 1994 the plaintiff/appellant, Mrs Rosellie Cole, aged 45, was struck and injured by a motor vehicle while walking alone on the highway about 100 metres from premises operated as a registered club by the defendant/respondent ("the club"). About 20 minutes before this accident, Mrs Cole had left the club premises in an intoxicated state after refusing management's offer of safe transport home and after her apparently sober companions had informed management that they would "look after her". After the accident, Mrs Cole's blood alcohol content indicated she had consumed 16 standard drinks. Mrs Cole had been on the club premises for about eight hours. She had consumed free wine supplied by the club at a "champagne breakfast". She later purchased a bottle of wine from the club at about 12.30 pm but was refused further service by the club at about 3 pm on account of her intoxicated state.

In a negligence action commenced by Mrs Cole in the Supreme Court of New South Wales to recover damages for personal injury, the primary judge (Hulme J) found that the club and the driver of the motor vehicle had been negligent, Mrs Cole had been contributorily negligent and responsibility for the accident should be apportioned as to 30 per cent each against the club and the driver of the motor vehicle and 40 per cent against Mrs Cole. The New South Wales Court of Appeal (Heydon and Santow JJA and Ipp AJA) set aside the trial judgment and entered judgment for the club and the driver of the motor vehicle. Mrs Cole's appeal to the High Court was limited to the liability of the club in negligence for the injury suffered by her when she was struck by the motor vehicle.

A majority of the High Court, comprising Gleeson CJ, Gummow, Hayne and Callinan JJ, found that the club was not liable for Mrs Cole's injury and dismissed her appeal. The dissenting judges, who, in separate judgments, would have allowed Mrs Cole's appeal on the ground that there had been breach of a relevant duty of care by the club, were McHugh and Kirby JJ. Gleeson CJ and Callinan J, in separate judgments, found that the club did not owe Mrs Cole a relevant duty of care and that, in any event in the particular circumstances of this case, there was no breach of duty. Gummow and Hayne JJ, in a joint judgment, found it unnecessary to decide whether the club owed Mrs Cole a relevant duty of care. In their Honours' view there had been no breach of duty by the club or, if there had been breach of a duty to monitor and moderate the amount of alcohol consumed by Mrs Cole, that breach was not a cause of the injury suffered by her.]

GLEESON CJ. [some footnotes in whole or part omitted] [472] 1. The appellant, having suffered personal injuries, claims that the ... respondent is liable to her in damages for negligence. In the circumstances of this case, it is of little assistance to consider issues of duty of care, breach, and damages, at a high level of abstraction, divorced from the concrete facts. In particular, to ask whether the respondent owed the appellant a duty of care does not advance the matter. Before she was injured, the appellant was for some hours on the respondent's premises, and consumed food and drink supplied by the respondent. Of course the respondent owed her a duty of care. There is, however, an issue concerning the nature and extent of the duty. To address that issue, it is useful to begin by identifying the harm suffered by the appellant, for which the respondent is said to be liable, and the circumstances in which she came to suffer that harm: cf *Modbury Triangle Shopping Centre Pty Ltd v Anzil* (2000) 205 CLR 254 at 262-263 [13]-[16]. As Brennan J said in *Sutherland Shire Council v Heyman* (1985) 157 CLR 424 at 487, "a postulated duty of care must be stated in reference to the kind of damage that a plaintiff has suffered". ...

[473] 2. The appellant was injured as a result of being run down by a motor car on a public road. ... The respondent had no connection with the motor car, or the driver. ... The appellant blames the respondent for her presence on the road in an intoxicated state, and for her injuries. Two aspects of the conduct of the respondent are said to involve fault. First, it is said that the respondent supplied the appellant with drink at a time when a reasonable person would have known she was intoxicated. Secondly, it is said that the respondent allowed the appellant to leave its premises in an unsafe condition, without proper and adequate assistance. ...

[475] 8. The harm suffered by the appellant was personal injury resulting from her careless behaviour as a pedestrian, the carelessness being attributable to her state of intoxication at 6.20 pm. The argument for the appellant must involve two steps: first, that the respondent, as a supplier of alcohol, owed her a duty to take reasonable care to protect her against the risk of physical injury resulting from her careless behaviour in consequence of her excessive consumption of alcohol; and secondly, that in the circumstances the conduct of the respondent, through its employees, amounted to a failure to take such care. ...

9. It is unnecessary, for the purposes of the present case, to endeavour to formulate, in abstract terms, some general proposition as to whether in any, and if so what, circumstances a supplier of alcohol, in either a commercial or a social setting, is under a duty to take reasonable care to protect a consumer of alcohol against the risk of physical injury resulting from consumption of alcohol. The question is whether there was such a duty in the circumstances of this case. The practical consequences of such a duty are worth noting.

10. Intoxication is an imprecise concept, but the laws concerning drink driving reflect the fact that a person in charge of a motor vehicle may be at risk of suffering, or causing, injury after three or four standard drinks. That is probably the best known and most clearly foreseeable risk of

injury that accompanies the consumption of alcohol. The risk does not necessarily involve a high level of intoxication. There are other forms of risk of physical injury which may accompany the consumption of alcohol, even in relatively moderate amounts. Consistently with the appellant's argument, if she had gone home in the early afternoon, tripped on a doorstep, and suffered a broken wrist, she may have had a cause of action against the respondent. ...

[476] 12. Some consumers of alcohol respond quickly to its effects, while others can consume a large quantity without much change of appearance or demeanour. People in both categories may be at risk of injury if they drive a car. To impose on suppliers of alcohol a general duty to protect consumers against risks of injury attributable to alcohol consumption involves burdensome practical consequences. It provides no answer to say that such a duty comes into play only when a consumer is showing clear signs of a high degree of intoxication. The risk sets in well before that. The appellant argued that there is a duty on a supplier to "monitor" alcohol consumption. The capacity of a supplier of alcohol to monitor the level of risk to which a consumer may be exposed is limited. If a restaurant proprietor serves a bottle of wine to two customers at a table, the proprietor may not know what either of them has had to drink previously, the proportions in which they intend to share the bottle, or what they propose to do when they leave the restaurant. Few customers would take kindly to being questioned about such matters.

13. There is a further question of principle bearing upon the reasonableness of the imposition of a duty of the kind for which the appellant contends. Most adults know that drinking to excess is risky. The nature and degree of risk may be affected by the extent of the excess, or by other circumstances, such as the activities in which people engage, or the conditions in which they work or live. A supplier of alcohol, in either a commercial or a social setting, is usually in no position to assess the risk. The consumer knows the risk. It is true that alcohol is disinhibiting, and may reduce a consumer's capacity to make reasonable decisions. Even so, unless intoxication reaches a very high degree (higher than that achieved by the appellant in this case), the criminal and the civil law hold a person responsible for his or her acts. If, in the present case, the appellant, deliberately or negligently, had damaged the respondent's property, or caused [477] physical injury to some third party, she would have been liable for the damage. There is no suggestion that she lacked the mental capacity to form the necessary intent. Save in extreme cases, the law makes intoxicated people legally responsible for their actions. As a general rule they should not be able to avoid responsibility for the risks that accompany a personal choice to consume alcohol.

14. The significance of a need for coherence in legal principle and values, when addressing a proposal for the recognition of a new form of duty of care, was stressed by this Court in *Sullivan v Moody* (2001) 207 CLR 562 at 581 [55]. Although there are exceptional cases, as Lord Hope of Craighead pointed out in *Reeves v Commissioner of Police of the Metropolis* [2000] 1 AC 360 at 379-380, it is unusual for the common law to subject a person to a duty to take reasonable care to prevent another person injuring himself deliberately. "On the whole people are entitled to act as they please, even if this will inevitably lead to their own death or injury." This principle gives effect to a value of the law that respects personal autonomy. It is not without relevance to ask what the appellant says the respondent should have done by way of monitoring and controlling her behaviour. Whatever exactly it might have been, it would seem to involve a fairly high degree of interference with her privacy, and her freedom of action. It is not difficult to guess what the appellant's response would have been if the person who sold her a bottle of wine at 12.30 pm and demanded to be told whether she intended to drink it all herself. A duty to take care to protect an ordinary adult person who requests supply from risks associated with alcohol consumption is not easy to reconcile with a general rule that people are entitled to do as they please, even if it involves a risk of injury to themselves. The particular circumstances of individual cases, or classes of case, might give rise to such a duty, but we are not here concerned with a case that is out of the ordinary.

15. Again, as a general rule a person has no legal duty to rescue another. How is this to be reconciled with a proposition that the respondent had a duty to protect the appellant from the consequences of her decision to drink excessively? There are many forms of excessive eating and drinking that involve health risks but, as a rule, we leave it to individuals to decide for themselves how much they eat and drink. There are sound reasons for that, associated with values of autonomy and privacy. ...

[478] 17. It is possible that there may be some circumstances in which a supplier of alcohol comes under a duty to take reasonable care to protect a particular person from the risk of physical injury resulting from self-induced intoxication: cf *Desmond v Cullen* (2001) 34 MVR 186 at 187. (It is to be noted that the Canadian case *Jordan House Ltd v Menow* [1974] SCR 239 involved knowledge of the plaintiff's propensities, and placing him in a situation of known danger.) However, the appellant cannot succeed in this case unless there is a general duty upon a supplier of alcohol, at least in a commercial setting, to take such care. I do not accept that there is such a general duty. I would add that, if there were, it is difficult to see a basis in legal principle, as distinct from legislative edict, by which it could be confined to commercial supply. When supply of alcohol takes place in a social context, there may be a much greater opportunity for appreciating the risks of injury, for monitoring the condition of the consumer, and for influencing the consumer's behaviour. In a social, as in a commercial, context, the risk of injury associated with the consumption of alcohol is not limited to cases where there is an advanced state of intoxication. Depending upon the circumstances, a guest who has had a few drinks and intends to drive home may be at greater risk than a guest who is highly intoxicated but intends to walk home. If there is a duty of the kind for which the appellant contends, it would be the degree of risk associated with the consumption of alcohol, rather than the degree of intoxication, that would be significant. In many cases the two would go together, but in some cases they would not.

18. The consequences of the appellant's argument as to duty of care involve both an unacceptable burden upon ordinary social and commercial behaviour, and an unacceptable shifting of responsibility for individual choice. The argument should be rejected. ...

[480] 26. The appeal should be dismissed with costs. ...

KIRBY J. [dissenting] ...

[493] The Club owed the appellant a duty of care ...

[494] 90. The reasons of Gummow and Hayne JJ ... prefer to postpone resolution of the issue of the duty of care although hinting at difficulties which their Honours see in its availability. The reasons of Gleeson CJ and Callinan J deny the existence of a duty of care. Their Honours' reasons are, with respect, replete with expressions reflecting notions of free will, individual choice and responsibility. ... Whatever difficulties free-will assumptions pose for the law in normal circumstances, such assumptions are dubious, need modification and may ultimately be invalidated having regard to the particular product which the Club sold or supplied to patrons such as the appellant, namely alcoholic drinks. The effect of that product can be to impair, and eventually to destroy, any such free will. This fact imposes clear responsibilities upon those who sell or supply the product in circumstances like the present to moderate the quantity of the supply; to supervise the persistent sale or supply to those affected; and to respond to, and ameliorate, the consequences of such sale or supply where it is clear that the recipient has consumed enough of the product to be in a temporary state of inability to take proper care for his or her own safety. ...

91. The law of tort exists not only to provide remedies for injured persons where that is fair and reasonable and consonant with legal principle. It also exists to set standards in society, to regulate wholly self-interested conduct and, so far as the law of negligence is concerned, to require the individual to act carefully in relation to a [495] person who, in law, is a neighbour: *Donoghue v Stevenson* [1932] AC 562 at 580. The Club had a commercial interest to supply alcohol to its members and their guests, including the appellant. Doing so tended to attract them to an early morning breakfast, to induce them to use profitable gambling facilities in the Club's premises and to encourage them to use the restaurant and other outlets where alcohol would continue to be purchased or supplied to the profit of the Club. As McHugh J points out in his reasons, with which I agree, the common law has long recognised that the occupier of premises owes a duty to take reasonable care for the safety of those who enter the premises. That duty arises from the occupation of premises. It extends to protection from injury from all of the activities on the premises, including, in registered premises such as the Club's, the sale of alcoholic drinks.

92. In such circumstances, to hold that the Club owed no duty of care by the standards of the common law of negligence, to patrons such as the appellant, is unrealistic. Such a patron was a person who, in the reasonable contemplation of the Club and its employees, was potentially

vulnerable to harm as a result of its commercial activities. Such harm was reasonably foreseeable in the given circumstances. The appellant was within the proximity of the Club in a physical sense. The policy reasons, concerned with free will and personal autonomy, that might in other circumstances justify withholding the imposition of a duty of care are overridden, in the case of the Club, by the commercial interest it had in the presence of the appellant on its premises and the known propensity of the alcoholic product, made available there, to expose at least some individuals to the risk of serious harm.

93. With all respect to those with doubts or holding contrary views, I therefore have no hesitation in concluding that the Club owed the appellant a duty of care of the kind posited. There is much support for this proposition in Canada: *Jordan House Ltd v Menow* [1974] SCR 239 and *Stewart v Pettie* [1995] 1 SCR 131. There are many decisions elsewhere that support the general proposition that a person in control of licensed premises owes a duty of care in negligence to take reasonable precautions in the circumstances not to contribute to a danger to others: *Chordas v Bryant (Wellington) Pty Ltd* (1988) 20 FCR 91 and *Munro v Porthkerry Park* **[496]** *Holiday Estates Ltd* [1984] TLR 138 per Beldam J. (See Orr, "Is an innkeeper her brother's keeper? The liability of alcohol servers", (1995) 3 Torts Law Journal 239; Solomon and Payne, "Alcohol liability in Canada and Australia: sell, serve and be sued", (1996) 4 Tort Law Review 188.) The withered view of community and legal neighbourhood propounded by Gleeson CJ and Callinan J is one that I would reject. ...

96. The Club, a registered purveyor of alcoholic drinks that began the day with a breakfast with the supply of free bottles of spumante in large quantities and thereafter tolerated the continued presence on its premises of a patron who became drunk, and who eventually was **[497]** obviously drunk (drinking at one stage directly from a bottle of wine and acting in a disordered, sometimes indecent and even offensive manner), cannot say that it owed no duty of care to her. It cannot do so when soon after she left its premises the virtually inevitable motor accident occurred with serious injuries to her person. ...

[498] The proper operation of the law of tort
104. Either this Court accepts that the law imposes a duty of care on those in effective control in such circumstances (the Club and its **[499]** employees) or it transfers responsibility solely to a person whose capacity to exercise responsibility had been repeatedly and seriously diminished over a very long time by the type of conditions that existed in the Club's premises, as described in the evidence. If responsibility – even partial – is imposed on the Club by the law of negligence a message is sent that control is not just a formal duty imposed on the Club and its officers by Parliament and by statutory offences [under the *Registered Clubs Act 1976* (NSW)] unlikely to be prosecuted often. A holding of liability in negligence would reinforce such duties (see Young, "Dram shop liability: a sobering thought for licensees", (1998) 18(1) Proctor 30 at 33) by visiting civil consequences that would sound in direct liability to the injured, with a resulting increase in insurance premiums that might stimulate a desirable change of culture and conduct. ...

Appeal dismissed

Stuart v Kirkland-Veenstra
(2009) 237 CLR 215; [2009] HCA 15
High Court of Australia

There is no general common law duty of care to rescue a person from harm, including self-harm. The fact that the defendant is a police officer with a statutory power to apprehend a mentally ill person who has recently attempted, or is likely to commit, suicide does not necessarily give rise to a common law duty of care.

[Sometime between mid-morning and 2.30pm on 22 August 1999 Mr Ronald Veenstra, the husband of the plaintiff (respondent), Mrs Kirkland-Veenstra, committed suicide at his home by fixing a hose to the exhaust of his car and starting the engine. Earlier that day, at about 5.40am, two experienced police officers, members of the Victorian police service, had approached Mr Veenstra while he was sitting in his car in a beachside carpark. Although the car engine was cold and not running, there was a hose leading from the exhaust into a rear window of the car. When questioned about the hose, Mr Veenstra said he had been sitting in the car park for two hours and that he had contemplated doing "something stupid". The police officers offered to contact a doctor, Mr Veenstra's family and a psychiatric crisis service. However, Mr Veenstra refused these offers of help and indicated that he wanted to return to his home and speak to his wife about his marital problems. The police officers allowed Mr Veenstra to leave after forming the view that he did not display any sign of mental illness and was rational and responsible. The police officers were aware that, under s 10 of the *Mental Health Act 1986* (Vic), they had power to "apprehend a person who appears to be mentally ill" if they (the police officers) had "reasonable grounds for believing that – (a) the person has recently attempted suicide ... or (b) the person is likely by act or neglect to attempt suicide ...".

The plaintiff contended that a cause of the death of her husband was the failure of the police officers to apprehend him and arrange for his medical examination. The plaintiff commenced, against the two police officers and the State of Victoria (the defendants), a fatal accidents action (under Part III of the *Wrongs Act 1958* (Vic)) in respect of her husband's death and an action to recover damages in respect of the nervous shock and post-traumatic stress disorder which she allegedly sustained as a result of this incident. The trial judge in the County Court of Victoria held that the police officers did not owe the plaintiff or her husband a relevant of care and entered judgment for the defendants. On appeal, the Court of Appeal of the Supreme Court of Victoria (Warren CJ and Maxwell P; Chernov JA dissenting) held that the police officers did owe a relevant duty of care to the plaintiff and her husband and remitted the case for retrial. On further appeal by the defendants, the High Court of Australia unanimously allowed the appeal and restored the judgment of the trial judge.]

GUMMOW, HAYNE and HEYDON JJ. [some footnotes in whole or part omitted]...

[244] The statutory framework

75. All parties to the appeal in this Court recognised the need to begin examination of the issues by reference to the relevant statutory framework. Although closest attention must be given to the relevant provisions of the *Mental Health Act* (and s 10 in particular) it is necessary to notice not only some other statutory provisions, but also some matters of history that lie behind them.

76. The proposition that, at common law, suicide was a "felony equivalent to murder" (Howard, *Australian Criminal Law*, 2nd ed (1970), p 123) has been seen as requiring some amplification or qualification. But the proposition was generally accepted in Australia for many years and it is not necessary to consider **[245]** whether it is complete or accurate. By the time of the events giving rise to this proceeding, suicide was no longer a crime in any State or Territory ... .

77. ... In 1967, the Victorian Parliament enacted that "[t]he rule of law whereby it is a crime for a person to commit or to attempt to commit suicide is hereby abrogated" (*Crimes Act 1967* (Vic), s 2, inserting s 6A in the *Crimes Act 1958* (Vic)). ...[A] new section, s 463B, was inserted in the *Crimes Act 1958* (Vic) (the Victorian *Crimes Act*) providing that:

Every person is justified in using such force as may reasonably be necessary to prevent the commission of suicide or of any act which he believes on reasonable grounds would, if committed, amount to suicide.

In 1983 legislation was enacted in New South Wales (*Crimes (Mental Disorder) Amendment Act 1983* (NSW).) and South Australia (*Criminal Law Consolidation Act Amendment Act 1983* (SA)) abolishing the rule of law that it is a crime to commit or attempt to commit suicide. And by the same legislation, provision was made in both New South Wales and South Australia justifying the use of force to prevent suicide. ...

78. It is to be noted that provisions like s 463B of the Victorian *Crimes Act* did not permit apprehension or arrest of a person who had threatened or was threatening suicide. The provisions authorised the application of force to prevent suicide.

79. That s 463B of the Victorian *Crimes Act* did not authorise apprehension or arrest was apparent from its text. If reinforcement for this construction was necessary (and it most likely was not) it was provided, in Victoria, by s 457 of the Victorian *Crimes Act* (113) which since 1972 has provided (in effect) that no person may be arrested without warrant except pursuant to the provisions of that Act or some other Act expressly giving power to arrest without warrant.

[246] 80. It is against this background that, in 1986, provision was made in Victoria, by s 10 of the *Mental Health Act*, for a police officer to have power if certain conditions are met to apprehend a person who appears to be mentally ill. Section 10 of the *Mental Health Act* (as in force in August 1999) provided:

> 10. *Apprehension of mentally ill persons in certain circumstances* (1) A member of the police force may apprehend a person who appears to be mentally ill if the member of the police force has reasonable grounds for believing that —
>
>> (a)   the person has recently attempted suicide or attempted to cause serious bodily harm to herself or himself or to some other person; or
>>
>> (b)   the person is likely by act or neglect to attempt suicide or to cause serious bodily harm to herself or himself or to some other person.
>
> (1A) A member of the police force is not required for the purposes of sub-section (1) to exercise any clinical judgment as to whether a person is mentally ill but may exercise the powers conferred by this section if, having regard to the behaviour and appearance of the person, the person appears to the member of the police force to be mentally ill.
>
> (2) For the purpose of apprehending a person under sub-section (1) a member of the police force may with such assistance as is required —
>
>> (a)   enter any premises; and
>>
>> (b)   use such force as may be reasonably necessary.
>
> (3) A member of the police force exercising the powers conferred by this section may be accompanied by a registered medical practitioner.
>
> (4) A member of the police force must as soon as practicable after apprehending a person under sub-section (1) arrange an examination of the person by a registered medical practitioner.
>
> (5) The registered medical practitioner may examine the person for the purposes of this Act."

Some aspects of s 10 should be noticed.

81. First, s 10(1) gives a member of the police force the power to apprehend a person "who appears to be mentally ill" if the member has reasonable grounds for believing one or more matters. What is meant by "appears to be mentally ill" is explained in s 10(1A), a sub-section that directs attention to the behaviour and appearance of the person, and the definition of mental illness in s 8(1A). Section 8(1A) provides that, subject to s 8(2) (which gives a long list of what is *not* sufficient to demonstrate mental illness), mental illness is "a medical condition that is characterised by a significant disturbance of thought, mood, perception or memory".

[247] 82. For present purposes, however, the critical observation that must be made about s 10(1) is that it gives *power* to police officers: "[a] member of the police force *may* apprehend …" (emphasis added). The sub-section does not in terms impose on police officers an obligation to exercise that power of apprehension if a person appears mentally ill and there are reasonable grounds for the officer to believe that the person has recently attempted or is likely to attempt suicide or to cause serious bodily harm to that person or to some other person. And there may very well be circumstances in which a police officer acting reasonably would not exercise the power even if the conditions for its exercise were met.

Framing the duty of care
[247] 83. … Argument in this Court focused upon whether the [police] officers owed Mr Veenstra a duty of care. It was accepted in this Court (as it had been in the Court of Appeal) that if no duty was owed to Mr Veenstra, the officers owed no duty to the plaintiff. …

84. …In this Court, the duty was said to be to take reasonable steps to prevent foreseeable harm to Mr Veenstra at his own hand. The scope of the duty was described as including apprehension and taking him to a medical practitioner for assessment. But it was accepted that the duty was not

absolute. That is, it was accepted that there may be cases in which it would be reasonable to do nothing, or to take some step short of apprehension.

85. The framing of the case in this way tended to obscure the distinction between the existence of a duty of care and the considerations which arise in the determination of what a reasonable man [sic] would do by way of response to the risk of injury to the plaintiff: *Wyong Shire Council v Shirt* (1980) 146 CLR 40 at 47-48. In part, this reflects the special nature of the posited duty as a duty to prevent harm to the deceased at his own hand, not at the hand of another.

86. The duty thus posited is novel. It has two particular features which require more detailed examination. First, although framed as a duty to take reasonable steps to prevent foreseeable harm, the particular kind of harm to be prevented is harm at the hand of the person to whom the duty is owed. Secondly, although the duty is framed in general terms **[247]** (to take reasonable steps to prevent foreseeable harm) it is evident that central to the concept of "reasonable steps" is exercise of an identified statutory power.

A duty to prevent self-harm?

87. The duty which the plaintiff alleged the police officers owed her late husband was a duty to control *his* actions, not in this case to prevent harm to a stranger, but to prevent him harming himself. On its face, the proposed duty would mark a significant departure from an underlying value of the common law which gives primacy to personal autonomy, for its performance would have the officers control conduct of Mr Veenstra deliberately directed at himself.

88. Personal autonomy is a value that informs much of the common law. It is a value that is reflected in the law of negligence. The co-existence of a knowledge of a risk of harm and power to avert or minimise that harm does not, without more, give rise to a duty of care at common law: *Graham Barclay Oysters Pty Ltd v Ryan* (2002) 211 CLR 540 at 596. As Dixon J said in *Smith v Leurs* (1945) 70 CLR 256 at 262, "[t]he general rule is that one man is under no duty of controlling another to prevent his doing damage to a third". See also *Modbury Triangle Shopping Centre Pty Ltd v Anzil* (2000) 205 CLR 254. It is therefore, "exceptional to find in the law a duty to control another's actions to prevent harm to strangers": *Smith v Leurs* at 262. And there is no general duty to rescue. In this respect, the common law differs sharply from civil law. The common law has been described as "individualistic", the civil law as "more socially impregnated": Markesinis and Unberath, *The German Law of Torts: A Comparative Treatise*, 4th ed (2002) at 90.

89. It may be said that the notion of personal autonomy is imprecise, if only because it will often imply some notion of voluntary action or freedom of choice. And, as Windeyer J pointed out in *Ryan v The Queen* (1967) 121 CLR 205 at 244, albeit in a different context, words like "voluntary" are ambiguous. But expressed in the most general way, the value described as personal autonomy leaves it to the individual to decide whether to engage in conduct that may cause that individual harm: *Agar v Hyde* (2000) 201 CLR 552 at 583-584. As Lord Hope of Craighead put it in *Reeves v Commissioner of Police of the Metropolis* [2000] 1 AC 360 at 379-380, "[o]n the whole people are entitled to act as they please, even if this will inevitably lead to their own death or injury". See also *Cole v South Tweed Heads Rugby League Football Club Ltd* (2004) 217 CLR 469 at 477. ...

[249] 91. Is the duty postulated in this case to be justified on the basis that the person to whom the duty is owed is not capable of exercising personal autonomy? The majority in the Court of Appeal concluded that it was to be inferred from s 10 of the *Mental Health Act* that it was the legislative view "that to attempt suicide is to be mentally ill". If that were right, it may be said that finding the alleged duty of care would not encroach upon the autonomy of the individual because autonomy presupposes full capacity to make choices. But the inference which the Court of Appeal drew is not open. Section 10 does not reveal any legislative view that to attempt suicide is to be mentally ill. ...

92. That s 10 does not reveal that legislative view is demonstrated by the requirement of s 10 that two conditions be met in order to enliven the power of apprehension: first, that the person appear to be mentally ill and second, that the person has recently attempted or is likely to attempt suicide, or has recently caused or is likely to attempt to cause serious bodily harm, whether to that person or to another. Perhaps an inference of the kind drawn by the majority might have been available if there were no separate requirement that the person concerned appear to be mentally

ill, but even then it would be a bold inference to draw that the Victorian legislature assumed that threatening serious harm to oneself or another will in every case suggest mental illness. ...

[250] 98. Contrary to the inference drawn by the majority in the Court of Appeal in this case, the premise for the provisions that now appear in s 10 of the *Mental Health Act* is that a person threatening suicide may or may not be suffering mental illness. ... **[251]** [T]he *Mental Health Act* reinforces the importance of that value of personal autonomy which must inform the development of the common law.

99. The duty which is postulated in the present case is expressed in terms which, on their face, would require every person who knows (perhaps every person who *ought* to know) that another is threatening self-harm to take reasonable steps to prevent that harm. ... So expressed the duty would be a particular species of a general duty to rescue. The common law of Australia has not recognised, and should not now recognise, such a general duty of care.

100. No doubt it was with that in mind that, despite the general terms in which the postulated duty was described, the plaintiff submitted that the duty was one which should be understood as arising from the "peculiar relationship" created by s 10 of the *Mental Health Act*. ...

101. Understood in this way, the duty alleged is revealed as being a duty to exercise a statutory power. This aspect of the matter merits separate consideration.

[252] A duty to exercise a statutory power? ...

[253] 108. ... The duty alleged in this case was said to arise out of the relationship created by the existence of the power given to police officers by s 10 of the *Mental Health Act*. ...

110. As noted earlier, the plaintiff had pleaded a claim for breach of statutory duty but that claim was not pressed at trial. Because s 10 of the *Mental Health Act* confers power but does not impose a duty to exercise the power, the abandonment of the claim for breach of statutory duty derived from that Act was inevitable and right: *Sovar v Henry Lane Pty Ltd* (1967) 116 CLR 397 at 404-405; *Byrne v Australian Airlines Ltd* (1995) 185 CLR 410 at 457-461.

[254] 111. Why, then, does the common law not impose a duty of care?

112. There can be no duty to act in a particular way unless there is authority to do so. Power is therefore a necessary condition of liability but it is not a sufficient condition. Statutory power to act in a particular way, coupled with the fact that, if action is not taken, it is reasonably foreseeable that harm will ensue, is not sufficient to establish a duty to take that action. Rather, as was pointed out in *Graham Barclay Oysters Pty Ltd v Ryan* (2002) 211 CLR 540 at 596-597, the existence or otherwise of a common law duty of care owed by a statutory authority (or in this case the holder of statutory power) "turns on a close examination of the terms, scope and purpose of the relevant statutory regime". Does that regime erect or facilitate "a relationship between the authority [here the holder of statutory power] and a class of persons that, in all the circumstances, displays sufficient characteristics answering the criteria for intervention by the tort of negligence" (at 596-597)? ...

114. In the present matter, as in a number of cases about the exercise of statutory power, it is the factor of control that is of critical significance. It was not the officers who controlled the source of the risk of harm to Mr Veenstra; it was Mr Veenstra alone who was the source of that risk. For the reasons that have been expressed in connection with consideration of the value of personal autonomy, this factor is of predominant importance.

[255] 115. The present case stands in sharp contrast to *Crimmins v Stevedoring Industry Finance Committee* (1999) 200 CLR 1. In that case the Court held that the Australian Stevedoring Industry Authority owed a waterside worker a common law duty to take reasonable care to protect him from reasonably foreseeable risks of injury arising from his employment by registered steve-dores. The conclusion reached by the majority of the Court was founded on considerations that were identified as finding close analogy with those which lead to an employer being responsible for providing a safe system of work and a safe place of work. The Authority had or should have had knowledge of the special risks to which the workers were subject and could control (or at least minimise) those risks by the exercise of its statutory powers. And it was the Authority that put the workers at risk of harm because it was the Authority that assigned the workers to particular stevedores. The Authority was held to control the source of the risk of harm to the workers.

116. No similar analogy with existing relationships giving rise to a duty of care can be drawn in the present case. More particularly, the police officers did not control the source of the risk to Mr Veenstra as would have been the case if he had been a prisoner in custody. No doubt it can be said that the police officers knew of the particular risk to Mr Veenstra. They had, after all, observed the preparations Mr Veenstra had made at the car park. No doubt it can also be said that they were in a position to control or minimise the occurrence of the observed risk (in this case because they had the power given by s 10 of the *Mental Health Act*). But considerations of the same kind will almost always be present when a passer-by observes a person in danger. The passer-by can see there is danger; the passer-by can almost always do something that would reduce the risk of harm. Yet there is no general duty to rescue. And unlike the case in *Crimmins*, it was not the officers who put Mr Veenstra in harm's way. They came upon the scene which Mr Veenstra had created. Were they to intervene to prevent *his* conduct? That question is not answered by pointing to what was decided in *Crimmins*. ...

[256] Conclusions and orders
121. For these reasons, the trial judge was right to hold that the police officers did not owe Mr Veenstra the duty of care upon which the plaintiff's claim under the *Wrongs Act* depended. It was not disputed that it follows that the officers did not owe the plaintiff the duty of care upon which her action for damages for psychiatric injury depended.

[257]The appeal should be allowed. ...

[In separate judgments, French CJ and Crennan and Kiefel JJ agreed that the defendants' appeal should be allowed.]

Appeal allowed

8. PUBLIC AUTHORITIES

Crimmins v Stevedoring Industry Finance Committee
(1999) 200 CLR 1; [1999] HCA 59
High Court of Australia

Whether a public authority owes a duty of care in respect of a failure to act (an omission) depends on factors such as whether the public authority was under an obligation to protect the specific class of persons to which the plaintiff belonged, whether the public authority was in a position of control over the relevant danger and the special vulnerability of the plaintiff.

GAUDRON J. **[14]** 10. The relevant facts and the history of these proceedings are set out in [McHugh J's judgment]. ...

[23] 42. Various tests have been propounded as to the factors which will stamp a relationship as one which calls a duty of care into existence. In some cases, emphasis has been placed on the notion of "general reliance". The concept of general reliance in its application to public authorities was explained by Mason J in *Sutherland Shire Council v Heyman* (1985) 157 CLR 424 in these terms (at 464):

[24] "Reliance or dependence in this sense is in general the product of the grant (and exercise) of powers designed to prevent or minimize a risk of personal injury or disability, recognized by the legislature as being of such magnitude or complexity that individuals cannot, or may not, take adequate steps for their own protection. This situation generates on one side (the individual) a general expectation that the power will be exercised and on the other side (the authority) a realization that there is a general reliance or dependence on its exercise of power".

His Honour cited the control of air safety, the safety inspection of aircraft and the fighting of fire in a building by a fire authority as examples of situations where general reliance may operate.

43. The notion of general reliance has been the subject of some criticism and more recent decisions of this Court have tended to focus on the vulnerability of the person who suffers injury,

on the one hand, and, on the other, the knowledge of risk and the power of the party against whom a duty of care is asserted to control or minimise that risk. And those precise considerations appear to underpin the notion of general reliance as explained by Mason J in *Sutherland Shire*.

44. In the present case, Mr Crimmins was not only vulnerable to injury by reason of the hazardous nature of his employment but he was less able than employees in most other industries to protect his own interests. The casual nature of his employment precluded the development of any longstanding employer-employee relationship in which he might usefully seek to secure his own health and welfare. And his relative powerlessness in that regard was magnified by the Authority's directions as to when and where he was to work in **[25]** circumstances in which he was at risk of having his registration as a waterside worker cancelled or suspended if he did not obey.

45. As already indicated, the Authority ought to have known from its inspectors of the frequency with which and the degree to which waterside workers at the Port of Melbourne were exposed to asbestos. Further, it knew that exposure to asbestos dust and fibres could be injurious to health. It was in a position to know what, if any steps, employers were taking to avoid the risks posed by asbestos. And more to the point, if employers were not taking adequate measures, the Authority was in a position to take various steps, short of making orders having the force of law, to control or minimise those risks.

46. Given the vulnerability of the late Mr Crimmins, the knowledge the Authority had or should have had, and its position to control or minimise the risks associated with the handling of asbestos, there was, in my view, a relationship between Mr Crimmins and the Authority giving rise to a duty of care on the part of the Authority to take those steps, short of making binding orders, which, in the circumstances, a reasonable authority with its powers and resources would have taken to avoid foreseeable risk of injury as a result of exposure to asbestos.

47. The appeal should be allowed with costs ... .

McHUGH J. ... **[26]** 52. The appellant, Mrs Maureen Crimmins, is the widow and executrix of the estate of Brian John Crimmins, who was the waterside worker in question and was the plaintiff in the action against the respondent. In or about May 1997, Mr Crimmins ("the plaintiff") was diagnosed as suffering from the lung disease mesothelioma which is caused by the inhalation of asbestos fibres. The disease is inevitably fatal. He died on 23 July 1998. His action was conducted on the basis that the relevant injury was not sustained until shortly before the manifestation of symptoms in May 1997. The respondent accepted that this was so.

53. Between April 1961 and November 1965, the plaintiff was employed as a registered waterside worker in the Port of Melbourne. At that time, stevedoring operations throughout Australia were regulated by the Australian Stevedoring Industry Authority ("the Authority") which was established by the *Stevedoring Industry Act* (Cth) ("the Act"). The Authority was later abolished and replaced by the respondent, the Stevedoring Industry Finance Committee ("the Committee") ...

[27] 54. The plaintiff contended at trial that the Authority was in breach of the duty of care that it owed to him to protect him from the harmful effects of asbestos dust and that that breach was one of the existing "liabilities and obligations of the Authority" assumed by the Committee ...

55. During the period from 1960 to 1965, 12 to 15 stevedoring companies were registered with the Authority at the Port of Melbourne where the plaintiff worked. The Act required the Authority to register employers who applied for registration and who satisfied the statutory requirements, one of which was that the employer was capable "of carrying out stevedoring operations ... in an expeditious, safe and efficient manner" (s 28(b)(i) of the Act). ...

56. During this period, about 5,000 waterside workers were registered with the Authority. Registration was governed by the Act and depended, *inter alia*, upon a medical examination and the satisfaction of the Authority's "reasonable requirements ... as to ... age, physical fitness, competence and suitability". However, the workers were employed not by the Authority, but by the stevedores (and occasionally the owner or master of a ship), employment being on a job by job basis. But the Authority's role was more than supervisory. The Authority allocated the waterside workers for work in accordance with the needs of the various employers – the workers having no say in the allocation. ...

57. The Authority's other functions included ... **[28]** the appointment of Port Inspectors who were empowered to make investigations and to report to the Authority and the Commonwealth Conciliation and Arbitration Commission regarding matters of safety and efficiency of stevedoring operations; the power to lay informations for offences by registered employers; the encouragement of safe working conditions including if necessary the provision of the proper safety equipment; and a general power to "regulate the performance of stevedoring operations" (s 17(1)(a) of the Act). ...

58. During his employment at the Port of Melbourne, the plaintiff was required (by unspecified stevedoring companies) from time to time to unload asbestos cargoes. The asbestos fibres were packed in loosely woven hessian bags, the handling of which resulted in the percolation of the fibres through the hessian and spillage from broken bags, creating clouds of airborne asbestos dust. Dust accumulated on clothes, hair and arms. At times, the dust was so pervasive that the plaintiff would have to blow his nose frequently to expel the dust from his nostrils. The plaintiff estimated that he worked approximately 20 days a year on asbestos cargoes. Neither the Authority nor any employer warned the plaintiff of the dangers of asbestos; nor was he provided with clothing or equipment to protect him from those dangers. ...

[29] The duty of care alleged by the plaintiff
61. Upon these facts, the question arises whether the Authority, as well as the individual employers, owed a common law duty of care to the plaintiff. In my opinion, it did. The correct approach in determining whether a statutory authority owes a duty of care is to commence by ascertaining whether the case comes within a factual category where duties of care have or have not been held to arise. Employer and employee, driver and passenger, carrier and consignee are a few examples of the many categories or relationships where, absent statute or contract to the contrary, the courts have held that one person always owes a duty of care to another. Frequently, a statutory authority will owe a duty of care because the facts of the case fall within one of these categories. The authority may, for example, be an employer or occupier of premises or be responsible for the acts of its employees, such as driving on a public street. ...

[32] The common law liability of statutory authorities in negligence
71. The present case has no factors which require it to be categorised as a case where a duty always exists or never exists, although the plaintiff asserts that the case is analogous to an employer-employee relationship and should be examined in that light. Nor is the case one where the factual situation is identical or nearly so with a situation where a common law court has held that the defendant owed no duty of care. It is a case where the plaintiff claims that a statutory authority owed him a duty to take affirmative action to protect him. The question of duty must therefore be determined by reference to what has been decided in similar cases.

72. Basic to that determination, as always, is the question: was the harm which the plaintiff suffered a reasonably foreseeable result of the defendant's acts or omissions? A negative answer will automatically result in a finding of no duty. But a positive answer then invites further inquiry and a close examination of any analogous cases where the courts have held that a duty does or does not exist. In determining whether the instant case is analogous to existing precedents, the reasons why the material facts in the precedent cases did or did not found a duty will ordinarily be controlling. ...

[34] 78. Sometimes, as in *Perre v Apand Pty Ltd* (1999) 73 ALJR 1190 at 1206-1207; 164 ALR 606 at 630-631, no case will be found which can reasonably be regarded as analogous to the instant case. Where such novel cases arise, the existence of a duty can only be determined by reference to the few principles of general application that can be found in the duty cases. My judgment in *Perre* (1999) 73 ALJR 1190 at 1214; 164 ALR 606 at 641-642 refers to the principles which are ordinarily applicable in cases of pure economic loss.

General principles concerning statutory authorities
79. Common law courts have long been cautious in imposing *affirmative* common law duties of care on statutory authorities. Public authorities are often charged with responsibility for a number of statutory objects and given an array of powers to accomplish them. Performing their functions with limited budgetary resources often requires the making of difficult policy choices and discretionary judgments. Negligence law is often an inapposite vehicle for examining those choices

and judgments. Situations which might call for the imposition of a duty of care where a private individual was concerned may not call for one where a statutory authority is involved. This does not mean that statutory authorities are above the law. But it does mean that there may be special factors applicable to a statutory authority which negative a duty of care that a private individual would owe in apparently similar circumstances. In many cases involving routine events, the statutory authority will be in no different position from ordinary citizens. But where the authority is alleged to have failed to exercise a power or function, more difficult questions arise.

80. In Australia, the starting points for determining the common law [35] liability of statutory authorities for breach of affirmative duties are the decisions of this Court in *Sutherland Shire Council v Heyman* (1985) 157 CLR 424 and *Pyrenees Shire Council v Day* (1998) 192 CLR 330. In *Heyman*, Mason J, speaking with reference to a failure to exercise power, said (at 459-460):

"Generally speaking, a public authority which is under no statutory obligation to exercise a power comes under no common law duty of care to do so ... But an authority may by its conduct place itself in such a position that it attracts a duty of care which calls for exercise of the power. A common illustration is provided by the cases in which an authority in the exercise of its functions has created a danger, thereby subjecting itself to a duty of care for the safety of others which must be discharged by an exercise of its statutory powers or by giving a warning ..."

Public law concepts and the policy/operational distinction

81. Common law courts have offered a number of different solutions to the problem of imposing an affirmative duty of care on a statutory authority. In *Stovin v Wise* [1996] AC 923 at 953 Lord Hoffmann (with whose speech Lord Goff of Chieveley and Lord Jauncey of Tullichettle agreed) said:

"In summary, therefore, I think that the minimum preconditions for basing a duty of care upon the existence of a statutory power, if it can be done at all, are, first, that it would in the circumstances have been irrational not to have exercised the power, so that there was in effect a public law duty to act, and secondly, that there are exceptional grounds for holding that the policy of the statute requires compensation to be paid to persons who suffer loss because the power was not exercised."

82. With great respect to the learned judges who have expressed these views, I am unable to accept that determination of a duty of care should depend on public law concepts. Public law concepts of duty and private law notions of duty are informed by differing rationales. On the current state of the authorities, the negligent exercise of a statutory power is not immune from liability simply because it was within power, nor is it actionable in negligence simply because it is ultra vires. In *Heyman*, Mason J rejected the view that mandamus could be "regarded as a foundation for imposing ... a duty of care on the public authority in relation to the exercise of [a] power. Mandamus will compel proper consideration by the authority of its discretion, but that is all" (at 465).

[36] 83. The concerns regarding the decision-making and exercise of power by statutory authorities can be met otherwise than by directly incorporating public law tests into negligence. Mr John Doyle QC (as he then was) has argued, correctly in my opinion, that there "is no reason why a valid decision cannot be subject to a duty of care, and no reason why an invalid decision should more readily attract a duty of care" (Doyle, "Tort Liability for the Exercise of Statutory Powers", in Finn (ed), *Essays on Torts* (1989) 203 at 235-236).

84. Another way in which courts in many jurisdictions have attempted to accommodate the difficulties associated with public authorities is the "policy/operational distinction". Mason J referred to this distinction in *Heyman* at 469:

"The distinction between policy and operational factors is not easy to formulate, but the dividing line between them will be observed if we recognize that a public authority is under no duty of care in relation to decisions which involve or are dictated by financial, economic, social or political factors or constraints. Thus budgetary allocations and the constraints which they entail in terms of allocation of resources cannot be made the subject of a duty of care. But it may be otherwise when the courts are called upon to apply a standard of care to action or inaction that is merely the product of administrative direction, expert or professional opinion, technical standards or general standards of reasonableness." ...

[37] 86. Recently, however, the distinction has come under attack. [In *Stovin v Wise*] a majority of the House of Lords held that the distinction was "inadequate" (at 951 per Lord Hoffmann, Lords Goff of Chieveley and Jauncey of Tullichettle agreeing). The Supreme Court of the United States in *United States v Gaubert* 499 US 315 (1991) has also pointed out that almost anything done by a public authority involves discretionary and policy judgments about priorities and resources. In *Pyrenees*, two justices of this Court expressed the view that the distinction was unhelpful on the facts of that case (at 358-359 per Toohey J, 393-394 per Gummow J; see also *Romeo v Conservation Commission of the Northern Territory* (1998) 192 CLR 431 at 484-485 per Hayne J).

87. Despite these criticisms, there is some support in this country for the distinction ... It may be that functions and powers which can be described as part of the "core area" of policy-making, or which are quasi-legislative or regulatory in nature, are not subject to a common law duty of care (*Sutherland Shire Council v Heyman* at 469 per Mason J, 500 per Deane J; *Pyrenees Shire Council v Day* at 393-394 per Gummow J). Outside this narrowly defined policy exception, however, as Professor Todd has argued, it seems preferable to accommodate the distinction at the breach stage rather than the duty stage (Todd, "Liability in Tort of Public Bodies", in Mullany & Linden (eds), *Torts Tomorrow – A Tribute to John Fleming* (1998) 36 at 46-47). ...

[38] 89. In *Pyrenees*, I said at 371 (see also at 394-395 per Gummow J):

"[T]he fact that the authority owes a common law duty of care because it is invested with a function or power does not mean that the total or partial failure to exercise that function or power constitutes a breach of that duty. Whether it does will depend upon all the circumstances of the case including the terms of the function or power and the competing demands on the authority's resources."

90. To highlight the different position of statutory authorities therefore, it also seems best to formulate an authority's duty by reference to what a "reasonable authority" – rather than a "reasonable person" – would have done (or not done) in all the circumstances of the case.

The obligation of a statutory authority to take affirmative action ...

[39] 93. In my opinion, therefore, in a novel case where a plaintiff alleges that a statutory authority owed him or her a common law duty of care and breached that duty by failing to exercise a statutory power, the issue of duty should be determined by the following questions:

1. Was it reasonably foreseeable that an act or omission of the defendant, including a failure to exercise its statutory powers, would result in injury to the plaintiff or his or her interests? If no, then there is no duty.
2. By reason of the defendant's statutory or assumed obligations or control, did the defendant have the power to protect a specific class including the plaintiff (rather than the public at large) from a risk of harm? If no, then there is no duty.
3. Was the plaintiff or were the plaintiff's interests vulnerable in the sense that the plaintiff could not reasonably be expected to adequately safeguard himself or herself or those interests from harm? If no, then there is no duty.
4. Did the defendant know, or ought the defendant to have known, of the risk of harm to the specific class including the plaintiff if it did not exercise its powers? If no, then there is no duty.
5. Would such a duty impose liability with respect to the defendant's exercise of "core policy-making" or "quasi-legislative" functions? If yes, then there is no duty.
6. Are there any other supervening reasons in policy to deny the existence of a duty of care (eg, the imposition of a duty is inconsistent with the statutory scheme, or the case is concerned with pure economic loss and the application of principles in that field deny the existence of a duty)? If yes, then there is no duty.

94. If the first four questions are answered in the affirmative, and the last two in the negative, it would ordinarily be correct in principle to impose a duty of care on the statutory authority. ...

[40] 95. [I]t may be helpful to say something about the second, third and fourth of these questions and their impact on the last two questions. ...

The grant of powers for the protection of a specific class of plaintiff ...

99. [S]ome powers are conferred because the legislature expects that they will be exercised to protect the person or property of vulnerable individuals or specific classes of individuals. Where powers are given for the removal of risks to person or property, it will usually be difficult to exclude a duty on the ground that there is no specific class. The nature of the power will define the class – eg, an air traffic control authority is there to protect air travellers. Furthermore, a finding that the authority has powers of this type will often indicate that there is no supervening reason for refusing to impose a duty of care and that no core policy choice or truly quasi-legislative function is involved.

Vulnerability

100. Except in cases where a statutory authority has assumed responsibility, taken control of a situation or is under a statutory obligation to act, it seems an essential condition for imposing a duty of care on an authority that the plaintiff is vulnerable to harm unless the authority acts to avoid that harm. I use the term "vulnerable" in the sense that, as a practical matter, the plaintiff has no or little capacity to protect himself or herself. In earlier cases, it was common to refer to the **[41]** concept of general reliance or dependence as a necessary condition for imposing a duty of care on a statutory authority (*Sutherland Shire Council v Heyman* at 464). As I remarked in *Perre v Apand Pty Ltd*, however, while the concept of general reliance has been criticised, properly understood, the concept was merely one way of testing for an important requirement in the determination of duty of care – how vulnerable is the plaintiff as the result of the defendant's acts or omissions (164 ALR 606 at 639-640). In the context of the common law liability of statutory authorities, general reliance is a combination of the requirements of the existence of powers in the statutory authority to ameliorate harm and the vulnerability of the plaintiff to that harm. ...

Knowledge

101. In *Perre v Apand Pty Ltd*, I said that "[t]he cases have recognised that knowledge, actual or constructive, of the defendant that its act will harm the plaintiff is virtually a prerequisite of a duty of care in cases of pure economic loss. Negligence at common law is still a fault based system ... It would offend current community standards to impose liability on a defendant for acts or omissions which he or she could not apprehend would damage the interests of another" (164 ALR 606 at 640-641). This applies no less to cases regarding the common law duty of public authorities – vulnerability and knowledge go hand in hand. ...

102. In *Perre*, I also discussed the issue of constructive knowledge, **[42]** saying that "[i]t would not be wise, or perhaps even possible, to set out exhaustively when it would be permissible to rely on constructive knowledge" (164 ALR 606 at 634). That statement also applies to this area of the law as much as to cases of pure economic loss. In my opinion, however, one must be very careful about using constructive knowledge in this area. ... Speaking generally, I think it is unlikely that a plaintiff could succeed because of the authority's constructive knowledge of an area of risk, unless it can be said that the defendant authority had an obligation to seek out the requisite knowledge in all the circumstances, including cases where the defendant authority already possesses certain actual knowledge, but fails to look further. It would be a far-reaching step to impose affirmative obligations on a statutory authority merely because it could have or even ought to have known that the plaintiff was, or was a member of a class which was, likely to suffer harm of the relevant kind.

The Authority owed a duty of care to the plaintiff

The risk of harm to the plaintiff was reasonably foreseeable

103. Safety on the waterfront was part of the Authority's general responsibilities. I do not understand the respondent to contend otherwise. Keeping in mind the generalised nature of the inquiry at the duty stage, it is clear that it was reasonably foreseeable that, if the Authority failed to perform its safety functions with reasonable care, then waterside workers would be liable to suffer injury, even if only because it was reasonably foreseeable that the employers might be derelict in performing their own duties.

The plaintiff was vulnerable as the result of the directions of the Authority

104. To my mind, the factor that points compellingly to the Authority owing an affirmative duty of care is that the Authority directed the waterside workers where they had to work and that the failure to obey such a direction could lead to disciplinary action and even deregistration as a waterside worker. That factor points so strongly to the existence of a duty of care that it should be negatived only if to impose the duty was inconsistent with the scheme of the Act. It can seldom be the case that a person, who controls or directs another person, does not owe that person a duty to take reasonable care to avoid risks of harm from that direction or the effect of that control. The police officer who directs traffic (See *O'Rourke v Schach* [1976] 1 SCR 53), the gaoler who has the **[43]** custody of the prisoner (See *Howard v Jarvis* (1958) 98 CLR 177) and the helpful bystander, who obligingly points the way to the traveller seeking guidance, all owe a duty to take care that their directions or control do not lead to harm. ...

107. What is required to discharge a duty arising from a direction or the control of a person's freedom of action will depend on the circumstances, and, in some cases, it may be very little. But usually the very fact of the direction or control will itself be sufficient to found a duty. Where the person giving the direction or in control of another person's freedom of action knows that there is a real risk of harm unless the direction is given or the control is exercised with care, the case for imposing a duty is overwhelming. I find it impossible to accept, for example, that, if the Authority knew that it was sending waterside workers to a ship where there was a high risk of death or injury, it owed no duty of care to those workers. ...

[46] The legislative scheme – the functions and powers of the Authority

114. No common law duty of care can be imposed on a statutory authority if to do so is either forbidden by the relevant Act or is inconsistent with the statutory scheme. To that question, I now turn.

[After referring to several provisions of the Act, his Honour concluded as follows:]

[50] 130. In my opinion, an examination of the scheme and purpose of the Act reveals that the Authority possessed the necessary powers and functions to protect the specific class of waterside workers by ensuring that certain minimum standards of safety were observed, either by direct action, or via its control and influence over employers. Furthermore, nothing in the Act forbade, or was inconsistent with the imposition of, a common law duty of care on the Authority.

"Core policy-making" and "quasi-legislative" functions

131. Section 20 of the Act declared that any orders made by the Authority had the "force of law". This section indicates that orders made by the Authority were part of the exercise of a "quasi-legislative" function and beyond the scope of any duty of care. This, however, does not exhaust the Authority's powers, even within s 18(1) itself. The Authority still retained sufficient powers to ameliorate the risk of injury to the waterside workers and those powers do not fall within the definition of "core policy-making". The "policy/operational" distinction has certain difficulties that attend it, but the nature of the other powers and functions exercised by the Authority with respect to safety clearly fall closer to the "operational" end of the spectrum. Although they involve considerations of convenience, discretion and budgetary allocation, they are matters appropriately considered as part of the breach question.

Other policy factors

132. There are no other reasons to deny a duty of care. There are no considerations ... **[51]** cutting across of a statutory scheme, the "delicacy" of the relationship between the parties or the fact that the officers of the Authority might adopt a "more cautious and defensive approach to their duties." Quite the opposite – in this case a recognition of a duty would likely have made the Authority more vigilant in its role. Nor do I think that the position of the Port Inspectors is analogous to the position of police officers (*Hill v Chief Constable of West Yorkshire* [1989] AC 53; *Elguzouli-Daf v Commissioner of Police of the Metropolis* [1995] QB 335), given that the Authority was charged with responsibility for the safety of a specific class – the waterside workers under its direction.

133. The Authority, as a reasonable authority in the exercise of its statutory functions, powers and duties (excepting the power to make orders), therefore owed a duty to the plaintiff to take

reasonable care to protect him from reasonably foreseeable risks of injury arising from his employ-ment. Whether it was open to the jury to find that there was a breach of that duty and that that breach was causally connected with the plaintiff's mesothelioma does not arise for consideration in this Court. ...

[56] 148. The appeal should be allowed ... .

[Gleeson CJ agreed with McHugh J. Kirby J and Callinan J in separate judgments also allowed the appeal. Gummow and Hayne JJ dissented.]

Appeal allowed

9. PURE ECONOMIC LOSS

Hedley Byrne & Co Ltd v Heller & Partners Ltd
[1964] AC 465
House of Lords

As a matter of principle, a duty of care may be owed in respect of a negligent misstatement on which the recipient reasonably relies to his or her financial loss.

LORD REID. [480] My Lords, this case raises the important question whether and in what circum-stances a person can recover damages for loss suffered by reason of his having relied on an innocent but negligent misrepresentation. I cannot do better than adopt the following statement of the case from the judgment of McNair J: "This case raised certain interesting questions of law as to the liability of bankers giving references to the credit-worthiness of their customers. The plaintiffs are a firm of advertising agents. The defendants are merchant bankers. In outline, the plaintiffs' case against the defendants is that, having placed on behalf of a client, Easipower Ltd, on credit terms substantial orders for advertising time on television programmes and for advertising space in certain newspapers on [481] terms under which they, the plaintiffs, became personally liable to the television and newspaper companies, they caused inquiries to be made through their own bank of the defendants as to the credit-worthiness of Easipower Ltd who were customers of the defendants and were given by the defendants satisfactory references. These references turned out not to be justified, and the plaintiffs claim that in reliance on the references, which they had no reason to question, they refrained from cancelling the orders so as to relieve themselves of their current liabilities." ...

The appellants now seek to recover this loss from the respondents as damages on the ground that these replies were given negligently and in breach of the respondents' duty to exercise care in giving them. ...

McNair J gave judgment for the respondents on the ground that they owed no duty of care to the appellants. ...

[482] This judgment was affirmed by the Court of Appeal both because they were bound by authority and because they were not satisfied that it would be reasonable to impose upon a banker the obligation suggested. ...

The appellants' first argument was based on *Donoghue v Stevenson* [1932] AC 562. That is a very important decision, but I do not think it has any direct bearing on this case. That decision may encourage us to develop existing lines of authority, but it cannot entitle us to disregard them. Apart altogether from authority, I would think that the law must treat negligent words differently from negligent acts. The law ought so far as possible to reflect the standards of the reasonable man, and that is what *Donoghue v Stevenson* [1932] AC 562 sets out to do. The most obvious difference between negligent words and negligent acts is this. Quite careful people often express definite opinions on social or informal occasions even when they see that others are likely to be [483] influenced by them; and they often do that without taking that care which they would take if asked for their opinion professionally or in a business connection. ...

Another obvious difference is that a negligently made article will only cause one accident, and so it is not very difficult to find the necessary degree of proximity or neighbourhood between the negligent manufacturer and the person injured. But words can be broadcast with or without the consent or the foresight of the speaker or writer. It would be one thing to say that the speaker owes a duty to a limited class, but it would be going very far to say that he owes a duty to every ultimate "consumer" who acts on those words to his detriment. ...

So it seems to me that there is good sense behind our present law that in general an innocent but negligent misrepresentation gives no cause of action. There must be something more than the mere misstatement. I therefore turn to the authorities to see what more is required. The most natural requirement would be that expressly or by implication from the circumstances the speaker or writer has undertaken some responsibility, and that appears to me not to conflict with any authority which is binding on this House. Where there is a contract there is no difficulty as regards the contracting parties: the question is whether there is a warranty. The refusal of English law to recognise any jus quaesitum tertii causes some difficulties, but they are not relevant here. Then there are cases where a person does not merely make a statement but performs a gratuitous service. I do not intend to examine the cases about that, but at least they show that in some cases that person owes a duty of care apart from any contract, and to that extent they pave the way to holding that there **[484]** can be a duty of care in making a statement of fact or opinion which is independent of contract.

Much of the difficulty in this field has been caused by *Derry v Peek* (1889) 14 App Cas 337. The action was brought against the directors of a company in respect of false statements in a prospectus. It was an action of deceit based on fraud and nothing else. But it was held that the directors had believed that their statements were true although they had no reasonable grounds for their belief. The Court of Appeal held that this amounted to fraud in law, but naturally enough this House held that there can be no fraud without dishonesty and that credulity is not dishonesty. The question was never really considered whether the facts had imposed on the directors a duty to exercise care. It must be implied that on the facts of that case there was no such duty. But that was immediately remedied by the *Directors' Liability Act 1890*, which provided that a director is liable for untrue statements in a prospectus unless he proves that he had reasonable ground to believe and did believe that they were true.

It must now be taken that *Derry v Peek* (1889) 14 App Cas 337 did not establish any universal rule that in the absence of contract an innocent but negligent misrepresentation cannot give rise to an action. It is true Lord Bramwell said (14 App Cas 337, 347): "To found an action for damages there must be a contract and breach, or fraud." And for the next 20 years it was generally assumed that *Derry v Peek* decided that. But it was shown in this House in *Nocton v Lord Ashburton* [1914] AC 932 that that is much too widely stated. We cannot, therefore, now accept as accurate the numerous statements to that effect in cases between 1889 and 1914, and we must now determine the extent of the exceptions to that rule. ...

[486] ... Lord Haldane [in *Robinson v National Bank of Scotland Ltd* (1916) SC(HL) 154 at 157] did not think that a duty to take care must be limited to cases of fiduciary relationship in the narrow sense of relationships which had been recognised by the Court of Chancery as being of a fiduciary character. He speaks of other special relationships, and I can see no logical stopping place short of all those relationships where it is plain that the party seeking information or advice was trusting the other to exercise such a degree of care as the circumstances required, where it was reasonable for him to do that, and where the other gave the information or advice when he knew or ought to have known that the inquirer was relying on him. ...

[492] But here the appellants' bank, who were their agents in making the inquiry, began by saying that "they wanted to know in confidence and without responsibility on our part," that is, on the part of the respondents. So I cannot see how the appellants can now be entitled to disregard that and maintain that the respondents did incur a responsibility to them. ...

[493] I am therefore of opinion that it is clear that the respondents never undertook any duty to exercise care in giving their replies. The appellants cannot succeed unless there was such a duty and therefore in my judgment this appeal must be dismissed.

LORD MORRIS of BORTH-Y-GEST. … **[502]** The guidance which Lord Haldane gave in *Nocton v Lord Ashburton* [1914] AC 932 was repented by him in his speech in *Robinson v National Bank of Scotland Ltd* 1916 SC (HL) 154. He clearly pointed out that *Derry v Peek* 14 App Cas 337 did not affect (1) the whole doctrine as to fiduciary relationship, (2) the duty of care arising from implied as well as express contracts, and (3) the duty of care arising from other special relationships which the courts may find to exist in particular cases.

My Lords, I consider that it follows and that it should now be regarded as settled that if someone possessed of a special skill undertakes, quite irrespective of contract, to apply that skill for the assistance of another person who relies upon such skill, a duty **[503]** of care will arise. The fact that the service is to be given by means of or by the instrumentality of words can make no difference. Furthermore, if in a sphere in which a person is so placed that others could reasonably rely upon his judgment or his skill or upon his ability to make careful inquiry, a person takes it upon himself to give information or advice to, or allows his information or advice to be passed on to, another person who, as he knows or should know, will place reliance upon it, then a duty of care will arise. …

[504] There was in the present case no contemplation of receiving anything like a formal and detailed report such as might be given by some concern charged with the duty (probably for reward) of making all proper and relevant inquiries concerning the nature, scope and extent of a company's activities and of obtaining and marshalling all available evidence as to its credit, efficiency, standing and business reputation. There is much to be said, therefore, for the view that if a banker gives a reference in the form of a brief expression of opinion in regard to credit-worthiness he does not accept, and there is not expected from him, any higher duty than that of giving an honest answer. I need not, however, seek to deal further with this aspect of the matter, which perhaps cannot be covered by any statement of general application, because, in my judgment, the bank in the present case, by the words which they employed, effectively disclaimed any assumption of a duty of care. …

I would therefore dismiss the appeal.

LORD HODSON. … **[513]** It was held in *Low v Bouverie* [1891] 3 Ch 82; TLR 582 CA that if a trustee takes upon himself to answer the inquiries of a stranger about to deal with the cestui que trust, he is not under a legal obligation to do more than to give honest answers to the best of his actual **[514]** knowledge and belief, he is not bound to make inquiries himself. I do not think a banker giving references in the ordinary exercise of business should be in any worse position than the trustee. I have already pointed out that a banker, like anyone else, may find himself involved in a special relationship involving liability, as in *Woods v Martins Bank Ltd* [1959] 1 QB 55, but there are no special features here which enable the appellants to succeed.

I do not think it is possible to catalogue the special features which must be found to exist before the duty of care will arise in a given case, but since preparing this opinion I have had the opportunity of reading the speech which my noble and learned friend, Lord Morris of Borth-y-Gest, has prepared. I agree with him that if in a sphere where a person is so placed that others could reasonably rely upon his judgment or his skill or upon his ability to make careful inquiry such person takes it upon himself to give information or advice to, or allows his information or advice to be passed on to, another person who, as he knows, or should know, will place reliance upon it, then a duty of care will arise.

I would dismiss the appeal.

LORD DEVLIN. … **[516]** Originally it was thought that the tort of negligence must be confined entirely to deeds and could not extend to words. That was supposed to have been decided by *Derry v Peek* 14 App Cas 337. I cannot imagine that anyone would now dispute that if this were the law, the law would be gravely defective. The practical proof of this is that the supposed deficiency was in relation to the facts in *Derry v Peek* 14 App Cas 337 immediately made good by Act of Parliament. Today it is unthinkable that the law could permit directors to be as careless as they liked in the statements they made in a prospectus.

A simple distinction between negligence in word and negligence in deed might leave the law defective but at least it would be intelligible. This is not, however, the distinction that is drawn in Mr Foster's argument and it is one which would be unworkable. A defendant who is given a car to overhaul and repair if necessary is liable to the injured driver (a) if he overhauls it and repairs it negligently and tells the driver it is safe when it is not; (b) if he overhauls it and negligently finds it not to be in need of repair and tells the driver it is safe when it is not; and (c) if he negligently omits to overhaul it at all and tells the driver that it is safe when it is not. It would be absurd in any of these cases to argue that the proximate cause of the driver's injury was not what the defendant did or failed to do but his negligent statement on the faith of which the driver [517] drove the car and for which he could not recover. ...

This is why the distinction is now said to depend on whether financial loss is caused through physical injury or whether it is caused directly. The interposition of the physical injury is said to make a difference of principle. I can find neither logic nor common sense in this. If irrespective of contract, a doctor negligently advises a patient that he can safely pursue his occupation and he cannot and the patient's health suffers and he loses his livelihood, the patient has a remedy. But if the doctor negligently advises him that he cannot safely pursue his occupation when in fact he can and he loses his livelihood, there is said to be no remedy. Unless, of course, the patient was a private patient and the doctor accepted half a guinea for his trouble: then the patient can recover all. I am bound to say, my Lords, that I think this to be nonsense. It is not the sort of nonsense that can arise even in the best system of law out of the need to draw nice distinctions between borderline cases. It arises, if it is the law, simply out of a refusal to make sense. The line is not drawn on any intelligible principle. It just happens to be the line which those who have been driven from the extreme assertion that negligent statements in the absence of contractual or fiduciary duty give no cause of action have in the course of their retreat so far reached. ...

[524] In his celebrated speech in ... [*Donoghue v Stevenson* [1932] AC 562] Lord Atkin did two things. He stated (at 580) what he described as a "general conception" and from that conception he formulated (at 599) a specific proposition of law. In between (at 584) he gave a warning "against the danger of stating propositions of law in wider terms than is necessary, lest essential factors be omitted in the wider survey and the inherent adaptability of English law be unduly restricted."

What Lord Atkin called (at 580) a "general conception of relations giving rise to a duty of care" is now often referred to as the principle of proximity. ...

Now, it is not, in my opinion, a sensible application of what Lord Atkin was saying for a judge to be invited on the facts of any particular case to say whether or not there was "proximity" between the plaintiff and the defendant. That would be a misuse of a general conception and it is not the way in which English law develops. What Lord Atkin did was to use his general conception to open up a category of cases giving rise to a special duty. It was already clear that the law recognised the existence of such a duty in the category of articles that were dangerous in themselves. [525] What *Donoghue v Stevenson* [1932] AC 562 did may be described either as the widening of an old category or as the creation of a new and similar one. The general conception can be used to produce other categories in the same way. An existing category grows as instances of its application multiply until the time comes when the cell divides. ...

It would be surprising if the sort of problem that is created by the facts of this case had never until recently arisen in English law. As a problem it is a by-product of the doctrine of consideration. If the respondents had made a nominal charge for the reference, the problem would not exist. If it were possible in [526] English law to construct a contract without consideration, the problem would move at once out of the first and general phase into the particular; and the question would be, not whether on the facts of the case there was a special relationship, but whether on the facts of the case there was a contract.

The respondents in this case cannot deny that they were performing a service. Their sheet anchor is that they were performing it gratuitously and therefore no liability for its performance can arise. My Lords, in my opinion this is not the law. A promise given without consideration to perform a service cannot be enforced as a contract by the promisee; but if the service is in fact performed and done negligently, the promisee can recover in an action in tort. ...

[528] I think, therefore, that there is ample authority to justify your Lordships in saying now that the categories of special relationships which may give rise to a duty to take care in word as well as in deed are not limited to contractual relationships or [529] to relationships of fiduciary duty, but include also relationships which in the words of Lord Shaw in *Nocton v Lord Ashburton* [1914] AC 932, 972 are "equivalent to contract," that is, where there is an assumption of responsibility

in circumstances in which, but for the absence of consideration, there would be a contract. Where there is an express undertaking, an express warranty as distinct from mere representation, there can be little difficulty. The difficulty arises in discerning those cases in which the undertaking is to be implied. In this respect the absence of consideration is not irrelevant. Payment for information or advice is very good evidence that it is being relied upon and that the informer or adviser knows that it is. Where there is no consideration, it will be necessary to exercise greater care in distinguishing between social and professional relationships and between those which are of a contractual character and those which are not. It may often be material to consider whether the adviser is acting purely out of good nature or whether he is getting his reward in some indirect form. The service that a bank performs in giving a reference is not done simply out of a desire to assist commerce. It would discourage the customers of the bank if their deals fell through because the bank had refused to testify to their credit when it was good. …

[533] On the facts of the present case Mr Foster [senior counsel for the respondents]… submits, first, that it ought not to be inferred that the respondents knew that the National Provincial Bank were asking for the reference for the use of a customer. If the respondents did know that, then Mr Foster submits that they did not intend that the reference itself should be communicated to the customer; it was intended only as material upon which the customer's bank could advise the customer on its own responsibility. I should consider it necessary to examine these contentions were it not for the general disclaimer of responsibility which appears to me in any event to be conclusive. I agree entirely with the reasoning and conclusion on this point of my noble and learned friend, Lord Reid. A man cannot be said voluntarily to be undertaking a responsibility if at the very moment when he is said to be accepting it he declares that in fact he is not. The problem of reconciling words of exemption with the existence of a duty arises only when a party is claiming exemption from a responsibility which he has already undertaken or which he is contracting to undertake. For this reason alone, I would dismiss the appeal.

LORD PEARCE. … [534] The reason for some divergence between the law of negligence in word and that of negligence in act is clear. Negligence in word creates problems different from those of negligence in act. Words are more volatile than deeds. They travel fast and far afield. They are used without being expended and take effect in combination with innumerable facts and other words. Yet they are dangerous and can cause vast financial damage. …

[536] How wide the sphere of the duty of care in negligence is to be laid depends ultimately upon the courts' assessment of the demands of society for protection from the carelessness of others. Economic protection has lagged behind protection in physical matters where there is injury to person and property. It may [537] be that the size and the width of the range of possible claims has acted as a deterrent to extension of economic protection. …

[539] If an innocent misrepresentation is made between parties in a fiduciary relationship it may, on that ground, give a right to claim damages for negligence. There is also, in my opinion, a duty of care created by special relationships which, though not fiduciary, give rise to an assumption that care as well as honesty is demanded.

Was there such a special relationship in the present case as to impose on the defendants a duty of care to the plaintiffs as the undisclosed principals for whom the National Provincial Bank was making the inquiry? The answer to that question depends on the circumstances of the transaction. If, for instance, they disclosed a casual social approach to the inquiry, no such special relationship or duty of care would be assumed (see *Fish v Kelly* 17 CBNS 194). To import such a duty the representation must normally, I think, concern a business or professional transaction whose nature makes clear the gravity of the inquiry and the importance and influence attached to the answer. … A most important circumstance is the form of the inquiry and of the answer. Both were here plainly [540] stated to be without liability. … They are part of the material from which one deduces whether a duty of care and a liability for negligence was assumed. If both parties say expressly (in a case where neither is deliberately taking advantage of the other) that there shall be no liability, I do not find it possible to say that a liability was assumed. …

I would therefore dismiss the appeal.

Appeal dismissed

L Shaddock & Associates Pty Ltd v Council of the City of Parramatta
(1981) 150 CLR 225
High Court of Australia

A duty of care may be owed in respect of a negligent misstatement made in relation to a "serious matter". It is not essential for the maker of the statement to possess or profess some special skill or competence in the subject matter of the statement.

[The plaintiffs had contracted to buy certain land in reliance on information supplied by the defendant Council to their solicitor that the land was not affected by road widening proposals. In fact road widening proposals had been approved in principle by the Council. The erroneous information was furnished initially over the telephone by an unidentified Council employee. It was reiterated in a certificate furnished under s 342AS of the *Local Government Act 1919* (NSW) which related to zoning and town planning matters. The practice was for the question to be asked, on the form requesting such a certificate, whether there were any such proposals, and for the Council to make a notation at the foot of the certificate if the land concerned was affected. If it was not affected no reply would be given to the question. No endorsement was made on the certificate issued to the plaintiffs' solicitor. The trial Judge and the New South Wales Court of Appeal found that negligence was established but held that the Council owed no duty of care.]

GIBBS CJ. ... **[230]** In the present case, having regard to the practice of the Council to indorse information as to road widening proposals at the foot of the certificates, its failure to do so when it had been asked, by the use of the form commonly employed, to supply the information for conveyancing purposes could reasonably have been understood by the recipient of the certificate as information that no proposal existed, and the Council ought to have known (although Mr Carroll had not expressly informed it of his awareness of the practice) that it would probably be so understood. The return of the certificate unindorsed was therefore tantamount to the giving of information that there were no proposals; clearly it was careless to give such a certificate.

The question then is whether there was a duty to answer carefully the questions put to the Council orally and in writing. It is now settled by the decisions in *Hedley Byrne & Co Ltd v Heller & Partners Ltd* [1964] AC 465 and *Mutual Life & Citizens' Assurance Co Ltd v Evatt* (1968) 122 CLR 556 (High Court) and (1970) 122 CLR 628; [1971] AC 793 (in the Judicial Committee) that a person can be liable for financial loss resulting from a negligent misstatement of fact or opinion, although the mis-statement was honestly made, and there was no fiduciary or contractual relationship between the parties. ...

[231] However, it was held by the majority of the Judicial Committee in *Mutual Life & Citizens' Assurance Co Ltd v Evatt* (1970) 122 CLR 628; [1971] AC 793 that this **[232]** duty of care is cast only on a person who carries on a business or profession which involves the giving of advice of a kind which calls for special skill and competence, or on a person who, although not carrying on such a business or profession generally, has let it be known that he claims to possess skill and competence in the subject matter of the particular inquiry comparable to those who do carry on the business or profession of advising on the subject matter and is prepared to exercise a similar skill and competence in giving the advice ((1970) 122 CLR, at pp 637-638; [1971] AC, at pp 805-806). ...

Lord Reid and Lord Morris of Borth-y-Gest, who dissented, took a broader view. They held that: "... when an inquirer consults a business man in the course of his business and makes it plain to him that he is seeking considered advice and intends to act on it in a particular way ... his action in giving such advice" ... [gives rise to] ... "a legal obligation to take such care as is reasonable in the whole circumstances." ...

On either view, the duty in my opinion can exist in relation to the giving of information as well as advice. ...

[234] The judgment of the majority in *Mutual Life & Citizens' Assurance Co Ltd v Evatt* has been much criticized by academic writers, and in at least two cases in the Court of Appeal a preference has been expressed for the minority view: *Esso Petroleum Co Ltd v Mardon* [1976] QB at p 837, per Ormrod LJ; *Howard Marine & Dredging Co Ltd v Ogden & Sons (Excavations) Ltd,* per Lord Denning MR [1978] QB at p 591 and per Shaw LJ [1978] QB at p 600. This Court, unlike the Court of Appeal of New South Wales, is free to adopt the view of the minority in the Judicial Committee rather than that of the majority. With all respect I find it difficult to see why in principle the duty should be limited to persons whose business or profession includes giving the sort of advice or information sought and to persons claiming to have the same skill and competence as those carrying on such a business or profession, and why it should not extend to persons who, on a serious occasion, give considered advice or information concerning a business or professional transaction. However, in the present case it does not seem to me to be necessary to decide whether the view of the majority or that of the minority in *Mutual Life & Citizens' Assurance Co Ltd v Evatt* should be accepted. ... [235] From the standpoint of principle there is no difference between a person who carries on the business of supplying information and a public body which in the exercise of its public functions follows the practice of supplying information which is available to it more readily than to other persons, whether or not it has a statutory duty to do so. ...

In the present case, Mr Carroll, as solicitor for the appellants, relied on the Council to exercise reasonable care in advising him whether the land was subject to local road widening proposals. It was reasonable for him to do so, because the Council was in a position to know better than anyone else whether any such proposals existed, and it commonly followed the practice of giving information as to that matter when requested. The Council ought to have [236] known that Mr Carroll's clients were relying on the information which he sought. The importance of certificates given under s 342AS for conveyancing purposes is obvious and well known. It is true that Mr Carroll did not expressly say what the purchasers intended to do with the land, but the Council ought to have known that the road widening, if carried out, would adversely affect the use of the land for most conceivable purposes. The Council was so placed that others could reasonably rely upon its ability to give accurate information as to any local road widening proposals, and it followed the practice, in the course of exercising its functions, of making such information available. The nature of the inquiry – made by a solicitor, for conveyancing purposes, on a form commonly used and prepared by law stationers – made clear the gravity of the inquiry and the importance attached to the answer. The Council therefore owed a duty of care to Mr Carroll's clients, the appellants, in answering the written inquiry.

It would not, however, have been reasonable for the appellants to have relied on an uncon-firmed answer given by an unidentified person in response to an inquiry made over the telephone. The Council therefore owed no duty of care in making response to such an inquiry. ...

[237] For these reasons I would allow the appeal . ...

STEPHEN J. ... [239] [I]s the Council liable in damages for supplying this admittedly erroneous information? The response to this would be clearly "Yes" if this were a case of advice given by someone in the course of their business or profession, the advice requiring the possession and exercise of special skill or competence – *Hedley Byrne & Co Ltd v Heller & Partners Ltd* [1964] AC 465 and *Mutual Life & Citizens' Assurance Co Ltd v Evatt* (1970) 122 CLR 628; [1971] AC 793. However the respondents contend that, as a result of the judgment of those of their Lordships comprising the majority in the latter of these two cases, no duty of care can be said to have arisen on the part of the Council in relation to the answer given by it to the appellants' question. Such a duty of care only arises, it is said, where advice or information is given by those who possess or profess some special skill or competence in the subject matter of the advice or information, as by being engaged in a business or profession involving the exercise of such skill or competence, and whose course of conduct involves the furnishing of advice or information to others. This is said to be the positive limitation imposed by *Mutual Life & Citizens' Assurance Co Ltd v Evatt.* ...

[240] But their Lordships were careful, on more than one occasion, to make it clear that it was no hard and fast rule which they were enunciating ((1970) 122 CLR, at pp 638, 642; [1971] AC, at pp 806, 809). They deplored the notion that *Hedley Byrne* should be regarded as laying down

"the metes and bounds of the new field of negligence to which the gate is now opened" ((1970) 122 CLR, at p 642; [1971] AC, at p 809). They **[241]** described their own decision as but one step in the step by step ascertainment of the limits of that new area. I do not understand their judgment as in any way suggesting that it is only those engaged in private enterprise, in particular trades or professions, who may attract such a duty of care. ...

For example, one who holds himself out as being, by reason of having set up a system for its gathering and collation, in possession of special knowledge, especially when he has a monopoly of that knowledge, and who further holds himself out as providing the fruits of that system to those who seek it, should be subject to such a duty. Such, I think, is the position of this Council; and, consistently with the views of the majority in *Mutual Life & Citizens' Assurance Co Ltd v Evatt*, that appears to me to be enough to attract to the Council a liability for negligent misstatement. ...

[243] It is for the foregoing reasons that I have concluded that nothing said by their Lordships who were in the majority in *Mutual Life & Citizens' Assurance Co Ltd v Evatt* denies the existence of a duty of care owed by the Council to the appellants. ...

[244] I would allow the appeal. ...

MASON J. ... **[248]** This Court must now decide for itself what is the common law for Australia upon the topic, unfettered by the Judicial Committee's decision in *Mutual Life & Citizens' Assurance Co Ltd v Evatt* (see *Viro v The Queen* (1978) 141 CLR 88). The decision to be made, broadly speaking, calls for a choice between the view of liability expressed by the majority (Lord Hodson, Lord Guest and Lord Diplock) and the wider view of liability favoured by the minority (Lord Reid and Lord Morris of Borth-y-Gest) and by this Court. ...

[250] According to the Chief Justice [in *Mutual Life & Citizens' Assurance Co Ltd v Evatt* (1968) 122 CLR, at pp 572-3], whenever a person gives information or advice to another upon a serious matter in circumstances where the speaker realizes, or ought to realize, that he is being trusted to give the best of his information or advice as a basis for action on the part of the other party and it is reasonable in the circumstances for the other party to act on that information or advice, the speaker comes under a duty to exercise reasonable care in the provision of the information or advice he chooses to give. ...

The Chief Justice, like the minority in the Privy Council, was in disagreement with the majority in the Privy Council who drew a distinction between those who bring, or profess to bring, professional knowledge or skill into the preparation of their statements and those who do not do so and are not expected to do so, the latter being under no duty of care in relation to their statements ((1970) 122 CLR, at p 637; [1971] AC, at p 805). ...

[251] I prefer the wider view to that expressed by the majority of the Privy Council in the *MLC Case*. I consider that this Court should now adopt Barwick CJ's statement of the conditions which give rise to a duty of care in the provision of advice or information. ...

[255] I would allow the appeal ...

MURPHY J. In general, a person who makes a negligent misstatement in circumstances where he knows or should know that the person or persons to whom the mis-statement is made may rely upon it, is liable in damages for loss sustained by the person or persons as a result of relying upon the mis-statement. The liability extends to economic as well as non-economic loss (see *Mutual Life & Citizens' Assurance Co Ltd v Evatt* (1968) 122 CLR 556; (1970) 122 CLR 628; [1971] AC 793 (the *MLC Case*); also *Caltex Oil (Australia) Pty Ltd v The Dredge "Willemstad"* (1976) 136 CLR 529).

The liability does not depend on the negligent mis-statement being of fact, it extends to negligent advice, but the information or advice **[256]** must be on serious matters. The liability is not confined to those who have special skill or competence. This reflects the approach of this Court in the *MLC Case* and departs from that of the Privy Council in the same case which restricted liability to those who possessed or professed special skill or competence on the subject of the mis-statement. For the purpose of this appeal, it is enough to hold that liability extends to those whose profession or business it is to give advice or information, whether gratuitously or not. ...

The appeal should be allowed.

[Aickin J agreed with Mason J. Stephen, Mason and Murphy JJ agreed that the oral statement by the Council in response to the telephone inquiry would not give rise to liability.]

Appeal allowed

Esanda Finance Corporation Ltd v Peat Marwick Hungerfords
(1997) 188 CLR 241
High Court of Australia

In the absence of reasonable reliance by the plaintiff (recipient of the statement) and an assumption of responsibility by the defendant (maker of the statement), an auditor of a public company does not owe a duty of care to potential creditors or investors to produce an accurate report of the company's financial position.

BRENNAN CJ. **[246]** The issues in this appeal arise on the pleadings in an action in which the appellant ("Esanda") sued the respondent company ("PMH") claiming, inter alia, damages for pure economic loss resulting from the negligence of PMH in connection with its auditing of the accounts of a corporation ("Excel"). In its pleading … Esanda alleged that PMH were the auditors of Excel and

> "furnished to the members of Excel a report stating that it had audited the accounts of Excel for the year ended 30 June 1989 in accordance with Australian Auditing Standards and reporting:
> 'In our opinion the accounts are properly drawn up in accordance with the provisions of the *Companies (South Australia) Code* and so as to give a true and fair view of:
> > (1) the state of affairs of the company as at 30th June 1989 and of the result of the company for the year ended on that date;
> > (2) the other matters required by Section 269 of that Code to be dealt with in the accounts;
> and are in accordance with Australian Accounting Standards and applicable Approved Accounting Standards.'"

Esanda was not a member of Excel; it was a financier which entered into a number of transactions involving Excel or corporations associated with Excel. The Full Court of the Supreme Court of South Australia, allowing an appeal from a Judge of that Court, struck out certain paragraphs from the **[247]** statement of claim on the ground that the statement of claim did not disclose a cause of action in negligence against PMH.

[His Honour then quoted the relevant paragraphs.]

[248] The question is whether in an action for negligence for pure economic loss it is sufficient to plead that it was reasonably foreseeable by an auditor that creditors and financiers of a corporation might rely on the audited accounts of the corporation, along with an unqualified auditor's report upon those accounts, in entering into their respective financial transactions. On those facts, does a duty of care arise which is owed to every member of the class comprising the creditors and financiers of the corporation? The fact that PMH foresaw or ought reasonably to have foreseen that a member of that class might rely on Excel's audited accounts and PMH's report thereon is pleaded in the statement **[249]** of claim but no other relevant factor is pleaded as a foundation of a duty of care. …

In actions for negligence occasioning economic loss suffered in consequence of a statement made or advice given by a defendant, foresight or reasonable foreseeability that a member of a class including the plaintiff might rely on the statement or advice and thereby suffer loss has never been held sufficient to support recovery. Something more is needed. …

[His Honour then quoted from Australian and English authorities.]

[252] The uniform course of authority shows that mere foreseeability of the possibility that a statement made or advice given by A to B might be communicated to a class of which C is a member and that C might enter into some transaction as the result thereof and suffer financial loss in that transaction is not sufficient to impose on A a duty of care owed to C in the making of the statement or the giving of the advice. In some situations, a plaintiff who has suffered pure economic loss by entering into a transaction in reliance on a statement made or advice given by a defendant may be entitled to recover without proving that the plaintiff sought the information and advice: *San Sebastian Pty Ltd v The Minister* (1986) 162 CLR 340 at 356-357. But, in every case, it is necessary for the plaintiff to allege and prove that the defendant knew or ought reasonably to have known that the information or advice would be communicated to the plaintiff, either individually or as a member of an identified class, that the information or advice would be so communicated for a purpose that would be very likely to lead the plaintiff to enter into a transaction of the kind that the plaintiff does enter into and that it would be very likely that the plaintiff would enter into such a transaction in reliance on the information or advice and thereby risk the incurring of economic loss if the statement should be untrue or the advice should be unsound. If any of these elements be wanting, the plaintiff fails to establish that the defendant owed the plaintiff a duty to use reasonable care in making the statement or giving the advice. The statement of claim does not plead these elements. Accordingly, the Full Court was correct in ordering the striking out of the relevant paragraphs of the statement of claim. ... [T]he appropriate order is ... that the appeal be dismissed.

TOOHEY and GAUDRON JJ. ... **[259]** The only question in the appeal is whether the facts pleaded in the contested paragraphs are capable of giving rise to a duty of care between Peat Marwick, as Excel's auditors, and Esanda, as a company providing finance to Excel and its associated companies. In essence, the pleaded facts are:
1. Peat Marwick were at all material times members of the Institute of Chartered Accountants in Australia and bound by the Australian Accounting Standards (par 84A).
2. At the relevant time, the Australian Accounting Standards required, in relation to a business entity, the disclosure in its audited accounts of financial information relevant to present and potential providers of equity or loan capital, and creditors (par 84B).
3. Esanda was at all relevant times a member of a class or classes of persons, namely creditors and financiers of Excel, whom Peat Marwick foresaw or ought reasonably to have foreseen might reasonably and relevantly rely on Excel's audited accounts for the year **[260]** ending 30 June 1989 and the report accompanying those accounts (par 84C).
4. Esanda relied on Excel's audited 1989 accounts and the auditor's report accompanying those accounts in deciding to enter into financial transactions with Excel and its associated companies, those transactions resulting in financial loss (par 87).

The question whether the pleaded facts are capable of giving rise to a duty of care falls to be decided in light of the law's insistence that a plaintiff who sues in negligence to recover pure economic loss must establish more than the foreseeability of loss. ... L]iability is frequently seen to depend on the plaintiff's reliance on the defendant or on the defendant's assumption of responsibility or both. Esanda relies on both considerations in this case.

Before considering Esanda's arguments with respect to reliance and assumption of responsibility, it is relevant to note some matters which are not pleaded. It is not pleaded that Esanda approached Peat Marwick for information or advice; it is not pleaded that Peat Marwick knew that Esanda was proposing to enter into the transactions in question or, indeed, any transaction with Excel or its associated companies; it is not pleaded that Peat Marwick knew that Excel's 1989 accounts or their report on the accounts would be communicated to Esanda or any other finance provider with respect to the obtaining of finance or for any other purpose. Had one or more of those matters been pleaded, Esanda might have brought itself within the duty of care recognised by Barwick CJ in *Mutual Life & Citizens' Assurance Co* **[261]** *Ltd v Evatt* (1968) 122 CLR 556 at 572-573 (note that the decision was overturned by the Privy Council in *Mutual Life & Citizens' Assurance Co Ltd v Evatt* (1970) 122 CLR 628, but the holdings of Barwick CJ have subsequently been held to be correct: see *Shaddock & Associates Pty Ltd v Parramatta City Council (No 1)* (1981) 150 CLR 225 at 251, 255-256) or that recognised by the House of Lords in *Hedley Byrne & Co Ltd v Heller & Partners Ltd* [1964] AC 465 at 497. ...

[262] It is not pleaded that Peat Marwick prepared the accounts and the audit certificate for the purpose of inducing Esanda or others to enter into financial transactions with Excel or its associated companies. Nor is it pleaded that they intended that Esanda or finance providers generally should act upon the accounts or the audit certificate in deciding to enter into financial transactions with Excel or its associated companies. Moreover, it is neither pleaded that Peat Marwick expressly or impliedly invited Esanda or finance providers generally to act on the basis that the accounts were accurate nor that they had an interest in Esanda so acting. Had one or more of these matters been pleaded, Esanda would have found support in this Court's decision in *San Sebastian Pty Ltd v The Minister* (1986) 162 CLR 340 at 357, see also at 372 per Brennan J. ...

[263] Esanda ... claims that Peat Marwick assumed responsibility to finance providers and creditors for the correctness of Excel's 1989 accounts. And as already indicated, it claims that it relied on those accounts. Moreover, it impliedly claims that it was reasonable for it to do so. ...

[265] The decided cases do not identify precisely what it is that results in liability for economic loss suffered in consequence of the voluntary [in the sense of non-requested by the recipient] provision of information or advice. However, commonsense requires the conclusion that a special relationship of proximity marked either by reliance or by the assumption of responsibility does not arise unless the person providing the information or advice has some special expertise or knowledge, or some special means of acquiring information which is not available to the recipient. Moreover, ordinary principles require that the relationship does not arise unless it is reasonable for the recipient to act on that information or advice without further inquiry. Similarly, ordinary principles require that it be reasonable for the recipient to act upon it for the purpose for which it is used. That is not to say that a special relationship of proximity exists if these conditions are satisfied. Rather, it is to say that the relationship does not arise unless they are.

There are, in our view, only two pleaded facts which are relevant to the existence of a special relationship of proximity between Esanda and Peat Marwick. The first is that Peat Marwick were Excel's [266] auditors and, inferentially, were in a situation of particular advantage to know or ascertain its true financial position. The second is that, by virtue of its membership of the Institute of Chartered Accountants in Australia, Peat Marwick accepted a general professional responsibility to ensure that Excel's audited accounts disclosed information relevant to Excel's present and potential creditors.

It was not argued that the facts pleaded are capable of sustaining a suggestion that Peat Marwick intended or encouraged Esanda to rely upon their audit of Excel's accounts. And in our view, they are not. Nor are they capable of giving rise to a relationship of proximity marked either by reliance or the assumption of responsibility for information or advice which is voluntarily provided. It may be accepted that, as Excel's auditors, Peat Marwick were in a particularly advantageous position to know or ascertain Excel's true financial position. However, there is nothing to suggest Esanda was not itself able to have accountants undertake the same task on its behalf as a condition of its entertaining the possibility of entering into financial transactions with Excel. And, which is much the same thing in the circumstances of this case, there is nothing to suggest that it was reasonable for Esanda to act on the audited reports without further inquiry.

The appeal should be dismissed.

McHUGH J. The issue in this appeal is whether the facts pleaded in a Statement of Claim are arguably sufficient in law to establish that Peat Marwick Hungerfords (Reg) ("Peat Marwick") owed a duty of care to the appellant, Esanda Finance Corporation Limited ("Esanda") in respect of the publication of an audit report commissioned by Excel Finance Corporation Limited ("Excel"). In my opinion they are not. The facts pleaded amount to no more than a claim of reasonable foreseeability of a risk of harm to Esanda which by itself is insufficient to establish that Peat Marwick owed a duty of care to Esanda. ...

[275] [T]he position in Australia to date with respect to liability for pure economic loss caused by negligent misstatement is that, absent a statement to a particular person in response to a particular request for information or advice or an assumption of responsibility to the plaintiff for that statement, it will be difficult to establish the requisite duty of care unless there is an intention to induce the recipient of the information or advice, or a class to which the recipient belongs, to act

or refrain from acting on it. Mere knowledge by a defendant that the information or advice will be communicated to the plaintiff is not enough. ... Nevertheless, the decisions have all emphasised that a lack of an intention to induce the plaintiff to act or refrain from acting is not necessarily fatal to a plaintiff's claim because other factors may be present that obviate the need for such an intention. (As Brennan J observed in *San Sebastian* (1986) 162 CLR 340 at 371, to hold otherwise would be to render "the tort of deceit otiose"; cf *R Lowe Lippmann* [1992] 2 VR 671 at 679 per Brooking J.)

In its statement of claim, Esanda does not allege an intention to induce it to rely on the audit. The question that arises therefore is whether the facts pleaded nonetheless give rise to a duty of care owed by Peat Marwick to Esanda. That is to say, does the duty of care owed **[276]** by an auditor extend to members of a class such as creditors or investors whom the auditor knows or ought reasonably to know will rely on the audit report. Alternatively, does the duty extend to members of such a class when the auditor belongs to a professional body which requires its members to consider the members of a class to be users of the audited accounts and report?

The overseas decisions
Significantly, the majority of courts that have considered the issue of auditor liability for negligent misstatement in England, Canada, New Zealand and the United States of America would hold that no duty was owed in the present case.

[His Honour then examined the course of authority in those jurisdictions.]

[281] This survey of authority in England, Canada, New Zealand and the United States shows that, absent some mutual relationship giving rise to an assumption of responsibility, the common law courts are reluctant to impose a duty of care on an auditor in favour of a third party unless the auditor intended that the audit report be given to the third party for a specific purpose. The trend is very much against expanding the liability of auditors for negligent misstatements. (This trend is apparent even in New Zealand: see *Jagwar Holdings Ltd v Julian* (1992) 6 NZCLC 68,040.)

The law in Australia
... Esanda concedes that reasonable foreseeability of harm to it from relying on the audit was not itself sufficient to impose a duty of care on Peat Marwick. But Esanda argues that a combination of circumstances exist in this and other audit cases which makes it proper to hold that an auditor in the position of Peat Marwick owes a duty of care to Esanda. The primary reason that Esanda gives for finding a duty of care in circumstances such as those pleaded in this case is that the auditor of a public company assumes a public position of trust and responsibility which demands the imposition of a duty of care. Esanda contends that by assuming responsibility for the task of auditing the accounts of public companies and providing audit certificates, auditors are representing to the world at large that the information contained in the audit and the certificate is accurate and can be relied upon. Moreover, auditors know or ought to know that persons in the position of Esanda will rely on the skill of the auditors to prepare accurate audit accounts and reports and that they may suffer loss if the audit **[282]** work is done negligently. Esanda argues that it is, therefore, reasonable to impose on auditors a duty of care in order to ensure that the information prepared and disseminated by them in fulfilling their duties, statutory or otherwise, is correct because this will encourage auditors to do their work properly. ...

In cases where audits are required by law, the law invariably imposes statutory duties on the auditors, breaches of which give rise to civil and criminal liability. Having regard to these sanctions, it is difficult to believe that giving third parties rights against auditors is likely to achieve any higher standard of care than is presently available. In cases where audits are not required by law, auditors have other incentives to maintain high standards. Clients are unlikely to retain or be attracted to an auditor who has a reputation for careless work. (These incentives to produce high standard work are of course also applicable to auditors carrying out audits that are required by law.) Negligent work in non-statutory areas may also result in the non-registration or de-registration of auditors in areas where such registration is required by law. In any event, the increased standard of care argument is only one of a number of factors to be weighed in determining whether a duty of care to outsiders should be imposed on auditors. At least six other factors arise for consideration.

Further factors relevant to the existence of a duty of care

First, whether or not imposing a duty in favour of third parties will deter auditors from being careless, extending liability will probably reduce the supply of their services. Courts often assume that insurance against extended tort liability is readily obtainable and that the increased cost of an extension of liability can be spread among clients by the payment of additional premiums for insurance. But insurance in this field may not be as readily obtainable as courts assume. Insurers are reluctant to insure against risks which are difficult to quantify, as they usually are when the number and amount of the claims arising from the risk are difficult to estimate. Lord Oliver addressed this factor in *Caparo Industries plc v Dickman* [1990] 2 AC 605 at 643 when he questioned the ability **[283]** of auditors to insure against such risks if liability depended on "only the foreseeability of possible damage without some further control".

Extending the liability of auditors for negligent misstatements may also reduce the demand for their services. Even when insurance is obtainable, increasing fees to pay for the cost of additional insurance may result in a reduction of demand for audit services in cases where the law does not require regular audits. Experience in the United States suggests that some of the smaller accounting firms may be forced out of business. If demand slackens because of unsuccessful attempts to pass on the cost of increased premiums, auditors must either lose the business or absorb the whole or part of the cost in an attempt to regain that business. Unless auditors are making excessive profits (which is not likely in a competitive field), absorbing the cost of insurance may force them to reduce other overheads such as the time spent or the number of personnel engaged in audits. Ironically, such cost cutting may lead to a reduction in the standard of care. Or, as Lucas CJ suggested in the Californian Supreme Court in *Bily v Arthur Young & Co* (1992) 834 P 2d 745 at 766, auditors may respond by reducing audit services to high risk businesses where there is a greater likelihood of failure and therefore of liability to investors and creditors.

Thus, the result of widening the circumstances in which auditors will owe a duty of care to third parties may be: (i) a significant increase in the cost of auditing services; (ii) a decrease in the competition for or the provision of such services; and (iii) a reduction in the standard of those services.

This would be detrimental to the interests of creditors, investors and business generally.

Second, no examination of the public interest should overlook the effect of an extension of auditor's liability on the administration of the court system. Experience of claims against auditors by public company liquidators (even claims in respect of proprietary companies or unincorporated businesses are likely to be reasonably lengthy) over the last thirty years in this country indicates that almost any claim is likely to take many months to hear, not to mention the time taken in interlocutory matters and appeals. ...

Any extension of auditor's liability to cover cases such as the present is likely to mean that courts and judges hearing such cases will be tied up for many months – sometimes for more than a year – to the detriment of other litigants. Only the most insistent demands of corrective justice should induce the common law courts to mould legal rules to cover cases that bring about this consequence in an era when court resources are already stretched to breaking point and courts are forced to send many cases out to private arbitrators for determination.

However, the need for a rule to correct perceived injustice to third party plaintiffs in audit actions is not compelling. If the liability of auditors was extended to third parties in circumstances such as those alleged here, the common law would be conferring rights on a sophisticated group who have the means in most cases to take steps to avoid the risk of loss. ...

It is by no means certain that the demands of corrective justice require auditors rather than these sophisticated creditors and investors to absorb the losses that flow from lending to or investing in the **[285]** auditor's client. ...

Creditors and investors ... are likely to be in a better position than auditors to know the likely extent of their losses. The investor or creditor knows the maximum extent of any likely loss. Unlike most plaintiffs in negligence cases, these investors and creditors can take steps to protect themselves against loss. ... [T]he question is whether investors and creditors, as one class, or auditors as the other can most efficiently absorb the losses which flow from the conduct of the clients of auditors.

Whichever class bears the loss, it is likely that the public will have to pay, directly or indirectly, for the risk of those losses. ...

[286] From the public's point of view, therefore, the primary question is, who is the more efficient absorber of the losses?

Esanda put no material before this Court establishing that auditors rather than the likely class of third party plaintiffs can more efficiently absorb the losses that flow to those plaintiffs as a result of their dealings with the audited client. That being so, this Court should be extremely cautious before extending auditor's liability to cover cases like this one.

Third, creditors and shareholders already have an indirect remedy against the auditors in many cases. The liquidator or receiver can bring an action on behalf of the audited client. ... [B]ecause of the liquidator's remedy, an extension of auditor liability may mean only that creditors and investors who relied on the audit report increase the amount that they will already receive from an action by the liquidator against the auditor.

Fourth, the client's conduct is the primary cause of the plaintiff's loss; the auditor's role is secondary. In addition, the accounts are ordinarily prepared by the client and, in any event, are that person's responsibility: *Bily v Arthur Young & Co* (1992) 834 P 2d 745 at 762. Each case must be judged on its own facts. But it would have to be an exceptional case for the client and all its servants and agents to be innocent of fraud or negligence in relation to the publication of accounts that are false or misleading. In most cases, one would think that the major cause of the plaintiff's loss was the [287] conduct of the client or its employees, rather than the auditor. Yet because auditors are sued only when the plaintiff cannot recover in full from the client, it is usually the case that the "auditor has now assumed center stage as the remaining solvent defendant and is faced with a claim for all sums of money ever loaned to or invested in the client" (*Bily* (1992) 834 P 2d 745 at 763) which have not been repaid. The auditor is left to foot the bill even though on a comparative basis the auditor may bear only a minor and secondary responsibility for the plaintiff's loss.

Fifth, the need for a plaintiff to prove that he or she relied on the audit report means that the auditor's liability is often problematical even when the auditor has been guilty of gross carelessness. Years after the event, a court has to decide what was the plaintiff's state of mind at the time of extending the credit or making the investment. ... At a trial, years after the event, these creditors and investors may honestly testify that they relied on the audit in making their credit or investment decisions. But if the truth could be known, it may turn out that the audit was no more than background material for their decisions. Sophisticated creditors and investors who study audit reports before making decisions are unlikely to regard that study as sufficient "due diligence".

Consciously or unconsciously, they are likely to be influenced by a myriad of other factors. ...

[288] Sixth, the factual issues that arise in auditor's liability cases – was the auditor's opinion negligent, did the plaintiff rely on the audit? – make it almost impossible for an auditor to avoid a trial or settlement even when the auditor is not liable to the plaintiff. ... [T]he likely length and expense of most audit actions will mean that an auditor has to settle a case that, if tried, would be found to be without merit.

The prospect of vexatious or near vexatious litigation is a matter to be considered in fashioning a legal rule ... .

[289] Although considered individually none of the six factors to which I have referred points decisively against imposing a duty of care to cover a case such as the present, collectively they support the conclusion that the demands of corrective justice do not require the imposition of such a duty.

In the end, the most powerful point for holding that auditors owe a duty of care in cases like the present is that investors and creditors suffer their losses because they have relied, as the auditor knew or ought reasonably to have known they would, on his or her report, and the auditor has made that report carelessly. As against that, however, is the fact that the auditor did not invite or intend them to rely on it and they have paid nothing to the auditor for the preparation of the work. They require the auditor to compensate them for the loss that arose from their self-induced reliance, but they were not prepared to pay for the auditor's work.

In addition, the result of extending liability will ordinarily be to impose a financial burden on the auditor out of all proportion to his or her comparative fault, and the risk of imposing that liability and burden may be contrary to the public interest. Moreover, the plaintiff has failed to prove that the demands of corrective justice require a remedy for the plaintiff. In these circumstances, the case for extending liability to cover cases like the present is not compelling. In the absence of cogent evidence that the public interest or corrective justice requires an extension of auditor's liability to cases where no more appears than that the auditor knows that the plaintiff might rely on the audited accounts and report, this Court should not extend the liability of auditors to such cases. ...

[292] The appeal should be dismissed with costs.

GUMMOW J. ...

[302] Auditor's negligence

[303] ... In framing any applicable principle in this area, including what have been called "control mechanisms", it is important to have regard to a number of considerations. First, in many cases the corporate client of the auditor will be insolvent and may be in receivership, liquidation or under some other form of administration; the third party seeks to elevate itself beyond the status of other creditors by seeking a solvent defendant from which to recoup the consequences of its poor business judgment in financing or otherwise dealing with the company. Secondly, the alleged negligence of the auditor necessarily will be subsidiary to the failures of the corporation which prepared the accounts the auditor certified.

Thirdly, the auditing process involves rather more than the statement of a verifiable fact, such as the zoning of a particular parcel of land. The discharge by the auditor of its statutory functions requires a complex process which may involve differences of professional opinion. Fourthly, the plaintiff in a case such as the present in substance seeks to render the auditor liable as if it had given, but without receipt of reciprocal value for doing so, a guarantee to a range of third parties who finance the operations of the corporation; this [304] guarantee is unlimited in amount and lacks the protection of various doctrines by which the courts have shown a tenderness to sureties.

Finally, the recipients of that guarantee, such as Esanda, are in quite a different league to the consumer in product liability cases. A financier such as Esanda would not lack power to deal from a position of strength in ordering its commercial relationship with the party to whom it provided financial accommodation. ...

[311] The appeal should be dismissed with costs.

[Dawson J delivered a concurring judgment.]

Appeal dismissed

Hill v Van Erp
(1997) 188 CLR 159
High Court of Australia

A lawyer drafting and in control of the execution of a will pursuant to a contractual retainer for a client may owe a duty of care in tort to an intended beneficiary of the client's estate.

[Mrs Currey, a client of the defendant (appellant) solicitor, wished to change her will, which had been prepared by the defendant. The defendant drafted a new will, as instructed, with a bequest of Mrs Currey's house to Mrs Currey's son and to her neighbour and friend, the plaintiff (respondent), as tenants in common in equal shares. The will also include a gift to the plaintiff of some household goods. The defendant brought the new will to Mrs Currey's house where it was duly signed by her, and signed as attesting witnesses by the defendant, and at the defendant's request, by the plaintiff's husband. The consequence of the plaintiff's husband attesting the will was that the testamentary dispositions to the plaintiff failed by virtue of s 15(1) of the *Succession Act 1981* (Qld) and the relevant property was instead received by Mrs Currey's next of kin entitled on intestacy. The plaintiff sued the defendant for negligence in the District Court of Queensland and was awarded damages. After the defendant's appeal to the Queensland Court of Appeal failed, she appealed to the High Court Australia. The parties were agreed as to negligence, causation of loss and damages, so that the only issue was whether the defendant owed a duty of care to the plaintiff, a third party to the contractual relationship between Mrs Currey and the defendant, to avoid causing her pure economic loss. A majority of the court, Brennan CJ, Dawson, Toohey, Gaudron, and Gummow JJ; McHugh J dissenting, held that she did. The judgment of Gummow J is extracted below. The decision in this case also marked the beginning of the end of the concept of proximity as the conceptual determinant of the existence of a duty of care, but Gummow J's judgment is not extracted on that point.]

GUMMOW J. [footnotes omitted in whole or in part] …

[223] *The legal framework*
I turn to consider the general framework of the legal relationships between the testatrix, her estate, the intended beneficiary, and the solicitor, within which the intended beneficiary makes the present claim in tort. One consideration of some significance when determining the existence of a duty of care is the provision already made, if any, by the general law in that regard. This is not with a view to supplanting by the tort of negligence other established principle, carefully developed in existing authority, but to determine whether there is a need consistently with the overall policy of the law to provide a coherent and comprehensive system of civil obligations, to supplement those established rules (*Hawkins v Clayton* (1988) 164 CLR 539 at 584).

One of the important functions of an effective law of personal obligations is to facilitate the operation of those elements of the law of **[224]** property which enable the transmission of ownership whether by a transaction inter vivos or post mortem. At least since the commencement of the *Wills Act 1837* (UK) (274), s 3, the law has favoured a full power of testamentary disposition. …

The legal profession plays, and is widely perceived to play, an important part in the exercise of the freedom of testation. In practice, the public relies on the legal profession for the preparation of effective wills, and a coherent law of obligations ought not to leave ineffectual, in a practical sense, the undoubted responsibility in that regard of the solicitor to the client. …

[T]he third party, here the intended beneficiary, seeks recompense which affords her protection against negligent performance by the promisor, the solicitor, of the solicitor's obligations to the promisee, the testator.

[225] In *White v Jones* [1995] 2 AC 207 at 223-224, in the Court of Appeal, Sir Donald Nicholls V-C said,
    The law of contract is unable to provide the remedy [against the solicitor]. In some cases, where the purpose of a contract is to confer a benefit on a third party, the purpose can be achieved, in the event of breach, by the court making an order compelling the party in breach specifically to perform his obligation to make a payment or confer some other benefit on a third party (See *Beswick v Beswick* [1968] AC 58). That route is not available here. The solicitor did not agree to confer a benefit on the intended beneficiary. He agreed to take steps to enable his client to do so. Specific performance of that agreement is no longer possible once the client has died. I have, indeed, considered whether a remedy for breach of contract could be shaped whereby, the client having lost the opportunity to make a gift to the intended beneficiary, (1) his estate should be regarded as having lost a sum equal to the amount of the intended gift, and (2) the executors should hold that sum, when recovered from the solicitor, upon trust for the intended beneficiary.

In the event, his Lordship did not shape any such remedy. In the House of Lords Lord Goff of Chieveley considered but rejected (at 266-267) the possibility of bringing the instant case within the group of decisions described in *The Albazero* [1977] AC 774 at 846-847. There a plaintiff may sue in contract and recover damages for a loss suffered by a third party on the footing that the plaintiff be accountable to the third party for the damages so recovered (cf in tort, as to recovery of the value of services to be gratuitously provided, *Griffiths v Kerkemeyer* (1977) 139 CLR 161). It should be borne in mind that whatever criticisms may fairly be made of the privity doctrine, there remains "a sensible concern not to allow every breach of contract to generate a tort claim by any third party who had an interest in the performance of that contract" (Stapleton, "Duty of Care: Peripheral Parties and Alternative Opportunities for Deterrence", *Law Quarterly Review,* vol 111 (1995) 301, at p 324).

Mrs Van Erp does not frame her complaint as one against the next **[226]** of kin, alleging their unjust enrichment at her expense. She is correct in not doing so. There has been some support in the academic literature for development of a remedy to force the party taking under the unaltered or unrevoked will to transfer the benefit in question to the intended beneficiary, at least where that party knew of the later and, in the event, unfulfilled intentions of the testator. But in the present case the qualifying or vitiating factor would be negligence of Mrs Hill, something for which the next of kin bore no responsibility. ...

[227] [T]he intended beneficiary usually will be a volunteer, unable to rely upon contractual rights in his or her favour. In *Seale v Perry* [1982] VR 193, Murphy J was a member of the majority which allowed the appeal by the solicitor against the award of damages to the plaintiffs, the testamentary gift to whom by the solicitor's client had failed because the will had not been attested according to law. His Honour said (at 220) that the plaintiffs were volunteers whom equity would not assist; nor would equity perfect the imperfect gift.

Nevertheless, in *Seale v Perry* consideration no doubt passed from the client to the solicitor. The plaintiffs would have benefited from proper performance of that contract but were strangers to it. It is true that the general principle is that equity does not assist volunteers. But, as Mason CJ and McHugh J pointed out *Corin v Patton* (1990) 169 CLR 540 at 588, the rationale for refusing to complete an incomplete gift is that the donor should not be compelled to do so, the decision to give being a personal one for the donor to make. That consideration does not apply where the complaint of the prospective donee is that the donor died with an **[228]** apparently unchanged intention to confer testamentary bounty, but that intention has miscarried for want of compliance with legal formalities. ...

[His Honour then considered whether any equitable principles or remedies would assist the plaintiff, and concluded that there were no circumstances that would attract equity's intervention.]

[229] Accordingly, the claim by Mrs Van Erp in negligence was made in circumstances where, as they presently exist, the other constituent elements comprising the general law of civil obligations afforded her no satisfactory remedy in respect of the failure of Mrs Currey successfully to implement her testamentary intentions in favour of Mrs Van Erp. The question then becomes one of the role, if any, of the law of tort, particularly negligence, to provide a remedy.

Known reliance and assumption of responsibility
The primary task of the courts is to quell controversy, not only as to matters of fact, but by appropriate development of principle. The goal must be that, so far as practicable, the rights of litigants, individual, corporate, or governmental, may be ascertained, and the correlative liabilities accepted, by reference to criteria of some specificity and without recourse to the courts at trial, let alone appellate, level. ...

It may be expressing the point too strongly to say that any attempts to establish a single general principle of liability for all negligence cases, "which run the gamut from physical injury to emotional distress to various kinds of economic loss", will be shown "to be as hopeless as it is unwise" (Christie, "The Uneasy Place of Principle in Tort Law", in Owen (ed), *Philosophical Foundations of Tort Law* (1995) 113, at p 123). Nevertheless, some such concern does appear to be reflected in the joint judgment in *Bryan v Maloney* (1995) 182 CLR 609 at 618-619, per Mason CJ, Deane and Gaudron JJ. There their Honours described as "special" the categories of case in which a duty to take reasonable care to avoid causing mere economic loss would arise. They added:

> Commonly, but not necessarily, they will involve an identified element of known reliance (or dependence) or the assumption of responsibility or a combination of the two.

The use of the imprecise and beguiling but deceptively simple terms "known reliance" and "assumption of responsibility" in a number of recent decisions in this field has been subject to stringent criticism by **[230]** judges (*Smith v Bush* [1990] 1 AC 831 at 864-865, per Lord Griffiths; *Caparo plc v Dickman* [1990] 2 AC 605 at 628, per Lord Roskill) and in academic writing. Doubt has been expressed that they have sufficient coherence to dispose of novel cases. Further, it has been said that the picture of liability, now hidden by the language of voluntariness and reliance, is particularly untidy and beset with a multiplicity of concerns, and that the law of negligence would benefit greatly were the courts to set aside these conceptual veils and confront this complex picture.

The objective of such confrontation should be that thereafter, on given facts, issues of liability will be susceptible of determination without recourse to the courts. However, the field of liability in negligence for pure economic loss is a comparatively new area. It also is a developing area. The case law will advance from one precedent to the next.

In the present case, the respondent, Mrs Van Erp, did not assert in her favour any identified element of known reliance or dependence by her upon the discharge by Mrs Hill of her professional obligations in seeing to the execution of Mrs Currey's will. However, it was contended that Mrs Hill voluntarily assumed responsibility for the making by the testatrix of a valid will reflecting her intentions, including the bounty to the respondent. The submission was that Mrs Hill did so by holding herself out as having and lending a professional skill for that purpose.

The difficulty with that submission is that the evidence does not disclose, in any specific sense, any assumption of responsibility by Mrs Hill other than to her client. In *Marc Rich & Co v Bishop Rock Ltd* [1996] 1 AC 211 at 238, Lord Steyn, speaking for the majority of the House of Lords, responded to the submission that the classification society had assumed responsibility to the cargo owners when conducting a survey of the vessel in question (which later sank) on instructions of the ship owners, by stressing that it was "not even suggested that the cargo owners were aware that [the society] had been brought in to survey the vessel". On the other hand, in *White v Jones* [1995] 2 AC 207 at 294, Lord Nolan said:

> A professional man ... who undertakes to exercise his skill in a manner which, to his knowledge, may cause loss to others if carelessly performed, may thereby implicitly assume a legal responsibility towards them.

[231] In *White v Jones* (at 274-275), Lord Browne-Wilkinson sought to meet criticism of the use in such contexts of the phrase "assumption of responsibility". His Lordship said that it should be understood as referring "to a conscious assumption of responsibility for the task rather than a conscious assumption of legal liability to the plaintiff for its careful performance". Any such general notion of "assumption of responsibility" by reference to the performance of services and without identification of those to whom or for whose benefit they are performed has attracted criticism, with which I agree.

The role of the law of tort

Bingham LJ has observed that, like equity, the law of torts may, in appropriate circumstances, fill what otherwise are perceived to be "gaps" in what should be one coherent system of law (*Simaan Contracting Co v Pilkington Ltd (No 2)* [1988] QB 758 at 782). Professor Francis Reynolds has written ("Contract and Tort: The View from the Contract Side of the Fence", *Canterbury Law Review*, vol 5 (1993) 280, at p 281):

> The aim of the law should be to devise principles which provide a way of solving disputes between private persons (including of course corporations); *rivalry* between principles, as opposed to a study of their interaction and interrelation, is unlikely to be productive. We are used to such interaction of the principles of restitution with contract and (subject to problems of integration) equity. We should accept it also in the case of tort.

That, of course, is not to assert that the function of the law of tort, with respect to recovery of economic loss caused other than by reliance upon deceitful statements, is limited to the filling in of gaps left by the law of contract. But it is a starting point for consideration of the present case. ...

[232] Does it matter that the result of so doing will be to compensate for failure in the mere expectation of receipt of the testatrix's bounty? A basic difference between the measure of damages recoverable in contract and tort often is said to be that it is only in contract that damages may be recovered for expectations or benefits not realised, as opposed to losses actually suffered or expenses incurred. The substance of the proposition is that the objective of damages in contract is to put the plaintiff in the position the plaintiff would have enjoyed if the contract had been performed whilst award of damages in tort seeks to place the plaintiff in the position that would have been occupied if the tort had not been committed. However, care is needed before accepting

any such propositions as universally applicable. In this case, the complaint of the plaintiff arises from failure to **[233]** perform services so that the testamentary benefit has not been provided. The allegation here of pure economic loss thus embraces (and may properly embrace) failure to provide the benefit, an "expectation interest".

The disposition of this appeal

One asks what there was in the circumstances, including the existence of Mrs Van Erp as the object (identified by Mrs Currey to Mrs Hill) of intended testamentary bounty, which was sufficient to generate, between Mrs Hill and Mrs Van Erp, a duty of care in tort to supplement the dry right of action by the estate against Mrs Hill (cf *White v Jones* [1995] 2 AC 207 at 276, 291, 295).

The matter may be approached by asking whether the relationship between Mrs Hill and Mrs Van Erp was "equivalent to contract". That term was used by Lord Shaw in *Nocton v Lord Ashburton* [1914] AC 932 at 972 and taken up by Lord Devlin in *Hedley Byrne & Co Ltd v Heller & Partners Ltd* [1964] AC 465 at 529-530. It was directed by their Lordships immediately to cases where there was an "assumption of responsibility" in circumstances in which, but for the absence of consideration, there would be a contract. Here there was a contract. But Mrs Van Erp was not a party to it, although if the contract had been duly performed she would have benefited therefrom. The use of contractual analogies in development of new duties of care may make little sense where what is involved is the attachment of responsibilities to relationships which in substance and form are non-contractual. However, that is not this case.

The expression "equivalent to contract", in the context of the present factual matrix, may be understood as embracing a situation where (a) the transmission of the property in question from the client of the defendant to the plaintiff was the objective sought to be accomplished by the contract, and (b) the plaintiff had no interest in the matter adverse to that of the client, yet default by the defendant in performance of her contractual obligations otherwise sounds only in ineffective legal remedies. The duty of the solicitor was one of imperfect obligation. The law of tort operates in such circumstances to complete and vindicate fulfilment of that contractual obligation.

Dean Prosser has pointed out (Prosser, *Selected Topics on the Law of Torts* (1982), Ch VII, "The Borderland of Tort and Contract", pp 391-402) that, in the development of the law relating, for example, to the duties of bailees to bailors and of occupiers of land to invitees and licensees, there have been other instances of extension of liability in negligence by reference to **[234]** concurrent contractual relationships. More recently, in *Al-Kandari v JR Brown & Co* [1988] QB 665 at 675, Bingham LJ said:

> A solicitor owes a duty of care to his client. If the client intends to confer a benefit on a third party, the solicitor may owe a duty to the third party to take reasonable care to see that effect is given to the client's intentions.

This is an illustration of the proposition espoused by Mason CJ, Deane and Gaudron JJ in *Bryan v Maloney* (1995) 182 CLR 609 at 621 that, in some circumstances, the existence of a contract will provide the occasion for, and constitute a factor favouring the existence of, a liability in negligence between one or other of the parties to the contract and a third party.

It is, as I have indicated, well understood that the trust may operate to protect the interests of those concerned in a contractual relationship and to vindicate rights derived therefrom. This was stressed by Mason and Deane JJ in *Gosper v Sawyer* (1985) 160 CLR 548 at 568-569. In a case such as the present, so also does the law of tort. That was the approach taken by Sir Donald Nicholls V-C in *White v Jones* [1995] 2 AC 207 at 223. The result is to assist the desirable coherence of the law of obligations.

Not only the foreseeability of harm to Mrs Van Erp as specific legatee and devisee but a complex of other factors combine to summon into existence a duty of care owed by Mrs Hill to Mrs Van Erp to ensure execution of the will in such a manner as not to attract the invalidating operation of s 15 of the Act. These matters include the extent to which the engagement of Mrs Hill by the testatrix plainly was designed to enhance the economic position of Mrs Van Erp as a particular individual, the control exercised (as a practical matter) over the realisation by the testatrix of her testamentary intentions towards Mrs Van Erp, and the closeness of the connection between the request by Mrs Hill to Mr Van Erp that he attest the will and the direct legal effect thereof, being the consequent failure of the gifts to Mrs Van Erp by the will. There is also the public interest in the promotion of professional competence and the avoidance of disappointment of the wishes and expectations of testators and beneficiaries by negligent actions of solicitors (*Gartside v Sheffield, Young & Ellis* [1983] NZLR 37 at 51).

Consequences
So to determine the present matter is ... **[235]** by no means to espouse any general proposition to the effect that if A promises B to perform a service for B which B intends, and A knows, will confer a benefit on C if performed, A owes to C a duty in tort to perform that service with reasonable skill and care. The question whether this or any variant of a proposition in such broad terms should be accepted must be left for another day. The present case lies in a narrower compass. Recently, in *Goodwill v Pregnancy Advisory Service* [1996] 1 WLR 1397 at 1403, Peter Gibson LJ said:

> It must be recognised that *White v Jones* belonged to an unusual class of cases. A remedy in tort was fashioned to overcome the rank injustice that the only persons who might have a valid claim (the testator and his estate) had suffered no loss and the only persons who had suffered a loss (the disappointed beneficiaries) had no claim.

In *Bryan v Maloney* (1995) 182 CLR 609 at 618, Mason CJ, Deane and Gaudron JJ said:

> One policy consideration which may militate against recognition of a relationship of proximity in a category of case involving mere economic loss is the law's concern to avoid the imposition of liability 'in an indeterminate amount for an indeterminate time to an indeterminate class'.

Their Honours were referring to the well-known passage in the judgment of Chief Judge Cardozo in *Ultramares Corporation v Touche* (1931) 174 NE 441 at 444. They continued (at 618):

> Another consideration is the perception that, in a competitive world where one person's economic gain is commonly another's loss, a duty to take reasonable care to avoid causing mere economic loss to another, as distinct from physical injury to another's person **[236]** or property, may be inconsistent with community standards in relation to what is ordinarily legitimate in the pursuit of personal advantage.

Neither of these considerations applies in the present case in a manner adversely to the recognition of liability in the appellant. The existence of a duty of care owed to Mrs Van Erp by Mrs Hill does not involve the creation of a liability which is indeterminate as to quantum, identity of plaintiff, or time. There is no occasion for imposition of the "control mechanisms" which have been seen as necessary curbs upon liability for negligent misstatement or for pure economic loss in such cases. See *Esanda Finance Corporation Ltd v Peat Marwick Hungerfords* (1997) 188 CLR 241.

Further, escape by Mrs Hill from financial responsibility for failure to exercise professional skill in accordance with her undertaking would be inconsistent with what might be thought ordinarily legitimate in the pursuit of personal advantage. Nor, as I have sought to demonstrate, does the law otherwise offer to a person in the position of Mrs Van Erp recourse in respect of the consequences of negligent performance by Mrs Hill as promisor of professional duties owed to Mrs Currey as promisee.

Lord Browne-Wilkinson pointed out in *White v Jones* that in a class of case (which includes this appeal) the consequences of the negligence of a solicitor usually will not immediately be apparent and will take effect only on the death of the testator. At that point in time the interest of the intended beneficiary would have matured beyond a spes, yet the error which will cause this not to come to pass will have become permanently incapable of direct remedy in jurisdictions where there is no statutory provision such as those found in South Australia, New South Wales and Victoria (*Wills Act 1936* (SA), s 12(2); *Wills, Probate and Administration Act 1898* (NSW), s 13; *Wills Act 1958* (Vic), s 13).

Moreover, in a case such as the present there can be no conflict of interest between the solicitor and the testatrix and the intended beneficiaries. To impose upon the solicitor a duty in tort towards the intended beneficiaries is not to mandate a conflict of interest. The duty owed by Mrs Hill to Mrs Currey involved the implementation of Mrs Currey's wish to bestow her property upon Mrs Van Erp. The existence of a duty of care in tort owed by Mrs Hill to Mrs Van Erp does not cut across the basic proposition that, subject to professional rules and standards, the solicitor owes duties to the court as well as its officers and to the client but not, in general, to the other parties with whom the client is dealing in the relevant transaction.

In *White v Jones* [1995] 2 AC 207 at 223, the Vice-Chancellor illustrated this basic **[237]** proposition by contrasting cases such as that before him with various examples. These illustrated such propositions as that the solicitor for the vendor does not normally become subject to a duty of care to the purchaser (cf *Gran Gelato Ltd v Richcliff Ltd* [1992] Ch 560 at 569-571). The solicitor acting for a party who is engaged in "hostile" civil litigation owes a duty to the client and to the court but normally does not owe any duty to the opponent of the client (*Al-Kandari v J R Brown & Co* [1988] QB 665 at 672, 675; cf as to prosecuting authorities *Elguzouli-Daf v Commissioner of Police* [1995] QB 335 at 348-349). ...

The imposition of liability upon the appellant in tort as sought by the respondent does not invade any area which the legislature has dealt with in the Act in a fashion intended to be exhaustive. The effect is not to gainsay the operation of s 15, but to reinforce the need for professional advisers to ensure compliance with it by testators. ...

[239]*Conclusion*
The appeal should be dismissed with costs.

Appeal dismissed

Caltex Oil (Australia) Pty Ltd v The Dredge "Willemstad"
(1976) 136 CLR 529
High Court of Australia

As a matter of principle, a duty of care may be owed in respect of pure economic loss suffered by another person as a result of the defendant's negligent act, as distinct from a negligent misstatement.

GIBBS J. **[535]** The appeals now before us are from judgments delivered in three of four actions which were heard together by Sheppard J in the Supreme Court of New South Wales.

The actions were brought to recover damage caused when a dredge, the "Willemstad", fractured a pipeline which was laid on the bed of Botany Bay and which connected an oil refinery at Kurnell, on the southern shore, with an oil terminal at Banksmeadow, on the northern shore. Both the refinery and the pipeline (which in fact comprised four pipes) were owned by Australian Oil Refining Pty Ltd ("AOR") and the terminal was owned by Caltex Oil (Australia) Pty Ltd ("Caltex"). The pipeline was used to carry products of the refinery to the terminal. By agreement between Caltex and AOR, Caltex supplied crude oil to the refinery for processing, and the product was delivered to Caltex either into a vessel at the AOR wharf or by way of the pipeline to the Caltex terminal. Although the product carried through the pipeline belonged to Caltex, the agreement provided that the risk of damage or loss rested with AOR. ...

[536] The dredge was able to navigate, not only by conventional means, but also by the use of equipment supplied by Decca Survey Australia Ltd ("Decca"), by which the position of the dredge could be fixed with great accuracy by receiving and plotting radio signals transmitted from the shore. To enable Decca's system to be used, there was prepared a track plotter chart showing the area to be dredged, and on which the track of the vessel could be seen and if necessary recorded. An employee of Decca had drawn on the track plotter chart parallel lines showing the western boundary of area A, beyond which dredging ought not to be carried out, lest it endanger the pipeline, and showing also the pipeline itself. The lines were incorrectly drawn ... .

AOR and Caltex each brought an action in rem in the Admiralty jurisdiction of the Supreme Court against the "Willemstad". Each also brought an action in the Common Law Division against Decca. ... The learned trial judge found that the damage to the pipeline was caused by the negligent navigation of the dredge and also by the negligence of a servant or agent of Decca in wrongly marking the lines on the chart. In the actions in rem he gave judgment for the plaintiffs against certain Netherlands companies who **[537]** were respectively the owner and the charterers of the dredge. ... However, in the action in rem brought by Caltex, the amount for which judgment was given was in respect of matters not involved in this appeal, and no damages were allowed to Caltex for economic loss which it suffered as a result of the damage to the pipeline. ... In the action by Caltex against Decca, judgment was given for the defendant, for the reason that the only loss suffered by Caltex as a result of Decca's negligence was economic loss which the learned trial judge held was not recoverable.

On these appeals three distinct questions fall for decision: ... (3) whether Caltex was entitled to recover damages for economic loss. ...

[543] (3) Damage for economic loss.
As a result of the damage to the pipeline some of the refined product then being carried through the pipes was lost. Although **[544]** that product was owned by Caltex, it was at the risk of AOR, which has been compensated for its loss. The loss in respect of which Caltex seeks to recover damages was entirely economic in nature, and did not flow from the loss of the product. By reason of the damage to the pipeline Caltex lost its normal means of obtaining deliveries of petroleum products at the Banksmeadow terminal while the pipeline was being repaired and restored to service. ... It is unnecessary to go into the details of the expense to which Caltex was put by reason of the breakage of the pipeline. It was admitted by the parties that if Caltex was entitled to judgment in respect of the damage to the pipeline which occurred on the night of 25th-26th October 1971 the proper amount to be awarded is $95,000, which, it was admitted, does not include any amount for the loss of the product of the refinery.

In these circumstances it becomes necessary to consider whether a person is entitled to be compensated in damages for economic loss sustained by that person as a result of damage negligently caused to the property of a third party. The further question arises whether a person whose property has been physically damaged as the result of a negligent act may recover compensation for economic loss which was not a consequence of that physical damage but which happened to be caused by the negligent act that caused the physical damage.

Of course it is clearly settled that where personal injury or physical damage to property has been caused by a negligent act, the damages which may be recovered include compensation for all pecuniary loss suffered as a result of the injury or damage. The assessment of the pecuniary loss suffered by an injured plaintiff is an everyday task performed by judges and juries hearing negligence cases. However, before the decision in *Hedley Byrne & Co Ltd v Heller & Partners Ltd* [1964] AC 465 it appeared to have been established that a plaintiff who sustained economic loss which resulted from loss or damage negligently caused to the property of a third person was not entitled to recover damages. The simplest explanation of these decisions appears **[545]** to be that it was thought that the wrongdoer owed the plaintiff no duty to take care to avoid causing him loss which was purely economic, although in some cases the reason given was that the damage was too remote, for in this as well as in other branches of the law of negligence questions of duty of care and remoteness of damage are difficult to disentangle. ...

[551] It may be right to say, as Lord Devlin said, that the distinction between recovery for economic loss and recovery for material loss is illogical, but that does not mean that the decisions that have drawn that distinction were erroneous, because the law aims at practical justice rather than logical consistency. However, I am in respectful agreement with Lord Denning MR in *SCM (United Kingdom) Ltd v WJ Whittall & Son Ltd* [1971] 1 QB, at p 344 that the distinction is not lacking in common sense. If a person committing an act of negligence were liable for all economic loss foreseeably resulting therefrom, an act of careless inadvertence might expose the person guilty of it to claims unlimited in number and crippling in amount. For example, if, through the momentary inattention of an officer, a ship collided with a bridge, and as a result a large suburban area, which included shops and factories, was deprived of its main means of access to a city, great loss might be suffered by tens of thousands of persons, but to require the wrongdoer to compensate all those who had suffered pecuniary loss would impose upon him a burden out of all proportion to his wrong. Similarly, the driver of a vehicle which collided with a pylon carrying electric power lines in an industrial area might dislocate the work of dozens of **[552]** factories. It is true that under modern conditions some claims arising from physical injury or material damage can be very large in amount – for example if a passenger train were derailed. Nevertheless, the extent of claims for loss that is purely economic is likely to be very much wider than that of claims arising out of physical injury and material damage. Further, a law which imposed a general duty to take care to avoid causing foreseeable pecuniary loss to others would, as Widgery J suggested, interfere greatly with the ordinary affairs of life. There are sound reasons of policy why economic loss should not be treated in exactly the same way as material loss.

One possible view of the decision in *Hedley Byrne & Co Ltd v Heller & Partners Ltd* [1964] AC 465 is that it allows the recovery of economic loss only if it was caused by negligent misrepresentations, and thus creates a limited exception to the general rule that there is no liability for unintentional negligent infliction of economic loss which is not itself consequential upon foreseeable physical injury or damage to property. That seems to have been the view of Winn LJ in *SCM (United Kingdom) Ltd v WJ Whittall & Son Ltd* [1971] 1 QB, at p 352. If this were correct, negligent misstatements, which were thought to give rise to no liability at all, now entail a liability for damages of a kind which cannot be recovered if the negligence consists in acts rather than in words. That would be a surprising result. It is often not easy to decide whether a particular act of negligence can rightly be described as a negligent misstatement or as negligent conduct. In the present case, for example, it would be possible to argue that Decca's action in making available an erroneously marked chart amounted to a misrepresentation as to the situation of the pipeline. I would not accept that argument, but it illustrates the fine distinctions that would arise if it were held that the rule in *Hedley Byrne & Co Ltd v Heller & Partners Ltd* [1964] AC 465 applied only to negligent misrepresentations. ...

[554] The majority of the Court of Appeal in *Spartan Steel & Alloys Ltd v Martin & Co (Contractors) Ltd* [1973] 1 QB 27 comprised Lord Denning MR and Lawton LJ. Lord Denning MR expressed his conclusion as follows ([1973] 1 QB, at p 37):

> The more I think about these cases, the more difficult I find it to put each into its proper pigeon-hole. Sometimes I say: "There was no duty." In others I say: "The damage was too remote." So much so that I think the time has come to discard those tests which have proved so elusive. It seems to me better to consider the particular relationship in hand, and see whether or not, as a matter of policy, economic loss should be recoverable, or not.

[555] I would, with respect, completely agree that it is necessary to consider the particular relationship in hand, but cannot think that the law leaves it entirely to the court to decide as a matter of policy whether the economic loss should be recoverable. The other member of the majority, Lawton LJ, said ([1973] 1 QB, at p 47): "In my judgment the answer to this question is that such financial damage cannot be recovered save when it is the immediate consequence of a breach of duty to safeguard the plaintiff from that kind of loss." The difficulty with this suggested answer to the problem is that it does not give any guidance as to when such a duty arises, although Lawton LJ made it quite clear that financial loss resulting from damage to electric cables, gas pipes and water mains is not recoverable.

In my opinion it is still right to say that as a general rule damages are not recoverable for economic loss which is not consequential upon injury to the plaintiff's person or property. The fact that the loss was foreseeable is not enough to make it recoverable. However, there are exceptional cases in which the defendant has knowledge or means of knowledge that the plaintiff individually, and not merely as a member of an unascertained class, will be likely to suffer economic loss as a consequence of his negligence, and owes the plaintiff a duty to take care not to cause him such damage by his negligent act. It is not necessary, and would not be wise, to attempt to formulate a principle that would cover all cases in which such a duty is owed; to borrow the words of Lord Diplock in *Mutual Life & Citizens' Assurance Co Ltd v Evatt* (1970) 122 CLR 628, at p 642; [1971] AC 793, at p 809: "Those will fall to be ascertained step by step as the facts of particular cases which come before the courts make it necessary to determine them." All the facts of the particular case will have to be considered. It will be material, but not in my opinion sufficient, that some property of the plaintiff was in physical proximity to the damaged property, or that the plaintiff, and the person whose property was injured, were engaged in a common adventure.

In the present case the persons interested in the dredge and the employees of Decca (in particular Mr Austin) knew that the pipeline led directly from the refinery to Caltex's terminal. They should have known that, whatever the contractual or other relationship between Caltex and AOR might have been, the pipeline was the physical means by which the products flowed from the refinery to the terminal. Moreover, the pipeline [556] appeared to be designed to serve the terminal particularly (although no doubt it would have been possible for it to serve other persons as well) and was not like a water main or electric cable serving the public generally. In these circumstances the persons interested in the dredge, and Decca, should have had Caltex in contemplation as a person who would probably suffer economic loss if the pipes were broken. Further, the officers navigating the dredge had a particular obligation to take care to avoid damage to the pipeline, which was shown on the drawing supplied to them for the very purpose of enabling them to avoid it. Decca had a similar obligation to draw the lines on the track plotter chart, in such a way that the navigators would not sail the dredge over the pipeline. In all these circumstances the particular relationship between the dredge and Decca on the one hand, and Caltex on the other, was such that both the dredge and Decca owed a duty to Caltex to take reasonable care to avoid causing damage to the pipeline and thereby causing economic loss to Caltex. It should therefore in my opinion be concluded that Caltex is entitled to recover the economic loss resulting from the breach of that duty of care. The quantum of damages is, as I have said, admitted.

For these reasons I would allow Caltex's appeals.

STEPHEN J. ... [567] Policy considerations must no doubt play a very significant part in any judicial definition of liability and entitlement in new areas of the law; the policy considerations to which their Lordships paid regard in *Hedley Byrne* [1964] AC 465 are an instance of just such a process and to seek to conceal those considerations may be undesirable. That process should however result in some definition of rights and duties, which can then be applied to the case in hand, and to subsequent cases, with relative certainty. To apply generalized policy considerations directly, in each case, instead of formulating principles from policy and applying those principles, derived from policy, to the case in hand, is, in my view, to invite uncertainty and judicial diversity. This suggests a need to search for some more positive guidance as to the entitlement, if any, to recover in negligence for solely economic loss than is provided by judicial policy making based upon a case-by-case consideration of whatever factors the particular court may deem relevant. ...

[568] No doubt to discard the element of physical injury to person or property as a prerequisite to the recovery of damages in negligence means that its effect of tending to ensure that compensable damage is restricted to that which is immediately consequential upon the tortious act also disappears; there then looms the spectre, described by Cardozo CJ in *Ultramares Corporation v Touche* (1931) 174 NE 441, at p 444; 74 ALR 1139, at p 1145 as that of "liability in an indeterminate amount for an indeterminate time to an indeterminate class". However to counter this spectre by rejecting all recovery for economic loss unless accompanied by and directly consequential upon such physical injury is Draconic; it operates to confer upon such physical injury a special status unexplained either by logic or by common experience. No reason exists for according to it such special status other than its character of tending to ensure a reassuringly proximate nexus between tortious act and recoverable damage; to this alone does it owe such merit as it may have as a necessary element in the recovery of damages in negligence.

In addition to the arbitrary nature of such a rule it also possesses the unattractive quality of being quite unresponsive to the grossness of the wrongdoer's want of care in its exclusion of non-consequential economic loss. Again, the outcome of applying such a rule may well depend upon the precise terms of a contract between the injured person and a third party; those terms, otherwise wholly irrelevant to the tortfeasor's wrongful act, will, if they determine whether the injured person possesses a sufficient interest of the requisite kind in property which has been damaged, either confer upon him or deny to him an entitlement to damages. The injured party will suffer the same loss in either event but his right to compensation will depend upon the particular contractual situation into which the effect of the tortious act has wrongfully intruded itself. ...

[570] Were the suggested rule that, whether or not associated with injury to person or property, economic loss was never recoverable it would at least have the virtue of consistency. However recovery for economic loss, so long as it is consequential upon physical injury, is well established; the law thus recognizes it is a kind of detriment which, if negligently caused, is not in

itself unsuitable for compensation. There is, indeed, nothing about economic loss which makes it inherently unsuited to compensation by an award of damages; on the contrary a detriment which manifests itself in monetary terms is especially suited to compensation by the award of a sum of money; in this respect it compares favourably with the case of personal injuries, so notoriously difficult of assessment in monetary terms. ...

[573] The need, in cases of purely economic loss, for some further control of liability apart from that offered by the concept of reasonable foreseeability arises in part because, in cases of physical injury to person or property, the concept has been given a very far-reaching operation, far more extensive than may be thought to have been conveyed by Lord Atkin's reference to that which one "can reasonably foresee would be likely to injure" a person in the relationship of neighbour (*Donoghue v Stevenson* [1932] AC 562, at p 580). This is perhaps well enough so long as what is in question is only liability for injury to person or property, the duty of care being fixed by reference to the plaintiff whose person or property is injured, those indirectly affected by the repercussions of the negligent act having suffered no such injury. But if economic loss is to be compensated its inherent capacity to manifest itself [574] at several removes from the direct detriment inflicted by the defendant's carelessness makes reasonable foreseeability an inadequate control mechanism. ...

The need is for some control mechanism based upon notions of proximity between tortious act and resultant detriment to take the place of the nexus provided by the suggested exclusory rule which I have rejected. Its precise nature and the extent to which it should restrict recovery for purely economic loss must depend upon policy considerations just as does the conclusion that for cases of economic loss such an additional control mechanism is necessary. ...

[575] The articulation, through the cases, of circumstances which denote sufficient proximity will provide a body of precedent productive of the necessary certainty; the gradual accumulation of decided cases and the impact of evolving policy considerations will reflect "the courts' assessment of the demands of society for protection from the carelessness of others" – per Lord Pearce in *Hedley Byrne* [1964] AC, at p 536 reiterated by Lord Diplock in *Dorset Yacht Co v Home Office* [1970] AC 1004, at p 1058. ...

[576] As the body of precedent accumulates some general area of demarcation between what is and is not a sufficient degree of proximity in any particular class of case of economic loss will no doubt emerge; but its emergence neither can be, nor should it be, other than as a reflection of the piecemeal conclusions arrived at in precedent cases. The present case contains a number of salient features which will no doubt ultimately be recognized as characteristic of one particular class of case among the generality of cases involving economic loss. This will be typical of the development of the common law in which, in the words of Barwick CJ in *Mutual Life & Citizens' Assurance Co Ltd v Evatt* (1968) 122 CLR, at p 569, the elements of the relationships out of which a duty of care is imposed by law "will be elucidated in the course of time as particular facts are submitted for consideration in cases coming forward for decision". The existence of these features leaves no doubt in my mind that there exists in this case sufficient proximity to entitle the plaintiff to recover its reasonably foreseeable economic loss.

These features comprise the following:

(1) the defendant's knowledge that the property damaged, a set of pipelines, was of a kind inherently likely, when damaged, to be productive of consequential economic loss to those who rely directly upon its use. To damage an item of productive equipment or an item used in conveying goods or services, such as power or water, is inherently likely to cause to is users economic loss quite apart from the physical injury to the article itself Moreover the nature of a pipeline, used in conveying refined products from a refinery to another's terminal, is such as to indicate very clearly the existence of something akin to Lord Roche's common adventure, the person to whom the petroleum products are being delivered through it having a very real interest in its continued operation as a means of conveyance, whether or not possessing a proprietary or possessory interest in the pipes themselves;

(2) the defendant's knowledge or means of knowledge, from certain charts then in use on the dredge, that the pipelines extended across Botany Bay from the AOR refinery to the plaintiff's Banksmeadow terminal, leading to the quite obvious inference that their use

was to convey refined products from refinery to terminal, the plaintiff being in this sense a user of the pipeline.

[577] These two factors lead to the conclusion that Caltex was within the reasonable contemplation of the defendants as a person likely to suffer economic loss if the pipelines were cut. ...

    (3)   the infliction of damage by the defendant to the property of a third party, AOR, as a result of conduct in breach of a duty of care owed to that third party.

There are two other relevant factors:

    (4)   the nature of the detriment suffered by the plaintiff; that is to say its loss of use, in the above sense, of the pipeline;

    (5)   the nature of the damages claimed, which reflect that loss of use, representing not some loss of profits arising because collateral commercial arrangements are adversely affected but the quite direct consequence of the detriment suffered, namely the expense directly incurred in employing alternative modes of transport. ...

[580] It is for these reasons that I would allow the appeals by Caltex. Before turning to the remaining questions I wish to make some concluding remarks on the topic of economic loss. In any reference to the writings on this topic, and articles abound in the law journals of the last fifteen years in the common law countries, frequent mention will be found of the important role to be played by insurance and of the significance which judicial policy considerations should accord to it and to what has come to be known as "loss spreading". If due weight be given to these two factors they will, it is sometimes said, point to the conclusion that liability in negligence should not be further extended and that, however logically unsatisfying may be the suggested exclusory rule, the correct pragmatic solution is to deny recovery for purely economic loss.

I have myself avoided reference to either of these two factors and I should explain my reasons for doing so. If loss-inflicting consequences of an act are reasonably foreseeable and the necessary proximity is shown to exist, the present state of the law of torts, unreformed by any fundamental departure from fault liability, suggests no reason why the tortfeasor should not bear the consequences of his conduct. The task of the court remains that of loss fixing rather than loss spreading and if this is to be altered it is, in my view, a matter for direct legislative action rather than for the courts. It should be undertaken, if at all, openly and after adequate public inquiry and parliamentary debate and not worked towards covertly, in the course of judicial decision, by the adoption of policy factors which assume its desirability as a goal and operate to further its attainment. ...

MASON J. **[584]** The common law has exhibited remarked reluctance to allow recovery of pure economic damage sustained as a result of negligence. Before *Hedley Byrne & Co Ltd v Heller & Partners Ltd* [1964] AC 465 in the long line of cases that commenced with *Cattle v Stockton Waterworks Co* (1875) LR 10 QB 453 no plaintiff succeeded in recovering economic damage which was not consequential upon physical damage – see *Simpson and Co v Thomson* (1877) 3 App Cas 279; **[585]** *Société Anonyme de Remorquage à Hélice v Bennetts* [1911] 1 KB 243; *Chargeurs Réunis Compagnie Française de Navigation à Vapeur v English & American Shipping Co* (1921) 9 Ll LR 464. It was otherwise if the plaintiff had a proprietary or possessory interest in property: in that event he could recover consequential financial loss (*The Okehampton* [1913] P 173; *Elliott Steam Tug Co Ltd v The Shipping Controller* [1922] 1 KB 127).

How *Morrison Steamship Co Ltd v Greystoke Castle (Cargo Owners)* [1947] AC 265 stood in this scheme of things is a question which has been much debated. Certainly the celebrated example given by Lord Roche [1947] AC, at p 280 of the owners of freight who incurred expense in making alternative transport arrangements when the lorry by which their goods were carried was damaged by the negligence of another indicated that there was no absolute rule inhibiting the recovery of pure economic damage for negligence. On the other hand Lord Simonds [1947] AC at pp 304-307 invoked the earlier decisions in support of the view that pure economic damage will not ground an action in negligence. However, in *Hedley Byrne* [1964] AC 465 three members of the House of Lords regarded *Greystoke Castle* [1947] AC 265 as an instance of recovery of damages for pure financial loss.

None the less before *Hedley Byrne* [1964] AC 465 the influence of the early cases was strong and it seems to have been generally considered that financial loss not consequential upon property damage could not be recovered. For the most part the cases concerned a claim by a plaintiff that he suffered a loss or lost a profit under a contract because the defendant's negligent conduct damaged or destroyed property of the other contracting party thereby putting an end to the contract or rendering it unprofitable. Yet the cases were thought to establish a general principle relating to the recovery of pure economic damage. This was because the judgments emphasized the far-reaching consequences which would flow if financial loss arising under a contract, divorced from any property damage suffered by the plaintiff, could be compensated in damages for negligence and because Blackburn J in *Cattle* (1875) LR 10 QB, at p 458 drew a distinction between financial loss caused by negligence and that caused by malicious intention, asserting that in the former case it was not sufficiently proximate and direct for the law redresses "only the proximate and direct consequences of wrongful acts".

Whether the refusal of relief in these cases was based on the absence of a duty of care (a concept by no means fully developed **[586]** at the time of *Cattle* (1875) LR 10 QB, at p 457) or remoteness of damage is perhaps not entirely clear. But Blackburn J's remarks which I have quoted and those of Hamilton J in *Bennetts* [1911] 1 KB, at pp 247-249, quite apart from the observations of Lord Simonds in *Greystoke Castle* [1947] AC, at pp 300-308, indicate that remoteness was thought to be the true foundation of the decisions.

It was to be expected that the speeches in *Hedley Byrne* [1964] AC 465, by acknowledging that a plaintiff who sustains financial loss, which is not consequential upon physical damage, as a result of a negligent misstatement, a view confirmed for Australia by *Mutual Life & Citizens' Assurance Co Ltd v Evatt* (1970) 122 CLR 628; [1971] AC 793, would open the way to liability for pure economic damage sustained in consequence of negligent conduct. So far the expectation has been disappointed.

The English decisions since *Hedley Byrne* [1964] AC 465 have not given much encouragement to the plaintiff who suffers pure economic damage through negligent conduct. No claim for pure financial loss has yet succeeded – see *The World Harmony* [1967] P 341; *Weller & Co v Foot and Mouth Disease Research Institute* [1966] 1 QB 569; *Electrochrome Ltd v Welsh Plastics Ltd* [1968] 2 All ER 205; *British Celanese Ltd v AH Hunt (Capacitors) Ltd* [1969] 1 WLR 959; *Margarine Union GmbH v Cambay Prince Steamship Co Ltd* [1969] 1 QB 219; *SCM (United Kingdom) Ltd v WJ Whittall & Son Ltd* [1971] 1 QB 337; *Spartan Steel & Alloys Ltd v Martin & Co (Contractors) Ltd* [1973] 1 QB 27. To these cases there should be added a reference to *French Knit Sales Pty Ltd v N Gold & Sons Pty Ltd* [1972] 2 NSWLR 132, where Asprey and Hardie JJA thought that financial loss is not recoverable if it is not consequential upon property damage. ...

[590] All this indicates that in England the foreseeability test which seemed to emerge after the decision in *The Wagon Mound* [1961] AC 311 as the ultimate touchstone of liability in negligence, has not been accepted as an exclusive criterion of liability for economic damage. There are a number of reasons which tend to support this conclusion. Some of them have to do with the various types of financial loss which are denoted by the expression "economic damage" and with the wide variety of circumstances in which financial loss may be sustained. I may suffer financial loss because I lose a profit or the benefit of expenditure under a contract the performance of which is affected due to the negligence of another. Or my business may be adversely affected by supervening circumstances attributable to the negligence of another (*Weller* [1966] 1 QB 569). Or I may be put to additional expense because I have been deprived of a service or facility through another's negligence. In many of these cases the loss will be foreseeable, though the degree of its connexion with the negligence will vary. ...

[591] Now that the recovery of economic damage not consequential upon property damage is recognized in the case of negligent misstatements, there is no sound reason for accepting the traditional rule that only financial loss which is consequential upon property damage can be recovered. The traditional rule is not only at odds with *Hedley Byrne*, it is based on an absolute distinction between property damage and economic damage which is difficult to justify (see *Hedley Byrne* [1964] AC, at pp 517, 538). ...

[592] It is preferable ... that the delimitation of the duty of care in relation to economic damage through negligent conduct be expressed in terms which are related more closely to the principal factor inhibiting the acceptance of a more generalized duty of care in relation to **[593]** economic loss, that is, the apprehension of an indeterminate liability. A defendant will then be liable for economic damage due to his negligent conduct when he can reasonably foresee that a specific individual, as distinct from a general class of persons, will suffer financial loss as a consequence of his conduct. This approach eliminates or diminishes the prospect that there will come into existence liability to an indeterminate class of persons; it ensures that liability is confined to those individuals whose financial loss falls within the area of foreseeability. ...

In the result, in my opinion the two appeals by Caltex should be allowed and it should recover judgment in each of the actions **[594]** against the dredge and Decca in the agreed amount of damages. ...

JACOBS J. ... **[597]** The relevant duty of care in the present case is the duty of care owed to those whose persons or property are in such physical propinquity to the place where an act or omission of the defendant has its physical effect that a physical effect on the person or property of the plaintiff is foreseeable as the result of the plaintiff's act or omission. The damages for the breach of such a duty of care are those which result from the physical effect on the plaintiffs person or property of the defendant's act or omission.

A question of central importance in the present case is whether the physical effect in this context is limited to actual physical injury. In my opinion it is not. Person or property may be injured not only physically but also by physical effect thereon short of physical injury: eg by an act or omission which prevents physical movement of a person or which prevents physical movement or operation of property.

The damages for immobilization of property may frequently be quantified as the cost of mobilizing the property and the loss of the use of the property during its immobilization. Such damage may be called pecuniary or economic loss. However, it is an **[598]** error to concentrate attention on the question whether a particular loss is pecuniary or economic. Rather it is necessary to examine the circumstances of the loss. If the loss arises from the physical effect of an act or omission on the person or property of a plaintiff and that physical effect is one which was foreseeable and that foreseeability gives rise to a duty in the defendant to take reasonable care to avoid that physical effect, it is no answer to the plaintiff's claim for damages that his loss was pecuniary or economic. ...

[599] Because economic loss commonly arises out of the loss of the benefit of a contract with a third party, and because the loss of the benefit of a contract with a third party is not a kind of injury which of itself gives rise to a duty of care, there has been a tendency of late to express the principle to be that in an action for negligence by a physical act or omission economic loss is not recoverable. Such an expression is incorrect because in every case it is necessary to go further and to examine how the so called economic loss arises. If it arises in a way which can only be characterized as the loss of the benefit of a contract with a third party it will not be recoverable. However, if it arises out of a physical effect on the person or property of the plaintiff, it will not be irrecoverable simply because it is economic loss. ...

[604] The defendants owed no duty of care to Caltex arising simply from a risk that AOR might by the physical injury to its property be unable to supply refined petroleum products to Caltex under a contract for the supply thereof. However that is not the end of the matter. There was a duty of care owed by the defendants to Caltex. The duty of care was that owed to a person whose property was in such physical propinquity to the place where the acts or omissions of the dredge and Decca had their physical effect that a physical effect on the property of that person was foreseeable as the result of such acts or omissions. ... **[605]** The physical effect on this property of Caltex was the immobilization through the pipeline of the crude oil and the products thereof. The risk of such a physical effect was foreseeable as the result of the act of breaking the pipeline. The damage suffered was the immobilization through the pipeline of the processed crude oil. ...

The appeals of Caltex should be allowed with costs, the verdicts set aside and in lieu thereof there should be verdicts with costs in favour of Caltex against all defendants in the sum of $95,000.

[Murphy J delivered a concurring judgment.]

Appeals allowed

Perre v Apand Pty Ltd
(1999) 198 CLR 180; [1999] HCA 36
High Court of Australia

A plaintiff faces a difficult but not impossible hurdle in establishing that the defendant owed the plaintiff a duty of care to avoid causing pure economic loss. This hurdle has not been made easier by the variance in the approaches ("proximity", "incremental", "salient features") of the members of the High Court of Australia to the determination of whether a duty of care exists in a novel case. When determining whether a duty of care exists in respect of pure economic loss caused by a negligent act, account may be taken of factors such as indeterminacy of the defendant's potential liability, unreasonable interference with the defendant's commercial autonomy, the defendant's knowledge of and control over the risk and the plaintiff's vulnerability to the risk.

GLEESON CJ. **[191]** 1. The issue to be decided is whether the respondent, whose careless conduct resulted in financial loss to others, unconnected with physical injury to their persons or property, owed them a duty of care such as to sustain an action for damages for negligence.

2. The facts of the case … are as follows. In a rural locality in South Australia, a number of farmers grew potatoes, some for export to Western Australia. The respondent negligently introduced a form of disease, known as bacterial wilt, onto the land of one farmer [the Sparnons]. The Western Australian regulations imposed a prohibition on the importation into Western Australia, not only of potatoes grown on land known to be affected by the disease, but also of potatoes grown on land within a certain distance of affected land. The appellants were involved, in various ways, in potato growing on such land, and claimed to suffer financial loss. The issue is whether the respondent, whose conduct is, for the purposes of argument, assumed to have caused harm to each of the appellants, owed a duty of care to all or any of them. In the Federal Court at first instance, and in the **[192]** Full Court, that question was answered in the negative as to all appellants.

3. Although the appellants, considered collectively, owned, or had other interests in, land which was in the neighbourhood of land directly affected by the respondent's negligent conduct, no property belonging to, or used by, the appellants suffered any physical harm. The loss allegedly suffered by each appellant was of a kind conventionally described as pure economic loss. …

4. In *Caltex Oil (Australia) Pty Ltd v The Dredge "Willemstad"*(1976) 136 CLR 529 all the members of the Court, except Murphy J, accepted that there is no general rule that one person owes to another a duty to take care not to cause reasonably foreseeable financial harm. The consequences of such a rule would be intolerable. However, as the decision in that case showed, and as had previously been shown in *Hedley Byrne & Co Ltd v Heller & Partners Ltd* [1964] AC 465, there are circumstances in which the law recognises a duty of care such as will permit recovery of pure economic loss.

5. There are at least three considerations which have been, and will remain, influential in restraining acceptance of such a duty of care in particular cases, or categories of case. First, bearing in mind the expansive application which has been given to the concept of reasonable foreseeability in relation to physical injury to person or property, a duty to avoid any reasonably foreseeable financial harm needs to be constrained by "some intelligible limits to keep the law of negligence within the bounds of common sense and practicality" (*Caparo Industries plc v Dickman* [1990] 2 AC 605 at 633 per Lord Oliver of Aylmerton). Secondly, to permit recovery of foreseeable economic loss, which may or may not occur in a commercial setting, for any negligent conduct, may interfere with freedoms, controls and limitations established both by common law and statute in many legal contexts. Thirdly, in those cases where the loss occurs in a commercial setting, a third party, C, may suffer financial harm as a result of conduct which is regulated by **[193]** a contract between A and B. It may be that the consequences of such conduct, as between A and B, are governed and limited by the contract. This is a problem which commonly occurs in relation to maritime claims, and may help to explain the strictness with which an exclusionary rule has been applied in shipping cases (see *Leigh and Sillivan Ltd v Aliakmon Shipping Co Ltd* [1985] QB 350 at 397 per Robert Goff LJ).

6. Another matter of concern is the lack of precision in the concept of financial or economic loss. Physical injury to person or property is usually readily identifiable, even if it may take time to manifest itself. However, the concept of financial or economic loss or harm is wide enough to comprehend a variety of circumstances or contingencies, some of which may be indirect and difficult to identify or measure. Suppose, for example, that a child's parents are killed as a result of the negligent conduct of another. In many jurisdictions there are statutory provisions which govern entitlement to compensation (for example, *Compensation to Relatives Act 1897* (NSW)). However, if the matter were at large, how would a court set about identifying, and estimating, the kinds of financial loss which might sound in damages? What kinds of detriment, harm, or disadvantage, would be treated as "financial loss"? The law of tort is a blunt instrument for providing a remedy for many kinds of harm which may be suffered as a consequence of someone else's carelessness, and which are capable of being described as financial.

7. If there once was a bright line rule which absolutely prevented recognition of a duty of care in any case where the negligent conduct of one person caused financial loss to another, not associated with injury to the other's person or property, and which assigned claims to recover such loss to the field of contract rather than tort, the line gave way in an area where there is a clear potential for carelessness to cause financial harm: negligent misstatements made to a person who, to the knowledge of the maker of the statement, relies upon the advice or information provided. However, there is no convincing reason why conveying advice or information should be treated as the solitary exception to an otherwise absolute exclusionary rule.

8. Once the exclusionary rule ceased to be a bright line rule, it lost one of its principal justifications. Nevertheless, the considerations underlying the rule remain cogent, even if they are no longer seen as absolutely compelling. Courts have found difficulty in proposing an alternative general rule which makes better sense and which, at the same time, pays due regard to the problems earlier mentioned. ...

10. **[194]** In *Caparo*, Lord Oliver (at 643) emphasised that, in this field of discourse, the mere foreseeability of possible damage, without some further control, (which he summarised as "proximity", after explaining what he meant by that term), would not be useful as the test of liability. At the same time, however, his Lordship made it clear that "in some cases the degree of foreseeability is such that it is from that alone that the requisite proximity can be deduced." (at 633). In relation to the giving of advice or information, questions of reliance and actual foresight of the possibility of harm, (or, what is the same thing, the foresight that a reasonable person would have), are closely related. Moreover, knowledge (actual, or that which a reasonable person would have) of an individual, or an ascertainable class of persons, who is or are reliant, and therefore vulnerable, is a significant factor in establishing a duty of care.

11. Vulnerability can arise from circumstances other than reliance. In *Caltex*, the obvious vulnerability of a specific plaintiff was influential in a number of the judgments (at 555, 576-577, 593). This was not merely an arbitrary method of solving the problem of potentially indeterminate liability. It was an application of what Lord Oliver later discussed as the idea that in a given case, the degree (and nature) of foreseeability may have an important bearing on whether there is a duty of care.

12. I agree with the reasons given by Gummow J for concluding that, in the present case, the respondent owed the appellants a duty of care. In particular, I would emphasise the following matters. ...

15. **[195]** The reasoning in the Federal Court was strongly influenced by the consideration that there was seen to be no rational basis for distinguishing between the position of the present appellants and that of an indeterminate number of other people. That was unquestionably an important issue to address. A decision that a duty of care is owed to some who suffer financial harm as a consequence of negligent conduct, but not to others, is only just if it is capable of being explained on a rational basis. As the judgments of other members of this Court show, to an extent the Federal Court's conclusion was based upon a view of the facts, and in particular of the critical aspect of the negligent conduct, which cast the net of potential liability too wide. Furthermore, the combination of circumstances involving the use and ownership or enjoyment of land, the physical propinquity of such land to the Sparnons' land, the known vulnerability of people in the position of the appellants,

and the control exercised by the respondent over the relevant activity on the Sparnons' land, is unlikely to apply to an extent sufficient to warrant an apprehension of indeterminate liability.

16. I agree that the appeal should be allowed ...

GAUDRON J. ... **[201]** 38. Where a person is in a position to control the exercise or enjoyment by another of a legal right, that position of control and, by corollary, the other's dependence on the person with control are, in my view, special factors or, which is the same thing, give rise to a special relationship of "proximity" or "neighbourhood" such that the law will impose liability upon the person with control if his or her negligent act or omission results in the loss or impairment of that right and is, thereby, productive of economic loss. ...

[202] 41. Although it would not be strictly accurate in this case to describe the respondent as being in a position of control, its relationship with the appellants is closely analogous to that which obtains where one person is in a position to control the exercise or enjoyment of a legal right by another person. In this case, the respondent knew that there was a class of persons who availed themselves of the right to sell potatoes in the Western Australian market and/or who used their property and equipment to produce potatoes for that market. It knew that those who did so would lose those rights or would have them impaired for a period of five years if bacterial wilt were discovered within 20 kilometres of the place or places in which their potatoes were grown, cleaned, washed, graded or packed. And the respondent knew or ought to have known that, if bacterial wilt were to be transmitted to potatoes grown within that 20 kilometre zone, those persons who grew potatoes for the Western Australian market or who used their land and equipment for that purpose were powerless to protect their own interests.

42. In my view, where a person knows or ought to know that his or her acts or omissions may cause the loss or impairment of legal rights possessed, enjoyed or exercised by another, whether as an individual or as a member of a class, and that that latter person is in no position to protect his or her own interests, there is a relationship such that the law should impose a duty of care on the former to take reasonable steps to avoid a foreseeable risk of economic loss resulting from the loss or impairment of those rights. ...

[203] 46. The appeal should be allowed ...

McHUGH J. ... **[208]** ... 71. Until 1963, the so-called "exclusionary rule" prohibited the **[209]** recovery of any damages for pure economic loss suffered as the result of the negligence of another. Yet even before then, courts recognised that the rigour of the rule, if it ever existed in a pristine form, often occasioned injustice to plaintiffs. To overcome those injustices, the courts allowed recovery in a number of exceptional situations (*Morrison Steamship Co Ltd v Greystoke Castle (Cargo Owners)* [1947] AC 265; *Woods v Martins Bank Ltd* [1959] 1 QB 55; *Schneider v Eisovitch* [1960] 2 QB 430). Denial of recovery for pure economic loss remains the rule, but, since *Hedley Byrne & Co Ltd v Heller & Partners Ltd* [1964] AC 465 was decided in 1963, many exceptions to the rule have been recognised. However, they have been developed in a haphazard and ad hoc fashion with no single principle underlying them. Indeed, Professor Feldthusen denies that such a principle may be divined, although he concedes that all cases of pure economic loss share certain characteristics (Feldthusen, "Liability for Pure Economic Loss: Yes, But Why?" (1999) 28 *University of Western Australia Law Review* 84 at 85-86).

72. No doubt one important reason why courts have felt the necessity to distinguish between liability for harm resulting in pure economic loss and liability for harm to person or tangible property is that pure economic losses frequently result in mere transfers of wealth. The plaintiff's loss is the defendant's or a third party's gain. Harm to person or property, on the other hand, ordinarily involves a net loss to social wealth. Furthermore, the risk of sustaining economic loss is "a burden which is much more often and easily spread than the risk of physical damage" (Atiyah, "Negligence and Economic Loss" (1967) 83 *Law Quarterly Review* 248 at 270). So even with the demise of the exclusionary rule, courts in most jurisdictions still require a plaintiff in a pure economic loss case to show some special reason why liability should be imposed on the defendant.

73. In *Murphy v Brentwood District Council* [1991] 1 AC 398 at 487, Lord Oliver said:

The infliction of physical injury to the person or property of another universally requires to be justified. The causing of economic loss does not. If it is to be categorised as wrongful it is necessary to find some factor beyond the mere occurrence of the loss and the fact that its occurrence could be foreseen. Thus the categorisation of damage as economic serves at least the useful purpose of indicating that something more is required ...

74. For some years in this Court, the "something more" was "proximity" which Deane J suggested in *Jaensch v Coffey* (1984) 155 CLR 549 at 584 "involves the notion of nearness or closeness". However, this Court no longer sees proximity as the unifying criterion of duties of **[210]** care. The reason that proximity can not be the touchstone of a duty of care is that it "is a category of indeterminate reference par excellence" (McHugh, "Neighbourhood, Proximity and Reliance", in Finn (ed), *Essays on Torts* (1989) 5 at 13). ...

The *Caparo* test

77. The continuing use of proximity as a duty indicator in England appears most clearly in *Caparo Industries plc v Dickman* [1990] 2 AC 605 at 617-618 per Lord Bridge where the House of Lords proposed a three stage approach for determining duty. That approach has been adopted in this Court by Kirby J (*Pyrenees Shire Council v Day* (1998) 192 CLR 330 at 419-420). Under the three stage approach, the plaintiff can establish a duty of care only when it can prove three matters: first, that the causing of the damage was reasonably foreseeable; second, that a relationship of "proximity" existed; third, that in all the circumstances of the case, it is fair, just and reasonable to impose a duty of care on the defendant. **[211]** However, in *Caparo* Lord Bridge (with whose speech Lords Roskill and Ackner agreed) went on to say (at 618) "that the concepts of proximity and fairness ... are not susceptible of any such precise definition as would be necessary to give them utility as practical tests, but amount in effect to little more than convenient labels to attach to the features of different specific situations which, on a detailed examination of all the circumstances, the law recognises pragmatically as giving rise to a duty of care of a given scope." The three stage approach formulated in *Caparo* was applied by the House of Lords in *Marc Rich & Co v Bishop Rock Marine Co Ltd* [1996] AC 211. In my respectful opinion, the *Caparo* formulation suffers from three defects.

78. First, proximity as the second stage in a three stage test has no more content than it did when it was used as the unifying criterion, a point which it is fair to say was recognised by Lord Bridge in *Caparo*. If the meaning of proximity is restricted to nearness or closeness, neither logic nor policy requires that it should always be elevated above other factors that are relevant in a particular case. I think that Dawson J was correct when he said in *Hill v Van Erp* that proximity is neither a necessary nor a sufficient criterion for the existence of a duty of care (at 176-177). Furthermore, proximity in the sense of nearness or closeness is hardly a useful concept in most cases of pure economic loss.

79. Second, there is a danger that the *Caparo* test will be used as the test of duty in every case where duty is in issue. That would deny the operation of the established categories and the certainty that they provide. Even at its zenith, proximity was a rationale to be applied in aid of the principled development of new categories. It was not meant to "invade" the existing categories and wreak havoc with accepted and unproblematic principles developed within those categories.

80. Third, almost everyone would agree that courts should not impose a duty of care on a person unless it is fair, just and reasonable to do so. But attractive as concepts of fairness and justice may be in appellate courts, in law reform commissions, in the academy and among legislators, in many cases they are of little use, if they are of any use at all, to the practitioners and trial judges who must apply the law to concrete facts arising from real life activities. While the training and background of judges may lead them to agree as to what is fair or just in many cases, there are just as many cases where using such concepts as the criteria for duty would mean that "each judge would have a distinct tribunal in his own breast, the decisions of which would be as **[212]** irregular and uncertain and various as the minds and tempers of mankind" (*Donaldson v Beckett* (1774) 2 Brown 129 per Lord Camden). Lord Devlin was surely right when he said: ("The Judge and Case Law" in Devlin, *The Judge* (1979) at 181.)

> For a judge to decide fairly and convincingly every case that comes before him in the light only of his own sense of justice, he would have to be a superman. I doubt if there have ever been more than a handful of men on the Bench who could do it, though doubtless there are slightly more who think that they could.

81. Furthermore, when legislatures and courts formulate legal criteria by reference to indeterminate terms such as "fair", "just", "just and equitable" and "unconscionable", they inevitably extend the range of admissible evidentiary materials. Cases then take longer, are more expensive to try, and, because of the indeterminacy of such terms, settlement of cases is more difficult, practitioners often having widely differing views as to the result of cases if they are litigated. Bright line rules may be less than perfect because they are under-inclusive, but my impression is that most people who have been or are engaged in day-to-day practice of the law at the trial or advising stage prefer rules to indeterminate standards.

82. No doubt in some cases judges cannot escape applying notions of "current ideas of justice or morality" in determining the duty question, any more than they can escape them in determining whether the foreseeable consequences of negligence should be regarded as too remote for liability to be imposed. As Cooke P pointed out in *South Pacific Manufacturing Co Ltd v NZ Security Consultants & Investigations Ltd* [1992] 2 NZLR 282 at 294 "whatever formula be used, the outcome in a grey area case has to be determined by judicial judgment. Formulae can help to organise thinking but they cannot provide answers." But if negligence doctrine is to escape the charge of being riddled with indeterminacy, ideas of justice and morality should be invoked only as criteria of last resort when more concrete reasons, rules or principles fail to provide a persuasive answer to the problem.

The *Anns* test

83. In *Anns v Merton London Borough Council* [1978] AC 728, the House of Lords formulated a two stage test for duty that is still applied in **[213]** Canada and New Zealand although it had been rejected in this Court (*Sutherland Shire Council v Heyman* (1985) 157 CLR 424) and now in England (*Murphy v Brentwood District Council*). Under the *Anns* test, the court will find that a duty existed if the defendant knew or ought to have known that its conduct might cause harm to the plaintiff and there is no policy reason for negating the existence of such a duty. To approach the duty question by holding that reasonable foreseeability of the relevant harm grounds a prima facie duty of care widens the scope of liability, probably enormously and of itself provides no principled formulation. To now adopt it in this country would also be contrary to the growing consensus, evidenced by recent cases, that, if there is to be an in-built bias in the determination of duty of care, particularly in cases of pure economic loss, it should be against imposing a duty of care. According to that consensus, any potential claimant in a novel situation should affirmatively demonstrate that its loss deserves vindication via the law of negligence. ...

86. So if proximity is not the unifying test for negligence, if the two stage and three stage tests are defective, if the "precise legal right" formula is unacceptable and if the categories and incremental approach is not accepted favourably by the majority of judges, is there any solution to the problems posed by the development of a tort of negligent economic loss? Or must we now accept that *Hedley Byrne* was a glorious mistake and retreat to the exclusionary rule of the common law?

87. The exclusionary rule is often justified on the ground that it is certain – which it certainly is. But its certainty is obtained by rejecting claims that most people would agree ought to sound in damages. As will appear, it is not necessary, in my view, to use the exclusionary rule to obtain stability and predictability in the law of negligently inflicted pure economic loss. Furthermore, in *Caltex Oil (Australia) Pty Ltd v The Dredge "Willemstad"* (1976) 136 CLR 529, this Court rejected the exclusionary rule, and nearly 25 years later there should be no turning back. ...

[215] The need for predictability

88. Law is one of the most important means by which a Western society remains socially cohesive while encouraging the autonomy of its individual members and the achieving of its social, political and economic goals. But the effectiveness of law as a social instrument is seriously diminished when legal practitioners believe they cannot confidently advise what the law is or how it applies to the diverse situations of everyday life or when the courts of justice are made effectively inaccessible by the cost of litigation. When legal practitioners are unable to predict the outcome of cases with a high degree of probability, the choice for litigants is to abandon or compromise their claims or defences or to expose themselves to the great expense and unpredictable risks of litigation. ...

91. **[216]** … If negligence law is to serve its principal purpose as an instrument of corrective justice, the principles and rules which govern claims in negligence must be as clear and as easy of application as is possible. Ideally, arguments about duty should take little time with need to refer to one or two cases only instead of the elaborate arguments now often heard, where many cases are cited and the argument takes days. The needs of the litigant or potential litigant, the legal practitioner and the trial judge should guide the formulation of the applicable principles. That does not mean, however, that the common law must adopt arbitrary "bright-line" rules for the sake of certainty at the expense of what most people including judges would regard as a desirable result.

92. In many areas of law, judges cannot realistically ignore the past or change legal rules. This is the case with constitutional law and statutes. In those areas, the doctrine of separation of powers requires that judges be faithful to the past decisions of legislators and the makers of the Constitution. But in the area of judge-made law, the duty of judges to be faithful to the past is weaker. While *stare decisis* is a sound policy because it promotes predictability of judicial decision and facilitates the giving of advice, it should not always trump the need for desirable change in the law. In developing the common law, judges must necessarily look to the present and to the future as well as to the past.

The further development of the common law of negligence

93. Having rejected arbitrary exclusions, proximity, impairment of precise legal rights and *Anns* and *Caparo* as suitable determinants of duty, where does one find a conceptual framework that will promote predictability and continuity and at the same time facilitate change in the law when it is needed? I think that the existing legal materials already contain part of the answer. We have the established categories, a considerable body of case law and the useful concept of reasonable foreseeability. If a case falls outside an established category, but the defendant should reasonably have foreseen that its conduct would cause harm to the plaintiff, we have only to ask whether the reasons that called for or denied a duty in other (usually similar) cases require the imposition of a duty in the instant case. No doubt that may sometimes mean that, whether or not a duty is imposed at a particular time, will depend on the extent to which the case law has progressed to that time. But that is the way of the common law, the judges preferring to go "from case to case, like the ancient Mediterranean mariners, hugging the coast from point to point, and avoiding the dangers of the open sea of system or science" (Lord Wright, "The Study of Law" (1938) 54 *Law Quarterly Review* 185 at 186). It is not an approach that appeals to grand theorists who prefer to decide cases by general principles applicable to all cases. But in an area of law such as awarding damages for negligently inflicted economic loss, which is still developing and which has been recently cast adrift from any unifying principle, there is no alternative to a cautious development of the law on a case by case basis (*Caltex Oil (Australia) Pty Ltd v The Dredge "Willemstad"* at 555 per Gibbs J, 576 per Stephen J). Perhaps another unifying principle may emerge and gain widespread acceptance. Past experience suggests that, if it does, its fall from favour will not be long in coming. Until a unifying principle again emerges, however, the best solution is to proceed incrementally from the established cases and principles.

The incremental approach is the most satisfactory approach

94. In my view, given the needs of practitioners and trial judges, the most helpful approach to the duty problem is first to ascertain whether the case comes within an established category. If the answer is in the negative, the next question is, was the harm which the plaintiff suffered a reasonably foreseeable result of the defendant's acts or omissions? A negative answer will result in a finding of no duty. But a positive answer invites further inquiry and an examination of analogous cases where the courts have held that a duty does or does not exist. The law should be developed incrementally by reference to the reasons why the material facts in analogous cases did or did not found a duty and by reference to the few principles of general application that can be found in the duty cases.

95. Further, I think that, so far as possible, the reasons for upholding or denying a duty in particular cases should be regarded as principles to be applied in determining whether a duty exists in cases within that category. Such reasons will reflect policies that the courts have recognised as relevant in determining the duty issue. In some cases, they will be so decisive in determining duty that they can be applied as rules or principles in other cases.

[217] 96. The present case is not one falling within any categories of liability hitherto recognised. The Canadian Supreme Court has adopted the categorisation of cases of pure economic loss proposed by Professor Feldthusen (*Winnipeg Condominium Corporation No 36 v Bird Construction Co* [1995] 1 SCR 85 at 96-97):

[218] 1. The Independent Liability of Statutory Public Authorities;

2. Negligent Misrepresentation;

3. Negligent Performance of a Service;

4. Negligent Supply of Shoddy Goods or Structures;

5. Relational Economic Loss.

97. The present case is not within any of these categories. It is perhaps closest to the last category. Professor Feldthusen has said that relational economic loss exists "when the defendant damages property owned by a third party and the plaintiff thereby suffers economic loss because of some relationship that exists between the plaintiff and the third party" (Feldthusen, "Liability for Pure Economic Loss: Yes, But Why?" (1999) 28 *University of Western Australia Law Review* 84 at 98). However, this case is not a typical case of relational economic loss as the relationship between the third party (the Sparnons) and the plaintiff (the Perres) is purely a matter of physical proximity. ...

99. The present case is therefore novel in terms of the categories. But that does not mean that no duty of care was owed to the Perres. "The categories of negligence", said Lord Macmillan, "are never closed" (*Donoghue v Stevenson* [1932] AC 562 at 619). The issue of duty must be decided by reference to the few general principles that appear to govern all cases of pure economic loss.

The reasons for denying or imposing a duty of care in cases of pure economic loss ...

[219] 101. Until 1963, the almost universal rule was that, absent contract or fiduciary relationship, a person owed no duty to avoid causing economic loss to another person, and, although no longer a universal rule, no duty is the general rule. Judges and academic commentators have subjected this exclusionary rule to an intense scrutiny which has yielded a broad consensus on the rationale for the rule. They generally agree that the theoretical underpinnings of the exclusionary rule are the need to avoid imposing indeterminate liability and the need to avoid imposing unreasonable burdens on the freedom of individuals to protect or pursue their own legitimate social and business interests without the need to be concerned with other persons' interests.

102. If the policy of the law is that indeterminacy of liability and conduct legitimately protecting or pursuing a person's social or business interests should not give rise to a duty of care, that policy should be translated into forms which can be applied as rules of law. I see no reason why that step should not be taken. However, indeterminacy and conduct legitimately protecting or pursuing a person's social or business interests are merely factors which negative the existence of a duty. That is an important limitation on their utility [220] as a principle for determining whether a duty exists. Recognition of that limitation also answers the criticism that indeterminacy of liability and conduct legitimately protecting or pursuing a person's social or business interests are not useful criteria in determining duty because they are not relevant to all cases of pure economic loss. On the contrary, they are useful because, when they apply, they provide valid reasons for rejecting a duty. It hardly needs to be said that, when they are absent, no duty, or even a prima facie duty, automatically arises.

103. Nevertheless, when a court is satisfied that the economic loss suffered by the plaintiff was reasonably foreseeable by the defendant, that no question of indeterminacy of liability arises and that the defendant was not legitimately protecting or pursuing his or her social or business interests, it will often accord with community standards and the goals of negligence law, as an instrument of corrective justice, to hold that the defendant should have had the plaintiff's interests in mind when engaging or refusing to engage in a particular course of conduct. However, the common law in its desire to give effect to the autonomy of each individual does not generally require a person to act as if he or she were "my brother's keeper". That is particularly so when the defendant would have to take affirmative action to save a person from suffering harm.

104. What is likely to be decisive, and always of relevance, in determining whether a duty of care is owed is the answer to the question, "How vulnerable was the plaintiff to incurring loss by reason of the defendant's conduct?" So also is the actual knowledge of the defendant concerning

that risk and its magnitude. If no question of indeterminate liability is present and the defendant, having no legitimate interest to pursue, is aware that his or her conduct will cause economic loss to persons who are not easily able to protect themselves against that loss, it seems to accord with current community standards in most, if not all, cases to require the defendant to have the interests of those persons in mind before he or she embarks on that conduct.

105. The principles concerned with reasonable foreseeability of loss, indeterminacy of liability, autonomy of the individual, vulnerability to risk and the defendant's knowledge of the risk and its magnitude are, I think, relevant in determining whether a duty exists in all cases of liability for pure economic loss. In particular cases, other policies and principles may guide and even determine the outcome. But I do not think that a duty can be held to exist in any case of pure economic loss without considering the effect of the application of these general principles. ...

[231] Apand owed a duty of care
133. Upon the facts of this case, whether or not Apand owed a duty of care depends on the answers to the following questions:
1. Was the loss suffered by the Perres or members of the group reasonably foreseeable?
2. If yes to question 1, would the imposition of a duty of care impose indeterminate liability on Apand?
3. If no to question 2, would the imposition of a duty of care impose an unreasonable burden on the autonomy of Apand?
4. If no to question 3, were the Perres or some of them vulnerable to loss from the conduct of Apand?
5. Did Apand know that its conduct could cause harm to individuals such as the Perres?

134. I do not think that any other factors are relevant in determining whether Apand owed a duty of care to the Perres. For example, no question of economic efficiency arises.

135. Apand does not dispute that the loss suffered by the Perres was reasonably foreseeable, and I think the rest of these questions should be answered favourably to the Perres or, at all events, to some of them.

136. Upon the facts of this case, therefore, Apand owed a duty of care to **[232]** the Perres to protect them from the loss of sales to the Western Australian market and diminution in the value of their farming lands. That is to say, Apand owed the Perres a duty to protect them from pure economic loss. ...

GUMMOW J. ... **[253]** 199. The case law will advance from one precedent to the next. Yet the making of a new precedent will not be determined merely by seeking the comfort of an earlier decision of which the case at bar may be seen as an incremental development, with an analogy to an established category. Such a proposition, in terms used by McCarthy J in the Irish **[254]** Supreme Court, "suffers from a temporal defect – that rights should be determined by the accident of birth" (*Ward v McMaster* [1988] IR 337 at 347).

200. The emergence of a coherent body of precedents will be impeded, not assisted, by the imposition of a fixed system of categories (see the observations of Lord Goff of Chieveley in *Westdeutsche Landesbank Girozentrale v Islington London Borough Council* [1996] AC 669 at 692) in which damages in negligence for economic loss may be recovered. ...

201. I prefer the approach taken by Stephen J in *Caltex Oil (Australia) Pty Ltd v The Dredge "Willemstad"* (1976) 136 CLR 529. His Honour isolated a number of "salient features" which combined to constitute a sufficiently close relationship to give rise to a duty of care owed to Caltex for breach of which it might recover its purely economic loss (at 576-7). In *Hill v Van Erp* (1997) 188 CLR 159 (at 233-4) and *Pyrenees Shire Council v Day* (1998) 192 CLR 330 at 389, I favoured a similar approach, with allowance for the operation of appropriate "control mechanisms". ...

[255] The salient features of the present case ...
[258] 213. [A]t the time of the supply of the seed to the Sparnons, Apand knew or ought to have known that Warruga grew commercial potato crops within the 20 kilometre buffer zone, and knew of the special requirements of the Western Australian law with respect to importation of potatoes grown in adjoining areas to those where there was an outbreak of the disease. ...

[259] 215. The evidence was that, leaving aside the Saturna seed, the only potato seed which Apand sent into South Australia had been certified under the Certification Scheme. Apand appreciated that the major cause of the spread of bacterial wilt was through growers buying non-certified seed. As a practical matter, Apand was in control of the initiation and conduct of the experimental activities using the Sparnons' property. Apand both selected and supplied the seed and chose the location for the experiment.

216. The Perres had no way of appreciating the existence of the risk to which they were exposed by the conduct of the Apand experiment and no avenue to protect themselves against that risk. They thus stood in quite a different position from that of the financier in *Esanda Finance Corporation Ltd v Peat Marwick Hungerfords* which had the power to deal from a position of strength in ordering its commercial relationship with the party to whom it provided financial accommodation (see (1997) 188 CLR 241 at 266, 284-285, 304). Here, the relevant risk to the commercial interests of the appellants was in the exclusive control of Apand. ... The effect of the Western Australian legislation upon the export market from South Australia was such that, within the **[260]** buffer zone, the economic loss would flow directly and inevitably and the possibility of its occurrence would not be speculative.

217. The characteristics of the present case to which I have referred combined ... to bring the Perres and Apand into such close and direct relations as to give rise to a duty of care owed by Apand for breach of which purely economic loss may be recovered. ...

KIRBY J. ... **[275]** 259. **The proper approach: foreseeability, proximity and policy**
... As an approach or methodology for deciding whether a legal duty of care in negligence exists, I suggested [in *Pyrenees Shire Council v Day* (1998) 192 CLR 330 at 419-420] that the decision-maker must ask three questions:
1. Was it reasonably foreseeable to the alleged wrongdoer that particular conduct or an omission on its part would be likely to cause harm to persons who have suffered damage or a person in the same position?
2. Does there exist between the alleged wrongdoer and such person a relationship characterised by the law as one of "proximity" or "neighbourhood"?
3. If so, is it fair, just and reasonable that the law should impose a duty of a given scope upon the alleged wrongdoer for the benefit of such a person? ...

[285] 285. Critics have complained that the three-fold approach is not helpful. If the courts have recognised as "control mechanisms" the avoidance of indeterminate liability and non-interference with ordinary business conduct, it is asked, why not say so directly? Why not simply adopt these considerations as legal rules?

286. The answer to this question depends upon the importance attached to returning legal liability for pure economic loss to a conceptual framework common to all other actions expressed in terms of the tort of negligence. It also depends upon the level of abstraction in which such concepts are to be stated for legal purposes. Considerations of indeterminacy of liability, vulnerability to risk, the autonomy of the individual and market competitiveness are not issues relevant to all negligence actions. It is therefore quite inappropriate to elevate them so that they are legal preconditions to the existence of a duty of care in negligence or "principles" to be applied in deciding whether the duty exists in the particular case. They are not even essential or relevant to every case framed in negligence where the damage claimed is purely of an economic character, without physical injury to the plaintiff's property or person. What is therefore needed is a more general or conceptual methodology or approach which provides the heading to which these considerations may be assigned when, in the particular case, they are considered relevant. Conceptually, they all belong to the evaluation of considerations of policy. Each of them is a powerful negative policy reason for inhibiting the extension of legal liability in negligence for pure economic loss.

287. Finally, it is said that the three-fold approach imposes upon lawyers advising clients, trial judges and even appellate courts unreasonable **[286]** burdens and upon clients intolerable uncertainties and costs. The answer to this complaint is that such burdens and uncertainties already exist. They do not disappear simply because the policy considerations are artificially squeezed into the "labels" of "foreseeability", "reliance" or "proximity". They certainly do not disappear because

new rules or "principles" are invented in the fond hope, once again, of establishing universal norms. The policy evaluation stubbornly remains. As it seems to me, it is better by far that it be addressed with candour and recognised for the legal function that it performs. I do not accept that such a function is beyond the evaluative powers of judges and lawyers. Indeed, they already perform that evaluation. *Caparo* and its methodology simply bring the judicial choices into the open. ...

Application of the three-stage approach

289. **Foreseeability:** When the problem in the present appeal is approached by the methodology which I favour, the answer to the first question (foreseeability) is readily given. It is beyond serious argument in this case that damage to the Perre interests of the type that occurred was, or ought reasonably to have been, foreseen by Apand. ... **[287]** Not only *ought* Apand to have foreseen damage of the kind that might occur to the Perre interests; the evidence discloses that it actually *did* foresee precisely the kind of damage that eventuated, even if it did not turn its attention to the particular individuals who would be afflicted with that damage if it occurred. ...

[288] 292. **Proximity:** ... As a matter of fact, the evidence showed that each of the Perre interests carried on their respective activities within extremely close physical proximity to the Sparnons' property. ...

[289] 296. The outer boundary was relevantly circumscribed by potato growing interests within a radius of 20 kilometres from a farm to which the non-certified seed was sent for planting. This was a risk which Apand took with its eyes open. Potato farmers within that radius were in a relationship of proximity or neighbourhood because of their vulnerability arising from an almost contiguous physical propinquity to a farm to which Apand decided to introduce the uncertified seed as part of its winter crop experiment. The second consideration is therefore also satisfied.

297. **Policy:** When I turn to the third consideration, it is necessary to weigh the two particular policy reasons which, in the past (and, it was suggested, in this case), have emerged to justify a rule excluding a legal duty of care to a plaintiff who has suffered no physical damage to its person or property but only pure economic loss.

298. I refer, first, to the concern to avoid imposing legal liability upon an indeterminate class for indeterminate amounts. This is a legitimate and justifiable concern. It would, for example, allow the law to draw a rational line which would deny recovery to the local store in the Perres' town whose income had dropped because of the loss to the Perre interests (and hence to the income of its principals and employees) following the loss of the export trade to Western Australia. It would permit exclusion of a legal duty of care to a trucking firm which, before the blight, carried the potatoes to Western Australia. It would exclude consumers in that State, forced to purchase potatoes, or **[290]** the crisps manufactured from them, from other more distant and expensive suppliers. A line must be drawn to limit indeterminate liability. What permits it to be drawn in this case, and not to exclude all of the Perre interests, is the specific foresight of potential damage to potato producers in the position of the Perres, operating in such close proximity to the Sparnons. In this sense the Perres were particularly vulnerable to the conduct of Apand, as it ought to have recognised and in a general sense did. ...

300. Nor is this a case where to hold Apand to a legal duty of care would be to interfere unreasonably with its economic freedom, its autonomy and the competitive operation of the marketplace (*Leigh and Sillivan Ltd v Aliakmon Shipping Co Ltd* [1985] QB 350 at 393). As a matter of policy, the law will generally uphold the right of a party lawfully to gain profit although doing so will occasion economic loss to others. That is often the very way in which the market operates in our form of economy. Apand certainly had an economic interest in disposing of the non-certified seed when its original Saturna experiment was called off. But Apand was not entitled to pursue that interest in a way that constituted a breach of the law. ...

[291] 302. I do not consider that any other reason of legal policy, derived by analogy from earlier decisions in claims for pure economic loss (or from the so-called "exceptions" to the exclusionary rule), warrants a denial of the existence of a legal duty to which the foregoing considerations strongly point. So I now look back and check this conclusion with the general objects of the law of negligence in mind. The conclusion is confirmed. The basic question that lies at the heart of the tort is asked: ought Apand to be under a legal obligation to observe care to prevent damage to the

Perre interests from the risk inherent in its activities, the nature of which Apand actually foresaw or which was reasonably foreseeable to it? The answer which I would give to that question is in the affirmative. Apand owed the Perre interests a duty of care. An action based on the tort of negligence lies to enforce that duty for a proved breach which results in damage. It is not excluded merely because the damage suffered by the Perre interests was purely economic loss.

[Hayne J and Callinan J, in separate judgments, also found that the respondent owed a duty of care not to cause pure economic loss to the appellants.]

Appeal allowed

Chapter 6

Negligence: Breach of Duty

1. STANDARD OF CARE

Council of the Shire of Wyong v Shirt
(1980) 146 CLR 40
High Court of Australia

The breach of duty inquiry involves two stages, the first being whether a reasonable person in the defendant's position would have foreseen that his or her conduct involved a "not far-fetched or fanciful" risk of injury to a person in the plaintiff's position. If the answer is in the affirmative, the second stage is to determine what a reasonable person in the defendant's position would have done by way of response to the risk.

[The plaintiff brought an action for negligence against the defendant Council and others for damages for personal injuries suffered in a water-skiing accident in Tuggerah Lakes in January 1967. The plaintiff had been skiing in a circuit which was habitually used by water-skiers, when he fell and struck his head on the bed of the lake, suffering quadriplegic paralysis. The depth of the water in the lake at the point where he fell was between three feet six inches and four feet. In May 1966 the Council had completed dredging a channel six to eight feet deep from the shore into the lake and erected four signs carrying the words "Deep Water" adjacent to the channel. The accident occurred in the vicinity of one of those signs. The plaintiff maintained that he was misled by the sign into thinking that the water in the area where he was skiing was deep. At the trial the jury found that the Council was negligent. The New South Wales Court of Appeal upheld the verdict and judgment in favour of the plaintiff.]

MASON J. ... **[44]** The issue ... is whether it was reasonably open to the jury to conclude, as they did, that the Council was in breach of its duty to take care. The majority in the Court of Appeal thought that this question should be answered in the affirmative when, as Glass JA put it, "allowance is made for the undemanding test of foreseeability" ([1978] 1 NSWLR, at p 641).

Glass JA described the test as "undemanding" because in his view in its application to breach of duty the test involves the defendant in liability for injury which, though foreseeable, is extremely unlikely and may be described as "only a remote possibility" ([1978] 1 NSWLR, at p 642). His Honour specifically rejected the notion that the test denotes only events which are "likely to happen" or "not unlikely to happen" ([1978] 1 NSWLR, at p 641). He relied on Lord Reid's observations in *Koufos v C Czarnikow Ltd* [1969] 1 AC 350 and comments made by the Judicial Committee in *The "Wagon Mound" (No 2)* [1967] 1 AC 617. But he made no reference to the opposing view expressed by Barwick CJ in *Caterson v Commissioner for Railways* (1973) 128 CLR 99, at pp 101-102, where the Chief Justice stated his preference for the "not unlikely to occur" formulation.

Despite the comment by the Chief Justice in *Caterson* (1973) 128 CLR, at p 102 on Lord Reid's observations in *Koufos* [1969] 1 AC, at pp 385-386, Lord Reid there asserted **[45]** that liability in tort extended to "any type of damage which is reasonably foreseeable as liable to happen even in the most unusual case". A later passage in Lord Reid's speech ([1969] 1 AC, at p 389) makes it plain that his Lordship was using the expression "liable to happen", not in the sense of "not unlikely to happen", but so as to include an event which may be described as "a very improbable result".

So understood, his Lordship's comments are entirely consistent with what his Lordship had earlier said in delivering the opinion of the Judicial Committee in *The "Wagon Mound" (No 2)* [1967] AC, at pp 642-643. I venture to think that some confusion has arisen as to what was said and decided in that case by reason of the quotation of a single sentence from the opinion which appears at p 642. This sentence, when read in isolation and divorced from the discussion which precedes and succeeds it, is apt to convey an impression different from that expressed by the opinion when read in its entirety, as it should be. The sentence is in these terms:

> In their Lordships' judgment *Bolton v Stone* [1951] AC 850 did not alter the general principle that a person must be regarded as negligent if he does not take steps to eliminate a risk which he knows or ought to know is a real risk and not a mere possibility which would never influence the mind of a reasonable man.

Taken in isolation this observation may lend itself to the interpretation that foreseeability extends only to that which is not unlikely to occur.

His Lordship's discussion of the foreseeability doctrine began earlier with a classification of the cases which preceded *Bolton v Stone* [1951] AC 850, and continued with an examination of that case. The examination was designed to show that the case raised a new problem, the problem being that posed by a risk of injury which was foreseeable, notwithstanding that "the chance of its happening in the foreseeable future was infinitesimal", so infinitesimal "that it was only likely to happen once in so many thousand years" ([1967] AC, at p 642). The House of Lords held that there was no breach of duty, not because the risk of injury was not foreseeable, but because the risk, though foreseeable, was so small that a reasonable man would have been justified in disregarding it and taking no steps to eliminate it. Lord Reid then went on to observe that a reasonable man would only neglect such a small risk if he had some valid reason for doing so, "eg that it would involve considerable expense to eliminate the risk".

[46] Following the critical sentence which I have quoted above, Lord Reid said ([1967] AC, at pp 642-643):

> What that decision [*Bolton v Stone*] did was to recognise and give effect to the qualification that it is justifiable not to take steps to eliminate a real risk if it is small and if the circumstances are such that a reasonable man, careful of the safety of his neighbour, would think it right to neglect it.

In this sentence his Lordship characterizes the risk in *Bolton v Stone*, earlier described as "infinitesimal" yet one which could not be described as "a fantastic or far-fetched possibility", as none the less constituting "a real risk".

Finally, Lord Reid went on to deal with the facts as they had been established in *The "Wagon Mound" (No 2)*. He said ([1967] AC, at pp 643-644):

> In their Lordships' view a properly qualified and alert chief engineer would have realised there was a real risk here and they do not understand Walsh J to deny that. But he appears to have held that if a real risk can properly be described as remote it must then be held to be not reasonably foreseeable. That is a possible interpretation of some of the authorities. But this is still an open question and on principle their Lordships cannot accept this view. If a real risk is one which would occur to the mind of a reasonable man in the position of the defendant's servant and which he would not brush aside as far-fetched, and if the criterion is to be what that reasonable man would have done in the circumstances, then surely he would not neglect such a risk if action to eliminate it presented no difficulty, involved no disadvantage, and required no expense.

It is beyond question that their Lordships positively rejected the view that a risk of injury which is remote is of necessity not a real risk and that it falls outside the concept of foreseeability. What is more, as I read the opinion, the rejection of this view was essential to the decision in the case. Although this Court is no longer bound by a decision of the Privy Council, we will accord it great weight (see *Viro v The Queen* (1978) 141 CLR 88) especially when it is unanimous and it has been given on appeal from an Australian court.

However, it is of some significance that this Court in *Chapman v Hearse* (1961) 106 CLR 112, at p 120, though acknowledging the importance of the question under consideration, refrained from deciding it. Since then, by way of contrast to the observations of Barwick CJ in *Caterson* (1973) 128 CLR, at pp 101-102, we have seen the acceptance and application by Windeyer and Walsh JJ in *Mount Isa Mines Ltd v Pusey* (1970) 125 CLR 383, at pp 398-400, 413 of the concept of foreseeability as explained in *The "Wagon Mound"* **[47]** *(No 2)* [1967] AC, at pp 642-643. This is not to say that Barwick CJ is without support on the point. On the contrary it seems that Dixon CJ ((1961) 106 CLR, at p 115) was inclined to a somewhat similar view – see *Mount Isa Mines Ltd v Pusey* (1970) 125 CLR, at p 398, and we know that earlier Walsh J had based his judgment at first instance on a similar view in *The "Wagon Mound" (No 2)*.

Notwithstanding this Australian support for a narrower version of the foreseeability doctrine as applied to breach of duty, this Court would be well advised to accept that the law upon the point was correctly stated and applied by the Judicial Committee in *The "Wagon Mound" (No 2)*. I say this not only because *The "Wagon Mound" (No 2)* was a unanimous decision given on appeal from the Supreme Court of New South Wales, but also because there are sound reasons for accepting it as a correct statement of the law.

In essence its correctness depends upon a recognition of the general proposition that foreseeability of the risk of injury and the likelihood of that risk occurring are two different things. I am of course referring to foreseeability in the context of breach of duty, the concept of foreseeability in connexion with the existence of the duty of care involving a more generalized enquiry.

A risk of injury which is quite unlikely to occur, such as that which happened in *Bolton v Stone* [1951] AC 850, may nevertheless be plainly foreseeable. Consequently, when we speak of a risk of injury as being "foreseeable" we are not making any statement as to the probability or improbability of its occurrence, save that we are implicitly asserting that the risk is not one that is far-fetched or fanciful. Although it is true to say that in many cases the greater the degree of probability of the occurrence of the risk the more readily it will be perceived to be a risk, it certainly does not follow that a risk which is unlikely to occur is not foreseeable.

In deciding whether there has been a breach of the duty of care the tribunal of fact must first ask itself whether a reasonable man in the defendant's position would have foreseen that his conduct involved a risk of injury to the plaintiff or to a class of persons including the plaintiff. If the answer be in the affirmative, it is then for the tribunal of fact to determine what a reasonable man would do by way of response to the risk. The perception of the reasonable man's response calls for a consideration of the magnitude of the risk and the degree of the probability of its occurrence, along with the expense, difficulty and inconvenience of taking alleviating action and any other conflicting responsibilities which the defendant may **[48]** have. It is only when these matters are balanced out that the tribunal of fact can confidently assert what is the standard of response to be ascribed to the reasonable man placed in the defendant's position.

The considerations to which I have referred indicate that a risk of injury which is remote in the sense that it is extremely unlikely to occur may nevertheless constitute a foreseeable risk. A risk which is not far-fetched or fanciful is real and therefore foreseeable. But, as we have seen, the existence of a foreseeable risk of injury does not in itself dispose of the question of breach of duty. The magnitude of the risk and its degree of probability remain to be considered with other relevant factors.

In this case, however, the argument was aimed at the foreseeability of the risk. ... It was contended that the jury could not reasonably find that a reasonable man in McPhan's [the Council's engineer] circumstances would have foreseen that the message conveyed by the sign placed in the position in which it was fixed might lead to a risk of injury by inducing an inexperienced water-skier unfamiliar with the area to ski in the water immediately beyond the sign in the mistaken belief that it was deep whereas in fact the depth was only three feet six inches.

Despite the force of Mr McHugh's [senior counsel for the defendant] argument I am not persuaded that a finding of breach of duty was beyond the jury's competence. A reasonable man might well have concluded that the sign was ambiguous and that it could be read as an indication that there was a zone of deep water beyond, rather than in front of the sign. A reasonable man might also have concluded that a waterskier, so reading the sign, might be induced to ski in that zone of water, mistakenly believing it to be deep. The possibility might also have occurred to a reasonable man that it would be unsafe for an inexperienced water-skier to ski in water having a depth of three feet six inches and no more. He might well contemplate the possibility of a skier being projected into the water at a relatively high speed in consequence of a mishap and thereby sustaining injury in striking the bed of the lake. ...

[49] I would dismiss the appeal. ...

[Murphy J delivered a concurring judgment. Stephen and Aickin JJ agreed with Mason J. Wilson J dissented.]

Appeal dismissed

[In *Council of the Shire of Wyong v Shirt* (above), Mason J at 47 sets out a number of matters that a court should take into account in determining whether the defendant's conduct was a breach of the duty of care. A factor that may be considered at common law and should be considered under civil liability legislation, eg s 5B of the *Civil Liability Act 2002* (NSW), is the social utility of the defendant's activity that creates the risk of harm. In *Zhi Ming Jiao v New South Wales* [2011] NSWCA 232, the plaintiff was partly blinded when he was attacked by a fellow inmate of a remand centre while he, the plaintiff, talked to his wife during visiting hours. The trial judge found that the attack occurred suddenly and without warning with no opportunity for anyone to intervene, nor was there any reason for the defendant, the State of New South Wales as the entity legally responsible for the Prison Service, to anticipate the attack. The existence of a duty of care owed by the State to its prisoners was admitted and the State also admitted that the risk of one prisoner assaulting another was reasonably foreseeable. The issue at the trial was whether the State breached its duty to the plaintiff. The plaintiff argued, inter alia, that the defendant should have provided boxes in which prisoners would be isolated while having visitor contact. Evidence was given by a prison officer that over a six-year period there had been 224,640 visits involving an estimated 1,296,000 visitors. During that period there had been only six incidents, including that involving the plaintiff, where force had been necessary to restrain or subdue inmates in the visiting area. The trial judge dismissed the plaintiff's claim. An appeal to the New South Wales Court of Appeal failed. McFarlane JA, in agreement with Handley, AJA and Young, JA, commented:

18. In considering in what way, if any, a reasonable person in the position of the prison authorities would have responded to such risk of injury to the appellant as there was, it is in my view important to take account, as the primary judge did, of the following evidence given by Assistant Superintendent Hannah. At the date of trial Superintendent Hannah was the officer in charge of inmate visits at the [remand centre]. The following evidence that he gave was, this Court was told, not challenged in cross-examination, nor contradicted by other evidence.

"If say for instance a decision was made to provide all inmates with only box visits then a minimum of 60 boxes would be necessary. The implementation of box visits only would certainly dramatically reduce the need for camera surveillance however other problems arise. That is to say, human contact for inmates with family and friends is an essential ingredient for humanising an inmate[']s time in gaol. The aspect of contact and non-contact box visits are respectively used to provide reward and punishment. My experience is that it is more common than not that inmates with box visits are more agitated and aggressive as a result. Having [in] mind that physical harm and other ill treatment such as possibly the withholding of food is illegal and because an inmate[']s freedom has already been removed then there is very little in the gaol system that enables reward and punish[ment]. Reward basically involves buy-ups, telephone calls and contact visits whilst punishment involves segregation, removal of buy-ups, removal of telephone calls and non-contact visits. Of the rewards contact visits are the most significant. Box visits to my way of thinking is just a further step towards dehumanisation of the inmate. Without contact visits behaviour of inmates would worsen considerably. Without contact visits one of the most significant methods for control and good management of the gaol would be lost. Bearing in mind that problems during contact visits are virtually negligible. I can only imagine the mayhem that would occur with the gaol system if contact visits were removed" (Statement of Gordon Hannah, 10 September 2009 at [15]).

19. This evidence indicated that there was considerable social utility in the activity that alleg-edly created the risk of harm (see *Civil Liability Act 2002* (NSW), s 5B(2)(d)).]

Romeo v Conservation Commission of the Northern Territory
(1998) 192 CLR 431; [1998] HCA 5
High Court of Australia

When determining what a reasonable person in the defendant's position would have done in response to a reasonably foreseeable risk of injury to a person in the plaintiff's position, account will be taken of factors such as whether the risk was obvious, the degree or magnitude of the risk, the seriousness of any potential injury, the practicability and cost of safety precautions and the social utility of the defendant's activity in question.

[The appellant (plaintiff), Nadia Romeo, fell off the cliff-edge in a coastal reserve which was controlled and managed by the respondent (defendant), a public authority. Earlier, the appellant had been drinking alcohol at the car park situated at the top of the cliff, the perimeter of which consisted of low log fencing. The appellant had no recollection of the circumstances in which she fell off the cliff and there was no other direct evidence as to the circumstances of her fall. The trial judge rejected her claim for damages in negligence. She appealed to the Court of Appeal of the Northern Territory primarily on the ground that the trial judge had applied the wrong test to determine whether the respondent had breached its duty of care. The Court of Appeal dismissed the appeal. On further appeal to the High Court, it was unanimously held that the respondent owed the appellant a duty of care. However, the court by a majority held that the respondent had not breached its duty of care and dismissed the appeal. The following extracts are from some of the majority judgments describing the exercise of determining the breach of duty question.]

TOOHEY and GUMMOW JJ. … **[454]** 50. Whether there was a breach of the duty of care owed by the respondent to those who came onto the Reserve depended on "the action that a reasonable person in the respondent's situation would have taken to guard against the foreseeable risk of injury which existed" (*Nagle* [v *Rottnest Island Authority*] (1993) 177 CLR 423 at 431). An assessment of that action must be on the footing that the respondent had to take into account "the possibility that one or more of the persons to whom the duty is owed might fail to take proper care for his or her own safety" (*Nagle* at 431). But this does not mean that the respondent was obliged to ensure, by whatever means, that those coming onto the Reserve would not suffer injury by ignoring an obvious danger. This is particularly so in the case of the cliff which did present an obvious danger.

51. Because the appellant was aware of the danger presented by the cliff and since she failed to exercise ordinary care for her own safety, Angel J held that the respondent was not in breach of its duty of care. This approach directs attention to the degree of probability of the occurrence of an accident. There is however some tension between this approach and decisions of this Court which place this factor on the scales, to be weighed against the seriousness of the foreseeable risk and the expense, difficulty and inconvenience of precautions which could be taken. …

[455] 53. The point from which the appellant fell was not a viewing point except in the sense that visitors used the car park in order to watch sunsets from their cars. It was an obvious part of the cliff, even allowing for the vegetation in the area. And the evidence does not support a conclusion that there was an appearance of a path leading to the edge. If reasonable foreseeability is isolated from any other consideration, there may have been a "risk" of someone falling over the edge of the cliff in the sense used by Mason J in *Wyong Shire Council v Shirt* (1980) 146 CLR 40 at 48:
"A risk which is not far-fetched or fanciful is real and therefore foreseeable."
But in the present case the risk existed only in the case of someone ignoring the obvious.

54. In putting the matter in that way, there is a danger of drawing in the question of contributory negligence of the plaintiff to what is a consideration of the duty of care on the defendant. For that reason we think it is preferable to approach the matter on the footing that there was a duty of care on the respondent to take any steps that were reasonable to prevent the foreseeable risk becoming an actuality. But reasonable steps did not extend to fencing off or illuminating the edge of a cliff which was about two kilometres in length. The relationship of the car park to the rest of the Reserve did not call for special precautions at the cliff face nearby. A sign might serve as a warning to someone unfamiliar with the area. But to someone who was familiar, as the [456] appellant was, a warning sign would serve no purpose. ...

55. In that case, for the reasons given earlier, any negligence on the part of the respondent in this respect would not have caused the appellant's injuries. In that regard the case stands in contrast to *Nagle* and also to *Shirt* where the sign was ambiguous.

56. The respondent was under a general duty of care to take reasonable steps to prevent persons entering the Reserve from suffering injury. But the taking of such steps did not extend to fencing off an area of natural beauty where the presence of a cliff was obvious. In other words, there was no breach of the respondent's duty of care in failing to erect a barrier at the cliff edge. ...

59. We would dismiss the appeal.

KIRBY J. ... [478] *Scope of the duty*
122. It is one thing to hold that a person owes a duty of care of some kind to another. But the critical question is commonly the measure or scope of that duty. The failure to distinguish these concepts can only lead to confusion.

123. The ordinary formulation of the common law is that a body such as the Commission must take reasonable care to avoid foreseeable risks of injury to persons entering an area such as the reserve, including the cliffs, as of common right (cf *Nagle v Rottnest Island Authority* (1993) 177 CLR 423 at 429-430). However, that expression of the duty must be elaborated if it is to be of any practical guidance. The entrant is only entitled to expect the measure of care appropriate to the nature of the land or premises entered and to the relationship which exists between the entrant and the occupier. The measure of the care required will take into account the different ages, capacities, sobriety and advertance of the entrants. While account must be taken of the possibility of inadvertence or negligent conduct on the part of entrants, the occupier is generally entitled to assume that most entrants will take reasonable care for their own safety (*McLean v Tedman* (1984) 155 CLR 306 at 311-312; *Nagle* at 431; cf *Phillis v Daly* (1988) 15 NSWLR 65 at 74). For example, it would be neither reasonable nor just to impose upon a body such as the Commission an obligation to erect secure climb-proof fencing along the entire elevated headland of the reserve against the risk of injury suffered by the occasional visitor bent on suicide. In judging the measure of the duty which is owed regard will certainly be had to any particular statutory obligations or powers enjoyed by a public authority. But where, as here, the statutory duties are stated in general and permissive terms, the scope of the duty of care imposed by the common law will be no more than that of reasonable care. Where a risk is obvious to a person exercising reasonable care for his or her own safety, the notion that the occupier must warn the entrant about that risk is neither reasonable nor just. In considering whether the scope of the duty extends, in a case such as the present, to the provision of fencing or a wire barrier, it is not sufficient to evaluate that claim by reference only to the area of the Dripstone Cliffs. An accident of the kind which occurred to the appellant might have occurred at any other elevated promontory in every similar reserve under the control of the Commission to which members of the public had access. The projected scope of the duty must therefore be tested,

not solely with the hindsight gained from the happening of the accident to the particular plaintiff but by reference to what it was reasonable to have expected the Commission to have done to respond to foreseeable risks of injury to members of the public generally **[479]** coming upon any part of the lands under its control which presented similar risks arising out of equivalent conduct (*Cekan v Haines* (1990) 21 NSWLR 296).

124. It must never be forgotten that, in defining the measure of the duty of care, a court is not only determining an element essential to the ascertainment of the rights of the particular parties. It is also giving expression to the standards which occupiers of land or premises generally must reach, and possibly insure against, in case similar mishaps befall them (*Cekan v Haines* (1990) 21 NSWLR 296 at 299-300).

125. The conclusion that a duty of care is owed to a class of persons including the plaintiff, is not, of itself, determinative of the negligence of the defendant. The critical question in many cases is whether the plaintiff has proved that the duty has been breached in the circumstances of the case.

126. In *Wyong Shire Council v Shirt* (1980) 146 CLR 40, Mason J expressed the test which is accepted in Australia for ascertaining whether a breach of a duty of care of the defined scope has occurred. He said that the tribunal of fact must ask whether a reasonable person in the defendant's position would have foreseen that the conduct complained of involved a risk of injury to the plaintiff or to a person in a similar position (at 47-48):

"If the answer be in the affirmative, it is then for the tribunal of fact to determine what a reasonable man would do by way of response to the risk. The perception of the reasonable man's response calls for a consideration of the magnitude of the risk and the degree of the probability of its occurrence, along with the expense, difficulty and inconvenience of taking alleviating action and any other conflicting responsibilities which the defendant may have. It is only when these matters are balanced out that the tribunal of fact can confidently assert what is the standard of response to be ascribed to the reasonable man placed in the defendant's position."

127. It was not contested that this was the test to be applied in the present case. Thus, it is the reasonableness of a defendant's actions or inactions, when faced with the relevant risk, which is critical in determining whether a duty of care has been breached. The question whether the defendant has met the requisite standard of the reasonable person must be assessed on the facts of each case with reference to considerations such as those collected by Mason J in *Shirt*. These considerations provide a framework for determining which risks the defendant should guard against and which it can safely ignore.

[480] 128. Insufficient attention has been paid in some of the cases, and by some of the critics, to the practical considerations which must be "balanced out" before a breach of the duty of care may be found. It is here, in my view, that courts have both the authority and responsibility to introduce practical and sensible notions of reasonableness that will put a brake on the more extreme and unrealistic claims sometimes referred to by judicial and academic critics of this area of the law. Thus, under the consideration of the magnitude of the risk, an occupier would be entitled, in a proper case, to accept that the risk of a mishap such as occurred was so remote that "a reasonable man, careful of the safety of his neighbour, would think it right to neglect it" (*Overseas Tankship (UK) Ltd v Miller Steamship Co Pty Ltd* [1967] 1 AC 617 at 642-643). It is quite wrong to read past authority as requiring that *any* reasonably foreseeable risk, however remote, must in *every* case be guarded against. Such an approach may result from the erroneous conflation of the three separate inquiries: duty, scope of duty and breach of duty. Although a reasonably forseeable risk may indeed give rise to a duty, it is the inquiry as to the scope of that duty in the circumstances and the response to the relevant risk by a reasonable person which dictates whether the risk must be guarded against to conform to legal obligations. Precautions need only be taken when that course is required by the standard of reasonableness (*Phillis v Daly* (1988) 15 NSWLR 65 at 73 per Mahoney JA). Although it is true, as the appellant argued, that an occupier is not entitled to ignore safeguards against dangers because of the absence of past mishaps, it is equally true that years of experience without accidents may tend to confirm an occupier's assessment that the risks of harm were negligible.

129. As to the expense of taking alleviating action, it is increasingly recognised that courts must "bear in mind as one factor that resources available for the public service are limited and that

the allocation of resources is a matter for" bodies accorded that function by law (*Knight v Home Office* [1990] 3 All ER 237 at 243 per Pill J). Demanding the expenditure of resources in one area (such as the fencing of promontories in natural reserves) necessarily diverts resources from other areas of equal or possibly greater priority (*Cekan v Haines* (1990) 21 NSWLR 296 at 314 per Mahoney JA). Whilst this consideration does not expel the courts from the evaluation of what reasonableness requires in a particular case, it is undoubtedly a factor to be taken into account in making judgments which affect the operational priorities of a public authority and justify a finding that **[481]** their priorities were wrong. I leave aside, but shall return to, the extent to which "true policy" decisions of a public authority are justiciable. But even in so-called operational decisions, which are subject to court assessment, it is necessary to evaluate more than simply the cost of preventing the particular accident. Inherent in the suggestion of the obligation of prevention is the cost that would be incurred in the measures necessary to prevent all equivalent accidents of a like kind and risk.

130. In the reference to "other conflicting responsibilities" regard may be had to considerations such as the preservation of the aesthetics of a natural environment and the avoidance of measures which would significantly alter the character of a natural setting at substantial cost and for an improvement in safety of negligible utility.

131. When, therefore, the considerations mentioned by Mason J in *Shirt* are given their full measure, the conclusion in this case that no breach was shown on the part of the Commission must be upheld. The important distinction between this case and *Nagle* is that there the danger of the submerged rocks was hidden from the ordinary users of the Basin. Here, the danger of the elevation of the cliffs was perfectly obvious to any reasonable person.

132. In determining what risks the defendant was required by law to respond to, it is necessary to have regard to what acts the defendant may have reasonably anticipated in the circumstances. Given the prominence of the danger, past usage of the site and accident experience it was not reasonable to expect the defendant to anticipate the inadvertence of the plaintiff in this case. So far as her complaint about the clearing of the vegetation and its appearance as a path is concerned, that appearance would not have deceived her, according to the primary judge's findings, but for her alcohol affected state. It is true to say that the Commission, acting reasonably, would have to anticipate a variety of visitors, including children, the elderly, the shortsighted, the intoxicated and the exuberant. However, because the risk was obvious and because the natural condition of the cliffs was part of their attraction, the suggestion that the cliffs should have been enclosed by a barrier must be tested by the proposition that all equivalent sites for which the Commission was responsible would have to be so fenced. The proposition that such precautions were necessary to arrest the passage of an inattentive young woman affected by alcohol is simply not reasonable. The perceived magnitude of risk, the remote possibility that an accident would occur, the expense, difficulty and inconvenience of alleviating conduct and the other proper priorities of the Commission confirm the conclusion that breach **[482]** of the Commission's duty of care to the appellant was not established. The Commission's failure to provide protection against the risk that occurred was not unreasonable. The decision of the Court of Appeal to that effect was correct. It should be confirmed. ...

[485] 142. The appeal should be dismissed.

HAYNE J. ... **[488]** 155. In this case the Commission owed visitors who lawfully entered land which it managed, a duty to take reasonable care to avoid foreseeable risks of injury to them. But the bare fact that the risk of the injury which in fact occurred was reasonably foreseeable (in the sense of not far-fetched or fanciful) does not conclude the enquiry about the scope of the Commission's duty. The duty is a duty to take *reasonable care*, not a duty to prevent any and all reasonable [sic] foreseeable injuries.

156. The fact that an accident has happened and injury has been sustained will often be the most eloquent demonstration that the possibility of its occurrence was not far-fetched or fanciful. Indeed, often it will be difficult, if not impossible, to demonstrate the contrary to a tribunal of fact. That is why it is of the first importance to bear steadily in mind that the duty is not that of an insurer but a duty to act reasonably.

157. What is reasonable must be judged in the light of *all* the circumstances. Usually the gravity of the injury that might be sustained, the likelihood of such an injury occurring and the difficulty and cost of averting the danger will loom large in that consideration. But it is not only those factors that may bear upon the question. In the case of a public authority which manages public lands, it may or may not be able to control entry on the land in the same way that a private owner may; it may have responsibility for an area of wilderness far removed from the nearest town or village or an area of carefully manicured park in the middle of a capital city; it may positively encourage, or at least know of, use of the land only by the fit and adventurous or by those of all ages and conditions. All of these matters **[489]** may bear upon what the reasonable response of the authority may be to the fact that injury is reasonably foreseeable. Similarly, it may be necessary, in a particular case, to consider whether the danger was hidden or obvious, or to consider whether it could be avoided by the exercise of the degree of care ordinarily exercised by a member of the public, or to consider whether the danger is one created by the action of the authority or is naturally occurring. But all of these matters (and I am not to be taken as giving some exhaustive list) are no more than particular factors which *may* go towards judging what reasonable care on the part of a particular defendant required. In the end, that question, what is reasonable, is a question of fact to be judged in all the circumstances of the case (*Herrington v British Railways Board* [1971] 2 QB 107 at 120 per Salmon LJ cited with approval in *Hackshaw* (1984) 155 CLR 614 at 663 per Deane J). ...

[490] 159. It is because the duty is a duty to take reasonable care that the suggestion that the liability of public authorities has been taken too far is a suggestion that should be rejected. As I have pointed out, it may be relatively easy to show that the risk of occurrence of an injury which a person has suffered in fact was a reasonably foreseeable risk, but if it was reasonable for the defendant authority to take steps to avoid such a risk there is no reason why it should not be held liable for its failure. And if it was not reasonable to take steps to avoid the risk the authority will not be liable.

160. It may be said that this analysis does not recognise, or even may be said to obscure, the forensic disadvantage which a defendant suffers once a court concludes that a risk of injury was reasonably foreseeable. Counsel for the Commission suggested, in effect, that some cheap solution can always be put forward after the event and that a finding of liability is then inevitable once foreseeability of the risk is accepted. This case is a good illustration of why that argument is flawed.

161. It was suggested in this Court, and below, that all that would have been necessary to stop the plaintiff walking off the edge of the cliff was two star pickets and one or two strands of wire across the part of the cliff which the trial judge inferred that she and her companion had mistaken for a path. Thus, so the argument ran, a cheap and obvious means of avoiding catastrophic injury was readily available. That attributes a false degree of precision to identification of the foreseeable risk; it attributes too high a probability to the occurrence of that risk and it fails to identify properly the response that would have had to be made to that risk to avoid it. ...

[492] 166. In this case the plaintiff failed to demonstrate that the Commission, in the exercise of reasonable care, should have fenced the area in some way that would have prevented her falling and suffering the horrific injuries which she has. Her claim against the Commission must therefore fail and her appeal be dismissed.

[Brennan CJ also dismissed the appeal but on the ground that the respondent, as occupier, had not been shown to have breached its duty of care owed to entrants according to the test propounded by Dixon J in *Aiken v Kingborough Corp* (1939) 62 CLR 179 at 210. That test imposes a duty on an occupier to exercise reasonable care to prevent injury from dangers arising from the structure or condition of premises which are not apparent and are not to be avoided by the exercise of reasonable care on the part of the entrant. Gaudron and McHugh JJ, in separate dissenting judgments, held that the respondent had breached its duty of care by failing to fence the cliff-edge at the point where the appellant fell.]

Appeal dismissed

[*Romeo v Conservation Commission of the Northern Territory* (above) illustrates the factors that may be relevant in a determination of whether a defendant occupier, in that case a public authority, has breached its duty of care to an entrant. Those factors were said to include an expectation on the part of an occupier that entrants will take reasonable care for their own safety. Taking reasonable care may involve entrants taking precautions to avoid, inter alia, obvious risks.

Since the High Court of Australia, in *Brodie v Singleton Shire Council; Ghantous v Hawkesbury City Council* (2001) 206 CLR 512, overturned the long-standing common law immunity enjoyed by highway authorities from liability for negligence arising from their failure to repair public roads, the role and weight of the obviousness of a risk and the validity of an expectation that pedestrians and other road users will take reasonable care for their own safety have become significant in cases involving defects in public foot-paths and other road facilities.

The obviousness of a risk has also proved significant in cases involving diving accidents in natural swimming areas where the alleged negligence was the failure of a public authority to warn of the risk of diving into water of unknown or variable depths. In two cases, heard together, *Vairy v Wyong Shire Council* (2005) 223 CLR 422 and *Mulligan v Coffs Harbour City Council* (2005) 223 CLR 486, the plaintiff ultimately failed to prove negligence by the defendant public authority. Individual judgments of members of the High Court of Australia gave varying emphasis to the significance of the obviousness of the risk, in the light of other circumstances, in the determination of breach of duty, with Heydon and Callinan JJ stating in *Mulligan* at 509 [75] "obviousness may be of such significance and importance, indeed of such a very high degree of importance as to be overwhelmingly so, and effectively conclusive in some cases", while in *Vairy*, Hayne J at 470 [163], with whom Gummow J at 441 [55] agreed, stated "the 'obviousness factor' is not to be elevated into some doctrine or general rule of law".

In *Neindorf v Junkovic* (2005) 222 ALR 631, Kirby J said (footnotes omitted) of his statement at 478 [123] in *Romeo* (above):

[649] 71. … In *Romeo*, I wrote that "[w]here a risk is obvious to a person exercising reasonable care for his or her own safety, the notion that the occupier must warn the entrant about that risk is neither reasonable nor just". However, that statement was particular to the circumstances of that case. The case involved a manifestly dangerous cliff edge in a nature [650] reserve with a large drop. The statement was qualified by the need of the occupier to take account of "the possibility of inadvertence or negligent conduct on the part of entrants". It could not constitute, and was not intended to constitute, a universal proposition of law, applicable whatever the facts and circumstances of a case. And it said nothing about precautions other than warnings – such as taking practical steps to prevent or reduce the risks of avoidable injury.

72. Based on a misunderstanding of dicta of the kind described in *Romeo*, the idea has spread through the courts of Australia that occupiers, with responsibilities for the safety of premises can totally ignore those responsibilities because of the alleged obviousness of the risk to entrants. In principle, that is not and cannot be the law. In a sense, the obviousness of risk speaks chiefly to those who are in charge of the source of the risk and who have the opportunity, and prime responsibility, to reduce or eliminate it. … In some circumstances, the more obvious the risk, the greater the responsibility of those with the relevant power to protect others from it.

73. Entrants might (like the respondent in the present case) be momentarily distracted. The occupier will generally have more time and occasion to consider issues of risk and safety than short-term entrants. Further, a danger of placing so much emphasis on suggested obviousness is that, in a given case, it will distort proper consideration of a defence of contributory negligence. It will take that factor of alleged carelessness on the part of the plaintiff up into the negation of a breach of duty, instead of reaching it at the conclusion of conventional negligence analysis.

74. The mischief of this approach, which is spreading like wildfire through the courts of this land and must be arrested if proper negligence doctrine is to be restored, is that it can effectively revive the ancient common law position so that effectively, contributory negligence, of whatever proportion, becomes again a complete defence to an action framed in negligence and debars that

action. That consequence would reverse the universal enactment of apportionment legislation. That legislation recognises that, in many cases, a plaintiff's inadvertence or momentary carelessness is much less significant in the responsibility for accidents than a defendant's indifferent neglect of considerations of accident prevention which are substantially the defendant's own obligation.

75. If I could expunge the quoted passage from my reasons in *Romeo*, I would gladly do so. I would take it out, not because it was incorrect as a factual observation in the context of that case but because it has been repeatedly deployed by courts as an excuse to exempt those with greater power, knowledge, control and responsibility over risks from a duty of care to those who are vulnerable, inattentive, distracted and more dependent.

It remained a matter of contention as to whether these factors were relevant to the determination of the existence or scope of the *duty* of care or rather, and only, to the determination of *breach* of duty. In *Thompson v Woolworths (Q'land) Pty Ltd* (2005) 221 CLR 234, the High Court of Australia, in a joint judgment of Gleeson CJ, McHugh, Kirby, Hayne and Heydon JJ, stated:

[246] 36. The obviousness of a risk, and the remoteness of the likelihood that other people will fail to observe and avoid it, are often factors relevant to a judgement about what reasonableness requires as a response. In the case of some risks, reasonableness may require no response … .

[247] 37. The factual judgement involved in a decision about what is reasonably to be expected of a person who owes a duty of care to another involves an interplay of considerations. The weight to be given to any of them is likely to vary according to circumstances. If the obviousness of the risk, and the reasonableness of an expectation that other people will take care for their own safety, were conclusive against liability in every case, there would be little room for a doctrine of contributory negligence. On the other hand, if those considerations were irrelevant, community standards of reasonable behaviour would require radical alteration.

In *United States v Carroll Towing* 159 F 2d 169 (1947) Learned Hand J at (173) set out what has become well known as "the Hand Formula" in American jurisprudence, in the course of a judgment concerning the liability of a barge owner for damage done when an unattended barge broke away from its moorings:

Since there are occasions when every vessel will break from her moorings, and since, if she does, she becomes a menace to those about her; the owner's duty, as in other similar situations, to provide against resulting injuries is a function of three variables: (1) The probability that she will break away; (2) the gravity of the resulting injury, if she does; (3) the burden of adequate precautions. Possibly it serves to bring this notion into relief to state it in algebraic terms: if the probability be called P; the injury, L; and the burden, B; liability depends upon whether B is less than L multiplied by P: ie, whether B less than PL ["B<PL"].

In *Mulligan v Coffs Harbour City Council* (2005) 223 CLR 486, Gleeson CJ and Kirby J (who, in the minority, would have upheld the plaintiff's appeal in *Vairy v Wyong Shire Council* (2005) 223 CLR 422) agreed with the other members of the High Court of Australia that the plaintiff's appeal in that case should be dismissed. In this context their Honours commented as follows on the use of the term "negligence calculus" in deliberations about breach of duty, and on the difference, as they saw them, between these two cases:

[490] 1. This appeal was heard together with *Vairy v Wyong Shire Council*. In our reasons in that case we made some general remarks about the role of precedent in decision-making on the issue of breach of duty in negligence actions. We would incorporate them by reference in these reasons, and would add the following in relation to arguments that were put to the Court by reference to what was described as a "calculus".

2. Reference is often made to the "*Wyong Shire Council v Shirt* calculus". In that case [(1980) 146 CLR 40 at 47-48], Mason J referred to the way in which a tribunal of fact might determine what a reasonable person would do by way of response to a foreseeable risk. As he made clear, he

was describing a process of factual judgment. He referred to such factors as the magnitude of the risk, the degree of probability of its occurrence, the expense, difficulty and inconvenience of taking alleviating action, and any other conflicting responsibilities of the defendant. These, he said, were matters to be balanced out in making a judgment about reasonableness. The later use of the word "calculus" to describe this passage is unfortunate. A calculus is a method of calculation. What is involved in the process to which Mason J was referring is not a calculation; it is a judgment. In *Ridge v Baldwin* [1964] AC 40 at 65, Lord Reid observed that "[t]he idea of negligence is ... insusceptible of exact definition". Moreover, depending upon what may be involved in the concept of conflicting responsibilities, in some contexts, of which the present is an example, to treat what was said in *Shirt* as an inflexible formula could produce a distinctly unreasonable result. Where the suggested alleviating action is putting up a single warning sign at a particular location in a public recreational area, the expense, difficulty and inconvenience involved may be made to appear negligible. The more important question may be why a public authority would choose to single out that particular spot, or that particular risk, as the subject of a warning. In *Vairy*, according to the evidence, there were clear reasons why the public authority would choose to single out the elevated rock **[491]** platform. There was an established risk that supported the factual conclusion of the primary judge that a prohibition, or warning, sign should have been erected. Fifteen years before Mr Vairy's injury a similar accident had occurred. A young man who dived from the platform had struck the ocean bed and had been rendered tetraplegic. Contemporaneous reports had indicated a beach inspector's recommendation that a sign be placed in position. Yet it was not. The public authority's employees knew, or ought to have known, of the continued practice of diving from the rock platform in conditions of established danger. No such features were present in the facts of Mr Mulligan's case.

3. This Court recently said, in *Thompson v Woolworths (Q'land) Pty Ltd* (2005) 221 CLR 234, that reasonableness may require no response to a foreseeable risk, and pointed out that householders do not ordinarily place notices at their front doors warning entrants of all the dangers that await them if they fail to take reasonable care for their own safety. That observation was not the product of a calculus; it was simply a statement about community standards of reasonable behaviour.

4. ...The appellant [plaintiff] and a friend were swimming in the waters of a tidal estuary adjoining the Pacific Ocean in the popular holiday resort of Coffs Harbour. They were not doing anything that was unusual or that was attended by any particular level of danger over and above that which exists whenever and wherever swimmers plunge head first into water of variable depth. The appellant, a capable and experienced swimmer, was standing about thigh-deep in water. He had been swimming in the locality for about half an hour. He could not see the sandy bottom. As he had done, safely, on a number of earlier occasions, he dived into the water. This time, he hit his head on the sand. The appellant knew that the water was of variable depth, and that diving into water of variable depth is risky. The trial judge, Whealy J, found that the variation in depth resulted from bedforms that were "within normal and naturally occurring limits" of such an estuary.

5. In terms of appellate review, a significant difference between this case and the case of *Vairy* is that, in this case, there are concurrent findings of fact by the primary judge, and the Court of Appeal, adverse to the appellant on the issue of negligence. ...

[492] 6. The reasoning of Whealy J on all the issues in the case was orthodox. His conclusion on the issue of breach of duty was amply supported by the evidence, and unsurprising. There were features of the place where the appellant was swimming that were distinctive, but the conditions that led to the appellant's injury were not unusual. The danger that materialised was one that exists at virtually every Australian beach, and in most waterways. It is one of many dangers involved in swimming. It is difficult to see how such common dangers can be addressed by particular warnings at particular locations.

7. This has not been shown to be a case of injustice or error such as would justify the interference by this Court in the concurrent findings on the issue of negligence made in the Supreme Court of New South Wales. In any case, having considered the reasons of the Court of Appeal, and of the primary judge, we find no error. ...

The effect and legitimacy of an expectation on the part of a defendant that a plaintiff would take reasonable care for his or her own safety were considered again by the High Court of

Australia in *Roads and Traffic Authority of New South Wales v Dederer* (2007) 234 CLR 330 (below). So too was the significance of concurrent findings of fact by the trial judge and the intermediate appellate court. It may be observed that, in *Dederer*, although the plaintiff's personal injury claim ultimately failed on the issue of breach of duty, a question of fact, five of the nine judges who considered the case at the various stages of the litigation process were of the view that the defendant, the Roads and Traffic Authority of New South Wales, had been negligent.]

Roads and Traffic Authority of New South Wales v Dederer
(2007) 234 CLR 330; [2007] HCA 42
High Court of Australia

In determining whether there has been a breach of duty, the statement of principle by Mason J in Council of the Shire of Wyong v Shirt (1980) 146 CLR 40 at 47-48 (the so-called "calculus" of negligence) remains authoritative. However, in the application of that statement of principle to the facts of a particular case, there may be an acute division of judicial opinion.

[The first respondent/plaintiff, Mr Philip Dederer, then aged 14, dived from the Forster-Tuncurry bridge into the waters of the Wallamba River about nine metres below and suffered catastrophic personal injury when he struck a submerged sandbar. Although there were signs on the approaches to the bridge (of which the first respondent was aware) prohibiting diving and this was the first reported diving accident, there was evidence of a long standing and widespread practice (of which the appellant/defendant was aware) of young persons diving from the bridge.

In an action by the first respondent in the Supreme Court of New South Wales to recover damages for personal injury, the primary judge (Dunford J) found that the appellant, the public authority responsible for the bridge, had been negligent in failing to erect signs warning of the variable depth of the water below the bridge and the presence of sandbars. The appellant also had been negligent in failing to replace the horizontal fence railings on the bridge with vertical railings and in failing to replace the flat top of the handrail with a triangular shaped one. The primary judge also found that the appellant's negligence was a cause of the first respondent's personal injury and that the first respondent was guilty of contributory negligence. These findings were affirmed by a majority of the New South Wales Court of Appeal (Ipp and Tobias JJA; Handley JA dissenting), although the New South Wales Court of Appeal increased the primary judge's finding of the first respondent's contributory negligence from 25% to 50%.

A majority of the High Court of Australia (Gummow J, with whom Heydon J agreed, and Callinan J; Gleeson CJ and Kirby J dissenting) allowed the appellant's appeal from the New South Wales Court of Appeal and held that there had been no breach of duty by the appellant. Some footnotes are omitted in the extract below.]

GLEESON CJ. **[333]** 1. The principal question to be decided is whether this Court should overturn findings on negligence and causation made in the Supreme Court of New South Wales by the primary judge (Dunford J) and the Court of Appeal (Ipp and Tobias JJA, Handley JA dissenting) in an action for damages for personal injuries brought by the first respondent.

2. ... It is not in dispute that the appellant owed the first respondent a duty to take reasonable care for his safety. That the first respondent's own serious carelessness contributed to his injuries is plain; a large deduction from the damages he was awarded was made on account of his contributory negligence. Nevertheless, the appellant owed him a duty of care, and there was an issue whether, by its acts or omissions, it failed to take reasonable care for the safety of the first respondent. There was also an issue whether such failure was *a* cause of his injuries. Those issues, essentially factual, were resolved by the primary judge, and the Court of Appeal, adversely to the appellant. The bridge

was not designed to be a platform from which people might, for their own amusement, jump or dive into the water below. That was not its intended use. Yet it was a use that was regularly made of it, even though diving was prohibited. A claim, by a young person who disregarded the prohibition, that the bridge authority failed to take reasonable care for his safety is not immediately attractive, and would not be accepted lightly. Its wider implications are obvious. Even so, the **[334]** first respondent succeeded in his claim for damages (subject to a substantial reduction for contributory negligence) and his success was affirmed on appeal.

3. It is to be noted that the evidence in the case deals with the bridge and the railings as they were at the time of the injuries to the first respondent. They were still the same at the time of the trial. The bridge, in its present state, is there for anyone to see. At the time of the injury to the first respondent, and at the time of the trial, the railings on the northern side of the bridge consisted of three flat horizontal members. It was not difficult for a young person to mount the top rail and thereby use the bridge as a platform for jumping or diving. That is what the first respondent, and, according to the evidence, many others before him, did. The primary judge, and the majority in the Court of Appeal, criticised the appellant for not having installed a barrier (such as pool-type fencing) that would have been much more difficult to mount and use for diving. The fact that, in 1998, the design of the railings made it comparatively easy to climb on to or over the railings was an important part of the case against the appellant. There is no foundation in the evidence, or in common experience, for inferring that the only way to deter people from climbing and jumping would have been to adopt extreme and fanciful measures such as erecting a very high fence topped with shards of glass or razor wire. If the appellant had attempted, in argument, to persuade the Court to that view then it might have been challenged by questions prompted by the design of the present barrier.

4. The conclusion of the trial judge and the Court of Appeal that the appellant was negligent turned upon findings of primary fact, some of which were disputed and some of which were undisputed, inferences from those primary facts, and judgment as to what reasonableness required in the circumstances. Similarly, the issue of causation turned upon primary facts, inferences, and judgment on questions of probability.

5. In an appeal of this nature, the function of this Court, as a second appellate court and a court of final resort, is not simply to give a well-resourced litigant a third opportunity to persuade a tribunal to take a view of the facts favourable to that litigant. "It is well settled that a second appellate court, such as this Court is in the present case, should not, in the absence of special reasons such as plain injustice or clear error, disturb such concurrent findings" (*Louth v Diprose* (1992) 175 CLR 621 at 634 per Deane J). This is a principle of long standing, and its importance has not been diminished, but rather has been increased, in the circumstances of modern litigation.

6. In *Graham Barclay Oysters Pty Ltd v Ryan* (2002) 211 CLR 540 at 568-569 [53]-[54], I referred to what was said about the principle by the House of Lords during the nineteenth century in *Owners of P Caland v Glamorgan Steamship Co* **[335]** *Ltd* [1893] AC 207. That case concerned a collision between two ships. The question which vessel was to blame turned upon evidence about lighting. The Lord Chancellor, Lord Herschell, said that, weighing the probabilities, he would have been disposed to accept a particular view of the evidence, but he declined to give effect to that disposition because of what the House of Lords had said previously as to "the importance of not disturbing a mere finding of fact in which both the Courts below have concurred" (at 215). Such a step should be taken, he said, only "when it can be clearly demonstrated that the finding was erroneous" (at 215). Lord Watson said that it was "a salutary principle that judges sitting in a Court of last resort ought not to disturb concurrent findings of fact by the Courts below, unless they can arrive at … a tolerably clear conviction that [those] findings are erroneous" (at 216). …

[336] 10. [In *Louth v Diprose* (1992) 175 CLR 621 at 634 (a case about unconscionable conduct)]… Deane J referred to what he had earlier said in *Waltons Stores (Interstate) Ltd v Maher* (1988) 164 CLR 387 at 434-435 (concerning findings about mistaken belief in a contractual setting) as to the modern rationale of the principle, and the importance of litigious finality as a means of preserving equitable access to justice:

> [I]t is in the overall interests of … the preservation of at least some vestige of practical equality
> before the law that, in the absence of special circumstances, there should be an end to the

litigation of an issue of fact at least when the stage is reached that one party has succeeded upon it both on the hearing before the court of first instance and on a rehearing before the court of first appeal.

11. ...It is a principle that stands alongside, and applies in addition to, the principle concerning appellate intervention in factual judgments where a primary judge enjoys some particular advantage (*Graham Barclay Oysters Pty Ltd v Ryan* (2002) 211 CLR 540 at 569 [54]). The principles exist for different reasons, although in many cases they work to the same end.

12. In past times, in most Australian jurisdictions, including New South Wales, a decision on the issue of negligence in an action for damages for personal injuries would be made by a jury as the tribunal of fact. Since no reasons would be given for such a decision, the practical possibility of an appeal on the issue would be very limited (*Swain v Waverley Municipal Council* (2005) 220 CLR 517 at 519-522 [1]-[8].). Nowadays, as in the present case, the issue of negligence is normally dealt with by a trial judge who sits without a jury and who delivers a fully reasoned decision. This procedure facilitates (and in some cases invites) appellate review. The decision of a court of appeal also takes the form of a reasoned judgment, or of reasoned judgments, delivered after a reconsideration of all the evidence and arguments. The law continues to value finality (*D'Orta-Ekenaike v Victoria Legal Aid* (2005) 223 CLR 1), which, as Deane J pointed out, is related to questions of reasonable and equal access to justice. The more litigation becomes a process of attrition, the greater will be the tendency for the outcome of litigation to depend upon the resources, or financial support, available to litigants. That is not good for the administration of civil justice. Given the substantial reduction of jury trials in the administration of civil justice, the respect which a second appellate court shows to concurrent findings of fact is an important **[337]** counterweight to the seemingly inexorable tendency to prolong litigation. As Isaacs J said [in *Major v Bretherton* (1928) 41 CLR 62 at 70-71], it does not mean that this Court abdicates its own responsibilities; but it discharges those responsibilities with an appreciation that, for good reason, it requires to be clearly convinced of error before it will disturb such findings.

13. Two examples involved in the findings on negligence and causation in the present case illustrate the point. The primary judge and the majority in the Court of Appeal found that the appellant was aware, over a period of years, of the propensity of many people to jump, and of some people to dive, from the bridge. That inference was based largely on two facts: first, a number of witnesses said they saw these things happen, and there is no reason to think such occurrences were not widely known; secondly, the appellant erected a sign which appeared to reflect an awareness of the practice. Again, the primary judge and the majority in the Court of Appeal inferred that a more expansive sign, and a differently constructed railing or fence on the bridge, would have prevented the first respondent from diving. Those inferences were contestable, but they were open on the evidence, and the appellant's arguments on those matters were considered and rejected, for cogent reasons, by a trial judge and an appellate court.

14. A conclusion that a differently designed railing or fence on the bridge, or a differently expressed warning sign, would have deterred an over-confident youth, prepared to disregard an existing prohibition, from diving is a matter on which judgments may differ. Yet it is a judgment of a kind routinely made in negligence actions. When, in a given case, such a finding is reviewed and affirmed by an intermediate appellate court, then this Court should reverse the finding only when it is clearly convinced of error.

15. ... I agree with Kirby J, for the reasons he has given, that the findings on the issues of negligence and causation should not be overturned.

GUMMOW J. ...18. The errors of which the appellant rightly complains, regarding both the reasons of the trial judge and those of the New South Wales Court of Appeal, did not turn on factual matters upon which reasonable minds might differ. Rather, they concerned the misapplication of basic and settled matters of legal principle. These principles may be restated shortly. First, the proper resolution of an action in negligence depends **[338]** on the existence and scope of the relevant duty of care. Secondly, whatever its scope, a duty of care imposes an obligation to exercise reasonable care; it does not impose a duty to prevent potentially harmful conduct. Thirdly, the assessment of breach depends on the correct identification of the relevant risk of injury. Fourthly, breach must be assessed prospectively and not retrospectively. Fifthly, such an assessment of breach must be made in the manner described by Mason J in *Wyong Shire Council v Shirt* (1980) 146 CLR 40 at 47-48. ...

[345] *The scope of the RTA's duty of care*

43. Although the existence of a duty of care owed by the RTA to Mr Dederer was not in dispute, two points must be made about the nature and extent of that obligation. First, duties of care are not owed in the abstract. Rather, they are obligations of a particular scope, and that scope may be more or less expansive depending on the relationship in question. Secondly, whatever their scope, all duties of care are to be discharged by the exercise of reasonable care. They do not impose a more stringent or onerous burden.

44. Regarding the first point, a duty of care involves a particular and defined legal obligation arising out of a relationship between an ascertained defendant (or class of defendants) and an ascertained plaintiff (or class of plaintiffs). Sometimes, the determination of that legal obligation is more complicated than it was at the time Lord Atkin announced his "neighbour" principle in 1932 (*Donoghue v Stevenson* [1932] AC 562 at 580). The law now recognises types of loss and kinds of relationships which are different from those of earlier days. ...

45. ...The result of [*Brodie v Singleton Shire Council* (2001) 206 CLR 512] is that a road authority is obliged to exercise reasonable care so that the road is safe "for users exercising reasonable care for their own safety" (at 581 [163]). The expression of the scope of the RTA's duty of care in those terms has long antecedents in the law relating to occupiers' liability. In *Indermaur v Dames*, giving the judgment of the Court of Common Pleas, Willes J held that ((1866) LR 1 CP 274 at 288):

> **[346]** we consider it settled law, that [a visitor], using reasonable care on his part for his own safety, is entitled to expect that the occupier shall on his part use reasonable care to prevent damage from unusual danger.

The modern form of that principle has been frequently affirmed in recent times, both with regard to occupiers and roads authorities. Of course, the weight to be given to an expectation that potential plaintiffs will exercise reasonable care for their own safety is a general matter in the assessment of breach in every case (*Thompson v Woolworths (Qld) Pty Ltd* (2005) 221 CLR 234 at 246 [35]), but in the present case it was also a specific element contained, as a matter of law, in the scope of the RTA's duty of care.

46. A road authority such as the RTA is not obliged to exercise reasonable care in the abstract; still less is it obliged to ensure that a road be safe in all the circumstances. So much was recently reaffirmed in *Leichhardt Municipal Council v Montgomery* (2007) 230 CLR 22. Such an expression of the duty's scope has an obvious and direct consequence when assessing breach. As Gaudron, McHugh and Gummow JJ stated in *Brodie* at 580 [160]:

> In dealing with questions of breach of duty, whilst there is to be taken into account as a 'variable factor' the results of 'inadvertence' and 'thoughtlessness', a proper starting point may be the proposition that the persons using the road will themselves take ordinary care. (Citations omitted.)

Their Honours went on to observe that persons exercising reasonable care will be able to avoid injury in some situations, whereas others will present "a foreseeable risk of harm even to persons taking reasonable care for their own safety" (at 581 [163]).

47. The RTA's duty of care was owed to all users of the bridge, whether or not they took ordinary care for their own safety; the RTA did not cease to owe Mr Dederer a duty of care merely because of his own voluntary and obviously dangerous conduct in diving from the bridge. However, the extent of the obligation owed by the RTA was that of a roads authority exercising reasonable care to see that the road is safe "for users exercising reasonable care for their own safety" (*Brodie* at 581 [163]). The essential point is that the RTA did not owe a more stringent obligation towards careless road users as compared with careful ones. In each case, the same obligation of reasonable care was owed, and the extent of that obligation was to be measured against a duty whose scope took into account the exercise of reasonable care by road users themselves. ...

[347] *Reasonable care, not prevention*

49. In simple and complicated cases alike, one thing is fundamental: while duties of care may vary in content or scope, they are all to be discharged by the exercise of *reasonable* care. In *Vairy v Wyong Shire Council* (2005) 223 CLR 422, McHugh J explained (at 432 [25]):

> [T]he duty in negligence is generally described as a duty to take reasonable care. In some areas of the law of negligence, however, the duty is expressed in more limited and specific terms. Until the decision of this Court in [*Australian Safeway Stores Pty Ltd v*] *Zaluzna* (1987) 162 CLR 479, for example, the duty owed to entrants upon privately owned land varied according to the category of the entrants. They were classified as invitees, licensees and trespassers. Similarly, the duty in respect of negligent statements is more specific and limited than a simple duty to take reasonable care in all the circumstances of the case. In negligence cases involving physical injury, however, the duty is always expressed in terms of reasonable care. As Prosser and Keeton have pointed out, 'the duty is always the same – to conform to the legal standard of reasonable conduct in the light of the apparent risk' (*Law of Torts*, 5th ed (1984), p 356).

His Honour dissented from the outcome in *Vairy*, but that does not qualify the cogency of the above observations.

[348] 50. Leaving aside matters such as vicarious liability and the potential existence of non-delegable duties of care – neither of which is presently relevant – the exercise of reasonable care is always sufficient to exculpate a defendant in an action in negligence. In *Blyth v Birmingham Waterworks* (1856) 156 ER 1047 at 1049, Alderson B laid down the nature of the action ...:

> Negligence is the omission to do something which a reasonable man, guided upon those considerations which ordinarily regulate the conduct of human affairs, would do, or doing something which a prudent and reasonable man would not do.

Blyth was a case in which the exercise of reasonable care was sufficient to exonerate the defendants notwithstanding the plaintiff's injuries. However, the standard of reasonable care also results in the inculpation, rather than exoneration, of defendants. In the earlier case of *Vaughan v Menlove* (1837) 132 ER 490 at 493, Tindal CJ was able to say that:

> The care taken by a prudent man has always been the rule laid down ...Instead, therefore, of saying that the liability for negligence should be co-extensive with the judgment of each individual ... we ought rather to adhere to the rule which requires in all cases a regard to caution such as a man of ordinary prudence would observe.

It was therefore insufficient, in the judgment of his Lordship, that the defendant had acted "honestly and bonâ fide to the best of his own judgment" (at 493).

51. Such an obligation to exercise reasonable care must be contrasted with an obligation to prevent harm occurring to others. The former, not the latter, is the requirement of the law. ...

[349] 53. The RTA correctly complains that this orthodox approach was not applied at trial or in the Court of Appeal. The trial judge and the majority in the Court of Appeal each fixed on the failure of the "no diving" pictograms and "no climbing" signs to *prevent* diving or jumping from the bridge. The trial judge was "satisfied" that the signs "were *not effective* in the sense that large numbers of young people continued to jump, dive, do somersaults, etc from the bridge into the water", and his Honour found it "not sufficient to ignore the fact that the signs were being disregarded". In the Court of Appeal, Ipp JA reasoned that the signs "were not serving the purpose for which they had been erected"; that is, they "were not *preventing* children and young adults from endangering themselves in relatively large numbers on what seems to have been a daily basis over the summer months" and they were being "ignored and the practice was continuing unabated". Tobias JA asked whether the "known fact" of continued jumping called "for different measures to be adopted by the RTA to *prevent* the practice at least of jumping off the bridge". His Honour concluded that it was unreasonable "to ignore the well-known practice of children jumping from the bridge in defiance of 'No Diving' signs".

54. The error in that approach lies in confusing the question of whether the RTA failed to prevent the risk –taking conduct with the separate question of whether it exercised reasonable care. ...

[353] *The proper assessment of breach*

65. Having dealt with the relevant risk, it is appropriate to return to the inquiry into the assessment of breach. Whether reasonable care was exercised in the particular case is a question of fact going to the breach of any duty owed, not to the existence of that duty. In each case, the question of whether reasonable care was exercised is to be adjudged prospectively, and not by retrospectively asking whether the defendant's actions could have prevented the plaintiff's injury. As Hayne J stated in *Vairy* (at 461 [126]):

> When a plaintiff sues for damages alleging personal injury has been caused by the defendant's negligence, the inquiry about breach of duty must attempt to identify the reasonable person's response to foresight of the risk of occurrence of the injury which the plaintiff suffered. That inquiry must attempt, after the event, to judge what the reasonable person would have done to avoid what is now known to have occurred. Although that judgment must be made after the event it must seek to identify what the response would have been by a person looking forward at the prospect of the risk of injury. ...

66. Each of these principles was misapplied by the trial judge and the majority in the Court of Appeal. As explained earlier in these reasons, their Honours erred by focusing in retrospect on the failure of the RTA to *prevent* Mr Dederer's dive, as opposed to asking what, in prospect, the exercise of reasonable care would require in response to a foreseeable risk of injury. The use of phrases such as "an accident waiting to happen" was redolent of a retrospective, not prospective, approach to the matter.

67. What, then, was the correct approach towards assessing breach? The particular trap into which the majority of the Court of Appeal fell was that warned against by Hayne J in *Vairy* (462 [128]):

> If, instead of looking forward, the so-called *Shirt* calculus is undertaken looking back on what is known to have happened, the tort of negligence becomes separated from standards of reasonable-ness. It becomes separated because, in every case where the cost of taking alleviating action at the particular place where the plaintiff was injured is markedly less than the consequences of a risk coming to pass, it is well nigh inevitable that the defendant would be found to have acted without reasonable care if alleviating action was not taken. ...

[354] 69. ... What *Shirt* requires is a contextual and balanced assessment of the reasonable response to a foreseeable risk. Ultimately, the criterion is reasonableness, not some more stringent requirement of prevention.

70. Here, the risk of injury consequent upon jumping or diving from the bridge into water of variable depth was reasonably foreseeable. Indeed, the Court of Appeal correctly found, contrary to the trial judge, that the risk was one that was obvious even to a 14 year old boy, and it beggars belief that the RTA could not foresee the very conduct [355] against which its signage warned. The RTA's evidentiary dispute about whether it did in fact know of the continued practice of diving is beside the point: reasonable foreseeability is to be determined objectively, and the present risk was plainly foreseeable on any objective standard.

71. The magnitude of the risk was self-evidently grave. Mr Dederer's partial paralysis is among the worst kinds of injuries imaginable. The probability of that injury occurring was, however, low. Despite the frequency of jumping and diving from the bridge, no-one was injured until Mr Dederer's unfortunate dive.

72. What, then, of the expense, difficulty and inconvenience of taking alleviating action? The erection of further warning signs should not have been expensive, but Mr Dederer provided no evidence that they would be reasonable. The installation of pool-type fencing and a triangular cap on the handrail would have been more expensive and intrusive. The estimate of the cost of the handrail modification was some $108,072, and it was accepted that the cost of new fencing would be around $150,000 but, again, the reasonableness of such measures is open to doubt. ...

[356] 78. Returning, then, to the assessment of breach mandated by *Shirt*, it becomes apparent that the RTA did not breach its duty of care. Though grave, the risk faced by Mr Dederer was of a very low probability, and a reasonable response to that risk did not demand the measures suggested by him. ...

79. This was not a case in which the defendant had done nothing in response to a foreseeable risk. To the contrary, the RTA had erected signs warning of, and prohibiting, the very conduct engaged in by Mr Dederer. … In the circumstances, that was a reasonable response, and the law demands no more and no less.

Conclusion
80. The appeal should be allowed with costs. The RTA did not breach the duty of care it owed to Mr Dederer. …

CALLINAN J. … **[406]** 271. All parties, as did the courts below, accepted that the well-known formulation of Mason J in *Wyong Shire Council v Shirt* (1980) 146 CLR 40 at 47-48 should be applied here:

> In deciding whether there has been a breach of the duty of care the tribunal of fact must first ask itself whether a reasonable man in the defendant's position would have foreseen that his conduct involved a risk of injury to the plaintiff or to a class of persons including the plaintiff. If the answer be in the affirmative, it is then for the tribunal of fact to determine what a reasonable man would do by way of response to the risk. The perception of the reasonable man's response calls for a consideration of the magnitude of the risk and the degree of the probability of its occurrence, along with the expense, difficulty and inconvenience of taking alleviating action and any other conflicting responsibilities which the defendant may have. It is only when these matters are balanced out that the tribunal of fact can confidently assert what is the standard of response to be ascribed to the reasonable man placed in the defendant's position.

272. The evidence shows that there was a basis for holding that … the appellant …should reasonably have foreseen that the bridge and the railing on it, in its current state might present these risks: that the latter might provide a platform for divers and jumpers; and that they might thereby injure themselves, severely, either by jumping or diving on to a passing boat or a submerged bank, or indeed in the water itself.

273. The question then becomes, what was an appropriate response to those risks? That has to be answered by balancing the magnitude of the risk, the degree of probability of its occurrence, and the expense, **[407]** difficulty and inconvenience of taking alleviating action, and any other conflicting responsibilities of the defendants.

274. In my opinion the trial judge and the majority of the Court of Appeal erred, by failing to undertake this balancing exercise in a sufficient and proper way. Had they done so they would have identified and given full weight to these matters. As to "magnitude", I accept that diving from a height of 8 to 10 metres was itself a risky activity. It was for this reason that it was discouraged by police and officials, banned, and the subject of the pictograph signs. But even so, and despite flagrant defiance of the ban, not one out of the many who had dived in the 40 or so years that had elapsed since the construction of the bridge had been injured, so far as anyone could recall, let alone severely injured. This is to say that the risk, although undisputedly present, had a very low degree of probability of realization. And although the first respondent's injuries were grave, that is of great magnitude, seemingly minor mishaps can sometimes cause grave injuries.

275. Also to be balanced, are the interests of the community in being able to walk across the bridge, to enjoy the view, and to pause and lean in comfort on a flat surface of a top rail as they do so. Only an extremely high unscaleable fence, with perhaps shards of glass embedded in its top, or barbed, or electric, or razor wire, might, on the evidence, have deterred determined and adventurous youths from climbing and jumping. Equally, the substitution of vertical bars for horizontal rails is unlikely to have been an effective deterrent. Other measures such as the provision permanently of a sufficient number of police or other officials would exceed the requirements of a reasonable response. …

276. In any event, the notion that the first respondent and other youths would have heeded a worded sign when they flagrantly disregarded a pictograph sign of unmistakeable import, strains credibility. Indeed, the making of the excruciatingly fine distinctions, as each of the courts below did, between the content of the signs actually erected, and other allegedly preferable ones, as to which those courts themselves were not in agreement, was quite unconvincing. …

[408] 278. A defendant is not an insurer. Defendants are not under absolute duties to prevent injury, or indeed even to take all such measures as might make it less likely to occur. They are obliged only to make such responses as can be seen to be reasonable in the circumstances. A proper balancing exercise which takes all of the relevant circumstances into account leads inescapably to the conclusion that the appellant, in responding to a risk that had not been realized for 40 years, by erecting the pictograph signs, acted reasonably and adequately. ...

282. ... I would allow the appeal. ...

Appeal allowed

Rogers v Whitaker
(1992) 175 CLR 479
High Court of Australia

In advising or informing a patient of inherent risks before carrying out a surgical procedure, the standard of care required of a medical practitioner involves disclosure of risks to which a reasonable person in the patient's position would be likely to attach significance.

[The respondent (plaintiff), a patient of the appellant (defendant), an ophthalmic surgeon, became almost totally blind following surgery performed by him on her right eye. The respondent had been nearly blind in her right eye since a penetrating injury at the age of nine but had lived a substantially normal working and family life despite this disability. In 1983, at the age of forty-seven, after a routine eye "check-up" in which reading glasses were prescribed, she was referred to the appellant for possible surgery. The appellant advised her that he could operate on her right eye to remove scar tissue, which would improve its appearance and would probably restore significant sight to that eye as well as assisting in the prevention of glaucoma. Following the operation, not only was there no improvement in her right eye but the respondent developed inflammation in that eye and inflammation and sympathetic ophthalmia in her left eye, which led to complete loss of sight in the left eye and thus almost total blindness. The respondent commenced proceedings against the appellant for negligence.

At the trial before Campbell J in the Supreme Court of New South Wales, the evidence was that there was slightly more than a one in 14,000 chance of sympathetic ophthalmia developing after such surgery.]

MASON CJ, BRENNAN, DAWSON, TOOHEY and McHUGH JJ. ... **[482]** There is no question that the appellant conducted the operation with the required skill and care ... .

In the proceedings commenced by the respondent, numerous heads of negligence were alleged. Campbell J rejected all save the allegation that the appellant's failure to warn of the risk of sympathetic ophthalmia was negligent and resulted in the respondent's condition. While his Honour was not satisfied that proper medical practice required that the appellant warn the **[483]** respondent of the risk of sympathetic ophthalmia if she expressed no desire for information, he concluded that a warning was necessary in the light of her desire for such relevant information. The Court of Appeal (Mahoney, Priestley and Handley JJA) dismissed all grounds of the appellant's appeal from the judgment of $808,564.38 on both liability and damages ... . [T]he appellant has appealed on the questions of breach of duty and causation. ...

The law imposes on a medical practitioner a duty to exercise reasonable care and skill in the provision of professional advice and treatment. That duty is a "single comprehensive duty covering all the ways in which a doctor is called upon to exercise his skill and judgment": (*Sidaway v Governors of Bethlem Royal Hospital* [1985] AC 871, at p 893, per Lord Diplock); it extends to the examination, diagnosis and treatment of the patient and the provision of information in an appropriate case (*Gover v South Australia* (1985) 39 SASR 543, at p 551). It is, of course, necessary to give content to the duty in the given case.

The standard of reasonable care and skill required is that of the ordinary skilled person exercising and professing to have that special skill (*Bolam v Friern Hospital Management Committee*

[1957] 1 WLR 582, at p 586; [1957] 2 All ER 118, at p 121; [see also *Whitehouse v Jordan* [1981] 1 WLR 246; [1981] 1 All ER 267, at p 277, at p 258, per Lord Edmund-Davies and *Maynard v West Midlands Regional Health Authority* [1984] 1 WLR 634, at p 638; [1985] 1 All ER 635, at p 648, per Lord Scarman]), in this case the skill of an ophthalmic surgeon specializing in corneal and anterior segment surgery. As we have stated, the failure of the appellant to observe this standard, which the respondent successfully alleged before the primary judge, consisted of the appellant's failure to acquaint the respondent with the danger of sympathetic ophthalmia as a possible result of the surgical procedure to be carried out. The appellant's evidence was that "sympathetic ophthalmia was not something that came to my mind to mention to her".

The principal issue in this case relates to the scope and content of the appellant's duty of care: did the appellant's failure to advise and warn the respondent of the risks inherent in the operation constitute a breach of this duty? The appellant argues that this issue should be **[484]** resolved by application of the so-called *Bolam* principle, derived from the direction given by McNair J to the jury in the case of *Bolam v Friern Hospital Management Committee* [1957] 1 WLR 582; [1957] 2 All ER 118. In *Sidaway v Governors of Bethlem Royal Hospital* [1985] AC, at p 881, Lord Scarman stated the *Bolam* principle in these terms:

The *Bolam* principle may be formulated as a rule that a doctor is not negligent if he acts in accordance with a practice accepted at the time as proper by a responsible body of medical opinion even though other doctors adopt a different practice. In short, the law imposes the duty of care: but the standard of care is a matter of medical judgement.

Before the primary judge there was evidence from a body of reputable medical practitioners that, in the circumstances of the present case, they would not have warned the respondent of the danger of sympathetic ophthalmia; there was also, however, evidence from similarly reputable medical practitioners that they would have given such a warning. The respondent, for her part, argues that the *Bolam* principle should not be applied if it entails courts deferring to the medical experts in medical negligence cases and that, in any event, the primary judge was correct in the circumstances of this case in not deferring to the views of those medical practitioners who gave evidence that they would not have warned the respondent.

The *Bolam* principle has invariably been applied in English courts (*Whitehouse v Jordan; Maynard v West Midlands Regional Health Authority; Hills v Potter;* [1984] 1 WLR 641; [1983] 3 All ER 716; *Sidaway; Blyth v Bloomsbury Health Authority;* (Unreported; Court of Appeal; 5 February 1987); *Gold v Haringey Health Authority* [1988] QB 481). In decisions outside the field of medical negligence, there are also statements consistent with an application of the *Bolam* principle (*Mutual Life and Citizens Assurance Ltd v Evatt* [1971] AC 793, at p 804; *Saif Ali v Sydney Mitchell & Co* [1980] AC 198, at pp 218, 220). At its basis lies the recognition that, in matters involving medical expertise, there is ample scope for genuine difference of opinion and that a practitioner is not negligent merely because his or her conclusion or procedure differs from that of other practitioners (see *Hunter v Hanley* [1955] SLT 213, at p 217, per Lord President Clyde); a finding of negligence requires a finding that the defendant failed to exercise the ordinary skill of a doctor practising in the relevant field. ...

[Their Honours then referred to *Sidaway v Governors of Bethlem Royal Hospital* [1985] AC 871 in which the majority of the House of Lords, Lord Scarman dissenting, held that the question whether an omission to warn a patient of inherent risks of proposed treatment constituted a breach of a doctor's duty of care was to be determined by applying the *Bolam* principle, although members of the majority differed in their application of the principle.]

[486] One consequence of the application of the *Bolam* principle to cases involving the provision of advice or information is that, even if a patient asks a direct question about the possible risks or complications, the making of that inquiry would logically be of little or no significance; medical opinion determines whether the risk **[487]** should or should not be disclosed and the express desire of a particular patient for information or advice does not alter that opinion or the legal significance of that opinion. The fact that the various majority opinions in *Sidaway* [1985] AC, at pp 895, 898, 902-903, for example, suggest that, over and above the opinion of a respectable body of medical practitioners, the questions of a patient should truthfully be answered (subject to the therapeutic privilege) indicates a shortcoming in the *Bolam* approach. The existence of the shortcoming suggests that an acceptable approach in point of principle should recognize and attach significance to the relevance of a patient's questions. Even if a court were satisfied that a reasonable person in the patient's position would be unlikely to attach significance to a particular risk, the fact that the patient asked questions revealing concern about the risk would make the doctor aware that *this patient* did in fact attach significance to the risk. Subject to the therapeutic privilege, the question would therefore require a truthful answer.

In Australia, it has been accepted that the standard of care to be observed by a person with some special skill or competence is that of the ordinary skilled person exercising and professing to have that special skill (*Cook v Cook* (1986) 162 CLR 376, at 383-384; *Papatonakis v Australian Telecommunications Commission* (1985) 156 CLR 7, at 36; *Weber v Land Agents Board* (1986) 40 SASR 312, at 316; *Lewis v Tressider Andrews Associates Pty Ltd* [1987] 2 Qd R 533, at 542). But, that standard is not determined solely or even primarily by reference to the practice followed or supported by a responsible body of opinion in the relevant profession or trade (see, eg, *Florida Hotels Pty Ltd v Mayo* (1985) 113 CLR 588, at pp 593, 601). Even in the sphere of diagnosis and treatment, the heartland of the skilled medical practitioner, the *Bolam* principle has not always been applied (see *Albrighton v Royal Prince Alfred Hospital* [1980] 2 NSWLR 542, at pp 562-563 (case of medical treatment). See also *E v Australian Red Cross* (1991) 27 FCR 310, at p 360). Further, and more importantly, particularly in the field of non-disclosure of risk and the provision of advice and information, the *Bolam* principle has been discarded and, instead, the courts have adopted (*Albrighton v Royal Alfred Hospital* [1980] 2 NSWLR, at pp 562-563; *F v R* (1983) 33 SASR 189, at pp 196, 200, 202, 205; *Battersby v Tottman* (1985) 37 SASR, at pp 527, 534, 539-540; *E v Australian Red Cross* (1991) 27 FCR, at pp 358-360) the principle that, while evidence of acceptable medical practice is a useful guide for the courts, it is for the courts to adjudicate on what is the appropriate standard of care after giving weight to "the paramount consideration that a person is entitled to make his own decision about his life" (*F v R* (1983) 33 SASR, at p 113).

[488] In *F v R* (1983) 33 SASR 189, which was decided by the Full Court of the Supreme Court of South Australia two years before *Sidaway* in the House of Lords, a woman who had become pregnant after an unsuccessful tubal ligation brought an action in negligence alleging failure by the medical practitioner to warn her of the failure of the procedure. The failure rate was assessed at less than 1 per cent for that particular form of sterilization. The Court refused to apply the *Bolam* principle. King CJ said at p 194:

> The ultimate question, however, is not whether the defendant's conduct accords with the practices of his profession or some part of it, but whether it conforms to the standard of reasonable care demanded by the law. That is a question for the court and the duty of deciding it cannot be delegated to any profession or group in the community.

King CJ considered, at pp 192-193, that the amount of information or advice which a careful and responsible doctor would disclose depended upon a complex of factors: the nature of the matter to be disclosed; the nature of the treatment; the desire of the patient for information; the temperament and health of the patient; and the general surrounding circumstances. His Honour agreed, at pp 193-194, with the following passage from the judgment of the Supreme Court of Canada in *Reibl v Hughes* [1980] 2 SCR 880, at pp 894-895; (1980) 114 DLR (3d), at p 13:

> To allow expert medical evidence to determine what risks are material and, hence, should be disclosed and, correlatively, what risks are not material is to hand over to the medical profession the entire question of the scope of the duty of disclosure, including the question whether there has been a breach of duty. Expert medical evidence is, of course, relevant to findings as to the risks that reside in or are a result of recommended surgery or other treatment. It will also have a bearing on their materiality but this is not a question that is to be concluded on the basis of the expert medical evidence alone. The issue under consideration is a different issue from that involved where the question is whether the doctor carried out his professional activities by applicable professional standards. What is under consideration here is the patient's right to know what risks are involved in undergoing or foregoing certain surgery or other treatment.

The approach adopted by King CJ is similar to that subsequently **[489]** taken by Lord Scarman in *Sidaway* and has been followed in subsequent cases (*Battersby v Tottman; Gover v South Australia* (1985) 39 SASR, at pp 551-552; *Ellis v Wallsend District Hospital* (Unreported; Supreme Court of New South Wales; 16 September 1988); *E v Australian Red Cross* (1991) 27 FCR, at pp 359-360). On our view, it is correct.

Acceptance of this approach does not entail an artificial division or itemization of specific, individual duties, carved out of the overall duty of care. The duty of a medical practitioner to exercise reasonable care and skill in the provision of professional advice and treatment is a single comprehensive duty. However, the factors according to which a court determines whether a medical practitioner is in breach of the requisite standard of care will vary according to whether it is a case involving diagnosis, treatment or the provision of information or advice; the different cases raise varying difficulties which require consideration of different factors (*F v R* (1983) 33 SASR, at p 191). Examination of the nature of a doctor-patient relationship compels this conclusion. There is a fundamental difference between, on the one hand, diagnosis and treatment and, on the other hand, the provision of advice or information to a patient. In diagnosis and treatment, the patient's contribution is limited to the narration of symptoms and relevant history; the medical practitioner provides diagnosis and treatment according to his or her level of skill. However, except in cases of emergency or necessity, all medical treatment is preceded by the patient's choice to undergo it. In legal terms, the patient's consent to the treatment may be valid once he or she is informed in broad terms of the nature of the procedure which is intended (*Chatterson v Gerson* [1981] QB 432, at p 443). But the choice is, in reality, meaningless unless it is made on the basis of relevant information and advice. Because the choice to be made calls for a decision by the patient on information known to the medical practitioner but not to the patient, it would be illogical to hold that the amount of information to be provided by the medical practitioner can be determined from the perspective of the practitioner alone or, for that matter, of the medical profession. *Whether* a medical practitioner carries out a particular form of treatment in accordance with the appropriate standard of care is a question in the resolution of which responsible professional opinion will have an influential, often a decisive, role to play; *whether* the patient has been given all the relevant information to choose between undergoing and not undergoing the treatment is a question of a different order. Generally speaking, it is not a question the answer to which depends upon medical standards or **[490]** practices. Except in those cases where there is a particular danger that the provision of all relevant information will harm an unusually nervous, disturbed or volatile patient, no special medical skill is involved in disclosing the information, including the risks attending the proposed treatment (see JG Fleming, *Law of Torts*, 7th ed (1987), p 110). Rather, the skill is in communicating the relevant information to the patient in terms which are reasonably adequate for that purpose having regard to the patient's apprehended capacity to understand that information.

In this context, nothing is to be gained by reiterating the expressions used in American authorities, such as "the patient's right of self-determination" (see, eg, *Canterbury v Spence* (1992) 464 F 2d, at p 784) or even the oft-used and somewhat amorphous phrase "informed consent". The right of self-determination is an expression which is, perhaps, suitable to cases where the issue is whether a person has agreed to the general surgical procedure or treatment, but is of little assistance in the balancing process that is involved in the determination of whether there has been a breach of the duty of disclosure. Likewise, the phrase "informed consent" is apt to mislead as it suggests a test of the validity of a patient's consent (*Reibl v Hughes* [1980] 2 SCR 880, at p 892; (1980) 114 DLR (3d), at p 11). Moreover, consent is relevant to actions framed in trespass, not in negligence. Anglo-Australian law has rightly taken the view that an allegation that the risks inherent in a medical procedure have not been disclosed to the patient can only found an action in negligence and not in trespass; the consent necessary to negative the offence of battery is satisfied by the patient being advised in broad terms of the nature of the procedure to be performed (*Chatterson v Gerson* [1981] QB, at p 443). In *Reibl v Hughes* the Supreme Court of Canada was cautious in its use of the term "informed consent" ([1980] 2 SCR 880, at pp 888-892; (1980) 114 DLR (3d), at pp 8-11).

We agree that the factors referred to in *F v R* by King CJ (1983) 33 SASR at pp 192-193 must be considered by a medical practitioner in deciding whether to disclose or advise of some risk in a proposed procedure. The law should recognise that a doctor has a duty to warn a patient of a material risk inherent in the proposed treatment; a risk is material if, in the circumstances of the particular case, a reasonable person in the patient's position, if warned of the risk, would be likely to attach significance to it or if the medical practitioner is or should reasonably be aware that the particular patient, if warned of the risk, would be likely to attach significance to it. This duty is subject to the therapeutic privilege.

[491] The appellant in this case was treating and advising a woman who was almost totally blind in one eye. As with all surgical procedures, the operation recommended by the appellant to the respondent involved various risks, such as retinal detachment and haemorrhage infection, both of which are more common than sympathetic ophthalmia, but sympathetic ophthalmia was the only danger whereby both eyes might be rendered sightless. Experts for both parties described it as a devastating disability, the appellant acknowledging that, except for death under anaesthetic, it was the worst possible outcome for the respondent. According to the findings of the trial judge, the respondent "incessantly" questioned the appellant as to, amongst other things, possible complications. She was, to the appellant's knowledge, keenly interested in the outcome of the suggested procedure, including the danger of unintended or accidental interference with her "good", left eye. On the day before the operation, the respondent asked the appellant whether something could be put over her good eye to ensure that nothing happened to it; an entry was made in the hospital notes to the effect that she was apprehensive that the wrong eye would be operated on. She did not, however, ask a specific question as to whether the operation on her right eye could affect her left eye.

The evidence established that there was a body of opinion in the medical profession at the time which considered that an inquiry should only have elicited a reply dealing with sympathetic ophthalmia if specifically directed to the possibility of the left eye being affected by the operation on the right eye. While the opinion that the respondent should have been told of the dangers of sympathetic ophthalmia only if she had been sufficiently learned to ask the precise question seems curious, it is unnecessary for us to examine it further, save to say that it demonstrates vividly the dangers of applying the *Bolam* principle in the area of advice and information. The respondent may not have asked the right question, yet she made clear her great concern that no injury should befall her one good eye. The trial judge was not satisfied that, if the respondent had expressed no desire for information, proper practice required that the respondent be warned of the relevant principle as we have stated it, that the risk was material, in the sense that a reasonable person in the patient's position would be likely to attach significance to the risk, and thus required a warning. ...

[492] For these reasons, we would reject the appellant's argument on the issue of breach of duty. ... [There was no argument before the court on the issue of causation.] ... We would dismiss the appeal.

[Gaudron J agreed that the appeal should be dismissed. In her Honour's view the practice of medical practitioners was not relevant at all to the issue of what information should be supplied to the patient, except in the cases of emergency or an impaired ability to receive, understand and evaluate the information.]

Appeal dismissed

2. PROOF OF NEGLIGENCE

Schellenberg v Tunnel Holdings Pty Ltd
(2000) 200 CLR 121; [2000] HCA 18
High Court of Australia

The maxim res ipsa loquitur has no application once the cause of the relevant occurrence has been established.

[The appellant (plaintiff) was a supervisor employed by the respondent (defendant), a company engaged in the supply and servicing of pumps. The appellant was injured in the respondent's workshop when an air compression hose separated from its special fitting and struck him.

He brought an action in negligence in respect of the ensuing physical injury. The trial judge, Muller DCJ, ruled in favour of the appellant on the basis of the maxim *res ipsa loquitur*. The Full Court of the Supreme Court of Western Australia overturned this ruling on the ground that the maxim was inapplicable in this case. On appeal to the High Court, a majority comprising Gleeson CJ, McHugh, Hayne and Kirby JJ (Gaudron J dissenting) agreed with the Supreme Court of Western Australia and dismissed the appeal.]

GLEESON CJ and McHUGH J. **[125]** 1. The principal question in this appeal is whether the plaintiff can rely on the doctrine of *res ipsa loquitur* to make out a case of negligence in circumstances where a hose, carrying compressed air, which he was using in the course of employment, became loose and swung upwards striking him on the face. In our opinion, the doctrine of *res ipsa loquitur* did not apply, but, even if it did, its operation was spent once the trial judge found that the cause of the occurrence was the hose separating from a coupling to which it was attached. Once that finding was made, the question in the case was whether the plaintiff had proved that the separation was the result of the defendant's negligence. Because there was no evidence that established that the defendant was negligent in the assembly, inspection or maintenance of the hose and coupling, the Full Court of the Supreme Court of Western Australia was right to hold that the plaintiff's action failed. ...

[132] The history of res ipsa loquitur

20. The term *res ipsa loquitur* appears to have been first used in a negligence context by Chief Baron Pollock during argument in *Byrne v Boadle* (1863) 2 H & C 722 on the return of a rule nisi for the entry of a verdict for the plaintiff in an action for negligence. At the trial, the evidence had proved only that a barrel of flour fell from a window in the defendant's house and shop. Because that was the state of the evidence, the trial judge had non-suited the plaintiff. The Court of Exchequer made the rule absolute. In giving the leading judgment, the Chief Baron said at 728 that "[a] barrel could not roll out of a warehouse without some negligence, and to say that a plaintiff who is injured by it must call witnesses from the warehouse to prove negligence seems to me preposterous." During argument, Chief Baron Pollock had said at 725:

"There are certain cases of which it may be said res ipsa loquitur, and this seems one of them."

21. Two years later in *Scott v London and St Katherine Docks Co* (1865) 3 H&C 596 at 601 (Ex Ch) Erle CJ enunciated the basis of the principle of *res ipsa loquitur* in terms which have been regarded as the "foundation of all subsequent authority" (*Moore v R Fox & Sons* [1956] 1 QB 596 at 611 per Evershed MR). His Lordship said:

"There must be reasonable evidence of negligence.

But where the thing is shewn to be under the management of the defendant or his servants, and the accident is such as in the ordinary course of things does not happen if those who have the management use proper care, it affords reasonable evidence, in the absence of explanation by the defendants, that the accident arose from want of care."

The principle of res ipsa loquitur

22. Although Australian and English courts have diverged as to the scope and effect of the principle of *res ipsa loquitur*, in this country its scope and effect have been decisively settled by a series of decisions of this Court. Those decisions make it clear that the trial judge **[133]** was correct when he said that the principle is not a distinct, substantive rule of law, but an application of an inferential reasoning process, and that the plaintiff bears the onus of proof of negligence even when the principle is applicable. ...

[134] 25. *Piening v Wanless* (1959) 101 CLR 298 and *Anchor Products Ltd v Hedges* (1968) 117 CLR 498 as well as other cases in this Court make it clear that a plaintiff may rely on *res ipsa loquitur* even though he or she has also pleaded particular acts or omissions of negligence on the part of the defendant provided that the tribunal of fact concludes that:

1. there is an "absence of explanation" of the occurrence that caused the injury;
2. the occurrence was of such a kind that it does not ordinarily occur without negligence; and
3. the instrument or agency that caused the injury was under the control of the defendant.

Absence of explanation

26. The defendant argued in this Court that:

"The evidence established, to the satisfaction of the trial judge and confirmed at appeal, that the hose had separated from the jamec coupling. The separation of the hose from the jamec coupling provides an explanation for the accident. Proof of that fact by either party excludes the operation of the maxim."

To support that argument, the defendant relied on *Mummery v Irvings Pty Ltd* (1956) 96 CLR 99 at 115 where Dixon CJ, Webb, Fullagar and Taylor JJ said that "once the cause of an accident has been established and the relevant circumstances proved, there is no further room for the operation of the principle."

27. In our opinion, the defendant's argument is correct in asserting that the principle of *res ipsa loquitur* had no application once the learned trial judge found that the hose separated from the jamec coupling. The question then became whether the plaintiff had proved that the separation of the hose from the jamec coupling occurred in **[135]** circumstances of negligence. The relevant occurrence in the present case was the accident – the detachment of a hose, carrying compressed air, swinging around and striking the plaintiff in the face. If accidents of that kind do not occur if those who have control of the hose and its attachments use proper care, the plaintiff was entitled to rely on *res ipsa loquitur* to make out a prima facie case of negligence and it was then for the judge to hold whether the occurrence constituted negligence having regard to all the other circumstances of the case. But once the cause of the occurrence was proved, the principle could play no part in the proceedings.

28. Here the trial judge held that the occurrence was caused by the separation of the hose from the jamec coupling. Once that was proved, *res ipsa loquitur* ceased to apply as a reasoning process. ...

[136] 31. *Res ipsa loquitur* is concerned with negligence arising from an unknown or unspecified cause. It is concerned with an external event whose cause is under the control of the defendant. It is a principle that is as much, perhaps more, concerned with proof that the defendant was causally responsible for the occurrence as it is with proof of a breach of duty. In *Mummery v Irvings Pty Ltd* at 116, Dixon CJ, Webb, Fullagar and Taylor JJ said that "[t]he requirement that the accident must be such as in the ordinary course of things *does not happen* if those who have the management use proper care is of vital importance and fully explains why in such cases *res ipsa loquitur*" (emphasis added).

32. Once the cause of the external event is identified, the question becomes whether the plaintiff has proved that that cause was the product of negligence. In *Barkway v South Wales Transport Co Ltd* [1950] 1 All ER 392 at 394-395, in a passage which was cited with approval in *Mummery v Irvings Pty Ltd* at 115, Lord Porter said:

"The doctrine is dependent on the absence of explanation, and, although it is the duty of the defendants, if they desire to protect themselves, to give an adequate explanation of the cause of the accident, yet, if the facts are sufficiently known, the question ceases to be one where the facts speak for themselves, and the solution is to be found by determining whether, on the facts as established, negligence is to be inferred or not."

33. In principle, we think the relevant cause must be the immediate cause of the occurrence, which means the occurrence must be defined with reasonable precision if the principle is to operate effectively. Definition of the occurrence will determine whether the accident is of a class that does not ordinarily happen if those who have the management use proper care. Definition of the occurrence will also determine whether the cause of the occurrence has been established. To a large extent, the definition of the occurrence will depend on how much the tribunal of fact knows about the accident. Thus, in *Mummery* **[137]** *v Irvings Pty Ltd* at 116, the Court pointed out that *res ipsa loquitur* would have applied if the evidence had established no more than that, upon entering the defendant's premises, the plaintiff had been "violently struck by a piece of wood flying through the air." However, the evidence tended to establish that the wood was thrown by a circular saw and this was not *res ipsa loquitur*. The Court said at 117:

"In these circumstances a court must ask itself, not whether negligence may be inferred from the mere fact that a piece of wood struck the appellant immediately after he had entered the respondent's premises, but whether it may be inferred from the fact that a piece of wood was thrown from the circular saw."

34. Definition of the occurrence will also depend upon at what level of abstraction it is defined and upon what facts and circumstances are taken into account in defining the occurrence. No doubt the occurrence may sometimes, perhaps often, be defined at particular levels of abstraction, and judges may disagree as to what are the facts and circumstances that constitute the occurrence. In the present case, for example, it is arguable that the occurrence was more concrete than we have defined it and that what we have described as the cause was in fact part of the occurrence. On that view, the occurrence was the striking of the plaintiff with a hose which had separated from its jamec coupling.

35. Once the occurrence is defined, however, we do not think that there can be an infinite regression in which each "cause" can be traced to its cause with the result that the plaintiff can continue to rely on a claim of unspecified negligence no matter how far back down the causal chain you go. Once what can be properly described as the cause of the occurrence has been identified, it is not necessary that every circumstance surrounding that cause or every cause of that cause also be identified.

36. As soon as the immediate cause of the accident is established, the focus of the case changes. The question then becomes whether that cause was the product of negligence on the part of the defendant. That is the effect of *Mummery v Irvings Pty Ltd* and *Piening v Wanless*.

37. That the principle of *res ipsa loquitur* ceases to operate once the cause of the occurrence is identified does not mean that the plaintiff cannot rely on inferential reasoning to prove negligence. Thus, in a case like the present, with sufficient evidence, it might be inferred that it was lack of reasonable maintenance that caused the hose to become [138] detached. There was nothing to stop the plaintiff in this case, for example, from relying on *res ipsa loquitur* and also adducing evidence that the defendant had no system for inspecting the couplings. If he had done so, he would have been entitled to argue that the lack of such a system was negligent and that, if the hose had separated from the jamec coupling, it was proper to infer a causal connection between the lack of an inspection system and the detachment of the hose.

38. In our opinion, therefore, once the trial judge determined the cause of the occurrence, the only question was whether that cause was the result of the defendant's negligence.

Occurrence of such a kind that it ordinarily does not occur without negligence
39. The learned trial judge did not specifically find that the separation of the hose and its swinging upwards out of control was an event which would not ordinarily occur without negligence. Nor for that matter did he find that the separation of the hose from the jamec coupling was such an event. In our opinion, both findings were precluded in this case because the only evidence before his Honour on this matter – from the plaintiff's expert witness – indicated that in fact this sort of thing was apt to occur without negligence. ...

41. The defendant also argued that it was not open to the learned trial judge to find that this sort of occurrence ordinarily happens only as [139] the result of negligence because it was outside the ordinary experience of the lay person. In *Piening v Wanless* Barwick CJ said at 508 that:

"If the occurrence is to provide evidence, it can only be that, within the common knowledge and experience of mankind, that occurrence is unlikely to occur without negligence on the part of the party sued. By that very statement, the occurrence is unlikely to provide evidence except in connexion with machines or machinery of whose working and use the ordinary man has knowledge and experience. I do not think that the mechanical make-up of, and the forces operating on or with, the steering mechanism of a car are within such knowledge or experience."

Similarly in *Franklin v Victorian Railways Commissioners* (1959) 101 CLR 197 at 204 Dixon CJ stated that:

"[U]nless adequate knowledge about railway engineering and practice would suggest otherwise, an unexplained sway or lurch or jerk or jolt in a train travelling in an ordinary way in ordinary conditions does not seem in itself to raise a presumption of negligence. It is not a matter of common knowledge that it would be so unlikely to occur without negligence on the part of the driver or some other servant of the commissioners as to point prima facie to negligence. If a knowledge of railway engineering and practice would suggest hypotheses which would make the lurch more suggestive of negligence than not, then the hypotheses should have been explained by evidence and not left to uninformed reasoning."

42. In our opinion, this case cannot be described as one falling within the "common knowledge and experience of mankind". That being so, on one view, the doctrine is inapplicable (*Mahon v Osborne* [1939] 2 KB 14 at 21-22). Whether the doctrine is strictly inapplicable or not, however, is to some extent a sterile controversy. As Dixon CJ explained in *Franklin*, expert evidence may be adduced to suggest that an unexplained occurrence would not ordinarily occur without negligence. Moreover, the expert evidence may be unable to isolate a single hypothesis suggestive of negligence. Nevertheless, the expert evidence may suggest a number of hypotheses, all of which indicate negligence but none of which indicate a greater likelihood of having occurred than any other of them. As is pointed out in Glass, McHugh and Douglas, *The Liability of Employers in Damages for Personal Injury*, 2nd ed, 1979, p 215, it is no more than a dispute about terminology to determine whether that sort of case is an instance of expert evidence facilitating the doctrine or a case of unspecified negligence based on affirmative **[140]** evidence. In our opinion, however, if the expert evidence suggests a number of causes that enjoy an equal probability of occurrence and all involve negligence, the occurrence should be regarded as an unexplained occurrence to which the doctrine applies. It is only when the expert evidence assigns a particular cause as the most probable cause of the occurrence that the case should be regarded as outside the doctrine of *res ipsa loquitur*.

43. In this case, where the occurrence is outside the experience of the lay person, and the evidence, expert or otherwise, does not establish that such an occurrence ordinarily does not occur without negligence, *res ipsa loquitur* is inapplicable. Moreover, although the cause was proved, there was insufficient evidence to determine whether the separation of the hose from the jamec coupling was the product of negligence for which the defendant was responsible. In finding that the "only definite fact established on the evidence is that the air hose became detached when it should not have" when all the possible causes of the separation were "speculative factors unsupported by any evidence" Muller DCJ was effectively imposing a standard of strict liability.

44. In *Mummery v Irvings Pty Ltd*, Dixon CJ, Webb, Fullagar and Taylor JJ stated that in that case at 117:

"[I]t is difficult, if not impossible, in these circumstances to attribute the accident to some act of negligence on the part of the operator. If the question is posed 'Was the accident such as in the ordinary course of things does not happen if those who have the management use proper care?' the answer, on the evidence in the case, must be 'We simply do not know.' One may but conjecture but cannot as a matter of inference attribute negligence to the respondent's foreman."

45. In our opinion, this statement applies in this case.

46. The plaintiff contends that the application of *res ipsa loquitur* has accumulated a number of "encrustations" in the course of its judicial history that have hardened the maxim into a rigid rule of law, when it is merely a factor to be weighed "with the direct evidence to determine whether the plaintiff had established, on a balance of probabilities, a case." The plaintiff urged the Court to follow the Supreme Court of Canada in *Fontaine v British Columbia (Official Administrator)* [1998] 1 SCR 424 at 435 and abolish the maxim "as a separate component **[141]** in negligence actions". To do so, it was said, would be "consonant with the steps taken by this court to absorb isolated pockets of technical law into a context appropriate to its original rationale" as this Court did in *Australian Safeway Stores Pty Ltd v Zaluzna* (1987) 162 CLR 479 and *Burnie Port Authority v General Jones Pty Ltd* (1994) 179 CLR 520.

47. In our opinion, this Court should not follow that course. The Court has affirmed time and again that *res ipsa loquitur* is merely a mode of inferential reasoning and is *not* a rule of law. The "encrustations" that the plaintiff alleges do not exist. The fact that a plaintiff falls outside the "proper scope" of the rule does not mean that he or she may not avail himself or herself of inferential reasoning. There is therefore no need to subsume the maxim into the general body of tort law: it is already fully consonant with it.

Exclusive control

48. It is well established that if "the defendant is not in control *res ipsa loquitur* does not apply. This follows from the fact that it is not sufficient for the facts merely to speak of negligence: the evidence must point to the defendant's negligence" (*Doval v Anka Builders Pty Ltd* (1992) 28 NSWLR 1 at 13 per Clarke JA.). In our opinion there is much force in the defendant's argument that Muller DCJ was wrong to find that the machine was under the exclusive control of the defendant. In this case, as the defendant's written submissions demonstrate:

"(i) the Plaintiff was in control of the equipment prior to the accident.

(ii) the Plaintiff inspected the equipment and connection prior to using the equipment on the day of the accident.

(iii) the Plaintiff's use of the equipment involved him pulling on the hose in the situation where it was likely that the hose would be caught between the Plaintiff's body and the rim of the [body] valve.

(iv) the Plaintiff was in charge of the air pressure system.

(v) it was part of the Plaintiff's duties to make up extra hoses." (appeal book references omitted)

49. These factors suggest that the defendant may not have had sufficient control to attract the principle of *res ipsa loquitur*. However, the question whether the defendant still has control for the purpose of the principle when an object or instrument is in the sole custody or possession of the plaintiff is a difficult one. In the United States, courts have often held that the principle applies although the plaintiff has sole custody or possession or de facto control where the defendant retains the legal right of control or where it is more probable than not **[142]** that the negligence occurred while the defendant had control (See eg *Mobil Chemical Company v Bell* 517 SW 2d 245 (Tex 1974); *Qualls v United States Elevator Corp* 863 P 2d 457 (Okl 1993)). In *Fletcher v Toppers Drinks Pty Ltd* [1981] 2 NSWLR 911, the New South Wales Court of Appeal held that a tribunal of fact was entitled, but not required, to draw an inference of unspecified negligence against the bottler of a soft drink when the bottle exploded as the plaintiff unscrewed its top. The Court so held notwithstanding that there was no evidence as to how the bottle was handled by a third party from the time it left the bottler's premises until the time it reached the plaintiff's home. As it is not necessary to decide the issue of control in this case, we need say nothing more about it.

There was insufficient evidence to support a finding that the compression equipment was negligently maintained

50. As the above discussion of expert evidence and *res ipsa loquitur* illustrates, the fact that a plaintiff cannot attract the operation of the maxim does not prevent him or her relying on an analogous process of inferential reasoning to establish a specific particular of negligence. In this case, the learned trial judge effectively found that the defendant had negligently failed to properly assemble, inspect or maintain the relevant equipment. That finding is outside the scope of *res ipsa loquitur* as it is a specific allegation of negligence, even though it was premised on the general finding that the hose was "insecurely fastened". The finding that the hose was "insecurely fastened", however, is either a statement of the obvious, flowing from the fact the hose actually separated – in which case it does not speak one way or the other – or it is an erroneous application of *res ipsa loquitur*. ...

[143] 53. It follows that the trial judge's finding with respect to the assembly, inspection and maintenance of the compression equipment could not stand, as there was insufficient evidence to support the findings, either directly or by inference.

54. The Full Court was therefore right to allow the appeal and dismiss the plaintiff's action.

KIRBY J. ...[162] Res ipsa in Australian courts

106. From its simple beginnings a number of propositions have been derived from the maxim *res ipsa loquitur*.

107. First, the plaintiff must show that the thing (*res*) which, without more, is said to indicate negligence was under the exclusive management and control of the defendant or someone for whom the defendant is responsible or whom it has a right to control. If someone else had control of, or access to, the thing, that person might be responsible for the suggested negligence. The plaintiff must then differentiate the liability of the defendant by direct evidence.

108. Secondly, the invocation of the manner of reasoning which the maxim describes does not, as it has been traditionally expounded, involve a shifting of the legal burden of proof from the plaintiff to the defendant, such that, unless the defendant establishes a want of any negligence on its part, it will be presumed to be liable. Some early dicta in this Court and in the English courts in this respect have been rejected by later decisions: *Anchor Products Ltd v Hedges* (1966) 115 CLR 493 at 495 per Taylor J; *Government Insurance Office of NSW v Fredrichberg* (1968) 118 CLR 403 at 417 per Windeyer J. Thus, the maxim does not import a legal presumption having such effect. The defendant can remain silent and still succeed. If, in the particular case, the manner of reasoning described as *res ipsa loquitur* is applicable, it merely renders it *permissible* for the tribunal of fact to draw the inference which the plaintiff invites. It is not *obligatory*, as it would be **[163]** if the maxim had the effect of creating a presumption which the defendant was obliged in law to rebut.

109. Thirdly, this does not mean that a failure on the part of a defendant to call evidence in a case where a plaintiff has invoked *res ipsa loquitur* is treated, in Australia (any more than elsewhere), as completely irrelevant. In some circumstances such an omission will have a telling forensic impact. From the earliest descriptions of the method of reasoning which *res ipsa loquitur* sanctions, reference has been made to the relevance of the "absence of explanation by the defendants" (*Scott v London and St Katherine Docks Co* (1865) 3 H & C 596 at 601 [159 ER 665 at 667]). The practical necessities of an adversarial trial might, in at least some situations, effectively compel a defendant to attempt to show that the accident happened without negligence on its part.

110. It was in this sense, as a matter of forensic rather than legal necessity, that this Court was willing in *Mummery v Irvings Pty Ltd* (1956) 96 CLR 99 at 120-121 to accept that "the defendant may, perhaps, be said, to carry an onus". However, the distinction between the *legal* burden (which remains throughout upon a plaintiff) and the *forensic* evidential burden of persuasion (which the state of the evidence may effectively impose upon a defendant) although elusive is important. The position consistently followed in this Court for more than half a century is that described by Barwick CJ in *Nominal Defendant v Haslbauer* (1967) 117 CLR 448 at 456:

> "If then all the evidence as to the occurrence (if accepted) would itself support an inference of want of care on the defendant's part, it can properly be said that the defendant must negative that inference. … [I]f he has given evidence as to the occurrence, which if accepted, and taken with the plaintiff's evidence, does not logically warrant an inference of his negligence, it is … quite erroneous to say that none the less he must go further and show that the occurrence was without want of care on his part. So to conclude would be to reverse the onus, placing it on the defendant whereas in truth and unquestionably it remains throughout with the plaintiff." …

[164] 112. Fourthly, there was for a time a belief that a plaintiff would lose any benefit of reliance on the maxim of *res ipsa loquitur* if an attempt were made to prove, by direct evidence, the *actual* cause of the injury giving rise to the proceedings. In Australia, this belief derived, understandably enough, from a remark in the reasons of the majority in *Mummery's Case* (1956) 96 CLR 99 at 122. The misunderstanding was corrected by this Court in *Anchor Products Ltd v Hedges*. In that decision the Court made it clear that the evidence might still give rise to an inference of negligence although a plaintiff has sought, but failed, to explain the specific cause as arising from the defendant's want of due care. For example, where a defendant drove his motor vehicle into the back of the plaintiff's vehicle the maxim would be given *prima facie* operation. However, when the defendant established explicitly that the cause of that action was an unexplained and unforeseen brake failure, the plaintiff could no longer rely on the maxim to prove negligence. If, as a result of evidence of a fact directly concerned with the cause of the incident, there is no room for inference, the method of reasoning which the maxim expresses was **[165]** unavailing. The plaintiff would have to convince the court that the cause actually established betokened negligence on the defendant's part or, with some other fact, directly proved such negligence.

Res ipsa is unavailing in this case

113. Assuming that the maxim *res ipsa loquitur* remains part of our law, I do not consider that it assisted the appellant in the circumstances of this case. …

116. … [T]he difficulty of invoking the maxim of *res ipsa loquitur* arises from the requirement that the occurrence must be such that it would not have happened without negligence. This was

not the present case. The air hose could have become disconnected from the coupling without any negligence on the part of the respondent. This would be so in a number of circumstances which are readily imaginable. They were in fact contemplated by the primary judge as a matter of "common sense". They would include: **[166]**

1. That there was some latent defect in the hose not discoverable by external inspection (whether on the part of the appellant or of another employee of the respondent performing routine inspection on its behalf).

2. That there was some defect in the clamp used or in the coupling which was similarly not discoverable by prior inspection.

3. That the process of using the equipment, and the friction of the pressure involved, caused the hose clip to work itself loose in a way wholly unpredictable and insusceptible to discovery by prior inspection.

4. That the disconnection occurred as a result of a sudden, unexplained surge of air pressure, either from its source or as a result of the appellant's manoeuvring of the grinder in a particular way.

5. That even if the failure of the manager, Mr Mills, to give evidence of regular inspections of the equipment were deemed to carry some forensic weight, this would have to be judged in the context of a case in which the appellant (whilst making many other allegations of negligence) omitted to complain that his injuries were caused by the want of regular and timely inspection of the grinder and of its connection to the compressed air supply. ...

118. In the end, therefore, there were various possibilities. All of them were "conjectural". ...

[167] Survival of the res ipsa loquitur maxim?

119. Faced with this conclusion, the appellant grasped at two possibilities which it is necessary to mention.

120. The first was an invitation that this Court should follow the lead of the Supreme Court of Canada, abolish the special exposition of *res ipsa loquitur* and substitute in its place an endorsement of the general principle that the trier of fact should weigh circumstantial evidence with direct evidence when judging whether, on the balance of probabilities, a *prima facie* case of negligence has been made out against the defendant.

121. There are various attractions in taking this course. This Court has emphasised many times, and for over 60 years, that the maxim *res ipsa loquitur* "should be regarded merely as an application of the general method of inferring one or more facts in issue from circumstances proved in evidence" (*Davis v Bunn* (1936) 56 CLR 246 at 268). In this respect, this Court has not been alone. Judges elsewhere have been at pains to deny to the maxim any "magic qualities" (*Roe v Minister of Health* [1954] 2 QB 66 at 87 per Morris LJ). They have expressed exasperation at the suggestion that the maxim amounts to a "principle", or even worse, a doctrine of law. Lord Shaw of Dunfermline remarked nearly 80 years ago that if it "had not been in Latin, nobody would have called it a principle" ([1923] SC 43 at 56). Its invocation "is no substitute for **[168]** reasonable investigation and discovery" (*McDonald v Smitty's Super Valu Inc* 757 P 2d 120 at 125 (1988)). Nor does it "relieve a plaintiff too uninquisitive to undertake available proof" (757 P 2d 120 at 125 (1988)).

122. As these reasons demonstrate, despite the foregoing criticisms, in Australia as in other countries, the maxim has proved most resilient. Doubtless this is because its brevity expresses a vivid idea which may occasionally promise hope to a plaintiff who, through no fault of his or her own, is unable to establish exactly what caused the damage said to be the result of the defendant's want of care in respect of matters wholly or largely within the knowledge and control of the defendant.

123. An advantage of abolishing the maxim would be that it might release judicial minds from the encrustations of authority that have gathered around the maxim and its multitude of attempted applications over the 130 years of its existence. But even if, in this case, *res ipsa loquitur*, as such, were overthrown and the facts analysed by reference solely to ascertaining the inferences available from the facts as found, this would make no difference. The position would remain the same. The

attempts at specific explanations of the disengagement of the air hose and the grinder coupling would remain rejected. The possibility that the disengagement occurred for other reasons not alleged would still be, as the primary judge described them, "speculative". The question would come back to whether, in this context, the tribunal of fact was justified in inferring that it was more probable than not that the hose and coupling were insecurely fastened. That inference would remain just one of many possibilities. Selection of it as more probable than not would be as impermissible if no Latin maxim were invoked as it is if the established jurisprudence of *res ipsa loquitur* was applied.

124. Whilst, therefore, I am inclined to favour the conclusion reached by the Supreme Court of Canada, it is unnecessary to decide the point in this appeal. Nothing turns on it in this case. Where a maxim of the law has endured for so long, its resilience suggests a measure of utility that should restrain needless abolition. Perhaps *res ipsa loquitur* will continue to linger for a time as yet another indication of the attraction of lawyers to exotic labels. This case may have the merit of acting as a reminder of its limitations, the danger of treating it as a rule of law and the necessity to limit its use to that of an aid to logical reasoning by inference when considering whether the plaintiff has, or has not, established a cause of action in negligence. ...

[Hayne J, in a concurring judgment, held that the maxim did not apply in this case.]

Appeal dismissed

3. ROLE OF JUDGE AND JURY

Swain v Waverley Municipal Council
(2005) 220 CLR 517; [2005] HCA 4
High Court of Australia

In a negligence trial conducted before a judge and jury, questions of law are decided by the judge and questions of fact, including breach of duty, are decided by the jury.

Although it is a question of law, reviewable by an appellate court, whether there is evidence on which a jury reasonably may find the defendant was negligent, an appellate court may not overturn a jury's verdict simply because, on a review of the evidence, the appellate court does not agree with that verdict.

[The appellant (plaintiff), Guy Swain, then aged 24, suffered serious spinal injury when he dived into a wave while entering the surf between the red and yellow safety flags at Bondi Beach and struck a sandbar. He commenced tort proceedings for negligence in the Supreme Court of New South Wales against the respondent (defendant), the local council responsible for the care, control and management of the beach including the positioning of the safety flags. At the trial before Taylor AJ and a four-person jury, the appellant alleged that the positioning of the safety flags had induced him to enter the surf where he did and that the respondent had been negligent in the positioning of the flags or in failing to warn swimmers of the presence of the sandbar. The jury found the respondent liable for negligence with a finding of 25 per cent contributory negligence on the part of the appellant. The New South Wales Court of Appeal, by majority, allowed the respondent's appeal from the jury's verdict in favour of the appellant. In separate judgments on further appeal to the High Court of Australia, Gleeson CJ, Gummow and Kirby JJ held that the New South Wales Court of Appeal should not have disturbed the jury's verdict. McHugh and Heydon JJ, in separate dissenting judgments, would have dismissed the appeal on the ground that there was no evidence on which a jury could find that there existed a reasonably practicable means of avoiding the relevant risk of injury.]

GLEESON CJ. **[519]** 1. Actions for damages for personal injury suffered by a plaintiff allegedly in consequence of the negligence of a defendant in the past were commonly tried before a judge and a civil jury, usually of four persons. In New South Wales, and in some other Australian jurisdictions, the use of civil juries in such cases has become less common. This appeal draws attention to the different considerations involved in appellate review of primary decision-making, according to whether the decision-maker is a judge or a jury.

2. In the common law system of civil justice, the issues between the parties are determined by the trial process. The system does not regard the trial as merely the first round in a contest destined to work its way through the judicial hierarchy until the litigants have exhausted either their resources or their possibilities of further appeal. Most decisions of trial courts are never the subject of appeal. When there is an appeal, the appellate court does not simply re-try the case. Depending on the nature of the appeal provided by statute, courts of appeal act according to established principles by which their functions are constrained. Those principles reflect the primacy of the trial process and the practical limitations upon the capacity of a court which does not itself **[520]** hear the evidence justly to disturb an outcome at first instance. Trial by jury carries with it significant limitations of that kind.

3. At a trial by jury, the functions of judge and jury are clearly distinguished. The judge decides issues of law; the jury decides issues of fact. A judge, whether sitting alone or presiding at a jury trial, gives reasons for his or her decisions. An appellate court, having the benefit of a statement of a judge's reasons for a decision, may be well placed to identify error. Juries give no reasons for their decisions. Leaving to one side cases where a special verdict is taken, ordinarily a jury at a civil trial will simply announce a verdict for the plaintiff or the defendant and, where necessary, an award of damages. The jury will reach that verdict after receiving directions from the trial judge as to the relevant principles of law, and their relationship to the evidence in the case and the arguments of opposing counsel. Where unanimity is required, the jurors need to be unanimous only in relation to the ultimate issue or issues presented to them for decision. So long as individual jurors act in accordance with the directions they are given, different jurors might be impressed by different parts of the evidence, or by different arguments of counsel. Jurors are instructed that they may take a selective approach to the evidence, and even to different parts of the evidence of a particular witness. They may arrive at their joint conclusion by different paths. There may be no single process of reasoning which accounts for a jury verdict.

4. In an action framed in negligence, the judge (if necessary) will decide, as a matter of law, whether the facts alleged by the plaintiff are capable of giving rise to a duty of care in the defendant towards the plaintiff. A legal issue of that kind is often capable of being decided on the pleadings. On the other hand, the alleged duty of care might depend upon contested facts that need to be resolved as part of the trial process. In order to be entitled to a verdict, the plaintiff will need to establish a duty of care, conduct on the part of the defendant in breach of that duty (negligent conduct), and consequential damage.

5. In legal formulations of the duty and standard of care, the central concept is reasonableness. The duty is usually expressed in terms of protecting another against unreasonable risk of harm, or of some kind of harm; the standard of conduct necessary to discharge the duty is usually expressed in terms of what would be expected of a reasonable person, both as to foresight of the possibility of harm, and as to taking precautions against such harm. Life is risky. People do not expect, and are not entitled to expect, to live in a risk-free environment. The measure of careful behaviour is reasonableness, not elimination of risk. Where people are subject to a duty of care, they are to some extent their neighbours' keepers, but they are not their neighbours' insurers.

6. Where an action for damages for negligence is tried before a jury, the question whether the conduct of the defendant has been negligent, that is, whether it has departed from what reasonableness requires, is presented as a question of fact for the jury. The jury's decision will ordinarily involve both a resolution of disputed questions of primary **[521]** fact and an application, to the facts as found, of the test of reasonableness. Depending upon the nature of the case, and the findings of primary fact, the application of the test of reasonableness might be straightforward, or it might involve a matter of judgment upon which minds may differ. Either way, it is a jury question. In 1845, in *Tobin v Murison* (1845) 13 ER 431, the Privy Council identified a fundamental error of procedure in a Canadian trial where a jury was asked to find particular facts and then it was left to the judge to decide whether, on those facts, the defendant was negligent. Lord Brougham said (at 438): "Negligence is a question of fact, not of law, and should have been disposed of by the

jury." Of course, it may be a complex question. To the extent to which it requires the application to disputed primary facts of a contestable standard of reasonable behaviour, it may require different kinds and levels of judgment.

7. The resolution of disputed issues of fact, including issues as to whether a defendant's conduct conforms to a requirement of reasonable care, by the verdict of a jury involves committing a decision to the collective and inscrutable judgment of a group of citizens, chosen randomly. The alternative is to commit the decision to a professional judge, who is obliged to give reasons for the decision. In one process the acceptability of the decision is based on the assumed collective wisdom of a number of representatives of the community, properly instructed as to their duties, deciding the facts, on the evidence, as a group. In the other process, the acceptability of the decision is based on the assumed professional knowledge and experience of the judge, and the cogency of the reasons given. In the administration of criminal justice in Australia, the former process is normal, at least in the case of serious offences. In the administration of civil justice, in New South Wales and some other jurisdictions, in recent years there has been a strong trend towards the latter process. Originally, there were no procedures for appealing against the verdict of a jury, reflecting what Barwick CJ described as "the basic inclination of the law towards early finality in litigation": *Buckley v Bennell Design & Constructions Pty Ltd* (1978) 140 CLR 1 at 8. He referred, in another case, to the move towards trial by judge alone in civil cases as an abandonment of "the singular advantage of the complete finality of the verdict of a properly instructed jury": *Edwards v Noble* (1971) 125 CLR 296 at 302. In many areas, the law seeks to strike a balance between the interest of finality and the interest of exposing and correcting error. In a rights-conscious and litigious society, in which people are apt to demand reasons for any decision by which their rights are affected, the trend away from jury trial may be consistent with public sentiment. Even so, **[522]** decision-making by the collective verdict of a group of citizens, rather than by the reasoned judgment of a professional judge, is a time-honoured and important part of our justice system. It also has the important collateral advantages of involving the public in the administration of justice, and of keeping the law in touch with community standards.

8. Although the question whether certain conduct is a departure from a requirement of reasonable care, notwithstanding its normative content, is treated as a question of fact for the jury, a related, but different, question is treated as a question of law. That is the question whether there is evidence on which a jury *could* reasonably be satisfied that the defendant has been negligent. To the extent to which the dispute in a particular case is about the objective features of a defendant's conduct, that will come down to a question whether there is any evidence from which a jury could reasonably reach a conclusion about those features. There may also be a dispute about what reasonableness requires in a given case. When a trial judge, or an appeal court, asks *as a matter of law* whether a judgment adverse to the defendant is reasonably open to a jury, the enquiry may be affected by the nature of the judgment required of the jury. A judgment about whether the evidence could support a certain finding of primary fact might require nothing more than attention to the detail of the evidence, and a consideration of its probative potential. A judgment about whether behaviour is reasonable might involve the application of a measure that is to be found, not in the evidence, but in the wisdom and experience of those who make the decision.

9. The present appeal provides an example of a case where the jury was required to engage in both kinds of decision-making. ... The jurors had to decide disputed facts about the conduct of the appellant and the circumstances in which he was injured, they had to consider substantially undisputed facts about the conduct of the respondent, they had to take into account circumstances relating to other people for whose safety the respondent also had to be concerned, and then they had to make a judgment about the reasonableness of the respondent's conduct. ... **[523]** One of the conclusions to which the jurors had to come was whether, on the facts and in the circumstances found by them, the conduct of the respondent exhibited a failure to take reasonable care for the safety of the appellant. ...

11. There was a dispute at trial about whether the appellant was between the flags when he was injured, or was outside the flags. There was ample evidence, including that of the appellant, upon which the jury could find that he was between the flags. The respondent having made an issue out of whether the appellant was outside the flags, the jury would be likely to have treated their

conclusion that he was between the flags as a substantial point in his favour. Nevertheless, it was far from conclusive.

12. There was some debate before this Court as to what the flags might reasonably be taken to have signified to a person such as the appellant. On the day in question, surf conditions were calm. No one could seriously suggest that the beach should have been closed to surfers. Undoubtedly, the flags were there to give guidance (indeed, instruction) to people as to where they should bathe. As to precisely what they represented concerning safety, somewhat different views may have been open. Safety is not an absolute concept. No reasonable person would understand flags on a beach to indicate a complete absence of risk. People who use beaches are of all ages, all degrees of competence as swimmers, all sizes, and all standards of physical fitness. The evidence was that, for some people, such as children, or elderly or infirm swimmers, sand banks can be a safety feature rather than a hazard. Furthermore, as was pointed out in the Court of Appeal, [524] flags are not placed in the water. No one could possibly think that it was safe to dive anywhere between the flags. That would be nonsense. It would not mean it was safe to dive at the water's edge. To say that the flags conveyed a representation that it was safe to swim or dive in a particular area requires consideration of the range of persons to whom the representation was made, and the conditions that might constitute a hazard to different classes of person. Swimming in the ocean is never entirely risk-free. For some people who are poor swimmers, the water itself may be a considerable hazard. For many people, swimming in water beyond a certain depth is dangerous, even if they are between the flags. For all people, diving in shallow water is risky. Flags do not indicate an absence of risk. Even so, considerations of comparative safety play an important part in where they are placed.

13. The respondent succeeded in persuading a majority in the Court of Appeal that, as a matter of law, there was no evidence upon which the jury could reasonably be satisfied that the conduct of the respondent Council exhibited a failure to exercise reasonable care for the safety of the appellant. That involved a finding, not that the jury's conclusion about reasonableness was wrong, but that it was not even open.

14. It was clearly open to the jury to accept the appellant's version of how he came to suffer his injury. That was that he was swimming between the flags, he was not affected by drink, the manner in which he dived, or attempted to dive, into the water was orthodox, and he struck a submerged obstacle in the form of a sand bank which was not visible to him. The facts relating to the conduct of the respondent, so far as the evidence went, were uncontroversial. The condition of the surf, the location of the flags, the size and shape of the sand bank, and the number of people at the beach were not in dispute. There was, however, one matter that was not the subject of evidence. The appellant's case criticised the respondent for placing, or leaving, the flags in such a location that a submerged sand bank was in the path of swimmers intending to go any significant distance into the water. There was evidence that this was not unusual. There was also evidence that a sand bank (assuming it is stable) can provide security to some swimmers as well as a possible hazard to others. There was no evidence as to whether it would have been possible to move the flags so that the hazard was removed without compromising other aspects of safety. Witnesses spoke of general practice in relation to placing and moving flags at beaches, but no witness addressed that particular question. An employee of the respondent who was on duty at the beach that day gave evidence, but he did not assume responsibility for deciding whether or not to move the flags, or go into the question of the availability of possible alternative locations on the day. ...

[525] 16. When counsel for the respondent, in final address, invited the jury to consider whether the flags should have been placed elsewhere, it might have occurred to the jury that no witness, and in particular no witness for the respondent, had given evidence about that possibility. It was open to the jury to consider that the sand bank was a danger, although not one that was either unusual or such as necessarily to require the respondent either to prevent people from swimming near it or to give them a warning about it. Yet a possible point of view was that an assessment of the reasonableness of the respondent's conduct would involve a consideration of whether, by moving the flags, the danger could have been avoided without the creation of any countervailing problems. The argument of the respondent invited such a consideration. On that matter, the evidence was silent. As the trial judge's summary of the argument for the respondent shows, the approach of the respondent came down to the proposition that, regardless of conditions to either side of the flags,

the sand bank did not constitute a sufficient danger to warrant moving, or even considering moving, the flags. Apparently, the jury did not accept that.

17. More than 200 years ago, Lord Mansfield said that "all evidence is to be weighed according to the proof which it was in the power of one side to have produced, and in the power of the other to have [526] contradicted": *Blatch v Archer* (1774) 98 ER 969 at 970. This basic principle of adversarial litigation is not a matter of esoteric legal knowledge; it accords with common sense and ordinary human experience. When the jurors in this case were asked to consider whether the flags should have been placed elsewhere, they may have thought that it was up to the respondent, rather than the appellant, to tell them what difficulty there would have been about moving the flags to avoid the sand bank, or to explain why nothing would have been gained by putting the flags in a different location. That is something they might reasonably have taken into account in making a judgment about the reasonableness of the conduct of the respondent.

18. Given a finding that the appellant was swimming between the flags, the argument for the respondent was that the sand bank was not really a danger, or at least not such a danger as could have affected a decision about where to place the flags. Faced with a quadriplegic plaintiff, and a jury, that was a strong line to take in the absence of any evidence to show that moving the flags would not have made a material difference, or improved overall safety.

19. Many judges, and many juries, might have accepted the respondent's argument. Some people, applying their standards of reasonableness, might have reflected that variable water depths are as much a feature of the surf as variable wave heights, that diving into waist-deep water without knowing what lies ahead is obviously risky, just as catching and riding a wave to shore is risky, and for much the same reason, and that, if the conduct of the respondent in this case constituted negligence, the only prudent course for councils to take would be to prohibit surfing altogether. To my mind, those are powerful considerations. However, under the procedure that was adopted at this trial, the assessment of the reasonableness of the respondent's conduct was committed to the verdict of a jury. The question for an appellate court is whether it was reasonably open to the jury to make an assessment unfavourable to the respondent, not whether the appellate court agrees with it. The Court of Appeal should have answered that question in the affirmative.

20. The appeal should be allowed ... .

Appeal allowed

Chapter 7

Causation and Remoteness of Damage

1. CAUSATION

March v E & MH Stramare Pty Ltd
(1991) 171 CLR 506
High Court of Australia

Causation is determined by applying the 'but for' test as well as common sense principles to the facts of the case. Value judgements and considerations of policy also have a role to play in the context of causation.

MASON CJ. **[508]** Like McHugh J, I would allow this appeal but my reasons for taking this course are rather different from those stated by his Honour as I do not accept that the "but for" (causa sine qua non) test ever was or now should become the exclusive test of causation in negligence cases. ...

The appellant sued to recover damages for personal injuries sustained when, on 15 March 1985, at or about 1.00 am, the offside of the front of his motor vehicle struck the nearside rear of the tray of a truck, owned by the first respondent, which was parked along the centre line of Frome Street, Adelaide. The second respondent had parked the truck in that position for the purpose of loading it with large wooden bins containing fruit and vegetables from premises in Frome Street where the first respondent carried on business as a wholesale fruit and vegetable merchant. The appellant was travelling south in the lane closest to the centre line of the road, there being three southbound lanes. The rear of the truck, with its parking and hazard lights illuminated, faced the southbound traffic and about one-half of the width of the truck projected into the lane in which the appellant was travelling.

The primary judge (Perry J) found that the appellant was intoxicated at the time to such an extent that his ability to judge speed (including his own speed) and distance, his eye functions, his co-ordination and reaction times, and his vision while attending to the controls of the car were impaired, some substantially so. The primary judge found that, although the parking and hazard lights of the truck were illuminated, the second respondent should have appreciated that the parked vehicle might, in some circumstances, constitute a danger to oncoming vehicles. Accordingly, his Honour found that the second respondent was negligent in parking the truck in the middle of Frome Street. His Honour went on the find the appellant guilty of contributory negligence in driving when his faculties were impaired by alcohol, in driving through the preceding intersection of Frome Street and Rundle Street at a speed exceeding 60 kilometres per hour, in failing to see the truck and in failing to veer past the truck. Liability was apportioned 70 per cent against the appellant and 30 per cent against the respondents.

In allowing the appeal, the majority in the Full Court (Bollen and Prior JJ) held that the second respondent's negligence was not causative of the appellant's injuries, the negligence of the appellant being the "real cause", to use the words of Prior J. It seems that **[509]** both Bollen and Prior JJ applied a doctrine of "last opportunity" or "last clear chance" against the appellant. On the other hand, White J, who dissented, concluded that the parking of the vehicle in the middle of the road caused the collision.

Causation in the context of legal responsibility
It has often been said that the legal concept of causation differs from philosophical and scientific notions of causation. That is because "questions of cause and consequence are not the same for law as for philosophy and science", as Windeyer J pointed out in *National Insurance Co of New Zealand Ltd v Espagne* (1961) 105 CLR 569, at p 591. In philosophy and science, the concept of causation has been developed in the context of explaining phenomena by reference to the relationship between conditions and occurrences. In law, on the other hand, problems of causation arise in the context of ascertaining or apportioning legal responsibility for a given occurrence. The law does not accept John Stuart Mill's definition of cause as the sum of the conditions which are jointly sufficient to produce it. Thus, at law, a person may be responsible for damage when his or her wrongful conduct is one of a number of conditions sufficient to produce that damage: see *McLean v Bell* (1932) 147 LT 262, at p 264, per Lord Wright; *Sherman v Nymboida Collieries Pty Ltd* (1963) 109 CLR 580, at pp 590-591, per Windeyer J.

Causation and the measure of damages
Some of the confusion surrounding the legal concept of causation has been occasioned by the terminology employed in the various attempts which have been made over the years to express the principles governing the measure of damages recoverable in tort or contract. Not infrequently these endeavours have invoked the language of causation with a view to limiting liability by reference to causal considerations. Thus, it has been said that a wrongdoer is liable for consequences of his or her wrongful conduct which have been variously described as "direct" (*In re Polemis and Furness, Withy & Co* [1921] 3 KB 560), "natural and probable" (*Haynes v Harwood* [1935] 1 KB 146, at p 156); *Dorset Yacht Co v Home Office* [1970] AC 1004, at pp 1028-1030, "direct and **[510]** natural" (*The Edison* [1932] P 52, at pp 62-64, 74; affd sub nom *Liesbosch, Dredger v Edison, SS (Owners)* [1933] AC 449), when the wrongful act is "the proximate cause" (*Yorkshire Dale Steamship Co v Minister of War Transport* [1942] AC 691) or "the real effective cause" (*Leyland Shipping Co v Norwich Union Fire Insurance Society* [1918] AC 350, at p 370).

Modern commentators take the view that these formulae, or at least some of them, conceal the making of value judgments or reliance on unexpressed policy reasons for refusing to allow liability to extend to the damage sustained in particular cases. The shortcomings of formulae of this kind were exposed in *Overseas Tankship (UK) Ltd v Morts Dock & Engineering Co Ltd (The Wagon Mound)* [1961] AC 388, where the "direct consequences" measure of damages in negligence endorsed by *Polemis* was discarded, and in *Overseas Tankship (UK) Ltd v Miller Steamship Co Pty ("The Wagon Mound (No 2)")* [1967] 1 AC 617, where the criterion of reasonable foresight was applied so as to enable the plaintiffs to recover damages for the kind of loss as the reasonable man should have foreseen.

However, in *Chapman v Hearse* (1961) 106 CLR 112, at p 122, this Court said, "the term 'reasonably foreseeable' is not, in itself, a test of 'causation'; it marks the limits beyond which a wrongdoer will not be held responsible for damage resulting from his wrongful act". More recently, in *Mahony v J Kruschich (Demolitions) Pty Ltd* (1985) 156 CLR 522, at p 528, the Court said:

> A line marking the boundary of the damage for which a tortfeasor is liable in negligence may be drawn either because the relevant injury is not reasonably foreseeable or because the chain of causation is broken by a novus actus interveniens: *M'Kew v Holland & Hannen & Cubitts* 1970 SC (HL) 20. But it must be possible to draw such a line clearly before a liability for damage that would not have occurred but for the wrongful act or omission of a tortfeasor and that is reasonably foreseeable by him is treated as the result of a second tortfeasor's negligence alone (see *Chapman v Hearse* (1961) 106 CLR, at pp 124-125). Whether such a line can and should be drawn is very much a matter of fact and degree.

Just as *Chapman v Hearse* rejected reasonable foresight as a test of causation, so *M'Kew* and *Mahoney* rejected it as an exclusive criterion of responsibility.

[511] The defence of contributory negligence

Another fertile source of confusion in the development of a coherent legal concept of causation has been the common law defence of contributory negligence. The existence of the defence, as well as the absence of any mechanism for apportionment of liability as between a plaintiff guilty of contributory negligence and a defendant and as between co-defendants who were concurrent tortfeasors, was a potent factor in inducing courts to embrace a view of causation which assigned occurrences to a single cause. So long as contributory negligence remained a defence, the adoption of this approach was more likely to produce just results. The approach was reflected in the question: what was the "effective cause" of the injury, being "the one to which may be variously ascribed the qualities of reality, predominance, efficiency" in the words of Lord Shaw of Dunfermline: *Leyland Shipping Co* [1918] AC at p 370. Although his Lordship was speaking in the context of a claim under a policy of marine insurance, this notion of effective cause came to be applied in cases of contributory negligence by means of the "last opportunity" or "last clear chance" rule. In ordinary circumstances, the plaintiff was defeated by the defence of contributory negligence when his or her negligence was an effective cause of his or her injury, notwithstanding that the defendant's negligence was also an effective cause of that injury: *Boy Andrew (Owners) v St Rognvald (Owners)* [1948] AC 140.

According to the "last opportunity" or "last clear chance" rule, the plaintiff was entitled to recover, despite his or her own negligence, if the defendant had the last opportunity of avoiding the accident but failed to do so due to negligence: see the discussion of the rule in *Alford v Magee* (1952) 85 CLR 437, at pp 450-464. Then the defendant's negligence was the effective cause of the plaintiff's injury. The result achieved by the application of the rule was explained in the language of causation; the defendant's later negligence broke the chain of causation so that the defendant's negligence was left as the effective cause of the plaintiff's injury. And it is in that sense that, in the present case, Prior J described the appellant's negligence as the "real cause" of his injuries. In this respect his Honour's description echoes the comments of this Court in *Alford v Magee* (1952) 85 CLR at p 461:

> [T]here are cases in which there is so substantial a difference between the position of the plaintiff and the position of the defendant at the material time that (although the accident could not have happened if the plaintiff's conduct had not been [512] negligent) it would not be fair or reasonable to regard the plaintiff as in any real sense the author of his own harm.

The last opportunity rule served only to confuse even further the legal concept of causation because it did not apply as between co-defendants, so that a failure by one defendant to avail himself or herself of a last opportunity to avoid the accident did not prevent the negligence of the other defendant from being the effective cause of the plaintiff's injury.

The effect of the legislation providing for apportionment of liability

The elimination of the defence of contributory negligence and the introduction by legislation (s 27a(3) of the *Wrongs Act 1936* (SA) providing for the apportionment between tortfeasors of damages in accordance with the degree of responsibility of the parties for the damage have meant that issues of causation could be approached afresh. True it is that there are to be found, since the enactment of the legislation, statements which indicate that the courts will still identify, in some situations, one or two preconditions to a consequence resulting in injury as the effective (and sole) cause of that injury, treating the other precondition as a causa sine qua non having merely the status of an incident preceding the critical occurrence and, hence, irrelevant: see *Sherman* (1963) 109 CLR, at pp 590-591, per Windeyer J; *Stapley v Gypsum Mines Ltd* [1953] AC 663, at p 687, per Lord Asquith of Bishopstone (dissenting). These statements echo the remarks of Lord Wright in *McLean v Bell* (1932) 147 LT, at p 264. Obviously, in the nature of things, there will be some cases in which a court concludes that a precondition does not play such a part in the consequence that it deserves to be characterized as a cause. ...

[513] This Court severely criticized the last opportunity rule in *Alford v Magee*. In so doing, the Court noted (1952) 85 CLR, at p 452, with apparent approval, Professor Glanville Williams'

comment (*Joint Torts and Contributory Negligence* (1951), p 223) that the rule was introduced to mitigate the hardship caused by the existence of the defence of contributory negligence and went on to point out that the effect of the rule was to preclude negligence of the plaintiff *found to be a cause of the damage* from affording a good defence. Subsequently, in *Chapman v Hearse*, the Court, after referring to *Alford v Magee*, observed ((1961) 106 CLR, at p 124):

> No doubt, in many cases, the rule has been treated as if it had assumed the role of a test of causation but not, as far as we can see, on any occasion when it was of importance to distinguish between its real and what may, perhaps, be called its apparent character.

This conclusion was fatal to the argument that the last opportunity rule survived the enactment of s 27a(3) of the *Wrongs Act* which requires an apportionment of damages where a person has suffered damage as the result partly of his or her fault and partly of the fault of any other person or persons. That argument depended upon the proposition that the rule was devised as a test of causation so that, when applied, its effect was to brand the defendant's negligence as the sole cause of the plaintiff's injuries. That proposition, as we have seen, was rejected in *Alford v Magee*. See also *Teubner v Humble* (1963) 108 CLR 491, at p 502, Windeyer J. In England also, the view has been taken that the rule did not survive the enactment of the apportionment legislation. In *Davies v Swan Motor Co (Swansea) Ltd; James, Third Party* [1949] 2 KB 291, at p 322, Denning LJ offered a different reason for the conclusion:

> [514] [T]he practical effect of the Act is wider than its legal effect. Previously ... the courts in practice sought to select, from a number of competing causes, which was *the* cause – the effective or predominant cause – of the damage and to reject the rest. Now the courts have regard to all the causes and apportion the damages accordingly.

So the end result of the apportionment legislation was to abolish not only the defence of contributory negligence but also the last opportunity rule. ...

[T]he law's recognition that concurrent or successive tortious acts may each amount to a cause of the injuries sustained by a plaintiff is reflected in the proposition that it is for the plaintiff to establish that his or her injuries are "caused or materially contributed to" by the defendant's wrongful conduct: *Duyvelshaff v Cathcart & Ritchie Ltd* (1973) 47 ALJR 410, at p 417, per Gibbs J; *Tubemakers of Australia Ltd v Fernandez* (1976) 50 ALJR 720, at p 724, per Mason J; *Bonnington Castings Ltd v Wardlaw* [1956] AC 613, at p 620, per Lord Reid; *McGhee v National Coal Board* [1973] 1 WLR 1, at pp 4, 6, 8, 12. Generally speaking, that causal connexion is established if it appears that the plaintiff would not have sustained his or her injuries had the defendant not been negligent: see *ICIANZ Ltd v Murphy* (1973) 47 ALJR 122, at pp 127-128. But, as the decision in that case illustrates, it is often extremely difficult to demonstrate what would have happened in the absence of the defendant's negligent conduct.

[515] Causation as a question of fact

The common law tradition is that what was the cause of a particular occurrence is a question of fact which "must be determined by applying common sense to the facts of each particular case," in the words of Lord Reid: *Stapley* [1953] AC, at p 681. That proposition is supported by a long line of authority in the United Kingdom: *Leyland Shipping Co* [1918] AC, at pp 363, 369-370; *Admiralty Commissioners v SS Volute* [1922] 1 AC 129, at p 144; *Yorkshire Dale Steamship Co* [1942] AC, at p 706; *Alphacell Ltd v Woodward* [1972] AC 824, at p 847; *McGhee v National Coal Board* [1973] 1 WLR, at pp 5, 11. It is supported also by this Court's decision in *Fitzgerald v Penn* (1954) 91 CLR 268 ... Commentators subdivide the issue of causation in a given case into two questions: the question of causation in fact – to be determined by the application of the "but for" test – and the further question whether a defendant is in law responsible for damage which his or her negligence has played some part in producing: see, eg; Fleming, *Law of Torts*, 7th ed (1987), pp 172-173; Hart and Honoré, *Causation in the Law*, 2nd ed (1985), p 110. It is said that, in determining this second question, considerations of policy have a prominent part to play, as do accepted value judgments: see Fleming, p 173. However, this approach to the issue of causation (a) places rather too much weight on the "but for" test to the exclusion of the "common sense" approach which the common law has always favoured; and (b) implies, or seems to imply, that value judgment has, or should have, no part to play in resolving causation as an issue of fact. As Dixon CJ, Fullagar and Kitto JJ remarked in *Fitzgerald v Penn* (1954) 91 CLR, at p 277 "it is all ultimately a matter of common sense" and "[i]n truth the conception in question [ie causation] is not susceptible of reduction to a satisfactory formula" (at p 278).

That said, the "but for" test, applied as a negative criterion of causation, has an important role to play in the resolution of the **[516]** question. So much was conceded by Dixon CJ, Fullagar and Kitto JJ in *Fitzgerald v Penn* (1954) 91 CLR, at pp 276-277 in their discussion of the unreported decision of this Court in *Skewes v Public Curator (Qld)* (6th September 1954) where A and B were driving their vehicles at excessive speeds in conditions of poor visibility so that their vehicles collided. A was on his correct side of the road, B was not. A's negligence was not causative of injury. Their Honours pointed out that, had the action been tried by a jury, it would have been correct for the judge to instruct the jury to "ask themselves the question whether they were satisfied that the collision would not have taken place with the same results if driver A had been driving at a reasonable speed". See also *ICIANZ Ltd v Murphy* (1973) 47 ALJR at pp 127-128; *Duyvelshaff v Cathcart & Ritchie Ltd* (1973) 47 ALJR, at pp 414-417, 419.

The commentators acknowledge that the "but for" test must be applied subject to certain qualifications. Thus, a factor which secures the presence of the plaintiff at the place where and at the time when he or she is injured is not causally connected with the injury, unless the risk of the accident occurring at that time was greater: see Hart and Honoré, at p 122. As Windeyer J observed in *Faulkner v Keffalinos* (1970) 45 ALJR 80, at p 86:

> But for the first accident, the [plaintiff] might still have been employed by the [defendants], and therefore not where he was when the second accident happened: but lawyers must eschew this kind of "but for" or sine qua non reasoning about cause and consequence.

The "but for" test gives rise to a well-known difficulty in cases where there are two or more acts or events which would each be sufficient to bring about the plaintiff's injury. The application of the test "gives the result contrary to common sense, that neither is a cause": *Winfield and Jolowicz on Tort*, 13th ed (1989), p 134. In truth, the application of the test proves to be either inadequate or troublesome in various situations in which there are multiple acts or events leading to the plaintiff's injury: see eg, *Chapman v Hearse*; *Baker v Willoughby* [1970] AC 467; *McGhee v National Coal Board*; *M'Kew* (to which I shall shortly refer in some detail). The cases demonstrate the lesson of experience, namely, that the test, applied as an exclusive criterion of causation, yields unacceptable results and that the results which it yields must be tempered by the making of value judgments and the infusion of policy considerations. That in itself is **[517]** something of an irony because the proponents of the "but for" test have seen it as a criterion which would exclude the making of value judgments and evaluative considerations from causation analysis: see Weinrib, "A Step Forward in Factual Causation", *Modern Law Review*, vol 38 (1975) 518, at p 530.

Novus actus interveniens

In similar fashion, the "but for" test does not provide a satisfactory answer in those cases in which a superseding cause, described as a novus actus interveniens, is said to break the chain of causation which would otherwise have resulted from an earlier wrongful act. Many examples may be given of a negligent act by A which sets the scene for a deliberate wrongful act by B who, fortuitously and on the spur of the moment, irresponsibly does something which transforms the outcome of A's conduct into something of far greater consequence, a consequence not readily forseeable by A. In such a situation, A's act is not a cause of that consequence, though it was an essential condition of it. No doubt the explanation is that the voluntary intervention of B is, in the ultimate analysis, the true cause, A's act being no more than an antecedent condition not amounting to a cause. But this explanation is not a vindication of the adequacy of the "but for" test.

The facts of and the decision in *M'Kew* 1970 SC (HL) 20 illustrate the same deficiency in the test. The plaintiff would not have sustained his ultimate injury but for the defendant's negligence causing the earlier injury to his left leg. His subsequent action in attempting to descend a steep staircase without a handrail in the normal manner and without adult assistance resulted in a severe fracture of his ankle. This action was adjudged to be unreasonable and to sever the chain of causation. The decision may be explained by reference to a value judgment that it would be unjust to hold the defendant legally responsible for an injury which, though it could be traced back to the defendant's wrongful conduct, was the immediate result of unreasonable action on the part of the plaintiff. But in truth the decision proceeded from a conclusion that the plaintiff's injury was the consequence of his independent and unreasonable action.

The fact that the intervening action is deliberate or voluntary does not necessarily mean that the plaintiff's injuries are not a consequence of the defendant's negligent conduct. In some situations a defendant may come under a duty of care not to expose the plaintiff to a risk of injury arising from deliberate or voluntary conduct or even to guard against that risk: see *Chomentowski v* **[518]** *Red Garter Restaurant Ltd* (1970) 92 WN (NSW) 1070. To deny recovery in these situations because the intervening action is deliberate or voluntary would be to deprive the duty of any content.

It has been said that the fact that the intervening action was foreseeable does not mean that the negligent defendant is liable for damage which results from the intervening action: see *Chapman v Hearse* (1961) 106 CLR, at p 122; *M'Kew* (1970) SC (HL), at p 25; *Caterson v Commissioner of Railways* (1973) 128 CLR 99, at p 110. But it is otherwise if the intervening action was in the ordinary course of things the very kind of thing likely to happen as a result of the defendant's negligence. In *Dorset Yacht* [1970] AC at p 1030, Lord Reid observed:

> But if the intervening action was likely to happen I do not think that it can matter whether that action was innocent or tortious or criminal. Unfortunately, tortious or criminal action by a third party is often the "very kind of thing" which is likely to happen as a result of the wrongful or careless act of the defendant.

Much the same approach was adopted by this Court in *Caterson* where Gibbs J (1973) 128 CLR 99, at p 110 (with whom Barwick CJ, Menzies and Stephen JJ agreed) pointed out that, if the plaintiff's action in jumping from the train was, in the ordinary course of things, the very kind of thing likely to happen as a result of the defendant's negligence and was not unreasonable, the jury was entitled to find that the plaintiff's injuries were caused by the defendant's negligence. The finding that the plaintiff's action was not unreasonable was then essential to that conclusion because contributory negligence was a defence in New South Wales at the relevant time. See also *Chapman v Hearse* (1961) 106 CLR, at pp 124-125; and note the reference in *Mahoney* (1985) 156 CLR, at p 529, to the acceptance by Gibbs J in *Dillingham Constructions Pty Ltd v Steel Mains Pty Ltd* (1975) 132 CLR 323, at pp 329-330, of the suggestion that, if a pedestrian were run over by two drivers consecutively and both were negligent, the injuries caused by the second driver would be damage for which both drivers were liable if those injuries were also the foreseeable consequence of the first driver's negligence.

As a matter of both logic and common sense, it makes no sense to regard the negligence of the plaintiff or a third party as a superseding cause or novus actus interveniens when the defendant's wrongful conduct has generated the very risk of injury resulting from the negligence of the plaintiff or a third party and that injury **[519]** occurs in the ordinary course of things. In such a situation, the defendant's negligence satisfies the "but for" test and is properly to be regarded as a cause of the consequence because there is no reason in common sense, logic or policy for refusing to so regard it.

Conclusion

Viewed in this light, the respondents' negligence was a cause of the accident and of the appellant's injuries. The second respondent's wrongful act in parking the truck in the middle of the road created a situation of danger, the risk being that a careless driver would act in the way that the appellant acted. The purpose of imposing the common law duty on the second respondent was to protect motorists from the very risk of injury that befell the appellant. In these circumstances, the respondents' negligence was a continuing cause of the accident. The chain of causation was not broken by a novus actus. Nor was it terminated because the risk of injury was not foreseeable; on the contrary, it was plainly foreseeable.

In the result I would allow the appeal.

DEANE J. ... **[520]** It is clear that the second respondent was in a relationship of proximity with other users of the road on which he left the truck. That relationship gave rise to a duty to take reasonable care to avoid foreseeable injury to such other road users. That relationship and that duty of care were not confined to persons who were careful and sober but extended to all foreseeable users of the road, including bad and inattentive drivers and those whose faculties were impaired either naturally or by reason of the effect of alcohol. In that regard, as was pointed out in *Bus v Sydney County Council* (1989) 167 CLR 78, at p 90, "the law has progressed" in recent years "by placing an increased emphasis upon the relevance of the possibility of negligence or inadvertence on the part of the person to whom a duty of care is owed". The progression of the law in that regard can, to a significant extent, be traced to the effect of apportionment legislation which precludes the approach that causative negligence on the part of a plaintiff forecloses the answer to any question of liability on the part of the defendant. ...

[521] The case is one in which there was fault on both sides and in which, in the context of apportionment legislation, the accident must be seen as the result not only of the negligence of the appellant in driving his own vehicle but also of the negligence of the second respondent in parking the truck in breach of the duty of care which he owed a class of persons of which the appellant was a member. Expressed in terms of causative fault, the effective causes of the appellant's injuries were the negligence of the second respondent in creating a hazard for a careless and inattentive driver and the negligence of the appellant in being such a driver. In these circumstances, it is not possible to isolate the fault of either the [522] appellant or the second respondent as the "sole" cause of the appellant's injuries. The injuries were caused by the fault of both and, that being so, the case called for apportionment of responsibility and reduction of damages pursuant to the provisions of s 27a(3) of the *Wrongs Act*. In the context of such an apportionment provision, it is unnecessary and unhelpful to seek further refinement by reference to catchcries of "last opportunity" or "direct cause": see *Chapman v Hearse* (1961) 106 CLR 112, at pp 122-124; *Teubner v Humble* (1963) 108 CLR, at p 502; *Harvey v Road Haulage Executive* [1952] 1 KB 120, at p 126; *Fitzgerald v Penn* (1954) 91 CLR 268, at p 284.

There are two further matters which I would mention. The first is that I do not subscribe to the view that, under apportionment legislation, causation is automatically established if a negative answer is given to the question whether the plaintiff's injuries would have been sustained "but for" the negligence of the defendant. Causation in the context of the elements of the tort of negligence is not the same thing as the "scientific term descriptive of sequence in physical phenomena" (*Clerk & Lindsell on Torts*, 16th ed (1989), par 1-103; and see, generally, the various papers in "Symposium on Causation in the Law of Torts", *Chicago-Kent Law Review* vol 63 (1987) esp Professor Wright, "The Efficiency Theory of Causation and Responsibility: Unscientific Formalism and False Semantics", pp 553ff). For the purposes of the law of negligence, the question of causation arises in the context of the attribution of fault or responsibility whether an identified negligent act or omission of the defendant was so connected with the plaintiff's loss or injury that, as a matter of ordinary common sense and experience, it should be regarded as a cause of it (cf *Barnes v Hay* (1988) 12 NSWLR 337, at p 339). The "but for" (or "causa sine qua non") test may well be a useful aid in determining whether something is properly to be seen as an effective cause of something else in that sense. In particular, the test will commonly exclude causation for the purposes of the law of negligence if the answer to the question it poses is that the accident which caused the injuries would have occurred in the same way and with the same consequences in any event: see eg, *Duyvelshaff v Cathcart & Ritchie Ltd* (1973) 47 ALJR 410, at pp 414-417, 419. There are however, in my view, convincing reasons precluding its adoption as a comprehensive definitive test of causation in the law of negligence. First, [523] the clear weight of authority is against the substitution of such a formularized test of causation for a "common sense ideal of what is meant by saying that one fact is a cause of another"; see, eg, *Fitzgerald v Penn* (1954) 91 CLR, at p 277; *National Insurance Co of New Zealand Ltd v Espagne* (1961) 105 CLR 569, at pp 590-592; *Stapley v Gypsum Mines Ltd* [1953] AC 663, at pp 681-682. Secondly, unqualified acceptance of the "but for" test as even a negative or exclusionary test of causation for the purposes of the law of negligence would lead to the absurd and unjust position that there was no "cause" of an injury in any case where there were present two independent and sufficient causes of the accident in which the injury was sustained. ... Thirdly, the mere fact that something constitutes an essential condition (in the "but for" sense) of an occurrence does not mean that, for the purposes of ascribing responsibility or fault, it is properly to be seen as a "cause" of that occurrence as a matter of either ordinary language or common sense. Thus, it could not, as a matter of ordinary language, be said that the fact that a person had a head was a "cause" of his being decapitated by a negligently wielded sword notwithstanding that possession of a head is an essential precondition of decapitation. Again, the mere fact that a person makes a gift of money to another is not, in any real sense, a "cause" of the damage sustained by that other person when his agent negligently loses the money notwithstanding that the loss would not have occurred "but for" the original gift. As Lord Reid pointed out in *Stapley* [1953] AC, at p 681:

> The question [of "what caused an accident from the point of view of legal liability"] must be determined by applying common sense to the facts of each particular case. One may find that as a matter of history several people have been at fault and that if any one of them had acted properly the accident would not have happened, but that does not mean that the accident must be regarded as having been caused by the faults of all of them. One must discriminate between those faults which must be discarded as being too remote and those which must not. Sometimes it is proper to discard all but one **[524]** and to regard that one as the sole cause but in other cases it is proper to regard two or more as having jointly caused the accident. I doubt whether any test can be applied generally.

It is true that, in the context of apportionment legislation which gives the latitude necessary to enable the relief to be fairly adjusted to fit the circumstances, the courts will be unlikely to deny causation in any case where the fault of a defendant contributed to an accident. Nonetheless, the question whether conduct is a "cause" of injury remains to be determined by a value judgment involving ordinary notions of language and common sense.

The other further matter is that it should be apparent that nothing in what is written above should be read as indicating a view that a plaintiff is entitled to recover compensation under apportionment legislation in circumstances where his or her own negligence was, as a matter of ordinary common sense, the sole real cause of the accident. Even under apportionment legislation, it is an element of the tort of negligence that the injury sustained by the plaintiff be caused by the defendant's breach of duty. In a case where, as a matter of ordinary common sense, the "sole" cause of the plaintiff's injury was his or her own negligence, that element of the tort will be lacking.

The appeal should be allowed.

McHUGH J. ... **[529]** In *Thom (or Simpson) v Sinclair* [1917] AC 127, at p 135, Viscount Haldane pointed out that in "strict logic the cause cannot be pronounced to be less than the sum of the entire conditions". This statement was derived from John Stuart Mill's theory that the cause of an event is the sum of the conditions which are jointly sufficient to produce it. But since the act or omission of a person charged with a wrongful act will be one only of the set of conditions or relations sufficient to produce the damage which gives rise to the proceedings, the common law has been forced to reject the application of scientific and philosophical theories of causation. They provide no answer to the question whether the person charged should be held legally responsible for the act or omission which constitutes his or her negligence. Lawyers, and particularly academic lawyers, however, have modified Mill's theory of causation and adapted it for legal purposes. The adaption of Mill's theory holds that every necessary member of the set of conditions or relations which is sufficient to **[530]** produce the relevant damage is a cause of that damage: *International Encyclopedia of Comparative Law*, vol XI, (1983), Ch 7, at p 27; Prosser, *Law of Torts*, 4th ed (1971), p 237; Fleming, *Law of Torts* 7th ed (1987), p 173; *Nader v Urban Transit Authority of NSW* (1985) 2 NSWLR 501, at p 531. Hence, for the purposes of the common law, a person may be causally responsible for damage even though his or her act or omission was one only of the conditions or relations sufficient to produce the damage. This is the basis of the "but for" test of causation which, apart from some exceptional cases, most writers and judges agree is the threshold test for determining whether a particular act or omission qualifies as a cause of the damage sustained. If the damage would have occurred notwithstanding the negligent act or omission, the act or omission is not a cause of the damage and there is no legal liability for it: *Duyvelshaff v Cathcart & Ritchie Ltd* (1973) 47 ALJR 410.

However, as I have already indicated, a powerful school of opinion asserts that the fact that a person's act or omission was a necessary condition of the occurrence of the damage is not itself sufficient to make that act or omission a legal cause of the damage. This school of opinion asserts that, to be a legal cause of damage, the act or omission charged must not only have been a sine qua non of its occurrence, but it must also have been a cause according to "common sense principles". This school of opinion has always had strong judicial support: see, for example, *Leyland Shipping*

Co v Norwich Union Fire Insurance Society [1918] AC 350, at p 362; *Fitzgerald v Penn* (1954) 91 CLR 268, at p 277; *Stapley* [1953] AC, at p 681. The view that the notion of "cause" in everyday speech and legal purposes means more than a necessary condition or causa sine qua non also has the powerful support of Hart and Honoré in the influential textbook, *Causation in the Law*, 2nd ed (1985).

But when the damage suffered by a plaintiff would not have occurred but for negligence on the part of both the plaintiff and the defendant, a conclusion that the defendant's negligence was not a cause of the damage cannot be based on logic or be the product of the application of a scientific or philosophical theory of causation. It has to be based upon a rule that enables the tribunal of fact to make a value judgment that in the circumstances legal responsibility did not attach to the defendant even though his or her act or omission was a necessary precondition of the occurrence of the damage.

Whatever label is given to such a rule – "common sense **[531]** principles", "forseeability", "novus actus interveniens", "effective cause", "real and efficient cause", "direct cause", "proximate cause" and so on – the reality is that such a limiting rule is the product of a policy choice that legal liability is not to attach to an act or omission which is outside the scope of that rule even though the act or omission was a necessary precondition of the occurrence of damage to the plaintiff. That is to say, such a rule is concerned only with the question whether a person should be held responsible for an act or omission which ex hypothesi was necessarily one of the sum of conditions or relations which produced the damage. ...

[532] [F]urther reflection on the matter has persuaded me that, if the "but for" test is applied in a "practical common sense way", it enables the tribunal of fact, consciously or unconsciously, to give effect to value judgments concerning responsibility for the damage. If the "but for" test is applied in that way, it gives the tribunal an unfettered discretion to ignore a condition or relation which was in fact a precondition of the occurrence of the damage.

Moreover, it is doubtful whether there is any consistent commonsense notion of what constitutes a "cause". As Dr Lloyd-Bostock has asserted in "The Ordinary Man, and the Psychology of Attributing Causes and Responsibility", *Modern Law Review*, vol 42 (1979) 143, at p 167, modern psychological research:

> illustrates how judgments of causes and responsibility [by an ordinary person] are reached by an active, constructive process which goes beyond the information given and is therefore subject to various forms of error and bias: are structured by as well as expressed in language: and are influenced by the motives, values, experiences, and other characteristics of the judger, the specific context, and the anticipated consequences. These various effects are interwoven and difficult to disentangle both conceptually and empirically, but in general talking about the ordinary man, common sense, and everyday judgments appear somewhat hazardous.

[533] Indeed, I suspect that what commonsense would not see as a cause in a non-litigious context will frequently be seen as a cause, according to commonsense notions, in a litigious context. This is particularly so in many cases where expert evidence is called to explain a connexion between an act or omission and the occurrence of damage. In these cases, the educative effect of the expert evidence makes an appeal to commonsense notions of causation largely meaningless or produces findings concerning causation which would often not be made by an ordinary person uninstructed by the expert evidence.

It is understandable that, in the days when any contributory negligence on the part of a plaintiff was sufficient to deprive him or her of a verdict, judges should sanction tests for determining causation which in practice allowed juries to avoid the consequences of a strict application of the doctrine of contributory negligence. In that context, instructions to determine whether a particular act or omission was a cause of damage according to commonsense notions were appeals to extralegal values to determine "hard cases". Significantly, this Court said in *Fitzgerald* (1954) 91 CLR, at p 276 that:

> there will not seldom be cases in which the attention of the jury ought to be called by the judge to the question whether a particular act or omission, which they may regard as negligence, can *fairly and properly* be considered a cause of the accident. (My emphasis.)

But now that contributory negligence is no longer an absolute bar, why should the courts continue to sanction the use of formulas which allow tribunals of fact, under the guise of using commonsense, to determine legal responsibility by applying their own idiosyncratic values? Directions to use commonsense notions of causation to find the "proximate", "real", "efficient" or "substantial" cause of an occurrence are invitations to use subjective, unexpressed and undefined extra-legal values to determine legal liability. To hold a person liable for damage resulting from a set of conditions or relations simply because his or her wrongful act or omission was a necessary condition of the occurrence of that damage would be an unacceptable extension of the boundaries of legal liability in some cases. But this truth does not justify the use of vague rules which permit liability to be determined by subjective, unexpressed and undefined values.

In my opinion, now that legislation allows liability for damage to be apportioned in accordance with what the court thinks is just and [534] equitable having regard to the comparative responsibility of the parties, the preferable course is to use the causa sine qua non test as the exclusive test of causation. One obvious exception to this rule must be the unusual case where the damage is the result of the simultaneous operation of two or more separate and independent events each of which was sufficient to cause the damage. None of the various tests of causation suggested by courts and writers, however, is satisfactory in dealing with this exceptional case. Perhaps no more can be done in this situation than to treat each wrongful act as an independent cause for legal purposes. The terms of a statute, legal rule or legal instrument may also require a different approach from the "but for" test. In general, however, the "but for" test should be seen as the test of legal causation. Any other rule limiting responsibility for damage caused by a wrongful act or omission should be recognized as a policy-based rule concerned with remoteness of damage and not causation.

[McHugh J concluded that, subject to the question of apportionment, the respondents were liable for the appellant's damage and that the appeal should be allowed.

Toohey J concurred with Mason CJ, and Gaudron J concurred with Mason CJ and Deane J.]

Appeal allowed

Adeels Palace Pty Ltd v Moubarak
(2009) 239 CLR 420; [2009] HCA 48
High Court of Australia

In the context of the statutory obligations of licensees of licensed premises to minimise harm from alcohol abuse and not to permit violent or quarrelsome conduct on the premises, and of their statutory entitlement to evict or refuse admittance to people who were violent or quarrelsome, a licensee may owe a common law duty to take reasonable care to prevent personal injury to a patron on the premises by the violent criminal act of another patron. However, the plaintiff must prove that any breach of that duty caused his or her damage. Civil liability legislation in most Australian jurisdictions requires a court determining breach of duty to consider various matters when deciding what security precautions a reasonable person in the position of the defendant would have taken. That legislation, in describing how a court is to determine whether any breach, in fact, caused the plaintiff's damage, requires the court to apply the "but for" test.

[The defendant (appellant), Adeels Palace Pty Ltd, carried on a reception and restaurant business on licensed premises. One New Year's Eve, the premises were full of patrons. There were no security personnel on the premises. An incident occurred on the dance floor, precipitating a fight in which a patron was punched in the face by Mr Moubarak, the first plaintiff (first respondent). The patron left the premises but soon returned with a gun with which he shot Mr Moubarak, and the second plaintiff (second respondent), Mr Bou Najem, who was a random victim unconnected with the earlier incident. Both Mr Moubarak and Mr Bou Najem sustained injuries and sued the defendant in negligence for not providing any or sufficient security at the function. They were awarded damages in the District Court of New South Wales and the defendant, after an unsuccessful appeal to the New South Wales Court of Appeal, was successful in its appeal to the High Court of Australia, which ordered that the judgments for the plaintiffs be set aside.]

THE COURT. [French CJ, Gummow, Hayne, Heydon and Crennan JJ] ...

[431] *The issues ...*

[432] 11. In considering each of the issues of duty, breach and causation, it is of the first importance to identify the proper starting point for the relevant inquiry. In this case there are two statutes which require particular consideration: the *Civil Liability Act 2002* (NSW) and the *Liquor Act*. If attention is not directed first to the *Civil Liability Act*, and then to the *Liquor Act*, there is serious risk that the inquiries about duty, breach and causation will miscarry.

The Civil Liability Act ...

13. Although ss 5B and 5C appear beneath the heading "Duty of care", that heading is apt to mislead. The sections provided:

"5B General principles

 (1) A person is not negligent in failing to take precautions against a risk of harm unless:

 (a) the risk was foreseeable (that is, it is a risk of which the person knew or ought to have known), and

 (b) the risk was not insignificant, and

 (c) in the circumstances, a reasonable person in the person's position would have taken those precautions.

 (2) In determining whether a reasonable person would have taken precautions against a risk of harm, the court is to consider the following (amongst other relevant things):

 (a) the probability that the harm would occur if care were not taken,

 (b) the likely seriousness of the harm,

 (c) the burden of taking precautions to avoid the risk of harm,

 (d) the social utility of the activity that creates the risk of harm. ...

[433] Both [ss 5B and 5C] are evidently directed to questions of breach of duty.

14. By contrast, Div 3 (ss 5D and 5E) is directed to the subject matter described in the heading to the division – Causation. Those sections provided:

"5D General principles

 (1) A determination that negligence caused particular harm comprises the following elements:

 (a) that the negligence was a necessary condition of the occurrence of the harm (*factual causation*), and

 (b) that it is appropriate for the scope of the negligent person's liability to extend to the harm so caused (*scope of liability*).

 (2) In determining in an exceptional case, in accordance with established principles, whether negligence that cannot be established as a necessary condition of the occurrence of harm should be accepted as establishing factual causation, the court is to consider (amongst other relevant things) whether or not and why responsibility for the harm should be imposed on the negligent party. ...

 (4) For the purpose of determining the scope of liability, the court is to consider (amongst other relevant things) whether or not and why responsibility for the harm should be imposed on the negligent party.

5E Onus of proof

In determining liability for negligence, the plaintiff always bears the onus of proving, on the balance of probabilities, any fact relevant to the issue of causation."

15. These provisions of the *Civil Liability Act* are central to the questions of breach of duty and causation.

The Liquor Act

16. Consideration of provisions of the *Liquor Act* is central to the question of duty of care. Why that is so is revealed by the nature of the claims that were made.

[434] 17. Each plaintiff sued Adeels Palace for damages for injury he had suffered on the premises of Adeels Palace. ...

18. The central complaint each plaintiff made was that Adeels Palace had not regulated who came on to its premises, who stayed on those premises, and how those who were on the premises conducted themselves towards other patrons. Adeels Palace, as occupier of the premises, could control who came into and who stayed on the premises. But in conducting licensed premises (of which one of its directors was licensee) Adeels Palace was much affected by the duties which the *Liquor Act* cast on the licensee. [Their Honours set out the relevant sections of the Act]...

20. It is next important to recognise that the particular provisions made in the *Liquor Act* for controlling violent, quarrelsome or disorderly conduct on licensed premises take their place in a context set by two considerations. First, sale of liquor is controlled because it is well recognised that misuse and abuse of liquor causes harm, including what the *Liquor Act* refers to as "violent, quarrelsome or disorderly" conduct. Section 2A of the *Liquor Act* provided:

[435] *"Liquor harm minimisation is a primary object of this Act* A primary object of this Act is liquor harm minimisation, that is, the minimisation of harm associated with misuse and abuse of liquor (such as harm arising from violence and other anti-social behaviour). The court, the Board, the Director, the Commissioner of Police and all other persons having functions under this Act are required to have due regard to the need for liquor harm minimisation when exercising functions under this Act. In particular, due regard is to be had to the need for liquor harm minimisation when considering for the purposes of this Act what is or is not in the public interest."

The second and related point to make is that the duties cast upon those responsible for the service of liquor on licensed premises can be understood as a part of the price that is exacted for the statutory permission granted under the *Liquor Act*. The permission granted is to do what otherwise the Act forbids (s 122) – sell liquor – and to do that on premises to which members of the public may resort only in accordance with the conditions on which the licence is granted.

21. In considering whether a common law duty of care should be held to exist in these cases, it is important to recognise that the provisions of the *Liquor Act* that have been mentioned have close analogies in other States and Territories. Though variously expressed, all States and Territories make provision for a licensee of licensed premises to remove from, or prevent the entry to, licensed premises of violent or quarrelsome persons. All State and Territory liquor legislation forbids the sale of liquor without a licence. All State and Territory liquor legislation provides for the licensing of premises on which liquor may be sold and consumed, and not only regulates the sale and service of liquor in such places, but also (as already noted) directly or indirectly regulates the conduct of persons who are on the premises.

22. It is against this statutory background that the question of duty of care must be considered, not for the purpose of developing the common law by analogy with statute law (cf *Esso Australia Resources Ltd v Federal Commissioner of Taxation* (1999) 201 CLR 49 at 59-63 [18]-[28]), but to ensure that the imposition of a common law duty of reasonable care of the kind now in question would not run counter to the statutory requirements imposed on licensees in all Australian jurisdictions.

Duty of care?

23. Contrary to the submissions on behalf of Adeels Palace, this Court's decision in *Modbury* [*Triangle Shopping Centre Pty Ltd v Anzil* (2000) 205 CLR 254] does not dictate the conclusion that Adeels Palace owed no relevant duty of care to the plaintiffs in the present cases. Like the claims now under consideration, the claim that was made in [436] *Modbury* was for damages for personal injury suffered as a result of a criminal assault. The injured plaintiff in *Modbury* had been attacked in a shopping centre car park at night when the lights in the car park were off. He

alleged that the shopping centre proprietor was negligent in not leaving the car park lights on. A majority of the Court ((2000) 205 CLR 254 at 266-267 [29], 268-269 [36] per Gleeson CJ; at 270 [42]-[43] per Gaudron J; at 291-294 [108]-[118] per Hayne J; at 302 [147] per Callinan J) held that the shopping centre did not owe the plaintiff a duty to take reasonable care to prevent injury to the plaintiff resulting from the criminal behaviour of third persons on the shopping centre's land. It is important to recognise, however, that the duty alleged in *Modbury* was said to be founded only on the defendant's position as occupier of the land controlling the physical state of the land (there the level of its illumination). What is said in *Modbury* must be understood as responding to those arguments. No complaint was made that the defendant should have controlled, but did not control, access by the assailants to the land it occupied.

24. It is, of course, important to recognise that the decision in *Modbury* forms part of a line of cases in which consideration has been given to whether and when one person owes another a duty to take reasonable care to control the conduct of a third person (See, eg, *Smith v Leurs* (1945) 70 CLR 256 at 262 per Dixon J; *Howard v Jarvis* (1958) 98 CLR 177; *New South Wales v Bujdoso* (2005) 227 CLR 1; cf *Stuart v Kirkland-Veenstra* (2009) 237 CLR 215; *CAL No 14 Pty Ltd v Motor Accidents Insurance Board* (2009) 239 CLR 390). And the fact that the conduct in question is criminal conduct is of great importance in deciding not only what, if any, duty is owed to prevent its commission, but also questions of breach and causation.

25. Several considerations set the present case apart from *Modbury* and point to the conclusion that Adeels Palace owed each plaintiff a relevant duty of care. First, the complaint that was made in these cases was that the occupier of premises failed to control access to, or continued presence on, its premises (cf *Modbury Triangle Shopping Centre Pty Ltd v Anzil* (2000) 205 CLR 254 at 293-294 [117]). Secondly, the premises concerned were licensed premises where liquor was sold. They were, therefore, premises where it is and was well recognised that care must be taken lest, through misuse and abuse of liquor, "harm [arise] from violence and other anti-social behaviour" (*Liquor Act 1982* (NSW), s 2A). And thirdly, the particular duty said to have rested on the occupier of the premises (who was the operator of the business that was conducted on the premises) is a duty to take reasonable care to prevent or hinder the occurrence of events which, under the *Liquor Act*, the licensee was bound to prevent occurring – violent, quarrelsome or disorderly conduct. (And although variously expressed in the legislation of other Australian jurisdictions, **[437]** the evident scheme of all liquor licensing laws in Australia is to minimise anti-social conduct both on and off licensed premises associated with consumption of alcohol.)

26. In the circumstances reasonably to be contemplated before the restaurant opened for business on 31 December 2002 as likely to prevail on that night, Adeels Palace owed each plaintiff a duty to take reasonable care to prevent injury to patrons from the violent, quarrelsome or disorderly conduct of other persons. The duty is consistent with the duty imposed by statute upon the licensee and which was a duty enforceable by criminal processes. No question arises of translating a statutory power given to a statutory body into the common law "ought" (cf *Pyrenees Shire Council v Day* (1998) 192 CLR 330 at 375 [122]). The duty is not absolute; it is a duty to take reasonable care. It is not a duty incapable of performance. It is a duty the performance of which is supported by the provision of statutory power to prevent entry to premises and to remove persons from the premises, if needs be by using reasonable force. Although it is a duty directed to controlling the conduct of others (for the avoidance of injury to other patrons) it is a duty to take reasonable care in the conduct of activities on licensed premises, particularly with regard to allowing persons to enter or remain on those premises.

Breach of duty?
27. The question of breach of duty must be considered by reference to the relevant provisions of the *Civil Liability Act* – in particular s 5B.

28. It may be accepted, for the purposes of argument, that there was a risk, of which Adeels Palace knew or ought to have known (s 5B(1)(a)), that there would be violent, quarrelsome or disorderly conduct in the restaurant. It may also be accepted that this risk "was not insignificant" (s 5B(1)(b)). The question then becomes whether a reasonable person in the position of Adeels Palace would have taken the precautions that the plaintiffs alleged should have been taken (ss 5B(1)(c),

5B(2)). Those precautions were the provision of licensed security personnel who would act as crowd controllers or bouncers.

29. Just how many security personnel the plaintiffs alleged should have been provided was not always made clear in argument. ...

[438] 30. Whether any, and how many, security personnel should have been provided to satisfy the duty of Adeels Palace to take reasonable care depended upon the considerations identified in s 5B(2) of the *Civil Liability Act*: the probability that the harm would occur, the likely seriousness of the harm, the burden of taking precautions to avoid the risk, and the social utility of the activity that created the risk. No doubt the chief focus of those inquiries in these cases would fall upon the first three of those considerations.

Many different matters were relevant to the questions that thus were posed. They included, but were not limited to, such matters as the number of patrons expected to attend the restaurant, the atmosphere that could reasonably be expected to exist during the function, and whether there had been any suggestion of violence at similar events held in comparable circumstances, either at this restaurant or elsewhere. And all of those questions fell to be answered, and the probability of harm and other considerations mentioned in s 5B(2) assessed, prospectively (41), not with the wisdom of hindsight. That is, they were to be assessed *before* the function began, not by reference to what occurred that night. ...

[439] 39. The absence of consideration at trial of the matters prescribed by s 5B of the *Civil Liability Act* may have been reason enough to conclude that the question of breach of duty was not determined properly by the trial judge. It is, however, not profitable to examine that issue further.

[440] 40. It is not profitable to do that because resolution of the issue of breach would necessarily depend only upon the evidence that was led at trial. The points to be made that are of general application are first, that whether a reasonable person would have taken precautions against a risk is to be determined prospectively, and secondly, that the answer given in any particular case turns on the facts of that case as they are proved in evidence. It follows from the second of these considerations that deciding the question of breach in these cases would not establish any rule about when or whether security personnel should be engaged by the operators of licensed premises. It is not useful (cf *Pokora v Wabash Railway Co* (1934) 292 US 98 at 105-106 per Cardozo J) in these circumstances for this Court to form a conclusion about whether breach was proved in these cases. In particular, it is not necessary to examine the evidence that was led at trial to determine whether the finding of breach could be supported. Instead, it is desirable to consider the question of causation. Examination of that issue reveals that the negligence found against Adeels Palace was not shown to have been a cause of the injuries suffered by the plaintiffs.

Causation

41. The first point to make about the question of causation is that, in these cases, it is governed by the *Civil Liability Act*.

42. Section 5D(1) of that Act divides the determination of whether negligence caused particular harm into two elements: factual causation and scope of liability.

43. Dividing the issue of causation in this way expresses the relevant questions in a way that may differ from what was said by Mason CJ, in *March v E and MH Stramare Pty Ltd* (1991) 171 CLR 506 at 515, to be the common law's approach to causation. The references (at 515, quoting from *Fitzgerald v Penn* (1954) 91 CLR 268 at 277) in *March v Stramare* to causation being "ultimately a matter of common sense" were evidently intended to disapprove the proposition "that value judgment has, or should have, no part to play in resolving causation as an issue of fact". By contrast, s 5D(1) treats factual causation and scope of liability as separate and distinct issues.

44. It is not necessary to examine whether or to what extent the approach to causation described in *March v Stramare* might lead to a conclusion about factual causation different from the conclusion that should be reached by applying s 5D(1). It is sufficient to observe that, in cases where the *Civil Liability Act* or equivalent statutes are engaged, it is the applicable statutory provision that must be applied.

45. Next it is necessary to observe that the first of the two elements identified in s 5D(1) (factual causation) is determined by the "but for" test: but for the negligent act or omission, would the harm have occurred?

[441] 46. In the Court of Appeal, Giles JA, who gave the principal reasons, pointed out, correctly, that the reasoning of the trial judge on the question of causation was "not fully articulated". The reasoning was reconstructed by Giles JA in the following terms:

> From the evidence, security staff would have been aware of a significant fracas on the dance floor. Even if [the gunman] had not been identified at the time as the man who had got into a fight with Mr Moubarak, the presence of blood on his face would have caused the security staff at the street entrance, particularly with knowledge of the fracas, to deny him entry, or at least to require that he submit to search as a condition of being permitted to enter. On the balance of probabilities, security staff at the street entrance would have deterred or prevented [the gunman's] re-entry, and he therefore would not have shot Mr Moubarak and Mr Bou Najem.

47. Security personnel may have been able to deter or prevent re-entry by the drunk or the obstreperous would-be patron willing to throw a punch. There was, however, no basis in the evidence for concluding that security staff at the entrance to the restaurant would have deterred or prevented the re-entry to the premises of a man armed with a gun when later events showed he was ready and willing to use the weapon on persons unconnected with his evident desire for revenge.

48. The evidence at trial did not show that the presence of security personnel would have *deterred* the re-entry of the gunman. That conclusion could have been reached only if it was assumed that the gunman would have acted rationally. But, as was pointed out in *Modbury* at 291 [107], "[t]he conduct of criminal assailants is not necessarily dictated by reason or prudential considerations". The gunman's conduct at the restaurant on this night was dictated neither by reason nor by prudential considerations. He shot the man who had struck him during the mêlée that broke out after the confrontation on the dance floor. And before shooting that man, the gunman had shot a man who had done nothing to him and who, defenceless, begged for mercy.

49. Nor did the evidence show that security personnel could or would have *prevented* re-entry by the gunman: a determined person armed with a gun and irrationally bent on revenge. The evidence given at trial by the plaintiffs' expert security consultant did not go beyond the assertion that a security person confronting the gunman at the entrance to the restaurant "would have at least altered the chain of events and thereby likely altered the outcome". The security consultant called on behalf of Adeels Palace emphasised that the overriding principle which should govern the conduct of security personnel confronted by a gunman is "safety for all parties" and that "once a determined gunman is targeting a victim or victims there [is] no guaranteed safe or effective option".

[442] 50. Recognising that changing any of the circumstances in which the shootings occurred *might* have made a difference does not prove factual causation. Providing security at the entrance of the restaurant *might* have delayed the gunman's entry; it might have meant that, if Mr Bou Najem was a random victim, as seemed to be the case, someone else might have been shot and not him. But neither plaintiff proved factual causation by pointing to possibilities that might have eventuated if circumstances had been different.

51. Nor was "but for" causation established in these cases by observing that the relevant duty was to take reasonable care to prevent injury to patrons from the violent, quarrelsome or disorderly conduct of other persons. That is, the question of factual causation was not answered in these cases by pointing out that the relevant duty of care was to take reasonable steps to prevent violent assault, that each plaintiff was the victim of a violent assault, and that the damage sustained by the plaintiffs was "the very kind of thing" which the relevant duty obliged Adeels Palace to take reasonable steps to prevent (cf *Home Office v Dorset Yacht Co Ltd* [1970] AC 1004 at 1030 per Lord Reid; *Stansbie v Troman* [1948] 2 KB 48 at 51-52). That observation may bear upon questions about scope of liability (cf *Travel Compensation Fund v Tambree* (2005) 224 CLR 627 at 638-639 [26]-[27], 641-642 [40]-[41]). Describing the injury as "the very kind of thing" which was the subject of the duty must not be permitted to obscure the need to prove factual causation. Unlike *Home Office v Dorset Yacht Co Ltd* [1970] AC 1004 and *Stansbie v Troman* [1948] 2 KB 48, these are not cases where the evidence demonstrated that the taking of reasonable care would probably have prevented the occurrence of injury to the plaintiffs … .

53. In the present case, … the "but for" test of factual causation was not established. It was not shown to be more probable than not that, but for the absence of security personnel (whether at the door or even on the floor of the restaurant), the shootings would not have taken place. That is, the absence of security personnel at Adeels Palace on the night the plaintiffs were shot was not a necessary condition of their being shot. Because the absence of security personnel was not a necessary condition of the occurrence of the harm to either plaintiff, s 5D(1) was not satisfied. Did s 5D(2) apply?

[443] 54. Section 5D(2) makes provision for what it describes as "an exceptional case". But the Act does not expressly give content to the phrase "an exceptional case". All that is plain is that it is a case where negligence cannot be established as a necessary condition of the harm; the "but for" test of causation is *not* met. In such a case the court is commanded "to consider (amongst other relevant things) whether or not and why responsibility for the harm should be imposed on the negligent party". But beyond the statement that this is to be done "in accordance with established principles", the provision offers no further guidance about how the task is to be performed. Whether, or when, s 5D(2) is engaged must depend, then, upon whether and to what extent "established principles" countenance departure from the "but for" test of causation.

55. At once it must be recognised that the legal concept of causation differs from philosophical and scientific notions of causation (*March v E and MH Stramare Pty Ltd* (1991) 171 CLR 506 at 509…). It must also be recognised that before the *Civil Liability Act* and equivalent provisions were enacted, it had been recognised (*Bennett v Minister of Community Welfare* (1992) 176 CLR 408 at 413; *Chappel v Hart* (1998) 195 CLR 232 at 257 [66]-[67]) that the "but for" test was not always a *sufficient* test of causation. But as s 5D(1) shows, the "but for" test is now to be (and has hitherto been seen to be) a *necessary* test of causation in all but the undefined group of exceptional cases contemplated by s 5D(2).

56. Even if the presence of security personnel at the door of the restaurant *might* have deterred or prevented the person who shot the plaintiffs from returning to the restaurant, and even if security personnel on the floor of the restaurant *might* have been able to intervene in the incident that broke into fighting in time to prevent injury to anyone, neither is reason enough to conclude that this is an "exceptional case" where responsibility for the harm suffered by the plaintiffs should be imposed on Adeels Palace. To impose that responsibility would not accord with established principles.

57. It may be that s 5D(2) was enacted to deal with cases exemplified by the House of Lords decision in *Fairchild v Glenhaven Funeral Services Ltd* [2003] 1 AC 32 where plaintiffs suffering from mesothelioma had been exposed to asbestos in successive employments. Whether or how s 5D(2) would be engaged in such a case need not be decided now. The present cases are very different. No analogy can be drawn with cases like *Fairchild*. Rather, it would be contrary to established principles to hold Adeels Palace responsible in negligence if not providing security was *not* a necessary condition of the occurrence of the harm but providing security *might* have deterred or prevented its occurrence, or might have resulted in harm being suffered by someone other than, or [444] in addition to, the plaintiffs. As in *Modbury*, the event which caused the plaintiffs' injuries was deliberate criminal wrongdoing, and the wrongdoing occurred despite society devoting its resources to deterring and preventing it through the work of police forces and the punishment of those offenders who are caught. That being so, it should not be accepted that negligence which was not a *necessary* condition of the injury that resulted from a third person's criminal wrongdoing was a cause of that injury. Accordingly, the submission that the plaintiffs' injuries in these cases were caused by the failure of Adeels Palace to take steps that *might* have made their occurrence less likely, should be rejected. …

Appeals allowed

[Section 5B of the *Civil Liability Act 2002* (NSW) is in the same terms as the *Civil Law (Wrongs) Act 2002* (ACT), s 43; the *Civil Liability Act 2003* (Qld), s 9; the *Civil Liability Act 1936* (SA), s 32 and the *Civil Liability Act 2002* (WA), s 5B. It is very similar in its terms to the *Civil Liability Act 2002* (Tas), s 11 and the *Wrongs Act 1958* (Vic), s 48. Section 5D of the *Civil Liability Act 2002* (NSW) is in the same terms as the *Civil Liability Act 2003* (Qld), s 11. It is very similar in its terms to the *Civil Law (Wrongs) Act 2002* (ACT), s 45; the *Civil Liability Act 1936* (SA), s 34; *Civil Liability Act 2002* (Tas), s 13; the *Wrongs Act 1958* (Vic), s 51 and the *Civil Liability Act 2002* (WA), s 5C.]

Jobling v Associated Dairies Ltd
[1982] AC 794
House of Lords

Where the defendant negligently has caused personal injury to the plaintiff, a supervening illness affecting the plaintiff (but unrelated to the defendant's negligence) may be taken into account as a vicissitude of life negating or reducing the extent to which the defendant's negligence remains a cause of the plaintiff's damage.

[In January 1973, the plaintiff sustained a back injury at work, which rendered him fit for sedentary work only. He commenced proceedings against his employers, the defendants, but in 1976, before the trial, it was discovered that he had spondylotic myelopathy which affected his neck and rendered him totally unfit for work. This condition was unrelated and would have been dormant at the date of the original accident.

When assessing damages for loss of earnings, the trial judge held that he was bound, on the authority of *Baker v Willoughby* [1970] AC 467, to leave out of account the illness supervening after the accident. The Court of Appeal, holding that *Baker v Willoughby* was not applicable to a case involving a non-tortious supervening event, set aside the assessment of damages and held that the damages should be reduced to take into account the disability suffered as a result of the disease.

The plaintiff appealed.]

LORD KEITH of KINKEL. **[811]** My Lords, this appeal raises a short but very difficult point in connection with the assessment of damages for personal injuries. ...

[T]he question arose whether the respondents were liable to pay damages for loss of earnings upon the basis of a partial incapacity continuing throughout the period, which, in the absence of the myelopathy, would have represented the balance of the appellant's normal working life, or whether their liability was limited to loss of earnings up to the time when the myelopathy resulted in total incapacity. ...

The facts of *Baker v Willoughby* were that the plaintiff suffered an injury to his left leg through the defendant's negligence, resulting in a continuing disability which reduced his earning capacity. Before his case came to trial he was shot by a robber in the same leg, which in consequence had to be amputated. As a result the plaintiff's disability was rather greater than it had been before. This House, reversing the Court of Appeal, held that the award of damages for loss of earnings did not fall to be diminished by reason of the later injuries, upon the view that they represented no more than a concurrent cause, along with the original injury, of the plaintiff's disability.

[812] It was argued for the respondent, defendant in the action, that the second injury removed the very limb from which the earlier disability had stemmed, and that therefore no loss suffered thereafter could be attributed to the respondent's negligence. In rejecting this argument Lord Reid, whose speech was concurred in by Lord Guest, Viscount Dilhorne and Lord Donovan, said at p 492:

If it were the case that in the eye of the law an effect could only have one cause then the respondent might be right. It is always necessary to prove that any loss for which damages can be given was caused by the defendant's negligent act. But it is a commonplace that the law regards many events as having two causes: that happens whenever there is contributory negligence for then the law says that the injury was caused both by the negligence of the defendant and by the negligence of the plaintiff. And generally it does not matter which negligence occurred first in point of time.

Lord Reid took the view that the appellant's disability could be regarded as having two causes, and he found support for this view in *Harwood v Wyken Colliery Co* [1913] 2 KB 158. That was a workmen's compensation case in which the Court of Appeal held the plaintiff entitled to compensation, notwithstanding that there had supervened upon the incapacity resulting from an accident at work an incapacity of similar extent resulting from heart disease. Lord Reid later went on to distinguish the case where damages might properly fall to be diminished by reason of the death of the plaintiff before trial, upon the basis that in such a case the supervening event had reduced the plaintiff's loss. He said at p 494:

> If the later injury suffered before the date of the trial either reduces the disabilities from the injury for which the defendant is liable, or shortens the period during which they will be suffered by the plaintiff, then the defendant will have to pay less damages. But if the later injuries merely become a concurrent cause of the disabilities caused by the injury inflicted by the defendant, then in my view they cannot diminish the damages. Suppose that the plaintiff has to spend a month in bed before the trial because of some illness unconnected with the original injury, the defendant cannot say that he does not have to pay anything in respect of that month: during that month the original injuries and the new illness are concurrent causes of his inability to work and that does not reduce the damages.

It seems clear from this passage that the principle of concurrent causes which Lord Reid selected as the ratio decidendi of the case would, if sound, apply with the same force where the supervening event is natural disease, as in the present case, as it does where the supervening event is a tortious act.

Lord Pearson's main reason for rejecting the respondent's argument was that it would produce manifest injustice. He said at p 495:

> The supervening event has not made the plaintiff less lame nor less disabled nor less deprived of amenities. It has not shortened **[813]** the period over which he will be suffering. It has made him more lame, more disabled, more deprived of amenities. He should not have less damages through being worse off than might have been expected.

Lord Pearson went on to illustrate the nature of the injustice by pointing out that, where the supervening event was a tortious act, the later tortfeasor, upon the principle that he takes his victim as he finds him, would be liable for damages in respect of loss of earnings only to the extent that the act had caused an additional diminution of earning capacity. If the earlier incapacity were treated, in a question with the first tortfeasor, as submerged by the later, the plaintiff would be left in the position of being unable to recover from anyone a substantial part of the loss suffered after the date of the second tort. So he would not be fully compensated in respect of the combined efforts of both torts. It is to be observed that this was the consideration which had been principally urged in the argument for the appellant.

A notable feature of the speeches in *Baker v Willoughby* [1970] AC 467 is the absence of any consideration of the possible implications of what may be termed the "vicissitudes" principle. The leading exposition of this principle is to be found in the judgment of Brett LJ in *Phillips v London and South Western Railway Co* (1879) 5 CPD 280, 291-292:

> ... if no accident had happened, nevertheless many circumstances might have happened to prevent the plaintiff from earning his previous income; he may be disabled by illness, he is subject to the ordinary accidents and vicissitudes of life; and if all these circumstances of which no evidence can be given are looked at, it will be impossible to exactly estimate them; yet if the jury wholly pass them over they will go wrong, because these accidents and vicissitudes ought to be taken into account. It is true that the chances of life cannot be accurately calculated, but the judge must tell the jury to consider them in order that they may give a fair and reasonable compensation.

This principle is to be applied in conjunction with the rule that the court will not speculate when it knows, so that when an event within its scope has actually happened prior to the trial date, that event will fall to be taken into account in the assessment of damages.

In *Harwood v Wyken Colliery Co* [1913] 2 KB 158, which was founded on by Lord Reid in *Baker v Willoughby* [1970] AC 467 as supporting the view which he took upon causation, Hamilton LJ was at pains to stress that compensation under the *Workmen's Compensation Acts* had nothing in common with an award of damages for personal injuries, being based on what the workman has earned in the past, not upon what he will be prevented from earning in the future. He fully recognised the application of the "vicissitudes" principle in the damages context, saying at pp 169-170:

> In assessing damages for injury caused to a plaintiff workman by the tortious negligence of the employer or his servants a jury would be directed that, their damages being a compensation once for all, **[814]** they must consider not merely past injury, pain and suffering endured, expenses incurred and earnings lost, but also future loss. They would have to measure in money the future effects of permanent or continuing disablement, but they must consider also the possibility of future diminution or loss of earnings arising independently of the cause of action, from increasing age, from accident or illness in futuro, and so forth. They would be directed that they had to give solatium for suffering and compensation for disablement, but so that the tort-sufferer should not make a profit out of the wrong done him, the object being by the verdict to place him in as good a position as he was in before the wrong, but not in any wise in a better one.

By way of contrast, under the *Workmen's Compensation Acts* the workman was given a guarantee of compensation on the statutory scale where he was subject to an incapacity resulting from personal injury by accident arising out of and in the course of his employment. The statute did not say that the incapacity must result *solely* from the injury. It was therefore irrelevant that the incapacity resulted also to some extent from heart disease. In the circumstances *Harwood v Wyken Colliery Co* [1913] 2 KB 158 must be regarded as an infirm foundation for the decision in *Baker v Willoughby* [1970] AC 467.

It is implicit in that decision that the scope of the "vicissitudes" principle is limited to supervening events of such a nature as either to reduce the disabilities resulting from the accident or else to shorten the period during which they will be suffered. I am of opinion that failure to consider or even advert to this implication weakens the authority of the ratio decidendi of the case, and must lead to the conclusion that in its full breadth it is not acceptable. The assessment of damages for personal injuries involves a process of restitutio in integrum. The object is to place the injured plaintiff in as good as a position as he would have been in but for the accident. He is not to be placed in a better position. The process involves a comparison between the plaintiff's circumstances as regards capacity to enjoy the amenities of life and to earn a living as they would have been if the accident had not occurred and his actual circumstances in those respects following the accident. In considering how matters might have been expected to turn out if there had been no accident, the "vicissitudes" principle says that it is right to take into account events, such as illness, which not uncommonly occur in the ordinary course of human life. If such events are not taken into account, the damages may be greater than are required to compensate the plaintiff for the effects of the accident, and that result would be unfair to the defendant. ...

[815] I am therefore of opinion that the majority in *Baker v Willoughby* were mistaken in approaching the problems common to the case of a supervening tortious act and to that of supervening illness wholly from the point of view of causation. While it is logically correct to say that in both cases the original tort and the supervening event may be concurrent causes of incapacity, that does not necessarily, in my view, provide the correct solution. In the case of supervening illness, it is appropriate to keep in view that this is one of the ordinary vicissitudes of life, and when one is comparing the situation resulting from the accident with the situation had there been no accident, to recognise that the illness would have overtaken the plaintiff in any event, so that it cannot be disregarded in arriving at proper compensation, and no more than proper compensation.

Additional considerations come into play when dealing with the problems arising where the plaintiff has suffered injuries from two or more successive and independent tortious acts. In that situation it is necessary to secure that the plaintiff is fully compensated for the aggregate effects of all his injuries. As Lord Pearson noted in *Baker v Willoughby* it would clearly be unjust to reduce the damages awarded for the first tort because of the occurrence of the second tort, damages for which are to be assessed on the basis that the plaintiff is already partially incapacitated. I do not consider it necessary to formulate any precise juristic basis for dealing with this situation differently from the case of supervening illness. It might be said that a supervening tort is not one of the ordinary vicissitudes of life, or that it is too remote a possibility to be taken into account, or that it can properly be disregarded because it carries its own remedy. None of these formulations, however, is entirely satisfactory. The fact remains that the principle of full compensation requires that a just and practical solution should be found. In the event that damages against two successive tortfeasors fall to be assessed at the same time, it would be highly unreasonable if the aggregate of both awards were less than the total loss suffered by the plaintiff. The computation should start from an assessment of that total loss. The award against the second tortfeasor cannot in fairness to him fail to recognise that the plaintiff whom he injured was already to some extent incapacitated. In order that the plaintiff may be fully compensated, it becomes necessary to deduct the award so calculated from the assessment of the plaintiff's total loss and award the balance against the first tortfeasor. If that be a correct approach, it follows that, in proceedings against the first tortfeasor alone, the occurrence of the second tort cannot be successfully relied on by the defendant as reducing the damages which he must pay. That, in substance, was the result of the decision in *Baker v Willoughby*, where the supervening event was a tortious act, and to that extent the decision was, in my view, correct.

[816] Before leaving the case, it is right to face up to the fact that, if a non-tortious supervening event is to have the effect of reducing damages but a subsequent tortious act is not, there may in some cases be difficulty in ascertaining whether the event in question is or is not of a tortious character, particularly in the absence of the alleged tortfeasor. Possible questions of contributory negligence may cause additional complications. Such difficulties are real, but are not sufficient, in my view, to warrant the conclusion that the distinction between tortious and non-tortious supervening events should not be accepted. The court must simply do its best to arrive at a just assessment of damages in a pragmatical way in the light of the whole circumstances of the case.

My Lords, for these reasons I would dismiss the appeal.

LORD BRIDGE of HARWICH. ... [820] The vicissitudes principle itself, it seems to me, stems from the fundamental proposition of law that the object of every award of damages for monetary loss is to put the party wronged so far as possible in the same position, no better and no worse, as he would be in if he had not suffered the wrong in respect of which he claims. To assume that an injured plaintiff, if not injured, would have continued to earn his full wages for a full working life, is very probably to over-compensate him. To apply a discount, in respect of possible future loss of earnings, arising from independent causes may be to undercompensate him. When confronted by future uncertainty, the court assesses the prospects and strikes a balance between these opposite dangers as best it can. But when the supervening illness or injury which is the independent cause of loss of earning capacity has manifested itself before trial, the event has demonstrated that, even if the plaintiff had never sustained the tortious injury, his earnings would now be reduced or extinguished. To hold the tortfeasor, in this situation, liable to pay damages for a notional continuing loss of earnings attributable to the tortious injury, is to put the plaintiff in a better position than he would be in if he had never suffered the tortious injury. Put more shortly, applying well-established principles for the assessment of damages at common law, when a plaintiff injured by the defendant's tort is wholly incapacitated from earning by supervening illness or accidental injury, the law will no longer treat the tort as a continuing cause of any loss of earning capacity.

It follows from the foregoing that I am, with the utmost respect, unable to agree with the opinion of Lord Reid in *Baker's* case [1970] AC 467 ... In particular, I cannot accept that the decision in *Harwood v Wyken Colliery Co* [1913] 2 KB 158, affords any authority in support of Lord Reid's conclusion, or that he was right to say that causation could not be different in tort and under the Workmen's Compensation Acts. In *Harwood's* case, Hamilton LJ, with whose judgment Cozens-Hardy MR, agreed, was at pains to stress the very different principles governing a tortfeasor's liability to pay damages at common law on the [821] one hand, and the statutory liability of an employer to compensate an injured workman on the other. With reference to the former, he clearly recognised the vicissitudes principle. He said at p 170:

> They [the jury] would have to measure in money the future effects of permanent or continuing disablement, but they must consider also the possibility of future diminution or loss of earnings

arising independently of the cause of action, from increasing age, from accident or illness in futuro, and so forth.

With reference to the latter, he founded his view that an injury at work could be a continuing cause of incapacity, which would continue to attract compensation notwithstanding supervening illness, entirely on the construction of the particular language of the statute to be applied.

Having reached the conclusion that the ratio decidendi of *Baker's* case [1970] AC 467 cannot be sustained, it remains to consider whether the case should still be regarded as authority, as a decision on its own facts for the proposition that, when two successive injuries are both caused tortiously, the supervening disability caused by the second tort should, by way of exception to the general rule arising from the application of the vicissitudes principle, be disregarded when assessing the liability of the first tortfeasor for damages for loss of earnings caused by the first tort. I find it difficult to attribute such authority to the decision, when both the Court of Appeal and this House were expressly invited to adopt that proposition, and both, in different ways, declined the invitation. There is a powerful, perhaps irresistible, attraction in the argument that, in the circumstances envisaged, the aggregate of the damages recoverable by the plaintiff, should, provided both tortfeasors can be found and can meet their liability, be sufficient to cover the aggregate loss of earnings, past and future, which results from the combined effect of both injuries. But whether this end is properly achieved as between the two tortfeasors, by apportioning liability [on one or other of the principles proposed in argument] seems to me a very difficult question. For the reasons I have indicated, I think the speeches in your Lordships' House, by going off on a different tack, ultimately left that question unanswered. In the instant appeal, Mr Lawton, for the respondent, was content to accept the decision in *Baker's* case as correct on its facts, so your Lordships have not heard argument on the question. In these circumstances, the proper conclusion seems to me to be that the question should remain open for decision on another occasion, if and when it arises.

However that may be, for the reasons indicated earlier in this speech, I would dismiss the appeal.

[Lord Wilberforce, Lord Edmund-Davies and Lord Russell of Killowen agreed that the appeal should be dismissed. While accepting that the causation principle applied in *Baker v Willoughby* may have achieved an acceptable solution on its own facts, none was prepared to treat it as of general application and all preferred the "vicissitudes" approach on the present facts.]

Appeal dismissed

2. LOSS OF CHANCE OR OPPORTUNITY

Tabet v Gett
(2010) 240 CLR 537; [2010] HCA 12
High Court of Australia

The plaintiff may argue that although he or she cannot prove that the defendant's negligence caused the damage on the balance of probabilities, the plaintiff has lost a chance of a better outcome. While the law sometimes recognizes loss of a commercial or financial opportunity as actionable damage, the loss of a chance of a better medical outcome is not treated as actionable damage in tort law.

KIEFEL J. [some footnotes omitted in whole or in part] **[575]** 104. Reema Tabet ("the appellant") was six years old when she was readmitted to hospital on 11 January 1991 with symptoms of vomiting and headaches. She had recently suffered from varicella (chickenpox). A CT scan taken on 14 January revealed that she had a large brain tumour. Differing opinions were given by expert witnesses as to whether a scan should have been ordered by the respondent, a specialist paediatrician, at an earlier point in time, given the symptoms exhibited by the appellant. The trial judge, Studdert J of the Supreme Court of New South Wales, was persuaded that one was necessitated ...

on the morning of 13 January. The finding of a negligent omission, on the part of the respondent, is not in issue on this appeal.

[576] 105. The appellant suffered brain damage as a result of a neurological event which occurred on 14 January and which led to the CT scan being performed. Studdert J found that the damage was ...produced by the pressure of the tumour and an excess of spinal fluid in the cranial cavity (hydrocephalus). That damage contributed to the severe, irreversible brain damage and consequent disability which the appellant now suffers. The other contributors were the tumour itself, the operation undertaken in an attempt to remove it and the treatment which followed. Studdert J attributed 25 per cent of the appellant's overall disability to that neurological event.

106. Studdert J was not persuaded, on the balance of probabilities, that if the respondent had ordered a CT scan on 13 January and the appellant was treated upon the discovery of the tumour, such brain damage as occurred on 14 January would have been avoided. Her claim that such damage was caused by the respondent therefore failed. However, his Honour considered that she had been deprived of the chance of a better outcome by reason of the delay in the treatment she could have received and was entitled to be compensated for that loss. Earlier detection of the tumour would have enabled treatment [which] would have had some beneficial effect ... . His Honour assessed "the chance of a better outcome, and of avoiding the brain damage that occurred on 14 January 1991" at 40 per cent. His Honour applied that percentage to the figure representing the contribution of the event of 14 January to the appellant's overall disability in arriving at an award of $610,000.

107. The Court of Appeal of the Supreme Court of New South Wales considered that [on the evidence], were damages to be assessed for the loss of the chance of a better outcome, they should be reduced to 15 per cent. ...However, the Court allowed the respondent's appeal and dismissed the claim. In its opinion to permit recovery for the claim for the loss of the chance involves a proposition which would revolutionise proof of causation of injury. A decision of that Court which had adopted a loss of chance [577] analysis (*Rufo v Hosking* (2004) 61 NSWLR 678 (and also *Gavalas v Singh* (2001) 3 VR 404)) was considered by the Court of Appeal to have departed from conventional principles and it declined to follow it.

Damage and causation in an action for medical negligence

108. The three elements of a cause of action in medical negligence, necessary to be established in order to recover compensation, are a duty owed by the medical practitioner to the plaintiff to avoid harm which is reasonably foreseeable, a breach of that duty and damage which results from that breach. It is the third element which is the focus of this appeal. It incorporates both the fact of loss or damage having been suffered and the cause of that damage being the medical practitioner's negligent act or omission. Those facts are ordinarily required to be proved to the general standard, on the balance of probabilities (*Sellars v Adelaide Petroleum NL* (1994) 179 CLR 332 at 355).

109. Damage is an essential ingredient in an action for negligence; it is the gist of the action (*Williams v Milotin* (1957) 97 CLR 465 at 474). The action developed largely from the old form of action on the case, in which it was the rule that proof of damage was essential to a plaintiff's case. In *Brunsden v Humphrey* (1884) 14 QBD 141 at 150 Bowen LJ pointed out that in certain classes of case the mere violation of a legal right imports damage, but that principle was "not as a rule applicable to actions for negligence: which are not brought to establish a bare right, but to recover compensation for substantial injury." Generally speaking "there must be a temporal loss or damage accruing from the wrongful act of another, in order to entitle a party to maintain an action on the case" (*Williams v Morland* (1824) 107 ER 620 at 622). Negligence in the abstract will not suffice: *Bourhill v Young* [1943] AC 92 at 116 per Lord Porter; *Haynes v Harwood* [1935] 1 KB 146 at 152).

110. An action in negligence, said Bowen LJ (*Brunsden* at 150), "is based upon the union of the negligence and the injuries caused thereby, which in such an instance will as a rule involve and have been accompanied by specific damage." Nevertheless the action on the case has itself been described as sufficiently flexible to enable judges to extend it to cover situations where damage was suffered in circumstances which called for a remedy (*Sidaway v Bethlem Royal Hospital Board of Governors* [1985] AC 871 at 883 per Lord Scarman). The Court of Appeal in this case observed that the common law has adapted to recognise different kinds of harm. But [578] nowhere is it suggested

that the requirement for damage itself can be dispensed with. Liability based upon breach of duty of care without proven loss or harm will not suffice.

111. The common law requires proof, by the person seeking compensation, that the negligent act or omission caused the loss or injury constituting the damage. All that is necessary is that, according to the course of common experience, the more probable inference appearing from the evidence is that a defendant's negligence caused the injury or harm. "More probable" means no more than that, upon a balance of probabilities, such an inference might reasonably be considered to have some greater degree of likelihood; it does not require certainty.

112. The "but for" test is regarded as having an important role in the resolution of the issue of causation, although more as a negative criterion than as a comprehensive test (*March v E & MH Stramare Pty Ltd* (1991) 171 CLR 506 at 515-516 per Mason CJ; at 522 per Deane J). The resolution of the question of causation has been said to involve the common sense idea of one matter being the cause of another. But it is also necessary to understand the purpose for making an inquiry about causation and that may require value judgments and policy choices.

113. Once causation is proved to the general standard, the common law treats what is shown to have occurred as certain (*Mallett v McMonagle* [1970] AC 166 at 176 per Lord Diplock; *Malec v JC Hutton Pty Ltd* (1990) 169 CLR 638 at 642-643 per Deane, Gaudron and McHugh JJ). The purpose of proof at law, unlike science or philosophy, is to apportion legal responsibility. That requires the courts, by a judgment, to "reduce to legal certainty questions to which no other conclusive answer can be given." (*Bank of New South Wales v The Commonwealth* (1948) 76 CLR 1 at 340 per Dixon J, cited in *Amaca Pty Ltd v Ellis* (2010) 240 CLR 111 at 137 [70] per French CJ, Gummow, Hayne, Heydon, Crennan, Kiefel and Bell JJ). The result of this approach is that when loss or damage is proved to have been caused by a defendant's act or omission, a plaintiff recovers the entire loss (the "all or nothing" rule).

The appellant's problem in proof of causation of physical damage

114. In actions involving medical negligence the loss or damage claimed to have been suffered is ordinarily physical or mental injury or harm. When such injury or harm is proved the question then is whether it was **[579]** caused by the negligent act or omission, such as a failure to diagnose or treat the disease or other condition from which the plaintiff then suffered. The difficulty which the appellant faced in this case was that the expert medical evidence did not establish the link between the omission of the respondent, with the consequent delay in treatment, and the brain damage which occurred on 14 January, necessary for a finding of causation. There was no evidence as to what harm might have been caused by the delay. It could not be said that "but for" the delay the appellant would not have suffered brain damage. It follows from Studdert J's findings that the probability was that the tumour would have caused it in any event. ...

[580] 118. [The] evidence does not support a finding that any chance of a better outcome was as high as 40 per cent. The Court of Appeal .... considered that, at the most, it could be said that the appellant "lost some chance of a better outcome which ranged between speculative and some effect", but went on to hold that even so, to permit recovery for the deprivation of the possibility, but not the probability, of a better outcome would be to significantly alter the existing law as to proof of causation of injury, in particular by redefining what is "harm".

The appellant's arguments

Redefining damage?

119. The question raised by this appeal is whether the common law of Australia should recognise the loss of a chance of a better outcome, in cases where medical negligence has been found, as actionable damage. In *Gregg v Scott* [2005] 2 AC 176 Lord Nicholls of Birkenhead observed (at 180 [1]) that it is "a question which has divided courts and commentators throughout the common law world."([2005] 2 AC 176 at 180 [1]) The same observation may be made with respect to civil law systems. ...

120. The argument for the appellant, for the acceptance by this Court of the loss of a chance of a better outcome as damage, seeks to draw support from the approach taken by courts of some common law countries, notably the United States of America, and some civil law countries, in

particular France, as relevant to what is submitted to be the choice now presented. It is not suggested that a review of other legal systems reveals that there is a correct solution. So much may be accepted. Decisions by courts of other countries, including common law countries, concerning cases of this kind are made in the framework of their substantive law, the principles and policies which inhere in it and the requirements for proof of causation and damage which may or may not be adaptable to accommodate such a claim. ...

[581] *Analogy with loss of commercial opportunity cases*
122. It was argued that the loss of an opportunity of a better outcome in a patient's illness or condition should not be seen as novel. The law in Australia already recognises the loss of a commercial opportunity as actionable damage. Accepting that there is a commercial interest in realising an opportunity, it was submitted for the appellant that a person likewise has an interest in their medical outcome.

123. It was recognised in *Sellars v Adelaide Petroleum NL* (1994) 179 CLR 332 that a loss of the opportunity to obtain a commercial advantage or benefit is loss or damage for the purposes of s 82(1) of the *Trade Practices Act 1974* (Cth), where the cause of action arose under s 52(1) of that Act [prohibiting misleading or deceptive conduct by a corporation in trade or commerce]. Previous decisions allowing for recovery had been based in contract, where the breach of the promise to provide the chance itself gave rise to the loss of that chance (*Chaplin v Hicks* [1911] 2 KB 786; *Fink v Fink* (1946) 74 CLR 127). But as Brennan J said, in cases under s 82(1), "as in cases of tort where damage is the gist of the action, a lost opportunity may or may not constitute compensable loss or damage" and it must be proved in some other way (*Sellars v Adelaide Petroleum NL* (1994) 179 CLR 332 at 359).

124. What cases in contract, such as *The Commonwealth v Amann Aviation Pty Ltd* (1991) 174 CLR 64 and *Sellars v Adelaide Petroleum NL*, have in common is that the commercial interest lost may readily be seen to be of value itself. The same cannot be said of a chance of a better medical outcome or a person's interest in it. Lord Hoffmann observed (at 197 [83]) in *Gregg v Scott* [2005] 2 AC 176 that most cases where there has been recovery for loss of a chance have involved financial loss, where the chance itself can be regarded as an item of property. And in *Sellars v Adelaide Petroleum NL* Brennan J observed that, "[a]s a matter of common experience, opportunities to acquire commercial benefits are frequently valuable in themselves". So long as an opportunity provides a substantial and not merely a speculative prospect of acquiring a benefit, it can be regarded as of value and therefore loss or damage (*Sellars* at 364). A loss of a chance of a better medical outcome cannot be regarded in this **[582]** way. As the assessment of damages in this case shows, the only value given to it is derived from the final, physical, damage. ...

Loss of chance as independent harm ...
[583] 128. There is a real question in this case whether the loss of a chance of a better outcome could be said to be independent of the physical harm suffered by the appellant. ...

130. Professor Khoury suggests that if loss of chance were a truly independent type of injury, defendants would be forced to compensate the plaintiff even if the lost chance resulted in no actual injury (Khoury, "Causation and Risk in the Highest Courts of Canada, England, and France" (2008) 124 *Law Quarterly Review* 103 at 126). ...**[584]** Because the loss of the chance is the relevant damage, in theory a claim may be made as soon as the chance is lost or reduced.

131. Another aspect of the problem identified may be seen in *Gregg v Scott* [2005] 2 AC 176, where, however, the chance had not played out. The statistical model relied upon by the plaintiff gave his chances of survival for 10 years at the time he consulted with the defendant, who failed to treat his tumour, as 42 per cent. The plaintiff was still alive at trial, when his chances were then assessed at 25 per cent, and he was still alive when the appeal was heard. Considerable uncertainty attended the question as to what his chances were. As Lord Phillips of Worth Matravers MR observed, statistically his prospects of surviving had been improving up to trial and were increasing daily thereafter. The model was inadequate to provide a conclusion as to his chances. By the time of the appeal it was not possible to reach the trial judge's conclusion. The likelihood that the delay in treatment had any effect diminished the longer the plaintiff survived.

[Kiefel J considered the decision of the Supreme Judicial Court of Massachusetts in *Matsuyama v Birnbaum* (2008) 890 NE (2d) 819 where recovery was allowed, noting that the statistical evidence was regarded by the court in that case as wholly reliable, while, in contrast there was no evidence of such a kind in the present case.]

[585] 136. Different standards apply to proof of damage from those that are involved in the assessment of damages. *Sellars v Adelaide Petroleum NL* confirms that the general standard of proof is to be maintained with respect to the issue of causation and whether the plaintiff has suffered loss or damage ((1994) 179 CLR 332 at 355 per Mason CJ, Dawson, Toohey and Gaudron JJ; at 367 per Brennan J). In relation to the assessment of damages, as was said in *Malec v J C Hutton Pty Ltd*, "the hypothetical may be conjectured" ((1990) 169 CLR 638 at 643 per Deane, Gaudron and McHugh JJ). The court may adjust its award to reflect the degree of probability of a loss eventuating. This follows from the requirement that the courts must do the best they can in estimating damages; mere difficulty in that regard is not permitted to render an award uncertain or impossible (*Commonwealth v Amann Aviation Pty Ltd* (1991) 174 CLR 64 at 83 per Mason CJ and Dawson J, citing *Fink v Fink* (1946) 74 CLR 127 at 143).

137. Thus in the case of the loss of a commercial opportunity, the plaintiff must first establish the fact of the loss, for example by reference to the fact that it had a commercial interest of value which is no longer available to be pursued because of the defendant's negligence. The damages assessed of that loss, the estimation of its value, reflect the chance, often expressed in a percentage, that the opportunity would have been pursued to a successful outcome. The award is proportionate in that sense. ...

[586] Causation in this case

140. The issue whether damage has been caused by a negligent act invites a comparison between a plaintiff's present position and what would have been the position in the absence of the defendant's negligence. Such an inquiry directs attention to all the circumstances pertaining to the plaintiff's condition at the time he or she sought the medical treatment which was not properly provided. The question of whether harm or damage has been suffered is bound up in the question of causation. ...

[587] The standard of proof

143. Resort to the language of "chance" cannot displace the analysis necessary for the determination of the issue of causation of damage. Properly analysed, what is involved in the chance referred to in this case is the possibility, to put it at its highest, that no brain damage would occur or that it would not be so severe. They are the "better medical outcomes" involved in the chance. Expressing what is said to be the loss or damage as a "chance" of a better outcome recognises that what is involved are mere possibilities and that the general standard of proof cannot be met. Thus the appellant could only succeed if the standard of proof is lower than the law presently requires.

144. *Gregg v Scott* confirmed for the United Kingdom that the general standard of proof should be maintained with respect to claims for damages for medical negligence. ... The Supreme Court of Canada in *Laferrière v Lawson* confirmed that if a case did not meet the test of causation applying the general standard of proof, then recovery should be denied ([1991] 1 SCR 541 at 608 per Gonthier J).

145. The general standard of proof required by the common law and applied to causation is relatively low. It does not require certainty or precision. It requires that a judge be persuaded that something was probably a cause of the harm the plaintiff suffered. Historically the standard may have been chosen in order to minimise errors in civil jury trials, but it nevertheless serves also to accommodate a level of uncertainty in proof. ...

[588] 148. The standard of proof required by the common law already admits of some uncertainty in proof of causation. As Lord Hoffmann observed (at 198 [90]) in *Gregg v Scott* [2005] 2 AC 176, the wholesale adoption of possible rather than probable causation as a condition of liability is radical. ...

[589] 151. It would require strong policy considerations to alter the present requirement of proof of causation. None are evident. The argument that there should be compensation where breach of duty is proved simply denies proof of damage as necessary to an action in negligence. I

am unpersuaded that denial of recovery in cases of this kind would fail to deter medical negligence or ensure that patients receive an appropriate standard of care. These matters appear to have been influential in *Matsuyama v Birnbaum* (2008) 890 NE (2d) 819. However, a feature of that case was that the defendant was called as a witness and gave evidence that an effect of the particular contract between Mr Matsuyama's medical insurer and the doctors' practice to which the defendant belonged was that doctors had difficulty in providing patients qualifying for treatment under it with the best medical care (at 825, fn 13).

Conclusion

152. The appellant is unable to prove that it was probable that, had treatment by corticosteroids been undertaken earlier, the brain damage which occurred on 14 January 1991 would have been avoided. The evidence was insufficient to be persuasive. The requirement of causation is not overcome by redefining the mere possibility, that such damage as did occur might not eventuate, as a chance and then saying that it is lost when the damage actually occurs. Such a claim could only succeed if the standard of proof were lowered, which would require a fundamental change to the law of negligence. The appellant suffered dreadful injury, but the circumstances of this case do not provide a strong ground for considering such change. It would involve holding the respondent liable for damage which he almost certainly did not cause.

153. The appeal should be dismissed with costs.

[In separate judgments, Gummow A-CJ, Hayne and Bell JJ, Heydon J and Crennan J agreed that the appeal should be dismissed, with Gummow A-CJ and Heydon J holding that the evidence as to causation and loss of chance was no more than speculative.]

Appeal dismissed

3. NEW ACT INTERVENING

Mahony v J Kruschich (Demolitions) Pty Ltd
(1985) 156 CLR 522
High Court of Australia

A tortfeasor who negligently has caused personal injury to the plaintiff may be liable for the exacerbation of that injury as the result of negligent medical treatment by a third party.

[A worker sued his employer for damages for personal injuries suffered in an accident which he alleged was caused by the employer's negligence. The injuries required considerable medical treatment. The employer, in this cross-claim, sought contribution, pursuant to s 5(1)(c) of the *Law Reform (Miscellaneous Provisions) Act 1946* (NSW) from Dr Mahony, alleging that the doctor's negligence in treating the worker had caused or contributed to the worker's continuing injuries and incapacities.

Section 5(1)(c) provides: "Where damage is suffered by any person as a result of a tort ... (c) any tortfeasor liable in respect of that damage may recover contribution from any other tortfeasor who is, or would if sued have been, liable in respect of the same damage, whether as a joint tortfeasor or otherwise".

Dr Mahony sought to have the cross-claim struck out, on the ground that s 5(1)(c) provides for contribution only between tortfeasors who have inflicted "the same damage". He argued that this was a case of different damage inflicted at different times and that therefore there should be no contribution. The Supreme Court of New South Wales allowed the cross-claim to stand. Dr Mahony appealed.

On appeal to the High Court of Australia, one of the issues was whether the allegedly negligent employer could be liable to the worker for the damage caused by the doctor's alleged negligence in treating him.]

THE COURT. [Gibbs CJ, Mason, Wilson, Brennan and Dawson JJ] …**[528]** A negligent tortfeasor does not always avoid liability for the consequences of a plaintiff's subsequent injury, even if the subsequent injury is tortiously inflicted. It depends on whether or not the subsequent tort and its consequences are themselves properly to be regarded as foreseeable consequences of the first tortfeasor's negligence. A line marking the boundary of the damage for which a tortfeasor is liable in negligence may be drawn either because the relevant injury is not reasonably foreseeable or because the chain of causation is broken by a novus actus interveniens: *M'Kew v Holland & Hannen & Cubitts* 1970 SC HL 20 at p 25. But it must be possible to draw such a line clearly before a liability for damage that would not have occurred but for the wrongful act or omission of a tortfeasor and that is reasonably foreseeable by him is treated as the result of a second tortfeasor's negligence alone: see *Chapman v Hearse* (1961) 106 CLR 112 at pp 124-125. Whether such a line can and should be drawn is very much a matter of fact and degree (at p 122). …

Where it is not possible to draw a clear line, the first tortfeasor may **[529]** be liable in negligence for a subsequent injury and its consequences although the act or omission of another tortfeasor is the more immediate cause of that injury: cf *Lothian v Rickards*, per Griffith CJ (1911) 12 CLR 165, at p 176. Thus Gibbs J in *Dillingham* (1975) 132 CLR at pp 329-330 accepted the suggestion that if a pedestrian were run over by two drivers consecutively, and both were negligent, the injuries caused by the negligence of the second driver would be damage for which both drivers are liable if those injuries were also the foreseeable consequence of the first driver's negligence.

In particular circumstances, minds may differ as to whether a subsequent injury was foreseeable or whether it is too remote to be regarded as a consequence for which an earlier tortfeasor may be held liable. When an injury is exacerbated by medical treatment, however, the exacerbation may easily be regarded as a foreseeable consequence for which the first tortfeasor is liable. Provided the plaintiff acts reasonably in seeking or accepting the treatment, negligence in the administration of the treatment need not be regarded as a novus actus interveniens which relieves the first tortfeasor of liability for the plaintiff's subsequent condition. The original injury can be regarded as carrying some risk that medical treatment might be negligently given: see *Beavis v Apthorpe* (1962) 80 WN (NSW) 852, at p 858; *Moore v AGC (Insurances) Ltd* [1968] SASR 389 at p 394; *Lawrie v Meggitt* (1974) 11 SASR 5 at p 8; *Price v Milawski* (1977) 82 DLR (3d) 130 at pp 141-142; *Katzman v Yaech* (1982) 136 DLR (3d) 536. It may be the very kind of thing which is likely to happen as a result of the first tortfeasor's negligence. cf per Lord Reid in *Dorset Yacht Co v Home Office* [1970] AC 1004, at p 1030. That approach is consistent with the view taken in workers' compensation cases that the total condition of a worker whose compensable injury is exacerbated by medical treatment, reasonably undertaken to alleviate that injury, is to be attributed to the accident (see *Lindeman Ltd v Colvin* (1946) 74 CLR 313 at p 321, per Dixon J; *Migge v Wormald Bros Industries Ltd* [1972] 2 NSWLR 29, at p 48, per Mason JA; on appeal (1973) 47 ALJR 236), although medical negligence or inefficiency can be held to amount to a new cause of incapacity in some circumstances: *Rothwell v Caverswall Stone Co* [1944] 2 All ER 350, at p 365; *Hogan v Bentinck* **[530]** *Collieries* [1949] 1 All ER 588, at p 592. In the last-mentioned case Lord Reid, in dissent, expressed the opinion that there is a break in the chain of causation when a doctor is guilty of such negligence as would make him liable in damages. We think, with respect, that that test is too rigid. Some degree of medical negligence in the treatment of an injury may well be a reasonably foreseeable result of the act or omission by which that injury was inflicted, and then no clear line can be drawn to limit the original tortfeasor's liability to exclude the consequences of medical negligence.

However, in the ordinary case, where efficient medical services are available to an injured plaintiff, the original injury does not carry the risk of medical treatment or advice that is "inexcusably bad" (*Martin v Isbard* (1946) 48 WALR 52, at p 56), or "completely outside the bounds of what any reputable medical practitioner might prescribe" (*Lawrie v Meggitt* (1974) 11 SASR at p 8) or "so obviously unnecessary or improper that it is in the nature of a gratuitous aggravation of the injury" (*South Australian Stevedoring Co Ltd v Holbertson* [1939] SASR 257, at p 264) or "extravagant from the point of view of medical practice or hospital routine": Hart and Honoré, *Causation in the Law* (1959), p 169. In such a case, it is proper to regard the exacerbation of a plaintiff's condition as resulting solely from the grossly negligent medical treatment or advice, and the fact that the plaintiff acted reasonably in seeking and accepting the treatment or in following the advice will not make the original tortfeasor liable for that exacerbation.

It is neither necessary nor possible to determine at this stage of the action whether any and, if so, what aspects of the plaintiff's present condition ought to be regarded as the foreseeable consequence of both Kruschich's negligence if that negligence be proved and Dr Mahony's negligence if that negligence be proved. At this stage of the action, the plaintiff's condition and the negligence of both Kruschich and Dr Mahony are matters of allegation only. There are no facts admitted or proved by which to determine those issues.

If, when the action comes to trial, it is proved that an aspect of the plaintiff's condition is properly to be regarded as a foreseeable consequence of both Kruschich's negligence and Dr Mahony's negligence, Kruschich will be entitled to seek contribution under s 5(1)(c) from Dr Mahony in respect of so much of the damages awarded against it as relates to that aspect. ...

[531] It follows that the cross-claim should not be struck out. ...

The appeal should be dismissed.

Appeal dismissed

4. REMOTENESS

Overseas Tankship (UK) Ltd v Morts Dock and Engineering Co Ltd (The Wagon Mound (No 1))
[1961] AC 388
Privy Council

Reasonable foreseeability of the kind of damage suffered by the plaintiff is the test of remoteness of damage in modern Australian law.

[The defendant (appellant) was the charterer of a vessel named the "SS Wagon Mound". While it was moored to take in furnace oil, some of the oil spilled into Morts Bay in Sydney Harbour due to the carelessness of the defendant. It spread to underneath nearby Sheerlegs Wharf, which was owned and used by the plaintiffs (respondents) for their ship repair business and where, at the time, their employees were using oxyacetylene welding equipment.

Some cotton waste or debris floating on the oil was set on fire by molten metal falling from the wharf, and the flaming waste in turn set the floating oil alight, either directly or by first igniting a wooden pile coated with oil. An extensive fire then developed which damaged the plaintiffs' wharf and equipment.

In their action against the defendant in negligence, the plaintiffs were successful at first instance. The defendant's appeal to the Full Court of the Supreme Court of New South Wales was dismissed and the defendant then appealed to the Privy Council.]

VISCOUNT SIMONDS delivered their Lordships' judgment. ... **[413]** The trial judge ... made the all-important finding, which must be set out in his own words: "The raision d'être of furnace oil is, of course, that it shall burn, but I find the defendant did not know and could not reasonably be expected to have known that it was capable of being set afire when spread on water." ...

One other finding must be mentioned. The judge held that **[414]** apart from damage by fire the respondents had suffered some damage from the spillage of oil in that it had got upon their slipways and congealed upon them and interfered with their use of the slips. He said: "The evidence of this damage is slight and no claim for compensation is made in respect of it. Nevertheless it does establish some damage, which may be insignificant in comparison with the magnitude of the damage by fire, but which nevertheless is damage which, beyond question, was a direct result of the escape of the oil." It is upon this footing that their Lordships will consider the question whether the appellants are liable for the fire damage. ...

It is inevitable that first consideration should be given to the case of *In Re Polemis and Furness Withy & Co Ltd* [1921] 3 KB 560 which will henceforward be referred to as *Polemis* ... .

[415] [I]n the years that have passed since its decision *Polemis* has been so much discussed and qualified that it cannot claim, as counsel for the respondents urged for it, the status of a decision of such long standing that it should not be reviewed.

What, then, did *Polemis* decide? ... [T]he case proceeded as one in which, independently of contractual obligations, the claim was for damages for negligence. It was upon this footing that the Court of Appeal held that the charterers were responsible for all the consequences of their negligent act even though those consequences could not reasonably have been anticipated. The negligent act was nothing more than the carelessness of stevedores (for whom the charterers were assumed to be responsible) in allowing a sling or rope by which it was hoisted to come into contact with certain boards, causing one of them to fall into the hold. The falling board hit some substances in the hold and caused a spark: the spark ignited petrol vapour in the hold: there was a rush of flames, and the ship was destroyed. The special case submitted by the arbitrators found that the causing of the spark could not reasonably have been anticipated from the falling of the board, though some damage to the ship might reasonably have been anticipated. They did not indicate what damage might have been so anticipated.

There can be no doubt that the decision of the Court of Appeal in *Polemis* plainly asserts that, if the defendant is guilty of negligence, he is responsible for all the consequences whether **[416]** reasonably foreseeable or not. The generality of the proposition is perhaps qualified by the fact that each of the Lords Justices refers to the outbreak of fire as the direct result of the negligent act. There is thus introduced the conception that the negligent actor is not responsible for consequences which are not "direct", whatever that may mean. It has to be asked, then, why this conclusion should have been reached. The answer appears to be that it was reached upon a consideration of certain authorities, comparatively few in number, that were cited to the court.

[Their Lordships discussed the cases relied upon in *Polemis* to support the decision of the Court of Appeal and several earlier cases which support the view that foreseeability is relevant to the issue of damage.]

[419] The impression that may well be left on the reader of the scores of cases in which liability for negligence has been discussed is that the courts were feeling their way to a coherent body of doctrine and were at times in grave danger of being led astray by scholastic theories of causation and their ugly and barely intelligible jargon.

Before turning to the cases that succeeded it, it is right to glance at yet another aspect of the decision in *Polemis*. Their Lordships, as they have said, assume that the court purported to propound the law in regard to tort. But up to that date it had been universally accepted that the law in regard to damages for breach of contract was, generally speaking, and particularly in regard to the tort of negligence, the same. Yet *Hadley v Baxendale* (1854) 9 Exch 341 was not cited in argument nor referred to in the judgments in *Polemis*. This is the more surprising when it is remembered that in that case, as in many another case, the claim was laid alternatively in breach of contract and in negligence. If the claim for breach of contract had been pursued, the charterers could not have been held liable for consequences not reasonably foreseeable. It is not strange that Sir Frederick Pollock said that Blackburn and Willes JJ would have been shocked beyond measure by the decision that the charterers were liable in tort: see Pollock on Torts, 15th ed, p 29. Their Lordships refer to this aspect of the matter not **[420]** because they wish to assert that in all respects today the measure of damages is in all cases the same in tort and in breach of contract, but because it emphasises how far *Polemis* was out of the current of contemporary thought. The acceptance of the rule in *Polemis* as applicable to all cases of tort directly would conflict with the view theretofore generally held.

If the line of relevant authority had stopped with *Polemis*, their Lordships might, whatever their own views as to its unreason, have felt some hesitation about overruling it. But it is far otherwise. ...

[Their Lordships referred to later cases in conflict with the *Polemis* rule.]

[422] Enough has been said to show that the authority of *Polemis* has been severely shaken though lip-service has from time to time been paid to it. In their Lordships' opinion it should no longer be regarded as good law. It is not probable that many cases will for that reason have a different result, though it is hoped that the law will be thereby simplified, and that in some cases, at least, palpable injustice will be avoided. For it does not seem consonant with current ideas of justice or morality that for an act of negligence, however slight or venial, which results in some trivial foreseeable damage the actor should be liable for all consequences however unforeseeable and however grave, so long as they can be said to be "direct." It is a principle of civil liability, subject only to qualifications which have no present relevance, that a man must be considered to be responsible for the probable [423] consequences of his act. To demand more of him is too harsh a rule, to demand less is to ignore that civilised order requires the observance of a minimum standard of behaviour.

This concept applied to the slowly developing law of negligence has led to a great variety of expressions which can, as it appears to their Lordships, be harmonised with little difficulty with the single exception of the so-called rule in *Polemis*. For, if it is asked why a man should be responsible for the natural or necessary or probable consequences of his act (or any other similar description of them) the answer is that it is not because they are natural or necessary or probable, but because, since they have this quality, it is judged by the standard of the reasonable man that he ought to have foreseen them. Thus it is that over and over again it has happened that in different judgments in the same case, and sometimes in a single judgment, liability for a consequence has been imposed on the ground that it was reasonably foreseeable or, alternatively, on the ground that it was natural or necessary or probable. The two grounds have been treated as coterminous, and so they largely are. But, where they are not, the question arises to which the wrong answer was given in *Polemis*. For, if some limitation must be imposed upon the consequences for which the negligent actor is to be held responsible – and all are agreed that some limitation there must be – why should that test (reasonable foreseeability) be rejected which, since he is judged by what the reasonable man ought to foresee, corresponds with the common conscience of mankind, and a test (the "direct" consequence) be substituted which leads to nowhere but the never-ending and insoluble problems of causation. "The lawyer," said Sir Frederick Pollock, "cannot afford to adventure himself with philosophers in the logical and metaphysical controversies that beset the idea of cause." Yet this is just what he has most unfortunately done and must continue to do if the rule in *Polemis* is to prevail. A conspicuous example occurs when the actor seeks to escape liability on the ground that the "chain of causation" is broken by a "nova causa" or "novus actus interveniens."

[Turning to the conclusion of the Full Court in the present case their Lordships continued:]

[424] Applying the rule in *Polemis* and holding therefore that the unforeseeability of the damage by fire afforded no defence, they went on to consider the remaining question. Was it a "direct" consequence? Upon this Manning J said: "Notwithstanding that, if regard is had separately to each individual occurrence in the chain of events that led to this fire, each occurrence was improbable and, in one sense, improbability was heaped upon improbability, I cannot escape from the conclusion that if the ordinary man in the street had been asked, as a matter of common sense, without any detailed analysis of the circumstances, to state the cause of the fire at Mort's Dock, he would unhesitatingly have assigned such cause to spillage of oil by the appellant's employees." Perhaps he would, and probably he would have added: "I never should have thought it possible." But with great respect to the Full Court this is surely irrelevant, or, if it is relevant, only serves to show that the *Polemis* rule works in a very strange way. After the event even a fool is wise. But it is not the hindsight of a fool: it is the foresight of the reasonable man which alone can determine responsibility. The *Polemis* rule by substituting "direct" for "reasonably foreseeable" consequences leads to a conclusion equally illogical and unjust. ...

[425] It is, no doubt, proper when considering tortious liability for negligence to analyse its elements and to say that the plaintiff must prove a duty owed to him by the defendant, a breach of that duty by the defendant, and consequent damage. But there can be no liability until the damage has been done. It is not the act but the consequences on which tortious liability is founded. Just

as (as it has been said) there is no such thing as negligence in the air, so there is no such thing as liability in the air. Suppose an action brought by A for damage caused by the carelessness (a neutral word) of B, for example, a fire caused by the careless spillage of oil. It may, of course become relevant to know what duty B owed to A, but the only liability that is in question is the liability for damage by fire. It is vain to isolate the liability from its context and to say that B is or is not liable, and then to ask for what damage is he liable. For his liability is in respect of that damage and no other. If, as admittedly it is, B's liability (culpability) depends on the reasonable foreseeability of the consequent damage, how is that to be determined, except by the forseeability of the damage which in fact happened – the damage in suit? And, if that damage is unforeseeable so as to displace liability at large, how can the liability be restored so as to make compensation payable?

But, it is said, a different position arises if B's careless act has been shown to be negligent and has caused some foreseeable damage to A. Their Lordships have already observed that to hold B liable for consequences however unforeseeable of a careless act, if but only if, he is at the same time liable for some other damage, however trivial, appears to be neither logical nor just. This becomes more clear if it is supposed that similar unforeseeable damage is suffered by A and C but other foreseeable damage, for which B is liable, by A only. A system of law which would hold B liable to A, but not to C for the similar damage suffered by each of them could not easily be defended. Fortunately the attempt is not necessary. For the same fallacy is at the root of the proposition. It is irrelevant to the question whether B is liable for unforeseeable damage that he is liable for foreseeable damage, as irrelevant as would the fact that he had **[426]** trespassed on Whiteacre be to the question whether he has trespassed on Blackacre. Again, suppose a claim by A for damage by fire by the careless act of B. Of what relevance is it to that claim that he has another claim arising out of the same careless act? It would surely not prejudice his claim if that other claim failed: it cannot assist if it succeeds. Each of them rests on its own bottom, and will fail if it can be established that the damage could not reasonably be foreseen. We have come back to the plain common sense stated by Lord Russell of Killowen in *Bourhill v Young* [1943] AC 92, 101. As Denning LJ said in *King v Phillips* [1953] 1 QB 429, 441: "there can be no doubt since *Bourhill v Young* that the test of *liability for shock* is foreseeability of *injury by shock.*" Their Lordships substitute the word "fire" for "shock" and endorse this statement of the law.

Their Lordships conclude this part of the case with some general observations. They have been concerned primarily to displace the proposition that unforeseeability is irrelevant if damage is "direct". In doing so they have inevitably insisted that the essential factor in determining liability is whether the damage is of such a kind as the reasonable man should have foreseen. This accords with the general view thus stated by Lord Atkin in *Donoghue v Stevenson* [1932] AC 562, 580: "The liability for negligence, whether you style it such or treat it as in other systems as a species of 'culpa', is no doubt based upon a general public sentiment of moral wrongdoing for which the offender must pay." It is a departure from this sovereign principle if liability is made to depend solely on the damage being the "direct" or "natural" consequence of the precedent act. Who knows or can be assumed to know all the processes of nature? But if it would be wrong that a man should be held liable for damage unpredictable by a reasonable man because it was "direct" or "natural", equally it would be wrong that he should escape liability, however "indirect" the damage, if he foresaw or could reasonably foresee the intervening events which led to its being done: cf *Woods v Duncan* [1946] AC 401, 422. Thus foreseeability becomes the effective test. In reasserting this principle their Lordships conceive that they do not depart from, but follow and develop, the law of negligence as laid down by Baron Alderson in *Blyth v Birmingham Waterworks Co* (1856) 11 Exch 781, 784. ...

[427] Their Lordships will humbly advise Her Majesty that this appeal should be allowed, and the respondents' action so far as it related to damage caused by the negligence of the appellants be dismissed with costs … .

Appeal allowed

[*Overseas Tankship (UK) Ltd v Miller Steamship Co Pty Ltd (The Wagon Mound (No 2))* [1967] 1 AC 617, also a decision of the Privy Council on appeal from New South Wales, arose out of the same incident as in *The Wagon Mound (No 1)*. The plaintiffs were the owners of two vessels, "Corrimal" and "Audrey D", which were undergoing repairs at Sheerlegs Wharf and were damaged in the fire. The plaintiffs claimed damages in public nuisance and negligence against the charterer of the "Wagon Mound" (the same defendant as in *The Wagon Mound (No 1)*). In these proceedings, the evidence and findings were "substantially different" from the evidence and findings in *The Wagon Mound (No 1)*. In particular, there was a finding that a reasonable person in the position of the chief engineer of the "Wagon Mound" would have been aware of "a real risk" of fire after the furnace oil spillage into Morts Bay. Accordingly, this risk of fire, although small, was reasonably foreseeable. As the elimination of this risk involved no difficulty, disadvantage or expense, the charterer of the "Wagon Mound" was liable for the damage to the plaintiffs' vessels. *The Wagon Mound (No 2)* confirmed that reasonable foreseeability of the kind of damage suffered by the plaintiff is the test of remoteness of damage in nuisance as well as in negligence.]

Chapter 8

Death or Injury to a Third Party

1. FATAL ACCIDENTS

Swan v Williams (Demolition) Pty Ltd
(1987) 9 NSWLR 172
Supreme Court of New South Wales, Court of Appeal

According to the "much criticised" common law rule in Baker v Bolton (now partially abrogated by fatal accidents or compensation to relatives legislation in each Australian State and Territory), the death of a human being may not be complained of as a legal injury in civil proceedings. Thus, where a wrongdoer causes the death of a third party (eg, an employee) no tort action is maintainable against the wrongdoer by a person (eg, the employer of the deceased) who has suffered financial loss as a result of the death.

SAMUELS JA. **[174]** On 24 August 1981 an employee of Williams (Demolition) Pty Ltd (Williams) was using an oxy acetylene cutting torch in premises at the corner of York and Barrack Streets, Sydney, occupied by Williams for the purposes of demolition. In consequence of the use of the torch, a sandstone block weighing 630 kilograms was dislodged and fell onto a car stationary in York Street. The occupants of the car, Mrs DE Swan (the deceased) and her parents, were killed.

Two actions were commenced in respect of this unfortunate occurrence. The first, by Mr WM Swan (Swan), the deceased's husband, claiming to recover against Williams for negligence and for breach of various regulations made under the *Construction Safety Act 1912*, was brought pursuant to the *Compensation to Relatives Act 1897* on his own behalf and on behalf of the two children of the marriage, namely Edwina Elizabeth Swan, born on 20 **[175]** January 1971 and Andrew Warren Swan, born on 8 June 1972. The claim made was for financial benefits lost by Swan and the children by reason of the deceased's death, funeral expenses, which were admitted at $1,699.50, and for damages for nervous shock suffered by Swan upon learning of the death.

In a second action, Swan Paper Agencies Pty Ltd (the company), of which both Swan and the deceased were directors, shareholders and employees, sued Williams for breaches of duty, claiming damages for the loss of the deceased's services, and of those of Swan while he was affected by the alleged nervous shock. ...

[I]n the company's action the defendant, while conceding negligence and breach of statutory duty, denied that any claim lay for loss of the deceased's services by reason of her death, and disputed liability for any nervous shock sustained by Swan. In Swan's action the admission of liability was maintained, only the quantum of damages under the *Compensation to Relatives Act* and for nervous shock being challenged.

Both actions were heard together by Lusher J who gave judgment on 9 July 1985. He held that no action lay at the suit of the company for loss of the deceased's services and that its claim for loss of services incurred by reason of Swan's nervous shock failed on the ground that Swan had not sustained any such injury. In Swan's claim under the *Compensation to Relatives Act* damages were assessed in the sum of $43,850 with $2,000 and $3,000 apportioned to Edwina and Andrew respectively; and Swan's claim for nervous shock was described as nominal and assessed in the sum of $400. Both Swan and the company have appealed.

Lusher J, in rejecting the company's claim for damages for loss of the deceased's services occasioned by her death, accepted and applied what has come to be known as the rule in *Baker v Bolton* (1808) 1 Cam 493; 170 ER 1033. There, the plaintiff brought an action for damages for loss of his wife's consortium, she having died soon after sustaining injuries in an accident caused by the defendant's negligence. Lord Ellenborough CJ, sitting at first instance, dismissing so much of the claim as accrued after the wife's death, said: "In a civil Court, the death of a human being could not be complained of as an injury." That statement, which was not embellished by any reasons, has been accepted as a binding statement of the law by courts of authority in both England and Australia. It has also been much criticised as depending upon dubious legal premises, as inconsistent with plainly perceived social requirements and as destructive of legitimate expectations and unjust on that account. It was originally adopted in the United States of America but has there now been denounced and abandoned: *Moragne v States Marine Lines Inc* 398 US 375 (1970). In addition its effect has been avoided by statute. First of all, by enactments such as *Lord Campbell's Act* (9 & 10 Vict c 93) passed in England in 1846 and adopted in New South Wales in the following year (11 Vict No 32), which provided, in the case of certain dependants, recovery of the loss of the expectations of pecuniary benefit caused by death. Secondly, by enabling the survival of causes of action after death, and by [176] establishing liability for mental or nervous shock occasioned by an act causing death: see the *Law Reform (Miscellaneous Provisions) Act 1944*, s 2(1) and s 4(1).

It may be that, to adapt the saying of Roger North which prefaces *Holdsworth's History of English Law*, it is necessary only to indicate how the doctrine which *Baker v Bolton* enunciated now stands resolved, rather than to set out its plausibility or history, or the route by which it became embedded (as it undoubtedly is) in the common law. However, the appellant submits that the case was wrongly decided and should not be followed. In the course of making and answering this contention counsel (for whose assistance and diligent research we are indebted) have placed before us a considerable quantity of material, including cases, statutes and learned articles designed, on the one hand, to disestablish *Baker v Bolton*, and, on the other, to authenticate its credentials. I should say at once that I have come to the conclusion, after perhaps immoderate consideration, that the appellant's argument on this point must be rejected. I base that opinion upon a simple ground, which, in the end, does not entail extensive examination of the sources and submissions presented to us. But out of deference to the careful arguments of Mr Gross QC for the appellants and Mr Grieve QC for the respondent, I think it desirable at least to adumbrate the parties' contentions.

I start with a general consideration. In *State Government Insurance Commission v Trigwell* (1979) 142 CLR 617, the question was whether the High Court should apply the decision of the House of Lords in *Searle v Wallbank* [1947] AC 341 which affirmed the common law rule that a landowner had no duty to prevent his animals from straying onto an adjoining highway. It was a case which had been much criticised; and the rule which it endorsed had been, by the time *State Government Insurance Commission v Trigwell* came before the court, abrogated in England and elsewhere. Barwick CJ said (at 623):

> ... Where the law has been declared by a court of high authority, this Court, if it agrees that that declaration was correct when made, cannot alter the common law because the Court may think that changes in the society make or tend to make that declaration of the common law inappropriate to the times. The maxim that when the reason for its making has ceased the law itself ceases to bind has no application in such circumstances ... It can, of course, decide that that declaration was erroneous when made and itself declare what the common law ought properly be held to be.

There was further discussion in *State Government Insurance Commission v Trigwell* about the propriety of judicial amendment of judiciary law on account of a perceived alteration in social, economic or circumstantial conditions (see at 627 per Gibbs J, as he then was, Stephen J at 628-629) (citing statements made by Bray CJ in *Bagshaw v Taylor* (1978) 18 SASR 564 at 579 and by Turner J in *Ross v McCarthy* [1970] NZLR 449 at 456) and by Mason J (at 633). However, questions of changed social and economic circumstances do not, to my mind, arise in this case in support of the appellant's contention. *Baker* was not concerned with questions of social value or utility. It proceeded upon a view of highly technical areas of the law and is unlikely to engage the passions of social engineers. Its only continuing influence in New South Wales or, so far as I know, everywhere else in the **[177]** common law world, is to exclude actions at the suit of an employer or spouse for damages for loss of services or consortium caused by the negligently occasioned death of employee or spouse. ...

[178] Professor WS Holdsworth ... in what has now become a celebrated article, ("The Origin of the Rule in Baker v Bolton" (1916) 32 LQR 431) evidently written after the decision of the Court of Appeal in *The Amerika* [1914] P 167, and in anticipation of the appeal to the House of Lords, ... commences his argument (at 432) by observing that the principle laid down by Lord Ellenborough is capable of two distinct applications. First, it covers part of the ground occupied by the maxim "actio personalis moritur cum persona", that is to say, the rule that the representative of the deceased victim of a tort which has caused the victim's death cannot sue in his representative capacity. Secondly, it prevents a plaintiff suing a defendant for a wrong committed by the defendant to the plaintiff which consists in injury causing the death of a person "in the continuance of whose life the plaintiff had an interest." As the learned author points out, the second application of Lord Ellenborough's principle has nothing to do with the maxim actio personalis because both plaintiff and defendant are still alive. But it is with this application that the present case is concerned.

Professor Holdsworth then advances the view that the second application originates in the doctrine that if a cause of action in tort disclosed a felony, the right of action in tort was affected; see *Osborn* (at 96) per Bramwell B, and for a fuller treatment of the point: Holdsworth *History of English Law* vol 3 at 272-273. *Higgins v Butcher* (1607) Yelv 89; 80 ER 61, is regarded as the authority for this proposition. There, Tanfield J, with the concurrence of Fenner and Yelverton JJ, said:

> ... if a man beats the servant of JS so that he dies of the battery, the master shall not have an action against the other for the battery and loss of the service, because the servant dying of the extremity of the battery, it is now become an offence to the Crown, being converted into felony, and that drowns the particular offence and private wrong offer'd to the master before, and his action is thereby lost.

The same principle appears to have been applied in *Smith v Sykes* (1677) 1 Freem 224; 89 ER 160. But, as Professor Holdsworth indicates, there was some doubt as to whether the cause of action in tort was wholly lost or whether it was only suspended. And although the argument was inconclusive during the seventeenth and eighteenth centuries and even later it was clearly established in *Smith v Selwyn* [1914] 3 KB 98 that an action for damages based upon a felonious act by the defendant committed against the plaintiff **[179]** was not maintainable so long as the defendant had not been prosecuted, or a reasonable excuse shown for his not having been prosecuted and the proper course was for the court to stay further proceedings until the prosecution had taken place. Furthermore, it is clear that the tort-felony merger rule did not apply in any respect to a wrongful act which was the foundation of the civil claim but which amounted only to a misdemeanour. Holdsworth therefore suggests that *Baker* is the product of confusion between the rule based upon the maxim actio personalis and that based upon the fact that the tortious act was a felony. There never was, he asserts, a principle in the terms which Lord Ellenborough enunciated. There were only the two principles covering different ground, one which concerned the survival of causes of action after death and the other the suspension or, as it might have been thought in the early nineteenth century, the loss of a cause of action based upon facts which amounted to a felony. The rule in *Baker*, of course, covers a much wider field. ...

[180] The industry of counsel and the general interest, even if of a somewhat antiquarian kind, led to our being referred to a good deal of other material dealing with the problem, its background and consequences. Digesting these sources has taken some time but I think, as I indicated at the commencement of this judgment, it is unnecessary for me to answer the question which I posed a little time ago, that is, whether *Baker* was correctly decided. My inclination, however, is to conclude, with the late Professor Winfield, that Lord Ellenborough's dictum was correct, that is to say, that it accurately stated the law as it was at the time. That law itself may have been produced by a misapprehension of the tort-felony merger rule, or of its relationship to the maxim actio personalis. But it is said in the articles to which I have referred that between *Higgins* in 1607 and *Baker* in 1808 no trace can be found in the reports of any claim for loss of the consortium of a wife, or the services of a servant, negligently killed.

What is of critical importance for my purposes is the unquestionable fact that *Baker* was adopted in subsequent decisions as representing the true doctrine of the common law. ...

[183] In my view *Woolworths Ltd v Crotty* (1942) 66 CLR 603 is authority for the proposition that the doctrine of *Baker* as affirmed in *Admiralty Commissioners v SS Amerika (Owners)* [1917] AC 38 is part of the common law of Australia. ...

[184] In my opinion, therefore, the company's claim for damages for the loss of the deceased's services occasioned by her death must be denied.

The next question is whether the learned judge was wrong to reject the company's claim for damages for loss of Swan's services caused by the nervous shock he suffered as a result of the deceased's death. Lusher J came to the conclusion that the company had not established that the injury alleged had been sustained, finding that Swan had suffered no more than grief in his bereavement. In my view, the judgments in *Jaensch v Coffey* (1984) [185] 155 CLR 549 establish that in order to recover damages for nervous shock, the claimant must show that the condition precipitated satisfies the description of psychiatric illness or psychiatric or psychological disorder. As Brennan J pointed out in *Jaensch v Coffey* (at 559-560) Lord Denning MR in *Hinz v Berry* [1970] 2 QB 40 at 42 used the description "any reasonable psychiatric illness" which was adopted by Windeyer J in *Mount Isa Mines Ltd v Pusey* (1970) 125 CLR 383 at 394. It may very well be that the lawyers' use of a terms such as "mental or nervous shock" indicates scant acquaintance with the subtleties of psychiatric medicine. However, as I have indicated, the evidentiary requirement seems to me quite clear. ...

I can see no basis ... for the finding that Swan suffered any medical disorder capable of amounting to mental or nervous shock as the law understands that term. In my view, therefore, the learned judge was right to reject this head of the company's claim.

I come now to the action brought by Swan himself. I can dispose at once of the claim for damages for nervous shock. There was an admission which his Honour correctly interpreted as requiring the award of some damages and having regard to his findings which, as I have said, I regard as correct, he awarded a nominal amount which should stand. ...

[His Honour then considered the assessment of damages under the *Compensation to Relatives Act 1897*.]

[189] Accordingly, in the company's action and appeal, I would dismiss the appeal with costs. In Swan's action, I would allow the appeal with costs; set aside the judgment below and substitute judgment for the plaintiff in the sum of $124,900 to take effect on 9 July 1985. Of that sum, bearing in mind the ages of the children, and the period for which provision has been made, I would apportion $10,000 to each of them ... .

PRIESTLEY JA. ... [190] In regard to the rejection of the company's claim for the loss of Mrs Swan's services Lusher J was of the view that he was bound by the rule in *Baker v Bolton* (1808) 1 Camp 493; 170 ER 1033, to reject it. That rule is to the effect that in a civil court the death of a human being cannot be complained of as an injury. It is a rule which was followed in *Osborn v Gillett* (1873) LR 8 Exch 88 and later held by the House of Lords to be a rule of the common law: *Admiralty Commissioners v SS Amerika (Owners)* [1917] AC 38. In *Osborn* however Bramwell B criticised the rule vigorously and since then the rule has been subjected to an unending stream of criticism. Very little has been said in its favour and as far as I can see that is because there is indeed very little to say, either as a matter of legal history or in terms of any policy understandable in present times at least. ... If this Court were in a position to overrule *Baker v Bolton* there would seem to me to be many reasons for doing so and few for refraining from doing so. However, in *Woolworths Ltd v Crotty* (1942) 66 CLR 603, it clearly appears that the High Court made the correctness of the rule in *Baker v Bolton* part of its ratio decidendi of the case. That being so, the authority not of *Baker v Bolton* but of the High Court requires this court to accept the continuing validity of the rule in *Baker v Bolton*. ...

[191] In regard to the nervous shock aspect of the company's claim, Lusher J held that it could lawfully claim damages from the defendant for the loss of Mr Swan's services resulting from the nervous shock caused to him by his wife's death caused by the defendant's negligence. ... He went on however to find that the company had not proved that it had suffered damages because of nervous shock caused to Mr Swan of the kind necessary before damages could be recoverable in respect of it. ...

[His Honour reviewed the medical evidence and reached the conclusion, contrary to the trial judge, that Mr Swan had suffered nervous shock in the relevant sense.]

[199] Notwithstanding my conclusion in considering the company's claim based on the nervous shock suffered by Mr Swan I reach the same end point as did Lusher J. This is however for the different reason that although in my opinion Mr Swan did suffer nervous shock no evidence was put before the Court in the company's case which would permit any finding that its operations were affected in any measurable way by the effect upon Mr Swan of the nervous shock that he suffered. In so far as the company proved damage to it flowing from the death of Mrs Swan that damage appears to me to have been from the loss of her services which the company did not recover for the reasons earlier discussed and not from nervous shock suffered by Mr Swan.

I therefore agree with Samuels JA that the company's appeal against the dismissal of its claim by Lusher J should be dismissed with costs.

The nervous shock matter arises also in the appeal by Mr Swan in his case. I have already given my reasons for concluding that Mr Swan did suffer nervous shock in the relevant sense. ... In my opinion an appropriate amount to allow for damages on this head is $10,000. ...

The third major area of argument at the hearing concerned the extent of the damages to be awarded under the *Compensation to Relatives Act* claim. On this aspect of the case I fully agree with the approach taken by Samuels JA and his calculations. ...

[McHugh JA agreed with Priestley JA.]

Appeal in the first action allowed. Appeal in the second action dismissed

Woolworths Ltd v Crotty
(1942) 66 CLR 603
High Court of Australia

Under the fatal accidents or compensation to relatives legislation in each Australian State and Territory, where the death of a person has been caused by the defendant's "act neglect or default", a tort action is maintainable against the defendant for the benefit of family members of the deceased who have suffered financial loss as a result of the death. In this context, the defendant's "act neglect or default" includes a breach of contract.

LATHAM CJ. [608] This is an appeal from a judgment of the Full Court of the Supreme Court of New South Wales refusing to set aside a verdict for the plaintiff (respondent in this appeal) in an action against the defendant (appellant) under the *Compensation to Relatives Act 1897-1928* (*Lord Campbell's Act*) to recover damages for herself and her husband caused by the death of her son. The question which arises upon the appeal is whether *Lord Campbell's Act* applies in cases where death is brought about by a breach of contract, or whether the Act is limited to cases where death is the result of a tort.

The jury answered certain questions, and it is not contended that there was not evidence to support the answers given. From these answers, read in the light of the evidence, it appears that the plaintiff's daughter bought an electric light globe from the defendant on behalf of her brother. Her brother used the globe. The globe was imperfectly constructed and the result was that the brother was electrocuted and died. The jury found that the defendant company impliedly warranted that the globe was fit for the purpose to which it was subsequently put by the deceased and that it was not reasonably fit for such purpose. Accordingly, the facts brought the case within the *Sale of Goods Act 1923-1937*, sec 19(1) – implied condition of reasonable fitness for a purpose made known to the seller, the facts **[609]** showing that the buyer relied on the seller's skill or judgment, the goods being of a description which it is in the course of the seller's business to supply. The jury gave a verdict for the plaintiff for £331 19s 6d. There was no finding of negligence or other breach of duty creating a liability in tort. Thus the verdict depends entirely upon breach of contract and not upon tort.

The Full Court held that the *Compensation to Relatives Act*, which reproduced *Lord Campbell's Act*, applied to cases of breach of contract, and accordingly that the verdict should stand. The appellant contests this decision, and this is the only question which is raised upon the appeal. ...

There is no direct authority upon the question. ...

It will be convenient in the first place to set out the words of sec 1 of the Act as enacted in *Lord Campbell's Act* (9 & 10 Vict c 93 – 1846) and as reproduced in 11 Vict No 32 – 1847 (NSW):-
"Whereas no action at law is now maintainable against a person who by his wrongful act neglect or default may have caused the death of another person and it is oftentimes right and expedient that the wrongdoer in such case should be answerable in damages for the injury so caused by him Be it therefore enacted by His Excellency the Governor of New South Wales with the advice and consent of the Legislative Council thereof That whensoever the death of a person shall be caused by a wrongful act neglect or default and the act neglect or default is such as would (if death had not ensued) have entitled the party injured to maintain an action and recover damages in respect thereof then and in every such case the **[610]** person who would have been liable if death had not ensued shall be liable to an action for damages notwithstanding the death of the person injured and although the death shall have been caused under such circumstances as amount in law to felony."

The recital contained in the section has not been reproduced in the *Compensation to Relatives Act 1897-1928*, but both parties to the appeal have argued the case (in my opinion rightly) upon the assumption that the recital may be considered for the purpose of resolving ambiguity, if any, in the enacting part of the Act (*Crowder v Stewart* (1880) 16 Ch D 368, at p 370; *Attorney-General v Lamplough* (1878) 3 Ex D 214, at p 227).

The argument for the appellant may be put in the following propositions:-

(1) The words of the Act are fully applicable to cases of tort, but are not applicable to cases of breach of contract.

(2) The Act applies only in cases where no action at law was maintainable against a person who had wrongfully (to use a general term) caused the death of another person. This appears both from the recital and from the enacting words of the section. If in any case such an action at law could have been maintained and damages could have been recovered in respect of the death, the Act has no application to that case.

(3) In the case of breaches of contract causing death, an action at law was maintainable by the legal personal representative of the deceased and damages could be recovered in respect of death. Death was never part of a cause of action in any action of contract, but only possibly an element in assessing damages.

(4) It was otherwise in cases of tort because in such cases the damnum, which might include death, was part of the cause of action, and any remedy was excluded both by the rule *actio personalis moritur cum persona* and by the principle declared in *Baker v Bolton* (1808) 1 Camp 493; 170 ER 1033 that at common law it was not a civil wrong to cause the death of a human being and that, if a tort did cause such a death, there was no remedy for any of the personal injuries suffered by the deceased in consequence of the wrongful act.

The respondent, on the other hand, contends:-

(1) The words of the Act, in their natural meaning, apply as well to breaches of contract as to torts.

(2) Even if the Act were limited to torts, certain breaches of contract, including, in particular, breaches of implied warranty upon the sale of goods, were, at the time when the Act was passed, actionable as torts, and the Act therefore gave a remedy (which did not before exist) in the case of such torts.

[611] The recital contained in sec 1 as originally enacted shows that the Act is dealing with cases in which, after the death of a person, no action was maintainable against the person who had caused the death by a wrongful act, neglect or default. The recital also stated that it was oftentimes right and expedient that the wrongdoer in such a case should be answerable in damages for the injury so caused by him. The Act was accordingly directed to giving damages in cases where otherwise the death of the person injured would have prevented any action being brought and any damages being obtained. ...

Thus conditions of the applicability of the Act are:–

(1) The case must be one where no action at law was maintainable.
(2) The wrongful act, etc, caused death.
(3) If death had not ensued the party injured would have been entitled both to maintain an action and to recover damages. ...

It is necessary first to determine whether and in what cases an action at law was maintainable at the time when the Act was passed against a person who, either by a tort or by a breach of contract, caused the death of another person. The Act was intended to deal with *other* cases, ie where no such action was maintainable, but where it was right and expedient that a wrongdoer should be answerable in damages. ...

[612] It is necessary in this connection to consider two rules of law which have been the subject of much controversy. ... The first rule is *actio personalis moritur cum persona* – a personal action dies with the person, whether that person be regarded as a possible plaintiff or as a possible defendant. ...

The second rule is the rule in *Baker v Bolton* (1808) 1 Camp 493; 170 ER 1033 that "in a civil court the death of a human being cannot be complained of as an injury." *Baker v Bolton* (1808) 1 Camp 493; 170 ER 1033 was a case in which a husband sued the proprietors of a stage coach for damages caused to him by the death of his wife. It was an action of tort (negligence), and the Lord Ellenborough CJ laid down the rule which I have stated, adding: "In this case the damages as to the plaintiff's wife must stop with the period of her existence". I propose to consider these two rules in relation to both tort and breach of contract.

I. The rule actio personalis moritur cum persona in relation to tort.– ... [613] the effect of the maxim *actio personalis* in relation to actions of tort was that the personal representatives of the deceased victim of a tort had no remedy in respect of the pain and suffering, or the death of the deceased, though, by common law exceptions and by statute they had certain rights to recover damages caused to his property by a tort, even though he had died. There was, obviously and admittedly, room for *Lord Campbell's Act* to operate by giving a remedy of some kind to some persons in relation to damages which were not damages to the estate of the deceased.

II. The rule actio personalis moritur cum persona In relation to breach of contract.– ... Whatever the true historical position may be, it is at least now clear that, as stated in *Williams on Executors*, 11th ed (1921), vol 1, p 619, the maxim does not apply (and for some centuries has not applied) to prevent the survival of causes of action on contracts, so that "the personal representative may sue, by the common law, not only for all debts due to the deceased by specialty or otherwise, but for all covenants and indeed all contracts with the testator *broken in his lifetime.*" ...

[614] In the case of personal injuries to a deceased person resulting from an act constituting a breach of contract, there was a limitation upon the damages recoverable. Damages were not recoverable in respect of personal injuries such as personal suffering or death, but only in respect of injury to the personal estate of the deceased. ...

[615] Thus there were cases of breach of contract causing personal injury in which there was no remedy in damages for certain damages which in fact flowed from the breach where death had resulted. There was accordingly in these cases scope for remedial action by legislation.

III. The rule in *Baker v Bolton* (1808) 1 Camp 493; 170 ER 1033, in relation to tort.– ... [616] consideration of the application of the rule in *Baker v Bolton* to cases of tort shows plainly that there was room for remedial action by way of legislation by giving a right of action for the benefit of some persons who had suffered damage from the death of another person caused by an act which was wrongful in relation to that person, but not wrongful in relation to other persons. Admittedly the Act deals with such cases.

IV. The rule in *Baker v Bolton* (1808) 1 Camp 493; 170 ER 1033, in relation to breach of contract.– ... I repeat that the death of a man can hardly in itself be a breach of contract (though, of course, it may be a condition upon which obligations arise under a contract, for example, in a contract of life insurance). There could, therefore, be no cause of action in contract for the death of a person as a breach of contract.

It would seem, at first sight, that the rule in *Baker v Bolton* (1808) 1 Camp 493; 170 ER 1033 would prevent a claim for any damages which arose from the death of a person brought about by a breach of contract. But the contrary has been held in the case of *Jackson v Watson & Sons* [1909] 2 KB 193, which has been favourably mentioned in *Rose v Ford* [1937] AC at pp 851, 854. In *Jackson v Watson & Sons* [1909] 2 KB 193 an action was brought for a breach of warranty that tinned salmon sold by the defendants to the plaintiff was unfit for human consumption. The plaintiff included a claim for damages for the loss of services of his wife, who had died in consequence of eating the salmon. It was held that the death was not an essential part of the cause of action, but only an element in ascertaining damages, and that *Baker v Bolton* (1808) 1 Camp 493; 170 ER 1033 did not prevent damages being recoverable for the loss of the services of the wife. ...

[617] But *Jackson v Watson & Sons* [1909] 2 KB 193 was a case of a living person suing a living person in respect of damages resulting from the breach of a contract made between the plaintiff and the defendant where the breach of contract caused the death of a third person. The case does not deal with the position which arises where the death of a person is caused by a breach of a contract with that person and where the death brings about loss to others – as in the case before the Court upon this appeal. The legal personal representatives of the deceased had no right of action in such a case for reasons which have been stated, unless the breach of contract caused damage to the estate of the deceased. The rule *actio personalis* did not apply to prevent the executors altogether from suing for damages in such a case, but it limited the damages to damage to the estate. There was obviously no right of action in other persons, such as the husband or wife of the deceased, who might suffer damage by the death, but who, even with the limitation or explanation of the rule in *Baker v Bolton* (1808) 1 Camp 493; 170 ER 1033 given in *Jackson v Watson & Sons* [1909] 2 KB 193, could not bring any action, for the simple reason that they were not parties to the contract which the deceased person had made with the defendant. ...

Accordingly, in the case of death resulting from breach of contract, the application of the rule in *Baker v Bolton* (1808) 1 Camp 493; 170 ER 1033 was such as to leave room for remedial action by way of legislation.

[618] The above analysis shows, in my opinion, that there were cases of breach of a contract made with a deceased person in which no action was maintainable for damages in relation to his personal injuries such as pain and suffering or in relation to his death. This obviously and admittedly has always been the position in the case of tort. The reality and the extent of loss suffered by relatives of a deceased man would be the same whether the act, neglect, or default which caused his death was a tort or a breach of contract. Thus there is no *a priori* reason why *Lord Campbell's Act* should not be equally applicable in both cases. ...

For the reasons which I have stated, the contention of the appellant that there was really no room for the operation of *Lord Campbell's Act* in cases of breach of contract because the law had already provided a remedy in such cases, so that it could not be said that an action was not maintainable for damages in those cases, is a contention which should not be accepted. ...

[619] In my opinion the language of the Act is capable of being applied to the case of death resulting from breach of contract. The words are very general. "Wrongful act" is a term which in a perfectly natural meaning can be applied to breaches of contract as well as to torts. ... So also a breach of contract may fall within the heading of neglect or default, as where a party either fails, that is neglects, to perform a contractual duty, or makes a default in performing it, either by completely failing to perform it, or by performing it in an insufficient or imperfect manner. ...

For these reasons I am of the opinion that the judgment of the Supreme Court was right. The appeal should be dismissed.

[Rich and McTiernan JJ agreed with Latham CJ.]

Appeal dismissed

2. LOSS OF SERVICES

Commissioner for Railways (NSW) v Scott
(1959) 102 CLR 392
High Court of Australia

The ancient common law right of an employer to maintain an action for loss of services against a wrongdoer who has injured his or her employee is not confined to cases of domestic or household employees but is available in all cases where there is the relationship of employer and employee.

[The appellant (plaintiff) sued the respondent (defendant) for damages alleging that the respondent by negligence had caused injuries to a train driver employed by the appellant in the railway service under the provisions of the *Government Railways Act 1912* (NSW) and through those injuries the appellant had lost the services of the driver over a period of time. Pursuant to s 100B of the Act the driver had been paid his salary during his absence from duty and the cost of medical treatment. The District Court of New South Wales found for the appellant and awarded him damages. The respondent appealed to the Full Court of the Supreme Court of New South Wales on grounds which raised only the question whether there was such a relationship between the appellant and the driver at the time the injuries occurred as would support the action *per quod servitium amisit*. The Full Court, by a majority, allowed the appeal. The appellant appealed to the High Court of Australia.]

KITTO J. ... **[410]** It is beyond **[411]** controversy that the action *per quod* is confined at least to cases in which the relationship between the plaintiff and the injured person was that of master and servant in the sense in which those terms are used in the common law. The respondent, however, asserts that it is still more narrowly confined, so that it is available in respect only of the services of a menial or domestic servant. If that be so the respondent must succeed, for it can hardly be suggested that the driver of a railway locomotive is a menial or domestic servant. ...

[417] In my opinion, the right course for us to pursue ... is to maintain in its integrity what Abbott CJ stated as "a principle of the common law": "that a master may maintain an action for loss of service, sustained by the tortious act of another, whether the **[418]** servant be a child or not": *Hall v Hollander* (1825) 4 B & C 660 at p 663. Accordingly, I am in favour of holding that the action *per quod* lies whenever the plaintiff and the person injured by the wrongdoing stood to one another at the time of the injury in the relation of master and servant. ...

[420] I am of opinion that employment by the Commissioner, as surely as employment by a private railway company, creates the relationship of master and servant which supports the action *per quod servitium amisit*.

For these reasons I would allow the appeal. ...

WINDEYER J. ... **[439]** These events in twentieth century Australia seem as remote as could be imagined from life in England in the Middle Ages. But the arguments we heard showed this case as illustrating Maitland's statement that "the forms of action we have buried, but they still rule us from their graves". The difficulty is that the voice from the grave has been heard differently by different people when it speaks the words "*per quod servitium amisit*". ...

In some recent discussion of the scope of the action for loss of *servitium* it has been stated that the action is out of harmony with the economic and social conditions of today. This seems to me to be, in the abstract, a questionable assertion, especially if by such an action an employer is entitled to recover from the wrongdoer medical expenses he paid for, and wages he paid to, an injured servant during his absence from duty. I shall refer later to the debatable question of the damages in such an action. But assuming medical expenses and sick pay to be recoverable, this seems to me not inconsistent with the social and industrial conditions of today. An employer's right to be indemnified by a wrongdoer for expenses he has been put to because of the injury of his employee is well **[440]** recognised in workmen's compensation law. There the amount of compensation paid is recoverable from anyone whose tortious act caused compensable injury. ... Many employers to-day are bound to pay their employees sick pay and provide their medical expenses if they be injured. Their obligations are largely covered by a widespread and partly compulsory system of insurances. There is no social advantage that I can see in discouraging the assumption by employers of straightforward obligations, or in encouraging resort to devices, described as loans or *ex gratia* payments, referred to in some of the cases. Moreover there seems to me to be no logic in measuring the total liability of a tortfeasor by whether the person harmed by his wrongful act is or is not a menial servant. ...

[458] The respondent's argument in this case seemed at one point to be: the action lies in respect of a servant; in the eighteenth century most servants lived with their masters; therefore the action lies today only in respect of servants who live with their masters. But this is illogical. No doubt in the eighteenth century, as now, the word servant unqualified ordinarily meant a personal domestic servant. ... During the course of the argument I thought that possibly the word servant when used in declarations in actions *per quod servitium amisit* might therefore have implied that the servant was a menial or domestic. But there is nothing to support this. The word has in law always embraced many persons who are not domestic servants. ... I can see no more reason than apparently did the judges of the nineteenth century for thinking that the *servitium* for the loss of which an action would lie is not coextensive with the ordinary legal relationship of master and servant. That is why with great respect to the [English] Court of Appeal I find the decision in *Hambrook's Case [Inland Revenue Commissioners v Hambrook]* [1956] 2 QB 641 unsatisfactory. Moreover I am not clear whether the result of their Lordships' judgments is that the action *per quod servitium amisit* is today restricted to servants who perform domestic tasks whether they live in or out of their master's home; or to servants who perform domestic tasks and live in; or to all servants who live *intra moenia* as part of the household, whatever the nature of their work may be. And I am not clear what is the position of hotel, club and boarding house servants, nor whether the fact that their employer is a company rather than a private individual affects the matter. Perhaps it is unnecessary to speculate on this; for clearly the engine driver is excluded. But the rules that the Court of Appeal has enunciated raise many questions, not so much in the case of industrial employees as in **[459]** cases more nearly akin to the conditions in which the action first developed. How for example would one classify a station manager, the overseer, jackeroos, station hands and stockmen, the groom, the gardener, the cook at the homestead and the cook in the shearer's hut or in a musterer's camp? And that about a boundary rider living miles from the homestead? Is he *intra moenia* if his hut is within the boundary of the run? Or does he differ from a man similarly employed but living near the homestead and doing odd jobs there when required? And what are the station owner's rights if the overseer, the boundary rider, the cook and the housemaid should all be hurt in a motor accident caused by the negligence of someone else? And does it matter that the legal owner of the station, the employer of the servants, is not an individual pastoralist but, as is so often the case, a family company, the head of the family living in the homestead? And is the situation different on a property conducted on a more modest scale where a farm hand sleeps at the homestead and eats in the kitchen, perhaps with the farmer's family? The varieties of rural employment, both pastoral and agricultural, are great; and the domestic arrangements associated with them vary too. I have mentioned some of them because they do have some resemblance to the work of hired men on a mediaeval manor in respect of whom the action *per quod servitium amisit* would lie; and I find it hard to see why in respect of such servants today loss of services should in some cases give rise to an action for damages while in other cases it is said it would not. It is possible to determine by legal criteria whether a man be a servant; but whether he is the sort of servant contemplated by *Hambrook's Case* [1956] 2 QB 641 would seem to be often a matter of uncertainty and debatable as a question of fact. No doubt these difficulties could be all removed if the action *per quod servitium amisit* were abolished. But, whether that course be desirable or not, we cannot deny any plaintiff a right of action which the law gives him. That anomalies will multiply if the law be as stated in *Hambrook's Case* cannot concern us; but it does, I think, justify an examination of the grounds of that decision in a more critical way than might ordinarily seem proper in the case of a decision of the Court of Appeal. ...

[461] No question of the measure of damages arises in this case. I therefore prefer to express no concluded opinion on what is I think a difficult question – certainly one on which there has been a difference of opinion – namely whether damages for loss of services can include wages paid to an injured servant during his absence and medical expenses borne by his employer. ... [462] I incline to the view that, in general, moneys which a master became legally obliged to pay to or for his servant by reason of an injury incapacitating the servant are recoverable by the master in an action against the wrongdoer – and that (apart from special statutory provisions) the only form which such an action could take would be the common law action *per quod servitium amisit*, such damages being consequential upon the loss of *servitium*. ...

[463] For the reasons I have given I respectfully agree ... with my brothers Kitto, Taylor and Menzies ... in thinking that the action *per quod servitium amisit* is not limited to the case of domestic servants in the way the [English] Court of Appeal has held it to be. ... [464] I would therefore allow the appeal.

[In separate judgments, Taylor and Menzies JJ agreed with Kitto and Windeyer JJ. In their separate dissenting judgments, Dixon CJ, McTiernan and Fullagar JJ would have confined the action per quod servitium amisit to the loss of the services of a domestic or household employee, a category which did not include a train driver.]

Appeal allowed

GIO Australia Ltd v Robson
(1997) 42 NSWLR 439
Supreme Court of New South Wales, Court of Appeal

The decision of the High Court of Australia in Commissioner for Railways (NSW) v Scott remains the authoritative statement of the common law of Australia on the right of an employer to recover damages for the loss of services of an injured employee.

[Nowlin Pty Ltd ("Nowlin"), which carried on the business of a taxi operator, employed Mrs Margaret Craig as a driver. While driving one of Nowlin's taxis, Mrs Craig was injured in a motor accident allegedly caused by the negligent driving of Mr Phillip Robson (the respondent).

Nowlin commenced proceedings against the respondent claiming that, as a result of the injuries suffered by its employee Mrs Craig, she had been unable to work for Nowlin and that Nowlin had been deprived of her services as a driver with consequent loss of income and profits.

The respondent was insured "against liability in respect of ... injury to a person" under a compulsory third party policy issued by GIO Australia Ltd (the appellant).

The appellant refused the respondent indemnity under the policy. The Supreme Court of New South Wales ordered a separate question to be tried: whether the third party policy issued by the appellant to the respondent entitled him to indemnity in respect of Nowlin's claim for the loss of Mrs Craig's services. Hamilton A-J answered this question in the affirmative. On appeal, the appellant contended that the law of New South Wales should no longer recognise the action for loss of services.]

STEIN JA. ... [444] On behalf of the appellant Mr Deakin QC submits that the law should no longer recognise the action per quod servitium amisit. He submits that it is anachronistic, derivative and arbitrary. Because of the authority of *Commissioner for Railways (NSW) v Scott* (1959) 102 CLR 392 Mr Deakin's submission is a formal one only. In addition, this Court confirmed the action in *Marinovski v Zutti Pty Ltd* [1984] 2 NSWLR 571. While an action for loss or deprivation of the consortium of a husband or wife was abolished [in New South Wales] by the *Law Reform (Marital Consortium) Act 1984* the action per quod servitium amisit was not. The law has been stated by the High Court in *Commissioner for Railways (NSW) v Scott*, with which we are bound and it is patently inappropriate for an intermediate appellate court to seek to re-state the common law contrary to the High Court. Any question about the abolition of the action or its continued existence at common law is a matter for the legislature or the High Court. ...

[Mason P and Handley JA agreed with Stein JA.]

Appeal dismissed

Roads & Traffic Authority v Jelfs
(2000) Aust Torts Reports ¶81-583; [1999] NSWCA 179
Supreme Court of New South Wales, Court of Appeal

The statutory abolition in New South Wales, Tasmania and Western Australia of the ancient common law right of a husband to maintain an action for loss of consortium against a wrong-doer who has injured his wife does not affect the right of the family members of a fatal accident victim to recover damages, under the fatal accidents or compensation to relatives legislation, for loss of the deceased's domestic services.

[Mrs Jelfs, the respondent's (plaintiff's) wife, died as the result of an accident caused by the appellant's (defendant's) negligence.

The respondent successfully brought two proceedings in respect of his wife's death: a claim under the *Compensation to Relatives Act 1897* (NSW) for the benefit of himself and the two teenage children of the marriage as dependants of the deceased and a claim for nervous shock (psychiatric injury) in respect of the depressive illness suffered by the respondent as a reaction to his wife's death. In respect of the claim under the *Compensation to Relatives Act 1897* (NSW), the trial judge awarded the respondent damages for "past and future care", comprising 20 hours per week of domestic services, including cooking, cleaning, washing and gardening, which would have been provided to the respondent by his wife.

On appeal, the appellant argued that the award of damages for "past and future care" or domestic services was contrary to the *Law Reform (Marital Consortium) Act 1984* (NSW).]

MASON P. ... **[64,269]** Section 3(1) of the *Law Reform (Marital Consortium) Act 1984* ("the Consortium Act") provides:

A person is not liable for damages in tort on the ground that the negligence, or other act or omission, of the person caused loss or impairment of the consortium of a husband and wife.

The appellant accepts that a claim under the *Compensation to Relatives Act* (which is statutory) is not an action for loss of consortium (which was a claim at common law). However, the submission is that s 3(1) of the Consortium Act went beyond abolishing this common law right of a husband. It is contended that it also precludes the Court from including any sum in respect of "services" as a component of a widower's damages in proceedings under the *Compensation to Relatives Act*.

The proposition appears not to have been advanced in any earlier case. ...

The submission should ... be rejected because it is without merit. It is contradicted by the proper construction of the Consortium Act. And it evaporates in the sunshine of a proper under-standing of the respective bases of the **[64,270]** common law action for loss of consortium and the statutory cause of action under the *Compensation to Relatives Act*.

A husband's action for loss of his wife's services (loss of consortium) derived from the same stream of principle as a master's action for loss of an employee's services (loss of servitium). The action was also a relic of the proprietary rights that a husband was once thought to possess in his wife. ...

The long title of the Consortium Act is "An Act to abolish actions for damages for loss of consortium". ...

The mischief identified in the Minister's second reading speech (New South Wales Parliamentary Debates, 29 February 1984, Assembly, pp 4871-2) was the archaic, discriminatory and patriarchal nature of the husband's action for loss of consortium. Nothing suggests the slightest intention to effect what would be a partial and discriminatory repeal of the *Compensation to Relatives Act 1897*.

The essential fallacy in the appellant's reasoning is that it ignores the fact that the Consortium Act addressed a single issue, the husband's common law action for consortium. That, and that alone, was abolished. Neither the mischief identified by the Minister, nor the language of the statute went further. The use of the technical term "consortium" in s 3 confirms the limited scope of the reform. The action for loss of or impairment to consortium was a single cause of action, unavailable in relation to the death of the wife, which compendiously recompensed the husband for loss of a congeries of rights or benefits. See *Best v Samuel Fox Ltd* [1952] AC 716 at 735; *Toohey v Hollier* (1955) 92 CLR 618; *Harris v Grigg* [1988] 1 QdR 514 at 517. The Act does not purport to interfere with other rights of husbands, even if they involve compensation for lost "services". ... [I]t cannot be read as effecting a partial repeal of the *Compensation to Relatives Act*.

The position is equally clear when looked at from the perspective of the *Compensation to Relatives Act*. A husband's statutory right to recover damages flowing from the death of his wife cannot be equated with the action for loss of consortium. The infamous case of *Baker v Bolton* (1808) 1 Camp 493, 170 ER 1033 established, in Lord Ellenborough CJ's words, that "in a civil Court, the death of a human being could not be complained of as an injury". Of present interest is the fact that *Baker v Bolton* was a husband's action for damages for loss of consortium. *Baker* established that such damages do not lie where the tort kills the wife rather than simply maims her. ... No reason was given by Lord Ellenborough for his ruling and it has frequently been said to have been wrong. Nevertheless it became accepted law (see *Woolworths Ltd v Crotty* (1942) 66 CLR 603). When John Campbell, the **[64,271]** reporter of *Baker v Bolton*, became Lord Campbell, he procured its partial overturning by the *Fatal Accidents Act 1846* (UK) which commonly bears his name. The cause of action which the Act created was conferred, in the first instance, upon the legal personal representative as fiduciary for all the dependants whose interests had been infringed. It was a cause of action which was "new in its species, new in its quality, new in its principle, in every way new" (*The "Vera Cruz"* (1884) 10 App Cas 59 at 70-71 per Lord Blackburn). ...

It can therefore be seen that the Consortium Act addresses an entirely different universe of discourse from the *Compensation to Relatives Act*. ...

[Handley and Giles JJA agreed with Mason P.]

Appeal dismissed

Chapter 9

Breach of Statutory Duty

1. LEGISLATIVE INTENTION

O'Connor v SP Bray Ltd
(1937) 56 CLR 464
High Court of Australia

It is a question of statutory construction involving identification of the legislative intention whether a statute which imposes a duty on one person for the protection or safety of another person creates a private right of action in tort, distinct from a common law negligence action and any criminal penalty, in the event of breach of the statutory duty. As a guiding principle, where a statute prescribes a specific duty for the safety of others in circumstances where the person on whom the duty is imposed is under a common law duty of care (eg, as in the case of an employer in respect of the workplace safety of an employee), the statutory duty will create a private right of action in tort in the event of breach unless a contrary legislative intention appears.

[This case is extracted only in respect of the exposition of principle by Dixon J. His Honour's remarks were directed at the question whether an action for breach of statutory duty was maintainable in respect of personal injury suffered by an employee, Mr Cornelius O'Connor, in a lift accident at his place of work where he was employed by SP Bray Ltd. The statutory duty was derived from clause 31(b) of regulations contained in a schedule to the *Scaffolding and Lifts Act 1912* (NSW). This clause required safety gear to be provided for certain lifts.

Dixon J and Evatt and McTiernan JJ, in a joint judgment, held, as a matter of legislative intention, that an action for breach of statutory duty was maintainable by an injured person against the person responsible for the care, control and management of a lift for non-observance of clause 31(b). Starke J, the other member of the court, did not consider this issue.

On appeal by Mr O'Connor from a judgment of the Full Court of the Supreme Court of New South Wales in favour of his employer, the High Court of Australia (Starke J dissenting) ordered a new trial.]

> DIXON J. ... **[477]** It is a question of some difficulty whether a civil remedy is given to a person injured in consequence of the breach of that clause. Such a person may, of course, maintain an action of negligence and rely upon the failure to comply with the statutory regulations as evidence of negligence. But it is a different question whether the enactment itself confers a distinct cause

of action. The received doctrine is that when a statute prescribes in the interests of the safety of members of the public or a class of them a course of conduct and does no more than penalize a breach of its provisions, the question whether a private right of action also arises must be determined as a matter of construction. The difficulty is that in such a case the legislature has in fact expressed no intention upon the subject, and an interpretation of the statute, according to ordinary canons of construction, will **[478]** rarely yield a necessary implication positively giving a civil remedy. As an examination of the decided cases will show, an intention to give, or not to give, a private right has more often than not been ascribed to the legislature as a result of presumptions or by reference to matters governing the policy of the provision rather than the meaning of the instrument. Sometimes it almost appears that a complexion is given to the statute upon very general considerations without either the authority of any general rule or law or the application of any definite rule of construction. An illustration may be found in a comparison of the decision and reasoning in *Phillips v Britannia Hygienic Laundry Co* [1923] 2 KB 832 with those in *Monk v Warbey* [1935] 1 KB 75. Perhaps in the end, a principle of law will be acknowledged as the foundation of the cases. In the absence of a contrary legislative intention, a duty imposed by statute to take measures for the safety of others seems to be regarded as involving a correlative private right, although the sanction is penal, because it protects an interest recognized by the general principles of the common law. ... Whatever wider rule may ultimately be deduced, I think it may be said that a provision prescribing a specific precaution for the safety of others in a matter where the person upon whom the duty is laid is, under the general law of negligence, bound to exercise due care, the duty will give rise to a correlative private right, unless from the nature of the provision or from the scope of the legislation of which it forms a part a contrary intention appears. The effect of such a provision is to define specifically what must be done in furtherance of the general duty to protect the safety of those affected by the operations carried on.

The difficulty in applying this view to clause 31 (*b*) of the schedule to the *Scaffolding and Lifts Act 1912* arises from the **[479]** fact that it is only one of many provisions widely differing in scope and character for the regulation of scaffolding and lifts. A great number of these provisions clearly does not create any private right. A civil remedy would be inappropriate to the duties prescribed by many of them and opposed to the general sense of many others. But I think that the nature of the specific duty imposed by clause 31 (*b*) makes the general rule prima facie applicable and that the fact that side by side with it are regulations creating no private right is no sufficient reason for denying a civil remedy for a breach of clause 31 (*b*). ...

Appeal allowed

Abela v Giew

(1965) 65 SR (NSW) 485

Supreme Court of New South Wales, In Banco

A statute directed at the control and regulation of motor traffic in the general public interest does not create a private right of action in tort for breach of statutory duty.

THE COURT. [SUGERMAN, TAYLOR and MOFFITT JJ] **[487]** This is a demurrer to three counts of the plaintiff's amended declaration which allege as causes of action breaches by the defendant, as the driver of a motor vehicle, of regs 67(2)(a), 67(2)(b) and 71(3), respectively, of the Regulations made under the *Motor Traffic Act 1909*, as amended, whereby, it is alleged, the plaintiff was injured. The demurrer is upon the ground that these regulations respectively impose public duties only and do not confer private rights of action upon persons injured by reason of non-compliance with their provisions. The Regulations in question are as follows:

67 (2) (a): "The driver of a motor vehicle approaching a marked footcrossing shall proceed at such a speed as to be able, if necessary, to stop before reaching such footcrossing."

67 (2) (b): "Where a motor vehicle is approaching or is travelling upon a marked footcrossing and a pedestrian is walking upon such footcrossing, so that if both continued they would arrive at

the same point together and collide, the driver of the motor vehicle shall lessen the speed of or stop the vehicle and allow such pedestrian to pass in front thereof."

71 (3): "Where the driver of a motor vehicle turns his vehicle to his right from one public street into another at an intersection ...

(c) he shall in all circumstances take adequate precautions to avoid danger of his vehicle colliding with any pedestrian who may be upon any portion of the intersection of the streets."

And it was alleged in the respective counts that the plaintiff was lawfully on the said crossing, or a pedestrian walking thereon, or upon the said intersection. ...

The regulations relied upon are parts of a substantial body of regulations made under the Act which deal with a diversity of topics, such as the registration of motor vehicles and licensing of drivers, traffic administration and control, regulations for drivers, the equipment and construction of motor vehicles, noise and other nuisances, and the loading and dimensions of vehicles. They appear under the general heading of "Regulations for Drivers"; reg 67 (2), (a) and (b), forms part of a regulation more specifically headed "Right of Way at Intersections and Marked Footcrossings", and reg 71 (3) is part of an elaborate regulation headed "Right-hand Turn at Intersection." ...

[489] Reference was made in *Dennis v Brownlee* [1963] SR (NSW) at p 721; 80 WN at p 1241, to a "long established reluctance to concede a right of action on the statute to the injured individual where the statutory duty has been imposed in the general public interest and has relation to the use of the highway for traffic". The general principles which have become settled law on this subject may be stated more fully and positively as follows: In an action arising out of a collision on the highway between two vehicles, or between a vehicle and a pedestrian, the circumstances that the collision has been caused or contributed to by a breach of a statutory regulation of traffic is evidence of negligence, or of contributory negligence, as the case may be. But it is evidence only, to be taken into consideration with all the other circumstances, and of varying weight according to the circumstances. It is not, that is to say, conclusive evidence. Nor is it in itself a cause of action, on the one hand, or, on the other hand, what may be termed "statutory contributory negligence" barring the action.

That is, in our opinion, the result of the Australian cases – *Henwood v Municipal Tramways Trust (SA)* (1938) 60 CLR 438; *Lopresto v Golding* (1957) 31 ALJ 851; *Foxcroft v Duncan* [1956] QSR 136; *Gillespie v Munro* [1959] SR (NSW) 200; 76 WN 191; *Pusell v Grabham* [1963] SR (NSW) 561; 80 WN 910; *Tucker v McCann* [1948] VLR 222; *Hopewell v Baranyay* [1962] VR 311. ...

[490] The *Motor Traffic Act* and the Regulations made thereunder are intended to secure, *inter alia*, the orderly movement of traffic and the safety of those engaged therein. To these ends they deal with a large variety of subject matters and form part of a body of legislation even more extensive. In various ways they impose upon drivers of vehicles duties ranging from such a general requirement as that they do not drive negligently, or furiously, or recklessly, or at a speed or in a manner which is dangerous to the public (Act s 4) to such specific requirements as that the reasonable direction of members of the police force be observed (reg 62) or as prescriptions of the method of driving in Queens Square (reg 77) or of the order of precedence at punts (reg 79); and, as has been said, duties are also imposed on pedestrians by the Regulation for Pedestrian Traffic. Penalties are provided which may include imprisonment for certain offences under the Act, or a fine not exceeding £100 for any offence against the regulations; and these may be accompanied by suspension of a driver's licence or disqualification from obtaining one (s 10). There is to be no liability for a penalty if it is proved that the offence was the result of accident or could not have been avoided by reasonable effort (reg 130, *supra*); and nothing in the Act shall affect any liability of any person by virtue of any statute or at common law (s 17).

The scope of this legislation indicates, in our opinion, that its purpose is the control and regulation of traffic by way of securing a measure of order which will promote its free movement, and in the interest of safety, these ends being sought to be secured by appropriate penal sanctions; it is not [491] the conferment of private rights of action upon injured individuals. Duties are not merely imposed upon one class of persons for securing the safety of another class of persons. The whole scheme of legislation is one of mutual and reciprocal obligations imposed upon all who engage in traffic for the benefit and safety of all others so engaged as well as for their own benefit and safety.

These have to be applied to an infinite number of and variety of constantly and rapidly changing situations as between two vehicles or as between a vehicle and a pedestrian. In these circumstances the prescription of pre-appointed regulatory measures cannot be regarded as more than an attempt to secure in the general interest that order will obtain and that safety will be preserved. ...

[494] We are of the opinion for the reasons stated that the regulations set out in the three counts demurred to do not confer private rights of action, and that therefore those counts disclose no causes of action. Accordingly in our opinion there should be judgment for the defendant upon the demurrer.

Judgment accordingly

JD Bell (Calool) Pty Ltd v Shortland County Council
(1991) Aust Torts Reports ¶81-139
Supreme Court of New South Wales

As a matter of principle, an action for breach of statutory duty may be available in respect of property damage.

[The plaintiffs, JD Bell (Calool) Pty Ltd and 13 others, were land-holders in the Upper Hunter River region. The defendant, Shortland County Council, was the local electricity supply authority.

The plaintiffs sued the defendant for damages in respect of a fire which the plaintiffs alleged was caused by an uninsulated high voltage aerial conductor on an overhead line coming into contact with a tree growing on the boundary of the property of certain plaintiffs. The fire caused damage to approximately 15,000 acres of grazing land, including the plaintiffs' land.

The plaintiffs' alleged breach by the defendant of a common law duty of care and breach of statutory duty based on reg 38 of the *Overhead Line Construction and Maintenance Regulations 1962* (NSW). The defendant conceded that it owed the plaintiffs a common law duty of care but disputed whether there was a breach of that duty and whether any contact between the overhead line and the tree was a cause of the fire. The defendant also conceded that liability for breach of statutory duty would be strict but disputed whether an action for breach of statutory duty was maintainable in the present case. The court ordered that there be determined the separate question whether breach of reg 38 conferred on the plaintiffs a civil right of action.]

COLE J. ... [69,317] The applicable legal principles are not in doubt. ... [His Honour cited the judgment of Dixon J in *O'Connor v SP Bray Ltd* (1937) 56 CLR 464 at 477-478.]

[69,318] As Dixon J indicated, if the statute or regulation prescribes a specific precaution for the safety of others, the statutory duty will give rise to a [correlative] civil right unless a contrary intention is found in the scope of the legislation. Whilst the cases generally deal with personal physical injuries, there is no reason in principle why the statement of law enunciated by Dixon J does not equally apply to the property of a person injured as a result of breach of statutory duty.

The task then is to determine whether, properly construed in its context, the intention of the legislature in regulation 38 was to care for the safety of persons, and thus to confer upon them a [correlative] civil right to sue for breach of the regulation, or whether, properly construed, the regulation imposes an obligation on the defendant council owed to the Crown, for breach of which only the penalty provisions of the regulations apply. ...

The regulation is in the following terms:

Contact between trees and aerial conductors

Where an aerial conductor of an overhead line ... is in contact or is likely to come into contact with any tree, steps shall be taken by the electricity supply authority to have such tree trimmed to prevent contact with the aerial conductor. ...

[His Honour referred to the *Electricity Development Act 1945* (NSW) under which the regulations were proclaimed.]

[69,319] It is clear the legislature was concerned with the safety of persons who may be affected by, inter alia, transmission of electricity. ...

[His Honour referred to the decision of the New South Wales Court of Appeal in *Tonelli v Electric Power Transmission Pty Ltd* (1967) 67 SR(NSW) 308 where it was held that no civil cause of action was conferred on a person injured by breach of reg 8 which imposed a standard for materials used in the construction of overhead lines.]

[69,320] There is nothing in *Tonelli* which detracts from the construction of regulation 38 as being a regulation concerned with the safety of persons and property and, as such, conferring a civil right of action upon a party injured by breach of that regulation. ...

[69,321] That being so, to adapt the words of Dixon J in *O'Connor v SP Bray Ltd*, regulation 38 is a provision prescribing a specific precaution for the safety of persons and their property in a matter where the council upon whom the duty is laid is, under the general law of negligence, bound to exercise due care, and thus the duty gives rise to a correlative private right to sue for breach of that duty. I can find nothing in the regulation, or the legislation under which it was made, which indicates any contrary intention. ...

Of course, even if breach of the regulation is found, there remains the issue of causation, namely, whether the fire was in truth caused in consequence of the breach of the regulation.

I accordingly answer the separate question in the affirmative. ...

Separate question answered in the affirmative

Byrne v Australian Airlines Ltd
(1995) 185 CLR 410
High Court of Australia

A statute with the public aim of promotion of industrial harmony and industrial relations, as distinct from the workplace safety of employees, does not create a private right of action in tort for breach of statutory duty.

[Mr George Byrne was employed by Australian Airlines Ltd ("the airline") under the Transport Workers (Airlines) Award 1988 ("the award") as a baggage handler at Sydney airport. He was dismissed by the airline for pilfering. Clause 11(a) of the award, which was made under the *Industrial Relations Act 1988* (Cth), provided: "Termination of employment by an employer shall not be harsh, unjust or unreasonable". Mr Byrne contended that his dismissal was in breach of this clause. A question for the High Court of Australia, on appeal from a decision of the Full Court of the Federal Court rejecting the claim, was whether Mr Byrne could maintain an action for damages for breach of statutory duty against the airline.]

BRENNAN CJ, DAWSON and TOOHEY JJ. ... **[424]** A cause of action for damages for breach of statutory duty arises where a statute which imposes an obligation for the protection or benefit of a particular class of persons is, upon its proper construction, intended to provide a ground of civil liability when the breach of the obligation causes injury or damage of a kind against which the statute was designed to afford protection: see *Sovar v Henry Lane Pty Ltd* (1967) 116 CLR 397 at 404, 405. The question is one of the construction of the statute, although as Dixon J pointed out in *O'Connor v SP Bray Ltd* (1937) 56 CLR 464 at 477-478, an examination of the statute "will rarely yield a necessary implication positively giving a civil remedy". One generalisation that can be made is that where the persons upon whom the statutory obligation is imposed are under an existing common law duty of care towards the persons whom the statute is intended to benefit or protect, the statutory prescription of a higher or more specific standard of care may, in the absence of any indication of a contrary intention, properly be construed as creating a private right: *O'Connor v SP Bray Ltd* (1937) 56 CLR 464 at 478. Thus it is that Factories and Shops Acts and other legislation designed to protect the health and safety of employees in the workplace have been held to impose duties the breach of which gives rise to a right to sue for damages: see, eg, *Groves v Wimborne* [1898] 2 QB 402 ... .

The legislation in this case, the *Industrial Relations Act* ... is of a very different kind. The **[425]** principal object of the Act is expressed in s 3 to be the promotion of industrial harmony and co-operation among the parties involved in industrial relations in Australia by the doing of a number of things which include the provision of a framework for the prevention and settlement of industrial disputes by conciliation and arbitration in a manner which minimises the disruptive effects of industrial disputes on the Australian community as a whole. ...

Having regard to the public aims of the legislation, its scope and purpose is not such as to disclose any intention to benefit or protect employees or any other class of persons by conferring on them a right of action at common law for breach of an award obligation. ...

[McHugh and Gummow JJ, in a joint judgment, agreed that an action for breach of statutory duty was not maintainable by Mr Byrne.]

Appeal dismissed

2. CAUSATION

Sherman v Nymboida Collieries Pty Ltd
(1963) 109 CLR 580
High Court of Australia

The defendant's breach of statutory duty must be a cause of the plaintiff's damage. Causation will be negatived where the cause of the plaintiff's damage was the plaintiff's "own separate and independent act".

[The plaintiff sued under the *Compensation to Relatives Act 1897* (NSW) to recover damages for the death of her husband, a mine deputy employed by the defendant, who was killed as a result of an explosion of methane gas in a mine owned by the defendant. The plaintiff alleged that the death of the deceased was caused by the negligence of the defendant and by its breach of a statutory duty imposed by the *Coal Mines Regulation Act 1912* (NSW) to provide proper ventilation in the mine. The jury having returned a verdict for the defendant, the Full Court of the Supreme Court of New South Wales refused to order a new trial.]

WINDEYER J. ... **[589]** Breach of a statutory duty to provide means for ensuring the safety of workmen must, contributory negligence having been excluded by statute as a defence, be regarded as a duty that is owed to the careless just as much as to the careful. All safety requirements enacted by statute are obviously meant to meet conditions in which, if they were not insisted upon, the careless, the inattentive, the tired, the clumsy and unskilful, and any workers ready to take risks, might come to harm. If a law of that sort gives **[590]** a civil right of action to persons injured in consequence of its breach, then that right is available to the careless and the unskilful as well as to the careful and skilled. Moreover, even when contributory negligence is a defence, it is not every heedless act that amounts to contributory negligence disentitling a plaintiff to succeed: *Davies v Adelaide Chemical and Fertilizer Co Ltd* (1946) 74 CLR 541; *Cadswell v Powell Duffryn Associated Collieries Ltd* [1940] AC 152. Nevertheless, when an accident occurs and harm ensues, the question is always, What, in a legal sense, caused the harm? That must be answered if responsibility is to be fixed upon some person. ... In the present case the immediate cause of the explosion – in the proper sense of the word "immediate" and on any ordinary meaning of the word "cause" – was the ignition of the gas. And I agree that it, and not the antecedent condition of the mine due to neglect to provide proper ventilation, if there were such a neglect, was, for the purposes of determining legal responsibility, the cause of the death: see *Stapley v Gypsum Mines Ltd* [1953] AC 663. There are no simple criteria of universal application by which that question can be resolved. Foreseeability and the ordinary man's conceptions of culpability enter into a determination of it. One consideration, however, is that in this case the opening of the safety lamp was not merely a careless act. It was an act positively prohibited by law. This is not a decisive consideration: see the judgment of Dixon and McTiernan JJ in *Henwood v Municipal Tramways Trust (SA)* (1938) 60 CLR 438, and see *National Coal Board v England* [1954] AC 404. But it is, I consider, a most relevant consideration when the duty said to have been neglected is part of a complex of duties imposed by statute on different persons, which are meant cumulatively to ensure the safety of persons working in a mine or factory. Then, it seems to me, a question arises whether a person who was himself required by the statute to perform part of that complex of duties can, when an accident occurs as the immediate result of his own default in carrying out his duty, attribute the consequences that befall him to the antecedent default of another. The question in such a case is not simply one of contributory negligence on the part of someone to whom a duty of care was owed.

The facts of the present case bring the question into sharp relief. The deceased man was a deputy. As such, he himself had statutory **[591]** duties for the ensuring of safe working conditions in the mine. Schedule 6 of the Act made it the duty of a deputy to examine the mine before the commencement of each shift. It was to perform this task that he had entered the mine. The object of the examination was, among other things, to see whether gas was present. A deputy also has duties (under pars 42 and 43 of Schedule 6) in relation to the safety lamps. It seems that a deputy who, in the course of making an examination to see whether gas be present, detonated gas, by striking a light or exposing the flame of his safety lamp, could not maintain an action for breach by his employer of a statutory duty to ventilate the mine. And the representative of a deputy who was killed in this way cannot, I think, in an action under *Lord Campbell's Act*, ask the tribunal of fact to disregard the conduct of the deceased man. He had, under the statute, a complementary statutory duty to see whether the ventilation, which it was his employer's duty to provide, was in fact sufficient to dispel gas from the mine to an extent to make it safe for men to work there. It is not contributory negligence that precludes him, or his representative, if he be killed, from recovering. It is that, in the circumstances, the accident was not, in the eye of the law, the result of his employer's failure to perform a statutory duty but of his own separate and independent act. The validity of the distinction may be debatable. But it has been said that, in law, questions of cause and consequence are to be resolved according to "the ordinary common sense of the matter" – and in order to allot responsibility, not to trace back from ultimate consequence to first cause. In *Norris v William Moss & Sons Ltd* [1954] 1 All ER 324, Vaisey J used words which I adopt as appropriate here: "It is not, I think, admissible to construct chains of causation in a case such as this where a single cause – simple, obvious and amply sufficient to account for what happened – is to be found in the inexcusably careless behaviour of the workman himself" ([1954] 1 All ER at pp 327, 328). This may sound harsh. But so far as the facts of this case can ever be known, it is unfortunately applicable. ...

[592] The appeal must, I consider, be dismissed.

[McTiernan, Kitto, Taylor and Owen JJ, in a joint judgment, also declined to order a new trial.]

Appeal dismissed

Pask v Owen

[1987] 2 Qd R 421

Supreme Court of Queensland, Full Court

In the context of causation, a breach of statutory duty may have a continuing effect not limited in time to the initial breach.

[Section 63(2) of the *Firearms and Offensive Weapons Act 1979* (Qld) ("the Act") provided that "a person shall not knowingly supply any firearm ... or ammunition to or for the use of a prevented person". For the purposes of the Act, a "firearm" included an air-gun and a "prevented person" was a person under the age of 17.

The plaintiff (respondent) Shaun Pask, aged 13, suffered damage to his right eye when a loaded air-gun he was handling discharged. The air-gun belonged to the plaintiff's friend Troy Owen, aged 15, who had been given the air-gun as a birthday present about eight months before this incident by his parents, the defendants (appellants) Mr and Mrs Owen.

At the time of the discharge of the air-gun the plaintiff was present as a visitor in Troy's bedroom. Mrs Owen called Troy to come to his evening meal. Just before Troy left his bedroom, the plaintiff, with Troy's permission, picked up the air-gun to look at it. The air-gun and its ammunition were stored in a wardrobe in Troy's bedroom with the knowledge and approval of the defendants. Shortly after Troy left his bedroom, the plaintiff loaded a pellet and, in some unexplained way, the air-gun discharged causing the plaintiff's injury.

The trial judge dismissed the plaintiff's action against the defendants for negligence but awarded the plaintiff damages in respect of his claim for breach of statutory duty founded on s 63(2) of the Act. The basis of this liability was that the defendants had "supplied" a firearm to Troy who was a "prevented person".

An issue in the defendants' appeal to the Full Court of the Supreme Court of Queensland was whether there was a causal connection between the defendants' breach of s 63(2) of the Act and the plaintiff's injury.]

ANDREWS CJ. ... [425] It is significant to note that the provision [s 63(2) of the Act] strikes against supplying a firearm or ammunition to, as well as for the use of, a prevented person; that possession and not merely use by a prevented person is something to be guarded against. ...

[His Honour referred to the primary purpose of the Act as being to ensure safety in the possession and management of firearms as well as their use, particularly by young persons.]

[426] It was urged on behalf of the defendants ... that there has not been shown to be a continuance of causality so as to enable the act of giving a firearm as a birthday present to the boy Troy to have created a danger still operative and which was shown to be effective in the circumstance in which the plaintiff took hold of the weapon and loaded it and by reason of his inexperience or immaturity discharged it in such a way that the pellet struck him in the eye. ...

[427] I would hold that this was a breach of statutory duty of continuing effect where the defendants permitted Troy Owen to keep the gun and ammunition in his room ... .

[431] I would dismiss the appeal ... .

THOMAS J. ... [433] The most common meaning of "supply" (in the context of supplying a chattel such as a gun) is the single act of giving possession or entitlement. If the supply is by gift, the supply is complete when the gift is complete. This gift was complete upon delivery. However the gravamen of Mr and Mrs Owen's conduct was in "supply ... *for the use*" of Troy who was a prevented person. Although their breach occurred some eight months before the accident, it was a breach that contemplated future consequences. It was a gift of the gun for Troy's use ... . If anyone were to be injured as a result of Troy's use of the gun, it would not be surprising to find the law holding Mr and Mrs Owen liable in damages for the consequences of their supplying the gun to him. On the other hand, if the injury were not the result of Troy's use of the gun, I would find it impossible to hold it to have been caused by any breach of the Act on the part of Mr and Mrs Owen. ...

[Thomas J considered the evidence and concluded that the plaintiff's injury was the result of the "use" of the air-gun by Troy within the meaning of s 63(2) of the Act in that Troy had permitted the plaintiff to handle the air-gun in his presence.]

[436] Without this finding of use of the gun by Troy, I would find it impossible to discern any causal connection between the plaintiff's injury and the breach by Mr and Mrs Owen. ...

The appeal must be dismissed ... .

[Andrews CJ, with whom Kelly SPJ agreed, also held that the defendants were negligent at common law in permitting Troy to keep the air-gun and ammunition unsupervised in his bedroom bearing in mind the defendants' knowledge that young visitors, including the plaintiff, were in that room for extended periods. Thomas J found it unnecessary to consider whether the defendants were liable for negligence.]

Appeal dismissed

3. KIND OF DAMAGE

Gorris v Scott
(1874) LR 9 Ex 125
Court of Exchequer

There will be no liability in tort for breach of statutory duty if the damage suffered by the plaintiff was damage of a kind the statute was not intended to prevent.

KELLY CB. **[127]** This is an action to recover damages for the loss of a number of sheep which the defendant, a shipowner, had contracted to carry [from Hamburg, Germany to Newcastle, England], and which were washed overboard and lost by reason (as we must take it to be truly alleged) of the neglect to comply with a certain order made by the Privy Council, in pursuance of the *Contagious Diseases (Animals) Act 1869* ["the Act"]. The Act was passed merely for sanitary purposes, in order to prevent animals in a state of infectious disease from communicating it to other animals with which they might come in contact. Under the authority of that Act, certain orders were made; amongst others, **[128]** an order by which any ship bringing sheep or cattle from any foreign port to ports in Great Britain is to have the place occupied by such animals divided into pens of certain dimensions, and the floor of such pens furnished with battens or foot-holds. The object of this order is to prevent animals from being overcrowded, and so brought into a condition in which the disease guarded against would be likely to be developed. This regulation has been neglected, and the question is, whether the loss, which we must assume to have been caused by that neglect, entitles the plaintiffs to maintain an action. ...

[His Lordship referred to the purposes for which orders under the Act could be made by the Privy Council and noted that all of the enumerated purposes were directed to the prevention of disease and none had any relation to the danger of loss of animals by the perils of the sea.]

[129] That being so, if by reason of the default in question the plaintiffs' sheep had been overcrowded, or had been caused unnecessary suffering, and so had arrived in this country in a state of disease, I do not say that they might not have maintained this action. But the damage complained of here is something totally apart from the object of the Act ... **[130]** and it is in accordance with all the authorities to say that the action is not maintainable.

[In separate judgments, Pigott, Pollock and Amphlett BB agreed with Kelly CB.]

Judgment for the defendant

Chapter 10

Public Nuisance

1. TITLE TO SUE

Walsh v Ervin
[1952] VLR 361
Supreme Court of Victoria

A member of the public (as distinct from the Attorney-General on behalf of the public generally) has title to sue for public nuisance only if he or she has suffered "particular damage", that is, damage "beyond that suffered by the public generally".

[The plaintiff and defendant were farmers whose respective properties were divided by a highway. The defendant ploughed up part of the highway for crops so that the plaintiff was unable to use one of his gates to obtain access to the highway. The defendant also constructed gates across the highway which caused the plaintiff inconvenience when moving sheep and passing along the highway. The plaintiff sought an injunction and damages.]

SHOLL J. ... **[362]** The plaintiff as the owner of freehold land adjoining the road, which was and is a public highway, had and has a right (subject to any statutory interference therewith) to free and uninterrupted access to the highway from any point on his land contiguous with the highway, and from the highway to any point on his land contiguous therewith. This is a private right, which the plaintiff enjoys as an adjoining landowner ... .

[364] It follows that in my opinion the plaintiff in this case can obtain at least nominal damages if there has been something sufficiently substantial to constitute an interference with his right. In my opinion, the prevention of the possibility of access for motor vehicles for some months does amount to such an interference. It was a substantial diminution of the effective content of the plaintiff's right ... .

[365] I turn now to the second question, *viz*, whether the ploughing and cropping of the road ... and the maintenance of obstructions thereon ... gave the plaintiff the right to sue in his own name, and not merely as relator, for an injunction and/or damages, notwithstanding that he has not proved any actual pecuniary loss, ascertained, or capable of being precisely ascertained, in money. ... The circumstances in which an individual plaintiff can sue alone for relief in respect of an obstruction of, or other nuisance to, a public highway have been the subject of many cases, and of some uncertainty, for more than four centuries. ...

[368] As the general principle is usually stated, an individual cannot sue alone for relief in respect of a nuisance to a public highway unless he has sustained some particular damage, in the sense of some substantial injury, direct and not merely consequential, beyond that suffered by the

353

public generally. It follows, of course, from this that there can be no question, in respect of such a claim, of recovering nominal damages for the mere fact of infringement of an absolute legal right of passing and repassing on such a highway, on the basis of such infringement constituting an *injuria* from which loss is presumed. For the legal right of passing and repassing is the same in all members of the public, and it is to avoid the multiplicity of actions which might result if many members of the public sued, without proof of actual damage, in respect of such infringement of their right, that the law requires that in such a case the Attorney-General must sue on behalf of all. It is only if particular damage *ultra* can be established that the individual can sue alone. ...

What, then, is particular damage? ... **[369]** In my opinion, delay and inconvenience of a substantial character, direct and not merely consequential, so long as not merely similar in nature and extent to that in fact suffered by the rest of the public, may amount to sufficient damage, particular to the individual plaintiff ... .

[370] It would, in my judgment, seem to any Australian countryman the negation of common sense to say that a person using a public Government road as this plaintiff used it would not suffer peculiar prejudice by its being closed, or rendered more difficult of use. So long as the delay and inconvenience is substantial, it can in my opinion make no difference that the way is not wholly closed, if it is effectively rendered unavailable for important **[371]** purposes of the plaintiff, even though it is not possible to infer actual pecuniary loss by him. ...

The conclusions of law which I have above stated on this branch of the case may now be summarised.

(1) An individual person or corporation cannot sue in his or its own name in respect of a nuisance to a public highway, except for "particular damage" occasioned to him or it thereby.

(2) "Particular damage" is not limited to "special damage" (in the sense of actual pecuniary loss).

(3) It may consist of proved general damage, *eg*, inconvenience and delay – as in the present case – provided that it is substantial, that it is direct and not consequential, and that it is appreciably greater in degree than any suffered by the general public.

(4) Since such particular damage must be thus proved, it follows that mere nominal damages cannot be recovered, since there is no presumption of particular damage.

(5) But I see no reason why exemplary damages might not in a proper case be awarded. ...

In stating proposition (3) above, I have adopted the view of Lord Penzance in *Metropolitan Board of Works v McCarthy* (1874) LR 7 HL 243, at p 263, that a difference in degree of damages is sufficient, notwithstanding the view expressed in *Clerk & Lindsell* [*on Torts*] (8th ed), p 359, that the authorities favour the requirement of a difference in kind, and not merely in degree. In the present case, even if the latter test were the proper one, I think the plaintiff would satisfy it ... by reason of the peculiar **[372]** situation of his allotments, the special character of his user of the road, and the absence of evidence of user by anyone else during the relevant period.

There can be no question in this matter of an injunction, since the obstructions were all removed in November 1949, two months after writ, and there is no threat of repetition. In such a case damages and costs are a sufficient remedy ... .

There will accordingly on the whole claim be judgment for the plaintiff ... .

Judgment for the plaintiff

2. HIGHWAY AND WATERWAY OBSTRUCTION

Silservice Pty Ltd v Supreme Bread Pty Ltd
(1949) 50 SR (NSW) 127
Supreme Court of New South Wales

Obstruction of a footpath or highway by an activity which involves gathering together a crowd may constitute a public nuisance. However, where a business does not engage in such an activity, the operator of the business will not be liable in public nuisance in respect of queues or crowds of customers seeking to do business provided that the business is conducted on "suitable premises and in a normal and proper manner".

ROPER CJ in Eq. **[128]** The plaintiff is the proprietor of a café situated at No 327 George Street, Sydney. The defendant bakes and sells bread on the adjoining premises, No 329 George Street. At times, and particularly on the Friday of each week and on the last business day before a public holiday, a queue of people seeking to buy the defendant's bread forms outside the defendant's shop and stretches along the footpath creating an obstruction to the entrance to the plaintiff's shop. This is a motion for an interlocutory injunction in the suit in which the plaintiff claims that the obstruction is a nuisance caused by the defendant, and causing particular damage to the plaintiff.

The questions of fact arising on the motion have caused me no difficulty. There is some dispute on the evidence as to the degree of the obstruction and the extent of damage, but this is an interlocutory application and I think that the plaintiff has shown a probability that it will be able, at the hearing of the suit, to establish an appreciable obstruction, and that it has caused appreciable damage. On the other hand, assuming that the evidence at the hearing is substantially the same as has been led on this motion, I think that it will not be able to establish that the defendant's premises are unsuitable for the carrying on of its business, or that the defendant does anything which is not necessary for the *bona fide* carrying on of its business for the purpose, or having the effect, of attracting or retaining crowds of people, or that it could take better, speedier, or other more effective steps in serving its customers so as to prevent the formation of the queues. The only unusual feature of the defendant's trade is, apparently, that the bread which it bakes is of good quality, and the queues are formed because many people wish to buy it, and find it convenient to make their purchases at about the same times of the day. It was put that the defendant should have an employee to control the queues, so as to make them form along the kerb side of the footpath instead of along the building line where they now form, and that, if this were done, the damage to the plaintiff would be obviated or diminished to the extent that it would be negligible; but, on the evidence, I think that the defendant would probably be prevented by the police from controlling and marshalling the queues in this way.

I turn then to the questions of law involved. Subject to the question of degree, which enters into all cases of nuisance, an obstruction of a highway by a crowd of people may constitute a public nuisance which would be actionable at the instance of an individual who suffers special damage because of it; but it does not follow in every case that where a crowd constituting a nuisance assembles outside a man's house or shop because of something therein, or something occurring therein, that that man is responsible for the nuisance. For instance, I think that no action could have been maintained against Mr Very in the circumstances set out in the report of *R v Curlile* (1834) 6 C & P 636, at 646(a), if he had not taken the drastic steps which he found necessary to end the nuisance. "Mr Very was a confectioner in Regent Street, and he had a daughter who attended to his shop, who was considered so beautiful that a crowd of three or four hundred persons used daily to assemble and stand at his shop windows for the purpose of looking at her. Police officers were obliged to be in constant attendance before Mr Very's house, and the **[129]** inconvenience was so great, both to Mr Very and to his neighbours, that he was obliged to send his daughter out of town."

The plaintiff's submission, shortly stated, is that this case falls within the principle of *Barber v Penley* [1893] 2 Ch 447 and *Lyons, Sons & Co v Gulliver* [1914] 1 Ch 631; and the defendant relies upon the decision in *Dwyer v Mansfield* [1946] KB 437 ... [approved by] ... a Divisional Court of three Judges in *Fabbri v Morris* [1947] 1 All ER 315 at 316, where Goddard CJ said, "If a person is selling in the ordinary way from a shop, he cannot be held responsible because a queue forms in the street of people anxious to go into the shop and buy. If he is carrying on business in the ordinary way, no offence is committed, as was recently pointed out by Atkinson J in *Dwyer v Mansfield*", and Lewis J said, "If the appellant had been carrying on business in a normal and proper manner there could have been no offence."

Barber v Penley and *Lyons, Sons & Co v Gulliver*, in the judgments in which all the previous cases are collected and examined, both dealt with the formation of theatre queues. ... [I]t appears that in cases of this kind if the defendant has available to him reasonable means of removing or avoiding the obstruction, he is responsible for the nuisance if he does not adopt those means. The test is not whether an obstruction has been caused, but whether the obstruction could reasonably have been avoided: 63 LQR 147, and cf *Fabbri v Morris*. I think, however, that this is not the sole test of whether a person is responsible for the nuisance caused by the assembly of a crowd of people, and that a more absolute liability rests upon the person whose business involves the gathering together of a crowd, or who, apart from any consideration of the *bona fide* conduct of his business, deliberately continues to gather the crowd.

An essential feature of the theatre cases appears to me to be that the business of the theatre proprietor requires and depends upon the collection of a crowd of people within the theatre. In bringing the crowd together the proprietor must, I think, ensure that neither the crowd, nor the process of collecting it, causes damage to his neighbours. I think that the judgments in *Barber v Penley* and *Lyons, Sons & Co v Gulliver* show that the defendants would have been held liable even if the earlier opening of the doors had not solved the difficulty.

Every case of nuisance depends upon its own facts, and general principles can only be stated broadly. I think, however, that the cases establish the following propositions in regard to nuisances arising from crowds or queues: (1) if the crowd is attracted by something done by a defendant which is not [130] necessary for the *bona fide* carrying on of his trade, or which is done for the purpose of bringing a crowd together, and is reasonably liable to have that effect, he is liable for any nuisance arising from the presence of the crowd: *R v Carlile* (1834) 6 C & P 636; (2) if a defendant whose business attracted a crowd could by some reasonable means within his control prevent the damage and does not adopt those means he is similarly liable: *Fabbri v Morris*; (3) if it is a necessary ingredient in the successful conduct of the business of a defendant that he should cause a crowd of people to assemble, as in the theatre and circus cases, he is liable for any nuisance caused by the assembly, or by the process of bringing it together: *Barber v Penley*; *Lyons, Sons & Co v Gulliver*; and (4), subject to the foregoing, a defendant carrying on business in suitable premises and in a normal and proper manner is not liable for the nuisance which may result from crowds of customers seeking to do business with him.

If the evidence as it stands at this stage remains substantially the same at the hearing, I think that the plaintiff will not establish that the defendant is liable for the nuisance complained of in the suit.

I, therefore, order that the motion be dismissed...

Motion dismissed

York Bros (Trading) Pty Ltd v Commissioner of Main Roads
[1983] 1 NSWLR 391
Supreme Court of New South Wales

Obstruction of a waterway, such as a navigable river, may constitute a public nuisance. In order to constitute a public nuisance an interference with the right of navigation must be "substantial and material". As a matter of principle, statutory authority may justify an activity which otherwise would constitute a public nuisance.

[The report of this case contains no statement of the facts. However the reporter for the New South Wales Law Reports has summarised the facts at the beginning of Powell J's judgment.]

POWELL J. [The plaintiffs were the owners of a shipyard at Swan Bay on the Richmond River, or were interested as principals in that shipyard. Downstream from that shipyard the defendant was constructing a road bridge at Woodburn, the effect of which when constructed would be to block the plaintiffs' use of the river for navigation purposes. The plaintiffs sought declarations that the Richmond River was a navigable river pursuant to the *Navigation Act 1901*, that they had a right of way upon the river, that the defendant could not interfere or obstruct the navigation of the river, that the river was a public highway and various injunctions to restrain the defendant from constructing the bridge or obstructing the rights of the plaintiffs in respect of their use by navigation of the river. His Honour having considered the evidence continued:]

[393] The right of navigation on tidal waters is simply a right of way thereover (*Orr-Ewing v Colquhoun* (1877) 2 App Cas 839), for all the public for all purposes of navigation, trade or intercourse. It extends prima facie over the whole space over which the tide flows and is not suspended when the tide is out. The right carries with it all rights necessary for the full use and enjoyment of the rights of convenient passage, such as the rights to pass and to ground and to anchor, to remain for a reasonable time for the purposes of loading and unloading or completing repairs; or of waiting till the wind or weather, or probably also the season, permits the vessel to leave. Such ancillary rights, however, may be exercised only in relation to the exercise of the particular ship's right of navigation; they do not, for example, extend to permitting a coal hulk to be moored in Portland Harbour so as to coal ships using the harbour (*Denaby and Cadeby Main Collieries Ltd v Anson* [1911] 1 KB 171). Further, since a navigable river is, in effect, a public highway navigable by all members of the body politic, the exercise of the right of navigation must be done for a reasonable purpose and in a reasonable way. But, although the right of navigation is common to all, the rights of all vessels are not coextensive. Thus, it has been said that it may be right and reasonable that a small vessel should go up to the farthest point she can **[394]** reach in order to give the public the benefit of the public way; but the same right does not exist in the case of a large vessel, and she is not entitled under extraordinary circumstances to get to a place where large vessels are not accustomed to go, and where there is no accommodation for mooring and unloading them (*Colchester Corporation v Brooke* (1845) 7 QB 339; 115 ER 518; *The Octavia Stella* (1887) 57 LT 632; 6 Asp MLC 182; *The Swift* [1901] P 168; *Hawkins v Rutter* [1892] 1 QB 668). Since, although the bed of all navigable rivers is prima facie vested in the Crown, the ownership by the Crown is for the benefit of the subject, that ownership cannot, without more, be used by the Crown, or a grantee from it, in such a manner as to derogate from or interfere with the exercise of the right of navigation which belongs, by law, to the members of the body politic (*Gann v Free Fishers of Whitstable* (1865) 11 HL Cas 192; 11 ER 1305; *Attorney-General v Earl of Lonsdale* (1868) LR 7 Eq 377).

What I have thus far written would not, I think, provoke much, if any, dispute on the part of the defendant. But, as the arguments which I have recorded above would seem to demonstrate, there is a significant dispute between the parties as to the degree of interference with the right of navigation which must be demonstrated in order to establish a public nuisance, and, further as to the relevance, whether as constituting a defence, or as a matter to be considered in evaluating whether or not there is a nuisance, of any benefit flowing to the public by reason of the obstruction or interference complained of.

Although the analogy between a public highway stricto sensu and a public navigable river is not complete (*The Calgarth; The Otarama* [1927] P 93, at 107 per Scrutton LJ; see also *The Swift* (supra) at 174) nonetheless it seems to me that the cases establish that, as is the case in obstructions to a public highway, it is not every interference, however slight, with the right of navigation which constitutes an actionable nuisance; rather, to constitute an actionable nuisance, the interference must be substantial and material. If authority for that view be needed it might be found in the decision of the Court of Appeal in England in *Attorney-General v Terry* (1874) 9 Ch App 423. ...

The question which then arises is, whether, assuming that there is an obstruction to navigation in the relevant sense, it may, nonetheless, be justified upon the ground that it is for the public benefit. As I have indicated, the plaintiffs would deny that "public benefit" can ever afford a justification for a public nuisance, an argument which they found upon the decisions in *R v Train* (1862) 2 B & S 640; 121 ER 1209, and *R v Ward* (1836) 4 Ad & El 384; 111 ER 832, whereas the defendant submits that there may be cases, of which it was submitted the present was one, in which "public benefit" may afford a justification. If I may, with respect, say so, such authorities as there are on this aspect of the law leave the matter in a singularly obscure position. ...

[396] After giving the matter much anxious consideration I have come to the conclusion that, in truth, the question of "public benefit" is but one matter to be weighed in the scale when determining whether or not an obstruction to navigation is substantial and material; it following that, if it be held that an obstruction is substantial and material, it matters not that some public benefit may flow from its **[397]** construction, but that if an obstruction, though technically a nuisance, does not significantly interfere with navigation, the fact that public benefits flow from its construction would lead a court not to intervene.

Adopting this approach I have come to the conclusion that the bridge, if constructed as designed, would constitute a substantial and material interference to the right of navigation, for this will not be a case in which, in general, the river up to Swan Bay will remain open for navigation to vessels of the type hitherto accustomed to use it, the only restriction on the right being that, in future, such vessels will not be able to utilize the whole surface of the river but must pass between piers set in the river bed; rather this will be a case in which some of the vessels, or vessels of a like type, will have denied to them – either totally, or until significant modifications (if they be feasible) have been carried out – passage up the river beyond the bridge. I conclude, therefore, that, notwithstanding the advantages which may flow from replacing the vehicular ferry – which, however, it should be recorded, had not significantly hindered navigation – and notwithstanding the other advantages flowing from the construction of the bridge, it is, prima facie, to be regarded in law as a public nuisance.

This view notwithstanding, the defendant nonetheless submits that, having been authorized and directed pursuant to the provisions of the *Main Roads Act 1924*, s 25, to build a bridge at Woodburn, and having acted with reasonable regard to the interests of all who might be affected by the construction of such a bridge, it is not liable to action at the suit of the plaintiffs.

The cases in which a nuisance may be justified by reference to a statutory duty imposed, or a statutory power or authority conferred, upon the constructor, or operator, of a work or thing said to be a nuisance are many – recent convenient collections and analyses of them may be found in the decision of the Court of Appeal in England in *Allen v Gulf Oil Refining Ltd* [1979] 3 WLR 523; [1979] 3 All ER 1008, and of Holland J in this Court in *Rudd v Hornsby Shire Council* (1975) 31 LGRA 120. I take the general principle to be that a nuisance may be justified by statute if that nuisance is "the inevitable consequence" of the performance of statutory duties or the exercise of statutory powers or authorities, and that, in such case, in the absence of some specific form of redress provided by the statute in question, those who may suffer by reason of the nuisance must go without remedy. Where such a justification is sought to be raised, the initial question must, so it seems to me, always be one of construction of the relevant statutory provision; if the provision either directs or permits the construction and/or operation of a precisely defined structure or work at or in a specified location, then it would seem hard to avoid the conclusion that the consequences naturally flowing from the construction and/or operation of that work were intended, and thus made lawful by the statute; in which event, unless the nuisance arose by reason of the work negligently constructed and/or operated, those affected by the nuisance would have no redress. Where, however, the duty is imposed, or the power or authority conferred, in general terms, then, prima facie, it was not the intention of the legislature that the rights of others should be invaded as a consequence of the performance of the duty or the exercise of the power or authority, and such an invasion may be justified only if it can be demonstrated that the work was **[398]** reasonably necessary, that it was properly performed in all respects, and that, if it resulted in damage, there was, in the light of the scientific knowledge then available no reasonable way in which the end directed or permitted could have been achieved without doing the damage which in fact resulted.

In the present case it seems to me that even if it is proper to equate an authority and direction (to carry out the work of construction and maintenance) given by his Excellency in Council pursuant to the provisions of the *Main Roads Act 1924*, s 25, to such an authority contained in the statute itself, the present case must fall for consideration into the second, rather than into the first, of the classes of case which I have discussed above, for not only were the site plan and the working drawings not before the Executive Council for consideration but the final working drawings appear not then to have been settled upon.

The questions thus are – the onus of so establishing being on the defendant (*Manchester Corporation v Farnworth* [1930] AC 171) – is the construction of the bridge reasonably necessary, and whether there was no reasonable way in which a road bridge could have been built over the river at or near Woodburn without obstructing navigation. ...

There can, I think, be little doubt – and no real argument to the contrary was put by the plaintiffs – that the construction of *a* road bridge at or near Woodburn was desirable and, within the meaning of that phrase as I understand the authorities, "reasonably necessary" – if only as a means of providing what the vehicular ferry did not, that is, a means of road access at times of flood. But the question remains: was it practically feasible to build a road bridge crossing the river without substantially interfering with the right of navigation upstream from the site of the bridge? There can be no doubt that, at least in the abstract, it was possible so to do by adopting the course previously adopted at Wardell, and by building a lift span bridge of appropriate size. However, such an answer is, in the defendant's submission, too simplistic; the test, in the words of Viscount Dunedin in *Manchester Corporation v Farnworth* at 183 is:

> ... not what is theoretically possible but what is possible according to the state of scientific knowledge at the time, *having also in view a certain common sense appreciation, which cannot be rigidly defined, of practical feasibility in view of situation and expense.* (my emphasis)

and, here, it was totally unreasonable to require the construction of a bridge, the cost of which would be some 66 per cent greater merely so that one **[399]** "person", the continued operations of which were under a cloud, and which could in any event, so design or build its ships as to avoid the consequences of any obstruction which might be caused by the building of the bridge as designed, could continue its operations. I do not, for one minute, doubt that the defendant, acting through its officers, has at all times, in relation to this bridge, endeavoured to carry out its duty in a proper way and, in particular, while endeavouring to achieve the most economic solution to the problem of providing a bridge at Woodburn, nonetheless sought to avoid there being created such a situation as had arisen. That, however, in my view, is not enough to justify me in holding that the defendant has "justified" the nuisance and that the proceedings should therefore be dismissed; for that result to follow I must, in my view, hold that the construction of a lift-span bridge "is some fantastic method really quite unsuited to the object in view, although it might to some extent perform the duty prescribed": *Provender Millers (Winchester) Ltd v Southampton County Council* [1940] Ch 131, at 138 per Farwell J (as he then was) and that, I believe, the evidence does not permit me to do.

This view notwithstanding, the defendant, nonetheless, submits that, as a matter of discretion, injunctive relief should not be granted, and that the plaintiffs' remedy should be limited to damages. ...

Even accepting that the grant of an injunction lies in the discretion of the court, there is, so it seems to me, a number of objections in principle to my adopting the course submitted by the defendant. They are these:

1. Such authorities as there are on the application of *Lord Cairns' Act* (*Dreyfus v Peruvian Guano Co* (1889) 43 Ch D 316; *Shelfer v City of London Electric Lighting Co* [1895] 1 Ch 287) lay down the principle that where, as here, what is sought is a quia timet injunction, the court has no jurisdiction to award damages in respect of the injury not yet committed but only threatened;

2. Even if it be otherwise, the principles laid down in relation to the manner in which the discretion to award damages ought to be exercised establish that, in contrast to the approach to be adopted where a mandatory injunction is sought (*Redland Bricks Ltd v Morris* [1970] AC 652) where what is prayed is a negative, or restrictive, injunction it is only in exceptional circumstances that damages should be awarded in lieu of an injunction (*Shelfer v City of London Electric Lighting Co* (supra)). Prima facie, once the plaintiff's legal right and its threatened infringement has been established the plaintiff is entitled to an injunction according to the ordinary principles upon which the court is in the habit of acting in such cases (*Martin v Price* [1894] 1 Ch 276, at 285; *Shelfer v City of London Electric Lighting Co* (supra) at **[400]** 321; *Redland Bricks Ltd v Morris* (supra) at 664). In the absence of exceptional circumstances, so it has been said, a departure from this general approach is justified, first, if the injury to the plaintiff's legal rights is small, secondly, if it is one which is capable of being estimated in money, thirdly, if it is one which can adequately be compensated by a small money payment, and, fourthly, if the case is one in which it would be oppressive to the defendant to grant an injunction (*Shelfer v City of London Electric Lighting Co* (supra) at 322, 323, per AL Smith LJ);

3. Even if one accepts that a plaintiff's laches, acquiescence and delay, may, where what is in suit is a private right, constitute such special circumstances as would justify the refusal of an injunction and an award of damages in its stead, where, as here, what is in suit – albeit at the instance of a private individual who claim to have suffered, or to be likely to suffer, special damage – is a

public right, I would question whether it is open to a defendant to raise, or legitimate for the court to permit a defendant to rely upon, defences, such as laches, acquiescence and delay, or estoppel, which are based upon the personal fault of the plaintiff, so as to prevent the vindication of the public right (see, for example *Attorney-General v Scott* [1905] 2 KB 160; *Attorney-General v South Staffordshire Waterworks Co* (1909) 25 TLR 408; *Southend-on-Sea Corporation v Hodgson (Wickford) Ltd* [1962] 1 QB 416; *Associated Minerals Consolidated Ltd v Wyong Shire Council* [1974] 2 NSWLR 681; [1975] AC 538);

    4. Even if it be otherwise, I would seriously doubt that, in such a case, it would be a legitimate exercise of the relevant discretion to permit any person – and, in the absence of a statutory authority so to do – and none is claimed here – the Crown has no greater right than any other member of the body politic to interfere with the right of navigation – in effect to buy the right to create and continue a public nuisance at the expense only of such damage, if any, as it may be held that one member of the public has suffered;

    5. Finally, so it seems to me, when one has, in determining whether or not the potential obstruction is likely to constitute a public nuisance, already considered the question of public benefit, to refuse an injunction on the ground that, notwithstanding that the obstruction will constitute a public nuisance, it will afford benefit to the public is – to borrow a commonly used phrase from the field of industrial arbitration – to indulge in an unjustified exercise of "double-counting".

[His Honour then reviewed the facts and concluded:]

[402] In the circumstances I have come to the conclusion that the plaintiffs have established an entitlement to relief of the kind prayed by them.

Orders accordingly

[The New South Wales Law Reports in an editorial note to this case notes that an appeal lodged by the defendant was allowed by consent, pursuant to a deed in which the parties agreed to the construction of the bridge on the payment of sufficient monetary compensation to allow the plaintiffs to move the shipyard downstream.]

Chapter 11

Defences

1. CONSENT

Giumelli v Johnston
(1991) Aust Torts Reports ¶81-085
Supreme Court of South Australia, Full Court

By participating in a body contact sport, a person may be taken to have consented to contact which otherwise would constitute trespass to the person.

KING CJ. **[68,708]** The respondent sued the appellant for damages for assault. The assault alleged was the unlawful application of force by the appellant to the respondent in the course of a football match in which they played on opposite sides. The action was tried by Judge Lunn in the District Court. He found proved an assault and battery and gave judgment against the appellant in the sum of $7,801.60. The appellant has appealed to this Court against that judgment. ...

[68,709] Assault, more properly battery, is for present purposes the unlawful application of force by one person to another without that other person's consent. The respondent's injury was sustained in the course of a bodily contact sport. The rules of Australian Rules Football permit bodily contact, including strong bodily contact, in the course of the game. Those who participate in a football match are taken to consent to the infliction on them of such physical force as is permitted by the rules of the game. It was accepted by the respondent in evidence, moreover, that some bodily contact outside the rules of the game is to be expected as an ordinary incident of a football match. The respondent in his evidence instanced "tripping, or grabbing someone's legs or pushing someone in the back" as applications of physical force which were to be expected in the course of a game. I think that it may be accepted that the consent which a participant in a football match gives to the application of physical force to him extends to physical force of that kind notwithstanding that it involves some infringement of the rules. There is no doubt, moreover, that as the respondent was in possession of the ball, a hip and shoulder bump, however forceful, would have been within the rules of the game. It is equally clear that a blow with the elbow to the face was an infringement of the rules of the game notwithstanding that the respondent was in possession of the ball.

Although a player's consent to the application of force to him in the course of the game extends not only to the application of **[68,710]** force within the rules of the game but also to certain commonly encountered infringements of the rules, such as those instanced by the respondent, such consent cannot be taken to include physical violence applied in contravention of the rules of the game by an opposing player who intends to cause bodily harm or knows, or ought to know, that such harm is the likely result of his actions.

The learned trial judge found on ample evidence that the appellant struck the respondent's face with his elbow intending to do so and intending thereby to cause him physical harm. Such an action was completely outside the scope of any consent implied from the respondent's participation in the game.

On the evidence accepted by the learned trial judge, the assault and battery were clearly proved and the appeal should be dismissed.

[Mohr and Prior JJ agreed that the appeal should be dismissed for the reasons given by King CJ.]

Appeal dismissed

Secretary, Department of Health and Community Services v JWB and SMB (Marion's Case)
(1992) 175 CLR 218
High Court of Australia

As a general principle, medical or surgical treatment involving body contact will constitute battery if carried out without the consent of the patient. The capacity of a minor to consent to medical or surgical treatment and the scope of parental power to consent to such treatment will depend on the particular circumstances of the case, such as the maturity and intellectual capacity of the minor and the nature of the proposed treatment. Arguably, the onus of proof of consent is on the defendant, that is, the person carrying out the medical or surgical treatment.

[Marion was the pseudonym of a person aged 14 years at the time of this appeal. She suffered from a severe intellectual disability and was unable to care for herself. Her parents applied to the Family Court for an order authorising the performance of sterilisation procedures for the purpose of preventing pregnancy and menstruation, with its psychological and behavioural consequences or, alternatively, for a declaration that it would be lawful for them to consent to such a procedure. The appeal to the High Court concerned, inter alia, two questions: whether Marion's parents could lawfully authorise the carrying out of a sterilisation procedure without an order of the court and, if not, whether the authority of the Family Court of Australia was required by law to enable the procedure to be carried out lawfully. The judgment of the majority, answering "No" and "Yes" to these two questions, is extracted below. Brennan, Deane and McHugh JJ gave different answers to these questions. The judgment of McHugh J is extracted for its discussion of the burden of proof with respect to consent.]

MASON CJ, DAWSON, TOOHEY and GAUDRON JJ. ... **[231]** Two major issues are **[232]** involved in the first question in the case stated. The first is the threshhold question of consent; whether a child, intellectually disabled or not, is capable, in law or in fact, of consenting to medical treatment on his or her own behalf. The second arises where a child is incapable of consenting. That issue is whether sterilisation is, in any event, outside the scope of a parent to consent to on behalf of his or her own behalf. ...

Assault, consent, medical treatment
In a case such as the present one, it is primarily the prospect of surgical intervention which attracts the interest of the law. This is because the law treats as unlawful, both criminally and civilly, conduct which constitutes an assault on or a trespass to the person. Therefore it is the legality of the specific medical treatment amounting to a hysterectomy and ovariectomy (or, it may be, tubal ligation or vasectomy) which must be the focus of inquiry. However, to characterize intervention comprising sterilization as "medical treatment" is already to make assumptions and to narrow the inquiry, perhaps inappropriately. As will become clear, it is the very fact that sterilization implies more than medical, or surgical, treatment that is crucial to the central issue in this appeal.

The *Criminal Code Act 1983* (NT) ("the Code") provides that an act is unlawful if it is done "without authorization, justification or excuse" (s 1. See also ss 24 and 25.) Section 26 of the Code provides:

"(1) An act, omission or event is authorized if it is done, made or caused –

(a) in the exercise of a right granted or recognized by law;

(b) ...

(c) ... ; or

(d) subject to subsection (3), pursuant to authority, permission or licence lawfully granted."

"Assault" is defined in s 187 of the Code to mean:

"(a) the direct or indirect application of force to a person without his consent ... ; or

(b) the attempted or threatened application of such force other than the application of force –

(c) ... when giving any medical treatment or first aid reasonably needed by the person to whom it is given"...

[233] Section 188 of the Code makes an unlawful assault an offence. A person who unlawfully causes grievous harm to another is guilty of a crime (s 181).

The corollary of these provisions, which embody the notion that, prima facie, any physical contact or threat of it is unlawful, is a right in each person to bodily integrity. That is to say, the right in an individual to choose what occurs with respect to his or her own person. In his *Commentaries*, 17th ed (1830), vol 3, p 120, Blackstone wrote:

"[T]he law cannot draw the line between different degrees of violence, and therefore totally prohibits the first and lowest stage of it; every man's person being sacred, and no other having a right to meddle with it, in any the slightest manner."

Consent ordinarily has the effect of transforming what would otherwise be unlawful into accepted, and therefore acceptable, contact. Consensual contact does not, ordinarily, amount to assault. However, there are exceptions to the requirement for, and the neutralizing effect of, consent and therefore qualifications to the very broadly stated principle of bodily inviolability. In some instances consent is insufficient to make application of force to another person lawful and some-times consent is not needed to make force lawful. For example, a person in the Northern Territory cannot render a killing lawful by consenting to be killed (The Code, s 26(3)) and at common law a comparable qualification exists with respect to assault in some circumstances. *Attorney-General's Reference (No 6 of 1980)* [1981] QB 715 held that those entering into a consensual fight were guilty of assault if they intended to inflict bodily harm: *R v Coney* (1882) 8 QBD 534; *R v Donovan* [1934] 2 KB 498.

The rationale for this exception appears to rest in the idea that some harms involve public, not just personal, interests: *R v Coney* (1882) 8 QBD, at p 549; and see Glanville Williams, *Textbook of Criminal Law*, 2nd ed (1983), pp 582-583, 586-587. Moreover, the absence of consent is irrelevant in a lawful arrest or in circumstances which amount to self-defence. A further exception of this kind is reflected in *Collins v Wilcock* [1984] 1 WLR 1172, at p 1177; [1984] 3 All ER 374, at p 378, where it was said that in respect of physical contact arising from the exigencies of everyday life – jostling in a street, social contact at parties and the like – there is an implied consent "by all who move in society and so expose themselves to the risk of bodily contact", or that such encounters fall "within a general exception embracing all physical contact which is generally acceptable in the ordinary conduct of daily life".

[234] Medical treatment of adults with full mental capacity does not come within any of the exceptions mentioned (*In re F* [1990] 2 AC 1, at pp 73-74, per Lord Goff of Chieveley; cf *Wilson v Pringle*, [1987] QB 237, at p 252). It may fall within s 187(c) of the Code. The factor necessary to render such treatment lawful when it would otherwise be an assault is, therefore, consent. The Code impliedly treats non-consensual medical treatment as an assault by making it a form of "grievous harm" which may be consented to (s 26(3)). This, again, reflects the principle of personal inviolability echoed in the well-known words of Cardozo J in *Schloendorff v Society of New York Hospital* 105 NE 92 (1914), at p 93:

"Every human being of adult years and sound mind has a right to determine what shall be done with his own body; and a surgeon who performs an operation without his patient's consent commits an assault."

Sterilization comes within the category of medical treatment to which a legally competent person can consent. ... But what of medical treatment of those who, because of incapacity, cannot consent? What, besides personal consent, can render surgical intervention lawful?

The reasons for, and circumstances of, incapacity differ greatly. An adult who is normally of full mental capacity may be temporarily unable to consent due to, for example, an accident resulting in unconsciousness. Or a child's parents may be temporarily unavailable to give or withhold consent to emergency medical treatment of their child. In the Northern Territory these circumstances are dealt with by the *Emergency Medical Operations Act 1973* (NT). ... The different nature and status of parental consent as opposed to personal consent is reflected in s 3(4)(b) of the Act which makes provision for a doctor to perform an emergency operation on a child even in the absence of parental consent ... . **[235]** In the case of medical treatment of those who cannot consent because of incapacity due to minority, the automatic reference point is the minor's parent or other guardian. Parental consent, when effective, is itself an exception to the need for personal consent to medical treatment ... .

[236] The scope of parental power
The two major issues referred to at the beginning of this judgment arise more specifically at this point in an examination of parental consent as an exception to the need for personal consent to medical treatment. As noted earlier, the first issue relates to the important threshold question of consent: whether a minor with an intellectual disability is or will ever be capable of giving or refusing informed consent to sterilisation on his or her own behalf. Where the answer to that question is negative the second question arises. Is sterilisation, in any case, in a special category which falls outside the **[237]** scope of a parent to consent to treatment? Is such a procedure a kind of intervention which is, as a general rule, excluded from the scope of parental power?

By virtue of legislation, the age of majority in all States and Territories of Australia is eighteen years ... . Every person below that age is, therefore, a minor and under the *Family Law Act* the powers of a guardian, generally speaking, cease at that age (s 63F). In some States a minor's capacity to give informed consent to medical treatment is regulated by statute (*Minors (Property and Contracts) Act 1970* (NSW) s 49(2) and *Consent to Medical and Dental Procedures Act 1985* (SA) s 6(1)) but in the Northern Territory the common law still applies. The common law in Australia has been uncertain as to whether minors under sixteen can consent to medical treatment in any circumstances ... However, the recent House of Lords decision in *Gillick v West Norfolk AHA* [1986] AC 112 is of persuasive authority. The proposition endorsed by the majority in that case was that parental power to consent to medical treatment on behalf of a child diminishes gradually as the child's capacities and maturity grow and that this rate of development depends on the individual child. Lord Scarman said (at pp 183-184):

> "Parental rights ... do not wholly disappear until the age of majority. ... But the common law has never treated such rights as sovereign or beyond review and control. Nor has our law ever treated the child as other than a person with capacities and rights recognised by law. The principle of the law ... is that parental rights are derived from parental duty and exist only so long as they are needed for the protection of the person and property of the child."

A minor is, according to this principle, capable of giving informed consent when he or she "achieves a sufficient understanding and intelligence to enable him or her to understand fully what is proposed" (at p 189, and see pp 169, 194-195).

This approach, though lacking the certainty of a fixed age rule, **[238]** accords with experience and with psychology. The psychological model developed by Piaget (Piaget and Inhelder, *The Psychology of the Child* (1969)), one of the leading theorists in this area, suggests that the capacity to make an intelligent choice, involving the ability to consider different options and their consequences, generally appears in a child somewhere between the ages of eleven and fourteen. But again, even this is a generalisation. There is no guarantee that any particular child, at fourteen, is capable of giving informed consent nor that any particular ten year old cannot. ... It should be followed in this country as part of the common law. ...

Of course, the fact that a child suffers an intellectual disability makes consideration of the capacity to consent a different matter. The age at which intellectually disabled children can consent will be higher than for children within the normal range of abilities. However, terms such as "mental disability", "intellectual handicap" or "retardation" lack precision. There is no essential cause of disability; those who come within these categories form a heterogeneous group. And since most intellectually disabled people are borderline to mildly disabled, there is no reason to assume that all disabled children are incapable of giving consent to treatment. ...

Any rule which purports to apply to the group of intellectually disabled children therefore involves sweeping generalization.

It may also be said, in this context, that not only are there widely varying kinds and consequences of intellectual disability but such handicaps, possibly more so than other forms of disability, are often surrounded by misconceptions on the part of others in society, misconceptions often involving an underestimation of a person's [239] ability. This applies particularly with respect to sexuality and sexual identity which are central to the question here. Although complex for everyone, these matters are especially complex for disabled persons, sometimes because of ignorance and misconceptions on the part of those on whose care disabled persons find themselves dependent. ...

To conclude this aspect, it is important to stress that it cannot be presumed that an intellectually disabled child is, by virtue of his or her disability, incapable of giving consent to treatment. The capacity of a child to give informed consent to medical treatment depends on the rate of development of each individual. And if *Gillick* is taken to reflect the common law in Australia, as we think it now does, these propositions are true as a matter of law in the Northern Territory.

[After considering the authorities in Australia, New Zealand, England and the United States, their Honours concluded that sterilization is a kind of intervention which should be excluded from the ordinary scope of parental power to consent to medical treatment. They concluded that court authority is necessary as a procedural safeguard. Their Honours emphasised that this was not a case where sterilisation was an incidental result of surgery performed to cure a disease or correct some malfunction].

McHUGH J. ...**[309] The need for consent to the carrying out of a surgical procedure**
It is the central thesis of the common law doctrine of trespass to the person that the voluntary choices and decisions of an adult person of sound mind concerning what is or is not done to his or her body must be respected and accepted, irrespective of what others, including doctors, may think is in the best interests of that particular person. To this general thesis, there is an exception: a person cannot consent to the infliction of grievous bodily harm without a "good reason" (*Attorney-General's Reference (No 6 of 1980)* [1981] 1 QB 715, at p 719). But save in this exceptional case, the common law respects and preserves the autonomy of adult persons of sound mind with respect to their bodies. By doing so, the common law accepts that a person has rights of control and self-determination in respect of his or her body which other persons must respect. Those rights can only be altered with the consent of the person concerned. Thus, the legal requirement of consent to bodily interference protects the [310] autonomy and dignity of the individual and limits the power of others to interfere with that person's body.

At common law, therefore, every surgical procedure is an assault unless it is authorized, justified or excused by law. The law draws no lines between different degrees of violence, "every man's person being sacred, and no other having a right to meddle with it, in any the slightest manner" (Blackstone, *Commentaries*, 17th ed (1830), vol 3, p 120). A person who inflicts harm upon another must justify the doing of the harm. He or she may do so by proving that the harm was lawfully consented to or that the harm occurred in circumstances which the law recognizes as a justification or excuse: *Collins v Wilcock* [1984] 1 WLR 1172, at p 1177; [1984] 3 All ER 374, at p 378. Because a surgical procedure necessarily involves the touching and usually the infliction of bodily harm on a patient, the carrying out of such a procedure is an assault unless the patient or that person's legally authorized representative has consented to the procedure: *In re F* [1990] 2 AC 1, at pp 55, 72.

In *Schloendorff v Society of New York Hospital* 105 NE 92 (1914), at p 93, Judge Cardozo said:
"Every human being of adult years and sound mind has a right to determine what shall be done with his own body; and a surgeon who performs an operation without his patient's consent commits an assault for which he is liable in damages."

Consent is not necessary, however, where a surgical procedure or medical treatment must be performed in an emergency and the patient does not have the capacity to consent and no legally authorized representative is available to give consent on his or her behalf.

In England, the onus is on the plaintiff to prove lack of consent: *Freeman v Home Office (No 2)*, [1984] QB 524, at p 539. That view has the support of some academic writers in Australia (see Balkin and Davis, *Law of Torts* (1991), pp 38-39; Luntz and Hambly, *Torts: Cases and Commentary*, 3rd ed (1992), pp 680-681; Blay, "Onus of Proof of Consent in an Action for Trespass to the Person", *Australian Law Journal*, vol 61 (1987) 25) but it is opposed by other academic writers in Australia (see Fleming, *Law of Torts*, 7th ed (1987), p 72; Trindade and Cane, *Law of Torts in Australia*, (1985), pp 39-40). It is opposed by Canadian authority: *Hambley v Shepley* (1967) 63 DLR (2d) 94, at p 95; *Kelly v Hazlett* (1976) 75 DLR (3d) 536, at p 556; *Allan v New Mount Sinai Hospital* (1980) 109 DLR (3d) 634. It is also opposed by Australian authority: *Hart v Herron* [1984] Aust Torts R 80-201; *Sibley v Milutinovic* [1990] Aust Torts R 81-013. Notwithstanding the English [311] view, I think that the onus is on the defendant to prove consent. Consent is a claim of "leave and licence". Such a claim must be pleaded and proved by the defendant in an action for trespass to land: *Kavanagh v Gudge* (1844) 7 Man & G 316 [135 ER 132]; *Wood v Manley* (1839) 11 Ad & E 34 [113 ER 325]; *Plenty v Dillon* (1991) 171 CLR 635, at p 647. It must be pleaded in a defamation action when the defendant claims that the plaintiff consented to the publication (see *Loveday v Sun Newspapers Ltd* (1938) 59 CLR 503, at p 525). The *Common Law Procedure Act 1852* (15 & 16 Vict c 76) (Sched B 44) also required any "defence" of leave and licence to be pleaded and proved. However, those who contend that the plaintiff must negative consent in an action for trespass to the person deny that consent is a matter of leave and licence. They contend that lack of consent is an essential element of the action for trespass to a person. I do not accept that this is so. The essential element of the tort is an intentional or reckless, direct act of the defendant which makes or has the effect of causing contact with the body of the plaintiff. Consent may make the act lawful, but, if there is no evidence on the issue, the tort is made out. The contrary view is inconsistent with a person's right of bodily integrity. Other persons do not have the right to interfere with an individual's body unless he or she proves lack of consent to the interference.

[Consequential orders were made, substituting the answers of the High Court for those of the Full Court of the Family Court to the case stated.]

Appeal allowed

2. VOLENTI NON FIT INJURIA

Rootes v Shelton
(1967) 116 CLR 383
High Court of Australia

The law of negligence applies as between the participants in a sport or game. However, participants in a sport or game voluntarily assume such risk of injury as is inherent in the activity.

BARWICK CJ. **[384]** The appellant [plaintiff], an experienced water skier, was skiing on the Macquarie River at Dubbo, performing in company with other experienced water skiers an operation known as "crossovers", in which three skiers being towed with ropes of different lengths pass from side to side across the wake of the towing boat and across each other's paths. The appellant at the material time was the middle of the three men and thus in crossing had to pass his tow rope over the skier ahead of him and crouch under the rope of the skier behind him.

The towing boat was being driven along a fairly straight and sufficiently wide stretch of river during the manoeuvre, travelling at thirty to thirty-five miles per hour. As the appellant was passing to the starboard side of the boat's wake he was temporarily blinded by spray and had need to clear his eyes before starting to turn inwards again. This may possibly have caused him to swing wider in executing his manoeuvre than otherwise he might have done. However, when he could see again he was faced with a stationary boat, as he says, about six feet away from him. He endeavoured to avoid colliding with it but was unable to do so. In the result he was severely injured. He sued the respondent [defendant] who was the driver of the towing boat for failure to take due care in the control of the boat and for failure to warn him of the presence of the stationary boat.

[385] It seems that it was usual, as the appellant, the respondent and the other participants conducted their water skiing, to have an observer as well as a driver in the towing boat: it was also usual for the driver or the observer to signal the presence of any obstacle which was seen in or on the water along which the tow was being made. Although on this occasion there was another person in the towing boat as well as the driver, as I read the evidence, that person was not acting as observer nor was any signal given by the driver warning of the presence of the stationary boat of whose presence or position it was conceded the driver at material times was aware.

The jury found for the plaintiff: but the Supreme Court (Court of Appeal Division) set aside the verdict on the ground that the respondent driver of the towing vehicle owed no relevant duty to the appellant, both being participants in a sport who had, by engaging in it, accepted the risks of injury which might be involved in taking part in it.

I am clearly of opinion that the Supreme Court was in error in setting aside the verdict of the jury and in the reasons expressed for doing so. I find it unnecessary to canvass these reasons in detail: it is sufficient in the circumstances if I set out my own conclusion as succinctly as possible.

By engaging in a sport or pastime the participants may be held to have accepted risks which are inherent in that sport or pastime: the tribunal of fact can make its own assessment of what the accepted risks are: but this does not eliminate all duty of care of the one participant to the other. Whether or not such a duty arises, and, if it does, its extent, must necessarily depend in each case upon its own circumstances. In this connexion, the rules of the sport or game may constitute one of those circumstances: but, in my opinion, they are neither definitive of the existence nor of the extent of the duty; nor does their breach or non-observance necessarily constitute a breach of any duty found to exist.

No doubt there are risks inherent in the nature of water skiing, which because they are inherent may be regarded as accepted by those who engage in the sport. The risk of a skier running into an obstruction which, because submerged or partially submerged or for some other reason, is unlikely to be seen by the driver or observer of the towing boat, may well be regarded as inherent in the pastime. Or that situation may be analysed by saying that that driver or observer owes no duty in respect of the unobservable obstruction. But neither the possibility that the driver may fail to avoid, if practicable, or, if not, to signal the presence of an observed or observable obstruction nor that the driver will tow [386] the skier dangerously close to such an obstruction is, in my opinion, a risk inherent in the nature of sport. In this connexion an observable obstruction is one which would be observed by reasonable attention by the driver and observer to their respective tasks. That there is a recognized practice amongst participants that the driver or the observer should signal the presence of an observed obstruction is no more than emphatic that the skier does not accept these possibilities as risks which he must run without recourse. There was, in my opinion, no evidence that any of the risks to which I have referred were inherent in the sport.

In my opinion, the appellant was entitled to have the respondent exercise reasonable care in carrying out his part of the operation in which they were co-operating: failure to signal the presence of the stationary launch and towing the appellant dangerously close to it, particularly if it was thought that the driver ought to have realized that the appellant might well be temporarily blinded at times by the spray from the wash of the boat during his manoeuvres, could clearly be regarded as breaches of that duty.

If it is said that a participant in a sport or pastime has voluntarily assumed a risk which is not inherent in that sport or pastime so as to exclude a relevant duty of care, it must rest on the party who makes that claim to establish the case in accordance with recognized principles. In the present case there was, in my opinion, no evidence whatever to support the view that the appellant voluntarily assumed any of the risks which I have described. ...

I would restore the jury's verdict.

KITTO J. ... **[390]** It seems to me that when a judge is directing a jury as to the acceptance of risk which a plaintiff's participation in a sport has implied, it is not satisfactory for him to confine their attention to the risks "inherent" in the sport, or the risks that are "recognized" (in the sense of "perceived") in it; for not only are these expressions imprecise – they may refer, for example, to risks necessarily incurred, or reasonably to be expected, or obviously possible – but the question to be decided is regarded by the common law rather from the defendant's point of view: was the defendant's conduct which caused injury to the plaintiff reasonable in all the circumstances, including as part of the circumstances the inferences fairly to be drawn by the defendant from the plaintiff's participation in what was going on at the time.

Accordingly I am of the opinion that the learned judges below should have held that on the evidence as to the nature of the skiing that was being carried on at the time of the accident it was open to the jury to find, first, that the appellant did not by his participation indicate to the respondent a willingness to accept either the risk of the respondent's steering a course which was closer to the stationary boat than was reasonable in the circumstances, or the risk of his omitting to take all reasonable measures to warn the appellant of the position of the stationary boat in time for him to avoid it; secondly, that the respondent did steer a course that was closer than was reasonable or omitted to take reasonable measures to warn the appellant, or both; and, thirdly, that that act or omission or each of them was a cause of the appellant's injuries. ...

I would allow the appeal and restore the [jury's] verdict.

[McTiernan J agreed with the conclusions of Barwick CJ. Owen J delivered a judgment along the same lines as that of Barwick CJ. Taylor J delivered a judgment in which he expressed substantial agreement with Owen J.]

Appeal allowed

3. CONTRIBUTORY NEGLIGENCE

(a) Conduct Amounting to Contributory Negligence

Caterson v Commissioner for Railways
(1973) 128 CLR 99
High Court of Australia

At common law, contributory negligence is a complete defence to a claim founded on negligence. Contributory negligence is the failure of a person to take reasonable care for his or her own safety. However, it is a question of fact whether, in response to a situation of danger or inconvenience created by the defendant's negligence, the plaintiff has been guilty of contributory negligence.

[The plaintiff (appellant), accompanied by his 14-year-old son, had driven a friend some 40 miles to a country railway station, in order that the friend might catch the Brisbane-Sydney express. The plaintiff carried the friend's luggage into the carriage, and as he was leaving the carriage he noticed that the train had started to move. No one in the carriage heard any warning that the train was about to depart. The next station at which the train was scheduled to stop was some 80 miles away. The train was not travelling very fast when the plaintiff, thinking of his son on the platform 40 miles from home, jumped on to the platform and was injured. There was no direct evidence that there was a communication cord in the carriage, but there was evidence from which it might have been inferred that there was such a cord.]

GIBBS J. **[105]** This is an appeal from a judgment of the Court of Appeal Division of the Supreme Court of New South Wales. An action was brought in that Court by the appellant against the respondent, the Commissioner for Railways, for damages for personal injuries sustained by the appellant by reason of the negligence of the respondent. The action was tried by a judge **[106]** sitting with a jury, and a verdict was entered for the appellant. The Court of Appeal ordered that the verdict be set aside and that in lieu thereof a verdict be entered for the respondent. ...

[His Honour then set out the facts and held that there was evidence on which the jury was entitled to find in favour of the plaintiff on the issues of duty of care, breach of duty and causation.]

[111] If, on the other hand, the appellant by jumping from the train failed to take reasonable care for his own safety he could not recover from the respondent damages in respect of his injuries because at the relevant time contributory negligence was still a complete defence in New South Wales. ... The question remains whether the appellant by the very act of jumping from the train failed to take reasonable care for his own safety, and thus acted unreasonably.

No doubt on the evidence it was open to the jury to find that the appellant did not take reasonable care for his own safety and that his injuries were caused by his own want of care. It was submitted by the respondent that it was not open to the jury to take any other view. It was said that the principle which is sometimes referred to as the doctrine of alternative danger, and of which *Jones v Boyce* (1816) 1 Stark 493; 171 ER 540 is an early example, has no application unless the plaintiff has been placed by the defendant's negligence in a position in which he has to choose between two dangers: it will never be reasonable, so it was said, to take a risk of injury merely to avoid an inconvenience, however great. I cannot agree with that submission which seems to me inconsistent with the decisions in *Robson v North Eastern Railway Co* (1875) LR 10 QB 271 (see especially (1875) LR 10 QB at p 275) and *Sayers v Harlow Urban District Council* [1958] 1 WLR 623. Where a plaintiff has by reason of the negligence of the defendant been so placed that he can only escape from inconvenience by taking a risk, the question whether his action in taking the risk is unreasonable is to be answered by weighing the degree of inconvenience to which he will be subjected against the risk that he takes in order to try to escape from it – cf per Lord Evershed MR in *Sayers v Harlow Urban District Council* [1958] 1 WLR, at p 626.

[112] No one could doubt that it would be negligent to jump from a train travelling at full speed simply to avoid the inconvenience of being carried on to another station. On the other hand, a person who wished to avoid being carried on to a distant station might not unreasonably jump out from a train which was travelling very slowly. The question at what speed the train was travelling was therefore in the present case a critical one. Having regard to the evidence to which I have referred it seems to me that the jury was entitled to conclude that the train had not attained any great speed when the appellant jumped from it. The jury then had to weigh the inconvenience which the appellant would suffer if he remained on the train against the risk of leaving a train which was moving at the speed at which they considered that it was travelling. They also had to consider the question whether the appellant failed to take reasonable care for his own safety by leaving the train instead of pulling the communication cord, assuming one had been provided. In this connexion they could have considered the appellant's evidence that he jumped instinctively and could have concluded that in the stress of the moment it was not to be expected that he would think of the possibility that the carriage would be provided with a communication cord or, alternatively, that it was not necessarily unreasonable for him to endeavour to leave the train immediately rather than to spend time looking for a communication cord, for if there had proved to be no cord the lapse of time would have increased the hazard of leaving the train, which was gaining speed. Bearing all the circumstances in mind I find it impossible to conclude that the jury was bound to find that the appellant's injuries were caused or contributed to by any negligence on his own part. ...

I consider that there was evidence on which the jury could reasonably find for the appellant, and that the respondent was not as a matter of law entitled to a verdict. ...

I would allow the appeal.

[McTiernan J delivered a concurring judgment. Barwick CJ and Menzies J delivered judgments in which they expressed agreement with Gibbs J. Stephen J agreed with the reasons for judgment of Barwick CJ and Gibbs J.]

Appeal allowed

(b) Apportionment Legislation

Pennington v Norris
(1956) 96 CLR 10
High Court of Australia

Under the apportionment legislation in each Australian State and Territory, the damages recoverable by a plaintiff guilty of contributory negligence shall be reduced by such extent as the court considers "just and equitable" having regard to the comparative degree to which the conduct of the plaintiff and the defendant departed from the standard of care of the reasonable person.

THE COURT. [DIXON CJ, WEBB, FULLAGAR and KITTO JJ] **[11]** This is an appeal from the Supreme Court of Tasmania (Crisp J). The appellant was the plaintiff in an action in which he claimed damages for personal injuries sustained when he was struck by a motor car driven by the respondent. His Honour found that the damage had been caused by negligent conduct on the part of both parties and that each was equally at fault. He assessed the plaintiff's damages at £9,178 8s 0d but, acting in pursuance of the *Tortfeasors and Contributory Negligence Act 1954* (Tas), he reduced these damages by one-half and gave judgment for £4,589 4s 0d. The plaintiff maintains that the learned judge was wrong in finding the plaintiff at fault, or at least in finding him equally at fault with the defendant, and he says that he should have had judgment for the full amount of £9,178 8s 0d, or at least for a sum substantially larger than one-half of that amount. ...

[Their Honours then referred to the facts.]

[13] The *Tortfeasors and Contributory Negligence Act 1954* (Tas) by s 4(1) provides: "Where a person suffers damage as the result partly of his own fault and partly of the fault of any other person, a claim in respect of that damage is not defeated by reason of the fault of the person suffering the damage, but the damages recoverable in respect thereof shall be reduced to such extent as the court thinks just and equitable, having regard to the claimant's share in **[14]** the responsibility for the damage". The word "fault" is defined by s 2 as meaning "negligence, breach of statutory duty, or any other act or omission that gives rise to a liability in tort, or would, but for this Act, give rise to the defence of contributory negligence". ...

[15] Mr Wright [counsel for the appellant] ... contended that, if there must be an "apportionment" under the Act, the learned judge took a view altogether too unfavourable to the plaintiff, and that his damages should be reduced by a very much smaller proportion than one-half. He suggested ten per cent as the maximum reduction that could properly be made.

It is clear that the Act intends to give a very wide discretion to the judge or jury entrusted with the original task of making the apportionment. Much latitude must be allowed to the original **[16]** tribunal in arriving at a judgment as to what is just and equitable. It is to be expected, therefore, that cases will be rare in which the apportionment made can be successfully challenged: see *British Fame (Owners) v Macgregor (Owners)* [1943] AC 197 and *Ingram v United Automobile Service Ltd* [1943] KB 612. But, giving full weight to these considerations in the present case, we are unable to avoid the conclusion that, in apportioning the responsibility equally, his Honour must have overlooked certain features of the case, and that the amount by which he reduced the assessed damages cannot really be supported.

The only guide which the statute provides is that it requires regard to be had to "the claimant's share in the responsibility for the damage". As to the effect of this see generally an article by Mr Douglas Payne, *Reduction of Damages for Contributory Negligence* (1955) 18 Mod LR 344. What has to be done is to arrive at a "just and equitable" apportionment as between the plaintiff and the defendant of the "responsibility" for the damage. It seems clear that this must of necessity involve a comparison of culpability. By "culpability" we do not mean moral blameworthiness but degree of departure from the standard of care of the reasonable man. To institute a comparison in respect of blameworthiness in such a case as the present seems more or less impracticable, because, while the defendant's negligence is a breach of duty owed to other persons and therefore blameworthy, the plaintiff's "contributory" negligence is not a breach of any duty at all, and it is difficult to impute "moral" blame to one who is careless merely of his own safety.

Here, in our opinion, the negligence of the defendant was in a high degree more culpable, more gross, than that of the plaintiff. The plaintiff's conduct was *ex hypothesi* careless and unreasonable but, after all, it was the sort of thing that is very commonly done: he simply did not look when a reasonably careful man would have looked. We think too that in this case the very fact that his conduct did not endanger the defendant or anybody else is a material consideration. The defendant's position was entirely different. The learned judge found only that he was negligent in not keeping a proper look-out, but there were several other important elements in the case, as Mr Wright pointed out. We think, indeed, that the equal allocation of responsibility by his Honour must have proceeded from an overlooking of these elements. The first matter is his speed. It could not on the evidence have been found to be less than thirty miles per hour. Again, there was a large number of people in the [17] vicinity, – the defendant himself says that he noticed "quite a number of people about". The hotels, of which there were three in the immediate vicinity, had closed a very short time previously. It was a misty night, and the road was wet. Visibility must have been impaired by these factors, and it was further impaired by mistiness on the inside and outside of the windscreen. To drive at thirty miles per hour in a town at night under these circumstances seems to us to have been to do an obviously dangerous thing, and to have amounted to negligence of far greater culpability than anything that can possibly be attributed to the plaintiff.

Having regard to these factors, and to all the circumstances or the case, we are of opinion that a fair and reasonable allocation of the responsibility for the damage done is to attribute it, as to eighty per cent to the defendant and, as to twenty per cent to the plaintiff. The appeal should be allowed, and the judgment of the Supreme Court of Tasmania varied so as to give effect to this apportionment.

Appeal allowed

[In *Podrebersek v Australian Iron & Steel Pty Ltd* (1985) 59 ALR 529, Gibbs CJ, Mason, Wilson, Brennan and Deane JJ made the following observation at 532-533:

[532] The making of an apportionment as between a plaintiff and a defendant of their respective shares in the responsibility for the damage involves a comparison both of culpability, ie of the degree of departure from the standard of care of the reasonable man (*Pennington v Norris* (1956) 96 CLR 10 at 16) and of the relative importance of the acts of the parties in causing [533] the damage: *Stapley v Gypsum Mines Ltd* [1953] AC 663 at 682; *Smith v McIntyre* [1958] Tas SR 36 at 42-49 and *Broadhurst v Millman* [1976] VR 208 at 219, and cases there cited. It is the whole conduct of each negligent party in relation to the circumstances of the accident which must be subjected to comparative examination. The significance of the various elements involved in such an examination will vary from case to case; for example, the circumstances of some cases may be such that a comparison of the relative importance of the acts of the parties in causing the damage will be of little, if any, importance.]

(c) Intentional Torts

Horkin v North Melbourne Football Club Social Club
[1983] VR 153
Supreme Court of Victoria

Contributory negligence is no defence in a claim for intentional battery.

[The plaintiff sued the defendant for battery alleging that he was violently ejected from the defendant's premises whereby he suffered personal injuries. The defendant maintained that the plaintiff was a trespasser who had been removed by its employees using no more force than reasonably necessary. Brooking J found for the plaintiff on this issue holding that the force used was excessive. The defendant also alleged that the plaintiff's damages should be reduced for contributory negligence. The judgment is extracted on this issue.]

BROOKING J. ... **[157]** I turn now to the matter of contributory negligence. ...

I find that the plaintiff was guilty of contributory negligence in that he became intoxicated while on licensed premises and failed to leave when asked in a proper manner to do so, and given a reasonable opportunity of doing so, by authorized employees of the defendant whom he knew or believed to be such, and instead of having attempted to push his way past one of the defendant's employees and penetrate further into the premises, so bringing about the situation in which the defendant's employees, acting lawfully by way of removing a trespasser, found it necessary to use, and did use, force to expel him by marching him to the door. His attempting to push past the defendant's employee did technically amount to a battery on his part. He was intoxicated and argumentative and speaking loudly and had tried to force his way through, and it was only natural and proper that he should be seized and removed from the premises as quickly as possible. He created a situation in which the use of force to expel him was the natural and lawful consequence of his own misbehaviour. The degree of force used was, in the end, after he had reached the door, unlawful, and was not the necessary consequence of his own condition and behaviour, but in my opinion a causal connection has been shown between his own negligence and his injury. ...

But does contributory negligence operate to reduce damages in an action for battery? Trespass to the person may be either intentional or negligent, **[158]** and accordingly there can be a negligent battery so far as the law of tort is concerned, although in the criminal law intention or recklessness is necessary: *R v Venna* [1976] QB 421; [1975] 3 All ER 788; *R v Bacash* [1981] VR 923, at p 935. In the present case, the application of force to the plaintiff's body constituting the battery was "intended" on any view of the meaning of that term. Although purists would in Australia (*Williams v Milotin* (1957) 97 CLR 465), but perhaps not in England (*Letang v Cooper* [1965] 1 QB 232; [1964] 2 All ER 929; cf *Gorely v Codd* [1966] 3 All ER 891; [1967] 1 WLR 19, at p 25), still speak of a negligent battery for civil purposes, I shall use the term "battery" to designate an intentional application of force.

"Fault" is defined in s 25 of the *Wrongs Act* 1958 as: "negligence breach of statutory duty or other act or omission which gives rise to a liability in tort or would, apart from this Part, give rise to the defence of contributory negligence". If the words, "negligence breach of statutory duty or other act or omission which gives rise to a liability in tort", which I shall call the first limb of the definition, apply to a plaintiff, then it will in the present case be necessary to consider whether the trespass to land of which the plaintiff was guilty (for he had become a trespasser) or the battery he committed by trying to force his way past Sexton was a cause of the damage which he suffered. If, on the other hand, the first limb of the definition is inapplicable to a plaintiff, the present plaintiff's damages are liable to reduction under the statute only if at common law contributory negligence afforded a defence to an action for battery.

The view that the first limb is not confined to defendants has the support of Bright and Jacobs JJ in *Venning v Chin* (1974) 10 SASR 299, at pp 324 and 327, Moller J in *Hoebergen v Koppens* [1974] 2 NZLR 597, at pp 601 and 605-6, and, it seems, Lord Denning MR, speaking for the Court of Appeal, in *Murphy v Culhane* [1977] QB 94, at p 99, where, however, the question is not shown to have received any real consideration. Luntz in *Assessment of Damages for Personal Injury and Death*, 1974, para 1.820, regards the question as an open one. In *Winter v Bennett* [1956] VLR 612, at p 622, Herring CJ and Barry J treat the first limb of the definition as concerned only with defendants. Whether or not this observation binds me, I am content to adopt it, for it accords with my own view and is supported by the opinions expressed in *Quinn v Burch Bros (Builders) Ltd* [1966] 2 QB 370, at p 378; [1966] 2 All ER 283, *AS James Pty Ltd v Duncan* [1970] VR 705, at p 726; *Venning v Chin, supra*, at pp 316-7, per Bray CJ; Glanville Williams, *Joint Torts and Contributory Negligence*, 1951, p 318; and Winfield and Jolowicz, *Tort,* 11th ed, p 135.

It follows that the defendant in the present case cannot rely on the torts of trespass to land and battery committed by the plaintiff to found an apportionment and that apportionment is not possible unless at common law the defendant to an action for battery could set up contributory negligence.

While in Australia the plaintiff in a running down case can still sue in trespass whether the injury was inflicted intentionally or negligently (*Williams v Milotin* (1957) 97 CLR 465), it is not to be thought that an Australian court would permit a plaintiff who sued in trespass to escape the consequences of his own negligence: at common law, and under the **[159]** apportionment legislation, the plea of contributory negligence is in a highway case available to a defendant sued for a negligent trespass. An examination of the cases and the old books on pleading and practice has led me, as it led Bray CJ (with whom Jacobs J agreed) in *Venning v Chin* (1974) 10 SASR 299, to the conclusion that the common law afforded the defence to a negligent defendant sued in trespass in respect of a highway accident; the case was carried to the High Court but not on that point ((1975) 49 ALJR 378). Indeed, it seems to me, as it seemed to Diplock J (as he then was) in *Fowler v Lanning* [1959] 1 QB 426, at pp 433-4; [1959] 1 All ER 290, that at common law contributory negligence was an answer in all cases of unintentional trespass to the person, on or off the highway. What does remain unresolved is whether the defence of contributory negligence formerly availed, and now by statute avails, the intentional trespasser. In *Venning v Chin, supra,* at p 317, Bray CJ, in a judgment to which I acknowledge my indebtedness, thought it clear that at common law the defence was not open if the trespass to the person was intentional.

Almost 100 years ago Higinbotham J had to deal with an application for particulars of the defence of contributory negligence pleaded in an action for assault and battery. His Honour described the plea as embarrassing to the last degree, saying, "I cannot conceive it possible that there should be contributory negligence in an action of this nature", and would have struck out the paragraph then and there had it not been for the fact that the defendant had not come prepared to meet an application to strike out; on that ground the summons was adjourned: *Reason v Knight* (1886) 8 ALT 15, a decision cited by Gillard J in *Belous v Willetts* [1970] VR 45, at p 50. With the exception of *Reason v Knight* I have been unable to find any reported case outside the United States in which the common law defence of contributory negligence was raised in an action for assault or battery. Nor have I discovered in any of the books on practice written when the old system of pleading was in force any suggestion that the defence is available in such an action. ...

[161] Textbooks on the law of torts published about the turn of the century contain no indication that contributory negligence may be availed of in an action for assault and battery. ...

It appears to be settled law in the United States of America that contributory negligence is no defence to assault and battery ... In Canada the view has been taken by Wells J of the High Court of Ontario that a plea of contributory negligence was never a defence to an action of trespass, whether or not the injury was intentional; *Hollebone v Barnard* (1954) 2 DLR 278, at p 286.

[162] Clearly provocation is no defence to an action for battery. ... In *Fontin v Katapodis* (1962) 108 CLR 177 the incident occurred on 10 December 1958 in the Northern Territory, where apportionment legislation had been in operation since 1956: *Law Reform (Miscellaneous Provisions) Ordinance 1956.* Contributory negligence was not pleaded, and the question was dealt with as part of the law relating to mitigation of damages. The judgments contain nothing dealing in terms with the matter of contributory negligence, yet one cannot avoid the impression that some reference would have been made to contributory negligence if in the opinion of the Court it would have been available had it been raised on the pleadings. ...

Two recent decisions of the [English] Court of Appeal must now be reviewed. ... In the first case, *Lane v Holloway* [1968] 1 QB 379, the defence relied upon an insult uttered and blows struck by the elderly plaintiff as "fault" which caused or contributed to the plaintiff's injury. The County Court Judge reduced the damages on the ground of the plaintiff's insult, challenge and blow, evidently treating those matters as going in mitigation. Lord Denning MR said nothing of contributory **[163]** negligence and followed *Fontin v Katapodis, supra.* Salmon LJ also applied the decision of the High Court, but at pp 392-3 did advert to contributory negligence, saying "As Winn LJ pointed out in the course of the argument, if the plaintiff on the facts of this case can be said to have been negligent, then before the statute what he did would have afforded the defendant a complete defence to the action – a somewhat surprising proposition. To my mind it is impossible to hold that what this old man did, however rude or silly or cantankerous, amounted to contributory negligence."

In the passage cited, Salmon LJ appears to accept that at common law contributory negligence is a defence to an action for battery and to treat the question as one of fact; on the other hand, since his Lordship considered that a finding of contributory negligence was not open on the facts, the question of law did not fall for determination. Winn LJ, who agreed with the other judgments, added, at ([1968] 1 QB) p 393, that there was in the case nothing that could constitute a fault within the statutory definition.

In *Murphy v Culhane* [1977] QB 94; [1976] 3 All ER 533 the victim of the assault was not "a rather cantankerous old man of 64 years of age", "rather infirm and full of beer", into whose face "this man 40 years younger than himself" had "smashed his fist"; he was one of the authors of "a wicked plot" to "beat up" another man. Faced with these different facts, the Court of Appeal considered that compensatory damages ought to be mitigated, and sought to distinguish *Lane v Holloway* and *Fontin v Katapodis, supra*, as cases where, on the facts, the trivial provocation could not be fairly regarded as responsible in part for the injury, an attempt bluntly criticized in *Landry v Patterson* (1978) 93 DLR (3d) 345. In *Murphy v Culhane* at ([1977] QB) pp 98-9 Lord Denning MR, with whose judgment the other members of the court agreed, went on to say that the defendant might be entitled to have the damages reduced under the apportionment legislation, evidently on the ground that the victim of the assault might well himself have been liable in tort. This appears to proceed on the footing that the first limb of the statutory definition of "fault" was the relevant, or at all events a relevant, part of that definition; his Lordship does not elaborate.

In 1974 Moller J of the Supreme Court of New Zealand, after considering the views of text writers and *Lane v Holloway, supra*, concluded that contributory negligence, constituted by insulting words, could lead to an apportionment in an action for battery: *Hoebergen v Koppens* [1974] 2 NZLR 597. It appears from a brief note in (1979) Australian Current Law 356 that on 4 April 1979 Sheahan J of the Supreme Court of Queensland held, in *Barley v Paroz*, that the apportionment legislation was applicable where the plaintiff failed to have due regard for his own safety in the circumstances leading up to the assault; but no report of the decision has been available to me.

Text writers are divided on whether the apportionment legislation applies to actions for assault and battery, and generally speaking the treatment is very brief. ...

[164] There has been much discussion of the basis of the doctrine of contributory negligence. ... **[165]** Over the years the doctrine of contributory negligence has often been explained in the cases simply in terms of causation, but it has for some time now been clear that it is wrong to refer the whole doctrine to the theory of causation ...

Once it is accepted (as it must in Australia, having regard to *Alford v Magee* (1952) 85 CLR 437) that contributory negligence is not wholly to be referred to the theory of causation, it becomes easier to ground in principle the view that contributory negligence affords no defence at common law to an action for battery. Given that one may consider whether it is fair or reasonable to regard the plaintiff as in any real sense the author of his own harm (*Alford v Magee*, at p 461), it is easy to understand why the law should, as a matter of policy, withhold the defence in cases of intentional as opposed to negligent trespass to the person and to say with Prosser, *Handbook on Torts*, 3rd ed, p 436 that the reason why contributory negligence is no defence where the defendant intended to inflict injury is to be found in the difference between the fault of the defendant and that of the plaintiff; the difference is not merely in degree but in kind, and the social condemnation attached to the fault differs markedly. Similarly, Glanville Williams, *supra*, article 55, suggests that the exclusion of the defence in cases of intentional wrongdoing is both a penal provision, aimed at repressing conduct flagrantly wrongful, and the result of the ordinary **[166]** human feeling that the defendant's wrongful intention so outweighs the plaintiff's wrongful negligence as to efface it altogether.

I have concluded that contributory negligence was not at common law and is not under the statute available in an action for battery.

Judgment for the plaintiff

New South Wales v Riley
(2003) 57 NSWLR 496; [2003] NSWCA 208
Supreme Court of New South Wales, Court of Appeal

In cases of intentional trespass to the person, the "contributory negligence" of the plaintiff is no defence. However, where there are indirect and unintended consequences of an intentional trespass, the plaintiff's contributory negligence is a defence in respect of those consequences.

[Police officers, for whom the defendant, the State of New South Wales, was vicariously liable, arrested and detained the plaintiff, Jonathan Riley, in circumstances constituting assault and false imprisonment. After the arrest in question, the plaintiff's hands were handcuffed behind his back and he was placed in a police "paddy wagon" and taken to a hospital for psychiatric assessment. In the course of the journey, which involved some sharp curves and steep grades, the plaintiff, who was very angry and in an agitated state, threw himself from side to side in the back of the police vehicle. As a result of the overly-tight application of the handcuffs and the police officers' lack of care in transporting the plaintiff, the plaintiff suffered a fractured wrist. In respect of this particular injury the primary judge (Phegan DCJ) found the plaintiff guilty of contributory negligence and, on this account, reduced the plaintiff's damages by 40%.

The New South Wales Court of Appeal agreed with the primary judge's finding on contributory negligence and the substantial award of compensatory damages made by the primary judge for the assault and false imprisonment.

Hodgson JA (with whom Sheller JA and Nicholas J agreed) observed (at [102]) that the plaintiff's wrist fracture was a foreseeable consequence of the false imprisonment.]

HODGSON JA. ... **[522]** 104. It seems clear that such a defence [contributory negligence] is not available at common law to a claim for damages for an intentionally inflicted injury: *Quinn v Leathem* [1901] AC 495 at 537, *Fontin v Katapodis* (1962) 108 CLR 177, *Horkin v North Melbourne Football Club Social Club* [1983] 1 VR 153. ...

105. However, the wrist fracture was not inflicted intentionally, and was not proved to be other than an indirect consequence of the false imprisonment. This gives rise to two questions: (1) as an indirect consequence of the imprisonment, could it in any event be compensated in an action for trespass to the person; and (2) if it could be compensated in such an action, would a defence of contributory negligence lie because the injury was not intended?

[523] 106. It seems clear that contributory negligence is available as a defence to an action for unintentional trespass: see *Venning v Chin* (1974) 10 SASR 299. And at 317 in that case, Bray CJ said:

It is clear that contributory negligence could never be a defence to an intentional tort, or perhaps it would be preferable to say to the intentional consequences of a tort.

Bray CJ then referred to Glanville Williams, *Joint Torts and Contributory Negligence* (1951) at 197-199. And in Fleming on *Torts* (9ᵗʰ edn), the following appears at 316:

Even at common law contributory negligence was not a defence to all torts. Thus it did not apply to intended injury as distinct from unintended consequences of wilful wrongdoing.

107. Returning to my two questions, I am inclined to the view that, once some direct interference is established so that an action for trespass does lie, even indirect consequences of that interference can be compensated in the action for trespass (although such action would not lie at all if there was no direct interference but only indirect consequences). However, where there are indirect and unintended consequences of the trespass, I think the better view is that the defence of contributory negligence is available in respect of those unintended consequences. This view has some support from the decision of the Court of Appeals of New York in *Sindle v New York City Transit Authority* (1973) 352 NYS 2d 183, which concerned a false imprisonment action brought by a schoolboy who sustained injuries attempting to escape from a moving bus. Jason J, with whom the other six judges agreed, said this:

Where the damages follow as a consequence of the plaintiff's detention without justification an award may include those for bodily injuries. And although confinement perceived to be unlawful may invite escape, the person falsely imprisoned is not relieved of the duty of reasonable care for his own safety in extricating himself from the unlawful detention.

[In the result, the New South Wales Court of Appeal, after detailed consideration of the conduct of the police officers who had arrested the plaintiff, allowed the defendant's appeal in respect of the award of aggravated and exemplary damages made by the primary judge. In this regard, Hodgson JA observed at 531 that the conduct of the police officers was not "beyond ordinary human fallibility".]

Appeal allowed in part

4. PLAINTIFF'S UNLAWFUL CONDUCT

Henwood v Municipal Tramways Trust (South Australia)
(1938) 60 CLR 438
High Court of Australia

There is no general principle that a person injured at a time when he or she is breaking some provision of the law is, on that account, precluded from recovering damages in negligence.

LATHAM CJ. **[443]** This is an appeal from a judgment of Napier J for the defendant, the Municipal Tramways Trust, in an action for negligence against the trust under the *Wrongs Act 1936* (*Lord Campbell's Act*) of South Australia. The action was brought by the parents of Alfred John Henwood in respect of his death as the result of an accident when he was travelling on one of the defendant's trams. He was a passenger on the tram on 26th March 1937. He became sick, left his seat in the tram, leaned out over a rail on the off side of the tram and vomited. His head struck in succession two steel standards, which were in the middle of the street, and he died shortly afterwards. The standards were seventeen inches from the side of the tram. The negligence alleged depends upon the construction of the tram without, it is said, sufficient barriers to prevent or discourage passengers from leaning out, taken in conjunction with the nearness of the standards. Negligence was denied, and contributory negligence on the part of the deceased was alleged.

A by-law was made by the trust under the *Municipal Tramways Trust Act 1906*, s 74, and duly confirmed by the Governor in Council, in the following terms:– "38A. No passenger shall project or lean his head or other portion of his body or limbs out of any window in any tram, or outside the barrier on the off side of the open portion of any tram. Penalty £5." ...

[444] The learned trial judge ... determined the case upon one point and one point only. He held that the existence and the breach by the deceased of the by-law prohibiting leaning outside the barrier on the off side **[445]** of the tram afforded "a conclusive answer to the claim in any form in which it could be presented." It is contended for the appellant that this decision of the learned judge is wrong in law.

This is an interesting and important question upon which there is not very much authority in English law. There is much to be said for the view that, where a provision of the law is directed towards securing the safety of persons by penalizing acts of carelessness, no person can recover damages when the injury of which he complains was directly brought about by his own act in breach of the law. ...

[446] But there are other considerations which are, in my opinion, sufficiently weighty to displace those to which I have referred. In the first place, there is no general principle of English law that a person who is engaged in some unlawful act is disabled from complaining of injury done to him by other persons, either deliberately or accidentally. He does not become *caput lupinum*. Other persons still owe to him a duty to take care, the extent of that duty being determined by the circumstances of the case which create the duty. The person who is injured in a motor accident may be a child playing truant from school, an employee who is absent from work in breach of his contract, a man who is loitering upon a road in breach of a by-law, or a burglar on his way to a professional engagement – but none of these facts is relevant for the purpose of deciding the existence or defining the content of the obligation of a motor driver not to injure them. Thus, it cannot be held that there is any principle which makes it impossible for a defendant to be liable for injury brought about by his negligence simply because the plaintiff at the relevant time was breaking some provision of the law. ...

[His Honour then held that there was no implication in the by-law of an intention to protect the Trust from liability.]

[449] As there has been no definite finding on the subject of the negligence of the defendant, and no finding at all on the subject of contributory negligence, in my opinion the case should be remitted to the learned judge for the purpose of making findings on these matters so that he may give judgment in accordance with his findings.

The appeal should be allowed and the case remitted for the purpose stated. ...

STARKE J. ... [452] In my opinion, the question is whether the prohibition contained in the by-law is imposed as a duty for the protection of the trust or really as a matter of policy for the protection generally of the travelling public. ... [453] The manifest purpose of the by-law is to prohibit acts that are or are regarded as dangerous or careless acts on the part of passengers. It is a punitive provision. It does not in so many words relieve or purport to relieve, and perhaps could not directly relieve, the tramways trust of the consequences of its own negligent or wrongful acts. Nor does it, in express words, deprive passengers of their civil rights against the trust in case of a breach of its duty to exercise care and forethought for securing their safety. All that can be inferred from the terms of the by-law is that it prohibits certain acts and provides a specific penalty. It no doubt creates a duty but not a duty upon which the trust can found any right of action or any conclusive defence for breach of any duty which it owed to the deceased. ...

[His Honour held that the appeal should be allowed and the case should go back to the trial judge for consideration of the questions of negligence and contributory negligence.]

DIXON and McTIERNAN JJ. ... [Their Honours' interpretation of the judgment of the trial judge was that he took the view that the defendant was negligent and that there was no contributory negligence on the part of the deceased. Thus if the case be considered apart from the by-law the plaintiffs should succeed.]

[457] When the harm complained of is otherwise the proximate consequence of the defendant's negligence, is it a sufficient answer to the cause of action that, but for the illegal act of the party sustaining the injury, it would not have happened? ...

[458] Little or no English authority is to be found upon the illegality of a plaintiff's own conduct as a disqualification from recovery for tort. But there is much case law upon the subject in the United States, and from it the directness of the connection between the illegality and the injury seems to have emerged as the *discrimen* more generally adopted. If the immediate cause of the injury is the unlawful act of the plaintiff, he cannot recover; but, if the unlawful act does no more than create a prior state of affairs upon which the defendant's negligence operates, he may recover. In Massachusetts the rule against recovery by a plaintiff himself acting unlawfully was carried to great extremes in the application of a law forbidding the driving of vehicles on Sunday. The decisions were not all consistent, but, for the most part, the plaintiff was held to have suffered no actionable wrong where, but for his driving on Sunday, the injury would not have occurred. Thus, a plaintiff who was injured by a defective highway was held disentitled to recover from the highway authority, because the injury arose from his driving upon the highway on Sunday (*Bosworth v Swansey* (1845) 10 Met (Mass) 363). ...

[460] In the present case the act constituting the breach of the by-law is not only an indispensable condition of the resulting injury, but it is the final act which produces it. The tram-car is rapidly moving with the posts alongside, and the passenger in that condition by leaning over completes the conditions necessary to cause the injury.

In *Canning v The King* [1924] NZLR 118; [1923] GLR (NZ) 595 Salmond J lays down a further condition which is also fulfilled. The condition is that a purpose of the statute broken by the plaintiff must have been to prevent the kind of accident which actually occurred.

We wish to make it clear that the facts of the present case fulfill the conditions which we have mentioned because, notwithstanding that they do so, we have formed the opinion that breach of the by-law on the part of the deceased does not disable the plaintiff from recovering in respect of his death. We do not think that, in the absence of English authority requiring us to do so, we ought to adopt as part of the law of torts a general principle that, if the damage suffered by the plaintiff has been directly brought about by an act of his which is unlawful, he can never complain of a wrongful or negligent act or omission on the part of the defendant from which the damage otherwise flows as a reasonable and probable consequence. It appears to us that in every case the question must be whether it is part of the purpose of the law against which the plaintiff has offended to disentitle a person doing the prohibited act from complaining of the other party's neglect or default, without which his own act would not have resulted in injury. ...

[462] [T]here is no rule denying to a person who is doing an unlawful thing the protection of the general law imposing upon others duties of care for his safety. ...

[467] In our opinion the true inquiry is whether it is the intention of the statute penalizing the particular conduct to affect civil responsibility. In the present case such an intention appears to us to be absent.

We think the appeal should be allowed: the judgment of the Supreme Court should be discharged and judgment in the action be entered for the plaintiffs for £250, the damages contingently assessed by the Supreme Court.

Appeal allowed. Case remitted to Napier J

5. NECESSITY

Southwark London Borough Council v Williams
[1971] Ch 734
English Court of Appeal

The defence of necessity is confined within narrow limits, such as situations of imminent peril.

LORD DENNING MR. [740] This case arises out of the extreme housing shortage in London. In September 1970 some people who were homeless and others who were living in bad conditions sought the assistance of a squatters' association. They made an orderly entry into some empty houses in the Borough of Southwark which were owned by the council. They squatted there. The council applied to the court under the new procedure which has been brought in to deal with urgent cases of squatting. RSC, Ord 113, enables the court to make an order for immediate possession. It is a summary procedure and should be used only when there is no arguable defence.

[741] The squatters here admit that they have no title to these houses. They admit that the houses belong to the Southwark London Borough Council. But they seek to justify or excuse their action on the ground that it is the duty of the borough council to provide temporary accommodation for persons who are in need thereof: and that it was of necessity that they entered the houses. ...

[His Lordship then held that s 21(1) of the *National Assistance Act 1948* did not assist the squatters in these proceedings.]

[743] I will next consider the defence of "necessity". There is authority for saying that in case of great and imminent danger, in order to preserve life, the law will permit of an encroachment on private property. That is shown by *Mouse's Case* (1609) 12 Co Rep 63, where the ferryman at Gravesend took 47 passengers into his barge to carry them to London. A great tempest arose and all were in danger. Mouse was one of the passengers. The defendant threw a casket belonging to the plaintiff (Mouse) overboard so as to lighten the ship. Other passengers threw other things. It

was proved that, if they had not done so, the passengers would have been drowned. It was held by the whole court " that in case of necessity, for the saving of the lives of the passengers it was lawful for the defendant, being a passenger, to cast the casket of the plaintiff out of the barges ..." The court said it was like the pulling down of a house, in time of fire, to stop it spreading; which has always been held justified pro bono publico.

The doctrine so enunciated must, however, be carefully circumscribed. Else necessity would open the door to many an excuse. It was for this **[744]** reason that it was not admitted in *R v Dudley and Stephens* (1884) 14 QBD 273, where the three shipwrecked sailors, in extreme despair, killed the cabin boy and ate him to save their own lives. They were held guilty of murder. The killing was not justified by necessity. Similarly, when a man, who is starving, enters a house and takes food in order to keep himself alive. Our English law does not admit the defence of necessity. It holds him guilty of larceny. Lord Hale said that "if a person, being under necessity for want of victuals, or clothes, shall upon that account clandestinely, and animo furandi, steal another man's food, it is felony ...": Hale, *Pleas of Crown,* i 54. The reason is because, if hunger were once allowed to be an excuse for stealing, it would open a way through which all kinds of disorder and lawlessness would pass. So here. If homelessness were once admitted as a defence to trespass, no one's house could be safe. Necessity would open a door which no man could shut. It would not only be those in extreme need who would enter. There would be others who would imagine that they were in need, or would invent a need, so as to gain entry. Each man would say his need was greater than the next man's. The plea would be an excuse for all sorts of wrongdoing. So the courts must, for the sake of law and order, take a firm stand. They must refuse to admit the plea of necessity to the hungry and the homeless: and trust that their distress will be relieved by the charitable and the good.

Applying these principles, it seems to me the circumstances of these squatters are not such as to afford any justification or excuse in law for their entry into these houses. We can sympathise with the plight in which they find themselves. We can recognise the orderly way in which they made their entry. But we can go no further. They must make their appeal for help to others, not to us. They must appeal to the council, who will, I am sure, do all they can. They can go to the Minister, if need be. But, so far as these courts are concerned, we must, in the interest of law and order itself, uphold the title to these properties. We cannot allow any individuals, however great their despair, to take the law into their own hands and enter upon these premises. The court must exercise its summary jurisdiction and order these people to go out.

EDMUND DAVIES LJ. Nobody of even ordinary sensitivity could have read the affidavit evidence presented in this case without experiencing a feeling of deep depression. It serves to illustrate afresh the extent of the grave social problem presented by the dire shortage of adequate housing accommodation. But in fairness it has to be remembered that the circumstances present great difficulties to the local authorities concerned as well as to the benighted who are living in deplorable conditions or who may even be lacking a roof over their heads. The one question presented by these appeals is whether the defendants have shown that a triable issue has been raised in answer to the action for possession brought by the plaintiffs – that and nothing else has now to be determined. If there be a triable issue, leave would have to be granted and the appeals allowed. ...

[745] These appeals raise in an acute form the questions as to whether a plea of necessity is a defence to otherwise unlawful acts, whether such a plea has any place in English law, and, if it does exist, what are the limits and extent of its application.

Firstly, then, does it exist? The matter has been learnedly treated by Professor Glanville Williams in *Current Legal Problems*, Vol 6 (1953), p 216, and also in his *Criminal Law*, 2nd ed (1961), para 229 and the succeeding paras, pp 722-746. That the plea may in certain cases afford a defence does emerge from the recorded decisions – see, for example, *Mouse's Case*, 12 Co Rep 63. In *Moore v Hussey* (1609) Hob 93, 96, Hobart CJ said: "All laws admit certain cases of just excuse, when they are offended in letter, and where the offender is under necessity, either of compulsion or inconvenience. ..."

But when and how far is the plea of necessity available to one who is prima facie guilty of tort? Well, one thing emerges with clarity from the decisions, and that is that the law regards with the deepest suspicion any remedies of self-help, and permits those remedies to be resorted to only in very special circumstances. The reason for such circumspection is clear **[746]** – necessity can very easily become simply a mask for anarchy. As far as my reading goes, it appears that all the cases where a plea of necessity has succeeded are cases which deal with an urgent situation of imminent peril: for example, the forcible feeding of an obdurate suffragette, as in *Leigh v Gladstone* (1909) 26 TLR 139, 142, where Lord Alverstone CJ spoke of preserving the health and lives of the prisoners who were in the custody of the Crown; or performing an abortion to avert a grave threat to the life, or, at least, to the health of a pregnant young girl who had been ravished in circumstances of great brutality, as in *Rex v Bourne* [1939] 1 KB 687; or as in the case tried in 1500 where it was said in argument that a person may escape from a burning gaol notwithstanding a statute making prison-breach a felony, "for he is not to be hanged because he would not stay to be burnt." (See Glanville Williams, *Criminal Law*, 2nd ed, pp 725, 726.) Such cases illustrate the very narrow limits with which the plea of necessity may be invoked. Sad though the circumstances disclosed by these appeals undoubtedly are, they do not in my judgment constitute the sort of emergency to which the plea applies. …

Finally, even if necessity could be invoked in such circumstances as the present, it could surely at most justify merely an initial entry into premises in such circumstances as those to which I have referred. I do not see how it could possibly be permitted to extend to and authorise continuing in occupation for an indefinite period of time, which was the understandable aim of the appellants when entering these premises. I therefore have to concur with Lord Denning MR in holding that the public weal demands that these appeals be dismissed. …

[Megaw LJ delivered a concurring judgment.]

Order for possession

In Re F
[1990] 2 AC 1
House of Lords

The principle of necessity may justify medical or surgical treatment, which otherwise would constitute trespass to the person, when the patient is incapable of giving his or her consent by reason of lack of consciousness in an emergency situation or mental disability. However, application of this principle is accompanied by stringent safeguards requiring that the proposed treatment be in the best interests of the patient in order to preserve his or her life, health or well-being.

[F, a woman aged 36, suffered from serious mental disability and possessed the general mental capacity of a child of four or five with no possibility of further development. She was a patient at a mental hospital where she had formed a voluntary relationship of a sexual nature with a male patient. There were practical and medical objections to the use by F of conventional methods of contraception. From a psychiatric point of view it was considered disastrous for F to conceive and give birth to a child. However, due to her mental disability F was incapable of giving consent to a sterilisation operation. F, by her mother and next friend, applied for a declaration that the performance of a sterilisation operation on F by means of ligation of the Fallopian tubes would not amount to an unlawful act by reason only of the absence of F's consent.

Scott Baker J made the declaration sought and an appeal by the Official Solicitor was dismissed by the Court of Appeal. The Official Solicitor then appealed to the House of Lords.]

LORD BRANDON of OAKBROOK. … **[55]** At common law a doctor cannot lawfully operate on adult patients of sound mind, or give them any other treatment involving the application of physical force however small ("other treatment"), without their consent. If a doctor were to operate on such patients, or give them other treatment, without their consent, he would commit the actionable tort of trespass to the person. There are, however, cases where adult patients cannot give or refuse their consent to an operation or other treatment. One case is where, as a result of an accident or otherwise, an adult patient is unconscious and an operation or other treatment cannot be safely delayed until he or she recovers consciousness. Another case is where a patient, though adult, cannot by reason of mental disability understand the nature or purpose of an operation or other treatment. The common law would be seriously defective if it failed to provide a solution to the problem created by such inability to consent. In my opinion, however, the common law does not so fail. In my opinion, the solution to the problem which the common law provides is that a doctor can lawfully operate on, or give other treatment to, adult patients who are incapable, for one reason or another, of consenting to his doing so, provided that the operation or other treatment concerned is in the best interests of such patients. The operation or other treatment will be in their best interests if, but only if, it is carried out in order either to save their lives, or to ensure improvement or prevent deterioration in their physical or mental health.

Different views have been put forward with regard to the principle which makes it lawful for a doctor to operate on or give other treatment to adult patients without their consent in the two cases to which I have referred above. The Court of Appeal in the present case regarded the matter as depending on the public interest. I would not disagree with that as a broad proposition, but I think that it is helpful to consider the principle in accordance with which the public interest leads to this result. In my opinion, the principle is that, when persons lack the capacity, for whatever reason, to take decisions about the performance of operations on them, or the giving of other medical treatment to them, it is necessary that some other person or persons, with the appropriate qualifications, should take such decisions for them. Otherwise they would be deprived of medical care which they need and to which they are entitled. ...

[68] I would dismiss the appeal ...

LORD GOFF of CHIEVELEY. ... [71] It is well established that, as a general rule, the performance of a medical operation upon a person without his or her consent is unlawful, as constituting both the crime of battery and the tort of trespass to the person. Furthermore, before Scott Baker J and the Court of Appeal, it was common ground between the parties that there was no power in the court to give consent on behalf of F to the proposed operation of sterilisation, or to dispense with the need for such consent. ...

It follows that, as was recognised in the courts below, if the operation upon F is to be justified, it can only be justified on the applicable principles of common law. The argument of counsel revealed the startling fact that there is no English authority on the question whether as a matter of common law (and if so in what [72] circumstances) medical treatment can lawfully be given to a person who is disabled by mental incapacity from consenting to it. Indeed, the matter goes further; for a comparable problem can arise in relation to persons of sound mind who are, for example, rendered unconscious in an accident or rendered speechless by a catastrophic stroke. All such persons may require medical treatment and, in some cases, surgical operations. All may require nursing care. In the case of mentally disordered persons, they may require care of a more basic kind – dressing, feeding, and so on – to assist them in their daily life, as well as routine treatment by doctors and dentists. It follows that, in my opinion, it is not possible to consider in isolation the lawfulness of the proposed operation of sterilisation in the present case. It is necessary first to ascertain the applicable common law principles and then to consider the question of sterilisation against the background of those principles ...

I start with the fundamental principle, now long established, that every person's body is inviolate. As to this, I do not wish to depart from what I myself said in the judgment of the Divisional Court in *Collins v Wilcock* [1984] 1 WLR 1172, and in particular from the statement, at p 1177, that the effect of this principle is that everybody is protected not only against physical injury but against any form of physical molestation.

Of course, as a general rule physical interference with another person's body is lawful if he consents to it; though in certain limited circumstances the public interest may require that his consent is not capable of rendering the act lawful. There are also specific cases where physical interference without consent may not be unlawful – chastisement of children, lawful arrest, self-defence, the prevention of crime, and so on. As I pointed out in *Collins v Wilcock* [1984] 1 WLR 1172, 1177, a broader exception has been created to allow for the exigencies of everyday life – jostling in a street or some other crowded place, social contact at parties, and such like. This exception has been said to be founded on implied consent, since those who go about in public places, or go to parties, may be taken to have impliedly consented to bodily contact of this kind. Today this rationalisation can be regarded as artificial; and in particular, it is difficult to impute consent to those who, by reason of their youth or mental disorder, are unable to give their consent. For this reason, I **[73]** consider it more appropriate to regard such cases as falling within a general exception embracing all physical contact which is generally acceptable in the ordinary conduct of everyday life.

In the old days it used to be said that, for a touching of another's person to amount to a battery, it had to be a touching "in anger" (see *Cole v Turner* (1704) 6 Mod 149, *per* Holt CJ); and it has recently been said that the touching must be "hostile" to have that effect (see *Wilson v Pringle* [1987] QB 237, 253). I respectfully doubt whether that is correct. A prank that gets out of hand; an over-friendly slap on the back; surgical treatment by a surgeon who mistakenly thinks that the patient has consented to it – all these things may transcend the bounds of lawfulness, without being characterised as hostile. Indeed the suggested qualification is difficult to reconcile with the principle that any touching of another's body is, in the absence of lawful excuse, capable of amounting to a battery and a trespass. Furthermore, in the case of medical treatment, we have to bear well in mind the libertarian principle of self-determination which, to adopt the words of Cardozo J (in *Schloendorff v Society of New York Hospital* (1914) 105 NE 92, 93) recognises that:

> Every human being of adult years and sound mind has a right to determine what shall be done with his own body; and a surgeon who performs an operation without his patient's consent commits an assault ...

This principle has been reiterated in more recent years by Lord Reid in *S v McC (orse S) and M (DS intervener)*; *W v W* [1972] AC 24, 43.

It is against this background that I turn to consider the question whether, and if so when, medical treatment or care of a mentally disordered person who is, by reason of his incapacity, incapable of giving his consent, can be regarded as lawful. ...

Upon what principle can medical treatment be justified when given without consent? We are searching for a principle upon which, in limited circumstances, recognition may be given to a need, in the **[74]** interests of the patient, that treatment should be given to him in circumstances where he is (temporarily or permanently) disabled from consenting to it. It is this criterion of a need which points to the principle of necessity as providing justification.

That there exists in the common law a principle of necessity which may justify action which would otherwise be unlawful is not in doubt. But historically the principle has been seen to be restricted to two groups of cases, which have been called cases of public necessity and cases of private necessity. The former occurred when a man interfered with another man's property in the public interest – for example (in the days before we could dial 999 for the fire brigade) the destruction of another man's house to prevent the spread of a catastrophic fire, as indeed occurred in the Great Fire of London in 1666. The latter cases occurred when a man interfered with another's property to save his own person or property from imminent danger – for example, when he entered upon his neighbour's land without his consent, in order to prevent the spread of fire onto his own land.

There is, however, a third group of cases, which is also properly described as founded upon the principle of necessity and which is more pertinent to the resolution of the problem in the present case. These cases are concerned with action taken as a matter of necessity to assist another person without his consent. To give a simple example, a man who seizes another and forcibly drags him from the path of an oncoming vehicle, thereby saving him from injury or even death, commits no wrong. But there are many emanations of this principle, to be found scattered through the books. These are concerned not only with the preservation of the life or health of the assisted person, but also with the preservation of his property (sometimes an animal, sometimes an ordinary chattel) and even with certain conduct on his behalf in the administration of his affairs. Where there is a pre-existing relationship between the parties, the intervenor is usually said to act as an agent of necessity on behalf of the principal in whose interests he acts, and his action can often, with not too much artificiality, be referred to the pre-existing relationship between them. Whether the intervenor may be entitled either to reimbursement or to remuneration raises separate questions which are not relevant in the present case.

We are concerned here with action taken to preserve the life, health or well-being of another who is unable to consent to it. Such action is sometimes said to be justified as arising from an emergency; in Prosser and Keeton, *Handbook on Torts*, 5th ed (1984), p 117, the action is said to be privileged by the emergency. Doubtless, in the case of a person of sound mind, there will ordinarily have to be an emergency before such action taken without consent can be lawful; for otherwise there would be an opportunity to communicate with the assisted person and to seek his consent. But this is not always so; and indeed the historical origins of the principle of necessity do not point to emergency as such as providing the criterion of lawful intervention without consent. The old Roman doctrine of negotiorum gestio presupposed not so much an emergency as a prolonged absence of the [75] dominus from home as justifying intervention by the gestor to administer his affairs. The most ancient group of cases in the common law, concerned with action taken by the master of a ship in distant parts in the interests of the shipowner, likewise found its origin in the difficulty of communication with the owner over a prolonged period of time – a difficulty overcome today by modern means of communication. In those cases, it was said that there had to be an emergency before the master could act as agent of necessity; though the emergency could well be of some duration. But when a person is rendered incapable of communication either permanently or over a considerable period of time (through illness or accident or mental disorder), it would be an unusual use of language to describe the case as one of "permanent emergency" – if indeed such a state of affairs can properly be said to exist. In truth, the relevance of an emergency is that it may give rise to a necessity to act in the interests of the assisted person, without first obtaining his consent. Emergency is however not the criterion or even a pre-requisite; it is simply a frequent origin of the necessity which impels intervention. The principle is one of necessity, not of emergency.

We can derive some guidance as to the nature of the principle of necessity from the cases on agency of necessity in mercantile law. When reading those cases, however, we have to bear in mind that it was there considered that (since there was a pre-existing relationship between the parties) there was a duty on the part of the agent to act on his principal's behalf in an emergency. From these cases it appears that the principle of necessity connotes that circumstances have arisen in which there is a necessity for the agent to act on his principal's behalf at a time when it is in practice not possible for him to obtain his principal's instructions as to do. In such cases, it has been said that the agent must act bona fide in the interests of his principal: see *Prager v Blatspiel Stamp & Heacock Ltd* [1924] 1 KB 566, 572 *per* McCardie J. A broader statement of the principle is to be found in the advice of the Privy Council delivered by Sir Montague Smith in *Australasian Steam Navigation Co v Morse* (1872) LR 4 PC 222, 230, in which he said:

> when by the force of circumstances a man has the duty cast upon him of taking some action for another, and under that obligation, adopts the course which, to the judgment of a wise and prudent man, is apparently the best for the interest of the persons for whom he acts in a given emergency, it may properly be said of the course so taken, that it was, in a mercantile sense, necessary to take it.

In a sense, these statements overlap. But from them can be derived the basic requirements, applicable in these cases of necessity, that, to fall within the principle, not only (1) must there be a necessity to act when it is not practicable to communicate with the assisted person, but also (2) the action taken must be such as a reasonable person could in all the circumstances take, acting in the best interests of the assisted person.

[76] On this statement of principle, I wish to observe that officious intervention cannot be justified by the principle of necessity. So intervention cannot be justified when another more appropriate person is available and willing to act; nor can it be justified when it is contrary to the known wishes of the assisted person, to the extent that he is capable of rationally forming such a wish. On the second limb of the principle, the introduction of the standard of a reasonable man should not in the present context be regarded as materially different from that of Sir Montague Smith's "wise and prudent man," because a reasonable man would, in the time available to him, proceed with wisdom and prudence before taking action in relation to another man's person or property without

his consent. I shall have more to say on this point later. Subject to that, I hesitate at present to indulge in any greater refinement of the principle, being well aware of many problems which may arise in its application – problems which it is not necessary, for present purposes, to examine. But as a general rule, if the above criteria are fulfilled, interference with the assisted person's person or property (as the case may be) will not be unlawful. Take the example of a railway accident, in which injured passengers are trapped in the wreckage. It is this principle which may render lawful the actions of other citizens – railway staff, passengers or outsiders – who rush to give aid and comfort to the victims: the surgeon who amputates the limb of an unconscious passenger to free him from the wreckage; the ambulance man who conveys him to hospital; the doctors and nurses who treat him and care for him while he is still unconscious. Take the example of an elderly person who suffers a stroke which renders him incapable of speech or movement. It is by virtue of this principle that the doctor who treats him, the nurse who cares for him, even the relative or friend or neighbour who comes in to look after him, will commit no wrong when he or she touches his body.

The two examples I have given illustrate, in the one case, an emergency, and in the other, a permanent or semi-permanent state of affairs. Another example of the latter is that of a mentally disordered person who is disabled from giving consent. I can see no good reason why the principle of necessity should not be applicable in his case as it is in the case of the victim of a stroke. Furthermore, in the case of a mentally disordered person, as in the case of a stroke victim, the permanent state of affairs calls for a wider range of care than may be requisite in an emergency which arises from accidental injury. When the state of affairs is permanent, or semi-permanent, action properly taken to preserve the life, health or well-being of the assisted person may well transcend such measures as surgical operation or substantial medical treatment and may extend to include such humdrum matters as routine medical or dental treatment, even simple care such as dressing and undressing and putting to bed.

The distinction I have drawn between cases of emergency, and cases where the state of affairs is (more or less) permanent, is relevant in another respect. We are here concerned with medical treatment, and I limit myself to cases of that kind. Where, for [77] example, a surgeon performs an operation without his consent on a patient temporarily rendered unconscious in an accident, he should do no more than is reasonably required, in the best interests of the patient, before he recovers consciousness. I can see no practical difficulty arising from this requirement, which derives from the fact that the patient is expected before long to regain consciousness and can then be consulted about longer term measures. The point has however arisen in a more acute form where a surgeon, in the course of an operation, discovers some other condition which, in his opinion, requires operative treatment for which he has not received the patient's consent. In what circumstances he should operate forthwith, and in what circumstances he should postpone the further treatment until he has received the patient's consent, is a difficult matter which has troubled the Canadian Courts (see *Marshall v Curry* (1933) 3 DLR 260, and *Murray v McMurchy* (1949) 2 DLR 442), but which it is not necessary for your Lordships to consider in the present case.

But where the state of affairs is permanent or semi-permanent, as may be so in the case of a mentally disordered person, there is no point in waiting to obtain the patient's consent. The need to care for him is obvious; and the doctor must then act in the best interests of his patient, just as if he had received his patient's consent so to do. Were this not so, much useful treatment and care could, in theory at least, be denied to the unfortunate. ...

I am satisfied that, for the reasons so clearly expressed by the judge, he was right to grant the declaration sought by the plaintiff in the present case. I would therefore dismiss the appeal. ...

[Lord Bridge of Harwich, Lord Griffiths and Lord Jauncey of Tullichettle agreed with the judgments of Lord Brandon and Lord Goff.]

Appeal dismissed

Malette v Shulman
(1990) 67 DLR (4th) 321
Ontario Court of Appeal

Where an adult patient of sound mind has refused life-saving medical treatment, the carrying out of that treatment against the wishes of the patient will constitute battery which cannot be justified under the principle of necessity.

The judgment of the court was delivered by ROBINS JA. **[322]** The question to be decided in this appeal is whether a doctor is liable in law for administering blood transfusions to an unconscious patient in a potentially life-threatening situation when the patient is carrying a card stating that she is a Jehovah's Witness and, as a matter of religious belief, rejects blood transfusions under any circumstances.

I

In the early afternoon of June 30, 1979, Mrs Georgette Malette, then age 57, was rushed, unconscious, by ambulance to the Kirkland and District Hospital in Kirkland Lake, Ontario. She had been in an accident. The car in which she was a passenger, driven by her husband, had collided head-on with a truck. Her husband had been killed. She suffered serious injuries.

[323] On arrival at the hospital, she was attended by Dr David L Shulman, a family physician practising in Kirkland Lake who served two or three shifts a week in the emergency department of the hospital and who was on duty at the time. Dr Shulman's initial examination of Mrs Malette showed, among other things, that she had severe head and face injuries and was bleeding profusely. The doctor concluded that she was suffering from incipient shock by reason of blood loss, and ordered that she be given intravenous glucose followed immediately by Ringer's Lactate. The administration of a volume expander, such as Ringer's Lactate, is standard medical procedure in cases of this nature. If the patient does not respond with significantly increased blood pressure, transfusions of blood are then administered to carry essential oxygen to tissues and to remove waste products and prevent damage to vital organs.

At about this time, a nurse discovered a card in Mrs Malette's purse which identified her as a Jehovah's Witness and in which she requested, on the basis of her religious convictions, that she be given no blood transfusions under any circumstances. The card, which was not dated or witnessed, was printed in French and signed by Mrs Malette. Translated into English, it read:

NO BLOOD TRANSFUSION!

As one of Jehovah's Witnesses with firm religious convictions, I request that no blood or blood products be administered to me under any circumstances. I fully realize the implications of this position, but I have resolutely decided to obey the Bible command: "Keep abstaining ... from blood." (Acts 15:28, 29). However, I have no religious objections to use the nonblood alternatives, such as Dextran, Haemaccel, PVP, Ringer's Lactate or saline solution.

Dr Shulman was promptly advised of the existence of this card and its contents.

Mrs Malette was next examined by a surgeon on duty in the hospital. He concluded, as had Dr Shulman, that, to avoid irreversible shock, it was vital to maintain her blood volume. He had Mrs Malette transferred to the X-ray department for X-rays of her skull, pelvis and chest. However, before the X-rays could be satisfactorily completed, Mrs Malette's condition deteriorated. Her blood pressure dropped markedly, her respiration became increasingly distressed, and her level of consciousness dropped. She continued to bleed profusely and could be said to be critically ill.

At this stage, Dr Shulman decided that Mrs Malette's condition had deteriorated to the point that transfusions were necessary to replace her lost blood and to preserve her life and **[324]** health. Having made that decision, he personally administered transfusions to her, in spite of the Jehovah's Witness card, while she was in the X-ray department and after she was transferred to the intensive care unit. Dr Shulman was clearly aware of the religious objection to blood manifested in the card carried by Mrs Malette and the instruction that "NO BLOOD TRANSFUSION!" be given under any circumstances. He accepted full responsibility then, as he does now, for the decision to administer the transfusions.

Some three hours after the transfusions Celine Bisson, who had driven to Kirkland Lake from Timmins, arrived at the hospital accompanied by her husband and a local church elder. She strongly objected to her mother being given blood. She informed Dr Shulman and some of the other defendants that both she and her mother were Jehovah's Witnesses, that a tenet of their faith forbids blood transfusions, and that she knew her mother would not want blood transfusions. Notwithstanding Dr Shulman's opinion as to the medical necessity of the transfusions, Mrs Bisson remained adamantly opposed to them. She signed a document specifically prohibiting blood transfusions and a release of liability. Dr Shulman refused to follow her instructions. Since the blood transfusions were, in his judgment, medically necessary in this potentially life-threatening situation, he believed it his professional responsibility as the doctor in charge to ensure that his patient received the transfusions. Furthermore, he was not satisfied that the card signed by Mrs Malette expressed her current instructions because, on the information he then had, he did not know whether she might have changed her religious beliefs before the accident; whether the card may have been signed because of family or peer pressure; whether at the time she signed the card she was fully informed of the risks of refusal of blood transfusions; or whether, if conscious, she might have changed her mind in the face of medical advice as to her perhaps imminent but avoidable death.

As matters developed, by about midnight Mrs Malette's condition had stabilized sufficiently to permit her to be transferred early the next morning by air ambulance to Toronto General Hospital where she received no further blood transfusions. She was discharged on August 11, 1979. Happily, she made a very good recovery from her injuries.

II

In June 1980, Mrs Malette brought this action against Dr [325] Shulman, the hospital, its executive director and four nurses, alleging, in the main, that the administration of blood transfusions in the circumstances of her case constituted negligence and assault and battery and subjected her to religious discrimination. The trial came on before Donnelly J who, in reasons now reported at 63 OR (2d) 243, 47 DLR (4th) 18, 43 CCLT 62, dismissed the action against all defendants save Dr Shulman. With respect to Dr Shulman, the learned judge concluded that the Jehovah's Witness card validly restricted his right to treat the patient, and there was no rationally founded basis upon which the doctor could ignore that restriction. Hence, his administration of blood transfusions constituted a battery on the plaintiff. The judge awarded her damages of $20,000 but declined to make any award of costs.

Dr Shulman now appeals to this court from that judgment. Mrs Malette cross-appeals the judge's dismissal of the action against the hospital and his order with respect to costs.

… I should perhaps underscore the fact that Dr Shulman was not found liable for any negligence in his treatment of Mrs Malette. The judge held that he had acted "promptly, professionally and was well-motivated throughout" and that his management of the case had been "carried out in a competent, careful and conscientious manner" in accordance with the requisite standard of care. His decision to administer blood in the circumstances confronting him was found to be an honest exercise of his professional judgment which did not delay Mrs Malette's recovery, endanger her life or cause her any bodily harm. Indeed, the judge concluded that the doctor's treatment of Mrs Malette "may well have been responsible for saving her life".

[326] Liability was imposed in this case on the basis that the doctor tortiously violated his patient's rights over her own body by acting contrary to the Jehovah's Witness card and administering blood transfusions that were not authorized. His honest and even justifiable belief that the treatment was medically essential did not serve to relieve him from liability for the battery resulting from his intentional and unpermitted conduct. …

[327] The right of a person to control his or her own body is a concept that has long been recognized at common law. The tort of battery has traditionally protected the interest in bodily security from unwanted physical interference. Basically, any intentional nonconsensual touching which is harmful or offensive to a person's reasonable sense of dignity is actionable. Of course, a person may choose to waive this protection and consent to the intentional invasion of this interest, in which case an action for battery will not be maintainable. No special exceptions are made for medical care, other than in emergency situations, and the general rules governing actions for battery are applicable to the doctor-patient relationship. Thus, as a matter of common law, a medical

intervention in which a doctor touches the body of a patient would constitute a battery if the patient did not consent to the intervention. Patients have the decisive role in the medical decision-making process. Their right of self-determination is recognized and protected by the law. As Justice Cardozo proclaimed in his classic statement: "Every human being of adult years and sound mind has a right to determine what shall be done with his own body; and a surgeon who performs an operation without his patient's consent commits an assault, for which he is liable in damages." *Schloendorff v Society of New York Hospital* 211 NY 125 (1914). …

The doctrine of informed consent has developed in the law as the primary means of protecting a patient's right to control his or her medical treatment. Under the doctrine, no medical procedure may be undertaken without the patient's consent obtained after the patient has been provided with sufficient information to evaluate the risks and benefits of the proposed treatment and other available options. The doctrine presupposes the patient's capacity to make a subjective treatment based on her [328] understanding of the necessary medical facts provided by the doctor and on her assessment of her own personal circumstances. A doctor who performs a medical procedure without having first furnished the patient with the information needed to obtain an informed consent will have infringed the patient's right to control the course of her medical care, and will be liable in battery even though the procedure was performed with a high degree of skill and actually benefited the patient.

The right of self-determination which underlies the doctrine of informed consent also obviously encompasses the right to refuse medical treatment. A competent adult is generally entitled to reject a specific treatment or all treatment, or to select an alternate form of treatment, even if the decision may entail risks as serious as death and may appear mistaken in the eyes of the medical profession or of the community. Regardless of the doctor's opinion, it is the patient who has the final say on whether to undergo the treatment. The patient is free to decide, for instance, not to be operated on or not to undergo therapy or, by the same token, not to have a blood transfusion. If a doctor were to proceed in the face of a decision to reject the treatment, he would be civilly liable for his unauthorized conduct notwithstanding his patient's life or health. The doctrine of informed consent is plainly intended to ensure the freedom of individuals to make choices concerning their medical care. For this freedom to be meaningful, people must have the right to make choices that accord with their own values regardless of how unwise or foolish those choices may appear to others: see generally, Prosser & Keeton, *op cit*, p 112 *et seq*; Harper, James & Gray, *The Law of Torts*, 2nd ed (1986), c. III; Linden, *op cit*, p 64 *et seq*; and *Reibl v Hughes* (1980), 114 DLR (3d) 1, [1980] 2 SCR 880, 14 CCLT 1.

IV

The emergency situation is an exception to the general rule requiring a patient's prior consent. When immediate medical treatment is necessary to save the life or preserve the health of a person who, by reason of unconsciousness or extreme illness, is incapable of either giving or withholding consent, the doctor may proceed without the patient's consent. The delivery of medical services is rendered lawful in such circumstances either on the rationale that the doctor has implied consent from the patient to give emergency aid or, more accurately in my view, on the rationale that the doctor is privileged by reason of necessity in [329] giving the aid and is not to be held liable for so doing. On either basis, in an emergency the law sets aside the requirement of consent on the assumption that the patient, as a reasonable person, would want emergency aid to be rendered if she were capable of giving instructions. …

On the facts of the present case, Dr Shulman was clearly faced with an emergency. He had an unconscious, critically ill patient on his hands who, in his opinion, needed blood transfusions to save her life or preserve her health. If there were no Jehovah's Witness card he undoubtedly would have been entitled to administer blood transfusions as part of the emergency treatment and could not have been held liable for so doing. In those circumstances he would have had no indication that the transfusions would have been refused had the patient then been able to make her wishes known and, accordingly, no reason to expect that, as a reasonable person, she would not consent to the transfusions.

However, to change the facts, if Mrs Malette, before passing into unconsciousness, had expressly instructed Dr Shulman, in terms comparable to those set forth on the card, that her religious convictions as a Jehovah's Witness were such that she was not to be given a blood transfusion under any circumstance and that she fully realized the implications of this position, the doctor would have been confronted with an obviously different situation. Here, **[330]** the patient, anticipating an emergency in which she might be unable to make decisions about her health care contemporaneous with the emergency, has given explicit instructions that blood transfusions constitute an unacceptable medical intervention and are not to be administered to her. Once the emergency arises, is the doctor none the less entitled to administer transfusions on the basis of his honest belief that they are needed to save his patient's life?

The answer in my opinion, is clearly no. A doctor is not free to disregard a patient's advance instructions any more than he would be free to disregard instructions given at the time of the emergency. The law does not prohibit a patient from withholding consent to emergency medical treatment, nor does the law prohibit a doctor from following his patient's instructions. While the law may disregard the absence of consent in limited emergency circumstances, it otherwise supports the right of competent adults to make decisions concerning their own health care by imposing civil liability on those who perform medical treatment without consent.

The patient's decision to refuse blood in the situation I have posed was made prior to and in anticipation of the emergency. While the doctor would have had the opportunity to dissuade her on the basis of his medical advice, her refusal to accept his advice or her unwillingness to discuss or consider the subject would not relieve him of his obligation to follow her instructions. The principles of self-determination and individual autonomy compel the conclusion that the patient may reject blood transfusions even if harmful consequences may result and even if the decision is generally regarded as foolhardy. Her decision in this instance would be operative after she lapsed into unconsciousness, and the doctor's conduct would be unauthorized. To transfuse a Jehovah's Witness in the face of her explicit instructions to the contrary would, in my opinion, violate her right to control her own body and show disrespect for the religious values by which she has chosen to live her life: see *In re Estate of Brooks*, 205 NE 2d 435 (1965, Ill); and *Randolph v City of New York* an unreported judgment of the Supreme Court of New York released July 12, 1984, Index No 17598/75; reversed 501 NYS 2d 837 (1986); varied 514 NYS 2d 705 (1987).

V

The distinguishing feature of the present case – and the one that makes this a case of first impression – is, of course, the **[331]** Jehovah's Witness card on the person of the unconscious patient. What then is the effect of the Jehovah's Witness card?

In the appellant's submission, the card is of no effect and, as a consequence, can play no role in determining the doctor's duty toward his patient in the emergency situation existing in this case. The trial judge, the appellant argues, erred in holding both that the Jehovah's Witness card validly restricted the doctor's right to administer the blood transfusions, and that there was no rationally founded basis for ignoring the card. The argument proceeds on the basis, first, that, as a matter of principle, a card of this nature could not operate in these circumstances to prohibit the doctor from providing emergency health care and, second, that in any event, as a matter of evidence, there was good reason to doubt the card's validity. The appellant acknowledges that a conscious rational patient is entitled to refuse any medical treatment and that a doctor must comply with that refusal no matter how ill-advised he may believe it to be. He contends, however, to quote from his factum, that "a patient refusing treatment regarded by a doctor as being medically necessary has a right to be advised by the doctor, and the doctor has a concomitant duty to advise the patient of the risks associated with that refusal". Here, because of the patient's unconsciousness, the doctor had no opportunity to advise her of the specific risks involved in refusing the blood transfusions that he regarded as medically necessary. In those circumstances, the appellant argues, it was not possible for the doctor to obtain, or for the patient to give, an "informed refusal". In the absence of such a refusal, the argument proceeds, Dr Shulman was under a legal and ethical duty to treat this patient as he would any other emergency case and provide the treatment that, in his medical judgement, was needed to preserve her health and life. In short, the argument concludes, Mrs Malette's religiously motivated instructions, prepared in contemplation of an emergency, directing that she not be given blood transfusions in any circumstances, were of no force or effect and could be ignored with impunity.

In challenging the trial judge's finding that there was no rationally founded evidentiary basis for doubting the validity of the card and ignoring the restriction contained in it, the appellant puts forth a number of questions which he claims compel the conclusion that he was under no duty to comply with these instructions. He argues that it could properly be doubted whether the card constituted a valid statement of Mrs Malette's wishes in this emergency because it was unknown, for instance, whether she **[332]** knew the card was still in her purse; whether she was still a Jehovah's Witness or how devout a Jehovah's Witness she was; what information she had about the risks associated with the refusal of blood transfusion when she signed the card; or whether, if she were conscious, she would refuse blood transfusions after the doctor had an opportunity to advise her of the risks associated with the refusal.

I do not agree [with the appellant] that the Jehovah's Witness card can be no more than a meaningless piece of paper. I share the trial judge's view that, in the circumstances of this case, the instructions in the Jehovah's Witness card imposed a valid restriction on the emergency treatment that could be provided to Mrs Malette and precluded blood transfusions. ...

[338] Finally, the appellant appeals the quantum of damages awarded by the trial judge. In his submission, given the findings as to the competence of the treatment, the favourable results, the doctor's overall exemplary conduct and his good faith in the matter, the battery was technical and the general damages should be no more **[339]** than nominal. While the submission is not without force, damages of $20,000 cannot be said to be beyond the range of damages appropriate to a tortious interference of this nature. The trial judge found that Mrs Malette suffered mentally and emotionally by reason of the battery. His assessment of general damages was clearly not affected by any palpable or overriding error and there is therefore no basis upon which an appellate court may interfere with the award. ...

[The other members of the court who concurred in this judgment were Catzman and Carthy JJA.]

Appeal dismissed

Chapter 12

Concurrent Liability

1. VICARIOUS LIABILITY

(a) Employees and Independent Contractors

Sweeney v Boylan Nominees Pty Ltd
(2006) 226 CLR 161; [2006] HCA 19
High Court of Australia

The critical distinction is to be maintained between employees, for whose conduct the employer generally will be vicariously liable, and independent contractors, for whose conduct the employer, ie the person engaging the independent contractor, generally will not be vicariously liable.

[The defendant (respondent), Boylan Nominees Pty Ltd, was the owner of a commercial refrigerator which was placed in the "convenience store" area of a suburban service station. At the request of the service station operator, the defendant, which was under an obligation as between itself and the service station operator to service and maintain the refrigerator, arranged for a mechanic, Mr Comninos, to repair a defect in the refrigerator door. The repairs were carried out negligently by Mr Comninos with the result that the plaintiff (appellant), Mrs Maria Sweeney, suffered personal injury when the door fell on her as she opened the refrigerator to buy a carton of milk. The evidence established that Mr Comninos carried on his own business and was not an employee of the defendant. His van carried his own company name and the defendant did not provide him with a uniform or equipment. Mr Comninos was paid by the defendant upon submitting an invoice for the work performed and for spare parts. The plaintiff commenced proceedings against the service station operator, as occupier of the premises, and the defendant to recover damages for personal injury. For reasons unexplained, Mr Comninos was not a party to the proceedings.

At the trial in the District Court of New South Wales, the claim against the service station operator was dismissed on the ground that the service station operator had done all that could reasonably be expected in the circumstances and had not been negligent. However, the District Court entered judgment against the defendant on the ground that it was vicariously liable for the negligence of Mr Comninos. On appeal, the New South Wales Court of Appeal set aside the judgment against the defendant on the ground that it was not vicariously liable for the negligence of Mr Comninos who was an independent contractor. An appeal by the plaintiff was dismissed by the High Court of Australia (Gleeson CJ, Gummow, Hayne, Heydon and Crennan JJ; Kirby J dissenting).]

GLEESON CJ, GUMMOW, HAYNE, HEYDON and CRENNAN JJ. [some footnotes in whole or part omitted] ... **[166]** 11. Three recent decisions of this court have examined questions of vicarious liability: *Scott v Davis* (2000) 204 CLR 333 (*Scott*), *Hollis v Vabu Pty Ltd* (2001) 207 CLR 21 (*Hollis*) and *New South Wales v Lepore* (2003) 212 CLR 511 (*Lepore*). It is unnecessary to rehearse all that is established by those decisions. It is important, however, to begin examination of the issues in this appeal from a frank recognition of some considerations that are reflected in those decisions. First, "[a] fully satisfactory rationale for the imposition of vicarious liability in the employment relationship has been slow to appear in the case law": *Hollis* at 37. Secondly, "the modern doctrine respecting the liability of an employer for the torts of an employee was adopted not by way of an exercise in analytical jurisprudence but as a matter of policy": *Hollis* at 37. That may suggest that the policy to which effect was given by "the modern doctrine" is clearly identified, but, as is implicit in the first proposition, the policy which is said to lie behind the development of the modern doctrine is not and has not been fully articulated. Thirdly, although important aspects of the law relating to vicarious liability are often traced to the judgment of Parke B in *Quarman v Burnett* (1840) 151 ER 509, neither in that decision, nor in other early decisions to which the development of the doctrine of vicarious liability may be traced, does there emerge any clear or stable principle which may be understood as **[167]** underpinning the development of this area of the law. Indeed, as is demonstrated in *Scott* at 386-408, the development of the law in this area has not always proceeded on a correct understanding of the basis of earlier decisions.

12. Nonetheless, as the decisions in *Scott, Hollis* and *Lepore* show, there are some basic propositions that can be identified as central to this body of law. For present purposes, there are two to which it will be necessary to give principal attention. First, there is the distinction between employees (for whose conduct the employer will generally be vicariously liable) and independent contractors (for whose conduct the person engaging the contractor will generally not be vicariously liable). Secondly, there is the importance which is attached to the course of employment. ...

13. Whatever may be the justification for the doctrine, it is necessary always to recall that much more often than not, questions of vicarious liability fall to be considered in a context where one person has engaged another (for whose conduct the first is said to be vicariously liable) to do something that is of advantage to, and for the purposes of, that first person. Yet it is clear that the bare fact that the second person's actions were intended to benefit the first, or were undertaken to advance some purpose of the first person, does not suffice to demonstrate that the first is vicariously liable for the conduct of the second. The whole of the law that has developed on the distinction between employees and independent contractors denies that benefit or advantage to the one will suffice to establish vicarious liability for the conduct of the second. ...

[168] 14. In the present case, the appellant's contention that the respondent was vicariously liable for the negligence of the mechanic fastened upon a number of statements found in the reasons for judgment of Dixon J in *Colonial Mutual Life Assurance Society Ltd v Producers and Citizens Co-operative Assurance Co of Australia Ltd* (1931) 46 CLR 41. It was submitted that those statements supported the conclusion that the mechanic did the work he did "as a representative" of the respondent. He was a "representative", so the appellant submitted, because the mechanic "represented" that he had an association with the respondent, and the respondent "represented" that same association. It was not said that these representations of association had in any way been relied on by the appellant. She knew nothing of these matters until after her accident. The "representing" was said to be constituted by what passed between the respondent and the service station operators before and at the time of the attempted repairing of the door. ...

17. In *Colonial Mutual Life*, Dixon J said, (1931) 46 CLR 41 at 50:

Some of the difficulties of the subject arise from the many senses in which the word 'agent' is employed. 'No word is more commonly and constantly abused than the word "agent". A person may be spoken of as an "agent" and no doubt in the popular sense of the word may properly be said to be an "agent", although when it is attempted to suggest that he is an "agent" under such circumstances as create the legal obligations attaching to agency that use of the word is only misleading' (per Lord Herschell in *Kennedy v De Trafford* [1897] AC 180 at 188). Unfortunately, too, the expressions 'for,' 'on behalf of,' 'for the benefit of' and even 'authorise' are often used in relation to services which, although done for the advantage of a person who requests them, involve no representation.

[169] In *Colonial Mutual Life* the person, for whose statements the appellant was sought to be made vicariously liable, had been engaged by the appellant to canvass for proposals for life insurance. The statements which it was alleged that he made, and which were slanderous of the respondent company, had been uttered in the course of his attempting to induce persons to make proposals for life insurance by the appellant. He was not a servant of the appellant company. Yet it was held that the appellant was vicariously liable for his statements because he made them in acting as the company's agent.

18. In soliciting proposals, the person who made the slanderous statements was acting in right of the company and with its authority. He had express authority to canvass for the making of contractual offers to his principal. Although he had no authority from his principal to accept any offers that were made, "the Company in confiding to his judgment, within the limits of relevance and of reasonableness, the choice of inducements and arguments, authorised him on its behalf to address to prospective proponents such observations as appeared to him appropriate" (at 50 per Dixon J). "[T]he very service to be performed consist[ed] in standing in [the principal's] place and assuming to act in [its] right *and not in an independent capacity*" (at 48-49 per Dixon J) (emphasis added) in a transaction with others. He acted in right of the principal, and not in an independent capacity, because he acted in execution of his authority to canvass for offers to contract with his principal.

19. In *Colonial Mutual Life* (at 49), Dixon J said that the rule imposing liability upon a master for the wrongs of a servant committed in the course of employment was (then) (See now, however, *Scott v Davis* (2000) 204 CLR 333 at 413 [239]) commonly regarded as part of the law of agency. ...

[170] 21. *Colonial Mutual Life* must be understood against the background of the development of this area of law by the assertion and application of conclusions whose ultimate roots are found in analogies which are no longer apt (if they ever were). But whatever may now be seen to be the imperfections in the ultimate roots of this area of the law, the conclusion reached in *Colonial Mutual Life* fits entirely within the explanation of vicarious liability identified by Pollock (*Essays in Jurisprudence and Ethics* (1882) p 122) and reflected in the subsequent decisions of this Court culminating in *Scott, Hollis* and *Lepore*.

22. *Colonial Mutual Life* establishes that if an independent contractor is engaged to solicit the bringing about of legal relations between the principal who engages the contractor and third parties, the principal will be held liable for slanders uttered to persuade the third party to make an agreement with the principal. It is a conclusion that depends directly upon the identification of the independent contractor as the principal's agent (properly so called) and the recognition that the conduct of which complaint is made was conduct undertaken in the course of, and for the purpose of, executing that agency. ...

[171] 26. But the wider proposition that underpinned the argument of the appellant in this case, that if A "represents" B, B is vicariously liable for the conduct of A, is a proposition of such generality that it goes well beyond the bounds set by notions of control (with old, and now imperfect analogies of servitude) or set by notions of course of employment.

27. These bounds should not now be redrawn in the manner asserted by the appellant. Hitherto the distinction between independent contractors and employees has been critical to the definition of the ambit of vicarious liability. The view, sometimes expressed (*Scott* at 370 per McHugh J; *Hollis* at 57-8 per McHugh J) that the distinction should be abandoned in favour of a wider principle, has not commanded the assent of a majority of this court.

28. In *Scott*, the majority of the court rejected the contention that the owner of an aircraft was vicariously liable for the negligence of the pilot of that aircraft if the pilot operated the aircraft with the owner's consent and for a purpose in which the owner had some concern. The argument that "a new species of actor, one who is not an employee, nor an independent contractor, but an

'agent' in a non-technical sense" (*Scott* at 423 per Gummow J) should be identified as relevant to determining vicarious liability, was rejected.

[172] 29. In *Hollis*, the court amplified the application of the distinction between independent contractors and employees to take account of differing ways in which some particular enterprises are now conducted. As was said in the joint reason, at 40:

> In general, under contemporary Australian conditions, the conduct by the defendant of an enterprise in which persons are identified as representing that enterprise should carry an obligation to third persons to bear the cost of injury or damage to them which may fairly be said to be characteristic of the conduct of that enterprise.

But neither in *Scott* nor in *Hollis* ... was there established the principle that A is vicariously liable for the conduct of B if B "represents" A (in the sense of B acting for the benefit or advantage of A). On the contrary, *Scott* rejected contentions that, at their roots, were no different from those advanced in this case under the rubric of "representation" rather than, as in *Scott*, under the rubric "agency". As was said in *Scott* of the word "agent", at 423, to use the word "representative" is to begin, but not to end, the inquiry.

30. It is as well to add something further about *Hollis*. *Hollis* hinged about whether the person whose conduct was negligent was to be identified as an employee of the principal. Seven considerations were identified in the facts of that case (at 42-5) as bearing upon the question. They included that the courier wore the principal's livery, that he was subject to close direction by the principal about not only the manner of performing the work (work which required only limited skills), but also both the financial dealings generated by the work and the times at which the work was done.

[173] 31. The circumstances of the present case are very different. The mechanic [Mr Comninos] was not an employee of the respondent. He conducted his own business: Cf *Hollis* at 42. It may be that it could be inferred that he did that through, and as an employee of, the company whose name provided the name advertised on his vehicle. But this was not a matter to which close attention was given in evidence at trial and it is not necessary to pursue it to its conclusion. That the mechanic was engaged in a business other than that of the respondent was demonstrated by a number of circumstances, but chief among them were his invoicing the respondent for each job he did and the respondent's concern to verify that the mechanic had proper workers' compensation and public liability insurance. The interposition of the mechanic's company would, of course, give further support to the conclusion that he was engaged in a business other than that of the respondent.

32. The mechanic or, if it were the case, his company, was engaged from time to time as a contractor to perform maintenance work for the respondent. Unlike the principal in *Hollis*, the respondent did not control the way in which the mechanic worked. The mechanic supplied his own tools and equipment, as well as bringing his skills to bear upon the work that was to be done. And unlike the case in *Hollis*, the mechanic was not presented to the public as an emanation of the respondent. ...

33. Whatever may be the logical and doctrinal imperfections and difficulties in the origins of the law relating to vicarious liability, the two central conceptions of distinguishing between independent contractors and employees and attaching determinative significance to course of employment are now too deeply rooted to be pulled out. And without discarding at least the first, and perhaps even the second, the appellant's claim against the respondent must fail. The mechanic was an independent contractor. He did what he did for the benefit of the respondent and in attempted discharge of its contractual obligations. But he did what he did not as an employee of the respondent, but as a principal pursuing his own business or as an employee of his own company pursuing its business.

[174] 34. The conclusion that the mechanic was an independent contractor is determinative of the issue that arises in the appeal. The appeal must be dismissed with costs.

Appeal dismissed

(b) Employment Relationship

Zuijs v Wirth Bros Pty Ltd
(1955) 93 CLR 561
High Court of Australia

An indicia of the relationship of employer and employee is that the employer lawfully may command the employee as to the manner in which the employee is to do his or her work. It is not material to the existence of the relationship of employer and employee that, in the case of employees who are employed to perform specialised functions, there may be little scope for the exercise by the employer of this power of command.

DIXON CJ, WILLIAMS, WEBB and TAYLOR JJ. **[566]** The respondents to this appeal are circus proprietors who in the Workers' Compensation Commission and in the Supreme Court of New South Wales have successfully resisted the claim of an acrobat for compensation in respect of injuries suffered in the circus. The acrobat, who is the appellant, performed upon the trapeze in conjunction with a colleague. During a performance in which the latter hung from a rope with his hands while the appellant grasped his feet and was thus suspended beneath him, his colleague slipped from the rope so that both fell, his companion falling on top of the appellant. It was in this way that the appellant sustained his injuries and there is no question that they arose out of, as well as in the course of, the work he was doing for the respondents. The ground upon which the respondents have escaped liability is that the appellant was not employed under a contract of service with the respondents and that he did not fall within any special provision bringing him within the *Workers' Compensation Act 1926-1948* (NSW). ...

[571] The terms of the often repeated statement of Bramwell LJ are: "A servant is a person subject to the command of his master as to the manner in which he shall do his work": *Yewens v Noakes* (1880) 6 QBD 530, at pp 532, 533.

The duties to be performed may depend so much on special skill or knowledge or they may be so clearly identified or the necessity of the employee acting on his own responsibility may be so evident, that little room for direction or command in detail may exist. But that is not the point. What matters is lawful authority to command so far as there is scope for it. And there must always be some room for it, if only in incidental or collateral matters. Even if Mr Phillip Wirth could not interfere in the actual technique of the acrobatics and in the character of the act, no reason appears why the appellant should not be subject to his direction in all other respects.

Assuming that the terms of the engagement fixed the character of the act and that from its very nature an acrobatic performance must be executed upon the unhampered responsibility of the performers, that does not remove the relationship from the category of master and servant. There are countless examples of highly specialized functions in modern life that must as a matter of practical **[572]** necessity and sometimes even as a matter of law be performed on the responsibility of persons who possess particular knowledge and skill and who are accordingly qualified. But those engaged to perform the functions may nevertheless work under a contract of service. In the present case what has been proved in evidence all points to the conclusion that the relation between the parties was that of master and servant. If the power of selecting the person engaged must exist in the master in order that the contract may be one of service, that element was certainly present. If the fact that the remuneration takes the form of wages is a mark of the relationship, that was the case here. If a right in the master to suspend or dismiss for misconduct is something to be looked for, then again there could be little doubt that the appellant was subject to that discipline. If a right to superintend and control the manner in which the servant fulfils his obligation must exist in some degree, a little consideration will show that the daily relations of a performer playing a regular part in the work of such an organization as a travelling circus would demand a large measure of control and superintendence. With reference to the act itself there are many subsidiary matters. The place it took upon the programme, the measures of safety to be observed, the number, time and manner of the rehearsals, the costume of the performers, the place where they dressed and their conduct both before the audience and otherwise, these are all matters naturally calling for control. The grand parade doubtless involved no inherent difficulty but one may suppose that it was necessary to exercise control and direction as to the manner in which it was done. Apart from the two central duties of performing the act and taking part in the grand parade, the incidents of the relation between a regular performer and a touring circus must cover a wide field of conduct calling for superintendence and control. No doubt it might all be dealt with by a contract for services, but unless the express terms of the contract of engagement specified the obligations of the performer in great detail in order to avoid reserving an extensive power of control, it would be likely to be treated as a contract of service. ...

[573] The first question which is reserved in the case stated should therefore be answered that upon the evidence before the commission the commission did err in law in holding that the applicant was not employed under a contract of service. ...

[McTiernan J delivered a concurring judgment.]

Appeal allowed

Hollis v Vabu Pty Ltd
(2001) 207 CLR 21; [2001] HCA 44
High Court of Australia

Where an employer conducts an enterprise in which persons are identified as representing that enterprise, this indicates that those persons are employees. On the other hand, an independent contractor carries out his or her work as a principal, not as a representative of the employer.

[Mr Hollis, the plaintiff/appellant, suffered personal injury when, as a pedestrian, he was struck by an unidentified cyclist negligently riding a bicycle on a footpath in breach of traffic regulations.

In an action by Mr Hollis to recover damages for personal injury, the trial judge in the District Court of New South Wales found that the cyclist was a bicycle courier "employed" by Vabu Pty Ltd ("Vabu"), the defendant/respondent, which conducted a parcel and document delivery business. The trial judge also found that (1) at the time of the accident the cyclist was on Vabu's business and was wearing the uniform bearing Vabu's trade name issued to him by Vabu and which Vabu required him to wear, (2) Vabu had known for some time before the accident that a significant number of its bicycle couriers disobeyed traffic regulations and posed a danger to pedestrians, and (3) Vabu set the rates of remuneration of its bicycle couriers without negotiation, such remuneration being in accordance with deliveries made rather than in the form of wages or salary, allocated work to its bicycle couriers, assumed responsibility as to the direction, training, discipline and attire of its bicycle couriers, provided its bicycle couriers with numerous items of accessory equipment (but not bicycles, which the couriers supplied themselves) and deducted the cost of insurance from the remuneration of its bicycle couriers. However, the trial judge rejected Mr Hollis' contention that Vabu was vicariously liable for the conduct of the negligent cyclist. In reaching this conclusion the trial judge considered himself bound by the decision of the New South Wales Court of Appeal in *Vabu Pty Ltd v Federal Commissioner of Taxation* (1996) 33 ATR 537 where, on substantially similar evidence as in the present case, the court held that, in the context of Commonwealth superannuation legislation, the bicycle couriers were independent contractors and not employees of Vabu.

In the present case the New South Wales Court of Appeal dismissed an appeal by Mr Hollis, who was granted special leave to appeal to the High Court of Australia.]

GLEESON CJ, GAUDRON, GUMMOW, KIRBY and HAYNE JJ. [some footnotes omitted] **[25]**
1. This appeal involves issues respecting the nature of the relationship of employment and the scope of the doctrine of vicarious liability. ...

[36] 32. ... It has long been accepted, as a general rule (see the observations of Brennan J in *Burnie Port Authority v General Jones Pty Ltd* (1994) 179 CLR 520 at 575), that an employer is vicariously liable for the tortious acts of an employee but that a principal is not liable for the tortious acts of an independent contractor (*Northern Sandblasting Pty Ltd v Harris* (1997) 188 CLR 313 at 329-330, 366). That general rule was not challenged in this appeal. ...

[38] 39. In *Colonial Mutual Life Assurance Society Ltd v Producers and Citizens Co-operative Assurance Co of Australia Ltd* (1931) 46 CLR 41, Dixon J explained [at 48] the dichotomy between the relationships of employer and employee, and principal and independent contractor, in a passage **[39]** which has frequently been referred to in this Court (*Kondis v State Transport Authority* (1984) 154 CLR 672 at 691-692; *Burnie Port Authority v General Jones Pty Ltd* (1994) 179 CLR 520 at 574; *Northern Sandblasting Pty Ltd v Harris* (1997) 188 CLR 313 at 329-330, 366). His Honour explained that, in the case of an independent contractor:

> [t]he work, although done at [the principal's] request and for his benefit, is considered as the independent function of the person who undertakes it, and not as something which the person obtaining the benefit does by his representative standing in his place and, therefore, identified with him for the purpose of liability arising in the course of its performance. The independent contractor carries out his work, not as a representative but as a principal.

40. This statement merits close attention. It indicates that employees and independent contractors perform work for the benefit of their employers and principals respectively. Thus, by itself, the circumstance that the business enterprise of a party said to be an employer is benefited by the activities of the person in question cannot be a sufficient indication that this person is an employee. However, Dixon J fixed upon the absence of representation and of identification with the alleged employer as indicative of a relationship of principal and independent contractor. These notions later were expressed positively by Windeyer J in *Marshall v Whittaker's Building Supply Co* (1963) 109 CLR 210 at 217. His Honour said that the distinction between an employee and an independent contractor is "rooted fundamentally in the difference between a person who serves his employer in his, the employer's, business, and a person who carries on a trade or business of his own". In *Northern Sandblasting* (1997) 188 CLR 313 at 366, McHugh J said:

> The rationale for excluding liability for independent contractors is that the work which the contractor has agreed to do is not done as the representative of the employer.

41. In *Bazley v Curry* [1999] 2 SCR 534 at 552-555, the Supreme Court of Canada saw two fundamental or major concerns as underlying the imposition of vicarious liability. The first is the provision of a just and practical remedy for the harm suffered as a result of the wrongs committed in the course of the conduct of the defendant's enterprise. The second is the deterrence of future harm, by the incentive given to employers to reduce the risk of accident, even where there has been no negligence in the legal sense in the particular case giving rise to the claim.

[40] 42. In general, under contemporary Australian conditions, the conduct by the defendant of an enterprise in which persons are identified as representing that enterprise should carry an obligation to third persons to bear the cost of injury or damage to them which may fairly be said to be characteristic of the conduct of that enterprise. In delivering the judgment of the Supreme Court of Canada in *Bazley v Curry* [1999] 2 SCR 534 at 548, McLachlin J said of such cases that "the employer's enterprise [has] created the risk that produced the tortious act" and the employer must bear responsibility for it. McLachlin J termed this risk "enterprise risk" and said that "where the employee's conduct is closely tied to a risk that the employer's enterprise has placed in the community, the employer may justly be held vicariously liable for the employee's wrong" (*Bazley v Curry* [1999] 2 SCR 534 at 548-549). ...

[41] 45. So it is that, in the present case, guidance for the outcome is provided by various matters which are expressive of the fundamental concerns underlying the doctrine of vicarious liability. These include, but are not confined to, what now is considered "control". ...

47. ... **[42]** The concern here is with the bicycle couriers engaged on Vabu's business. A consideration of the nature of their engagement ... indicates that they were employees.

48. First, these couriers were not providing skilled labour or labour which required special qualifications. … The notion that the couriers somehow were running their own enterprise is intuitively unsound, and denied by the facts disclosed in the record.

49. Secondly, the evidence shows that the couriers had little control over the manner of performing their work. …

50. Thirdly, the facts show that couriers were presented to the public and to those using the courier service as emanations of Vabu. They were to wear uniforms bearing Vabu's logo. …

[43] 53. Fourthly, there is the matter of deterrence. Reference has been made to the findings of fact in this case respecting the knowledge of Vabu as to the dangers to pedestrians presented by its bicycle couriers and the failure to adopt effective means for the personal identification of those couriers by the public. One of the major policy considerations said by the Supreme Court of Canada in *Bazley v Curry* [1999] 2 SCR 534 to support vicarious liability was deterrence of future harm. …

54. Fifthly, Vabu superintended the couriers' finances … . There was no scope for the couriers to bargain for the rate of their remuneration.

[44] 56. Sixthly, the situation in respect of tools and equipment also favours, if anything, a finding that the bicycle couriers were employees. … Although a more beneficent employer might have provided bicycles for its employees and undertaken the cost of their repairs, there is nothing contrary to a relationship of employment in the fact that employees were here required to do so. …

57. Finally, and as a corollary to the second point mentioned above, this is not a case where there was only the right to exercise control in incidental or collateral matters. Rather, there was considerable scope for the actual exercise of control (*Stevens v Brodribb Sawmilling Co Pty Ltd* (1986) 160 CLR 16 at 29). Vabu's whole business consisted of the delivery of documents and parcels by means of couriers. … [45] It was not the case that the couriers supplemented or performed part of the work undertaken by Vabu or aided from time to time; rather … to its customers they *were* Vabu and effectively performed all of Vabu's operations in the outside world. It would be unrealistic to describe the couriers other than as employees. …

[46] 61. The relationship between Vabu and the bicycle courier who struck down Mr Hollis was that of employer and employee. Vabu thus was vicariously liable for the consequences of the courier's negligent performance of his work. …

[47] 63. The appeal should be allowed with costs. …

[McHugh J, after a consideration of contemporary work practices, including the contracting out of work by employers, and the rationales for vicarious liability, found that Vabu was liable for the negligence of the bicycle courier on the basis that, although the courier was not an independent contractor or an employee, he was an agent of Vabu acting within the scope of his authority as Vabu's representative carrying out a contractual obligation of Vabu. Callinan J dissented.]

Appeal allowed

(c) Course of Employment

Joel v Morison
(1834) 172 ER 1338
Court of Exchequer

An employer is liable for a tort committed by an employee in the course of employment. However, an employer is not liable where an employee commits a tort while "on a frolic" of his or her own.

[While crossing a public road, the plaintiff was struck and injured by a horse-drawn cart driven by the defendant's employee. In the plaintiff's negligence action against the defendant for damages for personal injury, the defendant's witnesses stated that, in the ordinary course of things, the cart was not driven in the particular locality in the City of London where the accident occurred but was "in the habit of being driven between Burton Crescent Mews and Finchley". Extracted below is Parke B's summing up to the jury, which returned a verdict for the plaintiff.]

> PARKE B. [1338] This is an action to recover damages for an injury sustained by the plaintiff, in consequence of the negligence of the defendant's servant. There is no doubt that the plaintiff has suffered the injury and there is no doubt that the driver of the cart was guilty of negligence, and there is no doubt also that the master, if that person was driving the cart on his master's business, is responsible. If the servants, being on their master's business, took a detour to call upon a friend, the master will be responsible. If you think the servants lent the cart to a person who was driving without the defendant's knowledge he will not be responsible. Or, if you think that the young man who was driving took the cart surreptitiously, and was not at the time employed on his master's business, the [1339] defendant will not be liable. The master is only liable where the servant is acting in the course of his employment. If he was going out of his way, against his master's implied commands, when driving on his master's business, he will make his master liable; but if he was going on a frolic of his own, without being at all on his master's business, the master will not be liable. ...

Verdict for the plaintiff

Bugge v Brown
(1919) 26 CLR 110
High Court of Australia

Whether a given act of an employee is in the course of employment is a question of fact dependent on the circumstances of the case.

[The appellant (plaintiff) suffered damage in a fire which started on land belonging to the respondent (defendant). The fire had been lit by Winter, an employee of the respondent, in order to cook some food given to him by the respondent for his midday meal. Winter had been sent, with another employee, to a distant part of the respondent's property in order to cut thistles. He was instructed to cook at a deserted homestead about a mile or more away from the work, but, instead of going there, began to cook at an old chimney close to the operations. It seems that the purpose of the instruction with respect to the place of cooking was not to avoid the danger of the fire getting out of control, but to obviate the need to take a frying pan in which to cook the meat.

In an action by the appellant against the respondent the trial Judge gave judgment for the respondent on the ground that, though Winter was negligent, the lighting of the fire was not within the course of his employment.]

> ISAACS J. [some references omitted] ... [116] The responsibility of a master for the wrongful act of his servant does not depend merely on the question of authority, express or implied. He may be liable though the act be beyond any authority actually given by him. ...
>
> [117] The principle on which the responsibility rests is that it is more just to make the person who has entrusted his servant with the power of acting in his business responsible for injury occasioned to another in the course of so acting, than that the other and entirely innocent party should be left to bear the loss. The principle was enunciated about 1700 by *Holt* CJ in *Hern v Nichols* (1708) 1 Salk 289, was strikingly enforced by *Willes* J in *Limpus v London General Omnibus Co* (1862) 1 H&C 526 in 1862, was reaffirmed and acted on by the Court of Appeal in *Hamlyn's Case* [1903] 1 KB 81, see p 86, and has been definitely approved by the House of Lords in *Lloyd v Grace, Smith & Co* [1912] AC 716, see particularly pp 726-727, 732, 738. ...

The rule of law founded on that principle is that the master is responsible, provided the servant is acting in "the course of his employment." That phrase and various corresponding phrases, such as "scope of employment" and "sphere of employment" and other similar phrases, are used to indicate the just limits of a master's responsibility for the wrongdoing of his servant. We have seen that the narrow view of "limits of authority" whether actual or implied, or even where a definite prohibition against doing the act complained of exists, or where even the law itself forbids the act, does not determine the question of liability to answer for the wrong; for the act complained of may nevertheless be within the course of the employment. But the law recognizes that it is equally unjust to make the **[118]** master responsible for every act which the servant chooses to do. The limit of the rule – expressed in the widest form by the phrase "the course of their employment" or "the sphere of the employment" – is when the servant so acts as to be in effect a stranger in relation to his employer with respect to the act he has committed, so that the act is in law the unauthorized act of a stranger. ...

The act of the servant complained of is regarded as outside the relation, and as that of a stranger: (*a*) if he did not assume to act within the scope of his employment; or (*b*) if what he did was a thing so remote from his duty as to be altogether outside of, and unconnected with, his employment. ...

A prohibition, either as to *manner*, or as to *time*, or *place*, or even as to the very *act* itself, **[119]** will not necessarily limit the sphere of employment so as to exclude the act complained of, if the prohibition is violated. ...

An instruction or a prohibition may, of course, limit the sphere of employment. But to have that effect it must be such that its violation makes the servant's conduct complained of so distinctly remote and disconnected from his employment as to put him *quâ* that conduct virtually in the position of a stranger. This is the ultimately decisive consideration in this case. ...

[121] When proper regard is had to the legal considerations to which I have referred, the question of whether a given act of a servant is or is not within the course of his employment is a question of fact dependent entirely upon the circumstances of the particular case. ...

[122] I proceed now to consider the facts in evidence. ...

[Isaacs J reached the conclusion that the employee Winter had been acting in the course of employment and that the act of lighting the fire in disregard of the instruction to cook his meal at a particular place was not "a frolic of his own" unconnected with his employment.]

[129] The judgment appealed from should be reversed, and judgment entered for the plaintiff appellant for £1,022, with costs.

[Higgins J delivered a concurring judgment. Gavan Duffy J dissented.]

Appeal allowed

Deatons Pty Ltd v Flew
(1949) 79 CLR 370
High Court of Australia

An act of an employee which is unconnected with what he or she is employed to do will not be an act in the course of employment even though the act occurs on the employer's premises and while the employee is otherwise engaged in his or her employment duties.

DIXON J. **[379]** The question upon which this appeal appears to me to turn is whether the jury might properly find that an assault upon the plaintiff by the defendant Barlow, a barmaid in the employ of the defendant Deatons Pty Ltd, was committed in the course of her employment. The contents of a glass of beer, and the glass, left the hand of the barmaid and struck the plaintiff in the face. This is the assault. It resulted in the plaintiff's losing one eye.

The plaintiff's case was that he went into the public bar and asked by name for the publican. Thereupon the barmaid threw first the beer into his face and then the glass. According to his case it was an unprovoked and unjustified assault and his case was so left to the jury.

The case made for the defendants was that the plaintiff, who was drunk, did ask for the publican, that the barmaid said that he was in the saloon bar, that the plaintiff then pushed his way through **[380]** the customers in the wrong direction upsetting a number of glasses of beer, that the barmaid then asked him to go away, whereupon he used filthy expressions and struck the side of her face. She then threw in his face the beer in a glass she was holding, but the glass slipped out of her hand and also hit his face. The jury found a verdict against both defendants, the barmaid and the company employing her. On either version of the assault the barmaid would be liable. She made no case of self-defence and on the facts she could not make one. The provocation may have been great but that is no answer to the plaintiff's cause of action, whatever effect it might have upon damages.

In my opinion, however, it is clear that, upon the case made for the plaintiff, a finding could not be supported that the barmaid acted in the course of her employment so that the defendant company would be vicariously liable. For upon the plaintiff's case the assault was as unexplained as it was unprovoked and might have proceeded from private spite on the part of the barmaid or from some other cause quite unconnected with her occupation or employment. So far as the plaintiff's case went to show, nothing occurred which would in any way relate her action to the duties of her office or explain it by reference to anything incidental to what she was employed to do. As the jury had been instructed that the plaintiff was entitled to recover against both defendants if they took the view that the assault occurred as the plaintiff put his case, the Full Court of the Supreme Court set aside the verdict and rightly so.

But their Honours did not enter a verdict for the defendant company because, though not without considerable doubt, they thought there was evidence upon which a jury might find against the defendant company upon a basis described in the following passage from the judgment of Jordan CJ, viz:- "If a reasonable inference was that the barmaid's action was an instinctive act of self-defence against an assault made upon her whilst she was doing, and because she was doing, what she was employed to do, I think that it would be open to the jury to find that the employer was liable. A master who employs a servant in a capacity which exposes her to the risk of brutal violence may fairly be regarded as impliedly authorising her to defend herself against such violence" ((1949) 49 SR (NSW), at p 222; 66 WN, at p 99). In my opinion it would not be possible to support a verdict against the employer upon this basis. The circumstances were not such as to allow of the inference that the barmaid acted, however instinctively, through any motive of defending herself. She was behind **[381]** the bar, and the man was lurching about drunk among a crowd of men. Plainly she retaliated for a blow and an insult. She says her retaliation was limited to the contents of the glass and that she did not mean to throw the glass itself. But in either case it was a retort and not an act of self-protection.

It may be that acts of self-defence may so arise out of a servant's acts done in furtherance of his master's interests as to be considered incidental to the performance of his duties and so in the course of his employment. But from its nature self-defence is hardly a thing done by a servant on behalf of his master and I am not prepared to adopt the phrase in the foregoing passage which speaks of the master as impliedly authorizing the servant to defend herself against violence. However, for the reason I have given, it does not appear to me to fit the facts of this case. There is not in my opinion any other ground on which it could be found that the barmaid threw the beer or the glass or both in the course of her employment. The suggestion that it was her mistaken or improper manner of responding to an inquiry and that she was employed, among other purposes, to respond to inquiries is quite untenable.

There is scarcely any better foundation for the suggestion that a barmaid must take her part in keeping order in the bar and that she was doing in her own way. She did not throw the beer or the glass in the course of maintaining discipline or restoring order. Moreover she was not in charge of the bar. Over her there was another woman who was behind the same bar, and, it may be added, who at once said "You wicked girl." In the saloon bar close at hand was the publican.

The general and somewhat indefinite position was relied upon that the barmaid was there to deal with customers and with situations and this was the manner in which she dealt with the plaintiff and the situation which he caused. It is not a case of a negligent or improper act, due to error or ill judgment, but done in the supposed furtherance of the master's interests. Nor is it one of those wrongful acts done for the servant's own benefit for which the master is liable when they are acts to which the ostensible performance of his master's work gives occasion to or which are committed under cover of the authority the servant is held out as possessing or of the position in which he is placed as a representative of his master (see *Lloyd v Grace, Smith & Co* [1912] AC 716; *Uxbridge Permanent Benefit Building Society v Pickard* [1939] 2 KB 248).

The truth is that it was an act of passion and resentment done neither in furtherance of the master's interests nor under his express **[382]** or implied authority nor as an incident to or in consequence of anything the barmaid was employed to do. It was a spontaneous act of retributive justice. The occasion for administering it and the form it took may have arisen from the fact that she was a barmaid but retribution was not within the course of her employment as a barmaid.

I think that the appeal should be allowed with costs and a verdict entered for the defendant company, which should have its costs of the action. The cross appeal should be allowed against the respondent Barlow with costs and the verdict and judgment against her restored.

[Latham CJ, McTiernan, Williams and Webb JJ delivered judgments to a similar effect.]

Appeal allowed

Starks v RSM Security Pty Ltd
(2004) Aust Torts Reports ¶81-763; [2004] NSWCA 351
Supreme Court of New South Wales, Court of Appeal

An employer may be vicariously liable for a criminal assault committed by an employee where the act of the employee is an unauthorised mode of doing what the employee was employed to do. In such a case, the act of the employee is within the course of employment.

[The plaintiff/appellant, Mr Byron Starks, a patron at the Bondi Hotel, was asked to leave by a security officer, Mr Eugene Wilson, the first defendant. When the plaintiff/appellant, who was not acting in any way aggressively, questioned this request, the first defendant head-butted him causing personal injury. In respect of this incident, the first defendant was charged with the criminal offence of assault and pleaded guilty.

The plaintiff/appellant commenced proceedings in the District Court of New South Wales to recover damages for personal injury. The primary judge, Garling DCJ, awarded the plaintiff/appellant damages against the first defendant (the security officer). However, his Honour rejected the plaintiff's claims against (1) the security officer's employer, RSM Security Pty Ltd, the second defendant/first respondent, and (2) the hotel owner and occupier, Hotel Bondi Pty Ltd, the third defendant/second respondent, and the hotel licensee, Mr Cyril Maloney, the fourth defendant/third respondent.

The New South Wales Court of Appeal allowed the plaintiff/appellant's appeal in respect of the claim against the second defendant/first respondent (the security officer's employer) but dismissed the plaintiff/appellant's appeal in respect of the claims against the third defendant/second respondent (the hotel owner and occupier) and the fourth defendant/third respondent (the hotel licensee).]

BEAZLEY JA. ... **[65,989]** 4. ... [T]he matter to be determined raises two important questions. The first is the circumstances in which an employer can be vicariously liable for an unauthorised and illegal act of its employee. The second is the further question of when a party, in this case the hotel owner and the licensee, are vicariously liable for such acts of a third party. ...

[65,991] 12. An employer is vicariously liable for a tort or other actionable wrong committed by an employee in the course of employment. However, it is not every actionable wrong committed by an employee that will give rise to vicarious liability. Whether or not an employer is liable depends upon the scope of the employment. Thus, an employer will not be vicariously liable for a wrongful act of the employee if it is committed by the employee "on a frolic of his own": see *Morris v CW Martin & Sons Limited* [1966] 1 QB 716 at 733; *New South Wales v Lepore* (2003) 212 CLR 511 at [41]. ...

13. It is well settled that an employer is liable for a wrongful act of the employee if the employer has authorised it. An employer may also be liable for unauthorised acts. That is also well settled. The difficulty that arises in the latter case is determining the circumstances in which an employer will be so liable. This was the question under consideration in *Lepore*. There Gleeson CJ restated, at [42], Salmond's formulation of the principle in Salmond, *Law of Torts*, namely that:

> ... an employer is liable even for unauthorised acts if they are so connected with authorised acts as they may be regarded as modes – although improper modes – of doing them but the employer is not responsible if the unauthorised and wrongful act is not so connected with the authorised act as to be a mode of doing it, but is an independent act.

14. The employer [the second defendant/first respondent, RSM Security Pty Ltd] submitted that the case was indistinguishable from the facts in *Deatons Pty Limited v Flew* (1949) 79 CLR 370. In that case, a barmaid threw a glass of beer into the face of the plaintiff. The plaintiff was also hit by the glass. The plaintiff alleged that the barmaid had thrown it at him, the barmaid contending however that in throwing the beer at the plaintiff, the glass slipped out of her hand. There was also a dispute as to whether the plaintiff had spoken to the barmaid "using filthy expressions" and whether he had struck her on the side of the face.

15. The plaintiff sued the barmaid and her employer. The jury found a verdict against both. In the High Court, the employer was found not to be liable as the barmaid was not acting in the course of her employment or doing any act connected with or incidental to the work that she was employed to perform. ...

[65,992] 19. In the present case, Mr Wilson requested Mr Starks to leave the hotel. Although the terms of his employment were not in evidence, there was no issue in the case as to his entitlement to do so. That was part of his job if the circumstances called for it.

20. In his written submissions, counsel for the respondents pointed out that there was no evidence to indicate that Mr Wilson was required to make any physical contact with Mr Starks in order to carry out his duties. However, in argument before the Court, he dealt with the argument that force might be used. Section 103(1) of the *Liquor Act 1982* provides that a person employed in the position of Mr Wilson "may turn out, or cause to be turned out" persons acting, for example, in a disorderly or drunken way. As a matter of the plain language of the section and common experience, it might be expected that force could be used in such circumstances.

21. Counsel for the respondents accepted that there might be occasions when excessive force was used for which the employer would be liable. He accepted, for example, that if in the course of escorting a customer from the premises a security officer used excessive force, then the employer may well be liable. The employer submitted however, that Mr Wilson's action in head-butting Mr Starks was a gratuitous and unprovoked attack which had nothing to do with his duties as a security guard and was not simply an unauthorised mode of doing that for which he was employed. ...

22. There may of course be questions of degree as to whether an unexpected mode of the execution of an employee's duties will give rise to vicarious liability, as Gleeson CJ pointed out in *Lepore* at [54]:

> Where acts of physical violence are concerned, the nature and seriousness of the criminal act may be relevant to a judgment as to whether it is to be regarded as a personal, independent act of the perpetrator, or whether it is within the scope of employment. A security guard at business premises who removes a person with unnecessary force may be acting in the course of employment.

23. ... In *Lepore*, Gleeson CJ at [51] postulated that if, in *Deatons*, it had been established that part of the barmaid's duties was to keep order in the bar and "[i]f, on the facts, it had been open to regard her conduct as an inappropriate response to disorder, then the jury could properly have held the employer liable in trespass". However, an employer would be less likely to be held vicariously liable if, in addition to unnecessary violence there were other factors such as personal animosity.

In such a case, a conclusion might more readily be drawn that an attack was an independent act directed against the victim even though the employee was carrying out duties at the time.

24. In this case, there was no evidence that Mr Starks acted aggressively towards Mr Wilson. Counsel for the respondents relied upon this as indicating that the assault was unprovoked and had nothing to do with the employment. However, the fact that there was no evidence of aggression or other behaviour that might have provoked Mr Wilson's conduct, whilst relevant, is not determinative of whether Mr Wilson was acting in the course of his employment when he assaulted Mr Starks. Although Mr Wilson's action in head-butting Mr Starks was unreasonable, uncalled for, and not a usual mode for a security officer to use to persuade a customer to leave hotel premises, the fact is, Mr Wilson acted in that way in the course of seeking to have Mr Starks leave the premises. In my opinion, his action was so **[65,993]** directly connected with his authorised acts that this case is one that falls on that side of the line that makes the employer vicariously liable. ...

[Her Honour then considered Mr Sparks' claims against the hotel owner and occupier and the hotel licensee and concluded that, in the circumstances of the present case, there was no basis on which the hotel owner and occupier could be held vicariously liable for a tort committed by an employee (the security officer) of an independent contractor (RSM Security Pty Ltd). On this basis, her Honour found it unnecessary to consider separately the liability of the hotel licensee. In reaching these conclusions her Honour observed that there was no evidence of the precise relationship between the hotel owner and occupier and RSM Security Pty Ltd. For example, there was no evidence as to whether, in carrying out security arrangements, RSM Security Pty Ltd acted as the representative of the hotel owner and occupier or whether the security officers were subject to the directions of the hotel owner and occupier or wore a uniform which identified them with the hotel owner and occupier.

Sheller JA and Grove J agreed with Beazley JA.]

Appeal allowed in part and dismissed in part

[The High Court of Australia dismissed an application by RSM Security Pty Ltd for special leave to appeal from the decision of the New South Wales Court of Appeal extracted above: *RSM Security Pty Ltd v Starks* [2005] HCATrans 421. In the course of the special leave application, senior counsel for RSM Security Pty Ltd sought to draw an analogy between the conduct of the security officer, Mr Wilson, in the present case and the conduct of the beer glass-throwing bar attendant in *Deatons Pty Ltd v Flew* (1949) 79 CLR 370. This produced the following response from the Chief Justice:

GLEESON CJ: Hang on. Throwing a glass of beer in somebody's face is not an over enthusiastic way of serving beer, but exercising undue violence is a well-known, over enthusiastic way of ejecting people from premises.]

2. AGENCY

Scott v Davis
(2000) 204 CLR 333; [2000] HCA 52
High Court of Australia

The owner or bailee in possession of a motor vehicle who permits another person to drive the vehicle may be liable as principal for the negligence of the driver who, for this purpose, is treated as the owner's or bailee's agent. However, there is no such principle of agency where the chattel in question is another form of conveyance such as an aircraft or boat.

[The respondent (defendant), Mr Davis, was the owner of several restored vintage aeroplanes for private use, which were kept on his property at Jacob's Creek in South Australia. The appellants (plaintiffs), Mr and Mrs Scott and their 11-year-old son, Travis, attended a birthday party at Mr Davis' property. Another guest at the party was Mr Bradford, who held a pilot's licence. As between Mr Davis and Mr Bradford there was no contractual relationship of employment or agency.

After lunch on this social occasion, Mr Scott asked Mr Davis if Travis could have a ride in one of the aeroplanes. Mr Davis, through his wife, Mrs Davis, requested Mr Bradford to take Travis for a flight in a two-seater aeroplane. During the brief flight, with Mr Bradford as pilot and Travis as passenger, the aeroplane crashed. The cause of the crash was Mr Bradford's negligence. In the crash, Mr Bradford was killed and Travis suffered personal injury. Mr and Mrs Scott, who witnessed the crash, suffered nervous shock on seeing Travis's injured condition.

By majority (Doyle CJ and Nyland J, Millhouse J dissenting) the Supreme Court of South Australia, Full Court, reversing the judgment of the trial judge in the District Court of South Australia, dismissed the appellants' claim against the respondent. The issue on appeal by the appellants to the High Court of Australia was whether the respondent, as owner of the aeroplane, was vicariously liable for the pilot's negligence. In the High Court, the appellants did not contend that the respondent was personally negligent in any relevant respect or that he was subject to a non-delegable duty of care or that he had authorised or ratified any act of negligence on the part of the pilot.]

GUMMOW J. [some footnotes omitted] ... [373] 124. The issues which arise on the appeal require an examination of the foundation in principle of the proposition for which a passage in the joint judgment in *Soblusky v Egan* (1960) 103 CLR 215 is authority. In that passage, their Honours (Dixon CJ, Kitto and Windeyer JJ) referred (at 229-230) to what they took as having been decided in three decisions of the Court of Exchequer, *Chandler v Broughton* (1832) 149 ER 301, *Booth v Mister* (1835) 173 ER 30 and *Wheatley v Patrick* (1837) 150 ER 917. They then said that it was "from this line of [374] authority" that the decision of the Privy Council in *Samson v Aitchison* [1912] AC 844 had proceeded, and continued (at 231):

> It means that the owner or bailee being in possession of the vehicle and with full legal authority to direct what is done with it appoints another to do the manual work of managing it and to do this on his behalf in circumstances where he can always assert his power of control. Thus it means in point of law that he is driving by his agent. ... The principle of the cases cited is simply that the management of the vehicle is done by the hands of another and is in fact and law subject to direction and control. ...

126. *Soblusky* decided that the appellant, who had assumed liability under a hire-purchase agreement in respect of a motor vehicle and who was a passenger at the relevant time, was liable at common law for the negligence of the driver. Subsequently, in *Launchbury v Morgans* [1973] AC 127, the House of Lords rejected the proposition ... that, in the case of a "family car", the owner was responsible, as a matter of vicarious liability, for the use of it by other family members. This "doctrine" had its origin in certain jurisdictions in the United States and, in argument before the House of Lords, reference was made to the statement by Dean Prosser that there was an element of "unblushing fiction" in it (*Handbook on the Law of Torts* (3rd ed, 1964) at p 494). ... However, their Lordships did accept that liability might be incurred by the owner of a motor vehicle if it could be shown ... that the driver [375] was using it for the owner's purposes under delegation of a task or duty.

127. In Australia, authorities such as *Soblusky* and *Launchbury* still have significance for property damage cases, but retain little vitality in their application to personal injury caused by the negligent use of motor vehicles. The reasons for this state of affairs have been summarised as follows (Trindade and Cane, *The Law of Torts in Australia* (3rd ed, 1999) at pp 733-734):

> In most Australian jurisdictions the owner of a car must, as a prerequisite of registration, take out a policy of insurance covering the liability of the owner and the driver (whether the latter is driving with the authority of the owner or not) for personal injury or death caused by or arising out of the use of the motor vehicle. This provision by itself is wide enough to impose

liability on the owner (and thus tap the owner's insurance) whether or not the driver was the owner's common law agent. But in some jurisdictions there is a provision that deems the driver of a motor vehicle (whether with or without the authority of the owner) to be the agent of the driver for the purposes of the legislation. Where insurance is not taken out by the owner, the injured person has recourse against a statutory fund. So there are very few cases in which a plaintiff will need to appeal to common law principles to establish the liability of the owner of a car for the negligence of the driver. The common law principles may be relevant where the plaintiff seeks to recover for damage to property … .

[378] 132. In the present case, the majority in the Full Court held that the rationale for vicarious liability in relation to the use of motor vehicles did not extend to the use of other forms of conveyance such as privately owned aircraft not used for commercial purposes. Doyle CJ and Nyland J said ((1998) 71 SASR 361 at 377):

> If the wider approach is applied to other forms of conveyance, there seems to be no reason why it should not be applied to chattels generally, and we consider that that development would have an unsettling effect on the law. For those reasons, we consider that the wider approach should not be extended to a new area, even though we acknowledge that as a matter of logic it is capable of extension. Accordingly, we decline to do so.

Their Honours also decided that, in any event, the proposition in *Soblusky*, which has been set out earlier in these reasons, could not be applicable. This was because, at the relevant time, the piloting of the aeroplane was not under the control of the owner, nor did he have the ability to assert control. …

[Gummow J considered the three decisions of the Court of Exchequer referred to above (*Chandler v Broughton, Booth v Mister* and *Wheatley v Patrick*) and concluded that those cases did not provide a sound foundation for any general principle respecting "agency" and "vicarious liability". His Honour continued.]

[408] 227. The reliance by the present appellants upon agency affirms the force in Lord Herschell's observation in *Kennedy v De Trafford* [1897] AC 180 at 188 … that "[n]o word is more commonly and constantly abused than the word 'agent.'" There is considerable terminological confusion in this area. The term "agency" is best used, in the words of the joint judgment of this Court in *International Harvester Co of Australia Pty Ltd v Carrigan's Hazeldene Pastoral Co* (1958) 100 CLR 644 at 652 "to connote an authority or capacity in one person to create legal relations between a person occupying the position of principal and third parties". …

[409] 230. The common law derived the notion of vicarious liability, as Holmes ("Agency" (1891) 4 *Harvard Law Review* 345 at 364) and Wigmore ("Responsibility for Tortious Acts: Its History" (1894) 7 *Harvard Law Review* 315 (Pt 1), 383 (Pt 2)) explained, from mediaeval notions of headship of a household, including wives and servants, whereby their legal standing was absorbed into that of the master. The liability of the master for the wrongs of his servants thereafter became limited to acts **[410]** he had commanded or later ratified, then was supplemented by the notions of "the course of employment" and of "control". (See *Kooragang Investments Pty Ltd v Richardson & Wrench Ltd* [1982] AC 462 at 471-472.)

231. Writing at the time of *Soblusky*, Professor Fleming referred to the difficulty arising from the variety of meanings attached to the term "agent", saying (*The Law of Torts* (2nd ed, 1961) at p 325):

> It is frequently used either in the sense of a comprehensive category encompassing the two species of servant and independent contractor or to describe servants, properly so-called, whose employment is casual rather than more or less continuous.

He went on (*The Law of Torts* (2nd ed, 1961) at p 326) to refer to the decision in *Colonial Mutual Life Assurance Society Ltd v Producers and Citizens Co-operative Assurance Co of Australia Ltd* (1931) 46 CLR 41 as an exceptional case where an "agent" was not subject to controlled employment yet the principal incurred vicarious liability. The insurance agent in that case who solicited proposals acted in a genuinely representative capacity for the insurer which was treated as if it were conducting the transaction and as if it were the insurer's voice with which the agent defamed the competitor. …

[417] 250. *Burnie Port Authority v General Jones Pty Ltd* (1994) 179 CLR 520, in its treatment of **[418]** the rule in *Rylands v Fletcher*, shows the disfavour with which strict liability is viewed. The nature of the "vicarious liability" asserted by the appellants and found in their favour at the trial is open to criticism of a similar nature to that respecting non-delegable duties. Both would involve a species of strict liability by holding Mr Davis responsible for the wrongful act or omission of the pilot, where Mr Davis himself was not negligent. ...

253. The doctrine of vicarious liability in modern times derives support from the notion that a party who engages others to advance that party's economic interest should be placed under a liability for losses **[419]** incurred by third parties in the course of the enterprise. (See *Bugge v Brown* (1919) 26 CLR 110 at 117.) Further, the employer is seen as a suitable means for the passing on of those losses through such means as liability insurance and higher prices for the goods and services supplied by the enterprise. Such notions of economic efficiency have little part to play in supporting any broad principle respecting the bailment of chattels or in supporting the imposition of liability upon a party in the position of Mr Davis. ...

254. Here, one is left with the suggestion that Mr Davis may have or should have, by the means of insurance, a deeper pocket than the estate of Mr Bradford. However, the Court was told that, at the time of the accident which injured Travis in 1990, there was no statutory requirement for compulsory third party insurance by owners in respect of non-commercial flights, and that the registration system of private aircraft did not require evidence of such insurance. In the absence of such a requirement, it is difficult to impose an absolute liability upon a person such as Mr Davis in respect of non-commercial activities. ...

[423] 269. What the appellants seek to have this Court do is to introduce a new species of actor, one who is not an employee, nor an independent contractor, but an "agent" in a non-technical sense. They then seek to advance this indeterminacy by attaching vicarious liability to the defendant whose social connection with that actor occasioned their injuries. ...

272. Further, as the Chief Justice and Callinan J each explain in their reasons for judgment, to introduce notions of "agency" and "control" in the performance of social activities such as those involved here would be liable to chill ordinary social and familial intercourse. ...

[424] 274. I would dismiss the appeal with costs.

[In separate judgments, Gleeson CJ, Hayne J and Callinan J agreed, for substantially the same reasons as Gummow J, that the principles stated in *Soblusky v Egan* (1960) 103 CLR 215 should not be extended beyond motor vehicles. In a dissenting judgment, McHugh J said:

[373] 121. Once it is accepted that the owner of a motor car may be liable for negligent conduct of a driver who is not an employee and whose conduct was neither authorised, instigated nor ratified, that principle must also apply to planes and boats. Nothing about planes or boats provides any logical reason for pushing them outside the scope of the principle.]

Appeal dismissed

[In *Gutman v McFall* (2004) 61 NSWLR 599, a decision of the New South Wales Court of Appeal, Giles JA (with whom Mason P and McColl JA agreed) held that *Scott v Davis* (extracted above) had confined the principle stated by the High Court in *Soblusky v Egan* (1960) 103 CLR 215 at 231 to motor vehicles and, in that context, a dinghy with an outboard motor was not a motor vehicle in the relevant sense. Accordingly, the defendant Evian Gutman, who had hired a dinghy with an outboard motor for use for a few hours on Sydney harbour with four school friends aged 16 or 17, was not vicariously liable for the negligent navigation of the boat by another member of the party when the boat struck and injured a scuba diver, the plaintiff, James McFall.]

3. NON-DELEGABLE DUTIES

Kondis v State Transport Authority
(1984) 154 CLR 672
High Court of Australia

As a general rule, an employer is not liable for the negligence of an independent contractor. However, in respect of the workplace safety of his or her employees, an employer is under a non-delegable duty of care. Thus, if an employer delegates the performance of this duty to an independent contractor, the employer will be liable for the independent contractor's negligence.

[The appellant (plaintiff) was injured in the course of employment by the respondent (defendant) when part of a crane beneath which he was standing fell on him. The crane had been hired by the respondent from a third party and was being operated by the third party's employee, Clissold. The accident occurred while Clissold was manually extending the crane's jib. The trial judge found that Clissold was negligent and that the respondent was liable for that negligence. An appeal to the Full Court of the Supreme Court of Victoria was allowed.]

MASON J. ... **[678]** It is conceded by the respondent that Clissold was negligent in dropping the rod. Furthermore, it was found by the trial judge and is now accepted by the respondent that the appellant had been instructed to assist in the extension procedure by standing under the jib and that he was acting in accordance with his instructions when he was struck by the rod. Leaving to one side for the moment the possibility of the respondent being negligent independently of the negligence of Clissold, the question then becomes whether, in such circumstances, the respondent is liable to the appellant for an admitted act of negligence on the part of an employee of an independent contractor.

The extent of the liability of an employer for injury caused to an employee in the course of his employment through the negligence of another has been the subject of continuing debate. The formulation of the relevant principles has been beset by many problems. One problem, that caused by the doctrine of common employment, is no longer with us, though the law in the course of its development has had to take account of the doctrine. One legacy of the doctrine is the concept of the personal or non-delegable duty, a concept which was designed to circumvent the doctrine of common employment and has been invoked frequently in recent times. But the principal difficulty in formulating acceptable principles has been due to the dominating influence accorded to the so-called general rule that the **[679]** employer is not liable for the negligence of a person who is not a servant but an independent contractor. The area of operation of this rule has not been precisely defined. At times it seems to have been thought that the effect of the rule was to exclude liability on the part of an employer who engaged a competent independent contractor to engage in work on the employer's premises: *Haseldine v CA Daw & Son Ltd* [1941] 2 KB 343, an invitor-invitee case. At other times it has been suggested that the rule may mean no more than that there was no liability in the employer for injury caused in the execution of some activity or operation falling outside the employer's business activity or his skill and experience, involving the doing of work which he had no capacity or opportunity to inspect or check: *Davie v New Merton Board Mills Ltd* [1959] AC 604, at p 646. And from time to time in England it has been said that the rule excluded the employer's liability for casual acts of negligence on the part of the contractor or the contractor's servants. Moreover, it has been accepted that in many situations an employer will be liable for the negligence of his independent contractor, eg, when the injury is caused by an act which the contractor is employed to do or when the contractor's neglect involves the employer in a breach of his duty of care: see, eg, *Pickard v Smith* (1861) 10 CB (NS) 470, at p 480 [142 ER 535, at p 539].

However, to express the extent of the liability in the terms stated in the preceding sentence provokes the question: In what circumstances does the negligence of the contractor amount to a breach of the employer's duty of care? In recent times there has been a tendency to say that such a breach of duty arises when the employer's duty is "non-delegable". This is to say that the duty is of such a nature that its performance cannot be delegated to a contractor on the footing that delegation to a competent contractor is a sufficient compliance with the duty. ...

[680] If the employer's common law duty of care to his employees is no higher than the general duty to take reasonable care and skill for their safety, it imposes on him an obligation to take reasonable steps to provide adequate plant and equipment, a safe place of work and a safe system of work. If the duty or obligation of the employer requires no more than the exercise of reasonable care, it will often be satisfied by engaging a competent person to perform some service or work, particularly if the service or work calls for some skill or experience which the employer does not possess and cannot reasonably be expected to possess and the employer has no opportunity or capacity to inspect or check what the contractor does. It has been a reluctance to accept this result that has prompted judges to speak of the employer's duty as "personal" or "non-delegable" and to conclude that it cannot be satisfied by the appointment of a competent person to carry out the necessary task.

The leading example of this approach – and it has great importance for the present case – is the decision of the House of Lords in *Wilsons & Clyde Coal Co v English* [1938] AC 57, where it has been held that the duty of care owed by an employer to an employee was non-delegable with the consequence that the defence of common employment was not available to an employer who was the owner of a mine where injury was caused to a miner through the failure of the mine manager appointed as agent in charge of the employer's mining activities to provide a safe system of work. The employer was held liable because the system of work was not reasonably safe, although the system had been devised by the manager to whom the employer was obliged by statute to leave the matter and the employer had personally done everything that it could to provide a safe system. ...

[681] The concept of the employer's personal duty as explained by Lord Wright [in *Wilsons' Case*] amounts to a duty to see that care is taken, eg, in the provision of safe premises and of a safe system of work. Although in this respect it imposes on the employer a more stringent obligation than that imposed by the general duty to exercise reasonable care and skill, Lord Wright characterized it as a particular exemplification of the general duty in its application to an employer with respect to the safety of his employees. So it is said that the employer in order to discharge his general duty of care for the safety of his employees must ensure that reasonable care and skill is exercised in relevant respects. Lord Wright's approach is vulnerable to the criticism that he advances no reason or policy consideration for fixing the employer with the higher duty to see that care is taken instead of the duty that he himself take reasonable care.

In a later case, *Thomson v Cremin* [1956] 1 WLR 103n, Lord Wright treated *Wilsons' Case* as an application of the general rule stated by Lord Blackburn in *Dalton v Angus* (1881) 6 App Cas 740. After referring to the general rule that a person employing a contractor to do work is not liable for **[682]** the negligence of the contractor or his servants, Lord Blackburn continued ((1881) 6 App Cas, at p 829):

> On the other hand, a person causing something to be done, the doing of which casts on him a duty, cannot escape from the responsibility attaching on him of seeing that duty performed by delegating it to a contractor.

In *Dalton v Angus* a landowner and a contractor were held liable for the actions of a sub-contractor in carrying out excavations which caused subsidence on adjoining land in relation to which a right of support had been acquired. It seems that it was because they commissioned excavations which interfered, or tended to interfere, with the neighbour's right of support that they came under a personal duty to see that care was taken. It is impossible to regard Lord Blackburn's statement as extending generally to the ordinary case in which a duty to take reasonable care is owed.

In *Thomson v Cremin* itself it was held that an invitor was liable to an invitee for the negligence of an independent contractor on the ground that, as the duty was personal, he was under an obligation to see that care was taken, notwithstanding that he had no reason to think that there had been negligence on the part of the independent contractor. ...

In *Wilsons' Case* [1938] AC 57 the system of work was devised by an employee, not by an independent contractor. ... However, the concept of the personal duty which he [Lord Wright] expounded makes it impossible to draw a convincing distinction between delegation of performance of the employer's duty to an employee and delegation **[683]** to an independent contractor. On the hypothesis that the duty is personal or incapable of delegation, the employer is liable for its negligent performance, whether the performance be that of an employee or that of an independent contractor. ...

In Australia the approach taken by Lord Wright in *Wilsons' Case* was accepted and applied in *Cotter v Huddart Parker Ltd* (1941) 42 SR (NSW) 33. ...

[684] [S]tatements ... [explaining] the nature and consequences of a non-delegable duty ... have been criticized on the ground that they offered no criteria distinguishing those duties which are non-delegable from those which are not: see Glanville Williams, "Liability for Independent Contractors" [1956] *Cambridge Law Journal* 180, at pp 183-184. Indeed, it has been said that the classification of a duty as non-delegable in the circumstances of particular cases rests on little more than assertion: cf Fleming, *Law of Torts*, 6th ed (1983), p 360; *Salmond & Heuston on Torts*, 18th ed (1981), p 457. Lord Blackburn's statement gives no guidance upon this critical question because it assumes the existence of a personal duty on the part of the person engaging another to do **[685]** something and states that the first person cannot avoid compliance with the duty by delegating its performance to another. ...

Outside the realm of master and servant ... the concept of a personal duty has been applied to the common law duty of care owed by a hospital to its patient (*Gold v Essex County Council* [1942] 2 KB 293, at p 304; *Cassidy v Ministry of Health* [1951] 2 KB 343; *Samios v Repatriation Commission* [1960] WAR 219; *Toronto General Hospital v Matthews* [1972] SCR 435 and by a school authority to its pupils: *Ramsay v Larsen* (1964) 111 CLR 16, at p 28; *The* **[686]** *Commonwealth v Introvigne* (1982) 150 CLR 258, at pp 271, 274-275, 279; *Carmarthenshire County Council v Lewis* [1955] AC 549. ... The liability of a hospital arises out of its undertaking an obligation to treat its patient, an obligation which carries with it a duty to use reasonable care in treatment, so that the hospital is liable, if a person engaged to perform the obligation on its behalf acts without due care: *Gold* [1942] 2 KB, at p 304. Accordingly, the duty is one the performance of which cannot be delegated, not even to a properly qualified doctor or surgeon under a contract for services: *Cassidy* [1951] 2 KB, at p 364.

Likewise with the school authority. It is under a duty to ensure that reasonable care is taken of pupils attending the school. It is the immaturity and inexperience of the children and their propensity for mischief that lie at the basis of the special responsibility which the law imposes on a school authority to take care for their safety: *Introvigne* (1982) 150 CLR, at p 271. The child's need for care and supervision is so essential that it is a necessary inference of fact from the acceptance of the child by the school authority, "that the school authority undertakes not only to employ proper staff but to give the child reasonable care", to use the words of Kitto J in *Ramsay v Larsen* (1964) 111 CLR, at p 28. ...

The principal objection to the concept of personal duty is that it departs from the basic principles of liability in negligence by substituting for the duty to take reasonable care a more stringent duty, a duty to ensure that reasonable care is taken. The failure in *Wilsons' Case* [1938] AC 57 to acknowledge this departure and to advance a convincing reason for fixing the employer with a more stringent **[687]** duty made the reasoning in *Wilsons' Case* vulnerable to criticism. However, when we look to the classes of case in which the existence of a non-delegable duty has been recognized, it appears that there is some element in the relationship between the parties that makes it appropriate to impose on the defendant a duty to ensure that reasonable care and skill is taken for the safety of the persons to whom the duty is owed. As I said in *Introvigne* (1982) 150 CLR, at p 271 "the law has, for various reasons imposed a special duty on persons in certain situations to take particular precautions for the safety of others". ...

The element in the relationship between the parties which generates a special responsibility or duty to see that care is taken may be found in one or more of several circumstances. The hospital undertakes the care, supervision and control of patients who are in special need of care. The school authority undertakes like special responsibilities in relation to the children whom it accepts into its care. If the invitor be subject to a special duty, it is because he assumes a particular responsibility in relation to the safety of his premises and the safety of his invitee by inviting him to enter them. ... In these situations the special duty arises because the person on whom it is imposed has undertaken the care, supervision or control of the person or property of another or is so placed in relation to that person or his property as to assume a particular responsibility for his or its safety, in circumstances where the person affected might reasonably expect that due care will be exercised. ...

The foreseeability of injury is not in itself enough to generate the special duty. Before the special duty arises there must exist in the relationship between the parties an element of the kind already discussed.

That such an element exists in the relationship of employment is beyond serious challenge. The employer has the exclusive responsibility for the safety of the appliances, the premises and the system of work to which he subjects his employee and the employee has no [688] choice but to accept and rely on the employer's provision and judgment in relation to these matters. The consequence is that in these relevant respects the employee's safety is in the hands of the employer; it is his responsibility. The employee can reasonably expect therefore that reasonable care and skill will be taken. In the case of the employer there is no unfairness in imposing on him a non-delegable duty; it is reasonable that he should bear liability for the negligence of his independent contractors in devising a safe system of work. If he requires his employee to work according to an unsafe system he should bear the consequences. Indeed, there is a stronger case for concluding that the employer's duty is non-delegable than there is for reaching the same conclusion in the case of the invitor. It is not immediately obvious that it is appropriate to impose liability on the occupier of a house for injury caused to an invitee by the negligence of an independent contractor, eg, in making or repairing an electrical installation carelessly, when it is reasonable for the occupier to rely on the reputed competence of the contractor in a field in which the occupier has no expert knowledge. But this is by the way, for it is not an issue that needs to be decided in the present case. ...

If control of this operation was in the hands of Clissold then it was for him to adopt a safe system of work. The respondent is liable for his neglect, not on a vicarious basis, but because Clissold's omission to adopt a safe system is a breach of the respondent's duty. ...

Even if I had not concluded that the respondent was liable for the default of the independent contractor in failing to prescribe and adopt a safe system on the footing that the duty to provide a safe system was non-delegable, I should have concluded that the respondent was in breach of its duty on the ground that the appellant's foreman failed to direct him not to be under the jib of the crane during the extension procedure. ...

[689] The appeal should be allowed ...

[Deane and Dawson JJ agreed with Mason J. Murphy and Brennan JJ delivered concurring judgments.]

Appeal allowed

Burnie Port Authority v General Jones Pty Ltd
(1994) 179 CLR 520
High Court of Australia

In the common law of Australia, the rule in Rylands v Fletcher has been "absorbed by the principles of ordinary negligence". Thus, an occupier of premises who introduces a dangerous substance onto the premises, carries on a dangerous activity on the premises or allows an independent contractor to do either of those things, owes a duty of reasonable care to avoid injury or damage to the person or property of another, including a person or property lawfully in a place outside the premises.

MASON CJ, DEANE, DAWSON, TOOHEY and GAUDRON JJ. [some footnotes in whole or part omitted] [526] The respondent, General Jones Pty Ltd (General), suffered damage when a very large quantity of frozen vegetables which it owned was ruined by a fire which destroyed a building owned by the appellant, the Burnie Port Authority (the Authority), at Burnie in Tasmania. The frozen vegetables were stored in three cold rooms in the building. General occupied the cold rooms and an office area pursuant to an agreement with the Authority. The rest of the building, including the area between the ceiling and roof, remained under the occupation of the Authority.

At the time of the fire, work was being carried out to extend the building and install further cold storage facilities in the extension. The original building in which the vegetables were stored was known as "Stage 1" and the uncompleted extension was known as "Stage 2".

The Authority had not engaged a head contractor in relation to the work involved in erecting and equipping Stage 2. Through employees, it effected part of that work itself, including clearance of the site, the pouring of the concrete foundations and the design of the steel work. Other work involved in Stage 2, including the [527] erection of the steel frame and the installation of electrical and refrigeration equipment, was entrusted to independent contractors. One of those independent contractors was Wildridge & Sinclair Pty Ltd (W & S).

The work contracted to W & S included the installation of the additional refrigeration in Stage 2. It involved considerable welding and the use of a large quantity of expanded polystyrene (EPS) which is an insulating material. While EPS contains retardant chemicals to inhibit ignition, it can be set alight if brought into sustained contact with a flame or burning substance. Once ignited, the substance dissolves into a liquid fire which burns with extraordinary ferocity, at a rate which increases in geometric progression. The EPS to be used by W & S was marketed under the commercial name of "Isolite" and was contained in approximately 30 cardboard cartons which were, to the knowledge of the Authority, stacked together in an area or "void" under the roof of Stage 2 (the roof void) in close vicinity to where W & S would, again to the knowledge of the Authority, be carrying out extensive welding activities. Obviously, it was essential that care be exercised to ensure that sparks or molten liquid from those welding activities did not ignite the cardboard of one of the stacked containers. If that happened, the likelihood was that the Isolite in that container would ignite with the result that the whole of the Isolite would become an uncontrollable conflagration.

It is common ground that, at relevant times, the Authority was itself in occupation of Stage 2, including the roof void. The Authority took no steps to avoid the risk of conflagration which unguarded welding activities in the vicinity of the cartons of Isolite involved. On the findings of the learned trial judge, employees of W & S carried out the welding activities in such a negligent fashion that sparks or molten metal fell upon one or more of the cartons containing the Isolite. The cardboard was set alight and the Isolite itself commenced to burn fiercely. The conflagration spread from the roof void to the whole of Stage 2 and most of Stage 1, including those parts of the original building containing the cold rooms occupied by General. Within minutes of the commencement of the fire, the whole complex was engulfed in flames.

In due course, General sued both the Authority and W & S in the Supreme Court of Tasmania. ... The learned trial judge (Neasey J) found that General was entitled to judgment against the Authority and W & S for the damage (to be [528] assessed) which it had sustained by reason of the loss of its frozen vegetables. His Honour held that W & S's liability resulted from the application of the ordinary principles of the law of negligence (ordinary negligence) and from the application of a special rule relating to an occupier's liability for damage caused by the escape of fire from his or her premises (the "ignis suus rule"). His Honour held that the Authority's liability resulted from the application of the ignis suus rule. As between the Authority and W & S, his Honour found that the Authority was, by reason of W & S's negligence, entitled to be indemnified by W & S in respect of any damages which it paid to General. ...

The Authority appealed to the Full Court from the trial judge's order that judgment be entered in General's favour against it. The Full Court (Cox, Crawford and Zeeman JJ) affirmed the Authority's liability to General and ordered that the appeal be dismissed. However, the members of the Full Court concluded that the basis of the Authority's liability to General lay not in any special rule relating only to the escape of fire but in a more general common law rule, the rule in *Rylands v Fletcher* (1866) LR 1 Ex 265; affd (1868) LR 3 HL 330, relating to the liability of an occupier for damage caused by the escape of dangerous substances introduced to his or her premises. The present appeal is by the Authority from the judgment and order of the Full Court.

In this Court, General has argued that it is entitled to maintain the judgment in its favour on each of three distinct grounds, namely, (i) the ignis suus principle; (ii) *Rylands v Fletcher* liability; and (iii) ordinary (or *Donoghue v Stevenson* [1932] AC 562) negligence. A fourth ground, ordinary nuisance, was raised in General's written outline of argument but was abandoned in the course of oral argument. For its part, the Authority, while denying any liability to General, has not challenged the findings in the courts below to the effect that General sustained substantial damage caused by the spread of fire from premises occupied by the Authority (Stage 2 and the residue of Stage 1) to the premises occupied by General (the cold rooms) and that the fire was caused by negligence on the part of the Authority's independent contractor in carrying out unguarded welding operations on the premises occupied by the Authority in the close vicinity of the stacked cardboard cartons of Isolite. It is in the **[529]** context of those now undisputed findings of fact that the applicable principles of law must be identified. ...

[Their Honours then discussed the ignis suus principle, a special common law rule relating to the liability of an occupier for damage caused by the escape of fire from his or her premises, and held that the principle did not form part of the law in Australia.]

[535] The "true rule" in *Rylands v Fletcher*

In *Fletcher v Rylands* (1866) LR 1 Ex, at 279-280, a strong Court of Exchequer Chamber (Willes, Blackburn, Keating, Mellor, Montague Smith and Lush JJ), in a judgment delivered by Blackburn J, identified what was described as "the true rule of law":

> the person who for his own purposes brings on his lands and collects and keeps there anything likely to do mischief if it escapes, must keep it in at his peril, and, if he does not do so, is prima facie answerable for all the damage which is the natural consequence of its escape. He can excuse himself by shewing [sic] that the escape was owing to the plaintiff's default; or perhaps that the escape was the consequence of vis major, or the act of **[536]** God; but as nothing of this sort exists here, it is unnecessary to inquire what excuse would be sufficient.

Notwithstanding the many accolades which have been, and continue to be, lavished on Blackburn J's judgment that brief exposition of "the true rule of law" is largely bereft of current authority or validity if it be viewed, as it ordinarily is, as a statement of a comprehensive rule. Indeed, it has been all but obliterated by subsequent judicial explanations and qualifications. ...

The Court of Exchequer Chamber in *Fletcher v Rylands* itself **[537]** recognised that the above statement of the "true rule of law" is too wide, even as an exposition of a prima facie rule, unless it is accompanied by some overriding qualifications. Thus, Blackburn J commented (*Fletcher v Rylands* (1866) LR 1 Ex, at 280) that:

> it seems but reasonable and just that the neighbour, who has brought something on his own property which *was not naturally there*, harmless to others so long as it is confined to his own property, *but which he knows to be mischievous if it gets on his neighbour's*, should be obliged to make good the damage which ensues if he does not succeed in confining it to his own property. (Emphasis added.)

Again, however, Blackburn J's statement of those qualifications has long been overlaid and effectively displaced. ...

Unfortunately, the subsequent judicial alterations and qualifications of Blackburn J's statement of the "true rule" have introduced and exacerbated uncertainties about its content and application. ...

[540] If the problems of the rule in *Rylands v Fletcher* were confined to the uncertainties of its content and application, it would be necessary for the courts to continue their so far spectacularly unsatisfactory efforts to resolve them. The problems are not, however, so confined. In the more than a century and a quarter that has passed since its formulation by Blackburn J, the rule has been progressively weakened and confined from within and the area of its effective operation, in the sense of the area in which it applies to impose liability where it would not otherwise exist, has been progressively diminished by increasing assault from without. ...

[544] Ordinary negligence and the rule in *Rylands v Fletcher*

Much has been written in the past about precisely where, among the old forms of action, one should locate the source or sources of the rule in *Rylands v Fletcher*. However, the subsequent emergence of a coherent law of negligence to dominate the territory of tortious liability for unintentional injury to the person or property of another has deprived the question of much of its practical **[545]** significance. Regardless of the parental claims of nuisance, the rule has been increasingly qualified and adjusted to reflect basic aspects of the law of ordinary negligence. ...

[550] The "non-delegable" duty …
It has long been recognised that there are certain categories of case in which a duty to take reasonable care to avoid a foreseeable risk of injury to another will not be discharged merely by the employment of a qualified and ostensibly competent independent contractor. In those categories of case, the nature of the relationship of proximity gives rise to a duty of care of a special and "more stringent" kind, namely a "duty to ensure that reasonable care is taken" (see *Kondis v State Transport Authority* (1984) 154 CLR 672 at 686). Put differently, the requirement of reasonable care in those categories of case extends to seeing that care is taken. One of the classic statements of the scope of such a duty of care remains that of Lord Blackburn in *Hughes v Percival* (1883) 8 App Cas 443 at 446:

> that duty went as far as to require [the defendant] to see that reasonable skill and care were exercised in those operations. … If such a duty was cast upon the defendant he could not get rid of responsibility by delegating the performance of it to a third person. He was at liberty to employ such a third person to fulfil the duty which the law cast on himself … but the defendant still remained subject to that duty, and liable for the consequences if it was not fulfilled.

In *Kondis v State Transport Authority* (1984) 154 CLR, at 679-687 (and see also, *Stevens v Brodribb Sawmilling Co Pty Ltd* (1986) 160 CLR, at 44, per Wilson and Dawson JJ), in a judgment with which Deane J and Dawson J agreed, Mason J identified some of the principal categories of case in which the duty to take reasonable care under the ordinary law of negligence is non-delegable in that sense: adjoining owners of land in relation to work threatening support or common walls; master and servant in relation to a safe system of work; hospital and patient; school authority and pupil; and (arguably), occupier and invitee. In most, though conceivably not all, of such categories of case, the common "element in the relationship **[551]** between the parties which generates [the] special responsibility or duty to see that care is taken" is that

> the person on whom [the duty] is imposed has undertaken the care, supervision or control of the person or property of another or is so placed in relation to that person or his property as to assume a particular responsibility for his or its safety, in circumstances where the person affected might reasonably expect that due care will be exercised" (*Kondis v State Transport Authority* (1984) 154 CLR, at 687; see also, *Stevens v Brodribb Sawmilling Co Pty Ltd* (1986) 160 CLR, at 31, 44-46).

It will be convenient to refer to that common element as "the central element of control". Viewed from the perspective of the person to whom the duty is owed, the relationship of proximity giving rise to the non-delegable duty of care in such cases is marked by special dependence or vulnerability on the part of that person *Commonwealth v Introvigne* (1982) 150 CLR 258 at 271, per Mason J).

The relationship of proximity which exists, for the purposes of ordinary negligence, between a plaintiff and a defendant in circumstances which would prima facie attract the rule in *Rylands v Fletcher* is characterised by such a central element of control and by such special dependence and vulnerability. One party to that relationship is a person who is in control of premises and who has taken advantage of that control to introduce thereon or to retain therein a dangerous substance or to undertake thereon a dangerous activity or to allow another person to do one of those things. The other party to that relationship is a person, outside the premises and without control over what occurs therein, whose person or property is thereby exposed to a foreseeable risk of danger ("which he knows to be mischievous if it gets on his neighbour's [property]": *Fletcher v Rylands* (1866) LR 1 Ex, at 280). In such a case, the person outside the premises is obviously in a position of special vulnerability and dependence. He or she is specially vulnerable to danger if reasonable precautions are not taken in relation to what is done on the premises. He or she is specially dependent upon the person in control of the premises to ensure that such reasonable precautions are in fact taken. Commonly, he or she will have neither the right nor the opportunity to exercise control over, or even to have foreknowledge of, what is done or allowed by the other party within the premises. Conversely, the person who introduces (or allows another to introduce) the dangerous substance or undertakes (or allows another to undertake) the dangerous activity on premises which he or she controls is "so placed in **[552]** relation to [the other] person or his property as to assume a particular responsibility for his or its safety".

It follows that the relationship of proximity which exists in the category of case into which *Rylands v Fletcher* circumstances fall contains the central element of control which generates, in other categories of case, a special "personal" or "non-delegable" duty of care under the ordinary law of negligence. Reasoning by analogy suggests, but does not compel, a conclusion that that common element gives rise to such a duty of care in the first-mentioned category of case. There are considerations of fairness which support that conclusion, namely, that it is the person in control who has authorised or allowed the situation of foreseeable potential danger to be imposed on the other person by authorising or allowing the dangerous use of the premises and who is likely to be in a position to insist upon the exercise of reasonable care. It is also supported by considerations of utility:

> the practical advantage of being conveniently workable, of supplying a spur to effective care in the choice of contractors, and in pointing the victim to a defendant who is easily discoverable and probably financially responsible. (Thayer, op cit at p 809)

The weight of authority confirms that the duty in that category of case is a non-delegable one. ...

[555] Conclusion

Once it is appreciated that the special relationship of proximity which exists in circumstances which would attract the rule in *Rylands v Fletcher*. gives rise to a non-delegable duty of care and that the dangerousness of the substance or activity involved in such circumstances will heighten the degree of care which is reasonable, it becomes apparent, subject to one qualification, that the stage has been reached where it is highly unlikely that liability will not exist under the principles of ordinary negligence in any case where liability would exist under the rule in *Rylands v Fletcher*. It is true that one can point to a few cases, of which the most important are probably the 1934 case of *Hazelwood v Webber* (1934) 52 CLR 268 in this Court and the 1908 case of *West v Bristol Tramways Co* [1908] 2 KB 14 in the English Court of Appeal, in which *Rylands v Fletcher*. liability was held to exist notwithstanding a finding of, or to the effect of, no negligence by the defendant. However, close examination of those cases discloses that they lack validity as examples of circumstances where the application of the modern law of negligence and the rule of *Rylands v Fletcher* would produce different results. ...

[556] [T]here may remain cases in which it is preferable to see a defendant's liability in a *Rylands v Fletcher* situation as lying in nuisance (or even trespass) and not in negligence (see, eg, *Northwestern Utilities Ltd v London Guarantee & Accident Co* [1936] AC, at 119; *Cambridge Water Co v Eastern Counties Leather plc* [1994] 2 WLR 53; and, generally, Newark, op cit). It follows that the main consideration favouring preservation of the rule in *Rylands v Fletcher*, namely, that the rule imposes liability in cases where it would not otherwise exist, lacks practical substance. In these circumstances, and subject only to the above-mentioned possible qualification in relation to liability in nuisance, the rule in *Rylands v Fletcher*, with all its difficulties, uncertainties, qualifications and exceptions, should now be seen, for the purposes of the common law of this country, as absorbed by the principles of ordinary negligence. Under those principles, a person who takes advantage of his or her control of premises to introduce a dangerous substance, to carry on a dangerous activity, or to allow another to do one of **[557]** those things, owes a duty of reasonable care to avoid a reasonably foreseeable risk of injury or damage to the person or property of another. In a case where the person or property of the other person is lawfully in a place outside the premises that duty of care both varies in degree according to the magnitude of the risk involved and extends to ensuring that such care is taken. It is unnecessary for the purposes of the present case to express a concluded view on the question whether the duty of care owed, in such circumstances, to a lawful visitor on the premises is likewise a non-delegable one. The ordinary processes of legal reasoning by analogy, induction and deduction would prima facie indicate that it is. Like Windeyer J in *Benning v Wong* (1969) 122 CLR 249, we have added the qualifications "lawfully" and "lawful" to reserve the position of, rather than to exclude, the unlawful plaintiff.

The present case

... The critical question for the purposes of applying the principles of ordinary negligence to the circumstances of the present case is whether the Authority took advantage of its occupation and control of the premises to allow its independent **[558]** contractor to introduce or retain a dangerous substance or to engage in a dangerous activity on the premises. The starting point for answering that question must be a consideration of what relevantly constitutes a dangerous substance or activity.

In the context of the ordinary law of negligence, the character of "dangerous" is not confined to those classes of things, such as poison, a loaded gun or explosives, which are "inherently dangerous" or "dangerous in themselves". ...

The fact that a particular substance or a particular activity can be seen to be "inherently" or "of itself" likely to do serious injury or cause serious damage will, of course, ordinarily make characterisation as "dangerous" more readily apparent. That fact does not, however, provide a criterion of what is and what is not dangerous for the purpose of determining whether the duty of a person in occupation or control of premises to take care to avoid injury or damage outside the premises is or is not a delegable one. It suffices for that purpose that the combined effect of the magnitude of the foreseeable risk of an accident happening and the magnitude of the foreseeable potential injury or damage if an accident does occur is such that an ordinary person acting reasonably would **[559]** consider it necessary to exercise special care or to take special precautions in relation to it.

Similarly, a substance or activity entrusted to an independent contractor or other agent may be relevantly dangerous notwithstanding that foreseeable injury or danger will arise only in the event of what is commonly described as "collateral" negligence. If X engages an independent contractor to separately move two chemicals, which will cause a major explosion if they come into contact with one another, into separate storage areas, there may be no real risk of injury or damage at all if the independent contractor does what he or she is engaged to do. The activity is, however, obviously fraught with danger unless special precautions are taken to ensure that the independent contractor does not, through "collateral" negligence, transport the two chemicals together and in a way which causes contact between them. ...

In the present case, the particular qualities of EPS made the stacked cardboard containers of Isolite in the roof area of the Authority's premises a dangerous substance in the sense that, if one of the cardboard containers were accidentally set alight, an uncontrollable conflagration would almost inevitably result (cf Lord Sumner's description, in *Rainham Chemical Works Ltd v Belvedere Fish Guano Co* [1921] 2 AC, at 479, of dinitrophenol as a "dangerous explosive" notwithstanding that "a hot flame is needed to explode it"). Clearly, the introduction of more than 20 of those cardboard containers called for special precautions to be taken to avoid any risk of that happening. A fortiori, the carrying out of welding activities in the premises within which the cardboard containers of Isolite were stacked was itself a dangerous activity in that it was reasonably foreseeable that, unless special precautions were taken, sparks or molten metal might fall upon one of the containers and set the cardboard alight.

As has been seen, the evidence established that the Authority (through one of its employees) was aware that the cardboard containers of Isolite were being stored in the roof area near where welding work was to be carried out by W & S. It is, however, unnecessary that that was so. It suffices for present purposes that the Authority engaged and authorised its independent contractor to **[560]** carry out work within its premises which required both the introduction of such large quantities of EPS to the premises and the carrying out of extensive welding work within the premises. It has not been suggested that it was not reasonably foreseeable that the large quantities of EPS which W & S was authorised and required by the Authority to use would be contained in a combustible container such as cardboard. To the contrary, the evidence established that the Isolite had been used in Stage 1 of the building, and, as has been said, that an employee of the Authority actually saw the cardboard containers being raised into the roof of the premises. In these circumstances, the overall work which the independent contractor was engaged to carry out on the premises was a dangerous activity in that it involved a real and foreseeable risk of a serious conflagration unless special precautions were taken to avoid the risk of serious fire. It was obvious that, in the event of any serious fire on the premises, General's frozen vegetables would almost certainly be damaged or destroyed. In these circumstances, the Authority, as occupier of those parts of the premises into which it required and allowed the Isolite to be introduced and the welding work to be carried out, owed to General a duty of care which was non-delegable in the sense we have explained, that is to say, which extended to ensuring that its independent contractor took reasonable care to prevent the Isolite being set alight as a result of the welding activities. It is now common ground that W & S did not take such reasonable care.

It follows that the Authority was liable to General pursuant to the ordinary principles of negligence for the damage which General sustained. The appeal must be dismissed.

[Brennan and McHugh JJ delivered dissenting judgments in which they disagreed both with the majority judges' finding in favour of the plaintiff and with their reasoning. They held that the circumstances did not fall within the rule in *Rylands v Fletcher* (which still existed as an independent basis of liability, and into which the 'ignis suus' principle had been absorbed) because the use of the premises authorised by the defendant was an "ordinary" not a "non-natural" one.

Brennan J accepted the non-delegability of the duty owed by a person who employs a contractor to perform work the nature of which creates or increases a risk of injury to a third party. However, he thought that the law distinguishes between a risk of damage arising from the *nature* of the authorised work and a risk of damage arising from the *manner* in which the work is performed. In the circumstances here it was the *manner* in which the work was performed that caused the harm. The defendant had not authorised the risk-creating activity of welding in the vicinity of the Isolite. McHugh J rejected the negligence claim on the basis that *Stoneman v Lyons* (1975) 133 CLR 550 denied that an occupier of premises is liable for the negligence of an independent contractor merely because the work the contractor was employed to do involves a real and serious risk of injury unless precautions are taken.]

Appeal dismissed

New South Wales v Lepore
Samin v Queensland
Rich v Queensland
(2003) 195 ALR 412; [2003] HCA 4
High Court of Australia

Where a teacher employed by a school authority commits a sexual assault on a student at school during school hours, the school authority is not liable to the student for breach of a non-delegable duty of care unless there was negligence on the school authority's part. Save perhaps in exceptional circumstances where a teacher's employment responsibilities place the teacher in a position of power and intimacy in relation to a student, a sexual assault committed by the teacher on the student at school during school hours is outside the course of employment and, for that reason, is conduct for which the school authority is not vicariously liable.

GLEESON CJ. [some footnotes in whole or part omitted] **[415]** 1. If a teacher employed by a school authority sexually abuses a pupil, is the school authority liable in damages to the pupil? ...

2. One potentially important matter is fault on the part of the school authority. The legal responsibilities of such an authority include a duty to take reasonable care for the safety of pupils. There may be cases in which sexual abuse is related to a failure to take such care. A school authority may have been negligent in employing a particular person, or in failing to make adequate arrangements for supervision of staff, or in failing to respond appropriately to complaints of previous misconduct, or in some other respect that can be identified as a cause of the harm to the pupil. ...

3. We are not presently concerned with such a case. Our concern is with the more difficult problem of liability in the absence of such fault. The presence of fault on the part of the school authority, causally related to the harm to the pupil, will result in liability. In what circumstances may there be liability notwithstanding the absence of fault? ... The assumed relationship between authority and teacher is that of employer and employee. A further assumption is that there has been no want of care on the part of the authority, either in appointing or supervising the teacher, or in

any other relevant aspect of the arrangements made for the care of pupils. The teacher has been guilty of intentional criminal conduct that has caused harm to a pupil. An employer is vicariously responsible for the wrongful act of an employee in some circumstances, and not in others. Either the law imposes vicarious responsibility on the school authority, or it does not. Does that conclude the matter? It has been argued that there is another possible basis upon which the authority may be found liable, even though there has been no want of care on its part, and even though the law refused to treat it as vicariously responsible for the tort of its employee. If it exists, this must be a form of liability even more strict than vicarious liability. It must be, or at least encompass the possibility of, liability for the intentional **[416]** wrongdoing of an employee in circumstances where the ordinary principles of vicarious responsibility do not entitle a plaintiff to succeed. This, it is contended, is the legal consequence of what has been called the non-delegability of a school authority's duty of care. The argument is that the authority's duty to take reasonable care for the safety of pupils, because it is non-delegable, may become a source of liability for any form of harm, accidental or intentional, inflicted upon a pupil by a teacher.

4. Three appeals in cases involving sexual abuse of pupils by teachers were heard together by this court. The first is from a decision of the Court of Appeal of New South Wales: *Lepore v New South Wales* (2001) 52 NSWLR 420. Because of defects in the manner in which the case was decided at first instance, it was an unsatisfactory vehicle for the resolution of the issues involved. However, a majority of the Court of Appeal (Mason P and Davies AJA, Heydon JA contra) accepted in principle that the school authority (the New South Wales Government) was liable on the basis of non-delegable duty. The extent of the liability was expressed by Mason P (with whom Davies AJA agreed) as follows (at 432):

In my view the State's obligations to school pupils on school premises and during school hours extend to ensuring that they are not injured physically at the hands of an employed teacher (whether acting negligently or intentionally).

5. That is a proposition with wide implications. Because of the principle upon which it is said to rest, its significance extends beyond schools, and beyond activities involving the care of children. The ambit of duties that are regarded as non-delegable has never been defined, and the extent of potential tort liability involved is uncertain, but it is clearly substantial.

6. The other two appeals are from the Court of Appeal of Queensland, which heard the cases together, and which declined to follow the decision of the New South Wales Court of Appeal: *Rich v Queensland; Samin v Queensland* (2001) Aust Torts Reports 81-626. ...

The plaintiffs' claims

7. In the first matter, the first respondent sued the appellant (the State of New Wales) and the second respondent (the teacher) in the District Court of New South Wales. The events complained of occurred in 1978, when the first respondent, then aged seven, was attending a state primary school. He alleged that he was assaulted by the second respondent. The assaults were said to have occurred in the context of supposed misbehaviour by the first respondent, and the imposition of corporal punishment for such misbehaviour. On a number of occasions, the first respondent, after being accused of misbehaviour, was sent to a storeroom, told to remove his clothing, smacked, and then touched indecently. On some occasions, other boys would be present, also ostensibly being punished.

8. The behaviour of the second respondent was reported to the police. He was charged with a number of offences of common assault. He entered pleas of guilty. Sentence was deferred upon his entering into a recognisance to be of good behaviour. He was also fined $300. He resigned as a teacher.

9. The second respondent took no part in the proceedings in the District Court, or in the subsequent appeals. Judge Downs QC, who was about to retire, dealt **[417]** separately with the issue of the liability of the state and the teacher, and deferred questions as to damages to be heard by another judge. He heard evidence, and then delivered a judgment which found that the second respondent had assaulted the first respondent. Regrettably, the judgment left unresolved the nature and extent of the assaults. The learned judge did not accept all the evidence of the first respondent, but it was not disputed that the second respondent had struck the first respondent on his bare bottom.

This was found sufficient to justify a finding of assault, and it resulted in liability on the part of the second respondent.

10. As to the liability of the appellant, Judge Downs found that there was no failure on the part of the state to exercise proper care. ...

11. Regrettably, Judge Downs did not make any detailed findings about the nature of the teacher's conduct. That some assaults occurred was not in dispute. His Honour was apparently content to let the judge who was to deal with the issue of damages work out the extent of the assaults. The judge also failed to deal with an argument based on breach of a non-delegable duty. The first respondent appealed against the decision in favour of the appellant. The Court of Appeal was left with an unsatisfactory factual basis for a review of the decision. There was no challenge in the Court of Appeal to the factual findings absolving the Department of Education of negligence. The principal complaint was that the trial judge failed to address the issue of breach of a non-delegable duty of care.

12. Neither at first instance, nor in the Court of Appeal, was the case against the appellant put on the basis of vicarious liability. There may have been an arguable case based on vicarious liability, even on a narrow view of the potential scope of such liability. Chastisement of a pupil is within the course of a teacher's **[418]** employment: *Ryan v Fildes* [1938] 3 All ER 517. On the account given by the first respondent, the inappropriate conduct seems to have taken place in the context of punishment for misbehaviour. However, no such argument was advanced, and the factual findings necessary for the purpose of considering such an argument were not made. ...

13. The second and third matters both arose out of the conduct of a teacher (the third respondent) at a one-teacher state primary school in rural Queensland. In each case, the appellant was a young girl attending the school. At the relevant times (between 1963 and 1965) the appellants were aged between seven and ten. The third respondent has taken no part in the proceedings. He was sentenced to a lengthy term of imprisonment. Each appellant alleged serious acts of sexual assault by the third respondent. Those acts, as particularised in the statement of claim, occurred, at school, during school hours, and in a classroom or adjoining rooms. Because no evidence has been taken, the full circumstances of the alleged assaults are not apparent. For example, it is not clear whether the third respondent's behaviour allegedly occurred in front of other pupils, or how he came to be in intimate physical contact with the appellants.

14. In each case, the former pupil commenced action, in the District Court of Queensland, against the State of Queensland, the Minister for Education of Queensland, and the former teacher. We are not presently concerned with the action against the teacher. In relation to the claims against the state and the minister (which reflected some uncertainty as to the identity of the school authority) each statement of claim alleged, in terms of a non-delegable duty, that the state was under "a duty to ensure that reasonable care was taken of [the appellant] whilst she was at the school" and that, in breach of the state's duty, the teacher sexually assaulted the appellant. It then alleged psychiatric injury and other harm to the appellant. There was no allegation of fault on the part of the school authority in relation to its conduct of the school, or appointment of the teacher, or failure to respond to warnings or complaints. It was simply alleged that the teacher sexually assaulted the appellants at school, and that this constituted a breach of the duty owed by the school authority to the appellants.

15. Applications were made by the first and second respondents to strike out each statement of claim. Those applications failed in the District Court. There were appeals to the Court of Appeal of Queensland. The appeals were successful. The Court of Appeal (McPherson, Thomas and Williams JJA) ordered that each statement of claim be struck out, and that each plaintiff have leave to deliver a further statement of claim. The claims were argued solely on the basis of non-delegable duty. No reliance was placed on vicarious liability. In noting that fact, McPherson JA said:

> Nothing can be clearer than that the assaults alleged to have been committed here were independent and personal acts of misconduct by [the teacher]. They were in no sense capable of being regarded as methods of conducting his teaching function, but were done in utter defiance and contradiction of it and of his duties as an employee of the State.

[419] 16. The Court of Appeal of Queensland declined to follow the reasoning of the majority in *Lepore*, preferring the minority opinion of Heydon JA.

17. In this court, counsel for the appellants in the cases of *Samin* and *Rich* indicated that, pursuant to the leave to re-plead, reliance would be placed on vicarious liability. The court was shown the proposed form of amended statements of claim. The only difference from the original pleadings is that they assert that the school authority is vicariously responsible for the assaults perpetrated by the teacher, and give as particulars the opportunity which the school afforded the teacher to abuse his authority, the intimacy inherent in the relation between teacher and infant pupils, the power of the teacher and the vulnerability of the pupils, the fact that the teacher had sole control of the school, and the fact that the assaults occurred during school hours and at school premises. By reason of those matters, it is contended, the assaults "occurred in the course of or were closely connected with" the teacher's employment. Once again, there is no allegation of any act or omission of the school authority involving a want of care for the safety of the pupils. Apparently, the appellants did not, and do not, intend to take advantage of the opportunity to re-plead to seek to make out a case of direct liability based on some act or omission of the school authority.

18. In all three cases, the issue is whether, there being no allegation of any fault on the part of the school authority in its systems or procedures, its appointment and supervision of staff, its arrangements for responding to complaints or warnings, or any other matter which might have given rise to a claim that the authority itself was guilty of a want of care, the acts of the teacher make the authority liable. In this court, primary reliance is again placed on the principle of non-delegable duty, and the reasoning of the majority in the New South Wales Court of Appeal. However, in the alternative, it is now argued that the school authorities are vicariously liable. Recent decisions of the House of Lords (*Lister v Hesley Hall Ltd* [2002] 1 AC 215) and of the Supreme Court of Canada (*Bazley v Curry* [1999] 2 SCR 534; *Jacobi v Griffiths* [1999] 2 SCR 570) are said to support that alternative approach. …

The non-delegable duty of care

19. For more than a century, courts have described certain common law duties of care as "non-delegable" or "personal": *Kondis v State Transport Authority* (1984) 154 CLR 672 at 685. The purpose and effect of such a characterisation of a duty of care is not always entirely clear. However, in a number of cases, members of this court have so described the duty owed by a school authority to its pupils. …

[421] 24. The case of [*Commonwealth v*] *Introvigne* (1982) 150 CLR 258 raised an unusual problem. The plaintiff, a schoolboy aged 15, attended the Woden Valley High School in the Australian Capital Territory. One morning before class, he and some friends entertained themselves by swinging on the flagpole in the school grounds. As a result of their exertions, the truck of the flagpole became detached, and fell on the plaintiff's head. He was injured. The plaintiff's case was originally based on the allegedly defective condition of the flagpole. He sued the Commonwealth as occupier of the school premises. He also sued the designer of the flagpole. On the first day of the hearing, the plaintiff obtained leave to amend his statement of claim by alleging negligence on the part of the teachers. In particular, he alleged that the acting principal failed to arrange for adequate supervision in the school grounds. The plaintiff claimed that the Commonwealth was liable as a result of that failure. However, the Commonwealth was not the employer of the acting principal, or the other teachers. They were all employees of the New South Wales Department of Education which, at the relevant time, operated the Woden Valley High School on behalf of the Commonwealth pursuant to an inter-governmental arrangement. It was too late for the plaintiff to sue the State of New South Wales. The trial judge found no negligence. That finding was reversed on appeal. The factual issue is presently irrelevant. What was significant for future cases was the basis on which the court attributed responsibility to the Commonwealth for the negligence of the teachers.

25. Mason J, with whom Gibbs CJ agreed, said that, although the case had been presented by the plaintiff, and dealt with at first instance and in the intermediate appellate court, as one of vicarious liability, the plaintiff was entitled to succeed on a different basis. He did not reject the possibility that the Commonwealth might have been vicariously liable for the negligence of the teachers. However, he rested his decision on the ground that "[t]he duty … imposed on a school authority is akin to that owed by a hospital to its patient" (at 270). In *Gold* [*v Essex County Council*]

[1942] 2 KB 293, it had been held that the liability of a hospital arises out of an obligation **[422]** to use reasonable care in treatment, the performance of which cannot be delegated to someone else. This is a "personal" duty. It is more stringent than a duty to take reasonable care; it is a duty to ensure that reasonable care is taken. The reason for its imposition in the case of schools is the immaturity and inexperience of pupils, and their need for protection. This gives rise to a special responsibility akin to that of a hospital for its patients. ...

30. What was decided in *Introvigne* was that, even though it may have been doubtful that the Commonwealth was vicariously liable for the negligent failure of the teachers to provide adequate supervision, (the doubt arising from the inter-governmental arrangement), nevertheless the Commonwealth was under a duty to provide reasonable supervision;` it could not discharge that duty by arranging for the State of New South Wales to conduct the school; it had a responsibility to see that adequate supervision was provided; and the absence of adequate supervision meant that it had not fulfilled its responsibility and was in breach of its duty of care. ...

[423] 31. The failure to take care of the plaintiff which resulted in the Commonwealth's liability in *Introvigne* was a negligent omission on the part of the teachers at the school, acting in the course of their ordinary duties. ... A responsibility to take reasonable care for the safety of another, or a responsibility to see that reasonable care is taken for the safety of another, is substantially different from an obligation to prevent any kind of harm. Furthermore, although deliberately and criminally inflicting injury on another person involves a failure to take care of that person, it involves more. If a member of a hospital's staff with homicidal propensities were to attack and injure a patient, in circumstances where there was no fault on the part of the hospital authorities, or any other person for whose acts or omissions the hospital was vicariously responsible, the common law should not determine the question of the hospital's liability to the patient on the footing that the staff member had neglected to take reasonable care of the patient. It should face up to the fact that the staff member had criminally assaulted the patient, and address the problem of the circumstances in which an employer may be vicariously liable for the criminal acts of an employee. Intentional wrongdoing, especially intentional criminality, introduces a factor of legal relevance beyond a mere failure to take care. ...

32. As will appear, courts of the highest authority in England and Canada, and courts in other common law jurisdictions, have analysed the problem of the liability of a school authority for sexual abuse of pupils by teachers in terms of vicarious liability. If the argument based on non-delegable duty, said to be supported by *Introvigne*, is correct, their efforts have been misdirected, and the conclusions they have reached have unduly restricted liability. If the proposition accepted in the Court of Appeal of New South Wales is correct, and represents the law in Australia, then the liability of school authorities in this country extends beyond that which has been accepted in other common law jurisdictions. Moreover, in this country, where a relationship of employer and employee exists, if the duty of care owed to a victim by the employer can be characterised as personal, or non-delegable, then the potential responsibility of an employer for the intentional and criminal conduct of an employee extends beyond that which flows from the principles governing vicarious liability. It is unconstrained by considerations about whether the employee was acting in the course of his or her employment. It is enough that the victim has been injured by an employee on an occasion when the employer's duty of care covered the victim. The employer's duty to take care, or to see that reasonable care is taken, has been transformed into an absolute duty to prevent harm by the employee. ...

[424] 34. The proposition that, because a school authority's duty of care to a pupil is non-delegable, the authority is liable for any injury, accidental or intentional, inflicted at school upon a pupil by a teacher, is too broad, and the responsibility with which it fixes school authorities is too demanding. ...

[425] 38. There is no reason, either in principle or in authority, to treat the existence of a non-delegable duty of care as having the consequences held by the New South Wales Court of Appeal. In that respect, the reasoning of Heydon JA, and of the Queensland Court of Appeal, is to be preferred. ...

Vicarious liability

40. An employer is vicariously liable for a tort committed by an employee in the course of his or her employment. The limiting or controlling concept, course of employment, is sometimes referred to as scope of employment. Its aspects are functional, as well as geographical and temporal. Not everything that an employee does at work, or during working hours, is sufficiently connected with the duties and responsibilities of the employee to be regarded as within the scope of the employment. And the fact that wrongdoing occurs away from the workplace, or outside normal working hours, is not conclusive against liability. ...

[426] 42. ... It is clear that if the wrongful act of an employee has been authorised by the employer, the employer will be liable. The difficulty relates to unauthorised acts. The best known formulation of the test to be applied is that in Salmond, *Law of Torts* in the first edition in 1907 (at 83), and in later editions: an employer is liable even for unauthorised acts if they are so connected with authorised acts that they may be regarded as modes – although improper modes – of doing them, but the employer is not responsible if the unauthorised and wrongful act is not so connected with the authorised act as to be a mode of doing it, but is an independent act. ...

[428] 49. The leading Australian authority on the subject of vicarious responsibility for an assault by an employee is *Deatons Pty Ltd v Flew* (1949) 79 CLR 370. ... The plaintiff sued a hotel barmaid and her employer in trespass. The barmaid had thrown the contents of a glass of beer, and then the glass itself, into his face. He lost an eye. There was conflicting evidence as to what led up to the incident. The plaintiff's version was that he simply asked to speak to the publican, and the next thing he remembered was that he woke up in the eye hospital. There was other evidence that he was drunk and aggressive, and that he had quarrelled with the barmaid, striking her and calling her names. The jury found against both defendants. The employer appealed. The Full Court of the Supreme Court of New South Wales ordered a new trial. ...

50. The employer then appealed to this court, contending, successfully, that it was entitled, not merely to a new trial, but to a verdict by direction. The court considered that, on either version of the facts, the employer was not vicariously liable for the trespass: on the plaintiff's version what the barmaid did was a gratuitous, unprovoked act; the only alternative view open was that it was an act of personal retribution. Either way, it was not incidental to the work she was employed to do. It was emphasised that it was not the duty of the barmaid to keep order in the bar. There were other people to do that. Her job was merely to serve drinks. Her conduct was not an excessive method of maintaining order. It was "a spontaneous act of retributive justice" (at 382 per Dixon J). ...

[429] 53. It is the element of protection involved in the relationship between school authority and pupil that has given rise to difficulty in defining the circumstances in which an assault by a teacher upon a pupil will result in vicarious liability on the part of a school authority. ...

54. ... [430] Sexual abuse, which is so obviously inconsistent with the responsibilities of anyone involved with the instruction and care of children, in former times would readily have been regarded as conduct of a personal and independent nature, unlikely ever to be treated as within the course of employment. Yet such conduct might take different forms. An opportunistic act of serious and random violence might be different, in terms of its connection with employment, from improper touching by a person whose duties involve intimate contact with another. In recent years, in most common law jurisdictions, courts have had to deal with a variety of situations involving sexual abuse by employees.

55. In 1999, the Supreme Court of Canada dealt consecutively with two such cases. ... The first case was *Bazley v Curry* [1999] 2 SCR 534. A non-profit organisation, which operated residential care facilities for the treatment of emotionally troubled children, required its employees to perform parental duties, ranging from general supervision to intimate functions like bathing and tucking in at bedtime. It employed a man who was a paedophile. He sexually abused a child. The question was whether the organisation was vicariously liable for his wrongdoing. That question was answered in the affirmative.

56. McLachlin J, who delivered the judgment of the court, examined the considerations of policy underlying the concept of vicarious liability, and said (at 557):

> Underlying the cases holding employers vicariously liable for the unauthorized acts of employees is the idea that employers may justly be held liable where the act falls within the ambit of

the risk that the employer's enterprise creates or exacerbates. Similarly, the policy purposes underlying the imposition of vicarious liability on employers are served only where the wrong is so connected with the employment that it can be said that the employer has introduced the risk of the wrong (and is thereby fairly and usefully charged with its management and minimization). The question in each case is whether there is a connection or nexus between the employment enterprise and that wrong that justifies imposition of vicarious liability on the employer for the wrong, in terms of fair allocation of the consequences of the risk and/ or deterrence. ...

[431] 59. *Jacobi v Griffiths* [1999] 2 SCR 570 ... [the second case in the Supreme Court of Canada] concerned the vicarious liability of a non-profit organisation, which operated a recreational club for children, for sexual assaults upon two children by one of the club's employees. The employee was a program director, whose job was to organize after-school recreational activities. He cultivated an intimate association with the two victims, and assaulted them at his home. It was held that the club was not liable.

62. ... *Bazley* was distinguished as a case where the sexual abuse occurred in a special environment that involved intimate private control, and quasi-parental relationship and power. In *Jacobi*, on the other hand, the club offered group recreational activities in the presence of volunteers and other members. Those activities were not of such a kind as to create a relationship of power and intimacy; they merely provided the offender with an opportunity to meet children. ...

[433] 68. A recent decision of the House of Lords, *Lister v Hesley Hall Ltd* [2002] 1 AC 215, concerned a school, operated as a commercial enterprise, mainly for children with emotional and behavioural difficulties. Boarding facilities were provided for some of the pupils. A warden was in charge of the boarding annex. He and his wife, for most of the time, were in sole charge. The annex was intended to be a home, not a mere extension of the school environment, and the warden had many of the responsibilities of a parent. He sexually abused some of the pupils. The question was whether his employer was vicariously liable for his assaults. The House of Lords answered that question in the affirmative.

69. Lord Steyn, with whom Lord Hutton agreed, asked "whether the warden's torts were so closely connected with his employment that it would be fair and just to hold the employers vicariously liable", and answered in the affirmative. Lord Clyde also said that the issue to be considered was the closeness of the connection between the act in question and the employment. [Gleeson CJ referred to the judgment of Lord Hobhouse of Woodborough and continued.] ...

71. Lord Millett said (at 250):
In the present case the warden's duties provided him with the opportunity to commit indecent assaults on the boys for his own sexual gratification, but that in itself is not enough to make the school liable ...But there was far more to it than that. The school was responsible for the care and welfare of the boys. It entrusted that responsibility to the warden. He was employed to discharge the school's responsibility to the boys. For this purpose the school entrusted them to his care. He did not merely take advantage of the opportunity which employment at a residential school gave him. He abused the **[434]** special position in which the school had placed him to enable it to discharge its own responsibilities, with the result that the assaults were committed by the very employee to whom the school had entrusted the care of the boys.

72. I do not accept that the decisions in *Bazley*, *Jacobi*, and *Lister* suggest that, in Canada and England, in most cases where a teacher has sexually abused a pupil, the wrong will be found to have occurred within the scope of the teacher's employment. However, they demonstrate that, in those jurisdictions, as in Australia, one cannot dismiss the possibility of a school authority's vicarious liability for sexual abuse merely by pointing out that it constitutes serious misconduct on the part of a teacher. ...

74. If there is sufficient connection between what a particular teacher is employed to do, and sexual misconduct, for such misconduct fairly to be regarded as in the course of the teacher's employment, it must be because the nature of the teacher's responsibilities, and of the relationship with pupils created by those responsibilities, justified that conclusion. It is not enough to say that teaching involves care. So it does; but it is necessary to be more precise about the nature and extent of care in question. Teaching may simply involve care for the academic development and

progress of a student. In these circumstances, it may be that ... the school context provides a mere opportunity for the commission of an assault. However, where the teacher-student relationship is invested with a high degree of power and intimacy, the use of that power and intimacy to commit sexual abuse may provide a sufficient connection between the sexual assault and the employment to make it just to treat such contact as occurring in the course of employment. ...

The case of *Lepore* ...

[435] 77. Although the plaintiff's case against the state at the first hearing before Judge Downs ... was put in terms of breach of non-delegable duty rather than vicarious liability, and although vicarious liability was not argued in the Court of Appeal, nevertheless there is no reason in justice why, at a new trial, the plaintiff should not be permitted to amend his statement of claim and to seek to make out a case of vicarious liability.

78. The fact-finding at the first hearing was so deficient that it is not possible to form a clear view as to the strength of such a case. However, the maintenance of discipline is clearly within the employment responsibilities of the teacher, and much, perhaps all, of the alleged misconduct appears to have taken place in the context of administering punishment for supposed misbehaviour. It may be possible that some or all of it could properly be regarded as excessive chastisement, for which a school authority would be vicariously liable. The relatively minor criminal charges laid against the teacher, and the modest penalties imposed, may be consistent with this view of the matter. Whether excessive or inappropriate chastisement results from the sadistic tendency of a teacher, or a desire for sexual gratification, or both, it is conduct in the course of employment, for which a school authority is vicariously liable. ...

79. The proceedings at first instance comprehensively miscarried. There should be a new trial on all issues although, as will appear from the above, the argument based on non-delegable duty should no longer be treated as open, and the only potential basis for a case of vicarious liability depends upon finding that the relevant conduct amounted to excessive or inappropriate chastisement. ...

81. The appeal should be allowed in part. ...

The cases of *Samin* and *Rich*

82. The Court of Appeal of Queensland was correct to reject the only case advanced in argument before it, which was a case of strict and absolute liability based on non-delegable duty.

83. However, the plaintiffs now seek also to make out a case of vicarious liability. Unless such a case is unarguable, then they should have an opportunity to do so. The Court of Appeal gave them unqualified leave to deliver a further statement of claim.

[436] 84. All that this court knows about the alleged facts is what appears in the proposed amended statement of claim, which has been summarised earlier. ...

85. For the reasons given earlier, in order to make the State of Queensland vicariously liable for the teacher's sexual assaults, it would be necessary for the plaintiffs to show that his responsibilities to female pupils of the age of the plaintiffs at the time, placed him in a position of such power and intimacy that his conduct towards them could fairly be regarded as so closely connected with his responsibilities as to be in the course of his employment. That would involve making findings both as to his powers and responsibilities, and as to the nature of his conduct. It would not be enough that his position provided him with the opportunity to gratify his sexual desires, and that he took advantage of that opportunity.

86. The appeals should be dismissed. ...

[Gaudron and Kirby JJ, in separate judgments, and Gummow and Hayne JJ, in a joint judgment, agreed with Gleeson CJ's disposition of the three cases. McHugh J, in a dissenting judgment in which his Honour would have dismissed the appeal by the State of New South Wales in *Lepore* and allowed the plaintiffs' appeals in *Samin* and *Rich*, said at **[447]**:

136. In my opinion a State education authority owes a duty to a pupil to take reasonable care to prevent harm to the pupil. The duty cannot be delegated. If, as is invariably the case, the State delegates the *performance* of the duty to a teacher, the State is liable if the teacher fails to take

reasonable care to prevent harm to the pupil. The State is liable even if the teacher intentionally harms the pupil. The State cannot avoid liability by establishing that the teacher intentionally caused the harm even if the conduct of the teacher constitutes a criminal offence. It is the State's duty to protect the pupil, and the conduct of the teacher constitutes a breach of the State's own duty. It is unnecessary to decide whether the State is also vicariously liable for the tort of the teacher who assaults or sexually assaults a pupil. ...

Callinan J expressed the view that deliberate criminal conduct by a teacher was not conduct for which the teacher's employer was vicariously liable. As the primary judge in *Lepore* had made a finding that the teacher in that case had engaged in deliberate criminal conduct, there could be no vicarious liability on the part of the State of New South Wales. Accordingly, in Callinan J's view, the appeal by the State of New South Wales in *Lepore* should have been allowed with no order for a new trial. Callinan J agreed with Gleeson CJ, Gaudron, Gummow, Kirby and Hayne JJ, that the plaintiffs' appeals in *Samin* and *Rich* should be dismissed.]

New South Wales v Lepore
Appeal allowed in part. New trial ordered

Samin v Queensland
Rich v Queensland
Appeals dismissed

Leichhardt Municipal Council v Montgomery
(2007) 230 CLR 22; [2007] HCA 6
High Court of Australia

A roads authority, such as a local council, in which is vested a public road and a statutory power to carry out maintenance work on the road, does not owe a non-delegable duty of care to a road user who suffers personal injury due to the negligence of an independent contractor engaged by the roads authority to perform that work.

[The plaintiff (respondent), Mr Leslie Montgomery, suffered personal injury when he fell into a telecommunications pit which had a broken cover while walking along the footpath adjoining Parramatta Road, Leichhardt. The immediate cause of the plaintiff's personal injury was the negligence of an employee of an independent contractor, Roan Constructions Pty Ltd, which the defendant (appellant), Leichhardt Municipal Council, had engaged to perform maintenance work (which the parties to the present proceedings agreed was not of an extra-hazardous nature) on the footpath. This negligence consisted of the employee of the independent contractor carelessly putting carpet over the broken telecommunications pit into which the plaintiff fell.

In an action to recover damages for personal injury, the primary judge (Quirk DCJ) held that the defendant was liable to the plaintiff for the negligence of the independent contractor's employee without the need for the plaintiff to prove negligence on the part of the defendant, ie the defendant was under a non-delegable duty of care to the plaintiff to ensure that reasonable care was exercised by the independent contractor's employee. The decision of the primary judge was upheld by the New South Wales Court of Appeal. The High Court of Australia unanimously allowed the defendant's appeal, ordering that the plaintiff pay the costs of the appeal, and remitted the case to the New South Wales Court of Appeal for determination of the unresolved issue whether the defendant, in any relevant respect, had itself breached its duty of care to the plaintiff, eg in failing to supervise the independent contractor's activities.

In the remitted hearing, the plaintiff was unsuccessful and was ordered to pay the defendant's costs: *Leichhardt Municipal Council v Montgomery* [2007] NSWCA 361.]

GLEESON CJ. **[26]** 1. The appellant Council was the roads authority, within the meaning of the *Roads Act 1993* (NSW), for Parramatta Road, Leichhardt. That road is one of Australia's oldest and busiest public highways, and passes through densely populated suburbs of Sydney. On both sides of the road there are footpaths which, by definition, are part of the road for the purposes of the *Roads Act*. The *Roads Act* vested the road in the appellant. Section 71 conferred upon the appellant a power to carry out work on the road. The appellant engaged a contractor, Roan Constructions Pty Ltd (Roan Constructions), to perform work on the footpath. There is nothing unusual about that. Local councils commonly use their own staff for routine road maintenance, but they also commonly engage outside contractors to undertake substantial road works. ...

3. On the trial judge's finding about the conduct of Roan Constructions' employees, that company was clearly liable to the respondent. The respondent had sued both Roan Constructions and the appellant. The claim against Roan Constructions was compromised before hearing, and the case proceeded against the appellant. ...

4. ... Both [the trial judge and the Court of Appeal] accepted the respondent's alternative submission, which was recorded by the primary judge as being "that **[27]** the council owed to the plaintiff a non-delegable duty of care, notwithstanding the fact that the footpath reconstruction works ... were being carried out by a contractor ... Roan Constructions Pty Ltd".

5. Following a line of English authority (*Hardaker v Idle District Council* [1896] 1 QB 335; *Penny v Wimbledon Urban District Council* [1899] 2 QB 72; *Holliday v National Telephone Co* [1899] 2 QB 392; *Salsbury v Woodland* [1970] 1 QB 324; *Rowe v Herman* [1997] 1 WLR 1390), and earlier decisions of the New South Wales Court of Appeal (*Roads and Traffic Authority (NSW) v Scroop* (1998) 28 MVR 233; *Roads and Traffic Authority (NSW) v Fletcher* (2001) 33 MVR 215), Hodgson JA, with whom Mason P and McColl JA agreed, said:

> [W]here a road authority engages a contractor to do work on a road used by the public, such as to involve risk to the public unless reasonable care is exercised, the road authority has a duty to ensure reasonable care is exercised; and the road authority will be liable if the contractor does not take reasonable care. However, the road authority will not be liable for casual or collateral acts of negligence by the contractor.

6. A conclusion that, in given circumstances, a defendant who is sued in negligence owed a duty going beyond a duty to exercise reasonable care to avoid injury (or injury of a certain kind) to a plaintiff, and extending to a duty to ensure that reasonable care to avoid injury to the plaintiff was exercised, is commonly described as a conclusion that a defendant was under a non-delegable duty of care to a plaintiff. It is a proposition of law concerning the nature or content of the duty of care. A duty of this nature involves what Mason J described in *Kondis v State Transport Authority* (1984) 154 CLR 672 at 687 as "a special responsibility or duty to see that care is taken". Such a duty enables a plaintiff to outflank the general principle that a defendant is not vicariously responsible for the negligence of an independent contractor. The present case provides an example. No one doubted that, if causative negligence on the part of Council employees had been established, the Council would have been liable. No one doubted that the finding of causative negligence on the part of Roan Constructions' employees meant that Roan Constructions was liable. However, there being no suggestion of any fault in the choice of Roan Constructions as a contractor, if it had not been for the special duty held (as a matter of **[28]** law) to exist, the appellant would not have been liable for an injury caused only by the negligence of Roan Constructions' employees. ...

8. In considering the question of non-delegable duties of care it is convenient to put to one side other questions of law that may arise concerning the nature, or content, of a duty of care. Such questions might arise because of the kind of injury suffered by the plaintiff, or the circumstances of that injury, or the relationship between the parties, or the responsibilities of the defendant. For example, in *Graham Barclay Oysters Pty Ltd v Ryan* (2002) 211 CLR 540 actions were brought against a grower of oysters, a distributor of oysters, a local council and the State. As against the grower and the distributor, it was a product liability case. The defendants, who produced and supplied oysters, owed a duty to take reasonable care to avoid injury to consumers. The issue

was one of breach; an issue of fact. As against the council and the State, however, the issue was one of law. What would it have meant to say that the State of New South Wales owed a duty to take reasonable care to avoid injury to consumers of oysters? If a duty were formulated in that fashion, what would be the issues of fact to be decided on the question of breach? If there were a trial by jury, what matters would a judge direct a jury to consider? In a broadly political sense, it is plausible to assert that a government owes a duty to take care of its citizens, but when it comes to formulating a duty for the purposes of a claim for negligence, a duty expressed at that level of abstraction would lack practical content. In any action in negligence, a proposition about a duty of care must be capable of being expressed in a manner that would enable a judge to direct a jury how to set about deciding whether there had been a breach. This is not difficult in well-established areas such as litigation arising out of industrial accidents, motor vehicle accidents, occupiers' liability or professional negligence. It may be otherwise, however, in cases which lie at the boundaries of the law of negligence. There, the separation of issues of **[29]** law (affecting duty) from issues of fact (affecting breach) may be more problematic. (In this context I include among issues of fact questions of normative judgment that often affect decisions about reasonableness.) The decreasing use of juries in many Australian jurisdictions tends to obscure distinctions between questions of duty and questions of breach. Questions that would need to be kept separate at a jury trial may merge, or at least overlap, in the reasoning of a judge sitting alone. In this appeal, however, it is clear that we are concerned only with a question of law, that is, the nature of the duty of care owed by the appellant to the respondent.

9. In practice, the difference between a duty to take reasonable care and a duty to ensure that reasonable care is taken matters where it is not an act or omission of the defendant, or of someone for whose fault the defendant is vicariously responsible, that has caused harm to the plaintiff, but the act or omission of some third party, for whose fault the defendant would not ordinarily be vicariously responsible. If a negligent act or omission is that of a defendant, or a person for whose fault the defendant is vicariously responsible (such as an employee), no problem arises. Again, if the nature of a defendant's responsibility is such that it can be discharged lawfully or properly only by the defendant personally, an attempted delegation would be irrelevant. Some responsibilities are non-delegable in the sense that it is of their essence that they be performed by a particular person, perhaps because of trust or confidence reposed in that person. In some cases, a duty to take care involves a duty to act personally. That kind of non-delegability should not be confused with a case where the engagement of a third party to perform a certain function is consistent with the exercise of reasonable care by a defendant, but the defendant's legal duty is not merely to exercise reasonable care but also (if a third party is engaged) to ensure that reasonable care is taken. In such a case, the third party's failure to take care will result in breach of the defendant's duty. The legal consequence is that the circumstance that the third party is an independent contractor does not enable the defendant to avoid liability. It is because of its practical effect of outflanking the general rule that a defendant is not vicariously responsible for the fault of an independent contractor that the identification of this special responsibility or duty is important.

10. In the exercise of statutory functions, non-delegability of the first kind (strict non-delegability) would arise, for example, where a power or duty was conferred in terms, or in a context, such that it had to be performed or exercised personally by the repository of the power or duty or, if the repository were a corporation or other legal entity, by that corporation or entity. Non-delegability of the second kind would arise where there was nothing to prevent the engagement of a third party to perform the function, but it appeared from the terms of the statute that the legislature intended the repository of the power or duty to have a responsibility for ensuring the exercise of reasonable care **[30]** even if a third party were engaged to perform the function. That would involve a question of statutory construction. …

[33] 18. We are not here concerned with the non-delegable duty that arises from the conduct of extra-hazardous activities. When, in *Burnie Port Authority v General Jones Pty Ltd* (1994) 179 CLR 520, this Court decided that the rule in *Rylands v Fletcher* (1868) LR 3 HL 330 should be treated as subsumed in the ordinary law of negligence, part of the justification advanced for that decision was the protection afforded, within the law of negligence, by the concept of non-delegable duty (1994)

179 CLR 520 at 550-554. Road works could in some circumstances involve an extra-hazardous activity, but that is not this case.

19. The possibility of a special duty of care falling upon roads authorities extending beyond a duty to take reasonable care to a duty to see that reasonable care is taken, is accepted in North America (*Prosser and Keeton on the Law of Torts*, 5th ed (1984), p 511; *Restatement of Torts*, 2d (1965), vol 2, Ch 15, Topic 2, p 394). In *Lewis v British Columbia* ([1997] 3 SCR 1145), in 1997, the Supreme Court of Canada held that the statutory powers exercised by the British Columbia Ministry of Transportation and Highways, which employed an independent contractor to remove dangerous rocks beside a highway, were such that the Ministry was under a duty to ensure that its independent contractor took reasonable care. The Supreme Court attached importance to a statutory provision that not only placed the contractor's work under the Ministry's control, but also required the Ministry to direct the work (1997) 3 SCR 1145 at 1161 [25]). This provision was interpreted to mean that the Ministry was required to conform "to a statutory duty to personally direct [the] works", a duty imposed in the interests of public safety.

20. At the centre of this problem there is a question of statutory construction. The common law should define the duty of care to which a roads authority is subject by reference to the nature of the statutory powers given to the authority, and the legislative intendment discernible from the terms in which those powers are granted, considered in the light of the purposes for which they are conferred.

21. The first object of the *Roads Act*, stated in s 3, is to set out the rights of members of the public to pass along public roads. The first substantive provision of the Act is s 5, which provides that a member of the public is entitled as of right to pass along a public road whether on foot, in a vehicle or otherwise. Roads authorities are provided for by s 7. They are to have the functions conferred on them by the Act. Part 6 of the Act deals with road works. These may be carried out by roads authorities. Roads authorities are required, in certain **[34]** circumstances, to obtain approval for works from the Roads and Traffic Authority. By definition, road work includes any kind of work, building or structure (such as, for example, a roadway, footway, bridge or tunnel) that is constructed or installed on or in the vicinity of a road for the purpose of facilitating the use of the road as a road. Section 71 empowers a roads authority to carry out road work. Since such work will commonly affect the public right declared by s 5, this provision authorises what otherwise may be a nuisance. Roads authorities may construct tunnels or bridges (s 78). These, of course, may be major works, and often are undertaken by independent contractors who would be expected to apply extensive resources and expertise, including expertise that would not be available to a local council. In the present case we are concerned with a fairly basic form of construction, but operations within the purview of the Act include some which require a high level of technical skill. Section 145 vests a public road in a local government area in fee simple in the appropriate roads authority. Section 146 provides that the dedication of land as a public road does not constitute the owner of the road as an occupier of land.

22. It is consistent with that statutory scheme to conclude that there is a duty in a roads authority to take reasonable care to prevent physical injury to a person such as the respondent from the carrying out of road works. It is also consistent with the statutory scheme to conclude that, if an independent contractor is engaged to perform such works, the roads authority remains under a "personal" duty to take reasonable care to prevent such injury, and that such duty is not discharged *merely* by exercising care in the selection of the contractor. Reasonable care on the part of the roads authority may well involve a certain level of scrutiny of the contractor's plans and supervision of the contractor's activities. It is a different thing to say that the legislation imposes, or is consistent with the imposition of, a duty to *ensure* that no employee of the independent contractor act carelessly.

23. This raises a more general question concerning non-delegable duties. A "special" responsibility or duty to "see" or "ensure" that reasonable care is taken by an independent contractor, and the contractor's employees, goes beyond a duty to act reasonably in exercising prudent oversight of what the contractor does. In many circumstances, it is a duty that could not be fulfilled. How can a hospital ensure that a surgeon is never careless? If the answer is that it cannot, what does the law mean when it speaks of a duty to ensure that care is taken? It may mean something different. It may mean that there should be an exception to the general rule that a defendant is not vicariously responsible for the negligence of an independent contractor. The present case illustrates the

artificiality of attributing to the appellant a duty to ensure that care was taken. The failure to take care consisted in a workman, in the employment of Roan Constructions, placing a carpet over a telecommunications pit that had a defective cover, in circumstances where the workman should have noticed the defect. [35] Thus a trap was created and the respondent fell into it. To speak of a local council having a duty to ensure that such an apparently low-level and singular act of carelessness does not occur is implausible. It is one thing to find fault on the part of council officers where there has been a failure to exercise reasonable care in supervising the work of a contractor, or in approving a contractor's plans and system of work. It is another thing to attribute to the council a legal duty of care which obliges the council to do the impossible: to ensure that no employee of the contractor behaves carelessly. The problem is even more acute if the source of this duty of care is said to be found in statute. One of the things that is special about this duty is that it is a duty to do the impossible. That is unlikely to have been intended by the legislature.

24. If the law were frankly to acknowledge that what is involved is not a breach by the defendant of a special kind of duty, but an imposition upon a defendant of a special kind of vicarious responsibility, a different problem would have to be faced. It would be necessary to identify and justify the exceptions to the general rule that a defendant is not vicariously responsible for the negligence of an independent contractor, and to provide a means by which other exceptions may be identified when they arise. That, in turn, would require an explanation of the general rule so as to account for the circumstances in which it yields to exceptions. It may be difficult to justify those circumstances in terms of fixed categories. Within those categories there may be individual cases some of which may be thought to merit making them an exception and others of which may not. ...

26. In *Brodie*, the majority in this Court (Gaudron, McHugh and Gummow JJ, with whom Kirby J agreed) said that the liability of highway authorities should now be treated as covered by the modern law of negligence, into which public nuisance has been absorbed ((2001) 206 CLR 512 at 564-570 [116]-[129]). They formulated a duty of care, to apply in cases of non-feasance as well as misfeasance, being a duty to take reasonable care that the exercise of or failure to exercise the powers by such authorities does not create a foreseeable risk of harm to road users (at 577 [150]). We are here concerned with a case of misfeasance. The later statutory reinstatement of a measure of protection for non-feasance is irrelevant. For reasons already explained, I do not take *Brodie* to deny the importance of statutory construction. The formulation of the duty of care given in *Brodie*, in its application to cases of misfeasance, and to a case where a roads authority has exercised its powers by engaging an independent [36] contractor, is consistent with what I have already indicated is the construction I would place upon the *Roads Act*. It is not a special duty to ensure anything; certainly not a duty to ensure that no worker behaves carelessly. It is a duty to exercise reasonable care. It is not discharged merely by engaging a reputable contractor. The exercise of reasonable care for the protection of road users, in a case where an independent contractor is engaged, may be affected by the nature of the work involved and the resources respectively available to the roads authority and the contractor. What is required of a local council which engages a major construction company to build a bridge or tunnel may differ from what is required of another council in different circumstances. The content of a requirement of reasonable care adapts to circumstances, unlike the content of a requirement to ensure that care is taken. As was mentioned earlier, in this case there is an unresolved issue about an alleged failure by the appellant's officers to exercise reasonable care.

27. The concept of a non-delegable duty, elaborated as a duty to ensure that care is taken, may have a useful, if not entirely admirable, role in some cases involving the tort of negligence. We are concerned only with roads authorities. We are concerned particularly with the *Roads Act*, and the powers and responsibilities it confers. The appellant had a duty to take reasonable care, a duty that was not discharged merely by engaging the services of Roan Constructions. It did not have a duty to ensure that the employees of Roan Constructions did not behave carelessly. The basis upon which the case was decided against the appellant at first instance and in the Court of Appeal was incorrect.

28. The appeal should be allowed. ...

KIRBY J. ...[58] 98. The use of non-employee contractors has greatly expanded in Australia in recent times, due to the privatisation of many activities formerly performed by governments and their agencies, and the resulting "out-sourcing" of functions to independent contractors that operate for their own profit. The general rule is that the principal is not liable for the wrongs done by an independent contractor or its employees. It is not easy to see why an exception should be specifically carved out allowing the person injured to recover from a roads authority in addition to the normal rights that the person enjoys against the independent contractor posited as the effective cause of the wrong. In particular, it is difficult to see why the general policy of the law that the economic cost of the wrong should be borne by the legal [59] entity immediately responsible for it should not be enforced in this case given the strong reasons of economic principle and social policy that lie behind that rule. ...

Appeal allowed

4. MULTIPLE TORTFEASORS

XL Petroleum (NSW) Pty Ltd v Caltex Oil (Australia) Pty Ltd
(1985) 155 CLR 448
High Court of Australia

In proceedings against two or more joint tortfeasors where all the tortfeasors are liable for compensatory damages, exemplary damages may be awarded against one (or more) but not necessarily all the tortfeasors. The purpose of an award of exemplary damages is to punish and deter a defendant "for conduct showing a conscious and contumelious disregard for the plaintiff's rights".

GIBBS CJ. [451] In this appeal we are called upon to decide whether judgment was rightly entered for the appellant, XL Petroleum (NSW) Pty Ltd ("XL"), in a sum which included exemplary [452] damages and if so whether the Court of Appeal of the Supreme Court of New South Wales was right in reducing the amount of the exemplary damages awarded by the jury.

The appellant, XL, was a company formed in New South Wales in January 1970 for the purpose of engaging in the sale of petrol in that State. An associated company had for some years earlier been engaged in the sale of petrol in Victoria at a discount, ie at a price lower than that normally charged by other companies, and XL intended similarly to sell in New South Wales at a discounted price. There was, at 150 Princes Highway, Arncliffe, a piece of land owned since October 1969 by St Christopher Motors Pty Ltd which had previously been used as a service station for the sale of the petrol of the respondent, Caltex Oil (Australia) Pty Ltd ("Caltex") but which had not been used for that purpose since at least May 1968. XL entered into an agreement with St Christopher Motors Pty Ltd under which it acquired full rights of occupancy to the land from 9.00 am on 12 June 1970, and, as the jury found, XL had actual possession of the land on that date.

Three underground tanks, designed to hold petrol, were installed in the land. The tanks had been put in the land by Caltex in about the year 1953. Caltex was a company which engaged in the sale of petrol on a large scale; it had about 800 service stations in New South Wales. Caltex had at no time been the owner of the land in question, and the jury's findings (which were not challenged on this point) negatived a submission made at the trial that the tanks were not fixtures and that Caltex was the owner of them. At about 8.45 am on 12 June 1970 an employee of Caltex telephoned a company, Turnbull & Foster Pty Ltd, which carried on business as industrial plumbers, and instructed that company to spike the tanks on the land. The instruction was issued under the authority of Mr Braitling, then the manager for retail sales in New South Wales for Caltex. Mr Braitling said in evidence that he believed that the tanks were owned by Caltex and that he issued the instruction to render the tanks safe. In consequence of the instruction, Mr Peter Turnbull, a director of Turnbull & Foster Pty Ltd, went to the land that morning, between 9.00 and 9.30 am filled the tanks with water and by hammering a steel bar through the dip points made a hole in each tank and then concreted over the dip points. Mr Sykes, the Managing Director of XL, came on the scene while this was going on but despite his protests the spiking of the tanks was completed. The result was that the tanks were rendered unfit for use until 7 July 1970.

XL commenced in the Supreme Court of New South Wales an action against Caltex, Turnbull & Foster Pty Ltd and Peter **[453]** Turnbull for damages for trespass. The action was tried by a jury which returned a verdict for the plaintiff. The jury found that the damages to which XL was entitled in respect of the replacement of the tanks and the expenses incurred and profits lost as a result of the trespass was $5,527.90. The jury further found that XL was entitled to exemplary damages against Caltex in an amount of $400,000. The learned trial judge thereupon ordered that judgment be entered for XL against Caltex in the sum of $405,527.90 plus interest and costs and for XL against Turnbull & Foster Pty Ltd and Peter Turnbull in the sum of $5,527.90 plus interest and costs.

From this decision Caltex appealed to the Court of Appeal. ... First, it was submitted that it was not competent for the learned trial judge to enter judgment for XL against the three joint tortfeasors in different amounts. The Court of Appeal, by a majority (Hutley and Glass JJA, Mahoney JA dissenting) rejected this submission. Secondly, it was submitted that the award of exemplary damages was excessive to the point of perversity. ... [T]he majority of the Court held that the exemplary damages were excessive and reduced them from $400,000 to $150,000. ...

From the decision of the Court of Appeal, XL appealed to this Court seeking an order restoring the judgment of $405,527.90 (plus interest and costs) in its favour. Caltex cross-appealed, seeking primarily an order that judgment be entered against Caltex for the sum of $5,527.90 (plus interest and costs) or alternatively for an **[454]** order giving judgment in favour of XL for the amount of $5,527.90 together with such sum of exemplary damages as this Court should assess or in the further alternative that the proceedings be remitted to the Court of Appeal to reassess the amount of exemplary damages.

The first question for our decision is whether it is possible for a plaintiff who has brought one action against two or more joint tortfeasors to obtain separate judgments for different amounts, one including exemplary damages and the other limited to compensatory damages. It was a settled rule of the common law that where two or more tortfeasors were sued for damages for a joint tort, only one judgment for one sum of damages could be given in favour of the plaintiff. Although this rule had been established by the time of Sir Edward Coke (see *Sir John Heydon's Case* (1612) 11 Co Rep 5a [77 ER 1150]), the manner in which it should be applied when the circumstances justified an award of exemplary damages against one tortfeasor and not against the others was open to debate until the House of Lords decided the question in *Broome v Cassell & Co* [1972] AC 1027. Before that time it was not clear whether, in such a case, the plaintiff was entitled to judgment for the amount which could have been recovered from the most blameworthy tortfeasor, or that which could have been recovered from the least blameworthy, or some figure in between. ... **[455]** The House of Lords, in *Broome v Cassell & Co*, held that the amount to be awarded should be the least figure for which any of the defendants could be held liable. ...

The rule that only one judgment could be obtained in an action against a number of joint tortfeasors depended on the fact that there **[456]** was a single wrong and a single cause of action. ...

The same theory, that when two or more joint tortfeasors commit a tort there is only one cause of action, was also the foundation of the rule in *Brinsmead v Harrison* (1871) LR 7 CP 547 that a judgment obtained against one joint tortfeasor is a bar to an action against the others for the same cause of action, even if the judgment remains unsatisfied. ...

The rule in *Brinsmead v Harrison* was in effect abolished by s 5(1) of the *Law Reform (Miscellaneous Provisions) Act 1946* (NSW) which reproduced s 6(1) of the *Law Reform (Married Women and Tortfeasors) Act 1935* (UK). Section 5(1) provides as follows:

Where damage is suffered by any person as a result of a tort (whether a crime or not)–

    (a) judgment recovered against any tort-feasor liable in respect of that damage shall not be a bar to an action against any other person who would, if sued, have been liable as a joint tort-feasor in respect of the same damage;

    (b) if more than one action is brought in respect of that damage by or on behalf of the person by whom it was suffered, or for the benefit of the estate, or of the wife, husband, brother, sister, half-brother, half-sister, parent or child, of that person, against tort-feasors liable in respect of the damage (whether as joint tort-feasors or **[457]** otherwise) the sums recoverable under the judgments given in those actions by way of damages shall not in the aggregate exceed the amount of the damages awarded by the judgment first given; and in any of those actions, other than that in which judgment is first given, the plaintiff shall not be entitled to costs unless the court is of opinion that there was reasonable ground for bringing the action; …

The critical question in this case is whether the enactment of this provision affected the rule that only one sum may be awarded in an action brought against two or more joint tortfeasors.

The effect of s 6(1) of the *Law Reform (Married Women and Tortfeasors) Act* was not discussed in *Broome v Cassell & Co* [1971] 2 QB 354; [1972] AC 1027, but the effect of a statute of Singapore (s 11(1)(a) of the *Civil Law Act*) which was in the same terms as s 6(1)(a) of the *Law Reform (Married Women and Tortfeasors) Act* came to be considered by the Judicial Committee in *Wah Tat Bank Ltd v Chan* [1975] AC 507. In that case the plaintiff banks sued two joint tortfeasors – a ship owner and a shipping company – in one action for damages for conversion. It was ordered that judgment be entered against the shipping company for damages to be assessed, and that the liability of the ship owner be retried. The damages against the shipping company were assessed, and judgment was entered against it, but the judgment remained unsatisfied. The issue of the liability of the ship owner was then retried and it was held by the courts of Singapore that he was liable for the tort but that the action against him was barred by the judgment entered in favour of the plaintiffs against the shipping company. Those courts held that par (a) of the sub-section, on its true construction, does not apply where two or more tortfeasors are sued in the one action in respect of the same tort, and that in those circumstances judgment against one still bars the right of action against the others. This conclusion was, they thought, strengthened by the fact that par (b) clearly contemplates a number of actions and not a single action. However on appeal the Judicial Committee held that the plaintiffs were entitled to recover. Their Lordships held **[458]** that sub-s (a) had the effect that if, in a hypothetical action, judgment would have been given against joint tortfeasors A and B, then in actual proceedings B is deprived of the immunity which he would have enjoyed at common law as a result of the judgment already recovered against A. Their Lordships continued [1975] AC, at p 518:

This would follow whether in the actual action A were sued jointly with B (as in the present case) or whether the action against A had been instituted before or after the action against B.

Their Lordships accordingly conclude that paragraph (a) abolishes the old common law rule in its entirety …

They considered that this construction of par (a) accorded equally with the manifest intention of the legislature and with fairness and commonsense and that since par (b) was designed to prevent a multiplicity of actions there was no reason why its provisions should have been extended to apply to the case where more than one judgment is given in a single action.

Soon after that decision was given the Court of Appeal in England followed and applied it in *Bryanston Finance Ltd v de Vries* [1975] QB 703. …

Although the words of the sub-section are elliptical and somewhat obscure I respectfully agree with the result reached by the Judicial Committee and the English Court of Appeal. Neither court expressly dealt with the question whether the section affected the common law rule that only one sum can be awarded in a single **[459]** proceeding for the one tort committed by joint tortfeasors. …

Once it is accepted that more than one judgment may be given against joint tortfeasors for damages caused by a joint tort, whether damages are given in the same or in different proceedings, there can remain no foundation for the rule that only one sum can be awarded by the different judgments. The reason for the rule was that there was only one cause of action against the joint tortfeasors, but that is no longer the position – the statute has abolished, "in its entirety" **[460]** the old common law principle that a person who suffers damage by a joint tort has only one cause of action which merges in the first judgment recovered in respect of it. Surely the statutory provision was not intended to abolish only the doctrine of merger, for it was not primarily directed to the question of merger, and there is no reason for selecting one aspect of the principle rather than another as that which it was intended to affect; the whole principle should be held to have gone. It seems to me impossible now to hold that there is any principle that would prevent a plaintiff from recovering different sums from different joint tortfeasors if he brings separate actions against them, provided that some are liable for exemplary damages and others are not, and the same must be true if the joint tortfeasors are all sued in one action. …

[461] For the reasons I have given I hold that in the present case the Court of Appeal in New South Wales was right in concluding that it was competent for the learned trial judge to enter judgment against Caltex in a larger sum than that for which judgment was given against the other defendants.

The next question for decision is whether the Court of Appeal was justified in reducing the amount of damages. There were circumstances which justified a substantial award. It was open on the evidence for the jury to conclude that Caltex, a large company, decided to render the tanks unusable so that a smaller competitor, which intended to engage in discounting the price of petrol in a way that might prove detrimental to Caltex' business interests, might be impeded in its efforts to establish itself in New South Wales. At the least, this action was taken by Caltex without bothering to ascertain whether it was lawful; indeed the jury may well have thought that Caltex did not care whether it was lawful or not. The jury might well have regarded the action of Caltex as showing a high-handed and outrageous disregard for XL's rights, or, as Glass JA described it: "an act of vandalism of the most disreputable kind, calling for the most indignant censure". The jury was entitled to consider the financial circumstances of Caltex, and the amount awarded, $400,000, represented 1 per cent of the operating profit of Caltex after tax. In concluding that the award was excessive to the point of perversity, Glass JA in the Court of Appeal relied principally on three matters. First, it was said that the infamous conduct of the defendant was of short duration. I would not attach much significance to that fact in itself; much evil can be done in a moment. However, the damage was repaired, at no very great cost, within three weeks, and the actual loss to XL was fully compensated for by the award of $5,527.90, and there was no repetition of the trespass, which occurred about eleven years before the verdict of the jury was given. These circumstances, together, reduce the seriousness of the incursion. Secondly, Glass JA said that there was some belief in the mind of Mr Braitling that the tanks still belonged to **[462]** Caltex and that he was entitled to authorize their destruction, even though the jury found that such belief was ill-founded. I cannot agree that it was right to approach the matter in that way. It was open to the jury to conclude that Mr Braitling had no genuine belief that Caltex had any right to destroy the tanks and that the evidence given on behalf of Caltex that the spiking of the tanks was carried out as a routine operation in the interests of safety was no more than a spurious excuse. There is indeed, with all respect, some inconsistency between the tolerant view which Glass JA took of Mr Braitling's belief and the approach which the Court of Appeal took in making its re-assessment. Glass JA said that the court had demurred to the suggestion that it should re-assess exemplary damages when it had not seen and heard the witnesses. His Honour continued:

> Particular concern was expressed with regard to the state of mind of the Caltex officers for which it could be held vicariously accountable. In these circumstances it was ultimately accepted by Mr Bennett [who appeared for Caltex] that, if the Court felt unable to decide these questions for itself upon the evidentiary record, he would consent to a reassessment being made upon the footing that all those matters were taken to be established which the evidence was capable of proving on that view of it most favourable to the plaintiff. Mr Hodgson [for XL] naturally had no objection to this course.

If the court approached the re-assessment on that footing it should, as it seems to me, have acted on the assumption that the jury had rejected Mr Braitling's evidence that he believed that the tanks belonged to Caltex.

The third matter upon which the Court of Appeal relied was that XL could not lawfully use the storage tanks since it could not sell petrol from the site without the consent of the council and that an application which it made for consent on or about 16 June was refused on 26 June. It was later restrained from using the site for that purpose by declaratory order made on 26 November 1970. It was submitted on behalf of XL that this was an irrelevant consideration. Certainly the fact that the sale of the petrol would have been illegal neither provoked nor justified Caltex' actions; indeed it had no bearing on Caltex' decision to act as it did. XL had not used the site when the trespass occurred, and it was not known by Caltex, and could not have been assumed, that XL intended to use the site illegally; in fact XL was not shown to have had that intention and it promptly applied for the council's consent. Nevertheless these circumstances were not irrelevant. In deciding to what extent Caltex should be punished for its invasion of XL's rights, the **[463]** nature of those rights and the ability of the plaintiff to benefit from their exercise are matters properly to be considered. As events showed, XL was in fact refused the consent that it needed to entitle it to use the land for the purpose of selling petrol. Nevertheless, I would not have regarded these matters as of major consequence in deciding whether to reduce the jury's assessment.

I doubt whether the matters upon which the Court of Appeal principally relied would, in themselves, have justified an interference with the jury's award. However, in my opinion, when all the circumstances of the case are considered, the award of exemplary damages was so large as to be unreasonable, and an appellate court was entitled to interfere with the verdict within the established principles stated in *Precision Plastics Pty Ltd v Demir* (1975) 132 CLR 362 at p 369. Although the limitations which the House of Lords in *Rookes v Barnard* placed on the circumstances in which exemplary damages may be awarded are not part of the law in Australia, I nevertheless consider that in that case Lord Devlin was correct in pointing to the risk that exemplary damages might amount to a punishment greater than would be likely to be imposed if the conduct were criminal, and in suggesting that in making an award juries should display restraint ([1964] AC at pp 1227-1228). Lord Hailsham of St Marylebone LC, in *Broome v Cassell & Co* [1972] AC at p 1081, did not agree with the suggestion of Lord Devlin that appellate courts might more readily interfere with jury awards of exemplary damages than in other cases, but he did regard it as extremely important that judges make sure in their direction that the jury is fully aware of the danger of an excessive award. I respectfully agree with these pleas for moderation. The award in the present case seems to me to have been out of all proportion to the circumstances of the case and the Court of Appeal was right in reducing it.

Mr Bennett on behalf of Caltex then submitted that the amount selected by the Court of Appeal, $150,000, was itself excessive. Although, as I have indicated, I do not fully accept all that was said in the Court of Appeal as to the reasons for reducing the jury's verdict, I do not consider that we would be justified in interfering with the award made by the Court of Appeal. While the views expressed by the Court of Appeal were, if anything, too favourable to Caltex, the amount awarded was in my opinion at the upper end of the permissible range. It was certainly not too low, but, in the light of the circumstances which I have mentioned, which would justify a large award, I am not persuaded that it was excessive. ...

[464] For these reasons I would dismiss both the appeal and the cross-appeal.

[Mason and Wilson JJ agreed with the judgment of Gibbs CJ. Murphy and Brennan JJ agreed that the *Law Reform (Miscellaneous Provisions) Act 1946* (NSW) permits judgments against joint tortfeasors for different amounts, but (dissenting on this point) considered that the Court of Appeal was not justified in interfering with the jury's assessment of the amount of exemplary damages. The judgment of Brennan J on the issue of the exemplary damages is now extracted.]

BRENNAN J. **[471]** The appeal seeks the restoration of the jury's verdict of $400,000 exemplary damages in addition to compensatory damages (as to which there is no dispute). Though the assessment is large, that is not a sufficient reason for an appellate court to interfere. Before an appellate court can interfere with the verdict, it must be plain that no reasonable jury properly applying the relevant principles could have awarded so large a sum: *Coates v Carter* (1951) 82 CLR 537, at p 543, *Precision Plastics Pty Ltd v Demir* (1975) 132 CLR 362, at p 369. If some less rigorous test were applied and an order made for a retrial, the next jury might reasonably return the same verdict as that set aside as manifestly excessive (see per Lord Reid in *Broome v Cassell & Co* [1972] AC at p 1090). Where a jury is entitled to award exemplary damages it is very difficult for a defendant to show that the award is so disproportionate as to warrant the setting aside of the verdict: *Uren v John Fairfax & Sons Pty Ltd* (1966) 117 CLR at p 128.

As an award of exemplary damages is intended to punish the defendant for conduct showing a conscious and contumelious disregard for the plaintiff's rights and to deter him from committing like conduct again, the considerations that enter into the assessment of exemplary damages are quite different from the considerations that govern the assessment of compensatory damages. There is no necessary proportionality between the assessment of the two categories. In *Merest v Harvey*

(1814) 5 Taunt 442 [128 ER 761] substantial exemplary damages were awarded for a trespass of a high-handed kind which occasioned minimal damage, Gibbs CJ saying:

> I wish to know, in a case where a man disregards every principle which actuates the conduct of gentlemen, what is to restrain him except large damages?

The social purpose to be served by an award of exemplary damages is, as Lord Diplock said in *Broome v Cassell & Co* [1972] AC, at p 1130, "to teach a wrong-doer that tort does not pay". The purpose of restraint looms large in the present case. The jury were entitled to take into account that Caltex and XL were competitors in an industry in which, notoriously, competition for markets and for outlet sites has been intense. The jury were therefore entitled to **[472]** form the view that a risk of repetition of Caltex' conduct in spiking a competitor's tanks was quite unacceptable, for the intensity of commercial competition might lead to violence and counter-violence among competitors if legal process proved inadequate to suppress the use of force. And if the jury formed the view that it was desirable to ensure that Caltex did not again spike the tanks of a competitor, the jury were entitled to assess exemplary damages in an amount that would be likely to have a deterrent effect – sufficient to make Caltex smart. In *Uren v John Fairfax & Sons Pty Ltd* (1966) 117 CLR at pp 136-137, Taylor J cited with approval a passage from the judgment of Grier J delivering the opinion of the Supreme Court of the United States in *Day v Woodworth* (1851) 13 How 363, at p 320 [14 Law Ed 181, at p 185]. That passage included the following:

> In actions of trespass, where the injury has been wanton and malicious, or gross and outra-geous, courts permit juries to add to the measured compensation of the plaintiff, which he would have been entitled to recover had the injury been inflicted without design or intention, something farther [sic] by way of punishment or example, which has sometimes been called 'smart money'. This has been always left to the discretion of the jury, as the degree of punish-ment to be thus inflicted must depend on the peculiar circumstances of each case.

Where exemplary damages may properly be awarded to deter a tortfeasor, evidence of his means is material not only to show that he can afford to satisfy a substantial judgment or to show that he has acted on contumelious disregard of the plaintiff's rights by taking advantage of his wealth, but to show what sum will be a sufficient deterrent against repetition of the conduct that attracts the award. No doubt the width of the jury's discretion in assessing exemplary damages has evoked judicial expressions of concern about employing the civil law to inflict punishment. But it is now beyond argument that, by the law of this country, it is proper to award exemplary damages by way of punishment of the tortfeasor: see per Taylor J in *Uren v John Fairfax & Sons Pty Ltd* (1966) 117 CLR at pp 136-137; *Australian Consolidated Press Ltd v Uren* [1969] 1 AC at p 642; 117 CLR at p 239. Clearly the jury in the present case must have awarded exemplary damages for that purpose. Although the amount which the jury assessed is much greater than I would have thought appropriate, I am quite unable to hold that the jury were not entitled to take the view that an award of $400,000 was necessary to provide an effective deterrent against a repetition of Caltex' conduct. As that view is not shared by a **[473]** majority of the Court, I should say that, if I were to give effect to my own opinion, I would regard $150,000 as an appropriate award of exemplary damages.

I would allow the appeal and dismiss the cross-appeal.

Appeal dismissed. Cross-appeal dismissed

Chapter 13

Damages

1. COMPENSATORY DAMAGES FOR PERSONAL INJURIES

Skelton v Collins
(1966) 115 CLR 94
High Court of Australia

In the case of a young person rendered unconscious in an accident and with a very short post-trial expectation of life during which consciousness would not be regained, damages for loss of future earning capacity should be assessed by reference to the plaintiff's pre-accident expectation of life but subject to deduction of the plaintiff's living costs during the years in which he or she will be dead. In a case such as the present, damages for loss of amenities of life and loss of expectation of life should be limited to a modest amount.

[The appeal was from a judgment of the Supreme Court of Western Australia in which damages were awarded in respect of personal injuries sustained by the plaintiff (appellant) as a result of the defendant's (respondent's) negligence. The complaint was that the amount awarded was manifestly inadequate. The plaintiff, who was 17 years of age at the time when the injuries were sustained, suffered severe brain damage which rendered him unconscious. He had remained unconscious since the accident and, at the date of the trial, was expected to die within six months.]

KITTO J. ... **[96]** What I have to say will relate to the challenge that has been made to the trial Judge's allowance of £1,500 under the head of general damages. He allowed nothing for pain and suffering, either physical or mental; and in this he was plainly right, for the plaintiff was rendered unconscious by the collision, had remained unconscious ever since, and, as his Honour found, would never regain consciousness.

There are only two forms of loss for which the £1,500 could have been intended as compensation, namely those which are often described, conveniently if not very happily, as a loss of expectation **[97]** of life and a loss of amenity during the reduced life span. Each is a matter properly to be taken into account in assessing damages, but judicial opinion as to the way in which the task of allowing for them should be approached has not been unanimous. Obviously each may have a subjective as well as an objective aspect: the plaintiff may not only have sustained the loss itself but may also have to bear a sense of his loss. ...

In *Benham v Gambling* [1941] AC 157 the injured person was a child of two and a half. He was unconscious from the moment of the accident until his death, which occurred later on the same day. He had acquired at the time of injury a cause of action for loss of expectation of life. *Flint v Lovell* [1935] 1 KB 354 had so decided, and in *Rose v Ford* [1937] AC 826 the House had approved the decision. By statute the cause of action survived for the benefit of his estate, and his administrator accordingly sued. The subjective aspect of the loss did not have to be allowed for, the child having had a moment's realization of his loss; but it is implied clearly enough in the judgment of Viscount Simon LC that if the child had at any time a sense of loss the damages must have been increased by reason of it under the head of pain and suffering. The sole question was how much should be allowed as compensation for the objective element, the loss of such chance as the child had had, immediately before the accident, of living longer than he did. Should that chance be treated as having been worth much or little, when a judge or jury is trying to find an appropriate sum to award as fair compensation for the loss? It was a chance fraught with uncertainties – uncertainties not only as to how long the child would in fact have lived but also as to what causes for happiness and unhappiness the years would have given him. "The thing to be valued", said the Lord Chancellor in a speech with which all their Lordships concurred, "is not the prospect of length of days, but the prospect of a predominantly happy life … The ups and downs of life, its pains and sorrows as well as its joys and pleasures … have to be allowed for in the estimate" ([1941] AC, at p 166). The probable circumstances of the life which the injured person would have led, his character and habits, were recognized as relevant if calculated, on balance, to lead him to a positive measure of happiness or unhappiness. Then there is this passage: "I would further lay it down that, in assessing damages for this purpose, the question is not whether the deceased had the capacity or ability to appreciate that his further life on earth would bring him happiness; the test is not subjective and the right sum to award depends on an objective estimate of what kind of future on earth the victim might have enjoyed, whether he had justly estimated that future or not" ([1941] AC at p 167).

The emphasis throughout the speech is upon the objective nature of the inquiry that remains when any pain and suffering, physical or mental, have been put aside as being properly the subject of separate allowance. But it is made clear that under the head of loss of expectation of life the inquiry is not as to the value of a mere period of time – "not the prospect of length of days"; it is as to the value of the experiences that would have been lived through but for the injury. When it is said that the right sum to award **[98]** depends on an objective estimate of the kind of future on earth the victim "might have enjoyed", what is meant, as the immediate context shows, is the kind of total experience the future would have offered the victim, looking at the matter objectively and not concerning oneself with any question as to the amount of pleasure or misery that the victim would have derived in fact from the variety of situations in which he would have found himself.

The speech, having thus made clear what it is that has to be evaluated when compensation for loss of expectation of life is being considered, lays down the proposition, for the guidance of assessing tribunals and of the courts generally, and therefore as a proposition of law, that under this head of damages very moderate amounts only are allowable. The Lord Chancellor pointed to the extreme difficulty of fixing a solatium for a person who is dead ([1941] AC at p 165), and to the fact that to put a money value on a prospective balance of future happiness is to attempt to equate incommensurables ([1941] AC at p 168). Then he said that damages which would be proper for a disabling injury may well be much greater than for deprivation of life ([1941] AC at p 168). His Lordship was not, I think, saying anything so trite as that the fixing of a sum of money as compensation for what cannot be bought and sold is difficult because of the different natures of the things that are being weighed against one another. What I understand him to be pointing to as the fact which brings in its train a special consequence for a tribunal assessing damages is that, since none can form any opinion as to what would have been the experience through which the victim would have lived if he had not suffered the injury, that which has to be measured against money is not only different from money but cannot itself be known and therefore cannot be measured at all. For this reason it is simply impossible to select any substantial figure as compensation for the loss of years of living (as distinguished from the mental distress due to realization of the loss) and feel any degree of satisfaction with it as fair compensation. This the decision underlined quite dramatically by reducing an award of only £1,200 for the shortening of life to a mere £200. … **[99]** While it would be erroneous to allow an amount so small as to be illusory – for the presumption is, contra spoliatorem as Lord Devlin was to say in *West's Case* [1964] AC at p 363, that the experiences of life would have been such as to offer some balance of enjoyability – a tribunal which awards under this head a sum running into more than a very few hundred pounds must be failing to perform its function in accordance with law, because it purports to have what it cannot possibly have, namely a satisfaction that the selected sum of money is fair, or reasonable, or appropriate, as compensation for the loss of a balance of enjoyability as to which no man can have any idea whether it would have been great or small. The onus of proof as to damages is, after all, upon the claimant. ...

[102] I do not find myself able to put aside *Benham v Gambling* [1941] AC 157 as affording no guidance for such a case as the present. It treated of life not as a state of being, a mere physical phenomenon, but as a thing to be lived and lived consciously. Thus, what was meant by every reference to loss of expectation of life was, in truth, loss of the possibility of conscious experience. The whole burden of the Lord Chancellor's speech was the legal impropriety of attempting to place any but the most modest figure on a human being's capacity to experience the varied quality of life; and I cannot bring myself to say that although the law sees the impropriety where a person has died it does not see it where he has lost all capacity for thought and feeling. ...

[103] So far as this country is concerned, I think that *Benham v Gambling* [1941] AC 157 ought to be accepted as prescribing the correct approach in all cases where the matter for which compensation is to be given is, whether by reason of death or not, the fact that the plaintiff has been excluded for a period from the whole of the experiences that make up life. ...

[104] The figure which [the trial Judge] finally adopted to cover both the loss of expectation of life and the loss of enjoyment of life during the period of continuing existence was £1,500. Having regard to currency equivalents and changes in the value of money I am not able to say that by adopting this figure his Honour failed to give due effect to the principle of *Benham v Gambling* [1941] AC 157, and I would therefore not disturb it.

[His Honour agreed with Taylor J with respect to the assessment of economic loss.]

TAYLOR J. **[105]** This is an appeal from an order of the Supreme Court of Western Australia by which judgment was directed to be entered for the plaintiff, the present appellant, in the sum of £5,790. This amount was awarded as damages in respect of personal injuries sustained by the appellant as the result of the respondent's negligence and the complaint made upon this appeal is that the amount awarded is manifestly inadequate. ...

The argument upon the appeal was concerned with the amount assessed for general damages but before dealing with the points which were raised on behalf of the appellant I pause to observe that the inclusion in the award of practically the whole of the total amount that the appellant would probably have received for wages **[106]** up to the date of trial, if he had not been injured, and for six months thereafter, operated unduly to inflate the assessment in the circumstances of the case. In the ordinary run of cases it is no doubt proper to assess damages substantially by reference to the amount of wages actually lost up to the date of trial and by reference to the present value of any probable future loss of that character. But where, as here, there is nothing to suggest that, if the appellant had not been injured, his wages would have been more than sufficient to provide for his own maintenance during his shortened life, it was erroneous to award a sum for loss of wages in addition to a larger sum calculated to provide for his complete maintenance and care during that period. The respondent, however, has made no complaint on this score but it is a material matter to be borne in mind when we come to consider whether the total amount awarded was or was not inadequate.

In assessing £1,500 as general damages excluding future economic loss the learned trial judge proceeded upon the basis that he should award compensation "for what the plaintiff consciously suffers" and in doing so he departed from the principles acted upon in England by a majority of the Court of Appeal in *Wise v Kaye* [1962] 1 QB 638 and by a majority of the House of Lords in *H West & Son Ltd v Shephard* [1964] AC 326. ... What finally led him to disregard them was the fact that in 1964 two members of the Supreme Court of Western Australia had already done so and he thought that in the circumstances the Supreme Court "should speak with one voice and not a variety of voices". ...

[107] In the present case two main complaints are made. The first is that general damages for the plaintiff's injuries, excluding those assessed for physical pain and suffering, should have been assessed without regard to the fact that he had remained unconscious since the accident. They should, it is said, have been assessed on what has, somewhat unhappily, been called an "objective" basis. The second is that in assessing damages for the plaintiff's lost earning capacity regard should have been had to the probable period of the plaintiff's working life immediately before he sustained his injuries and not merely to the period of life which remained to him after that event. ...

[113] [I]n assessing damages for a loss of amenities of life resulting from the physical destruction or impairment of some part of the body, I find it impossible to ignore, or, to regard merely as a minimal factor, what has been referred to as the subjective element. The expression "loss of the amenities of life" is a loose expression but as a head of damages in personal injury cases it is intended to denote a loss of the capacity of the injured person *consciously* to enjoy to the full as, apart from his injury, he might have done. It may be said, of course, that a person who is completely incapacitated as a result of his injuries suffers such a loss whether or not his injuries are of such a character to render him insensible to his loss. But, in my view, a proper assessment can be made only upon a comparison of the condition which has been substituted for the victim's previously existing capacity to enjoy life and where the mind is, as it were, willing and the body incapable there is, in my view, a much higher degree of loss than where the victim is completely insensible to his lost capacity. Perhaps, in other words, it may be said that a person who is obliged for the rest of his life to live with his incapacity, fully conscious of the limitations which it imposes upon his enjoyment of life, is entitled to greater compensation than one who, although deprived of his former capacity is spared, by insensibility, from the realization of his loss and the trials and tribulations consequent upon it. In the result I am left with a firm view that the plaintiff's general damages in this case were assessed on a proper basis. This conviction coupled with the fact that a body of authority inconsistent with the decision of the majority in *West's Case* [1964] AC 326 has grown up in this country and the fact that there was a remarkable diversity of opinion in that case induces me to say that we ought not to follow it. Accordingly, I would reject the appellant's first contention.

The further question arises whether in assessing damages for the destroyed earning capacity of the appellant it was proper to have regard only to the period of life which remained to him after receipt of his injuries. *Oliver v Ashman* [1962] 2 QB 210 is, of course, an authority for the course which his Honour took. ...

[121] I need scarcely mention the anomaly that would arise if *Oliver v Ashman* [1962] 2 QB 210 is taken to have been correctly decided. An incapacitated plaintiff whose life expectation has not been diminished would be entitled to the full measure of the economic loss arising from his lost or diminished capacity. But an incapacitated plaintiff whose life expectancy has been diminished would not. Yet the recovery by him of damages that does not take into account his full economic loss will operate to prevent his dependants, in the event of his death, from recovering damages under the *Fatal Accidents Act*. However if he dies without having sued for damages his dependants will be entitled to recover damages assessed upon a consideration of what his economic prospects would have been had he survived for the full period of his pre-accident expectancy.

For the reasons I have given I find myself forced to the conclusion that the recognition which has been accorded to the right of an injured plaintiff to recover damages for "the loss of a measure of prospective happiness" in no way operates to displace or destroy his right to recover damages for economic loss resulting from his diminished earning capacity. Accordingly in my view damages in the present case should have been assessed under this head having regard to the plaintiff's pre-accident expectancy and not only to the expectancy of life remaining to him after the receipt of his injuries. Any assessment should, or course, take into account the vicissitudes and uncertainties of life and also the fact that if the plaintiff had survived for the full period it would have been necessary for him to maintain himself out of his earnings and, no doubt, his expenditure on his own maintenance would have increased as his earnings increased.

In considering what he called the plaintiff's economic loss the learned trial judge in the present case did not have regard to the plaintiff's pre-accident expectancy of life and he assessed an amount of £1,500 for general damages which I take to be the amount which he considered an appropriate award to compensate the plaintiff both for his loss of amenities of life during the period of life remaining to him after the accident and also for his diminished expectancy of life. In making this assessment he proceeded "on the basis that in assessing damages for personal injuries beyond economic loss the primary, although not the sole, ground for awarding damages is to be for what the plaintiff consciously suffers". Assuming, for the moment, that £500 of this amount was in effect a *Benham* **[122]** *v Gambling* [1941] AC 157 award merely for loss of expectancy of life, the question is whether the sum of £1,000 is manifestly inadequate to compensate him on an objective basis for his injuries and his loss of amenities of life during the residue of his life. In the circumstances I am not disposed to think that it is and, accordingly, that we should not interfere. So far as his economic loss is concerned the material before us indicates that the plaintiff at the time of the injury was earning approximately £13 a week, that at the age of twenty-one he would probably have earned something in excess of £20 a week and that by the time he attained the age of thirty his salary would have been, had it not been for the accident, some £2,000 or £2,500 per annum. In those circumstances it seems to me that on a balance of what his future income and expenditure on maintenance would have been the economic loss resulting from his destroyed earning capacity should not be rated highly. Particularly is this so when account is taken of the uncertainties and vicissitudes of life. Under this head of damages I would assess the sum of £2,000 as reasonable compensation. …

WINDEYER J. … **[130]** I am unable myself to understand how monetary compensation for the deprivation of the ability to live out life with faculties of mind and body unimpaired can be based upon an evaluation of a thing lost. It must surely be based upon solace for a condition created not upon payment for something taken away. …

[132] [T]he distinction between a loss of a thing on which a money value can be put and the distress of mind and sense of loss for which money is only a solace is, I consider, basic and real. …

[133] In my view, his Honour, having … held that on the evidence there was not even a chance that the additional sum [the £1,500 for non-economic loss] could be used for the advantage of the plaintiff, ought not to have awarded it. It could not bring any advantage or consolation to the plaintiff. Consolation presupposes consciousness and some capacity of intellectual appreciation. If money were given to the plaintiff he could never know that he had it. He could not use it or dispose of it. It would simply go to his legal personal representatives on his death. …

[136] I do not find the underlying assumptions of the judgment in *Benham v Gambling* [1941] AC 157 about the worth of life easy to make, even as mere assumptions. But putting that aside, I – for the sake of conformity with the views of most of my brethren, but not from conviction – agree that we can be guided in this case by what was said in that case. We can accept it as an ipse dixit of the law. I am grateful for the analysis of its meaning that my brother Kitto has proffered in his judgment, which I have had the benefit of reading and studying. Although it seems to me that the sum of £1,500 awarded in this case was more than was justified on the basis of *Benham v Gambling* [1941] AC 157, I, again for conformity, agree in the order proposed. I confess that I do so the more readily because it seems that the plaintiff lived for a longer time than the learned trial judge reckoned on when he estimated what should be allowed for future medical and nursing expenses. This, of course, only shows how unsatisfactory in an insurance age is the system of lump sum damages to cover future outgoings.

I can only hope that some day the law will provide some better way of meeting the consequences of day-to-day hazards than by actions for negligence and a measuring of damages by unprovable predictions, metaphysical assumptions and rationalized empiricism.

I agree that the appeal should be allowed and the judgment of the Supreme Court varied as proposed by Kitto J.

[Windeyer J agreed with Taylor J on the issue of economic loss. Owen J delivered a judgment in which he concurred with the majority on both issues. Menzies J agreed with Taylor J on the issue of economic loss but preferred the approach of the English courts on the issue of non-economic loss and therefore dissented on that point.]

Appeal allowed.
Judgment of the Supreme Court of Western Australia varied

Sharman v Evans
(1977) 138 CLR 563
High Court of Australia

Where, as a result of his or her injuries, the plaintiff will spend substantially the rest of his or her life in hospital (and be entitled to damages for future hospital expenses), a deduction should be made from damages for loss of future earning capacity to take account of saved outside expenses such as board and lodging and work-related outgoings. At the same time, it should be acknowledged that there are inherent difficulties in assessing damages for loss of amenities of life, "perfect" compensation being impossible.

GIBBS and STEPHEN JJ. **[569]** The defendant, Dennis Sharman, appeals against the dismissal, by a majority of the New South Wales Court of Appeal, of his appeal from a verdict for $300,547.50 in favour of the plaintiff, June Marilyn Evans.

Miss Evans, then aged twenty, was injured in a motor car accident in December 1971. She suffered very serious injuries including brain stem damage; she was unconscious for almost a month and is now a quadriplegic. This condition, disastrous enough in itself, is in her case aggravated by trauma-caused epilepsy, by unusually severe impairment to her respiratory function as a consequence of the brain injury and by an almost total loss of the ability to speak because of the injury to the larynx. She is fully aware of her plight. ...

[570] Before the accident the prospects for Miss Evans' future were bright; she was a healthy, out-going and intelligent girl who was trained for and was experienced in secretarial work ... She had an understanding with a young man, a fellow student, that they would marry in due course. After the accident their engagement was announced and but for her ultimate decision that she could not permit him to take as his wife a quadriplegic she would by the time of the trial have been married to him; he has a good position and a secure future in the Department of Civil Aviation. Had she resumed her secretarial work after finishing her two-year college course she could have earned at least $70 per week net.

In these circumstances the learned trial judge, in a most carefully reasoned judgment, assessed general damages at $275,000, the agreed special damages of some $25,500 making a total of just over $300,000.

Three consequences of her injuries account in large measure for the size of the award of general damages; her need for intensive nursing and medical attention in the future, her total loss of earning capacity and the gross impairment of the future enjoyment and amenities of her life. She has, in addition, experienced particularly severe pain and suffering and her life expectancy has been substantially reduced.

The learned trial judge did not essay any exact quantification of damages for every item of detriment suffered by the plaintiff. He arrived at a range of from $150,000 to $175,000 for the future cost of her nursing and medical care and at a sum of $6,000 for the shortened life expectancy of the plaintiff. ...

[571] A variety of difficulties, both of principle and of fact, surround the assessment of damages in this case. They stem from at least three distinct sources: the great increase in the cost of future nursing care should the plaintiff be cared for at home rather than in hospital; a variety of problems involved in assessing compensation for the plaintiff's loss of future earning capacity and, finally, the doubts as to the plaintiff's present life expectancy. ...

[572] In view of the attack made upon various aspects of his Honour's assessment of damages it is appropriate to examine the various heads of damages which presented themselves for assessment so as to appreciate and deal with the various criticisms raised by the appellant. First are those costs which the plaintiff will be obliged to incur in consequence of her injuries, principally although not exclusively, the cost of nursing and **[573]** medical care. It is clear that she will require such care for the rest of her life. It can be provided either in a hospital in Perth devoted to the care of persons incapacitated as she is or, at very much greater cost, in her own home. The plaintiff would much prefer the latter but the question is whether the defendant should be required to make compensation upon this much more expensive basis. The learned trial judge's award of damages contemplated that the plaintiff, while spending the greater part of her life in hospital, would spend some part of it being cared for at home.

Where the plaintiff is to be cared for in the future will not only directly affect the extent of nursing and medical expenses which are to be compensated for; it will also bear upon the extent of her loss of the amenities and enjoyment of life, a lifetime substantially spent in hospital will greatly aggravate that loss. In our view the medical evidence in this case does not justify the conclusion that the defendant should be required to compensate for future nursing and medical expenses on any basis other than that the plaintiff's future will be one substantially spent in hospital.

The appropriate criterion must be that such expenses as the plaintiff may reasonably incur should be recoverable from the defendant ...

[574] Assuming, for convenience and comparison, a life expectancy of twenty years, the future expenses of the plaintiff if confined to hospital would be of the order of a present value, computed on six per cent tables, of $108,500, inclusive of nursing, medical and physiotherapy services and cost of special beds etc. The provision to her of like services at her mother's home over that period would amount to a present value of about $390,000, to which would have to be added a weekly cost for medicaments etc of about $23 per week and a capital cost of some $11,750 for suitable alterations to her mother's home; moreover this is exclusive of the cost of food and of the cost of providing another home should her mother die during the period and the present home cease to be available to the plaintiff. The benefit to the plaintiff of being cared for at home rather than in hospital is not any benefit to her health but rather to her future enjoyment of life which would be enhanced by a home atmosphere; her life would not thereby be prolonged nor would her physical condition be at all improved; indeed she would be somewhat more at risk physically at home than in hospital. There is no evidence suggesting any likely psychiatric benefits, probable though these might appear to the layman.

In these circumstances the future cost of reasonable nursing and medical attention must, we think, be assessed on the basis of a lifetime substantially spent in hospital. ... For the purpose of our present examination of the award, and since we would regard the plaintiff's future as one involving permanent hospitalization in conditions of maximum nursing and medical care, we adopt thirty years as the appropriate period. For that period the present value, on six per cent tables, of the cost of hospital care, medical and physiotherapy treatment and the provision of a special bed and the like will amount to about $128,000.

There is another item of future expense which must enter into the assessment process. Because we conclude that the defendant [575] should not be required to compensate the plaintiff on any basis other than that of a lifetime in hospital it follows that the plaintiff's loss of the enjoyment and amenities of life will be the greater. She must be regarded as wholly deprived of the everyday pleasures of living in the environment of her own home. Instead she will be exposed to a lifetime of institutional life. Not only must this be reflected in the damages to be awarded under the conventional head of pain, suffering and the loss of enjoyment and amenities of life. In the present case it is also appropriate to reflect rather more positively one particular aspect of this situation of permanent hospitalization. The effect of the latter upon the plaintiff can clearly be somewhat mitigated if she is able to vary the monotony of the hospital ward by occasional day visits to her home and by other outings, possibly even by occasional weekends away from hospital. The medical evidence discloses that these would be possible provided that constant nursing attention was provided. Applying again the criterion or reasonableness but now weighing the expense of such attention against the clear benefits in amenity and enjoyment of life that such breaks in a lifetime in hospital would provide we are in no doubt that the plaintiff is entitled to compensation for the cost of such outings. ...

We turn next to the question of compensation for lost earning capacity and in particular to an examination of the deductions which should be made in assessing that compensation. ...

[576] Both principle and authority (*Skelton v Collins* (1966) 115 CLR 94, at p 106) establish that where, as here, there is included in the award of damages for future nursing and medical care the plaintiff's entire cost of future board and lodging, there will be overcompensation if damages for loss of earning capacity are awarded in full without regard for the fact that the plaintiff is already to receive as compensation the cost of her future board and lodging, a cost which but for

her injuries she would otherwise have to meet out of future earnings. If the true concept be that it is lost earning capacity to the extent to which it is likely to be exercised in the future, rather than loss of future earnings, that is to be compensated it may seem inelegant to speak of deducting from damages for that lost capacity an amount for some saving in outgoings. It would better accord with principle if the savings in board and lodging could be isolated from, and excluded from the damages to be awarded in respect of, hospital expenses. However so long as the true nature of the adjustment is understood no harm is done by making an appropriate deduction from the damages for lost earning capacity. What is to be avoided is double compensation and, as is apparent from what was said by their Lordships in *Shearman v Folland* [1950] 2 KB 43, it is not a question of estimating the plaintiff's likely future costs for board and lodging and treating them as an outgoing which the consequences of the defendant's tortious act have now spared her from making; that is a notion which is as distasteful as it is misconceived. Rather is it a matter of her already having been compensated for future board and lodging as a component of hospital expenses, so that to disregard this and award the full sum for lost earning capacity, part of which would be used to provide the very item of board and lodging already compensated for, would be to award compensation twice over. Accordingly some no doubt fairly arbitrary proportion of the present value of future hospital expenses regarded as attributable to board and lodging must be taken and deducted from the present value of lost earning capacity; it will be quite irrelevant how expensively or how frugally the plaintiff might in fact have lived had she not been injured.

Although it is only the cost of board and lodging which, unless subject to deduction in this way, will lead to actual double compensation there are other items which require **[577]** consideration as possible deductions when assessing damages for loss of earning capacity. ...

Where, as here, a plaintiff suffers a total loss of earning capacity he will not normally continue to incur all of the outgoings necessary for the realization of that capacity which would have been incurred had his capacity been unaffected; items such as the cost of clothing suitable to his particular employment and of transportation to and from work provide examples, no doubt there are others. Compensation for loss of earning capacity is paid only because it is or may be productive of financial loss (*Graham v Baker* (1961) 106 CLR 340, at p 347) and to compensate for total loss of earning capacity without making allowance for the cessation of these outgoings is to compensate for a gross loss when it is only the net loss that is in fact suffered.

On the other hand there are other types of saved expenditure upon which a defendant cannot rely in diminution of damages. It is now well established that no reduction is to be made, when awarding damages for loss of earning capacity, for the cost of maintaining oneself and one's dependants unless an element of double compensation would otherwise intrude, as in the case of hospitalization as a non-fee paying patient or where the cost of future hospital expenses is also awarded and necessarily includes, as in the present case, the patient's board and lodging ... .

[578] The present plaintiff is now denied many of the opportunities for pleasure-giving expenditure, as distinct from what may be regarded as expenditure on maintenance, which our society affords. Are the savings in expenditure, thus involuntarily thrust upon her by reason of the state to which her injuries have reduced her, to have the effect of reducing the damages awarded for her loss of earning capacity? We think not. They may be left out of reckoning, they neither produce double compensation nor compensate for gross rather than net loss. Indeed to treat them as items going to reduce damages is unjustifiably to assume that because pre-accident avenues of expenditure are now foreclosed to a plaintiff the necessary consequence is a corresponding non-expenditure. ...

The present plaintiff still possesses powers of enjoyment through the use of her senses; her sight, her hearing and her **[579]** taste are unaffected and in place of sport, entertainment, cosmetics and clothes she may find pleasure in recorded music, in a movie projector and the hire of films, in days spent on drives in a chauffeured car, perhaps in special foods. She can thus experience pleasure and ward off melancholia by such distractions as may be to her taste and within her means. Many of her former modes of enjoyment are closed to her but some new ones remain to be explored and from which she will be capable of deriving pleasure. ...

As to "lost years", the plaintiff is to be compensated in respect of lost earning capacity during those years by which her life expectancy has been shortened, at least to the extent that they are years when she would otherwise have been earning income (*Skelton v Collins* per Taylor J (1966) 115 CLR, at p 121). But, unlike the thirty years of her actual post-accident life expectancy, no outgoings whatever will be involved in respect of that period since it is assumed that the plaintiff will then be dead. ...

It is well established in Australia that there should be taken into account in reduction of damages for the lost earning capacity of "lost years" at least the amount that the plaintiff would have expended on his own maintenance during those lost years (*Skelton v Collins*, per Taylor J (1966) 115 CLR, at pp 121, 122, applied in *Jackson v Jackson*, per Sugerman P [1970] 2 NSWR 454, at p 460 and per Jacobs JA [1970] 2 NSWR at p 464, by Williams J in *Gannon v Gray* [1973] Qd R 411 and by Sheppard J in *Jackson v Stothard* [1973] 1 NSWLR 292). ...

[581] We ... have concluded that, properly regarded, *Skelton v Collins* (1966) 115 CLR 94 does not require that anything, other than the cost of a plaintiff's own maintenance, should go in reduction of damages for lost earning capacity for "lost years". ...

[583] Because in the ordinary case a plaintiff must maintain himself in the future out of his damages, the cost of doing so is not to go in reduction of an award for lost earning capacity during his remaining years of life; the converse of that proposition may well be, in the special case of lost earning capacity in "lost years", that because those years can involve him in no cost of maintenance the cost thus avoided must go in reduction of damages. Like reasoning does not apply to the cost of maintaining others. It is for a quite different reason that, in the ordinary case, that cost does not go in reduction of damages, that reason being that the courts do not concern themselves with the manner in which the plaintiff expends his income or damages. ...

There remains one future [sic] aspect of the assessment of damages for loss of earning capacity. Loss must depend upon the likelihood that there would have been a future exercise of that earning capacity, but what of a female plaintiff likely to marry and who may cease to exercise her earning capacity on, or at some time after, marriage? Despite recent changes in patterns of employment of married women this remains a not unusual situation, the woman in effect exchanging the exercise of her earning capacity for such financial security as her marriage may provide. The measure of the one of course bears no necessary relationship to the other and the whole situation must be full of [584] critical uncertainties such as whether the plaintiff marries, the extent if any of her employment after marriage, the success of that marriage and the extent to which it in fact provides her with economic security. Perhaps the only relatively certain factor will be her pre-injury possession of earning capacity and this in itself may be sufficient reason, absent any clear evidence pointing in a contrary direction, for the adoption of the expedient course of simply disregarding the prospect of marriage as a relevant factor in the assessment of such a plaintiff's future economic loss; this course at least recognizes the plaintiff's retention of capacity, which would have been available to her for exercise, in case of need, despite her marriage.

The last two heads of damages which call for particular mention are those conventionally described as pain, suffering and loss of the enjoyment and amenities of life and damages for shortening of life expectancy. As to the latter it bears no relationship to lost earning capacity during "lost years" but is rather the loss of a measure of prospective happiness (*Skelton v Collins*, per Taylor J (1966) 115 CLR, at p 121); it is not compensation for "the mental distress due to the realization of the loss" (per Kitto J (1966) 115 CLR at p 98). That forms instead a part of the general damages for pain and suffering ((1966) 115 CLR at p 100): compare Windeyer J ((1966) 115 CLR at pp 131-132). In the present case a figure "of the order of" £6,000 was allowed for this item in reliance upon the views expressed by Windeyer J in *Skelton v Collins* (1966) 115 CLR at p 132. If it be correct that compensation under this head is not to take into account the anguish of mind which any appreciation of the loss may cause, that being compensated for under another head, then Windeyer J's suggested maximum figure of £6,000, which reflected this very factor, may be thought to have been excessive at the time and to depart from the general standard of the "conventional sum" which the courts have quite arbitrarily fixed upon ever since *Benham v Gambling* [1941] AC 157. The amount awarded may properly take into account a fall in the value of money (*Yorkshire Electricity Board v Naylor* [1968] AC 529) but is to be no more than a quite conventional sum, very moderate in amount. In our view, despite the fall in the value of money, $6,000 departs from previous notions of what is appropriate under this curious and unsatisfactory head of damages. We would have thought that the sum of $2,000 is about the amount now appropriate as the conventional award under this head.

It remains only to say something about damages for loss of the enjoyment and amenities of life. It is in this field that there **[585]** exists the need to recall what has often been said about fairness, moderation and the undesirability of striving to provide an injured plaintiff with "perfect" compensation. The warning against attempting perfectly to compensate means, we think, in the case of pecuniary loss, no more than the need to make allowance for contingencies, for the vicissitudes of life, compensating for probable rather than for merely speculative detriments. But when a non-pecuniary detriment is in question the injunction against "perfect" compensation means rather more. It cannot refer to the exclusion of all question of punishment of the wrongdoer; the word "compensation" standing on its own would be sufficient to do this; rather is it designed to remind that the maiming of a plaintiff and its consequences cannot wholly be made good by an award of damages and that the recognition of this fact is to be no occasion for any instinctive response that no amount is too large to atone for the plaintiff's suffering. Such a response will be unfair to the defendant and may be of little advantage to the plaintiff; many consequences of injury are not capable of remedy by the receipt of damages, particularly those of the most personal character – the loss of the opportunity of a fulfilling marriage, of parenthood, of sexual satisfaction, of the realization of ambitions. It is very much at these detriments that the warning against any attempt at "perfect" compensation must be aimed. The authorities also require, as does good sense, that to the extent that damages awarded under other heads produce freedom from economic uncertainty and the availability of funds for pleasurable activities, the less will be the loss to be compensated under this head. This will be of particular relevance when a considerable sum is assessed for lost earning capacity. …

[586] The learned trial judge specified no precise amounts for lost earning capacity or for pain, suffering and loss of the amenities of life. …

[Their Honours considered a sum in the range of $34,000 to $43,000 for loss of earning capacity for the plaintiff's remaining years would not be erroneous. The estimate was increased to the range of $37,000 to $45,000 to include the "lost years".]

[587] The learned trial judge awarded a total of $275,000 for general damages, or $80,000 more than what we would regard as the maximum for heads of damage other than pain, suffering and loss of the amenities of life. …

[589] Pain and suffering and loss of the amenities of life is a head of damages which is peculiarly difficult to assess but when full compensation has been determined in respect of all other heads of damages, it appears to us that an additional sum of $80,000 exceeds what could properly be awarded under this last head. …

[590] We would accordingly allow this appeal and substitute for the present award an amount of $270,547.50.

[Barwick CJ agreed that overall the damages should be reduced to the degree suggested by Gibbs and Stephen JJ; but in his opinion the appropriate nominal sum for loss of expectation of life was $1250. Jacobs J (dissenting) concurred in the analysis made by Gibbs and Stephens JJ of the approach which a court should take to the assessment of damages in such a case as the present but considered the figures assessed by the trial Judge were not disproportionate. Murphy J (dissenting) considered that the award of the trial judge reflected a substantial under-assessment of the major economic and non-economic elements of the plaintiff's damages and therefore would have dismissed the appeal.]

Appeal allowed.
Order of the Supreme Court of
New South Wales, Court of Appeal varied

Todorovic v Waller
Jetson v Hankin
(1981) 150 CLR 402
High Court of Australia

In the assessment of damages for future economic loss "evidence as to the likely course of inflation, or of possible future changes in rates of wages or of prices, is inadmissible". However, a discount rate of 3 per cent, to be used in all cases in calculating the present value of a future loss, is intended to make appropriate allowance for these matters.

[The following statement as to the effect of these cases was read by the Chief Justice before judgment was delivered:

[**409**] Because of the practical importance of the decision in these cases, the Court now publishes this statement ...

In an action for damages for personal injuries, evidence as to the likely course of inflation, or of possible future changes in rates of wages or of prices, is inadmissible. Where there has been a loss of earning capacity which is likely to lead to financial loss in the future, or where the plaintiff's injuries will make it necessary to expend in the future money to provide medical or other services, or goods necessary for the plaintiff's health or comfort, the present value of the future loss ought to be quantified by adopting a discount rate of 3 per cent in all cases, subject, of course, to any relevant statutory provisions. This rate is intended to make the appropriate allowance for inflation, for future changes in rates of wages generally or of prices, and for tax (either actual or notional) upon income from investment of the sum awarded. No further allowance should be made for these matters.]

GIBBS CJ and WILSON J. These two appeals require the Court to consider the manner in which courts in Australia should approach the everyday task of assessing damages for personal injuries in cases in which the plaintiff, by reason of his injuries, has suffered a loss or impairment of his capacity to earn wages in the future, or will require in the future to be supplied with goods and services for which he will have to pay. ...

[**411**] The questions of principle that are raised by these appeals are whether, in the assessment of damages for loss of earning capacity, and for the cost of goods and services which the plaintiff will need in the future because of his injury, it is proper to make allowance for future inflation, and if so how this is to be done and whether evidence is admissible on the issue. ...

At the outset it is necessary to refer to the general principles which govern the assessment of damages, and the accepted method by which those principles are applied in Australia. We are not concerned with damages for pain and suffering and loss of amenities of life, but with damages for financial loss likely to be sustained in the future. There are two principal elements – the loss or diminution of earning capacity in so far as it is likely to cause financial loss in the future, and the need, caused by the injuries, for [**412**] services (such as medical treatment or nursing or domestic care) or goods (such as appliances designed to assist the disabled) in the future. ...

[**413**] Before one turns to consider the critical questions that arise in the case, it is convenient to discuss briefly the purpose and method of discounting in the assessment of damages, putting aside the effect of inflation. In *Nance v British Columbia Electric Railway Co Ltd* [1951] AC 601, a case under legislation corresponding to the *Fatal Accidents Act*, Viscount Simon ([1951] AC at p 615) pointed out that the sum to be awarded is not simply the annual loss multiplied by the number of years over which the loss will be suffered, "because that sum is a sum spread over a period of years and must be discounted so as to arrive at its equivalent in the form of a lump sum payable at his death as damages." The reason for discounting was explained by the Supreme Court of the United States in *Chesapeake & Ohio Railway Co v Kelly* (1916) 241 US 485, at p 489, as follows:

So far as a verdict is based upon the deprivation of future benefits, it will afford more than compensation if it be made up by aggregating the benefits without taking account of the

445

earning power of the money that is presently to be awarded. It is self-evident that a given sum of money in hand is worth more than the like sum of money payable in the future. ...

[414] If the award is not discounted, the plaintiff will necessarily be over-compensated. The process of discounting can only be dispensed with if some other consideration completely offsets the advantage that a plaintiff gains by receiving at the date of judgment a sum that if he had not been injured would have been paid to him at some time in the future, or a sum that he will be required to expend at some time in the future.

Different methods of discounting are used in different parts of the world, but they are of course intended to achieve the same result. The method that has been adopted in countless cases in Australia is to use tables, prepared by actuaries, which show the present value of a given amount, (eg a dollar) of income receivable periodically over a given number of years. The tables reveal the sum which, if invested at the discount rate, would suffice to enable periodic drawings of the given amount to be made from income and capital over the given number of years, so that at the end of that period both capital and income would be exhausted. Obviously the assumption is that the drawings will at first be made mainly out of income, but that there will be increasing resort to capital as time goes on.

There has been little judicial consideration of the rate at which the discount should be made, assuming that inflation is being ignored. Obviously the rate should be one obtainable from investments at the date on which the award is made. ... [415] Such authorities as there are seem opposed to the view that the discount rate is that which will be yielded by investments that are completely free of risk. It would seem to accord with the general approach of the common law that the rate should be that produced by reasonably safe investments – such investments as a prudent man in the position of the plaintiff, very much concerned to preserve his capital, but not over cautious, would make – such investments as loans issued by public authorities such as electricity commissions and water boards, or debentures issued by large well-established industrial companies. At the present time it would not seem unreasonable to suppose that an interest rate of at least 15 per cent would be obtainable on such securities.

In order to do justice to the plaintiff, it has been thought necessary, when discounting, to take account of the notional tax that would be payable on the notional issue of the invested fund. This was established in *Cullen v Trappell* (1980) 146 CLR 1 ... .

[416] Against this background, it is now possible to consider the question whether allowance should be made for inflation, and if so, in what manner. ... Before an attempt is made to consider the matter from the point of view of principle, it is convenient to see how it is dealt with by the authorities. In *O'Brien v McKean* (1968) 118 CLR 540, it was held by this Court that the Full Court of the Supreme Court of Queensland was not in error in setting aside the decision of a trial judge who had admitted evidence as to the future decline in the value of money and had allowed for future inflation in making an award of damages in respect of loss of future earning capacity and in respect of the necessity to make expenditure in the future. The decision, which was reached unanimously by five Justices, is clear authority for the proposition that direct evidence of inflation is not admissible on this issue. ...

[417] In Australia ..., at least since the 1950s, the courts have consistently made a modest allowance for inflation by adopting comparatively low discount rates. ... We have been informed by counsel in *Todorovic v Waller* that by the time *Barrell Insurances Pty Ltd v Pennant Hills Restaurants Pty Ltd* (1981) 145 CLR 625 came to be decided the discount rates applied in the various States tended to be as follows: Victoria 6 to 9 per cent, Queensland 8 per cent, Western Australia 6 to 6 1/2 per cent, South Australia 5 to 6 per cent and Tasmania 7 to 8 per cent. Of course this is an indication only of the range: there were variations in individual cases. In New South Wales, however, it was perceived that it was erroneous to increase the discount rate in line with rising interest rates. In *Lindsley v Hawkins* [1973] 2 NSWLR 581, at p 586, Jacobs P said:

> The consequence of the rule that one should not speculate on future inflationary trends is that, to avoid unfairness, one [418] should not take account of present high interest rates which are a symptom of the instability which inflationary trends bring. ...

At the time *Barrell Insurances* was decided the state of the law, having regard to authority and practice, might have been thought to be settled as follows: (1) in the assessment of damages for personal injuries, inflation could not directly be taken into account, and evidence of predictions of future inflation was inadmissible. (2) Some allowance for future inflation was made by taking a discount rate lower than that available from safe investments. The **[419]** trial judge had a discretion as to the rate selected. The rate originally taken, 5 per cent or sometimes less, had crept up without adequate consideration being given to the justification for the increase. ...

[420] We have already given reasons for adhering to the settled doctrine which requires the Court to reject evidence of inflation. Such evidence would be purely speculative, it would tend to prolong trials, and would introduce an additional element of uncertainty into awards. The only practicable alternative, if inflation is to be considered, is by taking it into account in fixing the discount rate. In the absence of evidence, that can only be done by an intuitive recognition that the chosen discount rate bears a just relation to the impact of inflation. ...

[423] In strictness perhaps this Court should not declare the rate at which discounts should be effected, but should leave that to the discretion of the courts of trial, as was done in *Hawkins v Lindsley* (1974) 49 ALJR 5. However, it is most desirable that awards of damages should be predictable, so that settlements may be facilitated, and the task of the courts eased. Moreover, while general economic circumstances remain as they are, there is no compelling reason why one judge should select a discount rate different from that selected by another. In the interest of securing uniformity throughout Australia this Court should therefore do what it has held that a Supreme Court of one State may not do, and that is to make an arbitrary ruling regarding interest rates of general application.

We consider that in future the courts in Australia, in States where the question is not governed by statute, should, in assessing damages, **[424]** arrive at the present value of a future loss by discounting at a fixed rate which will be applied in all cases and which will in itself reflect the effect of notional tax on notional income from the invested fund. To take this course may seem to involve some sacrifice of accuracy in the interests of predictability, but the whole process involves so much speculation that it is impossible to pretend to accuracy. In fixing the discount rate, the fact that for so long the rates applied by the courts in Australia have been at a level of 5 per cent and above should not be disregarded. Some downward adjustment is necessary to take account of notional tax. The actuaries' tables show that if the assumption is, as it must be, that the income is earned at the discount rate the necessary adjustment is quite small, particularly when the assumed income is within the range within which most employees' incomes fall in Australia. Now that the effect of inflation has become more apparent, it seems right to make a further moderate downward adjustment to the rate. Our own choice would be to adopt a discount rate of 4 per cent, but all that we have said indicates how arbitrary any choice must be and for that reason it is necessary for individual members of the Court to adjust their views in the interests of achieving a final and authoritative decision. We therefore concur in the view, to which we understand a majority of the Court is prepared to subscribe, that until this Court otherwise decides, a discount rate of 3 per cent should in future be applied and that no further allowance should be made for notional tax.

Our discussion of the questions involved indicates that the law relating to the assessment of damages for personal injury is far from satisfactory. However, any decision as to the way in which the law should be reformed depends on views as to social policy which can be formed only by the legislatures. ...

[Gibbs CJ and Wilson J then turned to the disposition of the two appeals before the Court and proposed certain orders. Mason, Aickin and Brennan JJ, in separate judgments, agreed that the Court should declare that the discount rate should be set at 3%, and concurred in the orders proposed by Gibbs CJ and Wilson J. Stephen and Murphy JJ dissented on the ground that, in their view, in assessing damages for future economic loss in a claim for personal injuries, there should be no discount for present payment.]

Appeal allowed

Wynn v NSW Insurance Ministerial Corporation
(1995) 184 CLR 485
High Court of Australia

In the assessment of damages for loss of future earning capacity, the court must take into account the contingencies or "vicissitudes" of life, that is, "the various possibilities which might otherwise have affected earning capacity".

[The appellant (plaintiff) brought proceedings to recover damages for injuries sustained in a car accident in 1986 when she was 30 years of age. She had been injured previously in an accident in 1972 but had surgery at that time and was virtually symptom-free by 1986. From 1981 she had a very successful, well-paid career with American Express where at the time of the accident she was one step below vice-president. The 1986 accident brought about a serious aggravation of the injury sustained in 1972. She was unable to continue her previous career and, at the time of the trial, worked part-time for a family business. Following an appeal by the respondent (defendant) against the trial judge's assessment of damages, the New South Wales Court of Appeal reduced the award to take into account the costs of child care and the likelihood that she would not have continued in such a demanding job. The appellant appealed against this decision to the High Court, which considered a number of issues relating to contingencies and vicissitudes of life, and varied the orders made by the New South Wales Court of Appeal.]

DAWSON, TOOHEY, GAUDRON and GUMMOW JJ. ... **[493] The trial judge's calculation of damages for future economic loss**
The trial judge found that, but for the aggravation of her earlier injury, the appellant "would have worked within the American Express organisation at least until the age of sixty years". In reaching that conclusion, his Honour found that it was not very probable that, having worked her way to the position of Director of Customer Services, she would retire by reason of marriage or motherhood.

The appellant's net weekly loss as at the date of hearing was assessed at $1,013. This figure was reached by deducting $440 for present earning capacity from the then net weekly salary package of $1,453 for Director of Customer Services. Calculation of that loss until the age of sixty (23.75 years) in accordance with Sch 3 to the *Motor Vehicles (Third Party Insurance) Amendment Act 1984* (NSW) produced an amount of $743,137. That sum was then discounted by 5 per cent to take account of contingencies or what are commonly called "the vicissitudes of life" (note the criticism of this expression in *Bresatz v Przibilla* (1962) 108 CLR 541 at 543-544, per Windeyer J who referred to contingencies as being "glibly called" the vicissitudes of life. See also *Jackson v Hamparsum* (1988) 7 MVR 80 at 87, per Hope JA who regarded it as "quaint and even discrimina-tory" to treat the prospect of a woman having a child as a "vicissitude"), resulting in the sum of $705,980 for future economic loss.

In deciding on a discount of 5 per cent for contingencies, the trial judge made allowance for the possibility that, had she remained in employment with American Express, the appellant might have taken maternity leave but considered that, except for ordinary transient illnesses, her work would not otherwise have been interrupted. In particular, his Honour considered that, although her 1972 injury would have produced symptoms by the time she was fifty-five, it would not have prevented her continuing in employment until the age of sixty. His Honour balanced against the possible need to take maternity leave the prospect that the appellant might have been promoted to a vice-presidential position.

[494] The approach of the Court of Appeal
In the Court of Appeal, Handley JA (with whom Clarke and Sheller JJA agreed) considered that the calculation of future economic loss should be deduced by amounts to allow for superannuation contributions and the cost of child care and domestic help. The reduction for superannuation contributions can be put to one side as the parties agree that the Court of Appeal was correct in this

regard. So far as concerns child care and domestic help, a deduction of $125 per week (the Court of Appeal calculated that the cost of child care and domestic help would be $250 per week, with the appellant and her husband bearing half each) was made for the whole of what would have been the appellant's working life. In the result, future economic loss was assessed at $571,320.34 before allowing for contingencies.

The Court of Appeal held that there should be a discount of 28 per cent for contingencies, of which 8 per cent was for two years' absence from the workforce to have two children. The balance of the discount was for the prospect that the appellant "would at some stage [choose] or [be] forced to accept a less demanding job" because she "would be unable or unwilling to remain in her job which placed such heavy demands on her time, energy and health and the love and patience of her husband".

At the conclusion of the appellant's argument in this Court, counsel for the respondent conceded that the approach taken by the Court of Appeal could not be supported. It is appropriate to observe that that concession was correct and to indicate why that is so. It is convenient in so doing to deal first with the separate aspects of the discount for contingencies, namely, the prospect of reduced participation in the workforce and the possibility that the appellant would take maternity leave.

So far as concerns the prospect of reduced participation in the workforce, there is nothing in the evidence to suggest that the appellant was any less able than any other career oriented person, whether male or female, to successfully combine a demanding career and family responsibilities. Rather, the evidence of her rapid promotion within the American Express organisation, her ambition to advance further and her desire to remain in the paid workforce, when considered in the light of the practice of American Express to promote from within the organisation, clearly justified the trial judge in forming the view that there was a prospect of her further advancement. As will later appear, the trial judge was correct to treat this as a positive factor to be taken into account in allowing for contingencies.

So far as maternity leave is concerned, the appellant gave evidence that, for her first child at least, she would have wished to take twelve months' maternity leave if she had continued to work with American Express. Even if allowance is made for two years' unpaid maternity **[495]** leave for two children – calculated by the Court of Appeal as 8 per cent of net loss after deduction for child care and domestic help – there is no reason to think that it was not adequately reflected in the trial judge's balancing exercise which, after allowing for the possibility of promotion and increased earnings, resulted in a discount of 5 per cent.

The position with respect to the deduction of child care expenses for the purpose of calculating net loss is, perhaps, not so clear. It is well settled that "[c]ompensation for loss of earning capacity is paid only because it is or may be productive of financial loss" (*Sharman v Evans* (1977) 138 CLR 563 at 577, referring to *Graham v Baker* (1961) 106 CLR 340 at 347. See also *Medlin v State Government Insurance Commission* (1995) 182 CLR 1 at 4-5, 16) Thus, it has been said that "outgoings necessary for the realisation of that capacity" (*Sharman v Evans* (1977) 138 CLR 563 at 577), such as transport costs, tools and equipment, must be deducted.

There is simply no basis for treating domestic help as necessary for the realisation of earning capacity and, to the extent that the Court of Appeal thought otherwise, it was clearly wrong. What a person does or does not do outside working hours may depend on whether he or she has domestic help, but domestic help has no relevant connection with the earning of income. There are, however, circumstances in which the cost of caring for very young children may properly be seen as an "essential prerequisite" to the earning of income (*Lodge v Federal Commissioner of Taxation* (1972) 128 CLR 171 at 175, per Mason J) and, in this sense, as an outgoing "necessary for the realisation of [earning] capacity". However, outgoings which are deducted for the purpose of calculating economic loss are those which are necessarily incurred in or in connection with the employment or undertaking by which earning capacity is realised (*Sharman v Evans* (1977) 138 CLR 563 at 577; *Lim v Camden & Islington Area Health Authority* [1980] AC 174 at 191), not those which are incurred, even as a "necessary prerequisite", merely to provide an opportunity to realise that capacity. In a sense, child care can be regarded as an opportunity cost. But even that mistakes its true nature.

Child care is a cost that may be incurred by men (see, eg, *Halstead v Condon* (1970) 46 Tax Cas 289; [1970] TR 91) or women. It may be incurred whether or not the child's mother is in the paid **[496]** workforce. On the other hand, not all women in the paid workforce incur a cost for the care of their young children. For example, one or more family members may provide care on a voluntary basis. Moreover, if costs are incurred they will vary according to the type of care decided upon and decisions in that regard are likely to take account of various matters besides those directly associated with participation in the paid workforce. These considerations lead to the conclusion that the cost of child care is simply one of various costs associated with having children. And as such, the cost is properly characterised for the purpose of calculating economic loss, as it is for the purposes of taxation law, as essentially private or domestic in character (see, as to the tax deductibility of child care expenses, *Lodge v Federal Commissioner of Taxation* (1972) 128 CLR 171; *Martin v Federal Commissioner of Taxation* (1984) 2 FCR 260; *Jayatilake v Federal Commissioner of Taxation* (1991) 101 ALR 11. See also *Bowers v Harding* [1891] 1 QB 560; *Wylie v Eccott* (1912) 6 TC 128; *Norman v Golder* [1945] 1 All ER 352; *Halstead v Condon* (1970) 46 TC 289). So characterised, it is no more to be deducted when calculating loss of earning capacity than are other items of expenditure for personal amenity.

In view of the Court of Appeal's apparent treatment of the cost of child care as a cost of earning income and the concession by the respondent that its approach was vitiated by error, it is neither necessary nor desirable to consider the circumstances in which deductions should be made for saved expenditure with respect to items of personal amenity (see *Sharman v Evans* (1977) 138 CLR 563 at 578. See also *Shearman v Folland* [1950] 2 KB 43 at 50; *Fletcher v Autocar & Transporters Ltd* [1968] 2 QB 322 at 336-337; *Lim v Camden & Islington Health Authority* [1980] AC 174 at 191; *Dews v National Coal Board* [1988] AC 1 at 14; *Toneguzzo-Norvell v Burnaby Hospital* [1994] 1 SCR 114 at 127; 110 DLR (4th) 289 at 296-297). Moreover, there is nothing in the evidence to suggest that the appellant's reduced participation in the workforce results in reduced or saved expenditure on child care.

The respondent's argument in this Court

The argument for the respondent in this Court was that allowance should have been made for the possibility that the appellant's 1972 injury would have prevented her working in a high level managerial position until age sixty even if the 1986 accident had not occurred. An argument to that effect was put in the Court of Appeal but not dealt with in its judgment (the issue was, however, recognised by Clarke and Handley JJA during the course of argument). As it was developed in this Court, the argument was that, overall, the appropriate discount was 38 per cent (the respondent added the cost of child care and domestic help, calculated by the Court of Appeal at $125 per week, to the discount of 28 per cent awarded for "vicissitudes" and calculated that this was effectively a discount for "vicissitudes" of 38 per cent), resulting after allowance for superannuation contributions, **[497]** in a verdict in the sum allowed by the Court of Appeal. More precisely, it was argued that no allowance should be made for the prospect of advancement and that 38 per cent fairly represents the possibility that the appellant would have taken unpaid maternity leave and the further possibility that her previous neck injury would have prevented her continued employment until age sixty.

It is necessary to say something as to contingencies or "vicissitudes". Calculation of future economic loss must take account of the various possibilities which might otherwise have affected earning capacity. The principle and the relevant considerations were identified by Barwick CJ in *Arthur Robinson (Grafton) Pty Ltd v Carter* (1968) 122 CLR 649 at 659 as follows:

"Ill health, unemployment, road or rail accidents, wars, changes in industrial emphasis, so that industries move their location, or are superseded by new and different techniques, the onset and effect of automation and the mere daily vicissitudes of life are not adequately reflected by merely – and blindly – taking some percentage reduction of a sum which ignores them."

It is to be remembered that a discount for contingencies or vicissitudes" is to take account of matters which might otherwise adversely affect earning capacity and as Professor Luntz notes, death apart, "sickness, accident, unemployment and industrial disputes are the four major contingencies which expose employees to the risk of loss of income" (*Assessment of Damages for Personal Injury and Death*, 3rd ed (1990), p 285. See also *Jones v Schiffmann* (1971) 124 CLR 303 at 305, per Barwick CJ; *Mitchell v Mulholland (No 2)* [1972] 1 QB 65 at 75). Positive considerations which might have resulted in advancement and increased earnings are also to be taken into account, (see, eg, *Lulich v Bell Bros Pty Ltd* (1967) 41 ALJR 268 at 268, 270; *Broadribb v Hanna* [1969] 1 NSWR 35 at 42; *Jones v Schiffmann* (1971) 124 CLR 303 at 315 where positive contingencies were taken into account. See also *Ritchie v Victorian Railways Commissioner* (1899) 25 VLR 272 at 276; *General Motors-Holden's Pty Ltd v Moularas* (1964) 111 CLR 234 at 258; *Murphy v Houghton & Byrne* (Q) Pty Ltd [1964] QWN 6 at 15-16; *Sinclair v Bonnefin* (1968) 13 FLR 164; *Mallett v McMonagle* [1970] AC 166 at 177; *Toneguzzo-Norvell v Burnaby Hospital* [1994] 1 SCR 114 at 124; 110 DLR (4th) 289 at 295 where it was recognised that contingencies can be favourable as well as adverse), for, as Windeyer J pointed out in *Bresatz v Przibilla* (1962) 108 CLR 541 at 544 (see also *Teubner v Humble* (1963) 108 CLR 491 at 508-509; *Blackstock v Patterson* [1982] 4 WWR 519 at 533), "[a]ll 'contingencies' are not adverse: all 'vicissitudes' are not harmful". Finally, contingencies are to be considered in terms of their likely impact on the earning capacity of the person who has been injured, not by reference to the workforce generally (*Lewis v Todd* [1980] 2 SCR 694 at 714; 115 DLR (3d) 257 at 271-272). Even so, the practice in New South Wales is to proceed on the basis that a **[498]** 15 per cent discount is generally appropriate (see, eg, *Moran v McMahon* (1985) 3 NSWLR 700 at 713-714. Note the criticism of Kirby P at 706. See also *Burnicle v Cutelli* [1982] 2 NSWLR 26 at 30; *Hobell v Leonard* (unreported; Supreme Court of NSW, Court of Appeal; File No 40209 of 1989; 29 May 1990)), subject to adjustment up or down to take account of the plaintiff's particular circumstances.

Leaving aside the appellant's previous neck injury and the possibility that she might have taken unpaid maternity leave, there was little, if anything, in her circumstances to suggest that her earning capacity was at risk from any of the four major items which Professor Luntz has identified as detrimentally affecting earning capacity. She was in good health, fit and energetic; she was employed in a position which would not seem to involve exposure to accident or disease; and as an employee in a managerial position with American Express, she would not seem to have been at particular risk of redundancy or the possibility of being involved in industrial disputes.

As already indicated, there was evidence upon which the trial judge might properly form the view that, had the accident not occurred, there was a prospect that the appellant would have been further promoted within American Express. The argument of the respondent to the contrary must be rejected. All that had to be established was "a real possibility" (*Wilson v Peisley* (1975) 50 ALJR 207 at 209; 7 ALR 571 at 574. See also *Malec v JC Hutton Pty Ltd* (1990) 169 CLR 638 at 639-640, 643; *Sellars v Adelaide Petroleum NL* (1994) 179 CLR 332 at 365-367; *Mallett v McMonagle* [1970] AC 166 at 176) of promotion. The evidence clearly permitted an inference to that effect. And once that inference was drawn by the trial judge, it was necessary for the prospect of advancement to be taken into account and balanced against the need to take maternity leave. If they were the only personal considerations to be taken into account, it could not be said that, in the circumstances of this case, a discount of 5 per cent was inappropriate.

However, the evidence clearly established that, following the injury in 1972 and notwithstanding the bone graft carried out in 1974, the appellant's spine was susceptible to further injury and was likely to suffer degenerative changes. If there was a chance that the 1972 injury would have reduced the appellant's ability to work in any event, that chance had to be assessed and allowed for in the calculation of future economic loss (*Malec v JC Hutton Pty Ltd* (1990) 169 CLR 638). Unless allowed for in that way, the defendant would be held responsible for loss which was not causally related to the injury suffered in 1986.

It is necessary to say something of susceptibility to further injury. It is not permissible in assessing the chance that an earlier injury may have resulted in impaired earning capacity to have regard to the possibility of further tortious injury. That possibility must be **[499]** disregarded because, in the event of further injury, damages would be assessed, as in this case, by allowing for any pre-condition resulting in or having the possibility of resulting in impaired earning capacity (see *Jobling v Associated Dairies Ltd* [1982] AC 794, especially per Lord Keith of Kinkel at 815-816, approving *Baker v Willoughby* [1970] AC 467 on this point. See also *General Motors-Holden's Pty Ltd v Moularas* (1964) 111 CLR 234 at 248-249; *Wilson v Peisley* (1975) 50 ALJR 207 at 209,

212; 7 ALR 571 at 574, 581-582). Only by disregarding the possibility of further tortious injury does the law ensure full compensation.

The trial judge clearly found that the probabilities were that, but for the 1986 accident, the pre-existing condition occasioned by the 1972 accident would not have affected the appellant's continued employment until age sixty. However, it was still necessary for his Honour to consider whether it might have done so. This he did not do. As the medical evidence is not really in dispute, the questions whether there was a chance of the appellant's pre-existing condition reducing her ability to work, and, if so, what allowance should be made for that chance may conveniently be dealt with by this Court.

The undisputed evidence was that the appellant had a better than average result from the spinal fusion carried out in 1974 but that, nevertheless, her spine was vulnerable to further injury. The evidence of Dr Bryan, the appellant's treating doctor, was that she was particularly at risk in the first four to five years after the spinal fusion but that "as the years passed ... she became much more able to handle the situation". That evidence did not exclude a continuing risk of injury. And it is fair to assume that risk was not restricted to tortious injury.

Moreover, the evidence clearly established the possibility of degenerative changes. The trial judge's finding, on the probabilities, that the changes would have produced symptoms at age fifty-five but would not have prevented continued employment until age sixty did not eliminate the possibility that symptoms might have occurred earlier, resulting in reduced earnings or in early retirement. This and the possibility of non-tortious injury should have been allowed for in determining the appropriate discount for contingencies (*Wilson v Peisley* (1975) 50 ALJR 207 at 209; 7 ALR 571 at 574).

As Brennan and Dawson JJ pointed out in *Malec v JC Hutton Pty Ltd* (1990) 169 CLR 638 at 640, "[d]amages founded on hypothetical evaluations defy precise calculation". The discount to be allowed for the possibility that the appellant's previous injury might have resulted in her impaired earning capacity can at best be a matter of impression. Having regard to the better than average result of the surgical fusion carried out in 1974 and the diminishing nature of the risk of further injury, the discount should not be great. In our view, the appropriate discount for maternity leave and the possible effects of the condition brought about by the 1972 **[500]** accident, balanced against the prospect of further advancement, is 12½ per cent. ...

[Brennan CJ agreed with the order proposed in the joint reasons for judgment.]

Appeal allowed in part

Kars v Kars
(1996) 187 CLR 354
High Court of Australia

Under the Griffiths v Kerkemeyer principle, a plaintiff who has suffered personal injury caused by the defendant's negligence may recover damages representing the value of necessary services, past and future, provided gratuitously to the plaintiff by a relative or friend. This principle applies where the services are provided to the plaintiff by the defendant tortfeasor.

[The plaintiff, Rebecca Kars, was seriously injured in a motor accident caused by the negligence of her husband, Mark Kars, the defendant. The plaintiff's injuries left her with a permanent disability and a need for continuing care. Much of that care was provided by family members, with more than half of the care provided by the defendant. In the plaintiff's action against the defendant for damages, the trial judge rejected the claim for damages for the value of gratuitous services which were likely to be provided to the plaintiff by the defendant in the future. The Queensland Court of Appeal reversed the decision of the trial judge. The defendant appealed to the High Court, which unanimously affirmed the decision of the Queensland

Court of Appeal allowing the claim. The court also held that a plaintiff does not hold damages awarded in respect of future care on trust for the person who may provide the services.]

DAWSON J. ...**[358]** The defendant accepts that, since the decision of this Court in *Griffiths v Kerkemeyer* (1977) 139 CLR 161, a plaintiff disabled as the result of another's negligence may recover a sum representing the value of necessary services provided gratuitously by a relative or friend. In *Griffiths v Kerkemeyer*, however, the services were not provided by the defendant tortfeasor and that, the defendant contends, distinguishes *Griffiths v Kerkemeyer* from this case. The argument which is advanced is that, to the extent that the defendant provides services, the need of the plaintiff for them is met and the defendant's liability is accordingly reduced. Put another way, the argument is that, having provided the services, the defendant cannot be required to pay, in addition, the cost of providing them. ...

In *Griffiths v Kerkemeyer* the plaintiff, who was rendered a quadriplegic as the result of the negligence of the defendant, recovered damages which included a sum representing the value of nursing and other services gratuitously provided for him in the past and to be provided in the future by his fiancee and members of his family. In upholding the award, this Court departed from its previous view that expenses in an action for damages for personal injuries could only be recovered where there was, or would be, a legal obligation to pay them (see *Blundell v Musgrave* (1956) 96 CLR 73.). Instead, it followed the decision of the English Court of Appeal in *Donnelly v Joyce* [1974] QB 454 and viewed the damages in question as damages for one component of the plaintiff's loss occasioned by his physical disability. The disability gave rise to the need for nursing and other care. The need was met by the services gratuitously provided. The value or cost of those services was, in the circumstances, an appropriate means of quantifying that aspect of the plaintiff's loss which was represented by the need (see *Nguyen v Nguyen* (1990) 169 CLR 245 at 261-262). ...

[360] Since the acceptance of the rationale in *Donnelly v Joyce* by this Court in *Griffiths v Kerkemeyer*, it cannot be said in Australia that the underlying rationale of awarding damages for services provided gratuitously is to enable the carer to receive proper recompense for his or her services. The damages are recoverable to compensate the plaintiff for the loss which is evidenced by the need for the services and it is a matter for the plaintiff whether they are used to recompense the person providing the services. Thus in *Griffiths v Kerkemeyer* the idea of a trust advanced by Lord Denning [in *Cunningham v Harrison* [1973] QB 942] was rejected by both Stephen J (at 176-177) and Mason J (at 193-194). Stephen J said (at 177):

"There is, I think, some difficulty in the concept of a trust in favour of a provider attaching to some perhaps wholly unquantified part of an award of damages and this will be the greater if the provider's services lie wholly or partly in the future. However, quite apart from difficulties of this sort, and from those additionally mentioned by Bray CJ in *Beck v Farrelly* (1975) 13 SASR 17 at 22, the plaintiff should, I think, be regarded as beneficially entitled to the judgment he obtains without question of the imposition of any trust in respect of some part of his damages in favour of one who has rendered, or may in the future render, gratuitous services to him."

Once it is recognised, as it must be, at all events after the decision of this Court in *Van Gervan v Fenton* (1992) 175 CLR 327, that a plaintiff receives the value of services voluntarily provided by way of damages as compensation for the loss suffered by reason of the injuries which manifests itself in the form of a need for those services, and that the need does not have to be productive of financial loss, then cases such as **[361]** as the present one are taken outside the area of special damages, such as loss of wages or out-of-pocket expenses which, at least for the past, may be calculated simply by adding them up. True it is that the value of services provided or to be provided gratuitously to satisfy a need will ordinarily provide a guide in quantifying the damages to be awarded for the loss giving rise to the need, but those damages are general damages which are incapable of precise mathematical calculation and remain at large until quantified. It has been conventional when juries are called upon to assess damages to classify general damages under three heads: economic loss, loss of enjoyment of life and pain and suffering. Economic loss is often said to be the future loss of wages or loss of income but in fact it is for the loss of earning capacity that such damages are awarded. As Fullagar J pointed out in *Paff v Speed* (1961) 105 CLR 549 at 559:

"Actual loss of wages or loss of income will have been already taken into account in assessing special damages, and what the plaintiff must receive in respect of the future is compensation for total or partial incapacity to earn income."

In the same way the damages which a plaintiff receives for the need for services is compensation for the loss or incapacity giving rise to the need.

That means that the voluntary provision of services to a plaintiff injured as a result of another's negligence is not to be regarded as relieving the plaintiff of expenses which he or she would otherwise have to bear. That is to say, the voluntary provision of services cannot be regarded as being in reduction of a financial loss sounding in damages. If it could be so regarded, damages awarded in respect of past services would fall within the category of special damages and, as was pointed out in *Van Gervan v Fenton*, that is denied in *Donnelly v Joyce* and *Griffiths v Kerkemeyer*. Rather, the provision of voluntary services is to be regarded as a benevolence which is prompted by the ties of friendship, or familial concern or duty. If the benevolence is not to be regarded as compensation, the underlying loss or disability giving rise to the need for the services remains to be compensated. That, then, carries one into an area which is sufficiently identified by the cases even if the principle which the cases lay down is not always susceptible of easy application.

In Australia the starting point is *National Insurance Co of New Zealand Ltd v Espagne* (1961) 105 CLR 569 where the problem which confronted the Court was identified by Dixon CJ in a passage which it is necessary to set out, though it is well-known (*Espagne* (1961) 105 CLR 569 at 573):

[362] "The reasoning begins with a distinction which I think is clear enough in general conception. There are certain special services, aids, benefits, subventions and the like which in most communities are available to injured people. Simple examples are hospital and pharmaceutical benefits which lighten the monetary burden of illness. If the injured plaintiff has availed himself of these, he cannot establish or calculate his damages on the footing that he did not do so. On the other hand there may be advantages which accrue to the injured plaintiff, whether as a result of legislation or of contract or of benevolence, which have an additional characteristic. It may be true that they are conferred because he is intended to enjoy them in the events which have happened. Yet they have this distinguishing characteristic, namely they are conferred on him not only independently of the existence in him of a right of redress against others but so that they may be enjoyed by him although he may enforce that right: they are the product of a disposition in his favour intended for his enjoyment and not provided in relief of any liability in others fully to compensate him. This is readily seen in the case of benevolence."

Dixon CJ went on to provide the example of a subscription taken up by neighbours to assist an injured plaintiff. Similarly, the proceeds of an accident insurance policy taken out by an injured plaintiff before he sustained the injury would not be taken into account in assessing the damages to be paid by the person who caused the injury. Of course, in the latter case, it might be said that the plaintiff purchased the benefit himself with the premiums paid for the policy (see *Bradburn v Great Western Railway Co* (1874) LR 10 Ex 1). And in the latter case, as in the former, there may be some qualification of the principle that damages are purely compensatory (see *Espagne* (1961) 105 CLR 569 at 598, per Windeyer J). However, as Deane J pointed out in *Redding v Lee* (1983) 151 CLR 117 at 167 "another anomaly in a field (damages for personal injury) where the existence of an anomaly is far from anomalous" should occasion no difficulty.

The provision of gratuitous services to an injured plaintiff by a friend or relative is, to my mind, clearly to be categorised as an act of benevolence where there is no intention that it should result in the reduction of damages recoverable by the injured person. In his judgment in *Espagne*, Windeyer J asked why the benefits of benevolence do not reduce the recoverable damages and concluded (*Espagne* (1961) 105 CLR 569 at 598-599):

"The most satisfying of the reasons that have been given for refusing to diminish damages because of voluntary gifts is that they are given for the benefit of the sufferer and not for the benefit of the [363] wrongdoer. That, it may be said, cuts across the principle that damages for negligence are compensatory and not punitive. It may be that, at all events since *Bradburn's Case* (1874) LR 10 Ex 1, there are some limits to strictly logical applications of that principle. But I do not think the two propositions necessarily come into collision. A donor can say who is to benefit by his generosity. If, out of sympathy for a man unfortunately responsible for a motor accident, someone gives money to the victim, stating that he does so in the interest of the tortfeasor and to diminish the damages he must pay, effect must be given to his intention. If, on the other hand, the donor's expressed intention is that the injured man shall enjoy his bounty in addition to whatever rights he may have to recover damages from the tortfeasor, effect must in my opinion, be given to that intention. And if nothing be said, the intention of the giver may be inferred from the circumstances."

Windeyer J went on to say (*Espagne* (1961) 105 CLR 569 at 599-600) that where personal injury is productive of private benevolence (and also some other forms of bounty), it is the intent of the donor which is crucial in deciding whether the benefit should be enjoyed in addition to and not in diminution of any claim for damages. If that is the purpose of the benevolence then the law will give effect to it. As Mason J and I put it in *Redding v Lee* (1983) 151 CLR 117 at 137:

"The subsequent decisions in this Court apply the principles expressed by Dixon CJ and Windeyer J in *Espagne*. They make it clear that the issue turns on the character and purpose of the particular financial benefit which the plaintiff receives: Was the benefit conferred on him independently of any right or redress against others and so that he might enjoy the benefit even if he enforced the right?"

There remains the problem whether such a test is capable of application where the benefit is in the form of gratuitous services provided by a friend or relative who is the tortfeasor whose negligence caused the plaintiff's injuries which, in turn, gave rise to the need for the services. I can see no relevant distinction between a financial benefit and a benefit in the form of services and, for my part, I am unable to see why the character and purpose of the benefit should not be determined by reference to the intent of the provider whether or not that person is also the defendant from whom the injured plaintiff is able to claim damages.

There is no reason in principle why a person who is sued by a friend or relative, to whom he has negligently caused injury, should not provide services gratuitously to that person with the intention that the **[364]** provision of those services should be in addition to and not in diminution of any damages which that person may recover against him. Perhaps such an intention would have been less common in the past, but now when, as Deane J put it in *Redding v Lee* (1983) 151 CLR 117 at 166, "[a]s a result either of statutory compulsion or accepted standards of business prudence, almost all defendants in actions for damages for personal injuries are insured", it should not be a matter of surprise that a defendant, particularly a relative or friend, should gratuitously provide services, needed by a plaintiff as a result of the defendant's negligence, without any intention of reducing his liability in damages. And, it may be added, where the person providing the services is a friend or relative who is uninsured, it is much less likely that an injured plaintiff would sue that person for damages. It may be correspondingly more likely that the services provided by the defendant are provided with the intention of diminishing his liability in damages.

Where someone other than the defendant provides gratuitous services to an injured plaintiff, it is, perhaps, theoretically easier to discern an intention that the provision of the services should not have the effect of relieving the defendant wrongdoer of any liability. As Lord Reid somewhat forcefully put it in *Parry v Cleaver* [1970] AC 1 at 14:

"It would be revolting to the ordinary man's sense of justice, and therefore contrary to public policy, that the sufferer should have his damages reduced so that he would gain nothing from the benevolence of his friends or relations or of the public at large, and that the only gainer would be the wrongdoer."

Whilst those considerations have no application here, that is not to say that it is impossible or, in this day and age, even unlikely, that a defendant should engage in benevolence towards a plaintiff for purposes other than the reduction of his liability to the plaintiff and if that is what occurs then there is no reason why the applicable principle should be any different.

There is no suggestion in this case that the services provided by the defendant were provided with the intention of reducing his liability to the plaintiff in damages and, accordingly, I would dismiss the appeal.

[In a joint judgment, Toohey, McHugh, Gummow and Kirby JJ agreed that the appeal should be dismissed.]

Appeal dismissed

Husher v Husher
(1999) 197 CLR 138; [1999] HCA 47
High Court of Australia

In the assessment of damages for loss of future earning capacity, the basic task is to identify "what earning capacity has been impaired or lost and what financial loss is occasioned by that impairment or loss". Thus, where the plaintiff was in a profit-sharing partnership for income tax purposes with his or her spouse before suffering the relevant injury, this fact should not obscure the true extent of the plaintiff's loss of future earning capacity.

[The appellant (plaintiff) was injured in a motor accident caused by the negligent driving of his wife, the respondent (defendant). Before the accident, he had carried on a business as a block layer in partnership with his wife. His skill and physical labour generated the entire income and his wife did the bookkeeping and similar tasks. Profits were divided equally for tax purposes. After the accident he was unable to continue with this work and the partnership ceased operation. In his action against his wife in negligence, he claimed damages for loss of earning capacity. The trial judge assessed damages on the basis that the partnership would have continued and the plaintiff would have received half the profits for the rest of his working life. The Court of Appeal of the Supreme Court of Queensland upheld this decision. The plaintiff appealed to the High Court.]

GLEESON CJ, GUMMOW, KIRBY and HAYNE JJ. … **[142] Impairment of earning capacity productive of financial loss**
6. A person who is physically injured by the negligence of another may suffer damage in a number of ways. As has long been established, the damages to be awarded to the victim are "that sum of money which will put the party who has been injured, or who has suffered, in the same position as he would have been in if he had not sustained the wrong for which he is now getting his compensation or **[143]** reparation": *Livingstone v Rawyards Coal Co* (1880) 5 App Cas 25 at 39, per Lord Blackburn. If the victim's pursuit of gainful employment is interrupted or affected because of the negligent infliction of physical injury, the victim is to be compensated by an amount that reflects the financial consequences that follow from the impairment.
7. Since at least *Graham v Baker* (1961) 106 CLR 340 it has been recognised that it is convenient to assess an injured plaintiff's economic loss "by reference to the actual loss of wages which occurs up to the time of trial and which can be more or less precisely ascertained and then, having regard to the plaintiff's proved condition at the time of trial, to attempt some assessment of his future loss": *Graham v Baker* (1961) 106 CLR 340 at 346-347, per Dixon CJ, Kitto and Taylor JJ. But damages for both past loss and future loss are allowed to an injured plaintiff "because the diminution of his earning capacity is or may be productive of financial loss" (*Graham v Baker* (1961) 106 CLR 340 at 347, per Dixon CJ, Kitto and Taylor JJ. See also *Arthur Robinson (Grafton) Pty Ltd v Carter* (1968) 122 CLR 649 at 658, per Barwick CJ; Atiyah, "Loss of Earnings of Earning Capacity?", *Australian Law Journal*, vol 45 (1971) 228). Both elements are important. It is necessary to identify both what capacity has been lost and what economic consequences will probably flow from that loss. Only then will it be possible to assess what sum will put the plaintiff in the same position as he or she would have been in if injury had not been sustained.
8. No doubt the past may provide important evidence about the plaintiff's earning capacity and what economic consequences will probably flow from what has happened: *Arthur Robinson (Grafton) Pty Ltd v Carter* (1968) 122 CLR 649 at 658, per Barwick CJ. What a worker earned in the past may provide very useful guidance about what would have been earned if that worker had not been injured. But the inquiry is an inquiry about the likely course of future events and evidence of past events does not always provide certain guidance about the future. There may be many reasons why an injured plaintiff's past work history provides no assistance in deciding what that plaintiff has lost through diminution of future earning capacity. The student who is yet to enter the workforce is an obvious case of that kind. That student may have no history of paid work.

Important as evidence of past events may be, that evidence is not determinative of an issue about loss of future earning capacity....

[146] 16. [T]he decisions reached in particular factual contexts must not be permitted to obscure what we have referred to as the basic principles.

17. Those principles require identification of what earning capacity has been impaired or lost and what financial loss is occasioned by that impairment or loss. In the present case there is no doubt that the [147] *capacity* that the appellant lost was a capacity to earn whatever he *could* have earned working as a block layer. But the inquiry does not stop at what the appellant *could* have earned. It is necessary to ask what loss the appellant suffered because of the diminution of that capacity and that invites attention to what *would* have happened but for the negligent infliction of injury (as best a court can predict that future course of events). The latter question (what *would* have happened but for the negligent infliction of harm) was said to be answered, in this case, by identifying that it was highly probable that the partnership at will would have been maintained but for the occurrence of the accident. But it is necessary to consider the content and consequences of that conclusion with some care.

Impairment causing loss
18. The financial loss occasioned by impairment of earning capacity is the loss of what (if there had been no accident) the injured plaintiff *would* (as opposed to could) have expected to have had under his or her control and at his or her disposal by exercising that capacity. We refer to "control" and "disposal" because what the plaintiff has lost are the financial rewards from work that are rewards the plaintiff would have been able to direct to whatever purpose or destination he or she chose.

19. The finding in this case about probable continuance of the partnership reveals how the appellant would, in all probability, have ordered his financial affairs – by an arrangement terminable at will under which, in return for services of negligible value, he would have shared with this wife 50 per cent of the net proceeds of his endeavours. But the finding about probable continuance of the partnership, standing alone, does not reveal how much the appellant would have had under his control and at his disposal.

20. There are two critical elements. First, the whole of the income of the partnership came from the efforts of the appellant and the exploitation of *his* earning capacity. As a matter of practical reality, his wife's contribution to the income was negligible. Secondly, the partnership was a partnership at will. The appellant would very probably have chosen to maintain those arrangements but that was *his* choice. If he chose to make some other arrangement concerning the fruits of his labour, effect would be given to that choice, whatever view his wife may have held. What the appellant would have had under his control and at his disposal but for the accident was, therefore, the whole of the fruits of his skill and labour. And it is, then, the whole of those fruits that he has lost. In this regard, the case is no different from the injured plaintiff who would probably have devoted some or all of the income earned in the future to charity (see, eg, *Turenne v Chung* (1962) 36 DLR (2d) 197). ...

[148] The importance of the facts in each case
23. Deciding what value is to be ascribed to the loss of future earning capacity of an injured plaintiff requires close attention to the facts of each case. The task is not one to be undertaken by seeking to classify cases as concerning "sole traders" or "partnerships" or "wage-earners" or "trading trusts", and then attempting to deduce some rule of general application to all cases falling within the classification thus of general application to all cases falling within the classification thus devised. Rather the inquiry is about what *could* the plaintiff have done in the workforce but for the accident and what sum of money *would* the plaintiff have had at his or her disposal. Only when those inquiries are pursued can a judgement be made about what capital sum to allow as damages for the impairment of the plaintiff's earning capacity. In doing so, regard must be had, of course, to all those contingencies of life that might reasonably be expected to affect the course of events in the future.

Adjustment for taxation consequences?
24. One other point, mentioned in the course of argument, but not falling for decision in this case, should be noted. Should any account be taken of the taxation consequences of income-splitting arrangements like those the appellant had made?

25. The assessment of damages for loss of future economic capacity involves questions of judgement and estimation. Being an attempt to predict what would have happened, the process can never be exact. The fact that calculations are made by multiplying present values of net income by the expected duration of remaining working life should not obscure that the process is necessarily inexact. Even so, the assessment of lost earning capacity requires some care in identifying (as best one can) what net income the plaintiff would have had at his or her disposal. That may require some consideration of the taxation consequences of different arrangements. ...

[Callinan J delivered a separate judgment in agreement.]

Appeal allowed

2. FATAL ACCIDENTS

Nguyen v Nguyen
(1990) 169 CLR 245
High Court of Australia

Damages in a fatal accident claim may include the value of the domestic services provided by the deceased even though the surviving spouse or other family members bringing the claim do not intend to replace those lost services with paid outside assistance.

DAWSON, TOOHEY and McHUGH JJ. **[258]** This action was brought under the Queensland equivalent of *Lord Campbell's Act*, namely, ss 12 to 15C of the *Common Law Practice Act 1867* (Q). The plaintiffs claimed damages arising from the death of Nu Thi Nguyen. The deceased died as a result of injuries received when a motor car, driven by the defendant, in which she was a passenger, **[259]** left the road and collided with a power pole. The plaintiffs were the husband of the deceased and their two children, born 20 May 1976 and 8 September 1980 respectively. Negligence was admitted and the action proceeded as an assessment of damages before a Master of the Supreme Court. Damages were awarded in the sum of $179,573 of which the sums of $28,000 and $34,000 were apportioned to the two children, the second and third plaintiffs, respectively. The total sum was arrived at as an assessment of the value of the housekeeping services lost to the family as a result of the death of the deceased, to cover a period ending upon the younger child attaining the age of sixteen years.

In fact the husband has not engaged anyone to perform housekeeping services for himself and the two children, nor does he intend to. Apart from a period when a relative helped out temporarily, the husband has himself performed the functions which had previously been performed by his wife. The family, who are of Vietnamese origin, arrived in Australia in November 1980. The wife was killed in July 1981. The husband had obtained work as a labourer at a brickworks for a short time but, apart from that, has not worked since his arrival in Australia. The wife never worked. The family has depended on unemployment benefits and, after the death of the wife, a supporting parent's benefit.

The defendant appealed against the award of damages to the Full Court. The point taken was that, save for a small amount of approximately $6,000, the plaintiffs were not entitled to any recompense for the loss of the wife's housekeeping services because those services have been and will be performed by the husband at no cost. This point was upheld by a majority in the Full Court and the damages were reduced to the sum of $6,079, apportioned as to $1,079 and $2,000 to the second and third plaintiffs respectively.

The majority applied the previous decisions of the Full Court in *Seymour v British Paints (Australia) Pty Ltd* [1967] Qd R 227, and in *Wiliams v Fleming* Unreported; 23 February 1979. In *Seymour*, a husband's claim under the *Common Law Practice Act* for damages for the loss of his wife's domestic services was rejected because the husband did not, and did not intend to, replace his wife by employing a housekeeper. It was held (Wanstall and Douglas JJ, Gibbs J dissenting) that: "... there being no prospect of the appellant's incurring expense in employing a housekeeper, it is impossible to quantify as 'a hard matter of pounds, shillings, and pence' the value to him of future domestic services which his wife may have performed if she had **[260]** survived" ([1967] Qd R, at p 227, per Wanstall J). In so holding, the majority appear to have thought that they were doing no more than applying the well-established principle that under *Lord Campbell's Act* damages are confined to compensation for the loss of material benefits, or the reasonable prospect of such benefits: *Baker v Dalgleish Steam Shipping Co* [1921] 3 KB 481 at p 485; *Horton v Byrne* (1956) 30 ALJ 583, at p 585. Indeed, the words quoted by Wanstall J are those used by Lord Wright in *Davies v Powell Duffryn Associated Collieries Ltd* [1942] AC 601, at p 617, where, in describing a claim by a widow in respect of the death of her wage-earner husband, he said:

> There is no question here of what may be called sentimental damage, bereavement or pain and suffering. It is a hard matter of pounds, shillings and pence, subject to the element of reasonable future probabilities.

But as Gibbs J pointed out in dissent, domestic services have a pecuniary value which is capable of assessment and deprivation of those services "is just as much a pecuniary loss as the deprivation of income or of contributions of food and clothing" ([1967] Qd R at p 230). He went on to make it clear that the fact that a husband does not intend to replace the services "does not mean that they had no value. It merely shows that he is prepared to use his own time and labour instead of expending money in replacing the services" ([1967] Qd R at p 230). ...

[261] In *Griffiths v Kerkemeyer* (1977) 139 CLR 161, it was held that the plaintiff, who was rendered a quadriplegic as the result of the negligence of the defendant, was entitled to recover by way of damages a sum representing the value of nursing and other services gratuitously provided for him in the past and to be provided in the future by his fiancee and members of his family. In reaching its conclusion, the Court followed the decision of the Court of Appeal in *Donnelly v Joyce* [1974] QB 454, and viewed the damages in question as damages for one component of the plaintiff's loss occasioned by his physical disability. The disability gave rise to the need for nursing and other care. The need was met by the services gratuitously provided. The value or cost of those services was, in the circumstances, an **[262]** appropriate means of quantifying that aspect of the plaintiff's loss which was represented by the need. As the need represented the loss, the value of the services required to fulfil that need served as a means of assessing the loss. The fact that there were persons, prompted by motives of concern for the plaintiff, who were prepared to provide the services gratuitously was, it was held, not something which should diminish the damages to the advantage of the defendant. It was only right in the circumstances that the plaintiff should benefit rather than the wrongdoer whose negligence was the cause of the plaintiff's loss.

This approach was a divergence from the view previously taken that expenses in an action for damages for personal injuries could only be recovered where there was, or would be, a legal obligation to pay them. ...

The claim in *Griffiths v Kerkemeyer* was, as we have said, a claim for damages for personal injuries. It was of a different nature from a claim under *Lord Campbell's Act*, which is a claim for the loss of a material benefit. The plaintiff's loss in *Griffiths v Kerkemeyer* was caused by his physical disability. It was in accordance with accepted principle to assess part of that loss by reference to the cost of the services which were required to satisfy the need to which the disability gave rise. What was novel about the decision was the application of that principle even though the plaintiff had not borne and would not bear the cost of the services. The novelty was not in valuing the necessary services, both retrospectively and prospectively; there was nothing new in that. The novelty lay in giving the plaintiff the cost of those services even **[263]** though he had not paid, and would not pay, for them, in order that he, and not the defendant, should reap the benefit.

By way of contrast, a claim for damages under *Lord Campbell's Act* is a claim for recompense for some tangible advantage which has been lost by reason of the death of the deceased. ... In this type of claim the loss can be identified directly and it is unnecessary to point to some need by which it is represented. Commonly the claim is based upon the loss of the financial contribution made by the deceased to the household and is referred to as a claim for the loss of a breadwinner. But the deceased may have made a contribution in services rather than money in which case damages are recoverable for their loss, whether or not they are, or are to be, replaced, provided that a pecuniary value can be placed upon them. And as Gibbs J pointed out in *Seymour* [1967] Qd R

227, if the services are housekeeping services there is no reason why a pecuniary value should not be placed upon them. Why the majority in *Seymour* should have reached the contrary conclusion merely because the housekeeping services were not to be replaced is far from clear. To deny that the services were a material benefit merely because they were not be replaced was plainly an error and it is the contrary view taken by Gibbs J rather than that of the majority which has prevailed elsewhere in Australia: *Tong v Purdy (No 2)* [1941] VLR 147; *Rowe v Scanlan* [1969] 1 NSWR 43; *Cornish v Watson* [1968] WAR 198; *Naum v Nominal Defendant* [1974] 2 NSWLR 14; *Doody v Federation Insurance Ltd* (1977) 16 SASR 173 at p 175; *Budget Rent-A-Car Pty Ltd v Van Der Kemp* [1984] 3 NSWLR 303; *Swan v Williams (Demolition) Pty Ltd* (1987) 9 NSWLR 172. …

[264] *Griffiths v Kerkemeyer* (1977) 139 CLR 161 has nothing to say about a claim under *Lord Campbell's Act* for damages for the loss of domestic services. As we have said, such a claim is not related to need. A husband claiming for the loss of housekeeping services by reason of the death of his wife may have no need of those services in that he may be able to perform them himself. But if he has suffered the loss he is entitled to recover for it and, as Gibbs J pointed out in *Seymour* [1967] Qd R at p 230, it does not matter whether he intends to use the damages to replace the services or not. …

[265] In evaluating the loss in these circumstances, "[c]ompensation for the loss of a wife's gratuitously rendered domestic services should not be confused with the actual cost to the bereaved husband [of] providing substitute services. This no doubt affords a guide to the amount but the actual expenses of the plaintiff for a limited period are not necessarily its measure": per Sugerman JA in *Rowe v Scanlan* [1969] 1 NSWR 43, at p 45. In practice evidence is often led of the cost of engaging domestic help between the date of death and the hearing of the action: see, for instance, *Budget Rent-A-Car Pty Ltd v Van Der Kemp* [1984] 3 NSWLR 303, at p 306. But the damages to be assessed are those suffered by the plaintiff and cannot always be equated with the cost of such help. The services formerly rendered by a deceased wife may not be capable of being reproduced faithfully by services which are commercially available and the scope and cost of the only services commercially available may be disproportionate in comparison with the scope and value of the services which were actually provided by the deceased wife. In circumstances such as that it will not be reasonable to regard the cost of substitute services as any more than a starting point in assessing a plaintiff's loss. Indeed, in cases where the disproportion is severe, the cost of commercially available services may offer no real guide at all. It must always be borne in mind that the damages to be assessed are those suffered by the plaintiff by reason of the death alone.

Where the services are likely to be replaced as a result of remarriage, the reasonable prospect of that remarriage will serve to reduce the compensation to which a plaintiff will be entitled, not because the plaintiff's need for the services will then be satisfied, but because the plaintiff's loss is thereby directly reduced. The prospect of remarriage has always been regarded in claims under **[266]** *Lord Campbell's Act* as providing a gain to the husband in the form of a revival of the capacity to marry. It is something which he would not have had, if his wife had not died: *Carroll v Purcell* (1961) 107 CLR 73, at p 79. In some families, the children might reasonably have been expected in the course of time to have taken up, to a greater or lesser extent, the household duties previously performed by a parent. In that event, the loss incurred by reason of the death of that parent is the less. Of course, if the children take up the household duties, not in the ordinary course of events, but only because of the death of the parent, that will not reduce the total loss and it is irrelevant that the services do not need to be replaced by someone outside the household.

Although the question must always be "what loss the claimant has in fact sustained by the death" (*Baker v Dalgleish Shipping Co* [1922] 1 KB 361, at p 372), courts have been reluctant to conclude that where someone outside the immediate family voluntarily takes over the care of the household, especially the care of infant children, a deduction should be made from the assessment of damages due to a plaintiff, and reluctant to recognise that the loss suffered by a plaintiff is thereby reduced. …

[267] Whatever be the true basis of the reluctance – and it may be partly the belief that voluntary unsolicited assistance cannot be permanently relied upon – it has been accepted that this form of assistance should not be brought into account in relief of the wrongdoer. But these are all questions of the extent of the loss suffered and are different questions from those raised in

Griffiths v **[268]** *Kerkemeyer* (1977) 139 CLR 161, where the problem was not so much the extent of the loss as its quantification by reference to the need for services to which the loss gave rise in circumstances where the services are provided without cost to the plaintiff.

The Full Court in the present case were unanimously of the view that *Seymour* [1967] Qd R 227 was wrongly decided. They were correct in that view. Nevertheless, the majority applied *Seymour* and *Wiliams v Fleming*, following what was said to be the prevailing practice in Queensland whereby the Full Court regards itself as bound by its own previous decisions. ...

[270] For the reasons which we have given, both *Seymour* [1967] Qd R 227 and *Williams v Fleming* should be overruled. Since it does not appear that the members of the Full Court accepted the assessment of damages made by the Master, apart from the fact that it was made in disregard of those decisions, it is appropriate that this matter should be remitted to the Full Court for reconsideration in accordance with these reasons, upon the basis that *Seymour* and *Williams v Fleming* no longer represent the law in Queensland. The appeal should be allowed and the matter remitted to the Full Court of the Supreme Court for this purpose.

[Brennan and Deane JJ delivered concurring judgments.]

Appeal allowed

3. COMPENSATORY DAMAGES FOR PROPERTY DAMAGE

Parramatta City Council v Lutz
(1988) 12 NSWLR 293
Supreme Court of New South Wales, Court of Appeal

As between the plaintiff and the defendant, considerations of reasonableness may require the defendant to pay compensatory damages amounting to the reasonable cost of reinstatement (rather than replacement) of a dwelling house destroyed as a result of the defendant's negligence.

[The facts were set out in the judgment of Kirby P as follows:

[296] The appeal is from a judgment of Smart J in an action brought in the Supreme Court by the respondent, Hilda Katerina Lutz (Mrs Lutz) against the appellant, Parramatta City Council (the Council) and Jixone Pty Ltd (Jixone). Mrs Lutz is the owner of land at 17 New York Street, Granville. She purchased that land in August 1980. She immediately commenced occupation of a modest weatherboard cottage built on the land. Almost one year later, on 9 August 1981, the cottage and many of Mrs Lutz's possessions were destroyed by fire.

The Council was the local authority for the relevant area under the *Local Government Act 1919* (the Act). As such, it was charged with the responsibility of implementing the provisions of the Act. Jixone was, at all relevant times, the owner of land at 19 New York Street which adjoined Mrs Lutz's property. Mrs Lutz alleged that, as a result of the negligence of Jixone and the Council, a fire had spread to her property causing the damage referred to. Jixone did not appear in the action. Judgment was entered against it. Although informed of the appeal, it did not appear. It may be inferred that it had few, if any, assets. The Council denied the allegations of negligence. It defended the action and, having lost, prosecuted this appeal.

At the trial Mrs Lutz's case against the Council relied on the fact that, at about the time she purchased the property at 17 New York Street, and on a number of occasions thereafter, she had drawn to the Council's attention the danger to her property threatened by the partly burnt, dilapidated remains of a dwelling situated on the property at 19 New York Street. Mrs Lutz claimed that, when drawing the matter to the Council's attention she had made it known to the Council, through its employees, that she was requesting the Council's advice and assistance and that she was relying upon the skill and expertise of the Council. She claimed that the Council had, in response to her approaches, promised her that it had the matter in hand and that it was exercising its statutory powers to ensure that the property at 19 New York Street, would not remain a danger to the plaintiff and her property. She claimed that such information and advice as was given by the Council was wrong, careless and negligent on its part. Furthermore, she claimed that it was because of her reliance upon the Council's advice that she took no further action or steps to rectify the state of affairs and as a result suffered loss, expense and damage as a result of the fire.

Deciding the action in Mrs Lutz's favour, Smart J found that the Council had been negligent in the circumstances in failing either to proceed to enter and demolish the building on Jixone's land within a reasonable time or to inform Mrs Lutz that it was cautious about doing so and that it was likely to take some considerable time. Had it so informed Mrs Lutz, she and certain [297] neighbours and friends of hers would have been alerted to the need to "pursue other courses of action promptly". Smart J held that the Council was liable in damages for negligence to Mrs Lutz. He entered judgment in her favour in the sum of $34,919. The Council has appealed to this Court against his Honour's finding that it owed Mrs Lutz a duty of care which it had breached thus causing her loss. Mrs Lutz has cross-appealed, claiming that the damages awarded by his Honour were inadequate.

The Court of Appeal unanimously dismissed the Council's appeal and by a majority (Kirby P and McHugh JA; Mahoney JA dissenting on this issue) allowed Mrs Lutz's cross-appeal on damages.]

KIRBY P. ... [311] Mrs Lutz by cross-appeal appealed from that part of Smart J's judgment relating to the assessment of the damages to which she was by law entitled. His Honour awarded her the sum of $34,919. This included $5,767 being the value of her possessions which were destroyed in the fire, $13,875, being the value of her cottage at the time it was destroyed and $15,277 being interest calculated on the foregoing as from 9 August 1981 to the date of the judgment.

Counsel for Mrs Lutz submitted that his Honour had erred in holding that she was entitled only to the replacement cost of her cottage rather than the reinstatement costs which was a substantially higher figure.

In determining the cross-appeal, it is important to remember the principle which applies to the award of damages in tort, namely restitutio in integrum. The High Court of Australia in a joint judgment delivered by Gibbs CJ, Mason, Murphy, Wilson and Brennan JJ, explained this principle in *State of South Australia v Johnson* (1982) 42 ALR 161 at 169-170: "... The object is to restore the plaintiff to the position in which he would have been placed if the wrongful act had not been committed." See also *Gates v City Mutual Life Assurance Society Ltd* (1986) 160 CLR 1 at 13. The application of the [312] principle to circumstances such as the present was discussed by this Court in *Evans v Balog; Evans v Progress & Securities Pty Ltd* [1976] 1 NSWLR 36.

Smart J certainly erred in holding that, because of English and Scottish authority to which his Honour referred, it was "not open" to him to take a different approach to the assessment of damages than that favoured in *Moss v Christchurch Rural District Council* [1925] 2 KB 750 at 751 and the majority in *Hutchinson v Davison* 1945 SC 395. It was upon this basis that his Honour refused to allow the cost of rebuilding the house as part of Mrs Lutz's home. ...

Mrs Lutz is entitled to recover the reasonable cost of reinstatement of her house. Taking into account her personal circumstances, her desire to have the home in which she was living reinstated is not unreasonable. It is certainly not excessive or extravagant. It is not an attempt by her to make a profit out of the loss or to secure something more than that which she lost. Such a home for a person such as Mrs Lutz is a necessity of life. Restoring it is the only way in which Mrs Lutz could be reinstated in the position she would have been in had she not suffered loss. Smart J assessed the reasonable costs of reinstatement at $27,750. That sum has not been disputed. ...

McHUGH JA. ... [335] The fundamental rule of the common law is that in an action for damages for tort the court awards: "that sum of money which will put the party who has been injured, or who has suffered, in the same position as he would have been in if he had not sustained the wrong for which he is now getting his compensation or reparation": *Livingstone v Rawyards Coal Co* (1880) 5 App Cas 25 at 39. When the choice is between damages which constitutes the value of the property destroyed or the cost of reinstating and restoring that property, a plaintiff is entitled to the cost of reinstatement only if it is reasonable to have the property reinstated and restored: *Evans v Balog*; *Evans v Progress & Securities Pty Ltd* [1976] 1 NSWLR 36 at 39-40 per Samuels JA.

Smart J held that the reasonable cost of reinstatement was $27,750 which was twice the value of the premises. However, I cannot see anything unreasonable in Mrs Lutz insisting that her home be restored. She wants a home, not a sum of money. A sum equivalent to the value of her home will not give her a home. The Council must pay the cost of reinstating her home. ...

Appeal dismissed. Cross-appeal allowed

4. DAMAGES FOR INTERFERENCE WITH GOODS

Butler v Egg and Egg Pulp Marketing Board
(1966) 114 CLR 185
High Court of Australia

The general principle that an injured party should receive the sum of compensatory damages which will put the injured party in money terms in the same position as if the tort had not been committed applies to an action for conversion.

[The plaintiff Board brought an action against the defendants claiming damages for the conversion of certain eggs, which, by virtue of the *Marketing of Primary Products Act 1958* (Vic), became the property of the Board when they came into existence. The producer was entitled to a proportion of the proceeds of sale after the Board had deducted expenses. The defendants, instead of delivering the relevant eggs to the Board, had sold them to a third party.

This was an appeal from the decision of Little J in the Supreme Court of Victoria that the plaintiff Board was entitled to the full value of the eggs converted.]

TAYLOR and OWEN JJ. ... [190] His Honour's reasons began with the proposition that in an action of conversion the general rule is that the plaintiff is entitled to recover the value of the goods converted. There are, he pointed out, exceptions to that general rule, as where the defendant, as between himself and the plaintiff, has an interest in the thing converted. This exception, he thought, had no application to the present case. The appellants had no interest in the eggs. All that they had were claims for payment which were conditioned upon delivery of the eggs to the Board, a delivery which in fact had not been made. For these reasons his Honour applied what he described as the general rule and held that the Board was entitled to recover the full value of the eggs.

If this be correct, it would mean that the appellants would have to pay to the Board, by way of damages, the amount which the Board would have received had the eggs been delivered to and sold by it. The amount so paid would become part of the Board's funds and as such would be available to meet a proportion of its costs and to provide payments to other producers who were entitled to share in the "pool" but the appellants would not be entitled to receive any such payments since the eggs had not been delivered by them to the Board. It would follow that the Board would be in a better position financially than would have been the case had the appellants complied with the Act since it would have received the [191] full value of the eggs, would have incurred no expense in handling and disposing of them and be under no obligation to make any payment for them. But such a result would not accord with the general principle upon which compensatory damages are assessed, whether in actions of contract or of tort. That principle is that the injured party should receive compensation in a sum which, so far as money can do so, will put him in the same position as he would have been in if the contract had been performed or the tort had not been committed: *Livingstone v Rawyards Coal Co* (1880) 5 App Cas 25 at p 39. And this principle is as much applicable to actions of conversion as it is to the case of other actionable wrongs. In most cases of conversion it is, of course, obvious that its application will result in the injured plaintiff recovering the full value of the property converted since that will usually represent the loss that he has sustained by the defendant's wrongful act. Hence the statement which appears so often in the books that the general rule is that the plaintiff in an action of conversion is entitled to recover the full value of the goods converted, but this statement should not be allowed to obscure the broad principle that damages are awarded by way of compensation. ... The Board's loss must, in our opinion, be determined by considering what sum of money would be required to place it in the same position as it would have been in if the appellants had performed their statutory obligation. Had they done so, the Board would, on the figures agreed upon by the **[192]** parties, have realized £4,000 by selling the eggs and out of that sum would have had to pay the appellants £2,900. Its loss resulting from the appellants' tortious act is therefore £1,100.

For these reasons we would allow the appeal.

MENZIES J. ... Damages should, I think, be assessed not on the basis of the value of the eggs at the time of the conversion but upon the actual loss sustained by the respondent because the appellants converted the respondent's eggs instead of delivering them in accordance with the Act.

There is no hard and fast rule that the value of the goods at the time of a conversion is always the measure of the damages to be assessed for the conversion. Often the application of such a rule would produce an obviously unjust result – for example, if goods converted by a defendant had since been recovered by the plaintiff-owner. The true rule is, I think, that stated by Bramwell B in *Chinery v Viall* (1860) 157 ER 1192, viz that the plaintiff is entitled to recover no more than the real damage he has sustained. Not only is the principle of that case applicable here, but the facts of the case afford an instructive application of the principle. Punishment for non-compliance with the Act is within the realm of the criminal, not the civil, law.

[193] It having been agreed that, if the appeal were to be allowed, the damages to which the respondent is entitled are $1,283.33 as against the appellant company and $916.67 as against the other appellants, I would allow the appeal and direct that damages in those sums should be entered for the plaintiff in the action.

Appeal allowed.
Order of the Supreme Court of Victoria set aside
and judgment entered for the respondent (plaintiff)
as agreed by the parties

5. AGGRAVATED AND EXEMPLARY DAMAGES

Fontin v Katapodis
(1962) 108 CLR 177
High Court of Australia

Although provocation is no defence or ground for the reduction of compensatory damages in an action for assault and battery, provocation may negative or reduce an award of exemplary damages. Where force is used in self defence, the degree of force must be proportionate to the threat to which the defendant is exposed.

McTIERNAN J. **[180]** These appeals arise out of an action for assault and battery. The plaintiff was Katapodis and the defendants were Fontin and his employers, Millars and Sandovers. Katapodis alleged that Fontin assaulted and beat him and that Millars and Sandovers were vicariously liable on the same cause of action. The defendants said in answer to the alleged cause of action that Katapodis first assaulted and beat Fontin and he necessarily assaulted and beat Katapodis in his own self-defence. Millars and Sandovers denied that Fontin committed the alleged assault and battery in the course of carrying out his employment as their servant. Bridge J, who was the trial judge, found that Katapodis first beat and assaulted Fontin and he thereupon assaulted and beat Katapodis, but in so doing Fontin exceeded his right of self-defence. Accordingly, he decided that Fontin was liable for the damage and loss which Katapodis suffered in the affray. The learned judge decided that Fontin did not assault and beat Katapodis in the course of Fontin's employment with Millars and Sandovers and accordingly dismissed the action as against them. The learned judge assessed the damages at £2,850 which Katapodis should recover from Fontin in respect of the personal injury he suffered and the expenses and financial loss he incurred in consequence of the assault and battery. He found that Katapodis provoked Fontin in to the assault and battery he sustained and on that basis mitigated the total damages of £2,850 to the extent of £850. There was, therefore, a verdict and judgment of £2,000 in favour of Katapodis against Fontin.

The appeal by Fontin raises the question whether Bridge J ought to have decided in his favour on the issue of self-defence; and the appeal by Katapodis raises the question whether the decision ought to have been that Millars and Sandovers were vicariously liable. Another question which is raised by Katapodis in his appeal is whether it was an error to mitigate or reduce the total damages assessed.

None of the findings of fact made at the trial is called into question. The facts which the learned judge found are as follows: Katapodis had purchased goods for cash at the store conducted by Millars and Sandovers. Fontin was a servant of this firm and worked in the glass department of the store. His principal duty was to cut glass to sizes suitable for louvres ordered by customers. He did his work at a table behind which the uncut glass was stacked. The tools which he used were a wooden T square and a small cutter operated by hand. When Katapodis purchased the goods Fontin, a fellow Greek, assisted him because Katapodis was not able to [181] converse in English. Katapodis paid cash and took the goods away with him, but the books of the firm contained no record of the payment. A few days afterwards Katapodis was at the store and Fontin pointed him out to the assistant manager as the customer who had not paid his account. This accusation enraged Katapodis who thereupon went home, found the receipt and produced it to the assistant manager at the store. The assistant manager apologized unreservedly to Katapodis and told him that the incident was closed. Katapodis insisted on his bringing the receipt to Fontin. Fontin was working at his table, attending to a customer. Katapodis and the assistant manager stood in front of the table and the receipt was shown to Fontin. The assistant manager apologized to Katapodis and repeated his assurance that the incident was closed. Katapodis called Fontin "a bad man". As the assistant manager turned to go away Katapodis began an altercation with Fontin and made an insulting remark to him. Fontin replied to Katapodis in similar fashion. Katapodis then grabbed the T square by the end without the cross-piece and hit Fontin with it once on the arm and once on a shoulder. Katapodis had raised the T square to hit Fontin again. Fontin, thereupon, picked up an off-cut of louvre glass fifteen inches long and two to three inches wide and threw it at Katapodis' face. Katapodis dropped the T square and raised one of his hands to fend off the missile. It cut the socket of the thumb and severed the ulna nerve. Serious and permanent injury was done to the hand. The assault and battery alleged in the action was that Fontin threw the piece of glass at Katapodis and wounded him with it. It is not contested in this Court that Fontin did so. The justification pleaded in defence is that Katapodis hit Fontin with the T square and was about to hit him again. Katapodis does not here contest the finding that he did this. Bridge J decided that Katapodis' attack on Fontin did not justify his throwing the piece of glass at Katapodis for the purpose of self-defence. It is clear that Fontin had a right to defend himself against being beaten by Katapodis. The question is whether, in the circumstances, it was reasonably necessary for him to throw the piece of glass at Katapodis in order to protect his right of personal safety. The piece of glass which he threw at Katapodis was capable of causing him serious injury. Aimed at the face it is clearly a very dangerous weapon. Apparently, Fontin realized this because he attempted to pitch it so that none of its edges would strike Katapodis. Katapodis had done only trifling harm to Fontin by hitting with the T square. Perhaps, Katapodis may have struck more severe blows if Fontin had not prevented [182] him. But to throw the piece of glass at Katapodis as a means of self-defence was out of all reasonable proportion to the emergency confronting Fontin. No other weapon was available to Fontin but instead of throwing the piece of glass at Katapodis he could easily have moved away from him and thus have avoided further blows from the T square. Fontin had no need to stand his ground and it was not reasonably necessary for him to throw at Katapodis the cruel and cutting missile which he did throw. It was somewhat of the nature of a deadly weapon. The conclusion of Bridge J that, in the circumstances, it was not reasonably necessary for Fontin to use it in self-defence, is right. The next question is whether Millars and Sandovers were responsible for the assault and battery committed by Fontin on Katapodis by throwing the piece of glass at him, Fontin being the servant of Millars and Sandovers. They were liable only if this trespass was committed by Fontin in the course of his service. The trespass was an unlawful act but Millars and Sandovers were nevertheless responsible if it was Fontin's mode of performing a duty which fell within the scope of his employment. The fight between Fontin and Katapodis was a sequel to the incident about the account. That incident generated the anger in Katapodis which lead to his abusing Fontin. However, the incident was then closed and what ensued cannot be held to be other than a personal quarrel. The need for Fontin to attack Katapodis by throwing the piece of glass at him did not arise from his employment. Katapodis did not, in the capacity of a customer, beat Fontin nor did Fontin, in the capacity of a servant, hit back. The fight occurred on the premises of Fontin's employers, but by throwing the piece of glass, at Katapodis he was not, in fact, serving his employers' interest or affecting to do so. In my opinion, it is not a reasonable conclusion from the evidence that Fontin was acting in the course of his employment while engaged in this altercation and affray between himself and Katapodis. The decision of Bridge J on the question of vicarious liability is right.

Katapodis, in his appeal, calls into question the deduction referable to provocation which the learned trial judge made from the total damages he assessed for damage and loss suffered by Katapodis as a result of his being hit by the piece of glass. The part of the judgment relevant to this question is: "Doing the best I can with this somewhat nebulous evidence as to the plaintiff's loss of earnings in consequence of his injury, I find that a fair figure to cover both past loss and possible future loss would be £1,500. I thus find the plaintiff's full pecuniary loss for expenses as well as past and future lost earnings to be £1,600. In respect of his general pain [183] and suffering and loss of amenities and enjoyment of life I find that a fair figure for compensatory damages would be a further £1,250. Normally this would result in a total verdict for the plaintiff against Fontin of £2,850. However, as I consider that Fontin, in the commission of his assault, was substantially provoked by the plaintiff, this sum should be mitigated, in my view, to £2,000". It is contended for Katapodis that it is an error to mitigate or diminish the damages as assessed even if it is accepted that Katapodis provoked Fontin, thus causing him to resort to violence. Assault and battery is actionable *per se* and damages are "at large", so far as the trespass itself is concerned. Such damages may be nominal or substantial, according to the circumstances in which the plaintiff's right is infringed. A defendant's conduct may be such that it is right to require him to pay exemplary or punitive damages to the plaintiff. In the present case exemplary or punitive damages were not awarded. Having regard to the conduct of Katapodis, he had no ground for claiming damages of that kind. The damages awarded are actual and compensatory damages, nothing else. It may be that for the mere trespass itself Katapodis could have been awarded nominal damages. The damages awarded are solely for personal injury and consequent economic loss. They may be called compensatory or actual damages to distinguish them from exemplary, punitive or aggravated damages. The question is whether it was right to mitigate the damages computed by the trial judge. He mitigated or reduced them by £850 for the reason that Katapodis provoked the assault that resulted in the injury and loss in respect of which he claimed damages of a compensatory character. There are conflicting views on the question whether in the case of assault and battery mitigation or reduction of damages on account of provocation by the plaintiff applies only to exemplary or punitive damages, not to compensatory or actual damages. ... [184] It would seem that the principle on which damages of all kinds are reduced or mitigated because of provocation in a case of assault and battery is that the plaintiff brought the trespass on himself. It is, as it were, contribution charged to him on account of his own fault. On the other hand, it is said that the law provides a remedy for any damage or loss occasioned by a wrongful act and, therefore, if provocation brings the defendant to do any act in excess of lawful self-defence which results in personal injury and economic loss to the plaintiff, he is entitled to just and adequate damages, and to mitigate or reduce actual or compensatory damages is to deprive the plaintiff *pro tanto* of a legal right. This would seem to place actual or compensatory damages for assault and battery on the same footing as damages for personal injury caused by negligence. I am inclined to the view that there ought to be no reduction of actual or compensatory damages for provocation in the case of assault and battery. It seems to me to be correct in principle to mitigate or reduce damages of the nature of exemplary damages if the plaintiff has provoked the assault and battery complained of. It follows that the judgment of the Supreme Court of the Northern Territory should be varied by substituting the sum of £2,850 for the sum of £2,000. I agree in the order proposed in the case of each appeal.

OWEN J. [His Honour declined to disturb the trial judge's rejection of Fontin's plea of self-defence and continued:]

[186] On the question of the defendant company's liability, his Honour [the trial judge] was of opinion that, in throwing the piece of glass to defend himself against the plaintiff' attack, Fontin was not doing something incidental to the performance of his duties and I think that finding was correct. It is true that the altercation between the plaintiff and Fontin had its origin in the fact that the latter had earlier reported to Miles [the assistant manager of the store] that the plaintiff had not paid for the goods which he had bought some days before, but the inference is clear that what precipitated the attack with the measuring stick was the insulting remark made to the plaintiff by Fontin and that his response to the attack that followed was not an act done in furtherance or supposed furtherance of his employers' interests.

There remains a question relating to damages. The learned trial judge found that, as a result of his injuries, the plaintiff had incurred expense for medical and hospital treatment amounting to £100. He assessed the damages for earnings lost up to the date of the trial and for reduced earning capacity in the future at £1,600 and went on to say "in respect of his general pain and suffering and loss of amenities and enjoyment of life I find that a fair figure for compensatory damages would be a further £1,250". This, as his Honour said, would normally result in a verdict against Fontin for £2,850. He was of opinion, however, that since Fontin's action in throwing the glass had been provoked by the plaintiff, that fact might be taken into account in mitigation of damages. Accordingly he reduced the amount which he otherwise would have awarded [187] to £2,000. In this respect, I think his Honour fell into error. In an action for assault, as in many other cases of tort, the conduct and motives of the parties may be taken into account either to aggravate or mitigate damages. In a proper case the damages recoverable are not limited to compensation for the loss sustained but may include exemplary or punitive damages as, for example, where the defendant has acted in a high-handed fashion or with malice. But the rule by which the defendant in an action in which exemplary damages are recoverable is entitled to show that the plaintiff's own conduct was responsible for the commission of the tortious act and to use this fact to mitigate damages has no application to damages awarded by way of compensation. It operates only to prevent the award of exemplary damages or to reduce the amount of such damages which, but for the provocation, would have been awarded. ...

In my opinion, the appeal by the defendant Fontin should be dismissed and that of the plaintiff should be allowed to the extent of increasing damages awarded to him to £2,850.

[Dixon CJ agreed with Owen J.]

Order of the Supreme Court of the Northern Territory
varied by increasing the amount of damages to £2,850

Henry v Thompson
[1989] 2 Qd R 412
Supreme Court of Queensland, Full Court

Aggravated damages may be awarded as compensation for conduct which causes emotional hurt, insult and humiliation to the plaintiff.

[The plaintiff was awarded damages in the District Court of Queensland against the defendants, three police officers, who had assaulted him while he was in custody. Damages were assessed at $5,000 for his physical injuries, $10,000 aggravated damages and $10,000 exemplary damages. The defendants appealed.]

WILLIAMS J. … **[413]** The learned trial judge found that the respondent, an Aboriginal, had attended a dance with his de facto wife on that Friday night at the Normanton Hall and was "probably under the influence of liquor to some extent when he was arrested for using obscene language" by the appellants Thompson and Doolan. The respondent was forcibly removed from the dance hall and taken to the watchhouse in a police Toyota motor vehicle. There was then a finding that the respondent was "pulled from the vehicle onto the ground by Thompson". The learned trial judge made findings with respect to the events which followed in these terms:

> The plaintiff was pushed into the watchhouse by Thompson and Doolan where he was punched by both of them and knocked down. While the plaintiff was on the floor Thompson and Doolan kicked him around the head and shoulders. The plaintiff covered his head and called out that he had had enough.
>
> During the assault, the plaintiff managed to get to his feet and make a break for the door of the watchhouse, but he was pushed back by Smith who had been standing at the doorway while the others were punching and kicking the plaintiff. Smith pushed the plaintiff down and back against the wire mesh in the communal area in front of the watchhouse.
>
> While the plaintiff was on the floor and against the mesh, Thompson took hold of the mesh to steady himself and jumped up and down on the head and shoulder area of the plaintiff. After Thompson stopped jumping on the plaintiff, he walked away. Not long after he had gone, Doolan went up to the plaintiff, stood over him and urinated on his stomach.

Counsel for the respondent submitted, obviously correctly, that such findings in the light of the evidence meant that the appellant Smith, the officer in charge of the police station, stood by whilst the other two were viciously assaulting the respondent and did nothing to exercise his authority over them. The appellant Smith had the power to prevent what was happening, but did not exercise that power, even to prevent (or stop) the appellant Doolan urinating on the respondent. Further, both Smith and Doolan stood nearby watching during the most violent part of the incident, that is when Thompson was jumping up and down on the respondent.

[After setting out the trial judge's findings that the defendants had acted in conscious and contumelious disregard for the plaintiff's rights and in a high handed fashion with malice, and considering the plaintiff's physical injuries, he continued:]

[415] It is in those circumstances that the assessments under each of the three heads were challenged as being manifestly excessive. Authorities establish that it was appropriate to award damages under each of the heads: Pain and suffering, aggravated damages, and exemplary damages (*Loudon v Ryder* [1953] 2 QB 202; *XL Petroleum (NSW) Pty Ltd v Caltex Oil (Australia) Pty Ltd* (1985) 155 CLR 448 and *Lamb v Cotogno* (1987) 164 CLR 1) …

Lamb clearly confirms, if authority be necessary, the compensatory nature of aggravated damages. The court there said at 8:

> Aggravated damages, in contrast to exemplary damages, are compensatory in nature, being awarded for injury to the plaintiff's feelings caused by insult, humiliation and the like. Exemplary damages, on the other hand, go beyond compensation and are awarded "as a punishment to the guilty, to deter from any such proceedings for the future, and as proof of the detestation of the jury to the action itself".

Whilst, as the court there noted, it may on occasion be difficult to differentiate between aggravated and exemplary damages, problems will be avoided if the differentiating factors referred to are kept in mind at the time of assessment. This was, in my view, a classic case for a high award of aggravated damages. Urinating on the respondent caused him no actual physical harm but, as was intended by the perpetrators, it caused him great emotional hurt, insult, and humiliation. The learned trial judge in his reasons referred to the fact that the respondent broke down and cried when relating that particular incident to the doctor the following day. He could also have referred to the unchallenged evidence with respect to the matter from the respondent and his de facto wife. The respondent was asked how the fact that he had been urinated upon affected him and he replied: "It upset me a lot. You can't say it in words." His de facto wife spoke of him being "close to tears" when he was telling her about that particular incident. She threw the clothes in the rubbish bin without washing them because they were "smelly". In any circumstances the act of urination in the course of an assault would, in my humble view, call for an award of aggravated damages. But when the guilty party is a police **[416]** officer, a person in authority, and the act is performed in the presence of other senior ranking police officers, the incident cries out for an even higher award. And finally, when one adds into the case the racial overtones present here, then a jury assessment of the appropriate award for aggravated damages is largely unrestrained. It hardly lies in the mouths of the appellants to complain that the award is too high. The conduct, as his Honour found, was "in conscious and contumelious disregard for the plaintiff's rights" and his findings clearly indicate that the inhuman conduct of these police officers was calculated to cause the greatest possible insult and humiliation to the respondent.

The learned trial judge found that the two most senior police officers stood by and took no steps to prevent or stop their junior colleague, Doolan, from urinating on the respondent. Further, Thompson facilitated the commission of that act by Doolan in that by kicking and jumping on the respondent he rendered him immobile. Thus even the act of urination was part of the "joint enterprise" as found by the judge which involved the "infliction of pain and humiliation" on the respondent. It follows that all three were equally responsible for those factors calling for a high award of aggravated damages and I can see no justification at all for interfering with an award of $10,000 under that head.

[His Honour then considered the award of damages for physical injuries, and the award of exemplary damages, applying the High Court's decisions in *XL Petroleum (NSW) Pty Ltd v Caltex Oil (Australia) Pty Ltd* and *Lamb v Cotogno*, above.]

[417] Whether looked at under the specific headings, or whether looked at as a global sum, I am of the view that the award of the learned trial judge was not manifestly excessive and was not such that a reasonable jury, applying proper principles, could not have awarded.

It follows that the appeal should be dismissed with costs.

[Connolly and McPherson JJ concurred.]

Appeal dismissed

Myer Stores Ltd v Soo
[1991] 2 VR 597
Supreme Court of Victoria, Appeal Division

A substantial award of aggravated damages for false imprisonment is justified where, after the tort was committed, the defendant persists with the assertion that he or she was justified in detaining the plaintiff.

[A department store's security camera recorded a person putting some crystal ware into his bag and pocket. While viewing the film with one Evans, the store's security officer, another employee from the store remarked that the person shown on the video film looked like a regular customer. A few days later, while the plaintiff (respondent) was shopping in the hi-fi department, Evans told the second and third defendants, police officers who happened to be in the store, that the plaintiff was the person shown in the film. The three men approached the plaintiff, explained that he matched the description of the person on the video and insisted that he accompany them to the store's security office. He was interviewed for about an hour. Evans later supplied the plaintiff's details to the fourth defendant, another police officer, who obtained a search warrant to conduct a search of the plaintiff's house, which revealed nothing. At all times, the plaintiff denied that he was the person who had stolen the crystal ware.

The plaintiff sued the first defendant, the owner of the department store, and the second to sixth defendants, all police officers, for, inter alia, false imprisonment, claiming damages for personal injury in the form of a severe adverse emotional reaction, and including aggravated damages. The trial judge found that the second and third defendants had falsely imprisoned the plaintiff in the store and that the first defendant's security officer, for whom it was vicariously liable, had procured this false imprisonment. The trial judge then found that no personal injury had been proved by the plaintiff, and awarded him nominal damages of $5000 for the false imprisonment. Although his Honour found that the false imprisonment was a significant insult to the plaintiff, he declined to award aggravated damages because the conduct of the defendants was not premeditated, malicious or deserving of sanction or punishment.

The defendants appealed and the plaintiff cross-appealed. The judgment of Murphy J is extracted on the issue of aggravated damages.]

MURPHY J. ... **[600]** Having viewed the video several times myself, I do not believe that it would have been reasonably open for anyone to identify the respondent as the person on the video to be seen handling the merchandise. It would seem implicit in the course of events that this latter view was accepted to be the fact, for no charge was ever laid against the respondent and Senior Constable Barrett said that the plaintiff could not be identified.

My own view is that the obtaining of a search warrant and the searching of the respondent's premises after this video had been seen by the police and after the respondent had been questioned and denied that it was he who was shown on it, was an undue assumption of power which seriously infringed the respondent's right to privacy in his home. It was however only carried into effect following the administrative decision of the magistrate, to whom the application for the issue of the warrant was made.

The circumstances of the earlier occasion, when Evans directed the second and third appellants to the respondent, whilst he was purchasing goods in the hi-fi department ... support the view that the first named appellant by its servants was directly responsible for the imprisonment.

The second and third appellants at this time knew nothing of the matter, save what Evans had told them a few minutes earlier. They not seen the video. It is not to be countenanced that they made an independent judgment. Their imprisonment of the respondent, with Evans' active assistance, is in my opinion clear. The learned trial Judge was not only entitled to form the view that they had, on approaching the respondent, made up their mind that he should not exercise his liberty, but, in my opinion, this was the only reasonable view open on the facts. They formed this intention on the basis of Evans' assessment of the material. This was not a case of asking the police to interview a person found in possession of goods in the store without a receipt, to ask him to explain how he came by them. It was a case of acting imprudently on the spurious authority of an incautious remark of a shop assistant, which must be seen to have been **[601]** unwarranted. Neither he nor Evans was called to give evidence at the trial, although Evans was identified during the hearing, sitting in the "well of the court".

Yet Evans told the first and second respondents [sic second and third appellants] that the thief seen on the video was in the hi-fi department.

In my opinion, the resultant detaining of the respondent from the moment he was approached until he was allowed to leave the Myer security room to which he was escorted, was a serious encroachment on his liberty, which Evans actively promoted and in which he participated, and for which the first respondent Myer Stores Limited is vicariously liable.

The respondent, who must be seen as an innocent victim of this rash behaviour, was naturally apprehensive. His request to be interviewed in the hi-fi department itself was dismissed by the police, and in my opinion having reviewed the whole of the facts, he was justified in concluding, as was the fact, that if he did not submit to do what was asked of him, he would have been compelled by force to do so. There was in my opinion no legal justification shown for this conduct (*Watson v Marshall* (1971) 124 CLR 621, 626; *Halsbury's Laws of England*, 4th ed vol 45 paras 1326, 1327).

Myer persisted in its assertion, presumably through Evans, that the respondent was the likely thief to be seen on the video, and it later left a message for Constable Barrett at Russell Street [police station] giving the respondent Soo's name and address.

Barrett, the fourth appellant, gave evidence that he then "decided to take a warrant to search for items in Mr Soo's house" (p 448).

I find this in the circumstances to have been a little alarming, having regard to the material available to Evans and to the police at that stage.

However, the validity of the warrant itself was not an issue argued at the trial. ...

The only relevance that the initiation of the warrant has on this appeal is to show that Myer continued, even after the false imprisonment of the respondent and his denial of involvement, to represent him as the thief, and to provide information to the police which led to the search warrant and its execution.

Whether it is relevant to damages to consider these facts may be a matter of debate.

The old cases seem to support the proposition that such conduct is relevant on the damages issue. "A man is taken up on a false charge of felony; surely he has a right to give evidence to show that it was not one lightly made and soon abandoned, but that it was seriously made, and persevered in to the last moment" (*Warwick v Foulkes* (1844) 12 M&W 507 Parke B). It is to be noted that even at trial, this slur was persisted in by counsel for Myer.

The learned Baron continued:

As to the damages being excessive, these are cases in which large damages are in general given, and properly so; if people choose to settle private disputes by giving others into custody; they must take the consequences (at 509 above ref).

[602] Again in *Walter v Alltools Ltd* [1944] WN 214 Lawrence LJ said after referring to *Warwick v Foulkes* (above):

That case laid down that any evidence in a case of false imprisonment which showed or tended to show that the defendant was persevering in the charge which he originally made might be given for the purpose of aggravating the damages, just in the same way as the defendant would be entitled to give any evidence which tended to show that he had withdrawn or had apologized for the charge on which the false imprisonment proceeded. False imprisonment affected not merely a man's liberty but his reputation, and damage to the latter continued until it was caused to cease by an avowal that the imprisonment was false.

It would appear that aggravated damages as distinct from exemplary damages (*Lamb v Cotogno* (1987) 164 CLR 1 at 8) may be invoked as a vindication of the reputation of the plaintiff in an action for false imprisonment, to make clear that there was no stain of any kind left on the character of the plaintiff. *Hook v Cunard Steamship Co Ltd* [1953] 1 WLR 682 at 686 per Slade J. They are compensatory damages and not punitive: *Dingle v Associated Newspapers Ltd* [1964] AC 371 at 419.

In *Dunphy v Moore* (1865) 13 LT 179 the Court of Queen's Bench held that actions taken consequent upon a false imprisonment, taken as a matter of practice and not in excess, are part of the transaction, and need not be specially pleaded. Thus the searching and stripping of the plaintiff in that case were relevant to aggravate the damages to be awarded.

Although I accept that Myer could not, on the evidence led in this case, be held responsible for the further indignities to which the respondent was subjected during the execution of the search warrant, the injury to the plaintiff's dignity and to his feelings consequent upon the initial false imprisonment may, I think, properly be seen to have been magnified by Myer's persistence, even up to trial, in harbouring and publicizing its continuous suspicions – perhaps its belief – that the respondent was the thief.

Evans told Constables Sterling and Mann [the second and third defendants] that "the person had been identified in the video and the same person was in the hi-fi section" (p 673). Evans was not called as a witness by Myer, though present in Court. Nor was the hi-fi salesman whom Barrett said had asserted that he recognized the person in the video called to give evidence and no explanation for not calling him was advanced. Barrett himself gave evidence at the trial. He was asked:

Q. And the film does not clearly identify anybody, does it? A. No, no it doesn't identify anyone. There was [*sic*] two members from the audio-visual section around with Jeff Evans and myself and Constable Bolton and I don't know who it was but one of them – it wasn't Jeff Evans but one of the two members said 'That looks like a regular customer of ours, his name is Sun or similar'.

It will be seen that the hi-fi man is alleged to have said "That *looks like* a regular customer", and not "That is a regular customer". It may be no wonder that he was not called to give evidence supportive of his damaging "throw away" line.

[603] This was the totality of the evidence to suggest that the respondent was the person in the video. It was simply that he was a person of Asian extraction, and it might have been a person of Asian extraction to be seen on the video.

Yet thereafter, Evans, so far as can be gathered from the evidence, promoted the respondent as the thief, even after his false imprisonment and questioning, and despite his denials – supplying his name and address to Barrett, which immediately prompted the police search of the respondent's home. Then, at trial, counsel for Myer did not desist from insinuating that the respondent could only have had certain information concerning the size of the crystal bowl, if he was in fact the thief who took it. He also cross-examined Dr Gibney concerning the respondent's reaction to his imprisonment at Myer, suggesting "his reaction is not really indicative of innocence, is it?"

The damages in an action for false imprisonment are generally awarded not for a pecuniary loss but for a loss of dignity, mental suffering, disgrace and humiliation. Any deleterious effect on the plaintiff's health will also be compensated.

As to the injury to dignity, mental suffering and the like, whilst the intervention of a judicial officer will usually make any consequent imprisonment too remote from the initial false imprisonment, yet damages for an initial false imprisonment may be aggravated by persistence in the assertion of facts which continue the slur on the plaintiff's reputation, damaged by the false imprisonment. Lawrence LJ in *Walter v Alltools* (above) stated that this continued "up to the moment when damages are assessed" (1944) 61 TLR 39, at 40).

By persevering in a charge which has brought about a false imprisonment, the damages are aggravated. See also *Warwick v Foulkes* (1844) 12 M & W 507.

The principle invoked appears to be analogous to that applicable in defamation claims. Persistence in the accusation is evidence of malice, not necessarily in the sense of spite or ill-will, though such would constitute malice, but rather in the enlarged sense of the jurist, as evidencing unreasoning prejudice or a motivation of which the law does not approve (cf *Mitchell v Jenkins* (1833) 5 B & Ad 588).

Particularly would this be so, when the defendant gave no evidence at the trial (*Simpson v Robinson* (1848) 12 QB 511 at 514). There Lord Denman CJ said:

The defendant's conduct in putting a justification on the record which he does not attempt to prove, and will not abandon, may be taken into consideration as proving malice and aggravating the injury and, if the defendant's conduct in that respect may at all affect the verdict, every other part of his conduct showing the same disposition may equally be laid before the jury; refusing to make reparation for unjustifiable slander may have that effect and the malice proved to exist at the time of the trial but connected with the subject matter of it, may well be believed to have existed at the time of speaking the words.

So also in my opinion in a case of false imprisonment, "the estimate of damages may be coloured, so to speak, by disapproval of the defendant's conduct (and in the opinion of the court legitimately so), though it be not a case for vindictive or exemplary damages in the proper sense". *Pollock on Torts* (15th ed) p 142.

[604] The present case is, in my opinion, just such a case.

In my opinion, for the reasons above stated, the persistence by Myer in its expressed suspicion (at the very least) was completely unsupportable in the circumstances. There was no reasonable ground shown for it. (*R v Newman* (1853) 1 E & B 558 at 581 per Erle CJ; cf *Darby v Ouseley* (1856) 25 LJ Ex 227 at 230 per Pollock CB; *Risk Allah Bey v Whitehurst* (1868) 18 LT 615 at 620 per Cockburn CJ).

No apology was forthcoming. No admission of any mistake was ever made by Myer.

The fons et origo of the accusation (the salesman in the hi-fi department) remained unknown, unidentified save as a Myer employee. The failure to call him as a witness, along with Evans, the "store detective" remained unexplained.

In these circumstances, the damages were in my opinion aggravated. (See generally *McGregor on Damages* 15th ed pp 1029-1030, 1057-1058). ...

[605] On the further consideration of the issue of damages the learned trial Judge said:

The plaintiff claims nominal and aggravated damages. It is my opinion that the failure of Evans to provide Sterling and Mann with the vital information, together with the failure by Sterling and Mann to realize that without the vital information they ought not to detain the plaintiff at all, was a matter of carelessness and perhaps negligence. However, it was not premeditated; it was not malicious, it was not deserving of sanction and punishment by this Court.

With so much of his Honour's reasons, I would not wish to disagree.

His Honour continued: I am of the opinion that the plaintiff, who has the burden of proof, has not proved any entitlement to aggravated damages.

However he is entitled to nominal damages for the tort of false imprisonment in a matter that is not 'trivial' and which was a 'serious wrong'. Reflecting as best I can a reasonable assessment of damages for the wrong committed upon the Plaintiff, I award the Plaintiff the sum of $5,000 damages against the first, second and third Defendants.

I am not altogether clear from reading the above remarks whether his Honour made the necessary distinction between aggravated damages, which are compensatory, and exemplary damages which are punitive. Exemplary damages were not pleaded (*County Court Rules 1989* and *Rules of the Supreme Court 1986* Rule 13.07(3)), nor sought, but aggravated damages were sought, and should in my opinion have been awarded, for the reasons above **[606]** set out. The important distinction between the two is clearly drawn in *Lamb v Cotogno* (1987) 164 CLR 1 at 8.

In my opinion, aggravated damages should have been awarded the respondent to compensate him for the added hurt to his feelings and the mental anguish perpetuated by the continued insinuations of suspicion of his guilt right up to verdict, the learned trial Judge then having found him to be "an innocent man" (p 692), as he must be seen to have been at all relevant times. ...

[610] I would dismiss the appeal by the appellants and allow the cross-appeal against the first, second and third appellants.

I would vary the order of the learned trial Judge by substituting the sum of $10,000 for the sum of $5,000, in the award of damages against the first, second and third appellants ... .

[O'Bryan and McDonald JJ delivered concurring judgments.]

Appeal dismissed. Cross-appeal allowed

Gray v Motor Accident Commission

(1998) 196 CLR 1; [1998] HCA 70

High Court of Australia

Exemplary damages are not to be awarded where the tortfeasor has been convicted of a criminal offence and sentenced to "substantial punishment" in respect of the conduct constituting the tort.

GLEESON CJ, McHUGH, GUMMOW and HAYNE JJ. **[3]** 1. The appellant, then aged 16 years, was seriously injured in September 1988 when he was struck by a motor car driven at him deliberately by Darren James Bransden. In March 1991, Bransden was convicted of causing grievous bodily harm with intent to cause grievous bodily harm to the appellant and was sentenced to seven years' imprisonment. The sentencing judge described the attack on the appellant as "brutal and cowardly" and one for which there was "no mitigating factor at all".

2. In 1993, in the District Court of South Australia, the appellant commenced an action against Bransden claiming damages for personal injury. The action was framed (at least principally) as a claim for damages for negligence. In January 1995, pursuant to certain provisions of the *Motor Vehicles Act 1959* (SA) the respondent, the compulsory third party insurer of Bransden, was substituted as defendant in the action. Although the respondent did not admit liability, there seems to have been no real dispute about that issue at **[4]** trial. A certificate of the conviction of Bransden and the sentencing remarks relating to him were tendered by consent of the parties as evidence of the truth of their contents.

3. The trial judge (Judge Pirone) assessed the appellant's damages at $72,206 comprising $15,000 for past economic loss, $30,000 for future economic loss, $18,190 for what is called in s 35A of the *Wrongs Act 1936* (SA) "non-economic loss" and $9,016 for special damages. The trial judge made no award of exemplary damages. He held that if the appellant were otherwise entitled to such an award, the fact that the respondent (the compulsory third party insurer) was defendant to the action, not Bransden, the tortfeasor, was no bar to making an award but, Bransden having already been punished in the criminal court, it was not appropriate to award exemplary damages. He indicated that if he had decided to award exemplary damages he would have assessed those damages at $10,000.

4. The appellant appealed, unsuccessfully, to the Full Court of the Supreme Court of South Australia: *Gray v State Government Insurance Commission* (10 September 1996, unreported). By special leave he now appeals to this Court.

5. Two issues arise. First, should exemplary damages have been awarded? Secondly, was the award of compensatory damages manifestly inadequate? ...

[5] The power to award exemplary damages

8. Exemplary damages have been awarded since at least the 18th century. Windeyer J (*Uren v John Fairfax & Sons Pty Ltd* (1966) 117 CLR 118 at 152) doubted "whether the famous cases concerning Wilkes and the *North Briton* should be regarded as the origin of the idea" conveyed by the expression "exemplary damages". Rather, the matter depended upon "how far you wish to go back and how much certainty you demand in the connecting links". In *Wilkes v Wood* (1763) Lofft 1; 98 ER 489, Lord Chief Justice Pratt said (1763) Lofft 1 at 18-19; 98 ER 489 at 498-499:

> I have formerly delivered it as my opinion on another occasion, and I still continue of the same mind, that a jury have it in their power to give damages for more than the injury received. Damages are designed not only as a satisfaction to the injured person, but likewise as a punishment to the guilty, to deter from any such proceeding for the future, and as a proof of the detestation of the jury to the action itself.

9. This Court has long recognised the power to award such damages. So, in *Herald and Weekly Times Ltd v McGregor* (1928) 41 CLR 254 it was assumed that "penal or vindictive damages" (at 262 per Knox CJ, Gavan Duffy and Starke JJ) or "exemplary damages" (at 266 per Isaacs J) might be awarded in a proper case. Several other examples are given in the judgments in *Uren*. (Taylor J refers ((1966) 117 CLR 118 at 139) to *Willoughby Municipal Council v Halstead* (1916) 22 CLR 352, *Triggell v Pheeney* (1951) 82 CLR 497, *Williams v Hursey* (1959) 103 CLR 30 and *Fontin v Katapodis* (1962) 108 CLR 177. Menzies J refers ((1966) 117 CLR 118 at 145) also to *Whitfeld v De Lauret & Co Ltd* (1920) 29 CLR 71.)

10. Neither party invited us to reconsider *Uren* or the considerable body of authority in this Court that lies behind it and to which effect was given in the later decisions of the Court in *XL Petroleum (NSW) Pty Ltd v Caltex Oil (Australia) Pty Ltd* (1985) 155 CLR 448 and *Lamb v Cotogno* (1987) 164 CLR 1. Notwithstanding, then, what are sometimes seen as the anomalies and difficulties that attend the awarding of exemplary damages, this appeal concerns when such an award may be made, not whether any anomalies are such as to invite some radical change to the law.

[6] 11. It is as well, however, to say something about some of those apparent anomalies. As Windeyer J said in *Uren* (1966) 117 CLR 118 at 149-150:

> Compensation is the dominant remedy if not the purpose of the law of torts today. But fault still has a place in many forms of wrongdoing. And the roots of tort and crime in the law of England are greatly intermingled. Some things that today are seen as anomalies have roots that go deep, too deep for them to be easily uprooted.

12. Exemplary damages are awarded rarely. They recognise and punish fault, but not every finding of fault warrants their award. Something more must be found. Although they are awarded rarely, they have been awarded in very different kinds of case: ranging from abuse of governmental power exemplified by *Wilkes v Wood* and its associated cases (*Huckle v Money* (1763) 2 Wils KB 205; 95 ER 768; *Benson v Frederick* (1766) 3 Burr 1845; 97 ER 1130), through defamation cases of the kind considered in *Uren*, to assault cases such as *Fontin v Katapodis* (1962) 108 CLR 177. And the examples could be multiplied. ...

[7] 14. Because the kinds of case in which exemplary damages might be awarded are so varied, it may be doubted whether a single formula adequately describes the boundaries of the field in which they may properly be awarded. Nevertheless, the phrase adopted by Knox CJ in *Whitfeld v De Lauret & Co Ltd* (1920) 29 CLR 71 at 77 of "conscious wrongdoing in contumelious disregard of another's rights" describes at least the greater part of the relevant field. (See also *XL Petroleum (NSW) Pty Ltd v Caltex Oil (Australia) Pty Ltd* (1985) 155 CLR 448 at 471 per Brennan J.)

15. In considering whether to award exemplary damages, the first, if not the principal, focus of the enquiry is upon the wrongdoer, not upon the party who was wronged. (The reaction of the party who is wronged to high-handed or deliberate conduct may well be a reason for awarding aggravated damages in further compensation for the wrong done. But it is not ordinarily relevant to whether exemplary damages should be allowed.) The party wronged is entitled to whatever compensatory damages the law allows (including, if appropriate, aggravated damages). By hypothesis then, the party wronged will receive just compensation for the wrong that is suffered. If exemplary damages are awarded, they will be paid in addition to compensatory damages and, in that sense, will be a windfall in the hands of the party who was wronged. Nevertheless, they are awarded at the suit of that party and, although awarded to punish the wrongdoer and deter others from like conduct, they are not exacted by the State or paid to it.

16. There is an appearance of tension between using civil proceedings to compensate a party who is wronged and using the same proceedings to punish the wrongdoer. But there is a tension only if it is assumed that "... a sharp cleavage between criminal law on the one hand and the law of torts and contract on the other is a cardinal principle of our legal system": Street, *Principles of the Law of Damages*, (1962) at 34. See also *McGregor on Damages*, 16th ed (1997), par 430. As Windeyer J points out in *Uren*, the "roots of tort and crime" are "greatly intermingled": (1966) 117 CLR 118 at 149. See also *Prosser and Keeton on The Law of Torts*, 5th ed (1984) at 7-9. And it is not only the roots of tort and crime that are intermingled. The increasing frequency with which civil penalty provisions are enacted (see, for example, *Corporations Law*, Pt 9.4B), the provisions [8] made for criminal injuries compensation (see, for example, *Criminal Injuries Compensation Act 1978* (SA)), the provisions now made in some jurisdictions for the judge at a criminal trial to order restitution (see, for example, *Criminal Law (Sentencing) Act 1988* (SA), s 52; *Sentencing Act 1991* (Vic), Pt 4, Div 1) or compensation to a person suffering loss or damage (including pain and suffering) as a result of an offence (see, for example, *Criminal Law (Sentencing) Act 1988* (SA), s 53; *Sentencing Act 1991* (Vic), Pt 4, Div 2) all deny the existence of any "sharp cleavage" between the criminal and the civil law. The tension we have mentioned may therefore be more apparent than real.

17. We do not mention these matters so that we might attempt to resolve any tensions that are thus identified; it is not necessary to do so in this appeal. But they are matters that may well bear upon when exemplary damages may be awarded. ...

[9] An exceptional remedy
20. If, as we have earlier suggested, the remedy is exceptional in the sense that it arises (chiefly, if not exclusively) in cases of conscious wrongdoing in contumelious disregard of the plaintiff's rights, at least two further questions arise: are exemplary damages available where the plaintiff's claim is for damages for negligence rather than some intentional wrong, and is the award of exemplary damages a matter of right or does it depend on the exercise of a discretion informed by some identifiable criteria?

Negligence and exemplary damages
21. Provoked by differing limitation periods for claims for damages for personal injury caused by negligence and other torts, there was a deal of debate in the 1960s about whether trespass to the person could be committed negligently: see, for example, *Kruber v Grzesiak* [1963] VR 621; *Letang v Cooper* [1965] 1 QB 232.

22. We do not think it necessary to revisit that debate. No question arises here of an intentional wrong being committed by inadvertence. For present purposes it is enough to note two things. First, exemplary damages could not properly be awarded in a case of alleged negligence in which there was no conscious wrongdoing by the defendant. Ordinarily, then, questions of exemplary damages

will not arise in most negligence cases be they motor accident or other kinds of case. But there can be cases, framed in negligence, in which the defendant can be shown to have acted consciously in contumelious disregard of the rights of the plaintiff or persons in the position of the plaintiff. Cases of an employer's failure to provide a safe system of work for [10] employees in which it is demonstrated that the employer, well knowing of an extreme danger thus created, persisted in employing the unsafe system might, perhaps, be of that latter kind: see, for example, *Midalco Pty Ltd v Rabenalt* [1989] VR 461; *Coloca v BP Australia Ltd* [1992] 2 VR 441; *Trend Management Ltd v Borg* (1996) 40 NSWLR 500. No doubt other examples can be found.

23. In many jurisdictions in the United States reckless indifference to the rights of others and other culpable conduct short of malicious intent is sufficient for the issue of an award of exemplary damages to be left to a jury: *Smith v Wade* 461 US 30 at 44-48, 52 (1983).

24. Secondly, the present proceeding, although said to have been framed as an action in negligence, appears to have been conducted at trial as if it were a claim in trespass. The allegation made in the appellant's statement of claim, and pursued at trial, was that Bransden drove his vehicle "deliberately towards [the appellant] without regard for the safety of [the appellant]" and such evidence of the events as was given at trial was all directed to showing Bransden deliberately inflicted injury on the appellant. Whatever may be the true characterisation of the pleading, the case was conducted as one of conscious wrongdoing by the tortfeasor.

A "discretionary" remedy?

25. Reported cases usually speak of a "discretion" to award exemplary damages: see, for example, *Lamb v Cotogno* (1987) 164 CLR 1 at 12-13; *Trend Management Ltd v Borg* (1996) 40 NSWLR 500 at 505. Standing alone, such a description, even if followed by the expression "to be exercised judicially" is of little assistance. At best, it invites attention to what are the criteria that are to inform the exercise of that discretion.

26. Because exemplary damages are awarded to punish, it is not surprising that their quantification should be treated as a matter for the discretion of the tribunal assessing damages. And for so many years that was a task for the jury, not the judge. Yet there is little to be found in the cases which would identify the proper instructions to a jury for performing this part of its function. Rather, it seems to be treated in a way not very different from what is called the jury's "constitutional right" to return a verdict of manslaughter notwithstanding proof of the elements of murder. That is, it is treated as if it is a power of the jury that is not to be hedged about by any more precise criterion for its use than the jury's intuitive conclusion that the defendant's conduct was sufficiently reprehensible to warrant punishment. Yet it is clear that there are thought to be limits on the power. ...

[12] 30. What is important is to consider what it is that entitles a plaintiff to an award of exemplary damages or (to put it in the language of power or discretion) permits or requires the making of an award.

31. No doubt the conduct of the wrongdoer is central to that enquiry: for exemplary damages are concerned to punish the wrongdoer and deter others from like conduct, not to compensate the party that was wronged. But there are other factors which must be considered. In this case, attention was directed to the fact that the defendant was a third party insurer, and that the tortfeasor had been convicted and punished for a criminal offence.

Insurance and exemplary damages

32. In *Lamb v Cotogno* the Court rejected the contention that "since the object of exemplary damages is to punish and deter, it is inappropriate that they should be awarded where the wrongdoer is insured under a scheme of compulsory insurance against liability to pay them": (1987) 164 CLR 1 at 9. The Court reached that conclusion for a number of reasons including that the deterrence intended by an award "extends beyond the actual wrongdoer and the exact nature of his wrongdoing" (at 9) and that their award appeases the victim and assuages any urge for revenge felt by the victim (at 9-10). ...

[13] 34. It follows that the fact that the tortfeasor was insured under a compulsory scheme of insurance against any liability for exemplary damages would not bar the award of such damages. ...

Significance of criminal punishment

38. The factor which weighed most heavily with the primary judge in considering whether to award exemplary damages was that Bransden **[14]** had been sentenced to a substantial term of imprisonment for the actions which gave rise to the appellant's claim.

39. The first aim adopted by the Law Commission spoke of reserving the award of exemplary damages for cases of wrongdoing "which would otherwise go unpunished by the law": United Kingdom Law Commission No 247, *Aggravated, Exemplary and Restitutionary Damages*, (1997), par 1.17. What significance should be attached to the fact of earlier criminal punishment?

40. Where, as here, the criminal law has been brought to bear upon the wrongdoer and substantial punishment inflicted, we consider that exemplary damages may not be awarded. We say "may not" because we consider that the infliction of substantial punishment for what is substantially the same conduct as the conduct which is the subject of the civil proceeding is a bar to the award; the decision is not one that is reached as a matter of discretion dependent upon the facts and circumstances in each particular case.

41. There are at least two reasons in principle why that is so.

42. First, the purposes for the awarding of exemplary damages have been wholly met if substantial punishment is exacted by the criminal law. The offender is punished; others are deterred. There is, then, no occasion for their award.

43. Secondly, considerations of double punishment would otherwise arise. In *R v Hoar* (1981) 148 CLR 32 Gibbs CJ, Mason, Aickin and Brennan JJ said that there is "a practice, if not a rule of law, that a person should not be twice punished for what is substantially the same act": at 38 citing *Connolly v Meagher* (1906) 3 CLR 682. (See also *Pearce v The Queen* (1998) 156 ALR 684.) That practice or rule would be breached by an award of exemplary damages in the circumstances described.

44. Because, in this case, substantial punishment was imposed on the tortfeasor for the conduct which was in issue in the civil proceedings, it is not necessary to decide whether the bar arises only where the punishment is "substantial" or how close must be the similarity between the conduct that is the subject of the two proceedings.

45. No doubt references to "substantial punishment" and to the need for "substantial identity" between the conduct that is the subject of the criminal and civil proceedings may lead to difficult questions of fact and degree. What is substantial punishment? Does it matter if the prosecuting authorities and the offender reach some arrangement about what will be charged and, if charged, admitted? Does it matter if for reasons personal to the accused (or for other reasons) only a nominal penalty is imposed in the criminal proceedings? Does it matter if the criminal offence charged is an offence of strict liability?

46. These, too, are not questions that fall for decision in this case. At first sight, however, if criminal charges, alleging the same conduct as **[15]** is alleged in a civil proceeding, have been brought and proved, it would be a most unusual case in which it was open to a civil court to conclude that the outcome of those criminal proceedings did not take sufficient account of the need to punish the offender and deter others from like conduct. There seems to be much to be said in favour of the views reached by a majority of the Court of Appeal of New Zealand in *Daniels v Thompson* that for a civil court to revisit a sentence imposed in a criminal court for the purpose of deciding whether the criminal received his or her just deserts is "contrary to principle" and must "undermine the criminal process": [1998] 3 NZLR 22 at 48 per Richardson P, Gault, Henry and Keith JJ; cf 76-77 per Thomas J.

47. Other considerations may well arise if relevant criminal proceedings ended in the accused's acquittal. But again those questions do not now arise and we do not deal with them: cf *Daniels v Thompson* [1998] 3 NZLR 22 at 50-52 per Richardson P, Gault, Henry and Keith JJ; cf 77 per Thomas J.

48. No doubt difficult questions may also arise where it is possible or probable that criminal proceedings will be brought but those proceedings have not been brought or, if started, have not been finished. The rule in *Smith v Selwyn* [1914] 3 KB 98 no longer applies in some jurisdictions: *Supreme Court Act 1986* (Vic), s 41; *Criminal Code Act 1924* (Tas), s 9; *Halabi v Westpac Banking Corporation* (1989) 17 NSWLR 26; *PT Garuda Indonesia Ltd v Grellman* (1994) 48 FCR 252. Thus it is possible for civil proceedings to be brought and concluded without there being any clear

indication about whether criminal proceedings will follow. It may be doubted, however, that the mere possibility of later criminal prosecution is reason enough not to award exemplary damages in a proper case. More difficult questions might arise if it were clear that such proceedings were probable or had been begun but it is likely that in such circumstances trial of the civil proceedings may, in any event, be delayed until conclusion of the criminal proceedings. But again these questions do not arise here: Bransden had been prosecuted and sentenced.

49. Although we consider the two matters of principle that we have mentioned (satisfaction of the purposes for an award and consideration of double punishment) are sufficient reason for the conclusion we have expressed, we consider that nothing in cases decided in this country or in other common law jurisdictions would suggest the adoption of a contrary view.

50. First, it is a conclusion consistent with such authority as there is on the point in this country: see particularly *Watts v Leitch* [1973] Tas SR 16. (*Lamb v Cotogno* is not to the contrary. Although the defendant in that case was convicted of an offence arising out of the incident the subject of the civil suit (see *Cotogno v Lamb (No 3)* (1986) 5 NSWLR 559 at 573) no point was made of that fact on appeal to this Court.)

51. Secondly, in Canada, courts have declined to award punitive **[16]** damages where the defendant has been imprisoned. ... We note, however, that the Ontario Law Reform Commission recommended (*Report on Exemplary Damages*, (1991) at 46) that the fact of prior criminal prosecution should not be a bar to an award of punitive damages but that in determining the extent, if any, to which punitive damages should be awarded, the court should be entitled to consider the fact *and adequacy* of any prior penalty imposed.

52. As might be anticipated, no single view of these questions has been uniformly adopted in the many jurisdictions of the United States. ... But in some of those jurisdictions the question is put in terms like those put forward by the Ontario Law Reform Commission namely: exemplary damages should not be awarded if the defendant has been *sufficiently* punished by the criminal justice system.

53. Putting the question in these terms emphasises the importance of addressing the underlying question of principle. How are the civil courts to set about a task of punishing a defendant when the criminal courts have already done so? In particular, how is the civil court to assess the adequacy of the punishment inflicted as the result of a criminal prosecution? If the criminal process has taken its course, why should it be open to a plaintiff in a civil proceeding to contend that the punishment inflicted is inadequate? Is it enough (as the Ontario Law Reform Commission, *Report on Exemplary Damages*, (1991) at 45 suggest) that the victim of a crime may bring forward at a civil trial matters that go to punishment but are not brought forward at a criminal trial? How does that proposition fit with provisions made for sentencing courts to consider victim impact statements?

54. No doubt, if the punishment inflicted by a criminal court is properly regarded as substantial (and a term of imprisonment would seem always to be so) no question of inadequacy should arise. But what if a financial or other non-custodial penalty is exacted? How is the adequacy of that penalty to be judged: see *Daniels v Thompson* [1998] 3 NZLR 22 at 52-53 per Richardson P, Gault, Henry and Keith JJ; cf 73 per Thomas J.

55. Again, none of these questions arises here. On any view, substantial **[17]** punishment has been inflicted on the wrongdoer in this matter. But to express the rule to be applied by a civil court in deciding whether exemplary damages may be awarded, simply as a discretion to be exercised according to whether, having regard to the nature of the defendant's conduct and the need to punish it and deter others from repeating it, exemplary damages should be awarded, may very well obscure deep-seated and difficult questions of principle.

56. Here, however, because substantial punishment was imposed on Bransden for the conduct that was the subject of this action exemplary damages could not be awarded. ...

[Kirby J and Callinan J, in separate judgments, agreed that the damages recoverable by the appellant should exclude exemplary damages. However, the Court also agreed that the compensatory damages awarded to the appellant were manifestly inadequate.]

Appeal allowed. New trial ordered on the issue of damages,
other than aggravated and exemplary damages